from Lilli[illegible]inson

to

Bonnie Robinson

May 1993

THE WORLD OF TWENTIETH-CENTURY MUSIC

THE WORLD OF TWENTIETH-

PRENTICE-HALL, INC., ENGLEWOOD CLIFFS, N.J.

CENTURY MUSIC

David Ewen

Fifth printing......March, 1970

The World of Twentieth-Century Music
by David Ewen

Library of Congress Catalog Card Number: 68–11358

Printed in the United States of America · *T*

Prentice-Hall International, Inc., *London*
Prentice-Hall of Australia, Pty. Ltd., *Sydney*
Prentice-Hall of Canada, Ltd., *Toronto*
Prentice-Hall of India Private Ltd., *New Delhi*
Prentice-Hall of Japan, Inc., *Tokyo*

PREFACE

The World of Twentieth-Century Music is a replacement for *The Complete Book of 20th Century Music* originally published in 1952—a *replacement,* not just a new edition. Less than ten percent of the material has been retained from the earlier volume. Hand in hand with such rewriting came expansion. In words alone, the present volume is almost double the size of the earlier one. Twenty-nine composers have been added, bringing the total up to almost one hundred and fifty. Some four hundred additional major works have been discussed, so that the present volume embraces about one thousand major works. In addition, the programmatic descriptions have been greatly extended, and the biographical matter and critical evaluations of composers that precede the analyses have been considerably amplified.

When *The Complete Book of 20th Century Music* was first published, its author felt it might fill a gap in musical literature by becoming the first book in any language to analyze today's musical compositions in all the major forms. Its continued success through the years has proved that there is a need for such a book. *The Complete Book of 20th Century Music* has gone through a dozen printings, and in 1959 was subjected to an updated edition. In 1965, when the idea for a replacement was first hatched, *The Complete Book of 20th Century Music* was still maintaining a healthy sales figure.

At first, both publisher and author discussed the possibility of bringing out just a new edition of the old book. Such a plan was soon discarded. So much has happened to the world of twentieth-century music since 1952—so sophisticated have music audiences everywhere become to twentieth-century music—that a much more ambitious volume now had to be planned. The decision was then reached to begin from scratch and to plan a book fully capable of meeting the needs of 1968. The aim now was to make the book as comprehensive and as informative as humanly possible. It is no longer desirable to discuss just the representative works of the major composers; now there is a need for an analysis of their lesser works as well, particularly early works, the better to point up the creative evolution of these masters. The new currents and crosscurrents in the music of our times had to be discussed and explained, such as serialism, chance music, directional music, neo-dadaism and so forth, just as these are now so liberally represented on concert programs and in recordings.

If the approaches, attitudes and content in *The World of Twentieth-Century Music* is almost totally different from those of the earlier book, the overall plan has been found still serviceable.

Here, as earlier, each section begins with a critical analysis of the composer's style. In many cases where a composer has initiated or popularized a new technique or a new movement, these are also clarified. (A convenient table of these techniques and movements will be found at the end of the volume.) A biography of the composer follows, now usually detailed enough to provide all the salient facts. Where dates and facts differ from those found in our earlier book—or, for that matter, in other reference books—it is because intensive research, usually from firsthand sources, has provided more accurate information. This is followed by a composer's works in chronological order to enable the reader to trace the development from apprenticeship through full maturity. Programmatic and analytical information on each of these works is now given in some detail. Wherever possible, the author has made use of programmatic analyses prepared by the composers themselves; in some instances these analyses were prepared expressly for this book. All discussions of operas and ballet include the plots.

The attempt has always been to be sufficiently informative to make this book of interest to the trained musician and sufficiently non-technical to make it useful for the layman.

David Ewen

INTRODUCTION

To a great many people, the term *modern music* implies much more than merely the music of our times. It signifies discordant, disordered music, often as disrespectful of reason as it is of discipline and tradition. Such people look upon this music as a twentieth-century phenomenon.

It is quite true that many composers today have gone to possible extremes in the presentation of unusual musical sounds within unusual contexts. At first, twentieth-century composers broke down the confining walls of structure to give music more *Lebensraum,* to allow their musical ideas to roam more freely in unrestricted spaces. Then composers freed themselves from the restrictions of consonance through unresolved discords, and from the tyranny of the key centre or tonic through atonality. From atonality some composers progressed to dodecaphony, from dodecaphony to serialism. Composers opened new areas of sound by combining tonalities, rhythms, meters and notes which never before had been joined for artistic ends. Some composers exploited noises from non-musical equipment such as sirens and whistles and motors, and after that by enlisting the seemingly limitless resources of electronic instruments to produce still newer noises and sounds. Richard Strauss manufactured a wind machine for *Don Quixote* as far back as 1897, and a thunder machine for *Ein Alpensinfonie* in 1914, both being noisemakers pure and simple. A few years before World War I, a band of futurists headed by Marinetti appeared in Milan, Italy, insisting that art called for a new set of aesthetics with which to express the modern world. The musical spokesman for this group was a composer named Luigi Russolo, who said in 1913: "Life in ancient times was silent. In the nineteenth century, with the invention of machines, noise was born." He then went on to maintain that even the extremes of the-then modern music were too limited for his aims and purposes. "We must break out of this narrow circle of pure musical sounds, and conquer the infinite variety of noise sounds." He formulated his ideas and principles in *The Art of Noises,* published in 1916. In his manifesto issued in Milan on March 11, 1913, he conceived of an orchestra made up of six families of noises produced mechanically—including whistles, screams, the voices of animals and so forth. For one of his compositions, he required the services of a snorer; for another, he invented a number of noisemaking instruments.

Music as an interpretation of the machine and industrial age was further advanced in the 1920s with Arthur Honegger's tribute to the locomotive in *Pacific 231,* in Alexander Mossolov's description of a factory in *Iron Foundry,* in Prokofiev's glorification of industrialization in *The Age of Steel,* and in Carlos Chávez's depiction of the machine age in *H.P.* Meanwhile, advances were also being made in the incorporation of noises within musical textures. In 1917, Erik Satie introduced into the scoring of his provocative ballet *Parade* the sounds of gunshots, clicking typewriters, whirring of roulette wheels, and the sounds of airplane motors and dynamos. In the 1920s, George Antheil scored his *Ballet mécanique* for anvils, airplane propellers, electric bells, and automobile horns. Edgard Varèse evolved "organized sounds" in which his search for new kinds of sonorities became a passion. He explored the extremes of register and sonorities. He reproduced the sounds of sirens and machines, and he simulated the jungle noises of birds and insects. He used all kinds of noisemakers including friction instruments, also sibilation instruments recreating hissing or whistling sounds. He also featured the sounds produced by metals and wood objects being smitten or beaten. Tubular chimes and low register tone clusters on the piano added to the din.

With the development of electronics, still newer sounds could be devised. With "musique concrète" in Paris, all kinds of noises were reproduced on tapes. These noises could breed still other kinds of noises by slowing down the tape or accelerating it, or by piling up one layer of sound upon another. This method was developed in the late 1940s under the auspices of the Club d'Essai of the Radiodiffusion française. Pierre Schaeffer, an engineer, was the pioneer in this movement. He concocted a ten-movement symphony, *Symphonie pour un homme seul,* in which sounds heard by a solitary man are recorded and arranged in rhythmic patterns.

After that came huge electronic machines, the medium through which sounds could be produced electronically. One such is the Mark II Electronic Synthesizer created in the middle 1950s by the David Sarnoff Research Centre and for which Milton Babbitt created a number of provocative compositions. As Richard Kostelanetz has explained in *The New York Times Magazine:* "In contrast to most electronic music, which is produced by tape doctoring, Babbitt's electronic pieces are composed directly on the Synthesizer. . . . Potentially, Babbitt says, the machine can create any sound known to man." Electronic laboratories in New York and Princeton (where Otto Luening and Vladimir Ussachevsky have done their experimentation); at Cologne, with Karlheinz Stockhausen; at Milan, with Luciano Berio; at Jerusalem, with Josef Tal—all have succeeded in extending the horizons of electronically produced sounds.

The computer has also been recruited for opening new vistas in musical composition. Its main spokesman is Iannis Xenakis, Greek-born architect, mathematician, physicist, philosopher and musician residing in Paris, who is responsible for the birth of "stochastic music." "Instead of thinking in terms of harmonics as musicians have for many centuries," Jan Maguire explains, "Xenakis thinks in terms of sound entities which possess the characteristics of pitch, intensity and duration as associated to each other by and within time." Xenakis creates his compositions on an electronic device known as IBM 7090, "whose routine schedule," says Maguire, "consists of planning movements for oil fleets, calculating the temperature of metal in furnaces and market research, and is capable of ten-decimal figures."

Electronics has also invaded the traditional symphony orchestra through the introduction of such instruments as the Thereminvox and Ondes Martenot. The Thereminvox is a device created by Leon Theremin in which the musical sounds are produced by electric oscillations varying in pitch as movement of the hands approaches or recedes from the instrument. Joseph Schillinger wrote an *Airphonic Suite* in which the Thereminvox is used, and Edgard Varèse incorporated it into the scoring of his *Equatorial*. The Ondes Martenot, the invention of Maurice Martenot, is a radio-electric instrument with a keyboard capable of producing definite sounds electronically in a tempered scale. Milhaud and Honegger, in search for new sound effects, have used the Ondes Martenot in their orchestras in several of their compositions; so has Samuel Barber in his opera, *Antony and Cleopatra*.

Hand in hand with this search for new sounds have come the exploitations of new rhythmic devices. To achieve rhythmic freedom, early modern composers like Erik Satie began writing barless music. Composers like Stravinsky and Ives utilized the most complex polyrhythms and rapidly changing meters, thereby emancipating rhythm and giving it the same creative importance as the Romantics had done to harmony and instrumentation, and the Classicists to melody. Possibly the greatest complexity and variety of rhythmic treatment can be found in Olivier Messiaen's ten-movement symphony, *Turangalîla*. Messiaen has made a lifelong study of Western and Eastern rhythms and has compiled a monumental dictionary of rhythm. In his symphony his rhythms are augmented, diminished, reversed; they are used canonically and combined contrapuntally. There are, in the awesome words of the composer himself, "non-reversible rhythms, asymmetric augmentations with several rhythmic identities, rhythmic modes, and the combinations of quantitative and sounding elements in reinforcing the values and the timbre of each percussion instrument by chords which form the resonance of these timbres."

Some composers have opened new horizons for melody. The success of Mussorgsky and Janáček in molding the melodic line from speech patterns—Mussorgsky with his "melodies of life" and Janáček with his "melodies of the language"—was the starting point for those who gave birth to a new kind of declamation or recitative, which culminated in the *Sprechstimme* of the atonalists. In *Sprechstimme,* melody is freed from formal intervals with the pitch being indicated rather than sung, and with the voice swooping up and down to the next indicated note. Others, not quite so ready to surrender the discipline of formal intervals, tried out intervals smaller than the half tone. Alois Hába, a Czech, devoted himself exclusively to the writing of quarter-tone music. His opera, *Die Mutter,* required not only quarter-tone singing but even quarter-tone instruments; for the première performance a special quarter-tone piano, quarter-tone clarinets, and quarter-tone trumpets had to be invented. A quarter-tone piano was also constructed by Hans Barth, an American, who wrote a library of piano music for that instrument, performing it throughout the United States for a number of years.

In shaping his chords, Scriabin used intervals of the fourth instead of the traditional thirds, baptizing his kind of chord as "Mystery." In the early 1920s,

Henry Cowell built his chords out of intervals of seconds. In those years, this practice was known as "tone clusters" but subsequently Cowell preferred to use the term "secondal harmonies." Cowell produced numerous works calling for the banging of fists, elbows and forearms on the keyboard. He was, however, anticipated by Charles Ives, who in his *Concord Sonata* for piano advised the performer to use a ruler or any other strip of wood for the projection of tone clusters.

Another iconoclastic way of using the piano—this time for experimentation with sonorities rather than harmony—was concocted by John Cage. Cage wrote a new kind of piano literature for an instrument he called the "prepared piano." Cage "prepares" his pianos by stuffing dampers of metal, wood, rubber, felt and other materials between the strings in carefully manufactured positions. This "preparing" gives the instrument percussive qualities unknown before; and each piece by Cage requires a different "prepared piano." When Virgil Thomson's mother first heard some of these Cage pieces for "prepared piano," she remarked, "It's pretty, but I never would have thought of doing it."

With other composers, a digression from melodic norm consists in building their compositions from unorthodox scales rather than unorthodox harmonies or intervals. Debussy popularized the whole-tone scale, in which the octave is divided into six equal parts. Numerous composers, including Respighi and Vaughan Williams, reverted at times to the old modes. Alexander Tcherepnin worked out a nine-tone scale devised by using passing tones in an augmented triad. A Californian avant-garde composer named Harry Partch formulated a forty-three tone scale, for which he had to construct his own instruments, many based on models from primitive music: elongated violas (played like the cello); kitharas with seventy-two strings (shaped like an ancient lyre); harmonic canons with forty-four strings (similar to the Japanese koto), and so on. In 1953, he invented an instrument which he named "The Spoils of War," constructed from artillery-shell casings, bellows, bowls, a 1912 auto horn, and something called a "whang-gun." His aim was "monophony" —a return to primitivism and ancient cultures. A return to primitivism was also achieved by Carl Orff, the opera composer, but in a different way, by dispensing with scenery, costumes, staging (leaving such matters to the discretion of producers) and reducing his musical writing to the basic essentials of rhythm and declamation, with minimal use of harmony and accompanying instruments.

But even such excesses appear almost normal in the face of some of the more recent extravagances of the avant-garde school. Taking a cue from Anton Webern, who gave almost as much significance to silence as to sound in his Symphony, Morton Feldman has filled many of his compositions with carefully planned periods of silence. John Cage has carried this practice to its ultimate conclusion in *Four Minutes Thirty Seconds,* a composition for the piano. Here the performer sits at the keyboard for four minutes and thirty seconds and plays nothing.

John Cage has also been one of many composers to explore the possibilities of "chance" in aleatory music. One of his piano compositions requires the performer to scatter the manuscript pages pell-mell on the floor. The performer picks up now one sheet, now another at random; when he has played the last sheet the composition is over. Other Cage compositions use a process called "I-Ching," meaning "Chinese Book of Changes." This process requires a pair of Chinese dice. Having previously worked out a system in which the numbers on the dice relate to elements in composition, Cage throws out the dice, and the outcome of the throw determines which elements he will employ in his writing. In Stockhausen's *Zyklus,* for percussion instruments, the performer can begin with any measure he wishes; from then on, he must play the work in the given order and finish with the first stroke of the measure with which he started. Boulez's Third Piano Sonata comprises five sections which can be performed in any order desired by the virtuoso. In 1957, Lukas Foss founded a small ensemble specializing in the presentation of chance music, and for it Foss created in 1960 the Concerto for Improvising Solo Instruments where only the broad outlines of the composition are suggested in a complex chart, while the details of creation are determined in spontaneous performances at the time of the concert. In *Time Cycle,* Foss created a merger between composed music and chance music, and so did Boulez in his *Improvisations on Mallarmé.*

John Cage has also explored fully the potential of dadaism, in which the avant-garde movement has carried the art of music well beyond the limits of absurdity. Dadaism in music is, of course, nothing new. It was anticipated by Erik Satie in 1913 in *Le Piège de Meduse* where the main character is made up to resemble Satie; where the action is always interrupted by the antics of a stuffed monkey; where all kinds of ridiculous episodes and situations transpire. Officially, dadaism was born on February 8, 1916, at 6 o'clock in the evening at the Terrace Café in Zurich, the creation of a man named Tristan Tzara. A product of war weariness that led to a cynical negation of all accepted values and standards, dadaism as an art form was first presented anywhere at the Cabaret Voltaire in Zurich on February 26, 1916, the collaborators including Picasso, Apollinaire, Modigliani, Kandinsky and Marinetti. The dadaistic movement in music flourished in the early 1920s with works like Milhaud's *Le Boeuf sur le toit,* William Walton's *Façade,* and Thomson's *Four Saints in Three Acts.* Then it went into discard, waiting for another period of disillusion and disenchantment and cynicism to demand another escape from realities into absurdities. Such a time came in the 1950s and 1960s, and with it neo-dadaism came into its own.

Here is a description in *The New York Times* of a neo-dadaistic composition, *Action Music,* by a Korean composer, Nam Jun Paik, presented in New York in 1965: "The opening consisted of the composer doing an action painting with black paint applied by both hands and hair entitled 'Homage to Cage.' After that, one of the upright pianos was smashed, eggs were broken, and roars came from loudspeakers through electronic means. This was followed by nails being driven into one of the pianos, with Mr. Paik cutting his hair, with bedecking several men and women with strips of shaving cream, with cutting off the tie and shirt with a scissors of one man. The high point of the performance came when Charlotte Moorman played the cello. She performed

Variations on a Theme by Saint-Saëns, wearing as her costume . . . a cellophane sheath. While she played, the composer held the end pin of the cello in his teeth. Midway in the performance of Saint-Saëns', *The Swan,* Miss Moorman climbed a six-foot ladder and immersed herself in an oil drum filled with water. Then she climbed out, her cellophane sheath clinging to her body, to complete playing *The Swan.*"

In *Mimetics* by an Argentine composer, Mauricio Klagel, one of the performers is instructed to bounce a rubber ball during one of the passages, while in another, two musicians are advised to engage in loud conversation. In John Cage's *Variations V,* a dancer, wearing red pants and gray shirt, rides a bicycle through a mass of electronic transmitters. As he rides, the movements of the bicycle encourage the electronic equipment to emit a cacophony of noises transmitted through the auditorium by means of loudspeakers. Cage's *Theatre Piece* requires a man to hang upside down in a black plastic cocoon; Charlotte Moorman to play a Cage composition on the cello, while the composer puts a cigar in her mouth and removes it from time to time; a tiny Japanese to wave silken banners from the top of a huge bamboo pole; an oil drum to be rolled down the stairs outside the audtorium; balloons to be punctured, buzzers to be sounded, and all kinds of electronic noises to be projected.

All such innovations call for new kinds of musical notation which, in many avant-garde compositions, resemble plans for guided missiles. In fact, numerous avant-garde compositions are as much a visual experience as they are an aural one. Innovations by avant-garde composers also call for a new method of musical performance, with emphasis on directional or spatial music to create a stereophonic effect. In the 1950s, Henry Brant wrote a number of works in which different groups of performers are placed in distantly separated positions in the concert hall. One such composition is *December,* where, in 1954, singers and instrumentalists were spotted all over Carnegie Hall in New York. Trombones occupied the second-tier boxes. Solo singers were placed on opposite sides of the dress circle. The chorus and percussionists and brass were placed on the stage. Stockhausen later conceived of a new kind of concert hall, shaped spherically, with the music converging on the audience from all parts of the hall through loudspeakers. The feasibility of directional or spatial music for artistic and aesthetic effect was strongly proved in two operas, *Don Rodrigo* by Ginastera and *The Visitation* by Gunther Schuller.

* * *

Experimentation, even excessive experimentation, is no aberration of the twentieth century.

When the late sixteenth-century *camerata* of Florence broke with polyphony to produce the "new art" of homophony—a single melody with harmonic accompaniment, in place of several simultaneously sounded melodies—this was a break with the past as decisive as Schoenberg's desertion of tonality. To sixteenth-century ears, the sound produced by this new art seemed as strange and acrid as that of Schoenberg to audiences in the 1910s and 1920s. When Rameau and Gluck turned their backs on the formalized opera of the Italians to produce the first music dramas, they were regarded by most of their contemporaries with the same kind of anger, ridicule and vituperation that met Wagner a century ago, and Debussy and Alban Berg after him. The learned Austrian Kapellmeisters of the eighteenth century went to their Emperor to denounce Haydn as a charlatan because he dared to tamper with, and thereby to amplify, existing forms. Mozart, Beethoven, Schubert, Schumann, Chopin, Liszt, Wagner, all struck new paths in one way or another, and all were denounced for it. But by striking new paths, they uncovered new worlds of musical sound, enriching the language of harmony, changing existing concepts of melody, developing the art and science of orchestration, and extending and sometimes creating musical forms.

That most of the great composers of the past were adventurous in their thinking and impatient with tradition has made it possible for music to grow and change, as every living organism must. It is, however, not without some element of paradox that at least a few of the so-called "new" techniques, which so horrified reactionary critics of our own generation, can be found in the music of the masters. Dissonance is almost as old as consonance itself. There were unresolved discords even in Monteverdi (1567–1643), a fact that inspired the sixteenth-century Artusi to remark acidly that music such as this could appeal to the senses but not to reason. Mozart's String Quartet in C major (K. 465) confused and astounded his contemporaries with its opening measures where chromatics create cross relations and where an obscurity of a definite key produces dissonant effects far in advance of Mozart's day. Even Haydn, who admired and loved Mozart without reservation, was puzzled by this strange music and could only remark: "If Mozart wrote it, he must have good reason to do so." Beethoven's first symphony, though in the key of C major, opens seemingly in F major, then goes on to the key of G, before finally settling down to its C major tonality. Such an unusual harmonic procedure was condemned by Beethoven's critics as outright stupidity, just as Beethoven's emphasis on brass and tympani inspired accusations of bad taste.

Nor is dissonance the only one of the much reviled twentieth-century practices to be found in the music of the past. Percy Scholes, in the *Oxford Companion to Music,* quotes an interesting canonic passage from one of Bach's works which is unmistakably polytonal. The whole-tone scale was used—before Debussy—by Mozart, Rossini and Berlioz. The shifting tonalities and daring voice-leading in Beethoven's last quartets give a hint, and a strong one, of atonality, while Wagner's chromatic harmonies is the soil out of which atonality grew. Polyrhythm and polymeters can be found in Brahms, unorthodox intervals and harmonies in Chopin and Schumann. Chopin's exquisitely fashioned music was described by the eminent critic, Rellstab, as "ear-rending dissonances, tortuous transitions, sharp modulations, repugnant contortions of melody and rhythm."

Once, in analyzing a piece of music, Eric Blom pointed to examples of so-called "modern writing" within the space of a few bars. He noted a "diminished seventh and a sweeping skip in the seventh bar, an unexpected transition to the tonic minor in the second, discordant suspensions in the next three, and a grinding false relation." It almost seems as if Blom were describing a piece of music by Bartók or some other twentieth-century rebel. Actually, he was discussing the ethereal slow movement of Mozart's C major Piano Concerto (K. 467)!

* * *

If not everything modern is new, then it is equally true that not everything that is modern is essentially "modern."

Innovation, iconoclasm, avant-gardism are intriguing facets of twentieth-century music—but not the only ones. For every composer who, like Bartók and Webern and Boulez and Stockhausen and Cage, looks fearlessly into the future, there are just as many who have thrown glances over their shoulders to the past. The middle-period Stravinsky, Casella, Respighi—as well as Americans like Norman Dello Joio and Roy Harris—have often gone to the seventeenth century for structures and occasionally even styles. Hindemith adopted the polyphonic style of the Baroque age, though, of course, in a modern linear version. The modality of the Gregorian chant has appealed to an American like Paul Creston. Henry Cowell used old American hymn tunes as a point of departure for many significant works.

A Sessions or an Ives may prefer excessive complexity; others have preferred the most stringent economy, barest simplicity, and a directness of expression. Jean Françaix and Francis Poulenc have made a fetish of simplicity in several compositions. At one period in his career, Aaron Copland consciously adopted a style easily assimilated by unsophisticated audiences. Erik Satie, and members of the "French Six," were spokesmen for an "everyday music" for "everyday audiences," while a corollary movement arose in Germany in the 1920s, with Kurt Weill, Krenek and others glorifying "contemporary art." Functional music also demands the most simple approach, and composers like Hindemith and Copland have produced a kind of music that can serve an educational or utilitarian function.

For every cerebral composer there is an Elgar or a Glazunov or a Rachmaninoff to prefer romantic, emotional, sensual, even passionate self-expression.

In other words, there are more approaches than one to the music of our times. Modern music has been subjected to the same forces of action and reaction which have always produced opposing styles in the past.

In the closing decades of the nineteenth century, German romanticism was perhaps the greatest single influence in music. The Wagnerian spell was irresistible. The younger men—under the enchantment of *Tristan,* the *Ring* and *Parsifal*—rivaled each other in the invention of gargantuan structures, elaborate orchestrations, overwritten harmonies and polyphony, gigantic climaxes, overpowering dramatic effects, passionate moods, sensuality—and music filled with symbolic or philosophic or mystical implications. Those who were not influenced by Wagner were followers of Brahms. With Mahler, Pfitzner, Dohnányi such romantic approaches were carried into the twentieth century.

Almost inevitably, forces were set into motion to counteract such an excess of romanticism. Erik Satie brought music down from its ivory tower and into the marketplace by using popular tunes, by glorifying simplicity, by indulging in whimsy and satire. Debussy wrote music, subtle in suggestion and delicate in effect, setting into motion the wave of impressionism under which composers everywhere became submerged. But impressionism bred indiscretions, as music became increasingly overprecious and overrefined. Reaction came with the expressionist abstractions of Schoenberg and his disciples: music was now stripped of all emotion and feeling, of all atmosphere and suggestive nuances, reduced to the barest of essentials, and given the exactness of a mathematical formula. Others combated romanticism and impressionism (and then the desiccated writing of the expressionists) by reverting to the classic forms and the stylistic procedures of the old composers, though with modern vocabulary and approaches; thus the neo-classic school came into being.

To a large extent, the birth of the Russian national school in the latter part of the nineteenth century was also an open challenge to German art forms and concepts in general, and to Wagnerism in particular. By realizing an idiom and style derived from their own folk sources, by reaching for subject matter in Russia's past history and culture, these Russian composers completely negated Germanic traditions. Out of the examples of the "Russian Five"—Mussorgsky, Rimsky-Korsakov, Cui, Balakirev and Borodin—came the national schools that sprouted so richly in many parts of the twentieth-century world.

With many expressionist and neo-classic composers, music was becoming too much of an esoteric art appealing only to the sophisticated few. A powerful movement away from this tendency was set into motion in different countries. In the Soviet Union, the attempt was made to create a proletarian art speaking to and for the masses. Elsewhere, popularism flourished—with Kurt Weill in Germany, with Gershwin and Morton Gould in the United States.

In the last analysis, movements and countermovements, actions and reactions, are only incidental forces in the work of important composers. The most significant influence is still the creative one: the production of works of art that are honest, forceful, original. To the historian or critic throwing a coup d'oeil over the first sixty-five and more years of the twentieth century, it may be illuminating to remark that trends were crystallized with Debussy's *Pelléas et Mélisande,* Strauss's *Salome* and *Elektra,* Stravinsky's *The Rite of Spring* and *Symphony of Psalms,* Berg's *Wozzeck* and Violin Concerto, Falla's *El Amor Brujo,* Hindemith's *Mathis der Mahler,* Ravel's *Daphnis and Chloe,* Scriabin's piano sonatas and symphonies, Gershwin's *Rhapsody in Blue,* Boulez's *Le Marteau Sans Maître,* Bartok's string quartets, and so on and so forth. To the same historian, it may be important to point out that in these works new creative areas were being fertilized. But to the lover of great music, the salient fact is only that these works are of major artistic importance, that this is music which brings aesthetic pleasure to many and belongs with the significant creations of all time.

BOOKS BY DAVID EWEN

The Complete Book of Classical Music
The Complete Book of 20th Century Music
The Home Book of Musical Knowledge
The World of Great Composers
Panorama of American Popular Music
Complete Book of the American Musical Theatre
A Journey to Greatness: *The Life and Music of George Gershwin*
Richard Rodgers
The World of Jerome Kern
The Encyclopedia of the Opera
The Encyclopedia of Concert Music
Milton Cross' Encyclopedia of Great Composers and Their Music (*with Milton Cross*)
Music for the Millions
Dictators of the Baton
Music Comes to America
The New Book of Modern Composers
Leonard Bernstein
The Story of America's Musical Theatre
The Book of European Light Opera
David Ewen Introduces Modern Music
The Life and Death of Tin Pan Alley
American Popular Songs: From the Revolutionary War to the Present

CONTENTS

Page numbers appear in italics

TO WILLIAM F. LEE—

scholar, educator, administrator, composer

but, most significantly to me, a most treasurable friend

ISAAC ALBÉNIZ 1860–1909

Quiescent for several centuries, Spanish art-music was reborn towards the end of the nineteenth century with the emergence of a nationalist school. Isaac Albéniz was its first significant composer. With him, and with his immediate followers (Granados, Turina, Falla), a musical renaissance took place in Spain.

Two significant influences molded the career of Albéniz. The first came in 1883 when he began an informal period of study with Felipe Pedrell. Felipe Pedrell (1841–1922) was a Spanish scholar whose researches into old Spanish music has profound musicological significance. His definitive editions of Spanish church and organ music and his rediscovery of the folk music of Andalusia, Catalonia and the Basque region, brought to light a rich but long neglected heritage of Spanish music. These researches (combined with his passionate belief in Spanish folk song and dance as vital creative forces for the Spanish composer) pointed a new goal.

Until Albéniz met and became Pedrell's student in composition, he was a musician of considerable natural aptitude but with no apparent direction or purpose. He was making his living as a pianist. As a composer, he had produced mostly minor, unoriginal pieces. It was Pedrell who first aroused Albéniz's thus-far latent ambition to become a serious and ambitious composer; who encouraged Albéniz to turn to Spanish backgrounds and idioms both for his inspiration and his materials. Inflamed by Pedrell's enthusiasm for the artistic potential of Spanish folk music, Albéniz completed a number of piano compositions which represented his first adventure into musical nationalism, beginning with the *Suite española,* op. 47, in 1886.

The second powerful influence in Albéniz's development came during a long residence in Paris beginning with 1894. Personal contact with Debussy, Chausson, Fauré, Dukas and d'Indy—and professional association with the Schola Cantorum as a teacher—compelled Albéniz to reevaluate himself and his music. As Gilbert Chase noted in *The Music of Spain:* "He was thrown into the company of 'serious' musicians with high ideals and complete mastery of medium, and it was natural that he should strive to emulate them." Growing increasingly ambitious in his thinking, Albéniz now began to seek out larger structures and to try arriving at an enrichment of harmonic writing and at a more personal melodic idiom. He also worked at the extension and perfection of his writing for the keyboard.

Although Albéniz wrote operas, operettas (zarzuelas), and various works for orchestra, his highest inspiration and his most original writing were reserved for the piano. In this field, he was a follower of Liszt, both in his rhapsodic style and in his skilful exploitation of piano technique. But Albéniz's compositions for the piano also owe a debt to French music: in their sensitively projected atmospheres; their occasional digression into impressionist writing; their delicacy and refinement of style.

The predominating trait of Albéniz's music is its Spanish personality, and specifically the personality of Andalusia. Albéniz believed he had Moorish blood in him; he often maintained that the one place he felt most at home was the Alhambra in Granada. Thus Andalusia exerted a powerful spell over him. Most of his music, and generally his best music, is of Andalusian inspiration. In his music, Albéniz spoke of the people of Andalusia, its folklore, its sights and sounds. He never yielded to quotation or adaptation. Nevertheless, the pulsing rhythms of Andalusian dances, the strumming quality of a guitar accompanying an Andalusian song, the haunting and sensual and oriental identity of the Andalusian *conte hondo,* or deep song (*see* Falla), the interplay of rhythm and the volatile alternation of mood from melancholy to gaiety found in Andalusian folk songs—all this, stylized and idealized, is found in Albéniz's music, of which the piano suite, *Iberia,* is his masterwork.

Albéniz was born in Camprodón, in the province of Gerona, Spain, on May 29, 1860. His formal education in music was begun at the age of six with piano lessons with Marmontel, and it continued two years later at the Madrid Conservatory. Albéniz ran away from school and home and traveled to such far-off places as South America, Puerto Rico and Cuba, earning his living by playing the piano. A craving for musical knowledge sent him to the Leipzig Conservatory in 1874, where his teachers included Jadassohn and Reinecke. Then he came to Brussels to study with François Gevaert. Subsequently, Albéniz devoted himself seriously towards perfecting his technique as pianist (a development inspired by his personal contacts with Liszt), after which he undertook a concert tour.

In 1883, Albéniz married Rosina Jordana, one of his pupils, with whom he eventually had three children. Marriage sobered him. He abandoned his former Bohemian ways to concentrate more seriously than ever on music study with Pedrell, and to earn his living in Madrid by giving concerts and teaching. For a while he resided in London, where he was the recipient of a generous annual subsidy from an English banker, Francis Money-Coutts, in return for writing music for Coutts's poetical dramas. This resulted in several operas, the most significant of which was *Pepita Jiménez,* introduced in Barcelona on January 5, 1896. Meanwhile, in 1893, Albéniz found a new permanent home in Paris, whose musical life and activities stimulated him no end. This influence can be detected in Albéniz's first large-scale work for piano and orchestra, *Catalonia,* introduced in Paris in 1899.

His own physical suffering as a victim of Bright's disease, the death of his daughter, and the chronic ailment of his wife all combined to darken his closing years. It was during this period of mental depression and physical disability that he completed his most significant composition, the piano suite, *Iberia.*

Though virtually an invalid, Albéniz managed in 1909 to leave Paris and make a trip with his family to the French Pyrenees. He died there on June 16, 1909, in the town of Cambo-les-Bains.

Outside of *Iberia,* most of Albéniz's popular compositions for the piano were written before 1900 and therefore are not discussed below. These compositions include the following:

Sevillañas, the third piece in *Suite española,* op. 47, the heart of which is a passionate melody, typical of those heard in the haunts of Seville, accompanied by rhythms suggesting the clicking of castanets.

Tango in D major, op. 164, no. 2, a prototype of all tango music, comprising a flamenco-like melody. Strange to say, the original piano version as written by the composer is rarely heard. What we do hear is an arrangement, also for the piano, by Leopold Godowsky, or transcriptions for a solo instrument and piano, or for orchestra.

Córdoba, the fourth and most famous number from the piano suite, *Cantos de España,* op. 232. This is a haunting nocturne opening with incisive chords, suggesting the plucking of guitar strings, and progressing towards an oriental-type melody evoking a picture of the Moorish-like city.

1905–1909 IBERIA, suite for piano. Book I: 1. Evocacíon. 2. El Puerto. 3. El Corpus Christi en Sevilla, or Fête-Dieu à Séville. Book II: 1. Rondeña. 2. Almería. 3. Triana. Book III: 1. El Albaicín. 2. El Polo. 3. Lavapiés. Book IV: 1. Málaga. 2. Jerez. 3. Eritaña.

NAVARRA, for solo piano.

Few tonal portraits of Spain penetrate so deeply into the heart of that country, or reproduce its pulse and heartbeat so authentically, as does *Iberia.* Though essentially of Andalusian inspiration, *Iberia* catches the spirit and soul of Spain down to its subtlest nuances and most elusive colors. Rich in imagery, varied in backgrounds, deft in the projection of atmosphere, sensitive in evoking sounds and smells, *Iberia* is truly Spain set to music.

The first performance of each of the four books took place between 1906 and 1909: Book I, in Paris on May 9, 1906; Book II, in St. Jean de Luz on September 11, 1907; Book III, in Paris on January 2, 1908; Book IV, in Paris on February 9, 1909. But for the grace of the performing artist, Blanche Selva, the world of music might have been robbed of this masterpiece. When Albéniz completed writing his first book he was seized by mental depression and discouragement. The fear haunted him that his music was far too difficult for performance. This lack of confidence made him determined to destroy his work. He might well have yielded to this impulse. Fortunately, Blanche Selva learned of his doubts and fears and prevailed on him to permit her to have the music before he destroyed it. In a few days' time she returned the music; but she also sat down at the piano to play it all from memory. Evidently the composer needed no further convincing, for he not only saved the composition but proceeded to create three more books of similar pieces.

BOOK I. Evocacíon (1905) was described by Gilbert Chase as a "little fandango with an intensely lyrical *copla* that appears first in the bass and later returns in the upper register marked 'very soft and distant.'" *El Puerto* (1907) describes a frenetic fiesta in a Spanish resort. Here we get the vital, pulsating rhythms of three Andalusian dances. "In the end," Chase explains, "all this exuberance and gaiety vanish in one of those fade-out codas to which Albéniz is so partial." *El Corpus Christi en Sevilla,* or *Fête-Dieu à Séville* (1905), dramatizes an ecclesiastical procession through the streets of Spain, with all its pomp and color, and accompanied by the majestic tolling of church bells. A march-like subject describes the approaching procession. This is followed by a "saeta" (an improvised song), sung by the onlookers as the procession passes by. At a climactic point, the march tune evolves into a fast dance figure; but it is with a final quiet statement of the "saeta" that the composition ebbs away. (This piece is often heard at orchestral concerts in transcriptions by either Enrique Fernández Arbós or Leopold Stokowski.)

BOOK II. *Rondeña* (1905) is a stately Spanish dance, a variant of the fandango. Its rhythm, points out Gilbert Chase, is "characterized by the alternation of measures in 6/8 time and 3/4 time, a nervous, staccato rhythm, interrupted at the section marked *Poco meno mosso* by the lyrical refrain of a *malagueña-rondeña,* which is later contrapuntally blended with the theme of the dance. *Almería* (1906) portrays the Mediterranean seaport in the rhythm of the *tarantas,* a dance with jota-like melody peculiar to that city. *Triana* (1906) depicts a suburb of Seville famous for its gypsies. This music is based on the *paso-doble* (two-step) and *marcha torera* (march for the bullring).

BOOK III. *El Albaicín* (1906) captures the melancholia, alternating with excitement, of a gypsy song heard in a Seville suburb. The passionate, throbbing sounds of a *cante hondo* are set against an accompaniment suggesting the strumming of a guitar. *El Polo* (1906) quotes a well-known Andalusian song of the same name which, the composer tells us, is to be played "with the spirit of a sob." *Lavapiés* (no year) interprets a popular quarter of Madrid. The composer suggests that it be played "joyfully and with freedom."

BOOK IV. *Málaga* (1907) blends the character of a *malagueña* (a dance typical of Málaga) with a graceful theme. *Jerez* (1909) is patterned after a gypsy dance known as a *soleares,* and consists of a main theme embellished with decorative filigree. *Eritaña* (1907) portrays a tavern on the outskirts of Seville in gay rhythms, and melodies subjected to interesting harmonic treatment and bold modulations. Here is how Claude Debussy described this music: "*Eritaña* is the joy of the morning, the happy discovery of a tavern where the wine is cool. An ever-changing crowd passes, their bursts of laughter accompanied by the jingling of tambourines. Never has music achieved such diversified, such colorful impressions: one's eyes close as though dazzled by beholding such a wealth of imagery."

Arbós orchestrated five sections from the four books: *Evocacíon, El Puerto, El Corpus Christi en Sevilla, Triana,* and *El Albaicín.* The music of *Iberia* was the inspiration for the ballet *Iberia,* introduced in Paris by the Ballets Suédois on October 25, 1920, choreography and scenario by Jean Borlin, who was also one of the principal dancers.

Navarra (1909) was Albéniz's last composition; he did not live to finish it, a chore accomplished for him after his death by Déodat de Séverac. This is a picture of a Spanish province below the Pyrenees. A sensual, languorous gypsy melody moves over an accompanying jota rhythm.

Navarra is heard most often today in a transcription for orchestra by Enrique Fernández Arbós.

HUGO ALFVÉN 1872–1960

Alfvén was Sweden's most significant symphonist. He was essentially a voice of German post-Romanticism. From Brahms, he derived his partiality for full-blooded melodies, well-sounding harmonies, a strong rhythmic pulse, and rhapsodic moods, all within clearly defined classical structures. From Richard Strauss came the brilliance and virtuosity of his orchestration. In his choral music, he betrayed still another influence, a return to the Baroque era, in his rich and at times complex polyphonic style; while in his three rhapsodies, he was a Swedish nationalist. But in every area, he was a traditionalist through and through, with little interest in experiment or innovation, and completely content with the status quo in music.

Alfvén was born in Stockholm on May 1, 1872. He received his music instruction at the Stockholm Conservatory, with private teachers in Stockholm, and after that with César Thomson in Brussels. His first symphony, in F minor, was introduced in Stockholm on February 9, 1897, and recognition came with his second symphony, in E major, heard in Stockholm on May 2, 1899. On a government stipend he then spent three years of travel and study in France and Germany. Upon his return to Sweden, he gained international fame with his first Swedish rhapsody, *Midsummer Vigil,* in 1904, and with his third symphony, in E major, in 1906. In 1908, he became a member of the Royal Academy. From 1910 to 1939, he was the musical director of Uppsala University. For many years, he directed its chorus. After retiring as University musical director, he led other Swedish choruses in performances throughout Europe up to 1947. In 1938, he visited the United States. Alfvén died in Falum on May 8, 1960.

1904 MIDSUMMER VIGIL (MIDSOMMARVAKA), Swedish Rhapsody No. 1, for orchestra, op. 19.

LA NUIT DE SAINT-JEAN (ST. JOHN'S EVE), ballet in one act, with scenario and choreography by Jean Borlin. First performance: Paris, October 25, 1920.

Alfvén's most popular composition, and the one which first made him known outside of Sweden, was also his first Swedish rhapsody. It is based not only on Swedish folk tunes and dance rhythms but also on two melodies from the Schleswig-Holstein region of Germany ("Von Hamburg gehts nach Ritze" and "Schoene Bertha Polka"). The music depicts a rustic revel celebrated in different parts of Sweden on June 24 during the festival of St. John's Eve, comprising songs, dances, bonfires, and so forth. In Germany, this festival is known as "St. Johannisfeier."

The rhapsody opens (Allegro moderato) with a delightful theme for clarinet accompanied by plucked strings. The bassoon arrives with the suggestion of a burlesque thought; this idea is then stated fully by bassoons and horns in unison. A slowing down of the tempo (Andante) brings on a melody for the English horn. This is followed by a light dance-like subject (Allegretto). The mood now grows in intensity (Allegro con brio) until a powerful climax suggests that the revel is at its height.

This music was adapted into the successful ballet, *La Nuit de Saint-Jean,* introduced by the Ballets Suédois. It was presented one hundred and thirty-four times during the first season, and one hundred and nineteen times during the next three years. Borlin, who prepared scenario and choreography, was also one of the two principal dancers (the other being Jenny Hasselquist). The synopsis of the ballet scenario appeared in the program of the première: "Following a very old tradition to which both young and old are strongly attached, the eve of St. John every year is the occasion for great rejoicing. From one end of the country to the other, it is one general festival of national character. Boys and girls, men and women, join around the flower-decked maypole and dance to the music of ancient folk songs. Between the dances they toast one another and clink glasses in a genuine Scandinavian *skol.* Only after sundown—and midsummer nights are very brief in Sweden—is there a brief respite, a moment of sweet nostalgia, which ends with the rising sun. Again the strains of folk music are heard, the dances are resumed, and the merry-makers continue their sarabande, dancing from village to village."

1906 SYMPHONY NO. 3 IN E MAJOR. I. Allegro con brio. II. Andante. III. Presto. IV. Allegro con brio.

The third is the most popular of Alfvén's five symphonies; it was introduced in Gothenburg, Sweden, on December 5, 1906. The music was written while the composer was vacationing in Italy and in the composer's description is "a paean in praise of all the joys of life, sunshine, and the joy of living."

The main theme of the first movement is immediately heard in the full orchestra, which also presents the second theme. In the second movement, a broad lyrical passage is stated first by the woodwind, then by muted strings; a secondary subject, equally lyrical, is offered by the clarinet. The third-movement Presto opens with a rapid, vigorous theme for first violins; after it has been developed, a second theme is presented by oboes and bassoons. The trumpet introduces the finale which, the composer explained, is "imbued with an intense longing for home; I dreamed I was a knight in a far-off land, who in a heedless gallop for home—a wild ride now through sunny landscapes, now through dark abysses—reaches the goal of my dreams. "The second theme is presented by the wind instruments over string tremolos. A passage for strings and the woodwind precedes the recapitulation, which concludes with the same trumpet call with which the movement opened.

1937 DALECARLIAN RHAPSODY, Swedish Rhapsody No. 3, for orchestra, op. 48.

This rhapsody differs from the popular *Midsummer Vigil,* which it followed by three decades, in several important respects. Unlike the earlier work, the *Dalecarlian Rhapsody* draws all of its melodies from a single province. Also, where the earlier composition was gay, lively and festive, the later one was subdued, at times even somber (all of its melodies, except one, being in the minor mode). Finally, where the *Midsummer Vigil* is in a three-part structure, that of the *Dalecarlian Rhapsody* is a quick alternation of slow and fast themes.

This is how the composer himself described the music: "The Rhapsody is imbued with the serenity of the lake forests north of Lake Siljan. The basic theme is gloomy, melancholy, full of yearning. I imagine a young shepherdess blowing her cow horn [soprano saxophone in the Introduction]. I am trying to describe her dreams, her yearning. She hears a bridal procession pass by far off in the distance. [This ancient wedding march is from the Orsa parish.]... Her imagination carries her back to her friends in the village. She remembers two happy dances [two polskas from the Orsa parish] and the mighty, serious melodies of the church services on Sundays [an old mountain hymn from the Alvdalen parish]. Finally she remembers with a shudder when a strange man made his way through the dancing couples, took the violin from the fiddler and played wild and bizarre melodies which made the people go mad. The man was the Evil One himself whose violent polska concludes the rhapsody."

1957 THE PRODIGAL SON, a ballet in one act, with choreography by Ivo Cramer. First performance: Stockholm, Spring, 1957

THE PRODIGAL SON, suite for orchestra. I. March. II. Polska. III. Festive March. IV. Polketta. V. Steak Tune. VI. Polka from Roslagen ("Roslag's Spring"). VII. Gössa Anders Polska.

The ballet, *The Prodigal Son,* was introduced at the Royal Swedish Opera to help celebrate the composer's eighty-fifth birthday. The scenario describes the departure of the prodigal son from his father's vineyard. His extensive travels bring him to Arabia, where he meets and is fêted by the Queen. He leads a sensual existence before returning home to receive the forgiveness of his father.

Subtitled *Five Danced Paintings from Dalarna,* the ballet tells its story with the same kind of simplicity and naïveté that characterized the religious paintings of Dalarna found in churches and homes. These were figures dressed like farmers, who enacted episodes from the Bible and legends from the Dalarna region.

The seven-movement symphonic suite from the ballet score has been played at concerts and has been recorded. The opening March is a tune from the Leksand parish. The composer described this brilliant movement as follows: "I wanted to make the march as magnificent and as colorful as possible.... I enjoyed immensely adding in chords which I knew would bring on the colors of gold, silver and rose." The second movement and the finale are polskas—a polska being a folk dance popular in Sweden from the sixteenth century on, a forerunner of the polonaise and the mazurka. The sixth movement is so melodious that the tune was used for a hit song that captured Sweden in 1957. The composer found this melody in Furusund at the turn of the century when he was gathering material for *Midsummer Vigil.*

GEORGE ANTHEIL 1900–1959

Though he had abandoned the musical indiscretions that had earned him the sobriquet of "bad boy of music" (a title he had used for an autobiography published in 1945), George Antheil will undoubtedly long be remembered for his once notorious *Ballet mécanique*. Scored for machines, anvils, bells, automobile horns, player pianos and percussion, *Ballet mécanique* created a mild sensation when introduced in Paris on June 19, 1926. On April 10, 1927, it was heard in Carnegie Hall, New York, conducted by Eugene Goossens. The rather vulgar publicity campaign preceding this performance succeeded in converting a provocative musical event into something resembling a circus. The performance itself was further vulgarized by its indulgence in sensational byplay not called for in the score. The audience was hostile. One wag, seated in the front row, attached a white handkerchief to his cane and rose, waving a symbol of surrender. The critics were equally vituperative.

The *Ballet mécanique,* and the other iconoclastic or jazz works completed by Antheil during the 1920s, are all gone and forgotten. Any attempt to revive them is futile, as was decisively proved on February 20, 1954, in New York City when the *Ballet mécanique* returned to Carnegie Hall in a new version (scored for four instead of eight pianos, and with the noise of a jet plane reproduced on a recording device). The work proved at that time that it had lost not only interest as a curiosity but also the capacity to arouse controversy. It fell flat completely.

Ballet mécanique was a pioneer not only in exploring the possibilities of non-musical sounds within serious contexts, but also in the use of rhythmic processes. To the latter practice, Antheil assigned the term "time-space." He further explained that he intended this music not as a glorification of machines but as an interpretation of the "barbaric and mystic splendor of modern civilization—mathematics of the universe in which the abstraction of the human soul lives." Antheil revised this composition in 1954.

In the late 1930s, Antheil began writing music in a vein entirely opposed to the provocative one he had produced a decade earlier. The day for experimentation was over, as far as he was concerned. Antheil now tried to write expressive or dramatic music according to classical rule and within traditional forms—and frequently music with an American background or identity. As Antheil himself said in the 1940s, in a communication to the program annotator of the Philadelphia Orchestra, his new objective was "to disassociate myself from the passé modern schools of the last half-century, and create a music for myself and those around me which has no fear of developed melody, real development itself, tonality, or understandable forms." It is with music Antheil wrote after 1939 that he has been represented most often on concert programs.

Antheil was born in Trenton, New Jersey, on July 8, 1900. After an extended period of study with Constantin Von Sternberg and Ernest Bloch, he was admitted to the Settlement School of Philadelphia (precursor of the Curtis Institute) as a scholarship pupil. During this period, while still under Bloch's influence, he wrote his first symphony.

In 1922, he toured Europe as a concert pianist, performing in leading cities and achieving more notoriety than fame for his passionate espousal of ultramodern piano music. A performance of his First Symphony in Berlin convinced him to choose composition over playing the piano. He settled in Paris where he wrote several works in an avant-garde idiom. They attracted attention and attack. The high point in this phase of his career was the performance of his *Ballet mécanique*. During this period in Paris, on October 4, 1925, he married Elizabeth (Boski) Markus, niece of the Austrian playwright and novelist, Artur Schnitzler; they had one son.

After achieving success with a jazz opera, *Transatlantic*—introduced in Frankfort-on-the-Main, Germany, on May 25, 1930—Antheil returned to the United States. His second opera, *Helen Retires* (libretto by John Erskine) was introduced in New York City on February 28, 1934, and pointed to a new direction for the composer towards lyricism, a lighter touch, and a calculated simplicity. In 1936, Antheil settled in Hollywood; for three years after that he did no composing. When he returned to writing symphonies, operas and ballets, he assumed the new romantic approach and more orthodox methods that would identify his writing from then on. One of Antheil's last compositions—a cantata, *Cabeza de Vaca*—was introduced posthumously over the television network of the Columbia Broadcasting Company on June 10, 1962. Antheil died in New York City on February 12, 1959.

1946 CONCERTO IN D MAJOR, for violin and orchestra. I. Moderato assai. II. Andante tranquillo. III. Ben ritmato a capriccioso.

This concerto was dedicated to Werner Gebauer, the concertmaster of the Dallas Symphony, who introduced it in Dallas on February 9, 1947, Antal Dorati conducting. The work is consistently rhapsodic, lyrical and romantic. The first movement is in the traditional sonata form with two full-blooded themes developed with amplitude. A poetic slow movement contains pages of tranquil, and at times, elegiac music. The spirited finale employs Latin-American themes and rhythms.

1948 SONATA NO. 4 FOR PIANO. I. Allegro giocoso-ironico. II. Andante. III. Vivo.

This is Antheil's last sonata for the piano, and his best. It passes flexibly from sentimental moods to ironic ones. The first movement makes a burlesque of salon piano playing. To make this point more apparent, this movement hastily quotes several measures by Chopin, darling of all salon performers. In the slow movement, Antheil becomes sentimental with an outpouring of tender lyricism. A powerful momentum gives the final movement its energy, while sharp contrasts provide continual interest. Of this concluding movement, Virgil Thomson said in the New York *Herald Tribune*: "It is one of the few brilliantly conceived toccatas in the whole modern repertory."

The sonata was introduced in New York City on November 21, 1948, by Frederick Marvin.

1948 SYMPHONY NO. 6. I. Allegretto. II. Larghetto. III. Allegro molto.

Antheil's sixth and last symphony was heard first in San Francisco on February 10, 1949; Pierre Monteux conducted the San Francisco Symphony.

The first movement, in sonata form, was inspired by the Delacroix painting, *Liberty Leading the People*. To his music Antheil brought, as he explained, "the smoke of battle, courage, despair, and hope, all marching into the future." A three-measure theme, heard in the introduction and repeated there four times, recurs throughout the symphony. The first subject in the main body begins with a fleet and accented figure in eighth notes in strings and woodwind, and ends in a more relaxed mood in first trumpet. The second subject is given by flutes and violins. A horn solo over plucked strings brings on the development, which, for the most part, is spirited and martial and in which the second subject receives ample treatment. The recapitulation is only ten measures in all.

The Larghetto is in the song form, with a middle section of unconventional length. After four measures of introduction, the first melody is heard in the violins. A short coda leads into the middle section, which opens with sprightly matter repeated several times; a second theme is offered by flute, oboe and violins. The composer described this movement as having "the breath of autumn, of sadness, and of optimism, all at once."

The closing movement, a rondo, suggests "the triumph of joy and optimism over despair, war, and annihilation," the composer has explained. This music is, for the composer, the natural follow-up to the "courage and hope-against-hope mood of the first movement." The first theme is vigorous. Without much ado, it is followed by two more vivacious ideas, the first in bassoons and cellos (the first violins then treating the same subject canonically), and the second in the strings. In the development, fragments of all three themes are combined effectively. A reminder of the first theme of the opening movement, played contrapuntally against the finale's second theme, leads into the recapitulation in which the first theme of the opening movement and the first theme of the rondo are played in counterpoint. A coda, in rapid tempo, brings reminders of the three themes of the finale, with a fragment of the movement's first theme serving to bring the symphony to its conclusion.

1952 VOLPONE, opera in two acts, with text by Albert Perry based on Ben Jonson's play of the same name. First performance: Los Angeles, California, January 9, 1953.

The idea to make an opera from Ben Jonson's comedy, *Volpone,* haunted Antheil for fifteen years before he began to work on it in earnest in 1950. When the opera was first introduced (at the University of Southern California in Los Angeles) it ran for almost four hours. Its excessive length invited tedium. Both composer and librettist realized that the opera needed cutting. It was compressed into two acts, which now required only about two hours for performance. When the new version was given in New York in July of 1953, Howard Taubman in *The New York Times* found that the plot was "first rate for a comic opera" and that the "current version is effective dramatically." He did, however, object to the light musical-comedy style of Antheil's music, which he felt robbed the work of "something of its sting."

The Ben Jonson play, on which the opera was loosely based, had for its central character a wily, avaricious Venetian nobleman dubbed "the fox." He goes into league with his servant Mosca to defraud his neighbors. By spreading the rumor that his master is dying, Mosca manages to get lavish gifts from the neighbors who hope thereby to gain recognition in the old man's will. Only after Mosca has tried to outwit his own master do the neighbors discover from Volpone himself of the way in which they had been duped.

"The music," wrote Albert Goldberg in a review for *Musical America,* "runs a gamut of style including a number of waltzes *à la Rosenkavalier,* but some of the arias and ensembles were extremely effective. The orchestration was remarkably diverse and the so-called 'extended recitativo' permitted the text to be clearly enunciated."

KURT ATTERBERG 1887–

Though his name does not often appear on American concert programs, Kurt Atterberg is one of Sweden's major living composers. Probably no other Swedish composer of the twentieth century has been so extensively published, performed and admired in his own country. Like his compatriot, Hugo Alfvén, Atterberg belongs with the more conservative men who prefer self-expression to innovation. He fills classical, well-disciplined structures with music that is romantic, though the romanticism is Nordic in its restraint. He achieves beauty with subdued colors and tight-lipped feelings, force through understatement. In such a vein do we find some of his later symphonies; the opera, *The Tempest,* introduced in Stockholm on September 19, 1949; the Cello Concerto, which Emmanuel Feuermann played in Berlin in 1923; and the Concerto for Violin and Cello (or Viola) and Orchestra, whose première took place in Stockholm in 1961.

Several of Atterberg's works have drawn their materials from Swedish folk music. Among these will be found the two compositions that have become most popular outside Sweden: the Fourth Symphony, and *A Värmland Rhapsody.*

Atterberg was born in Gothenburg, Sweden, on December 12, 1887. He was trained to be a civil engineer, but he combined engineering studies with musical pursuits. For eight months, between 1910 and 1911, he attended the Stockholm Royal Conservatory, a pupil of Andreas Hallén. A government subsidy then enabled him to travel to Germany for further music study with Max von Schillings and for the absorption of musical experiences.

While employed in the Royal Patent Office in Stockholm for over a quarter of a century, until 1940, Atterberg occupied himself with varied musical activities. He was a conductor at the Royal Dramatic Theatre from 1913 to 1922, music critic of the Stockholm *Tidningen* from 1919 to 1957, and a member of the Royal Academy of Music from 1940 to 1953.

In 1928, Atterberg was subjected to a good deal of publicity and unfavorable criticism. At that time his Sixth Symphony won the first prize of $10,000 in a worldwide competition among composers to honor the centenary of Franz Schubert's death, sponsored by the Columbia Phonograph Company. This symphony was introduced in Cologne, Germany, on October 15, 1928, Hermann Abendroth conducting. After that, it was played by major symphony orchestras the world over. Some critics took the work severely to task for its derivations, or "borrowings," from other composers. Ernest Newman suspected, in the Sunday *Times,* that Atterberg had deliberately appropriated the material of others to cater to the individual tastes of the members of the jury who had had given him the prize. Atterberg answered these charges by insisting that nothing in his symphony was quoted or borrowed—except for a passage in the finale movement, purposely taken from a Schubert string quintet to pay homage to that master. This issue, bitterly fought over pro and con, placed a cloud over Atterberg's reputation—but only temporarily. The tremendous success of *A Värmland Rhapsody,* in 1933, followed by a high level of creativity in his later compositions, have thrown this controversy into a welcome and now permanent obscurity.

1918 SYMPHONY NO. 4 IN G MINOR (SINFONIA PICCOLA), op. 14. I. Con forza. II. Andante. III. Scherzo. IV. Finale.

This "little" symphony, as Atterberg described it, freely utilized thematic material derived from Swedish folk music. The two basic themes of the first movement (the first played, beginning in the third measure, by the first violins and violas; the second, by the oboe) have a distinct folk-song character. A fermata leads to a beautiful slow movement in which a poignant melody for the clarinet is later subjected to variation. A gay dance tune, played by the first violins, sets the mood for the brief Scherzo. The finale is a spirited rondo vitalized by dance rhythms.

The Fourth Symphony was introduced in Stockholm in March, 1919.

1933 A VÄRMLAND RHAPSODY (VÄRMLANDSRHAPSODI), for orchestra, op. 36.

Atterberg wrote this rhapsody to honor the seventy-fifth birthday of Sweden's celebrated novelist, Selma Lagerlöf. For his musical ideas he went to the folk music indigenous to Värmland, the locale of Lagerlöf's masterpiece, *Gösta Berling's Saga.*

The work opens with a slow introduction. After a melody for violins, the tempo accelerates, then slackens; an eloquent melody for solo flute is now heard. The main section of the rhapsody then unfolds; the materials are two folk themes, the first played by the first violins, the second by the clarinet. After a climax is reached, the rhapsody ends with a soft, contemplative coda.

The Rhapsody was first heard over the Swedish Radio in Stockholm on November 20, 1933.

GEORGES AURIC 1899–

Of the six composers who had once been grouped under the convenient label of "The French Six" or "Les Six," only Georges Auric has more or less remained true to the approaches and style which first made the music of this group so popular and provocative in the early 1920s.

"The French Six" was an immediate outgrowth of a group of young French composers who called themselves "Nouveaux Jeunes." Its members were Germaine Tailleferre, Georges Auric, Roland-Manuel, Arthur Honegger and Francis Poulenc—a concert of whose works was given in Paris on January 15, 1918. "Nouveaux Jeunes" became "Les Six" by the elimination of Roland-Manuel and the inclusion of Darius Milhaud and Louis Durey.

Actually, "The French Six" was not a "school" in the accepted sense of the term—that is, a number of composers united by the same ideals and artistic purpose working together to achieve a single goal. And its birth was not due to the efforts of the composers themselves, but rather was the brainchild of a French critic. Reviewing an album of piano pieces by Tailleferre, Milhaud, Honegger, Poulenc, Durey and Auric, Henri Collet (in an article published in *Comoedia* on January 16, 1920) compared these composers to the earlier and more famous Russian nationalist school, "The Five." This was in spite of the fact that no similarity existed between these two groups. "The six Frenchmen," wrote Collet, "have by magnificent and voluntary return to simplicity brought about a renaissance of French music, because they understood the lesson of Erik Satie." One week after that, Collet once again discussed favorably the work of the six young French composers in *Comoedia,* and once again baptized them "The French Six." The label stuck to these six composers for a number of years, even though the men had little in common and tried their best to disassociate themselves from each other.

But there *was* a unanimity of style and purpose in some of the works of all six composers in the early 1920s. All six were influenced by Erik Satie, not only by his wit and whimsy, by his economy and simplicity, by his unorthodox techniques and iconoclasm, but also by his goal to create an "everyday music" for everyday people, a music stripped of grandiose pretensions and ivory-tower seclusion, a music that was plebian and down-to-earth. The members of "The Six" all wrote music with a light touch within slight structures; and many of them, like Satie, found their materials in popular music-hall tunes and in American ragtime and jazz.

Auric, for example, wrote a fox-trot for piano entitled *Adieu New York* (1920). In a similarly popular style, he wrote an orchestral overture, *The Fourteenth of July* (1921), and music for a ballet in a more or less popular idiom, *Les Mariés de la Tour Eiffel* (1921), whose score was a collaborative effort on the part of five of "The Six." Auric's ballet, *Les Matelots,* in 1925 was not only the finest and the most successful music he had written up to this time, but also the first full realization of his creative identity.

After this, Auric continued writing music for ballets which—however much they might increase in technical know-how and sophistication—nevertheless were extensions of the style he had crystallized in *Les Matelots.* These ballets included *La Pastorale* (1926), *Les Enchantements d'Alcine* (1929), *La Concurrence* (1932), *Les Imaginaires* (1934), *Phèdre* (1950), *Coup de Feu* (1952), and *Bal des Voleurs* (1959). He also wrote a good deal of music for the films, English produced as well as French, beginning with the René Clair motion-picture success, *À Nous la Liberté* in 1931. His most successful film score was for *Moulin Rouge,* the screen biography of Toulouse-Lautrec in 1952, out of which came the hit song "Where Is Your Heart?" (or "The Song from *Moulin Rouge*").

Auric was born in Lodève, France, on February 15, 1899. Between his twelfth and sixteenth years, he wrote about three hundred compositions—mostly songs and piano pieces; *Interludes,* a cycle of three songs, was performed at a concert of the Société Nationale in Paris when he was fifteen. Meanwhile, he had begun formal study at the Paris Conservatory, continuing it later with Vincent d'Indy and Albert Roussel at the Schola Cantorum. His first ballet score, *Les Noces de Gamache,* was written in 1917. Less than a year later, he became identified with four other young French composers as "Nouveaux Jeunes," when their compositions were performed at a concert at the Vieux Colombier. He achieved further recognition in 1920 when the critic Henri Collet banded him with five other young French composers under the nomenclature of "The French Six" or "Les Six."

Like the other five members of "The Six," Auric became interested in "everyday music," a vein which he tapped for his first important scores, all of them for ballets, the most significant being *Les Matelots,* in 1925. Auric continued writing music for ballet, and after 1931, he combined this activity with the creation of music for motion pictures. He also wrote some chamber, choral and piano music, an opera, some smaller pieces for orchestra and many songs. Between 1962 and 1967 he was the artistic director of the Paris Opéra and Opéra-Comique.

1925 LES MATELOTS (THE SAILORS), ballet in five scenes, with scenario by Boris Kochno and choreography by Léonide Massine. First performance: Ballet Russe de Monte Carlo, Paris, June 17, 1925.

The plot of Auric's most famous ballet reminds one, on the one hand, of Mozart's *Così fan tutte*, and, on the other, of the Jerome Robbins–Leonard

Bernstein ballet, *Fancy Free*. The setting is the dockside at Marseilles, France. Three sailors, on the eve of embarking on a long sea journey, visit a young girl, who becomes engaged to one of them. When the sailors return to Marseilles, they assume disguises to test the girl's fidelity. When every attempt to arouse her interest fails, the sailors remove their disguises and the lovers fall into each other's arms.

One of the most poignant scenes in the ballet—and one of the finest moments in Auric's score—comes in the second scene. The young girl, left alone, performs a solitary dance in which she expresses her longing for her absent lover. Auric's music here is built around a woodwind tune, which in its simplicity and poignancy is reminiscent of a French music-hall ballad.

Serge Lifar, appearing as one of the sailors, made his first appearance in a leading role in this ballet upon its première. *Les Matelots* was given for the first time in the United States on March 9, 1934, during a visit by the Ballet Russe to New York.

SAMUEL BARBER 1910–

Of Barber's many admirable qualities—his fine sense of musical design; the economy of his means; the inexorable logic of his thinking—the most significant perhaps is his highly developed lyricism. He has the gift of writing sustained melodies that flow easily and have a high degree of expressiveness. This melodic gift became evident with his earliest efforts: the two songs he wrote when he was about eighteen, "The Daisies," op. 2, no. 1, and "With Rue My Heart Is Laden," op. 2, no. 2; *Dover Beach,* for baritone and string quartet, which came three years later; the eloquent *Adagio for Strings,* and *Essay No. 1,* for orchestra, with which he first established his reputation in 1936 and 1937. As his talent ripened, he added poetic feeling to lyricism. And after that, while a growing intensity and strength of idiom entered his writing, his lyricism remained on a high plane of eloquence, the emotional factor rarely being sacrificed. "His work as a whole," says Nathan Broder, "is like a living organism with a clearly stamped individuality, enriching itself as it grows."

Barber was born in West Chester, Pennsylvania, on March 9, 1910. Precocious in music, he was filling a post as organist when he was only twelve years old. His musical education took place principally at the then newly founded Curtis Institute of Music in Philadelphia with Rosario Scalero (composition), Isabelle Vengerova (piano), and Emilio de Gogorza (voice). In his eighteenth year, he began composing seriously. When he was twenty-three, one of his orchestral works was performed by the Philadelphia Orchestra—the *Overture to the School for Scandal.*

Between 1935 and 1937, he won the Pulitzer Fellowship and the American Prix de Rome. In Rome, he wrote his first symphony, which was introduced there, and then was heard at the Salzburg Festival. Soon after returning to the United States, he became a member of the faculty of the Curtis Institute, where he taught orchestration and composition. He achieved additional prominence as a composer by becoming the first American to be performed by Arturo Toscanini and the NBC Symphony; on that occasion, the *Adagio for Strings* and *Essay No. 1* were introduced. During World War II, Barber served in the Army Air Corps, which commissioned him to write his Second Symphony. After the war, Barber lived in comparative seclusion at "Capricorn," a home near Mt. Kisco, which he shared with Gian Carlo Menotti. There most of his post-World War II works were written. In 1958 and 1963, he received the Pulitzer Prize in music—for the opera *Vanessa* in 1958, and for his Piano Concerto, in 1963. In 1959, he was given an honorary doctorate from Harvard University. For several years, he served as vice-president of the International Music Council of UNESCO in Paris. The world première of his opera *Antony and Cleopatra* opened the new auditorium of the Metropolitan Opera Association at the Lincoln Center for the Performing Arts on September 16, 1966.

1927–1953 SONGS, for voice and piano.

"Bessie Bobtail," op. 2, no. 3; "Daisies," op. 2, no. 1; "I Hear an Army," op. 10, no. 3; "Monks and Raisins," op. 18, no. 2; "Nuvoletta," op. 25; "The Queen's Face on the Summery Coin," op. 18, no. 1; "Rain Has Fallen," op. 10, no. 1; "Sleep Now," op. 10, no. 2; "With Rue My Heart Is Laden," op. 2, no. 2.

Hermit Songs, cycle of songs for voice and piano, op. 29, no. 1: 1. At Saint Patrick's Purgatory; 2. Church Bell at Night; 3. St. Ita's Vision; 4. The Heavenly Banquet; 5. The Crucifixion; 6. Sea-Santch; 7. Promiscuity; 8. The Monk and His Cat; 9. The Praises of God; 10. The Desire for Hermitage.

As the nephew of Louise Homer, the celebrated contralto, Samuel Barber came into contact with and learned to appreciate great singers and great songs at an early age. Subsequently, he himself studied voice and even gave Lieder recitals. His professional career as singer is now well behind him; but as a composer, Barber never quite gave up "singing"—particularly within the song form. He revealed his talent for song early, when, between 1927 and 1928, he issued a set of three songs (op. 2) comprising "Daisies" (James Stephens), "With Rue My Heart Is Laden" (A. E. Housman), and "Bessie Bobtail" (Stephens). Here, as later, Barber disclosed a partiality for the voice. He knows its potential and its limitations; he is able to make it a supple and effective instrument; and he revealed a natural bent for expressive lyricism.

Opus 3, while essentially instrumental, also emphasized the voice. This was Barber's first work in a form larger than the song. It was called *Dover Beach,* based on Matthew Arnold, scored for baritone and string quartet (or string orchestra). It was introduced in New York on March 5, 1933, by Rose Bampton and the New York String Quartet.

Three songs set to poems from James Joyce's *Chamber Music* followed, collected in op. 10 (1936). Here, as earlier, the Romanticism often springs from Brahms. "They reveal," says Robert Horan of these early songs, "an intimate, sensuous quality not always found in his larger works." James Hust Hall, however, finds that Barber's lyricism here "feeds on other than sugar and water"; he senses, for example, a "bitter strength" in "Bessie Bobtail," and an "overpowering drive and anguish" in "I Hear an Army."

Beginning with the 1940s—with songs like "The Queen's Face on the Summery Coin," text by Robert Horan (1942), "Monks and Raisins," text by José Garcia Villa (1943), and continuing through "Nuvoletta," text by Joyce (1947), as well as with the song cycle *Hermit Songs* to texts by anonymous Irish monks and scholars between the years 700 and 1300 (1952–1953)—Barber's lyricism is married to "Stravinskyan concepts," Hans Nathan notes. "Relinquishing the sweep of traditional cantability, it now relies on brief equal note values and adjacent pitches, and for its continuity, on the repetition of note patterns . . . with distinct shifting accentuations."

1933 COMPOSITIONS FOR ORCHESTRA:
Overture to the School for Scandal, op. 5.
Music for a Scene from Shelley, op. 7.

Barber's first two works for orchestra are by no means apprentice pieces, but compositions of uncommon talent and charm that first brought the young composer deserved praise and recognition.

The overture was introduced at the Robin Hood Dell in Philadelphia on August 30, 1933; it was the recipient of the Bearns Prize. While the music seeks to capture some of the mirth and gaiety of Richard Brinsley Sheridan's comedy, it singles out no episode or character for detailed programmatic treatment. The overture begins energetically in the entire orchestra to set the stage for a charming melody in first violins (Allegro molto e vivace). After this idea has been elaborated upon, we hear a haunting episode for solo oboe (Poco meno del tempo primo), followed by an equally effective theme for solo clarinet. Then the overture rushes to its conclusion with unbridled energy and gaiety.

Music for a Scene from Shelley was heard for the first time on March 24, 1935, Werner Janssen conducting the New York Philharmonic Orchestra. Barber's inspiration was Shelley's *Prometheus Unbound.* The composer explains: "The lines in Act II, Scene 5 (quoted on the title page of the score), where Shelley indicates music, suggested the composition. It is really incidental music for this particular scene, and has nothing at all to do with the figure of Prometheus." The quotation referred to above was spoken by Pantea to Asia:

> . . . Nor is it I alone
> Thy sister, thy companion, thine own chosen ear,
> But the whole world which seeks thy sympathy,
> Hearest thou not sounds i' the air which speak the love
> Of all articulate beings? Feelest thou not
> The inanimate winds enamored of thee?
> List! (*Music*).

Muted violins and violas project an atmosphere of mystery to which muted horns provide an ominous phrase in descending harmonies. After the colors have been enriched, and the mood has been dramatized, strings arrive with a new theme in octaves. An impressive climax is built up. The composition ends in the same air of mystery with which it began.

1936 SYMPHONY NO. 1, op. 9.

While Barber was in Rome on the American Prix de Rome, he wrote the *Symphony in One Movement*. On December 13, 1936, it was introduced in Rome by the Augusteo Orchestra, Bernardino Molinari conducting. After Artur Rodzinski had introduced this work to Cleveland on January 21, 1937, he conducted it successfully at the Salzburg Festival on July 25, 1937, the first time an American was represented there.

Barber revised his symphony in 1942. This new version was first heard on February 8, 1944, with Bruno Walter conducting the Philadelphia Orchestra.

The composer explained that the form of the symphony is "a synthetic treatment of the four-movement classical symphony. It is based on three themes of the initial Allegro non troppo, which retain throughout the work their fundamental character. . . . After a brief development of the three themes . . . the first theme in diminution, forms the basis of a Scherzo section (Vivace). The second theme (oboe over muted strings) then appears in augmentation in an extended Andante tranquillo. An intense crescendo introduces the finale, which is a short passacaglia based on the first theme (introduced by the violoncelli and contrabassi), over which, together with figures from other themes, the closing theme is woven, thus serving as a recapitulation for the entire symphony."

1937 ADAGIO FOR STRINGS, op. 11.

One of Barber's most popular works for the orchestra, the *Adagio for Strings*, originated as the slow movement of a string quartet (B minor); it was then transcribed by the composer for string orchestra. The latter version was introduced by the NBC Symphony under Arturo Toscanini on November 5, 1938. The music is built on a single melodic idea, heard immediately in the first violins. Then other groups of instruments take it over, treat it canonically, and finally carry it on to a compelling climax. The work subsides into the serenity with which it opened.

1937–1942 ESSAYS NOS. 1 and 2, for orchestra, opp. 12 and 17.

Barber's choice of a literary rather than a musical form for these two short orchestral works is significant. Each composition bears a strong resemblance to an essay in that a thought is projected in the beginning, and then is allowed to develop to a logical conclusion in the way a central thought is elaborated by an essayist.

The first *Essay* is somewhat slighter in texture than the second. It is a Scherzo, comprising a series of simple themes (Andante sostenuto, Allegro molto, Scherzando) which are allowed freedom to develop along rather slight dimensions. The quiet mood established by the opening subject is restored at the close of the work, which ends in a questioning attitude. Midway there is a vigorous martial subject for the horns.

The second *Essay* has more proportion and stature. The three themes (the first announced by a solo flute; the second by the violas; the third by the brass) are developed dexterously in a fugal section reaching a dramatic climax. A repetition of the main theme, fortissimo, is followed by a coda in which the third theme is suggested by the basses.

The first Essay was introduced by the NBC Symphony under Toscanini on November 5, 1938. The second Essay was first heard on April 16, 1942, in a performance by the New York Philharmonic Orchestra under Bruno Walter.

1940 CONCERTO FOR VIOLIN AND ORCHESTRA, op. 14. I. Allegro molto moderato. II. Andante sostenuto. III. Presto, in moto perpetuo.

Barber completed his concerto in July of 1940, while vacationing at Pocono Lake Preserve in Pennsylvania. It was introduced on February 7, 1941, by Albert Spalding and the Philadelphia Orchestra, Eugene Ormandy conducting. A flowing melodic thought for the solo violin is heard without preliminaries. A second subject, more sprightly in character, is introduced by the clarinet. When the solo violin takes it over, it embellishes it. A free fantasia rather than the usual development follows; but the recapitulation is given a formal presentation. A recitative for violin replaces the traditional cadenza. The movement ends with a brief recollection by the clarinet of the opening theme.

An extended oboe solo opens the slow movement. A contrasting rhapsodic theme is then assigned to the solo violin, following which it repeats the opening melody. The finale is in the style of a perpetual motion, its main figure heard first in unaccompanied tympani, then taken over by the solo violin.

1944 SYMPHONY NO. 2, op. 19. I. Allegro ma non troppo. II. Andante un poco mosso. III. Presto; Allegro risoluto; Allegro molto.

During World War II, Barber was a corporal in the Army Air Corps. There, on a commission from the Air Corps, he wrote his Second Symphony. In its original version, the program of the symphony gave every indication of having been inspired by, and written as a tribute to, the Air Force. In the second movement, for example, a climactic moment is suddenly interrupted by the voice of an electric instrument (manufactured expressly for this composition) to simulate the sound of a radio beam giving a code message to a pilot, instructing him on his course when he is flying "blind." Actually, this "theme" is given considerable prominence throughout the movement, being taken up rhythmically by the other instruments in projecting code signals.

The original version of this symphony was introduced by the Boston Symphony under Serge Koussevitzky on March 3, 1944. One week later, it was transmitted by shortwave throughout the world by the Office of War Information.

In 1947, Barber revised his symphony extensively, eliminating all programmatic intentions, and emphasizing the symphony's appeal as absolute music. The revised version was heard for the first time on January 21, 1948, with Eugene Ormandy conducting the Philadelphia Orchestra.

This symphony represents a departure from Barber's earlier preoccupation with the lyric element. Its dynamic power, rather than melodic content, is its principal attraction, though welcome contrasts of lyricism are provided. The first movement is in sonata form. "The intensely emotional opening movement," explained Max de Schauensee in his review in the Philadelphia *Evening Bulletin,* "with its smashing climaxes has a feeling of protest throughout its span." The second movement has a nocturnal character. "The affecting song of the strings and woodwind," says Mr. Schauensee, "bears the imprint of resignation." The finale opens with what the composer described as "introductory spiral-like figures" that lead to variations and to a fugato on an Allegro risoluto theme. "Mr. Barber has selected vigorous, insistent rhythms for his final section," concludes Mr. Schauensee, "and the massive climax is sincere and affecting."

1945 CONCERTO FOR CELLO AND ORCHESTRA, op. 22. I. Allegro moderato. II. Andante molto sostenuto. III. Molto allegro e appassionato.

On April 5, 1946, this concerto was introduced in Boston by Raya Garbousova and the Boston Symphony under Serge Koussevitzky. The New York Music Critics Circle singled it out as the most important new American work of the season.

The main theme of the first movement is heard on the English horn after two introductory measures, and is later taken up by the solo instrument. A second subject is also shared between orchestra (the strings) and the cello. Following a cadenza for the cello, the original material returns, and the movement ends with the two opening measures.

The slow movement is given up almost entirely to a sustained song, which begins after a single introductory bar and which engages the attention of both the orchestra and the cello. Brilliant material appears in the closing movement, which has particularly effective virtuoso passages for the cello. But the movement does not concern itself exclusively with virtuosity; one of its finest pages is an emotional passage chanted by the cello.

1946 MEDEA (CAVE OF THE HEART), op. 23, ballet, with choreography by Martha Graham. First performance: New York, May 10, 1946, under the title, *Serpent of the Heart.*

MEDEA, ballet suite for orchestra. I. Parados—Choros. II. Medea and Jason—The Young Princess. III. Jason—Choros—Medea—Kantikos Agonias—Exodos.

MEDEA'S MEDITATION AND DANCE OF VENGEANCE, for orchestra, op. 23a.

This ballet score was commissioned by the Ditson Fund of Columbia University for Martha Graham. The subject of Medea and Jason was chosen, but (as the composer has explained) "neither Miss Graham nor the composer wished to use the Medea-Jason legend literally. These mythical characters served rather to project psychological states of jealousy and vengeance which are timeless."

The composer wrote further about this work:

"The choreography and the music were conceived, as it were, on two levels, the ancient mythical and the contemporary. Medea and Jason first appear as godlike, superhuman figures of the Greek tragedy. As the tension and conflict between them increase, they step out of their legendary roles from time to time to become the modern man and woman, caught in the nets of jealousy and destructive love; and at the end reassume their mythical quality. In both the dancing and the music, archaic and contemporary idioms are used. Medea, in her final scene after the denouement, becomes once more the descendant of the sun."

Martha Graham and her group introduced the ballet at Columbia University under the title of *Serpent of the Heart*. After the ballet had been revised, it was renamed *Cave of the Heart* and given that way on February 27, 1947. Barber himself preferred *Medea* as a title. When, therefore, he prepared an orchestral suite drawn from the ballet score, in 1947, the work bore the preferred and now definitive title. The *Medea* Suite was introduced by the Philadelphia Orchestra under Eugene Ormandy on December 5, 1947.

"The suite follows roughly the form of a Greek tragedy," the composer explains. "In the Parados the characters first appear. The Choros, lyric and reflective, comments on the action which is to unfold. The Young Princess appears in a dance of freshness and innocence, followed by a heroic dance of Jason. Another plaintive Choros leads to Medea's dance of vengeance. Driven by mad jealousy, she rushes off the stage. The Kantikos Agonias, of menace and foreboding, is interrupted by her return. Her terrible crime, the murder of the Princess, and her own children, has been committed, announced by a violent fanfare of trumpets. In the Exodos, the various themes of the chief characters of the work are blended together; little by little the music subsides and Medea and Jason recede into the legendary past."

In 1955, Barber revised and rescored for full orchestra one section of the suite. Entitled *Medea's Meditation and Dance of Vengeance,* this excerpt was introduced by the New York Philharmonic under Mitropoulos on February 2, 1956. This episode, says Barber, "is directly related to the central character in Medea, tracing her emotions from her tender feelings towards her children, through the mounting suspicions and her decision to avenge herself. The piece increases in intensity to close in the frenzied Dance of Vengeance of Medea, the Sorceress, descended from the Sun God."

1947 KNOXVILLE: SUMMER OF 1915, for soprano and orchestra, op. 24.

This is a setting of a poem by James Agee, a motto from which appears under the title of the manuscript reading: "We are talking now of summer evenings in Knoxville, Tennessee, in the time that I lived there so successfully disguised to myself as a child." Barber completed his score on April 4, 1947. Its première took place on April 9, 1948, with Eleanor Steber as soprano soloist, and Serge Koussevitzky conducting the Boston Symphony. The composition is dedicated to the memory of Barber's father.

James Agee's poem describes the observations and memories of a child in an American town. The Barber setting is in four sections, played without interruption: Andante un poco mosso; Allegro agitato; Allegretto; and Maestoso.

"An initial motive," explains Hans Nathan, "provides musical and psychological unity. It carries as well a variety of meanings: it suggests the patter of the child; it indicates . . . the restfulness of the hour. . .; and like a fragment of a folk tune, evokes the locale. . . . The motive then transforms itself easily into what seems to be a recognizable melody (reminiscent of the music of the Southern Appalachian Mountains) but the prattling character of the story remains."

1949 SONATA IN E-FLAT MINOR, for piano, op. 26. I. Allegro energico. II. Allegro vivace e leggero. III. Adagio mesto. IV. Fuga.

Barber's piano sonata is one of his most important works. He wrote it on a commission from the League of Composers with funds provided by Richard Rodgers and Irving Berlin. It was introduced in New York City by Vladimir Horowitz on January 23, 1950.

In a modern idiom which has harmonic and rhythmic robustness, physical strength is combined with a fine-grained lyrical expression. This music, as Harriet Johnson remarked in her review in the *New York Post,* "encompasses realism and fantasy, conflict and resolution, poetry and power." Energy is set loose in the opening movement, whose interest is largely rhythmic. The third movement has poignancy and pathos: feelings deeply felt are voiced in expressive lyricism. The sonata closes with a monumentally conceived fugue, within whose formal construction majesty and grandeur find expression.

1954 PRAYERS OF KIERKEGAARD, for soprano solo, mixed chorus and orchestra, op. 30.

The text for this major choral work, which has the dimensions of an oratorio, was derived from various writings by the nineteenth-century Danish philosopher and theologian, Sören Aabye Kierkegaard: from his *Journals,* from *The Unchangeableness of God,* and from *The Christian Discourses*. In main, this text speaks of the infinity of God and His Love and of the yearning of Man to be at one with this Infinity and to be forgiven for his sins.

Describing Barber's music, Olin Downes wrote in the *New York Times:* "The unrhythmical and free-metered recitation in carefully shaped recitative has the flavor of the plainchant, reshaped, freely recast in forms of our own modern consciousness. Sometimes the music becomes nearly barbaric, and intensely dramatic in effect. Polytonality is used freely, logically, with destination." Mr. Downes then added: "The instrumentation is extremely dramatic. The final chord is no imitation of a Lutheran form, any more than the choral recitative comes from a Catholic direction. Universality is the suggestion, a universality that does not dismiss but includes inevitably the consciousness of the infinite mercy, the infinite tenderness, the cosmic design."

Prayers of Kierkegaard was introduced on December 3, 1954, Charles Munch conducting the Boston Symphony; Leontyne Price was the soprano soloist, and the orchestra was supplemented by the Cecilia Society.

1958 VANESSA, opera in four acts, op. 32, with text by Gian Carlo Menotti. First performance: Metropolitan Opera, New York, January 15, 1958.

Vanessa is Samuel Barber's first opera. Fruit of his full maturity, it is one of the most significant American operas of our time and one of its composer's major achievements. When it was first produced, Menotti served as stage director, while Cecil Beaton designed the sets and costumes; Dimitri Mitropoulos conducted.

Vanessa made Metropolitan Opera history on several counts. It became the first world première during the regime of Rudolf Bing, and the first new American opera mounted at the Metropolitan in eleven years; it became the second American opera given at the Metropolitan for three seasons (the first two in 1957–1958 and 1958–1959, the third in 1964–1965). *Vanessa* was also the first American opera ever given at the Salzburg Festival, where it made its European bow in 1958.

The setting is a Scandinavian city in 1905. In her funereal baronial manor, Vanessa has waited twenty years for the return of her lover. He is dead; but his son, Anatol, returns. Anatol seduces Vanessa's niece, Erika, offers to marry her, but is turned down because Erika knows he does not love her. Anatol finally marries Vanessa and takes her away with him. Now it is Erika's turn to inhabit the gloomy baronial manor and wait for her lover.

To his music, Barber brought not only his earlier command of writing for the voice and the breadth and dimension of his symphonic writing, but also a remarkable dramatic strength and a rare gift at projecting atmosphere and subtle moods. His style is eclectic, ranging from the sentimentality of a Puccini aria to the dissonances and atonality of an avant-garde composer; from the lilting music of the waltz and a country dance to the symphonic grandeur of a Wagner or Richard Strauss music drama. But the music always meets the demands of the text; and the result is an opera that has profound emotional impact without sacrificing the melodic and emotional values of Romantic opera.

One of the most memorable vocal pages in the score is the first-act waltz of the Old Doctor, "Under the Willow Tree"; it has become popular at song recitals. Equally distinguished is Erika's first-act air, "Must the Winter Come So Soon?"; the affecting song of Vanessa in the second act, "Our Arms Entwined"; the lyrical orchestral intermezzo (formerly in the fourth act, now a part of the third), which is sometimes heard at symphony concerts; and the five-voice fugue, which comes at the close of the opera, "To Leave, To Break, To Find, To Keep."

1960 DIE NATALI, chorale preludes for orchestra, op. 37.

Barber wrote these orchestral Christmas chorale preludes to honor the 75th anniversary of the Boston Symphony, which introduced them on December 22, 1960, Charles Munch conducting. The score is dedicated to the memory of Serge and Natalie Koussevitzky.

The title *Die Natali* is Latin for "Christmastide." Utilizing such contrapuntal devices as canon, double canon, and so forth, Barber developed his chorale preludes from celebrated Christmas carols. First, we hear "O Come, O Come, Emmanuel" in strings and brass; then, "Lo, How a Rose E'er Blooming" in strings and brass antiphonally, followed by three variations. When "We Three Kings of Orient Are" is heard, each of the kings is represented by a different prelude: the Caspar prelude heard in the bass clarinet; that of Melchior, in bassoon; that of Balthazar, in tuba. A rhythmic variation of "God Rest Ye Merry Gentlemen" is set against "Good King Wenceslas." "Silent Night" precedes the return of "O Come, Emmanuel." An ostinato crescendo based on two phrases of "Adeste Fideles" brings on "Joy to the World." The composition ends serenely with a recall of "Silent Night."

1962 CONCERTO FOR PIANO AND ORCHESTRA, op. 38. I. Allegro appassionato. II. Canzona. III. Allegro molto.

The publishing house of G. Schirmer commissioned Barber to write the piano concerto (his first such work) to celebrate the centenary of its founding. The world première took place on September 24, 1962, during the opening week festivities of the Lincoln Center for the Performing Arts at Philharmonic Hall, New York. John Browning was the soloist, and the Boston Symphony was directed by Erich Leinsdorf. In 1963, this concerto brought its composer the Pulitzer Prize in music for the second time in five years. During the late Spring of 1965, the concerto was featured prominently by the Cleveland Orchestra during its extensive tour of Europe; John Browning once again was the soloist, while the conductor was George Szell.

Three figures are introduced in the first-movement opening recitative of the solo piano. The first is declamatory, the second and third, rhythmic. When the orchestra intrudes, it brings sensual melody. This material is discussed before the oboe appears with a lyrical second subject (doppio meno mosso). An expansive development precedes the cadenza and recapitulation. In the second movement, a song is presented by the flute, then by the solo piano, and after that by muted strings. Several loud chords for orchestra bring on the finale, where an ostinato bass figure for the piano is used as the background for several themes. Two contrasting sections follow, one for clarinet solo (un pochettino meno), and the other for three flutes, muted trombones and harp (con grazia). But the ostinato figure keeps coming back, mainly in the piano.

1962 ANDROMACHE'S FAREWELL, for soprano and orchestra, op. 39.

The literary source of this moving work is, of course, Euripides's bitter indictment of war, *The Trojan Women*—specifically, that climactic moment in the drama when Andromache bids a poignant farewell to her son, Astyanax, who is doomed to die at the hands of the Greeks. An orchestral introduction presents the two main themes. The first is later connected with Andromache's heartrending resignation, in "So you must die, my son" (in John Patrick Creagh's new translation); the other is associated with Andromache's words, "He cannot come from the grave, nor any of his princes." A third theme, undulating in character, first heard in the orchestra, is later associated with the words "Oh dearest embrace, sweet breathing of your body." The composition ends with a return of the opening section, with modifications and alterations; its principal theme, stated loudly by the orchestra, serves to bring the work to a majestic conclusion.

Andromache's Farewell was commissioned by the New York Philharmonic Orchestra to celebrate its opening season at the Lincoln Center for the Performing Arts. It was introduced by that orchestra on April 4, 1963, with Thomas Schippers conducting, and Martina Arroyo, soprano.

1966 ANTONY AND CLEOPATRA, opera in three acts, with text by Franco Zeffirelli based on Shakespeare's drama. First performance: Metropolitan Opera, New York, September 16, 1966.

When the building of a new opera house for the Metropolitan Opera at the Lincoln Center for the Performing Arts became a reality, its general manager, Rudolf Bing, commissioned Barber to write an opera to open the theatre. Barber long hesitated before accepting. He finally gave an affirmative answer "only because I realized that none of my friends would talk to me anymore if I didn't," he confessed. Another thing led him to undertake the assignment: he had found a subject to excite and inspire him, Shakespeare's *Antony and Cleopatra.*

The job of reworking the Shakespeare drama into a functional libretto fell to Franco Zeffirelli (who had been engaged to stage and design the production). While keeping most of Shakespeare's lines intact, Zeffirelli took considerable liberties with the Shakespeare drama by rearranging scenes and episodes. Once Zeffirelli had finished writing his text, Barber went into monastic seclusion at his home in Mt. Kisco to work on his opera. He planned a work far different from *Vanessa. Vanessa* had been an intimate opera, rich in psychological probings, characterization and atmosphere. *Antony and Cleopatra*—to fit the gala occasion for which it was written—would be a grand opera in every sense of the term, with spectacular staging and costuming, with ballet and dramatic choral passages.

The opera was presented before a brilliant audience including leaders in American cultural, political and social life on September 16, 1966, this première coinciding with the opening of the new and magnificent auditorium that henceforth would serve as the home of the Metropolitan Opera. Leontyne Price was Cleopatra; Justino Diaz was Antony; Thomas Schippers conducted.

In his staging and costuming, Zeffirelli pulled out all the stops. He offered a lavish production calculated to stun the eye. But most of the critics found that he had been too pretentious to be effective, overdressing both stage and characters, and resorting to all kinds of stage tricks and devices, many of which failed to come off successfully. Harold C. Schonberg went so far as to describe Zeffirelli's stage effects in *The New York Times* as "so naive, so innocent, so delightfully childish, so unselfconsciously exhibitionistic—and, it must be confessed, sometimes so vulgar: artifice masquerading with a great flourish as art."

Most of the critical response to Barber's music felt that it played second fiddle to the staging. Some parts of the score were praised: the opening chorus of the opera (heard without the preliminaries of an overture or prelude), the vital and cogent ballet music in the first act, the suicide of Cleopatra and the lament of the people which closed the opera. But the high points were few and far between; melodic interest was at a minimum; and the overall determination to put on a good show, for ear as well as eye, frequently invited tedium. "Almost everything about the evening, artistically speaking, failed in total impact," was Schonberg's final judgment. "Good intentions cannot compensate for questionable taste and judgment."

BÉLA BARTÓK 1881–1945

Béla Bartók first became interested in Hungarian folk music late in 1904. While vacationing in the interior of Hungary, he overheard an eighteen-year-old peasant girl sing a strange, haunting melody far different from anything Bartók had heard before. On investigation, he discovered that this tune, and many others like it, were indigenous to the district. His curiosity aroused, Bartók decided to travel throughout Hungary to ascertain if other parts of the country had their own melodies. He visited remote regions, lived with the peasants, wrote down copious notes. This initial adventure—the first fruits of which were gathered in *Twenty Hungarian Folksongs* (1908), in collaboration with Zoltán Kodály—led to other expeditions, some of them in the company of his friend and colleague, Kodály. Bartók wandered from the Carpathian mountains to the Adriatic, from western Slovakia to the Black Sea. He unearthed several thousand folk songs and dances, then completely unknown to the rest of the world, put them down on paper, and finally issued them in monumental publications.

The folk literature uncovered by Bartók was far different from the sobbing, meretricious gypsy melodies that Brahms, Liszt and other composers had up to then exploited as authentic Hungarian music. The real folk music had a harder texture, was cruder in technique, more severe in line, more austere in spirit. The melodies, written in modal scales, had an exotic character. The rhythms were irregular.

Bartók's intensive study of this music influenced his own creative endeavors. Previously, he had written compositions derivative, on the one hand, from Debussy and, on the other, from Richard Strauss. He now became convinced that the folk art he had helped to discover could, as he said, "serve as the foundations for a renaissance of Hungarian art music." To help bring about such a renaissance, he assimilated into his own writing the stylistic traits and the personal idioms of Hungarian folk songs and dances, explaining: "The appropriate use of folk-song material is . . . a matter of absorbing the means of musical expression hidden in the treasury of folk tunes. . . . It is necessary for the composer to command this language so completely that it becomes the natural expression of his own musical ideas." Bartók now evolved his own idiom in which his melodic line assumed a declamatory character; in which the tonalities were so free as to give his composition the feel of atonality; in which modal harmonies introduced exoticism; in which brute force was gained through abrupt and shifting accents and complex rhythmic patterns.

The asperity of such compositions as the second and third string quartets, in 1917 and 1923 respectively, the *Dance Suite* for orchestra, in 1923, the fourth string quartet, in 1928, and the second piano concerto, in 1931, found few advocates among concertgoers. Despite the fact that here, and in other works, Bartók was one of the most original, independent and freshest voices in twentieth-century music, the bulk of his production was long neglected. Then, after making his home in the United States during World War II, Bartók completed several major works, of which the third piano concerto and the *Concerto for Orchestra* are sometimes singled out as the supreme achievements of his lifetime. It is true, as Halsey Stevens remarks, that here "no new tendencies are to be observed . . . but only the confirmation and continuation of the creative directions demonstrated by the scores which preceded them." Nevertheless, a certain amount of simplification did set in with this music, and with simplification a more personal viewpoint and a greater warmth of feeling than heretofore. This must surely explain the almost immediate and permanent acceptance these compositions received.

"In no other composer," maintains Halsey Stevens, "is there to be observed such an undeviating adherence to the same basic principles throughout an entire career." Amplifying on this point of view, Stevens continues: "With Bartók there were frequently additions to his creative equipment, but seldom subtractions; 'influences' were quickly assimilated, and no matter from what source, they became so personally a part of his style or his technique that their gravitation lost its pull and he continued undeviatingly in his own orbit."

Bartók was born in Nagyszentmiklós, Hungary, on March 25, 1881. He began to study music early and showed unusual talent. He was only nine when he began writing piano pieces; in his tenth year, he made public appearances as a piano virtuoso. Intensive study of music followed in Pressburg with László Erkel. After that, Bartók attended the Royal Hungarian Academy, a pupil of Stephen Thomán and Hans Koessler. In 1907, Bartók was appointed instructor of the piano at the Academy. Meanwhile, he had discovered for the first time the riches of Hungarian folk music.

A shy, modest, introverted artist, Bartók lived his life in Budapest quietly and unceremoniously, devoting himself to teaching, composition, playing the piano, and doing researches in folk music. Immediately after World War I, he was made a member of the Music Directorate in Hungary. He left Budapest to make a number of tours throughout Europe and the United States in performances of his own works; his American debut took place in 1927, when he appeared as soloist with the New York Philharmonic Orchestra, Willem Mengelberg conducting.

In 1940, with Europe at war, Bartók came to the United States to settle temporarily, as he then thought; actually, he lived in America the last years of his life. Though suffering from an incurable disease, as well as poverty and comparative neglect, Bartók nevertheless managed to be unusually productive; in fact, those last years saw the writing of compositions usually accepted as his masterworks. He died in a hospital in New York City on September 26, 1945. Paradoxically, death brought him the recognition and appreciation that life has for the most part denied him. Forty-eight major performances of his compositions took place within a few weeks of his death. Since that time, all his principal works have been frequently performed and recorded—familiarity with which has finally brought about a universal recognition that he was truly a Titan in twentieth-century music.

Bartók was married twice. The first marriage, with Marta Ziegler, entered upon in 1909, ended in divorce in 1923. That same year Bartók married Ditta Pásztory, a concert pianist. Bartók had a son by each marriage.

1904–1908 COMPOSITIONS FOR ORCHESTRA:
Scherzo, for piano and orchestra, op. 2.
Two Portraits, op. 5.

The Scherzo (or *Burlesque,* as it was at first identified) waited more than half a century to get heard. Written in 1904, probably under the influence of Richard Strauss's *Burleske* in D minor, it did not receive a world première until September 28, 1961, in a performance by E. Tusa and an orchestra directed by György Lehel, broadcast over the Hungarian Radio. Its American première followed in December of 1964, when William Steinberg conducted the New York Philharmonic Orchestra and Theodore Lettvin was the piano soloist.

While this music is in a burlesque spirit, it opens with a somewhat lugubrious subject for clarinet (Adagio ma non troppo). Orchestra and piano then given a hint of some of the themes to come. With the final measures of this introductory section, the pace quickens. The main body of the Scherzo (Allegro) begins with a graceful tune. There follow a variation of the opening clarinet melody in the piano and a contrasting subject for three solo violins accompanied by plucked strings and harp. After the development and recapitulation, we get the lyrical Trio (Andante) in which the solo piano is prominent. With a recall of the first section, earlier material receives radical transformations. The composition ends with a sonorous and vigorous restatement of the opening clarinet theme.

The *Two Portraits* (1907–1908) is derived from other Bartók compositions: notably, the first movement of his First Violin Concerto (which the composer withdrew) and the fourteenth Bagatelle, op. 6, where it is entitled *Ma Mie qui danse*. The two *Portraits* are studies in contrast. The first is slow and meditative, with the solo violin heard in the principal lyrical first theme, which subsequently receives fugal treatment. The second *Portrait* is a lively waltz, which terminates in an exciting accelerando. The *Two Portraits* were first heard in Budapest, in 1909, with László Kún conducting the Budapest Symphony.

1907–1917 STRING QUARTET NO. 1, op. 7. I. Lento. II. Allegretto; Introduzione; Allegro. III. Allegro vivace.

STRING QUARTET NO. 2, op. 17, I. Moderato. II. Allegro molto capriccioso. III. Lento.

The six Bartók string quartets produced between 1907 and 1939 are among the most significant in the entire repertory of present-day chamber music. Their frequent presentation, either singly or all six in a cycle, and their numerous recordings, have gone a long way to bring to Bartók the recognition he so well deserved, even if this recognition came posthumously. For variety of idiom, contrasts in sonority, daring in invention, resourcefulness in writing for the four instruments, independence of thought, these quartets are virtually unique in the music of the present century. For the Bartók student, they are particularly fascinating, since they epitomize the creative evolution of the composer.

The first quartet (1907) is still in a Romantic style, with the influence of both Brahms and Wagner visible in its chromaticism, its soaring melodic thoughts and sensuous harmonies, and its rhythmic vitality. But one is also made aware of the impact made on Bartók by his recent studies into Hungarian peasant music, particularly in the variety of rhythmic play.

The second quartet (1917) sheds derivative influences in favor of strength, brusqueness, primitivism—all three evident in the second movement. This quartet is unusual in structure in that it ends with a slow movement of almost funereal character.

The première of both string quartets was given in Budapest by the Waldbauer-Kerpely Quartet—the first, on March 19, 1910, the second, on March 3, 1918.

1908–1911 COMPOSITIONS FOR PIANO:

Evening in Transylvania (or *Evening with the Székelers*) and *Bear Dance* from *Ten Easy Pieces* (no opus number).

Two Romanian Dances, op. 8a.

Allegro barbaro (no opus number).

Two movements from the *Ten Easy Pieces* for piano (1908) have become popular through an orchestral transcription made by the composer in 1931, when they were used as the first two movements of a symphonic composition entitled *Hungarian Dances*. *Evening in Transylvania,* we are told by Halsey Stevens, "alternates two pentatonic tunes, one parlando, the other a sprightly tempo giusto tune to arrive at a rondo-like form." *Bear Dance* is "run through with rapidly repeated single notes, above and below which a rustic dance tune is blocked out in chords."

The *Two Romanian Dances* (1909–1910) is also more familiar in orchestral dress than in the original piano version—the transcription having been made by Leo Weiner in 1939. Within the casing of a three-part structure (A-B-A), Bartók has in each instance poured violent mood contrasts, sweeping folk melodies, percussive effects, and exciting rhythms. A point of relaxation is reached in the trio of the first dance, which boasts an improvisational melody over a rippling background of thirty-second notes.

Even more uninhibited in its emotional appeal and dynamic content is the *Allegro barbaro* (1911), with which, says Stevens, the composer first comes of age. Most of the early influences are now in discard, as a true Magyar style is evolved. Some commentators have interpreted the driving rhythms as the trampling hords of an Atilla or a Genghis Khan. To Halsey Stevens, the savage energy and primitivism of this music "has its roots in the East."

The composer himself gave the first performances of both the *Two Romanian Dances* and *Allegro barbaro*—the former in Paris on March 12, 1910, and the latter in Budapest on February 27, 1921. *Allegro barbaro* was transcribed for orchestra by Jenö Kenessey in 1946.

1911 BLUEBEARD'S CASTLE, opera in one act, op. 11, with libretto by Béla Balázs. First performance: Budapest, May 24, 1918.

This is Bartók's only opera. Both in text and music, it is a work rich in symbolism and in psychological implications. The main characters are Bluebeard and his latest bride, Judith. After a short somewhat grimly atmospheric prelude, the curtain rises on what the libretto describes as "a great circular hall in Gothic style" resembling "a dark, empty cavern." On a darkened stage, Bluebeard and Judith appear at the head of the stairway; this is Judith's first glimpse of her husband's castle. She is terrified, but she is determined to dispel her fears and bring happiness to her husband. She manages to get her husband to give her the keys to seven great doors in the castle. Despite Bluebeard's ominous warnings, she opens one door after another. The first five doors reveal among other things a garden, a torture chamber, a storehouse of jewels, a lake of tears, all dripping with blood. Convinced that the murdered bodies of Bluebeard's former wives can be found behind the last door, she rushes to open it. She finds there not dead women, but live ones, pale and bloodless. When Bluebeard adorns Judith with jewels, a crown and a cloak, she silently and helplessly joins the other women as the seventh door closes upon her."

Gerald Larner has pointed out that this text deals "with the long-term spiritual relationship of man and his wife, every man and any woman with whom he becomes involved more than temporarily through mutual love." He finds the "main import" of the opera to be as follows: "Just as Bluebeard has his castle, a man has his secrets, the private yield of active experience. Like Judith, a woman must possess entirely the man she loves, not only his body but also the innermost recesses of his soul. Just as Bluebeard has his seven locked doors, a man has a conscience, matters of shame and pride, all of them stained with the blood of others (and his own) and he has his sea of tears wept on his behalf."

Zoltán Kodály has said that "*Bluebeard's Castle* is for us what *Pelléas* is for France. If we can say that, in spite of the glorious past of the French lyrical theater, a type of musical declamation that suited the genius of the language did not exist before Debussy, how much truer such a statement is in our own case in relation to Bartók. . . . By respecting in his recitatives the natural music of our language and, in the more stylized parts of his opera, the tone of Hungarian folk music, Bartók opened a new road." Kodály also said: "The seven doors of Bluebeard's castle, opening one by one, give rise to musical images that are not externally descriptive but express the most intimate feeling." To this, Gerald Larner adds: "Bartók's music, with its wonderful variety so truthfully adapted to each vision, reached to the fundamentals of humanity. The tensions aroused as Judith turns the key in the locks is released in floods of emotion, never meretriciously but always irresistibly. These are the colorful highlights of the score; between them and behind them is the lyrical and passionate groundwork of the musical expression of Bluebeard's and Judith's love; before Judith's entry and after her departure is the tragic darkness of the castle, the desolation of Bluebeard's heart without the illumination of unquestioning feminine love. The musical symbols are as extensive and even more suggestive than those of the text."

Bartók's score here is still in the tonal, triadic and diatonic idiom of his early works; and derivative influences still abound. The influence of Debussy can be detected in the rejection of set pieces and the acceptance of a continuous dark and expressive recitative. Wagner's presence is felt in the discreet use of a Leitmotiv technique and the occasional chromaticism. Even a trace or two of Richard Strauss can be picked out. Nevertheless, we have here a good deal of Bartók as well, especially in the melodic line which suggests the Hungarian folk song in its austere and stark beauty.

Bluebeard's Castle was produced for the first time in the United States by the New York City Opera Company on October 2, 1952.

1919. THE MIRACULOUS MANDARIN, one-act danced pantomime, op. 19, with libretto by Menyhért Lengyel. First performance: Cologne, Germany, November 27, 1926.

THE MIRACULOUS MANDARIN, suite for orchestra, op. 19.

Bartók did not have much luck with this "danced-pantomime"—one of his three works for the stage. Hungary, immediately after World War I, was too emaciated by the recent conflict, and too torn apart by revolution, to mount new provocative ballets. *The Miraculous Mandarin* waited six years for a première performance, which finally took place in Germany. This presentation proved such a fiasco that the work was removed from the repertoire after only one performance. It hardly did better in Prague, where it also had to be withdrawn.

In an effort to make the work somewhat more palatable, Bartók, with the help of his librettist, removed some of the less agreeable episodes. A performance of the revised version was scheduled for performance in Budapest in 1931. Following the dress rehearsal, the projected production was canceled at the zero hour "owing to the illness of one of the principal dancers." When the ballet finally did reach the Hungarian stage, Bartók could not attend the performance. This was in 1945, when he was in America, seriously ill. On September 6, 1951, six years after Bartók's death, the work was introduced in the United States in a peformance by the New York City Ballet.

Much of the trouble confronted by this ballet was due to a sordid text, and the grim realism with which the story line was projected. The setting is a city street—a slum street in an unidentified metropolis. Here flourish prostitutes, thieves, blackmailers, dope fiends and other discredited members of society. Three gangsters compel a girl to lure men into her shabby room where they can be robbed and thrown back into the streets. The first two victims are a down-at-the-heels gentleman and a shy boy. The third is a Mandarin, sinister in appearance, with stark and staring eyes. The girl tries to arouse him with her dancing; then when he makes a move towards her, she shrinks in horror. He gets hot on her trail, but the thieves seize and rob him, then try to strangle him. He survives the attack, and still regards the girl with desire. Then the thieves try to stab him; but the Mandarin's desire for the girl keeps him alive. The thieves then try to hang him; still he does not die. At last, the girl takes the Mandarin in her arms and kisses him passionately. Suddenly, the blood oozes from his wounds; the Mandarin dies in an ecstasy of love.

This was stern stuff to exhibit on a stage, and much of it repelled audiences, in spite of Bartók's effective music. *Musical America* remarked in a report in 1926: "It is unpardonable that this displeasure should have allowed automatically to include the music, as it did in so many instances. For the music is inspired. Its clever combinations of instruments, and wonderful harmonic effects are completely fascinating."

Halsey Stevens finds much in Bartók's music to admire, particularly the musical characterizations. "As the girl ensnares the men, the successive clarinet cadenzas are the embodiment of erotic gesture; the elderly rake and the callow youth are painted in convincing colors; the Mandarin himself betrays his ancestry in a pentatonic theme harmonized by two lines of tritones." Stevens further singles out for special praise the waltz music accompanying the girl's seductive dance in front of the Mandarin; the Mandarin's pursuit of the girl, worked out musically in a fugue; the trembling of the orchestra to describe the Mandarin's lust.

Bartók prepared an orchestral suite from his ballet score, introduced by the Budapest Philharmonic under Dohnányi on October 15, 1928. It is made up roughly of the first half of the ballet score. The following excerpts are played without interruption: (1) Introduction, street noises, the orders of the ruffians to the girls; (2) the first siren call of the girl (clarinet solo), and entrance of the shabby gentleman who is robbed and thrown out; (3) second siren call of the girl, summoning the shy youth, who is likewise thrown out; (4) third call of the girl, and the appearance of the Mandarin (tutti fortissimo); (5) the girl dances before the Mandarin (very slow at first, then gradually hurrying waltz); (6) the Mandarin catches the girl after a wild chase.

1922 SONATA NO. 2 FOR VIOLIN AND PIANO. I. Molto moderato. II. Allegretto.

Less than a year separates Bartók's two violin sonatas. The first was completed late in 1921 and was introduced by Jelly d'Arányi and the composer in London on March 24, 1922. The second followed in November of 1922. Here, too, the première was given by Miss d'Arányi and the composer in London on May 7, 1923. The second sonata consists of two movements played without interruption. The first, in sonata form, is slow and deliberate; its main themes are in a Bartók idiom identified as "parlando-rubato." The second movement, in tempo giusto, is in rondo form. This is energetic music in which the violin sometimes simulates the off-pitch sounds produced by Hungarian village fiddlers. Towards the end of the sonata, the first theme of the opening returns to bring the music back to the slow and languorous pace with which it began. What distinguishes this sonata from its predecessor is the complete independence of the two instruments; there is no interchange of thematic material between them.

1923 DANCE SUITE, for orchestra. I. Moderato. II. Allegro molto. III. Allegro vivace. IV. Molto tranquillo. V. Comodo. VI. Allegro.

The *Dance Suite* was written for a music festival held in Budapest on November 19, 1923, to commemorate the fiftieth anniversary of the merging of the cities of Buda and Pesth. Mindful of this historic event, the composer produced a work with pronounced national leanings. All the themes are Bartók's own, yet their kinship with Hungarian and Romanian folk idioms is unmistakable. The work, while played without a break, is in six contrasting sections. A recurring refrain (a ritornello) serves as a connecting link between the first and second dances, and the second and third dances. Five of the sections represent dances (the first and fourth with an almost Arabian personality; the second and third, obviously Magyar; and the fifth, Romanian). The finale serves as a summation, being a skilful blend of all the disparate elements that had gone to make up the various dances.

Emil Haraszti suggests that the first movement is "suggestive of a dance of elves and gnomes"; the second describes "a wild revel, as though legions of gnomes had been let loose at the hour of midnight"; the third recreates "the fiery spirit of full-blooded peasant nature bursting into flame"; the fourth movement is "pastoral"; the fifth is filled with "floating shades . . . [whose] progress is leaden, incorporeal and bodiless." The finale, to Haraszti, is "a kind of summary of the preceding movements" starting with "a scarcely audible tap-tapping, and rises, through an orgy of rhythm, to the force of a hurricane."

When the *Dance Suite* was heard on November 19, 1923 in Budapest, the Budapest Philharmonic was conducted by Dohnányi.

1926–1939 MIKROKOSMOS (LITTLE WORLD), 153 progressive pieces for the piano gathered in six books.

BOOK I: 1–6. Six Unison Melodies; 7. Dotted Notes; 8. Repetition; 9. Syncopation; 10. With Alternate Hands; 11. Parallel Motion; 12. Reflection; 13. Change of Position; 14. Question and Answer; 15. Village Song; 16. Parallel Motion and Change of Position; 17. Contrary Motion; 18–21. Four Unison Melodies; 22. Imitation and Counterpoint; 23. Imitation and Inversion; 24. Pastorale; 25. Imitation and Inversion; 26. Repetition; 27. Syncopation; 28. Canon at the Octave; 29. Imitation Reflected; 30. Canon at the Lower Fifth; 31. Little Dance in Canon Form; 32. In Dorian Mode; 33. Slow Dance; 34. In Phrygian Mode; 35. Chorale; 36. Free Canon.

BOOK II: 37. In Lydian Mode; 38–39. Staccato and Legato. 40. In Yugoslav Mode; 41. Melody with Accompaniment; 42. Accompaniment in Broken Triads; 43. In Hungarian Style; 44. Contrary Motion; 45. Meditation; 46. Increasing—Diminishing; 47. Big Fair; 48. In Mixolydian Mode; 49. Crescendo—Diminuendo; 50. Minuetto; 51. Waves; 52. Unison Divided; 53. In Transylvanian Style; 54. Chromatic; 55. Triplets in Lydian Mode; 56. Melody in Tenths; 57. Accents; 58. In Oriental Style; 59. Major and Minor; 60. Canon with Sustained Notes; 61. Pentatonic Melody; 62. Minor Sixths in Parallel Motion; 63. Buzzing; 64. Line and Point; 65. Dialogue; 66. Melody Divided.

BOOK III: 67. Thirds Against a Single Voice; 68. Hungarian Dance; 69. Chord Study; 70. Melody Against Double Notes; 71. Thirds; 72. Dragon's Dance; 73. Sixths and Triads; 74. Hungarian Song; 75. Triplets; 76. In Three Parts; 77. Little Study; 78. Five-Tone Scale; 79. Hommage à J.S.B.; 80. Hommage à R. Sch.; 81. Wandering; 82. Scherzo; 83. Melody with Interruptions; 84. Merriment; 85. Broken Chords; 86. Two Major Pentachords; 87. Variations; 88. Duet for Pipes; 89. In Four Parts; 90. In Russian Style; 91–92. Two Chromatic Inventions; 93. In Four Parts; 94. Tale; 95. Son gof the Fox; 96. Stumblings.

BOOK IV: 97. Notturno; 98. Thumb Under; 99. Crossed Hands; 100. In the Style of a Folksong; 101. Diminished Fifth; 102. Harmonics; 103, Minor and Major; 104. Through the Keys; 105. Playsong; 106. Children's Song;

107. Melody in the Mist; 108. Wrestling; 109. From the Island of Bali; 110. Clashing Sounds; 111. Intermezzo; 112. Variations on a Folk Tune; 113. Bulgarian Rhythm I; 114. Theme and Inversion; 115. Bulgarian Rhythm II; 116. Melody; 117. Bourrée. 118. Triplets in 9/8 Time; 119. Dance in 3/4 Time; 120. Fifth Chords; 121. Two-Part Study.

BOOK V: 122. Chords Together and Opposed; 123. Staccato and Legato; 124. Staccato; 125. Boating; 126. Change of Time; 127. New Hungarian Folksong; 128. Peasant Dance; 129. Alternating Thirds; 130. Village Joke; 131. Fourths; 132. Major Seconds Broken and Together; 133. Syncopation; 134. Three Studies in Double Notes; 135. Perpetuum Mobile; 136. Whole-Tone Scale; 137. Unison; 138. Bagpipe; 139. Jack in the Box.

BOOK VI: 140. Free Variations; 141. Subject and Reflection; 142. From the Diary of a Fly; 143. Divided Arpeggios; 144. Minor Seconds, Major Sevenths; 145. Chromatic Invention; 146. Ostinato; 147. March; 148–153 Six Dances in Bulgarian Rhythm.

In these pieces it is Bartók's aim to instruct children in the many different idioms, techniques, methods and procedures of piano playing in general, and modern music in particular; also to introduce them to the folk music of the Baltic nations. Nicolas Slonimsky points out that "there is no insistence on C major as the fundamental tonality, which is characteristic of most piano courses, so that the student develops a C major complex and measures all modes and scale patterns against this chosen key. The reason for this is Bartók wants the child to get a feeling for modal writing from the very beginning." Slonimsky explains further: "There is no raising of the seventh in the minor mode, and the semi-cadences fall freely on different degrees of the modal scale." The rhythm is also freed from "symmetric rigidity of the common collections of piano exercise" being made up of "note values in changing patterns."

In the first four books, many specific technical problems are met and solved in most of these pieces, the problem involved being found in the title. In the fourth, fifth and sixth volumes, we also find many pieces that are descriptive or programmatic, while others are in a folk-song or folk-dance style.

Tibor Serly transcribed seven of these pieces for orchestra, assembling them into a *Mikrokosmos Suite*. The numbers he used were: *Jack in the Box* (No. 139), *Unison* (No. 137), *Bourrée* (No. 117), *From the Diary of a Fly* (No. 142), *Harmonics* (No. 102) and two *Bulgarian Dances* (Nos. 151, 153). As a prelude to these seven numbers, Serly used and orchestrated the third of Bartók's *Three Hungarian Folk Tunes* for the piano, written between 1914 and 1917.

Serly also transcribed for string quartet five of the *Mikrokosmos* pieces: *Jack in the Box* (No. 139), *Harmonics* (No. 102), *Wrestling* (No. 108), *Melody* (No. 116), and *From the Diary of a Fly* (No. 142).

Bartók himself transcribed seven of these pieces for two pianos: *Bulgarian Rhythm* (No. 113), *Chord Study* (No. 69), *Perpetuum Mobile* (No. 135), *Staccato and Legato* (No. 123), *New Hungarian Folksong* (No. 127), *Chromatic Invention* (No. 145) and *Ostinato* (No. 146).

1926 CONCERTO NO. 1 FOR PIANO AND ORCHESTRA. I. Allegro moderato. II. Andante. III. Allegro molto.

The first of Bartók's three piano concertos was written when he was in his full creative maturity. The world première took place at the festival of the

International Society for Contemporary Music in Frankfort, Germany, on July 1, 1927. The composer was the soloist, and the orchestra was led by Wilhelm Furtwaengler.

In his program analysis for the Los Angeles Philharmonic, Nicolas Slonimsky provided the following description: "The first movement introduces a discernible group of motives that corresponds to the first subject of a sonata; a second thematic configuration provides the contrast. Both groups are integrated in the recapitulation. Repeated dissonant chords in the piano part build up the cumulative energy. . . ."

Slonimsky points to a novel procedure in the second movement "by assigning thematic significance to a rhythmic pattern of three notes. The whole movement is a colloquy between the piano and a battery of drums as an antiphonal concertino. . . . String instruments are conspicuously absent . . . and wind instruments do not come in until the end. To compensate for the tenuousness of sonorous matter, Bartók attaches great importance to the dynamic minutiae, meticulously indicating the exact locus on the drumhead or on the suspended cymbal where the stick should strike. . . . "

Slonimsky describes the finale as "spontaneous motility. Distinctive rhythmic motives recur and vanish in the orchestra, while the piano contributes its share of sonorous, hard, desiccated strokes. There is no superfluity of variations; the statements are terse, crisp and sharp."

1927–1928 STRING QUARTET NO. 3. I. Moderato. II. Allegro. III. Moderato. IV. Allegro molto.

STRING QUARTET NO. 4. I. Allegro. II. Prestissimo con sordino. III. Allegro. IV. Allegretto pizzicato. V. Allegro molto.

In the third string quartet (1927), Bartók frees himself completely from academic restraints. Ten years had elapsed since he had last used the string-quartet form. Returning to it, he abandoned tonality (just as he now abandoned opus numbers); and at times his atonal writing comes close to the twelve-tone technique. Severity of line is matched by concentration of thought. The fourth quartet (1928) grows even more abstract in thought and more concise in technique. A terse six-note phrase (found in the seventh measure of the first movement) becomes the material from which the first and last movements are constructed. The finale is in a fiery Magyar spirit. The second, third and fourth movements are light in texture.

In both the third and fourth quartets, Bartók is no longer interested in contrapuntal writing. "In its place," writes Homer Ulrich, "comes preoccupation with brutal chords, running scale passages and with broken, hesitant rhythms." At the same time, Bartók increased his ability to arrive at new instrumental effects, "tight chordal formations, long glissandos, percussive bowing effects, concentrated tone clusters, new employment of pizzicato techniques—all are here . . . added to the emotional tension brought about by barbaric rhythms and unrelieved dissonance."

The Waldbauer-Kerpely Quartet gave the premières of both the third and fourth string quartets, the third in London on February 19, 1929, and the fourth in Budapest on March 20, 1929.

1928 RHAPSODIES, for violin and orchestra:

No. 1: I. Moderato. II. Allegro moderato.

No. 2: I. Moderato. II. Allegro moderato.

Both these compositions originated as music for violin and piano. (There is still another version of the first rhapsody—for cello and piano.) Both works follow the structural pattern established by Liszt in his Hungarian rhapsodies. Each opens with a slow introductory section, or *lassu*. The second movement is rhapsodic, vitalized by dance rhythms, or *friss*. A single subject is continually repeated. Each work concludes with a résumé of earlier material. An interesting feature of the orchestration of the first rhapsody is the inclusion of a cimbalom, an instrument long favored by Hungarian gypsies, and still frequently found in café and restaurant orchestras in Hungary.

The first and more popular of the two rhapsodies was written for and dedicated to Joseph Szigeti, who introduced it (in a violin and piano version) in Budapest on November 22, 1929. The second rhapsody was first heard in Amsterdam on November 19, 1928, in a performance by Zoltán Székely (to whom the work is dedicated), with Géza Frid at the piano.

1930 CANTATA PROFANA, for tenor, baritone, double mixed chorus and orchestra.

Bartók's most significant choral composition is based on Romanian folksong texts narrating the legend of nine sons. Pursuing a stag, they find themselves transformed into stags. The father comes looking for them, finds the nine stags at a spring, and almost shoots one who reveals himself to his father. The father entreats his sons to come home. But the oldest stag, speaking for his brothers, insists that they can live henceforth only in the forests and drink the waters of a cool spring.

The cantata is divided into three sections. The first describes how the sons are transformed into stags. The second tells of the confrontation of father and sons. In the third, the chorus retells the legend. These three parts are further divided into shorter segments, utilizing such musical forms as aria, canon, fugue and cadenza.

Modeling his vocal writing after peasant songs, Bartók here produced some of his most stirring and dramatic vocal writing. The world première of the cantata took place in London on May 25, 1934. Aylmer Buesst conducted the BBC Symphony, and the vocal soloists were Trefor Jones and Frank Phillips.

1931 CONCERTO NO. 2 FOR PIANO AND ORCHESTRA. I. Allegro. II. Adagio; Presto; Adagio. III. Allegro molto.

Five years separate Bartók's first two piano concertos. The second, like the first, was introduced in Frankfort, Germany, on January 23, 1933. Once again the composer was soloist, but this time the orchestra was conducted by Hans Rosbaud. The concerto was subsequently played all over Europe: in Amsterdam (at the festival of the International Society for Contemporary Music), London, Stockholm, Strassburg, Vienna, Winterthur, Zurich, Budapest. It was not, however, heard again in Germany until after World War II. With the rise of Hitler and the Nazi regime, Bartók refused to allow any of his works to be played in Germany.

Emil Haraszti has written that, in his opinion, this concerto represents "the highest pinnacle of pure music." It was written five years after the First Piano Concerto, and like other works of the same period is characterized by barbaric rhythmic force. The first movement (which dispenses with the strings) opens with an introductory motive for the trumpet. The solo piano then enters with the first theme, treated at some length. The second theme follows, also played by the solo instrument. Eight introductory bars in the piano preface the development section, in which the two major themes are developed with contrapuntal skill. The strings open the second movement with a chorale-like melody, after which the piano and tympani compete in percussive statements. The middle section erupts into an exciting Presto, based on a theme first heard in the piano. The Adagio returns, and with it the original tranquillity of the movement. In the final section, barbaric forces are set loose, with tympani and piano serving as the principal protagonists.

1934 STRING QUARTET NO. 5. I. Allegro. II. Adagio molto. III. Scherzo: alla bulgarese. IV. Andante. V. Allegro vivace.

In his fifth string quartet, Bartók begins to move back to a more or less consistent tonality. At the same time, his writing becomes simpler, clearer and more lyrical. "Architecturally less rigorous than the Fourth," says André Hodeir, "it also lacks the earlier work's expressive bit. It is most remarkable for the texture of its writing." Hodeir goes on to point out that in the first movement there can be found "another example of the use of a lowered dominant which so often typifies Bartók's tonal conception." The two slow movements are impressive chorales, while the finale—the most brilliant movement in the work—is an extraordinary exercise in polyphonic writing, climaxed by an extended fugue.

The first performance took place in Washington, D.C., on April 8, 1935 by the Kolisch Quartet.

1936 MUSIC FOR STRINGS, PERCUSSION AND CELESTA. I. Andante tranquillo. II. Allegro. III. Adagio. IV. Allegro molto.

The ensemble for which this composition is written is two string quartets (merged in the first movement, but treated independently thereafter), the percussion, double-basses and celesta. The violas are heard in the first theme, played pianissimo, with background embellishments by percussion; this theme is later taken up fugally by the other strings. The movement develops in sonority until it reaches a fortissimo; then it subsides. One principal theme of the second movement is heard pizzicato (second string group), while the first string group replies with the second subject. The third movement has been described by Lawrence Gilman as a "mystical nocturne," creating a hazy atmosphere of quiet and mystery. The work closes with an energetic Allegro molto, one of whose principal subjects is a peasant dance in the Lydian mode.

The composition was introduced in Basle, Switzerland, on January 21, 1937, with Paul Sacher conducting the Basle Chamber Orchestra which had commissioned it.

1938 CONTRASTS, for violin, clarinet and piano. I. Verbunkos. II. Pihenö. III. Sebes.

CAPRICHOS, ballet in four episodes, with choreography by Herbert Ross to the music of *Contrasts*. First performance: New York, January 29, 1950.

Joseph Szigeti, the eminent violin virtuoso, was searching for a composition for violin and clarinet which he might perform with Benny Goodman, the "king of Swing," then invading the world of the classics. He commissioned Bartók to write such a work for them, and they introduced it in New York on January 9, 1939. Strictly speaking, the composition is a quintet rather than a trio. The clarinetist is required to shift from a B-flat clarinet to one in A; and the violinist is required to use both a regular tuned instrument and a "mistuned" one (the four strings being G-sharp instead of G, D and A, as in a regular tuning, and E-flat instead of E); this "mistuned" violin approximated the instrument used by Hungarian peasants.

The title of the first movement can be freely translated as a "recruiting dance," popular in Hungary in the mid-eighteenth century. A stately march theme is heard in the violin, following which the clarinet offers the main theme. When the violin takes over this melody, the clarinet provides decorative arpeggios. A slow section precedes a cadenza for clarinet with which the movement ends.

The second movement, "Relaxation," is slow and meditative, made up of several brief subjects. The finale is a "Fast Dance" in which the "mistuned" violin is heard for thirty measures. The regular violin is used after that. This concluding movement is in three sections: a vigorous opening; a slow and lyrical part, introduced by the clarinet; and a robust third part, rhythmically similar to the first, in which a double canon in the piano is the highlight. After a cadenza for violin, the work ends with an outburst of energy.

The music of *Contrasts* was used for the ballet *Caprichos,* in which the choreography is based on four commentaries which the celebrated artist Goya made on his own series of etchings of that name. After the première, on January 29, 1950, the ballet was incorporated into the repertory of the American Ballet Theater.

1938 CONCERTO NO. 2 FOR VIOLIN AND ORCHESTRA. I. Allegro non troppo. II. Andante tranquillo. III. Allegro molto.

Bartók's first violin concerto was written in 1907–1908 and for a long time lay in total neglect, having been withdrawn by the composer. (Its première finally took place in Basle, Switzerland, on May 30, 1958.) Its first movement was used by the composer for the first of the *Two Portraits,* for orchestra. It took the composer almost thirty years to write another violin concerto. When he did so, he produced one of his masterworks, a composition that has won a permanent place in the violin repertory. This second concerto was introduced by Zoltán Székely (to whom it is dedicated) in Amsterdam on March 23, 1939, with Willem Mengelberg conducting the Concertgebouw Orchestra.

An illuminating analysis of this concerto was made by Georg H. L. Smith when it was introduced in Cleveland. It reads in part: "The solo violin announces the main theme after six introductory measures for harp and plucked strings, and continues with rhapsodical passage-work introducing a canonic statement of the theme by strings and woodwind. . . . The legato second subject is, according to the composer, 'a kind of twelve-tone theme, yet with pronounced tonality.' In the development section ... these themes are put to various uses. ... A varied recapitulation leads to a solo cadenza. ... The brief coda contains further developments of the principal subject."

The second movement is a theme and variations. "The theme is stated by the solo violin over a light accompaniment in the lower strings, punctuated by harp harmonies and strokes of the kettledrums. ... There are six variations, after which the solo instrument restates the theme in its original form."

The concluding rondo is "conceived as a free variation of the opening movement. The principal episode is based on the main theme of the first movement in new guises. Subsequent episodes, constructed from the transitional and second subjects of the first movement, are joined by a rapid connecting theme in triplets which finally brings the concerto to a close."

1939 STRING QUARTET NO. 6. I. Mesto: vivace. II. Mesto: marcia. III. Mesto: burletta. IV. Mesto.

In Bartók's last string quartet, we encounter not only the return to simplicity, clarity and unifying tonality of the fifth quartet, but even excursions into sardonic humor. This is found in passages in each of the first movements, and particularly in the third movement, which is in a burlesque mood. However, this jocular vein is abandoned in the finale, which begins poetically, then lapses into an indefinable sadness that, by the end of the movement, even succumbs to total depression. Thus touching sentiment, a quality not often encountered in earlier Bartók music, now asserts itself strongly. This quartet is interesting for a technique which André Hodeir describes as "the gradual exposition in one, two, three or four parts in each of its four movements, of a single theme subjected to various transformations."

The quartet was introduced in New York on January 20, 1941, by the Kolisch Quartet.

1939 DIVERTIMENTO, for string orchestra. I. Allegro non troppo. II. Molto adagio. III. Allegro assai.

The Divertimento, like the sixth string quartet, represents for Bartók a new attempt to abandon the complexity and dissonance of his previous works. Halsey Stevens describes it as "almost Mozartean in its buoyancy," and as "the most spontaneous and carefree work of Bartók since the *Dance Suite,* and without question the least problematical."

It was commissioned from the Basle Chamber Orchestra which introduced it under Paul Sacher's direction on June 11, 1940, in Basle, Switzerland.

In the first movement, passages for solo strings alternate with those for the entire ensemble. The principal material is an energetic theme that sticks closely to a central tonality; a loud and syncopated rhythm alternating with patterns in solo instruments is of secondary importance. In the slow movement, muted violins present a melody over accompanying basses. A climax is built up, following which the opening melody, made even more emotional than before through the use of tremolos, is heard again. The finale enters with a lively rhythmic idea. The second theme, equally vital, is first presented in octaves and then subjected to polyphonic treatment. A violin cadenza precedes the return of the first subject, which in turn is followed by a brief coda.

1940 CONCERTO FOR TWO PIANOS, PERCUSSION AND

ORCHESTRA. I. Assai lento; Allegro molto. II. Lento ma non troppo. III. Allegro non troppo.

Upon coming to the United States in 1940, Bartók needed a two-piano concerto for appearances with American orchestras with his wife. To fill the bill, he arranged a Sonata for Two Pianos and Percussion he had written in 1937 as a concerto for two pianos, percussion and orchestra. He and his wife, Ditta, introduced the concerto in New York on January 21, 1943, with Fritz Reiner conducting the New York Philharmonic Orchestra.

The concerto opens in a solemn vein, with a faint roll of the tympani and a low chromatic figure in the first solo piano. The Allegro that follows has principal subjects, described in this way by Edward Downes in his program notes for the New York Philharmonic Orchestra: "The first a series of sharply rhythmic piano chords punctuated by the tympani, the second a tranquil descending melody of irregular rhythm embellished by grace notes at a distance of parallel fifths," and the third leading off "with a series of fanfare-like, upward-leaping sixths. This last theme later becomes the basis of a dramatic fugal development." In the slow movement, "the lonely octave textures, and the rather bleak melodic line of the opening and closing sections contrast with a more colorful, nocturne-like mood of the central section." The finale "resembles a rondo. The dance-like refrain is hinted at first by the xylophone, and finally propounded by the second piano, the left and right hands playing the theme in canon."

1943 CONCERTO FOR ORCHESTRA. I. Andante non troppo; Allegro vivace. II. Allegro scherzando. III. Elegia: andante non troppo. IV. Intermezzo interrotto; Allegretto. V. Presto.

This was the first composition completed by Bartók, after he had made America his permanent home, that was not a transcription. At the time he wrote this orchestral concerto, he was at the lowest ebb of his health, spirits and fortune. His music was getting little recognition in America, a fact that so disturbed him that he found it hard to concentrate on serious creative work. His health had given way: he had to be hospitalized with a serious disease that was subsequently diagnosed as leukemia. It was at this low point in Bartók's life that Serge Koussevitzky came to him at the hospital with a commission from the Koussevitzky Music Foundation. This offer seemed to have a revitalizing effect on Bartók's spirit, though not on his health. Out of the hospital, and quartered at the Hotel Woodrow in New York City, he spent the summer of 1943 working on his orchestral concerto, which he completed by the fall. "It seemed," says Agatha Fassett, "as if the obstructed forces within him were released at last, and the entire center of his being had been restored and reawakened, even though he was still lying limp on his bed, hardly any stronger than he was before he went to the hospital."

The Concerto was introduced in Boston by the Boston Symphony under Koussevitzky on December 1, 1944. Despite his weakened condition, Bartók made the trip for the première. Thus he personally witnessed a major triumph —his first in many years.

The fact that this music was written while Bartók was so ill may perhaps explain why so much of it is in a lugubrious vein. It opens in a somber mood, the first theme presented at once in the dark lower strings; the second subject, tinged with melancholy, is later assigned to flute, and after that to trumpet. There is a brief respite from gloom in the light heart of the second movement, subtitled "The Game of the Couples." Here five pairs of winds (bassoons, oboes, clarinets, flutes and muted trumpets) are heard in five different themes representing five couples; the five themes are separated from each other by a short brass chorale. In the third movement, a funereal atmosphere is projected, for which the first subject of the first movement provides basic material. Once again we get an emotional respite in the fourth movement, a lyrical intermezzo. The concerto ends optimistically, as if in reaffirmation of life. This is music in a Hungarian style whose development section consists of a fugue.

Bartók has explained that the reason he called this work a concerto was because of its tendency "to treat the single instrument or instrument groups in concertante or soloistic manner." As for the structure, he went on to explain that the first and fifth movements were written "in more or less regular sonata form. Less traditional are . . . the second and third movements. The main part of the second consists of a chain of independent short sections. . . . Thematically, the five sections have nothing in common. . . . The structure of the fourth movement is likewise chain-like; three themes appear consecutively. These constitute the core of the movement."

1944 SONATA FOR SOLO VIOLIN. I. Tempo di ciaconna. II. Fuga. III. Melodia. IV. Presto.

In 1940, Yehudi Menuhin commissioned Bartók to write a sonata for solo violin. The composer's serious illness long delayed the fulfillment of this project. But while recuperating in Asheville, North Carolina, from his recent siege in the hospital, Bartók finally went to work. He completed his sonata on March 14, 1944, and Menuhin (to whom the work is dedicated) introduced it in New York City on November 26, 1944.

Robert Mann prepared an analysis of this sonata for his recording for Bartók Records. It reads in part: "The theme, in G, is stated in ciaconna style in 3/4 time with the stress on the second beat. Though the movement develops sectionally and motives are developed as variations, the organic growth takes precedence and the strict variation is seldom present. The second eight measures derive subtly from the theme and introduce a new element of two voices in contrary motion. . . . Bartók introduces a contrasting lyricism (in triple rhythm), still lightly stressing the second beat and creating a second voice from the material of the ciaconna theme. . . . The powerful fugue theme of the second movement derives its dramatic effect from the repetition and extension of the opening two-note motif, silence, and the chromatic of the theme from C to F-sharp, concluding on a descending legato measure. . . . The third movement is in three parts. A simple expressive melody and a distant cadence figure woven into a long line, starting and ending on B-flat, followed by a middle section of muted double stops and trills and a return to the melody, this time even softer and more ethereal. . . . The last movement is Bartók in a joyful mood. A special feature of this movement is the use of quarter tones, creating a more intense chromatic line."

1945 CONCERTO NO. 3 FOR PIANO AND ORCHESTRA. I. Allegretto. II. Adagio religioso. III. Allegro vivace.

When Bartók wrote his Third Piano Concerto, he knew that he did not have much longer to live. On the last bar of his sketches he wrote the Hungarian word *vege* ("the end")—the first time he had ever done so on a manuscript. He was writing finis not only to this composition, but to his entire creative life. Indeed, the composer did not live to complete the final measures. The last seventeen bars, for which he had left no notes, were developed and scored by his intimate friend, Tibor Serly.

Bartók had originally planned the work as a concerto for two unaccompanied pianos (he intended writing it for the duo-piano team of Bartlett and Robertson). As he realized that his days were growing fewer, he revamped the work as a loving and appreciative tribute to his wife, Ditta Pásztory Bartók, to whom he knew he could leave little except his creative works. The composition, therefore, became a deeply personal message from Bartók to his wife; and he felt that for such a message the proper medium was not two solo pianos but a single piano and orchestra.

While this concerto has virtuoso passages, and while it is often spiced with Bartók dissonances, it is essentially one of Bartok's most expressive works. It would be difficult to find among his compositions music of such serenity (occasionally jarred by the momentary invasion of turbulence, but serenity nevertheless) as that which appears in the second movement. These are the finest pages of the entire concerto; and they are among the most moving pages Bartók has written.

The first movement is in the conventional sonata form, with the main subject announced by the piano; the second theme is more decorative. In the second movement, the placidity of the principal subjects (an introduction for strings, followed by an almost Bach-like chorale for the piano) receives contrast from an agitated trio. The finale is an impulsive and fiery scherzo, in which the trio is a fugue.

The world première took place in Philadelphia on February 8, 1946. György Sándor was the soloist, and the Philadelphia Orchestra was directed by Eugene Ormandy.

1945 CONCERTO FOR VIOLA AND ORCHESTRA (completed, reconstructed and orchestrated by Tibor Serly). I. Moderato. II. Adagio religioso. III. Allegro vivace.

Bartók did not live to complete the concerto which William Primrose, the distinguished viola virtuoso, had commissioned. Bartók began writing it in the Spring of 1945, but his poor health impeded its progress. On August 5, he wrote to Primrose: "I am able now to tell you that I hope to write and finish at least its draft in four-five weeks, if nothing happens in the meantime which would prevent my work." On September 8, Bartók again wrote to Primrose: "I am very glad to be able to tell you that your viola concerto is ready in draft, so that only the score has to be written which means a purely mechanical work, so to speak. If nothing happens, I can be through in five or six weeks." Less than three weeks after this communication Bartók was dead.

The draft consisted of fifteen unnumbered pages. There was no indication as to orchestration, and the harmonies were suggested by a shorthand method devised by the composer. To Tibor Serly—Bartók's friend and musical executor—fell the task of deciphering the manuscript, establishing the sequence of the movements, and finding the proper places for the inclusion of material which Bartók had scrawled down haphazardly in different parts of this manuscript as they occurred to him at the moment. Serly was also required to complete unfinished harmonies, and work out various technical passages for the solo instrument. Finally, once the work had been fully reconstructed, there was the business of orchestrating it. In all, it took Serly two years to complete the assignment. The concerto was finally introduced in Minneapolis on December 2, 1949; William Primrose was the soloist with the Minneapolis Symphony conducted by Antal Dorati. "The concerto proved pronouncedly agreeable and much less problematical at first hearing than, for example, the violin concerto," reported Olin Downes in *The New York Times* when the concerto was first heard in New York on February 11, 1950. "But the first movement of the viola concerto is the biggest and boldest of the three in its harmonic structure. It is clearly and effectively orchestrated. . . . The second movement is short, poetical and in a romantic vein. In the dance finale, Hungarian rhythms share the stage with others which easily could be derived from American jazz."

Tibor Serly prepared a definitive analysis, of which the following is an excerpt: "Written in sonata form, the subject of the main theme starts with a solo viola accompanied by light rhythmic beat. . . . A short tutti of eight entrances in imitation ending with a vigorous passage in unison connects with the second subject. . . . The development which follows exploits fully the virtuoso resources of the solo violin in a typical concerto fashion, including a fairly elaborate cadenza that precedes the recapitulation of the main subject which now is heard in the horn and flute. . . . A brief interlude, Lento parlando, precedes the second movement. It is a sort of recitative, bringing to mind a cantor's improvisation . . . . The deeply expressive simplicity (of the slow movement) is unmatched in any of Bartók's other major works. Written in an extended A-B-A ternary song form, the solo viola predominates throughout the entire movement. . . . In utter contrast to the poignantly religious music of the slow movement, the Finale is a gay dance in rondo form . . . more Romanian than Hungarian in character."

LESLIE BASSETT 1923–

Leslie Bassett's interest in orchestral texture, in the organic growth of design and structure, and in the employment of a counterpoint of events or groups rather than of line, characterizes his mature writings. Though he has avoided systems or avant-garde innovations, he has consistently produced music with a modern sound and a thoroughly contemporary spirit, and music constructed with consummate skill and compelling logic.

Bassett was born in Hanford, California, on January 22, 1923. Piano study began when he was about five, and the trombone (in which he specialized) when he was fourteen. While attending high school and college, he played the trombone in various orchestras and jazz groups; he continued to do so in the 13th Armored Division Band during World War II. After the war, he received a Bachelor of Arts degree from Fresno State College in California in 1947. His musical training then continued at the University of Michigan, mainly with Ross Lee Finney in composition, from which he received a master's degree in music in 1949, and a doctorate in 1956. Between 1950 and 1951, he attended the École Normale de Musique on a Fulbright grant, where he was a pupil of Arthur Honegger; at the same time, he studied composition privately with Nadia Boulanger. In 1952, Bassett was appointed instructor of composition at the University of Michigan, where he subsequently was appointed to full professorship. Between 1961 and 1963, he was a recipient of the Prix de Rome; in 1964, of a grant and citation from the National Institute of Arts and Letters; and in 1966–1967, of a grant from the National Council of the Arts to devote himself to a year of composition.

His bow as a composer came on December 3, 1946, when his Suite in G was performed by the Fresno Symphony. After that, he completed two symphonies and numerous chamber-music and choral compositions. Several of his chamber-music works received significant awards, including that of the Concours Internationale pour Quatuors à Cordes in Brussels for his second string quartet. In 1966, he received the Pulitzer Prize in music for *Variations for Orchestra.*

1961 FIVE MOVEMENTS, for orchestra.

This was Bassett's first work for orchestra in five years, and his first fully mature achievement in symphonic music. It was completed at Ann Arbor on June 21, 1961. The first performance was given by the Radio Orchestra of Rome (RAI), Massimo Freccia conducting, on July 5, 1962.

The composer provides the following description: "The five movements are alternately slow and fast. In mood and function the first and fifth are related; so are the second and fourth. The middle movement serves as the apex of the five—the top, the highpoint. Just as the over-all form is arch-like, so are the forms of the slow movements, and, to a lesser extent, the fast ones as well. The arch concept is often present in the sections within movements and in many of the phrases, to the extent that a large number of them begin low, rise, and fall back. The opening of the first movement, where a pyramid of entries in the winds and brass rises from the opening sound of the gong, is a ready example of such a phrase.

"Each of the five movements has two or three readily describable elements that were primary and led subsequently to the choice of notes and rhythms. In the first movement these factors are pyramid sounds, tutti and solo lines, often descending to counteract the rising pyramids, and horn punctuations. The second movement opens with a middle-range sixteenth-note trill figure followed by high throbbing quarter notes and descending fast runs. This texture is interrupted by several digressions, but keeps returning. The third movement, more coloristic than the two previous ones, opens with low flutes alternating between two chords. The flutes are followed by horns, then trumpets, trombones and strings. The sixteenth-note alternations of the preceding movement are now broken into the interval of a fourth and are considerably slower. The somewhat impressionistic opening gradually becomes more involved, and complexity replaces the open simplicity of the beginning. In the fourth movement the throbbing quarter notes of the second movement return as basic musical material, as do several other factors, including the sixteenth-note alternation. The final movement rises from its opening in the low strings, through the brass, and on to a climax in the full orchestra. The work ends quietly with the strings echoing the opening phrases."

1963 VARIATIONS FOR ORCHESTRA.

Bassett wrote his *Variations* between November of 1962 and May of 1963 in Rome while holding the Prix de Rome at the American Academy. "I wanted to write a large, powerful, single movement work that would place the listener in the midst of a form he could perceive," says the composer, "and yet at the same time involve him in the gradual unfolding of a thematic-motivic web that would require his most thoughtful attention." The world première took place in Rome on July 6, 1963, Ferruccio Scaglia conducting the Radio Orchestra of Rome (RAI).

The composer describes his music as follows: "The *Variations* are not based upon a theme. The opening motivic introduction consists of four small areas or phrases, each of which is more memorable as color or mood than as theme, and each of which serves in some respect as the source of two variations. The first variation, for example, grows from the short repeated notes that appear early in the introduction, the second from a quintuplet figure and other minutiae from the second phrase, the third from a short but soaring clarinet line in the third phrase, and so forth.

"Naturally the early variations expose a significant amount of material that is not directly drawn from the introduction, but which I believed would be able to project and complete the sections. The later variations take up some aspects of the introduction that may have been overlooked or minimized in earlier sections. Some of the variations are attached to those that follow or precede them, others are not. A sizeable conclusion, opening rather like the beginning, completes the work, after revealing once again several of the motivic elements in climactic context."

After the *Variations* had been introduced in the United States—in a performance by the Philadelphia Orchestra under Eugene Ormandy on October 22, 1965—it received in 1966 the Pulitzer Prize in music.

SIR ARNOLD BAX 1883–1953

Early in his career, Arnold Bax was sympathetically drawn to the works of the great Irish poets and to Celtic lore. In the fantasies and legends of the Irish world of make-believe, he found room for his musical imagination to roam about freely.

Celtic influences abound in his music—symbolism, mystery, dream fantasy—together with the Celtic love for decoration and imagery. Bax's early tones (*In the Faëry Hills, The Garden of Fand, Tintagel*) were directly inspired by Celtic lore; and these were the works which first brought him to the attention of the music world. The romantic feelings and poetic ideas of some of his later works are also tinged with Irish green.

He was a romanticist whose artistic conscience compelled him to seek beauty and to capture it in his music. Sensitively projected, this beauty is not always on the surface; nor, for that matter, is the full impact of Bax's subtle thinking apparent on first contact. Bax's music demands from listeners, says Julian Herbage, "the same clear intellect and austere sense of lyrical beauty that the composer himself possesses."

What H. G. Sear has written about Bax's symphonies applies to all of this composer's music. "Bax has highly individual feeling for melody, but it is not always one that makes instantaneous appeal. Mental power is present, measuring, curbing, enhancing. His treatment of his melodies has a greater significance than the tunes themselves. He cannot bear literally to repeat them. He must clothe them afresh; and the new array implies a new attitude and approach." Bax's rhythms, Sear continues, "are extremely varied, ranging from the defined patterns which tempt the thoughtful listener to count them out in their detail, to a flexuous tune obtained by altering the time signature from bar to bar." As to Bax's harmony, it follows "no acclaimed system, new or old; it is his own."

Sir Arnold Trevor Bax was born in London on November 8, 1883. He entered the Royal Academy of Music when he was seventeen, and for several years was a pupil of Tobias Matthay (piano) and Frederick Corder (composition). While still a student, he began composing; by the time he was graduated in 1909, he had achieved a certain measure of recognition. With *Tintagel* in 1917 and his first symphony in 1922, his fame was secure, a fact established on November 13, 1922, with a successful all-Bax concert in London. In 1924, his first symphony and his Viola Sonata were represented at festivals of the International Society for Contemporary Music, at Prague and Salzburg respectively.

Financially independent, he did not have to earn a living from music and, consequently, could devote his entire energies to composition. A man of exceptional modesty, he lived in complete retirement in the little village of Storrington during the last decade or so of his life, never permitting publicity to invade his privacy. After 1939, he wrote little that added to his reputation. Besides contributing scores to two motion pictures (including *Oliver Twist*), he wrote a trumpet fanfare in 1949 for the wedding of Princess Elizabeth to the Duke of Edinburgh, and in 1953 a coronation march for Queen Elizabeth II.

Bax was knighted in 1937. In 1941, he was named Master of the King's Musick. He died in Cork, Ireland, on October 3, 1953.

1909–1917 TONE POEMS FOR ORCHESTRA:
In the Faëry Hills
The Garden of Fand

November Woods
Tintagel

Arnold Bax once noted that for him the problem of composition was one of translating ideas and impressions into music. His finest tone poems are programmatic.

In the Faëry Hill (1909) was his first successful orchestral composition in which Celtic colors and elements, dreams and fantasies are absorbed into his writing. It is based on an episode from *The Wanderings of Usheen*. The following program is followed literally by the music: Lured by a fairy girl to an island where revelry prevails, the poet Usheen, invited to sing of pleasure, plucks from his harp a melancholy strain. The harp is snatched from his hands and thrown into a pool. The poet then hurls himself unreservedly into the dancing and the revels.

The composer himself described the program of *The Garden of Fand* (1916). "The Garden of Fand is the sea. The earlier portion of the work seeks to create the atmosphere of an enchanted Atlantic. . . . Upon its surface floats a small ship. . . . The little craft . . . is tossed onto the shore of Fand's miraculous island. . . . Here is unhuman revelry . . . and the voyagers are caught away into the maze of the dance. After Fand sings of immortal love, a dance of revelry begins. The sea rises and submerges the entire island. Twilight falls, the sea becomes calm, and the Garden of Fand has disappeared." Lawrence Gilman found in this composition "the true tang and breath of Celtic poetry." Here were caught "dreams and witcheries and Celtic twilight . . . producing . . . music occupied with fairy spells and magic seas and haunted, melancholy woods."

November Woods (1917) is one of several tone poems inspired by Nature. Edwin Evans has explained that it presents "a picture of storms and driving leaves and the sere dank atmosphere of autumn. Mingled with this is the mood of human loneliness and regret, which is finally absorbed in the restlessness and turmoil of nature."

Tintagel is Bax's most famous tone poem; it contains the breath and heartbeat of Celtic lore and poetry. The composer explains: "Though detailing no definite program, this work is intended to evoke a tone picture of the castle-crowned cliff of Tintagel, and more particularly the wide distances of the Atlantic as seen from the cliffs of Cornwall on a sunny but not windless summer day. In the middle section of the piece it may be imagined that with the increasing tumult of the sea arise memories of the historical and legendary associations of the place, especially those connected with King Arthur, King Mark, and Tristram and Iseult. Regarding the last named, it will be noticed that at the climax of the more literary division of the work there is a brief reference to one of the subjects in the first act of *Tristan*."

1916 SYMPHONIC VARIATIONS, for piano and orchestra.

This major work for piano and orchestra waited four years for its première, which was given by Harriet Cohen in 1920 at a Promenade concert in London. The theme on which the variations are based is introspective; it is heard at once in the orchestra. The piano arrives in the tenth measure with cadenza-like passages accompanied by muted strings. The five variations that follow each carry a descriptive title providing the listener with a clue to their emotional or programmatic content: "Nocturne," "Strife," "The Temple," "Play," "Triumph." Between the fourth and fifth variations, there appears a brief intermezzo entitled "Enchantment," in which a poetic mood is projected by divided, muted strings over a persistent rhythm in the drums and by an extended undulating melody. At the close of the fifth variation, the full orchestra recalls the main theme loudly in its original form.

1923 QUINTET FOR OBOE AND STRINGS. I. Tempo molto moderato; Allegro moderato. II. Lento espressivo. III. Allegro giocoso.

This is one of Bax's finest chamber-music works. In the first movement, two subjects predominate: one for strings, the other (an oriental melody elaborately filigreed) for solo oboe. Both ideas are developed fully before the inclusion of further material.

Celtic flavors are prominent in the meditative second movement. An extended melody for violin opens this section and is its principal material. Throughout this movement there is a prevailing feeling of melancholy. But a more cheerful note is injected in the final movement, which comprises two bucolic themes, both introduced by the oboe.

1929 SYMPHONY NO. 3. I. Lento moderato; Allegro moderato. II. Lento. III. Moderato; Poco lento.

There are many reputable English critics who consider the symphonies of Arnold Bax as significant as those of Sibelius. They cover, wrote Wilfrid Mellers, "a wide and rapid emotional range, from the menacingly cruel to the lyrically beautiful, and each mood is conceived with the same dispassionate intensity."

Certain traits are common to all Bax symphonies. Though all utilize three movements, they are actually extended symphonic poems. An introduction is prominent in each, while all symphonies after the Second utilize a lyrical epilogue. Other qualities which identify them are their unusual color, their indulgence in Celtic moods and atmospheres, and their frequent use of motto themes.

The first two symphonies, completed respectively in 1922 and 1925, are steeped in pessimism. The third—introduced in London under Sir Henry J. Wood, on March 3, 1930—avoids melancholy and is filled with what one annotator happily described as "benevolent grace." This is music gentle, rather than somber, in character, dominated by the spirit of the Northern legends which, Bax acknowledges, influenced him subconsciously.

The symphony opens with a tender melody for bassoon. This subject is repeated by other instruments, then is enriched and extended until a highly rhythmic passage arrives (Allegro moderato). An expressive idea for first violins induces tranquillity which, for the most part, the movement maintains until the end. The solo horn opens the second movement, which, according to Robert H. Hull, "stands out as a tranquil utterance of strange beauty." Two major melodies provide the essential material: one for trumpet solo, the other for first violins. The burst of energy released in the third movement is arrested in the highly effective Epilogue, which contains some of the best music of the entire symphony: a noble passage for trombones precedes music of exceptional poignancy and arresting beauty.

1930 OVERTURE TO A PICARESQUE COMEDY, for orchestra.

Successfully introduced by the Hallé Orchestra, in November, 1931, this overture (as the composer has written) "does not pretend to be the prelude to any particular play. It is simply a piece of music associated with some character as d'Artagnan or Casanova."

There are two principal themes: one is mocking and impudent; the other is more dignified. The overture sparkles with bright-faced gaiety from first bar to last, and has been described by one nameless critic as "a swaggering piece of music."

1935 SYMPHONY NO. 6. I. Moderato; Allegro con fuoco. II. Lento molto espressivo. III. Lento moderato; Allegro vivace; Andante semplice; Lento.

In Bax's sixth symphony, we encounter a greater concentration of expression, a surer structural logic, and an increasing economy of means than we did in the third symphony, which had preceded it by six years. Here Bax is not only the master of his symphonic trade, but also the creator who reduces his thinking to essentials. In the first movement, an opening statement by horns and woodwind suggests the main theme. When that theme comes, it unfolds in woodwind and trumpets. The second subject, in flutes, introduces a moment of serenity, which is quickly dispelled by the tempestuous moods in the development.

Once again, in the slow movement, the nucleus of a main subject is found in the opening, in the six introductory measures. A temporary change of mood is introduced by the trumpets, but the earlier tranquillity is restored in the closing pages.

The finale is divided into three sections—an introduction, a scherzo with trio, and an epilogue. A basic theme is dominant, heard first in the clarinet. After that, the subject undergoes various transformations; and while this happens, new material of lesser importance is introduced.

To H. G. Spear the first movement suggests struggle; the lyrical second movement indicates a flight "to a realm of legend"; while the finale is a "land of music" in which the composer discovers "the tranquillity of absolute peace in an epilogue."

The symphony was introduced in London on November 21, 1935, Sir Hamilton Harty conducting.

PAUL BEN HAIM 1897–

Paul Ben Haim is the most important composer to come out of the new state of Israel. But his creative roots reach back to Germany in the early 1930s. Several impressive compositions completed in 1931—including *Pan,* a tone poem for soprano and orchestra, and a Concerto

Grosso—reveal a bent for effective lyricism and pastoral moods which would cling to much of his mature work in Palestine and Israel. After settling in Palestine, he began to work as pianist and arranger for several folk singers, but mainly for Braha Zephira, a Yemenite artist. This affiliation aroused his interest in the rich and varied folklore of Yemen, Bokhara, Persia and other regions in the Near East. This material provided him with a fresh source of stimulation, which led to the writing of his *Variations on a Palestinian Tune,* for piano, violin and cello (1939), whose main theme was of Bedouin origin. With his first symphony (1940) and continuing with other major works for various media and in sundry forms, Ben Haim was able to develop a style which, without deserting his former interest in gentle reflective moods and pastoral settings, tapped the rich folkloristic resources of his adopted country and its polyglot people.

Ben Haim was born Paul Frankenburger in Munich, Germany, on July 5, 1897. His music study took place at the Academy of Music in that city, with Friedrich Klose, Walter Courvoisier and Berthold Kellerman. For a while, after completing his studies, he conducted orchestral and operatic performances. But beginning with 1931, he devoted himself entirely to composition. With the rise of the Third Reich in 1933, he left his country for good, settled in Palestine, and adopted a Hebraic name. He soon became one of the country's leading musical figures, not only as a composer, but also as an educator. He taught composition in Conservatories in Tel Aviv and Jerusalem, becoming a prime mover and leader in the development of a musical educational system in Israel. In 1959, he paid a visit to the United States.

1939–1940 SYMPHONY NO. 1. I. Allegro energico. II. Molto calmo e cantabile. III. Presto con fuoco.

This is Ben Haim's first symphony; it is also the first significant symphony to come out of the region then known as Palestine (but now Israel). It is the work with which Ben Haim first achieved a distinctive creative identity, and to this day, it is one of his finest and most popular compositions. He wrote it during the somber months of 1939 and 1940, from the time in late August when Europe was drawing nearer to a world holocaust to that day in June of 1940 when France collapsed. While the composer had no intention of portraying in his music any of these tragic events, their dark shadow hovered over the composition. The first movement is turns intensely tragic by and passionate, while in the fiery finale—a tarantella whose force and energy are relieved by a calmer march-like episode—we find courage renewed and the spirit reborn. In between these two outer dramatic movements comes the slow movement with its lyricism of gentle beauty; this movement opens with a subject for strings that sounds like an oriental prayer, while it closes with an idyllic passage for flute and clarinet.

1945 PASTORALE VARIÉ, for clarinet solo, harp, and string orchestra.

The composition is based on a shepherd tune with a decidedly near-Eastern personality, which the composer had previously used in 1941 in the final movement of his Clarinet Quintet. There, too, it is subjected to variations, but the composer explains that his treatment in the later work differs from the earlier one "by giving more ample scope of solo virtuosity to the clarinet than in the chamber-music work."

All six variations in the *Pastorale varié* have a strong bond with the principal theme, and serve to present that theme in a variety of moods and feelings. The theme is given improvisational treatment in the epilogue. Following a brief cadenza for the clarinet, the composition ends in a gentle pastoral vein.

1949 CONCERTO FOR PIANO AND ORCHESTRA. I. Allegro. II. Andante. III. Rondo.

Ben Haim's piano concerto—which has received major performances not only in Israel but also in Europe and the United States—was first performed in Tel Aviv on February 6, 1950. The soloist was Frank Pelleg, who appeared with the Israel Philharmonic conducted by Charles Bruck.

The composer provided a title for each of the movements: "Vision," "Voices in the Night," and "Dance." Peter Gradenwitz describes the concerto as follows: "The first movement opens with a calm prelude: pianissimo arpeggios by the piano soloist are accompanied by soft tympani rolls and con sordino murmurings of cellos and double basses; a theme first takes shape with the entry of a trombone con sordino. The remaining brass instruments, and later the woodwind, build up a theme out of the motivic germs of the beginnings until the main section, Allegro con brio, of the movement begins with the piano solo. From here on, the movement develops in sonata form. There is a rhapsodic cadenza, preceding a soft-voiced coda; the rapid and fierce conclusion comes as a surprise.

"The second movement is a dainty and poetic nocturne in which the orchestration as well as the original melodic and rhythmic invention create a true 'Mediterranean-oriental' atmosphere; a viola d'amore solo creates an added dolce effect.

"The finale follows without break; it is a gay dance movement . . . in which the charming main theme gets an original orchestral coloring. Like a true oriental dance, the movement gains in momentum and tempo towards the end and concludes in frenetic ecstasy."

1953 THE SWEET PSALMIST OF ISRAEL, three symphonic movements for soprano and orchestra.

This work owes its origin to Serge Koussevitzky. On a visit to Israel, he conceived the idea of a monumental festival commemorating the three-thousandth anniversary of Jerusalem as the capital of the Hebrew world. For this festival, he commissioned several composers to produce works of religious or Biblical interest, and one of those whom he contacted was Ben Haim. Koussevitzky did not live to realize his giant project. Nevertheless, Ben Haim completed the commission by writing *The Sweet Psalmist of Israel,* whose world première took place in Tel Aviv in 1956 and in New York in 1959 with Leonard Bernstein conducting the New York Philharmonic and Jennie Tourel as soloist. Ben Haim, on his first visit to the United States, was in the audience.

The composition is in a concertante style. It describes King David, the musician, from several different points of view. The first section is based on a text from the Books of Samuel: "And it came to pass when the evil spirit from God was upon Saul that David took a lyre and played with his hand; so Saul refreshed, and was well, and the evil spirit departed from him." In this movement three main subjects are heard; towards the end of the movement they are combined polyphonically. Here the scoring is for harpsichord and wind.

The second movement was inspired by the following line from the Books of Samuel: "The sweet Psalmist of Israel said, The Spirit of the Lord spake by me and His word was on my tongue." This is an expressive lyrical section for strings and harp solo.

The concluding section is besed on the following lines from Psalm CXXXIV: "Behold, bless ye the Lord, all ye servants of the Lord, which by night stand in the house of the Lord. Lift up your hands in the sanctuary and bless the Lord. The Lord that made heaven and earth bless thee out of Zion." The structure here is a theme and variations, the theme given by the harpsichord. In each of the variations follows a wider range of instrumental color until, in the concluding climax, the fullest sonorous resources of the orchestra are exploited.

This composition received the Israel State Prize in 1957. It was subsequently chosen by the International Music Council to represent Israel in an anthology of contemporary music recorded under the auspices of UNESCO.

1958 TO THE CHIEF MUSICIAN, "Metamorphosis" for orchestra.

Ben Haim was commissioned by the Louisville Philharmonic to write this composition, which it introduced in Louisville, Kentucky, on October 28, 1958. The title comes from the heading to Psalm 49, which discusses the vanity of all things earthly.

In the same way that a psalm treats a basic subject with various poetic variations, this composition varies and transforms a single melodic idea. It is first heard in unaccompanied wind instruments and harp, to which strings and harpsichord make reply. Ten variations follow, the first three comparatively solemn. The tempo accelerates in the fourth variation until a climax is reached with the seventh, eighth and ninth variations—a march, toccata and wild dance, respectively. The tenth variation opens with a recitative in English horn, after which the composition ends with a dignified epilogue.

The composer described this work as a "metamorphosis" for orchestra, instead of "variations," because his transformations of the basic theme are freer and in a more unorthodox structure than they generally would be in the variation form.

ALBAN BERG 1885–1935

In 1904, Alban Berg met Arnold Schoenberg for the first time. What attracted each to the other was their mutual admiration for

Gustav Mahler. For the next six years, Schoenberg was Berg's teacher—his first teacher, and as it turned out, his only teacher. The older man helped release Berg's latent gift, while pointing out to him fresh new areas in which Berg's artistic personality could find root and bloom.

Berg had done some composing before his path crossed Schoenberg's—some seventy items, consisting mainly of songs and piano duets. Here the influence was Brahms, Wagner and Mahler. But while roaming about in these post-Romantic pastures, Berg came to a dead end. Instinctively he felt that the post-Romantic movement had exhausted itself; that, as a creator, he would only be repeating what others have said far better than he could were he to adopt their methods, techniques and aesthetic aims. He became convinced that, if he were to continue as a composer, he would have to adopt a new manner and a new idiom. And it was Schoenberg who first revealed to Berg what that new manner and idiom should be: the brave new world of atonality in which Berg could realize himself artistically.

While studying with Schoenberg, Berg completed three major compositions: the Piano Sonata, op. 1 (1908); the Four Songs, op. 2 (1909); and the String Quartet, op. 3 (1910). The Romantic influence still clung, even while Berg was finding the ways and means of freeing himself from the bonds of tonality. Though essentially polyphonic in style, the Piano Sonata was filled with Wagnerian chromaticisms; and (as Arthur Cohn suggested) while the op. 2 songs are "non Wagnerian," nevertheless "they resemble Wagner's composing habits, dressed up with additional sharps and flats." The String Quartet was the last work created by Berg as Schoenberg's pupil. Here Berg was beginning to think in his own terms and with his own formulas. "It is not surprising," says Cohn, "that some Wagnerian harmonies come forth, but none are of the sweet-tooth variety. Berg's tonal curves and ecstastic pronouncements are of a world which Wagner never knew."

The first work Berg completed after leaving Schoenberg's instruction was the *Five Orchestral Songs,* op. 4, in 1912. From this point on, his writing absorbed Schoenberg's atonal methods until finally and inevitably they brought him to the twelve-tone system (*see* Schoenberg). The twelve-tone system is found in some of the movements of the *Lyric Suite,* in 1926, and it is a dominant force in the Violin Concerto, in 1935. Berg's unfinished opera, *Lulu*—his last work—is entirely based on a twelve-tone row.

But where the twelve-tone row led Schoenberg to ever greater objectivity and abstraction, it failed to stifle Berg's natural romantic instincts. The very title *Lyric Suite,* and the descriptive words Berg appended here to each of the tempo markings ("*gioviale,*" "*amoroso,*" "*misterioso*" and so forth) point up that Berg the atonalist had no intention of avoiding subjective feelings. Such feelings so permeate his writing up to and including *Lulu*—so successful was Berg in endowing first atonality, and then the twelve-tone system, with human values and with a profound dramatic interest—that he has since been described as the Romantic of the twelve-tone school. For this reason, Berg has probably been the most palatable and the most popular of the Schoenberg group.

On two occasions, Berg interpolated fragments from the purely tonal music of other composers into his atonal fabric. This happened in the sixth movement of the *Lyric Suite,* where he quoted from the opening measure of the Prelude to *Tristan and Isolde.* It happened again in the second movement of his Violin Concerto, where he refers to the Bach chorale "*Es ist genug.*" These quotations underline a salient fact about Berg—namely, that, of the entire twelve-tone school, he was the one most successful in bridging the gap between the music of the past and the music of the future. "Alban Berg's significance as an artist lies—apart from his own creative genius—in his amazing gift for combining in his work all the elements of earlier and modern music, his ability to weld them into a convincing unity," said Emil Hertka, director of Universal Edition, in a memorial address. "For all their novelty, the connection between his works and the great Viennese tradition is always preserved. He resented particularly the accusation that his music was 'ruleless, chaotic, and atonal.' With his unusually developed sense of form and his feeling for law and order in music, he regarded such imputations as overwhelming proofs of misunderstanding."

The son of a merchant, Alban Berg was born in Vienna on February 9, 1885. Though he early showed a talent for music, and was encouraged by both his father and older brother in his music-making efforts, he received virtually no formal instruction until he reached maturity. Meanwhile, at the age of fifteen, he started composition: some songs and piano pieces in formal tonal systems. When he was twenty, he became Schoenberg's pupil. At this time, he earned his living by working in a government office, until a small family inheritance in 1908 enabled him to concentrate solely on music. In May of 1911, he married Helene Nahowski. He settled in a Vienna apartment and began to devote himself assiduously to composition. The first work completed at this period was the *Five Orchestral Songs,* which caused a riot when introduced in Vienna in 1913. Similar disturbances marked other of his premières. Nevertheless, Berg remained both undaunted and undiscouraged, continuing, under the stimulus of Schoenberg's example, to produce strikingly original compositions in an atonal style. A slow, fastidious workman, Berg required long periods of gestation for each composition. Thus, the only other principal works he completed up to the time of World War I were the *Four Pieces,* for clarinet and piano, op. 5, and the *Three Orchestral Pieces,* op. 6.

Found physically unfit for military duty during World War I, Berg helped the war effort by working in the War Ministry. Though he wrote nothing during this period, a major project was taking shape in his mind—the opera *Wozzeck.* He finally completed it in 1921, and its world première in Berlin in 1925 directed world interest on the composer.

Berg divided his chores as composer with the tasks of teaching and writing about music and promoting performances of avant-garde composers. In 1929, he was the recipient of one of the rare official honors to come his way when he was made a member of the Prussian Academy of Arts. After 1932, Berg divided his year between Vienna and a little summer place he had acquired on the Worthersee in Carinthia, to which he was particularly attached. His last years were spent in poverty and bad health. His death in Vienna on December 24, 1935, came from blood poisoning caused by a bee's sting. He died without completing his last major work, *Lulu,* upon which he had been at work for seven years.

1912 FIVE ORCHESTRAL SONGS (FÜNF ORCHESTER-LIEDER), after postcard texts by Peter Altenberg, op. 4. I. Seele, wie bist du schoener. II. Sahst du nach dem Gewitterregen. III. Ueber die Grenzen des Alls. IV. Nichts ist gekommen. V. Hier ist Friede.

This is Berg's first work after his period of study with Schoenberg—Berg's first attempt to fly on his own power, so to speak. This is also the first of his compositions to engage a symphony orchestra. On the other hand, this is also his last efforts within the song form; from this time on, his vocal writing would require the larger dimensions of opera or concert aria.

For his text, Berg selected the non-conformist ideas and sometimes erotic allusions expressed by the poet Altenberg on postcards sent to friends and enemies alike. Such a text had shock value, but this was not why Berg chose it. René Leibowitz explains that Berg was attracted to these verses because "they corresponded to the artistic and compositional needs of the inner structure of a work that in itself is 'shocking'." In all probability, the selection of this unusual literary material represented a further gesture of revolt on the part of an iconoclastic composer renouncing so many of the tenets by which music had been guided for so many years. For, as Leibowitz goes on to say, "the enthusiasm generated by those familiar with the resources of the new world of sound, free of tonal reminiscences, achieved full expression here."

The first song is noteworthy for its extended nineteen-measure orchestral prelude, whose germ motive is a five-note idea repeated frequently by piccolo, first clarinet and glockenspiel in unison. The second song is the shortest in the group (eleven measures). The third is in the A-B-A song form, elaborated mainly through orchestral means. The fourth is characterized by what Leibowitz describes as "extravagant effects" in the orchestra. The fifth and concluding song is a passacaglia; it is the longest in the group (fifty-five measures). Summarizing, Leibowitz says: "The most important characteristic of these songs in the spirit of structural and architectonic economy. . . .Berg, like Webern in the same period . . . succeeded in handling the variation technique with such rigorous mastery that he attained an astonishing equilibrium between abundance of invention and complete coherence."

Two of the five songs were heard for the first time in Vienna on March 31, 1913, at a concert sponsored by the Academic Society for Literature and Music. The program was made up entirely of works by Schoenberg and his followers. Throughout the concert, the angry reactions of the audience mounted, reaching a climax with the presentation of the Berg songs. A correspondent to the *Musical Courier,* on April 23, 1913, tells the rest of the story: "After the Berg songs the dispute became almost a riot. The police were sought and the only officer who could be found actually threw out of the gallery one noisemaker who persisted in blowing on a key for a whistle. But this policeman could not prevent one of the composers from appearing in a box and yelling to the crowd, '*Heraus mit der Baggage!*' ('Out with the trash!'). Whereat the uproar increased. Members of the orchestra descended from the stage and entered into spirited controversy with the audience. And finally the president of the Academic Society came and boxed the ears of a man who had insulted him while he was making an announcement."

1915 THREE PIECES FOR ORCHESTRA (DREI ORCHESTERSTÜCKE), op. 6. I. Praeludium. II. Reigen. III. Marsch.

In 1914, Berg set himself the task of writing a three-movement work for orchestra to honor Schoenberg on his fortieth birthday. Five days before the occasion, Berg despatched to Schoenberg two of the three movements (the first and the last), explaining that the middle part did not yet satisfy him. He completed the middle part in 1915. The Prelude and *Reigen* movements were performed for the first time in Berlin on June 5, 1923, Anton Webern conducting. A half-dozen years later, Berg revised the composition, altering some of the expression marks and removing some of the technical difficulties of the first trombone (a part sometimes now assumed by an E-flat bass trumpet). The new version was given in Oldenburg in 1930 under Johann Schueler's direction.

The opening prelude is brief, extending for only fifty-seven measures. It begins with percussion alone. Plucked strings, muted horns and solo flute are heard, after which the first bassoon presents a main thought, soon taken over by first trombone and horns. After the tempo is accelerated, a forceful climax is achieved. The principal thought is now presented in retrograde; the movement ends as it began, exclusively for percussion.

The *Reigen*, or Round Dance, is a dance movement in the tempo of an Austrian Ländler, which reveals the influence Mahler had upon Berg. A slow, quiet introduction precedes the presentation of the main thought by bassoon and trumpet. Ascending harp passages lead to a slow waltz tune. A descending passage for the oboe brings the movement to an end.

The concluding march movement also reveals the influence of Mahler, in the use of hammerblows ("*Hammerschlag*"), symbolic of the blows of fate, which Mahler had favored. Before the march tune appears, an important motive for the clarinet is repeated three times. The rhythm of the march melody enters in the brass in the twenty-fifth measure. The march is built up, while various brief motives are interjected, and the movement ends abruptly with a thunderous "hammerblow."

1921 WOZZECK, opera in three acts, op. 7, with book by the composer based on Georg Büchner's drama, *Woyzeck*. First performance: Berlin State Opera, December 14, 1925.

WOZZECK, three "fragments" for orchestra. I. Interlude—Langsam. II. Invention Theme—Marie's Remorse. III. Interlude—Epilogue to Wozzeck's Death—Langsam.

Early-twentieth-century Vienna rediscovered the dramas of Georg Büchner, written almost one hundred years earlier. It vibrated to their stark realism and acid indictment of social injustice. When Berg saw a performance of Büchner's *Woyzeck* in 1914, he immediately recognized its potential as an opera. His first problem was to compress twenty-five scenes into a workable three-act libretto. He did so in 1917, by assembling five scenes into each of the three acts.

There is no appreciable change in plot in the Berg version. The work remains a somber tragedy, hovering precariously between the world of reality and that of the subconscious, frequently having the distorted appearance of a nightmare. Wozzeck, a soldier, the object of ridicule in his regiment, is in love with Marie. But he has a rival in the drum major. Discovering Marie with a pair of earrings which the drum major had given her, Wozzeck passionately accuses her of infidelity. Confronting the drum major, Wozzeck is overwhelmed to hear the truth from the lips of his rival. He is further humiliated when, refusing a drink with the drum major, he is administered a sound thrashing. Repenting somewhat of the way she has treated Wozzeck, Marie consents to take a walk with him. Maddened by rage and jealousy, Wozzeck murders her. He seeks escape from his guilty conscience in drink; but, before stupefaction can set in, he suddenly remembers he has left the incriminating knife at the scene of the crime. He goes to search for it, finds it, and angrily throws it in a nearby pool. Then when he jumps into the pool to retrieve it, the water seizes him, and he is drowned.

His libretto completed, Berg set about the business of adapting play to music. He completed his score by 1920, and his orchestration was finished a year after that. When three fragments ("*Bruchstücke*") were introduced at the Frankfurt Music Festival on June 11, 1924, Hermann Scherchen conducting, the music drew ecstatic praises from the Schoenberg clique and equally excessive denunciations from most of the others. So much publicity was aroused by this performance that before long an operatic presentation was arranged, in spite of the formidable production difficulties posed by the work. On December 14, 1925, after one hundred and thirty-seven arduous rehearsals, Erich Kleiber conducted the world première at the Berlin State Opera. This event made music history. Some considered *Wozzeck* a landmark, the most significant twentieth-century opera since *Pelléas et Mélisande*. Many were horrified and shocked, failing to recognize either logic or artistic merit. "I had the sensation of having been not in a public theatre but in an insane asylum," wrote Paul Zsorlich in the *Deutsche Zeitung*. "On the stage, in the stalls—plain madmen." Indeed, so diverse were the critical reactions, so extreme in the presentation of their respective points of view, that a special booklet was published in Vienna quoting and analyzing these opposing opinions.

It is not too difficult to understand why the denunciations should have been violent, for *Wozzeck* is an opera such as none other in history. Atonal in style, the discordant music disgorged sounds from voices and orchestra that were strange, haunting and exotic. In place of melody, there was a stark, forbidding recitative, free in rhythm and unequal in measures, in which the pitch of a note was indicated, with the voice sliding up and down to the next indicated pitch (*Sprechstimme,* or *Sprechgesang*). What often resulted was an effect gruesome in intensity and harrowing in tension. "It had become plain," the composer wrote, explaining this brand of lyricism, "that this method of treating the voice in a music drama not only strengthened one of the best mediums for making such a work comprehensible—namely, words—but enriched the opera by the addition of a genuine means of artistic expression, created from the purest sources of music, ranging from a toneless whisper to the authentic *bel parlare* of far-reaching speech melodies."

Unorthodox, too, was the accompanying orchestra, which actually consisted of three different ensembles: a chamber orchestra; a military band; a restaurant orchestra of high-pitched violins. Instruments not usually encountered in traditional ensembles were used, among these being an out-of-tune upright piano, a bombardon (a kind of tuba), and an accordion.

Though on first contact *Wozzeck* might seem shapeless and structureless, it actually pursued a very rigid classical design with structures lifted from instrumental music. What Berg did was to plan the three acts along the outlines of the three-part song form (A-B-A). He called the first act "Exposition," the part in which is discussed Wozzeck "and his relation to his environment." Here Berg uses such traditional instrumental forms as the suite, the rhapsody, a military march, cradlesong, passacaglia, and a quasi rondo. Each structure is symbolic of some episode, character, or subconscious state. The second act is "Denouement," in which Wozzeck "is gradually convinced of Marie's infidelity." This is in the form of five-movement symphony (Sonata Form, Fantasie and Fugue, Largo, Scherzo and Rondo Marziale). The final act, "Catastrophe," describes how Wozzeck "murders Marie and atones through suicide." Structurally, what we have here are five Inventions: the first and second, on a theme; the third, on a rhythm; the fourth, on a key (D minor); and the fifth, on a persistent rhythm (or perpetual motion).

It is not always easy to uncover the precise structure being used at any given moment, just as it is not always easy to reduce Berg's complexity of style into ready comprehension. Nevertheless, as the drama of murder and death proceeds to its overpowering denouement—always dramatized and made compelling through Berg's hypertensioned musical language—it carries an overwhelming emotional impact. And the closing scene is one of the most heartbreaking episodes in contemporary opera. Marie's child is playing with a hobbyhorse, while the child's friends are going out to investigate Marie's death. Not comprehending the tragedy, the child rides faster and faster on his hobbyhorse with cries of "hopp, hopp," then goes off to join the others in their investigation, still calling "hopp" to the accompaniment of clarinet, drum, xylophone and pianissimo strings.

Other scenes have no less an emotional impact. One of these comes in the first scene of the third act where Marie reads the Biblical story of Mary Magdalen by candlelight, then laments over her own frailty. Structurally, this episode consists of an Invention—a theme and seven variations, with a fugue unfolding as she reads about Mary Magdalen and pleads to the Lord for His forgiveness. Structure and substance become one and indivisible to produce an unforgettable effect.

For telling tone painting, few incidents equal the drama and tensions of the fourth scene in the third act in which Wozzeck comes to the pond in search of his knife. Two solo violins are heard in a ghostly pianissimo with a downward descent of consecutive minor ninths. Below shudder the violas, playing tremolando on the bridge. This, Ernest Newman has written, "is the perfect, the inevitable realization, technical, pictorial and psychological, of the grisly horror of the scene in which the distracted Wozzeck searches in the moonlight for his knife."

Some of Berg's musical material springs from popular sources, however much these sources may be distorted. Marie's poignant lullaby to her child is rooted in German folk song; the music that accompanies the parade of the soldiers under Marie's window, in the same scene, reaches back to German military music; the dance music in the second-act inn scene is derived from the Austrian Ländler, while the song of the two young workmen stems from the waltz.

Ernest Newman pointed to the "unique oneness of the dramatic situations, the psychology of the characters and the musical expression" in explaining the effect of *Wozzeck* on audiences everywhere. "The first of these two elements is so consistently irrational that a certain irrationality (as the ordinary listener conceives it) in the music also seems right, especially in view of the fact that what revolts our harmonic sensibility in black and white can be made not only tolerable but gladly acceptable by means of orchestral color. . . . The non-technical listener . . . finds himself, perhaps for the first time in his life, taking a vast amount of non-tonal music and not merely not wincing at it but being engrossed by it. That simple fact is the true measure of Berg's achievement; whether the listener can account for his interest or not, the fact remains that he is interested in *Wozzeck* throughout, that he feels the music to be not only 'right' for the subject but the only musical equivalent conceivable for it."

Whether denounced or praised at its première, *Wozzeck* was a highly provocative, fiercely disputed art work that inspired curiosity and interest. This is the reason why it did not lack for performances. It was seen in Prague in 1926 (where the demonstrations were so bitter that the police removed it from the boards eighteen days after the first performance); in Leningrad, in 1927; in Vienna, in 1930. The American première took place in Philadelphia on March 19, 1931, Leopold Stokowski conducting, after which the same production was moved to New York City on November 24. By 1933, when the Nazis came to power in Germany and banned all further presentations, *Wozzeck* has been given twenty-one times in Berlin, and several hundred times in sixteen other German cities. Since then, *Wozzeck* has been produced in major music centers of the world. In 1951, it became one of the principal attractions at the Salzburg festival in Austria; that same year, Dimitri Mitropoulos conducted a concert version in New York with the New York Philharmonic, which was recorded in its entirety by Columbia. The opera was produced in English by the New York City Opera one year later, and it entered the repertory of the Metropolitan Opera for the first time on March 5, 1959. With such increasing familiarity, *Wozzeck* began to assume the status of a twentieth-century masterwork, a fact which the critics and audiences were now ready to concede universally.

Wozzeck is occasionally represented on symphony programs by three excerpts or "fragments." The first is taken from the close of Act I, Scene II, and includes the transition to and the beginning of Scene III. This at first is somewhat rhapsodic music, describing Wozzeck's melancholy state as he makes his way to the barracks. A martial note is introduced with the performance of a military march, heard offstage in the third scene, outside Marie's window. After that comes Marie's poignant lullaby to her child.

The second fragment comes from the opening of Act III. It is evening; Marie is in her room reading a Bible by candlelight. She is relating the story of Mary Magdalen to her own personal circumstances. Seven variations on her theme follow, ending in a brief fugue. Marie calls upon the Lord to forgive her for her frailty.

The third fragment contains the ending of Act III, Scene IV, and the closing music of the opera. Ascending chromatic passages for the woodwind and strings accompany the fall of the curtain where Wozzeck meets his doom in a pond. An extended three-part orchestral interlude follows (Adagio), described in the score as an "Invention on a Key." This is followed by the closing scene, designated in the score as "Invention on a Persistent Rhythm in Triplets." This is the scene in which Marie's child plays on his hobbyhorse, and continues playing, even when his friends run off to inspect Marie's dead body.

1925 CHAMBER CONCERTO (KAMMERKONZERT), for piano, violin and thirteen wind instruments. Epigraphe. I. Thema scherzoso con variationi. II. Adagio. III. Rondo ritmico con introduzione.

This is the first of Berg's compositions in a strict twelve-tone system; only one episode in Wozzeck had previously been built from that idiom. The key to understanding this concerto is the number "three." Berg wrote this concerto as a birthday gift to Arnold Schoenberg. Conscious that the trinity of the twelve-tone school was Schoenberg, Webern and himself, Berg constructed his music with fanatic mathematical precision with the number three in mind. There are three movements; the instrumental body comprises three groups (keyboard, strings, wind); the rhythmic and harmonic constructions carry out patterns of three.

In the *Epigraphe* that precedes the work, a kind of musical anagram is worked out, created out of those letters in the names of Schoenberg, Webern and Berg, that can be translated into musical notes (German notation); this anagram yields three themes that are utilized prominently throughout the composition. The structure is also created out of the number three, or its multiples. In the first movement (for piano and wind), there are six repetitions of the same idea (elaborated into a variation of thirty measures, divided into three sections). The Adagio, scored for violin and wind, is in three-part song form. And in the concluding movement (for piano, violin and wind ensemble), material from the first and second movements is repeated in three combinations.

1926 LYRIC SUITE (LYRISCHE SUITE), for string quartet. I. Allegretto gioviale. II. Andante amoroso. III. Allegro misterioso. IV. Adagio appassionato. V. Presto delirando. VI. Largo desolato.

"Lyric" is a happy description of this work. Despite the twelve-tone technique employed in some of the movements, the composition as a whole is filled with graceful melodic ideas and touching sentiment. The first movement opens brusquely with three chords in which are heard the twelve tones of the row employed in this movement. The basic material, however, is a flowing melody and the overall character of this music is joyful. The second movement carries strains reminiscent of an old Viennese waltz in music that bears nostalgic recollections of old Vienna. There are emotional outbursts in the third section. This is music generally delicate in its suggestions, though at times an eerie effect is produced by having its principal themes stated in plucked strings or *sul ponticello*. The fourth movement was described by Erwin Stein as having achieved "a summit of lyric expression through broad melody." The fifth movement is highly discordant, but the sixth (in which the Prelude to *Tristan and Isolde* is quoted) is pervaded by a dark, brooding melancholy.

Concerning the formal construction, Erwin Stein has written: "The sections are concerned with each other in a peculiar manner. For instance, a theme, idea, or passage from one movement always reappears in the next."

The première of the *Lyric Suite* took place in Vienna on January 8, 1927, in a performance by the Kolisch Quartet. In 1928, Berg arranged three movements from this suite for chamber orchestra, a version frequently performed. The three movements are: I. Andante amoroso. II. Allegro misterioso. III. Adagio appassionato. This chamber-orchestral adaptation was first heard in Berlin on January 21, 1929.

1929 WINE (DER WEIN), concert aria for soprano and orchestra.

Berg set three poems from Baudelaire's *Le Vin* (translated into German by Stefan George) and used them as three parts of a single, integrated and uninterrupted concert aria. In the first poem, "*L'Ame du vin*," the cork is drawn from the bottle and the soul of the wine is released. The second poem, "*Le Vin des amants*," tells how wine becomes the intoxicant of love. The third poem, "*Le Vin du solitaire*," describes how wine becomes the source of inspiration for a lonely poet lost in solitary dreams.

Robert Craft makes an interesting observation when he says that the three songs may be regarded as three parts of a one-movement symphony. Looked upon in this light, the first song becomes the exposition and development; the second, the scherzo; and the third (in which the first song returns telescoped) as the recapitulation.

Instrumental episodes serve as the transition from one song to the next—the first, short; the second, extended. The first song consists of an introduction and five episodes (one, a delightful tango); the second is in two parts, the first in 6/4 time and the second in fast waltz time, the waltz tune played twice; the third is an abbreviated version of the first.

The première of *Der Wein* took place in Königsberg, Germany, on June 4, 1930. Ruzena Herlinger was the soloist, and Hermann Scherchen conducted.

1935 CONCERTO FOR VIOLIN AND ORCHESTRA. I. Andante; Allegro. II. Allegro; Adagio.

Berg's special gift for endowing atonality in general, and the twelve-tone system in particular, with vibrant human values, deep emotion and romanticism is perhaps nowhere more evident than in this, his last complete work.

It had been commissioned by the concert violinist, Louis Krasner, in 1934. But Berg did not receive an inspirational incentive until a year later. It came with the death of one of his dear friends, Manon Gropius, a young girl (daughter of Gustav Mahler's widow by a second marriage), who died suddenly and unexpectedly just as she seemed to be making a remarkable recovery from a serious illness. Berg now conceived his concerto as a requiem to the girl, whom he described in his dedication as "an angel." The subject of death, with the young girl as its victim, naturally brings up a parallel in Schubert's song "Death and the Maiden." But where, in Schubert's song, it is Death who is first heard from, in the concerto, it is the maiden who appears first.

Once having found his inspiration, Berg worked intensively and passionately—putting aside for the time being his monumental labors on his opera *Lulu*. He completed the concerto in six weeks' time. Reporting the completion of the commission to Krasner, Berg wrote: "Yesterday I brought the composition of the violin concerto to its close. If you are perhaps astonished, I am still more so. I have never in my life worked with such constant industry, and I have taken increasing joy in it. I hope, indeed I believe, that this work will come out well."

Though based on the twelve-tone row, the concerto is a personal document, deeply felt, profoundly moving. Indeed, when the work was first introduced in England, Constant Lambert (who had little sympathy for atonality) described it as "the most beautiful and significant piece of music written since the war." It is now the general consensus of authorities on music that this is one of the most significant violin concertos in the twentieth century, and one of Berg's masterworks.

The composer intended the first movement as a description of the girl; in it, her ingratiating qualities are delineated in several graceful themes, one of them recalling an Alpine folk song, another suggesting a Viennese waltz. The movement opens in an improvisatory manner with a series of tones, a succession of fifths suggesting a violin's open strings; the interval of a perfect fifth is a motto that recurs throughout the concerto symbolizing the girl's purity. When the solo violin enters, it is heard in the principal theme, built from a twelve-tone series. The Allegretto that follows is a scherzo with two trios. This is music deriving its liveliness and joy from a Viennese waltz theme and a Carinthian folk song; here we get a personal portrait of the happy maiden in full bloom of youth and health.

The second movement is a more dramatic pronouncement, for it speaks of the tragedy of death, and it ends with the delivery of the girl's soul. A cadenza for solo violin suggests the death struggle; figures in horn simulate the relentless tread of Death. An intermezzo relieves the tension for a while, but then an emotional climax is built up and allowed to subside on a sustained F organ point in the basses. A recall of four notes of the motto theme develops into a presentation of the chorale melody "*Es ist genug*" from Bach's cantata *O Ewigkeit, du Donnerwort,* whose text speaks of resignation in the face of death. It is interesting to remark that Berg here first uses Bach's original harmonies before imposing on the melody his own harmonization derived from his twelve-tone row. A series of variations on his hymn melody for the solo violin now become a plangent elegy for the dead girl. After an effective climax, the coda finds the solo violin still engaging the requiem melody. The concerto ends as it began, with the fifths of open strings in the orchestra—ascending in the violins, descending in the basses.

The première of the concerto took place on April 19, 1936, at the fourteenth festival of the International Society of Contemporary Music in Barcelona. Louis Krasner was the soloist, and Hermann Scherchen conducted. The work was being heard posthumously, for Berg had died less than four months earlier. When the work received an ovation, Scherchen held up the score to indicate that the tribute belonged to the creator of this music, not to the performers.

1935 LULU, opera in three acts (unfinished), with libretto by the composer based on two plays by Frank Wedekind, *Erdgeist* and *Die Büchse der Pandora*. First performance: Municipal Theater, Zurich, June 2, 1937.

LULU, symphonic suite for orchestra. I. Rondo. II. Ostinato. III. Song of Lulu. IV. Variations. V. Adagio.

Berg labored seven years on an operatic successor to *Wozzeck*. He did not live to complete it. He left behind two finished acts, 268 measures of the third act, and a finale. He also had completed an orchestral suite, adapted from the opera score, made up of five excerpts (three of which have since enjoyed extensive performances at symphony concerts). This suite was introduced before the opera itself, in Berlin on November 30, 1934, Erich Kleiber conducting. On December 11, 1935, the suite was given in Vienna. Though seriously ill, Berg insisted on cooperating with the preparation of this performance and on attending the concert. It was his last appearance in a concert auditorium. Less than two weeks after that he was dead.

At the world première of the opera, in Zurich, in 1937, it was given in its incomplete version—two acts and two fragments—precisely as Berg had left it when he died. After that, the opera had to wait a dozen years to be staged again. In September 1949, it was presented at the Teatro La Fenice in Venice. The opera was produced for the first time in Germany, at Essen, in 1953, when the third act was filled out with spoken dialogue lifted from Wedekind. This was the same way the opera was given when it was first produced in the United States, at Santa Fé, New Mexico, on August 6, 1963.

The drama is a sordid one, comprising lust, murder, suicide, perversion, human degradation and the heroine's death by disembowelment at the hands of Jack the Ripper.

In discussing the German première for *The New York Times,* Henry Pleasants provided the following succinct summary of the plot: "Its heroine is palmed off by her lover on a physician who discovers her with a painter and dies of heart attack from the shock. She marries the painter, who is shortly driven to suicide by her promiscuousness. She then returns to her original lover, forcing him to break off his engagement with his fiancée and marries him. When he discovers her in a compromising situation with his own son, he hands her a revolver and suggests that she use it on herself. She playfully uses it on him, serves a term in prison and runs off with the son and a female lover to London where she becomes a professional prostitute. Among her customers is Jack the Ripper, who kills her."

The heroine, then, is a repulsive character whom Lawrence Gilman once described as "a symbol of human passion and agony and frustration and defeat." An unidentified critic in Prague said further: "Lulu is a heroine of four dimensional power in her endurance and her suffering, destroying all that she magnetizes. She is a phenomenon of nature, beyond good and evil, a complete cosmos whose secrets, altogether removed from ordinary comprehension, can be revealed only by the music. The way this glowing ball of fire scorches everybody that it touches and finally burns itself out, leaving all life about it extinguished or fading away, has led the metaphysician in the composer to make the transposition to those unearthly spheres, where figures flicker in death like dream images, illumined only by the last dying afterglow of a great irresponsible drama."

Berg's approach to structure in *Lulu* differs from the one he had adopted for *Wozzeck,* as the composer himself explained: "In contradistinction to *Wozzeck*, where the character and the completeness of the many short scenes necessitated the use of self-contained character pieces in the variety of musical forms, even those of pure instrumental music, *Lulu* called forth a preference for vocal forms like arias, duets, trios, and ensembles up to twelve voices. . . . I thought to make each scene complete in itself."

Where only one episode in *Wozzeck* had been in the twelve-tone technique, *Lulu* is entirely based on a twelve-tone row appearing at the very opening measures of the opera. In spite of its adherence to this rigid and austere tonal system, *Lulu* nevertheless is a more romantic opera than its predecessor, highlighted by modern dance rhythms when they fit the stage action. The score as a whole is characterized, as Lawrence Gilman said of it, by "a passionate sincerity" and an "uncompromising purity of intention." Gilman added that its "poignant intensity of feeling is as little to be resisted by the susceptible as the exalting tenderness of its pity and grief." Where *Wozzeck* had been distinguished by its apt atmospheric writing, its buildup of tensions, and its delvings in the subconscious of its main character, *Lulu* often resorted to literalism of musical action, in which music gives a realistic translation of what takes place on the stage—for example, the scene in which Lulu kills her husband with five bullets as the violins ascend the five notes of the chromatic scale.

Paul Collaer points out some of the outstanding pages in the opera: "The Lied in the second act which Lulu sings with disarming sincerity; the long duet song by Lulu and Alva, also in the second act; and Alva's hymn to Lulu's beauty. There are also three magnificent interludes." The three interludes Collaer speaks of, all for orchestra, are to be found in the five-movement suite Berg had prepared from his opera score. One is an "Ostinato," an intermezzo between the first and second scenes of the second act. Ernst Krenek describes this episode in the following way: "Berg has taken the rather complicated story of Lulu's imprisonment and liberation, hardly susceptible of treatment in a music drama, and has presented it in a silent film accompanied by orchestra. This central point of the work is also . . . the *peripeteia* in the fate of the heroine. Before, she has been an active element in the tragedy, destroying men by the passion she unleashed in them. Afterwards, she is a passive object, driven to destruction as a sacrifice to the bourgeois moralistic conception of guilt." This music begins quietly with imitative figures in low strings, piano and woodwind. A gradual crescendo leads to a climax, after which the fury subsides and the music recedes to a quiet fermata.

The second orchestral episode is "Variations," an entr'acte between scenes one and two in the third act. The variations are based on a street tune pointing up Lulu's moral disintegration. After a three-measure introduction (Moderato), there come four variations, marked *Grandioso, Grazioso, Funèbre* and *Affettuoso.* The tune itself is then heard in the woodwind, sounding as if it came from a hand organ.

The third instrumental excerpt is one of the most beautiful pages in the opera, the "Adagio" derived from the opera's finale. It opens Sostenuto—a spacious melody unfolding in the strings beginning with the forty-sixth measure (Grave). The song extends for thirty-six measures and is destroyed by an outcry in full orchestra describing Lulu's agony. The episode ends quietly and tenderly with a melody based on Countess Geschwitz' poignant farewell, "*Lulu, mein Engel.*"

LEONARD BERNSTEIN 1918–

Bernstein made his bow as composer with the Sonata for Clarinet and Piano (1941–1942), his first work to get published and to receive a public performance, which took place in Boston on April 21, 1942. This is music influenced by Hindemith's neo-classical idiom. That linear writing was just a passing phase became immediately evident with a composition of a completely different character and physiognomy, the rhapsodic symphony, *Jeremiah* (1942). The spare, lean, contrapuntal writing of the Sonata now gave way to romantic, even passionate episodes, with occasional leanings on Hebraic sources. The second symphony, *The Age of Anxiety* (1949), is more restrained and economical, though here, too, we frequently encounter intensity and ardor. This composition points a finger to Bernstein's eclecticism that has since characterized his work, passing as his style does from jazz to the twelve-tone row, from unashamed romanticism to the austerity of modern discords. A popular American idiom, found only in passing in this second symphony, is more strongly evident in his ballet, *Fancy Free* (1944), and in the little opera, *Trouble in Tahiti* (1952). The twelve-tone row is the basis of his third symphony, *Kaddish* (1963).

Here, then, is a composer who can and does employ many different styles. And he uses them equally well. He is extremely articulate, whatever the idiom; his writing is always in good taste and admirably projected; his moods are frequently vitalized with dramatic thrusts. Generally speaking, he is more effective with broad sweeps of sound and dramatic outbursts than with restraint, economy, or introspection; more convincing with the effect of his whole than with the subtlety of his parts.

Bernstein was born in Lawrence, Massachusetts, on August 25, 1918. He attended Harvard, where he took courses in music with Walter Piston and Edward Burlingame Hill, revealing extraordinary talent in everything pertaining to music. Following his graduation from Harvard in 1939, he studied conducting with Fritz Reiner at the Curtis Institute in Philadelphia, together with piano with Isabelle Vengerova and composition with Randall Thompson. Scholarships enabled him to attend the Berkshire Music Center at Tanglewood in 1940 and 1941. There he was a pupil of Serge Koussevitzky, who soon came to regard him as his protégé and who made him his assistant at Tanglewood in 1942. In 1943, Bernstein was appointed assistant conductor to Artur Rodzinski with the New York Philharmonic Orchestra.

On November 14, 1943, Bernstein made his official bow as conductor when he appeared as a last-minute replacement for Bruno Walter with the

New York Philharmonic. He created a sensation. Since then, he has conducted the major orchestras of the world, as well as opera at La Scala, the Vienna State Opera and the Metropolitan Opera. In 1958, he was appointed musical director of the New York Philharmonic, with which he made extensive tours of the United States, Europe, South America, the Orient, and countries behind the Iron Curtain. On November 2, 1966, Leonard Bernstein announced that at the termination of his contract with the New York Philharmonic, in the spring of 1969, he would resign as music director to devote most of his energies to composition. His association with the orchestra would continue through the creation of a lifetime post as "laureate conductor."

Bernstein also distinguished himself as a major composer for the popular Broadway stage, beginning with the musical comedy *On the Town* (1944) and climaxed with the worldwide success of *West Side Story,* first produced in 1957, and then made into an outstanding motion picture. In addition to his conducting and creative activities, Bernstein has been a significant personality on television, both in concerts and in lectures on musical subjects. Some of his television scripts were assembled into two best-selling books, *The Joy of Music* (1959) and *The Infinite Variety of Music* (1966).

On September 9, 1951, Bernstein was married to Felicia Montealegre, an actress of Costa Rican birth but American training. In 1965, Bernstein was awarded the Danish Sonning Prize of $7,200, one of the many honors that have come to him through the years.

1942 JEREMIAH SYMPHONY. I. Prophecy. II. Profanation. III. Lamentation.

"In the summer of 1939," wrote the composer, "I made a sketch for a *Lamentation* for soprano and orchestra. This sketch lay forgotten for two years until, in the spring of 1942, I began a first movement of a symphony. I then realized that this new movement, and the Scherzo that I planned to follow it, made logical concomitants with the *Lamentation*. Thus the symphony came into being, with the *Lamentation* greatly changed, and the soprano supplanted by a mezzo-soprano.

"The symphony does not make use to any great extent of actual Hebrew thematic material. The first theme of the Scherzo is paraphrased from a traditional Hebrew chant, and the opening phrase of the vocal part in the *Lamentation* is based on a liturgical cadence still sung today in commemoration of the destruction of Jerusalem by Babylon. Other resemblances to Hebrew liturgical music are a matter of emotional quality rather than of the notes themselves.

"As for programmatic meanings, the intention is again not one of literalness, but of emotional quality. Thus the first movement aims only to parallel in feeling the intensity of the prophet's pleas with his people; and the Scherzo, to give a general sense of destruction and chaos brought on by the pagan corruption within the priesthood and the people. The third movement being a setting of a poetic text is naturally a more literary conception. It is the cry of Jeremiah as he mourns his beloved Jerusalem, ruined, pillaged, and dishonored after his desperate efforts to save it. The text is from the *Book of Lamentations,* I, 1, 2, 3, 4; IV, 14, 15; V, 20, 21."

Leonard Bernstein himself introduced the symphony, with the Pittsburgh

Symphony on January 28, 1944; Jennie Tourel was the assisting artist. On February 18 and 19 of the same year, Bernstein conducted the work in Boston (his first appearance with the Boston Symphony); and on March 29, he led the New York Philharmonic in the symphony's New York première. The critical consensus was highly favorable. *Modern Music* said: "With unwavering simplicity and directness he has written not so much a literal expression of a Biblical excerpt as he has fashioned an emotional experience of his own.... The tense austerity of the first movement, the fresh charm of the . . . theme which opens the Scherzo, and the expressive simplicity of the final movement stand out." The New York Music Critics Circle gave the symphony its annual award, and in 1945 RCA Victor released a recording.

1944 FANCY FREE, ballet in one act with choreography by Jerome Robbins. First performance: Ballet Theatre, New York, April 18, 1944.

FANCY FREE, suite for orchestra. I. Dance of the Sailors. II. Scene at the Bar. III. Pas de deux. IV. Pantomime (Competition). V. Three Variations (Galop, Waltz, Danzon). VI. Finale.

Bernstein was commissioned by the Ballet Theatre in New York to write his first ballet score—to Jerome Robbins' first effort at choreography. Bernstein himself outlines the scenario as follows: "With the sound of a juke box . . . the curtain rises on a street corner with a lamp post, a side-street bar, and New York skyscrapers pricked out with a crazy pattern of lights, making a dizzying background. Three sailors explode on the stage; they are on shore leave in the city and on the prowl for girls. The tale of how they meet first one, then a second girl, and how they fight over them, lose them, and in the end take off after still a third, is the story of the ballet."

From the neo-classical style of the Clarinet Sonata and the Romantic-Hebraic tendencies of the *Jeremiah Symphony,* Bernstein proceeds here to a light, tuneful, saucy score with jazz melodies, rhythms and instrumental colors.

The première, at the Metropolitan Opera House in New York, with Bernstein conducting, was an enormous success. Edwin Fenby described *Fancy Free* in the *Herald Tribune* as "a perfect American character ballet," while John Martin in *The New York Times* called it a "rare little genre masterpiece." It was given 161 times in its first full season, and has since become a staple in the American ballet repertory. This ballet was also the source of, and the inspiration for, Bernstein's first musical comedy, *On the Town*, produced in 1944.

The symphonic suite adapted by Bernstein from the ballet score has been frequently performed by major American orchestras.

1946 FACSIMILE, "choreographic observation in one scene," with choreography by Jerome Robbins. First performance: Ballet Theatre, New York, October 24, 1946.

When *Facsimile* was introduced, the program quoted a motto by Ramón y Cajal explaining the theme of this second venture into ballet by Bernstein and Robbins. "Small inward treasure does he posses who, to feel alive, needs every hour the tumult of the street, the emotion of the theatre, and the small talk of society."

George Balanchine describes *Facsimile* as "a naturalistic ballet of ideas."

He goes on to explain that it deals with the basic problem of "what modern man shall do with his time. Often apparently immune to authentic feeling, he takes refuge in the constant company of his fellow men, where he can conceal his lack of security. He arranges his life not only to conceal his real identity from his friends, but to hide it from himself."

There are only three characters: a woman, a man and another man. The woman is on the beach alone, trying to amuse herself by dancing, and by playing with a toy in her hand. One man comes and tries to attract her interest, then a second. The first is a bore, but the second arouses her interest. When the two men begin to fight for her, she stops the brawl and sends them away. Once again she is alone on the beach, looking for distraction from boredom.

In his biography of Leonard Bernstein, this editor said: "This ballet represented for Bernstein a radical change of pace from *Fancy Free*. His first ballet had been realistic and satirical, modern and racy. The second was mainly melodramatic, atmospheric, at times nebulous. Ever resilient in adapting his musical style and thinking to the requirements of a text, Bernstein produced for *Facsimile* a score . . . utilizing the fullest resources of contemporary writing in music that was gripping in dramatic impact and high tensioned in mood."

1949 THE AGE OF ANXIETY, Symphony No. 2, for piano and orchestra.

Part I: The Prologue; The Seven Ages (Variations I-VII); The Seven Stages (Variations VIII-XIV). Part II: The Dirge; The Masque; The Epilogue.

The inspiration for Bernstein's Second Symphony was W. H. Auden's poem, *The Age of Anxiety*. The poet's concern with the insecurity of our times, and his search for a faith that can be accepted, even if blindly, impressed the composer, who tried to carry over the poem's message in his music. He began his symphony in 1947. His feverish activity as a conductor, which brought him to the four corners of the world, compelled him to write the work by fits and starts—in hotel lobbies and airplanes, wherever and whenever he could find a free hour. He completed the final orchestration on March 20, 1949, while on a month's tour with the Pittsburgh Symphony. On April 8, 1949, it was introduced by the Boston Symphony Orchestra, under Serge Koussevitzky, with the composer playing the piano part. The critics acclaimed it as a major work; a month later it received the Hornblit Prize as the best new work heard that year at the concerts of the Boston Symphony. The New York City Ballet presented it, with choreography by Jerome Robbins, on February 26, 1950.

The composer provided the following program for his music:

"Part I: (a) The Prologue (Lento moderato) finds four lonely characters, a girl and three men, in a Third Avenue bar, all of them insecure, and trying, through drink, to detach themselves from their conflicts, or, at best, to resolve them. They are drawn together by this common urge and begin a kind of symposium on the state of man. Musically, the Prologue is a very short section consisting of a lonely improvisation by two clarinets, echo-tone, and followed by a long descending scale which acts as a bridge into the realm of the unconscious, where most of the poem takes place.

"(b) The Seven Ages. The life of man is reviewed from four personal points of view. This is a series of variations which differ from conventional variations in that they do not vary any one common theme. Each variation seizes upon some feature of the preceding one and develops it, introducing, in the course of the development, some counter-feature upon which the next variation seizes. It is a kind of musical fission, which corresponds to the reasonableness and almost didactic quality of the four-fold discussion.

"(c) The Seven Stages. The variation form continues for another set of seven, in which the characters go on an inner and highly symbolic journey according to a geographical plan leading back to a point of comfort and security. The four try every means, going singly and in pairs, exchanging partners, and always missing the objective. When they awaken from this dream-odyssey, they are closely united through a common experience (and through alcohol) and begin to function as one organism. This set of variations begins to show activity and drive and leads to a hectic, though indecisive, close.

"Part Two: (a) The Dirge (Largo) is sung by the four as they sit in a cab en route to the girl's apartment for a nightcap. They mourn the loss of the 'colossal Dad,' the great leader who can always give the right orders, find the right solution, shoulder the mass responsibility, and satisfy the universal need for a father-symbol. This section employs, in a harmonic way, a twelve-tone row out of which the main theme evolves. There is a contrasting middle section of almost Brahmsian romanticism, in which can be felt the self-indulgent, or negative, aspect of this strangely pompous lamentation.

"(b) The Masque (Extremely Fast) finds the group in the girl's apartment, weary, guilty, determined to have a party, each one afraid of spoiling the others' fun by admitting that he should be home in bed. This is a scherzo for piano and percussion alone (including harp, celesta, glockenspiel, and xylophone) in which a kind of fantastic piano-jazz is employed, by turns nervous, sentimental, self-satisfied, vociferous. The party ends in anti-climax and the dispersal of the actors; the music of the piano-protagonist is traumatized by the intervention of the orchestra for four bars of hectic jazz. When the orchestra stops, as abruptly as it began, a pianino in the orchestra is continuing the Masque, repetitiously and with waning energy, as the Epilogue begins. Thus a kind of separation of the self from the guilt of escapist living has been effected, and the protagonist is free again to examine what is left beneath the emptiness.

"(c) The Epilogue (Adagio; Andante; Con Moto). What is left, it turns out, is faith. The trumpet intrudes its statement of 'something pure' upon the dying pianino; the strings answer in a melancholy reminiscent of the Prologue; again and again the winds reiterate 'something pure' against the mounting tension of the strings' loneliness. All at once the strings accept the situation, in a sudden radiant pianissimo, and begin to build with the rest of the orchestra, to a positive statement of the newly recognized faith."

Jazz, the twelve-tone system, a Brahmsian Romantic strain, an outpouring of lyricism, discords, polytonality and polyrhythmic methods are some of the ingredients in the eclectic score; yet always is there a feeling of unity, of singleness of purpose. With extraordinary taste and skill, Bernstein reaches for and finds the precise style or idiom called for by the varying moods, situations and concepts posed by Auden's provocative poem.

1952 TROUBLE IN TAHITI, opera in one act, with text by the composer. First performance: Waltham, Massachusetts, June 12, 1952.

Bernstein wrote both the text and the music for this light, witty, satirical little comedy in seven scenes which takes under forty minutes for performance. Like *Facsimile* and the Second Symphony, its theme is man's loneliness and emptiness, his search for lasting values. But the material is here treated with tongue in cheek, symbolized in the trite quarrels of a young married couple in a typical suburban community. After heated words had been exchanged at the breakfast table, the husband leaves home to attend to business and find relaxation in a gymnasium; the wife proceeds to town for a session with her psychiatrist and a movie show called *Trouble in Tahiti.* When both are back home that evening, their little quarrel and heated exchanges are resumed. After dinner, they come to the wise decision of abandoning their unpleasant squabble and going off to see *Trouble in Tahiti.*

The text is treated with sardonic humor and a bit of malice, with gaiety and occasionally a touch of bitterness. "Mr. Bernstein," wrote Howard Taubman in his review in *The New York Times,* "seeks to reach more deeply into the hearts of his principal characters and in a long aria for the wife his music becomes searching and affecting. . . . The music does not have much variety. There is a brief jazz figure that keeps recurring and that keeps haunting one with its insistent banality long after the show is over. No doubt, the banality is deliberate, but Mr. Bernstein has failed, as a composer, to comment on it and thus to rescue it from the low standards of its genre. Where he does comment, as in the scene in which the wife tells us what she thinks of a film called *Trouble in Tahiti* she has just seen, Mr. Bernstein writes with delicious and irresistible vitality."

The première of the opera was one of the features of the Festival of Creative Arts held at Brandeis University. The opera was then produced on a coast to coast television broadcast in the fall of 1952; was given at Tanglewood, in Lenox, Massachusetts; and on April 19, 1955, was seen on Broadway in a program entitled *All in One.*

1954 SERENADE, for solo violin, string orchestra, harp and percussion. I. Phaedrus; Pausanias. II. Aristophanes; III. Erixymachus. IV. Agathon. V. Socrates; Alcibiades.

This serenade, commissioned by the Koussevitzky Music Foundation, is a five-movement composition inspired by and based on Plato's *Symposium.* Each movement is devoted to one of five Greek philosophers or poets of the *Symposium,* who are involved in a heated discussion on love at the home of the poet, Agathon. The world première took place at the Venice Festival in Italy on September 12, 1954, with Isaac Stern as soloist, and Leonard Bernstein conducting. The same soloist and conductor officiated at the American première in New York on April 18, 1956. The music was subsequently used for a ballet entitled *Serenade for Seven,* choreography by Jerome Robbins; it was introduced at the Spoleto Festival in Italy in July 1959, with the American première following in the spring of 1960 in New York.

Bernstein provided the following programmatic notes: "The music, like the dialogue, is a series of related statements in praise of love, and generally follows the Platonic form through the succession of speakers at the banquet. The 'relatedness' of the movements does not depend on common thematic material, but rather on a system whereby each movement is evolved out of the elements in the preceding one. . . .

"I (Lento, Allegro). Phaedrus opens the symposium with a lyrical strain in praise of Eros, the god of love (Fugato, begun by solo violin). Pausanias continues by describing the duality of lover and beloved. This is expressed in a classical sonata-allegro based on the material of the opening fugato.

"II. (Allegretto). Aristophanes does not play the role of the clown in this dialogue, but instead that of the bedtime storyteller invoking the fairy tale mythology of love.

"III. (Presto). The physician speaks of bodily harmony as a scientific model for the working of love patterns. This is an extremely short fugato scherzo born of a blend of mystery and humor.

"IV. (Adagio). Perhaps the most moving speech of the dialogue, Agathon's panegyric embraces all aspects of love's powers, charms and functions. This movement is a simple three-part song.

"V. (Molto tenuto; Allegro molto vivace). Socrates describes his visit to the seer Diotima, quoting her speech on the demonology of love. This is a slow introduction of greater weight than any of the preceding movements; and serves as a highly developed reprise of the middle section of the Agathon movement, thus suggesting a hidden sonata-form. The famous interruption by Alcibiades and his band of drunk revelers ushers in the Allegro, which is an extended rondo ranging in spirit from agitation through jig-like dance music to joyful celebration."

1956 OVERTURE TO CANDIDE, for orchestra.

Candide is a musical play with book by Lillian Hellman, adapted from Voltaire's famous satire of the same name. It was produced on Broadway on December 1, 1956. It closed after only seventy-three performances—but it was far better than this unhappy history would suggest. The Hellman adaptation was bold, incisive, rich with Voltaire mockery and malice. And Bernstein's score was a cornucopia of riches, overflowing with all kinds of delightful tunes, tender and gay—parodies of opera arias, trios, quartets, choral numbers, a waltz, mazurka, ballad, tango, gavotte, and sundry other aural delights.

The Overture has survived, and makes its presence from time to time on serious symphony programs. It has opéra-buffa sparkle and vivacity, beginning with an exuberant, boisterous opening for full orchestra on a note of uninhibited gaiety and highlighting two delightful opéra-buffa melodies, one for the woodwind, the other for the strings.

1963 KADDISH, Symphony No. 3, for speaker (woman), soprano solo, mixed chorus, boys' choir and orchestra. I. Invocation (Kaddish I). II. Din-Torah (Kaddish II). III. Scherzo; Finale (Kaddish III).

In 1956, the Koussevitzky Music Foundation commissioned Bernstein to write a major orchestral work to help commemorate the seventy-fifth anniversary of the Boston Symphony. Bernstein did not get around to fulfilling this assignment until the summer of 1961, when he started work on it at Martha's Vineyard. The score was completed two years later, in August of 1963, and the orchestration was completed during a three-week period the following November. Bernstein was at work on the orchestration of the final Amen on November 22, the day President Kennedy was assassinated. Bernstein forthwith dedicated the *Kaddish* "to the beloved memory of John F. Kennedy."

At Bernstein's request, the world première took place not in Boston but in Tel Aviv, Israel. Bernstein conducted the Israel Philharmonic, and Jennie Tourel was soprano soloist. The date of the première was December 10, 1963. On January 31, 1964, the work received its American hearing, with Charles Munch conducting the Boston Symphony, Jennie Tourel as soprano soloist, and Felicia Montealegre (Mrs. Bernstein) as narrator. In Israel, Alexander Boskovitch described the symphony as "a great human and artistic document" revealing a "sublime mastery of musical values and techniques that made use of all the advantages of our musical age."

The composition is not actually a symphony but a hybrid product combining the best features of oratorio and spoken drama. Indeed, the spoken text assumes such a significant role in the overall context that the *Kaddish* is almost as much a literary production as a musical one.

The *Kaddish* is a Hebrew prayer for the dead, chanted at the grave, at memorial services, and in remembrance of the dead during synagogal worship. The prayer never makes mention of death or the dead, and so, actually, it is not a threnody at all. It is rather a hymn of praise to the Almighty, and at the same time it is an affirmation of life and the living. It is this dualistic nature of the prayer—the sanctification of the Lord and the affirmation of life—that Bernstein emphasized in this work.

The text employs the traditional words of the *Kaddish,* written and spoken in a mixture of Hebrew and Aramaic. Along with these traditional verses comes a long poetic text, written by Bernstein himself, which is an exhortation to God by a female narrator who identifies herself as Lily of Sharon. She is the embodiment, says Bernstein, of "that part of man that refuses death."

These Bernstein verses aroused considerable criticism in Jewish circles, since an intimate man-God relationship is established in which the narrator speaks to, upbraids, and accuses God the way she might another human being. It is in such a vein that she opens her first address to the Lord with the words: "Oh, Holy Father, ancient hallowed lonely disappointed Father, angry wrinkled Old Majesty, I want to pray." Later on, she addresses him angrily: "Listen, Almighty, with all your might you show me nothing at all!" Some felt strongly that words like these represented blasphemy. But Bernstein insisted that a man-God relationship has Biblical precedent (in the story of Job, for example) and was rooted in Hebrew folk tradition; that a "deep personal intimacy" always existed between religious Jews and their God "which allowed things to be said to God that are almost inconceivable in another religion."

The music also caused some eyebrows to rise: the rhythmic handclapping of the chorus and the monotoned choral passages, both suggesting a Negro

Shout rather than synagogal prayer; the excessive use of a tremendous battery of percussion for complex rhythmic effects; the persistent deployment of a twelve-tone row which endowed the musical writing with so much of its acidity and cerebralism; the one or two places where jazz rhythms and the blues rear their unexpected heads.

But there is also much in the score that is traditional, and much that has extraordinary emotional appeal. Ross Parmenter reported in *The New York Times*: "The music is decidedly more palatable than the text, where it had a good deal of rhythmic invention. There are exciting climaxes, a number of choral passages were lovely, and always the tone paintings, as in the vision of heaven and the contrasting chilly dawn, were vivid. . . . The reviewer kept wishing he could have had only the music, for so much of it was expressive and interesting."

1965 CHICHESTER PSALMS, for chorus and orchestra.

These psalms were commissioned from Bernstein by the Dean of Chichester, the Very Reverend Walter Hussey, in England. But its world première took place in New York City—on July 14, 1965—with Leonard Bernstein conducting the New York Philharmonic. Bernstein drew his text from three Psalms: "Make a Joyful Noise" (No. 100), "The Lord Is My Shepherd" (No. 23), and "Lord, Lord, My Heart is Not Haughty" (No. 131). Several verses from other psalms are also used "to throw these three in relief," as Raymond Ericson explained in *The New York Times*, "and unify the composer's philosophic intention, wherein the ideas of praise, meditation and strife lead to the ending: 'Behold how good and how pleasant it is for the brethren to dwell together in unity.' " The text is sung in Hebrew.

Here is how Alfred Frankenstein described Bernstein's music in *High Fidelity*: "The first movement . . . with its exhortation to make a joyful noise unto the Lord . . . is a powerful, pulsating, dancelike piece of music, full of shrewd invention in the colorful handling of choral and instrumental forces. The second movement . . . [is] a quiet, long-breathed pastoral solo for a boy's voice with much use of the harp in accompaniment; but these meditations of the adolescent David are contrasted at one point with an ironic resumption of the dance. . . . The finale . . . grows, to my taste, altogether too seraphic. Its idiom recalls the most angelic passages in the Fauré *Requiem*—but the wings of these angels are confected of whipped cream."

BORIS BLACHER 1903–

In some of his more traditional compositions, Blacher affiliated himself with the neo-classic school by combining a free atonal counterpoint with Baroque structures; here his writing is lean, spare, concise.

In this category, we find such works as the Concerto for String Orchestra, op. 20 (1940), the Partita, for strings and percussion (1945), and the two divertimenti, opp. 31 and 38 (1948, 1951). In other traditional compositions, he exploited a vein of irony and satire. A gift for these, as well as for parody, is encountered in his ballet-opera *Das Preussiches Märchen*, or *Prussian Fairy Tales,* op. 30 (1949), which reduces to the ridiculous the German love for uniforms and the pretentions of Prussian militarism, and in the ballet *Chiarina,* op. 33 (1946), set in a nineteenth-century German spa and caricaturing people and customs of the period.

But it is perhaps as an experimentalist and an innovator that Blacher has aroused most interest. In a few of his instrumental compositions, he originated a system of rhythm and meter which he dubbed "variable meters" (for an explanation see *Orchestral Ornaments*). In opera, too, he opened new vistas. *Fürstein Tarakanova,* op. 19 (Wüppertal, February 5, 1941), *Die Flut,* or *The Flood,* op. 24 (Dresden, March 4, 1947), and *Das Preussiches Märchen* (Berlin, September 23, 1952) are all made up of scenes, each of which is a self-contained entity dominated by a thematic motive or a rhythmic pattern. In *Abstrakte Oper Nr. 1* (1953), he delved into the world of abstraction; while in *Zweischenfälle bei einer Notlandung,* or *Incidents in a Crash Landing* (Hamburg, February 4, 1966), he made extensive use of electronic sounds reproduced stereophonically.

Though a German composer, Blacher was born in the Chinese town of Newchwang on January 19, 1903 (not January 6 as most reference books suggest), of Estonian-German parentage. His boyhood was spent in Irkutsk, Siberia, where he took his first lessons in harmony and violin. Later, he lived in Harbin, Manchuria. There he continued his study of harmony with the conductor of the local orchestra. In 1922, he settled in Berlin where he attended the High School of Music until 1927, a pupil of Friedrich Koch in counterpoint. Between 1927 and 1931, he worked with Schering and Blume in musicology at the University of Berlin. His Concerto for Two Trumpets and Two String Orchestra (1931) and *Kleine Marschmusik* (1932) were his first compositions to attract attention. He scored an impressive success with two major works—his first ballet, *Fest im Süden* (1935), and the *Concertante Musik*, the latter introduced by the Berlin Philharmonic under Schuricht on December 6, 1937.

Between 1938 and 1939, Blacher was a member of the faculty of the Dresden Conservatory. In 1945, he became director of the Berlin Radio. In 1948, he was appointed to the faculty of the Berlin High School of Music where he succeeded Werner Egk as director in 1953.

Blacher first visited the United States in 1955 to serve as guest professor of composition at the Berkshire Music Centre at Tanglewood. During this visit, his chamber opera, *Romeo and Juliet,* received its first American stage performance. (It had received its world première in 1947 in a concert version, and its first staged production anywhere at the Salzburg Festival in 1950.) Blacher returned to the United States during the summer of 1966, as composer-in-residence at the Hopkins Center Congregation of the Arts at Dartmouth College. At this festival, four concerts of Blacher's works were performed, including the American premières of his first and third piano concertos (1941,

1961). One year later, on August 19, 1967, the Hopkins Center Congregation of the arts presented the world première of his *Virtuose Musik*, for orchestra.

1947 VARIATIONS ON A THEME BY PAGANINI (ORCHESTERVARIATIONEN ÜBER EIN THEMA VON NICCOLO PAGANINI), for orchestra, op. 26.

This is one of Blacher's works in his precise, economical, neo-classic style, with emphasis on linear writing. It is one of his most successful compositions for orchestra. Its première took place on November 27, 1947, in a performance by the Leipzig Gewandhaus Orchestra.

The theme for these variations is that of the twenty-fourth caprice for solo violin by Paganini (which had been exploited for variation purpose by Brahms and Rachmaninoff; for Rachmaninoff's treatment, see *Rhapsody on a Theme by Paganini*). In Blacher's work, the theme is followed by sixteen variations, varied in rhythm and tempo.

1953 ABSTRACT OPERA NO. 1 (ABSTRAKTE OPER NR. 1), opera in seven scenes, op. 43, with text by Werner Egk. First performance: Frankfort, Germany, June 28, 1953 (concert version); Mannheim, Germany, October 17, 1953 (staged version).

In this opera, composer and librettist experimented with abstraction in opera. Scored for three soloists, chorus, wind, piano and percussion (with dancers miming the action on the stage) it exploits typical contemporary situations but arranged in an abstract design without any unifying plot. Titles are provided for each of the seven scenes to point up the emotion or state of mind employed. The opera begins and ends with "Fear." In between the opening and closing scenes come "Love—I," "Pain," "Negotiation," "Panic," and "Love—II." Most of the text consists of meaningless arbitrary sounds. In the "Fear" scene, for example, the dialogue consists entirely of the sounds "ah" and "ooh." The sound pattern of "laga, baba, nabuna" dominates another scene; "gurru, gurru," in a third; "adynazit, azit, azant, anitronit," in a fourth. On the rare occasion where the words are intelligible, they make little sense.

Here is how Klaus George Roy described some of the scenes in the *Christian Science Monitor*: "The opening scene shows three people in the throes of extreme anxiety, giving forth primeval wails . . . . A hilarious jealousy scene is caused by a dressmaker's dummy which gets shot. Most entertaining is a satiric negotiation scene between two diplomats . . . chanting English and Russian words at each other almost in the manner of Gertrude Stein. This is meaningfully followed by a scene of war and panic, at the end of which the world itself seems to topple. Romance again conquers; but the return of the opening fear scene suggests the futile merry-go-round of such modern life."

It was the unusual text, rather than the music, that inspired a major scandal when the opera was first staged. In a communication to *The New York Times,* Henry Pleasants reported: "The performance was greeted with laughter, catcalls, whistles and indignant 'pfuis!'. . . . Subsequent performances were given to similarly obstreperous audiences until the theatre director . . . resorted to a pre-performance appeal from the stage for tolerant silence, at least, during the show." However, when the opera was revived at the Berlin Festival in

1957, Hermann Scherchen conducting, it met with an enthusiastic response from both audience and critics.

1953 ORCHESTRAL ORNAMENTS (ORCHESTER-ORNAMENT), for orchestra, op. 44. I. Andante. II. Allegro. III. Presto.

STUDY IN PIANISSIMO (STUDIE IM PIANISSIMO), for orchestra, op. 45.

Blacher wrote two sets of *Ornaments* featuring "variable meters": a rhythmic and metrical device of his own invention. One was for the piano, a set of seven studies, op. 37 (1950); the second, three years later, was for orchestra.

In his compositions with "variable meters," Blacher selects a rhythm row very much in the way a twleve-tone composer chooses a tone row. The pattern of rhythm and meter is based on an arithmetical series: sometimes in strict succession (1, 2, 3, 4); sometimes by having the subsequent number become the sum of two preceding numbers (1, 2, 3, 5, 8); sometimes in cyclical variation (2–3–4–5, 5–3–2–4, 3–2–4–5).

Ornaments received its first performance at the Venice Music Festival on September 15, 1953, Hans Rosbaud conducting. When Dimitri Mitropoulos directed the American première with the New York Philharmonic on November 19, 1953, Howard Taubman wrote in *The New York Times*: "It has a certain energy and, in a few places where the spirit is almost jazz-like, it has a bit of life. . . . No doubt it is laid out with the utmost logic in accordance with the theory [of variable meters] and no doubt too Blacher was aiming after some communication that would go beyond displaying a formula."

The *Study in Pianissimo* was commissioned by the Louisville Orchestra in Kentucky, which introduced it under Robert Whitney on September 4, 1954. An orchestral nocturne, this is a study which throughout maintains the dynamic level of pianissimo. "The weight of the orchestra," the composer explains, "shifts from tutti to small ensemble groups." Structurally, the composition leads from a number of isolated tones to projected musical phrases, reaching towards the twelve-tone chords with which the piece ends; metrically, the work is characterized by a continually changing seven-bar pattern.

EASLEY BLACKWOOD 1933–

Beginning with his Opus No. 1, a Sonata for Viola and Piano (1953), Blackwood adopted an eclectic style which ranges from atonality and discords to expressive lyricism. He favors classical structures, and he prefers writing music free of programmatic or literary associations but which, as he has explained, is "an expression of musical ideas and nothing more." When in his later works he makes use of a serial technique, he uses it freely and only in passing. In general, he shuns avant-garde tendencies and avoids innovation for its own sake. He is not afraid, however, to adopt complex formal schemes, and he is always ready, as Alfred J. Frankenstein notes, to pursue that scheme "to its ultimate implications." In all of Blackwood's music, we are made aware of what Frankenstein has described as a "lively, original, uncompromising talent at work."

Blackwood was born in Indianapolis, Indiana, on April 21, 1933. His father is the world-famous authority on bridge, originator of the Blackwood Convention. Young Blackwood made successful appearances as a piano virtuoso in his boyhood. Music study took place for three summers at the Berkshire Music Centre at Tanglewood (composition with Oliver Messiaen in 1949), at Indiana University with Bernard Heiden and with Paul Hindemith at Yale. In 1953, Blackwood received his Bachelor of Music degree at Yale, and in 1954, his master's degree. After that, on a Fulbright grant, he went to France, where he was a pupil of Nadia Boulanger and where, in 1955, he received the Lili Boulanger Memorial Award.

His first two published compositions were the Viola Sonata and, in 1955, the Chamber Symphony, for fourteen instruments. Recognition came in his twenty-fifth year with a remarkable symphony. Later compositions fulfilled the high promises of this work. These included two string quartets (1958, 1959), a Concertino for five instruments (1959), the second symphony (1960), the Concerto for Clarinet and Orchestra (1964), the Concerto for Oboe and Orchestra (1966), and the Concerto for Violin and Orchestra (1967).

1955 SYMPHONY NO. 1, op. 3. I. Andante maestoso; Non troppo allegro ma con spirito. II. Andante comodo. III. Allegretto grotesco. IV. Andante sostenuto.

Blackwood wrote his first symphony in Paris during the period he was studying composition with Nadia Boulanger. He completed it in December of 1955. Its world première took place on April 18, 1958, in Boston, with Charles Munch conducting the Boston Symphony. The following November, Munch conducted it once again in Boston, and shortly after that introduced it to New York. Accolades by the critics in Boston and New York were followed by several honors, including first prize from the Koussevitzky Music Foundation, and a grant from the American International Music Fund for a recording. The jury that chose the symphony for this recording heard fifty-two entries. Blackwood's symphony was one of the last to get heard and, as one of the jurors—Alfred J. Frankenstein—later revealed, but "it all completely swept the field.

When the symphony was introduced in Boston, the composer provided his own analysis, of which the following is an extract:

"The first movement is a modified sonata form, with a slow introduction. From this introduction grows the first theme, which is then elaborately developed right away. The second theme is entirely new material, and is of much different nature. It too is developed immediately after its appearance. The unusual feature of the movement is that the development and recapitulation are combined. The development is actually a variation of the exposition, all in the proper sequence. The movement ends with a brief coda, the material of which is used to conclude each of the four movements. This motive also served as the starting point for several of the themes in the other movements: namely, the first theme of the second movement and the second theme of the third movement.

"The second movement consists of two themes which are much more alike in character than are those of the first movement. There is no real development of either theme. . . . The third movement is a scherzo, but in classical sonata form. The striking feature of this movement is that it is entirely built on ostinato figures which range in length from one to eighteen measures. The second theme is based on the material which concludes each movement. This is heard near the beginning played by a single horn, unaccompanied. The first part of the development is canonic; later the two themes are heard together. . . .

"The last movement is much freer in form than are the other three. This movement is in large part a variation of the first, although it contains some new material which has not been heard before. . . . This movement is quiet throughout, except for a brief climax near the end. There is a coda immediately following the climax which makes extensive use of the material which concludes all the movements. . . . The work concludes on the progression of two chords reiterated by muted violins pianissimo."

1960 SYMPHONY NO. 2, op. 9. I. Grave; Rapido e volubile; Tempo primo. II. Allegretto; Meno mosso; Tempo primo. III. Presto.

Hardly had he completed writing his first symphony when Blackwood began planning a second one. Ideas began coming thick and fast, but other projects kept him from developing this material into a symphony. Then he received a commission from the publishing house of G. Schirmer for a symphonic work commemorating the centenary of the firm's founding. This commission sent Blackwood back to his neglected symphony, which was finally written between July and November of 1960. The second symphony was introduced in Cleveland on January 5, 1961, with George Szell conducting the Cleveland Orchestra.

This is the composer's own description:

"The first movement is actually two movements combined: a slow movement and a fast movement. These are not heard consecutively, however. The slow section is interrupted by the fast part, but it returns later to end the movement. There is no thematic connection between the two parts, or between any two of the movements. The slow section is not characterized by formal rigor, but is a broad rhapsodic piece making great use of pedal points. The main theme appears at the beginning in the brass. The slow section concludes with a long oboe solo based on themes heard earlier. . . . The second theme is characterized by two elaborate oboe solos surrounding a broad tune in the violins. . . . There is a lengthy coda containing elements from all the themes, which ends the movement quietly.

"The second movement is a scherzo and trio. The scherzo part is made up of variations of two short themes which are heard alternately. . . . The trio is in a much slower tempo than the body of the movement, and is a formless rhapsody consisting of a broad line in the upper strings accompanied by a variety of sustained chords and staccato outbursts.

"The last movement is in the style of a brilliant toccata. Almost every instrument of the orchestra is called upon to play a prominent virtuoso part, both alone and with other members of the section. In form this movement is essentially a rondo; but themes appearing in the couplets are interrelated and the rondo theme itself is transformed considerably near the end of the movement. . . . A single note, 'E,' played by the tympani and the low strings pizzicato concludes the symphony."

1964 CONCERTO FOR CLARINET AND ORCHESTRA, op. 13. I. Allegro. II. Molto lento. III. Vivace.

This concerto was commissioned for the Cincinnati Symphony by a patron who prefers to remain anonymous. The world première took place in Cincinnati on November 20, 1964. Richard Waller was the soloist, and the Cincinnati Symphony was conducted by Max Rudolf.

The composer explains that the first movement is "made up essentially of two basic theme groups, each one of which undergoes two variations. In the first theme the clarinet plays an angular tune, while the orchestral accompaniment consists of staccato chords placed irregularly in the measure. In the second theme the clarinet melody is lyrical and freely expressive, while the accompaniment falls into regular patterns. The variations which follow take the two themes in their original order, but with considerable alterations and transformations."

The elegiac movement was written in memory of Paul Hindemith, to whom it is dedicated. "I have not attempted to write a piece strictly within the confines of Hindemith's own style or mannerisms, nor did I intend a paraphrase." However, certain aspects of this movement "are deliberately reminiscent of Hindemith."

The finale is "fast and bright, and makes considerable use of polyrhythmic counterpoint. It consists mainly of contrasting sections played by the solo instrument interspersed with brief orchestral interludes. These interludes are all made up of the same material, but it is juxtaposed and transformed so that they are never the same. The final transformation emerges as a brief parody of a military march."

1965 SYMPHONIC FANTASY, op. 17.

Commissioned by the Indianapolis Symphony Orchestra, the *Symphonic Fantasy* received its world première in Indianapolis on October 30, 1965. Izler Solomon (to whom the work is dedicated) conducted. Subsequently, the composer led a performance of the work in Berlin, Germany, during a festival of contemporary music.

When the *Symphonic Fantasy* was introduced, the composer provided the following analysis: "The *Fantasy* begins with a sustained line played by three trumpets in unison accompanied by strings and winds in the extreme high register. . . . Following this initial presentation comes a syncopated rhythm by the full orchestra in the low register. Shortly after this, there is added a jagged tune in the violins, flutes and E-flat clarinet. This leads to the sustained line in the three trumpets; and then the section, which to here is loud and agitated, suddenly becomes much more calm. There is a transition wherein the English horn refers indirectly to the trumpet line. The next section is somewhat in the nature of a development, although new material is still being introduced. This part is less violent than the beginning, but is much more stable. . . . After a brief 'recitativo' consisting of high strings and trumpets punctuated by brass and percussion, and followed by oboe and clarinets, there is a long flute solo accompanied by an undulating figure in the strings. This ends with a reference to the syncopated rhythm introduced near the beginning, but pianissimo this time. Beyond this point, no new material is introduced. The following section becomes stable once again and is characterized by a gradual build-up of excitement and orchestral forces. . . . The coda . . . is slow and meditative, and an oboe-piccolo duet recalls several of the less exploited motive. The work ends quietly with a slow progression of full chords."

SIR ARTHUR BLISS 1891–

Bliss began composing music seriously while he was still a student at the Royal College of Music in London. Then, during his army service in World War I, he had two chamber-music works published. These, and other earlier efforts, were destroyed immediately after the war, feeling as Bliss did that they no longer represented him. He now embarked upon an experimental period in which he undertook the writing of music on unusual subjects or with unusual material or unusual approaches. One was the Rhapsody, for soprano, tenor and instruments—an introspective and poetic piece of music in which the soprano was not so much a vocal soloist as a member of the instrumental ensemble, her role being to chant a wordless melody on the syllable "ah." This Rhapsody was Bliss's first mature composition to attract attention, initially at its world première in London in October of 1920, then at the festival of the International Society for Contemporary Music at Salzburg on August 5, 1923. Then, in 1920, there came a composition with an altogether different style and mood: *Rout*, for soprano and chamber orchestra. Here Bliss released his pronounced gift for comedy and satire; here, as in the Rhapsody, the vocalist sang not words but meaningless syllables. *Rout* proved a major success when it was heard in London in December of 1920, and it scored once again at Salzburg, Austria, on August 7, 1922. Humor was also present in *Conversations,* a set of five pieces for a quintet of instruments (1921). And in the *Color Symphony* (1922), new avenues were explored in associating various colors with various moods or events or episodes, and finding a correlation between all of them and musical sound.

After 1925, experimentation was relegated to a secondary place in Bliss's musical thinking. The striving for new media, effects, or procedures was not ended by any means; his intelligence was far too restless to become static. But intensity of feeling, poetic moods, refined speech were now the prevailing and identifying traits of his music. A more classical approach—with a respect for classical structures and a partiality for objectivity—became apparent in works like the Introduction and Allegro for orchestra (1926), the Oboe Quintet (1927), the Clarinet Quintet (1931), the Viola Sonata (1932) and the *Music for Strings* (1935). In works like these, he achieved the mission he had set for himself when he said: "If I were to define my musical goal it would be to try for an emotion truly and clearly felt, and caught forever in a formal perfection." But other of his mature works are more romantic, more subjective, more concerned with human values. In such a group we can find the moving choral symphony, *Morning Heroes,* dedicated to the memory of his brother who had been killed during World War I. This work proved extraordinarily successful when introduced at Norwich, England, on October 6, 1930.

Bliss was born in London on August 2, 1891. He received degrees in the arts and in music at Pembroke College, Cambridge. For a brief period, he attended the Royal College of Music, where he was a pupil of Vaughan Williams and Holst. During World War I, he saw combat duty in France as a commissioned officer; he was wounded at the Somme and gassed at Cambrai. For two years after the war, from 1923 to 1925, he lived in Santa Barbara, California, where he married Gertrude Hoffman, an American. He returned to the United States several times after that. In 1935, he came to Hollywood to write the score for the motion picture *The Shape of Things to Come,* based on H. G. Wells; and during World War II, he was a member of the music faculty at the University of California. From 1942 to 1944, he was affiliated with BBC in London, first as assistant director of overseas music, then as musical director. From 1946 to 1950, he was chairman of the Music Committee of the British Council. In 1950, he was knighted; in 1952, was made Master of the Queen's Music; and in 1963, was awarded the Gold Medal of the Royal Philharmonic Society.

1927 QUINTET FOR OBOE AND STRINGS. I. Allegro. II. Andante. III. Finale.

This is one of the early compositions in which Bliss assumed a classic pose and aimed for objectivity of expression. He dedicated this quintet to Mrs. Elizabeth Sprague Coolidge, the distinguished American patroness of music, who arranged for its first performance in Venice on September 11, 1927. One of the unusual features of this work is that the composer reverses the usual procedure of having the first movement dramatic and rhapsodic, and the second movement lyrical. In this Quintet, the emphasis in the opening Allegro is on lyricism, while in the slow movement there is a notable passage in which tensions and high drama are achieved. In the finale, the composer makes use of an old Irish fiddle tune, "Connolly's Jig." "It is not allowed to gain the upper hand," explains Edwin Evans, "but is a tasty ingredient in a well-seasoned dish, and supplies contrast to the earlier portions of the work, which are pensive and serious."

1935 MUSIC FOR STRINGS. I. Allegro moderato energico. II. Andante molto sostenuto. III. Allegro molto.

There is an intimate kinship between this work and Elgar's *Introduction and Allegro.* Both employ the string orchestra sensitively and effectively; both are romantic within a classical context; both are built on the foundations of English musical tradition.

Bliss's *Music for Strings* was heard first on an all-British program presented at the Salzburg Festival during the summer of 1935, Sir Adrian Boult conducting. The writing is free of any program; the thematic ideas are permitted flexibility of movement. This work is particularly notable for the skill with which the thematic material is distributed among different parts of the orchestra, and developed. No less admirable is the rich writing for the strings. Now, the players of one section are assigned different lyric parts, to the further enrichment of the musical texture; now, striking contrast is achieved by elevating the first-desk men to the status of solo performers.

1937 CHECKMATE, dramatic ballet in one scene and prologue, with choreography by Ninette de Valois and scenario by the composer. First performance: Sadler's Wells, Paris, June 15, 1937.

CHECKMATE, suite for orchestra. I. Dance of the Four Knights. II. Entry of the Black Queen. III. The Red Knight. IV. Ceremony of the Red Bishops. V. Death of the Red Knight. VI. Finale—Checkmate.

One of Bliss's greatest successes was achieved with this ballet, which he wrote for the British Week of Music at the Paris International Exposition. When Sadler's Wells toured the United States in 1949, *Checkmate* was its first modern production.

In the prologue, Love and Death, fighting for the lives of their subjects, play a game of chess. The ballet proper takes place on the chessboard. The struggle of the pawns, culminating in the murders of the Red Knight and the Red King by the Black Queen, is used by the composer as a symbol of the cruelty and lust of human beings in the game of life. This intriguing scenario draws from the composer a richly orchestrated score which is, by turns, dramatic, sensuous, and imaginatively pictorial.

1939 CONCERTO IN B-FLAT MAJOR FOR PIANO AND ORCHESTRA. I. Allegro con brio. II. Adagio. III. Andante maestoso; Molto vivo.

In 1939, the British Council commissioned Bliss to write a piano concerto for the New York World's Fair. Dedicated to "the people of the United States," this concerto was introduced in New York on June 10, 1939. Solomon was the soloist, and the orchestra was directed by Sir Adrian Boult.

The middle movement is one of Bliss's most poignant creations, a page of lyricism of rare sensitivity. It opens in an atmosphere of classic serenity before the first subject, a theme almost of waltz-like character, is announced by the solo piano; the second subject is dreamy and diaphanous.

The first and third movements are virile. The first contains a great deal of bravura writing for the piano, together with some dramatic utterances. It opens with an upward surge of strings and woodwind towards three virile chords. After some bravura passages for the piano, the full orchestra appears with the vigorous main subject. The second theme, a lyrical idea for the violins, comes after a brief cadenza for solo piano. The middle movement is dominated by an expansive waltz-like melody, first heard in solo piano. Contrasts in rhythm and dynamics are found in the closing movement, which has the structural characteristics of a scherzo. The highlight of this movement is an exquisite passage for solo cello, for which the piano provides a delicate background.

1949 THE OLYMPIANS, opera in three acts, with text by J. B. Priestley. First performance: Covent Garden, London, September 29, 1949.

Before attempting an opera, Bliss had proved his mastery in virtually every other area in music. The libretto (the work of one of England's most distinguished novelists and dramatists) concerns Olympian gods of Greek antiquity. Having fallen on difficult times with a decline of their fortunes and influence, they decide to come down to earth as strolling players. One night each year, however, they are allowed to return to their one-time glory.

A cabled report to *The New York Times* said: "Such a scenario provided the composer with many opportunities for the richest music—a dance for . . . Mercury; the prayer to Venus to reveal her beauty; and the voices of the Bacchantes offstage—indeed, one episode after another, in which Bliss writes a more lyrical, a more spontaneous music than would be expected by those who knew only his sinewy and sometimes astringent style. . . . Furthermore, he writes with frank romanticism . . . for the two lovers who wander in and out of this comedy of discomfiture by the aforesaid transmuted deities. . . . The opera provided also the scope for much fine choral writing, notably the bridal chorus at the end. The first act begins with a crisp, gay prelude, and is concerned with comedy. The author's intention is to vary realistic, down-to-earth dialogue with the happy fantasy of a midsummer night's dream, which needs poetry. His conception is admirable and well suited to operatic treatment."

1950 STRING QUARTET NO. 2 IN F MINOR. I. Allegro con spirito. II. Sostenuto. III. Vivo e con brio. IV. Larghetto; Allegro; Larghetto; Cantabile; Allegro largamente.

A decade separates Bliss's two string quartets. The second was written as a tribute to the Griller String Quartet to celebrate the twentieth anniversary of its founding. The composer explains that the first movement has a "forceful" opening, with "an energetic theme played in unison by the three upper strings." Throughout the movement this robust subject undergoes various transformations, as several other ideas are introduced. The most important of these is a fluid, lyrical seventeen-measure subject begun by the first violins over a pedal bass. The second movement, "slow and contemplative," begins with a "quiet dissonance, the rhythm and spread of which is characteristic of the first theme." The second section here is in a faster tempo, its principal thought announced by first and second violins. The third movement is in the form of a scherzo, and is played with lightning speed. The finale presents slow and fast sections alternately. Here the main theme is given by the viola, a melody that also serves as the basis for the quiet coda with which the movement ends.

1957 DISCOURSE, for orchestra.

This composition, as the title informs us, is a musical dissertation on a subject announced in the first four measures. The work has six sections, thus described by the composer: 1. Preliminary survey (Moderato; Larghetto); 2. A more disturbing view (Con moto e risoluto); 3. A gayer one (Vivace); 4. A contemplative one (Andante tranquillo); 5. An emphatic restatement of the subject, and a brief return to "3"; 6. A peroration, followed by a quiet coda.

The work was commissioned by the Louisville Orchestra in Kentucky, which introduced it, under Robert Whitney's direction, on October 23, 1957.

MARC BLITZSTEIN 1905–1964

Marc Blitzstein's greatest commercial success in the musical theatre came with Kurt Weill's *Three-Penny Opera* to which, in 1954, he contributed a modernized American text based on the original libretto by Bertolt Brecht. That production, born off-Broadway on March 10, 1954, had a New York run of some six years; it was also seen throughout the United States in performances by two national companies. This affiliation of Blitzstein with Weill—and of Blitzstein with the *Three-Penny Opera*—is not without significance in explaining and interpreting Blitzstein's career as a composer. For Blitzstein has often been described as an American Kurt Weill. Blitzstein's most famous and provocative operas are in the style, idiom and direction of the "song play"—a medium that Weill had originated in Germany in the late 1920s in an effort to make opera an everyday form of stage entertainment for the masses, its music springing from popular and music-hall sources. In addition, as his own librettist, Blitzstein (like Brecht) was a commentator on the social and political scene—an often angry and bitter commentator, with pronounced left-wing leanings, who used words and music as an instrument for propaganda.

While the influence of Weill (and coincidentally of Brecht) is unmistakable, Blitzstein was no imitator. In his strong dramatic instinct as a librettist, and in his remarkable skill in adapting an eclectic musical style to the requirements of his text, he was a significant creative force in his own right. Nor was he exclusively a polemicist. His social and political thinking was frequently just a means towards an artistic end.

Another significant fact about Blitzstein's career is worth noting. While he lived, his principal operas were first produced in the theatre and not in the opera house (even though some of them were subsequently presented by opera companies). This, perhaps, is as it should have been. Blitzstein's operas belong in the theatre, derive their significance and impact from the theatre. His music serves the stage and was not intended to have an independent existence of its own. Consequently, Blitzstein used any and every musical means at his disposal, however questionable some of them might have been from an artistic point of view. When a cheap or cliché-ridden melody served to heighten theatrical effect, when stage business was improved by an obvious comic effect in the orchestra, when a mood was best evoked through ragtime or jazz—Blitzstein never hesitated to use such material. In all of his produced operas, we find a strange mélange of different styles, ranging from Handelian recitatives and formal arias, to jazz, torch songs, pop tunes. It is not always excellent music, nor original music, by any means; and taken out of context, it leaves much to be desired. But it always helped to make for excellent theatre.

He was, to be sure, the apostle of social revolt—the angry man of the Depression, labor unrest and political storms of the 1930s. But as Minna Lederman said: "Marc Blitzstein was perhaps the most extravagantly gifted, certainly the most durable artist of our age of social unrest. . . . His multiple talents were catalyzed by the tensions of the Thirties. In the Sixties he was still carrying the flaming torch of protest. . . . With experience he learned to dim its intensity to a diffused candle glow. But in general, he preferred it at neon strength; and that is how it persists in memory, piercing and shadowless."

Blitzstein was born in Philadelphia, Pennsylvania, on March 2, 1905. After attending the public schools, and for two years, the University of Pennsylvania, he enrolled in the Curtis Institute of Music, where he studied composition with Rosario Scalero. At the same time, he commuted from Philadelphia to New York to take piano lessons with Alexander Siloti. Subsequently, his musical training was completed in Europe, with Nadia Boulanger in Paris and Arnold Schoenberg in Berlin.

His early compositions belong to the *Sturm und Drang* school of the ultramodern music of the 1920s—interesting for its experiments in structure, dynamics, tonality and discords. Not until his growing social consciousness dominated his musical thinking did he succeed in evolving his own creative personality. In his effort to reach a large audience, he abandoned his earlier experiments and complexity to arrive at a simplified idiom, often rooted in the soil of popular music. His first major work in this direction was his opera *The Cradle Will Rock*, in 1937, and it made him famous.

On the strength of two Guggenheim Fellowships, in 1940 and 1941, he completed a second opera, *No for an Answer,* produced in New York on January 5, 1941. It had a short life because the New York Commissioner of Licenses virtually censored the work by threatening the revocation of the auditorium's license on the specious grounds that it was unfit for operatic productions. (After this, the theatre was often used for opera without interference.)

During World War II, Blitzstein volunteered and served in the Eighth Air Force. He was assigned musical tasks, one of which was the writing of a symphony, *The Airborne,* dedicated to the Army Air Forces. Following his separation from the armed forces, he continued producing major works for the opera house, with *Regina,* in 1949, being the most significant.

In his last years, Blitzstein worked on three operas. One was a major project, based on the controversial Sacco and Vanzetti case of the 1920s, for which he had received a grant from the Ford Foundation, and in which the Metropolitan Opera expressed interest. Two others were shorter operas based on stories by Bernard Malamud, *Idiots First* and *The Magic Barrel.* He failed to complete any of these. While vacationing in Martinique, he was beaten by three sailors. He died in a hospital in Fort-de-France twenty-four hours later, on January 22, 1964. Excerpts from his three unfinished operas were heard at a memorial concert presented in New York City on April 20, 1964.

1937 THE CRADLE WILL ROCK, an opera (or musical play) in two acts, with text by the composer. First performance: New York City, June 15, 1937 (concert version); New York, February 11, 1960 (staged version).

In December of 1935, Bertolt Brecht, librettist of Kurt Weill's *Three-Penny Opera,* visited Marc Blitzstein at his apartment on Jane Street in New York's Greenwich Village. Biltzstein performed for his visitor a song he had recently written about a streetwalker, "The Nickel Under My Foot." Brecht liked it, and suggested that Blitzstein write a complete opera about prostitution in all its forms—sex, press, clergy, big business, and so forth. Blitzstein picked up the idea and started work the following week. For a while he wrote only by fits and starts, since his wife was bedridden with a fatal illness and he had to care for her. When she died, in the summer of 1936, Blitzstein sought escape from grief by absorbing himself completely with his opera. Before the end of the year, the work was finished and was accepted for performance by the WPA Federal Theatre.

The history of *The Cradle Will Rock* is surely one of the dramatic episodes in the American theatre. It was scheduled as a production of the WPA Theatre, directed by Orson Welles, and produced by John Houseman. On June 15, 1937, it was seen in a dress rehearsal. Meanwhile, the left-wing libretto had been creating uneasiness in certain influential government circles, which used pressure on the Federal Theatre to have the production banned. The ban was not announced until virtually the zero hour of opening night, with the result that the audience began gathering at the Maxine Elliott Theatre, unaware that the show had been called off. Members of the cast proceeded to entertain the audience, while director, producer, and composer scouted the nearby vicinity for another auditorium. When the nearby Venice Theatre was found available, the audience was directed there. And—denied the use of scenery, costumes, or orchestra—the opera was presented in oratorio form: the actors and chorus went on the bare stage dressed in their regular street clothes; and the composer, also on stage, played the score on the piano and informally explained to the audience, between scenes, what was taking place.

Thus, through accident, *The Cradle Will Rock* was presented in this unorthodox manner. The powerful impact it made on the audience was due not only to the intrinsic theatrical merits of the work but also to this unique manner of presentation.

Sam Grisman, a Broadway producer, attended that performance and, impressed by the dramatic appeal of the opera, offered to finance a Broadway run. Scenery, costumes and orchestra were now dispensed with, not through necessity, but out of purely artistic considerations. In this unique presentation, *The Cradle Will Rock* became not only an outstanding artistic success, but a resounding box-office attraction. It ran for 124 performances. "The most versatile artistic triumph of the politically insurgent theatre," was the way Brooks Atkinson described it. Virgil Thomson called it the "most appealing operatic socialism since *Louise*."

Ten years later, on November 24, 1947, the opera was revived by the New York City Symphony Orchestra, directed by Leonard Bernstein. In this performance it was heard with orchestra for the first time. The thunderous acclaim accorded the work after each of the two scheduled performances, and the chorus of approval by the critics (Olin Downes did not hesitate to describe it as a work of "genius") proved that it had lost little of its freshness and vitality. Once again an attempt was made to transfer the opera to the Broadway theatre, with the hope of duplicating the success of a decade past; but this time the box-office appeal was negligible, and the opera "folded" after thirteen performances.

Finally, on February 11, 1960, *The Cradle Will Rock* was presented as Blitzstein had originally intended it to be, not only with the orchestra, but also with scenery and costumes. This was also the first time the work was given by an opera company—the New York City Opera. At this revival, Howard Taubman noted in *The New York Times* that the opera was essentially a period piece whose subject, however exciting and provocative it might have been in 1937, had become "dated and corny." However, Taubman also remarked that even in 1960 the opera "bursts with vitality. It fills a theatre with excitement rare in an era when labor and capital argue their differences in comfortable hotels with high government officials to whisper impartial sweet talk in their ears."

The text is by the composer himself. The plot unfolds in a night court, and is built around the attempt of steel workers to create a union, and the devious methods of their employers to frustrate the attempt. Capitalism is symbolized by Mr. Mister, who controls Steeltown, and who has the town judge, newspaper editor, college president, doctor, and clergy under his thumb. By bribery and coercion, Mr. Mister brings the leading citizens of Steeltown together into a "Liberty Committee" organized to smash the union, which, of course, it fails to do.

The score Blitzstein wrote carries great momentum. Through recitatives, arias, patter songs, parodies, chorales—all in a style that blends popular elements with the harmonic and contrapuntal devices of serious music—the composer evolved a new kind of musico-dramatic art form in which the music performs as important a part as the spoken word in projecting dramatic situations; at times the music even displaces the word. Sometimes the music appears in the background, contributing strokes of characterization, tonal comment, satirical asides. Sometimes it carries forth the dramatic sweep of the action with impulsive rhythms and dynamic chords. Sometimes it injects a note of mockery into very serious proceedings with parodies of blues songs, torch songs, a Hawaiian song, and so forth.

"The musical tissue is neither subtle nor sophisticated," said Taubman in 1960. "Its only object is to add a dimension of pressure to a pressing theme. And it frequently succeeds—particularly in the stirring finale." Taubman concludes: "*The Cradle Will Rock* has lost its inflammability as an incitement to the barricades. But it blows up a storm in the theatre that you should appreciate whatever your political allegiance."

And Lewis Funke remarked (also in *The New York Times*) when the opera was revived in an off-Broadway production on November 9, 1964: "That it contains its indigenous vitality is a tribute to Mr. Blitzstein who composed a work of startling versatility. The music is stirring, it is also laden with that undercurrent of bite, disillusion and pathos."

1944 SYMPHONY: THE AIRBORNE. I. Theory of Flight; Ballad of History and Mythology; Kittyhawk; The Airborne. II. The Enemy; Threat of Approach; Ballad of the Cities; Morning Poem. III. Ballad of Hurry Up; Night Music; Ballad of the Bombardier; Recitative and Chorus of the Rendezvous; The Open Sky.

While serving with the Eighth Air Force in England, Blitzstein was commissioned to write a large symphonic work about the history of aviation. He wrote his own text, then composed the symphony. The orchestration was completed later, after the composer had been separated from the armed forces. On April 11, 1946, it was introduced in New York by the New York City Symphony under Leonard Bernstein.

The composer provided the following description:

"I call *The Airborne* a symphony (even though none of its three movements is strictly in the same form) in the same way that Liszt named the *Faust Symphony* and Stravinsky the *Symphony of Psalms*.

"There are twelve more-or-less self-contained sections that occur as subdivisions of the three larger movements. The work is about fifty-five minutes in length; and it is scored for a Speaker (I call him a Monitor, since nearly all his lines are couched in the imperative mood), male chorus, solo tenor (this part was conceived for Negro voice, because of what it might lend to the quality of the Ballad of History and Mythology), solo baritone, and full orchestra."

In text and music, Blitzstein offers not only a vivid description of the evolution of aviation from Icarus to World War II, but also points up as a commentary the futility of war and destruction. The symphony ends with a paean of praise to the open sky as a symbol of human freedom.

1949 REGINA, opera in two acts and prologue, with text by the composer based on Lillian Hellman's play, *The Little Foxes*. First performance: New York, October 30, 1949.

Lillian Hellman's bitter play, *The Little Foxes,* about the predatory Hubbard family in the South, whose members devour each other through hate, deceit, theft and even murder, only to devour themselves as well, was re-created by Blitzstein in a musical play of great force. All of Hellman's vitriol is retained—her devasting characterizations have lost none of their knife-edged sharpness. But through his music, Blitzstein seems to have brought a new dimension and perspective to these disagreeable people; and he did this—as Leonard Bernstein pointed out in an article in *The New York Times*—by bringing to his musical writing "sweetness and directness." Bernstein writes further: "Regina, herself perhaps one of the most ruthless characters in show business, sings melodies of enormous gentility and suaveness precisely at the moment when she is being most unscrupulous and heartless. There is a kind of urbanity involved in the musical treatment of this character, which results in a theatrical coup. . . . I might say that this is the underlying technique of the whole piece: coating the wormwood with sugar, and scenting with magnolia blossoms the cursed house in which these evils transpire."

To some of the drama critics, the contribution of softness to a hard play represented dilution. As Brooks Atkinson said, "What Blitzstein has added to it does not compensate for the loss in force, belligerence, and directness." But the music critics were more impressed by the results. Howard Taubman described the opera as "exciting musical theatre, in which the composer has "intensified the sinister mood of the central theme by setting it against an atmosphere that is more wholesome."

As in his other operas, Blitzstein blends many different styles of writing in *Regina*; each situation dictates the style that best suits its interpretation. There is music derivative from spirituals, sung by the colored servants, and there is ragtime music for a colored band. Formal dances help to evoke the period. Some recitatives have Handelian majesty, while others are as austere and forbidding as *Sprechstimme*. There are lilting tunes, and there are melodies of broad design. There are joyful choruses that in their bright-faced beauty make one think of madrigals; and there is a great deal of bitter music that brings up tonally the hatred and evil that permeate the entire household.

Among the most effective arias or songs are the two sung by Regina in which she reminisces about her past and describes her sufferings; also, the one sung by Alexandra, Regina's daughter, at the end of the play. Other memorable pages include an exciting "Galop"; Addie's mystical song, "Night"; the remarkable vocal quartet, "Listen to the Sound of the Rain," which Ross Parmenter described as "gentle and almost childlike . . . [characterizing] the innocents involved in the family warfare"; and Birdie's long scene that follows her confession that she is addicted to alcohol.

Regina has been frequently revived by the New York City Opera. Discussing the opera in 1959, Virgil Thomson said in the *Saturday Review*: "Time has already told us that Regina . . . is a repertory piece. Its story line is strong; its characters have reality; its music animates and enlarges them all, as good opera music must. Here is a work that fills an operatic stage and fulfills the listener."

ERNEST BLOCH 1880–1959

In his first mature compositions, Bloch wavered between Brahmsian romanticism within classical structures and subtle impressionism within the more flexible mould of the tone poem. In the first category, he produced his Symphony in C-sharp minor (1902); in the second, the tone poem *Hiver-Printemps* (1904-1905), and *Poèmes d'automnes* (1906). Then in his most ambitious work of this period, the opera *Macbeth*—first produced at the Paris Opéra-Comique on November 30, 1910—he was a carry-over of traditions established in nineteenth-century grand opera to which he contributed a dramatic passion and an intensity all his own.

Beginning with 1912, when he began working on his *Two Psalms* for soprano and orchestra, Bloch arrived at an artistic mission with which a new style became crystallized. As a composer, he now became conscious of his racial origins. What he now wanted to do in his music was to interpret his race. His works began to mirror, as he said, "the Jewish soul . . . the complex agitated soul that I feel vibrating through the Bible. I am a Jew. I aspire to write Jewish music . . . because it is the only way in which I can produce music of vitality—if I can do such a thing at all." Some of Bloch's most famous works were written at this time with such an aim in mind: *Schelomo*, the *Israel Symphony,* the *Baal Shem Suite*. Without digging into the past of Hebrew music and without reaching for liturgical materials, he created music that is Semitic in personality, in melodic contour, in intervallic structure; music whose racial identity was revealed in its high-strung nerves, brooding emotion, elegiac sadness, and most of all rhapsodic surge and sweep.

After the *Baal Shem,* in 1923, Bloch only occasionally and intermittently returned to the Hebraic fold. For the most part, he abandoned Hebraic programs and titles for major works. Nevertheless, the stylistic traits of these compositions remained ummistakably Semitic. Bloch's writing remained rhapsodic; his forms, spacious; his speech, passionate and intense. In his more introspective pages, he gave expression to the kind of poetry and mysticism we find in the noblest pages of his Hebrew masterworks.

During the last decade and a half of his life, Bloch veered more and more towards objectivity and classicism, to compositions concerned with what Olin Downes described as "the principles of sound workmanship, and the increasing devotion . . . to form, balance of parts and classic relations of tonality and movements. Polytonality is there. Oriental imagery is there, and intense feeling and drama. But the overall design is as classic as Brahms or Beethoven of the middle period."

"If asked to describe the style that is peculiarly Bloch's and no other composer's," writes John Hastings, "I should emphasize one attribute that stands out above all others. It is, I think, his spiritual reach, that intense quality so peculiarly intrinsic to his music: the quality of aspiration. . . . In having fought the 'geometry of tragedy' with an art that brought man into 'transfigured union with the tragedy of all things,' Bloch has asserted a spiritual integrity that places him with the masters."

The son of a Swiss merchant, Bloch was born in Geneva on July 24, 1880. Early music study took place with Jaques-Dalcroze and Louis Rey in Geneva. After that, he studied with Eugène Ysaÿe and François Rasse at the Brussels Conservatory, and with Ivan Knorr and Ludwig Thuille in Germany.

In 1902, Bloch wrote his Symphony in C-sharp minor. Disappointed by his inability to get it performed (except for an excerpt heard in Basle in 1903), and convinced he could not make a living out of music, he became a businessman in Geneva. Music, however, was not abandoned. His spare time was devoted to composing and to conducting orchestral concerts.

His opera, *Macbeth,* produced at the Opéra-Comique in Paris in 1910, was hailed by some of the critics. One of these was Romain Rolland, who made a special trip to Geneva to meet the composer and encourage him. It was largely due to Rolland's persuasion that Bloch finally gave up business for music. For several years he taught composition and aesthetics at the Geneva Conservatory.

In 1916, Bloch visited the United States as the conductor of the Maud Allen troupe scheduled to tour the country. The troupe, however, went bankrupt, leaving Bloch stranded in a strange country without funds or friends. Several important musicians rallied to his aid by bringing about performances of his major works. Through these concerts—and through the winning in 1919 of the Elizabeth Sprague Coolidge prize of one thousand dollars for his Suite for Viola and Piano—Bloch became comparatively famous.

In 1924, Bloch became an American citizen. Between 1920 and 1925, he served as director of the Cleveland Institute of Music. From Cleveland, he went to San Francisco to be director of its Conservatory. There he wrote the symphonic rhapsody *America,* which won the first prize of three thousand dollars in a contest sponsored by the magazine *Musical America.* In 1930, a San Francisco patron created a special endowment enabling Bloch to give up teaching and to devote himself entirely to creative work. For a few years, he lived in retirement in a little village in Switzerland, working on his *Sacred Service.* Bloch returned to the United States to direct its American première on April 11, 1934.

After 1950, Bloch was exceptionally prolific, despite the fact that in the last half of the decade he was suffering from a fatal sickness. In 1953–1954, he became the first composer to receive top awards from the New York Music Critics Circle in two categories—for his third string quartet, and his second

Concerto Grosso. A resident of Agate Beach, Oregon, since 1945, Bloch died of cancer in Portland, Oregon, on July 15, 1959.

1905 HIVER-PRINTEMPS (WINTER-SPRING), tone poem for orchestra.

Bloch's early interest in impressionism, in the seeking out of sensitive and delicate suggestions and moods, is found in this, one of his earliest compositions to survive. He wrote it while pursuing a business career in his father's shop in Geneva. Its première took place in Geneva on January 27, 1906.

In *Winter,* the principal elegiac theme is presented by the English horn accompanied by muted lower strings and harp, while violas and clarinet contribute a syncopated rhythmic background (Molto lento e dolente). This thought is followed by a lament in the strings, soon taken over by solo violin. A third subject is heard in muted trumpet (Dolce ed espressivo). Towards the end, the flute assumes this trumpet theme (Molto calmo), following which the English horn recalls the opening elegiac subject.

Where *Winter* has a melancholy character, *Spring,* by contrast, is joyous and ebullient (Moderato). The first subject is a vivacious little tune for the piccolo. This is followed immediately by a second sprightly staccato melody. A quieter episode (Molto espressivo e sostenuto) brings on a reflective melody for the strings, material that is developed into a climax. A loud E major chord and a rapid diminuendo precede a restatement of the opening theme, this time in the flute, while a brief recollection of the trumpet theme from *Winter* provides a gentle hint that, though spring is here, winter is not too far off.

1916 ISRAEL SYMPHONY. I. Allegro agitato. II. Andante moderato.

In planning this symphony, Bloch intended an interpretation of the symbolic meaning of Jewish holidays. Romain Rolland induced Bloch to extend his objective to embrace the entire race and to change Bloch's original title of *Fêtes juives* (*Jewish Holidays*) to *Israel Symphony.*

But as he wrote his music, Bloch continued to think about the holiday idea. He identified his first movement with the Day of Atonement—the holiest day in the Hebrew calender. The moods in this movement are turbulent, disturbed by inner doubts and conflicts. Repose comes with contrition. The second movement (which follows without interruption) brings peace to the repentant sinner. A climax is reached as human voices join the orchestra in intoning the phrases of a Hebrew prayer: "Adonoi, My Elohim, O My Elohim, Alleluia, O My Elohim, Hear My Voice, My Elohim, Hear My Prayer!" Bloch suggested that the voices be placed among the instruments, or at the rear of the platform.

Bloch has explained that there are three sections in the symphony. "A slow introduction, Adagio molto ("Prayer in the Desert"), is immediately followed by the Allegro agitato ("Yom Kippur"), with main theme of bold, barbaric character. A short transition leads into the second part, Moderato, which, after a fierce climax, brings in the voice. The second part of the work is more contemplative, serene, a kind of prayer."

This is what Paul Rosenfeld said of this symphony: "There are moments when one hears in this music the harsh haughty accents of the Hebrew tongue, sees the abrupt gesture of the Hebrew soul, feels the titanic burst of energy that created the race and carried it intact across lands and times, out of the eternal Egypt and through the eternal Red Sea. There are moments when this music makes one feel as though an element that had remained unchanged throughout three thousand years; an element that is in every Jew and by which every Jew must know himself and his descent were caught and fixed there."

The première of the symphony took place in New York City on May 3, 1917, at a concert of the Society of Friends of Music, Artur Bodanzky conducting.

1916 STRING QUARTET NO. 1. I. Andante moderato. II. Allegro frenetico; Molto moderato. III. Andante molto moderato. IV. Vivace.

The composer confessed that this work was written during a period of double crisis. There was personal crisis: at this time (1916), Bloch was stranded in this country, penniless and friendless, faced with a difficult orientation to a new environment. There was crisis, too, in the world around him: Europe was in the midst of a war. Whatever unrest, uncertainty or confusion Bloch felt is found in the nervous pages of this music, particularly in the cruel force of the last movement.

The composer has explained that the music of the quartet represented "a kind of synthesis of my vision of the world at that period." We have here a portrait of the world of serenity and dreams Bloch had known in his native Switzerland (third movement) as well as of the anguish of the dreamer who sees his reveries shattered by the cruel impact of reality (fourth movement).

While classical in form, the quartet is free in its rhythmic and harmonic writing. The first three movements were written while Bloch was still in Europe; the last movement was the first piece of music he wrote in America. It was introduced by the Flonzaley Quartet in New York on December 29, 1916.

Bloch provided his own analysis: "The first movement opens with a few measures of hesitant, questioning introduction. Then the initial motive, incisive and tense, is announced by the first violin and cello, lamentoso (Agitato doloroso). . . . It asserts itself and leads to a motive . . . treated freely. A quieter passage, tranquillo, combined with a fragment of the initial motive, serves as a transition to the second motive. . . . The development proper [is] based first on the initial theme presented alternately by all instruments, then by a new short motive of anguished rhythm, and character. . . . The coda [is] based on a fragment of the initial theme.

"The second movement bursts out with a brisk peremptory motive, ejaculated fortissimo by the four instruments in unison. After the exposition of this motive and its development in varied rhythms . . . several new themes appear, all of cruel, barbarous character. . . . All these elements are worked into a paroxysm of growing exacerbation."

In the third movement, "another world is evoked: nature, contemplation and dreams, far away from men's struggles. The opening motive is introduced by the viola, echoed by the second violin and continued by the viola, cello, and so forth. A new motive appears (Poco pìu animato) of Swiss, pastoral character, intoned by the viola and second violin. . . . A coda leads us into a conclusion of silence and absolute peace.

"Harsh, crushing accents break forth, instantly followed by a tense utterance of the initial motive of the Quartet ending abruptly. . . . Memories of part episodes are evoked. Then the movement proper starts (Agitato molto, Allegro con fuoco), a theme of inexorable character. . . . A new figure appears, of abrupt rhythm at first, evolving into a kind of . . . free melisma, while the cello obstinately persists in a figuration of the initial motive. . . . After a short silence comes the second theme, setting forth a rhythm of great future importance, a lamentation utterly desolate. . . . [In the] Epilogue . . . funereal music is heard interrupted here and there by recollections of previous motives, all very far away from another world. . . . The Quartet ends with accents of resignation, of acceptance."

1916 SCHELOMO (SOLOMON), for orchestra with cello obbligato.

"Schelomo" is the Hebrew name for Solomon, the wise king of the Bible; and Bloch's rhapsody is a portrait of the king.

In 1915, the cellist Alexander Barjansky asked Bloch to write a work for his use. Steeped in the Bible at the time, Bloch decided to draw his inspiration from it. A figurine of Solomon, the work of Barjansky's wife, provided Bloch additional stimulation.

A solo cello speaks for Solomon and re-creates him in music that is, by turns, dramatic, rhapsodic, introspective, brilliant, devotional. The instrument is used much in the way a voice might be, as a kind of wordless singing obbligato. There are two principal melodic subjects, the first heard in the solo cello (Più animato), and the second played by the reeds (Allegro moderato).

"The entire discourse of the soloist, vocal rather than instrumental, seems like musical expression intimately conjoined with the Talmudic prose," wrote Guido M. Gatti. "The pauses, the repetitions of entire passages, the leaps of a double octave, the chromatic progressions, all find their analogues in the book of Ecclesiastes—in the versicles, in the fairly epigraphic reiteration of the admonitions ('and all is vanity and vexation of the spirit'), in the unexpected shifts from one thought to another, in certain crescendi of emotion that end in explosions of anger or grief uncontrolled."

Schelomo was first heard at an all-Bloch concert of the Society of Friends of Music in New York, on May 3, 1917.

1919 SUITE FOR VIOLA AND PIANO (also for viola and orchestra). I. Lento; Allegro. II. Allegro ironico. III. Lento. IV. Molto vivo.

This suite does not belong with Bloch's Hebrew works of this period, "though perhaps," the composer said, "in spite of myself, one may perceive here and there, in a very few places, a certain Jewish inspiration." The inspiration for this music is the Far East: Java, Sumatra, Borneo—countries which the composer had visited only in his imagination. Originally, Bloch planned providing each of the four movements with the following programmatic titles: I. In the Jungle; II. Grotesques; III. Nocturne; IV. The Land of the Sun. "But," the composer explained, "those titles seemed incomplete and unsatisfactory to me; therefore I prefer to leave the imagination of the hearer completely unfettered."

The Suite received the Elizabeth Sprague Coolidge Award of $1,000 at the Berkshire Chamber Music Festival in Pittsfield, Massachusetts, where it was introduced by Louis Bailly and Harold Bauer on September 25, 1919. Bloch then rescored the work for viola and orchestra, in which form it was heard on November 5, 1920, at a concert of the National Symphony Orchestra, conducted by Artur Bodanzky, once again with Louis Bailly as soloist.

The composer's own description of this music follows:

"The first movement is the most complicated in inspiration and in form, aiming to give the impression of a very wild and primitive Nature. . . . The second movement is rather difficult to define. It is a curious mixture of grotesque and fantastic characters, of sardonic and mysterious moods. . . . The musical form follows closely the expression in its alternating moods. . . . The very simple page of the third movement expresses the mystery of tropical nights. . . . There is first a dreamy melody in the solo viola, above dark chords; then a second and third motive; and, as if from far away, reminiscences of motives from the first movement. The last movement is probably the most cheerful thing I have ever written. The form is extremely simple—an obvious A-B-A—the middle part being a more lyrical episode, built on motives from the other movements, treated in a broad and passionate mood."

1923 QUINTET NO. 1 FOR PIANO AND STRINGS. I. Agitato. II. Andante mistico. III. Allegro energico.

Impressed by the potentialities of quarter-tone music for certain specific effects, Bloch conceived the idea of writing a cello sonata employing this technique. As he began planning the work, and as his thematic ideas developed, he realized that a larger frame was called for. He finally decided on a piano quintet.

This quintet, of course, is not quarter-tone music. But it does utilize quarter-tone intervals in passages calling for high tensions. Quarter-tone writing endows the melodic line with intensified expressiveness. Novel colorings, barbaric rhythms, complex harmonic patterns make further modern contributions. The form, however, remains classical.

Perhaps in no other of Bloch's works does he maintain so consistent a level of eloquence as here. The work opens in an atmosphere of awe and mystery as the piano sounds a theme faintly suggestive of the *Dies Irae*, set against a quarter-tone harmonic background. This theme recurs throughout the work. Varied moods follow: primitive, passionate, intense, sensitive. Mystery and an all-pervading melancholy are sounded throughout the second movement: the unrelieved gloom at times develops into a kind of tortured despair. The poignancy is intensified until, towards the end of the movement—as the violins exclaim in piercing notes against the dark and brooding chords of the piano—it becomes virtually unbearable. The opening theme of the quintet returns in the beginning of the third movement; it is now strong and dramatic. Agitation persists, gaining momentum all the time, until the music becomes the chant of primitives, accompanied by percussive-like rhythms. Then the violence is over. The viola raises its voice in a poignant melody to restore serenity. (Bloch once described this last section as an "escape," a release of oneself from material considerations into spiritual values.)

On November 11, 1923, the Quintet was introduced in New York by the Lenox String Quartet and Harold Bauer; this performance took place at the inaugural concert of an organization then making its bow—the League of Composers.

1923 BAAL SHEM: THREE PICTURES OF HASIDIC LIFE, suite for violin and piano (also violin and orchestra). I. Vidui. II. Nigun. III. Simchas Torah.

One specific sect of the Hebrew religion is the inspiration of this suite: that known as Hasidism, founded by a mystic seer named Baal Shem, which developed and flourished in Poland in the late eighteenth century. The Hasids believed in goodness, joy, and pleasure. Religious worship was an occasion for feasting, revelry, and ecstatic music and dance. The Hasids believed that whatever God made is good. Consequently, even in evil there is some goodness; and there is no evil that is beyond redemption.

Hasidic folk songs and dances are as ecstatic and intense as the sect that gave them birth. Certain qualities of Hasidic music are found in this suite: its sense for improvisation (a carry-over from the synagogal chant); the intervalic construction; the throbbing rhythmic pulse.

The first movement, entitled "Contrition," is a mobile melody speaking of the return of a repentant sinner to the fold. In the second part, "Melody," an improvised song is heard, one such as a cantor develops as he intones his prayer in the synagogue. The music then passes from delicate and tender moods into a veritable orgiastic outburst of joy ("Simchas Torah"), as the Hasid celebrates his most joyous holiday—the commemoration of the handing down of the Torah to Moses and the Jewish people at Mount Sinai.

1925 CONCERTO GROSSO NO. 1, for piano and string orchestra. I. Prelude. II. Dirge. III. Pastoral and Rustic Dances. IV. Fugue.

Many contemporary composers have reverted to the musical forms of the classical past; but in doing so they have usually endeavored to return to classic simplicity and objectivity. With Bloch, reversion to the concerto-grosso style of Corelli and Handel did not encourage classical writing. The resources of modern music were not abandoned. The aesthetic aim here was to incorporate modern thinking and techniques within the framework of older forms. Bloch's composition pupils were given to writing rebellious works which ruthlessly swept aside all traditions. Bloch wished to prove to them that a composer can remain vibrantly contemporary in his speech without sacrificing classical structure.

Bloch wrote the Concerto Grosso in his last year as director of the Cleveland Institute of Music. It was introduced at the Institute on June 1, 1925, the composer conducting.

The harsh sounds of the first movement (Allegro energico e pesante), with its massive sequence of strident chords, is an exercise in modern writing. This is music of ungovernable strength, whose effect is created through ponderous sonorities and bold rhythmic movement. Relief comes in the second movement (Andante moderato) with a threnody. A group of pleasing rustic dances follows (Assai lento); shifting meters provide a piquant contemporary flavor. A robust fugue (Allegro) filled with modern harmonies brings the work to a close.

1927 AMERICA, symphonic rhapsody. I. 1620: The Soil—The Indians—The Mayflower—The Landing of the Pilgrims. II. 1861–1865: Hours of Joy—Hours of Sorrow. III. The Present—The Future.

In 1927, *Musical America* announced a contest for a symphonic work on an American subject, with a first prize of $3,000 and simultaneous performances by several major American symphony orchestras. The idea of writing a large orchestral work as a tribute to the land of his adoption had long interested Bloch. But it remained only a plan for almost a decade until a rereading of Walt Whitman provided Bloch with necessary stimulation. Bloch finally completed his symphonic rhapsody in February of 1927; it won first prize by a unanimous decision of the judges. The world première took place in New York City on December 20, 1928, at a concert of the New York Philharmonic. The following day, the rhapsody was performed by the major orchestras of Chicago, Philadelphia, Boston and San Francisco.

A quotation from Walt Whitman appears on the published score: "O America, because you build for mankind, I build for you." The score also provides the following information: "Though this symphony is not dependent on a program, the composer wants to emphasize that he has been inspired by this very ideal (the ideal of America). The anthem which concludes the work as its apotheosis, symbolizes the destiny, the mission of America. The symphony is entirely built on it. From the first bar it appears, in root, dimly, slowly, taking shape, rising, falling, developing and finally asserting itself victoriously in its complete and decisive form."

The first movement opens with a tremolo in divided strings (Poco lento, misterioso). The principal theme, with the personality of an American-Indian melody, emerges from this shimmering background; in the last movement, this melody will provide the material for a patriotic anthem. The main part of the movement (Animato) is launched with still another subject with an American-Indian identity. When this material has been exhausted, the setting changes to England with a march tune. A sea chantey in the cello and horn suggests the sailing of the *Mayflower*, material that is carried to a climactic peak, probably expressing the joy of the pioneers at the first sight of land. Once again, the American Indian is suggested through the rhythm of an Indian drum, while the religious spirit of the Pilgrims is projected through a quotation of the hymn "The Old Hundredth." The movement ends serenely.

In the second movement, the Civil War period is evoked with thematic fragments of patriotic songs, war songs, Negro spirituals, Creole folk songs and even a memory of Stephen Foster's "Swanee River." A southern ballad, in English horn, opens the movement (Allegretto). A Negro tune "Row after Row" follows in the violins. In short order, the orchestra presents hasty quotations from "Swanee River," "Pop Goes the Weasel," and "Hail Columbia." Later material includes snatches of such Civil War songs as "Dixie," "John Brown's Body," "The Battle Cry of Freedom," and "Tramp, Tramp, Tramp." Again and again, the motto theme of the first movement is recalled.

The finale begins with a syncopated version of the motto theme, Bloch's concession to the jazz age of the 1920s. Once again the rhapsody indulges in quotations—Negro tunes, the "Old Hundredth," and "Yankee Doodle," among other melodies. Climaxes rise and ebb. The feeling grows rhapsodic. At the peak of one of the climaxes, the patriotic anthem emerges in its entirety, sung by a chorus. (The composer suggests that the audience join in the singing.) This is the focal point of the rhapsody. The text begins with the lines: "America, America, Thy Name is in My Heart, My Love for Thee, Arouses Me, to Nobler Thoughts and Deeds."

1933 SACRED SERVICE (AVODATH HAKODESH), for baritone, mixed chorus and orchestra.

Bloch spent over two years working on the most spacious and ambitious of his Hebraic compositions, a musical setting of the Sabbath morning service in American Reform Temples. "The texts," the composer explained, "embody the essence of Israel's aspirations and its message to the world. Though Jewish in roots, this message seems to me above all a gift of Israel to the whole of mankind. It symbolizes for me more than a 'Jewish service,' for in its great simplicity and variety, it embodies a philosophy acceptable to all men."

The work, while in five sections, is performed without interruption, following the order of synagogue liturgy. Short preludes and interludes serve to connect the various parts and to provide the work with unity; they are also intended as a replacement for the customary "responsive readings" and to provide worshipers with an opportunity for silent meditation.

The composer provided the following analysis:

"The short orchestral prelude, 'Meditation,' sets forth the initial (Mixolydian) motive, which permeates the whole work, and two other melodic forms, which recur here and there. 'How Goodly Are Thy Tents' is a kind of invocation, in the desert perhaps, depicting the Temple of God in Nature. More liturgical is 'Sing His Praise' that follows. The short interlude that leads to 'Oh, Hear, Israel' is more cosmic. . . . 'Oh, Hear, Israel' is the great profession of the Jewish faith—the essential affirmation. Then comes 'And Thou Shalt Love Him" characterizing the union of religion and everyday life. . . . 'Who Is Like Thee?' is the crowd's response, and it expresses its exultation in the section 'And the Lord Shall Reign.' The tragic accents of 'Rock of Israel' succeed this short-lived joy, however, to end Part I on a mournful note."

The second part consists of music "from another world, seraphic and mysterious." It begins with "Kodosh, Kodosh, Kodosh" ("Holy, Holy, Holy"). Two bars of the "cosmic motive" lead into "One Is He Our God." This part ends with a hymn of joy, "Thou Shalt Reign."

The third part deals symbolically "with the law, its order, discipline and limitations." A short prelude, "Silent Devotion," precedes the a cappella chorus, "May the Words of My Mouth." The cantor now intones the words "Lift Up Your Heads, O Ye Mortals." Bloch explained: "I wanted to express the wish that man may free himself from hate, from dark instinct, and all that prevents him from rising above himself and seeing the Truth." A symphonic interlude then describes the removal of the Scroll from the Ark. A crescendo and an ascending progression reach towards a choral exultation, "Thine, Adonoi, Is the Greatness."

The fourth part represents a return to earth. "The Cantor calls to the people, and the crowd, expressing its joy, intones 'Earth Sees His Glory.' Then the Cantor, alternating with the chorus, proclaims the wisdom and perfections of the Law and reminds the people not to forsake it. A song of peace, 'Tree of life,' ends the fourth part."

The fifth part is an Epilogue beginning with an "Adoration" describing the peace of the Sabbath. "Now the Cantor addresses the people in a recitative (spoken voice) in which he prays that before long virtue may reign. . . . The chorus answers, 'On that Day the Lord Shall be One, and His Name One.' Suddenly the color changes, and the Cantor in tragic accents intones, 'And Now, Ere We Part'. . . . From afar is heard again the supplication of mankind. . . . 'O God of Israel, Arise to Help Israel.' After an ominous silence . . . a kind of collective voice rises slowly, mysteriously. . . . The beautiful poem, 'Adon Olom' ('Eternal God') is used here. . . . Thus, as a last resort, he commits himself, soul and body, into God's hands; or, if one prefers it, he relies humbly upon the vast forces, the laws, the everlasting and higher Truth of the Universe, and upon their ultimate wisdom. After this 'cosmic' dream we come back to earth again, with the 'Three Benedictions' and the 'Three Amens.' And the last expression of the Cantor to the Assembly is the beautiful word 'Shalom,' which means 'Peace.'"

Sacred Service was written in the little Swiss town of Ticino, Roveredo, to which Bloch had come in 1930. The world première took place in Turin, Italy, on January 12, 1934, the composer conducting. After a three-year absence, Bloch returned to the United States later in 1934 to direct the American première in New York on April 11, 1934.

1936 A VOICE IN THE WILDERNESS, for cello obbligato and orchestra.

This is Bloch's second major work for orchestra and obbligato cello, the first being *Schelomo*. But here the cello serves a different function. It is a kind of commentator, appearing between each of the six short movements, offering a terse discourse on the preceding section.

Bloch's original intention in writing this work was to present a group of short sketches for orchestra under the collective title of *Visions and Prophecies*. But as he began writing, contrapuntal solo melodies came to his mind, inspired by the music he was putting down on paper. Sensing the aesthetic value of these melodies in the larger concept of the composition, Bloch decided to employ the rather unique idea of a "commentator" cello.

The composer has described the six movements (played uninterruptedly) as "meditations," and has explained that the work as a whole is descriptive of the "apparently unhappy destiny of man." The composer has stated further: "The various movements follow and link each other quite naturally. They are sometimes bound together by a barely perceptive thematic relationship or 'reminiscence,' but each has its own clearly defined character."

The suite was introduced in Los Angeles by the Los Angeles Philharmonic, Otto Klemperer conducting, on January 21, 1937.

1938 CONCERTO FOR VIOLIN AND ORCHESTRA. I. Allegro deciso. II. Andante. III. Deciso.

American-Indian music, which plays such a significant role in the first movement of *America,* is also given some attention in the principal theme of the first movement of this concerto. But the music of the concerto is in no single style, just as it refuses to adhere to a single tonality. At times the writing has the rhapsodic character of Bloch's earlier Hebraic works; at times the music gives suggestions of impressionism, as in parts of the exquisite slow movement; at times it is severely modern in the freedom of its rhythmic movement and in the acerbity of its harmonies, as in the barbaric opening of the third movement.

The concerto was begun in 1930. At that time the composer wrote down some random ideas and sketches; these subsequently became the thematic materials for the concerto, which did not take actual shape until 1935, when Bloch wrote down the first part of the introduction. The necessity of completing other works delayed the writing of the concerto, and it was not finished until January, 1938. The world première took place in Cleveland on December 15, 1938. Joseph Szigeti was the soloist, and the Cleveland Orchestra was directed by Mitropoulos.

The first movement opens with a theme of American-Indian character in horns and woodwind. A cadenza with ascending chords leads into a section (Moderato assai) in which the solo violin recalls the American-Indian theme, while the trumpets provide a "call" motive and a rhythmic background in the harp. The solo violin is then heard in a new melody (Dolce espressivo). This material is elaborated while the mood becomes highly agitated. After the turmoil subsides, the solo violin is heard in a tranquil melody, which receives contrapuntal treatment from the woodwind. A new section (Moderato misterioso) introduces a theme reminiscent of the *Dies Irae* in plucked strings and bassoons over sustained notes in the trombone. A giant climax is built up; then the movement sustains a rhapsodic character for its duration through a dramatic coda, which ends with a forceful chord.

The second movement is dominated by a diatonic melody in three-four harmony, shared by flute and bassoons. A second thought is later presented by the solo violin.

A fortissimo sets into motion the storm and stress of the finale. When the tempest is over, the solo violin recalls the main subject of the opening movement. New material includes a pastoral motive, a joyful hymn in the horns, and a haunting melody for the solo violin.

1944 SUITE SYMPHONIQUE (OVERTURE, PASSACAGLIA, AND FINALE), for orchestra.

In the *Suite Symphonique,* the composer encases the passion and intensity of his earlier works within a classical architectonic structure. The work received its première in Philadelphia on October 26, 1945, in a performance by the Philadelphia Orchestra. For this occasion Bloch provided the following description: "The Overture starts with a Maestoso, followed by a quicker fugato, rather free, as the several entrances occur in the variations of the theme." A climax in full orchestra is succeeded by a Maestoso. "It dies out and connects immediately with a Passacaglia . . . a quite regular one on a motive of eight measures, starting in the Dorian mode, introducing the Neapolitan sixth and ending in a true minor. There are about twenty-two variations ending in all kinds of canons, motif inverted, and a great climax of lyrical character. After a little pause comes the Finale, a kind of moto perpetuo of exuberant character, constructed in the regular sonata form, the second theme being a grotesque, sardonic fugue." Just before the end of the work, the *Dies Irae* is quoted.

1945 STRING QUARTET NO. 2. I. Moderato. II. Presto. III. Andante. IV. Finale.

Almost thirty years elapsed between the writing of Bloch's first two string quartets. The second was completed in 1945, when Bloch was at the height of his creative powers. Less tortured in its struggle and less rebellious than its predecessor, the second quartet has an incandescence and spirituality of speech, a concentration and forcefulness of thinking that inspired Ernest Newman to compare it with the last quartets of Beethoven.

In reviewing the quartet for the *London Times*, Ernest Newman analyzed its unusual structure: "From an embryo in the second of the four movements, there comes into being an entity which from that point onward moulds the whole quartet from the inside into a single organic substance; differently accentuated or rhythmed as the work goes on, it assumes one personality after another till it expands in the finale into first of all the theme of a mighty passacaglia, then, re-rhythmed yet again, into the subject of a mighty fugue; while the whole work is rounded off in unexpected but inevitable rightness with a serene reminiscence, in the final bars of a tiny melisma with which the first movement had opened."

The quartet was introduced in London by the Griller Quartet on October 9, 1946. It received the New York Music Critics Circle Award in 1947.

1948 CONCERTO SYMPHONIQUE, for piano and orchestra. I. Pesante. II. Allegro vivace. III. Allegro deciso.

Bloch's only piano concerto was introduced by Corinne Lacomble, under the composer's direction, at the Edinburgh Festival, on September 3, 1949. It is a powerful and intense work, large in dimension, restless in its questioning doubts, tragic in expression.

When the concerto received its first American performance over the NBC network (with the soloist who had introduced the work in Edinburgh, but with Ansermet conducting), Olin Downes described it as follows in *The New York Times:*

"The first two movements in particular made a strong impression. The piano alone, in the deeep unisons and the swinging chords of the opening, without the orchestra, has the manner of deep tolling bells. When this unison motive is answered by the brass the mode of dark prophecy, as it were, is reinforced. The movement is almost monothematic, though there is a short lyrical counter-theme of a more tender nature. By far the greater part of the score hovers over the central theme, varies it, develops it with the aid of the solo instrument. . . .

"The second movement has much of the scherzo quality, with rapid figurations and developments on the first part, and a long contrasting section with new melodic thoughts and a melancholy reflective mood. . . . Its contrast to the first movement only serves to accentuate the difference of mood within the frame of a unit that has its various facets of emotions and of thought.

"The third movement was . . . given to the episodic and the sequential. But it may well be that the very mood of restlessness and inconclusiveness in this music necessitated just such fitful procedure on the part of the composer."

1951 STRING QUARTET NO. 3. I. Allegro deciso. II. Adagio. III. Allegro molto. IV. Allegro.

Bloch's third string quartet was dedicated to and introduced by the Griller String Quartet in New York on January 4, 1953. In the same year it received the New York Music Critics Circle Award. Unlike the composer's first two string quartets—which are rhapsodic in style, spacious in form, and alternate between spiritual and dynamic statements—the third quartet is for Bloch a singularly compact work making use of economical materials within a classic structure. While the Adagio movement finds Bloch in a recognizably introspective and poetic mood, the ensuing third movement has a light, whimsical feeling not often encountered in Bloch.

In his review in *The New York Times,* Olin Downes described the quartet as follows: "The vigor and forthrightness of the opening movement sweep the ideas to an irrefutable conclusion. The slow movement is a reverie within a man's spirit, above the earth. Its final measures, especially, are unforgettable. The scherzo, in true classic fashion, is a dance movement and very refreshingly of the earth and the good soil. . . . The finale is not a movement so easy to grasp at a first hearing or to be listened to with the same degree of certainty on the hearer's part as the earlier movements."

1952 CONCERTO GROSSO NO. 2, for string orchestra. I. Maestoso; Allegro; Maestoso. II. Andante. III. Allegro. IV. Tema con variazioni.

Bloch's second concerto grosso was introduced in London by the BBC Symphony under Sir Malcom Sargent on April 11, 1953. It received the New York Music Critics Circle Award. As in all traditional concerto-grosso writing, the technique of alternating and combining a smaller group of instruments with a larger one is followed. In the first movement an expressive Maestoso precedes and follows a dramatic fugal section. A lyrical slow movement follows without interruption. In the third movement the solo quartet is briefly separated from the main string section. The finale consists of a descending chromatic theme subjected to four variations.

Bloch planned a third concerto grosso but finally expanded it to symphonic dimensions and called it *Sinfonia brève* (1953). The *Sinfonia brève* received its première performance in London on April 11, 1953, with the BBC Symphony.

1955 STRING QUARTET NO. 5. I. Grave; Allegro; Grave. II. Calmo. III. Presto. IV. Allegro deciso; Calmo.

The concentration, compression and classicism which Bloch had achieved in his third string quartet are also present in the fourth (1954), which received its world première in Lenox, Massachusetts, on July 28, 1954, at the hands of the Griller String Quartet. The fifth string quartet, Bloch's last in this form, was more romantic in nature, and more subjective. Here, said Olin Downes in *The New York Times,* we can detect "the spirit of the late Beethoven quartets" together with suggestions of Brahms, Wagner, and the Schoenberg of *Verklaerte Nacht.* "In short, this half-hour work . . . is a big post-romantic piece of writing with a big romantic sweep. . . . Even at first hearing . . . one is struck by its strength and tenderness." The first movement opens and closes in a solemn vein (in the key of C minor), to find contrast in a vigorous middle section in triple meter. A broad melody dominates the second movement, through which courses a syncopated accompanying figure with which the movement had opened. The sprightly scherzo leads without a break into the finale in which material from earlier movements is recalled.

KARL-BIRGER BLOMDAHL 1916–1968

In the early 1940s, a group of young Swedish composers, all pupils of Hilding Rosenberg, used to meet regularly each Monday to discuss musical problems in general, and their own problems as composers in particular. These men included Sven-Erik Bäck (1919–) and Ingvar Lidholm (1921–). Karl-Birger Blomdahl was their acknowledged leader. This younger school of Swedish composers, which called itself "the Monday Group," was fed and nurtured on Hindemith's theoretical text, *Unterweisung im Tonsatz.* The twentieth-century composers they regarded as models for emulation were Hindemith, Bartók and the Stravinsky of the neo-classic period. The neo-classic influence—the linear writing and the partiality for Baroque or classical structures—is found in several major works by Blomdahl in the 1940s. These included two symphonies (1943, 1947); two concertos, one for the viola (1941), and the other for the violin (1947); a Concerto Grosso (1944).

Then, beginning with his third symphony in 1950, Blomdahl veered away from neo-classicism towards expressionism. The world of Schoenberg, Berg and particularly Webern opened up for him, as Bo Wallner noted, "the rich resources of the new expressionism with its immense possibilities of serial technique as a shaping force." From atonality, Blomdahl progressed to the twelve-tone row, and from the twelve-tone row to serialism. At the same time, he began exploring the artistic possibilities of concrete music and electronics.

"The basis of everything which Blomdahl has created," wrote Ingemar von Heijne, "is a striking rhythmic pulsation, overgrown with imaginative syncopated patterns. His rhythm is seldom neutral, sometimes it is playful, but mostly it is hard and driving. Equally striking is Blomdahl's ability to think architecturally and in large forms and a determination to set up broad bridges with long arches. . . . In his scores there is seldom any luxuriance of tone color, the orchestral texture is first and foremost harsh, while laying open the nerve fibers of the music right into the angry climaxes."

Blomdahl was born in Växjö, Sweden, on October 19, 1916. His principal music study took place in Stockholm, privately with Hilding Rosenberg (counterpoint, composition, orchestration) and with Tor Mann at the Royal High School of Music (conducting). His training was completed on the Continent. He first attracted interest in Sweden with several large-scale works in a neoclassic idiom, including his Concerto for Viola and Orchestra and his Concerto Grosso, introduced over the Swedish Radio in 1944 and 1945 respectively, and his first symphony introduced in Stockholm in 1945. With his Third Symphony in 1950, he gained an international stature for the first time, a stature that grew by leaps and bounds by virtue of the success of his opera *Aniara* in 1959. In 1953, Blomdahl became a member of the Royal Academy of Music where, a few years later, he was appointed professor of composition. Blomdahl died in Stockholm on June 16, 1968.

1950 SYMPHONY NO. 3, "FACETTER" ("FACETS").

Blomdahl's third symphony received its world première at the festival of the International Society for Contemporary Music at Frankfort-on-the-Main, Germany, in 1951. Performances of this work by several major European orchestras focused the limelight of international interest on its composer for the first time. In this work, Blomdahl had not yet freed himself completely from his earlier dependence on Hindemith and Bartók, but already his interest in atonality and expressionism becomes marked. Though in several sections, the symphony is in a single unified movement.

Here is how Halsey Stevens described the symphony in *Notes*: "The opening is especially touching, with solo flute over a tympani roll, gradually drawing in all the winds to reach a great climax and recede before the violins and violas are called upon. These first fifty bars symbolize the form of the whole work, whose inner sections—Prestissimo, the other Allegro molto deciso e ritmico—generate a furious energy which is only slightly tempered by the quieter pages that connect them. The Symphony comes full circle and closes with the quiet music of the opening."

1959 ANIARA, "a revue of mankind in space time," in two acts, with text by Erik Lindegren adapted from a drama of the same name by Harry Martinson. First performance: Royal Opera, Sweden, May 31, 1959.

Aniara excited world attention for several newsmaking reasons. It marked the first significant invasion of science fiction into opera. Its subject was vibrant front-page material—space travel. And it was the first successful opera to incorporate concrete music and electronic sounds within more formal textures and procedures.

The setting is the spaceship, *Aniara*. The opera opens on the third day of its voyage to Mars. The chief engineer reminds his passengers of mankind's cruelties and of the devastation caused by a recent atomic holocaust. A week later, while the passengers are celebrating their imminent arrival on Mars, *Aniara* is suddenly thrown off course. The ship can neither reach Mars nor return to earth. She is doomed to pursue an aimless course through space. Hesitantly, the passengers resume their dancing, but a fierce desperation soon seizes them as they realize that for the rest of their lives they must remain on the ship. Years of hopeless, helpless travel in space follow, the oppressiveness of space weighing heavily on one and all. Curious sects spring up; totem pole worship and human sacrifice are not far off. A group of penitents and prophets-of-doom perform a "Repentance Mass." A Cult of Light is proclaimed by a Blind Poetess, her words echoed enthusiastically by an invisible chorus. The twentieth anniversary of the flight is celebrated in song and dance, but most participants are haggard and weary, yearning pathetically for some miracle to save them. Then, on the last night, one after another of the passengers breaks down and vanishes from sight. The voice and the spirit of the Blind Poetess can be heard singing the praises of Death.

This play, of course, is symbolic, as its author, Harry Martinson, explained. The journey, he said, is basically "a pretext for presenting a vision of our own day, of how we ourselves go through life in a spiritual void. Its perspective is that of enlarged reflection, with the narrator's instruments transferred to a symbolic world. The symbols employed in *Aniara* derive from the world of modern science. . . . Surrounded by desolate space and banished from the community of our solar system, the *Aniara* people begin to discover the full extent of their human misery. Life acquires a different and hitherto unknown meaning for them. Death takes on an unsuspected immensity, becoming synonymous with space itself, while the protective walls of *Aniara* symbolize the brevity of life. At the same time, however, these walls mercilessly reflect the spiritual poverty within their confines. Where the soul's cravings are concerned, galaxies of light years become no more than gigantic majesties that one is swallowed up in but never reaches. The human soul and the cosmic infinity never find each other. What man longs for most profoundly lies within himself. Should he neglect this inner life it, too, will produce a void—and one that is far worse than the emptiness of outer space."

In commenting upon his music approach to this unusual symbolic drama Blomdahl says: "It seemed clear to me that Martinson's epic called for music of the same stylistic 'simplicity' as the text. . . . Accordingly I have refrained from developing my musical ideas symphonically, and concentrated instead on evoking 'simplicity,' emphasizing the scenic and dramatic elements. On the other hand, I have felt free to resort to musical allusions to create certain idea associations. Similarly, I have recognized the pronounced *vocal* idiom of the opera by treating the melodic elements in traditional vocal style rather than treating the voice in an instrumental style."

Every means at the composer's command was used: dance, church, and folk music; jazz; the ultramodern idioms of atonality, polytonality and the twelve-tone row. In addition to all this, extraordinarily effective use was made of noises and eerie electronic sounds reproduced on tape. This served to emphasize the hypertensions, the atmosphere of terror, the awesomeness of infinite space, the ghostly sound of far-off voices describing earthly cruelties and disasters. "This is the first time," said Kajsa Rootzén, "I have become convinced that electronic music has great possibilities for use in special cases." Commenting further on this use of electronic sounds, Harold Rogers noted in the *Christian Science Monitor*: "Here is at least one instance when electronic music can be aptly used to achieve dramatic effects not producible by the usual orchestral instruments. . . . The tapes are cleverly produced in that they take over where Blomdahl's orchestra leaves off and then amplify and compound the eerie confusion to the point of utter chaos."

H. H. Stuckenschmidt summed up the significance of the opera as follows: "I would not hesitate to call *Aniara* an artistic message of singular boldness and power. Here, at last, is a stage work which scorns the modish flight into the past and which concerns itself with the deepest problems of contemporary society."

Aniara was performed by the Royal Opera of Stockholm at Expo 67 in Montreal on May 31, 1967.

PIERRE BOULEZ 1925–

Pierre Boulez, one of the most influential composers to come out of France since the end of World War II, has been in the vanguard of the avant-garde movement in music. He has experimented with "concrete music." Concrete music was originated in Paris by Pierre Schaeffer, an engineer for Radiodiffusion française, who experimented with the production of non-musical sounds on tape, or distortions of such sounds; street noises, radio commercials, conversations, the banging of doors, and so forth. He then ran the tape backwards, sometimes increasing, sometimes decreasing the speed, thereby manufacturing still other sounds. These different qualities of noises or sounds were then integrated and assembled into musical "compositions." This innovation is found in Boulez's *Polyphonie x* (1951), which created a stir when introduced at the Donaueschingen Festival on October 6, 1951. He continued to work with electronics as a means of musical composition, notably in *Poésie pour pouvoir,* a spatial composition introduced at Donaueschingen on October 18, 1958, in which electronic sounds on tape were combined with the more formal and familiar sounds of two synchronized orchestras led by two conductors.

Boulez has produced improvisational music in *Improvisations on Mallarmé*, which received its initial hearing in Rome on June 14, 1959. Then he took a step beyond this by creating aleatory music, or music of chance, in this Third Piano Sonata (1961), where the performer is free to rearrange its five parts in any order he wishes, or to omit any of the parts.

But Boulez's greatest significance as a powerful and original creative force came mainly with his twelve-tone compositions. He started out as such a passionate member of the Schoenberg school that he was led to exclaim that "since the discoveries of the Viennese all composition other than twelve tones is useless." But Boulez soon became convinced that the same mathematical discipline that governed pitch through the use of the twelve-tone row had to apply to all other areas of musical creation. He consequently developed the serial technique—a *total* serialization of musical means whereby a preconceived mathematical order governed every area of music: note values, volume, density of note sequence as well as pitch, rhythm and color. It is quite true that attempts at total serialization had preceded Boulez in experiments by Milton Babbitt (1916–), a brilliant American mathematician-composer who had clarified his ideas in a monograph published in 1946, *The Function of Set Structure in the Twelve-Tone System*, and who then put theory into practice in his *Three Compositions,* for piano, and *Compositions for Four Instruments,* both completed in 1947. Nevertheless, working independently of Babbitt, Boulez worked out his own ideas of serialism in Paris, first in his Second Piano Sonata (1948)—a turning point in his creative development—and then in a succession of compositions culminating with his masterwork, *Le Marteau sans maître,* in 1954.

Boulez was born in Montbrison, in central France, on March 26, 1925. He originally planned being a mathematician and completed preliminary studies at Lyons. But finally deciding on music as his life's work, he entered the Paris Conservatory in 1944, where he studied harmony and composition with Olivier Messiaen, whose researches into rhythm exerted a potent influence on him. Boulez also studied counterpoint with Andrée Vaurabourg-Honegger. In 1945, he was introduced to the twelve-tone system through private study with René Leibowitz. Beginning with 1946, Boulez earned his living for a decade directing a theatre orchestra in Paris. Meanwhile, he set into motion his career as composer with provocative innovations and experiments that electrified, and often shocked, the world of music. In 1954, he founded the "Domaine musical," an annual series of concerts in Paris for the performance of avant-garde music. Here he proved his extraordinary gift at conducting, a talent which he soon revealed to the rest of Europe in guest appearances with major orchestras. He came to the United States in 1963 to deliver lectures at Harvard University. On May 1, 1964, he made his American debut as conductor in New York by directing the BBC Symphony of London. In 1966, he made front-page news by disavowing all further official affiliation with the French government—a gesture of protest against the appointment of Marcel Lewandowski, a conservative composer, to the newly created bureau in the Cultural Ministry.

1955 LE MARTEAU SANS MAÎTRE (THE HAMMER WITHOUT A MASTER), for contralto and six instruments. I. Avant "L'Artisanat furieux";

II. Commentaire I de "Bourreaux de solitude"; III. L'Artisanat furieux; IV. Commentaire II de "Bourreaux de solitude"; V. Bel édifice et les pressentiments; VI. Bourreaux de solitude; VII. Après "L'Artisanat furieux"; VIII. Commentaire III de "Bourreaux de solitude"; IX. Bel édifice et les pressentiments, *double*.

With *Le Marteau sans maître,* Boulez achieved international renown; and it is from this point on that he assumed leadership in the avant-garde movement in music. It was introduced at the festival of the International Society for Contemporary Music, at Baden-Baden, Germany, on June 18, 1955. In 1957, it received the prize of the Académie Charles Cros. Performances in major European capitals—as well as in New York and Los Angeles—helped make it one of the most significant creations of the musical avant-garde of the 1950s. Performed in New York on May 24, 1963, *Le Marteau* profited from the long and detailed verbal commentary provided by the composer himself, then on a visit to the United States.

Le Marteau is based on three poems by René Char: *L'Artisanat furieux* (*Furious Artisans*), *Bel édifice et les pressentiments* (*Beautiful Building and Premonition*) and *Bourreaux de solitude* (*Hangmen of Solitude*). Though we have here only three songs, the entire work is divided into nine movements. Three represent the sung versions of the three poems; the other six movements are instrumental commentaries on these poems. The composer has explained: "I have tried to find the deep roots of poetry in music, in the instrumental parts even more than in the vocal sections." The nine movements are split up into three "cycles" of three movements each, to include one sung movement and two instrumental ones. The composer took pains to point out that each cycle can be so split up as to allow the instrumental commentary on one poem to be followed by another poem. "The chronological order of composition," the composer said, "is not always the best way to hear a work. This way of working is fresher and more meaningful."

There is a relation in timbre and intervalic structure among the first, third and seventh movements; between the fifth and ninth movements; and among the second, fourth, sixth and eighth movements.

The work is scored for contralto and the following instruments: a xylorimba (a cross between the xylophone and the marimba); a vibraphone (since become an instrument favored by the avant-garde); a flute in G; a viola; a guitar; and a varied group of percussion instruments played by a single person (the reason why the percussion is regarded as a single instrument), consisting of tambourine, two pairs of bongos, maracas, claves, bell, triangle, high and low tam-tam, gong, suspended cymbal, and two little cymbals. The six instruments never play at a single time. They are divided among the nine movements in different combinations. The first movement (Rapide) is for flute, vibraphone, guitar and viola; the second (Lent) for flute, xylorimba, tambourine and muted viola; the third (Modéré sans rigueur) for contralto and flute; the fourth (Assez rapide) for xylorimba, vibraphone and small cymbals, guitar and viola; the fifth (Assez vif) for voice, flute, guitar and viola; the sixth (Assez lent) for voice and flute, xylorimba, vibraphone, maracas, guitar, muted viola;

the seventh (Rapide) for flute, vibraphone, guitar; the eighth (Assez lent) for flute, xylorimba, vibraphone, maracas, claves; and the ninth (Free tempo) for xylorimba, vibraphone, percussion, guitar, voice and viola.

Arthur Cohn described *Le Marteau* as "neo-impressionistic serialism"—remotely related to Schoenberg "by fantasy," and to Webern through its use of "sonic pulverization." Cohn adds: "The fluid result is pure Boulez—a music of perpetual variation in color and pitch. *Le Marteau sans maître* is a plastic transformation of strict serial composition. Its music stings while it expresses a Freudian world of sound."

1957 DOUBLES, for orchestra.

We encounter the term "double" in the classical suite of Johann Sebastian Bach. It refers to a variation of and an embellishment upon a dance movement that had preceded it. Boulez revived the term in this work for large orchestra, explaining: "The basic, rather simple, musical figures of the work have 'doubles' (that is, variations or new aspects of the basic figures) grafted upon them. These different figures, or their doubles, pass each other's prisms, or, to put it differently, they modify each other. The style of orchestral writing brings about a magnification of the writing itself, in order to achieve more massive as well as more differentiated results."

One of the unusual features about this composition is that it calls for a seating arrangement in the orchestra far different from the traditional one—"not so much for the sake of a more or less superficial stereophony," the composer explains, "but rather with the aim of organizing the sound more clearly."

Doubles was introduced in Paris on March 16, 1958. Its American première took place on May 2, 1965, when Boulez made his American debut as conductor—with the visiting BBC Symphony of London, at Carnegie Hall, New York.

Doubles is the middle part of a three-section work for orchestra entitled *Figures, Doubles, Prismes*; the entire work received its world première in Brussels on December 13, 1964, the composer conducting.

1964 ÉCLAT, for fifteen instruments.

Éclat is an elaboration of a piece of music called *Don*, which Boulez used to perform on the piano as the opening movement of his large work for orchestra, *Pli selon pli*. It was played for the first time in Los Angeles, on March 26, 1965, the composer conducting.

G. W. Hopkins called this work "an exercise in controlled improvisation." He added: "The composition is episodic, and reaches its greatest degree of freedom in a long central section in which both conductor and instrumentalists are given a certain amount of latitude. As if to provide a sufficiently stark contrast, Boulez has written out a closing coda in which freedom is at a minimum. . . . The 'concert ending' is complemented by a 'concert beginning,' in this case a piano solo, written mainly in regular values with free rather than written-in fluctuations. The material used here, as in the central section, relies to a great extent on permutational pattern-making. . . . Most interesting is the central section . . . in which the freedom of all performers interacts and coheres in a convincing way."

BENJAMIN BRITTEN 1913–

There are some English critics who look upon Benjamin Britten as England's greatest composer since Purcell. This may sound like excessive enthusiasm to those who admire Vaughan Williams or Sir William Walton. Nevertheless, there can be little doubt that no English composer—and few contemporary composers anywhere—have had the limelight of world interest and admiration flashed upon them the way Britten has. He is one of the most widely performed and recorded composers of our time. As a colleague of his once remarked wryly: "Britten has only to sneeze and it's immediately published, performed and recorded."

His popularity is well deserved. If he is not the greatest English composer since Purcell, he is surely one of the greatest—as well as one of the most versatile. There is no area of composition to which he has not made significant contributions; in some areas—notably opera—his contributions have been monumental, possibly unique in our times.

Though he was early attracted to the atonal music of Schoenberg and somewhat later was influenced by Mahler's post-Romanticism, Britten has adhered to no single style. He is essentially an eclectic composer whose manner of writing is influenced by the aesthetic requirements of the work he is producing. He has written in many different veins—sometimes even in the same work—and always with a brilliant command of his technique, complete facility, and lack of inhibitions in his self-expression. At his best, he has engaging warmth and a fine poetic speech.

He has been especially successful in the writing of realistic music set to a definite verbal text, whether in song or in opera. His talent for re-creating atmospheric backgrounds in his music, for evoking the exact mood of his text, and for projecting dramatic climaxes has been exceptional. What F. Bonavia wrote about *Peter Grimes* might aptly apply to all of Britten's best works: "He has found the right symbol for every situation, and every page bears evidence of distinction and originality."

In *The New York Times Magazine,* Charles Reid points out that in the opinion of most critics Britten's "salient gift is musico-dramatic—his knack of inventing themes, tunes, rhythms, harmonies, orchestral colors and so forth which, as well as being fascinating in their own right, hit off the scene, situation, sentiment or mood of nature of the moment. He is thus able to convey in musical terms the sniggers and anguish of corrupt young souls (*The Turn of the*

Screw), the din and tension of sea battle (*Billy Budd*), the pomp and cruelty of a Tudor court (*Gloriana*), the parching malaise of a sultry Roman night (*The Rape of Lucretia*), and the murmurous enchantments of the forest where Oberon reigned (*A Midsummer Night's Dream*)."

Mr. Reid then goes on to point out how similar felicitous "delineatory strokes" abound in Britten's concert music. "Whether devising such vast tonal canvases as the *Sinfonia da Requiem* and the *Spring Symphony* or pieces for voice and piano . . . Britten is always concerned with producing sounds that serve a specific emotional purpose, preferably a purpose outside his own personality."

Britten was born in Lowestoft, Suffolk, England, on November 22, 1913. From earliest childhood he revealed phenomenal gifts in music. He began composing when he was five. By nine, he had written his first string quartet and oratorio; and by fourteen, his works included a symphony, half a dozen quartets, ten piano sonatas, and some songs, In 1934, Britten published a *Simple Symphony*, for strings, in which he incorporated material from the music he had writetn during his boyhood.

His academic study took place at South Lodge, and at Gresham's School in Holt, Norfolk. His music study began at the piano when he was seven, followed by instruction on the viola a few years later, and lessons in theory with Frank Bridge, who influenced him greatly. In 1930, Britten entered the Royal College of Music on a scholarship. There his teachers included John Ireland in composition, and Arthur Benjamin in piano. Britten received the Ernest Farrar prize for composition, and because of his piano ability was given the title of Associate of the Royal College of Music.

His first works to get performed were a *Phantasy Quartet,* for oboe and strings, and three two-part songs, all heard in London on December 12, 1932. The quartet was repeated at the festival of the International Society for Contemporary Music at Florence on April 5, 1934. His first publication was a Sinfonietta, for chamber orchestra (1932). With the *Variations on a Theme by Frank Bridge* (heard first at the the Salzburg Festivel in 1937), Britten was represented on symphony programs throughout Europe and the United States.

Just before the outbreak of World War II in Europe, Britten came to the United States, where he attended the American première of his *Variations on a Theme by Frank Bridge.* He remained in America until 1942, completing a number of works that added to his reputation. The most significant was the *Sinfonia da Requiem.* A passionate pacifist, and a conscientious objector, Britten was officially exempted from military service following his return to England; but he cooperated in the war effort by giving numerous concerts in bombed areas and hospitals.

His major creative undertaking during the war was the opera *Peter Grimes,* which the Koussevitzky Music Foundation had commissioned him to write. Its première proved so successful that before long the major opera houses of the world included it in their repertory. *Peter Grimes* placed Britten among the major composers of England, a position he solidified with subsequent works, not only for the stage but also for the concert hall. He was the recipient of honorary doctorates in music from the University of Belfast in 1954 and

Cambridge University in 1959. He was also the first composer commissioned to write an opera for a coronation in England: *Gloriana,* introduced in London during the coronation festivities, on June 8, 1953, and earning for its composer the Companionship of Honor from Queen Elizabeth. In 1953, Britten received the Freedom of the Borough of Lowestoft. In 1964, he won the first Aspen (Colorado) Award of $30,000 for his contribution "to the advancement of the humanities." One year later, he was given Britain's highest award with the appointment as member of the Order of Merit.

In 1947, Britten helped found the Aldeburgh Festival—Aldeburgh being the coastal town in Suffolk where he makes his home. This festival, since then held annually in June, has become one of the most distinguished in England. In 1967, the twentieth anniversary of its founding was celebrated with the opening of a new concert auditorium, a ceremony attended by the Queen. Through the years, this festival has been dominated by Britten's personality and music, world premières of important Britten works often being basic to its program, which includes painting exhibits, poetry readings, dramatic presentations and lectures, as well as musical performances.

1937 VARIATIONS ON A THEME BY FRANK BRIDGE, for orchestra, op. 10.

For many years, Britten was a pupil of Frank Bridge, whom he greatly admired both as composer and as teacher. In 1937, Britten was inspired by a theme in the second of Bridge's *Three Idylls* to write a series of orchestral variations. Introduced at the Salzburg Festival on August 27, 1937, by the English String Orchestra under Boyd Neel, it was an immediate and unqualified success. One year later, it was repeated—and no less successfully—at the festival of the International Society for Contemporary Music held in London.

Following a brief introduction, in which certain elements of the Bridge theme are only suggested, the theme proper is introduced and then repeated without ornamentation. Ten variations follow, their subtitles giving us a clue to their musical or programmatic content: Adagio, March, Romance, Aria Italiana, Bourrée Classique, Wiener Waltz, Moto Perpetuo, Funeral March, Chant, and Fugue.

Though there are several undercurrents of sardonic humor (such as the suggestion of the goose step in the March, the tongue-in-cheek simulation of a Viennese waltz, and the parody of the operatic coloratura style in the Italian Aria), it is rather the deep emotional pages of this work that have made the most forceful impression upon listeners. The opening Adagio and the magnificent Funeral March are singularly moving The closing fugue is treated in a somewhat unorthodox manner: the entire exposition is in unison.

The music of the *Variations* was used for *Le Rêve de Léonore,* a ballet produced in 1949 by Roland Petit's Ballets de Paris, with choreography by Frederick Ashton.

1938 CONCERTO NO. 1 FOR PIANO AND ORCHESTRA, op. 13. I. Toccata. II. Waltz. III. Impromptu. IV. March.

This concerto was originally written in 1938 and was introduced in London on August 18 of the same year, with the composer as soloist and an orchestra conducted by Sir Henry J. Wood. In 1945, Britten rewrote the concerto, making minor revisions in three of the movements and replacing one of them completely (the third movement, originally, was a Recitative and Aria). In June, 1946, the revised version of the concerto was heard at the Cheltenham Festival.

The composer has prepared the following descriptive notes:

"The pianoforte starts the first movement (Allegro molto e con brio) with an energetic leaping motif which sets the mood for its own side of the argument. This is the principal subject of the movement. The orchestra continues with a subsidiary phrase which reaches an angry climax in the alternation of two not very closely related chords—an idea which has, however, significance throughout the work. After some discussion, the orchestra introduces hesitantly the second principal subject—a longer flowing tune on the woodwind. This the pianoforte mocks in brilliant fashion, and the orchestra tries to further its cause with the tune in the strings. The second section of the movement presents a grimmer aspect of this material.

"The second movement (Allegro, alla valse) is quiet throughout, as if overheard from the next room. The viola solo and clarinet suggest the first tune, and the pianoforte adds the chordal motif from the first movement as a codetta. After a slightly more defined repetition, the pianoforte starts a running theme, supported by waltz rhythms in the whole orchestra. This grows louder and louder, and eventually the first waltz tune returns energetically and forte, as if the door had been slightly opened. But it is soon shut again, and to the end of the movement the mood is that of the beginning. The chordal motif is used again and again rather ominously.

"A set of variations on a theme first announced by the piano comprises the third movement (Andante; Lento). Suggestions of marching rhythms follow directly from the previous movement and lead to a series of march tunes played full of confidence by the pianoforte and then by the orchestra."

1939 CONCERTO FOR VIOLIN AND ORCHESTRA, op. 15. I. Moderato. II. Vivace. III. Passacaglia.

This is Britten's first major work to get written on the other side of the Atlantic Ocean. He completed it in 1939 during a stay at St. Jovite in Quebec, Canada. This is also the work with which he was introduced to the American public, its world première taking place in New York on March 28, 1940; John Barbirolli conducted the New York Philharmonic, and the soloist was Antonio Brosa. In 1958, Britten revised the concerto.

It opens with a brief introduction in which a figure for tympani becomes the accompaniment to the main subject when it is given in the ninth measure by the solo violin. This is a quiet, introspective melody. Following a short cadenza, the orchestra repeats it. A more dramatic incident is introduced with the second theme (Agitato ma espressivo), which is presented by the solo instument over a chorale-like accompaniment in muted horns. Following an elaboration of this material, the recapitulation begins with a recall of the first subject in upper strings, which the solo instrument joins by repeating the tympani figure of the introduction. A serene coda brings the movement to its conclusion.

The second movement is a scherzo. A strong rhythmic figure, first in solo violin, then in bassoon, sets the stage for the main subject, a virile thought for solo violin. A calmer mood is projected in the middle trio. An extended cadenza leads into the finale, a ten-section passacaglia. The variations offer contrasts in mood, atmosphere and emotion, reaching their peak in a vigorous alla marcia section. The concerto then ends calmly.

1939 LES ILLUMINATIONS, song cycle for high voice and string orchestra, op. 18. I Fanfare. II. Villes. IIIa. Phrase. IIIb. Antique. IV. Royauté. V. Marine. VI. Interlude. VII. Being Beauteous. VIII. Parade. IX. Départ.

Britten's exceptional gift for writing songs that embrace a wide gamut of emotions with the greatest ingenuity of expression was first made strikingly evident in this cycle of ten decadent songs on prose poems by the French symbolist, Rimbaud. Poetry and music achieve integration as Britten catches in tones the subtlest nuances and the most delicate imagery of Rimbaud's poetry. In the perfection of characterization of each song, and in the balance of the ten, Erwin Stein finds an example of Britten's gift for building large forms by "co-ordination rather than integration" as he concerns himself with "neatly fitting together of a diversity of shapes" rather than "connecting and cementing them."

The cycle was written while Britten was in the United States, and was introduced in London on January 30, 1940. It was adapted into a one-act ballet by Frederick Ashton, choreographer of Sadler's Wells Ballet, the first commission which the New York City Ballet gave to a foreign artist. The ballet was introduced by the New York City Ballet on March 2, 1950, when it was described by John Martin in *The New York Times* as "a work of rare and delicate poetic beauty, a ravishingly romantic ballet."

1940 SINFONIA DA REQUIEM, op. 20. I. Lacrymosa. II. Dies Irae. III. Requiem Aeternam.

Though this symphony utilized the Latin titles of a Catholic Requiem Mass, its relation to the mass was intended by the composer to be emotional rather than liturgical.

The death of the composer's father was the inspiration for this strongly felt music. Britten wrote it in 1940 in the United States. On March 29, 1941, the New York Philharmonic Orchestra under John Barbirolli introduced it.

Britten has provided the following analysis:

The first movement (Andante ben misurato) is a "slow marching lament. There are three main motives: (1) a syncopated, sequential theme announced by the cellos and answered by the solo bassoon; (2) a broad theme, based on the interval of the major seventh; (3) alternating chords on flute and trombones, outlined by piano and harps. The first section of the movement is quietly pulsating; the second, a long crescendo, leads to a climax based on the first cello theme."

Without a pause, the work proceeds to the second section (Allegro con fuoco), "a form of Dance of Death, with occasional moments of quiet marching rhythm. The dominating motif of this movement is announced at the start by the flutes and includes an important tremolando figure. . . . The scheme of the movement is a series of climaxes of which the last is the most powerful, causing the music to disintegrate and to lead directly to the final section."

The closing movement (Andante piacevole) begins "very quietly over a background of solo strings and harps," after which the flutes "announce the quiet. . . . tune which is the principal motif of the movement. There is a middle section in which the strings play a flowing melody. This grows to a short climax, but the opening tune is soon resumed and the work ends quietly in a a long sustained clarinet note."

1941 SCOTTISH BALLAD, for two pianos and orchestra, op. 26.

This was another significant work for solo instruments and orchestra, completed by Britten during his residence in the United States in the early years of World War II. The work received its première in Cincinnati on November 28, 1941. Eugene Goossens conducted the Cincinnati Symphony, and the soloists were Ethel Bartlett and Rae Robertson.

The composer went to old Scottish tunes for his thematic material. But, as he explained, he had no intention of writing a medley, but "to evoke a sequence of ideas and emotions that have been characteristic of the life of the Scottish people during centuries of stormy history."

There are three sections played without interruption. The work begins with a short introduction (Lento) in which a psalm tune, "Dundee," is heard. This leads into a funeral march based on the lament, "The Flowers of the Forest." A recall of the psalm tune of the introduction, delicately harmonized, is the transition to the concluding part (Allegro). This is a Scottish reel, which starts out pianissimo, but is worked up into an exciting climax. The placement of the lively music of a reel after a recollection of a funeral march is characteristically Scottish, since after Scottish military funerals, pipers always returned to camp playing lively tunes.

1942 A CEREMONY OF CAROLS, for treble voices and harp obbligato, op. 28.

A Ceremony of Carols consists of an opening "Procession" (the choristers march up the church aisle chanting of Christ's birth), nine carols, and a "Recession" (a repetition of the opening "Procession," as the choristers march down the aisle again to leave the church). The carols are of medieval origin: five are of anonymous authorship; four are by James, John, and Robert Wedderburn; others are by Robert Southwell and William Cornish.

The music has a unanimity of style, even though there is contrast of mood from one carol to the next, as Britten re-ceates in modern terminology the style of the medieval plainchant. The simple and seemingly spontaneous music is filled with poetic beauty and religious feeling. The background of a single harp provides a remarkably effective accompaniment, and only on one occasion (between the two carols by Southwell) does it provide an instrumental interlude.

This work was introduced in London by the Fleet Street Choir, T. B. Lawrence conducting, on December 5, 1942.

1943 SERENADE, for tenor solo, horn, and string orchestra, op. 31.

This delightful setting of English lyrics by Cotton, Tennyson, Blake, Ben Jonson and Keats was introduced in London by Peter Pears, Dennis Brain, and an orchestra conducted by Walter Goehr, on October 15, 1943.

The Serenade opens with a prologue of a horn solo, which is repeated offstage at the conclusion of the work, the Epilogue.

Edward Sackville West, to whom this work is dedicated, described it as follows: "The subject is Night and its prestigia, the lengthening shadow, the distant haze at sunset, the Baroque panoply of the starry sky, the heavy angles of sleep; but also the cloak of evil—the worm in the heart of the rose, the sense of sin in the heart of man. The whole sequence forms an elegy or Nocturnal (as Donne would have called it) reviewing the thoughts and images suitable to the evening."

1944 PETER GRIMES, an opera in three acts, prologue and epilogue, op. 33, with libretto by Montagu Slater based on George Crabbe's *The Borough.* First performance: Sadler's Wells Theatre, London, June 7, 1945.

In 1941, the Koussevitzky Music Foundation commissioned Britten to write a full-length opera. The composer selected as a text George Crabbe's *The Borough*, a subject that appealed strongly to his sense of humanity and compassion. Peter Grimes, as Crabbe saw him, was an uncouth villain, turned hard and callow through the misunderstanding of his neighbors. Two apprentices work under him in slave conditions, both dying from maltreatment. In this theme Britten saw a symbol of man's struggle against a narrow society: the conflict of the individual against unreasoning masses.

The subject of *The Borough* was amplified and changed by Montagu Slater to emphasize the helplessness of Grimes against the fury of the masses. Though he is innocent, he is doomed to inevitable disaster. Thus Grimes becomes—in spite of his cruelty, brusque manners, and explosive temper—a sympathetic character. As the opera opens, he is brought to trial for a crime he did not commit: the death of his apprentice. The trial absolves him of his guilt; but ugly suspicions persist. The antagonism between Grimes and society persists. Overwhelmed by this antagonism, Grimes becomes surly; even the one who would give him sympathy and unquestioning allegiance—Ellen Orford, with whom he is in love—is rewarded with blows as Grimes refuses to accept pity. Grimes acquires a second apprentice; the mob, wondering if another "murder" is about to take place, marches to Grimes' lonely hut to see what is happening. Grimes flees to his boat; the apprentice, who follows him, slips and falls. A few days later, the sweater of the apprentice is found on the beach, proof to the townspeople that Grimes has committed murder. With fear and anger tormenting him, Grimes loses his mind. Rather than face an angry mob, he takes to the sea, never to return.

The première of the opera took place at the Sadler's Wells Theatre in London on June 7, 1945. This was a gala event for more reasons than one. The theatre was being reopened for the first time in five years, having been closed in 1940 by the Blitz. Besides, this was the first new opera heard in London in several years.

The opera proved to be a gripping emotional experience, and it scored a phenomenal success. There was a five-minute ovation for the composer. The critical reaction was equally enthusiastic. The correspondent of *The New York Times* called the event " a milestone in the history of British music." Ernest Newman described the opera as "a work of great originality. . . . The whole texture, musical and dramatic, of the opera is admirably unified, in spite of the many genres it employs, ranging from almost naked speech to music at its fullest power."

The success of *Peter Grimes* spread rapidly. In a short period, it was heard more than a hundred times in Sweden, Denmark, Switzerland, Italy, Germany, Holland and Hungary, and was translated into eight languages. On August 6, 1946, it received its first American performance at Tanglewood, in Lenox, Massachusetts, under the direction of Leonard Bernstein. On February 12, 1948, it entered the repertory of the Metropolitan Opera Association.

With a variety of style—lyricism and piercing dissonance, simple jigs and complicated contrapuntal sea chanteys, polytonal duets, and starkly realistic tone-painting—Britten achieves a score of great dramatic force. The full strength of the implacable tragedy befalling Peter Grimes, and his psychological conflicts are subtly delineated in the music. With grim atmospheric verity the composer imaginatively catches the feeling of fatalism pervading the drama. The score has gripping tensions; but on occasion it also has tenderness and compassion.

Five orchestral episodes, a Passacaglia and four interludes, are sometimes heard independently on symphony programs. They were introduced on June 13, 1945, at the Cheltenham Festival, with the composer conducting the London Philharmonic Orchestra.

The Passacaglia is played between the scenes in the second act. Where passacaglias are traditionally in 3/4 times, this one is in 4/4. Erwin Stein has explained that the theme from the Passacaglia comes from Peter's fateful cadence which dominates the music of the ensuing scene. "The theme," he explains, "is stubbornly repeated by the bass instruments and its irregular rhythm is frequently at cross purposes with the common time of the music which is built upon it. This is a set of variations on a new theme, played by the solo viola."

The *Four Interludes* comprise the following sections:

I. "Dawn" (between the Prologue and Act I). As Ernest Newman wrote, this section is descriptive of the "gray atmosphere of the hard-bitten little fishing town." The fishermen quietly go about their respective tasks. Three themes are used. The first suggests the bleak seascape in its austerity; the second represents the call of sea gulls; and the third, which is quiet and idyllic, paints a picture of the rise of the dawn over the water.

II. "Sunday Morning" (leading into Act II), a description of the village streets on a peaceful Sunday as church bells ring. Four horns are sounded. At the sixth measure, a syncopated melody is heard.

III. "Moonlight" (leading into Act III), depicting the street scene at night. Bassoons, horns and strings (minus the violins) offer us an almost impressionistic nocturnal portrait. The sensual web of tone is, from time to time, punctuated by soft chords in flutes and harp.

IV. "The Storm" (between Scenes 1 and 2 of Act I), a picturesque tonal setting of a storm as it rises and gathers force. The snarling trumpets and trombones moving in parallel fifths, the angry horns giving reply in octaves, point up the fact that the sea is in ferment. The mood is established for the storm that dominates the second scene of the first act, which is set in an inn, where the storm spills over into the inn whenever the door opens and somebody enters.

1945 THE YOUNG PERSON'S GUIDE TO THE ORCHESTRA, variations and fugue, op. 34.

Commissioned by the Ministry of Education in England to write music for an educational film describing the various instruments of the orchestra, Britten hit upon the happy idea of writing a series of variations on a theme, each variation featuring a different instrument or group of instruments. For his theme he selected a subject by Henry Purcell (taken from the Rondeau in the incidental music to *Abdelazar*). This theme is stated by the full orchestra in eight measures. The next four sections offer the instruments in choirs, first the woodwinds, then the brasses, the strings, and the percussion. Once again, the Purcell theme is stated by the full orchestra. Now we get thirteen variations on the theme, presenting the instruments in the following order: flutes and piccolo; oboes; clarinets; bassoons; strings; violas; cellos; double basses; harp; French horns; trumpets; trombones; tympani and other members of the percussion family, ending up with the xylophone. The composition concludes with a fugue in which the instruments enter, one by one, in the order in which they were heard in the variations; they then unite in a climactic enunciation of the Purcell theme for the last time.

1945 STRING QUARTET NO. 2, op. 36. I. Allegro calmo senza rigore. II. Vivace. III. Chacony.

In 1945, musical England celebrated the 250th anniversary of the death of Henry Purcell. To honor Purcell, Britten wrote several commemorative works, one of which was this string quartet.

The quartet opens with the traditional sonata-allegro movement built around three themes, each of which is characterized by an interval of the tenth. The second movement is a lugubrious Scherzo for muted strings. It is in the third movement that Britten pays homage to Purcell by writing a "chacony," or chaconne, a form which the master utilized with great technical mastery. Britten's chaconne consists of a theme and twenty-one variations, divided into four distinct groups, each separated from the others by a cadenza.

1946 THE RAPE OF LUCRETIA, opera in two acts, op. 37, with text by Ronald Duncan based on André Obey's play, *Le Viol du Lucrèce*. First performance: Glyndebourne, England, July 12, 1946.

In contrast to the almost Wagnerian proportions of *Peter Grimes, The Rape of Lucretia* (which came one year later) is of chamber-music dimensions. The artistic expression becomes lean as the composer tries to penetrate to essentials. There are only six principals in the cast. The two "choruses" consist respectively of one man and one woman who, in the manner of the Greek chorus, explain and interpret the action of the play. The musical writing is most spare, too. Subdued atmospheric writing provides a background that is rarely assertive and allows the play on the stage to assume first importance. The writing for the voices is direct, usually melodic. Generally speaking, the opera is lyrical, though an occasional excursion into dissonance is allowed for the sake of dramatic effect.

The opera is concerned with Lucretia, wife of the Roman general Collatinus, who is seduced by the Etruscan prince Tarquinius during the Etruscan domination of Rome.

The Rape of Lucretia, when introduced, was so successful that soon after the première it was performed about 130 times in England, before being heard in Holland, Belgium, Switzerland and the United States. The American première took place in Chicago on June 1, 1947. On December 29, 1948, it was brought on the Broadway stage, where it enjoyed a brief run, though with considerably less success than it had known in the opera house. In 1950, it was produced at the Salzburg Festival, and on October 23, 1958, it was given by the New York City Opera.

Britten's talent for giving the precise musical setting required by a text and interpreting musically the psychological conflicts of his characters is as evident in this opera as in *Peter Grimes*. A memorable section is the interlude accompanying Tarquinius's ride. Here is not only the sweep of the horse's movement conjured with vivid strokes of sound, but the mental turmoil of Tarquinius suggested in subtle overtones, as well. Equally memorable is a funeral march in passacaglia form over whose ostinato a remarkable sextet is built, in which, as Eric Walter White says, "each vocal part is developed with full regard for the characters of the various persons concerned." One of the finest vocal pages is found in the poignant lullaby of Tarquinius ("Within this Frail Crucible of Light") that opens the second act.

1947 ALBERT HERRING, opera in three acts, op. 39, with text by Eric Crozier based on Guy de Maupassant's story, *Le Rosier de Madame Husson*. First performance: Glyndebourne, England, June 20, 1947.

As an artistic (and possibly emotional) respite from the writing of such stark tragedies as *Peter Grimes* and *The Rape of Lucretia,* Britten wrote an opera buffa in the operatic project following these two works.

Albert Herring, written to launch the first independent season of the English Opera Company, was planned along economical lines to facilitate tours in England and Europe. The opera calls for a small cast and orchestra and limited scenery.

In adapting the story by Guy de Maupassant, Eric Crozier changed the locale from France to Suffolk, England. Madame Husson becomes Lady Billows, a lady with great reverence for virtue. Deciding to revive the May Day Festival, she offers a prize of twenty-five guineas for a May Queen of unquestionable morality. A search among local young ladies fails to uncover a single person capable of fulfilling the necessary qualifications. It is then decided to compromise on a May King, the choice falling on Albert Herring, a notoriously shy fellow. At the High Tea of the Festival, Albert Herring's friend, a practical joker, substitutes a glass of rum for Albert's glass of lemonade. Intoxication slowly sets in. Late that night, the young man's dormant emotions are stirred. He goes forth in search of debauchery and disappears into the night. The following day his whereabouts is a mystery. The wreath of orange blossoms which he had worn the day before is found crushed in the road, inspiring the belief that Albert is dead. His neighbors intone a moving dirge to his passing. Suddenly he appears—ill-kempt, ragged, but proud of his new-found freedom.

The realism of *Peter Grimes* gives way in this opera to wit and lusty satire. In his utilization of arias, duets, and ensemble numbers, Britten remains true to the traditions of opera buffa; but the writing is ever piquantly modern. Broad comedy, as in Albert Herring's return in the final scene, is developed with a healthy respect for burlesque. Parody is occasionally indulged in, as, for example, in the sly quotation of the love-potion music from Wagner's *Tristan* when Herring drinks the rum.

"It is the opera's special glory," says Eric Walter White, "that frequently a character or episode is treated with a mixture of satire and sentiment that produced as unforgettable a vignette as a drawing by Rowlandson or a poem by Betjeman. There is the bland and hesitant Vicar trying to reassure Lady Billows on the subject of virtue; the twittering of Miss Wordsworth nervously rehearsing the schoolchildren in the festive song, 'Time to Try Our Festive Song'; Mrs. Herring clutching the faded framed photo of her son as a little boy; and Albert himself when, returning in the evening from the feast, he enters the greengrocer's shop in the dark and looks round for matches to light the gas to the accompaniment of the exquisite nocturne for bass flute and bass clarinet first heard in the previous interlude."

The American première of *Albert Herring* took place at the Berkshire Music Center at Tanglewood during the summer of 1949.

1949 SPRING SYMPHONY, for soprano, tenor, mixed chorus, boys' chorus and orchestra, op. 44. Part I: 1. Shine Out, Fair Sun; 2. The Merry Cuckoo; 3. Spring; 4. The Driving Boy; Whenas the Rye; 5. The Morning Star. Part II: 1. Welcome Maids of Honour; 2. The Shower; 3. Out on the Lawn. Part III: 1. When Will My May Come?; 2. Fair as Fair; 3. Sound the Flute. Part IV: 1. London, to Thee I Do Present; 2. Summer Is Icumen In.

The composer has explained how he came to write this choral symphony in praise of the vernal season. "For two years I had been planning such a work, a symphony not only dealing with Spring itself, but the progress of Winter to Spring and the reawakening of earth and life to what that means. Originally, I had wanted to use medieval Latin verse and had made a selection of fine poems; but a re-reading of much English lyric verse and a particularly lovely Spring day in East Suffolk, the Suffolk of Constable and Gainsborough, made me change my mind."

This composition is more of an elaborate choral suite than a symphony. While the four sections are intended to suggest the four movements of the symphony, the suggestion is more psychological than structural, and the similarity remains vague. There is none of the organic growth and development of ideas one expects in a symphonic work, and the essential forms of the symphony are not utilized.

The composer has here set fourteen English poems of springtime, both of the past and the present. His musical approach is a poetic one as well. He is concerned primarily in evoking the mood of each poem in atmospheric music. He draws his spirit from the old English madrigalists and, like them, has succeeded in bathing his music with radiant warmth, a joyousness of expression, and ebullient feelings.

Each section of the symphony comprises several poems sung without interruption. The introduction (Lento) is based on *Shine Out, Fair Sun, with All Your Heat* (author unknown), sung by a mixed chorus. There then follow, in the first part, *The Merry Cuckoo, Messenger of Spring,* by Edmund Spenser (Vivace) for tenor solo and three muted trumpets; *Spring, the Sweet Spring,* by Thomas Nashe (Allegro con slanico) for mixed chorus, soloists, and full orchestra; *Whenas the Rye Reach to the Chin,* by George Peele; and *The Driving Boy,* by John Clare (Allegro molto), sung by soprano solo, a boys' chorus, and orchestra. John Milton's *The Morning Star* (Molto moderato ma giocoso), for mixed chorus, brass, and percussion, ends this section.

The second part opens with *Welcome Maids of Honour* (Allegretto moderato), by Robert Herrick, for alto solo, woodwinds, and divided strings. *The Shower,* by Henry Vaughan (Molto moderato), for tenor solo and violins, and *Out on the Lawn,* by W. H. Auden (Adagio), for alto solo, chorus, winds, and percussion, complete this section.

In the third part we hear *When Will My May Come?* by Robert Barnfield (Allegro impetuoso), for tenor solo and strings; *Fair as Fair,* by George Peele (Allegro grazioso), a duet for soprano and tenor, accompanied by strings and woodwinds; and *Sound the Flute,* by William Blake (Allegretto), for chorus and full orchestra.

The symphony concludes with *London, to Thee I Do Present,* by Beaumont and Fletcher (Moderato alla valse), for full orchestra and chorus, and a single line from the famous round, *Summer Is Icumen In* (Allegro pesante), interpolated into the preceding number.

Though the symphony was commissioned by the Koussevitzky Foundation, its world première took place not in America but in Holland, on July 9, 1949, during the Holland Music Festival. The Concertgebouw Orchestra was directed by Eduard von Beinum. The work received an ovation; it was generally conceded that this performance was the most distinguished event of the entire festival. A few weeks later, on August 13, Serge Koussevitzky directed the American première at the Berkshire Music Festival at Tanglewood.

1951 BILLY BUDD, opera originally in four acts, later rewritten as two acts, op. 50, with text by E. M. Forster and Eric Crozier based on Herman Melville's novel of the same name. First performance: Covent Garden, London, December 1, 1951; revised version, Covent Garden, London, April 26, 1963.

In *Billy Budd,* Britten returns to the sea, the setting of his first and, up to now, his most successful opera, *Peter Grimes.* There are other points of similarity between these two works. *Billy Budd* is the first of Britten's operas since *Peter Grimes* to revert to ambitious structural dimensions, calling for large musical and stage forces; *The Rape of Lucretia* and *Albert Herring* were both intimate and economical. And the central theme of *Billy Budd* is once again the brutality of injustice, of man's inhumanity to man. Billy Budd is a sailor compelled to serve in the British navy during the British-French wars in the eighteenth century. He is a lovable, happy-go-lucky lad, ready to do his duty.

But he inspires the hate of the master-of-arms, John Claggart, who manufactures a false charge of treason against him. Aroused by this monstrous accusation, and too poor in words to defend himself against it, Budd loses his temper, strikes Claggart, and kills him. He is court-martialed and hanged. Captain Vere realizes the just provocation that led Budd to murder Claggart, but naval justice must be fulfilled.

If there are resemblances between *Billy Budd* and *Peter Grimes,* there are also differences. Indeed, these differences distinguish *Billy Budd* from most other operas. For one thing, *Budd* is scored entirely for men's voices (there is no love interest whatsoever). For another, it dispenses almost entirely with melodic arias and aurally pleasing ensemble numbers. Except for some sailor chanteys (and they represent some of the finest pages in the score) and one or two lyrical pages, such as Billy's poignant resignation to his sad fate in the final act, the vocal score is confined to dramatic recitatives with the principal musical interest and variety found in the orchestration. It is the drama, rather than the music, that is Britten's first concern; every musical means at his command is employed to heighten and intensify that drama. Thus a passage like the series of disconnected triads heard after Budd has been condemned to die (the stage is empty) is of greater theatrical interest than musical; so is the effective unaccompanied monologue of Captain Vere, a discourse on good and evil, with which the opera ends.

Billy Budd was commissioned by the Arts Council of Great Britain for the Festival of Britain. It was introduced at Covent Garden, under the composer's direction. Most leading English critics hailed it as one of Britten's most important (and most human) operas. Scott Goddard described the score as "insidiously haunting"; Richard Capell remarked that its "incidental felicities are innumerable and many things are in the best vein"; and Stephen Williams referred to it as a "challenging, stimulating work of art." On May 26, 1952, *Billy Budd* was introduced to France as one of the major attractions of the Exposition of Masterpieces of the 20th Century held in Paris. The American première (a truncated version) took place over the NBC-TV network on October 19, 1952. In 1961, Britten revised the opera, principally by reducing the four acts into two. This version was performed in America for the first time on January 4, 1966, in a performance by the American Opera Society in New York.

1954 TURN OF THE SCREW, opera in two acts and prologue, op. 54, with text by Myfawny Piper based on the novel of the same name by Henry James. First performance: Venice, September 14, 1954.

Henry James's eerie and at times gruesome horror story is the source of one of Britten's most powerful operas, a work of extraordinary musical invention and dramatic impact. Britten wrote this opera for the Venice Festival, where it was introduced. Its première in the United States took place in New York on March 19, 1958.

James's strange tale has been followed here with only minor and unimportant deviations. A curse of evil has descended upon two children, protected by a neurotic governess, and abetted by the presence of two ghosts of former servants. All efforts to protect the children result only in arousing the morbid terror of the little girl and in bringing the little boy to his death. Thus a theme familiar in so many of Britten's operas—the struggle between good and evil—is here translated into a life-and-death clash between innocence and guilt, with innocence finally sacrificed.

One of the original procedures in this opera is the preface of an orchestral sequence before each of the sixteen scenes. These interludes are actually variations on a twelve-note theme ("The Screw") arranged in fourths and thirds, and serve the dramatic purpose of commenting orchestrally on what is transpiring on the stage. "Frequent ostinato, ingenious percussive effects and the tendency to polarize round easily recognizable chords," wrote Cynthia Jolly, "produce an almost hypnotic effect of terrifying persistence."

Turn of the Screw—like the composer's *Rape of Lucretia*—is a chamber opera of small dimensions. There are only six in the cast; and the orchestra numbers just fifteen. But economy and the reduction of all musical materials to their essentials make no sacrifice of dramatic values. In few of his operas has Britten written such high-tensioned music, so vivid in atmosphere and characterization; in few of his operas does he reveal such remarkable inventiveness of melodic and harmonic writing and such extraordinary variety of orchestral effects.

The North American première of the opera took place at the Stratford Shakespeare festival in Ontario, Canada, on August 20, 1957. At that time, Ross Parmenter wrote in *The New York Times*: "Whatever one might think of the work as an opera, one thing is clear: it is a remarkably sensitive piece of music. It is sensitive in its scoring, in the delicacy of its musical impressionism, and in the way each note, each stroke of the instrumentation mirrors the emotions of the text. It gives the same sense of being a single piece of music by the interweaving of its motifs, by its success in sustaining and developing a mood and by the way the orchestral interludes and the dramatized scenes form a continuous musical texture."

The United States première took place in New York City on March 19, 1958.

1956 THE PRINCE OF PAGODAS, ballet in three acts, op. 57, with scenario and choreography by John Cranko. First performance: Covent Garden, London, January 1, 1957.

Though several of Britten's compositions had previously been adapted for the ballet, *The Prince of Pagodas* was his first to get produced as a ballet score. In his music, Britten succeeded in unfolding "a pageant of music," in the words of Donald Mitchell, "whose wide range of mood . . . encompasses . . . the tender, the fantastic, the sinister, the joyous, the satirical, the heroic." A brief orchestral overture opens with several fanfares serving as a catalyzing agent for the entire score. This is followed by a formal gavotte. To Irving Kolodin, the high point of the music comes with a "well-imagined sequence in Act II, when Britten evokes a pagoda atmosphere with a mingling of bells, percussion and chimes." In the finale, which opens with a fugato, there is a résumé of earlier dances.

The ballet combines elements from *Cinderella, Beauty and the Beast* and *King Lear*. Its complicated plot is summarized by John Martin as follows: "A doddering king is removed from the throne by his evil elder daughter (Belle Epine), while his misunderstood younger daughter (Belle Rose) finds her romantic prince, by falling in love with what she assumes to be a monster."

1959 CANTATA ACADEMICA (CARMEN BASILIENSE), for soprano, contralto, tenor, bass, mixed chorus and orchestra, op. 62.

Britten was commissioned to write this cantata to help commemorate the five-hundredth anniversary of the founding of the University of Basel, Switzerland's oldest university. The composition was heard on July 1, 1960, during a festival in Basel celebrating this event. Britten's text was *Carmen Basiliense,* by Bernhard Wyss, which, in Latin, described the influence that the University had had on the people of Basel over a five-hundred-year period.

Here is how Britten described the work: "Although festive in style it is also—as seemed to me appropriate for the auspicious occasion—formal, with plenty of academic, technical devices: canons, fugues, mirrors, ostinatos, pedals, and so forth. In fact, each of the thirteen short sections into which the Cantata is divided is over (or under) a pedal, and these pedals make up a twelve-tone series sung by the chorus to a straightforward and chordal accompaniment in No. 8. I have made use in several of the numbers of a Canto Populare, a Basel tune (suggested to me by Dr. Sacher), *zBasle a mym Rhy.* This appears finally on bells in No. 13."

1960 A MIDSUMMER NIGHT'S DREAM, opera in three acts, op. 64, with text by the composer and Peter Pears based on the Shakespeare comedy. First performance: Aldeburgh, England, June 11, 1960.

In setting Shakespeare to music, Britten made no attempt to re-create the setting or atmosphere of Shakespeare's time through the quotation or imitation of folk songs and dances of old England. As Howard Taubman remarked in *The New York Times* in reviewing the opera at its world's première: "Mr. Britten has elected to seek an atmosphere of timelessness. . . . His idiom derives from impressionism, but his style is his own. He combines voices and orchestra in veils of shimmering song. . . . Bottom, Quince and the other characters are treated in a contrasting manner. Mr. Britten manages to characterize them and to underline their oafish humors without resorting to obvious effects. And for the performance of the 'tedious brief' tale in the third and final act he has written music that has the juiciness of the operatic style at its richest." Mr. Taubman sums up by calling this opera Britten's "happiest."

The librettists made extensive cuts in the Shakespeare comedy, keeping only about half of the original text; but, except for a single line of transition, only Shakespeare's lines were used. The opera, as the play, is poised on three levels: the world of the fairy kingdom; the world of the rustics; the world of the lovers. For each, Britten has found the appropriate musical equivalent. "Fairyland," said Taubman, "is immersed in the musical devices of impressionism." For the rustics, Britten produced "a kind of arioso style that bursts into full operatic bloom in the final act in a way reminiscent of the Italian lyric theatre of the early nineteenth century." And the lovers are "delineated in a conventional neo-romanticism."

The American première was given by the San Francisco Opera on October

10, 1961. On April 25, 1963, the opera was produced by the New York City Opera.

1962 A WAR REQUIEM, for soprano, tenor, baritone, mixed chorus, boys' choir, full orchestra and chamber orchestra, op. 66.

A War Requiem is its composer's most deeply moving, most eloquent, and most durable achievement for the concert hall, and possibly one of the greatest works he has produced in any medium. He wrote it on a commission for a festival celebrating the Consecration of the restored St. Michael's Cathedral at Coventry, the occasion upon which it was introduced on May 30, 1962. Its first performance in London took place at Westminster Abbey on December 6 of the same year, while the first American hearing took place at the Berkshire Music Festival at Tanglewood, on July 27, 1963, Erich Leinsdorf conducting.

The text is based partly on the traditional Missa Pro Defunctis (Requiem Aeternam, Dies Irae, Offertorium, Sanctus, Agnus Dei and Libera Me); and partly from the poems of Wilfred Owens, killed in World War I just one week before the Armistice, and after he had received the Military Cross for bravery. As an avowed pacifist, Britten was particularly struck by these Owens lines, which appear as a motto on the title page of his published score: "My subject is War, and the pity of War. The Poetry is in the pity. All that a poet can do is warn." Britten's procedure is to follow each section of the Latin Missal text with English verses by the soldier-poet, who protested the futility of war, its needless cruelty, and pity for those whose lives were shortened in this mass carnage.

The score is made up of three performing groups. The first is for full chorus and orchestra, with soprano solo. These perform the traditional Mass. A second group consists of a boys' choir, which chants parts of the Requiem service in its sweet, innocent voice to provide a refreshing relief and contrast from the turbulent sounds produced by the larger chorus. The third group conveys the personal message of the poet (and the composer). This is made up of solo tenor and solo baritone, accompanied by a small chamber orchestra. These voices are heard both separately and together, in close alternation with passages from the Mass, declaiming Owens's verses in a free recitative style.

Much of the overwhelming impact of the work lies in this juxtaposition of a ritual Mass with English poems: the poet's tragic contemplation of war and death—his protests, sorrows, despair—with the outcries of the anguished prayers from the Missal text. Thus ritual and lay elements are fused into a unified musical discourse.

First we get the ritual, the Requiem Aeternam section of the Mass. An augmented fourth (an interval Britten used frequently throughout the score) is heard in the first choral phrase to answering bells. The orchestra then develops a solemn and somber march, relieved from time to time by the ethereal chanting of a boys' choir, "The Decet hymnus." The Requiem Aeternam returns and dies away as bells peal. Now a tenor breaks in with a fast, agitated section to bitter lines by Owens ("What passing-bells for these who die as cattle? Only the monstrous anger of the guns"). The section ends with a return of the chorus singing the "Kyrie eleison."

The "Dies Irae" offers an ominous atmosphere with a funereal march subject interrupted by brass fanfares. Then the baritone begins a chant to an Owens verse beginning with the line, "Bugles sang, saddening the evening air." A soprano solo, and a reduced chorus, are now heard in the anguished plea of "Libera scriptus," followed by tenor and baritone solos beginning with the Owens line, "Out there, we've walked quite friendly up to Death." A choral setting of "Recordare" is succeeded by a baritone solo denouncing the stupidity of war, dramatized by fanfares, "Be slowly lifted up, thou long black arm." A return of the "Dies Irae" in chorus and soprano solo precedes the tenor solo, "Move him into the sun." This section ends with a choral setting of "Pie Jesu Domine."

The "Offertorium" begins with a two-part boys' chorus accompanied by organ ("Domine Jesu Christe"), preceding a fugal section for full orchestra ("Sed Signifer Sanctus Michael"). Tenor and baritone solos describe Abraham's sacrifice of his son in "So Abram rose." This part ends with the boys' choir intoning the lines of "Hostias et preces tibi Domine," followed by the full chorus returning quietly with the last part of their fugue to the words "Quam olim Abrahae."

The "Sanctus" opens with music of grandeur and magnificence as soprano solo and chorus hymn the glory of God in "Sanctus, Sanctus." A more poignant section ensues as the baritone solo intones a verse which opens with the line "After the blast of lightning from the East." To John Culshaw "the ending of the poem is the pivot point of the whole work, the moment when the juxtaposition of formalized aspiration and the poetic vision of despair is at its extreme."

The "Agnus Dei" is tranquil music in which chorus, the two orchestras and the tenor solo are collaborators. The tenor solo now is heard in lines beginning with "One ever hangs where shelled roads part," followed by the chorus in "Agnus Dei," and by tenor solo and chorus in "Dona nobis pacem."

The finale, "Libera me," is set into motion with a slow, stately march, whose emotion is heightened and intensified by a crescendo in the drums. Chorus and soprano solo offer the "Libera me, Domine," after which tenor solo intones the lines beginning with "It seemed that out of battle I escaped," and the baritone solo in, " 'None,' said the other, 'save the undone years.' " These are two men in battle, but on opposite sides, one of whom is killed by the other. Their enmity ends with death, as both sing "Let us sleep now" to the accompaniment of tolling bells. Finally, the boys' chorus, the full chorus and soprano solo join forces in "In paradisum deducant te angeli" as a final benediction over the dead.

1963 CANTATA MISERICORDIUM, for tenor, baritone, mixed chorus and orchestra, op. 69.

This cantata was written to commemorate the centenary of the International Red Cross. As part of this celebration, this work received its world première in Geneva on September 1, 1963, Ernest Ansermet conducting, with Peter Pears and Dietrich Fischer-Dieskau, vocal soloists.

Britten here uses a Latin text which dramatizes the parable of the Good Samaritan. This parable (adapted for Britten by Peter Wilkinson) enabled the pacifist-composer to speak out once again against the inhumanity of war. "It has been set with equal shrewdness, the simplicity of the parable matched by the simplicity of the scoring and its relative brevity." So wrote Raymond Ericson in *The New York Times* following the New York première. "Although there are some dramatic outbursts from the chorus and soloists, the work is pervaded by a sweetness and gentleness that echo the ending of the *War Requiem*." At times, the writing is highly descriptive: the excited passage for solo cello and orchestral cellos and double basses that describes the terrible loneliness of the road from Jerusalem and Jericho; the harrowing effect produced by strings and percussion with bitonal chords to depict the attack of the Traveler by the bandits. Frequently, too, the music passes from the atmospheric and pictorial to the lyrical, as in the beautiful arioso of the Good Samaritan, accompanied by piano, harp and double bass, "Ah, di boni! Quid audio?"; and the eloquent chorus that follows, in which the people speak their admiration for the compassion of the Good Samaritan in "Vincit ecce vincit"; also the beatific closing choral pages, where the chorus admonishes people everywhere to emulate the Samaritan. "Vade et tu fac similiter."

1964–1966 CURLEW RIVER, a parable for church performance in one act, op. 71, with text by William Plomer. First performance: Aldeburgh, England, June 13, 1964.

THE BURNING FIERY FURNACE, a parable for church performance in one act, op. 75, with text by William Plomer. First performance: Aldeburgh, England, June 9, 1966.

In 1956, Britten attended a performance of a "Noh" play in Japan, a stylized, impersonal religious spectacle. He then hit upon the idea of creating a similar work for the Western World in Western terms. William Plomer, an authority on Japan and a librettist who had worked with Britten in *Gloriana,* adapted an early fifteenth-century work called *Sumidagawa,* transformed it into a medieval miracle play, and called it *Curlew River*. Every part was to be enacted by monks—not only the performers on the stage but even the instrumentalists. They all enter the church in a procession while chanting a plainsong, "Te Lucis ante terminum." The singers take their place on the stage; the seven instrumentalists assume places next to the singers. Then the abbot announces that what is about to be performed is the true story of a miracle. A play within a play unfolds in which a demented mother searches for her son, who had been kidnapped across the Curlew River, only to find his grave, which has become a holy shrine. She regains her mind after seeing a vision in which her boy appears before her. The play ended, the monks move out of the church, once again chanting a plainsong.

"The work is almost hypnotically compelling in its concentration," reported Charles Osborne. "It opens with the austere beauty of the plainsong hymn . . . and then, urgent and colorful, Britten's orchestration strikes in, contriving to sound at once medieval, late sixteenth century, and modern."

For their second church parable, *The Burning Fiery Furnace* (1966), librettist and composer went to the Bible, instead of oriental drama—to the Book of Daniel. The text was based on the story of the three children of Israel who refused to deny their faith and survived the ordeal of Nebuchadnezzar's fires.

Once again, as in *Curlew River,* the parable is enacted by a company of monks, who open and close the church performance by singing a plainsong. The reviewer for the *Times* of London regarded the processional march as "one of the musical highlights of the score." Another "is the song of the three young men in the furnace, the Benedicte. . . ." And when, at the end of the play within a play, the Babylonian court unites in a reprise, the effect is climactic, a moment of musical as well as dramatic glory." The reviewer also found that this was "outwardly a less surprising work than the earlier Britten parable. . . . Visually it is much less austere—the golden image, a blaze of purpureal radiance, the fire, the vision of the four men and the fabulous sinister splendour of Nebuchadnezzar's appearance, his face and fingers masked in gold and orange."

To Eric Mason, writing in the London *Daily Mail,* what stands out particularly in the score are two "extraordinarily imaginative representations of Babylonian music. One is a procession of instrumentalists playing a small harp, glockenspiel, Babylonia drum and other exotic-sounding instruments. The other is a great pagan hymn like a wailing incantation, at the climax of which the alto trombone . . . howls like some demented beast, an exciting effect."

Both *Curlew River* and *The Burning Fiery Furnace* received their American premières at the Caramoor Festival in Katonah, New York—the former during the summer of 1966, and the latter, one year later.

FERRUCCIO BUSONI 1866–1924

To composing, Busoni brought the same trenchant and restless intellect which made him so fine a classical scholar, philosopher, poet, painter, essayist—and one of the aristocratic interpreters of piano music of his generation. His musical thinking was profound (sometimes even abstruse), as perhaps only those who listened to his discussions on aesthetics can best appreciate. Though he was dissatisfied with the restrictions imposed on him by conventions and academicism, he did not altogether break with the past in his indefatigable search for new musical expression. He invented new scales, and new harmonic schemes growing out of these scales; he tried to evolve a new system of musical notation; he experimented with quarter-tones. Frequently, he used composition as a kind of laboratory in which to test or prove his theories or solve a specific technical problem. Since a great many creative theories and problems occupied his mind, he did not achieve a single style, but went from one manner to another, following the dictates of the musical problem at hand. His music, consequently, is often an exercise in intellectual powers, in which the form is dictated by the idea, in which emotion is avoided, and in which new musical resources are continually explored. It is not the kind of music that can have a wide and permanent appeal, and for this reason is not often heard; but it is the kind of music that exerts a far-reaching influence on musical development.

His greatest influence came about through the introduction of neo-classicism, a movement of which he can be said to have been the father. Years before Prokofiev wrote the *Classical Symphony*, and Stravinsky the *L'Histoire du soldat*, Busoni sought to arrive at precision, clarity, lucidity, economy. "What he sought to achieve," wrote his biographer, Edward J. Dent, "was a neo-classicism in which form and expression may find their perfect balance." Busoni called this style "classicism of youth." As he wrote to Richard Strauss in a letter dated May 12, 1909: "Unwittingly we moved out of the domain of music little by little to enter that of philosophy. We lost the sense of pure expression. We are saturated with great thoughts. We prolonged Wagner's very difficult victory beyond its time. . . . We must erect a new classic art. . . . Let us open the windows." As a new classicist, or neo-classicist, Busoni returned to the old dance forms of sarabande, gavotte, minuet and gigue and to the old Baroque structures of fugue, toccata and divertimento. He wrote for small chamber-orchestral ensembles, reviving the concertante methods of the concerto grosso. He made polyphony once again a basic creative tool, even to the extent of producing a mammoth contrapuntal work, *Fantasia contrappuntistica,* which was derived from Bach's *The Art of the Fugue* and which may be described as Busoni's own *Art of the Fugue.*

"This constant refining, this spirituality and concentration, this absence of everything unessential and commonplace, this simple presentation of extremely difficult and complicated problems gives his style a certain severity and exclusiveness," wrote Hugo Leichtentritt. "Popular traits are almost entirely absent, save in the occasional allusion to some gay Italian tune. . . . The Italian vivacity and gaiety, simplicity, perspicuity, grace and beauty of form, and the Germanic Faustian intellectualism, idealism, weight of contents, and emotional fervor are blended in his art into a unique compound that has almost no parallel. His ultimate ideal was a neo-classicism founded on Bach and Mozart, the masters he most ardently revered, in which there should be combined Bach's constructive art, the logic of his polyphony, Mozart's clearness, grace, and elegance, and all the achievements of modern harmonic and orchestral art."

Busoni's influence was absorbed in Germany as well as in Italy, as Leichtentritt notes. "One can perceive this tendency in the music of Hindemith and Ernst Toch, and of the Italian artists, Casella, Malipiero, and Pizzetti. Paul Hindemith, the most successful of this group, shows the anti-romantic tendency, the strict construction, the linear polyphony of Busoni, to which he adds other traits still more modernistic."

Busoni was born in Empoli, Tuscany, on April 1, 1866. He began to study the piano with his mother when he was still a child. At eight, he made his debut with a recital at Trieste, and at nine, he made a highly successful concert appearance in Vienna. Though he was essentially self-taught, he eventually became one of the world's foremost piano virtuosos. He was the youngest musician since Mozart to become a member of the Bologna Philharmonic

Society. This took place in 1881, the same year that the city of Florence struck a gold medal in his honor. In 1913, he became the third Italian composer ever to receive the French Legion of Honor (the other two being Rossini and Verdi).

Busoni also distinguished himself as a teacher of the piano. He became a member of the faculty at the Helsinki Conservatory in 1889, where Jean Sibelius was his pupil. During this period, Busoni married Gerda Sjöstrand, daughter of an emiment Swedish sculptor. Later teaching posts brought him to the Moscow Conservatory, the New England Conservatory in Boston, Weimar (where he carried on the traditions of Liszt) and the Vienna Conservatory (where in 1908 he succeeded Emil Sauer). In 1913, he became the director of the Liceo Musicale in Bologna, and after World War I, he was appointed professor of composition at the Academy of Arts in Berlin.

During World War I, Busoni sought refuge in Zurich, Switzerland, where he completed two comic operas, *Arlecchino* and *Turandot,* which received their première performance on the same bill in Zurich on May 11, 1917. The last years of his life were devoted to the writing of an opera he regarded as his masterwork, *Doctor Faust,* which he did not live to complete. In 1920, Busoni returned to Berlin, where he died on July 27, 1924.

1904 CONCERTO IN C MAJOR FOR PIANO AND ORCHESTRA, with final chorus for male voices, op. 39. I. Prologo e introito. II. Pezzo giocoso. III. Pezzo serioso. IV. All' Italiana. V. Cantico.

Busoni worked on his piano concerto between 1901 and 1904. Its world première took place in Berlin on November 10, 1904, the composer at the piano, and Karl Muck conducting. It was a failure. Largely due to the efforts of such later virtuosos as Egon Petri and Pietro Scarpini, the Concerto has gained circulation in both Europe and America after a long period of neglect.

The composer described his composition as follows: "The present concerto differs from its predecessor, first, by its outward form, which for the first time is extended to five movements. The first to be composed were Nos. 1, 3, 5, which are all tranquil in general feeling. Nos. 2 and 4 naturally supplied livelier rhythms; and of these No. 2 illustrates to a high degree of energy that the fundamental spirit of the work would have been destroyed without the fifth movement to restore it. This fifth movement is, therefore, indispensable; it completes the circle through which we have travelled and joins the end to the beginning. And the music has taken us through so manifold a variety of human feelings that the words of a poet are necessary to sum them up in conclusion. [The text used by the composer is by the Danish poet, Adam Gottlob Oehlenschlaeger, who lived from 1779 to 1850.]

"The addition of human voices (an invisible chorus of men) is the second novelty of the work. The chorus does not break away from the previous mood to an opposite extreme of feeling, as it does in the Ninth Symphony; it resembles rather some original inborn quality in a person which, in the course of years, comes out again in him purified and matured as he reaches the last phase of his transformations. A third characteristic of this work is the insistence on the melodies and rhythms of Italy. Besides three actual Italian folk songs there are many turns of phrase that are definitely Italian. The fourth movement—a sort of Neapolitan carnival—is a highly developed form of tarantella."

The tempo markings of the five movements are: I. Allegro, dolce e solenne; II. Vivacemente, ma senza fretta; III. Andante sostenuto, pensoso; Andante, quasi adagio; IV. Vivace; V. Largamente, più moderato. In the concluding movements, earlier thematic material is recalled.

1909 BERCEUSE ÉLEGIAQUE (ELEGIAC BERCEUSE), for orchestra, op. 42.

In 1907, Busoni wrote a short, tender piece for the piano which he called simply *Berceuse*. This was music completely different from Busoni's neo-classical efforts. It surprised Busoni's admirers not only for its romantic spirit and emotion, but also because of a strange macabre atmosphere that pervaded the entire piece. Apparently, this music meant a good deal to its composer. When his mother died, he transcribed and elaborated it for orchestra as a memorial, providing it the subtitle of *Des Mannes Wiegenlied am Sarge seiner Mutter* (*A Man's Berceuse at the Coffin of His Mother*).

The title page of the published score has a picture of a mother at the cradle of her child; in the background is a man following a coffin. The following lines are added to explain the picture, and presumably the music: "The man sings to the dead mother the same song he had heard from her as a child and which had followed him through a lifetime and had undergone a transformation."

Berceuse élegiaque was performed for the first time anywhere in New York on February 21, 1910, Gustav Mahler conducting. Arturo Toscanini was partial to this composition and conducted it frequently in both Europe and the United States.

1910 FANTASIA CONTRAPPUNTISTICA, for piano (also for two pianos).

Busoni's veneration for the music of Johann Sebastian Bach is, of course, reflected in his transcriptions for the piano of numerous Bach compositions, transcriptions since become basic to the concert repertory. This veneration is also found in a monumental polyphonic work for the piano in which Busoni derives his material from Bach's *Art of the Fugue*. The contrapuntal skill and technique is of Bach's time; but there is here a good deal that belongs to twentieth-century music—discordant trills, vague tonalities, experimentations with new scales, the use of seven-tone arpeggios derived from these new scales, and so forth. Thus, the *Fantasia* is a marriage not only of two masters but also of two centuries, and, as such, it is one of several Busoni works to usher in the neo-classic movement.

How highly Busoni regarded this composition may be gauged from the fact that he wrote three versions for solo piano, the first in 1910, the next two in 1912. Then, a decade later, he arranged it for two pianos. The two-piano version was featured at the festival of the International Society for Contemporary Music at Salzburg on August 6, 1923.

The work is made up of a number of independent sections. The first is a prelude based on the Bach chorale "*Ehre sei Gott in der Hohe*." The next four sections consist of four three-part fugues, once again based on Bach material—this time from the unfinished final fugue (Contrapunctus No. 19) in the *Art of the Fugue*. The last of these four fugues has for a subject the four tones representing the letters in Bach's name (in German notation "B" stands for B-flat and "H" for B-natural). Before the fourth and concluding fugue, Busoni interpolated five other sections: an Intermezzo, three variations, and a cadenza. All use material from the preceding fugues.

"Busoni started from Bach," wrote Harold C. Schonberg in *The New York Times*, "and without losing the contrapuntal character of the music seemed to move through the nineteenth century into the twentieth. Through it all, from the first note to the last, came the feeling of a strong intellectual, inquisitive, sardonic mind and a perfect technician." Time and again, Busoni's personality comes to the fore. When it does, says Schonberg, "the harmonies become dry and slightly dissonant, and the entire feeling passes from Bach Baroque to something almost alien superimposed on it."

1913 INDIAN FANTASY (INDIANISCHE FANTASIE), for piano and orchestra, op. 44.

Natalie Curtis (Natalie Curtis Burlin), author of *Songs of Ancient America* (1905) and *The Indians' Book* (1907), brought to Busoni's attention several melodies and rhythms of the American Indian. During the summer of 1913 in Berlin, Busoni adapted some of this material into a work for piano and orchestra, which he himself introduced in Berlin the following year. The American première was also given by the composer—in Philadelphia on February 19, 1915, with Leopold Stokowski conducting.

Mrs. Burlin provided a programmatic guide and analysis of this composition when it was first heard in the United States. "The work conjures to the mind pictures of the endless prairies of North America: the Father of the Streams, the majestic Mississippi, the melancholy of the broad plains, on the distant horizon the picturesque profile of the redskins. . . . There is a savage war-whoop. . . . Like steel in their sharp outlines are the motives that are mostly derived from actual Indian songs. Their strange exotic character is based on their five-tone scale."

Though played without interruption, the *Fantasia* is in three parts. The fantasia proper comes first, its opening measures based on a song of the Hopi Indians. After the orchestral introduction, the piano is heard unaccompanied. A brief return of the orchestral introduction then precedes a series of variations on the Indian melody. The middle part is a Canzona based on two Indian songs. The finale is made up of three motives (one of which appeared first in the opening fantasia), and an original theme characterized by the persistent alternation of 3/4 and 4/4 time. The finale ends with a coda.

1917 RONDO ARLECCHINESCO, for orchestra, op. 46.

In 1916, Busoni wrote a one-act comic opera, *Arlecchino,* or *Die Fenster* (*Arlecchino,* or *The Windows*). Partly opéra-comique, and partly commedia dell' arte, *Arlecchino* (text by the composer) is set in eighteenth-century Bergamo. Matteo, his wife Columbine, and Harlequin form a love triangle. Harlequin manages to elope with Columbine, while Matteo is at home reading Dante and waiting for his wife to come home. The gay text was matched by an infectious score in which Busoni proved that his touch could be light and gay. *Arlecchino* received its world première in Zurich on May 11, 1917. The first performance in the United States was a concert version heard in New York on October 11, 1951, with Dimitri Mitropoulos conducting the New York Philharmonic.

While still working on his opera, Busoni developed one of his sketches into an orchestral composition which he named *Rondo arlecchinesco*. It became one of his more popular orchestral compositions. Busoni dedicated it to Frederick Stock, who conducted it in Chicago on April 5, 1929.

Busoni provided his own programmatic guide in the published score. At the head there appears a motto reading:

> "In motley garb
> A supple body,
> A sprightly and darting spirit. . . ."

Then the guide offered the following information:

"Harlequin's discourse is various. Now he insists with the trumpet: again he whistles across the world in the voice of the piccolo, threatens with the basses, languishes with the cellos, seeks the freedom of the wild through nimble paces of the violin.

"The three thoughts embodied in the motto will be found reflected in the music. Thus: 'In motley garb' may be understood as referring to the free and fantastic form of the composition. 'A supple body' indicates the tempi and rhythms. 'A sprightly and darting spirit' relates to the content of the piece, so far as the composer's ability has availed to achieve it."

1920 TANZWALZER (DANCE WALTZES), for orchestra, op. 53.

One day in 1920, soon after he had returned to postwar Berlin after a long residence in Zurich, Busoni heard the strains of a Johann Strauss waltz coming from a nearby café. This casual incident led him to write an orchestral composition based on the waltz, which he dedicated to the memory of Johann Strauss. This composition later served as a study for his ballet music to the opera *Doctor Faust*.

Before the waltzes are heard, there is a brief introduction in 4/4 time for muted horns, trumpets and low strings. Four waltzes follow. The first waltz tune is shared by oboe and clarinet, accompanied by plucked strings; the second, a livelier melody, is presented by the orchestra; the third, more sentimental than the first two, is heard in the violins playing in unison on the G string; the fourth is vivacious and witty. In the concluding coda, the first waltz melody is remembered.

1924 DOCTOR FAUST, opera in three scenes, with two prologues and an interlude (completed by Philip Jarnach), with text by the composer based on the Faust legend and Christopher Marlowe's *Dr. Faustus*. First performance: Dresden, Germany, May 21, 1925.

SARABANDE and CORTÈGE, two orchestral studies for *Doctor Faust*, op. 51.

In this opera, Busoni summed up his whole *Weltanschauung*. It is a tremendous intellectual achievement which—despite its many pages of spiritual beauty and nobility of spirit—can never achieve universal popularity because of its fastidious avoidance of emotion, love interest, and theatrical effect.

Busoni's designation of this opera as a "puppet-play" might suggest a work of limited dimensions. But *Doctor Faust* is nothing of the kind. It calls for live actors and is built along spacious lines. A work of formidable proportions, it utilizes a large cast of singers and instrumentalists and demands the fullest technical resources of the modern stage. What Busoni tried to emphasize was the opera's divorce from everyday reality and sentimentality; he attempted to project its monumental tragedy—an epic of disillusion and disenchantment, as F. Bonavia once described it—in a distant make-believe world.

Edward J. Dent has pointed out that Busoni identified himself completely with the character of Faust. Faust surrounded by his students was Busoni surrounded by his disciples; Faust the magician, calling up visions of Solomon and Samson, was really Busoni the magical interpreter at the piano, calling up the spirit of Bach and Beethoven; Faust exclaiming, "Give me genius with all its sufferings," was Busoni articulating one of his strongest beliefs.

The opera begins with two prologues and an interlude. In the first prologue, Faust is in his study when three students enter to bring him a magic book. In the second, also in Faust's study, Faust uses the magic book to invoke Mephistopheles. Faust wishes to taste of all human experiences, and Mephistopheles stands ready to grant the wish if Faust, in return, signs a pact to serve him forever after that. Faust complies eagerly. The interlude that follows takes place in a cathedral chapel where, through the powers of Mephistopheles, a young soldier, suspected of having killed his captain, is murdered by his fellow soldiers.

And now the main part of the opera begins, with a scene at the court of the Duke of Parma, where preparations are being made for the Duke's wedding. Faust is one of the guests. To amuse the guests, he conjures up visions, in each of which the characters resemble Faust and the Duchess. When Faust takes his leave, the Duchess expresses her love for Faust. Then Mephistopheles, disguised as a chaplain, arrives to inform the Duke that the Duchess has eloped with Faust.

At an inn in Wittenberg, Faust tells a group of students how, one year earlier, he had made love to the Duchess on the day she was married to the Duke. Just then Mephistopheles appears with the news that the Duchess is dead. As Faust, left to himself, contemplates the tragedy, three dark figures emerge from the shadows to demand the return of the magic book. Faust dismisses them impatiently, then begins to yearn for death.

In the next scene, Faust comes upon a beggar woman and child in a street in Wittenberg. To his horror, he recognizes her as the Duchess. His horror mounts when she pushes her child, a corpse, into his arms. He places the child reverently on the ground and prays that he can atone for his sins by having his spirit revive the dead child. Faust dies. From the body of the dead child there arises a naked young man who walks away.

Musically, *Doctor Faust* represents to Guido Pannain a synthesis of all of Busoni's stylistic methods. "It is," says Pannain, "the history of his musical soul." The man who derived so much inspiration and direction from Bach was represented by the eloquent choral pages that often reach towards a Bach-like grandeur: the "Credo," sung offstage, just as Faust signs his pact with

Mephistopheles; or the "Gloria," which the chorus of the Catholic and Protestant students sing in the Wittenberg inn (the Catholics singing a "Te Deum Laudamus" and the Protestants, "Ein' feste Burg"). Almost Bach-like, too, is the wonderful Sarabande heard just before the tavern scene.

But a good deal in the score belongs to the twentieth century rather than to the eighteenth. As H. H. Stuckenschmidt said: "Hindemith's canonic style is anticipated, and Busoni writes certain combinations of quartal harmony and parallel seconds at the same time that Alban Berg is evolving them. . . . The strict forms of absolute music are employed: as variations in the scene of the spirits; as a rondo in the murder of Gretchen's brother in the chapel, filled with organ music; as a dance suite in the Parma act. Besides these stand specific vocal forms, such as the superb and powerful aria of the Duchess, the song of Mephistopheles in the tavern, and the last monologue of Faust."

Busoni did not live to finish *Faust*, a chore accomplished for him by Philip Jarnach, using sketches and notes left behind by the composer. When first performed, less than a year after Busoni's death, *Doctor Faust* was poorly received. The libretto seemed too confused, and the music too complex. The opera lay in discard for the next fifteen years or so. Then, in 1942, it was revived at the May Music Festival at Florence. In 1955, it received a magnificent production at the Berlin State Opera and was acclaimed. On December 1, 1964, the opera was heard for the first time in the United States, in a production by the American Opera Society in New York.

Busoni composed two orchestral studies for *Faust*, which are sometimes given at orchestral concerts: the *Sarabande* and *Cortège*, op. 51. The *Sarabande* accompanies Faust's last entrance and gives a premonition of his death. The *Cortège* is music for the procession of the guests at the wedding of the Duke and Duchess of Parma. These two studies were first heard in Berlin on January 13, 1921.

JOHN CAGE 1912–

From his creative beginnings, John Cage felt that the music of the Western world had come to a dead end; that a composer now was compelled to seek out new media, new materials, new instruments, new sounds—in short, a new language. "I'm devoted to the principle of originality," he has said. "Not originality in the egotistic sense, but originality in the sense of doing something which it is necessary to do. Now, obviously, the things that it is necessary to do are not the things that have been done, but the ones that have not yet been done. This applies not only to other people's work, but seriously to my own work; that is to say, if I have done something, then I consider it my business not to do that, but to find what must be done next."

He started out, somewhat tentatively, as a twelve-tone composer in several compositions that included *Metamorphosis,* for the piano (1938). Feeling that even the twelve-tone system was still tied to the past, he soon deserted it for experiments in percussion music which relied exclusively on rhythm and rhythmic patterns and which dispensed completely with the melodic, harmonic and contrapuntal practices of the past. *Living Room Music* (1940) was for percussion and speech quartet (the percussion here being made up of things found in the living room, such as furniture, paper, window, walls, doors, and so forth). *Imaginary Landscape No. 2,* was for percussion quintet; *Credo in US* (1942), for percussion quartet including piano. His fascination for rhythm and percussive effects led him to invent the "prepared piano" and to write a library of music for it. Then he went on to explore the possibilities of extra-musical sounds, concrete music, aleatory music, and neo-dadaism.

The sounds he has incorporated in some of his compositions come from varied sources, usually from whatever noisemaking implement Cage can put his hands on. *Third Construction in Metal* (1941) is scored for rattles, drums, tin cans, cowbells, and even a lion's roar, among sundry other percussive instruments, many of exotic origin. In *Water Music* (1952) sounds are created by pouring water from a full container to an empty one and by shuffling a deck of cards.

To the field of "concrete music," he has contributed *Williams Mix* (1952) and *Fontana Mix* (1958), in which the sounds are reproduced on magnetic tape; the tapes for *Fontana Mix* were made by the composer at the Studio di Fonolgia of the Italian Radio, in Milan, with the technical assistance of Marino Zuccheri. In *Williams Mix,* the element of chance is introduced (as it is in other of Cage's works) by a process called I-Ching (the Chinese Book of Changes). This process calls for a pair of Chinese dice. Having first worked out a system relating the numbers on the dice to elements in a composition, Cage throws out the dice, and the outcome of the throw determines which elements he is to use and how. In other compositions—such as *Variations I* (1958) and *Variations II* (1961)—chance is incorporated by having the performer select at random, and wherever he may desire, sounds of his own choosing.

Cage has also been in the forefront of the neo-dadaistic movement come to prominence in the early 1960s. He has done this with various compositions. Of particular interest are *Variations V* (1965) and *Theatre Piece* (1965). *Variations V*—introduced in New York City on July 23, 1965—is an "audio-visual" composition whose score requires electronic equipment, noisemakers, loudspeakers, as well as orchestral instruments. Distorted images from TV and film clips were flashed on a screen. The principal performer (a dancer dressed in red pants and gray shirt) produced weird sounds by riding a bicycle through electronic transmitters, noises which were amplified and spread through the auditorium by several loudspeakers in different parts of the hall.

Theatre Piece (first performance in New York on September 11, 1965) had the following unusual attractions, as described by Richard D. Freed in

The New York Times: "A man hanging upside down and wrapped in a black plastic cocoon; a watermelon sliced in the sling that had held the man upside down; a film of Charlotte Moorman playing one of Mr. Cage's other works on the cello, as the composer placed a cigar in her mouth and removed it now and then; a tiny Japanese waving silken banners on a huge bamboo pole; an oil drum rolled down the stairs outside the auditorium; and the usual assortment of balloons, buzzers, and electronic sounds."

Cage was born in Los Angeles, California, on September 5, 1912. His music study comprised piano lessons, first with Fannie Charles Dillon, then with Lazare Lévy in Paris; and composition with Henry Cowell, Edgard Varèse, Arnold Schoenberg and Adolph Weiss. In 1936, he joined the music faculty of the Cornish School in Seattle, Washington, where he organized concerts of percussion music, his first major experiments in this direction. This was the first of many teaching posts held through the years in many different institutions. He began giving concerts of his experimental compositions in New York in the early 1940s. In 1949, he received a Guggenheim Fellowship, and an award from the National Academy of Arts and Letters. A panoramic concert of his creative achievements over the period of a quarter of a century was given in New York on May 15, 1958, and was recorded in its entirety. In 1963, Cage was the American representative at the Zagreb Biennale in Yugoslavia.

1942–1951 IMAGINARY LANDSCAPE NO. 2 (MARCH), for percussion quintet.

IMAGINARY LANDSCAPE NO. 3, for percussion sextet.

IMAGINARY LANDSCAPE NO. 4 (MARCH 2), for twelve radios.

Imaginary Landscape No. 2 (1942) is one of Cage's experiments in "rhythmed sound." It is scored for a variety of percussion instruments as well as for noisemakers capable of yielding unusual sounds. These include tin cans, a conch shell, a ratchet, bass drum, buzzers, water gong, a metal wastebasket, a lion's roar, and an amplified coil of wire.

The percussion and noisemaking family is extended in the *Imaginary Landscape No. 3* (1942) to include such electronic and mechanical devices as audio frequency oscillators, variable speed turntables for the playing of frequency recordings and generator whines, and a buzzer. An amplified coil of wire and a marimbula amplified by means of a contact microphone are also used.

Imaginary Landscape No. 4 (1951) derives its unusual sound textures from twelve radios manipulated by twenty-four performers, two performers to each radio. One of the two men at each set manipulates the tuning dial, while the other adjusts the dynamics. Wave lengths are indicated in Cage's score, also time values. But the sounds produced by the radios at any given time depend upon the stations that are pulled in at the time and the sounds that are being transmitted. This composition, consequently, consists of an indeterminate amalgamation of music, speech, radio static, squeals—and silences.

Imaginary Landscape No. 2 had its first performance in San Francisco in

1942, Lou Harrison conducting; the third *Imaginary Landscape* was first heard in Chicago on March 1, 1942, the composer conducting; the fourth, in New York City on May 2, 1951, the composer conducting.

1946–1948 SONATAS AND INTERLUDES, for "prepared piano."

As a pupil of Henry Cowell, John Cage became impressed with the experiments his teacher had conducted at the piano in the early 1920s to extend the sound qualities of the instrument through tone clusters and by plucking and manipulating the strings on the soundboard. In his search for new sounds, Cage extended Cowell's innovations by "preparing" the piano. He did so for the first time in 1938 with a six-minute composition, *Bacchanale,* written as background music for a dance by Syvilla Fort. "The need to change the sound of the instrument," the composer explained, "arose through the desire to make an accompaniment without employing percussion instruments, suitable for the dance."

A "prepared" piano is one in which all kinds of material is stuffed between the strings: nuts, bolts, screws, leather, felt, wood, spoons, clothespins, aspirin boxes, and so forth and so on. Thus a precise pitch is eliminated; formal scales are dispensed with; new sonorities and sound qualities are created, made up of varieties of gong-like sounds, pings, plucks, thuds. Cage regarded the "prepared" piano as a one-instrument percussion ensemble performed by a single player. Arthur Berger compared the "prepared" piano to a one-man jazz band.

After a concert of Cage's music for the "prepared" piano in New York City on December 10, 1945, Lou Harrison wrote in *Modern Music:* "The tension and strength that a few quiet tones can convey . . . are a sign of a completely new and authentic creative power." A dissenting opinion was expressed by J. Fred Lissfelt in the Pittsburgh *Sun Telegraph* when he wrote that the "prepared" piano sounds like "an old piano that should be thrown away"; also by Oscar Thompson in the *Christian Science Monitor,* who described Cage's pieces for the "prepared" piano as just "children's games for adult ears."

The *Sonatas and Interludes* which Cage wrote between 1946 and 1948 is the composer's most ambitious work in this field. It takes seventy minutes to perform, and the preparation of the piano is so complex and elaborate that between two and three hours are needed for the operation. The composer explained that this music was "an attempt to express . . . the 'permanent emotions' of Indian tradition: the heroic, the erotic, the wondrous, the mirthful, sorrow, fear, anger, the odious, and their common tendency toward tranquillity. The first eight, the twelfth, and the last four are written in the A-A-B-B rhythmic structures of varying proportions, whereas the first two interludes have no structural repetitions. This difference is exchanged in the last two interludes and the sonatas nine through eleven which have respectively a prelude, interlude, and postlude."

Four of these *Sonatas and Interludes* were introduced by Marjo Ajemian in New York on April 14, 1946, and four more on December 10, 1946. The entire work received its first hearing at Black Mountain College in Black Mountain, North Carolina, in the spring of 1948, in a performance by the composer.

1958 CONCERT FOR PIANO AND ORCHESTRA.

The *Concert* was introduced in New York on May 15, 1958, on a program tracing a quarter of a century of John Cage's development and evolution as a musical innovator. The *Concert* is one of its composer's most complex works, combining as it does percussive sounds, electronic sounds, and aleatory music. The composer has written: "The *Concert for Piano and Orchestra* is without a master score, but each part is written in detail in a notation where space is relative to time determined by the performer and later altered by a conductor. Both specific directives and specific freedoms are given to each player including the conductor." The work can be performed "in whole or part, any duration, any number of . . . performers, as a solo, chamber ensemble, symphony, concerto for piano and orchestra, aria, etc."

The solo pianist is required to play the keyboard in the normal fashion. At other times, he plucks and strums the strings on the piano soundboard; or he goes under the piano to thump the instrument from below. Occasionally, he leaves the piano to manipulate electronic machines. The pianist's part is made up of eighty-four different compositions, which the performer is free to play in whole, in part, or in any sequence he may desire.

The accompanying orchestra is also required to do unexpected things. One wind player is asked to perform two tubas at once. A trombone player is called upon to make sounds exclusively from the mouthpiece of his instrument. A violist is instructed to place his instrument between his knees and play on it as if it were a cello.

"The result of all this variety," wrote Virgil Thomson, "and also of the aristocratic, inherently 'musical' character of the instruments and players producing it, is a far cry from the poverty of electronic sound. It is human, civilized, and sumptuous. And if the general effect is that of an orchestra just having fun, it is doubtful whether any orchestra ever before had so much fun or gave such hilarity to its listeners." Thomson adds that this concert work "carries chance to its ultimate. . . . Its subject is its palette of sounds, nothing else. And if these express through their choice the gaiety and sweetness of Cage's temperament and through their manipulation his high capacity for inventing games, this composer can be said here to have, like many another, expressed himself."

1962 ATLAS ECLIPITICALIS, for orchestra and electronic instruments.

This composition (whose name was found by Cage, one day, in an astronomical atlas) was described by its composer as "'live' electronic music." He explains: "Most electronic music is dependent on magnetic tape for its performances and so becomes a recording. This music uses electronic circuits (microphones, amplifiers, loudspeakers) in connection with musical instruments." He wrote it on a commission from the Montreal Festivals Society; its world première took place at Montreal, Canada, on August 3, 1961. Chance plays a significant role in the performance of this music. The composer has suggested that the work may be performed as a whole, or in part, or for as long a duration as the performers wish. The eighty-six conventional instruments of the orchestra, with various unspecified non-pitched percussion instruments, may all be used, or only some. An electronic version is made possible "by use of contact microphones with associated amplifiers and loudspeakers operated by an assistant to the conductor."

JOHN ALDEN CARPENTER 1876–1951

Carpenter was essentially a conservative composer who was satisfied with traditional forms and techniques which, nevertheless, he endowed with the imprint of his own personality. It is not easy to identify him with any one school or style, for he wrote in many different veins with equal success. His first important work was programmatic music spiced with wit and satire: the *Adventures in a Perambulator,* written in 1915. A change of style took place with the ballet *Krazy Kat* (1921), in which the influence of jazz is strongly felt; the jazz style found its culmination in the ballet *Skyscrapers.* In a work like *The Birthday of the Infanta* with its pronounced Spanish character, a new facet in Carpenter's creative idiom was uncovered. In the last decade and a half of his life, Carpenter turned to impressionistic writing. This manner identifies some of his finest works, notably *Sea-Drift* and parts of the Second Symphony.

Carpenter was born in Park Ridge, Illinois, on February 28, 1876, a descendant of the Aldens of colonial Plymouth. At Harvard University he took music courses with John Knowles Paine. After his graduation in 1897, Carpenter studied music privately with Edward Elgar in Rome and Bernhard Ziehn in Chicago.

For many years (until his retirement in 1936), Carpenter combined music with business by serving as vice-president of the prosperous Chicago, shipping supply firm of George B. Carpenter & Co. At the same time, he composed numerous works. His first success came with a Violin Sonata introduced by Mischa Elman in 1912 and a song cycle on poems by Tagore, *Gitanjali* (1913). His fame grew with the orchestral suite, *Adventures in a Perambulator* in 1915, and with his first ballet, *The Birthday of the Infanta,* in 1919. In 1922, he received an honorary doctorate from Harvard, and in 1933, another one from Wisconsin University. In 1947, he was honored with a gold medal from the National Institute of Arts and Letters "for distinguished services to music." Carpenter died in Chicago on April 26, 1951.

1915 ADVENTURES IN A PERAMBULATOR, suite for orchestra. I. En Voiture. II. The Policeman. III. The Hurdy-Gurdy. IV. The Lake. V. Dogs. VI. Dreams.

This work has a definite story to tell. Carpenter has stated that he tried to reproduce in music the varied impressions gathered by a child as he is being wheeled about in his carriage by his nurse. The detailed program, provided by Carpenter, follows in part:

"I. En Voiture. Every morning—after my second breakfast—if the wind and sun are favorable, I go out. . . . My nurse is appointed to take me. . . . I am wrapped in a vacuum of wool, where there are no drafts. I am placed in my perambulator, a strap is buckled over my stomach, my nurse stands firmly behind me—and we are off!

"II. The Policeman. Out is wonderful! . . . It is confusing, but it is Life! For instance, the Policeman. . . . He walks like Doom. My nurse feels it too. She becomes less firm, less powerful. My perambulator hurries, hesitates, and stops. They converse. They ask each other questions. . . . When I feel that they have gone far enough, I signal to my nurse, and the Policeman resumes his enormous Blue March. He is gone, but I feel him after he goes.

"III. The Hurdy-Gurdy. Then suddenly there is something else. I think it is a sound. . . . I find that the absorbing noise comes from a box—something like my music-box. . . . Suddenly, at the climax of our excitement, I feel the approach of a phenomenon that I remember. It is the Policeman. He has stopped the music. . . . Delightful forbidden music.

"IV. The Lake. My nurse firmly pushes me on. . . . The land comes to an end, and there at my feet is The Lake. I feel the quiver of the little waves as they escape the big ones and come rushing over the sand.

"V. Dogs. We pass on. . . . It is Dogs! We are coming upon them without warning. . . . They laugh, they fight, they run. At last, in order to hold my interest, the very littlest brigand starts a game of 'Follow the Leader,' followed by all the others. It is tremendous!

"VI. Dreams. My mind grows numb. . . . The wheels of my perambulator make a sound that quiets my nerves. I lie very still. . . . In order to think more clearly, I close my eyes. My thoughts are absorbing. I deliberate upon my mother. . . . I hear her voice quite plainly now, and feel the touch of her hand. It is pleasant to live over again the adventures of the day. . . . It is pleasant to lie quite still and close my eyes and listen to the wheels of my perambulator."

In the beginning of the first movement, the cellos are heard in the theme identifying the Nurse. Strings and celesta later describe the perambulator, while a motive for the flute represents the child. A brisk opening leads into the slow and stately measures of the policeman on his beat. Represented by a solo bassoon, the policeman engages the Nurse in small talk, reproduced by the violins. The third part begins with a brief recall of the child theme. Then the sounds of a hurdy-gurdy are imitated by two xylophones and a harp in several tunes including a quotation from Irving Berlin's "Alexander's Ragtime Band." The "perambulator theme" of the first part serves as the basis for a waltz. In the fourth section, the ripple of the waters in the lake are suggested by moving figures, first in the flute and then in strings and horn. Amusing quotations from two popular tunes ("Where, Oh Where, Has My Little Dog Gone?" and "Ach du lieber Augustin") appear in the fifth section, in which a fugal episode serves to show how dogs chase each other. In the sixth part, a tender melody brings up the image of the baby's mother. This section ends with a cradlesong, whose melody is derived from the baby theme, and its accompaniment from the perambulator motive.

Adventures in a Perambulator was introduced by the Chicago Orchestra under Frederick Stock on March 19, 1915.

1919 THE BIRTHDAY OF THE INFANTA, ballet in one act, with scenario and choreography by Adolf Bolm based on a story of the same name by Oscar Wilde. First performance: Chicago, December 23, 1919.

THE BIRTHDAY OF THE INFANTA, ballet suite for orchestra. I. The Guests. II. The Infanta. III. Games.

The Birthday of the Infanta was Carpenter's first ballet. It told the story of a surprise birthday party given to a sixteen-year-old Spanish Infanta. During the festivities, jugglers and tightrope walkers provide entertainment. One of the performers is a grotesque dwarf, who so delights the Infanta that she throws him her handkerchief. But later on the dwarf comes to realize how ugly he really is. He dies of a broken heart, clutching to the handkerchief.

In 1930, the composer adapted the ballet score into a three-movement symphonic suite. Here, the composer said, "I have tried merely to build a piece of music which might be of interest as music without essential dependence on the original story."

Here is how the composer described the three movements:

"I. The Guests. This movement conforms closely to the opening of the original ballet with its variegated procession of arrivals for the Infanta's party. The guests are of all sizes, colors, and shapes, young and old, grave and gay, pompous and simple. They all bear gifts, appropriate and inappropriate. The movement ends with dancing by a band of gypsies brought in for the entertainment of the guests.

"II. The Infanta. In this section is assembled most of the musical material which was used in the original ballet in association with the varied moods and movements of the little Infanta, and closes on the note of her sadness at the death of her beloved and fabulous dwarf.

"III. Games. Here we return to the excitement of the birthday party. It is without doubt an expensive entertainment. A juggler and a tightrope walker have been provided—a curious team—and for a climax there is a mock bullfight. Surely no Infanta could ask for more."

1924 SKYSCRAPERS, ballet in six scenes, with scenario and choreography mainly by the composer. First performance: Metropolitan Opera, New York, February 19, 1926.

In 1924, Serge Diaghilev planned to tour the United States with his Ballet Russe de Monte Carlo. For this visit he commissioned Carpenter to create a ballet about American life. Carpenter completed his assignment in 1924, but the Ballet Russe tour did not materialize at this time. Nevertheless, Diaghilev was so interested in what Carpenter had done that he proposed mounting the ballet in Monte Carlo in March of 1925. However, as negotiations between Diaghilev and Carpenter dragged on, Carpenter responded to a request by the Metropolitan Opera Company that it be allowed to introduce the work. Robert Edmond Jones, the distinguished Broadway scenic designer, and Sammy Lee, famous dance director for Broadway musical comedies, were recruited to help Carpenter design the production and develop the choreography.

A note in the published score explains: "*Skyscrapers* is a ballet which seeks to reflect some of the many rhythmic movements and sounds of modern American life. It has no story, in the usually accepted sense, but proceeds on the simple fact that American life reduces itself to violent alternations of work and play, each with its own peculiar and distinctive character. The action of the ballet is merely a series of moving decorations reflecting some of the obvious external features of this life."

In reviewing the première of the ballet for *Musical America,* Oscar Thompson provided the following summary of the ballet action:

"With the parting of the curtains for *Skyscrapers,* blinking red lights are revealed at either side of the stage, that are at once understood to represent traffic signals. These, as the program makes clear, are 'symbols of restlessness.' A fantastic 'drop' is lifted, and reveals 'an abstraction of the skyscraper' and 'the work that produces it—and the interminable crowd that passes by.' Girders in angular confusion are etched against vacancy, men in the semblance of overalls go through the motions of violent labor, while shadows in human shape move listlessly, meaninglessly by.

"The whistles blow, the workers emerge, each steps into the arms of a short-skirted, bare-legged partner, and there is a dancing exodus for the resorts of pleasure. The stage picture that follows is one of striking illusion, representative of 'any Coney Island' with its Ferris wheels, its scenic railways, its street shows, its heedless fun-mad, dance-addled crowds, swirling through rhythmic gestures and formations, glorifying the American girls' nether extremities, with no particular thought as to whether she has brain or heart.

"There is a 'throw-back,' as movie parlance has it, to the idea of work, with a sudden cessation of the dancing, and a return in the midst of the Coney Island revelry, to the men in overalls swinging their ledges and crouched about their riveting fires. This is followed by an equally violent reversion to play, in which flappers, sailors, minstrel-show end men, comic policemen and characters of a midway plaisance are manipulated in colorful, but on the whole, orderly succession of dances.

"The fifth scene brings the transition from play to work, as the men in overalls surrender their dance partners to return to the labors of the skyscraper. Gigantic shadows, suggesting Herculean power behind the building of a great city's business edifices, are cast upward against the girders as the ballet ends."

Skyscrapers is Carpenter's most modern score, often resorting to discords to interpret the confusions and disorders of contemporary city life. But its principal attraction is its discreet use of a jazz idiom. This was not Carpenter's first attempt at writing jazz music within serious forms and media; the ballet pantomime, *Krazy Kat,* based on George Herriman's popular cartoon, had preceded *Skyscrapers* in 1921. But in *Skyscrapers,* jazz is more often suggested than realized. The composer himself explained that here his jazz writing is "filtered through an orchestra. . . . It is jazz once removed. Jazz itself depends on the sonority of the jazz band. To get something of this sonorous jazz effect we have used the saxophones and a banjo." To add to the American and popular flavors of this score, Carpenter occasionally resorted to the quotation of popular melodies. Among those he used were "Yankee Doodle," "Massa's in the Cold, Cold Ground," "Dem Goo-Goo Eyes" and a Negro blues melody.

Basically, the music, as a ballet, is a realistic interpretation of modern American life—the sounds and sights of a big city. But it also conveys feelings of gentle irony and pity; in short, the music is not only a portrait but also a commentary.

The ballet was successfully produced at the Munich Opera in 1929, with new choreography by Heinrich Kröller.

The orchestral suite, which has been frequently heard at symphony concerts, uses the basic material from the ballet score.

1933 SEA-DRIFT, symphonic poem for orchestra.

This orchestral poem, one of Carpenter's most sensitive works, derives its inspiration from the sea poems of Walt Whitman. It is particularly effective in its use of dynamics to suggest the roll and swell of the sea.

The composition is in two sections, each culminating in a dramatic climax. The opening of the piece (Lento tranquillo) beautifully suggests the shimmer and quiver of the waters as the first theme is heard in the lower strings. In the first section, most of the principal thematic subjects are assigned to the horn. In the second section, the most effective subject is a *dolente* theme, heard in the English horn and then repeated by the strings.

Sea-Drift was introduced by the Chicago Orchestra under Stock on November 30, 1933.

1942 SYMPHONY NO. 2. I. Moderato. II. Andante. III. Allegro.

When this symphony was introduced by the New York Philharmonic under Bruno Walter on October 22, 1942, the composer explained: "The work . . . derives some of its basic thematic material from a piano quintet which I composed in 1934 during a stay in Algiers. Some of the native tunes heard there 'rubbed off' to some extent in the coloring of the last movement of my work, which is otherwise devoid of programmatic intent."

The composer provided the following analysis:

"The opening measures of the first movement offer a broad statement of one of the three themes which dominate it. At the seventh bar the kettledrums establish the vigorous 5/4 rhythm which characterizes much of the movement.

The second theme follows in the strings. The ensuing development employs the basic elements of both themes in alternation and leads to a third subject.

"With a barely perceptible pause the kettledrums open the second movement with an echo from the closing bar of the first movement, introducing the broad opening theme of the second movement in the first violins and English horn. With a short development leading to a pause, the second subject is introduced in the strings with a solo oboe. This leads in turn to a sombre contrasting subject, which reappears at the close of the last movement. The movement ends with a reminiscence of the opening theme in a muted horn.

"The principal themes of the last movement are three in number, heard respectively in strings, in trombones, in horns. This varied material is developed in a loose and lively pattern leading finally to a broad restatement of the theme heard in the second movement. It then presses on to a vigorous close."

ELLIOTT CARTER 1908–

Elliott Carter is one of the most significant composers to arise in the United States since the end of World War II. He is a creator absorbed by intellectual processes. Each new work poses for him a new set of problems which he proceeds to solve with inexorable logic. Each work demands an individual approach and, consequently, a new set of rules to work by. Each new work is a model for the way in which basic material is shaped and formed along highly original lines. Though he often displays an extraordinary polyphonic gift, his main preoccupation is with polyrhythm, or with what William Glock has described in *Score* as "metrical modulation." Contrasting rhythms abound horizontally and vertically. Tempo changes are frequent and varied and so interrelated as not only to create a continuity with few points of repose but also to provide a specialized atmosphere and character. Yet Carter's significance rests not upon his individuality nor upon his technical skill nor upon the success with which new problems receive fresh solutions. It springs from the fact that in spite of the unquestioned complexity of his writing he manages to endow his music with mystery, sensitive communication, controlled wit, whimsy and tenderness; and when he reaches for a climax, he reveals a powerful feeling for drama. As Howard Taubman said in *The New York Times*, Carter's best work manages to evoke "a fresh world of sensibility which may seem strange upon first encounter but which is increasingly rewarding upon rehearing. . . . Whatever the composer's technical ingenuity, this is not an exercise in acoustics or mathematics; it is an ardent, tender, humorous, intense and grave voyage into the secret places of the heart."

Carter was born in New York City on December 11, 1908. After preliminary study at the Longy School of Music in Cambridge, Massachusetts, he attended Harvard, where in 1930 he received his Bachelor of Arts degree, and where he took graduate courses in music with Walter Piston, Edward Burlingame Hill and Gustav Holst. In 1932, Carter went to Paris to complete his study with Nadia Boulanger and at the École Normale de Musique. After he returned to the United States, his first ballet, *Pocahontas,* was produced in New York in 1939, and an orchestral suite based on this score received a publication award from the Juilliard Foundation.

Between 1937 and 1939, he was music director of the Ballet Caravan, and from 1939 to 1941, he was on the faculty of St. John's College in Annapolis, Maryland. A symphony was introduced by the Eastman Rochester Orchestra under Howard Hanson April 27, 1944. This was followed by his *Holiday Overture* which was successfully played by the Baltimore Symphony on January 7, 1946, after which it was performed by several European orchestras. In 1945, on a Guggenheim Fellowship, he completed a piano sonata which Webster Aitken introduced in New York on February 16, 1947. Between 1946 and 1948, he was a member of the faculty of the Peabody Conservatory in Baltimore. After that, he held a teaching assignment at Columbia University and from 1960 to 1962 was professor of composition at Yale. A second Guggenheim Fellowship, in 1950, enabled him to write his first string quartet, his most successful work up to that time. He achieved international renown with his second string quartet in 1960, which brought him the Pulitzer Prize in music. In 1953, Carter was also the recipient of the Prix de Rome and was elected member of the National Institute of Arts and Letters. He received the Sibelius Medal for Music in London in 1961, and the Creative Arts Award from Brandeis University in 1965; he was also the recipient of honorary doctorates from the New England Conservatory and Swarthmore College. In 1962, he was composer-in-residence at the American Academy of Rome; he later held the same position in Berlin at the invitation of the Berlin Senate and the Ford Foundation.

1951 STRING QUARTET NO. 1. I. Allegro scorrevole. II. Allegro scorrevole; Adagio. III. Variations.

Carter emerged as an important composer with his first string quartet. It is a highly complex composition in which Carter perfected his use of polyrhythms and a technique which William Glock described as "metrical modulation." The process of metrical modulation, Glock explained, is the idea "of having continual change of speed and character and linking them into a convincing and novel continuity. . . . To achieve this 'metrical modulation' the music breaks off only twice and both times in the middle of the movement." Throughout the composition the hearer is impressed by the freedom with which the music moves. Much of this freedom comes from the fact that each of the four instruments seemingly moves with complete independence of the other three. For this reason, the work appeared to Virgil Thomson "less a classical quartet than like four intricately integrated solos, all going at the same time."

The basic source-material in this quartet is a four-note chord (E, F, A-flat, B-flat) in which are found all the intervals from a minor second to a diminished fifth. "These intervals," Slonimsky says, "are used thematically in contrapuntal and harmonic groups . . . essentially a serial procedure."

Carter wrote this quartet in Tucson, Arizona, after having received the Guggenheim Fellowship a second time. He submitted the work to the Concours International de Quatuors à Cordes, in Liège, Belgium, capturing first prize from among one hundred and fifty contestants from twenty countries. The Walden String Quartet introduced the work in New York in February of 1953, and in 1954, the quartet was heard at the Rome Festival.

When the Juilliard String Quartet performed this work at the Institute of Contemporary Arts in London in 1955, Desmond Shawe-Taylor wrote: "That only an intellectual type of composer could have conceived and carried through the vast structural plan of this Quartet is undeniably true, and it is also true . . . that a powerful intellectual ferment seethes throughout the long work. But it is neither dry nor pedantic; on the contrary, it is impassioned and vigorous, the music of a man intensely aware of the sensuous possibilities of sound . . . and some of the most exciting and original passages occur when each of the players appears to be improvising to his heart's content, regardless of his neighbor, yet is also mysteriously contributing to the massive onward drive and logic of the whole movement."

1955 VARIATIONS FOR ORCHESTRA.

This composition was the consequence of a commission from the Louisville Orchestra which gave the world première in Louisville, Kentucky, on May 19, 1956, Robert Whitney conducting. It comprises several sections played without interruption: an introduction (Allegro); the statement of the theme (Andante); and ten variations (Vivace leggero; Pesante; Moderato; Ritardando molto; Allegro misterioso; Accelerando molto; Andante; Allegro giocoso; Andante; Allegro molto).

Here is how the composer describes his music:

"I conceived this one as a large, unified musical action of gesture. In it, definition and contrast of character decrease during the first variations, arriving at a point of neutrality in the central variation, then increasing again to the finale, which comprises many different speeds and characters. This work was thought of as a series of character studies in various states of interaction with each other both within each variation and between one and the next. Activity, development, type of emphasis, clearness or vagueness of definition, I hoped, would contribute to characterization. Form, rhythmic and development processes as well as texture and thematic material differ in each for this reason."

Though the work was not given in the United States for about four years after its Louisville première, it was frequently played in Germany, England, Italy and Sweden. It returned to the United States in 1960, when Enrique Jorda conducted it in San Francisco.

When the *Variations* was first introduced, William Mootz said in the Louisville *Courier-Journal*: "I found myself during its performance in the middle of an experience that at times held me in suspense and kept me anxiously awaiting the next twist in Carter's ingenious score. I heard sonorities that in the sheer realm of sound evoked a nervous reaction more pleasant than unpleasant. And I also became convinced that the composer is a more accomplished craftsman and a man more passionately devoted to the art of composition than most of the music makers the Louisville Orchestra commissions these days."

1959 STRING QUARTET NO. 2.

This is the string quartet that made the composer front-page news by virtue of winning three major awards: the Pulitzer Prize in music; the New York Music Critics Circle Award; and the first prize of the International Rostrum of Composers sponsored by UNESCO. Previous to that, it had earned the unanimous acclaim of the New York critics when it received its first performance—in New York City by the Juilliard String Quartet on March 25, 1960. Howard Taubman opened his review in *The New York Times* by saying: "With the Second String Quartet, Elliott Carter rivets his right to be regarded as one of the most distinguished of living composers."

It is not often that a string quartet gets such immediate recognition; less often, if the work is as complex as this one is. Here the composer assigns even greater individuality to each instrument than he had done in his first quartet, endowing each with its own "behavior patterns." In fact, to emphasize this individuality, Carter instructed the members of the Juilliard String Quartet to sit as far apart from one another as possible during the performance; but the Juilliard, after some experiments, found that this was not feasible. Each instrument is assigned specialized intervals of its own: the first violin, thirds and its multiples; the second violin, minor seconds and minor sevenths; the viola, minor sevenths and tritones; the cello, fourths and minor sixths.

Here, too, the composer pursues further and perfects his earlier techniques in rhythm and polyrhythms and "metrical modulation." All these methods, which had served the composer so well in his first string quartet, become the means by which he is able to express in the second quartet "fantasy, humor, passion, tension, and affecting gravity," as Howard Taubman said. Taubman then pointed to the section marked Andante espressivo as music of "rare originality and beauty, and the final measures are filled with a sense of sad mysticism. At the end one feels one has completed a momentous journey into a wholly new and magical land."

The work is in five sections played without interruption: Introduction, Allegro fantastico, Presto scherzando, Andante espressivo, and Allegro. Accompanied cadenzas for viola and for the cello, and an unaccompanied cadenza for the first violin, serve as transitions between the sections.

1961 DOUBLE CONCERTO FOR HARPSICHORD AND PIANO WITH TWO CHAMBER ORCHESTRAS.

This composition was commissioned by the Fromm Music Foundation. Its world première took place in New York on September 6, 1961, with Ralph Kirkpatrick and Charles Rosen as soloists, the orchestra being conducted by Gustave Meier; this performance took place before the Eighth Congress of the International Society for Musicology. The Concerto received the New

York Music Critics Circle Award. Between 1962 and 1965, it was performed in London, Berlin, Rome and Warsaw.

The work is in seven sections: Introduction; Cadenza for Harpsichord; Allegro scherzando; Adagio; Presto; Cadenza for Piano; and Coda. "It is one of a series of works in which I was concerned with the dramatic interplay of different musical characters presented by a dialectic that takes full advantage of the possibilities of dynamic and coloristic contrasts present in the different types of musical instruments," the composer has written. "With this vocabulary I have tried to present a musical analogue to the human experience of time both in brief moments and in the longer pattern of evolving events."

The composer explains further: "In this work each of the two chamber orchestras is associated with one of the soloists, and each is differently characterized not only in tone color but also in musical material and in musical expression. It is out of the interplay of these two musical organisms that the seven sections of the work, played without interruption, are formed."

Reviewing the Concerto for *The New York Times,* Eric Salzman wrote: "It is nothing less than an astonishing conception; a breathtaking panorama of flashing textures and rhythms that curve from opening to end with the most extraordinary, imaginative pulse."

1965 CONCERTO FOR PIANO AND ORCHESTRA. I. Fantastico. II. Molto giusto.

Carter's piano concerto was commissioned by Jacob Lateiner (through the auspices of the Ford Foundation). Lateiner introduced it on January 6, 1967, with the Boston Symphony, Erich Leinsdorf conducting.

For the première, the composer provided the following analysis:

"Technically the work is based on twelve different three-note groups (triads): six, used exclusively by the piano and concertino, and six, by the orchestra. Each triad is associated with one or more tempi and expressive characters. Musical ideas are formed out of constantly changing uses of these fundamental materials.

"At the outset, the piano and concertino state ideas derived from the triad shape exemplified by C, F-sharp, G and the three speeds and characters associated with it. This is answered briefly by the orchestra using material from one of the triads (shape: G, D-flat, F). Later these two triads, which are the primary ones for the orchestra and piano, each join three others from their respective instrumental groups to form one twelve-note chord for the soloists and another of different character for the orchestra, the alternation of which constitutes the conclusion of the first movement, summarizing in brief all the various expressive characters that have been brought into increasingly sharp focus and contrast.

"The second movement starts where the first ends with the orchestra introducing bit by bit its two main new features: regularly accented beats of many different speeds and ever-changing soft string chords which form the background of the piano's increasingly impulsive and passionate recitative which emerges from the material of the first movement. This recitative is interrupted here and there by the concertino, particularly the cadenzas of the three wind soloists who, like Job's friends, sympathize and comment. This large section is brought to an end by a coda of fast altercations between the piano with concertino and the orchestra. The work concludes with a brief passage by the soloist."

ALFREDO CASELLA 1883–1947

Casella was one of the most trenchant minds, and one of the most influential forces, in contemporary Italian music. He worked indefatigibly for Italian music, old and new, and for the Italian composer. And he devoted himself with equal fervor to the cause of contemporary music. Every important new trend found him as its stout protagonist. He organized societies, concerts, festivals, periodicals to promote the interests of the present-day composer.

Never a highly original composer—though always writing with facility and skill—Casella too easily assimilated the styles of others. He began as a romanticist. Then he tried impressionism. After that, he turned to polytonal writing. Finally, as his analytical mind absorbed and dissected the styles of major contemporaries, he found himself writing in many different veins. In one of his last works, the *Missa Solemnis Pro Pace* (1944), Casella even began experimenting with the twelve-tone system, which leads us to suspect that he might have embraced dodecaphony had he lived beyond 1947.

Perhaps his most agreeable and effective music was produced in the neo-classical style. Here the scholar of old music and the ardent protagonist of new music found a common meeting ground. But whatever the style, as Massimo Mila has written, "what unites all his styles (and no one is definitive, yet all are definitive at least in some works) is just this eagerness of novelty, this constant need to surpass himself, this barometric sensibility to the oscillations of contemporary taste."

Casella was born in Turin, Italy, on July 25, 1883. After studying the piano with his mother, and the cello with his father at the Liceo Musicale, he came to Paris in 1896. There he attended the Paris Conservatory; as a pupil of Diémer, Leroux and Fauré, he won first prizes in piano playing and harmony. He served as the harpsichordist for the Société des Instruments Anciens in Paris from 1906 to 1909. During this period, he completed the writing of two symphonies, the first of which marked his debut as a conductor, in Monte Carlo in 1908. On April 23, 1910, he conducted an all-Casella program in Paris that included his second symphony, the Suite in C major, and his first successful composition, the rhapsody *Italia*. In 1915, he returned to Italy where he assumed a dominating position in its musical life. He divided his seemingly inexhaustible energies among piano playing, conducting, composing, teaching, writing criticisms, editing, research, and the founding of musical societies. He made his American debut on October 28, 1921, when he appeared with the Philadelphia Orchestra as conductor, composer and pianist. After that, he made frequent appearances as conductor with American orchestras. Just before and during World War II, he allied himself to the cause of Fascism, a fact that discredited him with many of his former colleagues and admirers. He died in Rome on March 5, 1947, after a long illness.

1909 ITALIA, rhapsody for orchestra, op. 11.

Italia was one of Casella's first successful works, and has maintained its popularity. It was introduced in Paris on April 23, 1910, the composer conducting.

Though the rhapsody has no specific program, it was intended to reflect Sicilian and Neapolitan life. Sicilian life, we learn from a note in the published score, is "tragic, superstitious, passionate, as it is found under the scorching sun or in the inferno of the sulphur mines"; the life of Naples is a "turbulent, careless, frenetic existence which may be lived amid the magic of the Gulf of Naples."

For his melodic material, Casella drew from Sicilian and Neapolitan melodies. The rhapsody opens (Lento) with a song heard in the province of Caltanissetta. Following some development, this song is succeeded by a work-tune popular in the Sicilian sulphur mines. (Wolf-Ferrari later quoted the same melody in his opera *The Jewels of the Madonna.*) An English horn then is heard chanting a hymn heard on Good Friday in religious processions in Caltanissetta. After a theme for the bassoon (based on a work-song from the Catitu marble quarries) comes the finale, in which three popular melodies are heard: *Funiculi, Funiculà;* Costa's *Lariulà;* and Tosti's *Marechiare.*

1924 LA GIARA (THE JAR), ballet in one act, with choreography by Jean Borlin based on Pirandello's tale. First performance: Swedish Ballet, Paris, November 19, 1924.

LA GIARA, ballet suite for orchestra. Part I: 1. Prelude; 2. Sicilian Dance. Part II: 1. Nocturne; 2. Dance of Nela; 3. Entrance of Peasants and Brindisi; 4. General Dance; 5. Finale.

Casella composed the score of this, his best-known ballet, on a scenario based upon a Sicilian tale of Pirandello. The composer explains that the music "was composed in obedience to the fundamental idea of uniting in modern synthesis the old fundamental musical comedy of the Neapolitan school with the elements of Italian folklore, more particularly the Sicilian."

The text is an amusing one, and concerns the miser Don Lollo Zirafa, who is inordinately proud of a huge jar in his possession. Broken by a clumsy peasant (to the fury of Don Lollo) the jar is put into the hands of a local hunchback for repair. The hunchback enters the jar and repairs it, only to discover that now that his job is done he cannot get out. Don Lollo stoutly refuses to have his precious jar broken again. The hunchback takes the decision philosophically, sits placidly in the jar, smokes his pipe, watches the moon, and listens to a Sicilian song sung in the distance. A farmer's daughter enters the scene and dances around the jar. Peasants enter, make merry, and create such a hubbub that they awaken Don Lollo. In an uncontrolled fit of anger, Don Lollo sends the jar rolling down the hill until it smashes against an olive tree. The liberated hunchback is carried on the shoulders of the peasants in triumph.

An orchestral suite based on the ballet score is divided into two sections: I. Prelude (Andantino dolce quasi pastorale); Sicilian Dance (Allegro vivace). II. Nocturne (Lento; Calmissimo); Dance of Nela (Vivacissimo e leggiero); Entrance of Peasants and Brindisi (Allegro deciso); General Dance (Allegro rude e selvaggio); Finale.

1925 PARTITA for piano and orchestra. I Sinfonia. II. Passacaglia. III. Burlesca.

This partita is one of Casella's successful efforts in fusing old classical forms with contemporary idioms. It was introduced by the composer in New York City on October 29, 1925, at a concert of the New York Philharmonic Orchestra.

The composer has provided the following comments:

"I. Sinfonia. The ensemble results from fusion of the sonata form, bithematic, the suite of the Seventeenth Century, and the instrumental concerto and the concerto grosso. The chief themes are: the first given to the strings; one for the oboe with piano; and a subsidiary one.

"II. Passacaglia. While it evokes a more sombre atmosphere and is always loyally 'Spanish,' after the manner of the old varied dance form, it solves in a new and modern manner the problem of the varied theme. This reorientation of the old passacaglia is obtained by the successive introductions of contrasting rhythms, by the differing character given to the diverse instruments, and by a progressive variation of the persisting theme itself. . . . The eleventh variation is in the folk form of a Siciliana. The twelfth is a mysterious chorale of religious, distant solemnity. After some measures of piano and oboe, the clarinets bring back gently the first measure of the Passacaglia, which ends as it began.

"III. Burlesca. This is a frank and joyous rondo in which one can find a typical result of the influence beginning to be exercised in the field of pure music by Scarlatti, Rossini, and Verdi's *Falstaff*."

1942 PAGANINIANA, divertimento for orchestra, on themes of Niccolò Paganini, op. 65. I. Allegro agitato. II. Polachetta. III. Romanza. IV. Tarantella.

Casella wrote this divertimento to commemorate the centenary of the founding of the Vienna Philharmonic, which introduced it in March of 1942, Karl Boehm conducting. The orchestral writing is brilliant and pyrotechnical throughout, as might perhaps be expected from a composition whose material was derived from one of the greatest violin virtuosos of all time, famous for his digital pyrotechnics. In the first movement, string virtuosity is emphasized while four themes are being utilized, one each from the fifth, twelfth, sixteenth and nineteenth of Paganini's solo-violin *Caprices*. In the second movement, a little polonaise, we are reminded that Paganini was also a guitarist, its main subject coming out of Paganini's Quartet, for violin, viola, guitar and cello, op. 4. This theme is heard in the oboe, with the trumpet contributing a subsidiary thought. In the third movement (Larghetto cantabile, amoroso), the material is derived from an unpublished Paganini piece for violin and orchestra, *The Spring,* which Casella found in a library in Mannheim. After four introductory measures and a pause, the solo violin is heard in a broad melody, which is carried on in turn by clarinet and violin. In this movement, Casella makes a brief and passing reference to the Allegro molto vivace of Beethoven's C-sharp minor String Quartet, op. 131, and to melodies from Verdi's *La Traviata* and Bellini's *Norma*—the reason for these quotations never having been explained. The concluding movement is an exciting tarantella (Presto molto). Material from Paganini's *Tarantella* is used in the opening measures, while the main theme is lifted from the Paganini Guitar Quartet, op. 4.

MARIO CASTELNUOVO-TEDESCO 1895–1968

Several important influences have been brought to bear on Castelnuovo-Tedesco's music. The first is his native city of Florence, described in some of his earlier works. Indeed, Guido M. Gatti is convinced that the personality of that city has molded the composer's overall style. Another influence has been Shakespeare, whose plays and sonnets have inspired numerous songs, duets, eleven concert overtures, and two later operas, *The Merchant of Venice* (1956) and *All's Well that Ends Well* (1958). A third influence has been the composer's Jewish heritage and the Bible, reflected in such compositions as his second violin concerto entitled *The Prophets,* the *Sacred Service for the Sabbath Eve* (1943) and various cantatas and oratorios based on Biblical subjects and texts.

Castelnuovo-Tedesco is essentially a neo-romantic, who indulges in fine, rich sounds, and seeks out poetic ideas in whatever medium he chooses or whatever subject he selects. He may from time to time reveal the impact that other composers have had on his music, notably Richard Strauss, Ildebrando Pizzetti, Respighi, and at times even Puccini. But as Francis Toye once said, what Castelnuovo-Tedesco writes always has "character," and his finest works are the productions of a "musician full of taste and skill with a delicate touch and a considerable range of fancy in writing for the orchestra, and with quite an exceptional gift for writing for the voice."

Castelnuovo-Tedesco was born in Florence, Italy, on April 3, 1895. At the Cherubini Royal Institute in Florence, he studied with Ildebrando Pizzetti, who made a lasting impression on him. Castelnuovo-Tedesco began composing early. In 1926, he gained recognition with his opera, *La Mandragola* (his own libretto based on Machiavelli), which won the Italian Prize and was successfully produced in Venice on May 4, 1926. During the next decade, his stature grew and his reputation spread across the Atlantic to the United States, where performers like Toscanini, Jascha Heifetz and Gregor Piatigorsky introduced major works.

After Italy embarked on an anti-Semitic program, inspired by its Axis partner, Nazi Germany, Castelnuovo-Tedesco came to the United States. On November 2, 1939, he made his American debut in New York by appearing as soloist in his Second Piano Concerto with the New York Philharmonic conducted by John Barbirolli. He then settled in Beverly Hills, California, where for a while he wrote music for the movies, and for many years devoted himself to teaching composition to an entire generation of young composers for the screen. In 1958, his opera *The Merchant of Venice* won first prize in an international competition. He died in Hollywood on March 15, 1968.

1932 CONCERTO NO. 2 FOR VIOLIN AND ORCHESTRA ("THE PROPHETS"). I. Grave e meditativo. II. Espressivo e dolente. III. Fiero ed impetuoso ma sostenuto e ben marcato il ritmo.

Castelnuovo-Tedesco wrote three violin concertos. The first was influenced by the composer's native land, particularly the city of his birth, and was appropriately named *Concerto Italiano*. It was introduced in Rome on January 31, 1926. The second owes its subject matter and inspiration to the Bible, specifically the Prophets. "I sought to evoke the Biblical period," the composer explains, "and to suggest the flaming eloquence of the ancient prophets among the surrounding voices of the people and the voices of Nature." The first movement, in which lyricism and dramatic interest alternate, is based on Isaiah. The second finds its inspiration in Jeremiah. This is a lament in which the solo violin represents the prophet, while the orchestra speaks for the Hebrew people. The finale, in which a spirit of exaltation predominates, is a tonal portrait of Elijah.

The Prophets received its world première in New York on April 12, 1933. Jascha Heifetz was the soloist with the New York Philharmonic, conducted by Toscanini.

1933 OVERTURE TO *TWELFTH NIGHT*, for orchestra.

Castelnuovo-Tedesco's passion for the plays of Shakespeare has inspired him to write concert overtures for many of them. The *Twelfth Night* overture received its first performance in Rome on January 6, 1935, with Vittorio Gui conducting the Augusteo Orchestra. In this overture, the characters, not the dramatic action, are of central interest. A slow introduction (Andantino malinconico) brings up Prince Orsino, while a mocking and gay passage for bassoon (Vivo e burlesco) evokes Malvolio. These two principal themes and several subsidiary ones (describing the heroine and the clown) are developed astutely. An ancient dance (galliard) provides rhythmic and atmospheric interest.

1937 CONCERTO NO. 2 FOR PIANO AND ORCHESTRA. I. Vivo. II. Romanza. III. Vivo e impetuoso.

This concerto was introduced in New York City on November 2, 1939. The composer was the soloist and the New York Philharmonic Orchestra was conducted by John Barbirolli.

The music is direct in its appeal, making brilliant effects and containing a great deal of fine virtuoso writing for the piano. The first movement has graceful, sometimes sparkling, music; both principal themes are first introduced by the orchestra before being taken over by the soloist. A slow and dreamy Romanza follows. After a cadenza, the impetuous and headstrong closing movement arrives to provide excitement.

1940 CIPRESSI, for orchestra (also for piano).

Behind Castelnuovo-Tedesco's home in Florence there stood a row of majestic cypress trees, tracing the rise of a hill. Glancing out of his window one day in 1920, the composer was so impressed by this vista that he decided to interpret it musically in a short piece for the piano. Twenty years later, he returned to it nostalgically—it reminded him of his lost home—and decided to give it orchestral dress. In this form it was introduced by the Boston Symphony Orchestra under Serge Koussevitzky on October 25, 1940.

1958 THE MERCHANT OF VENICE, opera in three acts, with text by the composer derived from the Shakespeare drama. First performance: Florence, Italy, May 25, 1961.

The composer was on a visit to his native city of Florence where he planned to work on his opera based on Shakespeare's *All's Well that Ends Well.* There the director of the Opera told Castelnuovo-Tedesco of his pressing need for new operas to present at the annual Florence May Music Festival. He urged Castelnuovo-Tedesco to consider writing one for him with large dimensions; he also informed the composer about a prize of $8,000 being offered by La Scala in Milan (with funds provided by David Campari) for a new opera. Castelnuovo-Tedesco decided then and there to put aside *All's Well that Ends Well* for the time being and to go to work on a more ambitious and spacious operatic project. His final selection was Shakespeare's *The Merchant of Venice.* He began his first sketches in January of 1956, devoting four months to each of the three acts, and completing the entire opera early in 1958. Out of the sixty-four operas submitted to the La Scala contest, Castelnuovo-Tedesco's opera was the one to win the prize, because, as the citation read, it "was the one which showed the greatest understanding of the original text, and most unusual mastery in the texture of the score, and the greatest abundance and variety of musical ideas."

The composer prepared his own libretto. While every word of it is Shakespeare's, the original drama was reduced to one-fifth its original size. Five acts were compressed into three. The first and third acts in the opera were set in Venice; and second, at Portia's home in Belmont. Other basic changes were described by Albert Goldberg in the Los Angeles *Times*: "The three casket scenes interspersed throughout the play have been condensed into one, and the two foreign suitors have become miming parts on the assumption that they did not know the language. The Prince of Morocco does a barbaric dance and the Prince of Arragon, a stately Sarabande, while making the choice of the caskets containing Portia's likeness. Only the successful suitor, Bassanio, sings during this scene.

"Shylock's return to his home after Jessica's elopement, which is only narrated in Shakespeare, becomes the dramatic close to the first act, and the opera ends with the trial. The chorus comments in both scenes and signs madrigals during the selection of the casket. Shakespeare's fifth-act love passage between Lorenzo and Jessica becomes the close of the second act."

The composer provides the following description of his musical style: "It is my own idiom. I employ all the resources of modern technique, but there are only three times when a twelve-tone chord is used. When the three suitors are puzzled in their choice of the caskets, the orchestra plays a dissonant twelve-tone chord built up in intervals of fourths. For the losers it remained unresolved; for the winner it resolves into a C major chord. There are no set arias but rather what Verdi called ariosos—free but singable." Nevertheless, as Francis Toye remarked in a review, Castelnuovo-Tedesco is not ashamed "to write a straightforward duet, as for example that very pretty one at the end of Act II . . . and writes it without apology."

CARLOS CHÁVEZ 1899–

"Mexican music," Chávez has written, "is largely the product of a mixture of influences, that is, of crossbreeding. This mixed ancestry, chiefly Indo-Spanish, is never found to be in exact proportions of half and half. In the majority of cases, one basic element is altered by the other in a proportion much smaller than fifty percent."

From the native music of Mexico, particularly that of the Mexican Indian, Chávez acquired some of his stylistic traits: the austerity and stark simplicity of melodic line; the percussive harshness of sound; the primitive rhythmic force; the archaic-like idioms; the sudden, abrupt contrasts. Fusing such elements with the harmonic and instrumental techniques of a twentieth-century composer, Chávez arrived at a personal style, a style that is Mexican to the core, even when native Mexican materials are not used.

"Carlos Chávez," wrote Aaron Copland, "has faced in his music almost all the major problems of modern music: the overthrow of German ideals, the objectification of sentiment, the use of folk material in its relation to nationalism, the intricate rhythms, the linear as opposed to vertical writing, the specifically 'modern' sound images. It is music that belongs entirely to our own age. It propounds no problems, no metaphysics. Chávez's music is extraordinarily healthy. It is music created not as a substitute for living but as a manifestation of life. It is clear and clean-sounding, without shadow or softness. Here is contemporary music if there ever was any."

Chávez was born in Mexico City on June 13, 1899. He studied the piano with Manuel Ponce and Pedro Luis Ogazon, and he took some lessons in harmony from Juan B. Fuentes. But most of his musical education came out of textbooks and published musical scores, which he studied painstakingly by himself. His first works revealed European influences. But immersion in the folk music of his native land brought him freedom from such derivative influences and permitted his own creative individuality to express itself. The first important such work was the ballet *New Fire* (*El Fuego nuevo*), written in 1921 and introduced in Mexico City on November 4, 1928. In 1922–1923, Chávez traveled about in Europe, where he became acquainted for the first time with the music of Stravinsky and Schoenberg, among others. Back in Mexico in 1923, he organized and conducted concerts of new music, which introduced to Mexico the principal creative figures in twentieth-century music. For two years, beginning with 1926, he lived in New York. Then in 1928, he returned to Mexico to become its most powerful musical figure. He organized a symphony orchestra, the first such to give regular concerts in Mexico; he rehabilitated Mexico's educational system as director of the National Conservatory; he became head of the Department of Fine Arts. Single-handedly, he created a significant musical culture for his country, while enriching that culture with his own numerous compositions deeply rooted in Mexico's folk music. *H. P.*, a ballet inspired by the machine age, was staged for the first time on March 31, 1932, in Philadelphia, Leopold Stokowski conducting. Other important early works included his first two symphonies—*Sinfonía de Antígona* and *Sinfonía India*—and several works in which Mexican instruments were used prominently, of which *Xochipilli Macuilxochitl* (1940) is a significant example. He also distinguished himself as a conductor, appearing since 1936 as guest of practically all the major symphonic organizations in the United States. In 1958–1959, he was appointed Charles Eliot Norton Professor at Harvard University, lectures from which were gathered into the book *Musical Thought* (1960). He has received important decorations from France, Belgium, Sweden, as well as Mexico; he was made honorary member of the American Academy of Arts and Sciences in Boston, and of the American Academy and National Institute of Arts and Letters in New York.

1933–1935 SINFONÍA DE ANTÍGONA (SYMPHONY NO. 1), for orchestra.

SINFONÍA INDIA (SYMPHONY NO. 2), for orchestra.

A projected performance of Jean Cocteau's *Antigone* in Mexico City brought Chávez a commission from the Department of Fine Arts to write its incidental music. This music was adapted by Chávez into a one-movement "symphony" (1933), which he himself introduced with the Orquesta Sinfoníca de México on December 15, 1933.

This music mixes Indian styles with ancient Greek modes, thus acquiring a character all its own. The composer explains that this work is a "symphony, not a symphonic poem—that is, it is not subject to a program. Antigone, her self-confidence, defiance, heroism, and martyrdom are expressed by the music as a whole, not successively. The most elementary musical materials serve for this music, which could not be grandiloquent. Bare and elemental, it could not be expressed by laconic strength, just as what is primitive is reduced to its elements because it is primitive. The work has the basic structure of the sonata, and is strictly a symphony, though in one movement. . . . The score breathes a certain archaic quality because of the use of rhythmic, harmonic, and melodic elements essential to ancient Greek music; the themes are all modal, and the harmony is in fourths and fifths, thirds having been avoided because the Greek musical system treated them as dissonant."

There are three major thematic ideas: the first is introduced by the solo oboe; the second is given by the violins; the third appears in bass flute.

The *Sinfonía India* (1935) is a one-movement work in which Mexican-Indian themes are utilized, collected among the Seris of Sonora, the Huicholes of Nayarit and the Yaquis of Sonora. Chávez completed this work while on a visit to New York; he himself conducted its world première, with the Columbia Symphony Orchestra, over the CBS radio network, on January 23, 1936.

A brief introduction (Vivo) precedes a strongly rhythmed subject in oboes and violins, a melody of the Huichole Indians. After this has been elaborated upon, the clarinet is heard in a beautiful song of the Yaqui Indians of Sonora (Allegretto cantabile). This material is varied and sweeps towards a climax before another haunting Sonora-Indian melody is presented, this time in flutes and horns, and after that in the strings (Adagio). After a formal recapitulation of all this material, a vigorous, strongly accented dance tune of the Seri Indians introduces a feeling of tension and excitement that becomes intensified as the symphony rushes towards its final climax.

1940 CONCERTO NO. 1 FOR PIANO AND ORCHESTRA. I. Allegro agitato. II. Molto lento. III. Allegro.

In this highly percussive and austere music, Chávez's style arrives at its fullest development. It is music of persuading power, original in its harmonic texture, varied in its acoustic effects. The piano and the orchestra are treated as an integrated musical body, neither part of which is subsidiary to the other. The composer has said that his intention was to write virtuoso music for both the piano and the orchestra; but rather than virtuosity, what impresses us is the personal character of Chávez's melodic ideas (some of them written modally), and the individual way he develops them rhythmically, acoustically, harmonically.

The first and third movements derive their force and strength from the rhythms of native Indian music. Between these two energetic movements comes a lyrical section, exotic in its use of archaic idioms.

On January 1, 1942, this concerto was introduced by Eugene List, pianist, and the New York Philharmonic Orchestra under Dimitri Mitropoulos.

1942 TOCCATA FOR PERCUSSION INSTRUMENTS.

This unusual work is scored for eleven types of percussion instruments (played by six performers), some of them indigenous to Mexico: Yaqui drums; tenor and side drums; bells; xylophone; cymbal; chimes; hardwood sound sticks; rattles; kettledrums; bass drum; gongs. Different groups of instruments are used in different movements: high and low drums predominate in the first; xylophone, chimes, cymbal, gongs, are heard in the second; and rattles, hardwood sound sticks, and the small Indian drum in the third.

The *Toccata* is in three movements played without interruption: Allegro sempre giusto; Largo; Allegro un poco marziale. The variety of dynamics, rhythm, and color provides continual interest.

This work was introduced in Mexico City on October 31, 1947, Eduardo Hernandez Moncada conducting.

1950 CONCERTO FOR VIOLIN AND ORCHESTRA.

Chávez was deep at work upon his violin concerto when he received a commission for just such a work from Viviane Bertolami. Miss Bertolami introduced it in Mexico City, with the composer conducting, on February 28, 1952. A number of years later, the composer revised his score and changed the orchestration. This new version was performed by Henryk Szeryng and the New York Philharmonic under Leonard Bernstein in the fall of 1965.

The work has eight sections played without interruption. Four sections comprise the Exposition (Largo; Allegro; Adagio; Scherzo). Four others form the recapitulation (Scherzo; Adagio; Allegro; Largo). A cadenza for the solo violin separates the two scherzos. "Each movement," the composer reveals, "includes its own development both in the exposition and in the recapitulation. Otherwise the recapitulation is not literal and for the most part consists of a great 'mirror' of the exposition. The violin is seen here in the light of its possibilities, as an instrument of lyrical expression and rhythmic flexibility." The main melodic material of this concerto is an eloquent song for the solo violin which opens the work and also prefaces the closing Largo; also, an affecting thought for solo violin in the Exposition Adagio. The first scherzo consists of a theme and three variations.

1953 SYMPHONY NO. 4, "ROMANTICA" I. Allegro. II. Molto lento. III. Vivo non troppo mosso.

SYMPHONY NO. 5, for string orchestra. I. Allegro molto moderato. II. Lento. III. Allegro con brio.

The fourth symphony was commissioned by the Louisville Orchestra in Kentucky, which introduced it under the composer's direction on February 4, 1953. The composer's descriptive title of "Romantic" points up the lyric and emotional character of the work as a whole, a departure from the more discordant and percussive writing of some of his earlier symphonies. "The piece is tonal, melodic, agreeably worked out and scored," reported Howard Taubman in his review in *The New York Times*. "The first and second movements are expansive and just a shade sentimental and the last generates more momentum and excitement."

The main theme of the first movement, heard first in the English horn, recurs throughout the symphony, though frequently altered and varied. This is a comparatively brief idea, and so is the second theme, first presented by bassoon, flute and clarinet. The second movement opens with fragments of the first-movement theme, after which an extended aria is heard (this aria is also derived from the first theme of the preceding movement). The finale is a double rondo with two main themes, the first of which is related to the first theme of the opening movement.

Where the fourth symphony is romantic, the fifth is neo-classic. An interesting feature of the instrumentation of this work is the way in which Chávez creates new sound effects by writing for some of the instruments in registers to which they are not generally accustomed; the double basses, for example, climb to high treble registers. In addition, points out Edward D. Cole, "calculated overtones sounding 'accidentally' here produce effects just as important as those which may be noted."

The fifth symphony was first heard in Los Angeles on December 1, 1953, the composer conducting.

1963 SYMPHONY NO. 6. I. Allegro risoluto ma non troppo mosso. II. Adagio (At Ease). III. Con anima.

After completing his fifth, Chávez sought to write a symphony "within classic limitations." He added that by classic he was not referring to neo-classicism. A commission from the New York Philharmonic gave him the necessary stimulus. Most of this symphony was written between 1961 and 1962, but additional revisions delayed its completion until 1963. The world première took place in New York on May 7, 1964, with Leonard Bernstein conducting the New York Philharmonic.

The first theme of the opening movement is an extended thought; it is first offered by violins and violas. A contrasting mood is provided by the second subject, described by Edward Downes in his program notes for the New York Philharmonic as "a gently rocking figure for woodwinds over a slow octave tread of cellos and string basses." Downes describes the short slow movement as "a lyric interlude between the two vigorous outside movements" based upon a "melodic curve traced in the opening measures by two soft trumpets." Towards the end of this movement, the string basses suggest a subject which will be the basis of the third-movement passacaglia. This passacaglia consists of forty-three variations on a six-bar subject announced by solo tuba. Despite changes of tempo and key signature, the theme "retains its basic shape throughout," says Downes. "Only towards the end are a very few of the variations lengthened by the traditional devices of canon and fugue to build up a great contrapuntal climax."

1964 RESONANCES (RESONANCIAS), for orchestra.

Chávez was commissioned by the Secretariat of Public Education in Mexico to write a new work to help inaugurate the Museo Nacional de Arqueologia in Chapultepec. The world première took place in that Mexican city in September of 1964. At that time, the composer provided the following information: "*Resonancias* is a musical work more abstract than not, one which seems to encompass the manifold echoes that resound in me of an era that is past yet whose spirit is forever present in the immortal monuments of secular art and other manifestations as deep as they are dramatic. This work is not attached to any classified 'technique,' either past or present. The musical thought evolves without restrictions or academic help of any kind, and continues its course unencumbered for the duration of the piece."

AARON COPLAND 1900–

In the first of his works to attract attention—the *Music for the Theatre,* and the Concerto for Piano and Orchestra—Copland explored the potentialities of jazz as a serious medium for musical expression. This interest in jazz structure and style soon waned. In the music that followed—notably the *Dance Symphony,* the *Piano Variations,* the *Short Symphony,* and *Statements*—there can be heard the voice of a modernist whose skilful employment of advanced techniques of harmony, counterpoint, and rhythm was admired and praised by that esoteric circle of music lovers who went in for modern music. But the public at large failed to respond to this music.

Dissatisfied with his failure to please audiences, and feeling that he had been working in a sort of vacuum, Copland now made a conscious effort to speak "in the simplest possible terms." Not only did he simplify his writing, but he also adopted a speech which he felt was more easily assimilable. He began writing functional music: music for school children (the opera, *The Second Hurricane,* and *The Outdoor Overture,* for orchestra), music for the movies (*Of Mice and Men, Our Town, The City, North Star, The Heiress, The Red Pony*), music for the theatre (*Quiet City*), music for radio (*Music for Radio*). He adopted popular idioms even in his most serious efforts: that of Mexico in *El Salón México* and Cuba in *Danzón Cubano.* He drew inspiration for ballet music from the rich mine of American folk music: *Rodeo, Billy the Kid,* and *Appalachian Spring.* Even in works like the Third Symphony and the opera *The Tender Land,* which made little or no attempt to absorb materials from outside sources, the tendency towards simplification is still present, and the influence of American folk music is continually suggested in subtle overtones of expression.

There has been no cheapening of style or artistic concession in this conscious effort to write music that can be appreciated by the many instead of the few. On the contrary, in his later works Copland has grown in artistic stature. His language has become personalized, his speech has acquired subtler emotional nuances.

"Whatever Copland does," Arthur Berger has written, "has the recognizable virtues of a genuinely creative artist. With the same limitations peculiar to many composers of our time, he can accomplish much more than most of the others. He is at last an American that we may place unapologetically beside the recognized creative figures of any other country. Viewed with respect to the most representative, and perhaps the most successful, work of each period of his career, his contribution is its own justification. . . . We are not obliged, therefore, to credit Copland merely with what he has done to establish an indigenous style, for his achievements go deeper."

Copland was born in Brooklyn, New York, on November 14, 1900. He began studying the piano when he was fourteen and in 1917 took lessons in harmony from Rubin Goldmark. Subsequently, he attended the Fontainbleau School of Music in France, and from there he went on to Paris for three years of private lessons in composition and orchestration with Nadia Boulanger.

Just before returning to the United States in 1924, Copland was asked by Boulanger to write something she could use during a forthcoming tour of the United States as organist. Copland wrote the Symphony for Organ and Orchestra, which Nadia Boulanger introduced on January 11, 1925, with Walter Damrosch conducting the New York Symphony. One month later, it was repeated in Boston by the Boston Symphony under Koussevitzky.

A generous patroness interested herself in Copland at this time. This, and Guggenheim Fellowships in 1925 and 1926, relieved Copland of financial problems, enabling him to devote himself intensively to composition. In 1929, he won a prize of five thousand dollars for his *Dance Symphony* in a contest sponsored by RCA Victor. The subsequent winning of a Pulitzer Prize, awards from the New York Music Critics Circle, the Academy Award for *The Heiress,* and numerous other honors emphasized that he had truly become "the dean of American music." These other honors include election as a member to the American Academy of Arts and Letters (1954); an honorary doctorate from Princeton University (1956); and the Presidential Medal of Honor from President Johnson (1964).

Copland has toured the music world as pianist and conductor. One such tour took him to the Soviet Union in 1960, where he led several of his major works. From 1940 to 1965, he was head of the composition department at the Berkshire Music Center at Tanglewood, and from 1957 to 1965, he was chairman of the faculty. During the summer of 1967, he was composer-in-residence at Dartmouth College's Congregation of the Arts at Hopkins Center.

No résumé of Copland's career would be complete without considering his tireless, sustained efforts on behalf of American music. He was instrumental in bringing about performances of new American works and promoting the interests of American composers through the organization of the Copland-Sessions Concerts in New York, the American Festival of Contemporary Music at Saratoga Springs, New York, and the American Composers Alliance. He was chairman of the executive board of the League of Composers. He has been affiliated with the Koussevitzky Music Foundation and the United States section of the International Society for Contemporary Music. His books, articles for magazines, and lectures have also proved powerful instruments of propaganda for present-day American music.

1925 MUSIC FOR THE THEATRE, for chamber orchestra. I. Prologue. II. Dance. III. Interlude. IV. Burlesque. V. Epilogue.

Serge Koussevitzky was invited by the League of Composers to direct a concert of contemporary chamber-orchestral works in New York in 1925. For this concert, Koussevitzky asked young Copland (whose symphony he had recently performed in Boston) to write a new work. At that time, Copland was fascinated by the possibilities of jazz in serious composition. In planning a new work for Koussevitzky's use, he decided to explore jazz's artistic capabilities. *Music for the Theatre* was introduced by the Boston Symphony Orchestra under Koussevitzky in Boston on November 20, 1925, before receiving its New York performance at the League of Composers concert eight days later.

In writing this music, Copland had no specific play in mind. The title was intended to convey the idea that the music has the dramatic and atmospheric qualities of the theatre.

In the Prologue (Molto moderato), a solo trumpet announces the first theme. After a second subject is heard in the oboe, there follows a development, rising to a climax, then subsiding into the serenity of the opening measures. The Dance (Allegro molto) is a nervous, highly rhythmic piece of music in a popular style. This is followed by the lyric melody of the Interlude section (Lento) in clarinet, accompanied by strings, piano and glockenspiel. The Burlesque movement (Allegro vivo) is in A-B-A form, its middle part highlighted by a wailing subject for the trumpet. In the closing Epilogue (Molto moderato), material from the first and third sections is recalled. The composition ends as it began, in a peaceful atmosphere.

1926 CONCERTO FOR PIANO AND ORCHESTRA. I. Andante sostenuto. II. Molto moderato.

The Concerto was the second and the last of Copland's significant attempts to write in a jazz style within ambitious symphonic structures. He worked on his concerto during a trip to Europe in the summer of 1926, completing it in New York the following October. It received its world première in Boston on January 28, 1927, with the composer as soloist and Koussevitzky conducting the Boston Symphony. "When I premièred my concerto," Copland told an interviewer many years later, "the reactions were quite violent. They called me an 'ogre'; Boston listeners claimed that Koussevitzky programmed it with the malice of a foreigner who wanted to show how bad American music is." Early in 1964, the concerto was revived in New York by the New York Philharmonic under Leonard Bernstein; and the concerto was heard again during the summer of 1965, when the same orchestra gave its first series of free concerts in the New York City parks. On both occasions, the concerto was received well. Time had not diminished its inherent vitality and spontaneity, nor the skilled use of popular (though by now dated) materials.

Though in two movements, the work is played without interruption. The following analysis is by the composer:

"A short orchestral introduction announces the principal thematic material. The piano enters quietly and improvises around this for a short space, then the principal theme is sung by a flute and clarinet in unison over an accompaniment of muted strings. . . . A few transitional measures lead directly to the second part, which, roughly speaking, is in sonata form without recapitulation. The first theme, announced immediately by the solo piano, is considerably extended and developed before the second idea is introduced by a soprano saxophone.

The development, based entirely on these two themes, contains a short piano cadenza, presenting difficulties of a rhythmic nature. Before the end, a part of the first movement is recalled. This is followed by a brief coda."

1930 PIANO VARIATIONS. *See*: 1957. Orchestral Variations.

1935 STATEMENTS, for orchestra. I. Militant. II. Cryptic. III. Dogmatic. IV. Subjective. V. Jingo. VI. Prophetic.

Copland worked on *Statements* from 1933 to 1935, having been commissioned by the League of Composers for the Minneapolis Symphony. Two of the movements (*Jingo* and *Prophetic*) were played for the first time in a broadcast over the NBC radio network by the Minneapolis Symphony under Ormandy. The entire work was heard first in New York on January 7, 1942, with Dimitri Mitropoulos conducting the New York Philharmonic.

In choosing his title, the composer had in mind short, concentrated orchestral episodes, each with a well-defined character. The programmatic headings for each of the six movements give the listener a clue to the intent of the music.

The composer's succinct analysis follows:

"The 'militant' statement is based on a single theme, announced in unison at the beginning by three flutes, two oboes, bassoon and strings. The 'cryptic' statement is orchestrated for brass and flute alone with an occasional use of bass clarinet and bassoon. The 'dogmatic' statement is in tri-partite form; the middle section quotes the theme of the composer's *Piano Variations*. The 'subjective' statement is scored for strings alone, without double basses. The 'jingo' statement utilizes the full orchestra. It is built in rondo form on a chromatic melody with occasional bows to a well-known tune. The final section, a 'prophetic' statement, is rhapsodic in form and centers about a choral-like melody sung by the solo trumpet." The "well-known tune" Copland refers to is "The Sidewalks of New York," presented over a hurdy-gurdy type of accompaniment and intended to poke fun at Tammany Hall.

1936 EL SALÓN MÉXICO, for orchestra.

In the fall of 1932, Copland visited Mexico and carried away with him vivid impressions of its life and its music. One year after that, he came upon two scholarly works devoted to Mexican song which aroused in him the desire to write a work in Mexican style. Suddenly he recalled the impressions of his Mexican visit, particularly experiences in a popular dance hall called the "Salón México." He set to work on a musical composition about that dance hall which would portray the Mexico that the tourists saw and knew rather than the Mexico of ancient civilizations.

Adopting a form which was, as he put it, a "kind of modified potpourri in which Mexican themes and their extensions are sometimes inextricably mixed for use of conciseness and coherence," Copland created a vivid picture in which the smoke-filled and noisy dance hall is seen with all the exotic color of its background and clientele. The seductive rhythms of Mexican folk music pulse throughout the score and give it its greatest charm and appeal. Some authentic Mexican tunes are quoted, the most important being *El Mosco*, which is heard in the solo trumpet soon after the introduction (where *El Palo Verde* and *La Jesuita* are also quoted briefly).

"Expressively," says Julia Smith in her biography of the composer, "the work represents a series of moods or impressions which appear somewhat in this order: the lyrical, the sentimental, the garish, the lusty, the improvisatory, the humorous, and the frenetic—the latter with its whipped-up rhythmic verve (Copland style)." A good deal of the impact of this music springs from its "frenetic rhythmic sections" and particularly from its "frequent changes of meter . . . as applied to bits of Mexican tunes that flit about in the orchestra, at times producing a 'hopped-up' atmosphere."

The first performance of *El Salón México* took place in Mexico City on August 27, 1937; Carlos Chávez conducted the Orquesta Sinfonica de México. The piece was heard in the United States for the first time over the NBC radio network on May 14, 1938, with Adrian Boult conducting the NBC Symphony.

1938 BILLY THE KID, a ballet in one act, with scenario by Lincoln Kirstein and choreography by Eugene Loring. First performance: Ballet Caravan, Chicago, October 16, 1938.

BILLY THE KID, ballet-suite, for orchestra. I. The Open Prairie. II. Street in a Frontier Town. III. Card Game at Night (Prairie Night). IV. Gun Battle. V. Celebration Dance (after Billy's Capture). VI. Billy's Death. VII. The Open Prairie Again.

Billy the Kid, says Walter Terry in *Ballet,* "has long remained one of the most distinguished examples of ballets based upon American folk themes. Its movement, technique, though stemming from the classical ballet, is augmented by actions and gestures idiomatic to America or evocative of the American spirit."

Though named after the famous outlaw, the ballet is not so much a biography as it is "a perception of the pioneer West in which a figure such as Billy played a vivid role." Here is how the composer described the principal action, which begins and ends on an open prairie:

"The central portion of the ballet concerns itself with the significant moments in the life of Billy the Kid. The first scene is a frontier town. Familiar figures amble by. Cowboys saunter, some on horseback, others with their lassos. Some Mexican women do a Jarabo, which is interrupted by a fight between two drunks. Attracted by the gathering crowd, Billy is seen for the first time as a boy of twelve, with his mother. The brawl turns ugly, guns are drawn, and in some unaccountable way Billy's mother is killed. Without an instant's hesitation, in cold fury, Billy draws a knife from a cowhand's sheath and stabs his mother's slayers. His short but famous career has begun.

"In swift succession we see episodes of Billy's later life. At night, under the stars, in a quiet card game with his outlaw friends. Hunted by a posse led by his former friend Pat Garrett, Billy is pursued. A running gun battle ensues. Billy is captured. A drunken celebration takes place. Billy in prison is, of course, followed by one of Billy's legendary escapes. Tired and worn in the desert, Billy rests with his girl. Starting from a deep sleep, he senses movement in the shadows. The posse has finally caught up with him. It is the end."

The composer's tendency in the 1930s and 1940s to draw his melodic ideas from American folk-sources prevails in *Billy the Kid*, whose source is the cowboy. With his customary supple technique, the composer ingeniously incorporates into his score several familiar cowboy songs, notably *Git Along Little Dogie; Old Chisholm Trail; Goodbye, Old Paint;* and *O Bury Me Not*. Yet he never gives the impression that this music is just a potpourri of familiar tunes. The variety of mood and pace, the inventiveness of harmonic language, the picturesque re-creations of places and people bring to *Billy the Kid* both artistic scope and originality.

Most of the music from the ballet was incorporated by the composer into an orchestral suite which received its first hearing at a concert by the NBC Symphony under William Steinberg on November 9, 1940.

1938 AN OUTDOOR OVERTURE, for orchestra.

In the 1930s, Copland produced several works which young people could perform, and to which young people could enjoy listening. In 1937, he had written a children's opera, *The Second Hurricane,* described as a "play opera for high school performance." Its première took place in New York April 21, 1937 (staged by Orson Welles). A year later, the director of music at the New York High School of Music and Art suggested that Copland write a short single-movement orchestral piece "optimistic in tone" and "appealing to the adolescent youth in this country." Copland liked the idea so much he interrupted work on his ballet, *Billy the Kid,* to write this functional piece for young people. *An Outdoor Overture* was introduced at the High School of Music and Art in New York on December 16, 1938. It is simple, straightforward music with readily assimilable themes. It has four sections, alternating slow and fast movements. Its basic material consists of two march-like subjects and an extended lyrical thought for trumpet solo.

1941 SONATA FOR PIANO. I. Molto moderato. II. Vivace. III. Andante sostenuto.

The distinguished American playwright Clifford Odets commissioned Copland to write a piano sonata, a task Copland began in 1939 and completed in 1941 during a tour in South America. The première took place in South America—in Buenos Aires on October 21, 1941, the composer appearing on an all-American music concert. It was first heard in the United States on January 9, 1943, when the performer was John Kirkpatrick.

The composer explains that the first movement is an "Allegro closely allied to the usual sonata-allegro form, beginning and ending in the key of B-flat minor and containing the customary slow material . . . in G minor. The development section is somewhat free in character and is climaxed by the first thematic material in the original key and in a grandiose statement." The second movement is a scherzo, which the composer says "alternates wistful and poetic moods with sudden violent outbursts. There is no trio in the usual sense, although some contrasting material is introduced two-thirds of the way through the movement." The third movement is in a free form. "The opening chords start quietly and gradually build to a powerful climax, return to the bell-like sonorities of the opening, and finish on a note of complete serenity."

1942 LINCOLN PORTRAIT, for narrator and orchestra.

Soon after the entrance of the United States into World War II, André Kostelanetz, the orchestra conductor, commissioned several American composers to write orchestral works descriptive of great Americans which "could be employed to mirror the magnificent spirit of our country." To Copland went the assignment of writing music about an American statesman, and—as the composer tells us—"the choice of Lincoln as my subject seemed inevitable."

The composer explains further:

"The composition is roughly divided into three main sections.

"In the opening section I wanted to suggest something of the mysterious sense of fatality that surrounds Lincoln's personality. Also near the end of that section, something of his gentleness and simplicity of spirit. The quick middle section briefly sketches in the background of the times he lived in. This merges into the concluding section where my sole purpose was to draw a simple but impressive frame about the words of Lincoln himself."

The text, read by a narrator, is drawn from the letters and speeches of Lincoln which "seemed particularly apposite to our own situation today"; and it concludes with the closing lines of the Gettysburg Address.

Copland quotes two songs of the period to give his music contemporary flavor: Stephen Foster's "De Camptown Races" and the ballad "Springfield Mountain." In neither case is the treatment a literal one. Otherwise, the melodic material is entirely Copland's.

André Kostelanetz directed the first performance of the *Portrait* with the Cincinnati Symphony Orchestra on May 14, 1942.

1942 RODEO (or THE COURTING AT BURNT RANCH), ballet in one act, with choreography and scenario by Agnes de Mille. First performance: Ballet Russe de Monte Carlo, New York, October 16, 1942.

RODEO, ballet-suite for orchestra. I. Buckaroo Holiday. II. Corral Nocturne. III. Saturday Night Waltz. IV. Hoe Down.

Rodeo was commissioned by the Ballet Russe de Monte Carlo which (impressed by *Billy the Kid*) wanted a cowboy ballet for its own repertory. It proved an enormous success, receiving twenty-two curtain calls on opening night. As Edwin Denby reported, the audience was delighted with the "cowgirl-gets-her-cowboy plot." He said further: "Somehow the flavor of American domestic manners is especially clear in that peculiar desert landscape, and that is its fascination. The dance, the music, the decor . . . are each drawn to the same local fact with affection; and so they have a mysterious unity of a touching kind."

The ballet scenario (as the program explained) deals "with the problem that has confronted every American woman, from earliest pioneer times, and which has never ceased to occupy them throughout the history of the building of our country; how to get a suitable man." The plot traces the adventures of a cowgirl at Burnt Ranch, who competes with the city girls for the attention of local cowboys. The story carries her to a rodeo, then to a Saturday night dance at the ranch house. A roper and a wrangler fight for her. The girl then realizes she is in love with the roper and goes off with him; the wrangler finds consolation with the rancher's daughter.

Rodeo is a ballet filled with action. Walter Terry described it as a "danced dream." He said: "The movements of the ensemble support, enhance and color the activities of the principals, and the lesser characters are all a part of the choreographic fabric, which captures with brilliance, humor and touches of pathos an episode from life in the hearty, healthy, happy West."

In the fall of 1942, Copland adapted four dance episodes from his ballet score into an orchestral suite which received its first performance at a concert of the Boston Pops Orchestra, Arthur Fiedler conducting, on May 28, 1943. The first movement utilizes motives from two American folk songs, "Sis Joe" and "If He'd Be a Buckaroo by His Trade," which the composer found in *Our Singing Country,* edited by John A. and Alan Lomax. In the fourth movement, two square-dance tunes are quoted, "Bonyparte" and "McLoed's Reel."

1942 DANZÓN CUBANO, for orchestra.

The *Danzón* was originally written for two pianos as a birthday salute to the League of Composers; in this form it was introduced in New York in December of 1942, performed by Leonard Bernstein and the composer. The orchestral version was completed in Mexico during the summer of 1944, and was first heard on February 17, 1946, performed by the Baltimore Symphony under Reginald Stewart. Melodies and rhythmic elements elaborated in this score were heard and recorded by the composer during several visits to Cuba. A "danzón" is a highly popular Cuban dance. The composer explains that it "is normally constructed in two halves, which are thematically independent." However, the composer had no intention of writing an authentic "danzón" but only "an American tourist's impression of an absorbing Cuban dance form."

1944 APPALACHIAN SPRING, ballet in one act, with scenario and choreography by Martha Graham. First performance: Washington, D.C., October 30, 1944.

APPALACHIAN SPRING, ballet-suite for orchestra. I. Very Slowly. II. Sudden Burst of Unison Strings. III. Moderate. IV. Quite Fast. V. Still Faster. VI. Very Slowly. VII. Calm and Flowing. VIII. Moderate.

The composer has provided a history of this, one of his most successful works: "The music of the ballet takes as its point of departure the personality of Martha Graham. . . . At long intervals, Miss Graham and I planned to collaborate on a stage work. Nothing might have come of our intention if it were not for the lucky chance that brought Mrs. Elizabeth Sprague Coolidge to a Graham performance for the first time early in 1942. With typical energy, Mrs. Coolidge translated her enthusiasms into action. She invited Martha Graham to create three new ballets for the 1943 annual fall festival of the Coolidge Foundation in Washington, and commissioned three composers—Paul Hindemith, Darius Milhaud, and myself—to compose scores especially for the occasion.

"After considerable delay, Miss Graham sent me an untitled script. I suggested certain changes, to which she made no serious objections. I began work on the music of the ballet in Hollywood in June, 1943, but didn't complete it until a year later, in June, 1944, in Cambridge, Mass.

"The title, *Appalachian Spring,* was chosen by Miss Graham. She borrowed it from the heading of one of Hart Crane's poems, though the ballet bears no relation to the text of the poem itself."

The scenario is a simple presentation of a Pennsylvania housewarming party in the Appalachian mountains by a husbandman and his bride in pioneer times. Assisting in the ceremony are a pioneer woman, a revivalist and four of his followers. But as John Martin explained in his review in *The New York Times,* "the Spring that is being celebrated is not just any Spring but the Spring of America; and the celebrants are not just half a dozen individuals but ourselves in different phases." Then Martin adds: "It is completely simple, homely, dedicated, and a lovelier work you would have to go far to find. . . . The work has a rare unity and an irresistible winsomeness."

Appalachian Spring received the New York Music Critics Circle Award. In the spring of 1945, Copland arranged some of the best passages into an orchestral suite. After being introduced by the New York Philharmonic under Artur Rodzinski on October 4, 1945, this composition brought its composer the Pulitzer Prize in music. It has since become one of Copland's most frequently heard symphonic works.

The following is a terse description of the eight sections, which are played without interruption:

I. Very Slowly—The Introduction of the Characters.

II. Sudden Burst of Unison Strings, marking the beginning of the action. The sentiment here expressed combines elation with religious feeling.

III. Moderate (Duo for the Bride and Her Intended), a tender and passionate scene.

IV. Quite Fast (The Revivalist and His Flock). The feeling is folklike, with echoes of country fiddlers and suggestions of square dances.

V. Still Faster (Solo Dance of the Bride). The extremes of joy and fear are here voiced.

VI. Very Slowly (as at first). This is a transition scene in which the music brings up recollections of the introduction.

VII. Calm and Flowing (Scenes of Daily Activity for the Bride and her Farmer-Husband). A Shaker theme is heard, followed by five variations. The theme (solo clarinet) is derived from an actual Shaker melody entitled *Simple Gifts.*

VIII. Moderate (Coda). The married couple is left alone in their new home. Music that is almost reverent is intoned by muted strings. The final measures recall the opening pages.

1946 SYMPHONY NO. 3. I. Molto moderato, with simple expression. II. Allegro molto. III. Andantino quasi allegretto. IV. Molto deliberato (Fanfare); Allegro risoluto.

In the summer of 1944, during a stay in a small Mexican village, Copland began working on a new symphony that had been commissioned by the Koussevitzky Music Foundation. The first movement was completed the following April, the second in August of the same year. The third and fourth movements were written between January and September of 1946. On October 18, 1946, the symphony was introduced in Boston by the Boston Symphony Orchestra under Koussevitzky. The New York Music Critics Circle gave it its annual award for the best new work by an American composer.

Unlike so many other works by Copland written in this period, the symphony does not call upon ideas from folk-music sources, American or foreign. Except for the fact that it occasionally borrows brief subjects from earlier Copland works (in the opening movement a tonal device stems from *Appalachian Spring,* while the last movement quotes from *Fanfare for the Common Man*), the symphony contains only original material, all of it of compelling force and vitality. Serge Koussevitzky described it as "the greatest American symphony—it goes from the heart to the heart."

Copland has described the work in the following way:

"The opening movement, which is broad and expressive in character, opens and closes in the key of E major. . . . The themes—three in number—are plainly stated: the first in strings at the very start without introduction; the second, in related mood, in violas and oboes; the third, of a bolder nature, in trombones and horns. . . . The form [of the second movement] stays closer to normal symphonic procedure. It is the usual Scherzo, with the first part, trio, and return. . . . The third movement is the freest of all in formal structure. Although it is built sectionally, the various sections are intended to emerge one from the other in continuous flow, somewhat in the manner of a closely knit series of variations. . . . The final movement follows without pause. It is the longest movement of the symphony, and closest in structure to the customary sonata-allegro form."

1948 THE RED PONY, suite for orchestra. I. Morning on the Ranch. II. The Gift. III (a) Dream March (b) Circus Music. IV. Walk to the Bunkhouse. V. Grandfather's Story. VI. Happy Ending.

Early in 1948, Copland wrote the background music for the motion picture *The Red Pony,* based on John Steinbeck's story. The movie was produced by Lewis Milestone and starred Myrna Loy and Robert Mitchum. Later the same year, Efrem Kurtz commissioned Copland to adapt his movie score into a symphonic suite. Kurtz conducted the première with the Houston Symphony on October 30, 1948.

The motion picture described the life of a ten-year-old boy, Jody, on a California ranch. There is little action. Most of the interest in the film rises from the character sketches of the boy, his grandfather, Billy Buck (a cowhand) and the Tiflins (Jody's parents). "The kind of emotions that Steinbeck evokes in his story are basically musical ones," Copland has said, "since they deal so much with the unexpressed feelings of daily living."

The composer described the six movements as follows:

"I. *Morning on the Ranch.* Sounds of daybreak. The daily chores begin. A folklike melody suggests the atmosphere of simple country living.

"II. *The Gift.* Jody's father surprises him with the gift of a red pony.

Jody shows off his new acquisition to his school chums, who cause quite a commotion about it.

"III. *Dream March* and *Circus Music*. Jody has a way of going off into daydreams. Two of them are pictured here. In the first, Jody imagines himself with Billy Buck at the head of an army of knights in silvery armor; in the second, he is the whip-cracking ringmaster at the circus.

"IV. *Walk to the Bunkhouse*. Billy Buck was a 'fine hand with horses,' and Jody's admiration knows no bounds. This is a scene of the two pals on their walk to the bunkhouse.

"V. *Grandfather's Story*. Jody's grandfather retells the story of how he led a wagon train 'clear across the plains to the coast.' But he can't hide his bitterness from the boy. In his opinion, 'Westering has died out of the people. Westering isn't a hunger anymore.'

"VI. *Happy Ending*. Some of the title music is incorporated into the final movement. There is a return to the folklike melody of the beginning, this time played with boldness and conviction."

1948 CONCERTO FOR CLARINET AND STRING ORCHESTRA. I. Slowly and Expressively; Cadenza. II. Rather Fast.

Since this work was commissioned by Benny Goodman, "The King of Swing," it was to be expected that popular elements would be introduced into its musical texture. And the popular ideas employed by the composer stem not only from American but also from South American sources: the secondary material, for example, is based on a popular Brazilian melody. The first movement, in simple song form, is ingratiatingly melodic throughout. A cadenza for the solo instrument is the transition to the second and final movement, which comes without interruption and is in the form of a free rondo. This cadenza anticipates thematic material to be used in the ensuing movement. "Some of this material," the composer explains, "represents an unconscious fusion of elements obviously related to North and South American popular music. (For example, a phrase from a . . . popular Brazilian tune, heard by the composer in Rio, becomes embedded in the secondary material in F major.) The overall form of the final movement is that of a free rondo, with several side issues developed at some length. It ends with a fairly elaborate coda in C major."

The world première of the Concerto took place in New York on November 6, 1950. Benny Goodman was the soloist with the NBC Symphony conducted by Fritz Reiner.

The Concerto was adapted into a ballet, *The Pied Piper*. With choreography by Jerome Robbins, it was produced by the New York City Ballet on December 4, 1951. The central character here is not from Hamelin but is a clarinetist whose music has a hypnotic effect on all those who hear him.

1950 QUARTET FOR PIANO AND STRINGS. I. Adagio serioso. II. Allegro giusto. III. Non troppo lento.

The String Quartet, commissioned by the Elizabeth Sprague Coolidge Foundation, received its first performance at the Library of Congress in

Washington, D.C., on October 29, 1950. The New York Quartet performed. This is the first work in which Copland used the twelve-tone system. In the first movement, which has an overall fugal character, the first theme is in a twelve-tone row, while the second is a retrograde of that row. The lively second movement has a jazz-like vitality, while the finale has a quiet, introspective character "in the regions of immobility," says Lawrence Morton, out of which comes "some of Copland's most characteristic and beautiful music."

1950 TWELVE POEMS OF EMILY DICKINSON, for voice and piano. 1. Nature, the Gentlest Mother. 2. There Came a Wind Like a Bugle. 3. Why Do They Shut Me Out of Heaven? 4. The World Feels Dusty. 5. Heart, We Will Forget Him. 6. Dear March, Come In. 7. Sleep Is Supposed to Be. 8. When They Come Back. 9. I Felt a Funeral in My Brain. 10. I've Heard an Organ Talk Sometimes. 11. Going to Heaven! 12. The Chariot.

Emily Dickinson's poems have philosophic overtones, as they touch on such subjects as Nature (Nos. 1, 2, 6, 8), Death (Nos. 4 and 9), Life (Nos. 5, 7 and 10) and Eternity (Nos. 3 and 11). The twelfth song, which Julia Smith describes as the most abstract of the group, recalls a passage from No. 7 about sleep, "a quality of life." Miss Smith remarks: "Lending a cyclic summarization to the form, the composer eloquently closes his song cycle, combining the thoughts of Life, Death and Eternity."

Since Miss Dickinson's concepts are essentially intellectual, Copland, in his music-writing, reverted to the more abstract and objective manner he had crystallized in the late 1920s. "Almost completely homophonic in texture," says Miss Smith, "the piano accompaniments are exceedingly expressive, having captured the mood and introspective quality of the poems."

1954 THE TENDER LAND, an opera in three acts, with libretto by Horace Everett. First performance: New York City Opera, April 1, 1954.

To help celebrate the thirtieth anniversary of the League of Composers, Richard Rodgers and Oscar Hammerstein II commissioned Copland to write his first adult opera. He complied with *The Tender Land,* which (like the composer's earlier ballets) was thoroughly American in personality, spirit and musical content. The libretto is set in a farm in America's Midwest. The time is the early 1930s, during the spring harvest. The main characters are Laurie, a farm girl (about to be graduated from high school) and Martin, a young harvester. They meet, fall in love, and decide to elope. But Martin reconsiders, loses heart and makes his escape. Heartbroken at being deserted, Laurie deserts the security of family and home to go out into the world in search of Martin.

Copland's score vibrates continually with folklike overtones, as in the atmospheric opening measures of the first act and the square-dance music and the quotation of the folk song "Courtin' Song" in the second. But the opera does not strum on a single string. Copland's harmonic and rhythmic writing has powerful dramatic effect, as in the love music of Laurie and Martin in the third act, with what Julia Smith describes as its "bitter-sweet polytonal harmonies enhanced by the composer's skilful use of dissonance"; also, in the extraordinarily effective quintet that brings the opera to its end, "The Promise of

Living." The score, as a whole, notes Miss Smith, is "sincere, indigenous, gay, lusty, at times powerfully beautiful, poignantly nostalgic, and emotionally moving."

Following the première in New York, librettist and composer revised their opera to tighten up the dramatic action and further develop character delineation. Some of these revisions were used when the opera was given at the Berkshire Music Center at Tanglewood on May 20, 1955. In 1959, the revised opera was revived at the Juilliard School of Music, and in 1965, Copland led a concert performance with the New York Philharmonic at the Lincoln Center for the Performing Arts.

1957 PIANO FANTASY, for solo piano.
ORCHESTRAL VARIATIONS.

The Piano Fantasy was written on a commission from the Juilliard School of Music to celebrate its fiftieth anniversary. It was dedicated to the memory of the brilliant young American pianist William Kapell (who had died in an airplane crash in 1953). The first performance was given by William Masselos in New York on October 25, 1957. This is absolute music which does not derive any of its materials or personality from American folk-song sources. "His aim," said Howard Taubman in *The New York Times,* "was to let his fancy roam in the rarest regions, concerned only with bringing back the choicest and deepest musical thoughts." Occasionally, Copland uses the twelve-tone technique, in spite of which the composition does not lack a feeling of tonality.

The *Orchestral Variations* originated as a composition for the solo piano—back in 1930 when it was called *Piano Variations* and was performed for the first time by the composer at a League of Composers concert in New York on January 4, 1931. At the request of the Louisville Orchestra in Kentucky, Copland orchestrated it a quarter of a century later. The Louisville Orchestra, led by Robert Whitney, introduced the orchestral version on March 5, 1958. Since the *Piano Variations* originated in 1930, it belonged to that period when Copland was interested in a complex, abstract style. To the audiences of 1930, the *Piano Variations* was cerebral and austere music. A quarter of a century later, as variations for a symphony orchestra, it appeared much less so. "What seemed unyielding has become malleable," said Howard Taubman. "The music has not changed; our capacity to respond has. . . . [It has] breadth and vigor, economy and transparency and . . . dignity and becoming richness of effect."

1960 NONET, for three violins, three violas, and three cellos.

In this one-movement chamber-music work, the composer reaches back to the Baroque era by adapting freely the form of the ricercare. Like the old ricercare, the Nonet often utilizes a contrapuntal style; and, also like the ricercare, it begins slowly, with long notes, and increases its tempo with shorter notes to reach towards a climactic peak. The way in which Copland uses his three groups of stringed instruments in opposition to one another once again suggests a Baroque structure—this time the concerto grosso. But, as Edward Downes explained in his program notes for the New York Philharmonic, "what is unlike the early Baroque form is a certain built-in symmetry . . . which instead of ending with its climax, recedes in volume, grows rhythmically quieter, and in its last pages brings back certain thematic sections of the beginning, but in their reverse order." The vigorous, at times acrid, harmonic language is also not of the Baroque period but of our own times.

The Nonet was commissioned by the Dumbarton Oaks Research Library to celebrate the fiftieth wedding anniversary of Mr. and Mrs. Robert W. Bliss. The work was introduced at Dumbarton Oaks, near Washington, D.C., on March 2, 1961. The composer explains that this work can also be performed by a large string ensemble, by doubling the number of violas and cellos and quadrupling the violins; or tripling the number of violas and cellos and sextupling the violins. As many as forty-eight players can be used.

1962 CONNOTATIONS, for orchestra.

This is Copland's first purely orchestral composition since his Third Symphony of 1946. It is also his first orchestral composition to use the twelve-tone technique. "The row," says the composer, "is first heard vertically in terms of three four-voiced chords with, needless to add, no common tones. When spelled out horizontally, these chords supply me with various versions of a more lyrical discourse."

Connotations was written on a commission from the New York Philharmonic for its first concert in its new auditorium, Philharmonic Hall at the Lincoln Center for the Performing Arts. Leonard Bernstein conducted its world première on that occasion—on September 23, 1962.

Here, as in the Nonet of 1960, Copland reveals an interest in old Baroque structures. In the Nonet, he had made free use of the ricercare. In *Connotations,* he returns to the chaconne. "A succession of variations based on the opening chords and their implied intervals supplies the framework," the composer explains. "The variations are sometimes recognizably separate, one from another, sometimes not. The problem . . . was to construct an overall line that had continuity, dramatic force and an inherent unity."

1964 MUSIC FOR A GREAT CITY, for orchestra. I. Skyline. II. Night Thoughts. III. Subway Jam. IV. Toward the Bridge.

The London Symphony Orchestra invited Copland to write a symphonic work to honor its sixtieth anniversary. In doing so, the composer decided to use some of the materials he had formerly employed in 1961 for a motion picture score, *Something Wild,* starring Carroll Baker. "The nature of the music in the film seemed to me to justify extended concert treatment," he said. "The four movements of the work alternate between evocations of big-city life with its external stimuli, and the more personal reactions of any sensitive nature to the varied experiences associated with urban living."

This suite was introduced in London on May 26, 1964, the composer conducting the London Symphony. A London correspondent to *The New York Times* reported that the composer's attitude in his music was "one of ironic and exasperated affection experienced in music that is both tense and tender."

1967 INSCAPE, for orchestra.

Inscape was commissioned by the New York Philharmonic to help celebrate its 125th anniversary. The world première took place at the University of Michigan on September 13, 1967, Leonard Bernstein conducting the New York Philharmonic. The title (a word borrowed from Gerard Manley Hopkins) meant to Copland a "quasi-mystical illumination" governing musical creation. This short composition, lasting only ten minutes, is built out of two twelve-tone rows. The composer explains that his writing here has "greater leaning toward tonal orientation than is customary in serial composition." To Allen Hughes, reviewing the work for *The New York Times,* "the music is slow for the most part and so skilfully fashioned that it has a familiar ring despite its dodecaphonic nature."

HENRY COWELL 1897–1965

In his thousand or so compositions (over two hundred of which were published), Henry Cowell cultivated four areas successfully. The first was that of experimentation, beginning with his fourteenth year, when he instinctively sought to create a new language and a new sound for music. This is the period in which he developed the tone-cluster technique (or, as he later preferred to designate it, the technique of "secondal harmonies"). Then there was the music he wrote on stimulation from his Irish ancestry: early piano pieces like *Lilt of Reel* and *Jig*, and later larger compositions like his *Gaelic Symphony* (1942), or symphonies like the Sixth (1955) where an Irish-like jig takes the place of the conventional scherzo. In the 1940s, Cowell discovered American rural hymnology, with which he had first become acquainted as a boy in Kansas. This was his third area of creative activity, the source of numerous compositions, most significantly the sixteen *Hymn and Fuguing Tunes* which he wrote for various instrumental or vocal combinations; this was also a form which he incorporated into some of his symphonies (Nos. 4, 5, 6, 7, 10, 12 and 15) and string quartets (Nos. 4 and 5), besides other works. A fourth development in his creative evolution was inspired by the Orient and the Near and Middle East: the *Persian Set,* for twelve instruments (1957); *Ongaku,* two Japanese pieces, for orchestra (1958); the *Madras Symphony* (No. 13), based on North and South Indian elements (1959); *Homage to Iran* (1959); and the Concerto for Koto and Orchestra (1964), the koto being a Japanese instrument similar to the ancient European table-harp.

Whatever direction his creativity took, Cowell's aesthetic philosophy, as Hugo Weisgal wrote, was "neither Americanism, nor internationalism, nor orientalism, but the expression of a profound *humanism*. He feels no personal responsibility for the continuity of any one inherited tradition, because he sees each of the world's great musical cultures as a part of a worldwide Art of Sound, within which no one tradition is 'better' or 'more important' than any other, and whose basic unity is discoverable behind the immense variety of man's musical imagination. . . . By his highly creative appropriation of basic forms and ideas from other parts of the world, Cowell has . . . significantly widened the horizons of Western symphonic art."

Cowell was born in Menlo Park, California, on March 11, 1897. Study of the violin began when he was five, and two years after that he appeared in a sonata recital. Compelled by illness to abandon the violin, he turned to composition. By the time he was fourteen, he could afford to buy a second-hand piano on which he began experimenting with new sounds. In his first piano piece, *Adventures in Harmony,* he already began using tone clusters (or secondal harmonies). This and other compositions were heard at the San Francisco Musical Club on March 11, 1912, when he made his debut as pianist-composer.

For three and a half years, beginning when he was seventeen, Cowell attended music classes at the University of California, where his most significant influence was Charles Seeger. Following an interruption of more than a year, during which he was bandmaster in the Army in World War I, Cowell spent two additional years of study at the Institute of Applied Music in New York.

Between 1923 and 1933, Cowell toured America and Europe in performances of his avant-garde piano music, which often inspired riots and annihilating criticisms. But several leading composers and musical scholars—including Bartók and Schoenberg—regarded Cowell's music seriously and invited him to make special appearances. Between 1930 and 1932, by virtue of Guggenheim Fellowships, Cowell devoted himself to musicological studies of non-European folk and primitive music. Later in life, he did a considerable amount of firsthand study and research in the music of the Near East, the Middle East and the Orient through funds provided by the Rockefeller Foundation under the sponsorship of the American Department of State.

Cowell was consistently a champion of new music. He founded organizations which published and performed new works; he edited magazines propagandizing new music; he wrote numerous articles and several books, delivered lectures, and taught at important schools and universities. From 1932 on, and for the next thirty years, he lectured and presented concerts of new music at the New School for Social Research in New York; from 1949 to 1965, he was adjunct professor of music at Columbia University.

During World War II, he served in the Office of War Information in charge of shortwave broadcasts of music. In 1948, he received a grant from the American Academy of Arts and Letters, becoming a member in 1951, and a vice-president in 1961. He received honorary doctorates from Wilmington College in 1954 and Monmouth in 1963. In 1962, he was presented with the Henry Hadley Medal for distinguished services to American music by the Society of American Composers and Conductors.

Cowell's last work was the Trio for Violin, Cello and Piano, completed in 1965. He died in Shady, New York, on December 11, 1965.

1912–1930 COMPOSITIONS FOR SOLO PIANO:
The Tides of Manaunaun; Dynamic Motion; Amiable Conversation; Advertisement; The Voice of Lir; Fabric; The Aeolian Harp; The Banshee; Lilt of Reel; The Harp of Life; Sinister Resonance.

There were two ways in which Cowell, early in his career, revolutionized piano music. The first was through the development of tone clusters (or secondal harmonies). This consists of harmonies built from simultaneous minor seconds, produced by banging fists, forearms or palms of the hands on the piano keys. Tone clusters were not Cowell's invention (though he knew nothing of other and earlier such attempts at discords). They had been utilized by Rebikoff and Charles Ives. But Cowell was the one who named this discordant harmonic scheme as tone clusters, and it is with Cowell that this term is invariably associated.

He achieved another revolution by standing at the side of the piano, bending towards the sounding board, and strumming on the strings with his fingers, or using his hands on the strings in various ways to produce unusual sound effects, and even at times stuffing objects between the strings.

Cowell produced tone clusters for the first time in 1911, when he was fourteen. He called the piece *Adventure in Harmony*. Another interesting feature of this composition is that it anticipated the composer's later fascination for the exotic music of the East, since one of its sections is entitled *Oriental.*

The Tides of Manaunaun (1912) was one of several piano pieces not only using tone clusters but also anticipating still another of Cowell's later creative trends, his dependence for his subject matter on Irish lore and backgrounds. In Irish mythology, Manaunaun was the god of the ocean and of the waves of the sea. Tone clusters produced by fists and forearms in low register accompany a Celtic-like tune. Irish lore was also the source for such other tone-cluster pieces as *The Voice of Lir* (1915), *Lilt of Reel* (1925) and *The Harp of Life* (1925). Wilfred Mellers points out that in *Lilt of Reel,* Cowell uses tone clusters as "an overflow of animal high spirits; they do not disguise, and are not meant to disguise, the fact that this is a jolly conventional Irish reel with no harmonic or rhythmic surprises."

In *Dynamic Motion* (1913), Cowell explored effects of high, dissonant overtones. *Amiable Conversation* (1914) was inspired by a conversation in a laundry between two Chinese which the composer overheard, one Chinaman speaking in a high-pitched voice, the other talking in a low register. In *Fabric* (1917), Cowell developed chords formed by several different rhythms; each of the three voices is here in an independent rhythm. *The Aeolian Harp* (1923) and *The Banshee* (1925) explored new piano sonorities, achieved by having the performer manipulate the strings on the soundboard. In the first piece, the sound is intended to simulate tones produced by the wind blowing through the strings of an Aeolian harp; in the second, the sound suggests the wailing of a ghost of Irish legend. In *Sinister Resonance* (1930), Cowell experimented with new piano sounds by simulating resonances and effects of a violin or cello (harmonics, pizzicati and so forth) on the soundboard strings.

Between 1923 and 1933, Cowell made five tours of Europe besides making appearances in the United States, offering recitals of his unusual pieces. Riots sometimes broke out at his performances. In Leipzig, in 1923, the police had to be called in. For a New York concert, the editor of a leading newspaper sent its sports writer to report on the "bout" between "Battling Cowell" and "Kid Knabe." But eventually the shock wore off: by 1940, over two hundred and fifty pianists gave public performances of Cowell's formerly provocative pieces in America and Europe.

1938 TOCCANTA, for flute, soprano, cello and piano. I. Allegro quasi Andante. II. Larghetto. III. Moderato pomposo ma vivo. IV. Andante con moto. V. Allegro.

The term "toccanta" was coined by Cowell to connote a composition which combined identifiable qualities of a cantata and a toccata: in short, a toccata with vocal implications. The vocalise for soprano—a sinuous, rhapsodic vocal line with ostinato accompaniment—suggests the nasal singing of the Near East. "A discreet exoticism gives the work its color," said the critic of the New York *Herald Tribune,* "while its technical means depends upon an occasional polytonal statement, a series of rhythmic ostinati and a sweeping lyric line of considerable poignancy and refinement." Three of the movements use all four instruments; the second and fourth movements, both Interludes, dispense with the piano.

1940 TALES OF OUR COUNTRYSIDE, suite for piano and orchestra. I. Deep Tides. II. Exultation. III. The Harp of Life. IV. Country Reel.

In its original form, the *Tales* consists of a series of piano pieces composed between 1922 and 1930. In 1940, they were expanded by the composer, integrated as a four-movement suite, and scored for piano and orchestra. Each of the four movements was written in a different state in this country: the first in California; the second in the hills of the Hudson River Valley; the third in Iowa; and the fourth in Kansas.

The origin of the *Tales* as a work for solo piano has influenced its style. Tone clusters are utilized (though discreetly) in the solo piano part and inject dramatic color into the entire composition. However, though the spice of dissonance is present, the suite is romantic and for the most part conservative. American country tunes exert a strong, if possibly unconscious, influence on the thematic material, which is folkloristic in character, even though entirely original with the composer.

The first performance took place in Atlantic City, New Jersey, on May 11, 1941. The composer was at the piano, and the All-American Orchestra was conducted by Leopold Stokowski.

1944 HYMN AND FUGUING TUNE NO. 2, for string orchestra.

In or about 1941, Cowell came across William Walker's collection of hymns by the old singing-school masters, *Southern Harmony*, which suddenly brought back memories of the music he had heard as a boy sung by the Primitive Baptists in Kansas and Oklahoma. "Cowell began to wonder," his wife has written, "what the result would have been if our musical culture had not cut itself off from its living roots as it did during the last century, overawed by the achievements of Europe. Suppose the musical elements which formed the style of the shaped-note hymns had been allowed to develop and to penetrate our art music, what might they have become in the modern symphonic fabric?

"The result of this query has been a series of pieces for various instrumental combinations, all under the title of *Hymn and Fuguing Tune.* Among these are two for strings, one for full orchestra, one for symphonic band, several for piano, one for voice or instruments in three parts, and another in five parts for viola and piano, another for string quartet. . . .

"The famous New England tanner, William Billings, is credited with the invention of what he called 'fuguing tunes.' Their polyphony consists of an innocent kind of approximate imitation, but the separate entries of the voices lend interest, so the idea was widely adopted, and 'fuguing tunes' are still sung with enthusiasm at least as far west as the Ozarks."

Cowell's first composition in the style of American rural hymnology was the *Hymn and Fuguing Piece,* for piano (1942). This was followed by the *Hymn and Fuguing Tune No. 1*, for band (1943), which the Goldman Band introduced in New York during the summer of 1943.

The *Hymn and Fuguing Tune No. 2*, for string orchestra, was his first successful work of this style. It is music of intense expression, occasionally exalted in mood, written with almost severe simplicity and classic purity. Its effect comes from its sustained contrapuntal eloquence. Here is how *Modern Music* described this music following its première: "Cowell's piece is fundamentally based on the English-Kentucky mountain modal system as set forth in the shaped-note hymns. However, this is only local color; the music itself indicates a new, serious and satisfying development in Cowell's long list of stylistic adventures. He has avoided the perils of folksong style and developed a pure and rich piece bearing a close relationship to the 17th-century English Fancy. . . . The characteristic form in this work is also similar to that of a Fancy in two parts and indicates that some sort of law must operate during the cultivation of a polyphonic styleout of just this kind of material."

Hymn and Fuguing Tune No. 2 received its first performance over the radio network of the National Broadcast Company in March of 1944, Henri Nosco conducting the NBC Symphony. The first public performance followed in New York on October 8, 1944, with Daniel Saidenberg conducting the Saidenberg Little Symphony.

1945 SONATA NO. 1 FOR VIOLIN AND PIANO. I. Hymn. II. Fuguing Style. III. Ballad. IV. Jig. V. Finale.

This violin sonata is one of many works in the rural American hymn style which Cowell favored during this period. In two of its movements, it also betrays the Celtic influence on the composer. Cowell wrote the sonata for the eminent virtuoso, Joseph Szigeti; but its première was not given by Szigeti but by Sol Babitz, in Los Angeles on November 10, 1947.

The work opens with a solemn hymn followed by a fuguing tune in sonata form. The slow movement is based on an old Irish-American ballad, "Come All Ye." The Jig that follows is in scherzo form in which, as the composer explains, "piano and violin counteract each other in canon at the start . . . and play as if they hadn't properly started together at several points." The finale "focuses the forces initiated in the other four into a short and energetic statement that falls apart just before the end as if momentarily distracted; then the music gathers itself together and broadens to a full close that recalls the initial Hymn."

1946 SHORT SYMPHONY (NO. 4). I. Hymn. II. Ballad. III. Dance. IV. Fuguing Tune.

Like Cowell's *Hymn and Fuguing Tunes,* this symphony is inspired by old hymns. These hymns are not imitated or reproduced, but are developed—as the composer's wife has explained—"with increased variety of rhythm and tempo, modal modulation, contrast of tonal color, and more extended polyphony."

Mrs. Cowell has also analyzed the symphony:

"The first movement (Allegro) presents without any introduction the melodic material on which the entire composition is based. The movement consists of three contrasting hymn-like tunes. The first is in chorale or psalm-tune style, with variations; next comes a flowing Andante melody, and last an energetic modal melody more strictly in the shaped-note hymn tradition than the first two. Each of these is repeated with extended melodic development.

"In accordance with symphonic convention, the next two (Andante and Vivace) are in song form and in dance form, based on secular American rhythmic and melodic elements. The second movement is built on a melody of the unaccompanied, narrative-ballad character, set in a tonal atmosphere suggestive of a backwoods landscape rather than a literal instrumental accompaniment. The dance movement, an elaborately developed jig melody, has a strong Irish flavor and a strong family resemblance to the tunes played for square dancing and for the solo jig competitions among loggers from Maine to Washington across the northern United States. . . .

"The last movement (Moderato con moto) consists of an introduction, a fuguing tune, and coda; the fullest development of the thematic material has been reserved for this moment. The fuguing tune is a development from the shaped-note style, with the addition of occasional dissonant notes in passing, retaining, however, the plainness of form and the polyphonic vigor of the style."

Richard Burgin and the Boston Symphony Orchestra introduced the *Short Symphony* in Boston on October 24, 1947.

1947 SYMPHONY NO. 7, for small orchestra. I. Maestoso. II. Andante. III. Presto. IV. Maestoso.

The Seventh Symphony was one of Cowell's most successful and widely played symphonic works up to that time. His wife explains the reason: "With the Seventh Symphony, the various facets of his creative activities fall into place, not as random bits of experiment but as steps in the inevitable expansion and integration of a powerful musical personality." The symphony was introduced in Baltimore by the Baltimore Symphony under Reginald Stewart on November 25, 1952.

The symphony represents a blending of several styles that had distinguished Cowell's earlier works: the modal writing of his *Hymn and Fuguing Tune* compositions; the dissonant polyphonic and harmonic schemes of his experimental works; and the Celtic style. Mrs. Cowell provides the following analysis:

"The opening treads firmly with a bright, rising melodic line and a sunny, early morning air. A subsidiary theme is lyrical, moving by contrast within a small range and the second theme is a see-saw reel tune, 'in fiddling style.' Out of the subsidiary theme there grows a fine swinging melody, introduced by the English horn and expanded as it goes to and fro in the orchestra. All three themes are developed together for a while. . . . In the concluding section of the movement the last two themes appear in reverse order, the reel concluding securely with a flourish.

"The second movement saunters in with a gently persistent pentatonic figure against which one of Cowell's fine Celtic-American ballad tunes is set. . . . The third movement is the characteristic Cowell scherzo movement which makes sophisticated use of a country dance style (jig). A broad sentimental episode several times interrupts the orchestra's interplay with the elements of the dance tune; this latter turns unexpectedly emphatic for a moment, then whimsical, disappearing as the music winds about mysteriously. Next the sentimental form of the tune recurs, just before the last form of the sentimental bit leads the music to slither decrescendo into a high-pitched silence.

"The Finale uses material from all three of the preceding movements, climbing steeply in the manner of the symphony's opening. . . . There are interruptions by episodes of busy discontinuity until the music gathers its forces and voices the initial theme in an augmented and alerted rhythm expressive of the great determination. . . . It climbs strongly to a satisfying height at the end."

1954 SYMPHONY NO. 11, "SEVEN RITUALS OF MUSIC." I. Andantino. II. Allegro. III. Lento. IV. Presto. V. Adagio; Vivace; Andante.

"There are seven rituals of music in the life of man from birth to death," says the composer. The first movement is gentle music describing the ritual of a child's sleep; towards the end we get a premonition of grief. In the second movement, we get the ritual of work, with prophetic hints of war; this music makes effective use of percussion instruments. The third movement is for the ritual of love, with premonition of magic. This is followed by music for the ritual of dance and play, with reminiscences of music for work; music for the ritual of magic and mystical imagination, with remembrance of music for magic and love; and music for the ritual of dance preparing for war, including a fragment of the music for the ritual of work. The finale begins with a fugal exposition of themes from the preceding parts. This leads to the music for the ritual of death, which opens as a lament and grows in intensity and passion until the end of the symphony.

The Eleventh Symphony received its world première in Louisville, Kentucky, on May 29, 1954.

1956 STRING QUARTET NO. 5. I. Lento. II. Allegro. III. Andante. IV. Presto. V. Largo; Allegro marcato.

Cowell's Fifth String Quartet was commissioned by the Elizabeth Sprague Coolidge Foundation. It was introduced by the Juilliard String Quartet in Washington, D.C., in October of 1956. Cowell revised the work in 1962.

Like so many of Cowell's earlier instrumental works, this one is based on the style and personality of old American hymn and fuguing tunes. The opening slow movement is a hymn in greatly modified form in which the voices, as the notes in the published score explain, "start together, low in the bass and high in the treble, moving toward each other as they approach the ends of phrases, and descending together into unison at the end of the movement." The second movement is a vigorous stretto, making use of secondal counterpoint. A contrast comes in the gentle third movement, a soft, tender melody colored by chords in seconds. The Presto is a fast scherzo in asymmetrical rhythm, and the finale is in the style of a hymn and fuguing tune, which begins in a slow hymn-like manner before progressing to the fast fuguing tune. "The fast fuguing tune reverts twice to the slower pace of a hymn phrase before it acquires the momentum that carries its development of themes from earlier movements forcefully ahead to the work's conclusion."

1961 SYMPHONY NO. 15, "THESIS." I. Largo; Andante; Presto; Allegretto; Allegro. II. Moderato.

Like the Eleventh Symphony, this one was given its world première by the Louisville Orchestra under Robert Whitney—on October 7, 1961, in Murray, Kentucky. The work is unusual for a symphony in that it is made up of brief movements: a chorale-like introduction; a passionate melody; a scherzo; a longer quiet melody; an irregular rhythm dance which the composer explains "leads to recapitulation of these elements in one movement; and at the end, a sonata form movement based on an extension of the primary motive (a descending whole step followed by a half step) which is the mainstay of all the movements." Actually, the composition is more like a suite than a symphony, but the composer tells us he decided to call the work a symphony because the last movement is in sonata form.

1963 CONCERTO GROSSO, for five instruments and orchestra. I. Maestoso; Allegro; Maestoso. II. Allegretto. III. Andante. IV. Allegro. V. Allegro.

Cowell here reverted to the old Baroque structure of the concerto grosso to focus attention upon a different solo instrument in each of the five movements, including a cadenza for that instrument. A hymn-like introduction opens the first movement, in which the cello is prominent. Sprightly motives suggesting a cakewalk, contrasted by a slower waltz-like section, appear in the second movement, in which the solo oboe is featured. This is followed by a slow section featuring the harp. A scherzo in the style of an Irish jig makes use of the solo flute, while the finale, built from Oriental and West-African modes, throws attention to the clarinet. In the finale, material from all earlier movements is recalled.

The première took place in Miami, Florida. Fabien Sevitzky conducted the University of Miami Symphony, on January 12, 1964.

PAUL CRESTON 1906–

Early in his career, Creston expressed a belief that the two fundamentals of all music were song and dance. The juxtaposition of song and dance, or prelude and dance, long intrigued him as a musical structure. It is found in works like the *Prelude and Dance*, op. 25 (1941), *Pastorale and Tarantella,* op. 28 (1941), *Prelude and Dance,* Nos. 1 and 2, op. 29 (1942), the Second Symphony, op. 35 (1944), *Invocation and Dance,* op. 58 (1953), and *Janus*, op. 77 (1959). He has shown little interest in experiments with new techniques; those evolved from past procedures serve him well. Yet he always maintains a personal point of view and a strong individuality—these and what John Rosenfeld once described as "the broadness and freshness of viewpoint that has encompassed the spirit of our times without disturbing the past." Rosenfeld then described Creston's music as a combination of "the Italian gift for song or lyricism with an arresting self-taught use of all that has been accomplished by expansive orchestral study."

Creston was born in New York City on October 10, 1906. Much of his music study took place autodidactically, by poring into texts, by memorizing published scores and by playing the piano. In 1932, Creston wrote his first composition, a set of five dances for the piano. Two years later, he became the organist of St. Malachy's Church in New York, where he stayed many years. The playing of the organ and teaching composition were the principal sources of his income for a long time after that.

His *Threnody* and the *Two Choric Dances,* in 1938, were his first compositions to attract attention, while his First Symphony, in 1940, gave him a high status among the younger composers in America. He received Guggenheim Fellowships in 1938 and 1939, and Citations of Merit from the National Association of American Composers and Conductors in 1941 and 1943. In 1943, he got a grant from the American Academy of Arts and Letters, as well as a Ditson Fund Award. From 1956 to 1960, he was president of the National Association of American Composers and Conductors. A grant from the United States Department of State enabled him to travel in Israel and Turkey in 1960. In 1961, he became a member of the board of directors of ASCAP, and in 1962, he was made Fellow of the International Institute of Arts and Letters.

1938 THRENODY, for orchestra, op. 16.

TWO CHORIC DANCES, for orchestra, op. 17. I. Slow. II. Majestic; Fast.

Though the composer suggests that this work is autobiographical, he gives no clue about the specific event in his life that inspired the emotional music of the *Threnody*. The first performance took place in Pittsburgh on December 2, 1938, Fritz Reiner conducting the Pittsburgh Symphony.

Muted strings introduce the first theme, which is in the style of a plainsong. Following the statement of the second subject by the violas, the emotional intensity increases until a climax is reached. From this point on, the work repeats preceding material, but in reverse: the second theme (slightly varied) appears before the first. The work ends elegiacally with a flute solo sounding a tender strain against a background of muted strings.

Creston originally wrote the *Two Choric Dances* for chamber orchestra, in which form it was introduced in 1938 at the Yaddo Music Festival, at Saratoga Springs, New York, under the direction of Arthur Shepherd. Creston soon rescored the work for full orchestra, and Arthur Shepherd once again conducted the première performance, this time in Cleveland with the Cleveland Orchestra, also in 1938.

The intention of the composer was to suggest through music the movements of a group of dancers rather than tell any specific story. While the composer suggests that the music might be adaptable for choreographic treatment, he insists that it is to be heard as pure music.

The first movement consists of an introduction and dance. "The unifying element in the dance," the composer writes, "is the undulating figure in the strings forming the accompaniment to the melody in the woodwinds. This figure is later transferred to the piano and tom-tom and becomes the basis of the climax with the whole orchestra taking part in it."

The second movement also begins with a brief introduction before a pronounced rhythmic figure is presented by the piano to introduce the dance. The second dance moves at a whirlwind pace (in contrast to the slow dance of the first movement), marked by frequent changes of rhythm, color and mood.

1940 SYMPHONY NO. 1, op. 20. I. With Majesty. II. With Humor. III. With Serenity. IV. With Gaiety.

Creston's Symphony No. 1 received its first performance in Brooklyn, New York, on February 22, 1941, with Fritz Mahler conducting the N.Y.A. Symphony Orchestra. Two years later, on March 23, 1943, Eugene Ormandy and the Philadelphia Orchestra performed it, at which time it aroused considerable enthusiasm. The New York Music Critics Circle selected it as the most important new symphonic work by an American heard that season. In 1952, it received the first prize in the Paris International Competition.

Creston has provided the following analysis:

"The opening movement is in free sonata-allegro form, the thematic material of which is presented in two distinct sections. Within the first six measures are announced three separate motives, rhythmic and vigorous in character, comprising the first group of themes; at measure sixteen is presented the contrasting lyric theme. During the development of this material the themes are intertwined, combined, fugally treated, and varied in many ways, and at times change their initial aspect so that the rhythmic themes become lyric and the lyric become dramatic.

"The second movement is a scherzo. Rhythm is the reigning element, with overlapping and subdivisional patterns abounding throughout. The middle section is cast in a lyric vein, but the rhythmic aspect of the movement is maintained in the alternating figure played by the cellos and the basses.

"In the third movement, the cellos present in its complete form the main theme which was suggested in the introduction by muted strings. The oboe takes up this theme and develops it differently. This leads to the second theme, which is passed from flute to clarinet to oboe to bassoon to trumpet, each time varied. After the climax, the movement returns to its original serenity with muted strings.

"The final movement is based on two themes, the first being again subdivided into two sections: one presented at the opening by the oboe and the other by the clarinet in the ninth measure. The second theme is presented by the brass choir in chordal structure. No new material is introduced at any time during the movement. Each time the first theme appears it does so in a different texture, is varied, and is treated in a different style. The conclusion presents a fragment of the second theme in augmentation with a fragment of the first against it."

1944 SYMPHONY NO. 2, op. 35. I. Introduction and Song. II. Interlude and Dance.

In Creston's Second Symphony, the song-and-dance form, which the composer so favored, receives its most ambitious treatment and its fullest realization up to that time.

The symphony was introduced in New York on February 15, 1945. Artur Rodzinski conducted the New York Philharmonic Orchestra.

The following analysis is by the composer:

"In the opening of the Introduction are presented four themes as a cumulative ground bass, i.e., successively superimposed. Theme one, played by the cellos, and theme two, played by violas, are the main bases of the entire symphony. Whatever new thematic material emerges is either a ramification or a development of these two themes.

"The Song is largely built on a variation of theme one, tender and simple in character, presented first by the flute and then by the horn. . . .

"The Interlude opens with a completely transformed theme one, quite aggressive and defiant, leading to a rather quiet section, but soon returning to the aggressive character. This last merges into the Dance without pause, which after a rhythmic introduction begins with another variant of theme one (muted trumpet). Each appearance of this variation of theme one alters further the rhythm and contour of the melody. As the excitement mounts, theme two soars above the ever-recurrent rhythmic pulses, developing to a climax and into the next section of the Dance. In the second section, based on a variation of theme one inverted, the rhythmic pattern has changed and there is a greater sense of driving forward. This theme variant goes through several metamorphoses as the section builds into a major climax and then subsides to an altered version of the original cumulative ground bass. Above the three concurrent rhythms which were presented earlier in the Dance, the flute theme of the Song (now played by the violins), becoming more and more intense, brings the composition to a close."

1949 CONCERTO FOR PIANO AND ORCHESTRA, op. 43. I. Allegro maestoso. II. Andante tranquillo. III. Presto.

Creston completed his piano concerto in July, 1949, and dedicated it to the memory of Joseph D. Malkin, a Philadelphia music lover. It was introduced in the same year in France by Earl Wild and the Radiodifussion française de Lille, Chauncey Kelley conducting.

Creston has prepared the following analysis of his concerto:

"The first movement opens with a vigorous presentation of the main theme by the full orchestra, soon taken up by the piano in a rather rhapsodic style and leading to the second theme (cellos and basses) with arabesque figurations in the solo. This second theme in augmentation forms the basis of a quietly lyric section which ensues. After a short orchestral interlude, a fuller development of the two themes and moods is presented, closing in brilliant style.

"The second movement is pastoral in mood and is also based on two principal themes, the first tranquil and lyric, and the second slightly agitated. The development of these themes is entrusted largely to the solo instrument.

"The third movement is quite rhythmic in character and has much the feeling of a tarantella, although several un-Italian rhythms make their appearance here and there. The rhythmic drive is maintained throughout, even in the less impetuous section."

1950 SYMPHONY NO. 3 ("THREE MYSTERIES"), op. 48. I. The Nativity. II. The Crucifixion. III. The Resurrection.

Creston was commissioned to write his Third Symphony by the Worcester Music Festival to honor the memory of Aldus C. Higgins. It was completed in July, 1950, and was introduced in Worcester, Massachusetts, by the Philadelphia Orchestra under Eugene Ormandy on October 27, 1950.

The symphony, inspired by the "three mysteries," draws generously from the melodic storehouse of the Gregorian chant. It is not, the composer insists, a narrative or a painting, but rather "a musical parallel of the inherent emotional reactions" aroused by these religious events.

The first movement (Lento; Allegro moderato) is based on two Gregorian themes: the first is heard in the horn in the middle of the slow introduction; the second appears in the flute in a subdued section which follows the main climax. The movement ends with a fugato on the first theme.

Another Gregorian melody, played on the solo cello against a brass accompaniment, opens the second movement (Adagio). This melody is transformed into a passacaglia-like theme for the cellos, and against it is set the fragments of a second Gregorian theme. The spiritual calm passes into a brief section of great agitation, but soon returns with a restatement of the two subjects.

In the third movement (Lento moderato; Allegro ma calmo), a Gregorian melody is present in its entirety (cellos and basses). This leads to the second theme, a Gregorian theme heard in the horns. The introduction ended, the Allegro section emerges with animation. This section, says the composer, is "based primarily on the sequence for Easter, *Victimae paschali laudes,* perhaps the best known of all the themes utilized in this work. The original rhythmic structure of the Gregorian melodies is more closely retained in the second and third movements than in the first, although the actual melodic contour is evident in all of them."

1951 SYMPHONY NO. 4, op. 52. I. Maestoso. II. Andante pastorale. III. Allegretto giocoso. IV. Vivace saltellante.

This symphony was commissioned by Viola Malkin as a memorial to her husband, Joseph D. Malkin. It was introduced by the National Symphony Orchestra under Howard Mitchell on January 30, 1952, in Washington, D.C.

The first movement opens with an introduction which leads to the Allegro, in which the first principal theme is announced by the clarinet, and the second by the violins. Fragments of the thematic material are tossed from choir to choir, resolving into a full orchestral presentation of the first theme. The lyrical and gay elements are alternately presented in an increasing measure of excitement until the final triumphant outburst of the second principal theme in the brasses against the first principal theme in the rest of the orchestra.

The second movement is in three-part form, the first consisting of a pastoral melody, the second of a slightly restrained shepherd's dance, and the third a recapitulation of the pastoral song. The third movement is also in three sections, the outside parts featuring a jesting theme in various solo instruments and a muted pizzicato section for strings, with the middle portion devoted to a legato and lyric passage for strings. The fourth and concluding movement has the character of a tarantella. The pitch of excitement is almost constantly high, with intricate rhythms abounding throughout. The concluding section is a rapid résumé of all themes previously presented.

1955 SYMPHONY NO. 5, op. 64. I. Con Moto. II. Largo. III. Maestoso; Allegro.

Creston's Fifth Symphony was written for the twenty-fifth anniversary of the National Symphony Orchestra of Washington, D.C., which introduced it on April 4, 1956, Howard Mitchell conducting. "The keynote of the emotional basis of this symphony," explains the composer, "is intensity, and the feeling is generally one of spiritual conflicts which are not resolved until the final movement." The composer goes on to explain the construction as follows: "All the thematic material stems from the series of tones presented at the very beginning by cellos and basses, evenly measured, but irregularly grouped. From these tones three definite, rhythmically patterned themes evolve: the first, aggressive and defiant; the second, lyric and impassioned (an inversion of the first theme); and the third, tender and poignant (played by the flute)."

1957 TOCCATA, for orchestra, op. 68.

The Cleveland Orchestra commissioned Creston to write a symphonic work for its fortieth anniversary. The Toccata was the result, completed in

June of 1957, and introduced on October 17 of the same year. This is a brilliant showpiece exploiting sonorities and highlighting the virtuoso capabilities not only of the orchestra's component choirs but also of individual instruments. "Notice," wrote Arthur Loesser in his program notes for the Cleveland Orchestra, "the solo clarinet, not long after the beginning, sweeping way up high: a dancing, squirming skyrocket. Two interlocked flutes follow it presently, in a similar but shorter gyration. After a time the dignified tenor trombone breaks into an unexpected nimbleness, while the grave tuba is made to swing sweetly, and richly accompanied, in a still later slower middle section." Loesser explains that the composition may also well be regarded as a study in rhythm: "An examination of the composer's tabulation of possible single rhythms, that is, excluding polyrhythms, would reveal well over one hundred rhythms available in 3/4, but it would be sheer folly to attempt to include all of them in one composition. The listener is advised to direct the attention to the overall resultant sounds rather than trying to count the rhythms as they occur."

1959 JANUS, for strings, piano, and percussion, op. 77.

The title, the composer reveals, "is merely a means of identification and not descriptive of the composition. Any resemblance to the two-faced ancient Italian deity is purely coincidental, although the bipartite form of the work suggested the title. This two-part form follows the composer's favorite procedure of coupling a song or prelude with a dance. *Janus* opens with a slow, lyric first section (the prelude) and continues with a fast, highly rhythmic second section (the dance). A single theme is the basis of both parts; it is presented at the beginning by the oboe.

"Although it is written in 3/4 meter throughout," the composer explains, "there are multimeters, polymeters, various rhythmic structures and polyrhythms. The rhythmic element is predominant, not in the sense of merely strong accentuation, but in the basic structure of the work."

Janus was commissioned by the Association of Women's Committees for Symphony Orchestras. It was introduced by the Denver Symphony under Saul Caston on July 17, 1959.

1960 CONCERTO NO. 2 FOR VIOLIN AND ORCHESTRA, op. 78. I. Allegro. II. Andante. III, Presto.

This concerto was commissioned by the Ford Foundation for the violinist Michael Rabin, who introduced it on November 17, 1960, in Los Angeles as a soloist with the Los Angeles Philharmonic, Georg Solti conducting.

The composer provides the following analysis:

"The first movement, in modified sonata-allegro form, opens with a statement of the principal theme by two horns at a rather leisurely pace but gaining momentum through smaller units of the measure, culminating in the dramatic and rhapsodic entrance of the solo violin. After five measures, the solo violin calms down to the lyrical principal theme, singing with passion and abandon, and leading to the second, running and rhythmic, theme punctuated by pulsating passages in the orchestra. . . .

"The solo violin opens the second movement with a statement of the principal theme, which is picked up first by the flute, then the horn, and finally the violins, brought to a minor climax until the reentry of the solo violin. The development of this principal theme leads to the second section of the three-part form: a scherzo-like pastoral dance which leads to a forty-six measure cadenza for the soloist. At the end of the cadenza, the oboe enters with the principal theme, the solo violin later taking it up and bringing the movement to a quiet close.

"The final movement, in rondo form (A-B-A-C-A), begins with a six-measure orchestral introduction to the "A" section in the solo violin. The "B" theme, presented by flute and oboe in fourths, is actually an augmented, rhythmically altered "A" theme. The "C" theme is first presented by the two oboes with an undulating accompaniment in the solo violin, continued by two flutes, developed to a major climax and taken up by the solo violin in triumphant style. . . . In this movement, rhythm is the most important element, while form was most important in the first and melody in the second. Consequently, within the duple meter (two pulses to the measure) various musical and rhythmic structures are employed: regular, irregular, overlapping, polymetric and polyrhythmic. The final movement ends, naturally, with a brilliant passage in the solo violin."

1963 CORINTHIANS: XIII, for orchestra, op. 82.

For a number of years, Creston had been impressed with the musical possibilities of the apotheosis of love as expressed in the thirteenth chapter of St. Paul's Epistle to the Corinthians. He finally fulfilled this project in December of 1963 on a commission from Bruce Irwin for the Phoenix Symphony, which introduced it under the direction of Guy Tayloron on March 30, 1964. The published score explains that this composition "is neither an exegesis nor a painting, but an emotional parallel of three manifestations of love: the love between mother and child, between man and woman, and between man and mankind." It has three sections, together with an introduction and an episode bridging the first and second sections. To point up his belief that all manifestations are "in essence, *one*," Creston uses only a single theme, heard in the introduction in the bassoon. "The theme, however, is transformed and developed differently in the second and third sections to fit the particular moods," the published score explains. "Midway in the second section a short love dance is incorporated. In its transformation for the third section—love between man and mankind—the theme becomes, almost naturally and logically, the Gregorian melody, *Salve Regina,* which is utilized with a minimum of alteration."

1966 PAVANE VARIATIONS, for orchestra, op. 89.

This fifteen-minute composition was commissioned by the Men's Advisory Board of the La Jolla Musical Society. The first performance was given by the La Jolla Orchestra, Milton Katims conducting, on August 21, 1966. The composer explains that the composition consists of twelve variations on four twelve-tone rows with the accompaniment of the Pavane rhythm. He emphasizes, however, that the work is not in a serial technique.

LUIGI DALLAPICCOLA 1904–

Dallapiccola is the first significant Italian composer to use the twelve-tone technique; and he is still the most significant one. Though his allegiance to dodecaphony has for many years been unshakable, he has, nevertheless, succeeded in retaining his Italian identity through his strong predilection for the voice and the lyric line; through his bent for romantic or dramatic expression; and through his frequent ties to and reflections of the Italian past of the Renaissance and the Baroque eras. He started out with strong Romantic leanings before experimenting tentatively with the twelve-tone technique in the finale of his *Divertimento in quattro esercizi* (1934) and more decisively in parts of his *Canti di Prigionia* (1941). His first composition to be entirely based on a twelve-tone row was a cycle of songs on ancient Greek poems, *Sex Carmina Alcaei* (1943). From then on, he continued for a number of years to work with the twelve-tone system according to his own principles and ideas until in or about 1950, when his approach and technique became stricter and more faithful to the principles of Anton Webern. But even then, his Italian background and temperament asserted themselves.

Dallapiccola, the son of a professor of classical languages, was born in Pisino, Istria, on February 3, 1904. He began studying the piano when he was five. With Istria then under Austrian rule, Italians were placed in detention camps when World War I broke out. The Dallapiccolas were confined with them, then shipped to Graz, Austria, where they stayed for about two years. There Dallapiccola became convinced, by hearing and learning the operas of Mozart and Wagner, that he wanted to be a composer. After the war, the Dallapiccolas returned to Istria, where Luigi studied piano and harmony. In 1922, he entered the Cherubini Conservatory in Florence, graduating in piano playing in 1924, and composition in 1931. In 1934, he was appointed professor of piano at the Conservatory.

Dallapiccola first attracted interest as a composer with his Partita for Orchestra (1932), introduced in Florence on January 22, 1933, and then featured at the festival of the International Society for Contemporary Music on April 2, 1934. After that, major works for chorus (*Cori di Michelango,* in 1933), for voice (*Divertimento in quattro esercizi,* in 1934 and *Tre Laudi,* in 1937), and for the stage (*Volo di notte,* in 1939) gave him a front rank among the younger Italian composers. On April 30, 1938, he married Lauro Coen Luzzato, a Jewish girl, even though he himself was a Roman Catholic. With Mussolini embarked on an anti-Semitic program just before World War II, and with the Nazis occupying Florence during the war, the Dallapiccolas felt the full force of persecution and oppression, often having to go into hiding to escape imprisonment—an experience that stirred Dallapiccola both as man and as artist. Under this impact, he produced a number of works dominated by the subject of liberty, the most significant being the *Canti di prigionia,* or *Songs of Captivity,* in 1941, and the opera *Il Prigioniero,* in 1948.

Dallapiccola paid his first visit to the United States in the summer of 1951 to teach a master class in composition at the Berkshire Music Center at Tanglewood. He returned there the following summer. On August 16, 1952, he made his American debut as pianist by appearing as soloist with the NBC Symphony in the American première of his *Piccolo concerto,* for piano and orchestra. In 1956–1957, and again in 1959–1960, he was professor of music at Queens College, in Queens, New York, and in 1962–1963, he occupied the Chair of Italian Culture at the University of California in Berkeley. All-Dallapiccola concerts, first in Mexico City on September 22, 1952, then in New York City in 1959 and 1964, offered a cross section of his creative activity over a thirty-year period. Among the many honors he has received are the Grosser Musikpreis in Düsseldorf in 1962 and the Ludwig Spohr Preiz in Braunschweig in 1964.

1943 MARSIA, ballet in one act, with scenario by A. M. Milloss. First performance: Teatro Fenice, Venice, September 9, 1948.

MARSIA, ballet-suite for orchestra. I. Danza Magico. II. Danza di Appollo. III. Ultima Danza di Marsia. IV. La Morte di Marsia.

This was Dallapiccola's first major success for the stage. The music combined the tensions and the severity of an atonal style with dramatic power, but was softened from time to time by poetic moods. The story is as follows:

Marsia discovers sound by blowing into a flute. Excited by the music he is making, he goes into a feverish dance, at the climax of which he comes upon Apollo. Challenged by Marsia to a contest in producing beauty of sound, Apollo calls on the Muses to act as judges. Marsia plays and dances, and with such fire that the forest nymphs come to join him in his dance. But when Apollo goes into his music and dance, there can be no question that he is the superior. The Muses condemn Marsia to death by being skinned alive, and they raise Apollo high on their shoulders. Marsia dies in the arms of the forest nymphs, who grieve at his passing until their bodies become tears and mingle with Marsia's blood to form the Marsia River.

A symphonic suite derived from the ballet has been performed frequently in Europe and America—in America, for the first times, in 1950 with performances by the NBC Symphony under Guido Cantelli and the New Orleans Symphony under Massimo Freccia.

1946 DUE PEZZI (TWO PIECES), for orchestra. I Sarabande. II. Fanfare and Fugue.

These *Two Pieces* originated as *Two Etudes* for violin and piano (1946). Their inspiration was the frescoes of Pierro della Francesco in the church of St. Francis in Arezzo. As Dallapiccola recalled these frescoes, they emphasized two colors: white in the *Entry of the Queen of Sheba,* and red in the *Defeat of*

Chosroes, King of the Persians. Consequently, he tried to re-create in his two pieces the tonal qualities of these two colors. Soon after he himself had introduced the etudes for violin and piano (with Sandro Materassi), in Basle, Switzerland, Dallapiccola orchestrated them—the orchestral version heard first in 1947 in a radio performance by the BBC Symphony in London; the concert performance followed later the same year, by the Brussels Philharmonic in Belgium.

In this work, the twelve-tone technique is used freely. Two twelve-tone rows are used, the first opening the first-movement Sarabande. "I wanted to call it White Sarabande," says the composer, "but dropped the adjective at the last minute in order not to fall into literature." By contrary motion, this row becomes the countersubject of the fugue, while the second tone row serves as a second theme; this, in turn, is used as the principal subject of the fugue. The brief Fanfare that serves to introduce the Fugue is based on the second tone row. "In the Sarabande," the composer says, "the general shading is pianissimo (one single passage of three notes is written mezzo forte, and diminuendo, at that); but in the Fanfare and Fugue, the general shading is forte to fortissimo. No mezzo-forte."

1948 IL PRIGIONIERO (THE PRISONER), opera in one act and prologue, with text by the composer based on *La Torture par l'Espérance,* by Conte Villiers de l'Isle Adam, and Charles de Coster's *La Légende d'Ulenspiegel.* First performance: Turin Radio, November 30, 1949; first public performance, Teatro Communale, Florence, May 20, 1950.

On the very day in September of 1938 when Dallapiccola first began working on this opera, his wife lost her job at the National Library in Florence because she had been born Jewish—Mussolini then having embarked on an official anti-Semitic campaign. Thus the evils of Fascism, over which Dallapiccola had long been brooding, penetrated his home. During the decade that followed, the decade in which he worked on his opera on and off, Dallapiccola was to experience the full horrors of war, of persecution, of the loss of human dignity and freedom—particularly after September 11, 1943, when the Nazis marched into Florence. There were times after that when the Dallapiccolas had to go into hiding to evade house arrest. Thus *The Prisoner*—with its message of freedom—had deep personal implications for the composer. This is undoubtedly the reason why, without abandoning the twelve-tone technique, he was able to fill his writing with such a wealth of drama and humanity. Like Beethoven in *Fidelio,* Dallapiccola used his opera to sing a paean of praise to human liberty.

The setting of the opera is Flanders during the sixteenth-century Inquisition. In the prologue, a mother reveals to her son, the prisoner, that she has been troubled in her dreams by the appearance of Philip II. The first scene finds the prisoner expressing to his mother his hope for liberation. The guard has been calling him "Brother." His hopes mount in the second scene when the guard describes to him the outbreak of revolt among the Protestants and prognosticates the imminent downfall of Philip II. The guard, having left the cell door unlocked, provides the prisoner with an opportunity for escape. In the third scene, the prisoner passes as a monk. In the concluding scene, the prisoner encounters the Grand Inquisitor; he is none other than the cell guard himself, who had concocted the whole story about the revolt, in order to torture his prisoner with false hopes. Broken in spirit, his mind giving way, the prisoner offers no resistance as he is being led to the stake. He can only mutter the single word: "Freedom."

On March 15, 1951, *The Prisoner* was introduced in the United States by the Juilliard School of Music in New York. Describing the opera in his review for *The New York Times*, Howard Taubman wrote: "It is a work that, in its music and its bare, symbolic action, projects the horror of a fear-ridden world. . . . His music . . . seems to be an amalgam of the newest and oldest trends in music. . . . Dallapiccola reserves his most eloquent writing for the orchestra. He is a master of vivid and moving tonal combinations. And when he combines his orchestra with chorus toward the end, he achieves a shattering effect. . . . In sum, this is a composer and a work of individuality."

1950 JOB, dramatic oratorio for solo voices, chorus and orchestra.

Dallapiccola described his oratorio as a "*sacra rappresentazione*," or "sacred drama." He wrote it upon being stimulated by a photograph of a sculpture by Jacob Epstein, *Behold the Man*. Like other of the composer's works, this one is in a twelve-tone technique, based on a single row. But, as Frederick Prausnitz pointed out, the composer "allows himself such latitude in the manipulation and permutation of its tones that it turns into a practically new row when it pleases him."

There is very little action, with a good deal of the Job story commented upon by the choral groups representing God (the group used both in unison and canonically) and Satan. Other voices speak for Job, the Four Messengers, and Job's friends. A narrator serves as a catalytic agent. In giving this musical setting, the composer had human problems uppermost in mind. "The purely symbolic, unreal quality of its actors, except Job, brings the humanity of this Man of Sorrows into high relief," says Prausnitz.

Job received its world première in Rome on October 31, 1950. When first given in the United States (in New York on December 19, 1958), it was performed twice during the same evening, to provide the audience with an opportunity to become better acquainted with the composer's complex technique and idiom.

1951 TARTINIANA, for violin and orchestra. I. Larghetto. II. Allegro assai. III. Andante affettuoso. IV. Presto assai.

As the title suggests, *Tartiniana* is based on melodies by Giuseppe Tartini (1692–1770). Dallapiccola's work was commissioned by the Koussevitzky Music Foundation, its world première taking place in Berne, Switzerland, on March 4, 1952.

The composer's method here is similar to the one he had previously (1943) used in *Sonate-Canonica,* for solo piano, which had been based on Paganini's Caprices. This method is to use the diatonic melodies of the older composer, conceived along the lines of the basso-continuo technique, and to employ them in the strict canonic style allowed by the twelve-tone system. All of Dallapiccola's themes come out of Tartini's violin sonatas: the first movement, from the Sonata in D; the second, from the Sonata in G minor; the third, from the Sonata in G minor; and the fourth, from the Sonata in G major.

The composer wrote a second work for violin and orchestra based on Tartini—*Tartiniana seconda* (1956), introduced in Turin in 1957, then heard at the festival of the International Society for Contemporary Music on June 13, 1959.

1954 VARIAZIONI (VARIATIONS), for orchestra.

In 1952, while traveling in Canada, the United States and Mexico, Dallapiccola completed a composition for solo piano entitled *The Musical Notebook of Annalibera.* Annalibera was his then eight-year-old daughter, to whom that work is dedicated. He wrote it for the Pittsburgh International Contemporary Festival, where it was introduced in 1952. Then, commissioned by the Louisville Orchestra in Kentucky to write a symphonic work, he decided to orchestrate his piano composition. He retained the tempo markings of the eleven sections but omitted the descriptive titles he had affixed to each of these parts.

The composer has explained that his variations "are not at all variations in the traditional sense of the word. At the base of the whole composition, there is the same twelve-tone row that I used for my *Songs of Liberation* (1952–1955) and that I used for the *Musical Notebook of Annalibera.* . . . There are eleven variations built on the twelve-tone row."

The following are the eleven variations (the titles previously used in the piano work appear in parentheses to provide a clue to the musical content of each section):

1. Quasi lento misterioso (Symbol); 2. Allegro con fuoco (Accents); 3. Mosso scorrevolo (Contrapunctus primus); 4. Tranquillamente mosso (Lines); 5. Poco allegretto (Contrapunctus secondus); 6. Molto lento, con espressione parlante (Friezes); 7. Andantino amoroso esitando (Contrapunctus tertius); 8. Allegro, con violenza (Rhythms); 9. Affettuoso, cullante (Colors); 10. Grave (Shadows); 11. Molto lento fantastico (Quatrain constructed like a strophe of four verses).

The world première of the orchestral *Variations* took place in Louisville, Kentucky, on October 3, 1954, with Rober Whitney conducting the Louisville Orchestra.

1955 AN MATHILDE, cantata for female voice and orchestra. I. Den Strauss II. Gedächtnisfeier. III. An die Engel.

The text for this cantata is made up of three ironic poems by Heinrich Heine: "The Bouquet," "Commemoration" and "To the Angels."

The cantata was introduced at the Donaueschingen Festival in Germany on October 16, 1955. When it was first heard in the United States—in New York on May 7, 1956—Jay Harrison described it in the New York *Herald Tribune* as a "wholly romantic number . . . which, despite its occasional nervousness and violence, is essentially brooding and introspective. Even its score, elegant to a fault, suggests that the piece must stand or fall on the sparks of emotion it gives off. Thus . . . it is in no way cerebral music; it is meant to be felt, not merely understood."

1957 CONCERTO PER LA NOTTE DI NATALE DELL'ANNO 1956 (CHRISTMAS CANTATA), for soprano and orchestra.

There are two solos for soprano and three instrumental movements in this cantata, the vocal parts coming in the second and fourth sections. The music is sometimes a visual as well as aural translation of the text, which was derived from *Laude* by Jacopone da Todi. As Eric Salzman explained in *The New York Times*: "Jacopone da Todi . . . speaks of love as a 'cerchio rotondo,' a perfect circle; sure enough, the instrumental patterns diverge and converge to form circles on the page. This, of course, makes a perfectly legitimate aural effect, too; but its full significance comes home when we realize that each of the movements has a circular form and, indeed, so does the work as a whole."

Here is how Salzman described the music: "[It] becomes complex and fragmented, yet still it is firm and clear. Technique is subsumed in the structure within which the composer lets loose a powerful play of invention and expression. In a moment, he can fly from the ecstatic to the contemplative, yet never lose the thread of a musical discourse that is both lyrical and logical. Instead of merely looking inward, he looks inward and sees the world outside. Instead of a tree or flower, we get a whole landscape; a landscape in which men and gods can be perceived."

CLAUDE DEBUSSY 1862–1918

When Debussy was a young man, the artistic cults most frequently discussed in the cafés of Paris were those of the Impressionists in painting (Manet, Monet, Renoir, Degas, Cézanne, Seurat), and the Symbolists in poetry (Mallarmé, Baudelaire, Verlaine). Their artistic theories, and ideas of ways and means of achieving those theories, struck a responsive chord with Debussy, who, truth to tell, had also been drifting (though instinctively) in their direction.

The term "impressionism" was coined in the mid-nineteenth century. In 1867, some canvases by Édouard Manet were exhibited in Paris. At that time, the catalogue explained that Manet's aim was to render "impressions." At about this same time, Claude Monet did a canvas of a sunrise at sea entitled *Une Impression*. From either one of these two sources—perhaps from both—came the word "Impressionism" to identify a new way of painting.

Impressionist painters tried to create subjects or images not as others saw them but rather as they, the painters, saw them. Not the subject itself was important to the Impressionist but the feeling or impression that this subject aroused in him. The Impressionist painter emphasized design, color, light values, rather than form and substance. Skies may be blue or gray, but if the sky suggested to the painter feelings of deep purple, then the Impressionist painted his sky deep purple. To the Impressionist, what was of first importance in a painting was not the figure or the scene but—light. The vibrations of light, the Impressionist felt, gave life to every image and scene. He, therefore, tried to get down those vibrations of light on a canvas by means of commas and dots of pure color (using a smaller brush for this purpose), leaving it to the eye of the beholder to mix and blend the colors.

The Symbolists represented for French literature what the Impressionists did for French painting. Like the Impressionist, the Symbolist poet tried to appeal to senses rather than to intellect. Where the Impressionist emphasized light, color and shadows, rather than subject matter, the Symbolist accented the sound of words rather than their meaning. Words became important as the instruments of musical sounds. The Symbolist tried to impart the essence of a poetic experience not by reproducing facts but by presenting the symbol and by exploiting the metaphor. These became the means by which to suggest the mystery at the heart of human existence. The Symbolists rebelled against the Romantic movement in poetry—just as the Impressionist painter had revolted against heroic attitudes and sentimental landscapes in Romantic painting. The Symbolists rejected storytelling, moral preachings and passionate emotional outpourings. In this rejection, the poet turned inward, exploring and expressing the shifting subtle states of the human psyche.

The seeds of such ideas fell on fertile soil as Debussy listened to the Impressionists and Symbolists, as he absorbed those ideas and made them a part of his own *Weltanschauung.*

His own musical ideas had been undergoing several changes up to this time. After a visit to Bayreuth, he had become a passionate disciple of Wagner. Then a second visit to Bayreuth the next year dissipated his enthusiasm and changed him into a non-believer. Painstakingly, he now tried to free himself from the influence that the Wagnerian music drama had exerted on him. In Erik Satie he found a kindred spirit who was even more articulate than he in expressing his resentment against Wagnerian ideals and principles. More than ever, the German Romantic school repelled Debussy with its indulgence in excessive sentiments within inflated structures utilizing Gargantuan forces, with its weakness for expounding metaphysical ideas and Faustian struggles in music. Debussy's goal was now the production of a French music as opposed to the German; his new musical gods were old French masters like Rameau and Couperin. In them he found the clarity, precision, understatement, economy and refinement to which his own sensitive nature reacted instinctively. Debussy now called himself "*musicien français*"—a French musician—and his aim was to achieve a *French* music, exquisite in detail, objective in outlook, suggestive and controlled. His conversations with Satie clarified his thinking, just as some of Satie's harmonic and rhythmic innovations provided him with a new musical equipment.

From his contacts with the Impressionists and the Symbolists—from his association with Satie and his music—Debussy finally arrived at those artistic principles which henceforth were to give shape, form and substance to his own compositions. His was to be a new kind of music—no longer concerned with romantic effusions or dramatic force or programmatic realism, but rather with colors, nuances, moods, sensations, atmosphere. Chords became the means of projecting color and were used individually for their own specific effect rather than for their relationship to chords that preceded or followed them. Unresolved ninth and eleventh chords moved about freely without concern for a tonal center, evoking a world of shadows and mystery. The fourths, fifths and octaves, moving in parallel motion, the avoidance of formal cadences, the using of rapidly changing meters and rhythms created elusive moods and evanescent sensations. A new kind of sensitive, seemingly remote melody was realized through the use of the oriental pentatonic scale, the old Church modes and, most significantly, the whole-tone scale. The last of these, while occasionally appearing in works of earlier composers, is always identified with Debussy, for it is Debussy who used it so extensively and with such extraordinary effect.

Orchestration served not to achieve stirring and dramatic effects or to arrive at overpowering climactic points, but for subtle colorations. Individual timbres were made to stand out with wonderful clarity. A new kind of shimmering orchestral painting was realized by the flutes and clarinets in low registers, violins in upper registers, muted trumpets and horns, the delicate and at times esoteric sounds of harp, celesta, triangle, glockenspiel, muffled drums, a cymbal brushed ever so lightly by the drumstick. Debussy saw to it that basic timbres did not lose their identity even when grouped and massed; and he thought of different parts of the compass of any given instrument as if these parts were actually different instruments. His preference, like that of many other Frenchmen, was for the woodwinds; he bears the same relation to the reeds that Wagner did to the brass. He was also partial to the harp, giving it an important rather than a subsidiary role in the orchestration.

Intimacy was frequently arrived at through the use of themes built up from fragmentary and often repeated phrases, in place of the broadly spun out melodies of the Romantic school. In rhythm, a continuous stream was effected in which the beat was hidden and where the tyranny of the bar line was at times removed. Finally, in Debussy's rebellion against the grandiose architecture of the post-Wagnerian period, he sought forms that were fluid and plastic, in which structural landmarks were avoided, creating an uninterrupted flow of dream-like sounds where phrases, periods, sections overlapped.

All such technical features were absorbed into Debussy's impressionist art, opening up vistas of sensitive, delicate, exquisite impressions and textures rarely before realized in music.

Debussy, the father of musical Impressionism, was born in Saint-Germain-en-Laye, on the outskirts of Paris, on August 22, 1862. At the age of eleven, he entered the Paris Conservatory, where for the next eleven years he studied harmony with Durand and Lavignac, composition with Guiraud and piano with Marmontel. Despite his insistence on seeking out new chord combinations, and disconcerting his teachers with his unorthodox methods and techniques in defiance of textbook law, Debussy was an excellent student, winning prizes in solfeggio and sight-reading. In 1884, he acquired the much-coveted Prix de Rome with his cantata *L'Enfant Prodigue*.. In Rome, Debussy chafed under the restrictions imposed upon him by the academicians of the Conservatory. In addition, he hated Italy—its weather, food, people and music. He did not wait to complete his three-year residence, returning precipitously to Paris in the spring of 1887, where he completed the cantata *La Damoiselle Élue* (*The Blessed Damozel*), based on the poem of the same name by the pre-Raphaelite Dante Gabriel Rossetti as translated into French by Gabriel Sarrazin. Here color effects are given precedence over structural requirements; clarity makes way for vagueness and mystery; unusual modulations and unrelated chords replace Conservatory formulas. Since Prix de Rome winners were required to submit musical works, known as "envois," Debussy sent in *La Damoiselle Élue*. The judges found its departures too radical to permit its performance, which finally took place (without their blessing) at a concert of the Société Nationale in Paris on April 8, 1893. At this time, several prominent musicians acclaimed it, notably Vincent d'Indy and Julien Tiersot; and since then, it has been accepted as Debussy's earliest work of significance.

By 1893, Debussy had crystallized his thinking and arrived at his own manner of writing music. He now produced a series of masterpieces which forthwith placed him with the great creative men of his time and established him as one of the most provocative.

First came the Quartet in G minor for Strings, op. 10, written in 1893 and introduced by the Ysaÿe Quartet at a concert of the Société Nationale on December 29 of the same year. The audience was at turns puzzled and irritated by its daring style. The critics were outright denunciatory, one of them speaking derisively of its "orgy of modulations." Recognition was not to come for another decade; but in the early twentieth century, it was recognized as one of the most important and original string quartets since Brahms. It set into motion musical Impressionism as a compositional style; its influence on younger composers everywhere was incalculable.

Then came one of Debussy's most exquisite works, the orchestral *Prélude à l'Après-Midi d'un Faune* (*The Afternoon of a Faun*), written between 1892 and 1894, and introduced on December 22, 1894, by the Société Nationale, Gustave Doret conducting. Inspired by the delicate poem of Stéphane Mallarmé (dean of the Symbolists), it is a complete realization in music of the artistic concepts of both the Symbolists and the Impressionists.

With the three orchestral *Nocturnes,* written between 1897 and 1899, Debussy's tone-painting achieves the very quintessence of perfection. Debussy himself explained that this title of "Nocturne" was intended "to have a more general and, above all, a more decorative meaning," and that he was not concerned with the form of the nocturne, but with "everything that this word includes in the way of diversified impression and special lights." The first two *Nocturnes,* "*Nuages*" ("Clouds") and "*Fêtes*" ("Festivals"), were introduced by the Lamoureux Orchestra, Chevillard conducting, on December 8, 1900. The following year, on October 27, 1901, all three *Nocturnes*—the third of which was "*Sirènes*" ("Sirens"), scored for women's voices as well as orchestra —were performed at a Lamoureux concert.

The above-mentioned Debussy masterpieces were all written before 1900 and, consequently, are not discussed in detail in the pages that follow. There was, however, no diminution of creative power in the music Debussy produced after 1900. On the contrary! One after another, masterworks left his pen to make him the dominating figure in French music, one of the most inventive contributors of new techniques and aesthetics that the music of his day produced.

On October 19, 1899, Debussy married Rosalie Texier (whom he nicknamed "Lily-Lilo"), a dressmaker of plebian mind and tastes. For a while, Debussy was deeply attached to her, as his dedication to his *Nocturnes* proves. Then in 1904, he abandoned her for Emma Bardac, the wife of a banker. In 1905, they had a daughter, Claude-Emma, playfully known as "Chouchou." After her birth, Debussy and Emma Bardac were married, on October 15, 1905.

With the outbreak of World War I, ill health began to sap Debussy's energy to a point where composition required Herculean willpower. Nevertheless, he kept on writing. His music was now uneven in quality, occasionally suggesting his one-time originality and inventiveness but occasionally relying for its effect on technique and the repetition of tried and true mannerisms.

The growth of a cancer (for this was Debussy's ailment) necessitated an operation in 1915. Thereafter he was only a shadow of himself, usually in terrible pain. After 1917, he never left his apartment. He died there on March 25, 1918, only eight days after he had applied for a recently vacated chair at the Académie des Beaux-Arts. The war had so completely absorbed the attention of France that few at the time noticed that her greatest musician had passed away.

1902 PELLÉAS ET MÉLISANDE, opera in five acts, text being the play of the same name by Maurice Maeterlinck, only slightly altered. First performance: Opéra-Comique, Paris, April 30, 1902.

With *Pelléas et Mélisande,* Debussy's career as a composer of opera began and ended. It may be that *Pelléas* proved so complete, so perfect a realization of his Impressionist art within the operatic structure that Debussy might have felt any other work of his for the lyric theatre could only be duplication. It may also be that Debussy had found in *Pelléas* a libretto so perfectly suited to his sensitive art that all other librettos approached thereafter appeared unsympathetic by comparison.

Debussy had specific ideas on the role of the librettist: He must be "one who only hints at things and will thus enable me to graft my thought on his; one who will create characters whose history and abode belong to no particular time or place; one who will not despotically impose set scenes on me, but will allow me now and then to outdo him in artistry and perfect his work."

He also had definite ideas on the part music should play within the operatic framework: "I shall not follow the usual plan of the lyric drama in which the music insolently predominates, whilst the poetry is relegated to the background and smothered by elaborate musical trappings. There is too much singing in musical dramas. The characters should sing only when it is worthwhile, and the pathetic note should be held in reserve. The intensity of the expression should vary in degree. At times it is necessary to paint in monochrome and limit oneself to gray tones. . . . Nothing should retard the progress of the dramatic action: all musical development that is not essential to the text is incorrect. Apart from the fact that any musical development which is at all protracted cannot possibly correspond to the mobile words . . . my dream is to find poems that will not condemn me to perpetrate long, ponderous acts; poems that will provide me with ever-changing scenes, varied as regards place and atmosphere, in which the characters will not argue, but live their lives and work out their destinies."

Debussy acquired a copy of Maurice Maeterlinck's play in 1892. It enchanted him from the very first. The theme was as old as literature itself. Golaud, King Arkel's son, discovers Mélisande at a fountain. Falling in love with her, he brings her back to his castle to become his wife. In the castle, however, Golaud's brother, Pelléas, meets Mélisande; almost at once they both fall deeply in love with each other. When Golaud discovers that he has been betrayed, he kills Pelléas. Soon after this, Mélisande dies, after having given birth to a child. Golaud is at her side begging for a forgiveness that can no longer be forthcoming.

It was the simplicity with which the poet developed this age-old triangle, and the enchantment which the story evoked, that delighted Debussy. He knew at once that this was the text for his opera, and forthwith he began to sketch out some ideas (one of which was ultimately utilized in the fourth act, fourth scene, and became one of the melodic embryos of the entire work).

But the opera did not come easily. He wrote and destroyed; wrote and revised. Again and again, he felt that he was succumbing to the pernicious influence of "the phantom of old Klingsor, alias R. Wagner," from which he had to free himself completely before he could arrive at his own personal idiom.

Finally, on April 30, 1902, *Pelléas* was introduced at the Opéra-Comique. The première was preceded by a scandal that rocked artistic Paris. Maeterlinck had intended his mistress, Georgette Leblanc, as Mélisande. But Albert Carré, manager of the Opéra-Comique, had other ideas: he wanted Mary Garden for the role. Maeterlinck was furious. He threatened to cane Debussy, whom he suspected of having influenced Carré. He wrote a heated letter to *Le Figaro,* sixteen days before the première, denouncing the Opéra-Comique management and maintaining that the work "is now strange and hostile to me. I can only wish its immediate and emphatic failure." There was even talk of a duel between Maeterlinck and Carré, though nothing came of that.

At the dress rehearsal, a witty parody on the play was published and distributed at the entrance of the theatre—said to be the work of Maeterlinck himself, though this has never been proved. Thus hilarity was injected into the already confused situation. The rehearsal went badly. Disturbances (possibly inspired by the poet) were introduced by members of the audience, with Mary Garden as their particular victim.

In any event, the première proceeded on schedule, and was awaited in Paris with no little electrified anticipation. As the unorthodox music progressed—rarefied, disembodied, seemingly amorphous—hisses and loud-voiced denunciations rose audibly in the theatre. On the other hand, in the stalls and gallery pronounced enthusiasm gave answer to the skeptics. The critics, too, were divided in their opinion. "His music is vague, without color or nuance, without motion, without life. It is not even declamation, but a continual dolorous melopoeia without vitality or vigor, deliberately shunning all semblance of precision." Thus wrote Arthur Pougin in *Le Menéstrel.* The Paris correspondent of a London paper reported: "The composer's system is to ignore melody altogether, and his personages do not sing, but talk in a sort of lilting voice to a vague musical accompaniment of the text. The effect is quite bewildering, almost amusing in its absurdity." But other critics sensed that a new world had been opened for opera with this masterpiece; Gustave Bret, André Corneau and Henry Bauer spoke highly of Debussy's achievement.

Possibly because it was a *cause célèbre,* and possibly because its beauty began to cast a spell, *Pelléas* soon began to interest the Parisian public. By the seventh performance, the house could not accommodate all those ready to buy a ticket. It was performed fourteen times in May and June of that year, and ten times the following season—surely a formidable achievement for a new, revolutionary opera.

Since its première, *Pelléas* has acquired a permanent place in the operatic repertory as one of the supreme achievements of the twentieth century. In its magic fusion of word and sound, it has evoked for opera lovers the world over an enchantment whose spell is irresistible, unbroken from first bar to last. The marriage of text and music is as complete and perfect as any to be found in all opera. Recognizing that the drama was all important, Debussy was able to make his music subservient to the requirements of the text, a kind of shimmering background curtain for the stage action. To realize the remote, amorphous, mysterious personality of the Maeterlinck drama, Debussy enlisted all the tools of his Impressionist shop. Modal, pentatonic and whole-tone scale melodies and harmonies proved uniquely apt in projecting the misty, dreamlike character of the play. The seventh and ninth chords, moving often in organum-like parallel motion, gave the tonality a blur and a haze just right for the nebulous, vaporous and often obscure way in which the drama progressed towards its tragic denouement.

Some things Debussy took from Wagner, however much he may have wished to free himself from Wagner's influence. Like Wagner, he avoided arias and ensemble numbers, substituting for them a fluid flow of the most expressive declamation. Like Wagner, he took advantage of a leitmotiv technique (even though he had once scornfully referred to that technique as the "visiting cards" for the characters!). From Wagner, he learned to dispense with unnecessary appendages—choruses, dances, processions, and so forth. We are reminded of Wagner even in one or two details, as, for example, in the first orchestral entr'acte which could not have been written if Wagner had not created the *Transformation Scene* for *Parsifal.*

Some things Debussy took from Mussorgsky. From *Boris Godunov* he appropriated the use of ostinati figures in the bass, moving through the score like a parade of ghosts towards an impending doom. More significantly, Debussy used his expressive declamation the way Mussorgsky had done, but a declamation thoroughly French where Mussorgsky's had been Russian. The places where pure melody is allowed to overflow in *Pelléas* are few and far between. One such is Mélisande's third-act song. A calm, sweet orchestral prelude sets the mood. Mélisande is at the window, combing her hair. As she combs, she sings an unaccompanied chant which in its modal formation, melodic phraseology and curiously floating rhythm suggests an old folk song. She is in a half-dream state, which her murmuring chant suggests magically. But it is declamation rather than song that dominates the overall musical texture of the opera—a declamation moving freely and fluidly. By using a highly limited range and small intervals, and often by confining the voice to a single note—and at times by dispensing with bar lines—Debussy was able to evolve an uninterrupted melodic line which became the spine of the opera and which gained a good deal of its effect through understatement. The same kind of understatement prevailed in Debussy's dynamics. If Maeterlinck's play is spoken in a hushed whisper, so is Debussy's music. The full orchestra is hardly ever used, except in the entr'actes. There are no instrumental doublings to speak of, with small combinations and solo timbres the rule rather than the exception. Strings are often muted. In the whole score, there are only four fortissimos. These orchestral whisperings contribute immeasurably to the mysterious, symbolic and spiritual elements of the drama.

Two scenes in the opera derive their powerful dramatic impact through this gift of understatement. In the fourth act, Pelléas has come to tell Mélisande he must leave for a long journey. He kisses her, saying simply, "I love you," to which she replies softly and simply, "I love you too." This is the climax of the drama, and its immense effect springs from the way in which the whole scene is underplayed by the composer. All we get is a simple exchange of love, words which are almost spoken, over an elementary accompaniment; at one point, the orchestra is silent. Debussy asks us to supply our own reactions to this deeply moving episode.

In the closing scene, understatement once again is the secret of the emotional impact. Mélisande is dead. The grief-stricken Golaud is being led away by King Arkel, who then describes how Mélisande is lying silent, tranquil, in peace at last. In the closing measures, the orchestra spreads a veil of sweetness and tenderness over the scene. We hear flutes in the high register, muted strings and then the strumming of the harp. The last voice we hear is the sound of the harp, dropping its tones as if they were tears.

Of the influence of *Pelléas et Mélisande,* Herbert F. Peyser has written: "[It], like *Tristan,* is one of those creations after which the art of music can never again be exactly what it was before. It contributed an idiom that became an integral part of the language of tone and that promises to remain as permanent as any element of expression in music can be said to have permanence. Moreover, it embodies the quintessence of Debussy's artistic bequest. If everything else he composed were destroyed, it would be possible, in a manner of speaking, to reconstruct a tolerably faithful counterpart out of the opera or, for that matter, out of any scene of it. This is not to imply that the whole of Debussy's achievement . . . is a variant or a lesser reflection of *Pelléas,* but simply that in *Pelléas* we find the most distinctive flowering of his genius."

When *Pelléas et Mélisande* was first heard in the United States, the principals were the same ones who had created their roles—Mary Garden and Jean Périer. This première took place at Oscar Hammerstein's Manhattan Opera House on February 19, 1908. *Pelléas* came to the Metropolitan Opera House on March 21, 1925, when the title roles were sung by Lucrezia Bori and Edward Johnson.

1903–1905 COMPOSITIONS FOR PIANO:

ESTAMPES. I. Pagodes. II. Soirée dans Grenade. III. Jardins sous la Pluie.

L'ÎLE JOYEUSE.

SUITE BERGAMASQUE. I. Prelude. II. Minuet. III. Clair de Lune. IV. Passepied.

Estampes (1903), a set of three portraits for piano, was introduced by Ricardo Viñes at a concert of the Société Nationale, on January 9, 1904, and was well received: so great was the enthusiasm at the end of the work that the third piece had to be repeated. Since then it has become one of Debussy's best known works for the piano, one of his most successful efforts in projecting impressionistic effects through descriptive music.

In *Pagodes* Debussy employs the oriental pentatonic scale (which he heard at the Paris Exposition in 1889, performed by Javanese and other Far Eastern musicians) with considerable skill; an exotic picture emerges. Bell-like effects are sounded throughout the piece.

The "Evening in Granada" (the most famous of this trio of pieces) describes the Spanish city with its Moorish backgrounds as dusk descends. In the distance is heard the strum of a mandolin as a Spaniard raises his voice in a serenade. The rhythm of a habanera is here employed so felicitously that Manuel de Falla has called this piece "characteristically Spanish in every detail." It conjures, wrote Falla, "the effect of images mirrored by the moonlight upon the limpid waters of the large cisterns adjoining the Alhambra."

Two French folk songs appear in the "Gardens In the Rain" (*Nous n'irons plus au Bois* and *Do, Do, l'Enfant, Do*), which describes a garden drenched by the rain and combed by the fingers of the wind.

Though originally planned for the *Suite Bergamasque, L'Île Joyeuse* (1904) was published independently. It interprets Watteau's *Embarquement pour Cythère* in as sensual a piece of music as Debussy has written. Its ingenious deployment of rhythm and its use of orchestral timbres are particularly interesting. It was introduced by Ricardo Viñes on February 18, 1905.

The *Suite Bergamasque* had been begun as far back as 1889, but it was not completed until 1905. In it Debussy attempted for the first time to create music with the grace and charm of the seventeenth-century French clavecinists, without sacrificing his own harmonic experiments. This combination of the old and the new gives the music its greatest fascination.

The most famous movement of the four is the *Clair de Lune,* a sensuous picture of a moonlit night. Guido Gatti said about this exquisite piece of music: "What an airy flowering of arpeggios ascends the keyboard, to leap up again like a fountain jet which scatters its water on the air, then relapses into calm again in solid tonic and dominant undulations, on which the theme spreads out, ample, sonorous, expressive."

About the first movement, Edward Lockspeiser said: "It has an abundance of lyrical ideas and a freedom of form that is nevertheless wholly convincing. The diatonic harmony, despite some arresting modulations, is, however, still orthodox." The *Minuet* that follows displays "much freedom and spontaneity within the accepted tonal framework." The concluding *Passepied* is "a sophisticated pastiche of an eighteenth-century dance."

1904 FÊTES GALANTES, second set, for voice and piano. I. Les Ingénus. II. Le Faune. III. Colloque Sentimental.

In 1892, Debussy had composed the first set of *Fêtes Galantes* to poems by Paul Verlaine. This series included "*En Sourdine,*" "*Clair de Lune*" (not to be confused with the more celebrated piece for the piano in the *Suite Bergamasque*) and "*Fantoches.*" These were Debussy's first significant contributions to song literature.

The second set came twelve years later. In the first song, Debussy's good humor is in evidence as he carries over in his music Verlaine's delightful description of youthful lovers. The second song imitates the timbre of the flute (voice) and the tambourine (piano) in this description of the faun who guards the enchanted woods where lovers meet. In the final number, the feeling of disillusionment is caught beautifully as two former lovers meet again in a lonely park and recall their now dead rapture.

1905 LA MER, three symphonic sketches. I. De l'Aube à Midi sur la Mer. II. Jeux de Vagues. III. Dialogue du Vent et de la Mer.

Debussy's love of the sea is revealed in these effective tone pictures which present three facets of its personality. "I was intended for the fine career of a sailor," he wrote to a friend in 1903. And in 1905, following the crossing of the Channel, he wrote to his publisher: "The sea has been very good to me. She has shown me all her moods."

Debussy worked on *La Mer* from 1903 to 1905. On October 15, 1905, its first performance took place in Paris, with Camille Chevillard conducting the Concerts Lamoureux. M. D. Calvocressi, writing in the *Guide Musicale,* felt that the work marked a new phase in Debussy's development, with a "more robust inspiration, stronger colors, and more definite lines than his preceding works." But there were antagonistic reviews as well. "I neither hear, nor see, nor feel the sea," wrote Pierre Lalo with finality in *Le Temps.*

It is not easy to append a definite program to this nebulous music. And while it is possible to say with Lalo that one cannot specifically hear, see or feel the sea in the music, it is impossible to deny that the personality of the sea is magically suggested. It is the poet's conception of the sea that is invoked in this music—the reveries, moods and nostalgic longings which it inspires in a sensitive lover of Nature.

The mystery of the sea is suggested in the first sketch, with undulating figures bringing us a picture of the playing waves. Muted trumpet and English horn present the principal subject. As the music grows and swells, different images of the sea at different times of the day are projected. The section ends with a chorale for brass. In the second part, melodic fragments are varied in rhythm and color to portray the play of the waves as they are caressed by gentle winds. The music grows more dramatic in the closing section as the sea becomes more restive and engages the wind in a dialogue. The sea's immensity is suggested by figures in the strings, in the whole-tone scale. Some of the material from earlier movements is recalled with the chorale melody of the first part built into a formidable climax. Then the work ends with undulating figures recalling the movements of the sea.

Each of the three sections is a fully and completely realized tone poem, not just a sketch or an image. But so thoroughly integrated are the three parts that it is impossible to perform any one section by itself. A close bond among the three parts is maintained by having a movement take over where an earlier one had left off. The first two parts are played without interruption.

1905–1908 COMPOSITIONS FOR PIANO:

IMAGES, first set. I. Reflets dans l'Eau. II. Hommage à Rameau. III. Mouvement.

IMAGES, second set. I. Cloches à travers les Feuilles. II. Et la Lune Descend sur le Temple qui fut. III. Poissons d'Or.

CHILDREN'S CORNER. I. Doctor Gradus ad Parnassum. II. Jimbo's Lullaby. III. Serenade for the Doll. IV. Snow Is Dancing. V. The Little Shepherd. VI. Golliwogg's Cakewalk.

Debussy wrote two sets of *Images* for the piano, the first in 1905, the second in 1907. He regarded these pieces highly. In dispatching the first set to his publisher, he wrote: "I think I may say without undue pride that I believe that these three pieces will live and will take their place in piano literature . . . either to the left of Schumann . . . or to the right of Schumann."

Reflets dans l'Eau, of the first set, etches the shimmering reflections of figures and outlines in water with floating chords. Debussy said that this, one of his most famous pieces for the piano, incorporates "the newest discoveries in harmonic chemistry." In the second piece, Debussy pays tonal tribute not only to Rameau (as the title indicates) but also to the music of Rameau's time. The concluding piece creates a "perpetual motion" in a succession of gay triplets, relieved midway by a slow subject.

In the first piece of the second set, we hear delicate echoes of the murmur of forest leaves as they vibrate to the sounds of ringing bells. The title of the second number was conceived by Louis Laloy after the music had been written. An exotic atmosphere is here created, somewhat archaic and remote. *Poissons d'Or* was inspired by a piece of oriental lacquer on which was painted goldfish swimming in a stream.

Debussy wrote *Children's Corner* (1908) for his little daughter "Chouchou" (then only four years old). In the entire literature of music for children, there are few works which re-create a child's world so simply and charmingly.

The composer himself provided the work with English titles, thereby suggesting that each section was a game played by a little French girl and her English governess.

In the first movement the struggles of a child with the Clementi piano exercises are amusingly reproduced. There follows a lullaby to a stuffed elephant named Jimbo, one of the most cherished possessions of Chouchou, with which she shared her bed. Chouchou tells bedtime stories to Jimbo and sings her elephant to sleep. After the lullaby comes a child's piquant serenade to her doll. In the fourth movement, the child watches the falling snow from her window and waits for the return of the sun. A pastoral piece in Debussy's most refined manner is the fifth number, and the sixth is an American cakewalk, revealing Debussy's interest in American popular music; the interpolation of a phrase from Wagner's prelude to *Tristan* injects a satiric note.

1910 TROIS BALLADES DE VILLON, for voice and orchestra. I. Ballade de Villon à s'Amye. II. Ballade que Feit Villon à Requeste de Sa Mère pour Prier Nostre-Dame. III. Ballade des Femmes de Paris.

Debussy's fascination for musical medievalism—expressed in his use of Gregorian modes and in his love of old liturgical music—found satisfaction in his setting of three Villon poems. Modal writing is here utilized extensively; and to Léon Vallas the "restrained art attains its highest perfection" in this music.

On February 5, 1911, the three *Ballades* were introduced (with piano accompaniment) by Poule de Lestang. The orchestral version was heard for the first time on March 5 of the same year, with Charles W. Clark as soloist and the composer conducting.

The first song is declamatory, conveying the bitterness of the poet in discovering that his loved one is a hypocrite. The second creates a medieval atmosphere through modal writing, and is contrapuntal. The third (one of Debussy's most spirited songs) describes the chattering of Parisian women in gay and infectious music.

1910–1913 PRELUDES, for piano.

Book I: I. Danseuses de Delphes. II. Voiles. III. Le Vent dans la Plaine. IV. Les Sons et Les Parfums Tournent dans l'Air du Soir. V. Les Collines d'Anacapri. VI. Des Pas sur la Neige. VII. Ce qu'a vu le Vent d'Ouest. VIII. La Fille aux Cheveux de Lin. IX. La Sérénade interrompue. X. La Cathédrale Engloutie. XI. La Danse de Puck. XII. Minstrels.

Book II: I. Brouillards. II. Feuilles Mortes. III. La Puerta del Vino. IV. Les Fées sont d'Exquises Danseuses. V. Bruyères. VI. General Lavine—Eccentric. VII. La Terrasse des Audiences au Clair de Lune. VIII. Ondine. IX. Hommage à S. Pickwick, Esq., P. P.M.P.C. X. Canope. XI. Les Tierces Alternées. XII. Feux d'Artifice.

There are many authorities—Ernest Newman is among them—who consider Debussy's twenty-four Preludes as the quintessence of his art. All the technical and artistic devices with which he had been experimenting up to this time are completely realized, as new resources of color and resonance are explored for the piano.

Each of these pieces is a miniature—a brief improvisatory sketch—in which, to paraphrase Newman, infinitely delicate auditory and visual sensations are suggested in music. The form is free. Inspired by the fragment of a theme, or a rhythmic device, or an original chord combination, the composer develops the most refined mood portraits.

The Preludes are in two volumes, the first of which was completed in

1910, and the second three years later. It is interesting to note that the title of each piece was placed by the composer not at the head of each, but at the end—possibly because the titles did not occur to him until after he had completed the music.

BOOK I: I. "Dancers of Delphi." A greek sculpture representing three women in a slow dance was the composer's inspiration for this tranquil, mysterious music.

II. "Veils" or "Sails." Sailboats are anchored in port as the wind gently flutters the sails. This piece is one of the most successful in utilizing the whole-tone scale.

III. "The Wind on the Plain." A picture is here evoked, as Alfred Cortot has described it, of wind "gliding over the grass, fastening on the bushes, tumbling the hedges and sometimes in the young ardor of the morning, with a more brusque breath, bowing the springing corn with a long trembling wave."

IV. "Sounds and Odors Blend in the Evening Air." (The title is drawn from a poem by Baudelaire.) This is one of the most voluptuous pieces of music that Debussy wrote. Sound and fragrance draw intoxication from the evening air.

V. "The Hills of Anacapri." The piece has a folklore character, with a tarantella-like rhythm and a Neapolitan-style melody.

VI. "Steps on the Snow." Debussy himself indicated that the rhythm should "have the sonorous value of a melancholy snow-bound landscape." The entire piece has a subtle melancholy character.

VII. "What the West Wind Saw." A vivid description of a hurricane suggested in whirling arpeggios and in discords.

VIII. "The Girl with the Flaxen Hair." This exquisite melody is deservedly one of the most famous written by Debussy, a portrait of a maiden in diaphanous lines. The inspiration for this piece came from Leconte de Lisle's *Chanson Écossaise*.

IX. "Interrupted Serenade." A Spanish atmosphere is evoked through the suggestion of a strumming guitar and Andalusian rhythms.

X. "The Engulfed Cathedral." A mystic representation of an old Breton legend which told that on clear mornings, when the sea is transparent, the Cathedral of Ys rises to view; clearly audible are its tolling bells and chanting priests. Slowly the vision is dissipated. The cathedral returns to its sleep in the depths of the sea.

XI. "Puck's Dance." A roguish sketch, with ironic shadows, of the Shakespearean character in *A Midsummer Night's Dream*.

XII. "Minstrels." A music hall is depicted, in which suggestions of an old-time shuffling Broadway song gives basis to the belief that Debussy had black-faced minstrels in mind.

BOOK II: I: "Fogs." Vague tonalities—said to be the precursor of polytonality—create an amorphous picture.

II. "Dead Leaves." A series of melancholy ninth chords describe the descent of dead leaves to the ground.

III. "Puerto del Vino." The famous gate of the Alhambra in Granada—which Debussy saw on a picture post card—is described in dance rhythms and Andalusian ornamented melodies.

IV. "Fairies Are Exquisite Dancers." With quicksilver movement, the grace of fairy dancing is re-created.

V. "Heaths." An unforgettable picture of natural beauty, of sunlight streaking through leaves in a woodland.

VI. "General Lavine—Eccentric." A wooden puppet, famous at the Folies Bergère for his ungainly steps, is immortalized in this ironic piece, which has the character of an American cakewalk.

VII. "Reception in the Moonlight." A phrase from a letter by René Puaux, published in *Le Temps*, provided Debussy with this title. Echoes of the famous French song *Au clair de la lune* are heard in sevenths in this tonal picture of a "moon-drenched scene."

VIII. "Ondine." A water nymph is the heroine of this vaporous piece of music.

IX. "Homage to S. Pickwick." The celebrated Dickens character is here caricatured as amusing quotations are made from *God Save the King.*

X. "Egyptian Vase." A brief, melancholy threnody which, as Oscar Thompson put it, "is that of an impersonal sort of reverie."

XI. "Alternating Thirds." Debussy's predilection for the music of the old clavecin composers is here reflected.

XII. "Fireworks." This is a musical picture of a display of pyrotechnics, possibly one for Bastille Day, since strains of the *Marseillaise* are heard.

1912 IMAGES, for orchestra. I. Gigues. II. Ibéria. (1. Par les rues et par les chemins; 2. Les Parfums de la nuit; 3. Le Matin d'un jour de fête.) III. Rondes de Printemps.

It is the contention of Léon Vallas that the three Images which Debussy created for orchestra were each based on the folk songs of different countries. He finds that "*Gigues*" was derived from the English, with emphasis on the English jig; "*Ibéria,*" from the Spanish; and "*Rondes des Printemps,*" from the French.

"*Gigues*" (originally called "*Gigues Tristes*"—"Sad Gigues") was completed on January 4, 1909 in a piano version. André Caplet completed the orchestration in 1912, and on January 26, 1913, introduced it at a Colonne concert. Caplet saw in this music "the portrait of a soul in pain, uttering its slow lingering lamentation on the reed of an oboe d'amore." The gigue—the theme of which is believed to have been borrowed from a song by Charles Bordes—is heard in an unaccompanied solo by the oboe d'amore after twenty measures of introduction. A second principal theme is Scottish in character, and is heard in the bassoons.

"*Ibéria*" is the most famous section of this suite, and the one most frequently performed separately. Few portraits in music have caught so authentically the color and exotic charm of Spain. It is quite true that Debussy (as he himself insisted) did not try to write Spanish music, though suggestions of the Spanish idiom are recognizable. What he wanted to do, what he accomplished with telling effect, was to express in music the impressions that Spain made on him. It might be added, for further clarification, that the sum total of Debussy's experiences in Spain was a one-hour excursion to Saint-Sebastian. But, as Manuel de Falla remarked, "he preserved a lasting remembrance of the impression made on him by that peculiar light of a Plaza de Toros: the striking contrast between the part flooded by sunlight and that covered by shadow. 'The Morning of a Fête-Day' in '*Ibéria*' might perhaps be accepted as an evocation of that afternoon spent on the threshhold of Spain."

"*Ibéria*" has three sections:

I. "In the Streets and Byways" (Assez animé). The garish sunlight that floods the streets of Spain is suggested in the luminous orchestral colors that open this section. In the background is heard the persistent throb of castanet rhythms. The music grows in intensity, ebbs, develops into powerful climaxes and subsides as numerous thematic ideas are skilfully intertwined. The principal subjects are a jaunty theme for two clarinets, accompanied by oboes and bassoons and a pulsing tambourine, and a beautiful melody for viola and oboe.

II. "The Odors of the Night" (Lent et rêveur). An evocative picture, dreamlike and diaphanous, emerges in the glissandi of violins and chromatic runs of the woodwinds; it is nighttime in Spain. A note of melancholy is interpolated by the oboe. After the music becomes agitated, a solo horn restores an atmosphere of mystery and enchantment. Bells peal in the distance.

III. "The Morning of the Festival Day" (Dans un rhythme de marche lointaine, alerte et joyeuse) proceeds from the second movement without interruption. Thematic material from the preceding movement is recalled as the orchestra collects its strength and joyously injects power and brilliance to describe a characteristic festival day; people dance in the streets.

Though begun in 1906 (as a piece for two pianos), "*Ibéria*" was not completed until two years later as a work for orchestra. On February 20, 1910, Gabriel Pierné conducted the première at a concert by the Colonne Orchestra.

The French folk tune *Nous n'irons plus au bois* is the basic subject of the third of the *Images*—"*Rondes de Printemps*." This single idea, Laloy tells us, "now glides, now runs through light fronds of melody, till it joins in a breathless dance, whirls wildly for a moment, then grows calm and vanishes in clear air."

Debussy began the "*Rondes de Printemps*" in 1909. The première performance took place on March 2, 1910, with the composer conducting one of the Concerts Durand. The published score quotes the following line from the *Maggiolata:* "*Vive le mai! Bienvenu soit le mai avec son gonfalon sauvage!*" ("Long live the month of May! Welcome to May with its savage banner!")

1914 SIX ÉPIGRAPHES ANTIQUES (SIX ANCIENT EPIGRAPHS), for piano four hands (also orchestrated by Ernest Ansermet). I. Pour invoquer Pan, dieu du vent d'été. II. Pour un tombeau sans nom. III. Pour que la nuit soit propice. IV. Pour la danseuse aux crotales. V. Pour l'Égyptienne. VI. Pour remercier la pluie au matin.

In 1899, Debussy wrote incidental music for a set of Grecian poems by Pierre Louÿs, *Chansons de Bilitis,* to be recited and mimed. This reading, with Debussy's music, took place on June 7, 1901, in Paris. Thirteen years later, Debussy lifted six of the ten items from this score, arranged them for piano four hands, and assigned them a new overall title of *Six Épigraphes Antiques,* together with descriptive subtitles. This four-hand suite was heard in Paris on March 15, 1917, performed by the composer and Roger-Ducasse.

The first number invokes Pan, who is heard playing a tune in the pentatonic scale on his pipe. The second is music for an unnamed tombstone. "Hyper-chromatic melismas color the music," says Nicolas Slonimsky. "The ending is raucous, transitory and volatile in its dissonant substance." The third piece, a prayer for a propitious night, "is accentuated by distant drumbeats and chromatic arabesques," says Slonimsky. In the fourth number, the dancer with castanets is Cybèle, Greek goddess of nature. Slonimsky explains: "Debussy sees Cybèle through the mist of legend and the music is almost tranquil in Grecian modalities. But there are furious, though brief, explosions of passion." The next epigraph is an oriental piece entitled "For an Egyptian." "The melody is sinuous in its wistful arabesques. The rhythm is nervously dotted; the harmonies are austere in their open fifths. The ending is a static aureole." The concluding piece represents gratitude for a morning rain. Slonimsky here notes: "Rapid streamlets descend in chromatic passages; then the raindrops are more widely spaced, presently assuming pentatonic configurations. The ending is a reminiscence of the pipes of Pan of the opening."

The above suite is not to be confused with the song cycle, *Chansons de Bilitis,* once again to Pierre Louÿs's poems, which Debussy completed in 1897. The material in song cycle is completely different from that used in the incidental-music score.

1915 EN BLANC ET NOIR, for two pianos. I. Avec emportement. II. Lent, sombre: sourdement tumultueux. III. Scherzando.

Each of these three pieces (intended to suggest a picture in black-and-white) carries a motto which provides a clue to its meaning. The first piece, dedicated to Serge Koussevitzky, quotes a line from the Gounod opera *Roméo et Juliette*: "He who keeps his place and does not join in the ring silently confesses to some disgrace." A waltz melody is here developed with fervor.

The second number carries a motto from a François Villon ballad, and is dedicated to a French lieutenant killed in World War I. It begins solemnly, then develops into an agitated mood, when suddenly the strains of Luther's hymn *Ein feste Burg* are injected. The music finally, as Debussy put it, "cleanses the atmosphere of the poisonous fumes of the chorale, or rather of what it represents."

The third piece (dedicated to Stravinsky) quotes Charles, the Duke of Orleans: "Winter, you are nothing but a villain!" This is a fanciful scherzo written in rather slow tempo. It is believed to describe an old chateau standing bleakly in solitary splendor as a storm rages; this is the scene for a legend recounted by an old castellan. The storm subsides, and the setting becomes peaceful.

1915 ÉTUDES, for piano.

Book I. I. Pour les Cinq Doigts. II. Pour les Tierces. III. Pour les Quartes. IV. Pour les Sixtes. V. Pour les Octaves. VI. Pour les Huit Doigts.

Book II. I. Pour les Degrés Chromatiques. II. Pour les Agréments.

III. Pour les Notes Répétées. IV. Pour les Sonorités Opposées. V. Pour les Arpèges. VI. Pour les Accords.

More than any composer since Chopin, Debussy opened up new resources for the piano. In these Études (dedicated, appropriately enough, to Chopin), Debussy explored, as he has written, "a thousand ways of treating pianists according to their deserts."

Each Étude faces a technical problem and attempts its solution. The first book opens with a five-finger exercise (a somewhat satiric commentary on Czerny) and continues with exercises in thirds, fourths, sixths and octaves, ending with an eight-finger exercise. The second book treats problems of chromatic intervals, grace notes, reiterated notes, contrasted sonorities, arpeggios and chords.

But these two books are more than a *Gradus ad Parnassum* for pianists. They actually embody all of Debussy's experiments in harmony, counterpoint, tonality and rhythm and highlight his melodic idiosyncrasies.

1917 SONATA NO. 3, FOR VIOLIN AND PIANO. I. Allegro vivo. II. Intermède. III. Finale.

In 1915, Debussy planned the writing of a series of six sonatas for various instruments, in which a conscious effort would be made to return to the traditional classical forms of the seventeenth- and eighteenth-century French instrumental masters. Only three of these six sonatas were completed. The first, for cello and piano, was written in 1915. The second sonata, for flute, viola and piano, followed several months later. The third, though begun in 1915, was not completed until two years later. This last work was written under great duress. The composer was seriously ill, and had to undergo a serious operation for cancer which sapped his energy and strength. Besides his illness, there was the harrowing fear that at any day the advancing German armies might enter Paris. Only by dint of Herculean effort was he able to complete his violin sonata. On May 5, 1917, it was introduced in Paris by Gaston Poulet; the now-emaciated composer was at the piano.

Though some of the material sounds labored, the entire work is exemplary for mastery of workmanship. The first movement has particular rhythmic interest. It is followed by a scherzo-like movement of faun-like grace. The Finale is the most effective of the three movements, binding the whole work into an integrated unity by quoting at the very end the main theme of the first movement.

FREDERICK DELIUS 1862–1934

Refinement of speech, delicacy of touch, restrained emotion, tranquillity, poetic suggestions and subtle atmospheres are some of the qualities of Delius's music. It is impressionistic tone painting of the subtlest kind. A. K. Holland wrote: "His is a rhapsodic art but it is also an art of pure contemplation. He relies very much on the use of evocative associations, both in his actual vocabulary and in his choice of texts. His poetic principle is that of Keats, in that he strives to 'load every rift with ore,' to avoid all that is merely redundant, and all that is the product of barren musical reason. His sensitiveness to the finer shades of musical feeling, and his expression of them in a language that is as discriminating and various as it is personal and distinct, gives him a unique place in the music of our time."

Bernard van Dieren said: "To all that he touched he gave a new meaning, a new color, a new outline, a new loveliness, and a new poignancy. Music is greater, richer, and deeper for what he gave it."

Delius was born on January 29, 1862, in Bradford, England. Though he showed marked musical talent, his father intended him for the wool business, in which he worked for two years. In 1884, Delius escaped from the drudgery of the business world by emigrating to Solano, Florida, to take care of an orange plantation his father had bought for him. In Florida, he studied the violin by himself and began composing. At last, he received the belated permission of his father to study music seriously. He went to Europe in 1896 and studied under Jadassohn and Reinecke at the Leipzig Conservatory. After Leipzig, Delius went to Paris to assimilate its cultural life and to devote himself there more actively to creative work. In 1892, his first published work appeared, a *Légende* for violin and orchestra. This was followed by his first opera, *Irmelin* (1892), the fantasy overture *Over the Hills and Far Away* (1895) and the Piano Concerto in C minor (1897).

After marrying Jelka Rosen in 1897, Delius settled in Grez-sur-Loing, which was to remain his home for the remainder of his life. For the next decade and a half following 1899, he produced a series of masterpieces which placed him with the foremost composers of his time, the most important of which were a series of sensitively beautiful tone poems for orchestra, the opera *A Village Romeo and Juliet* and *A Mass of Life*.

Success and recognition came slowly. The elusive beauty of his music required intimacy before it could be appreciated, and performances of Delius's works were sporadic. It was in Germany that Delius's music first found a receptive public, following several important performances there of major works. However, there were a few disciples in England who fought Delius's battle patiently, the most notable of whom was Sir Thomas Beecham. It was through their indefatigable efforts that Delius ultimately achieved acceptance. When, in 1929, a festival of six concerts devoted entirely to Delius was launched in London, there were few to deny that he was one of England's great creative figures.

Meanwhile, soon after World War I, Delius began to disclose alarming symptoms of physical disintegration. At first, he suffered only from intense fatigue and attacks of inertia; but by 1922, he was a hopeless paralytic. Paralysis was followed, in 1925, by total blindness. Delius accepted his crushing fate with a calm and serenity that amazed those near him. Nor did he abandon composition. With the aid of Eric Fenby, who came to live with him and served as his amanuensis, Delius wrote several works, patiently dictating them note by note.

Delius died at his home in Grez-sur-Loing on June 10, 1934. One year later, his body was transported to its final resting place, in a churchyard in Limpsfield, in southern England.

1901 A VILLAGE ROMEO AND JULIET, opera in three acts and prologue, with text by the composer based on a story by Gottfried Keller. First performance: Komische Oper, Berlin, February 21, 1907 (in German); London, February 22, 1910 (in English).

Though Delius is not known as a composer of operas, he wrote six works in that form, the fourth of which is his most important. Delius himself referred to this opera—*A Village Romeo and Juliet*—as a "lyric drama in six pictures." He aimed for a work in which the stage action served merely to elucidate the music—to suggest through words and gesture what the music had realized completely. One commentator has referred to the opera as a kind of symphonic poem in which the play serves as the program.

Delius himself prepared the libretto (assisted by his wife), adapting a tale of Gottfried Keller, *Die Leute von Seldwyla*. The daughter of one family falls in love with the son of another—even though a bitter feud exists between the households. The lovers decide to escape. On the road they meet a vagabond fiddler who tries to induce them to follow him to a life of abandoned delights. The lovers are not interested; they prefer going their own way. That way eventually leads to suicide on a river barge.

The opera is written with subdued strokes: there are no climaxes, no emotional peaks, no dramatic thrusts. It is an amazingly quiet work, which, however, "burns with such white heat at the center [wrote Bernard van Dieren] that it seems little else than a bewildering number of lost opportunities."

One of the orchestral interludes has become familiar through performances at symphony concerts: "The Walk to the Paradise Garden." This intermezzo, occurring between the fifth and sixth "pictures," is said by Philip Heseltine to be an epitome of the whole opera. The episode begins with a waltz-like subject for cellos and bassoons. This is the introduction to the main part, which is dominated by two deeply affecting melodies, the first for horns and bassoons, the other for oboe set against a countersubject in the basses. "The Walk to the Paradise Garden" was not originally in Delius's score. He wrote it when his opera was first being produced in England, at the request of Thomas Beecham, who needed an interlude to allow for time in which to make a change of scenes.

1903 SEA DRIFT, for baritone, chorus and orchestra.

The first poem in Walt Whitman's *Sea Drift* provided Delius with his text. The shape of the music, as the composer told Eric Fenby, "was taken out of my hands, so to speak, as I worked, and was bred easily and effortlessly of the nature and sequence of my particular musical ideas, and the nature and sequence of the particular poetical ideas of Whitman that appealed to me."

Except in some of his shorter orchestral works, Delius rarely achieved such a consistently high level of inspiration as he did in this music. He absorbed the wind-swept rhythms of Whitman's poetry and the pathos and solemnity of its emotions; music and poem seem magically one, almost as if they had been created together, and by the same man.

Arthur Hutchings has pointed out that the work is not essentially a "seascape," even though the presence of the sea is felt; that the principal concern of the composer was to reproduce in music the emotions of such lines as:

Soothe! Soothe! Soothe!
Close on its waves soothes the wave behind,
And again another behind embracing and lapping,
    every one close,
But my love soothes not me, not me.

"The form of the music," writes A. K. Holland, "is a continuous web, following closely the pattern of the poem in its rise and fall of emotion, with few repetitions of phrase, except where the chorus echoes the words of the soloist and is pitted against him, or where the voices overlap." Holland adds: "Though it possesses a homogeneity as consistent as that of Whitman's poem, it relies comparatively little on formal thematic relationships and allusions. It is rather in its complete and single-minded absorption of the poem that it achieves a unity as powerful as any of Delius's works."

Sea Drift was introduced in Germany—at the Tonkünstlerfest in Essen in 1906. Its first performance in England followed in 1908, at the Sheffield Festival, Henry J. Wood conducting.

1905 A MASS OF LIFE, for double chorus, quartet and orchestra.

A Mass of Life was developed out of *Night Song of Zarathustra,* which Delius had composed in 1898. The *Night Song* is suggested in the early part of the *Mass*, and appears in the last movement as the principal theme.

The *Mass* was introduced in London on June 7, 1909, under Beecham's direction. Delius thought highly of this work, an expression of his almost religious fervor for the philosophy of Nietzsche.

The music, which gives the impression of improvisatory writing, is ideally suited to the mystical writings of Nietzsche. The music is, as Hugh Ross remarked, a series of mood pictures, in which a mood of revery alternates with dramatic passages.

To Sir Thomas Beecham, *A Mass of Life* is "the climax of Delius's creative achievement" and a "monumental masterpiece." He adds that "everything here is vibrating, ethereal and floating in soft-colored harmonies." Sir Thomas finds this music to be "full of thought and poetry," and he concludes by saying: "But not only beauty is represented in this music. The score of the Mass has its powerful moments as well as its lyrical. There the composer tightens the rhythm and unites orchestra and chorus in grand dramatic climaxes."

1907 BRIGG FAIR: AN ENGLISH RHAPSODY, for orchestra.

"Brigg Fair" is a famous English folk song rediscovered and arranged by Percy Grainger. It is the basic material which Delius enlarges and develops in his rhapsody. *Brigg Fair* was written one year after Grainger had published his setting of the song and was introduced by the Liverpool Philharmonic under Granville Bantock on January 18, 1908.

A slow improvisatory introduction precedes the statement of the folk song—in the oboe. Variations follow, some light and gay, some solemn, even funereal. A climax is reached, after which the folk tune is recalled and allowed to subside gently. Neville Cardus finds in *Brigg Fair* "no drama, no psychological transition." He describes the rhapsody as "a nature piece recollected in passionate tranquillity. The changes or variations are not dynamic or dramatic; they are variations of subjective emotion or poetry."

1908 IN A SUMMER GARDEN, fantasy for orchestra.

Two mottoes appear in the printed program, providing clues to both the emotional and programmatic implications of the music.

The first of these is by Dante Gabriel Rossetti:

All are my blooms; and all sweet bloom of love
To thee I give while Spring and Summer sing.

The other, of unknown authorship, appears in a German text and might serve as the program: "Roses, lilies, and a thousand scented flowers. Bright butterflies flitting from petal to petal, and gold-brown bees humming in the warm, quivering summer air. Beneath the shade of ancient trees, a quiet river with water-lilies. In a boat, almost hidden, two people. A thrush is singing in the distance."

A moody, atmospheric introduction opens with a soft subject for the woodwind and continues with a phrase in the English horn which receives significant treatment later in the work. In the main part, a livelier mood is immediately introduced, following which the strings are heard in a jaunty subject. The heart of the fantasy is an intense melody, which is worked up dramatically. A passage marked "mysterious" comes after this, with earlier material soon recalled. The fantasy lapses into serenity before ebbing away into silence.

In a Summer Garden was introduced on December 11, 1908, by the London Philharmonic, the composer conducting.

1908–1916 DANCE RHAPSODIES, NOS. 1 and 2, for orchestra.

Eight years separated the two *Dance Rhapsodies*. The first (1908) was introduced at the Hereford Festival in England on September 7, 1909. It opens with a subdued introduction before the first dance theme is heard in the oboe. This is the principal idea of the work. The rest of the composition consists of repetitions of this melody with various harmonic changes.

The second rhapsody (1916) makes effective use of the variation method. The work begins with a theme in the flute in a mazurka-type rhythm. This is subjected to considerable transformation throughout the piece. Midway, the oboe arrives with a new thought—a four-measure tune. After a climax, the mood grows serene; but the work ends with a forceful chordal statement.

1911 A SONG OF THE HIGH HILLS, for chorus and orchestra.

In a prefatory note within the published score of this composition, the composer wrote: "I have tried to express the joy and rapture felt in the High Mountains and to depict the lonely melancholy of the highest altitudes and of the wide expanses. The vocal parts typify Man in Nature."

Although written for chorus and orchestra, the work is essentially an orchestral composition, the choral parts being used as color background. It received its première in London nine years after its composition, on February 26, 1920, under Albert Coates's direction.

When *A Song of the High Hills* was introduced in the United States, under Percy Grainger, the conductor provided the following description of the music, published in the program:

"The entire work, from start to finish, is singularly solemn and uplifted in mood, and full of that rare quality of freshness and purity that is so striking a characteristic of things born of the hills—their flowers, their poets, their painters, etc. . . . Nothing is consciously descriptive on the composer's part, yet the analogy between much of the music and certain nature impressions is easily recognized. . . . Noteworthy is the scale in which the musical form of the work is cast—vast dimensions that recall little else in music except certain creations of Bach."

"The opening strikes a moaning, plaintive note," describes Philip Heseltine, "soon followed by a melody of winsome charm first heard in the woodwind, and continued in the strings. . . . The chief theme of the composition is ushered in on high violins in the slowest 4/4 time—a folk-like melody. . . . Out of the stillness emerges an alto solo (wordless, as in all the singing throughout the work) bearing the previously mentioned folk-like melody with which, a few measures later, the full chorus, a cappella, makes its first massed entry. . . . The third and topmost climax of the composition is gained in a blaze of almost demoniacal passion. . . . From here on, to the close of the composition, we witness the very gradual ebbing away of the dynamic force."

1912 ON HEARING THE FIRST CUCKOO IN SPRING, tone poem for orchestra.

SUMMER NIGHT ON THE RIVER, tone poem for orchestra.

These two tone poems are companion pieces. They were written in the same year and introduced at the same concert—in Leipzig, Germany, on October 2, 1913.

Delius often spent his summer vacations in Norway, in the hills of Jotenheim, where he was happiest surrounded by its natural beauties. In *On Hearing the First Cuckoo in Spring,* he transfers to music not only the feelings of a composer upon the awakening of springtime (a feeling magically suggested with the opening luminous chord) but also his own nostalgic yearnings for Norway. Thus, the second theme is a Norwegian folk song, "In Ola Valley." The first theme, however, has a character recognizably English, and recognizably Delius. This tone poem is one of Delius's masterworks, an unforgettable portrait of the vernal season, and one of the happiest examples of Delius's sensitive style and gift at atmospheric suggestions.

Summer Night on the River was not intended to be the kind of impressionistic setting that *The First Cuckoo* is. The pictorial description is direct rather than suggestive. The vague harmonies bring up a picture of mists settling over the river; the rhythms suggest the rocking of small boats. A cello solo is the main melodic idea—a beautiful song, creating an atmosphere of peace and mystery that embraces the river on a summer night.

1916 CONCERTO FOR VIOLIN AND ORCHESTRA.

Delius was not altogether happy in the concerto structure. He produced a piano concerto in 1897, a concerto for violin and cello in 1916, a violin concerto in 1916 and a cello concerto in 1921. Of these, the violin concerto is the most satisfactory. But it is hardly a concerto. In a single movement, it is more of a rhapsody, with the solo violin presenting a monologue from beginning to end. This monologue is heard after two introductory measures for orchestra—first with the principal subject in a moderate tempo, later with a secondary subject no less lyrical and expressive. Both ideas are amplified before a reflective section intrudes; later on, a second pastoral episode is heard. Then the opening theme returns for the last time, to bring the concerto to a subdued conclusion.

The concerto was introduced in London in January of 1919. Albert Sammons was the soloist with the Royal Philharmonic, conducted by Adrian Boult.

1917 EVENTYR (ONCE UPON A TIME), for orchestra.

Eventyr (like *On Hearing the First Cuckoo in Spring*) reflects its composer's love for Norway. In *Eventyr* it is Norwegian folklore rather than geography that provides creative stimulation: a collection of Norwegian fairy tales entitled *Eventyr* (*Legends*), published in 1841. Here the Norwegian love of fantasy, superstition and rustic humor predominate in tales peopled by spirits, giants, trolls, hobgoblins and other legendary creatures.

Though an integrated one-movement tone poem, *Eventyr* can, nevertheless, be divided into five sections. The first is a slow, mysterious introduction extending for twenty measures. Lower strings present a theme to which the woodwind offer reply. Then comes a broad melody of strings "with easy movement," which evokes an eerie atmosphere. This is followed by a theme in triplets for the bassoons, one of the main themes. The legendary atmosphere is evoked in the second part where a new lyrical thought is projected by the strings. In the third part, earlier material is varied and transformed, and a first climax is reached. This is succeeded by the fourth part, the development, where an even greater climax is achieved, at whose conclusion comes a majestic statement in broad chords for strings, harp and celesta. The concluding part consists of recapitulation, a kind of summation of what has previously been said. The work ends in serenity, with just a touch of mystery.

1919 REQUIEM, for solo voices, chorus and orchestra.

During World War I, Delius wrote and completed only a single major work for chorus and orchestra. This was a threnody "to the memory of all young soldiers fallen in the war," as the dedication reads. The Requiem received its first performance in London on March 23, 1922, Albert Coates conducting.

The Requiem opens with a majestic section for double chorus and orchestra ("Our Days Here Are As One Day"). The baritone solo appears with a bitter denunciation ("Why Dissemble We?"). A return of the opening chorus develops into an extended funeral march, interrupted by cries of the crowd. This crowd is made up of a double chorus: a woman's chorus representing the Christians shouting "Hallelujah," and a male chorus representing the Mohammedans exclaiming "Allah." When the hubbub subsides, the baritone returns ("And the Highways of Earth Are Full of Cries"), soon supplemented by the chorus, which eventually comments reflectively on death ("For All Who Are Living Know").

Where the first section had been essentially dramatic, the second is elegiac and lyrical. First, we hear a baritone solo in praise of his beloved. This is followed by another tender exhortation, this time for soprano ("I Honor the Man Who Can Love Life"). Now comes a rhapsody to Spring and to the awakening of Nature after her long winter sleep. The baritone raises his voice in praise of the vernal season ("The Golden Corn Awaits the Hand of the Reaper"). The Requiem ends with a glorious hymn to Spring by the chorus ("Springtime, Summer, Fall and Winter").

The Requiem is not a religious work but a work about death filled with an encompassing humanity. The composer himself explained: "Its underlying belief is that of a pantheism that insists on the reality of life. It preaches that human life is like a day in the existence of the world, subject to the great laws of All-Being. . . . Independence and self-reliance are the marks of a man who is great and free. He will look forward to death, with high courage in his soul, in proud solitude, in harmony with nature and the ever-recurrent sonorous rhythm of life and death."

1930 A SONG OF SUMMER, tone poem for orchestra.

During the last years of his life, Delius (now totally blind) dictated his music to his amanuensis, Eric Fenby. In this way the *Song of Summer* was written, based on sketches which Delius had written out many years earlier for a projected piece to be called *Poem of Love and Life*.

To Fenby, Delius provided the following description of this music: "I want you to imagine that we are sitting on the cliffs in the heather and looking out over the sea. The sustained chords in the high strings suggest the clear sky and stillness and calm of the scene. . . . You remember that figure that comes in the violins when the music becomes more animated. I'm introducing it there to suggest the gentle rise and fall of the waves. . . . The flutes suggest a sea gull gliding by."

A Song of Summer was introduced in London on September 17, 1931.

1931 PRELUDE TO "IRMELIN."

In 1892, Delius had completed the writing of his first opera. It was *Irmelin,* text by the composer—a love story involving a princess, Irmelin, and Nils, a prince disguised as a swineherd. (The long belated world première of this opera took place at Oxford, England, on May 4, 1953.)

Almost forty years after the opera had been written, Delius (now blind, paralyzed and at the dusk of his life) dictated to Eric Fenby, his faithful amanuensis, a new orchestral prelude for his first opera. The première of this prelude was given by Sir Thomas Beecham in London in 1935, when he used it as entr'acte music in a revival of Delius's third opera, *Koanga*. The music is typically Delius. It is a mood picture (Lento), whose main subject is presented in imitation first by flute and clarinet, then by oboe and clarinet, and after that by bass clarinet and bassoon. After this idea is amplified, the imitative scheme of the opening subject is repeated by solo violin and viola. The bass clarinet quietly reflects on the theme, whose last dying notes bring the prelude to a gentle conclusion.

NORMAN DELLO JOIO 1913–

By his own admission, Dello Joio has been influenced most strongly by his teacher, Paul Hindemith. The younger man belongs in the neo-classic camp which aims to revive old classical forms and styles and adapt them for the twentieth century. He may write a ricercare or a passacaglia or a chaconne—forms that flourished in the seventeenth century—but his writing remains contemporary in its harmonic and rhythmic freshness. Within this blending of old and new, Dello Joio has been able to create music that is forcefully motivated, frequently poetic, usually personal.

Other influences have affected his development. The traditional liturgical music of the Catholic Church, which he had heard and absorbed from his childhood on—the Gregorian chant particularly—has been a bountiful source of inspiration. This influence was early betrayed in his first work to get recognition, a *Magnificat* for orchestra (1942), for which he received the Town Hall Composition Award. Virgil Thomson described this music as a "transubstantiation into modern instrumental terms of the Vesper Canticle," whose melodic inspiration is "freely modeled after the style of the Gregorian chant." Some of Dello Joio's later works also spring from liturgical sources, notably the *Fantasia on a Gregorian Theme,* for violin and piano (1943); the orchestral *Variations, Chaconne, and Finale* (1947), whose basic material is derived from a Gregorian chant; and the *Meditations on Ecclesiastes* (1956), with which he received the Pulitzer Prize in music.

At the same time, his strong bent for rich lyricism that we encounter in his operas, and his interest in a grand manner of operatic writing, is a by-product of his lifelong interest in Italian opera, and particularly in Verdi.

As for structure, Dello Joio has continually been drawn to the form of theme-and-variations, the mold into which he poured some of his most successful creative inventions.

Singling out the basic earmarks of Dello Joio's style, Edward Downes points to his "strong melodic vein, rhythmic vitality, a relatively restrained harmonic vocabulary, an infectious brio and a freshness of invention."

Dello Joio was born in New York City on January 24, 1913. His initial music study took place with his father, a church organist, and was continued at the Institute of Musical Art, the Juilliard Graduate School, privately with

Pietro Yon, and with Paul Hindemith at the Berkshire Music Center at Tanglewood. His Trio for Flute, Cello and Piano received the Elizabeth Sprague Coolidge Award in 1939. There followed performances of major works throughout the country, and the receipt of many honors. Among the latter were two Guggenheim Fellowships (1944, 1945); a grant from the American Academy of Arts and Sciences (1947); two awards from the New York Music Critics Circle (1949, 1959); the Pulitzer Prize in music (1957), and an "Emmy" Award for his score for the NBC television production *The Louvre* (1965).

Between 1941 and 1943, he was musical director of The Dance Players, a company for which he wrote his first ballet scores in 1942 (*The Prairie* and *The Duke of Sacramento*). From 1944 to 1950, he was a member of the music faculty of the Sarah Lawrence College in Bronxville, New York, and in 1956, he was appointed professor of composition at the Mannes College of Music. He was the subject of a television program, "Profile of a Composer," over the CBS network on February 16, 1958, when he introduced a new work, *A Ballad of the Seven Lively Arts*, for piano and orchestra. In 1964, Dello Joio made an extensive tour of the Soviet Union.

1944 CONCERT MUSIC, for orchestra.

CONCERTO FOR HARP AND ORCHESTRA. I. Introduction and Passacaglia. II. Scherzo: March.

These were the first orchestral works by Dello Joio to receive significant performances. The *Concert Music* was written during the summer of 1944 and was introduced by the Pittsburgh Symphony under Fritz Reiner in January of 1946. Soon after this, the work was performed not only by the New York Philharmonic but also in three Polish cities. The composer has described this work as a "symphonic rondo." He adds: "A bold statement of the main germinal motive, played by the tympani *ff* opens the composition. An extended prologue follows for divided string choirs and commenting wind instruments, which anticipate, by suggestion, coming thematic material. The work plunges into a pulsating first theme for high woodwind supported by the full orchestra. A second theme, whose line is a continual dovetailing of different instruments, follows in a more relaxed and traditionally contrasting manner. . . . A dramatic prologue introduces the second part . . . the section's main characteristic being antiphonal brasses. . . . The third section is a kaleidoscopic treatment of all previous material."

The Harp Concerto was first heard in New York on November 3, 1947. Carlos Salzedo was the soloist and Thomas Scherman conducted the Little Orchestra Society.

The following information about this work is by the composer:

"The first movement is a passacaglia whose entrance is prepared by an extended introduction. This introduction has in it the melodic elements that emerge into the full passacaglia theme set forth by the cellos and basses. The movement closes with direct references to the introduction.

"The second movement is an amiable Scherzo. The rhythmic character of this movement affords the harp the opportunity for a varied virtuoso display. Most of the characteristics of the instrument are exploited to their maximum degree of sonority. The two contrasting themes that serve as the frame for the movement are in a constant state of kaleidoscopic treatment between the harp and the orchestra."

1946 RICERCARI, for piano and orchestra. I. Allegretto giocoso. II. Adagio. III. Allegro vivo.

A ricercare is a sixteenth- and seventeenth-century musical form in which the vocal motet is adapted to instrumental music. Generally speaking, the form presents a germinal idea (originally, the ricercare employed several ideas) which it develops fugally.

Dello Joio restores the old form to contemporary usage, retaining the classical structure but endowing it with modern writing. The three movements represent three different ways of developing the germinal idea: the first, harmonically; the second, melodically (a seven-measure theme for solo clarinet being the principal motive); the third, rhythmically.

This work was introduced on December 19, 1946, by the New York Philharmonic Orchestra. George Szell conducted, and the composer was at the piano.

1947 VARIATIONS, CHACONNE, AND FINALE, for orchestra.

When this work was introduced by the Pittsburgh Symphony Orchestra under Fritz Reiner, on January 30, 1948, it was called *Three Symphonic Dances*. The composer soon felt that to describe a work so serious in character as "dances" was something of an incongruity. He affixed a new title, by which the composition is now known. It has been extensively performed in both Europe and America; in 1949 it won the New York Music Critics Circle Award.

The basis of the entire work is a theme of liturgical character (first heard in the oboe) which the composer derived from the Kyrie of the *Missa de Angelis*. In the first movemement, following a brief prologue, the theme experiences six variations: Semplice grazioso; Andante religioso; Vivacissimo; Allegro pesante; Amabile; Funèbre. The chaconne that follows is built around the framework of the first four notes of the theme (in chromatic form). A veritable orgiastic outburst of energy marks the finale, in which the theme repeatedly asserts itself. This is joyous music—the religious music of the first two movements here becomes secular!—in which an almost carnival spirit of merrymaking prevails. With a thunderous enunciation of the first four notes of the theme, fortissimo, the music comes to a triumphant close.

1948 SONATA NO. 3, for piano. I. Theme and Variations. II. Presto e leggiero. III. Adagio. IV. Allegro vivo e ritmico.

Dello Joio's third piano sonata is one of his most significant works for solo piano and has enjoyed wide circulation. The first movement opens with a simple melody and continues with five brief variations. A sprightly scherzo movement follows, occasionally spiced with jazz condiments. The serene atmosphere of the opening movement returns in the third, a seven-minute Adagio, while the finale reverts to the lighthearted manner of the second movement. The opening and closing movements of this sonata borrowed some of its thematic material from the *Variations, Chaconne, and Finale,* for orchestra, described above.

1949 NEW YORK PROFILES, suite for orchestra. I. The Cloisters. II. The Park. III. The Tomb. IV. Little Italy.

This work was commissioned by Augustus L. Searle, honorary Vice-President of the Musical Arts Society of La Jolla, California. The première performance took place in La Jolla on August 21, 1949, under the direction of Nikolai Sokoloff.

Dello Joio provides, in this charming suite, four vignettes of New York City. In the first piece, the composer draws from the Gregorian chant to describe the magnificence of The Cloisters as it overlooks the Hudson. The second movement captures the spirit of fun and play among children in Central Park. A chorale fantasy next evokes Grant's Tomb, culminating in a brief quotation from *The Battle Hymn of the Republic.* The suite ends with a spirited Italian dance such as might be witnessed in the streets of New York's Italian neighborhoods. The composition ends with a reference to the Gregorian chant first heard in the initial movement.

1950 A PSALM OF DAVID, for mixed chorus, strings, brass and percussion.

Josquin des Prés' fifteenth-century setting of the Psalm, "Miserere mei, Deus," was the inspiration for one of Dello Joio's most impressive works for chorus, *A Psalm of David.* Dello Joio here borrows Josquin's cantus firmus and follows Josquin's three-part structure. This cantus firmus is heard six times in the slow introduction, and twenty-one times in the next three parts. In the first part, the cantus firmus is assigned to the basses. Here we encounter a good deal of a cappella writing for four-part chorus—"in a texture," Edward Downes explains, "recalling both the freely imitative and 'familiar' styles of the 16th century." The second part to Downes seems "episodic and even a bit disjointed." The third part develops into a "continuous hymn of praise. . . . The result is that the musical thought seems to flow more spontaneously; only the brief coda, Molto maestoso, seems a more rhetorical than musical flourish."

The first performance took place in Potsdam, New York, in 1951.

1951 THE TRIUMPH OF ST. JOAN SYMPHONY. I. The Maid. II. The Warrior. III. The Saint.

The subject of Joan of Arc had fascinated Dello Joio from his boyhood days on. He was only twelve, holding a post as church organist, when in his loft he came across a child's picture book of the saints. "I read for the first time of the maid from Lorraine and since that still vivid meeting with the girl, she has played . . . an important role in my musical thinking and career. . . . Always . . . it seems I was reading about some aspect of St. Joan and also discovering that the literature on her was endless."

In 1949, in writing his first opera on a commission from the Whitney Foundation, Dello Joio exploited the subject of Joan of Arc. He called the opera *The Triumph of St. Joan* (libretto by the composer in collaboration with Joseph Machlis), and it was produced at the Sarah Lawrence College in Bronxville, New York, on May 9, 1950. Despite the fact that the work was well received by the critics, Dello Joio refused to allow the work to be published, and discarded it for good. A number of years later he wrote a second opera about Joan with an entirely different libretto and score (*see*—1958).

But the music of *The Triumph of St. Joan* was not altogether abandoned. In 1950, Dello Joio was commissioned by the Louisville Orchestra to write an orchestral work for that organization. He adapted material from his deserted opera score into a three-movement symphony. When this symphony was first given, it bore the title of *Seraphic Dialogue* and was used in conjunction with a dance by Martha Graham; this was on December 5, 1951, in Louisville, Kentucky. But since then the music has been divorced from ballet and, under the title of *The Triumph of St. Joan Symphony,* has been extensively performed.

The first movement presents a folk song, "*Le Rossignol,*" intended to depict the simple, homespun personality of Joan, maid of Domrémy. This tune is followed by a set of variations, setting forth Joan's thoughts as she listens to the voices summoning her to lead the armies of France against England. The second movement describes Joan's military exploits, reaching a climax with the festive music attending the coronation of Charles VII. The finale touches upon Joan's martrydom. Its principal theme is a serene and exalted melody with religious overtones. The symphony ends not on a tragic note but in a spirit of "triumphant serenity," the composer says, explaining: "Joan must have welcomed the fire, for it was the final test which led to her salvation."

1954 LAMENTATION OF SAUL, for baritone, flute, oboe, clarinet, viola, cello and piano (also for baritone and orchestra).

Dello Joio wrote the *Lamentation* for the late Leonard Warren, the distinguished baritone, on a commission from the Elizabeth Sprague Coolidge Foundation. Warren introduced the work with the Pittsburgh Symphony Orchestra in August of 1954. The text was drawn from D. H. Lawrence's play *David.* Though Dello Joio here avoids the direct use of any liturgical material, his writing has, as Howard Taubman noted in *The New York Times,* "the feel of the Biblical world. There are grief and despair in this music, but these qualities do not become oppressive because the bitter self-knowledge of Saul is touched with poetry. . . . The solo and instrumental parts are fused with sententiousness of chamber music. The total effect is highly personal and eloquent."

1956 MEDITATIONS ON ECCLESIASTES, for string orchestra.

In its original version, this music was intended to accompany dance. It was written for José Limon when it bore the title *There Is a Time,* and was introduced by that dancer in New York in May of 1956. As a concert work, renamed *Meditations on Ecclesiastes,* it was first heard in Washington, D.C., on December 17, 1957, Howard Mitchell conducting the National Symphony. The orchestral composition received the Pulitzer Prize in music in 1957.

This music interprets the famous verses from chapter three of the Book of Ecclesiastes: "To everything there is a season . . . and a time for every purpose." The composition has twelve sections, each in a different tonality; structurally, it consists of a theme and variations.

The sections are as follows: I. Introduction (Largo), "to everything there is a season and a time for every purpose under the heaven"; II. Theme (Adagio con sentimento), "a time to be born"; III. Variation I (Solenne), "and a time to die"; IV. Variation II (Soave e leggiero), "a time to plant and a time to pluck up that which is planted"; V. Variation III (Grave), "a time to kill"; VI. Variation IV (Larghetto), "and a time to heal"; VII. Variation V (Animato), "a time to break down and a time to build up"; VIII. Variation VI (Adagio), "a time to weep and mourn"; IX. Variation VII (Spumante), "a time to dance and laugh"; X. Variation VIII (Adagio liberamente), "a time to embrace and a time to refrain from embracing"; XI. Variation IX (Con brio, deciso), "a time of hate and of war"; XII. Variation X (Semplice), "a time to live and a time of peace."

1958 THE TRIUMPH OF ST. JOAN (originally, THE TRIAL AT ROUEN), opera in two acts, with text by the composer. First performance: NBC-TV, April 8, 1956 (under the title, *The Trial at Rouen*); New York City Opera, April 16, 1959 (first stage performance, revised, with the definitive title of *The Triumph of St. Joan*).

This opera should not be confused with one similarly entitled *The Triumph of St. Joan* which Dello Joio had written in 1949 (*see*—1951, *The Triumph of St. Joan Symphony*). That opera had been abandoned. When Dello Joio decided to write another opera on his beloved subject of Joan of Arc, he used an entirely new libretto and score. This happened in 1955 with *The Trial at Rouen,* which was given its world première in a telecast by the NBC Opera Company. The composer subsequently revised his television opera to make it suitable for stage presentation, and after completing the revision, he borrowed the title (and nothing else) from his first opera. In making the transition from the TV screen to the stage, Dello Joio added a scene for Friar Julien and a sentry, to precede the first act, and interpolated an extended narrative for Joan at the stake. The revised opera received the New York Music Critics Circle Award in 1959.

In preparing his own libretto, the composer recognized that "the timelessness and universality of Joan as a symbol lay in the eternal problem of the individual's struggle to reconcile his personal beliefs with what he is expected to believe. . . . In a sense, she epitomizes the struggle of the artist, his fulfillment by sacrifice." The plot concentrates on the trial at Rouen. In the first scene, a corridor in the Rouen fortress, inquisitors are intoning a medieval prayer. Bishop Cauchon and Friar Julien exchange words. The Bishop is bent on destroying Joan, while the Friar is sympathetic to her. The scene then shifts to Joan's cell where the Friar is entreating her to submit to the ecclesiastical authorities. But Joan is intransigent, even though the Friar at times proves singularly persuasive. The second act consists of the trial in which Joan relives her military triumphs and is condemned to die at the stake by the fanatical judges. As this scene dissolves, a pyre is seen, into whose flames Joan mounts with pride and courage.

"Dello Joio has written an effective score," reported Frank Milburn, Jr., in *Musical America,* "one that underlines constantly the dramatic implications of the libretto. . . . The music gains in intensity as the drama progresses; in fact, so much so, that when Joan denies her voices—the climax of the work—the orchestra can be only silent while she speaks her words. The music's style is mildly dissonant and often Puccinian, but the music seems subordinate to the drama."

1961 FANTASY AND VARIATIONS, for piano and orchestra.

This work was commissioned by the Baldwin Piano Company of Cincinnati, and its première took place in that city on March 9, 1962. Lorin Hollander was the soloist, and Max Rudolf conducted the Cincinnati Symphony. The entire work is based on a four-note call (G, F-sharp, B and C). It opens with a three-part Fantasy (Adagio; Allegro vivo; Adagio), which is quiet and mysterious at the beginning. "A six-bar introduction by the solo piano is followed by an orchestral fortissimo," the composer explains. "Gradually the piano develops a melodic line which is carried on by the orchestra before the music fades away." In the second section, which begins in the orchestra, the main motive is reversed (B, C, F-sharp, G), and the third section is slow and short.

Six variations follow. In the first (Adagio), the piano states the four-note call after four measures, to which the orchestra gives reply. In the second (Allegro scherzando), the orchestra offers a new version of the call, which soon is assumed by the piano. The third variation (Andante amabile) has a "lilting rhythm" according to the composer, while the fourth (Spumante) is "effervescent." A slow section follows (Adagio mesto). "Characteristic of this variation," explains the composer, "is a series of piano arabesques taken up in the orchestra by the celesta." The concluding variation (Allegro gioioso) is in 12/8 meter and "is carried on with an uninterrupted pulsating rhythm. Here piano and orchestra achieve a vigorous cooperation. The ending comes abruptly with a vehement passage for piano and full orchestra."

1965 ANTIPHONAL FANTASY ON A THEME OF VINCENZO ALBRICI, for organ, brass, and strings. I. Moderato e deciso. II. Adagio. III. Gioioso.

Dello Joio dedicated this composition to the memory of his teacher, Paul Hindemith. The theme on which it is based—by Vincenzo Albrici (1631–1696)—had been previously used by the composer for his background music to the NBC television "special" *The Louvre* (winner of an "Emmy" in 1965). "The form of the work," the composer explains, "can be loosely described as a three-part form, after a lengthy introduction that indicates the thematic material. The manipulation of the three distinct groups has its roots in the antiphonal music of the early Italian church composers, particularly the Gabrielis." The three movements are played without interruption.

DAVID DIAMOND 1915–

In his earlier works—the *Psalm*, for orchestra (1936), the first violin concerto (1936), the *Elegy in Memory of Maurice Ravel* (1938), and the First Symphony (1940)—Diamond was the romanticist who spoke his heart freely and fully with emotional outbursts, rich harmonic textures, vivid orchestral colors. In the 1940s, he tended to simplify his writing and economize on his materials, but the romantic vein was still a significant trait. A tendency towards abstraction with an increasing concern for rhythmic vitality has been apparent in his later compositions beginning with *The World of Paul Klee,* for orchestra (1957). Yet even here a romantic element is present, and even here emphasis is placed on a strong and individual lyricism.

Diamond was born in Rochester, New York, on July 9, 1915. His basic training in music took place first at the Cleveland Institute of Music, the Eastman School of Music in Rochester, and the New Music School in New York. In 1936 he visited Paris where he subsequently studied with Nadia Boulanger, and wrote the *Psalm*, for orchestra, introduced in Rochester, New York, on December 10, 1936, and recipient of the Juilliard Publication Award in 1937. In the spring of 1938, he returned to Paris on a Guggenheim Fellowship, where he stayed until the outbreak of World War II. Back in America, he attracted attention with several orchestral works, the most notable being the First Symphony, which was performed by the New York Philharmonic under Mitropoulos on December 21, 1941. In 1941, he received a Guggenheim Fellowship (for the second time); in 1943, his Piano Quartet (1941) brought him the Paderewski Prize; and in 1944, he was given a grant by the National Academy of Arts and Letters. From then on, Diamond wrote prolifically in all the major forms of music except opera. Significant performances by leading American orchestras, chamber-music groups, and artists established him as one of America's important younger composers. His *Rounds,* for string orchestra, received a special citation from the New York Music Critics Circle, from which he also received an Award for his third string quartet (1947). Between 1951 and 1965, Diamond lived in Italy. In 1951, he was a Fulbright Professor at the University in Rome; and after that, he made his home in Florence where he proved uniquely productive. He returned to the United States at periodic intervals, serving as Slee Professor at the University of Buffalo, New York, in the spring of 1951, and again in the fall of 1963. He came back to the United States for good in 1965. In the fall of that year, he became a member of the music faculty at the Manhattan School of Music. In 1966, he was the recipient of the Stravinsky-ASCAP Award and was elected to the department of music of the National Institute of Arts and Letters.

1942 SYMPHONY NO. 2. I. Adagio funèbre. II. Allegro vivo. III. Andante espressivo, quasi adagio. IV. Allegro vigoroso.

Diamond's Second Symphony followed the first by about two years. It received its première in Boston on October 11, 1944, Serge Koussevitzky conducting the Boston Symphony.

In a detailed analysis of his symphony, the composer provided the following information. The opening Adagio funèbre is "a lyric movement of elegiac character consisting of two subjects: a long melody for the violins in unison (heard immediately after a short introduction by violas and cellos, *divisi*) and accompanied by an ostinato figure in cellos and basses; and a plangent melody for oboe solo accompanied by trilling violas—heard midway during the movement."

The Scherzo "has for its basic material a rhythmic figure mockingly tossed back and forth between cellos and basses and one bassoon. The rhythmic figure out of which the movement is built is derived from the second subject in the first movement. There is no trio section by itself."

The slow third movement "makes use of rhythmic harmonic and melodic elements heard in the first movement. After a short introduction utilizing the dirge-like motif (heard at the outset of the first movement in bases and tympani) there grows a short theme for muted violas (later to be developed in the fugato section). A clarinet solo follows, leading directly into a chorale-like section for strings which, for the main part, is played in unison by the first violins unaccompanied."

The function of the finale is "definitely that of the lively rondo-finale. The movement opens with a vigorous march-like subject for unison strings. Several of the episodes have important thematic functions; especially so the lyric folk song-like B section and the pizzicato C episodes for strings alone."

1944 ROUNDS, for string orchestra. I. Allegro molto vivace. II. Adagio. III. Allegro vigoroso.

The round—of which the twelfth-century *Sumer Is Icumen In* is both a classic example and a prototype—is more generally associated with vocal than with instrumental music. But in this work for string orchestra, Diamond demonstrates how its artistic possibilities can be extended. Diamond wrote it on a commission from Dimitri Mitropoulos, then conductor of the Minneapolis Symphony Orchestra, who introduced it in Minneapolis on November 24, 1944.

In the first movement, the different choirs of strings enter canonically as a kind of prelude to the main melody, which is played by the violas. The Adagio is a page of sustained lyricism, "a resting point between the two movements," in the words of the composer. The finale is a kind of fugal movement in the rondo form, in which the rhythmic device of the first movement is repeated, "so helping," wrote the composer, "to 'round' out the entire work and unify the formal structure."

Rounds received a special citation from the New York Music Critics Circle Award in 1945. It was then performed extensively by major American orchestras to become Diamond's most successful work up to that time.

1945 SYMPHONY NO. 3. I. Allegro deciso. II. Andante. III. Allegro vivo. IV. Adagio assai.

SYMPHONY NO. 4. I. Allegretto. II. Andante. III. Allegro.

Diamond's Third Symphony, dedicated to his parents, was given its first performance in Boston by the Boston Symphony Orchestra under Charles Munch, on November 3, 1950.

The composer explains that the symphony consolidates the cyclic form "by amalgamating all thematic, harmonic, and rhythmic material throughout the five movements." The composer adds further: "Apart from the principal thematic materials and their development in all movements, two 'motival' themes link together the entire symphony cyclically, appearing in their disguised forms . . . completely or in fragments."

Diamond's Fourth Symphony was the result of a commission from the Koussevitzky Music Foundation. On January 23, 1948, it was heard for the first time in a performance by the Boston Symphony Orchestra under Leonard Bernstein. Its première took place before that of the Third Symphony.

The work is of comparatively small dimensions. The first movement (in sonata form) opens with a tender theme which is projected in two sections, the first stated by muted strings and clarinets, and the second in the strings with a bassoon accompaniment. The second theme is gay and carefree (oboe solo). After a rather extended development in which the two themes are skilfully transfigured, there comes a powerful climax in which both of them are joined. The movement ends with a return of the first theme and a brief coda.

The introduction of the second movement is a chorale-like melody heard first in the brass and then repeated in the strings. The main idea of the movement is then unfolded, a long and sustained melody for viola. The third movement—full of dynamic power—opens with a vigorous subject for the brass. A rhythmic figure which follows in the tenor drum recurs throughout the movement and acquires increasing significance. This third movement has been described by its composer as combining the features of the scherzo and the rondo.

1946 STRING QUARTET NO. 3.

Diamond wrote his third string quartet in memory of a young American painter, Allela Cornell—the reason why there prevails in the first and last movements an elegiac character. The quartet was introduced at a concert of the League of Composers in New York on March 16, 1947. The quartet received the award of the New York Music Critics Circle.

This is the composer's succinct description: "The first movement is in the nature of a eulogy, modest and restrained in content and expressiveness, utilizing one theme which is fully developed and distributed in two formal sections. The second movement is a vigorous Allegro, akin to the scherzo, cast in the sonata-allegro form. The third movement combines formal features of an intermezzo and scherzo. The last movement is, in essence, the slow movement of the work, its dignified and elegiac character adding to the perorative and eulogistic aspect of the quartet."

1947 ROMEO AND JULIET, symphonic suite. I. Overture. II. Balcony Scene. III. Romeo and Friar Laurence. IV. Juliet and Her Nurse. V. Death of Romeo and Juliet.

This suite was commissioned by Thomas Scherman, conductor of the Little Orchestra Society, and was heard for the first time on October 20, 1947, in New York City, at a concert in which the Little Orchestra Society made its debut.

In writing this suite, the composer has informed us, he wished to "convey as fully and yet as economically as possible the innate beauty and pathos of Shakespeare's great drama without resorting to a large orchestral canvas and a definite musical form."

Describing his suite further, Diamond adds: "The Overture holds all the characteristics of the play in a very concentrated formal structure. The second movement needs no explanation. The third movement depicts those scenes of the drama in which the characters of Romeo and Friar Laurence appear, and in the music, thematic material of two distinct styles is used to describe them. The fourth movement is similarly descriptive. The last movement is the death of Romeo and Juliet."

1950 CONCERTO FOR PIANO AND ORCHESTRA. I. Andante; Allegretto; Allegro. II. Adagio, molto expressivo. III. Allegramente.

Diamond's Piano Concerto had to wait over a decade for its world première. This took place on April 28, 1966, in New York at a concert of the New York Philharmonic, the composer himself conducting, which also presented the world première of Diamond's Fifth Symphony, under Leonard Bernstein. The soloist in the concerto was Thomas Schumacher.

At its première, Diamond provided the following analysis of his concerto: "The first movement opens with the principal melodic idea in the strings. This is followed by a more emphatic three-note figure at the entry of the piano solo. The soloist restates the opening theme a fifth lower, leading to a short section of flowing sixteenth notes. The remainder of the movement is a working out of these materials. . . .

"The second movement opens with a theme of which the first two notes are important in the development of this movement. The first theme is presented by the strings, oboes, then solo oboe. Thereafter the solo piano enters with the second theme. Both themes are developed and reach a full orchestral climax, ending with a restatement of the opening, this time in the solo piano. The strings have a final, devotional, cadential comment.

"The third movement, a spirited rondo, takes off with a gay piccolo solo. The piccolo theme is immediately restated by the piano solo. A descending scale figure, in two different rhythmic forms, binds together the various sections of the rondo. The first contrasting section is built around a slowly rising arch-like figure announced by the piano solo. After a full orchestral climax and a short but brilliant technical display for the solo piano (not quite a cadenza), a slow, serious, metamorphosed version of the opening gay Allegro is heard in the solo piano and strings. The coda follows, returning to the gaiety of the opening—a brilliant display of virtuosity and velocity for both piano and orchestra."

1954 SYMPHONY NO. 6. I. Introduzione: Adagio interrotto; Allegro, fortemente mosso. II. Adagio interrotto. III. Deciso; Poco allegro.

Diamond's Sixth Symphony received its world première in Boston, Charles Munch conducting the Boston Symphony, on March 8, 1957. The most dramatic of the composer's symphonic compositions, this one utilizes the cyclic form in that all themes of all movements are related to the two themes of the first movement. The first theme, slow and stately, is heard at the very opening in oboe and English horn; the second appears in cellos and is faster and more sharply accented. The second movement is unusual in that it continually alternates slow and fast sections, its thematic material closely related to that of the introduction of the first movement. The third movement is in the form of an introduction, passacaglia and fugue. The fugato subject in the finale is based on the opening theme of the first movement, and so is its countersubject.

1963 ELEGIES FOR FLUTE, ENGLISH HORN AND STRINGS. I. Andante. II. Tempo moderato ma agitato; Adagio.

Diamond wrote the two *Elegies* in memory of two famous American writers: the first movement, for William Faulkner; the second, for the poet, E. E. Cummings. The first elegy is scored for English horn and string orchestra; the second, for flute and string orchestra. Each section takes about eight minutes to perform, and, though occasionally spiced by discords, is expressively melodic, all within a tonal framework. Eugene Ormandy conducted the Philadelphia Orchestra in the world première performance, on September 23, 1965, to help celebrate belatedly Diamond's fiftieth birthday.

1964 SYMPHONY NO. 5. I. Adagio; Allegro energico. II. Andante; Fuga: allegretto; Adagio.

Diamond's Fifth Symphony was written *after* he had produced Symphonies Nos. 6. 7, and 8. He had started working on his Fifth Symphony in 1947, intending it for Leonard Bernstein, who had given outstanding performances of Diamond's Fourth Symphony with the Boston Symphony. Diamond's plan at that time was to write a dramatic symphony inspired by *Oedipus Rex*. "I began the symphony that way," Diamond later revealed to an interviewer, "and after about three months I found that it was a bore. So I let the Fifth lie, and I went on to the Sixth, which I already had sketches for." During the next decade, Diamond kept thinking about and making sketches for his fifth symphony, while devoting himself to other projects, including two more symphonies. Then, on prodding from Bernstein, Diamond began an intensive campaign to finish the work. He did so in September of 1964. Leonard Bernstein and the New York Philharmonic introduced the symphony on April 28, 1966, on the same program featuring the world première of Diamond's Piano Concerto.

This is Diamond's analysis of his symphony:

"The slow introduction to the first movement holds the important thematic materials. . . . It opens with an unaccompanied English horn solo. There follows in plucked cellos and basses a pregnant motival idea, which becomes the principal theme of the Allegro section of this movement. The English horn melody is then expanded to fifteen bars by the strings. The pizzicato bass figure returns with a crescendo in which the tympani (two players) join, leading directly to the Allegro section. . . .

"The second movement opens with a strongly articulated thematic idea in cellos and basses. This is immediately followed by a very long melody in the first violins derived from the third theme of the first movement. This theme consists of motives and figures to be utilized in the ensuing fugue. The fugue subject is announced by the violas. Among the counter-subjects and in the episodes will be heard thematic ideas from the first movement. The fugue reaches its climax with the entry of the solo organ, then subsides to an Adagio (a coda) which ends in a long melody for solo cello amalgamating thematic ideas from both movements."

ERNST VON DOHNÁNYI 1877–1960

The admiration—adulation might be the apter word—which young Dohnányi had for Johannes Brahms had a marked influence on his musical writing. There were those facetious critics who referred to Dohnányi's op. 1, the Piano Quintet in C Minor (1895), as "Brahms' Second Piano Quintet." Indeed, there is no mistaking the Brahmsian romanticism, spaciousness, and emotional climaxes in this first Dohnányi composition. But even in subsequent Dohnányi music, the Brahmsian fingerprints are still in evidence. Yet, for all its debt to the master, these Dohnányi compositions have a charm of their own, due largely to Dohnányi's sound technique, inventive and often spontaneous lyricism, and (in the orchestral music) particularly interesting instrumentation.

Dohnányi never did succeed in achieving a personal identity in his music. He never allowed himself to be influenced by the new ideas and techniques and idioms springing up all around him. Even on those less frequent occasions when he derived his materials from Hungarian folk music—following the lead of his celebrated compatriots, Bartók and Kodály—his music never assumed a distinguished personality. He simply never outgrew his love for German post-Romanticism; and by the same token, he never quite developed from an interesting and a charming composer into a great one.

Dohnányi was born in Pressburg, Hungary, on July 27, 1877. After some study of the piano and organ with Karl Forstner in his native city, he entered the Royal Academy in Budapest in 1894. There, during the next three years, he made rapid strides both in piano, with Stefan Thomán, and composition, with Hans Koessler. His youthful Symphony in F major and *Zrinyi Overture* jointly won the Hungarian Millennium Prize in 1896. In 1897, he began his career as a concert pianist, a career that soon gathered notable successes the world over; his American debut took place with the Boston Symphony on March 22, 1900.

His concert career, however, did not stem the tide of his creativity. When only eighteen, he wrote an admirable Piano Quintet in C minor, op. 1, which inspired the praise of Brahms, who was responsible for getting it performed in Vienna. In 1899, he received the Hans von Bülow Prize for his first piano concerto, in E minor, op. 5. This was followed by his Symphony in D minor, op. 9, successfully introduced in Manchester, England, on January 30, 1902. In all these compositions Dohnányi was noticeably influenced by Brahms.

From 1905 to 1915, Dohnányi taught piano at the Berlin High School for Music, filling the rank of professor from 1908 on. In 1919, he was made associate director of the Budapest Academy of Music, becoming full director there in 1933. From 1918 to 1944, he was the conductor of the Budapest Philharmonic; in 1931, he was made head of the Hungarian Broadcasting Service. As conductor, he made guest appearances in Europe and the United States; in 1925, he was appointed principal conductor of the short-lived State Symphony in New York.

In 1947, Dohnányi left his native country for good. He first came to England where he himself introduced his Second Piano Concerto in B minor, op. 42, in Sheffield, in 1947. On November 23, 1948, there took place in London the première of his Symphony in E major, op. 40. In 1948, he came to the United States. One year later, he was appointed to the music faculty of the Florida State College in Tallahassee, where he remained for the rest of his life. He died in New York City, where he had come to supervise some recordings of his compositions, on February 9, 1960.

1907 STRING QUARTET NO. 2 IN D-FLAT MAJOR, op. 15. I. Andante; Allegro. II. Presto acciacato. III. Molto adagio; Animato.

In this, Dohnányi's second string quartet, there is such expressiveness, and at times such dramatic content, that the composition has sometimes been said to have fused the best elements of the sonata form and the tone poem. The first movement alternates between a pensive mood and an energetic one, the first theme of which has the kind of autumnal sadness and the feeling of resignation we associate with so many of Brahms's themes. This subject occupies Dohnányi's main interest in this movement. The second movement is a vigorous scherzo, its trio boasting a solemn chorale. A majestic slow movement precedes the concluding Animato section, which quotes material previously heard in the two earlier movements.

The D-flat major String Quartet followed the composer's first quartet (A minor, op. 7) by eight years. The première of the second quartet took place in Berlin in 1907 in a performance by the Klinger Quartet.

1909 SUITE IN F-SHARP MINOR, for orchestra, op. 19. I. Andante. II. Scherzo. III. Romanza. IV. Rondo.

This Suite is in Dohnányi's best Romantic vein. The influence of Brahms is obvious—as, for example, in the unmistakably Brahmsian song in the first movement, heard first in the woodwind, soon supplemented by strings. It is the subject of six variations that run the gamut from gentle tranquillity to gay animation, from quiet introspection to passionate romanticism. The often subtle and elusive relationship of variations to their theme is once again reminiscent of Brahms's use of the variation form.

Dohnányi's bent for wit is found in the Scherzo, a piquant little movement that moves with quicksilver grace. It opens with a sparkling thought for the woodwind, to which the strings give reply. A contrasting section emphasizes the note "A" in varying harmonies. Plucked strings introduce the Romanza, in which the principal subject is spoken by the solo cello (once again the image of Brahms is reflected). An energetic rondo brings gaiety to the closing pages of the score. Its main subject is vigorously presented by the strings.

The première of the Suite took place in 1910 at a concert of the Budapest Philharmonic, the composer conducting.

1913 VARIATIONS ON A NURSERY SONG, for piano and orchestra, op. 25.

The nursery song exploited here in a series of witty variations is a familiar one. It is the old French song, *Ah, Vous Dirai-Je, Maman,* which Mozart also used for variations, and which in the United States is sung with the alphabet.

Dohnányi's *Variations* opens with the utmost sobriety which seems to set the stage for the entrance of an impressive and dignified melody; then the gay little tune is introduced by the piano. The nine variations that follow are full of lighthearted, satiric and gay ideas. It becomes understandable why the composer dedicated this work "to the enjoyment of lovers of humor, and to the annoyance of others." In the finale, a robust fugue develops into a climax, after which the nursery theme returns in a slightly altered form.

The *Variations* was introduced in Berlin on February 17, 1916, with the composer at the piano, and the orchestra conducted by Karl Panzner.

1914 PIANO QUINTET IN E-FLAT MINOR, op. 26. I. Allegro non troppo. II. Allegretto e Presto, rubato e capriccioso; Vivace. III. Moderato.

As a young man of eighteen, Dohnányi had written his first Piano Quintet in C minor, which became his Opus No. 1. It was a youthful, romantic work unashamedly imitative of Brahms, and it had attracted the interest and support of that master. In his second piano quintet, some nineteen years later, a mature craftsman and a fully integrated creative artist is speaking—but still speaking with unmistakable Brahmsian accents. The work opens with a characteristic broad Brahmsian statement in unison violin and cello. The two contrasting themes that follow are broadly lyrical in German post-Romantic style. Brahmsian, too, is the gentle, and at times playful intermezzo, the second movement. The finale begins with a solemn-like fugue characterized by skilful contrapuntal writing, after which themes from the earlier two movements are remembered and discussed.

The Piano Quintet was performed for the first time in Berlin in 1914 by the Klinger Quartet, with Dohnányi at the piano.

1924 RURALIA HUNGARICA, for orchestra, op. 32b (also for piano, op. 32a, and for violin and piano, op. 32c). I. Andante poco moto, rubato. II. Presto ma non tanto. III. Allegro grazioso. IV. Adagio non troppo. V. Molto vivace.

Only infrequently did Dohnányi stray from the Brahmsian fields to graze in those Hungarian pastures cultivated by Bartók and Kodály. And when he did, his efforts were usually not rewarded with success. *Ruralia Hungarica* is an exception. Three versions exist. The original one is for solo piano, and it is found in the *Seven Pieces for Piano.* An orchestral version is one of the movements in *Five Pieces for Orchestra,* while an adaptation for violin and piano appears in *Three Pieces for Violin.* The orchestral version was given its première in Budapest in 1924, with the composer conducting the Budapest Philharmonic. Elements of Hungarian song and dance are charmingly utilized.

The first movement features a haunting melody for solo viola over an accompanying triplet figure in the oboe; a livelier tune for clarinet in triple time follows. The second movement is made up of three ideas: a march-like tune in full orchestra; a more reserved subject in the woodwind; a gay folk-tune melody, which is first presented by the clarinets before it passes on to other sections of the orchestra. The third movement alternates solo and tutti groups almost in the style of the Baroque concerto grosso. In the fourth movement, the composer touches a melancholy mood in both the opening and the closing sections, but provides contrast with occasional outbursts of passion midway. The finale, a kind of tarantella, has rhythmic interest and is dominated by a single theme.

PAUL DUKAS 1865–1935

No more than a handful of Paul Dukas's works have survived, the most of these being the delightful and witty programmatic scherzo, *L'Apprenti sorcier,* written before 1900. At different times in his career Dukas reacted creatively to different stimuli: to Wagner, in his first symphonic works, the concert overture *Polyeucte* (1891) and the Symphony in C major (1896); to the realism and literalness of Richard Strauss's programmatic details, in *L'Apprenti sorcier* (1897); to Beethoven and César Franck, in his two most significant works for the piano, the E-flat minor Sonata (1901) and the *Variations, Interlude et Final* (1903); and lastly, in his two all-important works for the stage—*Ariane et Barbe-bleue* and *La Péri*—to Debussy and Impressionism. But however close his spiritual ties may be now to one composer and now to another, he remains himself, in the mastery of his technique, in his fastidious workmanship, in the elegance of his style, in good taste and sensitivity, in his classic repose and serenity. Few though his works may be, and indebted as they may be to other masters, they have earned their composer the right to belong with the significant French composers of the twentieth century.

Dukas was born in Paris on October 1, 1865. After pursuing classical studies at the Lycée Charlemagne at Turgot, he entered the Paris Conservatory in 1882. There he was a pupil of Mathias (piano), Dubois (harmony) and Guiraud (composition). He won first prize in counterpoint, and in 1888, the second Prix de Rome for his cantata *Velléda*.

After a period of military service, he returned to Paris to devote himself to composition. He first attracted interest with his concert overture, *Polyeucte,* performed by the Lamoureux Orchestra on January 23, 1892. His reputation grew with his Symphony in C major, its première conducted in Paris by Paul Vidal on January 3, 1897. Then world recognition was focused on Dukas with the triumph of his orchestral scherzo, *L'Apprenti sorcier* (*The Sorcerer Apprentice*), now acknowledged to be his best symphonic composition. Dukas wrote it in 1897, inspired by the Goethe ballad, *Der Zauberlehring,* which in turn was an adaptation of an old folktale. With Richard Strauss's vividly realistic tone poems as his example, Dukas here produced an orchestral scherzo which re-creates graphically all the details of a charming tale, so much so that it is almost possible to follow the progress of the story without recourse to a program analysis. *The Sorcerer Apprentice* (this is the more accurate translation of the French title, as opposed to the more frequently used, *The Sorcerer's Apprentice*) was an immediate success when it was played for the first time, at a concert of the Société Nationale in Paris on May 18, 1897, the composer conducting.

Dukas wrote only two works for the stage, each representing him at the height of his powers: *Ariane et Barbe-bleue* in 1907, and *La Péri* in 1910. After 1910, his works were few and far between, and some of these he destroyed just before his death. He now concentrated for the most part on teaching, though he also wrote music criticisms for journals. From 1910 to 1912, he taught orchestration at the Paris Convervatory; from 1927 until his death, he was the professor of composition there. In 1918, he succeeded Debussy as a member of the Conseil de l'Enseignement Supérieur.

Paul Dukas died of a heart attack in Paris on May 17, 1935. A few months before his death, he was invited to occupy the chair at the Académie des Beaux-Arts vacated by Alfred Bruneau.

1907 ARIANE ET BARBE-BLEUE (ARIADNE AND BLUEBEARD), opera in three acts, with Maurice Maeterlinck's drama as text. First performance: Opéra-Comique, Paris, May 10, 1907.

It is the opinion of many French authorities that Dukas's only opera (though rarely heard) is one of the two great achievements of the French lyric theatre of the twentieth century, the other being Debussy's *Pelléas et Mélisande*. Comparison between these two masterpieces is inescapable. Both are derived from plays by Maeterlinck. Both have a unanimity of style and mood. Both have a few similar situations and episodes. Both are negations of the Wagnerian principles so much in vogue in the early twentieth century. Both are impressionistic in their utilization of symbolism, indulgence in atmospheric writing, and preference for subtle suggestion rather than outright statement.

But if these are similarities, there are also differences. Martin Cooper points out a few: "Dukas's orchestration alone would be enough to distinguish his music from Debussy's. It is full and brilliant, the brass is used with conventional effectiveness and the coloring is bright and dramatic in contrast. . . . The recitative is less fluid than in *Pelléas* and in Ariane's farewell there is an amplitude and a direct emotional appeal which is rhetorical in the best sense. . . . Dukas has not Debussy's personality and he was weak in melodic invention; but musical craftsmanship and nobility of sentiment are characteristic of *Ariane et Barbe-bleue*."

Maeterlinck wrote his drama expressly for Dukas, modestly describing it as a "short poem, of the genre which goes by the unfortunate name of opéra-comique, meant to provide musicians . . . with a theme suitable for musical development. It was not designed as anything more ambitious and my intentions are entirely mistaken by those who try to find in addition some moral or philosophic message." For his heroine, Maeterlinck selected the sixth wife of Bluebeard, Ariadne, who refuses to believe that Bluebeard has killed his other wives and that a similar fate awaits her. She is given seven keys by her husband: six are silver, giving access to vaults containing precious jewels—and these she may use at will. The seventh, of gold, opens a strange door; the use of that key is strictly denied her.

In that seventh room are Bluebeard's wives, huddled in rags. Ariadne arranges for their escape, brings them to her castle, and decks them out in fine clothes and lavish jewels. Meanwhile, Bluebeard engages in a fight with the villagers, is beaten, tied, and brought back to his home as captive. There, freed of the bonds that tie his wrists, he is astonished to find his beautiful wives. Ariadne decides to leave Bluebeard forever; but her entreaties to the other wives to follow her fall on deaf ears.

While the composer's indebtedness to Debussy and *Pelléas* cannot be denied, Dukas also takes from Wagner whatever could serve his own artistic ends—most notably the use of a *Leitmotiv* technique, and the building up of these motives into a rich and expressive symphonic texture, employing the fullest resources of instrumental virtuosity. More Wagnerian than Debussyan is Dukas's gift at descriptive writing, which, in the words of Richard Aldrich, "stands him in good stead in the episodes of the first act, where successively the several doors are opened, and the cascades of jewels are shown. For these he has used different transformations of one and the same theme, ingeniously wrought. There are few passages in the work more striking than that in which Ariadne hears for the first time the distant chanting of the imprisoned wives, a song that takes on clearer and clearer definition, and assumes the character of one of the mournful French folk tunes of medieval origin.

"The flood of light let in upon the gloom of the subterranean dungeon of the second act when Ariadne breaks the panes of the darkened window is accompanied by a splendidly sonorous burst of orchestral music, all the more effective from its contrast with the lugubrious pages that have preceded it. The picture of the smiling Spring landscape, with the sea beyond, seen through the open door and framed in the blackness of the groined vault, is delightfully illuminated by the music.

"The one scene in which gaiety enters into this opera, that with which the third act opens, is charmingly expressed in the music, after a long and sombre prelude, which has a dark and singular beauty of its own. The end of this act is developed with a sure touch in delineating the feverish excitement of the woman watching the combat without the castle, the entrance of the throng of awed and embarrassed peasants, the revived affection of the wives."

Ariane et Barbe-bleue was a substantial success when it was introduced at the Opéra-Comique in Paris. By the time it reached the stage of the Paris Opéra (on January 25, 1935), it had been given over a hundred times at the Opéra-Comique. Meanwhile it was introduced in the United States—at the Metropolitan Opera on March 29, 1911, Toscanini conducting, and Geraldine Farrar assuming the role of Ariadne.

1910 LA PÉRI, dance-poem for orchestra.

La Péri was written for the dancer Mlle. Trukhanova, to whom it was dedicated. It was introduced at the Châtelet Theatre in Paris on April 22, 1912, with the composer conducting.

The original program contained the following story-outline of the music:

"It happened that at the end of his youthful days. . . . Iskender went about Iran seeking the flower of immortality.

"The sun sojourned thrice in its dozen dwellings without Iskender finding the flower. At last he arrived at the end of the earth. . . . There, on the steps that lead to the hall of Ormuzd, a Peri was reclining, asleep in her jewelled robe. A star sparkled above her head; her lute rested on her breast; in her hand shone the flower.

"Iskender noiselessly leaned over the sleeper and, without awakening her, snatched the flower, which suddenly became between his fingers like the noonday sun over the forests of Ghilan. The Peri, opening her eyes, clapped the palms of her hands together and uttered a loud cry, for she could not now ascend toward the light of Ormuzd.

"Iskender, regarding her, wondered at her face, which surpassed in deliciousness even the face of Gurda-ferrid. In his heart he coveted her. The Peri knew the thought of the King, for in the right hand of Iskender the lotus grew purple and became as the face of longing.

"Thus the servant of the Pure knew that this flower of life was not for him. To recover it, she darted forward like a bee. The invincible lord bore away from her the lotus.

"But the Peri danced the dance of the Peris; always approaching him until her face touched his face; and at the end he gave back the flower without regret. Then the lotus was like unto snow and gold, as the summit of Elbourz at sunset. The form of the Peri seemed to melt in the light coming from the calix and soon nothing more was to be seen than a hand raising the flower of flame, which faded into the realm above, Iskender saw her disappear. Knowing from this that his end drew near, he felt the darkness encompassing him."

Gustave Samazeuilh points out that in this "dance-poem" Dukas realizes a new concept of the relationship between music and dance. "Inspired by a poetic oriental legend, preceded by a striking fanfare for brass instruments, the music unites . . . the deep feeling and ardor of perception with the originality of a form which is always plastic and symphonic, the result of intense poetic feeling."

WERNER EGK 1901–

When Werner Egk conceived the idea of an abstractionist opera and wrote the libretto (*Abstrakte Oper Nr. 1*), he asked Boris Blacher to write the music. This fact is not without significance, in view of the fact that Egk in his own right is a distinguished composer of operas. Though Egk occasionally employed modern idioms, he was essentially a conformist and a romanticist—and avant-garde opera just was not his meat. He is in his element—whether in serious or comic opera—when he sings lusty tunes and spins inviting dance rhythms; when he can fully exploit his remarkable gifts at orchestration; when he can draw from folk sources (preferably Bavarian); when he can be vividly descriptive. His spiritual predecessor is Richard Strauss—but the Strauss of *Der Rosenkavalier* and *Arabella* rather than the Strauss of *Salome* and *Elektra*. "Egk's music," said Arthur Honegger, "is direct, sometimes racy, frequently full of charm. It directly touches the listener and is broadly intelligible."

Egk was born in Auchsesheim, near Augsburg, Germany, on May 17, 1901. Except for some piano lessons from Anna Hirzel-Langenhan in Augsburg and a brief period of study of composition with Carl Orff in Munich, he has been self-taught. In 1929, he started writing music for a puppet theatre in Munich, besides launching his career as a conductor. Between 1929 and 1933, he wrote several operas—librettos as well as the music—for radio transmission. One of these radio operas, *Columbus,* he later revised for stage production, and it was introduced by the Frankfort Opera on January 13, 1942.

His first successful composition for the concert hall was *Georgica,* for orchestra, in 1934. Less than a year later came his first opera written directly for the stage—*Der Zaubergeige,* with which he achieved his first major success. This was followed by other operas that attracted considerable interest and aroused considerable enthusiasm: *Peer Gynt,* based on Ibsen, produced by the

Berlin State Opera on November 24, 1938; *Irische Legende,* derived from a story by William B. Yeats, and heard at the Salzburg Festival on August 17, 1955; *Der Revisor,* his most famous comic opera, produced in 1957; *Die Verlobung in San Domingo,* based on a story by Heinrich von Kleist, mounted in the-then newly rebuilt National Theatre of Munich on November 27, 1963.

From 1936 to 1940, Egk was a conductor of the Berlin State Opera. When Egk's ballet *Abraxas*—produced at the Munich Opera on June 6, 1948—was banned on moral grounds, Egk returned to Berlin from his home in Munich to serve as director of the Berlin High School for Music until 1953. He then reestablished his home in Munich, where he has since served as President of the Association of German Composers.

1934 GEORGICA, "peasant pieces" for orchestra.

Egk came from Swabian-Bavarian peasant stock. Bavarian folk songs and dances were close to his heart. He used three of these in his first successful work for orchestra, whose première took place in New York, at a concert of the New York Philharmonic, on November 14, 1934. The first of the pieces is a march. A subdued introduction prepares the rhythm for the march melody which erupts loudly in the strings. The second piece is an old Bavarian love song, first heard in the flute, then repeated by the trumpet. The closing piece, according to an unidentified annotator, "awakens memories of the pantomimic dances of the mountaineers, in which jealousy and the contests for the possession of the peasant maidens play the leading roles. A rough humor is especially apparent."

1935 DER ZAUBERGEIGE (THE MAGIC VIOLIN), opera in three acts, with text by Ludwig Andersen and the composer based on a puppet play by Count Pocci. First performance: Frankfort Opera, May 20, 1935.

Bavarian folk song and dance is a storehouse from which Egk drew a delectable score for this, his first work for the operatic stage, and the first work to bring him international recognition. *Der Zaubergeige* is a folk opera whose score overflows with infectious folk tunes and such folk dances as the Ländler and the Polka; it is a score continually brightened by a robust peasant humor and at times by delicate irony. It is easy to see why this opera became such a formidable success when first introduced, and why it has sustained its appeal through the years—after having gained a new lease on life through a revision first seen in Stuttgart on May 2, 1954.

The action takes place in some fairy-tale kingdom. Kaspar, a male servant, leaves his employer to seek his fortune. All he has with him are three coins, which the maid, Gretl, had presented to him. He parts with one of them when he meets a beggar. The beggar turns out to be Cuperus, king of the spirits, who rewards Kaspar by granting him any wish. Kaspar asks for and gets a magic violin which has the power to enchant anybody who listens to it; but in return for this gift, Kaspar must renounce all love. After encountering various adventures with his violin, Kaspar finally meets Gretl again. She is in despair at finding he has grown so cold to her, and goes off sobbing. But Kaspar is not so successful in withstanding the seductive charms and advances of Ninabella. For this reason, the violin loses its magic powers and Kasper is doomed. He is about to be executed when Cuperus suddenly appears and frees him. Happily, Kaspar gives up the magic violin for good and returns to a peaceful and uneventful life with Gretl.

1957 DER REVISOR (THE INSPECTOR GENERAL), comic opera in five acts, with text by the composer based on a story by Nikolai Gogol. First performance: Schwetzingen, Germany, May 9, 1957.

In adapting Gogol's famous satire on political and military corruption in provincial Russia for the musical stage, Egk was compelled to make a number of significant changes in the story. As he said: "It was self-evident that it was impossible with a play so rich in words, to compose word by word." Egk solved the problem by abandoning lyricism for a parlando style in which the dialogue could move swiftly and flexibly in a brisk tempo. "It was impossible to preserve in an opera all twenty-four persons of the play and, in addition to them, the whole male and female chorus, and merchants, petty bourgeoisie, and the petitioners." Egk consequently reduced the number of characters to a mere half-dozen singers and three dancers.

The opera, then, became a concise and compressed work made up mainly of secco-recitativos, interrupted by set numbers, ensembles and dances. A Russian atmosphere is realized through the interpolation of various Russian songs and dances. The most celebrated of these is the folk tune, "A Birch Tree Stood in the Field," which Tchaikovsky had once borrowed for the finale of his fourth symphony. In the opera it is heard at the end of the third act and in the beginning of the fourth.

In a small Russian town, in the middle of the nineteenth century, the rumor is spread that a government inspector is due from St. Petersburg to make a report. Clestakov, a stranger in the town inn, is suspected of being that inspector and is treated with pomp and ceremony that he soon comes to enjoy. He moves into the captain's house, where he fleeces the servants, makes love to the captain's wife, borrows huge sums of money from the captain, and then becomes engaged to the captain's daughter. An intercepted letter from Clestakov to a friend reveals to the horrified townspeople—and especially to the captain and his family—that they had been duped. Hardly have they all had time to recover from the shock, when they get word that the real Inspector from St. Petersburg has arrived and wishes to begin the research for his report—at which point the final curtain descends.

"In treating this subject," wrote Everett Helm in his review in *Musical America,* "Egk has concentrated on those scenes that lend themselves to ensemble numbers. These constitute the opera's framework and are on the whole extraordinarily effective. They alternate with passages in quick, rhythmic parlando recitative and with occasional scenes in pantomime with orchestral accompaniment. . . . Egk keeps things moving from start to finish."

The American première of *Der Revisor* took place in New York on October 19, 1960, in a performance by the New York City Opera conducted by the composer.

GOTTFRIED VON EINEM 1918–

Though he has been productive in the symphonic field in which he produced a good deal of excellent music, von Einem is essentially a musical dramatist. In fact, he is one of the most significant opera composers to come out of Austria since Alban Berg. He represents a compromise between past and present procedures. As a post-Romantic, he is a spiritual heir of Mahler and Richard Strauss. He reveals himself as a child of his own times in the expressiveness of his declamation, in his skilful use of dissonance, atonality and even jazz, when these idioms serve his artistic purposes. His music is essentially diatonic, placing importance on rhythmic vitality and occasionally on lyricism. It has passion, and it has tenderness. Most of all, however—whether he is writing for the concert hall or for the theatre—it has dramatic impetus.

Deszoe Hajas has explained that von Einem's style is "not a type of neoclassicism, or coquetry with traditional form, but a conquering of new possibilities of expression in tonality. It is not a formal, but a substantial, regeneration because it does not renew simply an outer form, but the ideal intention of classical music, to find a musical language which combines the author's individuality with that of the recipient, creating common understanding."

Von Einem was born in Bern, Switzerland, on January 24, 1918. He was the son of the Austrian military attaché. His boyhood was spent in Holstein, where he attended public school and first showed an interest in and a talent for music. When he was eleven, he completed two orchestral compositions. His musical training, however, remained sporadic until 1938, when he studied composition with Boris Blacher. In 1941, he worked as assistant conductor and coach at the Berlin State Opera and the Bayreuth Festival. His Opus No. 1 appeared in 1944, the ballet *Prinzessin Turandot,* produced in Dresden that year. His first successful work for orchestra was the *Capriccio,* op. 2, performed by the Berlin Philharmonic on March 12, 1943.

His early successes in Germany notwithstanding, von Einem was not regarded favorably by the Nazis. In fact, on one occasion, he and his mother were imprisoned by the Gestapo. In 1945, he left Germany for good and established residence in Salzburg, where, one year later, he married Lianne von Bismarck. His first operas were produced successfully at the Salzburg Festival: *Dantons Tod* in 1947 and *Der Prozess* in 1953. In 1953, he paid a visit to the United States as a guest of the State Department. During his stay, his *Orchestra Music* was performed by the New York Philharmonic under Mitropoulos.

Several of his most important works for orchestra after that were commissioned in the United States, and some of these received their world premières there. These included the *Meditations for Orchestra* in 1954; *Symphonic Scenes* (Boston Symphony, October 11, 1957); *Ballade* (Cleveland Orchestra, 1958); the *Philadelphia Symphony* in 1960; and *Night Music* (Vienna Philharmonic, April 27, 1963).

In 1954, von Einem was appointed a member of the artistic board of the Vienna State Opera. Since then, he has been the President of the Austrian section of UNESCO, and counsellor to the Vienna Konzerthausgesellschaft. In 1960, he was awarded both the Theodor Körner Prize and the Prize of the City of Vienna. In 1965, he received the Austrian State Prize for music.

1943 CAPRICCIO, for orchestra, op. 2.

CONCERTO FOR ORCHESTRA, op. 4. I. Allegro. II. Largo. III. Allegro.

The *Capriccio* was its composer's first success. It was introduced by the Berlin Philharmonic under Leo Borchard on March 12, 1943. Romantic in its outlook, and poetic in content, the work was obviously influenced by Mahler and Strauss, particularly in its indulgence in passionate statements, in rich orchestral sonorities and in its chromaticisms. It has three compact sections, played without interruption (Allegro, Adagio, Allegro), dominated by a unifying theme heard early in the violins. This subject is heard throughout the work in various tranformations, finally appearing in inversion in the concluding part. A secondary subject for clarinet has spiritual kinship with this main melody.

To Everett Helm, the *Concerto for Orchestra* represented "an amazing advance over his *Capriccio*." Herbert von Karajan introduced it in Berlin with the Berlin State Opera Orchestra on April 3, 1944. Here is how Helm described the composition in *Musical America*: "The opening Allegro is energetic and exciting except for a brief middle section in a quieter vein which contains some excellent contrapuntal writing." In the slow movement, "the opening melody, which is later developed and extended, is contrasted and then combined with a somewhat quicker, more rhythmic melody, and the movement contains two effective well-built climaxes." The finale is "amusing and vigorous. After a brief fortissimo introduction, comes the principal melody, which like many of von Einem's, hovers around a few recurring notes. After a section employing an ingenious rhythmic pattern, various elements suggesting jazz are introduced."

1947 DANTONS TOD (DANTON'S DEATH), opera in two parts, op. 6, with text by Boris Blacher and the composer based on a drama by Georg Büchner. First performance: Salzburg, Austria, August 6, 1947.

DANTONS TOD, symphonic suite for orchestra, op. 6a. I. Presto. II. Molto sostenuto. III. Im Tempo des französichen Geschwindmarsches. IV. Molto allegro.

Dantons Tod was its composer's first opera, and the work that focused international attention upon him. It was a major success when introduced at the Salzburg festival in 1947—in fact, it was regarded by most critics as the crowning achievement of that festival. Combining a highly effective declamatory style, which often follows speech patterns, with remarkable choral passages, which practically dominate the musical scheme, von Einem here merges as a musical dramatist of first importance.

The emphasis which Georg Büchner placed in his drama on political ideology is carried over into the opera, where the live interest between Danton and his wife, and between the secondary characters (Camille and Lucille), receive only passing attention. The high points of the opera, as in the Büchner play, lie in the Tribunal scene where Danton is tried and sentenced, and in the closing guillotine scene where he is executed. Here the chorus becomes the dominant character, as it exploits French revolutionary song materials. "As the people sound forth with the song of revolution of the 'Carmagnole' and Danton and his comrades sing the 'Marseillaise,'" reported Helmut Schmitt-Garre in *Merkur,* "interspersed with shouts from the masses of 'Down with him' and 'Traitor' in a fortissimo which is enveloped by the storm of the orchestra, dramatic turbulence and almost deafening sound are united in a powerful theatrical effect."

In the opening scene, in which Danton is playing cards with his friends and wife, we sense his growing disenchantment with the Revolution and his concern over the Reign of Terror to which it had given birth. The second scene finds Danton coming into direct conflict with Robespierre after one of the latter's inflammatory speeches. Robespierre now becomes convinced that his dear friend, Danton, must be disposed of, for the good of the Revolution, and orders his arrest. The chorus now takes over, crying out first for Danton's release, then, having been swayed by Danton's enemies, to demand his death. At the Tribunal, Danton makes a passionate but futile defense of his position and ideas. Finally, in the public square, the crowds are celebrating Danton's execution with song and dance. The crowds then disperse, leaving the stage empty except for Lucille, who has gone mad, because her beloved Camille had also been a victim of the guillotine. Sitting at the foot of the guillotine she moans sadly, as the final curtain descends: "There is a reaper and he is called Death."

The composer made no attempt at integration through the use of recurrent motives or to recall in later scenes significant musical thoughts from earlier ones. Each scene is self-sufficient. Even the opening prelude, which begins with an effective chorale for the brass and continues with an expressive subject for the strings, uses material never again heard in the opera itself. Rather, unity is achieved by having the orchestra provide the transition from one scene to the next and anticipating the coming mood and atmosphere of the drama. Four of these orchestral interludes were adapted by the composer into a four-movement symphonic suite, that has been played by major orchestras in Europe and America. The initial movement, performed between the first and second scenes, reflects Danton's growing anxiety at the direction the Revolution is taking. The second episode is funereal, presenting a mournful subject for the woodwind; the music in the opera separates the Tribunal scene from that of Danton's execution. The third part is a vigorous and somewhat grotesque march tune played between the second and third scenes; it tells of Danton's arrest. The fourth interlude, which comes between the fourth scene and the Tribunal scene, also has rhythmic interest and rises to a tumultuous climax.

The composer has revealed that, in writing his music for *Danton's Death,* he was profoundly influenced by the political and international storms and stresses of the period. He began writing his opera just a few days after July 20, 1944, when the German officers' plot to assassinate Hitler had failed. "Experiences with the Gestapo and of the times," he has said, "much youthful impetuosity, hope and expectations for the future flowed together into the work. . . . The Nuremberg trials and many personal hardships may have also lent color to the work."

The American première of *Danton's Death* was given by the New York City Opera in March of 1966; the composer was present at this performance.

1953 DER PROZESS (THE TRIAL), opera in two parts, op. 14, with text by Boris Blacher and Heinz von Cramer based on Franz Kafka's novel of the same name. First performance: Salzburg, August 17, 1953.

Kafka's abstruse, fragmentary, symbolic and grotesquely unreal story of Joseph K. is filled with inner probings, frustrations, anxieties, self-guilt, injustice and despair. In making this material suitable for opera, the librettists adhered strictly to Kafka's own words, though certain cuts and changes in the original text had to be made. Von Einem explained: "It seemed essential to us to project the story around Joseph K. . . . in the sharpest possible outlines. For this purpose we availed ourselves, among other things, of an old dramaturgic expedient, i.e. double casting. Thus Fräulein Buerstner, wife of the Law Court Attendant and Leni are all three represented by the same singer, for it seemed to us that these Kafka figures are not so much separate beings as the embodiment of woman, of her influences on K., and her task in his life. For the same reason, the individuals connected with the Court . . . are again represented by a single singer."

Von Einem then discussed his aims as a composer: "My object was to find a form that would be adequate to the course of dramatic events. Neither an illustrating, 'verismo' technique, nor a symphonic one, nor numbers seemed advisable. The single scenes represented unities which develop according to musical not to literary principles."

The two parts, or acts, are divided into nine tableaux, four in the first part, five in the second. Each tableau carries an identifying title.

I. *The Arrest.* Two men dressed in black enter the bedroom of Joseph K. and tell him he is under arrest. "You will not be prevented from living your life as you normally would," the Inspector informs him. "You are merely under arrest, and nothing more."

II. *Fräulein Buerstner.* That evening Joseph K. informs Fräulein Buerstner about his arrest. At first he succumbs to sobs. Then he embraces her and kisses her passionately.

III. *The Summons.* Joseph K. sees a soldier in the street, is met by a passerby who then vanishes into the darkness, and sees a man leaning against a nearby wall. He is convinced that everybody is out hunting for him.

IV. *The First Hearing.* Joseph K. has come late to court for his hearing, and the judge expresses anger. Bitterly, Joseph K. protests against the charges leveled against him. The proceedings are interrupted by a cry: the wife of a court attendant has been embraced by a student. With the hearing thus interrupted, judge and jury retire. During the recess, Joseph K. gets assurance from the attendant's wife that she will do what she can to help him. Before she can intercede for him with the judge, she is dragged away by the student. When the court reconvenes, the judge announces that Joseph K. has forfeited whatever chance he has had for clemency. Joseph K. is contemptuous and makes a hurried retreat.

V. *The Whipper.* In the second act, a whipper is required to flog Joseph K. The two men in black who had arrested him in the first tableau come pleading that he put in a good word for them, and the passerby that Joseph K. had seen in the third tableau comes to tell the prisoner that he must report at once to the office of the court.

VI. *The Advocate.* Joseph K. consults a lawyer, an old friend of his uncle, who maintains that the case has been jeopardized through the client's behavior.

VII. *The Manufacturer.* In his office, Joseph K. is unable to concentrate on his work since the trial has by now become an obsession. The manufacturer appears and advises Joseph K. to seek the help of Titorelli, a painter who has done the portraits of the judges.

VIII. *The Painter.* Joseph K. has come to the studio of Titorelli, who provides him with advice on the outcome of the trail. Titorelli suggests that the best procedure might be to get an adjournment. To this, Joseph K. replies: "If my trial is adjourned, I shall never be free."

IX. *In the Cathedral.* A priest tells Joseph K. in a dark cathedral that the case has gone against him because he has sought the help of too many strangers. Two men in frock coats and top black hats grasp Joseph K. under the arms and lead him into the street, and into a stone quarry. The darkness becomes intensified as one of the two men opens his frock coat and removes a butcher's knife. He passes it over K.'s head to his companion, who raises his hand and spreads his fingers. The darkness now becomes impenetrable.

Donald Fuller, writing in the New York *Herald Tribune,* explained that the opera consists of "dramatic scenes strung together, but they add up to a brilliant whole. Musical continuity and unity are achieved by the use of continuous rhythmic patterns that run throughout part of each scene rather than by the adoption of leitmotivs. An example of this is the passacaglia at the very opening of the work. Set pieces alternate with more recitative-like sections."

The American première of *The Trial* was given in English by the New York City Opera on October 20, 1953.

The American composer Gunther Schuller also wrote an opera based on Kafka's *The Trial,* calling it *The Visitation*; it is discussed in the section on Schuller.

1954 MEDITATIONS (MEDITATIONEN), two pieces for orchestra, op. 18. I. Allegretto. II. Adagio.

Written on a commission from the Louisville Orchestra, *Meditations* was introduced by that organization under Robert Whitney, in Louisville, Kentucky, on November 6, 1954. The composer says that the term "meditations" refers to the "musical result that comes from meditating on certain simple musical principles." There are two movements, or pieces. The first, though not in the sonata form, comprises two contrasting themes. The second is dominated by a gently flowing cantabile melody.

1960 PHILADELPHIA SYMPHONY, for orchestra, op. 28. I. Allegro giusto. II. Andante. III. Allegro vivace.

As the title indicates, this symphony was commissioned by the Philadelphia Orchestra and its conductor Eugene Ormandy—to help commemorate the one hundred and fourth anniversary of the Academy of Music in Philadelphia, the orchestra's home. That première (planned for January of 1961) had to be delayed, because Ormandy had been hurt in an automobile accident and could not perform. The world première, consequently, took place not in the United States but in Austria, with Georg Solti conducting the Vienna Philharmonic on November 14, 1961. The American première followed on November 9, 1962, in Philadelphia, Ormandy conducting. On that occasion John Briggs, annotator for the Philadelphia Orchestra, described the music as follows:

"The first movement opens with what might be a festival overture, that begins to develop into a full-fledged symphony. . . . The . . . second movement opens with a lovely clarinet solo. . . . This leads into a scherzo middle section, first introduced by the strings, then developed by the full orchestra. . . . The last movement is a sort of Festive March. It opens with full orchestra, soon to be followed by a development section for the strings, with woodwinds added later, then returning to the opening March. The middle section returns again, in the form of a dialogue between the strings and clarinet or horns. There is a sudden reappearance of a coda for full orchestra leading up to a stirring finish."

1963 NIGHT PIECE (NACHTSTÜCK), for orchestra, op. 29.

Edward B. Benjamin, a New Orleans patron, has made it a practice to commission composers to write pieces of "restful music," with the hope of building up a repertory of soft, gentle, slow works. Von Einem was one of the composers whom he contracted for this purpose, and the composer responded with *Night Piece*. This brief composition was intended for the Philadelphia Orchestra, but a series of delays in its performance necessitated a change of scene for the première. This took place in Vienna on April 27, 1963, with Mario Rossi conducting the Vienna Philharmonic. The Philadelphia Orchestra, under Ormandy, presented it on February 4, 1966.

The composition opens with a gentle lyrical thought in first violins (Adagio). This subject is taken over and amplified by other strings. A change of tempo brings contrast with a vigorous theme in solo clarinet and bassoon. A forceful episode is built up towards the return of this second theme over string harmonics. Muted first violins then introduce the closing section, in which the opening melody is recalled by second violins, violas and cellos and the second theme in the woodwind. The serene atmosphere is suddenly broken with a loud chord for full orchestra, with which the composition ends.

SIR EDWARD ELGAR 1857–1934

Elgar's severest critics have often said that he lacks originality, profundity, a personal style; that too much of what he has written is derivative from other composers (Schumann and Wagner, particularly). Yet it should not be denied that his language, at its best, has beauty. The charm of his lyricism, the distinction of his form, the robustness of his orchestration, together with the poetry and mysticism that touch his best pages, do not fail to enchant the ear and senses. It is music with attributes like those of the man who wrote them: suave, genial, witty, sentimental, polished, cultured. Unfortunately, it is also the kind of music that ages quickly; much of it has already worn a bit thin. But while its day is brief, this music, nevertheless, spreads the warmth of sunshine to those who come into contact with it for the first time.

He is probably best remembered and most admired as the musical spokesman of the Edwardian age. As Neville Cardus noted: "Elgar's music emerged from the period as the plant from the fruitful soil. . . . Here is music of peace and plenty. Pomp and circumstance, and Buckingham Palace, and the Mall, and Westminster—all poised in a crescendo and cadence of fulfillment—*nobilemente*. The flag is unfurled, waving possession not belligerence; the trumpet and the drum of satisfied conquest are alternated with the cathedral's thanksgiving for all the good things vouchsafed to His chosen people by the Lord. . . . So the pageant of Elgar's music passes."

Elgar was born at Broadheath, near Worcester, England, on June 2, 1857. His father was a church organist in Worcester, and the proprietor of a music shop. Though Edward showed pronounced talent for music, and occasionally substituted for his father as organist, he was first trained for the law. His love for music eventually drove him away from his legal studies. After devoting himself to a variety of musical activities, he came to London and took some violin lessons from Adolf Pollitzer. Then convinced that he was not destined to be a virtuoso, he returned to Worcester, where he became a bandmaster, filled various jobs as violinist and conductor, and started composing. His first work to get performed was an orchestral Intermezzo, which Stockley's Orchestra performed in Birmingham on December 13, 1883.

In 1885, Elgar succeeded his father as organist of the St. George Cathedral in Worcester. Four years after that, he married Caroline Alice Roberts, who got him to give up his varied musical activities and concentrate on composing. Transferring his home to London, Elgar began writing in larger forms. His first significant productions were the *Froissart* overture, op. 19, successfully performed on September 9, 1890; the cantata, *The Black Knight,* op. 25, featured at the Worcester Festival on April 18, 1893; and the oratorio, *The Light of Life,* op. 29, heard at the same festival on September 10, 1896.

Early in 1899, Elgar completed his first important work for orchestra, the *Variations on an Original Theme*, op. 36, better known today as the *Enigma Variations*. Elgar possibly referred to these variations as an "enigma" because of a "concealed theme," which is never actually heard but which is suggested in each of the variations, sometimes as "a silent accompaniment." Another enigmatic feature was the imposition of a set of initials before each variation, these initials identifying some Elgar friend, or Elgar's wife, or Elgar himself, of whom the variations were intended as a tonal characterization.

Hans Richter, the conductor, was delighted with this work, and introduced it in London on June 19, 1899. Its success not only in London, but also in Germany and Austria, brought Elgar recognition for the first time. To this day, it remains one of Elgar's best and most popular works.

His fame made further secure with the triumph of his oratorio, *The Dream of Gerontius,* Elgar now proceeded to identify himself as an *English* composer by writing a set of five nationalistic marches entitled *Pomp and Circumstance,* and an Ode for the coronation of Edward VII. In 1904, Elgar was honored with knighthood and a three-day festival of his music at Covent Garden. He received the Order of Merit in 1911. In 1924, he was appointed Master of the King's Musick, and seven years later received the highest honor that the Crown could offer a composer—a baronetcy.

During World War I, Elgar served, first, in the Hampstead Division as special constable; then, in the Hampstead Volunteer Reserve. The war over, he returned to serious writing. His vein now became more personal. He turned to chamber music, producing several intimate works, which are rarely performed.

The death of his wife in 1920 was a major blow. He swore he would never again write a bar of music. In 1929, however, his patriotism brought him back to his music. King George V was stricken by a serious illness. As a hymn of prayer for his recovery, Elgar wrote a Christmas carol—his first piece of music in nine years. Thus reawakened, his creative urge led him to plan a new symphony—his third.

He was never destined to complete that symphony. In 1934, a serious illness from which he never recovered sent him to bed. He died at his home in Marl Bank on February 23, 1934. His last request was that no one should meddle with the sketches of his Third Symphony, that it remain permanently unfinished and unpublished.

1900 THE DREAM OF GERONTIUS, oratorio for solo voices, chorus and orchestra, op. 38.

If the *Enigma Variations* first brought Elgar to the limelight in 1899, the oratorio, *The Dream of Gerontius,* kept him there. Based on the celebrated poem of Cardinal Newman, this oratorio consisted of a series of lyric and dramatic episodes portraying the doctrine of Purgatory as taught by the Catholic Church. Elgar had received Newman's poem as a wedding gift, and as he himself explained, it has "been soaking in my mind at least eight years while I have been gradually assimilating the thoughts of the author into my own musical promptings."

Here is how the text has been summarized: "The dying Gerontius beholds in a trance the mysteries of the unseen world. His soul is accompanied in its passage through infinite space to the throne of the Omnipotent by his Guardian Angel, who expounds to him the meaning of the changes that have come upon this spirit, and prepares him for the final agony of delight, that 'keen and subtle pain' that shall befall him, sick with love and yearning when he sees his Judge. At last they come 'into the veiled presence of our God,' and intercession is made for the soul of Gerontius by the Angel of the Agony. Finally, the soul, admitted into the presence of its Creator, is 'consumed, yet quickened by the glance of God,' and, after its ecstatic agony, given again into the enfolding arms of its Guardian Angel, who sings over it a tender, consolatory song of farewell."

"The strength of *The Dream of Gerontius,*" wrote Robert H. Hull, "lies in its convincing sincerity; the embodiment of a satisfying vision presented through finely controlled imaginative powers; and above all, an unerring sense of beauty. The orchestral writing excels both in content and design. From a vocal standpoint there are few departures from success. . . . For the most part the detail is excellently contrived. Elgar appreciates minutely the emotional characteristics of the text, and brings to it an exalted loveliness beyond anything which it may be said otherwise to possess."

An eloquent orchestral prelude introduces us to some of the important thematic material of the score. First, we hear the stately motive of Judgment (Lento mistico), followed by a feverish subject suggesting Gerontius's fear. A new motive points up his religious convictions. "The work now proceeds in a restless, undulating manner," writes Elgar's friend, A. J. Jaeger, "rising to a passionate outburst, being the appeal for mercy. This dies away and is succeeded by an eloquent passage, full of poignant feeling. It rises to a great fortissimo statement of Prayer. This, too, dies away and soon a lovely, soothing melody is heard, later used as the theme of the Priests and Assistants sending the Soul on its journey from earth. It is repeated twice, the second time being of great power and very impressive. As before, the outburst dies away; this time a stroke of the gong is given, and the earlier motives are heard very subdued."

Time and again in his score, Elgar rises to a lofty plane of spirituality and radiant exaltation. One such passage is the opening of the second part: quiet music which scarcely seems to move or even breathe and which Ernest Newman once described as the perfect tonal expression of felicity. Another passage is the one in which the Angel, in veiled words, describes the Stigmata of St. Francis. This is followed by probably the most famous page in the entire score, music of rare grandeur in which the chorus of angels sings out "Praise to the Holiest of the Height" and concludes with a mighty outcry of praise.

The Dream of Gerontius was introduced at the Birmingham Festival under

Richter on October 3, 1900. It was, at first, something of a failure. A few discerning musicians (among whom was Bernard Shaw) recognized it as a masterpiece, and were strongly moved by the mysticism and poetry of the music, the beauty of the sounds, the effective choral writing, the vivid musical imagery, the high-minded sincerity. But the public had come expecting a traditional oratorio with arias, choruses and ensemble numbers in the style of Handel. Elgar's unconventional form proved puzzling. For Elgar had molded his music to his text in the Wagnerian manner, creating a continuous musical flow which received its shape and form from the demands of the poem.

On December 19, 1901, *The Dream of Gerontius* was heard at the Lower Rhine Festival. It was immediately and immensely successful. This was possibly the first time that the work of an English composer inspired such enthusiasm in Germany. Richard Strauss did not hesitate to describe it as a "masterpiece." The German acclaim inevitably encouraged repeat performances in England. Eventually, the beauty and the poetry of the music impressed themselves on the English music public. *The Dream* now became one of the most frequently heard and one of the best-loved oratorios on the English concert stage, exceeded in popularity only by Handel's *Messiah* and Mendelssohn's *Elijah.*

1901–1930 POMP AND CIRCUMSTANCE, five marches for orchestra, op. 39. I. D major. II. A minor. III. C minor. IV. G major. V. C major.

In 1901, Elgar planned a set of stately marches to prove that march music need not necessarily be banal. He had in mind the same serious approach to the march that other composers had brought to other popular forms, such as the waltz or the polonaise. He completed five such marches, entitling the set *Pomp and Circumstance.* (The phrase "pomp and circumstance" was taken from Shakespeare's *Othello.*)

He was as proud of these marches as he was of his major works. While they are not all of equal merit, they are rousing without being pompous, filled with vigorous melodic ideas and rhythmic strength.

Of the five marches, it is the first (1901) that is the most famous, and the one that is usually referred to when the name of *Pomp and Circumstance* is mentioned. Probably no other single piece of music—except, perhaps, *God Save the King*—is so inextricably associated with the British Empire. In strict, three-part march form, the piece opens with a restless, strongly rhythmic theme, which serves to introduce the stately melody (in strings) which has become for the English people something of a second national anthem. Today, this middle section is frequently heard separately, sung to the words of Laurence Housman, *Land of Hope and Glory.* The melody also appears in the *Coronation Ode,* op. 44 (1901), which Elgar wrote to honor the Coronation of Edward VII.

The second *Pomp and Circumstance* was also written in 1901; the third, in 1905; the fourth, in 1907; and the last, in 1930. Of these, the most often heard is the fourth, known as the *Song of Liberty.* It opens and closes with spirited march music, while midway, a broad and stately melody unfolds in the strings. This tune receives extended treatment which culminates with a rousing statement by full orchestra, before the opening march theme is recalled.

The first two marches were introduced by the Liverpool Orchestra on

October 19, 1901. The third was heard first in London on March 8, 1905; the fourth, in London on August 24, 1907; and the fifth, in London on September 30, 1930.

1901 COCKAIGNE, concert overture, op. 40.

The title "Cockaigne" is here used to identify the city of London—a city of cockneys; the clue is found in the subtitle, "In London Town." The music is a realistic and sometimes witty picture of the city: its scurrying crowds and busy streets; its sights and sounds. Two lovers are taking a stroll. Their aural and visual impressions of the goings-on in the city streets are colorful as re-created in the music. The hubbub of the city is depicted realistically in the opening measures. Then comes a romantic passage, the core of which is an expansive melody for the strings; here we find reflected the feelings of the lovers as momentarily they stop off to rest in a public park. They continue their walk, hear the sounds of an approaching brass band, then enter a church where organ music is being played. The lovers then continue their leisurely stroll. The animated life of the city streets is once again reproduced, and the earlier romantic melody telling of the inmost feelings of the lovers is repeated.

Cockaigne was first heard at the concert of the Royal Philharmonic in London on June 20, 1901.

1903 IN THE SOUTH (ALASSIO), concert overture, op. 50.

A springtime holiday in the lovely Ligurian resort of Alassio was the inspiration for a sunny concert overture in which the composer's love of Nature is reflected. *In the South* was first played during a three-day Elgar festival in London on March 16, 1904. The following quotation appears in the published score: "A land which *was* the mightiest in its old command and *is* the loveliest; wherein were cast the men of Rome. Thou art the garden of the world."

A lively tune for clarinets, horns, violins and cellos projects a happy atmosphere without preliminaries. This is elaborated vigorously, then a pastoral section is presented by the woodwind and muted strings to describe a shepherd and his flock. Gaiety and tranquillity now take turns, the latter represented by the shepherd's melody. A viola solo leads into the recapitulation section. The concluding coda has been described by Donald Francis Tovey as "one of the best of all Elgar's perorations, its rhetoric entirely unspoiled by tub-thumping, and leaving us with a magnificent impression of punctuality at its end."

1905 INTRODUCTION AND ALLEGRO, for strings, op. 47.

One day while on a visit to Wales the composer heard the distant music of singing. The cadence of a falling third caught his ear and suggested to him the idea for a theme, characteristically Welsh. Subsequently, he heard in the valley of the Wye a true Welsh song, which, in his own words, "reinforced my Welsh impressions and led me to the completion of the work." It was first given in London on March 8, 1905.

The work—*Introduction and Allegro*—is scored for solo string quartet and string orchestra, and is vaguely in the style of the old concerto grosso, which utilized the solo quartet as a "concertante" with the rest of the orchestra as "tutti."

In the Introduction (Moderato), the solo quartet and strings pronounce the opening subject, and a second theme of contrasting character is posed by the quartet itself. After the development comes the Welsh melody that inspired the entire work, heard in the solo viola. The Introduction ends, and the second of the two opening themes returns, transformed from minor to major, in the Allegro section that follows, and is allowed to develop. After the solo quartet presents a new subject, an ingenious development grows into a powerful climax. Still another new idea becomes the germ of a fugato movement. The work ends in a recollection of the opening theme of the Allegro, in a resounding restatement of the Welsh melody by quartet and orchestra (Molto sostenuto), and in a final recapitulation of the opening theme of the Allegro movement.

1908 SYMPHONY NO. 1 IN A-FLAT MAJOR, op. 55. I. Andante nobilmente e semplice. II. Allegro molto. III. Adagio. IV. Lento; Allegro.

Elgar's First Symphony was several years in the planning. He had originally intended it as a tribute to General Gordon, whom he admired profoundly. But the subject restricted his musical thinking and he dropped the idea. When the symphony was finally completed in 1908, the composer provided the following clue to its emotional and spiritual content: "It is written out of a full life-experience and is meant to include the innumerable phases of joy and sorrow, struggle and conquest, and especially between the ideal and actual life." But the symphony, as Basil Maine suggests, is neither a tribute to any one man nor even an autobiographical document, but—in its majestic strides, epical structure and melodic grandeur—is actually the glorification of an entire era.

Power is generated throughout the entire work; but introspection and deep thinking are also present. After the first movement, with its heroic breadth and grandeur which tempted one critic to speak of it as "the British Empire in tones," a somber mood pervades the music, most strongly assertive in the slow movement, which reaches stirring emotional depths. Structurally, the symphony is well integrated, with the principal thematic ideas of the entire work posed in the introduction of the first movement, and returning as a summation in the closing movement.

It was introduced in Manchester by Hans Richter on December 3, 1908, and was received so successfully that within the next twelve months it was repeated many times.

1910 CONCERTO IN B MINOR FOR VIOLIN AND ORCHESTRA, op. 61. I. Allegro. II. Andante. III. Finale: allegro molto.

Elgar completed the writing of his violin concerto with the technical advice and assistance of his violinist-friend, William H. Reed. It was heard for the first time at an informal social gathering at Gloucester, with Reed playing the solo part and the composer accompanying him on the piano. On November, 10, 1910, Fritz Kreisler introduced the work officially with the London Philharmonic Orchestra, conducted by the composer.

On the flyleaf of the published score appears the following brief motto: "Here is enshrined the soul of. . . . " Without question, the concerto is a personal work into which the composer poured his most intimate feelings, thoughts, reveries, emotions. In few other works is his romanticism more ardent than it is in the spacious opening movement, built around four themes developed into passionate, intense and sensitive moods. In few other works is his feeling spoken with such warmth and tenderness as in the slow movement, a veritable poem recited alternately by orchestra and the solo instrument. Rarely does his flair for light-paced wit achieve such grace as in the Finale.

The concerto occasionally exploits interesting devices. One of these is the *accompanied* cadenza in the third movement; another (in the same section) is the novel effect achieved by the violinists in the orchestra drumming their fingers on the strings. In the very opening movement an ingenious method is realized when the solo violin plays the concluding bars of the orchestral introduction. But, for all such novel turns, the concerto is traditional in its form, faithful to the romantic concepts of the late nineteenth century, of which it is both a characteristic and a successful product.

1911 SYMPHONY NO. 2 IN E-FLAT MAJOR, op. 63. I. Allegro vivace e nobilmente. II. Larghetto. III. Rondo: presto. IV. Moderato e maestoso.

The Second Symphony, which followed the first by almost three years, is on a different emotional level. Where the earlier work is both grandiose and somber, the second (though beginning on a note of despair) achieves increasing good spirits as the symphony progresses. It erupts with veritable joyousness in the Rondo, and ends on a triumphant note of undisguised optimism. In comparing the two symphonies, Robert H. Hull finds that the second "is more immediate in its attractions," while the first is "more urgent in its ultimate meaning." To Hull, the general impression of the Second Symphony is one "of spontaneous gaiety. This atmosphere is common to each of the four movements, notwithstanding the sense of tranquil reflection discernible in the Adagio."

Elgar dedicated this symphony to "the memory of His Late Majesty King Edward VII." Its première took place in London on May 24, 1911.

1913 FALSTAFF, symphonic study, op. 68.

Though this is an integrated single-movement composition, *Falstaff* has four divisions, following each other without a break. They are provided the following programmatic headings: I. Falstaff and Prince Henry; II. Eastcheap—Gadshill—The Boar's Head—Revelry and Sleep; III. Falstaff's March—The Return to Gloucestershire—The New King—The Hurried Ride to London; IV. King Henry's Progress—The Repudiation of Falstaff, and his Death.

In the opening section (Allegro), Basil Maine finds the equivalent of a first movement symphony or suite "developed from the opposition of a three-fold theme-group and, as second subject, the Prince Henry motive." The tavern scene (Allegro molto) and the exploit at Gadshill together "introduce the scherzo element. . . . After so much breathless activity, the music, no less than Sir John himself is now in need of rest. The quiet regularity of a gavotte measure lulls him to sleep to dream of his boyhood. The next episode (Allegro) is a combination of march and song; and after the Gloucestershire Interlude, the underlying rhythm of which is that of the Gigue (remembered in tranquillity) there comes a finale of true symphonic grandeur (Grandioso) based on a transformation of earlier themes."

The source of Elgar's symphonic study is not *Falstaff* nor *The Merry Wives of Windsor* but *Henry IV* (Parts 1 and 2) and *Henry V*. The study was first performed at the Leeds Festival in England on October 1, 1913.

1918 PIANO QUINTET IN A MINOR, op. 84. I. Moderato. II. Adagio. III. Andante; Allegro.

Of the three chamber-music works Elgar completed in 1918 (the Violin Sonata in E minor, op. 82; the String Quartet in E minor, op. 83; and the Piano Quintet, op. 84), it is the last of these three—the Quintet—which is the most ambitious structurally, and the one most consistently gratifying in its material. Dedicated to Ernest Newman, it was introduced in London on May 21, 1919.

The quintet opens in an air of mystery (Serioso) with a piano subject that plays a prominent role throughout the work. After a change of key, we hear a haunting melody with an oriental personality, in a slow, undulating dance rhythm. The mood changes rapidly from dramatic animation to foreboding. "With alternations and elaborations of these moods," says W. H. Reed, "this remarkable movement proceeds through the development and recapitulation sections until it ends in rather a gloomy manner, leaving the listener with an uncanny feeling of awe." The slow movement throws its main weight on an exalted song for the viola. The finale opens with a questioning figure, first heard in the opening movement, which is developed climactically. A broad melody follows in unison strings, accompanied by piano chords, which is given detailed treatment. This is followed by a new oriental melody reminiscent of the one in the first movement. The tempo quickens, the sonority increases until a climax is achieved, after which the quintet ends on a note of triumph.

1919 CONCERTO IN E MINOR FOR CELLO AND ORCHESTRA, op. 85. I. Adagio; Moderato. II. Lento; Allegro molto. III. Adagio. IV. Allegro; Moderato; Allegro, ma non troppo.

The Cello Concerto is not only the last of Elgar's major works; it is also one of his most significant creations. Its world première took place in London on October 27, 1919, with Felix Salmond as soloist, and the composer conducting the London Symphony.

From Michael Maxwell's valuable annotations for the Cleveland Orchestra we learn that in the opening movement "the solo cello introduces a solemn recitative . . . of just four measures, which leads to the statement by the viola of the pincipal theme of the movement. It is repeated by the lower strings and then taken up by the cello. . . . The atmosphere lightens with the introduction of the second subject by the clarinet which is repeated by the cello."

Two measures by the solo cello, pizzicato, is the transition to the second movement, which is opened once again with a recitative in the solo cello. "There follows an upward rush of strings, and the cello sets out with single-minded purpose on a scherzo in G major, a kind of perpetuum mobile of scurrying semiquavers."

In the slow movement "an expressive mood of meditation and tranquillity is held by the cello and orchestra for sixty measures that reveal an impassioned song, searching, questioning."

The finale opens with eight measures of "dignified introduction . . .

followed by a statement of the principal theme, Moderato, by the cello, leading into a brief (two measures) cadenza. A dialogue between cello and orchestra ensues . . . the subject being the principal theme, and the rondo form of the movement is established. The mood is one of vigor restrained, continued through the lyrical second subject by solo cello. . . . The movement then turns away from the formal rondo and . . . the meditative mood of the Adagio returns, the cello rhapsodizing against a light orchestral fabric. A hushed atmosphere of calm is interrupted by the unexpected restatement of the opening recitative of the first movement by the cello. . . . The cello is pulled by the orchestra into a final pronouncement of the rondo theme to conclude the work."

GEORGES ENESCO 1881–1955

Enesco's most popular compositions are those in which the personality of his native Roumania is reflected through the exploitation of folk-music elements. With considerable vitality, Enesco transferred to his writing some of the vivid harmonic schemes, the oriental atmosphere, the irresistible dance rhythms of Roumanian folk music. In such a style we find not only Enesco's two most famous works, the *Roumanian Rhapsodies,* but also his Opus No. 1, *Poème roumain* (1897), the third violin sonata in A minor, op. 25 (1926), and the *Overture on Motives in the Roumanian Character,* op. 32 (1948).

But not all of Enesco's music is in a national style. Many of his early works are post-Romantic and Brahmsian, for example, his Symphony No. 1 in E-flat major, op. 13 (1905). The Suite No. 2, in C major, op. 20 (1915) is neo-classic. Still others are experimental, such as the opera *Oedipe,* op. 23 (1932), where he uses half-sharps and half-flats to approximate quarter tones. But whatever the manner, style or idiom, Enesco was always an aristocratic musician of high purpose and unblemished integrity, a composer, as Lawrence Gilman once said of him, "of depth and power and intensity."

Enesco was born in Liveni-Virnav, in the Dorohoï district of Roumania, on August 19, 1881. He took his first violin lessons as a child with local teachers. Then, when only seven, he was admitted to the Vienna Conservatory, where he studied with Joseph Hellmesberger. One of his most important contacts in Vienna was with Brahms, whom he came to adulate, and whom he later came to imitate.

After winning prizes in Vienna, Enesco completed his studies at the Paris Conservatory, which he had entered in 1894. His teachers (who included

Fauré, Massenet and Gédalge) used superlatives to describe his talent, which won for him first prizes in virtually every department. A concert devoted entirely to his compositions took place in Paris in June of 1897, and between 1898 and 1899, Édouard Colonne directed the premières of Enesco's first two orchestral compositions, the *Poème roumain* and the *Fantaisie pastorale*. Enesco also put into high gear a brilliant and worldwide career as a virtuoso violinist on February 11, 1900, when as a soloist with the Colonne Orchestra he performed two concertos. Success as a composer arrived with the premières of his two *Roumanian Rhapsodies* in 1903, and of his first symphony, in Paris on January 21, 1906.

Just before the outbreak of World War I, Enesco returned to his native land, settling in Bucharest. At once, he became the dominating figure in the musical life of Roumania. He was appointed conductor of the Bucharest Philharmonic; he organized concerts of modern music; he gave cycles of violin recitals tracing the history of music for the instrument; he did everything he could to promote the interests of young Roumanian composers, including the establishment of a Georges Enesco Prize.

The war over, Enesco returned to Paris, where he lived for the next few decades, filling a triple role in the music world as a violinist, conductor and composer. His American debut took place with the Philadelphia Orchestra on January 5, 1923. Once each year, he returned to Roumania for a visit, and in 1935, he married Marie Rosetti-Tescano, a Roumanian princess.

During the period of World War II, Enesco lived on a farm near Bucharest, tending to his animal stock and occasionally composing. After the war, Enesco resumed his activity as conductor and violinist throughout the world. He paid his first return visit in a decade to the United States in the fall of 1946, when he was honored with the Grand Cross of the Order of Loyal Service by the Roumanian Ambassador to the United States. In 1948, he conducted a master class in chamber-music performance at the Mannes College of Music in New York. His last public appearance in the United States, in New York on January 21, 1950, commemorated the sixtieth anniversary of his concert debut. On this occasion, he was heard not only as a violinist, conductor and composer, but also as a pianist.

Enesco suffered a paralytic stroke in the summer of 1954, and on May 4, 1955, he died in Paris. His last composition was the *Chamber Symphony,* for twelve solo instruments, op. 33 (1954). His native land honored him by making museums out of his homes in Liveni and Bucharest; by naming the town of his birth, a street in Bucharest, and the Bucharest Philharmonic after him; and by instituting a Georges Enesco international festival and competition in 1958.

1900 OCTET IN C MAJOR, for four violins, two violas, and two cellos, op. 7.

Though presumably in the key of C major, the Octet—Enesco's first significant composition—does not reach its tonal home base until the end of the composition. The changing tonalities is only a single facet of this fresh and provocative music which, as Nicolas Slonimsky has explained, "is embellished by the multicolored festoons of Enesco's Roumanian scales."

The work, while in a single movement, has several sections. "It opens," writes Slonimsky, "with a dynamic theme in propulsive rhythm. . . . The episodic material contains a recurrent motive that sounds like glorified fiddle-tuning. The dynamic potential mounts until a climax is reached. The theme returns with the accompaniment in throbbing tremolos. There follows a quiet section in swaying polyrhythms of two, three, and four notes to a beat. A lyrical melody appears in the low register of the violins. The succeeding recession leads to a long sustained pause. The movement is slowly resumed, and the melorhythmic pendulum begins to swing wider. . . . There is a fugal section. Then the movement subsides in a sudden pianissimo. The mood changes completely. The low strings play a voluptuous melody against gurgling streamlets of Roumanian scales, while in the upper region the violins play slowly descending chromatics skipping downwards by octaves. . . . The last section of the Octet is announced in slow tempo with muted strings. A mournful theme creates an air of premonition. Thematic fragments combine in a polyrhythmic polyphony that reaches the ultimate complexity of modern octuple counterpoint. In a final acceleration, the conclusion is reached in a sonorous C major."

What probably was the world première of the Octet, took place in New York on January 26, 1924, in a performance by the combined forces of the London and the Lenox String Quartets.

1901–1902 ROUMANIAN RHAPSODIES, NOS. 1 and 2, op. 11. I. A major. II. D major.

Though Enesco has written profounder and more original music than these two rhapsodies, none has equalled them in popular appeal. The world première of both rhapsodies took place in Bucharest on March 9, 1903; their international fame began with their performance in Paris on February 7, 1908, Pablo Casals conducting.

It is easy to see why these rhapsodies became so famous. In their ever-changing moods, abundance of spirited and wistful folk melodies, utilization of exciting folk-dance rhythms (principally those of the *hora* and *sirba*), these two works cast an irresistible spell. There is nothing either subtle or elusive about their charms. They wear their effects on their sleeves, for all to see at first glance.

The first Rhapsody (1901), by far the more popular of the two, treats a varied assortment of folk melodies in variation form: the melodies are now boisterous and gay, now sensuous, now languorous, now nostalgic. It opens with a languorous subject for clarinet which is soon repeated by the woodwind, then by the strings, and finally (in quickened tempo) by the orchestra. Next we hear a gypsy tune in the strings; an exciting dance melody in first violins and woodwind; an oriental-type improvisation in solo flute. The mood grows increasingly frenetic, as a rapid succession of whirling folk-dance melodies and rhythms is built up to a climax. Relaxation comes with a tender oriental theme in clarinet, but this is only a passing phase. The rhapsody ends in a renewed outburst of vitality.

The second rhapsody is more melancholy. A solemn declaration by the strings precedes a sober, restrained folk melody in strings. The dark mood thus projected is intensified by a theme for English horn over tremolo strings. Except for a brief interpolation of a lively dance tune in solo viola, the melancholy atmosphere is maintained throughout the rhapsody.

1905 SYMPHONY NO. 1, IN E-FLAT MAJOR, op. 13. I. Assez vif et rhythmé. II. Lent. III. Vif et vigoureux.

The composer once had this to say about the influences shaping his early creative life: "The god of my own youthful adoration was Brahms, and I wrote my early work quite flagrantly in the manner of the immortal Johannes." Enesco actually proved what he said in his First Symphony. It is obviously the work of a composer who adored Brahms, for many of Brahms' recognizable traits as a composer—the warmth of his romanticism, the spacious melodies, the luxurious harmonic and contrapuntal language, the adherence to classic form—are found here. But though the speech emulates that of Brahms, it still has personal accents of its own; and in this symphony, classic form is combined with freedom of expression without sacrificing the feeling of spontaneity. Consequently, though this is the earliest of Enesco's symphonies, it is the one most frequently heard.

The symphony received its première in Paris on January 21, 1906, in a performance by the Colonne Orchestra. Its success, the composer has written, "awakened an interest among my colleagues in my abilities as a composer, as heretofore they had regarded me only as a fiddler. . . . Ysaÿe wanted it immediately for Brussels, but I had already promised it to another conductor in London. That performance was so poor that . . . it took many years after this initial failure to achieve success in London. Since those early days, the symphony has been printed and performed throughout the world."

1915 SUITE NO. 2 IN C MAJOR, for orchestra, op. 20. I. Overture. II. Saraband. III. Gigue. IV. Minuet. V. Air. VI. Bourrée.

The neo-classical bug which bit and infected so many contemporary composers did not pass by Enesco. He composed this Second Suite in an attempt to re-create in modern terms the classical dance suite of Bach; it is possible that Bach's third orchestral suite was Enesco's immediate model. Since this suite originated in 1915, it must be regarded as one of the earliest example of neo-classicism.

The orchestral writing is modern throughout, but the rigid rhythmic pattern of the respective dances is respected. In spite of the frequent employment of present-day harmonic techniques, a classic spirit prevails and provides the work with much of its charm.

The suite opens with a robust Overture for full orchestra and piano. The stately dance of the Saraband follows (solo violin, flutes, horns). The strings then present the lively Gigue. The Minuet is first suggested by bassoons, celli and bass, then finally presented by full orchestra. After the beautiful song of the fifth movement (first played by oboe, then taken up by flute and clarinet) the work ends with a vivacious Bourrée, the longest and most complex of the six movements, and the only one to suggest even faintly a folk character.

This suite was introduced in Bucharest on April 9, 1916, the composer conducting.

1926 SONATA NO. 3 (IN A POPULAR ROUMANIAN STYLE), for violin and piano. I. Moderato malinconico. II. Andante sostenuto e misterioso. III. Allegro con brio.

Enesco's third and last violin sonata is his best, a product of his full maturity. Its première took place in Paris on March 28, 1927, performed by the composer with Nicolae Caravia at the piano.

The composer provided the following programmatic analysis:

"The mood of the first movement is . . . mainly one of plaintive melancholy. The undulating figure introduced by the piano at the outset, with its characteristic interval of the augmented second, so familiar in gypsy music, may be regarded as the principal theme. The violin replies to this with a phrase ending in mournful cadences. Presently, the piano introduces a new theme and energetic motive, which the violin also answers in the same manner as at first. These various thematic ideas are all treated in free rhapsodic style, with many elaborations of cadence and subtleties of nuance.

"The character of the first part of the second movement . . . is that of a nocturne, with its delicate wisps of sound for both instruments. Beginning with right-hand tremolandi for the piano, against harmonics for the violin, the music, while keeping its soft elusive character, gradually becomes more elaborate, with vague, fanciful figures. Eventually, the violin begins a melodic line, finally expanding into an impassioned utterance, and after a big climax the movement ends almost as calmly as it began.

"The finale is in free rondo form, upon the jaunty freakish little tune given out by the piano, while open fourths and fifths from the violin give a hint of the carousal suggested above. The rhythm is kept going energetically, until we come to an ingenious variation, *a poco meno mosso,* where the violin transforms it first into a declamatory recitative, then into a new dance figure. The movement increases in animation with the various returns of the rondo tune, and finally broadens out into *a largamente,* where eloquent and impassioned phrases for the violin are heard over an elaborate piano accompaniment."

MANUEL DE FALLA 1876–1946

No major composer in the twentieth century produced as little as did Manuel de Falla; and no major composer in the twentieth century maintained throughout his career such a consistently high level of production as did Falla. A lifetime of creativity yielded Falla only a handful of compositions, for Falla was hypercritical of his efforts, and creation for him was a long and arduous process. But most of what he has written are masterworks—fastidious in workmanship, rich in poetic beauty, evocative of the colorful personality of Spain.

Like Albéniz before him, Falla had been inspired and directed by Felipe Pedrell, the *grand homme* of Spanish music and one of Spain's foremost musical scholars. For it was Pedrell who first interested Falla in using his music to interpret Spanish backgrounds and subjects through the utilization of techniques, methods and styles of Spanish folk music. Falla's first works as a mature composer were already products of his pronounced national interests: the four *Pièces Espagnoles* (1908). Falla's first significant achievement, the opera *La Vida Breve* in 1915, was even more successful in deriving its spirit and inspiration from Spanish folk music (though all the thematic material is Falla's own). Virtually everything he wrote thereafter was intimately concerned with the backgrounds, the people, the folklore of his native land, though once in a while only through subtle suggestion.

What Falla once said about national Spanish music in general provides an illuminating insight into Falla's own music in particular. "Our music must be based on the natural music of our people, on the dances and songs that do not always show close kinship. In some cases, the rhythm alone is marked by clapping and drumsticks, without any melody; in others, the melody stands out by itself; so that no one should employ vocal melody alone as a manifestation of folk music, but everything that accompanies it or exists without it, never losing sight of the milieu wherein all this has its being. . . . It has occasionally been asserted that we have no traditions. We have, it is true, no written traditions; but in our dance and our rhythm we possess the strongest traditions that none can obliterate. We have the ancient modes which, by virtue of their extraordinary inherent freedom, we can use as inspiration dictates."

The exploitation of Spanish folk songs and dances—whether by assimilation and imitation, or much more rarely by quotation—was basic to Falla's art. His music is recognizably Spanish in the sinuous line and sensual content of his flamenco-like melodies; in his adoption of the old-world modalities of Spanish church music; in his electrifying and varied rhythms that are carry-overs from Spanish folk dances, rhythms now simulating the clicking of castanets and now the strum of the guitar. But the perfection and the refining of an essentially Spanish style of composition could never be an end in itself with Falla. It could only be the means by which to carry over into music the essence of Spain and its culture, geography and people. Falla was the mystic who sought out the soul of Spain; he was not just a literal tone painter interpreting specific or vague programs. The Spaniards have a word for Falla's kind of musical mysticism—"*evocación.*" Falla's music was a vibrant *evocación* of Spain rather than a picture of the country. As he himself said: "You must really go deep so as not to make any caricature. . . . You must go to the natural, living sources, study the sounds, the rhythms, use their essence, not their externals."

The essence of Falla's melody is in the *cante hondo* of Andalusia—meaning "deep song" which has the tortuous contours and throbbing vibrations of oriental chant, a song that speaks of the tragedies of life rather than of its joys. The *cante hondo* was the property of Andalusian gypsies, and since Falla was the voice of Andalusia, the *cante hondo* became his property as well.

Falla was born in Cádiz, Spain, on November 23, 1876. After preliminary music study with his mother and local teachers, he went to the Madrid Conservatory, where he came under the influence of Felipe Pedrell. After completing his studies at the Conservatory (where he won highest honors in piano playing), he earned his living by composing light musical scores for the theatres (*zarzuelas*) and teaching the piano. But he also devoted time to serious composition. His first important work was the opera *La Vida Breve,* which in 1905 won first prize in a competition among Spanish composers sponsored by the Academy of Fine Arts of Madrid.

In 1907, Falla went to Paris for a seven-week visit. He remained seven years. He moved in a musical circle that included some of the great names in French music (Debussy, Dukas, Ravel, Satie, Schmitt, Roussel). During his long stay in Paris, he wrote little; he was too busy gathering impressions, absorbing musical experiences, and studying the forms and techniques of French music. However, he did complete two works: the *Pièces Espagnoles,* for piano (1908), introduced by Ricardo Viñes at a concert of the Société Nationale in 1908, the year in which it was also published; and the *Trois Mélodies,* on texts by Gautier, (1909), heard and published in 1910.

In 1922, Falla settled in Granada, in the shadow of the Alhambra, where he lived for seventeen years in a retirement only infrequently interrupted by visits to European capitals to attend performances of his works. He detested publicity, avoided attention, refused to woo fame. His was the life of a recluse.

Intensely religious, he was at first drawn sympathetically to Franco during the Spanish Civil War, feeling that in Franco's victory the antireligious tendencies of the then new democracy would be aborted. But disenchantment with the Franco regime set in after the war. Now ill, Falla expatriated himself, living the last five years of his life at Alta Gracia, in the province of Córdoba, in Argentina. There he worked on and off on a "scenic cantata," *La Atlantida,* which had been occupying his thoughts for over a decade, and which he did not live to complete. He died at Alta Gracia on November 14, 1946.

1905 LA VIDA BREVE (BRIEF LIFE), opera in two acts, with libretto by Carlos Fernández Shaw. First performance: Nice, France, April 1, 1913.

Falla's first ambitious attempt to create a Spanish national art in his music came with his opera *La Vida Breve*. It has not survived in the repertory. But the two Spanish dances from this opera are among the composer's most popular compositions. The very heart of Spanish flamenco song and dance is found in these two pieces; *Spanish Dance No. 1* is especially popular. In this number, an arresting rhythmic opening precedes a bold and sensuous gypsy melody for horns and strings. The piece ends with rich chords for full orchestra. Fritz Kreisler made a fine transcription for violin and piano.

Though *La Vida Breve* won first prize in 1905 in a national competition sponsored by the Academy of Fine Arts of Madrid for a Spanish work by a a native composer, it was denied performance at that time. One reason may have been its unimpressive libretto. It told the story of a Granada gypsy girl, Salud, who was forsaken by Paco. During the wedding ceremony of Paco and Carmela, Salud arrives to denounce her lover and to fall dead at his feet.

La Vida Breve was finally performed at the Casino in Nice in 1913, with a production following at the Opéra-Comique in Paris on December 13, 1914. The Spanish première came on November 14, 1914, in Madrid. In the United States, the opera was heard first at the Metropolitan Opera on March 6, 1926. But the opera never caught on, and it is rarely heard today. To Gilbert Chase, Falla failed to solve "the problem of finding a characteristically Spanish declamation and melody for the more lyrical and dramatic situation . . . in which he had recourse to a more or less conventional idiom reminiscent of Massenet." However, Chase finds strength as well as weakness in the music. "In evoking the Andalusian background of his opera, and in the marvelously effective dances of the second act, Falla achieves a higher degree of artistry and ethnic authenticity than is to be found in any previous manifestation of the Spanish lyric drama."

1908–1919 COMPOSITIONS FOR PIANO:

PIÈCES ESPAGNOLES. I. Aragonesa. II. Cubana. III. Montañesa. IV. Andaluza.

FANTASIA BÉTICA.

The four *Spanish Pieces,* which Falla completed in 1908 while he was still in Paris and which he dedicated to Isaac Albéniz, was the composer's first published work. It was introduced by Ricardo Viñes at a concert of the Société Nationale in Paris in November of 1908. The first piece is stately in its lyricism, while the rhythms simulate the clicking of castanets and the pounding of dancing heels on the floor. In *Cubana,* guitar-like effects are imitated. The third number begins slowly and sedately (Andante tranquillo) before proceeding to a delicate passage (Più animata), which tries to capture the feeling generated by the high thin air of a Spanish mountain peak. The suite ends with a virtuoso piece energized by Andalusian rhythms and sensualized by a flamenco-like melody.

The *Fantasia Bética* (1919) has been described by some Spanish critics as Falla's most ambitious composition for solo piano. "*Bética*" is the ancient Roman name for Andalusia. The work as a whole is an extended portrait of the southern region of Spain from which the composer drew so much of his inspiration and stimulation. The piece is divided into three sections, but played without interruption: Allegro moderato, Lento, and Andantino. In the concluding part, material presented in earlier sections is repeated. The *Fantasia* was commissioned by Artur Rubinstein, the world-famous virtuoso, to whom it is dedicated.

1915 EL AMOR BRUJO (LOVE, THE SORCERER), ballet-pantomime in one act, with scenario by Martinez Sierra based on an old Andalusian legend. First performance: Madrid, April 15, 1915.

EL AMOR BRUJO, ballet suite for orchestra. I. Introduction and Scene. II. The Gypsies—Evening. III. Scene of Sorrowing Love (with voice). IV. The Homecomer. V. Dance of Terror. IV. The Magic Circle. VII.Ritual Fire Dance. VIII. Scene. IX. Song of the Will-o'-the-Wisp (with voice). X. Pantomime. XI. Dance of the Game of Love (with voice). XII. Morning Chimes.

Pastora Imperio, distinguished Spanish dancer, asked Falla to write a ballet for her in which she could sing as well as dance. Imperio's mother suggested a possible theme—an old Andalusian legend which Sierra proceeded to develop into a scenario for Falla. When *El Amor Brujo* was first produced, the following note was published in the program as an explanation: "The composer, whose feeling for and command of his country's folk music are well known, saw that it would be impossible to write true gypsy music by restricting himself to instrumental dances alone, and without resorting to the gypsies' most characteristic feature—their songs. But he has by no means used actual melodies. Every song is of his own invention, and it is his particular glory that he has succeeded in making it almost impossible to believe that the songs are not actual popular material."

The action of the ballet involves a sensuous gypsy, Candela, and the gypsy, Carmelo, with whom she falls in love after her husband's death. The love affair is troubled by the husband's ghost, which comes to haunt the pair. In despair, Candela decides on a happy solution. Knowing that her husband, while alive, was unable to resist the wiles of a beautiful gypsy, she calls on her friend Lucia to flirt with the ghost. Candela's husband succumbs to Lucia's beauty, leaving the lovers free, at last, to devote themselves to each other.

The première of the ballet was only moderately successful; and the ballet has proved hardly more successful in subsequent revivals. But the orchestral suite which the composer adapted from the ballet score—which Fernández Enrique Arbós introduced in Madrid in 1916—has become a twentieth-century classic, as well as Falla's most frequently performed symphonic work.

The suite has twelve numbers, three with contralto. The voice is sung backstage; it is an occasional practice of some conductors to dispense with the voice and to substitute a wind instrument, preferably the horn.

The suite opens with a fiery theme (Allegro furioso ma non troppo vivo) which serves as a motto that recurs throughout the score. Andalusian gypsy life then unfolds in music that is at turns atmospheric, passionate, languorous, dynamic—vividly oriental in coloring, its *cante hondo* melodies trimmed with imaginative ornaments, its dance rhythms vitally alive and continually exciting. Gypsy song is highlighted in the three vocal episodes, laden, says Gilbert Chase, "with that fatalistic quality which imbues the deep song of Andalusia." Of the dances, the most popular, of course, is *The Ritual Fire Dance* (*Danza Ritual del Fuego*), to whose hypnotic strains Candela dances at midnight to drive off the evil spirits. Dramatic, searing trills set the stage for a sensual Spanish melody in the oboe, moving over an irresistible rhythm. A second passionate subject follows, given by unison horns, then quietly repeated by muted trumpets. The dance gains in effect through repetitious phrases, ostinato rhythms and powerful dynamics arriving at a savage-like ferocity that is continually punctuated by piercing chords. The *Ritual Fire Dance* is often heard not only in it original orchestral versions but also in various transcriptions for solo instruments, the most popular being that for solo piano.

1915 NIGHTS IN THE GARDENS OF SPAIN (NOCHES EN LOS JARDINES DE ESPAÑA), symphonic impressions for piano and orchestra. I. In the Gardens of the Generalife. II. A Dance Is Heard in the Distance. III. In the Gardens of the Sierra de Córdoba.

"If these 'symphonic impressions' have achieved their object," said Falla of this work, "the mere enumeration of their titles should be a sufficient guide to the hearer. Although in this work—as in all which have a legitimate claim to be considered as music—the composer has followed a definite design regarding tonal, rhythmical, and thematic material . . . the end for which it was written is no other than to evoke places, sensations, and sentiments. The themes employed are based . . . on the rhythms, modes, cadences, and ornamental figures which distinguish the popular music of Andalucía, though they are rarely used in their original forms; and the orchestration frequently employs, and employs in a conventional manner, certain effects peculiar to the popular instruments used in those parts of Spain. The music has no pretensions to being descriptive; it is merely expressive. But something more than the sounds of festivals and dances have inspired these 'evocations in sound,' for melancholy and mystery have their part also."

These picturesque tone-portraits of Spanish gardens at night are not only among the most poetic works produced by Falla but, as Turina pointed out, among his saddest. "In the peculiar flavor of the orchestral sonority, one can in fact discern a feeling of bitterness, as if the composer had striven to express a drama of an intimate and passionate nature."

Since the composer has provided no specific program for his three nocturnal pictures, W. R. Anderson has admirably filled the gap with the following description: "We hear the first nocturne, 'In the Generalife'—the hill garden at Granada with its fountains and ancient cypresses contemplating the city below. . . . In the influence of the night, the fountains, dreamy patios, melancholy thickets and flowering pomegranates in the summer palace of the Moorish sultan, we can feel a sense of mystery and the ghosts of the past. . . . The hazy sound of the orchestral horn ceases, and we move in imagination to another garden, for the second nocturne, the 'Dance in the Distance.' About us again are the orange trees, the myrtles and the palms, the splashing waters. Mandolines and guitars play scraps of oriental-sounding tunes, coming nearer in the gentle wafts of tone now upborne, now falling, on the light breeze. In the last piece, we are 'In the Gardens of the Sierra de Córdoba,' on the mountainside, at a party where surely the gypsies are playing, singing, and dancing. Here is music wilder, rougher than before, still more deeply rooted in the East, in impassioned feeling and primitive power."

Nights in the Gardens of Spain was composed between 1909 and 1915, and was introduced on April 9, 1916, by the Orquesta Sinfónica of Madrid with Fernandez Arbós conducting and M. Cubiles as piano soloist.

The first nocturne (Allegretto tranquillo e misterioso) opens with a shimmering subject for solo viola supported by harp. Chords for strings and brass accentuate the first beat of each measure. The piano arrives with an inversion of the opening theme decorated by arpeggios. After that, a second subject is heard in the orchestra. This material is assumed by the piano (again in inversion) and repeated by the orchestra in its original form. A brief piano cadenza precedes the recall of the opening subject. In a brief coda, the horn reminds us of the opening theme, played over a soft string background.

The principal melody of the second nocturne (Allegretto giusto) is given by flute and English horn. Another dance tune follows in flute and strings, followed by a brief piano episode. The concluding nocturne (Vivo) enters without pause, a transition being effected by tremolos in the violins in the highest register. This concluding movement is demoniac music vitalized by exciting gypsy dance rhythms. The excitement mounts as one idea follows the next, energetic pages alternating with throbbing gypsy-like melodies. The mysterious and foreboding atmosphere projected in the opening of this nocturne returns at the end.

1919 THE THREE-CORNERED HAT (EL SOMBRERO DE TRES PICOS, or LE TRICORNE), ballet in one act, with book by Martinez Sierra based on a novel of the same name by Antonio de Alarcón. First performance: London, July 22, 1919.

THE THREE-CORNERED HAT, ballet suite for orchestra. I. The Neighbors. II. The Miller's Dance. III. Final Dance.

On a visit to Falla in Spain, Serge Diaghilev, the artistic director of the Ballet Russe de Monte Carlo, listened to parts of a score which Falla had written for a "pantomime" with text by Sierra. Diaghilev's talent for sensing a potential masterpiece did not betray him now. He recognized the potentialities for a Spanish ballet which would synthesize all Spanish folk arts and which would provide a novel and significant addition to his repertory; and he commissioned Falla to develop and enlarge his score for that purpose.

The first performance of Falla's ballet, which took place in London on July 22, 1919, was extraordinarily successful. Besides Falla's music, which evoked a new world of mystery and magic for London's ballet enthusiasts, there were Pablo Picasso's imaginative scenery and costumes (some of them based on paintings of Goya), Léonide Massine's choreography, and the dancing of Massine and Karsavina to create an artistic conception of striking originality, beauty, passion, exotic charm, and even wry humor.

At that première performance, the following synopsis of the scenario was published: "Over the whole brisk action is the spirit of a frivolous comedy of a kind by no means common only to Spain of the eighteenth century. A young miller and his wife are the protagonists, and if their existence be idyllic in theory, it is extraordinarily strenuous in practice—choreographically. . . . The miller and his wife between them, however, would hardly suffice even for a slender ballet plot. So we have, as well, an amorous Corregidor, or Governor (he wears a three-cornered hat as badge of office), who orders the miller's arrest so that the way may be cleared for a pleasant little flirtation—if nothing more serious—with the captivating wife. Behold the latter fooling him with a seductive dance, and then evading her admirer with such agility that, in his pursuit of her, he tumbles over a bridge into the mill-stream. But, as this is comedy and no melodrama, the would-be-lover experiences nothing worse than a wetting, and the laugh, which is turned against him, is renewed when, having taken off some of his clothes to dry them, and gone to rest on the miller's bed, his presence in discovered by the miller himself, who, in revenge, goes off in the intruder's garments after scratching a message on the wall to the effect that 'Your wife is no less beautiful than mine!' Thereafter, a 'gallimaufry of gambols' and—curtain!"

This amusing text had also been utilized by Hugo Wolf, for his opera *Der Corregidor,* composed in 1895.

An orchestral suite from this ballet score, comprising three major dances, is frequently heard at symphony concerts. The second dance, that of the miller, is perhaps the best of the three, successfully combining Andalusian rhythms with an ornamental Moorish melody. The final dance is a jota.

1926 CONCERTO FOR HARPSICHORD, FLUTE, OBOE, CLARINET, VIOLIN AND CELLO. I. Allegro. II. Lento. III. Vivace.

During a visit to Falla in Granada, the celebrated harpsichordist Wanda Landowska discussed with the composer the artistic possibilities of her instrument. Actually, Falla had been sufficiently interested in the harpsichord to incorporate it into the orchestra of his little opera for puppets, *El Retablo de Maese Pedro* (1919). But Landowska now intensified his enthusiasm to a point where he decided he would write a major work for it. He spoke of a concerto, and he promised Landowska that she would give the première performance.

As always with Falla, composition went slowly; the concerto took him three years. When it was completed, it did not prove to be a virtuoso work glorifying any one instrument, but a chamber-music work in which six instruments had equal importance.

Wanda Landowska introduced the concerto in Barcelona on November 5, 1926, the composer conducting.

Gilbert Chase, the eminent authority on Spanish music in general and Falla's music in particular, considers this concerto Falla's masterpiece, the one in which the "eternal essence" of Spain has been most completely embodied. The Spanish characteristics of this work are readily recognizable. In the first movement, the harpsichord suggests the subtle guitar performances of Spanish gypsies, weaving an intoxicating rhythmic background to melodies richly evocative of folk music. The second movement describes a religious processional, with plainsongs providing some of the melodic material. "In this movement," wrote Ralph Kirkpatrick, "are all of Spain, the harsh bitter fervor, the restraint of ceremony, the intellectual esctasy that are the inseparable constituents of the Spanish character." Spanish dance rhythms give the final movement of the concerto an engaging vitality.

Otto Mayer-Serra notes a strong affinity between Falla's concerto and the eighteenth-century harpsichord sonatas of Domenico Scarlatti. He notes "the revival" in Falla "of certain of Scarlatti's melodic and harpsichordist formulas, such as the 'angular' cut of the themes, the pedal effects, and the use of two keyboards, the quick repetitions of a single note, the multitude of appoggiaturas, etc." More important still, maintains Mayer-Serra, Falla derived from Scarlatti "the highest stylization in his epoch, of Spanish folkloric material, the intimate assimilation of popular elements that penetrated and completely transformed the original character of Scarlatti's idiom. This crystallization of the popular element finds its best expression in Scarlatti's rhythmic work; from this Falla derives his own concept of *internal rhythm*."

1946 LA ATLANTIDA (ATLANTIS), scenic cantata in three parts and prologue, with text by the composer based on Jacinto Verdaguer's epic poem of the same name (score completed by Ernesto Halffter). First performance: Barcelona, November 24, 1961 (concert version); La Scala, Milan, June 18, 1962 (staged version).

La Atlantida is structurally Falla's most ambitious project. It occupied him for over a quarter of a century, and he was still at work on it when he died in Argentina. He left behind so many sketches and excerpts and notations for the parts that still had to be written that it took Falla's pupil, Ernesto Halffter, five years to coordinate this material and to adapt and prepare the score for performance.

The nineteenth-century Catalonian epic poem by Verdaguer was based on the myth about the lost continent of Atlantis submerged by flood—with considerable additions and amplifications. The poem goes on to describe how Hercules saves Spain from the monster who wants to rule it; how he builds a port which came to be called Barcelona; how Columbus dreams of solving the mystery of the Atlantic Ocean; and how he helps to discover the New World.

A tug of war developed between Spain and Italy for the privilege of presenting the world première of Falla's last and most ambitious creation. The rights had been sold to the Italian publishing house of Ricordi, who had assigned the first performance to La Scala. But Spain insisted that the première of so great a national epic belonged to its own country. Finally (for a price) a compromise was reached. A concert version of excerpts was assigned to Spain before the staged version of the entire work was seen at La Scala.

Though in some of its Spanish identification, and in its modal writing, *La Atlantida* represents a carry-over for Falla of older creative practices, it also represents a significant departure. Enrique Franco noted: "There emerges a sacred polyphony, both vocal and instrumental, more beautiful than anything we have had since Vittoria. One may even say that the religious—or mystical—aspects of *Atlantida,* as musical entities are among the most attractive and moving to be found in European music." Franco also said: "As the music unfolds, from the grandiose to the detailed and finely wrought, Atlantida takes its sure place as the only Spanish work of such great magnitude, duration, quality, and depth of conception."

The distinguished Swiss conductor, Ernest Ansermet, summed up the principal textual and musical action in *Opera News* as follows: "The Prologue . . . shows that Falla has returned to the large orchestra. . . . Entirely a narrative, it uses a homophonic style except in orchestral episodes or certain lyrical moments, when it becomes polyphonic. . . .The Prologue begins with the orchestra evoking the sinking of Atlantis. This is followed by a summary of the action. It ends in a hymn of exaltation that God has preserved Spain and assured her future.

"During the first act, chorus and soloist describe the burning of the Pyrenees and Hercules' discovery of the dying Pyrene. . . . A hymn to the future of Barcelona concludes the act. The second act . . . depicts Hercules' arrival at the Garden of the Hesperides, the death of the dragon and the rage of the Atlanteans. . . . Atlantis sinks, and Hercules inscribes Gibraltar. In the third act, Columbus climbs the road leading to Isabella while the chorus recalls the prophecy of Seneca. The chorus rejoices on hearing Isabella relate her vision. A mystic choir utters liturgical words confirming the prophecy, and the chorus then sings of the ship's departure. Columbus is seen in mid-ocean surrounded by his men, singing a salute to the Virgin Mary. Then comes the 'Supreme Night' in which Columbus, alone, on the bridge of his ship, searches the heavens and the future, surrounded by mysterious and prophetic voices. The land is in sight and seems to welcome him in a Hosanna, followed by a jubilant Alleluia—as if on this new earth there appeared, in Columbus's eyes, an immense cathedral, symbol of Iberian grandeur and the triumph of Christianity."

Ernest Ansermet was the conductor who introduced parts of *La Atlantida* to the United States—in a concert version performed by the Metropolitan Opera company at Philharmonic Hall at the Lincoln Center for the Performing Arts on September 29, 1962.

GABRIEL FAURÉ 1845–1924

The delicacy and refinement of Fauré's style, his classic restraint and tendency towards understatement, his purity of expression, his fastidious attention to detail, and his exquisite workmanship—all these qualities betray the nationality of the composer. Indeed, so French is Fauré's art that it is sometimes said that only a Frenchman can properly appreciate it. His is an intimate art which does not wear its heart on its sleeve. In his music, modern technique is beautifully blended with the classic spirit of ancient Greece (twenty years before Debussy, he wrote impressionistically, while the harmonic language of his later works is an independent one). As Julien Tiersot once said of Fauré, "It is the spirit of Hellenism, as well as its forms, which is reborn in him."

A good deal of the Fauré music heard today was written before 1900. These works include the A major Violin Sonata, op. 13 (1876); the *Ballade,* in F-sharp minor, for piano and orchestra, op. 19 (1881); the G minor Piano Quartet, op. 45 (1886); the *Requiem,* op. 48 (1887); the *Pavane,* for orchestra, op. 50 (1887); the orchestral suite, *Pelléas et Mélisande,* op. 80 (1898); and such songs as "*Après un Rêve*" (c. 1865), "*Le Secret*" (1882), "*Les Roses d'Ispahan*" (1884), and the cycle *La Bonne Chanson* (1892); and, for the piano, the Barcarolles, opp. 41 and 66 (1885, 1894), Impromptus, op. 31 (1883), and the Nocturne, op. 74 (1898). All this music is sensitive in its lyricism, gentle in manner, whispering intimate confidences in a style which Aaron Copland once described as "delicate, reserved and aristocratic." After 1900, and up through his last work, the E minor String Quartet in 1924, Fauré's poetic temperament and French sensibility remained predominant. But he persisted in seeking an ever greater restraint and economy in his writing, an ever greater objectivity, while, occasionally, exploring the potential of new idioms and approaches. In these later works, as Martin Cooper notes, "the appeal to the senses is reduced to a minimum, the appeal to the emotions almost absent. . . . Fauré exposes in his later works a lean, muscular figure, slight in build but perfectly proportioned, statisfying to the senses without a hint of voluptuousness."

Fauré was born in Pamiers, Ariège, on May 12, 1845. From 1854 to 1865, he attended the École Niedermeyer, a period in which his first publication appeared, *Trois romances sans paroles,* for piano (1863). He began his professional career in 1866 as organist at the Saint-Sauveur Church in Rennes in Brittany. There, in 1868, Marie Miolan-Carvalho sang one of his earliest songs, "*Le Papillon et la Fleur,*" op. 1, with the composer at the piano. He came to Paris in 1870, and assumed an organ post at the Notre Dame de Clignancourt Church. During the Franco-Prussian War, he saw active service. Then he resumed his activity at the organ by occupying the bench at the Saint-Honoré d'Eylau Church. He also turned to teaching, becoming a professor at the École Niedermeyer. Later in life, in 1895, he became professor of composition at the Paris Conservatory, before becoming director of the Conservatory in 1905. A generation of French musicians studied with him and were influenced by him, including Ravel, Schmitt, Roger-Ducasse and Nadia Boulanger.

His early chamber-music works pointed up his growing maturity as a composer, notably the A major Violin Sonata in 1876 and the C minor Piano Quartet in 1870. These were followed by other important compositions climaxed by his monumental *Requiem,* in 1887, still regarded as one of his unqualified masterworks, written as a memorial to his father and introduced at the Madeleine Church in 1888.

Fauré married Marie Fremiet, daughter of a famous sculptor, in 1883. It was, for the most part, a marriage of convenience, but it seemed to have brought him a contented home life. He continued producing masterworks in all media, including the stage. His most important opera was the lyric drama, *Pénélope,* in 1913.

In 1909, Fauré was elected to the Académie des Beaux-Arts, and in 1910, he was made Commander of the Legion of Honor; in 1920, he was promoted to the highest class in the Legion. During the last years of his life, Fauré suffered from deafness which compelled him to resign his directorship of the Conservatory in 1920. He died in Paris on November 4, 1924.

1908–1922 NOCTURNES NOS. 9–13, for piano, opp. 97, 99, 104, 107, 119. IX. B minor-major. X. E minor. XI. F-sharp minor. XII. E minor. XIII. B minor.

In his earliest piano works (he composed his first three nocturnes, op. 33, in 1883), Fauré was strongly influenced by the style and stylistic mannerisms of Chopin and Schumann. Perhaps this was inevitable. But it was not long before he evolved his own style. The Nocturnes nos. 9 through 13 are among his finest creations for the piano. These are not gentle pieces of the night—as the nocturne frequently was with John Field and Chopin—but lugubrious music filled with despair and gloom. The ninth Nocturne (1908) is restless and febrile; this atmosphere is created by the unusual modulations. The eleventh Nocturne (1913) is a funeral elegy inspired by the death of Pierre Lalo's young wife. The thirteenth Nocturne (1922)—Fauré's farewell to the piano—is one of the most eloquently tragic pieces of music he ever put to paper.

1910 LA CHANSON D'ÈVE, song cycle for voice and piano, op. 95. I. Paradis. II. Prima Verba. III. Roses Ardentes. IV. Comme Dieu Rayonne. V. L'Aube Blanche. VI. Eau Vivante. VII. Veilles-tu Ma Senteur de Soleil? VIII. Dans un Parfum de Roses Blanches. IX. Crépuscule. X. O Mort, Poussière d'Étoiles.

It is indeed appropriate that an early published work of one destined to become France's greatest living master of the art song should have been a set of songs. Few composers of our time—few composers of any time, for that matter—have equaled Fauré's fresh and tender melodic vein, refinement of style, sensitivity to the poetic text, and gift for translating the subtlest atmospheres or feelings into tones. His more than one hundred songs are among his greatest achievements, and are among the most treasured items in the repertoire of French music.

In the songs written in the closing two decades of his life, Fauré had a simpler and more individual approach to both melody and harmony. His means are more economical; his harmonic language subtler and more suggestive. There is not a wasted phrase or a misspent note.

The best of his later songs are found in song cycles. *La Chanson d'Ève* is a setting of ten pantheistic poems by Charles van Lerberghe. In these poems, young Eve looks around the newly created world and interprets what she sees. The poems are vivid in their imagery and touched with mysticism; and to these poems Fauré always brought the musical *mot juste*. The cycle is prefaced by a five-bar motto phrase in the piano which resembles a plainchant, and which, so to speak, sets the stage for the cycle and creates the mood. The songs are delicate in feeling and fragile in construction.

1910 9 PRELUDES, for piano, op. 103. I. D-flat major. II. C-sharp minor. III. G minor. IV. F major. V. D minor. VI. E-flat minor. VII. A major. VIII. C minor. IX. E minor.

One French critic (who is anonymous) spoke of these preludes as the "purest and strongest music" written by Fauré. The preludes have a singleness of mood and a unity of form; the melodic ideas do not come fully developed, but are allowed to grow out of germinal ideas.

The finest of these nine preludes are the first (D-flat major), which has a wonderful serenity; the second (C-sharp minor), with its exotic atmosphere produced by the whole-tone scale; the fifth (D minor), which is in a stormy mood; and the exquisite sixth (E-flat minor), considered by Aaron Copland to be comparable to any one of the preludes in Bach's *Well-Tempered Clavier*.

1913 PRELUDE TO PÉNÉLOPE, for orchestra.

Pénélope is Fauré's most significant work for the stage. The score describes it as a "poème lyrique" ("lyric poem"), the three-act libretto by René Fauchois based on the classical story of Ulysses and Penelope derived from Homer's *Iliad.* Fauré's opera was introduced in Monte Carlo on March, 1913. About two months after that, it was produced for the first time in Paris, at the Théâtre des Champs Elysées. What is believed to be its American première took place at Harvard University on November 29, 1945, in a festival honoring the centenary of Fauré's birth.

The orchestral Prelude consists of two themes. The first, heard at once in the strings, describes Penelope; the other, stoutly announced by the horns, speaks for Ulysses. To Charles Koechlin, the prelude depicts "the heroism of noble expectancy, the sublime fidelity of the wife with her invincible hope .... At the peak of the exaltation of Penelope there appears at first from afar the motive of Ulysses—of a Doric simplicity.... And the development grows entirely from these two themes."

1917 SONATA NO. 2 IN E MINOR, for violin and piano, op. 108. I. Allegro non troppo. II. Andante. III. Allegro non troppo.

Fauré wrote two violin sonatas. The earlier one, in A major, op. 13 (1876) is the more popular—and understandably so. Its lyricism has surpassing charm, and its emotional content is consistently appealing. The second sonata, which came some forty years later, is a more subtle work, with its interest lying more in structure and workmanship than in melodic or harmonic writing. Each movement has some prevailing element to serve as a kind of catalytic agent. In the first, it is the appoggiatura rhythm that appears in the first theme and in the bass of the second. The second movement involves a device favored by the composer: having the melody move in octave leaps before or after it moves in single degrees of the scale. In the concluding movement, both themes are characterized by their quaver and semiquaver figurations. To provide an overall unification to the sonata, the composer quotes the main themes of the first movement in the finale.

1919 FANTAISIE, for piano and orchestra, op. 111.

In his biography of Fauré, Norman Suckling suggests that this *Fantaisie* "stands to the piano music of Fauré's old age in much the same relation of the *Ballade,* for piano and orchestra, op. 19 (1881) to that of his youth." Suckling goes on to say: "Its spareness of texture, in comparison with the earlier work, is a feature it shares with many of the other productions in those last years."

Suckling finds in the *Fantaisie* procedures that characterize the last manner of the composer. "The form is his familiar ternary one, and many of the old devices of figuration recur, such as the scale passages crossing and recrossing the melodic line and the indispensable broken chords; these, however, are of a thinner texture and modified by suspensions and passing notes, as in the piano writing of the later chamber works."

The piano is immediately heard in the principal theme (Allegro moderato), which the orchestra repeats a tone lower. This material is developed and varied. In the middle section (Allegro molto), the piano is heard in a strong, aggressive two-measure motive, which is repeated four times. After the orchestra gives response, the piano embarks on a broad melody in E minor. The opening Allegro moderato section returns with its material often embellished by decorative figurations in the piano.

1920 MASQUES ET BERGAMASQUES, suite for orchestra, op. 112. I. Ouverture. II. Menuet. III. Gavotte. IV. Pastorale.

Early in 1919, Fauré completed incidental music for a stage entertainment by René Fauchois, *Masques et Bergamasques,* which was produced in Monte Carlo on April 10, 1919. He adapted some of this music into an orchestral suite, and preceded it with an altogether new overture. The orchestral score is throughout characterized by an archaic atmosphere through the use of old song and dance forms in a Baroque-like style that is colored and dramatized by touches of modern harmonies. The composer transcribed his suite for piano, four hands.

1921 QUINTET NO. 2 IN C MINOR, for piano and strings, op. 115. I. Allegro moderato. II. Allegro vivo. III. Andante moderato. IV. Finale: allegro molto.

Fauré composed his first piano quintet, in the key of D minor, in 1906. Koechlin described it as "the first classic work of our times." Even more successful, and a much more integrated masterpiece, is the second quintet which came fifteen years later.

The first movement opens with a single bar for the piano, after which the viola enters with a fragment of the first principal theme. One by one the strings enter, until the theme is completely and fully realized. Sharp and agitated chords make up the second principal idea of the movement. The Scherzo, which follows, is in one of Fauré's vivacious moods: the touch is light; the movement, mercurial. Music of great emotional stress is found in the slow movement. A four-bar theme, speaking of unfathomable grief, is brought up by the strings. A dialogue of exquisite tenderness then takes place between violin and piano, after which a second melody—no less melancholy than the first—is heard in the piano. The sadness is completely dissipated in the agitation and rhythmic force of the last movement.

1922 L'HORIZON CHIMÉRIQUE, song cycle for voice and piano, op. 118. I. La Mer est Infinie. II. Je Me Suis Embarqué. III. Diane, Séléné. IV. Vaisseaux, Nous Vous Aurons Aimés.

Fauré's last work for voice and piano was based on four poems written by Jean de la Ville de Mirmont (a young poet killed in World War I). These poems use the sea as a symbol of the undiscovered. To the seventy-seven-year-old composer in the shadow of death, the sea becomes a symbol of the great Beyond. The songs are filled with a quiet and dignified pathos.

An unidentified annotator describes the first song as "quietly animated" and points to the ostinato rhythm in the second which "suggests quiet undulations." The third, he says, "fulfills the function of a slow movement, so to speak, after which the fourth, written in Fauré's favorite barcarolle rhythm, brings the cycle, with its last phrase, to an unexpected happy climax."

1924 STRING QUARTET IN E MINOR, op. 121. I. Allegro moderato. II. Andante. III. Allegro.

Fauré's last composition for a chamber-music ensemble, his only string quartet, is often compared to the last quartets of Beethoven. Fauré's work, like that of Beethoven's last period, is rich in spiritual content. As in Beethoven, the expressiveness of the melodic ideas transcends the music itself and seems to speak of mystic and philosophic concepts. One other point of resemblance is important. Both composers were completely deaf when they wrote these works, and, in their isolation from the world of actual musical sound, were led to employ unusual progressions, modulations and thematic sequences.

However, in Fauré—as is not often the case in the later Beethoven—the concentration of writing is so great that the music is stripped down to essentials. There is no diffuseness; no superfluity. Every line, every phrase, has its calculated mission; each is indispensable to the design of the whole.

The greatest of the three movements (and here, once again, we are reminded of Beethoven) is the slow one. This is music of quiet and gentle melancholy, music of autumnal moods—the introspection of a mature man who knows he has not much longer to live. Fauré's poetic speech here rises to a plane of eloquence rarely realized even by him. What Julien Tiersot said of Fauré in general applies most strongly to music such as this: "He . . . thrusts himself beyond the spheres in order to bring back pure beauty."

CARLISLE FLOYD 1926–

Carlisle Floyd has described his principles and attitudes as a composer of opera in *Musical America*: "My first consideration in attempting an opera is whether or not the subject is one in which the emotional, psychological, and philosophical concepts of the story can be externalized through action and visible situation and style retain absorbing, multidimensional characters. For the very reason that opera must be primarily externalized we have erred too often, I feel, in favor of situation, leaving character development in a rather primitive, elementary state. . . . Also I feel it is time that we who write operas attempt to make some commentary on timeless human problems in a contemporary way, and that it is not inappropriate that an opera have a 'theme' so long as it is not tiresomely didactic."

Floyd's musical style is eclectic. Much of its power is generated through expressive declamations, and his strong harmonic language. But he has not neglected lyricism altogether, which, from time to time, springs from his music like some geyser eruption. And he is not afraid of emotion, or of romantic attitudes, when the text calls for them. His extraordinary success stems from the fact that he is at one and the same time a supremely articulate and versatile musician and a telling and consummate dramatist in his librettos.

Floyd was born in Latta, South Carolina, on June 11, 1926. After studying the piano with private teachers, he received in his sixteenth year a scholarship in piano for Converse College. There he was a pupil of Ernst Bacon, with whom he continued his music study while attending Syracuse University, where he received his Bachelor of Arts and Masters degrees. He also studied piano privately with Rudolf Firkusny. In 1947, he became a member of the music faculty of the Florida State University in Tallahassee, where he has remained since as professor. He wrote two operas—*Slow Dark* (1949) and *Fugitives* (1951)—before achieving formidable success with *Susannah* in 1954. He received a Guggenheim Fellowship in 1956, and in 1957, a citation from the National Association for American Composers and Conductors. His later operas placed him with the most successful American composers of our time. Besides *Wuthering Heights* and *The Passion of Jonathan Wade,* discussed below, Floyd wrote *The Sojourner and Mollie Sinclair* to help celebrate the 300th anniversary of North Carolina; it was produced in Raleigh, North Carolina, on December 2, 1963. *Markheim,* based on the famous story of Robert Louis Stevenson, was produced in New Orleans on March 31, 1966.

1954 SUSANNAH, a musical drama in two acts, with text by the composer. First performance: Tallahassee. Florida, February 24, 1955.

Susannah was the opera with which its composer achieved national success. That success came after the opera's première in New York, where it was produced by the New York City Opera on September 27, 1956. The critics were lavish in their praises, and the opera became a strong box-office attraction. In addition, it received the New York Music Critics Circle Award and it represented American opera at the Brussels World's Fair Exposition in Belgium during the summer of 1958. Since then it has become a fixture in the repertory of American operas.

The composer wrote his own libretto. The central theme is, as the composer explained, "persecution and the concomitant psychological ramifications." The setting is a farm in New Hope Valley, in the mountains of Tennessee, in the present day. The heroine lives with her brother, Sam. She is held in suspect by her townspeople because she is so seductively beautiful, and because one day she is caught bathing nude in a nearby creek. Susannah thus is victimized by merciless gossip until it begins to destroy her spirit. Concerned over her soul, Reverend Blitch calls on her. Relieved at being able to pour out her grievances and bitterness to the Reverend, Susannah becomes sympathetic to his suddenly bold advances. When Susannah's brother, Sam, learns what has happened he kills the preacher, even as the latter is praying for Susannah's understanding and forgiveness. The crowd advances menacingly on Susannah to destroy her with its hatred, but is kept in check by Susannah with a shotgun. As the final curtain descends, Susannah is left alone, standing in the doorway of her farm, a forlorn and tragic figure.

Through the consistent use of hymn tunes, arias with a folk-song identity, and square dances, Floyd endowed his score with a rich American flavor, which is perhaps its main appeal. The opera opens with a hoedown; the first appearance of Reverend Blitch is greeted with a four-part American hymn; Sam's "Jaybird Song" is in the recognizable idiom of an American folk song. But Floyd's operatic style is also often rooted in the more traditional style of Puccini and Wagner: Puccini in some of the arias (as in Susannah's moving refrain, "Ain't it a Pretty Sight," for example), Wagner in the exploitation of the *Leitmotiv* technique. Floyd also owes a debt to the moderns, in his skilful use of the *Sprechstimme,* in his use of sung dialogue against a persistent musical background by the orchestra, and in his equally effective employment of polytonality and dissonance to heighten the dramatic impact of some of the more tragic episodes of his opera. "The story as I conceived it," said the composer, "seemed to me to be explosive with theatrical potential and foreseeable situations which would lend themselves to musical treatment and exploitation." The strength of Floyd's opera, and the reason for its immense popularity, is that he always found the proper musical treatment and exploitation for the demands of his play and its characters and situations.

1958 WUTHERING HEIGHTS, opera in three acts and prologue, with text by the composer based on Emily Brontë's novel. First performance: Santa Fe, New Mexico, July 16, 1958.

Floyd's opera was written on a commission from the Santa Fe (New Mexico) Opera Association which presented the world première. There it met with a mixed reaction. Some critics praised its moments of "moving lyricism" but found the score as a whole uneven and derivative, and the libretto full of clichés. This reaction led Floyd to revise his opera extensively with the third act being rewritten entirely. The revised version was produced by the New York City Opera on April 9, 1959. This time the critical response was most favorable. Virgil Thomson wrote in the *Herald Tribune:* "From first to last the familiar story is handled in a manner that compels attention and strong sympathy." Robert Sabin reported in *Musical America* that it was "a wholly successful and deeply moving opera—one of the best from an American composer."

Floyd took some liberties with the novel, mainly by shifting the time forward by some three decades and placing it in the nineteenth century. Some of the plot details were also altered, one or two episodes having been invented to intensify dramatic action. In the opera, the prologue shows Heathcliff as the master of Wuthering Heights, with his wife, Isabella, as its mistress. Then in a flashback, the first act shows Heathcliff as an orphaned boy of fifteen living with the Earnshaws. The plot traces Heathcliff's love for Cathy Earnshaw and his despair when she becomes engaged to Edgar. Heathcliff flees, and does not return to Wuthering Heights until many years later. Cathy dies before she can give birth to a child. Heathcliff marries Isabella, Edgar's sister, wins Wuthering Heights in a game of chance with Cathy's impoverished brother, and becomes its new master.

"The burden of the music," said Howard Taubman, "falls on the orchestra. . . . Note the charming Allegro giocoso that opens the second act. Note the minuet in the third act and especially the waltz which is pointed in its wry energy. Note the tender passage at the end of the first scene of the second act where Cathy binds Heathcliff's wounds."

In his vocal writing, the composer relies mainly on a declamation that Taubman finds "gray and undifferentiated." But Taubman also adds that "there are some touching moments for the singers—ariosos, bits of duet, a quartet and an agreeable chorus." Taubman concludes: "Mr. Floyd has not dominated his theme only because he has chosen one so overwhelming. What he has accomplished deserves respect. For this *Wuthering Heights* has warmth and sincerity. It is the work of a composer whose metier is the lyric theatre."

1962 THE PASSION OF JONATHAN WADE, opera in three acts, with text by the composer. First performance: New York City Opera, October 11, 1962.

Once again, as in *Wuthering Heights,* Floyd uses a large canvas. In this instance, the setting is the South during the Reconstruction period following the Civil War. But Floyd explores moral issues as well as political and social ones, by describing the tragedy incurred by the passions and hates the war had ignited, and whose flames refused to die down after peace; the destruction of a high-minded and idealistic man as a result of these hatreds.

The hero is an idealistic Northern colonel who commands the occupation forces in South Carolina after the end of the war. His mission is to help bind up the wounds caused by the recent conflict. There are some Southerners who are more moderate in their outlook. These take kindly to him. One of them is an aristocratic judge. Brooks Townsend, with whose daughter, Celia, Jonathan falls in love. But the radical Republicans—who are more intent on getting vengeance for their recent defeat—regard him as an arch-enemy. The wedding ceremonies of Jonathan and Celia are interrupted by a raid from the Ku Klux Klan. In time, the judge's pride in the South and in his social class leads him to join the Ku Klux Klan, which, just before the final curtain, is responsible for Jonathan's murder.

In projecting the drama, Floyd neatly balances expressive declamation (which helps explain the motivations of the characters and carry on the development of the story) with fully developed melodies (some of which are conventional arias). One of the best of his melodies is a spiritual sung by a Negro servant during the marriage ceremonies. This tune is then taken over by a chorus, which in turn is succeeded by a deeply affecting love duet. Ross Parmenter, in his review in *The New York Times,* remarked that the opera was at its best and most convincing when it indulged in such pages of lyricism. "In fact," he adds, "there was so much that was pretty and melodious that one was inclined to wish it had been more purely a love story, and less encumbered with a sense of dramatic history with philosophical overtones."

The opera was commissioned and produced by the New York City Opera on a grant from the Ford Foundation. Phyllis Curtin (who had appeared in the leading female roles in Floyd's earlier operas, *Susannah* and *Wuthering Heights*) once again assumed the role of the heroine.

ARTHUR FOOTE 1853–1937

The New England school of composers, which included George Chadwick, Frederick Converse, Henry Gilbert, Horatio Parker and Arthur Foote, was a conservative group which never outgrew the traditions of its teachers. These composers believed in using the sound forms of classical and romantic music and filling them with robust melodies, attractive harmonies, and the accepted contrapuntal techniques of the textbook.

Although Foote lived into the fourth decade of the twentieth century and saw composers everywhere shattering long-accepted rules and evolving new styles, he kept on producing the kind of music he had written in the closing years of the nineteenth century. For Foote, major innovations in musical style ended with Wagner and Brahms. The influence of Wagner—under whose spell he came in 1876, when he attended the first of the Bayreuth festivals—is found in such early choral works as *The Farewell of Hiawatha* (1886) and *The Wreck of the Hesperus* (1888); that of Brahms, in the chamber music he produced in the 1890s, which the Franz Kneisel Quartet introduced. Maturity and experience, of course, brought to his music enrichment of speech and refinement of writng, as well as a personal viewpoint and an individual manner. But they did not alter the essential character of his compositions, which remained romantic and emotional rather than academic or experimental.

Foote was born in Salem, Massachusetts, on March 5, 1853. He studied piano and harmony as a boy, and took music courses at Harvard, which he had entered in 1870. But serious music study did not begin until after he had been graduated from Harvard in 1874. At that time, he studied organ and piano with B. J. Lang, and composition with John Knowles Paine. Foote received his Master of Arts degree from Harvard in 1875.

The first important performance of one of his works came with the overture, *In the Mountains,* presented by the Boston Symphony on February 5, 1887. The Boston Symphony continued to introduce his major orchestral works, and the Kneisel Quartet, his chamber-music compositions, until he became one of the most highly regarded composers in America. During this period, he served as organist of the First Unitarian Church in Boston from 1878 to 1910, and he taught piano privately in Boston from 1883 to 1933. In 1899, he was elected a member of the National Institute of Arts and Letters, and a Fellow of the American Academy of Arts and Sciences. He also helped found the American Guild of Organists, serving as its president from 1909 to 1912.

He remained active in many different areas of music up to the end of his life. To celebrate his eightieth birthday, in 1933, the Boston Symphony presented a program devoted entirely to his music. Arthur Foote died in Boston on April 8, 1937.

1907 SUITE IN E MAJOR, for string orchestra, op. 63. I. Prelude. II. Pizzicato. III. Fugue.

This is one of Foote's best-known works. It was introduced by the Boston Symphony under Max Fiedler on April 16, 1909.

This short Prelude which opens the suite is built on an eight-note phrase heard at the outset. The plucking of the strings in the Pizzicato is only briefly interrupted by a melody for muted strings (Adagietto) played with the bow. The suite ends with a conventional fugue, the first four notes of whose theme are often heard by themselves before the projection of a fugue in a strictly Baroque style.

1912 FOUR CHARACTER PIECES, for orchestra, op. 48. I. Andante commodo. II. Allegro. III. Commodo. IV. Più allegro.

This was the last work that Foote wrote directly for the symphony orchestra (a later orchestral work, *A Night Piece,* was an adaptation of a composition tion for flute and string quartet.)

Each of the four episodes is inspired by verses from Omar Khayyám's *Rubáiyát.* The first ("Iram, indeed, is gone with all his Rose") is dominated by a haunting melody for solo clarinet over a persistent, throbbing rhythm. The second ("They say the lion and the lizard keep") presents a strongly accented theme, introduced by first violins. Midway in this section comes a gentle tune for clarinet and flute, softly accompanied by strings ("Yet ah, that Spring should vanish with the rose!"). The first part then returns, to rise towards a climax. In the third episode ("A book of verses underneath the bough"), the main thought is given immediately in the strings and then is subjected to various transformations. The concluding part ("Yon rising moon that looks for us again") offers its main melody in solo horn and cello. This is a romantic theme, built up sonorously, then allowed to die down. A contrasting scherzo section follows ("Waste not your hour, nor in the vain pursuit"), at whose conclusion we get a loud recollection of the theme of the first episode. After a pause, the first theme returns, accompanied by divided strings, after which the movement end in quiet solemnity.

1918 A NIGHT PIECE, for flute and string quartet (also for flute and string orchestra).

Foote wrote few works so pure in their musical expression, so completely deriving their effect from beauty of sound, as this nocturne. Marked *Andante liquido,* this piece is music diaphanous in harmonic texture, tender in melody, touched with the most delicate tone colors. Philip Hale wrote that the listener "is not conscious of anything but charming sounds, skilfully and logically succeeding each other, so that there is a thing of beauty."

This composition originated as a chamber-music work, in which form it was introduced by the San Francisco Chamber Society on January 28, 1919. Pierre Monteux asked the composer to adapt the music for flute and string orchestra. In the new version, the work was introduced by the Boston Symphony under Monteux on April 15, 1923.

LUKAS FOSS 1922–

As a young student in Paris, Lukas Foss, then in his early 'teens, began writing music in Hindemith's linear style. Less than half a dozen years later he became Hindemith's pupil in composition, first at the Berkshire Music Centre at Tanglewood and then at Yale, only to find that his musical thinking was turning sharply away from Hindemith towards a more romantic and emotional expression. Hindemith himself had nothing whatsoever to do with this change. What had taken place was the natural evolution of a young composer who had to write as he felt.

Foss first made his mark as a composer in a work in which an American identity was forcefully projected—the cantata *The Prairie* in 1943. More and more in the late 1940s and early 1950s, his style became increasingly melodic and harmonic rather than contrapuntal. This is in spite of a work like the *Symphony of Chorales* (first heard on October 24, 1958, with William Steinberg conducting the Pittsburgh Symphony), each of whose movements is based on a Bach chorale. But such reversions to neo-classical procedures and contrapuntal practices are the exceptions rather than the rule. "Dramatic power," wrote his friend Robert Strassburg in describing Foss's later style, "is matched by lyric warmth and spaciousness of concept." Humanity, deeply felt personal sentiments, and a rich romantic outlook are qualities which distinguished Foss's later compositions.

Since 1957, however, Foss has been experimenting with improvisation and with controlled chance. In the improvisational method, he produced first a *Concerto for Improvising Instruments and Orchestra,* which the Philadelphia Orchestra under Ormandy introduced in the fall of 1960. Here the orchestra provided a frame for a series of spontaneous improvisations by solo instruments. Foss's most significant creative attempt to use improvisation within a planned pattern is found in *Time Cycle,* in 1960, which is discussed below. Controlled chance governs a composition like the choral *Fragments of Archilochos,* which can be performed in many different ways at different performances.

"By following an intricate diagram," explains Brock McElheran, "the music is marked so that only a small amount of possible combinations is actually heard at any one time. At other concerts different combinations are used. There are actually hundreds of different compositions possible with the material assembled under this title, all predetermined by the composer when designing his diagram." Foss himself has offered an explanation as to why it is desirable to have a composition sound differently at different performances. "The answer . . . is simple: for the pleasure of surprise—not so much the audience's, who may hear the piece but once, but the performer's. He will experience surprise at every performance (a) because the detail is always different, (b) because, though always different, the music remains somehow curiously the same."

Foss was born in Berlin on August 15, 1922. After preliminary study of piano and theory with Julius Goldstein, Foss came to Paris in his eleventh year. There he attended the Conservatory, a student of Lazare Lévy (piano), Noël Gallon (composition) and Felix Wolfes (orchestration). In 1937, he made his permanent home in the United States, and in 1942, he became an American citizen. For three years, he attended the Curtis Institute of Music, from which he was graduated with highest honors. He also studied conducting and composition, the latter with Paul Hindemith, at the Berkshire Music Centre; he continued as Hindemith's pupil in composition at Yale between 1940 and 1941. In 1942, he became the youngest musician ever to receive a Pulitzer Traveling Scholarship. Three years later, he was the youngest musician ever to get a Guggenheim Fellowship. Meanwhile, several of his works were getting important performances in New York and Philadelphia, climaxed by the resounding success of his cantata, *The Prairie,* in 1943.

With major choral and orchestral works, he solidified his place in American music. His second piano concerto (1949) received the Hornblit Award in Boston, and following its revision in 1953, the award of the New York Music Critics Circle. His fantasy opera, *Griffelkin,* proved an outstanding success over television in 1955. At the same time, he was distinguishing himself as a pianist, conductor and teacher. He had made his conducting debut with the Pittsburgh Symphony in 1939. Between 1944 and 1950, he was the official pianist of the Boston Symphony, with whom he made numerous notable appearances as a soloist. During this period he was often heard as guest conductor with major orchestras. He began his teaching career as a member of the Berkshire Music Centre in 1946. From 1953 to 1963, he was professor of composition at the University of California in Los Angeles, whose orchestra he conducted. In 1957, he organized the Improvisation Chamber Ensemble with which he toured the United States in performances of improvised music. He toured the Soviet Union and Poland as a conductor of his own music in 1960, sponsored by the State Department of the United States. In 1963, he became artistic director of the Ojai Festival in California, where for two seasons he led highly successful performances. In 1965, he was director of the American-French Festival of the New York Philharmonic at the Lincoln Center of the Performing Arts. As the musical director of the Buffalo Philharmonic, to which he was appointed in 1963, and as co-director of the Buffalo Center for the Creative and Performing Arts, he has encouraged experiments in and performances of avant-garde music.

1943 THE PRAIRIE, cantata for solo voices, chorus and orchestra.

In the summer of 1941—four years after coming to this country—Foss conducted a performance of Copland's Suite from *Billy the Kid.* Copland's use of cowboy melodies, and the apt way in which the music interpreted America, intrigued Foss. The young man now felt the impulse to write a work of his own dedicated to and inspired by the land of his adoption. The reading of Carl Sandburg's poem *The Prairie* provided the neccessary stimulus. The reflection of the soil and spirit of America in Sandburg's poem—with the prairie, as Foss puts it, as a "symbol for the all-embracing principle of *growth* itself"—called for music. Foss set to work on a large cantata in 1943. On October 15 of that year, an orchestral suite from the score was introduced by the Boston Symphony under Koussevitzky. On May 15, 1944, the entire cantata was heard for the first time in New York City, performed by the Collegiate Chorale under Robert Shaw. It was selected by the New York Music Critics Circle as the best new American work of the season.

Spacious in its design, with broad, wind-swept melodies and sweeping sonorities suggestive of "vast open landscapes and lots of fresh air," *The Prairie* is American music without once quoting or even simulating American folk music.

Foss's description of the work follows:

"The opening movement, which has the nature of a prologue, speaks of the prairie, as we are accustomed to visualize it. The author, in a pastoral tenor solo, sings of open valleys and far horizons, and the music breathes fresh air. After this pastoral introduction, a fugue is heard in the orchestra, above which the chorus takes up a new theme in the manner of a chorale. This is the voice of the prairie. . . . As a complete contrast, a folk-like movement follows, but the melodies remain original throughout the work. . . . With the re-entry of the chorus, the prairie becomes 'mother of men, waiting.' Then the author reaches far back into the past and we see the cities rising on the prairie, out of the prairie, while the chorus chants of the years when the red and white men met. . . . In rugged . . . rhythms follows what may be styled the industrial section, ending with a fugue for male voices. . . . A lyrical intermezzo brings us back to the prairie. This consists of a short a cappella chorus, a soprano song, and a scherzando duet . . . held together by a dreamy little shepherd's lay, a nostalgic woodwind refrain of the prairie. The tenor's voice introduces the seventh and last section, and everyone joins in the final hymn to the future, expressing the healthy and sunny optimism unique to this country."

1944 ODE, for orchestra.

The original title for this short and deeply moving composition was *Ode to Those Who Will Not Return.* As this title suggests, the music was written in memory of those who fell during World War II. An immediate stimulation for the composer was this line from John Donne's *Devotion:* "Any man's death diminishes me."

The composer's analysis follows: "The beginning of the piece is austere and somber in mood. A dark, bell-like theme of even quarter notes is developed throughout, tolling and telling about this time of crisis and war. An Appassionato middle section contains fugato and variation elements, subsiding only to rise again to greater tension, climaxing in fanfare of moaning trombones. There returns the first theme of even quarter notes, but here it has none of the tranquillity of the opening. . . . Agitated now, and breathless, it calms down only after the trumpets and finally the violins sing out a nostalgic and consoling melody, until all motion comes to an end in the peace of a C major chord."

The first performance of the *Ode* was given by the New York Philharmonic under George Szell on March 15, 1945. In 1958, Foss revised this composition, the new version being given by the Philadelphia Orchestra under Ormandy the same year.

1945–1946 TWO BIBLICAL CANTATAS:

THE SONG OF ANGUISH, for baritone and orchestra.

SONG OF SONGS, for soprano and orchestra. I. Awake, O North Wind. II. Come, My Beloved, Let Us Go Forth into the Field. III. By Night on My Bed. IV. IV. Set Me a Seal Upon Thine Heart.

Foss wrote two biblical cantatas, the first being *The Song of Anguish* (1945), on a text from Isaiah. This cantata was written on a commission from the Kulas Foundation in Cleveland. The music was first heard as background for a dance performed by Pauline Kohner at Jacob's Pillow in Massachusetts during the summer of 1948. The first concert performance took place in Boston, with Foss conducting the Boston Symphony Orchestra on March 10, 1950. Marko Rothmüller was the assisting artist.

A long orchestral prelude (Andante sostenuto; Allegro) sets the mood of the music, which fluctuates from the poetic to the dramatic, from the elegiac to the passionate, following the demands of the text.

The passages from lsaiah open with the following lines:

> Woe unto them that call evil good and good evil,
> That put darkness for light and light for darkness,
> Woe unto them that are wise in their own eyes
> That are prudent in their own sight.
> Woe—Woe—Woe.

Foss's second biblical cantata, drawing its text from the Song of Solomon, was commissioned by the League of Composers for the soprano Ellabelle Davis. Completed in the summer of 1946, it was introduced by Ellabelle Davis and the Boston Symphony Orchestra, Serge Koussevitzky conducting, on March 7, 1947. Koussevitzky's enthusiasm for this new work was so great that he broke all precedent by performing it eight times in nine days: twice in Boston, twice in New York City, and once each in Philadelphia, Brooklyn, New Haven and Northhampton, Massachusetts.

The music—sensuous in style and containing many pages of great emotional intensity—has caught the essence of the text. It is at turns joyous and tragic, ecstatic and religious, delicately sweet and acrid. The opening section, intended as an introduction to the whole work, opens with a free fugue before the entrance of the voice. The second part is a broad and elastic melody—a *da capo* aria. The third part, in contrast, is a recitative, intermittently interrupted by orchestral interludes. The concluding movement, which follows the third section without a pause, is in the nature of a prayer.

1948 RECORDARE, for orchestra.

The title is taken from one of the sections of the traditional Requiem Mass. This tragic music, however, has no ritual connotations but has borrowed the name to suggest an act of remembrance. The person here being remembered is Gandhi, the writing of the composition having been begun on the day of Gandhi's death on January 30, 1948. The composition is in three-part form. The first and last are funereal, while the middle part is agitated. A single theme dominates the entire composition, a somber subject first heard in the clarinet; it undergoes numerous transformations of structure and changes of mood.

The *Recordare* received its first performance in Boston on December 31, 1948, the composer conducting the Boston Symphony.

1952 A PARABLE OF DEATH, cantata for narrator, tenor and chorus.

The Louisville Orchestra commissioned this work for Vera Zorina, dancer turned narrator. For his text, the composer went to a story and several poems by Rainer Maria Rilke. He uses the narrator, as he explains, to tell "quietly and intimately what appears to be an old legend about a man, a woman, and death. Chorus and solo tenor comment on the story. Their lines are taken from poems by the same author." The cantata was introduced in Louisville on March 11, 1953. Robert Whitney conducted, and Vera Zorina was the narrator.

The work has a prologue and six sections. Joseph Machlis explains that the prologue utilized "archaic harmonies in the orchestra" for the purpose of establishing "the quality of restlessness essential to the tale." A spirited chorus follows (Molto sostenuto) to a text beginning, "O God, give until every man his death." Then there comes a romantic, almost rhapsodic tenor solo (Allegretto), "There once were two people, a man and a woman, and they loved one another." A chorale follows to the words "Who built this house where the heart has led" (Con moto). The ensuing section, for narrator, accompanied by orchestra, describes the house that this man and woman have built. A high-tensioned chorus comes in the fourth part (Agitato ma sostenuto) to the words, "Listen! This might have been your heart's epiphany." This part concludes with another chorale, to which the orchestra provides comment (Maestoso). In part five, the tenor solo is heard in a sensitively lyrical part, "Tears, tears rising to drown me." A polyphonic chorus, "We know him not, this lordly caller," precedes the concluding section in which narrator and chorus bring the work to an eloquent ending.

1955 GRIFFELKIN, fantasy opera in three acts, with text by Alastair Reid based on a German fairy tale. First performance: NBC-TV, November 6, 1955.

When the NBC Opera commissioned Foss to write an opera for television, he recalled a fairy tale his mother had often narrated to him when he was a child. He decided to use this story for an operatic fantasy, or "miracle play," and asked Alastair Reid, of the faculty of Sarah Lawrence College, to prepare a libretto.

The main character, Griffelkin, is a kindly little devil, who is celebrating his tenth birthday in hell. He is given the gift of a bottle with a magic liquid that can turn live people to stone, and stone to live people. With this bottle, the devil is permitted to go down to earth for a single day. On earth he brings to life such inanimate objects as a statue, a couple of stone lions, and some toys. He also meets a girl, from whom he learns the meaning of love and pity. With the last drops of his magic liquid, he saves the life of the girl's mother. His fellow devils regard this as heresy, banish him from their world, and compel him to spend the rest of his life as a boy in the family he had saved.

This delightful little fairy tale is told, in text and music, simply and poignantly, with a directness and lack of pretension that makes it enjoyable listening for young and old. In *Musical America,* Robert Sabin found that "the most notable characteristics of this score are its rhythmic ingenuity and transparence of texture. Foss has absorbed the bounce, the syncopation and dance impulse of the popular music of our day into his bloodstream and his music reflects them in ways that are natural, unforced and delightful."

Formal operatic structures are used—arias, duets, choral numbers—together with a canon and a waltz. In the opening party scene, a bravura aria is parodied and Mozart's C major Piano Sonata is wittily quoted. "Cleverly, Foss saves his first strokes of pure lyricism for Griffelkin's discovery of the wonders of the earth," writes Sabin. "As he looks at the sky, the trees, the building, a sense of beauty that is in human life steals over him. . . . Later, when Griffelkin asks the little girl and boy what mother means, what love means, and what death means, the music again takes on a melodic intensity and simple harmonic beauty that bespeak a profoundly gifted composer."

1960 TIME CYCLE, for soprano and orchestra (also for soprano, piano, clarinet, cello and percussion). I. We're Late. II. When the Bells Justle. III. Sechzehnter Januar. IV. O Mensch! Gib Acht!

In 1957, Lukas Foss began experimenting with the possibilities of ensemble improvisations—an informal, spontaneous kind of music produced by performers who do not play composed music but evolve the music through the process of improvisation. Foss formed the Improvisation Chamber Ensemble which made appearances throughout the United States in concerts of spontaneous music-making. For this group, he created a *Concerto for Improvising Solo Instruments and Orchestra* which was introduced by the Philadelphia Orchestra in the fall of 1960. In this work, Foss only suggested the broad outlines of the composition in a kind of chart suggesting a germ motive or a rhythmic pattern, entrances and exits of individual instruments, and other basic ideas. The working out of this material was left to mere chance, details having been left to spontaneous improvisation.

Time Cycle is a unique experiment in combining composed music with improvisation. The work is made up of four songs. The first is based on a poem by W. H. Auden; the second, on a poem by A. E. Housman; the third, on lines from Kafka's diairies; and the fourth, on an excerpt from Nietzsche's *Thus Spake Zarathustra*. A unifying element among all four songs is the literary motive of time, each one of the poems or lines referring either to time, clocks or bells. Musical unity is achieved through the repetition of a single chord (C-sharp, A, B, D-sharp) in various alterations. This much consists of composed music. Chance comes in interludes for piano, clarinet, cello and percussion that separate one song from another. They are intended as a kind of commentary on time but created spontaneously. During the performance of the songs, the improvising instruments are silent. Then when the song is over, it is the turn of singer and orchestra to remain silent while the improvising quartet takes over.

When this work was first performed (by the New York Philharmonic under Leonard Bernstein on October 20, 1960), Bernstein told his audience: "I think so highly of Foss's *Time Cycle* that we would like to make a proposal. If you wish, we will repeat the whole piece for you. And if there are only twelve people in the house who want to hear it again we will play it for those twelve." In Boston, two years later, the audience walked out on the performance; while at the Stratford Festival in Ontario, Canada, it inspired an ovation, with Glenn Gould, the festival director, calling it "the most important work in the last ten years." The composition received the award of the New York Music Critics Circle in 1961, was choreographed by the Canadian National Ballet, and was recorded by Columbia.

Foss prepared a second version of this composition, by removing the improvised interludes and having only the quartet of instruments (piano, clarinet, cello, percussion) accompany the voice in place of the orchestra. This version was heard first at Tanglewood on July 10, 1961, and was recorded by Epic.

1964 ELYTRES, for eleven solo performers (also for orchestra).

"*Elytres*" is the French term for elytra or wingsheaths, the heavier exterior wings that protect the lighter under ones in certain insects. When performed as a chamber-music composition, *Elytres* calls for the following instruments: solo flute, two solo violins, distant violins and pitchless percussion, harp, vibraphone, piano. The piano is played not only on the keyboard but also on the strings of the soundboard, the percussionist using tape-covered vibraphone mallets. All instruments play only in their high registers. In a performance by an orchestra, the distant violins are tripled and some of the percussion parts are doubled. *Elytres* was given its world première in Los Angeles on December 8, 1964.

1966 PHORION, for strings, electronic organ, electronically amplified harpsichord (or piano) and amplified harp (or electric guitar).

This work was commissioned by the Association for Women's Committees for Symphony Orchestras, which not only gave the composer a cash payment but also the guarantee of performances by ten major American orchestras within a two-year period. The world première took place in New York City on April 27, 1967, with Leonard Bernstein conducting the New York Philharmonic. This is a curious compostion in that Foss took his notes from the Prelude of Bach's E major Partita for solo violin. (The title "Phorion" comes from the Greek meaning "stolen goods.") He explains that the idea came to him in a dream when he saw "torrents of the Baroque sixteenth-notes washed ashore by ocean waves, sucked in again, returning ad infinitum." Foss uses Bach's notes "as if no other notes were available." In *Saturday Review,* Irving Kolodin remarks: "What he does, in effect, is to derive strength from Bach's cascading invention, while indulging his vanity in subjecting it to any distortion, intrusion—eventually commotion—that occurs to him."

JEAN FRANÇAIX 1912–

Jean Françaix is as Gallic in his music as in his name. Lightness of touch, effervescence of spirit, irony that sometimes touches malice, grace, proportion are found in most of Françaix's works. He has been influenced by the neo-classic manner of Stravinsky, to the point where slender form, conciseness, brevity, simplicity, clarity and objectivity become almost a fetish. He is also strongly indebted to the French classic style. But there is enough acidity in his harmony and robustness in his rhythm to contribute contemporary spice to his writing. A few of his works are in a grand manner, and aspire towards nobility rather than wit, majesty of utterance rather than levity. In such a style, we encounter his opera, *La Main de gloire* (1945), introduced at the Bordeaux Music Festival on May 7, 1950; also his most ambitious choral composition, the oratorio, *L'Apocalypse de Saint Jean* (1939), text derived from the Book of Revelation, a work first heard in Paris on June 11, 1942. But profundity of thought and emotions deeply felt are exceptions rather than the rule with Françaix. Generally speaking, his most familiar works are slight in aesthetic intent but with a continual sparkle that makes for delightful listening.

Françaix was born in Le Mans on May 23, 1912, the son of the director of the Le Mans Conservatory. He began composing early—a piano suite written when he was nine was published by Maison Senart. He was first a pupil in his father's class at Le Mans, then a private student of Nadia Boulanger, and after that was enrolled at the Paris Conservatory. He won numerous prizes. *Eight Bagatelles,* for string quartet and piano, played at the International Society for Contemporary Music Festival in Vienna on June 21, 1932, gave strong evidence of his rapidly developing creative talent.

On November 6 of the same year, the Orchestre Symphonique de Paris under Pierre Monteux introduced his Symphony. Thereafter, Françaix was frequently represented on major concert programs, and was often referred to as the "white hope" of French music. He visited the United States in 1938. Among his more significant later works are *L'Horloge de flore,* for oboe and orchestra (1959) and the opera, *La Princesse de Clèves,* which received its world premiere in Rouen in 1966.

1932 CONCERTINO FOR PIANO AND ORCHESTRA. I. Presto leggiero. II. Lent. III. Allegretto. IV. Rondo: allegretto vivo.

The neo-classicist's ideal—music reduced to its very essentials—is realized successfully in this early and ingratiating work. The simplicity and directness of this music almost approaches the ingenuous. The solo piano presents a brief headstrong theme in the first movement, which is immediately taken up by the orchestra. This theme is the spine of the entire movement, which is light and capricious throughout. The second movement is only thirty bars long. Against a hauntingly tender background of strings, the piano presents a nostalgic melody. The trumpet injects a rakish and jazzy melody in the Allegretto that follows—to be answered soberly by the piano; but the mood throughout is carefree and abandoned. The last movement in the gayest of the four, effervescent in its good spirits.

The Concertino was introduced on December 15, 1934, by the Lamoureux Orchestra under Jean Morel, with the composer at the piano.

1933 SCUOLA DI BALLO (THE DANCING SCHOOL), ballet in one act, with scenario and choreography by Léonide Massine based on a comedy by Goldoni. First performance: Ballet Russe de Monte Carlo, Monte Carlo, April 25, 1933.

SCUOLA DI BALLO, ballet suite for orchestra. I. Leçon; Menuet. II. Larghetto; Rondo; Dispute. III. Presto; Pastorale; Danse allemande. IV. Scène du notaire; Finale.

In his first successful ballet, Françaix adapted music by Luigi Boccherini (1743–1805), from several of his rarely heard Quintets and from his Sinfonia No. 2 in B-flat. Cyril Beaumont informs us: "The choreography is pleasing and well adapted to Boccherini's flowing melodies, and many little touches of comedy and character—suggesting Longhi's paintings have been studied to some purpose—are adroitly introduced." The ballet tells about the efforts of a dancing master to convince an impresario to hire one of his backward pupils. When this pupil dances, the impresario realizes he has been duped. With the aid of a notary, the impresario manages to get back the money he had paid out to the dancing master.

An unidentified program annotator points to the following highlights in the ballet suite which the composer adapted from his score, and which have become popular at symphony concerts. "An occasional stern note in the 'Leçon' and the strong chords in the 'Menuet' suggest the teacher. The violin and bassoon play a duet which very clearly pictures the inept pupil. Further atmosphere is furnished by a guitar-like accompaniment heard on the harp from time to time. One is soon acquainted with the characters who appear in the various sections. The Larghetto closely resembles a movement in one of Haydn's symphonies, which suggests a tempting line of speculation."

1936 CONCERTO FOR PIANO AND ORCHESTRA. I. Allegro. II. Andante. III. Scherzo. IV. Allegro.

The usual spacious dimension and bigness of style found in concerto music are not to be encountered in this work. The texture is thin; the design fragile. There is no development of thematic material to speak of.

There are four little themes in the first movement, which is rhythmic and sprightly. A pensive note is injected in the Andante, the piano presenting a tender melody out of which the entire section is built. The mercurial Scherzo has three basic ideas, each introduced by the piano before being taken over by the orchestra. The vertiginous finale exploits four ideas with brilliant effect, the healthy animal spirits of the composer are allowed full freedom of movement and expression.

This concerto (with which, incidentally, Françaix made his American debut on February 11, 1938) was first heard in Berlin on November 8, 1936, the composer as soloist.

1947 L'APOSTROPHE (THE ATTACK), comic opera in one act, with text by the composer based on a story by Balzac. First performance: French Radio, 1947; Amsterdam, July 1, 1951 (first staged presentation).

The gaiety and mockery of Françaix's style leads itself naturally to the requirements of comic opera. The text of *L'Apostrophe* was derived from one of Balzac's *Droll Tales*, and concerns the futile love of the hunchback Darandas for the lovely and coquettish Tascherette, a love that brings him doom at the hands of Tascherette's husband.

The opera was first staged at the Holland Music Festival in Amsterdam. Reviewing the work, a correspondent for *The New York Times* described the score as follows: "The music is the essence of theatricalism . . . with an utter lack of inhibition in rhythm, melody, and orchestration. . . . The score is more ingenious than important, but since Françaix is attempting no more that a broad satire, the result is completely effective—so much so that even the non-French speaking section of the audience often was lured into laughter solely by the caprices of the score."

1948 LES DEMOISELLES DE LA NUIT (LADIES OF THE NIGHT), dramatic ballet in three scenes, with scenario by Jean Anouilh and choreography by Roland Petit. First performance: Paris, May 20, 1948.

This is one of the most scintillating and vividly pictorial scores that Françaix produced for ballet. The scenario describes the problems of a young man who marries a cat. The three scenes then show how he meets the cat; how he falls in love with it; how his love transforms the cat into a beautiful young girl; how he marries her; and how the wife is unable to resist her feline tendencies to scamper on rooftops. In the end both the young man and the cat die; and in death they finally find happiness together.

When the ballet received its world première, the two principal dancing roles were assumed by Margot Fonteyn and Roland Petit. The ballet was introduced in the United States by the Ballet Theatre, in New York, on April 13, 1951. At that time, the leading female role was danced by Colette Marchand.

GEORGE GERSHWIN 1898–1937

It is mainly since Gershwin's death that complete awareness of his musical importance has become almost universal. The little defects in his major works—those occasional awkward modulations, the strained transitions, the obscure instrumentation—no longer appear quite so important as they did several decades ago. What many did not realize then—and what they now know—is that the intrinsically vital qualities of Gershwin's works reduce these technical flaws to insignificance. The music is so alive, so freshly conceived, and put down on paper with such spontaneity and enthusiasm that its youthful spirit refuses to age. The capacity of this music to enchant and magnetize audiences remains as great today, even with familiarity, as it was yesterday, when it came upon us with the freshness of novelty.

Gershwin lacked the technical adroitness and the *savoir-faire* that come with a conservatory education. What he did have—and what no conservatory can teach—was an infallible musical instinct.

That he had a wonderful reservoir of melodies was, of course, self-evident when Gershwin was alive. What was not quite so obvious then was that he had impressed his identity on those melodies—his way of shaping a lyric line, his use of complex rhythmic patterns and changing meters, the piquant effect of some of his modulations and accompaniments—so that they would always remain recognizably his. His best songs sound as fresh today as they did when first written. Their piquancy, wistfulness, charm and tenderness have not been dissipated by time. And those lyric outbursts in his larger works—the rhapsodic slow middle section of the *Rhapsody in Blue,* the slow movement of the Concerto in F, the blues melody in *An American in Paris,* the best songs of *Porgy and Bess*—are the creations of a born melodist.

Beyond the fact that he produced several works that are among the treasured contributions to present-day music in America, Gershwin's significance lies in his influence on contemporary musical writing. When Gershwin came upon the musical scene, our popular music was a rather disreputable idiom, even though several major composers like Debussy, Satie, Stravinsky and Milhaud had experimented with it. It was Gershwin, however, more than any other single composer who brought artistic respectability to it. He set the example which encouraged composers throughout the world to emulate him. Ravel, Krenek, Weill, Lambert, Walton, Copland, Gould—to mention a few—owe a considerable debt to Gershwin which they readily conceded.

Gershwin was born in Brooklyn, New York, on September 25, 1898. He was by no means a prodigy, and his musical education was spasmodic. He took lessons at the piano (his first important teacher being Charles Hambitzer), and later studied harmony with Edward Kilenyi, then briefly with Rubin Goldmark. In his teens, he acquired a job as song plugger at Remick's, one of Tin Pan Alley's major publishing houses. Before long, he was writing songs of his own; and, in 1919, he was the proud parent of a "hit" song that swept the country, "Swanee." In 1920, he began writing the music for George White's annual revue, *Scandals*. Thereafter, his rise as one of the most successful composers for the Broadway stage was swift. In 1919, he composed his first serious work in a popular idiom, a *Lullaby,* for string quartet. (Its world première was given by the Julliard String Quartet in Washington, D.C., on December 19, 1967.) In 1922, he composed a one-act opera, *135th Street*. Two years after that came the *Rhapsody in Blue,* whose success made Gershwin famous throughout the world of music. After that, he divided his activities between writing popular music for the Broadway stage (and later for the Hollywood cinema) and serious works for concert-hall consumption. In both fields, he was extraordinarily successful. He died in Hollywood on July 11, 1937, after an exploratory operation on the brain that revealed a tumor. In 1945, the story of his life was told in the motion picture, *Rhapsody in Blue*.

1922 135TH STREET (BLUE MONDAY), one-act opera, with text by Bud De Sylva. First performance: New York, August 29, 1922.

Gershwin's first experiment in the use of jazz materials within an ambitious format was a one-act opera which he wrote to Bud De Sylva's libretto for the George White *Scandals of 1922*. There it had only a single performance under the title of *Blue Monday*. After opening night, George White felt that the little opera was too somber for a revue and that it made the audience unreceptive to the attractions that followed it. But though gone so quickly, the opera was not forgotten. It was revived by Paul Whiteman and his orchestra at a Carnegie Hall concert on December 29, 1925, the occasion upon which it was baptized *135th Street,* the name by which it was henceforth to be identified. Parts were subsequently interpolated into the George Gershwin screen biography, *Rhapsody in Blue,* and then, on March 29, 1953, the whole opera was presented over television on the "Omnibus" program.

The text tells of the rivalry of Joe and Tim for Vi. Joe leaves town to visit his mother, but ashamed of such a sentimental journey, he invents the fiction that he is going on business. Vi is suspicious of Joe's trip, and soon becomes convinced he is having a rendezvous with another woman. In a jealous rage, Vi shoots and kills Joe. Only then does she discover the truth.

It is a feeble plot, and Gershwin's score was not strong enough to carry it. This is by no means an integrated opera, but a series of popular tunes connected by a recitative with jazz inflections. There are some fine melodies ("Blue Monday Blues," "Has Anybody Seen My Joe?" and the spiritual, "I'm Going to See My Mother"); and at times jazz is effectively used for comic effect. But the material is not well integrated into the overall dramatic content, and the score, as a whole, lacks atmospheric or dramatic interest, while most of the recitatives are stilted. Nevertheless, *135th Street* remains of interest, not only because it is Gershwin's pioneer attempt to make artistic use of jazz, but also because it is the ancestor of *Porgy and Bess*.

1924 RHAPSODY IN BLUE, for piano and orchestra.

Paul Whiteman asked Gershwin to write a large work in the jazz idiom for a concert of popular music he was planning to give at Aeolian Hall in New York on February 12, 1924. The work Gershwin finally wrote (and which Ferde Grofé orchestrated for him) was the *Rhapsody in Blue,* which not only proved to be the tour de force of Whiteman's concert—the work that gave point and significance to Whiteman's experiment—but was also the turning point in Gershwin's career. It made him world-famous and rich. Royalties from the sale of sheet music and records, and from public performances on stage and screen, were astronomical. It was heard in every possible arrangement, even adapted into a ballet, and prepared for a tap dance. Its principal theme became Paul Whiteman's identifying signature on the radio. Its name provided the title for Gershwin's later screen biography, produced by Warner Brothers (with Robert Alda as the composer) and released in 1945. Few serious works in contemporary musical history enjoyed such a fabulous success in so short a period.

But the *Rhapsody* accomplished even more than making Gershwin rich and famous. By "making a lady out of jazz," it set into motion an entire new trend in modern music. Composers in many different parts of the world were encouraged by it to write serious works in the jazz idiom, often with great artistic success.

The *Rhapsody in Blue,* besides being very good music, has the additional strength of being very good *American* music. Few works written by Americans before 1924 have such an unmistakable national identity as this one. It is American to its very core, just as rodeos, baseball and tabloids are American. The nervousness, energy, youth, optimism, strength and infectious charm of this country are caught in its infectious rhythms. The color and background of America are reflected in its harmonies. The *Rhapsody* is music about an age of steel and speed; it is the voice of the great modern metropolis. Surely future historians will come to know what we were during the fabulous era of the 1920s by listening to the *Rhapsody,* just as today we know what Vienna was a century ago by hearing the waltzes of Lanner and Johann Strauss, and what France of the Second Empire was by listening to the *opéra-comique* of Offenbach.

The rhapsody opens with a low trill in solo clarinet, the beginning of a seventeen-note ascent towards the first theme, a jaunty subject that establishes the mood for the entire work. A transition in the winds carries the suggestion of the second main theme. This is a sprightly tune that finally emerges in the piano. This second subject is discussed at length, then becomes the basis for an extended narrative by solo piano. A few ascending chords in the piano now point to the main part of the entire work, the rhapsodic melody for strings, which has become one of the most famous melodies in all serious American music and which became Paul Whiteman's signature. The full orchestra repeats it. Then a hurried recall of its opening phrase in a fast tempo brings the concluding section. The opening clarinet theme becomes a climactic point in full orchestra, after which the piano remembers the second theme wistfully. The Rhapsody ends abruptly with a brief coda in which the opening phrase of the first clarinet theme is thundered by full orchestra.

1925 CONCERTO IN F, FOR PIANO AND ORCHESTRA. I. Allegro II. Andante con moto. III. Allegro con brio.

The tremendous success of the *Rhapsody in Blue* in 1924 brought Gershwin a major commission: to write a concerto for piano and orchestra for Walter Damrosch and the New York Symphony Society. Gershwin knew so little about the concerto form that before beginning work he had to buy a textbook to guide him. He planned to write a work more ambitious in form and scope than his *Rhapsody;* besides, he intended to orchestrate it himself, instead of relying on Ferde Grofé, as had been the case with the *Rhapsody.*

The première of the concerto took place in New York on December 3, 1925, with the composer playing the piano part and Damrosch conducting the orchestra. The work met a mixed reaction. Samuel Chotzinoff used the word "genius" without reservation; but other critics felt that too much of the concerto was derivative (from Debussy, for the most part), and too much of it was marred by technical flaws.

Since that first performance, the concerto has grown in popularity, and today it is one of Gershwin's best-loved works. Several years after it had been introduced, Albert Coates—the eminent English conductor—included it as the only American composition in a list of fifty of the most important musical works of our generation.

A Charleston motive appears in the introduction of the first movement, after which the bassoon presents the first major theme. This is developed. A second theme, more lyrical than the first, is introduced by the solo piano. The major part of the movement is devoted to discussing these two ideas. A brief coda, in which the rhythmic fragment of the introduction returns, brings the movement to a close. The second movement is poetic music, bringing up a moody subject for muted trumpet, followed by a sprightlier secondary theme for piano. After a development, a new melody comes forth, first in the strings and woodwinds, then in the piano, finally in the full orchestra. After an impressive climax, the first theme returns, and the movement ends in an atmosphere of questioning and mystery. In the final movement, Gershwin unleashes his rhythms and sprightliest jazz themes, then throws a reminiscent glance towards his first movement by repeating its second theme. A new idea for muted trumpet and strings is imposed. After some development, a fugato passage—based on the second theme of the finale—comes as a kind of summation. After the return of the main theme, the movement ends with a brief but effective coda.

1926 THREE PRELUDES, for piano. I. B-flat major. II. C-sharp minor. III. E-flat major.

On December 4, 1926, at a concert at the Hotel Roosevelt, George

Gershwin shared the platform with the contralto Marguerite d'Alvarez, who included on her program of art songs and arias several Gershwin numbers. Gershwin was her accompanist for his songs. He also appeared as a piano soloist, and in this capacity he gave the first performance of five preludes for piano. Three of these have become extremely popular; the other two are rarely heard.

The first prelude (Allegretto ben ritmato e deciso) is of rhythmic interest, a marriage of the tango and the Charleston. The second and most famous number in the group (Andante con moto e poco rubato) is a three-part blues, its melody set against a rich and exciting harmony. Rhythm is once again the predominant element in the third prelude (Allegretto ben ritmato e deciso), and helps to create a joyous, abandoned feeling.

The three preludes have been orchestrated several times. Jascha Heifetz transcribed them for violin and piano. Other arrangements include those for saxophone and piano, and trumpet and piano.

Of the two other preludes heard in 1926, now in comparative discard, one is a thirty-two bar blues, while the other is a tender melody in narrative style. The latter, when heard today, is given in a transcription for violin and piano, made by Samuel Dushkin, and entitled *Short Story*.

1928 AN AMERICAN IN PARIS, tone poem for orchestra.

In the spring of 1928, Gershwin escaped from his many business and social commitments in the United States for a European vacation. He hoped to devote himself to serious music study. He never did get around to studying, but he did succeed in writing a major work for orchestra. The exhilaration and intoxication of being in Paris inspired him to re-create these moods in his music, together with the inevitable feeling of homesickness which every American inevitably experiences. Gershwin completed his sketches in Paris, began his orchestration in Vienna, then completed the entire work on a return visit to Paris. On December 13, 1928, it was introduced in New York by the New York Philharmonic Orchestra, Walter Damrosch conducting.

A brisk and energetic theme for strings and oboe at the opening of the composition suggests the light-footed pace of the American walking through the Parisian streets. The noise of taxicab horns (the score calls for four actual taxi horns) assails his ears. A brief theme in the trombone suggests a music hall which the American passes. A second walking theme is then heard in the clarinet. After some development of both walking themes, a solo violin introduces a brief melody—it is a young lady who is approaching our American. But for all his exhilaration, our American cannot suppress a measure of homesickness. A plangent blues song—the principal melodic idea of the entire work—unfolds in muted trumpet. The walking themes and the blues return, and then a vigorous finale proclaims the fact that while it will be good to be home again, it is even better to be in Paris.

The tone poem provided the title for a motion-picture musical in 1951, which received the Academy Award as the best release of the year; it starred Leslie Caron and Gene Kelly. Here the music of the tone poem was used for a twenty-minute modernistic ballet that is the climax of the production, the dance conceived by Kelly, and danced to by Kelly and Miss Caron.

1931 SECOND RHAPSODY, for piano and orchestra.

In 1930, Gershwin came to Hollywood to write music for the screen musical *Delicious,* starring Charles Farrell and Janet Gaynor. His music included a six-minute sequence for orchestra describing the sounds and movements of a city and emphasizing the rhythm of riveting. Only a minute of this material was used a background. Gershwin liked the unusual material and decided to develop it into a symphonic work to be named *Rhapsody in Rivets.* He completed it by May of 1931. Fearing that the word "rivets" might include a disturbing aural image to listeners and raise programmatic interpretations he did not intend, Gershwin then changed the title of his composition to *Second Rhapsody.* Its first performance took place in Boston on January 29, 1932; Serge Koussevitzky conducted the Boston Symphony, and Gershwin was the piano soloist.

The initial idea of the rivets is discerned in the opening measures in a rhythmic subject for solo piano. This idea is then developed by the full orchestra after which it is heard in a rhumba melody. Following a detailed development of both themes, solo piano provides the transition to a blues song that is the heart of the composition. First it is played by a string choir; then it is taken over by the brass; and finally, it is elaborated upon by solo piano and orchestra. After a recall and embellishment of the two main themes, the rhapsody ends on a dramatic note.

1932 CUBAN OVERTURE, for orchestra.

Early in 1932, Gershwin spent a holiday in Cuba, where he became fascinated with the rhythms of Cuban dances and with native percussion instruments. The idea was then born to write a work which could exploit this material. He completed his composition in three weeks' time, initially using the title of *Rhumba;* it was introduced under that name on August 16, 1932, at an all-Gershwin concert at the Lewisohn Stadium, Albert Coates conducting. (This was the first time that an all-Gershwin concert had been given anywhere.) The following winter, on November 1, the composition was heard at a benefit concert at the Metropolitan Opera. For this performance, it was renamed *Cuban Overture.* Gershwin explained the reason for the change of title: "When people read *Rhumba* they expect 'The Peanut Vendor' or a like piece of music. *Cuban Overture* gives a more just idea of the character and intent of the music."

In his biography of George Gershwin—*A Journey to Greatness*—this editor provided the following description of this music:

"The overture is in three sections. A provocative rhythm, partly rhumba, partly habanera, opens the work. The first theme, Cuban in identity, makes its appearance in the strings. A three-part contrapuntal episode then leads to the second theme, which is soon combined contrapuntally with fragments of the first theme. A clarinet cadenza leads to the middle section, which is mostly a gradually developed canon in a melancholy vein. This canon is in two voices and is unusual in that (unlike traditional canons) it has a harmonic background. After a climax is built out of the ostinato theme of the canon, the finale makes its appearance. The finale uses themes of previous sections, but treated in a stretto-like manner. The composition ends with a dynamic and exciting rhumba in which native Cuban instruments of percussion are used. In his conductor's score, Gershwin specified that these instruments be placed in a row in front of the conductor's stand: first the Cuban stick, then the bondo, the gourd, and the maracas."

1934 VARIATIONS ON "I GOT RHYTHM," for piano and orchestra.

"I Got Rhythm" is the song that catapulted Ethel Merman to stardom in her Broadway debut—in the Gershwin musical comedy, *Girl Crazy* (1930). In his frequent sessions at the piano at parties, Gershwin enjoyed performing this song with improvised variations, a tour de force which has not been forgotten by those who heard it. In 1934, Gershwin embarked on an extended tour of one-night stands with the Leo Reisman Orchestra conducted by Charles Previn, featuring all-Gershwin programs. It was for this tour that Gershwin wrote down a formal set of variations for piano and orchestra on "I Got Rhythm," and introduced it in Boston with the Leo Reisman Orchestra on January 14, 1934, just eight days after he had finished writing it.

The work opens with a four-note ascending phrase taken from the first measure in the chorus of the song; it is played by the solo clarinet. After the theme has been taken over first by the solo piano, then by full orchestra, the piano presents the full chorus of the song. The variations then follow, in which not only the structure, melody and rhythm of the song are changed but also the mood and atmosphere. In the first variation, we get a release of dynamic energy; in the second, the virile tune is toned down to become a melancholy threnody. By turns, now, the melody becomes muscular and aggressive, or splendiferous, or transformed into a deep-throated blues.

1935 PORGY AND BESS, folk opera in three acts, with text by DuBose Heyward based on *Porgy,* a play by Dorothy and DuBose Heyward, and lyrics by DuBose Heyward and Ira Gershwin. First performance: Boston, September 30, 1935.

SYMPHONIC PICTURE, tone poem for orchestra based on melodies from *Porgy and Bess,* adapted and orchestrated by Robert Russell Bennett.

Having successfully tackled the forms of the rhapsody, concerto, overture, prelude and variations, Gershwin began thinking of writing an opera. But the problem of suitable libretto had to be solved. He remembered a Theatre Guild production he had seen some years earlier, a play called *Porgy* by DuBose Heyward. The American flavor of this play, and the poignant story of the love of Bess for the crippled Porgy, impressed themselves strongly on Gershwin's consciousness. The more he thought of it, the more he felt that this was the ideal subject for an opera, a *native* American opera, possibly a folk opera.

The libretto was prepared by DuBose Heyward in collaboration with Ira Gershwin. Then George Gershwin set to work on his music. To get the proper feel of the locale of his story, he went for several weeks to Charleston, South Carolina, living in a shack on the waterfront. There he absorbed the music of the Gullah Negroes. Thus saturated with the music and ritual of the Charleston Negro, Gershwin began collating his melodic ideas. Within the texture of his writing, he incorporated something of the piquant melodies of Charleston's street-cries, something of the savage rhythms of Negroes at work or in prayer, something of the plangent melody of a sad race. His writing did not go easily by any means. It took him eleven months to put his opera down on paper; and an additional nine months were consumed in the orchestration.

The première of the opera took place in Boston on September 30, 1935. On October 10, it began its run in New York City. It cannot be said that the opera was successful at first. The critics felt that though there were lovely songs in it, the work was neither opera nor musical comedy, but a sort of hybrid product. Olin Downes said that it did not "utilize all the resources of the operatic composer or pierce very often to the depths of the simple and pathetic drama."

But like all genuinely important works, *Porgy and Bess* did not have to wait indefinitely for full recognition. In 1937, it received the David Bispham Medal as an important contribution to native American opera. In 1938, it was produced in Los Angeles and San Francisco with outstanding success. Four years after that, on January 22, 1942, it was revived in New York, this time to become one of the great theatrical successes of the season and to enjoy the longest run ever known by a revival. The Music Critics Circle now embraced the work, selecting it as the most important musical revival of the year. Some of the leading critics, reevaluating it, now sang its praises. Between 1952 and 1956, an American-Negro company toured with *Porgy and Bess* throughout Europe, the Middle East, the Soviet Union and Latin America, scoring triumphs everywhere equaled by few contemporary operas, if any. It became the first opera by an American-born composer performed at the historic La Scala in Milan. In 1959, Samuel Goldwyn produced a motion-picture adaptation of the opera, starring Sidney Poitier, Dorothy Dandridge, Diahann Carroll, Sammy Davis and Pearl Bailey. In 1965, *Porgy and Bess* entered the regular repertory of the Volksoper in Vienna.

The setting is a Negro tenement in Catfish Row, in Charleston, South Carolina. While a crap game is taking place, Clara is lulling her baby to sleep with the lullaby, "Summertime." Jake, Clara's husband, takes the child from Clara, and sings to it a cynical ditty, "A Woman Is a Sometime Thing." Meanwhile, the crap game is gaining heat. A quarrel erupts between two of the participants, Robbins and Crown, in which Crown kills his adversary. To flee from the law, Crown goes into hiding, but leaves behind Bess, his girl friend. She accepts the protection and hospitality of the cripple, Porgy, who is devotedly in love with her.

In Robbins's room a wake is taking place. The widow, Serena, sings of her grief in "My Man's Gone Now," and the mourners raise their voices in a touching spiritual.

In the second act, we find Bess happy in her new life with Porgy. He, of course, is exultant that Bess is his, and he expresses his joy in "I Got Plenty o' Nuthin'," while the lovers exchange tender sentiments in the duet, "Bess, You Is My Woman Now."

The people of Catfish Row go off to a lodge picnic on Kittiwah Island. Bess goes along with them. There the folks make merry. Sportin' Life entertains the people with "It Ain't Necessarily So," his cynical attitude towards religion.

When the picnic is over, the people make for the boat. Crown, who has been hiding on the island, seizes Bess and takes her off with him to the woods.

A few days pass. The fishermen of Catfish Row are off at sea. Bess returns from the island, sick, worn and feverish. She is gratefully accepted by Porgy, who asks no questions and demands no explanations now that his beloved is back. They repeat their avowal of love in "I Loves You Porgy." Suddenly, a hurricane erupts. The women folk gather in Serena's room to pray for the safety of their husbands. Crown appears suddenly, in search of Bess; he introduces a mocking, sacrilegious note into the religious proceedings with his ditty, "A Red-Headed Woman Makes a Choo Choo Jump Its Tracks." From a place at the window, Clara notices that her husband, Jake, has fallen out of the boat into the raging waters. Crown mocks Porgy for being a cripple and unable to provide any help. Crown then rushes out in a futile attempt to save Jake. Upon his return, Crown is murdered by Porgy.

While Porgy is in the hands of the police for questioning, Sportin' Life induces Bess to go off with him to New York and its gay life, his bait being a package of "happy dust." Back from prison, Porgy looks about eagerly for Bess. When he learns that she has gone to New York with Sportin' Life, he jumps into his goat cart to follow her and bring her back.

The score, to be sure, is most memorable for its succession of wonderful songs, choral chants, folk tunes, street melodies—many strongly racial in character and idiom. As this writer noted in his Gershwin biography, *A Journey to Greatness*: "To portray this people in all the varied facets of their personality, Gershwin made extensive use of musical material basic to the Negro people. His recitatives are molded after the inflections of Negro speech. His songs are grounded either in Negro folk music or in those American popular idioms that sprang out of Negro backgrounds. His street cries emulate those of Negro vendors in Charleston. His choral pages are deeply rooted in spirituals and 'shouts.' . . . The pages that stir one most profoundly, and which bring to the opera its artistic importance, are those most deeply rooted in Negro folk culture: the wake scene, beginning with the lament, 'he's a-gone, gone, gone' and continuing with the stirring choral, 'Overflow, Overflow' to Bess's ecstatic spiritual, 'Oh the train is at the station'; the ecstatic 'shout' of Serena in her prayer for Bess's recovery; the piquant street cries of the honey man, crab man, and strawberry man; Jake's work-song, 'It takes a long pull to get there'; the moving choral exhortation to Clara on the death of her husband, 'Oh Lawd, Oh My Jesus Rise Up An' Follow Him Home'; and the final hymn of Porgy, 'Oh, Lord, I'm On My Way.' "

An excellent orchestral tone poem was made from the basic melodies of *Porgy and Bess* by Robert Russell Bennett. He called it *Symphonic Picture,* and he wrote it at the request of the conductor, Fritz Reiner, who introduced it with the Pittsburgh Symphony Orchestra on February 5, 1942. Since then, this composition has often been heard on symphony programs. The following sequences go to make up Bennett's tone poem, in the following order: Scene of Catfish Row with the peddlers' calls; Opening of Act II; "Summertime" and Opening of Act I; "I Got Plenty of Nuthin' "; "Storm Music"; "Bess, You Is My Woman Now"; "It Ain't Necessarily So"; and the finale, "Oh, Lawd I'm on My Way."

Five of the principal songs were transcribed for violin and piano by Jascha Heifetz, and recorded by him for RCA Victor.

HENRY F. GILBERT 1868–1928

A hearing of Charpentier's opera *Louise* in 1901 was a crucial hour in the life of Henry F. Gilbert. That performance motivated him to return to composition, which he had abandoned for a few years. Equally important, it convinced him of the necessity of deriving his materials and inspiration from American folk and popular styles, in much the same way that *Louise* was influenced by Parisian street cries. From then on, Gilbert went to American sources—popular and serious—for ideas and techniques. His first major symphonic work, *Americanesque* (1903), developed three minstrel-show tunes; renamed *Humoresque on Negro Minstrel Tunes,* it was introduced in Boston on May 24, 1911. Subsequently, Negro, Creole, ragtime, cakewalk music—as well as other minstrel melodies—played vital roles in his compositions.

His historic importance cannot be disputed: at a time when most American composers were feeble imitators of French impressionism or Germanic post-Romanticism, he pointed the way to a robust Americanism that was sincere and artistically valid. His music is vigorous, sometimes unconventional, made vital by rhythmic energy, and given humanity by an engaging sense of humor. Its American identity is unmistakable; and therein, perhaps, lies its greatest strength.

Born in Somerville, Massachusetts, on September 26, 1868, Gilbert received his musical education first at the New England Conservatory and then with Edward MacDowell. The necessity of earning a living made it difficult for him to devote himself to composition. During the years when he worked as a printer, arranger, and engraver, he became a student of American cultural backgrounds. This brought him into contact with American folk and popular music, which he came to admire. He was fired with the ambition of encouraging the emergence of an American nationalist school of music. With Arthur Farwell he founded the Wa-Wan Press, devoted to the publication of native American music. In his own compositions he became one of the first serious American composers to utilize American popular idioms successfully.

During most of his life, Gilbert suffered not only from intense poverty but also from miserable health. He had been born with an abnormally large right ventricle which sent forth a great amount of blood through the skin capillaries. His heart condition was further aggravated when he became a victim of typhoid fever in Paris in the early 1900s. With this deformity, the doctors insisted, Gilbert could not be expected to live beyond his thirtieth year. He lived twice that number of years, but they were years of great physical suffering.

Despite his poor health, he continued composing and produced several works of distinction. In 1927, he was one of two American composers (the other was Aaron Copland) represented at the International Society for Contemporary Music Festival, held in Frankfort, Germany. Though now an invalid, he went to Europe to attend the performance of his *The Dance in the Place Congo*. He died one year later at his home near Cambridge, Massachusetts, on May 19, 1928.

1905 COMEDY OVERTURE ON NEGRO THEMES, for orchestra.

For many years, Gilbert worked on an opera based on the Uncle Remus tales of Joel Chandler Harris. He had completed a great part of the score before he discovered that the operatic rights had been assigned to another composer. Gilbert's opera was therefore never published or produced.

From the music of this score he was able to create two independent works. One of these was his *American Dances,* for piano. The other was this overture. Renamed *Comedy Overture on Negro Themes* (and rescored for large orchestra), it has become one of Gilbert's most famous compositions.

The overture develops several authentic Negro melodies. One of them is of Bahaman origin. Another is a roustabout tune frequently heard and danced to along the Mississippi River (*I'se Gwine to Alabamy, Oh!*). The third, a spiritual named *Old Ship of Zion,* was utilized by the composer as the theme for a sprightly fugue.

The first performance of the overture took place at an open-air concert in Central Park, New York City, on August 17, 1910. It was not particularly successful; nor did it create a much deeper impression when it was repeated by the Boston Symphony Orchestra the following April. The serious treatment of native American tunes was still too novel for audiences (and even the critics) to allow recognition of the wit and skill with which the composer developed this material. Since then, however, native American idioms and themes have often been exploited in serious musical forms. Gilbert's overture is no longer new or original; but it remains to this day music of considerable charm.

1906 THE DANCE IN THE PLACE CONGO, tone poem for orchestra.

The music of the Creoles of Louisiana provided Gilbert with thematic subjects for this successful work. Five Creole songs are utilized "much after the manner of Grieg or Tchaikovsky," as the composer frankly pointed out. An atmosphere of eerie unreality is created for the frenetic slave dances, which pass from nimbleness to outright savagery. A bell tolls funereal sounds to call the slaves back to their tasks. The composition ends on a note of despair.

Gilbert composed his orchestral work in 1906. A decade later he decided to transform it into a ballet, and wrote his own scenario. The ballet was introduced at the Metropolitan Opera House on March 23, 1918 (on the same evening that Cadman's opera, *Shanewis,* was first performed). It was excellently received.

It was the symphonic poem, not the ballet, that represented American music at the International Society for Contemporary Music Festival in 1927. The Germans, who referred to Gilbert as the "*Uramerikaner*" ("primary American"), received the work with outstanding enthusiasm.

ALBERTO GINASTERA 1916–

Ginastera's first mature compositions—the ballet *Panambi,* and the *Argentine Dances,* for piano, both completed in 1937—reveal him as a nationalist composer interested in projecting Argentine backgrounds and culture through music filled with passionate chants of Argentine folk music and the frenetic rhythms of Argentine folk dances. He continued to cultivate this nationalist area for many years, and he cultivated it most successfully. But he always brought to his folkloristic writing a dynamic primitivism that betrayed his indebtedness to the early Stravinsky, together with a tart harmonic language that allied him to the modern school. Then, by degrees, he passed from a parochial nationalism towards internationalism by adopting a neo-classic approach, and after that by progressing towards serialism, which he employed with extraordinary skill and effect in such later works as the Violin Concerto in 1963, and his opera, *Don Rodrigo,* in 1964. With the cantata, *Bomarzo,* in 1964, he entered further into the camp of the avant-garde. This is a work, introduced in Washington, D.C., on November 1, 1964, that is partly in a serial technique, partly aleatory, partly *Sprechstimme,* and in part employs electronic means for special effects.

Ginastera was born in Buenos Aires on April 11, 1916. His musical training took place at the Conservatorio Williams in his native city, then with Athos Palma and José André at the National Conservatory. While in attendance at the latter school, he wrote music for the ballet, *Panambi,* which won the National Prize in 1940, and an orchestral suite derived from the ballet score, which became his first composition to receive major performances. He was graduated from the Conservatory with honors in 1938, and in 1941, he joined the faculties of the Conservatory and the Liceo Militar. His first symphony, *Sinfonia Porteña* (named after the port of Buenos Aires), introduced in Buenos Aires on May 12, 1942, advanced his career as composer. Between 1946 and 1947, he visited the United States on a Guggenheim Fellowship when concerts of his works were given in Washington, D.C., and in New York. Upon returning to Buenos Aires he founded the Conservatory of Music and Drama, serving as its director for a number of years. His first string quartet (1948) received the prize of the Asociación Wagneriana de Buenos Aires in 1948, was introduced in Buenos Aires on October 24, 1949, and represented Argentina at the festival of the International Society for Contemporary Music at Frankfort, Germany, in 1951. Significant commissions resulted in some of his most important compositions after that and helped make him a world figure in music. In 1962, he was appointed director of the-then newly organized Latin American Center for Advanced Musical Studies in Buenos Aires, sponsored by the Rockefeller Foundation. In 1962, Ginastera also organized the first of an annual series of festivals in Buenos Aires devoted to contemporary music.

1937 PANAMBI, ballet suite for orchestra. I. Moonlight on the Paraná. II. Invocation of the Powerful Spirits. III. Lament of the Maidens. IV. Round of the Maidens. V. Dance of the Warriors.

The one-act ballet, *Panambi,* based on a story about the Indians of north Argentina, was Ginastera's first significant attempt at musical nationalism and turned out to be his first major success as a composer. He wrote it when he was about twenty-one. The ballet (choreography by Margarita Wallmann and scenario by Felix L. Errico) was first staged at the Teatro Colón in Buenos Aires, on July 12, 1940, when it won the National Prize. But before this had happened, a five-movement orchestral suite derived from the ballet score had been introduced in Buenos Aires on November 27, 1937, Juan José Castro conducting. It proved a major success, and since then it has been frequently played by major orchestras everywhere.

The main interest in this music lies in the effective way in which Ginastera adapts the physiognomy of Argentine folk songs for his thematic material; also for the way in which the folk material is combined with the dynamic harmonic and rhythmic techniques of the twentieth cetury. The impact of Stravinsky's neo-primitivism is particularly evident, significantly so in the second movement, which is scored exclusively for percussion and brass, and in the finale, a vertiginous dance of the warriors built up into an overpowering climax.

1952 SONATA FOR PIANO. I. Allegro marcato. II. Presto misterioso. III. Adagio molto appassionato. IV. Ruvido ed ostinato.

In this piano sonata, the composer takes a significant step towards the polytonal and twelve-tone procedures that would characterize so many of his later significant works. But an Argentine profile is not lacking. Ginastera wrote his sonata on a commission from the Carnegie Institute and the Pennsylvania College for Women for a modern-music festival held in Pittsburgh, where it was introduced by Johana Harris on November 29, 1952. The sonata was then heard at the festival of the International Society for Contemporary Music at Oslo in May of 1953, performed by Marjorie Mitchell.

The first movement is basically in the sonata form, with two principal contrasting themes. The first is built from complicated rhythmic cells; the second has a lyrical character. In the second-movement scherzo, the main theme is built from a twelve-tone row. This movement is unusual in its dynamics in that it is played pianissimo throughout. The third movement approximates a three-part song form, the theme of the first and third parts corresponding to a melodic improvisation, while the middle section has the passionate lyricism of an Argentine folk tune. The finale is in the structure of a five-part rondo, and is in the style of a toccata.

1953 VARIACIONES CONCERTANTES, for orchestra.

This set of orchestral variations was commissioned by the Society of Friends of Music in Buenos Aires. It was introduced in that city on June 2, 1953, Igor Markevitch conducting. The composer has explained that this work, while having "a subjective Argentine character" does not utilize any basic folkloristic material. "The composer," he says, "achieves an Argentine atmosphere through the employment of his own thematic and rhythmic elements."

While performed without interruption, the composition is in twelve sections: Theme; Interlude; Giocoso; Scherzo; Dramatic Variation; Canonic Variations; Rhythmic Variation; Perpetual Motion; Pastorale; Interlude; Theme Reprise; and Rondo-Finale.

The theme, on which the variations are based, is heard in cello and harp. This is followed by an interlude for strings before the variations begin. Each variation features a different instrument or instruments, and the personality of each variation is derived from the character and quality of these instruments. The first variation has a jubilant character, highlighting the flute; the second, a scherzo, presents the clarinet; the third, pronouncedly dramatic, offers the viola. The fourth is a canonic variation for oboe and bassoon, while the fifth emphasizes rhythm and throws the limelight on trumpet and trombone. In the sixth, a solo violin is the protagonist in a perpetual motion, while the seventh presents the French horn in music of pastoral character. Now we get a recapitulation of the theme in double bass and harp, following which the concluding variation, in rondo form, is presented by full orchestra.

The music of these variations was used for two ballets. One, entitled *Tender Night,* was produced by the New York City Ballet on January 20, 1960, with choreography by John Taras. Another, called *Surazo,* had choreography by Patricio Bunster, and was mounted in Santiago, Chile, on July 13, 1961.

1954 PAMPEANA NO. 3: PASTORAL SYMPHONY, for orchestra. I. Adagio contemplativo. II. Impetuosamente. III. Largo con poetica esaltazione.

"Pampeana" is a term used by Ginastera to denote a national composition in which the melodic and rhythmic elements of the music of the Argentine plains are created, but with the composer's own musical vocabulary. Ginastera produced two earlier compositions in this form, the first for violin and piano in 1947 (first performance in New York on February 23, 1947, at a concert of the League of Composers), and the second in 1950, for cello and piano (first performance in Buenos Aires on May 8, 1950).

The third, a pastoral symphony, was commissioned by the Louisville Orchestra in Kentucky, which introduced it under Robert Whitney on October 20, 1954. The symphony was subsequently heard at the festival of the International Society for Contemporary Music on June 10, 1956, in Stockholm, Hans Schmidt-Isserstedt conducting.

Through the three movements a pastoral character is maintained. The first movement is in five closely knit sections (A-B-C-B-A). This is followed by a scherzo-like movement in which the central section has a bucolic personality (Intermezzo quasi trio: Un poco meno mosso). The finale is in three parts. The first offers the theme, which is carried through a crescendo towards the second subject. By contrast, the third and concluding part is made up mainly of a diminuendo until the symphony ebbs away into silence.

1960 CANTATA PARA AMERICA MAGICA (CANTATA FOR MAGIC AMERICA), for dramatic soprano and percussion. I. Prelude and Song of Dawn. II. Nocturne and Love Song. III. Song of the Warriors' Departure. IV. Fantastic Interlude. V. Song of Agony and Desolation. VI. Song of Prophecy.

The text for this, one of Ginastera's most significant compositions, was derived from Mayan, Aztec and Inca poems of unknown authorship. The term "magic" is here used in its primitive pre-Columbian sense, as the first of two stages of cultural and spiritual developments on the American continent. A program note goes on to explain: "The primitive man inhabiting Latin America before its discovery was essentially poetic in his concept of life, his spontaneous imagination, and his symbolic interpretation of the mysteries of nature. His poetry is strong and fascinating as are his sculptures and his pagan temples. The first Christian priests who came to America as missionaries were the affectionate compilers of the Mayan, Aztec and Inca civilizations. These are the collections from which Ginastera has drawn the text for his cantata, a work which is a long song in homage to America's primitive man."

The cantata was commissioned by the Fromm Foundation and received its world première at the second Inter-American Music Festival at Washington, D.C., on April 30, 1961. Howard Mitchell conducted sixteen percussion players, and Raquel Adonaylo was the soprano soloist. In his review in the Washington *Post*, Paul Hume wrote: "Ginastera has given voice to the thoughts of men and women who lived centuries ago, thoughts sometimes mirrored in our own time, often in terror as penetrating as that which shook those who first held them. . . . The resources are limitless and the savage sound shattering. . . . The Cantata seizes its hearers fast because it is the irresistibly logical product of a profound musical intellect, working on a level of intensity of overwhelming attraction." In the *Evening Star,* Irving Lowens said: "There was an almost frightening feeling that one was being transported to a new and enchanting world of fantastic sound. . . . So far as I can tell, it is stylistically unique. . . . This is unmistakably music of the Americas. It is bold, free, utterly magnificent music, composed by a man who takes pride in his heritage and who is brave enough to walk his own lonely path."

1961 CONCERTO FOR PIANO AND ORCHESTRA. I. Cadenza e varianti. II. Scherzo allucinante. III. Adagissimo. IV. Toccata concertata.

Like the cantata described above, the piano concerto received its world première at the second Inter-American Music Festival in Washington, D.C., on April 22, 1961. The soloist was Joao Carlos Martins and the National Symphony was conducted by Howard Mitchell; they repeated this performance in New York on March 11, 1962. The concerto had been commissioned by the Koussevitzky Music Foundation.

The concerto (which is in a serial technique) opens with a serial chord, a melodic transposition of which then appears in a piano cadenza. The variations are varied in mood, consisting of ten successive micro-structures, and lead to a coda. The second movement is played as quietly and as quickly as possible. Lyricism dominates the third movement, which is in a ternary form. The finale, a toccata, is a display piece with forceful rhythms. Structurally, the movement is made up of a seven-section rondo, beginning with an introduction and ending with a coda.

1963 CONCERTO FOR VIOLIN AND ORCHESTRA. I. Cadenza e Studi. II. Adagio per 22 Solisti. III. Scherzo pianissimo e perpetuum mobile.

The New York Philharmonic commissioned Ginastera to write a symphonic work to celebrate its opening season at the Lincoln Center for the Performing Arts. Though the composer went to work without delay, the violin concerto he produced in fulfillment of this commission was not completed until September 1963, and thus was too late for the occasion for which it had been intended. It was introduced by the New York Philharmonic under Leonard Bernstein on October 3, 1963, with Ruggiero Ricci, soloist.

In a serial technique (though employed freely, and in a personal way), this concerto makes an interesting effort to explore the sonorous capacities not only of the solo violin but also of individual instruments in the orchestra. The first movement has two sections, a rhapsodic opening, a cadenza in which material of the entire concerto is introduced—the series or tone row on which the work is based. This is followed by a set of six studies and a coda. Each study is a kind of variation of the previously stated tone row in chords, arpeggios, pizzicati, and even quarter tones. The flowing lyrical slow movement is intended by the composer to pay tribute to some of the first-desk men in the New York Philharmonic. A scherzo of lightning speed, and the quietest possible dynamics, opens the finale. This is followed by a quotation from themes from Paganini's Caprices for solo violin—"as if," explains the composer, "the shadow of this great violinist were passing through the orchestra." The coda, with which the concerto ends, is in the style of a perpetual motion.

1964 DON RODRIGO, opera in three acts, with text by Alejandro Casona. First performance: Teatro Colón, Buenos Aires, July 24, 1964.

Ginastera's first opera came late in his career; it is one of his supreme achievements. In the twelve-tone technique, it is a formidable work requiring enormous forces (about one hundred singers, nineteen soloists, eighty-four instrumentalists including eighteen French horns (six in the pit, the rest distributed around the balconies to produce a stereophonic effect) and a large conglomeration of bells of all sizes, sorts and weights.

The text is set in Toledo, Spain, in the eighth century. The hero is the last of the Visigoth kings, whose defeat at the battle of Guadalete brought about the downfall of Spain. The opera opens with the crowning of Rodrigo as king. He falls in love with, and rapes, the lovely Florinda, daughter of Don Julian, governor of Ceuta. To avenge the dishonor of his daughter, Don Julian invades Spain and defeats Rodrigo's army. Rodrigo escapes to a monastery where he has come to do penance. Florinda follows him to forgive him. But it is too late. Rodrigo, fatally ill, dies in her arms.

In reviewing the world première, John Vincent did not hesitate to call *Don Rodrigo* "a landmark similar to *Wozzeck*." This association of *Don Rodrigo* with Alban Berg's masterwork is significant, since *Wozzeck* served as the prototype for Ginastera's opera. For one thing, like Berg, Ginastera used instrumental structures for each of his scenes—such as the rondo, scherzo, suite, nocturne, canon, and so forth. For another, Ginastera relied heavily on *Sprechstimme,* or song-speech, even as did *Wozzeck*. Finally, atonality is a basic language of both operas, though the twelve-tone technique appeared only tentatively in *Wozzeck,* while it dominates the creative thinking of *Don Rodrigo*.

Dramatic interest, striking contrasts, and an overall symmetry is achieved in *Don Rodrigo* by pairing scenes opposite in mood and atmosphere. Scene one stands in contrast to scene nine; scene two to scene eight; scene three to scene seven; scene four to scene six. Scene five is the apex of what Vincent calls an "emotional arch—all upward to the capstone, then all down. This dramatic structure is reflected in the musical structure. Whatever the ultimate significance of the elaborate architectural engineering, it is nevertheless a neat package."

Here are some of the high musical moments in the opera as singled out by Vincent: the "dynamic intensity" of the opening scene, when the crowds gather to cheer Rodrigo; the "lyrical expressiveness" of Florinda's song with her handmaidens in the second act; and the final scene of Rodrigo's death in Florinda's arms as bells of all sizes and pitches peal from the stage, from the pit, from the balconies. Effective, too, says Vincent, is the second-act fanfare for twelve horns "representing Rodrigo at the chase," which becomes converted into "a stunning stereophonic depiction of the same Rodrigo searching frantically for Florinda who has run away from him in terror."

The New York City Opera entered its new home at the Lincoln Center for the Performing Arts by presenting the American première of *Don Rodrigo* on Februry 22, 1966. The critics were virtually unanimous in hailing the event as one of prime importance, and in pointing to *Don Rodrigo* as a major contribution to the operatic repertory. "It is a stunningly impressive work that is going to be in the opera repertoire for a long time," said a critic for *Life*. Harold C. Schonberg in *The New York Times* reported: "Mr. Ginastera is a professional all the way through. He knows his voice and he knows his orchestra. Regarded as a big, sweeping pageant . . . *Don Rodrigo* is quite a spectacle." Said Harriet Johnson in the *New York Post:* "*Don Rodrigo* is the work of a master craftsman who understands the theatre. . . . It represents a composer of big gifts and broad experience."

1965 CONCERTO FOR HARP AND ORCHESTRA. I. Allegro giusto. II. Molto moderato. III. Liberamente capriccioso; Vivace.

Ginastera began writing this concerto in 1956, intending it for the harpist, Edna Phillips (who had commissioned it) and who wanted to perform it at the Inter-American Music Festival in Washington, D.C., in 1958. However, it was not until 1965 that the concerto was completed. By that time, Edna Phillips had retired from the concert stage. The world première, therefore, was assigned to the harpist Nicanor Zabaleta, appearing with the Philadelphia Orchestra under Eugene Ormandy on February 18, 1965.

The composer provided the following brief guide to his composition: "My harp concerto is divided into three movements. The first one . . . is built in a kind of sonata form, concentrating more elements at the end of the re-exposition and coda. The second movement . . . is a juxtaposed form in four sections, A-B-C-A. The last movement . . . has a form equivalent to that of an Introduction and Rondo. The Introduction is a long cadenza for harp alone. The Rondo, in which one can recognize some rhythmic elements of Argentine music, is the last part of the movement. It has five sections—A-B-A-C-A." In his orchestration, the composer uses a percussion section made up of twenty-eight different instruments "to underline the strong rhythmic pulsation of the work."

1965 CONCERTO PER CORDE (CONCERTO FOR STRINGS). I. Variazione per solisti. II. Scherzo fantastico. III. Adagio angoscioso. IV. Finale furioso.

This string concerto was written for the 1966 Inter-American Music Festival at Caracas, Venezuela, where it received its world première on May 14, 1966, in a performance by the Philadelphia Orchestra under Ormandy. The same orchestra and conductor presented the American première—in Philadelphia on February 10, 1967.

The first movement is a series of variations for solo instruments. First, we hear a rhapsodic theme in the solo violin. Four variations follow: the first for solo cello; the second for a solo second violin; the third a Lento episode for solo viola accompanied by muted strings; and the last for solo double bass. The second movement is a "fantastic scherzo." It opens with tremolo strings before the scherzo idea is presented by the violins; solo viola later introduces a subsidiary thought. In the third part, an ascending subject in first violins is soon taken over by the other instruments in imitation. A powerful, dissonant climax is built up. The storm subsides and the music ebbs away into "nothingness," as the score indicates. Rapidly alternating rhythms endow the finale with its dynamism.

1967 BOMARZO, opera in two acts, with text by Mujica Lainez. First performance: Washington, D.C., May 19, 1967.

This opera should not be confused with a cantata of the same name for narrator, baritone and chamber orchestra which Ginastera wrote in 1964 to Lainez's text, and which received its world première in Washington, D.C., on November 1 of that year. The opera is an entirely different work, though on the same theme and much in the spirit of the cantata.

Both works have the same origin. One day in 1958 Lainez visited Bomarzo's gardens, fifty miles north of Rome. Throughout the gardens were huge stone monsters, the work of the sixteenth-century Duke of Bomarzo (Pier Francesco Orsini). Seeing these horrible figures, sculptured from huge volcanic boulders, Lainez came to the conclusion that their creator must have been a monster in his own right. He decided to explore this character for a novel, which he wrote in the form of an autobiography by the Duke. Lainez created as his central character a hunchbacked monster with mind as warped and deformed as his body, who went through violent experiences, many of his own making. Lainez's novel, called *Bomarzo,* was an enormous success, and won several Argentine literary prizes.

In 1964, Ginastera was commissioned by the Library of Congress in Washington, D.C., for a chamber-music composition. Ginastera's wife suggested the *Bomarzo* novel as a possible theme. The result was the cantata, for which the novelist provided a six-part Spanish text in prose and verse. Feeling that this material was even better suited for the operatic stage than for the concert hall, both librettist and composer decided to deal with it that way in a completely new work. Lainez now prepared a two-act text comprising fifteen scenes and a prelude. The story was told in a series of flashbacks. Dying from poison, Bomarzo recalls the highlights of his sordid career that was self-destructive, with degenerate episodes involving lust, narcissim and homosexuality. The libretto was crowded with shocking episodes. "In addition to murder by stabbing," wrote Allen Hughes in his review for *The New York Times,* "the screams of a young man who splits his head on a rock when diving into a river, and Bomarzo's own death agonies resulting from poisoning, there are ghostly apparitions, including an oversized skeleton that dances. There are near approaches to both male and female nudity; there is a seduction scene in a bordello, a scene of love-making observed by a crowd of voyeurs; and there is the possibility of some sort of relationship between Bomarzo and his slave. There are mysterious predictions and ceremonies of an astrologer, and a grandmother's mysterious references to protection by a 'she-bear.'"

Ginastera worked on his score between September of 1966 and April of 1967. He used every technique and means at his command to carry over into sound the torment of the hero and the degrading episodes in which he is involved: serial technique, electronic music, tone clusters, aleatory music, microtonal music. The chorus is placed in the pit with the orchestra, serving as a Greek kind of commentator. "The chorus hissed, gurgled, sighed, moaned and shrieked its way through the score," wrote Nan Robertson, adding: "In the spooky nocturnal prelude, which chillingly evokes the mysterious garden of the monsters, Ginastera had the chorus mouth only guttural consonants, which came out sounding like 'puh,' 'key,' 'luh,' 'guh'—and the distinct impression of mutes struggling for intelligible speech. This was precisely what Ginastera was aiming for—the stone ogres trying vainly to speak."

Together with the vocal episodes, there are fourteen orchestral interludes. Among the less usual instruments in the orchestra are a harpsichord, mandolin, viola d'amore, Japanese wood chimes, and a Japanese percussion instrument used in the Kabuki theatre called "hyoshigo." Often the orchestra is called upon to reproduce with conventional instruments non-musical sounds, such as the scream of a peacock. Other unusual sounds are reproduced electronically.

Allen Hughes singles out the following "more impressive vocal passages": "extended arias given to the grandmother and to the courtesan, and a trio involving Bomarzo, his future wife, and his brother at the beginning of Act

Two." Hughes then sums up: "*Bomarzo* already has adherents who think it is a masterpiece, and the curtain calls went on and on after the première. Nevertheless, it is possible to see and hear the opera more as a skilful fabrication of effects and sensations than as a sinewy work of art of enduring value. In any case, it is a fascinating theatre piece that is certain to win popular success."

Ginastera himself described his opera as a work of "sex, violence and hallucination." He also added: "For me, Bomarzo is an antihero. He is a man of our times. The Renaissance was like ours. It too was an age of violence of sex, of anxiety. Bomarzo is of our time and I had to compose music of our time."

Bomarzo was scheduled to receive its Argentine première in Buenos Aires on August 8, 1967. The municipal authorities, headed by the Mayor, prohibited the performance on the grounds that the work was obsessed with sex and violence and therefore was not fit to be produced. The reaction of the intellectual community was one of shock and outrage, expressing itself in a deluge of letters to the press and public protests. The Academy of Fine Arts insisted that banning the opera threatened artistic freedom.

ALEXANDER GLAZUNOV 1865–1936

Glazunov was one of the last of the Russian masters to carry on the traditions of the school of the "Five," and to bring those traditions forcefully to the attention of the Western world. When Prokofiev's *Scythian Suite* was introduced in St. Petersburg in 1916, Glazunov is said to have rushed out of the hall in horror, holding his hands over his ears to deafen them to Prokofiev's dissonances. This gesture was symbolic of Glazunov's career as a composer. He lived through the years in Russia which saw the changing of traditions and the making of epochs. Throughout his own life he saw and heard composers around him—beginning with Mussorgsky and continuing with Prokofiev and Stravinsky—adventurously striking out in new directions. Yet to all these new styles and sounds he closed his ears and went his own way, unaffected by the powerful oceanic surges of musical movements that swept so many composers along in their tide. Glazunov was certainly no revolutionist, no experimenter. He often confessed that he was most strongly influenced by Brahms. By this he meant that, like Brahms, he had a healthy respect for (and extraordinary skill in) architectonic construction. But with his remarkable technique he combined feeling for beauty; and for this reason some of his works continue to be heard and admired.

Most of Glazunov's important works were written before 1900. These included the tone poem, *Stenka Razin,* op. 13 (1885); the *Five Novelettes* for string quartet, op. 15 (1888); the Fourth, Fifth and Sixth Symphonies—in E-flat major, op. 48 (1893), in B-flat major, op. 55 (1895), and in C minor, op. 58 (1896); the *Scènes de Ballet,* for orchestra, op. 52 (1895); and the two highly successful ballets—to this day his most popular scores—*Raymonda,* op. 57 (1896), produced in St. Petersburg on January 7, 1898, and *The Seasons,* op. 67 (1899), introduced in St. Petersburg on February 23, 1900. These works do not come within the scope of the present volume.

Glazunov was born on August 10, 1865, in St. Petersburg. He began studying the piano in his ninth year, and was only thirteen when he started composing. Balakirev, impressed by his talent, urged him to study with Rimsky-Korsakov, under whose vigilant eye young Glazunov composed his First Symphony, in E major, op. 5 (1881). Introduced by Balakirev at a Free School concert in St. Petersburg on March 29, 1882, this symphony was outstandingly successful; Cui described it as an "amazing work, frightening in its precocious maturity." The symphony was no flash in the pan, as young Glazunov proceeded to prove by writing the excellent String Quartet in F major, op. 10 (1884), the brilliant *Overture on Greek Themes,* No. 2, op. 6 (1885), and the tone poem, *Stenka Razin.* Though he was only twenty, he was already considered by some to be one of Russia's foremost composers.

But his reputation was not confined to the boundaries of his own country. In 1884, his First Symphony was successfully performed by Franz Liszt in Weimar. *Stenka Razin* scored decisively at the Paris Universal Exhibition of 1889. So famous had Glazunov become throughout the world of music that, in 1893, he even received a commission from across the ocean: to write a *Triumphal March* for the Chicago Exhibition.

In 1899, he was appointed professor of instrumentation at the St. Petersburg Conservatory, beginning a long and eventful career as teacher, which was to influence an entire generation of Russian composers. In 1909, he became director of the Conservatory, holding the office with great distinction until 1928.

Well before the outbreak of World War I, Glazunov went into artistic decline as a composer—a fact which he himself obviously recognized. He lived on for two more decades, producing little of lasting interest. Though he was not in sympathy with the Revolution, he remained in Russia until 1928, even holding official positions. In 1928, he transferred his home to Paris. Now a sad and tired musician, he lived for the remainder of his life in the French capital. Occasionally he visited other countries to conduct his music. He made his first appearance in the United States on November 21, 1929, as a guest conductor of the Detroit Symphony.

Glazunov died in Paris on March 21, 1936.

1901 OUVERTURE SOLENNELLE, for orchestra, op. 73.

This festival overture opens with a rich proclamation of chords in strings and brass. Soon the woodwind and horns are heard in a romantic effusion which the violins take over—as violas, cellos and bassoons give reply with episodic phrases. A return of the opening rich chords marks the end of the introduction; and a spacious melody for violins (completed by the woodwind) is the beginning of the main body of the overture. This, and a second lyrical subject, are discussed along the traditional and spacious lines of the post-Romantic school.

1903 FROM THE MIDDLE AGES, suite for orchestra, op. 79. I. Prelude. II. Scherzo. III. Serenade. IV. The Crusaders.

Glazunov had a specific program in mind for each of the four movements of this suite. The first describes a castle by the sea, home for two lovers. In the scherzo, Death is playing the violin, urging people to dance to his lively tune. The third movement is a troubadour's serenade. The suite ends with a march accompanying the Crusaders' departure, as priests chant a farewell blessing.

1905 CONCERTO IN A MINOR, FOR VIOLIN AND ORCHESTRA, op. 82. I. Moderato. II. Andante. III. Allegro.

This concerto finds Glazunov at his romantic best, and for this reason it has established itself as one of the best-loved concertos in the twentieth century. It is consistently lyrical, its melodies always fresh and spontaneous. Its architectonic structure is sound and impressive. The writing for the violin is throughout effective.

The concerto was written for the eminent violinist and teacher, Leopold Auer, who introduced it in St. Petersburg on March 4, 1905. One day (so goes a familiar story), Glazunov visited Auer's class and heard one of Auer's prodigies perform. The composer was so impressed with the playing that he urged Auer to allow the pupil to introduce the concerto outside Russia. Auer consented. This is how the prodigy Mischa Elman (then only fourteen) came to give the Glazunov's concerto in London on October 17, 1905.

Though in three traditional movements, the concerto is played without pause. The principal subject of the first movement is heard in the opening announced by solo violin accompanied by clarinets and bassoons; it is a sentimental, even melancholy melody. The second theme, less elegiac and more romantic, is also presented by the solo instrument, this time with string accompaniment. The slow movement is made up principally of a broad and beautiful melody performed by the solo violin on the G string. An agitato section intrudes, with the violin providing figurations. Following a protracted cadenza, the main theme of the finale is heard. This is a dialogue between solo violin and trumpets. After a second melody, the music moves joyously to a spirited closing.

1906 SYMPHONY NO. 8 IN E-FLAT MAJOR, op. 83. I. Allegro moderato. II. Mesto. III. Allegro. IV. Moderato sostenuto; Allegro moderato.

This was Glazunov's last symphony. It was introduced in the year of its composition in St. Petersburg, and about a year later—on November 14, 1907—was heard in New York in a performance by the Russian Symphony Orchestra.

In the first movement, two introductory measures set the stage for the principal theme, forcefully announced by bassoons and horns. A more lyrical episode comes as a contrast—partly in the oboe, partly in the flute. This is the second subject, and it is given extensive treatment. A restatement of the opening theme, in brass and cellos, precedes the development section, while the recapitulation opens with the same theme, in the brass, but in augmentation.

There are two melodious passages in the second movement: the first comes in the strings, the second in the flute. A vivacious scherzo movement assigns its principal subject to the violas, while the secondary subject is begun by the second violins and continued by the flutes. A majestic finale is the crown of the entire symphony. The winds are heard first in an impressive introduction. Lower strings, horns and bassoons then enter with the main subject, which bears a spiritual kinship to the first theme of the second movement. After this idea has been worked out, the clarinet gives the second theme. Following a brief return of the introductory material, the principal theme receives considerable attention until a forceful climax is worked out. Now we get the recapitulation; then the coda devotes itself to the movement's introductory material.

REINHOLD GLIÈRE 1875–1956

Glière's style was subjected to a number of influences. In the early years of his creative life, he carried on the style and traditions of the Russian nationalist school. Later, his music became more romantic and epical, the impact which a two-year stay in Germany had made upon him. Subsequently, he returned to Russian subjects and idioms through the exploitation of autochthonous songs and dances of various regions of Russia where he had done intensive research: Azerbaijan folklore in the opera *Shah-Senem* (1925), produced for the first time in Baku on May 4, 1934, after the composer had revised it extensively; Uzbek folklore in his incidental music to *Hulsara* (1936), first performance at Tashkent on December 25, 1949. He also used his music to serve the social and political ideologies of the Soviet Union and to further the war effort during World War II.

He was never a particularly original composer. This was the reason why he was able to avoid the blazing fire of the Central Committee of the Communist Party in 1948, when it attacked most of the leading Soviet composers for their decadent tendencies (*see* Prokofiev). He was a craftsman, with a particular gift for striking orchestral effects; he had a rare gift for utilizing native materials for his own artistic ends. His romantic attitudes, his fulsome melodies, and his striking dramatic sense make his best works a rewarding aural experience.

Glière was born in Kiev on January 11, 1875. He attended the Kiev

Conservatory for three years; then, from 1894 to 1900, he was a pupil of Taneiev, Arensky and Ippolitov-Ivanov at the Moscow Conservatory. His First Symphony, op. 8 (1900) was received so apathetically when introduced in Moscow on January 3, 1903, that Glière became convinced of the need for more study. He spent two years in Berlin for that purpose. His Second Symphony, op. 25 (1907)—introduced in Berlin on January 23, 1908, in a concert at which Serge Koussevitzky made his baton debut—reveals the influence of this German period. In 1913, Glière became professor of composition at the Kiev Conservatory, rising to the post of director a year later. In 1920, he returned to Moscow to become professor of composition at its Conservatory; he kept this post until the end of his life. After the Revolution in Russia, he became one of the leading musical figures in the new regime, holding several high musical offices, and the recipient of many honors including the Order of the Red Banner, the Order of Merit and the title of Peoples Artist of the U.S.S.R. He also wrote a good deal of proletarian music, achieving a triumph with his ballet *The Red Poppy*, the first successful Soviet ballet on a revolutionary theme. During World War II, he turned out several compositions dedicated to the war effort, culminating with his *Victory Overture* celebrating the defeat of Nazi Germany. He received the Stalin Prize twice—in 1948, for his fourth string quartet, and in 1950, for his ballet *The Bronze Knight*. A month before he died, he toured the Soviet Union in concerts of his own works. He died in Moscow on June 23, 1956.

1911 SYMPHONY NO. 3 IN B MINOR (ILIA MOUROMETZ), op. 42. I. Wandering Pilgrims: Ilia Mourometz and Sviatogor. II. Solovei the Brigand. III. The Palace of Prince Vladimir. IV. The Feats of Valor and the Petrification of Ilia Mourometz.

Glière's most important work to date is his Third Symphony, introduced by the Russian Musical Society in Moscow under Emil Cooper on March 23, 1912. It received the Glinka Prize.

Inspired by ancient Russian folk legends and tales, Glière has here glorified the hero Ilia Mourometz, who is believed to have lived in the twelfth century, and whose exploits in war and peace were fabulous. Ultimately, Ilia was converted to Christianity.

Glière's symphony calls for a detailed program, which the composer supplied in his published score:

First movement: Ilia Mourometz, son of a peasant, is selected by two gods, disguised as wandering pilgrims, to become a bogatyr. He joins the all-powerful bogatyr Sviatogor to wander over the Holy Mountains. When Sviatogor dies, his heroic force passes on to Ilia, who now goes on to Kiev.

Second movement: In a dense forest lives Solovei the mighty Brigand. Ilia comes to the forest, wounds Solovei with his giant arrow, and drags him tied to the palace of Vladimir, the Sun.

Third movement: There is a royal feast at the palace of Vladimir, at which the mighty have gathered. When Ilia arrives, he commands Solovei to raise his ferocious cry, which causes the palace to shake and overcomes all the great men within. Ilia now slices off Solovei's head. Vladimir invites Ilia to the feasting table where he is royally welcomed.

Fourth movement: Batyagha the Wicked and his pagan army arise in Orda, the land of gold. Ilia, at the head of twelve bogatyrs, comes to do them battle. For twelve days the mighty battle continues, until the enemy is finally destroyed. Ilia, with seven bogatyrs, now goes forth to the limpid land. Two warriors come to challenge them. When they are destroyed, four rise in their place; when the four are overcome, there appear eight. The bogatyrs flee to the mountains, one after another of them being turned to stone, even the great Ilia. And since that day bogatyrs have disappeared from Holy Russia.

Several themes recur throughout the symphony, almost like leitmotifs. There is a chorale-like subject, written in free meter, which opens the symphony and suggests the Christian faith that drives Ilia Mourometz to his heroic deeds. This subject appears in several alterations, and is heard climactically at the end of the symphony, symbolic of the victory of Christianity over the bogatyrs. Two other major themes describe the hero, Ilia Mourometz, and appear throughout the work: the first is heard in the strings (low register) and bassoons; the second, more grandiose in character, is played by the trombones.

In the introduction (Andante sostenuto), we hear the chorale-like church chant, in the woodwind. After it has been developed, two themes portray the hero, Ilia: the first in low strings and bassoons (Allegro risoluto); the other in trombones. Both Ilia subjects recur throughout the symphony. The second movement opens with a tremolo figure in muted strings that project an eerie atmosphere. A motto is enunciated by the double bassoon. Then a melody arises out of a murmuring background, derived from the first Ilia theme; it is strong and assertive. But the movement ends softly and mysteriously.

The third movement is a lighthearted scherzo built up mainly out of a motive first heard in clarinet and a broad, flowing melody played by the cellos. Ilia's two themes are briefly recalled, as well as the double bassoon motto of the preceding movement.

The finale begins in an air of mystery, which is soon dissipated with an outburst of strength and power in a fugato episode. Ilia's theme is developed into a thunderous climat.

1927 THE RED POPPY, ballet in three acts, op. 70, with scenario by M. T. Kurilko. Fisrt performance: Moscow, June 14, 1927,

What is generally accepted as the first successful Soviet ballet employing a revolutionary subject was introduced, to outstanding acclaim, at the Bolshoi Theatre in Moscow. Since that time, it has been performed frequently in the Soviet Union, where it is regarded in high favor for its spirited music, so vibrant with melody and color, its vital dances, and the dramatic thrust of M. T. Kurilko's book.

The first act takes place in a Chinese port. Soviet propaganda appears in the depiction of the exploited Chinese coolies, an exploitation which is relieved by the sailors of a Soviet ship in the harbor. This act reaches a whirlwind climax with a series of dances for sailors of different nationalities. It is here that there appears the celebrated "Russian Sailors' Dance" ("*Ekh Yablochko*"). For the rest of the ballet, the port commander, enraged by the action of the Soviet sailors, tries to kill their captain. A maneuver to kidnap him fails. Meanwhile, beautiful Tai-Hao has fallen in love with the Soviet captain and is fired with the ideal of fighting for the freedom of the masses. Realizing that a plot is afoot to poison her beloved, she thwarts it. The port commander eventually shoots and kills Tai-Hao, who is now aboard the Soviet vessel. With her dying words she urges the children around her to fight for liberty, giving them a flower that is symbolic of that liberty—a red poppy. An epilogue, which hails the ultimate victory of the Chinese proletariat, utilizes for its principal melodic material a fragment of the *Internationale*.

The popular "Russian Sailors' Dance"—a frequent visitor to symphony programs—opens with a simple Russian melody in lower strings. A number of variations follow in which the tune gains momentum through acceleration of tempo and expanding sonorities until a climax is reached.

Though less popular than the "Russian Sailors' Dance," the "Dance of the Chinese Girls" from the same act is also sometimes heard at symphony concerts. A repeated descending interval leads to an oriental dance in the pentatonic scale; in this dance, percussion instruments and the xylophone are used with telling effect.

MORTON GOULD 1913–

Among the composers who have utilized popular styles of American music in serious forms, Gould has been one of the most important and successful. He has been a singularly prolific writer but, despite his abundance, haste is rarely evident in his music. He has a fine compositorial technique which occasionally succeeds in bringing to some of his works greater interest than their comparatively second-rate material would warrant. A natural gift for orchestration gives additional luster to his writing. Frequently, his works are purely functional, adequately serving the purposes for which they were intended. All this does not mean that Gould is a minor creative personality. His music at times achieves genuine distinction; several of his major works are original in concept and effectively written.

Gould was born in Richmond Hill, New York, on December 10, 1913. His unusual musical gift became apparent early: when he was only six, he wrote a waltz that was published; and not much later, he made appearances as a prodigy virtuoso of the piano. His musical studies took place at the Institute of Musical Art and at New York University. Following this, he held several musical jobs, the most important of which was that of staff pianist for the Radio City Music Hall. When he was eighteen, he made a significant bow as a composer, when on January 2, 1936, Leopold Stokowski introduced his *Chorale and Fugue in Jazz*.

He became associated with the radio for the first time when he was twenty-one—as conductor of an orchestra. For the next few years, he conducted a radio orchestra on a national hookup, becoming famous for his dynamic performances and brilliant orchestral transcriptions. He subsequently continued his conducting career both on records and as a guest with leading orchestras. At the same time, he produced major works, mainly for orchestra, which have been performed by the foremost orchestras under leading conductors.

1940 LATIN AMERICAN SYMPHONETTE, No. 4 I. Rhumba. II. Tango. III. Guaracha. IV. Conga.

The *Latin American Symphonette,* as the title suggests, is indebted to the melodies and rhythms of Latin America. Gould wrote four symphonettes, three of which (completed between 1933 and 1937) are based on popular North American idioms and ideas. The fourth is the only one inspired by the infectious dance rhythms of Latin America. Its première performance took place on a Mutual network broadcast beamed to South America under the composer's direction. The first concert performance took place in New York on February 22, 1941. Since then, it has been performed and recorded many times and has also been choreographed as a ballet.

While the materials of the fourth Symphonette are Latin American, the structure is classical. In effect, it is a little symphony, combining the classical with the exotic. The first movement is in orthodox sonata form with two contrasting themes and their development. This is followed by a languorous nocturne in which the Argentine influence can be detected. The third movement, instead of being the customary Scherzo, is built on a typical Latin dance-song style—the *Guaracha.* The last movement utilizes the propulsive rhythms and colors of this dance form and brings the work to a climactic finish.

1940 SPIRITUALS, for orchestra. I. Proclamation. II. Sermon. III. A Little Bit of Sin IV. Protest. V. Jubilee.

The idiom which Gould utilized in this highly successful work does not stem from Tin Pan Alley but from the treasury of American folklore: specifically spirituals, black and white. Actual spirituals are not reproduced; what Gould tried to do was to create melodies of his own which have the mood and the structure of authentic spiritual music. Since spirituals are varied in their emotional content, the melodies of Gould's work traverse a wide gamut, from lighthearted gaiety to tragedy, from wistfulness to deep feeling.

Structurally, the work is interesting for its utilization of a string choir as if it were a vocal chorus. Thus string choir and orchestra are often used antiphonally.

The five movements are sharply contrasted in atmosphere and mood. The first, described by the composer as "slowly rhapsodic and intense," is declamatory in character. A lighter mood is created through syncopated rhythms in the second section, which is "in a simple story style." The accoutrements of the dance orchestra are enlisted to project a gay and devilish mood in the third part (Moderately Fast, Piquant), while the fourth (Brutal and Crying Out) is a powerful utterance which increases in intensity as the section comes to a close. The last part, "Jubilee" (Fast, Vigorous, with Drive) is in three sections, the first a hoedown heard in the strings alone, the second with a kind of boogie-woogie bass against a sustained melody for violins and violas, and the third for the entire orchestra, with which the work comes to an exciting culmination.

The première took place in New York City on February 9, 1941.

1943 INTERPLAY (AMERICAN CONCERTETTE), for piano and orchestra. I. With drive and vigor. II. Gavotte. III. Blues. IV. Very fast.

Interplay was written for a radio concert conducted by Gould, which presented the pianist, José Iturbi, as soloist. Its original title was *American Concertette*. The composer, in his description of the music, informs us that "the first movement is . . . very rhythmic and brash in the accepted classical form of two contrasting themes and a short development. The second movement . . . is a gay, short dance with a sly glance back to the classical mode. The third movement is a Blues and what the title implies—a very simple and, in spots, 'dirty' type of slow, nostalgic mood. The fourth and last movement brings the work to a rousing close."

Soon after the première of the work, Jerome Robbins, the choreographer, utilized the music for a ballet called *Interplay,* which was first seen in Billy Rose's *Concert Varieties* in the summer of 1945. On October 17 of the same year, it was presented at the Metropolitan Opera House by the Ballet Theatre. The ballet, divided in four parts (I. Free Play. II. Horseplay. III. Byplay. IV. Team Play), contrasts the classic ballet with present-day dances with such freshness that it has become one of the outstanding successes in the Ballet Theatre repertoire, and was played on the Theatre's tour through the United States, Europe and South America.

1947 FALL RIVER LEGEND, ballet in eight scenes with prologue, with scenario and choreography by Agnes de Mille. First performance: Ballet Theatre, New York, April 22, 1948.

In August of 1892, in Fall River, Massachusetts, Lizzie Borden was accused of murdering her father and his second wife with an axe. Her trial made the front pages, and so did her ultimate acquittal. The celebrated case has been the subject of stories, plays and books. It was also used by Agnes de Mille for a ballet in which Lizzie Borden is identified as The Accused, and where she is not acquitted but meets death at the gallows. The ballet was an outstanding success; Francis Herridge said that it was "the best thing that Agnes de Mille has done to date, and one of the finest ballets in the modern idiom."

"The ballet," we are informed by the composer, "deals with the psychological motivations that led Lizzie Borden to commit murder, and its structure alternates between dramatic sequences and set-pieces, so that, in a sense, it combines the qualities of both pure and pantomimic dance."

An orchestral suite, consisting of six movements, was prepared from the ballet score by the composer and has been heard at orchestral concerts. "The suite," the composer explains further, "consists of the music for the more strictly balletic portions of the work; the composer feels that the freely dramatic sequences would lose some of their effect without the accompanying stage action, and, therefore, has limited the suite to the less literal parts of the score. The music makes many idiomatic references to New England hymns and dances of the '90s. The composer does not quote any such tune literally, but has fashioned his own thematic material in their guise in order to achieve an appropriate stylization."

1947 PHILHARMONIC WALTZES, for orchestra.

This light and infectious piece of music is Gould's apotheosis of the three-quarter time of the waltz. Though played as an integrated unit, it is in three sections. In the first, the composer recalls, and amplifies, the old-fashioned, sentimental waltz of the Gay Nineties. In Gould's own words: "The character is very bawdy and gay, and the orchestra echoes the colors of a player-piano and the old-time picnic and street music." There follows a straightforward romantic waltz, which, in turn, gives way to a continental-type waltz, with its "swirling patterns and broad lyrical lines."

Gould wrote these waltzes at the request of the Philharmonic League of New York, to be performed at the annual ball and Pension Fund concert of the New York Philharmonic. The première performance was conducted by Dimitri Mitropoulos on November 16, 1948.

1947 SYMPHONY NO. 3, for orchestra. I. Rhapsodic and intense. II. Moderately slow and relaxed. III. Moderately fast. IV. Slowly moving—fast.

One of Gould's most important works, the Third Symphony was given its world première in Dallas, Texas, with the composer conducting the Dallas Symphony, on February 16, 1947. Some time after this première Gould subjected the symphony to revision, writing an entirely new last movement for it. The revised version was introduced by the New York Philharmonic Orchestra, with Dimitri Mitropoulos conducting, on October 28, 1948.

As in so many other works of Gould, the symphony reaches to American popular idioms—jazz and blues—for its materials, developing them with breadth and considerable dexterity.

Gould's own analysis of the symphony follows:

"The first movement is rhapsodic and dramatic. Rather than self-contained themes, the melodic line is sort of long and unwinding and there are two contrasting sections which are developed. The movement ends on a grim and driving sort of funereal processional.

"The second movement is simple and lyrical and almost 'sweetness and light' as compared to the first. There are singing melodies throughout, and the harmonic and melodic scheme stays pretty close to the Blues tonality.

"The third movement corresponds to the Scherzo. It opens on a jazz fugue which grows wilder and wilder. The trio is blatant and humorous. There is a short return to the first theme and then a driving coda.

"The last movement is a Passacaglia and Fugue. The opening Passacaglia theme is austere and reserved. The whole passacaglia section is dynamically very soft, the variations changing in texture rather than impact. There are allusions to the thematic material of previous movements. The fugues opens with a sudden attack. Thematically the fugue is derived from the passacaglia, and the movement ends with the passacaglia theme announced double forte."

1953 DANCE VARIATIONS, for two pianos and orchestra.

This series of symphonic variations is made up of dance forms. The first is in the Baroque structure of a chaconne, and thus is in a pseudo-classical style; it is developed into a forceful climax. In the second, entitled "Arabesques," several set dance forms, old and new, are projected in a light, entertaining manner; these forms include the gavotte, the pavane, the polka, the quadrille, the minuet, the waltz and the can-can. The third movement, named "Pas de deux: Tango" is lyrical in a South-American way, while the finale, a Tarantelle, is virtuoso music.

The *Variations* was introduced on October 24, 1953, by the New York Philharmonic under Mitropoulos, with Whittemore and Lowe as piano soloists.

ENRIQUE GRANADOS 1867–1916

One searches in vain in Granados for some of the originality and personal attitudes of a Manuel de Falla. Granados was content to write in the traditional manner of the nineteenth-century Germans. But he did this with elegance and stately grace, and his best works make up in charm and appeal what they lack in individuality. He was first and foremost a romantic, a romantic often given to sentimental attitudes. Only after that was he a nationalist. He derived his stimulation from the city of Madrid the way Manuel de Falla did from Andalusia—but the Madrid of the distant past, the Madrid of the painter Goya, who had inspired Granados to achieve his highest creative altitudes. "The dominant aesthetic trait of Granados," says Gilbert Chase, "is his *madrilenismo,* his feeling for the spirit of Madrid at the most colorful and romantic moment in history." Then Chase adds: "His imagination is stimulated not so much by the impact of sensuous imagery and primitive feelings as by the visions of sublimated love and tragic passion viewed in the emotional perspective of the past."

"He may be said to represent in modern Spanish music the dramatic element which finds fluid expression in the melodic flow and poetic themes of the Malagueñas," says Leigh Henry, "and in the rhythmic nuances and movements of the popular Spanish dances. In so treating Spanish characteristics, however, Granados was objective and concerned with tonal and rhythmic-dynamic effects, not subjective, as the folk-cult 'nationalists' are."

Granados was born in Lérida, Spain, on July 27, 1867. His early music study took place at the Barcelona Conservatory. In 1884, he came to Madrid and enrolled in its Conservatory. There (like his famous compatriots, Albéniz and Falla), he came under the influence of Felipe Pedrell, who fired him with the mission of creating music in an authentic Spanish style rooted in Spanish folk songs and dances. In his twentieth year, Granados visited Paris for two years, and for a while studied with Charles de Bériot. Returning to Barcelona in 1889, he gave a highly successful piano recital that set him off on a career as virtuoso. But despite his achievements in the concert hall, he did not abandon composition. He worked industriously on piano pieces that combined the resources of Lisztian piano technique with traits of Spanish folk music—and so effectively that he is sometimes considered the creator of modern Spanish music for the piano, the immediate precursor of Albéniz. Among Granados's most distinguished piano works written before 1900 are his *Spanish Dances,* twelve pieces gathered into four sets, published in 1893. Here many of the familiar elements of Spanish folk dances are incorporated into music characterized by grace, elegance and poetic feeling. The fifth dance in E minor (called *Andaluza* or *Playera*) is the most celebrated, and probably the most famous single piece of music Granados ever wrote. But the sixth in D major, *Rondalla aragonesa,* is also popular.

On November 12, 1898, Granados's first opera, *Maria del Carmen,* was produced in Madrid. He wrote several more operas after that, the most significant being *Goyescas.* Its world première bought Granados to the United States in 1916. Invited to play for President Wilson at the White House, he delayed his return to Europe by a week. He was aboard the *Sussex,* sailing from Folkstone to Dieppe, when it was destroyed by German torpedoes on March 24, 1916. He met his death in the waters, a victim of World War I.

1912 GOYESCAS, suite for piano. Book I. 1. Los Requiebros. 2. Coloquio en la reja. 3. El Fandango del Candil. 4. Quejas o la maja y el Ruiseñor. Book II. 1. El Amor y la muerte. 2. Epilogo: La Serenada del espectro.

The two books which Granados collectively entitled *Goyescas,* or *Pieces after Goya,* are not only his most significant contribution to music, but one of the finest fruits of contemporary Spanish music. Each of the six numbers represents a scene from a Goya painting or tapestry, describing the picturesque Goyesque period of eighteenth-century Madrid. Lisztian technique and breadth of style are brilliantly blended with the rhythmic and melodic materials of Spanish folk music. Pianistically effective, these pieces are also atmospherically subtle, full of the most delicate poetic suggestion.

The most celebrated of the six pieces is the fourth, "The Maja and the Nightingale." This is music that is as singularly poetic as it is deeply personal. "Rarely," said Pedro Morales, "has the Spanish soul manifested itself so clearly in culture music as in the initial theme."

To Gilbert Chase, the "most dramatic and brilliant" of all the pieces is the first in the second volume, "Love and Death." Here the composer recalls some of the themes he had used in earlier numbers.

Discussing *Goyescas* in the *Musical Times* of London, Ernest Newman wrote: "The music, for all the fervor of its passion, is of classical beauty and composure. The harmony is rich but never experimental. The melodies have new curves, the rhythms new articulations. In forming it all is a new grace, a new pathos, a new melancholy. Not only the separate pieces themselves but the themes of them have a curious poetic individuality, so that to meet in a later piece with a theme from an earlier one is like seeing a definite personality step across the scene; but, above all, the music is a gorgeous treat for the fingers. . . . It is difficult, but so beautifully laid out that it is always playable: one has the voluptuous sense of passing the fingers through masses of richly colored jewels. . . . It is piano music of the purest kind."

Granados himself introduced both volumes of *Goyescas* at a recital at the Palais de la Musique Catalane on March 11, 1911.

1915 GOYESCAS, opera in one act, with text by Fernando Periquet, and music based upon Granados's piano suite of the same name. First performance: Metropolitan Opera, New York, January 28, 1916.

Soon after he had performed the world première of his piano suite, *Goyescas,* Granados became convinced that the Goya period in Madrid, and the music he had written about it, might serve as effective material for an opera. Without considering any libretto in particular, he went to work on an operatic score. When his music was completed, he called on Periquet to provide some suitable text for his music.

Periquet set his libretto in nineteenth-century Spain. Don Fernando, captain of the guards, is in love with beautiful Rosario. When he learns that Rosario has been invited by Paquita, the toreador, to a ball, Fernando is so overcome by his jealousy that he is driven to invade the ballroom. There Paquita challenges him to a duel and wounds him mortally. Fernando dies in the arms of his beloved Rosario.

Though the score contains at least one famous aria, "The Lover and the Nightingale," it is probably most notable for the skilful way in which Spanish dances are incorporated into the overall texture. But if any single excerpt can be said to be the most popular piece in the opera, it is the frequently played Intermezzo, a sensuous Spanish melody, richly harmonized. This fragment—through which the name of the opera is kept alive today—was not originally a part of the score. During rehearsals at the Metropolitan Opera, the opera house directors felt the need for an instrumental interlude. Granados hurriedly wrote out his Intermezzo and incorporated it into the opera.

The world première of the opera, at the Metropolitan Opera, brought Granados to the United States. Thus he was personal witness to its immense success. The critic of *The New York Times* praised "this full-blooded, passionate utterance, sometimes stirring in its characteristic rhythms and frank melody, sometimes languorous, poetical, profoundly pathetic, subtly suggestive. . . . This music has haunting power."

Despite this enthusiastic response on the part of public and critics, the opera was dropped from the Metropolitan Opera repertory after five performances and has never been revived. It was first produced at the Paris Opéra in 1919, at La Scala in Milan in 1937, and in London in 1951. Revivals, however, have been few and far between, even in Spain.

ALEXANDER GRETCHANINOFF 1864–1956

The field which Gretchaninoff tilled with greatest fertility—indeed, he made that field his own—was that of church music for the various services of the Russian Orthodox Church. It is here that he is most authentically Russian in inspiration, most original in thinking. His Liturgies—two of them of St. John Chrysostom, and the third entitled *Domestic Liturgy* (op. 13, 1897; op. 29, 1902; and op. 79, 1917)—are among the most significant contributions to Russian religious music since 1890. In addition to these three liturgies, Gretchaninoff produced numerous a cappella choruses and several outstanding Masses, including the *Missa Oecumenica* in 1936, and the *Missa Festiva,* op. 154, in 1937. Gretchaninoff's skill in writing for voices, his remarkable technique in polyphony, his ability to produce powerful choral effects, and his profound religious conviction are the qualities that place his best church music on such a high artistic plane.

Apart from his church music, Gretchaninoff was most famous for his songs, of which he has written over two hundred and fifty. As Sabaneyev has said, he knows "ideally and to perfection the properties of the human voice," knows how to realize the fullest potential of the voice for artistic expression. More important still, he had an abundant and varied melodic gift (often made piquant with Russian flavors) and a vein of tenderness all his own. He could be passionate, elegiac and romantic. His most celebrated songs—and they are among the best written by a Russian—were all composed before 1900. His first opus was a group of five songs written between 1887 and 1892. Here we find two numbers that to this day are treasured by singers and audiences: "O My Country" (poem by A. Tolstoy), and "Cradle Song" or "Lullaby" (words by Lermontov). A second group of songs followed in 1893, op. 5; this one included the familiar "Night" (poem by Kursky) and "On the Steppe" (words by Pleschchev).

Gretchaninoff was born in Moscow on October 25, 1864. His musical training came comparatively late. After casual study of the piano, he entered the Moscow Conservatory when he was seventeen. As a pupil of Safonov, Arensky and Laroche he proved to be a mediocre student, so much so that Arensky advised him to give up all thoughts of becoming a musician. Nevertheless, he went on to the St. Petersburg Conservatory, where he studied with Rimsky-Korsakov, and under whom he developed quickly and remarkably. A *Concert Overture* in D minor, written while he still attended the Conservatory became his first piece of music to get performed—in March of 1893. His first success came in 1895 with *North and South,* a choral composition. In 1901, he completed his first opera, *Dobrynia Nikitich,* which was a triumph when produced at the Bolshoi Theatre in Moscow on October 27, 1903; it entered the repertoire of virtually every Russian opera company. He continued writing operas, but specialized in producing church music, songs and piano pieces—achieving such importance that in the early 1910s, he was given a handsome pension by the Czar. In 1925, Gretchaninoff left Russia for good. He settled in Paris, where he was active as conductor, composer and teacher of the voice. He also made many tours in performances of his compositions, his American debut taking place in New York on January 17, 1929. Immediately after his fifth tour of the United States in 1939, he made New York his permanent home, and in 1946, he became an American citizen. On October 25, 1954, his ninetieth birthday was celebrated in New York with a concert of his music. He died in New York a few months later, on January 3, 1956.

1908 SNOWFLAKES, song cycle of children's songs, op. 47. I. Flocons de neige. II. Les Rameaux. III. Le Petit veau. IV. Au bois. V. Le Petit poucet. VI. Gnomes. VII. La Nuit, VIII. Gel. IX. La Perce-Neige. X. Chanson de la fée.

Gretchaninoff, who never had any children, had a flair for writing music for children. He wrote three children's operas and numerous piano pieces and songs for children. All enter the child's world without condescension or self-consciousness. He produced a whole library of children's songs where, with unaffected lyricism and a warm and ingratiating heart, he speaks of childhood impressions and experiences in a language children can readily understand. *Snowflakes,* all of them to poems by Bryusov, contains two numbers that are so exquisite that they have become concert favorites with singers the world over: the first, "Snowflakes," and the ninth, "Snowdrops."

1936 MISSA OECUMENICA (ECUMENICAL MASS), for soloists, chorus, orchestra, and organ, op. 142. I. Kyrie. II. Gloria. III. Credo. IV. Sanctus. V. Benedictus. VI. Agnus Dei.

In writing this mass, the composer did not intend a religious service for any one church, but a service embodying the universal meaning of all churches. In his own words, he intended a mass "in which there could be combined the musical character of the Eastern and Western churches. . . . The text—in Latin—is the one used in Catholic Churches."

Though in his liturgical music Gretchaninoff is most identifiably a Russian composer, this work reaches for its style not to the school of the "Russian Five," but to Franz Liszt. It is built along massive lines, is more rhapsodic and dramatic than lyrical, and is Germanic in its romanticism. Powerful and massive climaxes predominate (e.g., in the "*Gloria*" and "*Sanctus*"), and even in the "*Benedictus*" and "*Agnus Dei*" the effect is more dramatic than poignant.

There are no separate solo numbers. The chorus is utilized throughout the entire work (often with stunning effect), with the music for solo voices sometimes alternating with the chorus and sometimes integrated with it.

The tempo markings for the five sections are: I. Largo; Moderato; II.

Moderato; III. Moderato; IV. Allegro moderato e poco maestoso; V. Andante poco marciale; VI. Andante non troppo.

The Mass was written between 1938 and 1943, begun in Paris and completed in the United States. On February 25, 1944, it was introduced by the Boston Symphony under Koussevitzky.

1939 SYMPHONY NO. 5 IN G MINOR, op. 153. I. Allegro. II. Andante. III. Allegro. IV. Allegro moderato.

Gretchaninoff wrote five symphonies which are melodious, harmonically pleasing and structurally sound. While agreeable to listen to, they are not of outstanding artistic importance. Stylistically, they depend more upon German post-Romanticism than upon the idioms of the Russian school; emotionally, they are reminiscent of Tchaikovsky. The Fourth Symphony in C major, op. 102 (1924), as a matter of fact is dedicated to Tchaikovsky's memory. The best of his five symphonies is the last, which Leopold Stokowski and the Philadelphia Orchestra introduced on April 5, 1939.

The symphony opens with a majestic chorale for brass. Eight measures later the main body of the movement unfolds with a vibrant and rhythmic first theme and a soulful and lyrical second theme. The rhythmic first theme gets attention in the development section, a fragment of which returns in solo oboe in the coda. The second movement has a rhapsodic character. The first main melody is heard in horn quartet, bass clarinet and cello, while the flute provides a fetching contrapuntal theme. The heart of the movement is the middle section—a broad and stately melody. The third movement is an intermezzo made up of several intriguing ideas; it has grace and humor. The finale—also made up of episodes, of which the most significant is a lilting tune for the violins—has motor energy.

CHARLES T. GRIFFES 1884–1920

There can be little doubt that the early death of Griffes, at the premature age of thirty-six, robbed American music of a major creative figure. With each succeeding work, Griffes demonstrated increasing creative powers, growing imagination, stronger individuality, and an increasing gift for projecting beauty in music with sensitivity and poetry. His three masterworks came during the last five years of his life and represent him at the height of his achievements: *The White Peacock, The Pleasure Dome of Kubla Khan* and the *Poem*, for flute and orchestra. They suggest how much higher he could have risen had he lived to write more works.

He tapped two veins. Some of his compositions show a strong predilection for oriental subjects, oriental-type melodies, and oriental colors. Of such oriental interest are two dance-dramas written in 1917, *The Kairn of Koridwen* and *Sho-Jo*; also the *Five Poems of Ancient China and Japan* (1917). But the compositions which won him his fame, and a permanent place in American music, are those in which he is the Impressionist given to subtle suggestions, delicate atmosphere, sensitive moods and poetic speech.

Griffes was born in Elmira, New York, on September 17, 1884. He began the study of the piano early, and showed such talent that he was encouraged to prepare for a concert career. He went to Berlin in his nineteenth year to complete his piano studies. There he came under the influence of Humperdinck, who steered him away from a virtuoso career and towards composing. In Berlin, Griffes wrote his first works (some songs and a few piano pieces), in which the influence of German post-Romanticism is marked.

Returning to the United States in 1907, he became a teacher of music at Hackley School in Tarrytown, New York, a position he held until the end of his life. His salary was so meager that he had to supplement this job with hack work. But he did not neglect serious composition. A slow worker, he labored painstakingly on each composition, producing only a few scores. But these scores are all sensitive in construction, and of a fragile—and sometimes exotic—beauty.

A few friends recognized his talent and worked for his recognition. Through them there came about several performances of major works. Griffes realized a major triumph just before his death with the première of *The Pleasure Dome of Kubla Khan* in Boston in 1919. So successful was this performance that Griffes became famous overnight. Unfortunately, this recognition came too late. Always delicate in health, he had strained his sensitive constitution to the breaking point by working night after night copying out the parts of his score for the Boston performance. He never completely recovered from this setback. Death came in New York on April 8, 1920, following an unsuccessful operation for empyema. In November of 1964, Elmira College in New York held a three-day Griffes festival to commemorate the composer's eightieth birthday.

1917 THE WHITE PEACOCK, tone poem for orchestra (also for the piano).

Peacocks—white peacocks especially—held a strange fascination for Griffes. When he was in Berlin, where he visited the Zoological Gardens, he wrote: "Among the peacocks was a pure white one—very curious." It is said that whenever he came upon pictures of white peacocks he clipped and saved them. It is, therefore, not surprising that the poem of William Sharpe should have impressed him profoundly.

He wrote the piece originally for piano. It was published as the first of a set of four piano pieces entitled *Roman Sketches,* op. 7. In 1918, the composer introduced these *Sketches* at the MacDowell Club in New York.

Griffes orchestrated *The White Peacock* for a performance scheduled in—of all places!—a motion-picture theatre in New York. It was to serve as background music for a stage ballet at the Rivoli Theatre, and (to add to the incongruity) the ballet was interpolated between a Mack Sennett comedy and a picture about the Civil War. The orchestral version of *The White Peacock* received its concert première in Philadelphia with Leopold Stokowski conducting the Philadelphia Orchestra on December 19, 1919.

The tone poem creates a most delicate mood, sustained uninterruptedly throughout the composition. It is dominated by a haunting song for the flute, accompanied by an undulating theme in clarinet describing the strutting peacock. The following lines, from the poem of William Sharpe that inspired the piece, probably provide the best clue to the emotional and pictorial intentions of the music:

Here as the breath, as the soul of this beauty
Moveth in silence, and dreamlike, and slowly,
White as a snowdrift in mountain valleys
When softly upon it the gold light lingers:
Moves the white peacock, as tho' through the noontide
A dream of the moonlight were real for a moment.
Dim on the beautiful fan that he spreadeth. . . .
Dim on the cream-white are blue adumbrations. . . .
Pale, pale as the breath of blue smoke in far woodlands,
Here, as the breath, as the soul of this beauty,
Moves the white peacock.

Harlan Cozad McIntosh wrote a novel called *This Finer Shadow* in which this Griffes work plays a vital part in the plot development.

1918 THE PLEASURE DOME OF KUBLA KHAN, tone poem for orchestra.

The following lines from the celebrated poem by Coleridge are quoted in the published score of Griffes's tone poem:

In Xanadu did Kubla Khan
  A stately pleasure-dome decree;
Where Alph, the sacred river, ran
Through caverns measureless to man
  Down to a sunless sea.
So twice five miles of fertile ground
With walls and towers were girdled round:
And here were gardens bright with sinuous rills. . . .
Enfolding sunny spots of greenery.

The shadow of the dome of pleasure
  Floated midway on the waves;
Where was heard the mingled measure
  From the fountains and the caves.
It was a miracle of rare device,
A sunny pleasure-dome with caves of ice.

In translating the poem to music, Griffes explained: "I have given my imagination free rein. . . . The vague, foggy beginning suggests the sacred river, running 'through caverns measureless to man down to a sunless sea.' The gardens with fountains and 'sunny spots of greenery' are next suggested. From inside come sounds of dancing revelry which increases to a wild climax and then suddenly breaks off. . . . There is a return to the original mood suggesting the sacred river and the 'caves of ice.'"

The tone poem opens with a chord in divided cellos and double basses suggesting the "sacred river." A sequence of quiet chords then precedes the arrival of a poignant melody for flute and oboe describing the gardens and fountains. This melody is taken over by the strings. A dance revelry ensues, but after a wild climax the vigorous rhythmic passages are interrupted by a contemplative mood, with which the tone poem ends."

The Boston critics acclaimed the work when it was introduced by the Boston Symphony under Monteux on November 28, 1919. The critic of the Boston *Globe* puts Griffes in the same class as Ravel, Rachmaninoff and Stravinsky. Philip Hale, the most important of these critics, praised Griffes's "gift of expression . . . as he has found new harmonic and orchestral colors. . . . The music, from the strange, unearthly beginning, which at once arrests the attention, to the exquisitely fanciful close, is fascinating throughout."

1919 POEM, for flute and orchestra.

Griffes wrote the *Poem* for Georges Barrère, the famous flutist, who introduced it with the New York Symphony Society, Walter Damrosch conducting, on November 16, 1919. Because the composer provided no program for his music, it inspired a number of different interpretations. Walter Damrosch found it to be Grecian in spirit; one of the critics said it had the "naive and elemental qualities of an Irish folk song."

The work needs no descriptive program for appreciation. The languorous melody spun by the solo flute into an exquisite fabric cannot fail to enchant the discriminating ear. Impressionism is combined in this music with a Russian personality. The impressionism is found in the subtle atmosphere projected throughout the work, while the main melody has a Russian identity.

FERDE GROFÉ 1892–

Grofé has been a contributor to the movement which developed American jazz as a serious idiom. He is not one of our great composers. The area of his creative activity is a highly restricted one. But it is pleasantly landscaped and adds to the variety of our musical scene. On the credit side are his inventiveness in orchestral colors, his ability to exploit unusual timbres, his broad, likable melodies, his pleasing verve; on the debit side, a sometimes naive literalness in translating his program into tones, and superficiality in his musical thinking. He established his reputation with two entertaining musical works, *Mississippi Suite* and the *Grand Canyon Suite,* the popularity of which he has never quite equaled in his subsequent compositions (*Tabloid, Hollywood Suite, Metropolis, Hudson River Suite, San Francisco Suite*, etc.).

Grofé was born in New York City on March 27, 1892. He studied the piano, violin and harmony with his mother, and the viola with his grandfather. For ten years, he played the viola in the Los Angeles Symphony; during the later years of this period, he also played in jazz bands and wrote novel instrumentations of popular songs. Paul Whiteman heard one of his arrangements in 1919 and engaged Grofé to work for him as pianist and arranger. Thereafter, Grofé's name was intimately linked with that of Whiteman in the development of jazz music. All of Whiteman's orchestral arrangements were written by Grofé. It was Grofé, too, who wrote the orchestration for the world première of Gershwin's *Rhapsody in Blue.*

From orchestration, Grofé soon passed on to original composition, writing his first work in the larger form, *Broadway at Night,* in 1924. With the *Grand Canyon Suite,* in 1930, Grofé had arrived as a composer. He has conducted his own music in concert halls and over the radio, has worked in Hollywood writing music for the screen, and has appeared in concerts of two-piano music with his wife, Anne.

1924 MISSISSIPPI SUITE, for orchestra. I. Father of Waters. II. Huckleberry Finn. III. Old Creole Days. IV. Mardi Gras.

Mississippi Suite was Grofé's first serious work to achieve popularity. He wrote it for Paul Whiteman, who introduced it with his orchestra at Carnegie Hall in 1925.

A stately melody, with traces of Indian character, unfolds in the first movement to portray the mighty river. Jazz intrudes in the second section to provide a saucy and impudent flavor to this tonal characterization of Huckleberry Finn. The theme is first suggested by the tuba and is later taken up by the strings. A nostalgic picture is brought up in the third movement as a melody, suggestive of a Negro song, is carried from muted trumpet to strings, and from woodwinds again to the strings. The last movement—the most famous of all—is a gay carnival. The excitement and fever of the Mardi Gras is re-created in the opening through a brisk and rhythmic subject, which soon makes way for a beautiful song for strings—for the Mardi Gras is not only the time for frenetic merrymaking but for romance as well. The opening jaunty subject returns briefly, but the movement ends with the recapitulation of the song by the full orchestra.

1930 GRAND CANYON SUITE, for orchestra. I, Sunrise. II. The Painted Desert. III. On the Trail. IV. Sunset. V. Cloudburst.

Grofé's utilization of the jazz idiom is much more discreet in this work than it is in his other compositions, and is found in such subtle rhythmic and melodic suggestions that its presence might not be detected by the casual listener. It is only the spice giving piquancy to the dish Grofé is preparing; and the dish is an American recipe compounded, for the most part, of sound classical ingredients.

Grofé has here achieved vivid pictorial writing; the Suite is an unforgettable travelogue in tones. Five pictures are evoked with a brush of many colors—four different facets of the awe-inspiring beauty of the Grand Canyon and the emotions they stir in the composer.

The first picture is that of the sunrise. A roll of the kettledrums suggests the rising sun as dawn breaks. Against a background of chords, the principal theme is given by the muted trumpet. The music then grows and develops, gaining luster and brilliance much as the sun does when dawn grows into daytime.

An atmosphere of mystery and grandeur is next etched. Ominous chords suggest an eerie picture. A beautifully lyric middle section brings relief, but the movement ends as it began, in mystery.

The third picture is the most famous of the entire set. A halting rhythm describes the gait of a burro as he carries the visitor down the rim of the Canyon. Against the first subject a cowboy tune is introduced contrapuntally. The trip is interrupted when the visitors go off for refreshment, then continues.

After a series of distant animal calls, a beautiful melody emerges in the fourth section. It is sunset, and the peace and melancholy of dusk descend on the Canyon. Suddenly the clouds darken and gather, lightning flashes streak across the sky, and Nature erupts with thunder and showers. A summer storm is presented with vivid realism. Then all is peace again, and the Canyon is once again touched with indescribable grandeur.

The *Grand Canyon Suite* received its première performance in Chicago on November 22, 1931, with Paul Whiteman conducting his orchestra.

LOUIS GRUENBERG 1884–1964

In the early 1920s, Gruenberg's style was influenced by jazz. In a series of excellent compositions, he employed a jazz style with dignity and artistic validity. He was, in fact, one of the first Americans to uncover the artistic potential of jazz idioms and techniques for serious concert music. He did so most effectively in *Daniel Jazz,* for tenor and eight instruments (1923), introduced in New York on February 22, 1925; also in the *Jazz Suite,* for orchestra, which was performed by the Cincinnati Symphony on March 22, 1929. He also did so in a variety of other compositions, such as the *Jazzettes* for violin and piano; and for solo piano, *Jazzberries, Jazz Masks* and *Six Jazz Epigrams.*

Two of his later major works—one in the 1930s, the other in the 1940s—employed, in varying degrees, American idioms other than jazz. The opera *Emperor Jones* included an original Negro spiritual, while the Concerto for Violin and Orchestra was inspired by spirituals and hillbilly music.

Whatever his style—from the Impressionism of his apprentice days, through the jazz period of early manhood, and up to the utilization of advanced harmonic, rhythmic and tonal practices of his late works—Gruenberg was a master technician and an extraordinarily articulate artist.

Born in Brest-Litovsk, Russia, on August 3, 1884, Gruenberg came to the United States when he was two. He began to study the piano early, continuing it with Adele Margulies. Later on, he was a pupil of Ferruccio Busoni in Berlin, and he attended the Vienna Conservatory. In 1912, his professional career began in two fields: he made his debut as pianist by appearing as soloist with the Berlin Philharmonic; and he won a prize of $1,000 for a tone poem, *The Hill of Dreams*. He returned to the United States in 1919. From this time on, he devoted himself intensively to composition. In 1930, he won the RCA Victor prize of $5,000 for his First Symphony (which he had first written in 1919, then revised in 1929). From 1933 to 1936, he was head of the composition department of the Chicago Musical College. He then settled in California, where, for a while, he wrote music for the movies. On three occasions, he won Academy Awards. In 1947, he was elected a member of the National Institute of Arts and Letters. Though he devoted himself assiduously to composition up to the end of his life—and was producing what he felt was his most important music—he suffered almost complete neglect during the last decade of his life, a fact that made him extremely bitter. He died in Los Angeles on June 9, 1964.

1932 THE EMPEROR JONES, opera in seven scenes, with text by Kathleen de Jaffa based on Eugene O' Neill's drama of the same name. First performance: Metropolitan Opera, New York, January 7, 1933.

Though for the climax of the opera, Gruenberg wrote a Negro spiritual, *Standin' In the Need of Prayer,* not the style of Negro music but that of an ultramodern composer prevails in this work. To translate into music the high tensions, savagery and terror of Eugene O'Neill's famous play, Gruenberg had recourse to modern techniques. His melodic line, rather than imitating the *melos* of the Negro, is midway between song and speech; in its unorthodox line, it sometimes even simulates the *Sprechstimme* of Alban Berg. A complicated and subtle use of rhythm, and harmonic effects of the most intense kind, generate a driving power that sweeps through the entire opera, and—as in the final orgy—carries the listener through a profound emotional experience. The piercing interludal cries of the chorus are of an almost brutal strength. To these vital elements of modern writing, Gruenberg brought what one critic described as a "dramatic instinct and intuition for the theater" which was "unfailing," and a musical technique characterized by "a very complete modern knowledge and a reckless mastery of his means."

The libretto follows the Eugene O'Neill drama closely. Brutus Jones, a Pullman porter, having murdered a friend in a crap game, escapes to a distant Caribbean island where he becomes an "emperor." Overthrown, he escapes into the nearby forest, equipped with a pistol that has six bullets, one of them (a silver one) reserved for his own suicide if all else fails. Distant voodoo drums are heard in the forest as Jones sees fantastic phantoms of people he has killed. He fires at five of them. Terror-stricken, he suddenly remembers an old spiritual, *Standin' in the Need of Prayer,* which he sings to God in his appeal for forgiveness. The following morning, the natives catch up with him. Jones presses the pistol to his body and releases the silver bullet. As he stretches out, dead, the natives dance around his body, and then pass out of the forest.

The opera, which was fourteen months in the writing, was introduced at the Metropolitan Opera with great success. Lawrence Tibbett sang the part of Emperor Jones. The critics, the following morning, echoed the report of *The New York Times* that the opera was "swift, tense, emotional, with fantastical music and spectacular finale"; they considered it one of the major American operas of our time.

The Emperor Jones was produced in San Francisco on November 17, 1933. It was mounted in Europe for the first time, in Amsterdam in 1934. When the opera was seen in Rome in 1952, the principal character of Brutus Jones was changed into an Italian emperor. From time to time, the opera has been revived in various American cities.

1944 CONCERTO FOR VIOLIN AND ORCHESTRA, op. 47. I. Rhapsodic. II. With Simplicity and Warmth. III. Lively and with Good Humor.

Jascha Heifetz, seeking a major American composition to add to his repertoire, asked Gruenberg to write one for him. Gruenberg completed his concerto on August 7, 1944. A few months later, on December 1, Heifetz introduced it in Philadelphia; Eugene Ormandy conducted the Philadelphia Orchestra.

To endow his music with American flavors, Gruenberg incorporated into the second movement fragments of two spirituals, while in the third movement he introduced thematic ideas suggesting hillbilly music and the prayer music of revival meetings.

The first movement is, as marked, rhapsodic in character—a free fantasy, along elaborate lines, on several original themes. After a pyrotechnical cadenza for the solo instrument, the movement comes to a placid close. In the second movement, the violin is heard in two Negro spirituals, *Oh, Holy Lord* and *Master Jesus*. In the final movement, the scene passes from the world of the Negro to that of rural America. Strains of *The Arkansas Traveler* mingle with those of a fox-trot to bring up the picture of a barn dance. Suddenly, a shift is made to a revival meeting, with whose passionate, frenetic music the concerto ends.

CAMARGO GUARNIERI 1907–

From the time he assumed a place of importance among contemporary Brazilian composers, Guarnieri has inevitably invited comparison with his more distinguished colleague, Heitor Villas-Lobos. To

Donald Fuller, in *Modern Music,* Guarnieri "lacks the sudden, new-sounding flashes of a Villa-Lobos, but then it is not primarily for his coloristic nationalist traits that we appreciate him. He moves in a more universal sphere, though he is completely of his country." Guarnieri's style is partial to polyphony, which he skilfully blends with native folk elements of Brazil without resorting to quotations. Actually, despite his national leanings, Guarnieri is more interested in the flow of his counterpoint and in his rhythmic inventiveness than in his folkloristic strains.

Guarnieri was born in Tiété, in the state of São Paulo, Brazil, on February 1, 1907. He studied with local teachers, then attended the São Paulo Conservatory, where he was an honor student under Antonio de Sá Pereira and Lamberto Baldi. His first work to get published was a piece called *Rêve d'artiste,* written when he was eleven; the first in which his creative individuality becomes recognizable was *Curuçà,* introduced in São Paulo on July 28, 1930; and the first to gain him an audience outside Brazil, was the *Dansa Brasileira,* for orchestra. In 1927, he became a member of the faculty of the São Paulo Conservatory, where he was promoted to assistant professorship in 1932. He resigned from the Conservatory in 1938, to become director of the Cultural Department of the Municipality of São Paulo. Later the same year, he won a State prize that enabled him to spend three years in Europe. In Paris, he studied composition and orchestration with Charles Koechlin and conducting with François Ruhlmann. The outbreak of World War II sent him back to his native land. In 1940, his violin concerto won first prize in an international competition sponsored by the Fleisher Music Collection in Philadelphia. This brought him an invitation to come to the United States in 1942, where the League of Composers sponsored a concert of his works in New York. During this visit, he conducted the American premières of several of his major orchestral works in Boston and Rochester. Back in São Paulo, Guarnieri was appointed musical director of the São Paulo Orchestra. He now completed his First Symphony, whose world première took place in Boston during his second visit to the United States. His second piano concerto (which was introduced over the CBS radio network on April 16, 1947) received the Luiz Peanteado de Rezende prize of Brazil in 1946, while in 1947, he was awarded the second prize of $5,000 for his Second Symphony in a competition sponsored by the Detroit Symphony. Among later awards were the Fourth Centennial Prize for his Third Symphony in 1954; the first prize in an international contest sponsored in Caracas for his Chôros, for piano and orchestra (world première at the Caracas Music Festival on March 19, 1957); and two medals from the Association of Theatrical Critics in São Paulo, for his Concertino for Piano and Orchestra and his third string quartet, both in 1963. In 1960, Guarnieri returned to the faculty of the São Paulo Conservatory, where for one year, in 1960–1961, he served as director. In 1964, he became a member of the faculty of the Municipal Conservatory in Santos.

1942 ABERTURA CONCERTANTE, for orchestra.

This short orchestral work—introduced by the São Paulo Orchestra on June 2, 1942—was designated by its composer as a "concertante" because it features an alternation of wind and strings in the exposition section, much in the same way the concerto grosso of old alternated solo instruments and orchestra. "Abertura" means "overture."

The vigorous principal theme appears in the flute in the fifteenth measure. After a dialogue between strings and wind, the tympani introduces a transitional passage which precedes the second part of the work. This consists of an extended development of old material. A new transition restores the first part, after which recapitulation and coda follow. At the close of the work, the tympani project the rhythm of the main theme.

The *Abertura concertante* was Ginastera's first mature work for orchestra to get heard in the United States. The composer conducted it at a concert of the Boston Symphony on March 26, 1943.

1944 SYMPHONY NO. 1. I. Rude. II. Profondo. III. Radioso.

This symphony received first prize in a significant contest in Brazil for authentic Brazilian music. Dedicated to Koussevitzky, the symphony was heard in the United States on November 29, 1946, with the composer directing the Boston Symphony.

All themes are of folk origin, and are often written in the ancient modes characteristic of many Brazilian folk songs. The rhythmic patterns are also Brazilian in their complex variety and dynamic surge. The construction of the symphony is traditional, the first and third movements being in sonata form, and the second in the A-B-A song form (with coda).

1945 SYMPHONY NO. 2. I. Energico. II. Terno. III. Festivo.

Like its predecessor, the First Symphony, the Second was the recipient of an important award, this time in an international contest sponsored by the Detroit Symphony, where it received second prize of $5,000. Eleazar de Carvalho, the eminent Brazilian composer-conductor, who has often conducted this work (including ten performances in Israel in a single season) provides the following programmatic information:

"The work is written in modern musical language, although its melodic line, influence and atmosphere have their roots in Brazilian folk music, in which Indian influence is evident. . . . The first movement (Allegro) is in sonata form, beginning with a theme, Energico, of rhythmic character. The second theme, in B major, is of north-eastern (Brazilian) character, constructed on two contrasting elements—the first being the subject itself, and the second a contrapuntal variant of the first. . . . The Development begins with a working over of the first theme in augmentation, followed by canonic imitations until the entrance of the second theme. . . . Recapitulation is a normal one.

"The second movement is an Andante lento of poetic character beginning with a long melody played by the English horn. . . . What might be termed a contrasting section still is made up of material derived from the same subject. . . . "The third movement (Allegro vivo) is in sonata form and is descriptive of a holiday in Brazil. Although the themes are the composer's own, they are impregnated with Brazilian folk atmosphere. The first subject is imbued with the native syncopated style. . . . The second theme has Indian influences. . . . In the course of the development, the composer introduces a new subject—a beautiful melody in the Brazilian 'Nodinha' style. . . . The Recapitulation uses the same material as the Exposition, and in it the brass and woodwind instruments play an important part. A large and important coda closes the work."

HOWARD HANSON 1896–

As a conductor, and as the director of the American music festivals in Rochester, New York, Hanson has always been both receptive and encouraging to advanced musical thinking. But as a composer, he has preferred to hew to the traditional line. As he put it: "Though I have a profound interest in theoretical problems, my own music comes from the heart and is a direct expression of my own emotional reactions." He has the traditionalists' respect for classical form and his satisfaction with the accepted harmonic and tonal structures of the past. Hanson is at his best writing in a romantic vein, giving freedom of movement to his supple and expressive lyricism; but even then—possibly because of his Nordic blood—his feelings are held in check, and are subdued.

It is the comparative restraint with which Hanson speaks his heart—his restraint in the use of color, dynamics and tender melodies—that has tempted some commentators to describe him as "the American Sibelius." This characterization will serve. He is American to the core—no question about that. As for being another Sibelius, the somber moods and melancholy strains so often found in his music, the bleak effects he achieves through use of modal harmonies, the dramatic thrusts of his climaxes, the objective beauty of his melodies, all have a kinship with the symphonies of the Finnish master.

Hanson was born in Wahoo, Nebraska, on October 28, 1896. After studying at the School of Music of Luther College, he came to New York and became a pupil at the Institute of Musical Art. His academic and musical studies were completed at Northwestern University. In 1915, he became professor of theory and composition at College of the Pacific in San José, California, becoming the dean of its Conservatory of Fine Arts three years later. In 1921, he won the Prix de Rome of the American Academy. During his three-year residence in Rome, he composed his first major works: his first symphony, *Nordic,* which he himself introduced with the Augusteo Orchestra in Rome on May 30, 1923; also the orchestral tone poems written in 1923, *North and West,* with choral obbligato, and *Lux Aeterna,* with viola obbligato.

In 1924, he returned to the United States where he received an appointment as director of the Eastman School of Music, in Rochester, New York, a post he held for forty years. He has been a cogent force in American music—as an educator, propagandist for new music, conductor and composer. The number of musical organizations with which he has been associated—and whose mission it has been to develop musical education and culture in America—is legion. As the artistic director of the modern American music festival in Rochester, he has, through the years, performed some fifteen hundred works by about seven hundred composers; most of these compositions were being heard for the first time. Hanson has been the recipient of numerous honorary degrees and other honors. Among the latter are the Pulitzer Prize in music in 1944; the Alice M. Ditson Award in 1945; the George Peabody Award in 1946; the Laurel Leaf Award from the American Composers Alliance in 1957; and the Huntington Hartford Foundation Award in 1959. Between November of 1961 and February of 1962, he toured with the Eastman School Philharmonic Orchestra, under the auspices of the State Department, giving concerts throughout Europe, the Middle East and the Soviet Union.

1922 SYMPHONY NO. 1 IN E MINOR ("Nordic"), op. 21. I. Andante solenne; Allegro con fuoco. II. Andante teneramente con semplicita. III. Allegro con fuoco; Finale.

Though a youthful work (it was written when Hanson was twenty-five), this symphony is music of impressive beauty and sound structural logic. It has been widely performed. The world première took place in Rome on May 30, 1923, with the composer conducting the Augusteo Orchestra. Though the Italian audiences were not usually partial to new American works, they acclaimed this symphony.

The material for the entire symphony is found in the first movement—"strongly Nordic in character," as the composer described it, singing of the "solemnity, austerity, and grandeur of the North, of its restlessness and surging and strife, of its somberness and melancholy." The first principal theme is heard without preliminaries—in the cellos, with interruptions by the trumpet. Two other major subjects follow: the first (Pochissimo più animato) in the cellos, and the other (Poco meno mosso) in violins. The second movement, inscribed to the composer's mother, is gentle in character, touched with sadness, opening with an elegiac statement by the violas, with an expressive melody for the oboe following. The third movement (for his father) is more virile; it utilizes several thematic subjects suggestive of Swedish folk songs: the first in the woodwind, a second in the strings, and a third (preceded by an outburst in the percussion) in the cellos. The finale proceeds without pause, its principal theme heard immediately in the basses accompanied by tremolo violins.

1925 THE LAMENT OF BEOWULF, for mixed chorus and orchestra, op. 25.

The sagas of the North always appealed strongly to Hanson. While on a visit to England, he came upon a copy of *Beowulf,* translated by William Morris and A. J. Wyatt. He decided to set some of it to music, choosing the scene of Beowulf's death. Except for the brief orchestral introduction, which sets the somber mood of the entire work, the music is entirely choral. "My intention," Hanson has said, "has been to realize in the music the austerity and stoicism and the heroic atmosphere of the poem. This is true Anglo-Saxon poetry and may well serve as a basis for music composed by an American."

The music follows the text closely. A summary of the text has been provided by the composer: "There is a brief picture of the great burial mound by the sea on which the funeral pyre of the hero is built. A great beacon mound is constructed and on it are placed the trophies of the hero, mementos of his famous battles and victories. The women lament as the mound is built by the warriors. Then follows an episode in which the wife of the hero and her handmaidens voice their grief. The young warriors in a group surround the bier of their dead king and tell of his prowess. The work ends with the eulogy of the great hero."

Hanson began writing his work in Scotland "in an environment rugged, swept with mist, and wholly appropriate to the scene of my story." He continued it in Rome, and completed it on his return to the Uuited States. It was heard for the first time at the Ann Arbor Festival in Michigan in 1926.

1930 SYMPHONY NO. 2 ("Romantic"), op. 30. I. Adagio; Allegro moderato. II. Andante con tenerezza. III. Allegro con brio.

Hanson's Second Symphony followed his First by eight years. It was commissioned by Serge Koussevitzky for the fiftieth anniversary of the Boston Symphony Orchestra, which introduced it on November 28, 1930.

The composer's analysis of this symphony follows: "The first movement begins with an atmospheric introduction in the woodwinds, joined first by the horns, then the strings, and finally the brass choir, and then subsiding. The principal theme is announced by four horns with an accompaniment of strings and woodwinds, and is imitated in turn by the trumpets, woodwinds, and strings. An episodic theme appears quietly in the oboe and then in the solo horn. A transition leads into a subordinate theme, with the theme itself in the strings and a countersubject in the solo horn. The development section now follows. . . . The climax of the development section leads directly to the return of the principal theme in the original key by the trumpets. . . . The movement concludes quietly in a short coda.

"The second movement begins with its principal theme announced by the woodwinds with a sustained string accompaniment. An interlude in the brass, taken from the introduction of the first movement and interrupted by florid passages in the woodwinds, develops into a subordinate theme, which is taken from the horn solo of the first movement.

"The third movement begins with a vigorous accompaniment figure in strings and woodwinds, the principal theme of the movement—reminiscent of the first movement—entering in the four horns and later in the basses. The subordinate theme (Molto meno mosso) is announced first by the cellos and then taken up by the English horn; its development leads into the middle section. A brief coda . . . leads to a final fanfare and the end of the symphony."

1933 MERRY MOUNT, opera in five acts, with text by Richard L. Stokes based on Nathaniel Hawthorne's *The Maypole of Merry Mount.* First performance: Ann Arbor, Michigan, May 20, 1933 (concert version); Metropolitan Opera, New York, February 10, 1934 (staged version).

MERRY MOUNT, suite for orchestra. I. Overture. II. Children's Dance. III. Love Duet. IV. Prelude to Act II and Maypole Dances.

In 1932, Richard Stokes published a poem based on Nathaniel Hawthorne's *The Maypole of Merry Mount.* This poetic description of Puritan life in New England made such a deep impression on Hanson that he forthwith planned to use it as the basis of an opera. The libretto was prepared by the poet himself. When the opera was presented by the Metropolitan Opera, with Lawrence Tibbett in the principal role, it was well received (there were fifty curtain calls at the première performance) and was given twelve performances that season. Despite the fact that the critics spoke highly of it and the audience found the opera appealing, it was withdrawn from the Metropolitan repertory.

The plot revolves around the sensual dreams of Pastor Bradford in old New England. Though he is engaged to a Puritan girl, his restless fancies send his amorous thoughts in another direction. When the Cavaliers arrive, bringing with them beautiful Lady Marigold Sandys, Bradford is overwhelmed by his desire for her. On Merry Mount, Lady Marigold is to be married to Gower Lackland. But the Puritans, provoked by Bradford, arrive to disrupt the proceedings. When Indians come upon the scene there ensues such confusion that Bradford is able to abduct Lady Marigold to a nearby forest where he confesses to her his passion. Gower finds them; in the struggle that follows he is killed by Bradford. Sleep finally overtakes the murderer, who dreams that he is in Hell, that Gower is Lucifer, and that he kills Gower in order to take Lady Marigold for himself. Awakened by his own betrothed, Bradford is told that the Indians have ravaged their village. The villagers are aroused against Lady Marigold because they feel she is the cause of all their misfortunes. Sensing that a terrible doom awaits Lady Marigold, Bradford seizes her and drags her with him through the leaping flames of the burning church.

"*Merry Mount,*" the composer has written, "is essentially a lyrical work, and makes use of broad melodic lines as often as possible. There is less parlando than one might expect to find in a contemporary opera, and a greater tendency toward the old arioso style. The form of each small scene within the larger scene is considered as an entity in itself, a series of small forms within a large form, almost as if in symphonic structure. Both harmonically and rhythmically, the listener will hear certain Americanisms. In orchestration, too, use has been made of certain orchestral colors and devices which were born on this side of the Atlantic. . . . A word might be said concerning the rather frequent use of modal writing, especially in the music of the Puritans. It seemed to me that the characteristics of such melodic modes as the Aeolian, Dorian, Phrygian, and, in exalted moments, the Mixolydian, are very much in keeping with the Puritan character."

Hanson prepared an orchestral suite from the opera score which was heard for the first time in Rochester, New York, on December 17, 1936, with the composer conducting the Rochester Philharmonic. It contains four sections. In the first (Lento), the Puritan character of the score is briefly forecast. The second (Allegro molto) is descriptive of a children's dance. The children, left by their elders who go to church, are taught games by Prence, a Cavalier mountebank—games which bring trouble both to the children and to Prence. In the third part (Largamente molto expressivo), the passionate outburst of Bradford for Lady Marigold in Act III is reproduced. In the concluding part (Allegro grazioso), the christening of Merry Mount and the erection of a maypole takes place, a ceremony that includes Puritan dances.

1936 SYMPHONY No. 3, op. 33. I. Andante lamentando; Agitato. II. Andante tranquillo. III. Tempo scherzando. IV. Largamente e pesante.

The Third Symphony bears a closer affinity with the First than the Second. It was commissioned by the Columbia Broadcasting System, and three movements were introduced over the CBS radio network under the composer's direction on September 10, 1937. The entire symphony was given its first performance by the NBC Symphony, the composer conducting, on March 26, 1938.

The composer explains that his symphony "Pays tribute to the epic qualities of the pioneers" who founded the first Swedish settlement on the Delaware in 1638, and who in a later period forged westward to open up new territory. "The first movement," he explains, "is both rugged and turbulent in character, alternating with a religious mysticism." A brooding and quiet introduction in lower strings, interrupted by horns, precedes the statement of a chorale in basses and cellos. After this, we get the main theme in the woodwinds. In the development, a new thought is suddenly introduced, a delightful dance tune (Agitato). The movement ends with the chorale theme in muted horns and trumpets. "The second movement," the composer goes on to explain, "is, as its name implies, for the most part peaceful and brooding." Two lyrical and highly expressive subjects are prominent within an extended song form. "The third movement is in the tempo of a fast scherzo, and is vigorous and rhythmic." The first rhythmic subject is first announced by solo tympani. This is followed by another rhythmic and dance-like tune in solo oboe. "The fourth movement begins with the brooding character of the first movement, developing into an extended chorale in antiphonal style, rising to a climax in the full orchestra out of which appears the principal theme of the second movement, the symphony ending on a note of exultation and rejoicing."

1943 SYMPHONY NO. 4, op. 34. I. Kyrie. II. Requiescat. III. Dies Irae. IV. Lux Aeterna.

The Fourth Symphony was inspired by the death of the composer's father, to whose memory it is dedicated. It is an elegiac work, and one of the most personal and emotional of Hanson's symphonies. The four movements draw their subtitles from the Requiem Mass. On December 3, 1943, it was publicly introduced in Boston by the Boston Symphony Orchestra, the composer conducting.

The composer asked his former pupil, William Bergsma, to prepare an analysis of this symphony. The analysis, which has been widely quoted and can be considered definitive, is repeated here in part:

"The work . . . is concise and highly elided, taking barely twenty minutes to perform. The four movements can be characterized briefly; the first (Andante inquieto) is a turbulent and varied movement, a Kyrie theme alternating with dance and song-like sections, and a chorale statement preceding a stormy coda. The second (Largo) is a simple and tender treatment of a scale-like theme in eighth notes, given a first statement in the solo bassoon. The third (Presto) is a furious and bitter scherzo. The last (Largo pastorale), a pastorale with stormy interpolations, has a simple 2/4 ending, dying off on the second inversion of a major triad."

In 1944, the symphony was awarded the Pulitzer Prize in music, the first such work ever to win this honor.

1954 SYMPHONY NO. 5, "SINFONIA SACRA," op. 43.

In his Fifth Symphony, Hanson interprets musically the story of the first Easter as told in The Gospel According to St. John. The composer, however, does not tell this story programmatically, but, as he explains, attempts "to invoke some of the atmosphere of tragedy and triumph, mysticism and affirmation of this story which is the essential symbol of the Christian faith." In a single movement, this symphony is in the style of the Gregorian chant, but no chants are quoted directly. "Mr. Hanson," explained Olin Downes, in *The New York Times,* "is not trying to go archaic. . . . He has himself invented his themes, integrating them, technically speaking in a more or less contrapuntal style throughout. . . . The somber and mysterious introduction—the thought of Mary Magdalene peering into the sepulchre, to behold the two angels therein, and the later thought of the voice of Jesus, answering Mary in her need—these things dictate the expression of the music, which, at its climax, becomes very dramatic, and in the simplicity and serenity of the conclusion, nobly affirmative."

Though played without interruption, the symphony has three sections. The first consists of three introductions; the second presents three themes. Theme One (Pesante) achieves a climax in full strings and woodwind in unison and subsides into a gentle passage for strings. Theme Two (Gregorian) is characterized by long sustained phrases within a broad flowing melody for violas and violins successively, with woodwinds joining in later. Theme Three (Pastorale) comes in the English horn. A development of the third theme rises towards a climax. The third section of the symphony includes a return of Theme One, a new theme (Agitato), a return of Theme Two in the form of a Chorale (Largo), and Codetta.

The symphony was introduced on February 18, 1955, by the Philadelphia Orchestra under Eugene Ormandy.

1956 ELEGY (IN MEMORY OF SERGE KOUSSEVITZKY), for orchestra, op. 44.

Hanson was commissioned by the Boston Symphony Orchestra and the Koussevitzky Music Foundation to write a work for the seventy-fifth anniversary of the orchestra. Hanson decided to do a musical tribute in memory of that orchestra's celebrated conductor, Koussevitzky, as an expression of his own deep devotion to the man and the artist. The *Elegy* was introduced in Boston on January 20, 1956, Charles Munch conducting. The entire work is based on a single theme, an elegiac subject for the strings with which the composition opens. This melody is developed and brought to a climax in the winds before the work ends serenely and tenderly.

1957 MOSAICS, for orchestra.

The composer's aim here was to create musically some of the visual and spiritual effects from the mosaics in the Cathedral at Parma. "Just as a mosaic is a design made by inlaying bits of colored stone, glass, or some other substance," explains Ruth Watnabe, "the musical composition consists of a number of short melodic motives, related to each other, which are developed to make a total work. In keeping with the mosaic plan, there are contrasts in tempo and orchestral texture throughout the composition, creating musical lights, shadows, and a variety of color in an aural effect similar to the visual one of inlaid pattern."

The composition is in the form of variations. It opens with a passacaglia theme, but the variations that follow are not based on that subject but, as the composer explains, "on the specific relationship, harmonic and melodic, which occurs in that theme. In the strictly theoretical standpoint it might be called a variation on the relationship of (the intervals of the) major third, minor third, and minor second." The composer then points out that "the puckish quality of the first variation and the very somber quality of the next to the final variation are actually made out of the same material. The light simply strikes the mosaics in a different way."

Mosaics was commissioned by the Cleveland Orchestra to celebrate its fortieth anniversary. That orchestra, under George Szell, introduced it on January 23, 1958.

ROY HARRIS 1898–

Few American composers of our time have achieved so personal a style as Roy Harris. His music is easily identified by many stylistic traits to which he has clung through his creative development. The extended themes which span many bars before pausing to catch a breath, the long and involved developments in which the resources of variation and transformation are utilized exhaustively, the powerfully projected contrapuntal lines, the modal harmonies, and the asymmetrical rhythms are a few of the qualities found in most Harris works.

Though Harris has frequently employed the forms of the past (toccata, passacaglia, fugue, etc.), has shown a predilection for ancient modes, and on occasion has drawn thematic inspiration from Celtic folk songs and Protestant hymns, he is modern in spirit. His music has a contemporary pulse, the cogent drive and force of present-day living; there is certainly nothing archaic about it. More important still, it is essentially American music, even in those works in which he does not draw his ideas from our folk or popular music. The broad sweep of his melodies suggests the vast plains of Kansas, the open spaces of the West. The momentum of his rhythmic drive is American in its nervousness and vitality. But in subtler qualities, too, Harris's music is the music of America. "The moods," Harris once wrote, "which seem particularly American to me are the noisy ribaldry, the sadness, a groping earnestness which amounts to suppliance toward those deepest spiritual yearnings within ourselves; there is little grace or mellowness in our midst." Such moods—noisy ribaldry, sadness, groping earnestness—are caught in Harris's music; and to these moods are added other American qualities: youthful vigor, health, optimism and enthusiasm.

Harris was born in Lincoln County, Oklahoma, on February 12, 1898. He was the son of pioneers who had set out in an ox-cart for Oklahoma, and there staked a claim. While still a child, he learned to play the clarinet and the piano. But not until after World War I did he consider music as a career. He enrolled as a student of philosophy and economics in the Southern Branch of the University of California, where he also attended classes in harmony. After that, he studied music privately with Arthur Farwell. His first composition was an Andante for orchestra, introduced in Rochester, New York, on April 23, 1926, after which it was performed at the Lewisohn Stadium in New York and the Hollywood Bowl in California. In 1926, he went to Paris, where he profited from his associations with Nadia Boulanger. He stayed in Paris three years (two of them on a Guggenheim fellowship) and completed several major works. Of these, the Concerto for Piano, Clarinet and String Quartet was the most successful, being first heard in Paris on May 8, 1927. After returning to the United States, he produced several other important works in which a personal style was crystallized. These included the String Sextet (1932), the Symphony (1933), and the Second String Quartet (1936). The symphony, Harris's first, was played by the Boston Symphony under Koussevitzky on January 26, 1934, and then became the first American symphony to be commercially recorded. International success was not slow in coming, and it was first realized with his remarkable Third Symphony.

From 1934 to 1938, Harris headed the composition department of the Westminster School of Music in Princeton, New Jersey; and from 1938 to 1943, he was composer-in-residence at Cornell University, in Ithaca, New York. During World War II, he served as chief of the Music Section of the Office of War Information. After World War II, he held various musical posts with colleges and schools, including Colorado College, the Pennsylvania College for Women in Pittsburgh, the University of Illinois and Indiana University. In 1960, he was appointed director of the International Institute of Music, a division of the Inter-American University in Puerto Rico; and in 1961, he joined the music faculty of the University of California at Los Angeles.

In 1958, Harris became the first American to conduct his own music in the Soviet Union. He has been the recipient of numerous honors, including an honorary doctorate from Rutgers University, the Elizabeth Sprague Coolidge Medal, and the Award of Merit from the National Association of Composers and Conductors. In 1965, the government of Sweden bestowed on him the Military Order of Saint Savior and of Saint Bridget.

Since 1936, Harris has been married to the former Johana Duffy, a concert pianist.

1937 STRING QUARTET NO. 3.

QUINTET FOR PIANO AND STRINGS: I. Passacaglia. II. Cadenza. III. Fugue.

In his Third String Quartet, Harris's predilection for modal writing is revealed most strongly and, in certain ways, achieves its highest degree of artistic expressiveness. The quartet (it is actually a suite) comprises four preludes and fugues, in which is utilized what Slonimsky calls "the spectrum of modes," ranging from infradark to ultrabright. The preludes all have a medieval character, their remoteness and exoticism being their most ingratiating qualities. The fugues are the last word in contrapuntal dexterity, but they make their impression on the listener not for their technical ingenuity but for the driving power of their momentum.

The Roth Quartet—which had introduced this work in Washington D.C., on September 11, 1939, and then had made it a permanent part of its repertory—chose it as the only contemporary composition by an American heard at the International Congress of Musicologists in New York in 1939.

The Piano Quintet, like the third string quartet, represents a successful attempt to modernize old forms and stylistic methods. Modal writing here, too, contributes a distinctive, piquant flavor. A beautiful and highly personal modal subject is the kernel of the Passacaglia which, as the form demands, undergoes a number of transformations. With a virtuoso passage for the violin, the Cadenza is launched. Its highlight is a kind of recitative for string quartet, which is among the most tranquil pages ever written by Harris. The closing fugue has dramatic impact, containing some of the most vigorous passages in the entire work.

The Quintet was first heard in New York City on February 12, 1937.

1938 SYMPHONY NO. 3.

Though a comparatively early work, and though a handful of symphonies by Harris followed it, the Third is not only Harris's most successful work in this form but possibly the best. To this day, the Third remains one of the most significant symphonies by an American. It was introduced by the Boston Symphony Orchestra under Serge Koussevitzky in February 1939. At that time, Dr. Koussevitzky told an interviewer that he considered it one of the greatest American works he knew. This verdict was soon echoed by many leading critics throughout the country, as the symphony was performed by practically every major American orchestra. The critic of *Modern Music* wrote: "For significance of material, breadth of treatment, and depth of meaning; for tragic implication, dramatic intensity, concentration; for moving beauty, glowing sound, it can find no peer in the musical art of America."

The symphony, in a single uninterrupted movement, contains five sections. The following convenient outline, prepared by the composer himself, is a valuable guide for the work:

"I. Tragic (bow-string sonorities).

"II. Lyric (strings, horns, woodwinds).

"III. Pastoral (emphasizing woodwind color).

"IV. Fugue—dramatic. (brass, percussion predominating; canonic development of Section II material constituting background for further development of fugue; brass climax, rhythmic motif derived from the figure subject).

"V. Dramatic—tragic. (Restatement of violin theme of Section I. Tutti in strings in canon with tutti woodwinds. Brass and percussion develop rhythmic motif from climax of Section IV.)"

The symphony opens with a long-breathed thought for the cello, its rhythm mindful of old American psalmody. A chorale passage follows for full orchestra. This is the tragic part, and it is followed by a lyric one where, as Joseph Machlis explains, "his songful counterpoint asserts itself in the fluent, overlapping lines and in his antiphonal treatment of strings and winds." In the pastoral section, "the warblings of the strings and the mounting animation of the brass conjure up a lovely landscape." The fugal passage is based on a loud and strongly accented subject, building up into a brass climax. The chorale-like theme of the opening then returns and leads into the coda which the composer designated as both dramatic and tragic. "This processional," says Machlis, "strikes the epic tones and justifies those of Harris's admirers who find in his Third Symphony echoes of 'the dark fastness of the American soul, of its despair and its courage, its defeat and its triumph.'"

1939 SYMPHONY NO. 4 ("Folk Song"), for chorus and orchestra. I. Welcome Party. II. Western Cowboy. III. Interlude. IV. Mountain Love Song. V. Interlude. VI. Negro Fantasy. VII. Finale.

This functional work, whose explicit purpose was to provide practical music for symphony orchestras desiring to collaborate with their local high school or college choruses, is so effective in its utilization of American folk-song materials and so genuinely American in its atmosphere and spirit that it ranks among the composer's major efforts. The chorus, the writing for which is simple and direct, is heard in five of the seven movements.

Numerous familiar folk and popular songs are skillfully woven into this elaborate fabric. "When Johnny Comes Marching Home" is heard in the finale (not to be confused with the overture of the same name, also by Harris). Delightful cowboy songs are interpolated into the second movement, notably "Oh Bury Me Not on the Lone Prairie." Western fiddle tunes are introduced into the third movement, while in the fifth, such popular folk ditties as "Jump Up My Lady" and "The Blackbird and the Crow" are skillfully exploited.

The Symphony was introduced (in parts) by the Eastman-Rochester Symphony Orchestra under Howard Hanson on April 25, 1940. On December 26 of the same year, the entire symphony was heard in Cleveland, Rudolf Ringwall directing the Cleveland Orchestra. Following this performance, the work received a prize of five hundred dollars from the National Federation of Music Clubs as the best symphonic work of the year. Subsequently, Harris reshuffled the order of his movements. In this now definitive version, it was presented by the New York Philharmonic under Mitropoulos on December 31, 1942.

1941 SONATA FOR VIOLIN AND PIANO. I. Fantasy. II. Pastorale. III. Andante religioso. IV. Toccata.

This sonata was written for the Elizabeth Sprague Coolidge concerts in

Washington, D.C., where it was given its first performance at the hands of William Kroll and Johana Harris. The sonata received the Elizabeth Sprague Coolidge Medal.

The composer has explained that the first movement is a fantasia "to illustrate the freedom of melodic qualities on the four different strings of the violin." The second movement is in free folk-song style, and consists of an adaptation of the American-English folk song, "I'll Be True to My Love, If My Love Will Be True to Me." The third movement was conceived "to emphasize the singing potential of the violin," while the finale is a toccata "planned as a display of technical facilities of both instruments."

1942 SYMPHONY NO. 5. I. Prelude. II. Chorale. III. Fugue.

This symphony is closely identified with the political temper of the year in which it was written. At the time, the Soviet army was savagely resisting the invading Nazi armies, which, for the first time since the outbreak of the war, introduced hope and optimism for the cause of the Allied countries. Excited by this turn of events, Harris dedicated his Fifth Symphony to "the heroic and freedom-loving people of our great ally, the Union of Soviet Socialist Republics." It was introduced by the Boston Symphony Orchestra under Koussevitzky on February 26, 1943, a performance which incidentally, was transmitted by shortwave to the Soviet Union. The work was also heard by shortwave eleven times by American armed forces around the world during World War II. Harris led a performance of this symphony over the Moscow Radio on October 15, 1958.

A martial note is injected into the first movement with a theme played by the horns that resembles an army bugle call, a theme out of which the entire movement is developed. It is powerful and highly rhythmic music. By way of contrast comes the lyrical second movement, something of a rhapsody, melancholy in character; of particular poignancy is a melodic middle passage for violin (Maestoso). A complicated and brilliantly contrived double fugue ends the work with irresistible force.

1944 SYMPHONY NO. 6. ("Gettysburg Address Symphony"). I. Awakening. II. Conflict. III. Dedication. IV. Affirmation.

Harris was born on Lincoln's birthday, and in a log cabin. "The shadow of Abe Lincoln has hovered over my life since childhood." The Sixth Symphony reflects the composer's great admiration for and spiritual affinity with the Great Emancipator. It was written on a commission by the National Broadcasting Company, was dedicated "to the Armed Forces of Our Nation," and was introduced on April 14, 1944, by the Boston Symphony Orchestra under Koussevitzky.

The symphony draws its program from the Gettysburg Address. "In Lincoln's *Gettysburg Address,*" wrote the composer, "I find a classic expression of that great cycle which always attends any progress in the intellectual or spiritual growth of the people: (1) awakening, (2) conflict of the old against the new, (3) terrible suffering resulting from the conflict, and (4) the triumph of the new over the old, which is the affirmation of the eternal youth of the human spirit."

The first movement of the symphony expresses the opening of the speech. The second reflects on the passage, "Now we are engaged in a great civil war, testing whether that nation, or any nation so conceived and so dedicated can long endure." The third part, a chorale to the dead, begins with "We are met on the great battlefield of that war," and ends with "The world will little note nor long remember what we say here, but it can never forget what they did here." The concluding section, which is in fugal form, is devoted to the final lines of the Address, beginning with: "It is for us, the living, rather, to be dedicated here to the unfinished work which they who have fought here have thus far so nobly advanced."

1949 KENTUCKY SPRING, for orchestra.

To the composer, the state of Kentucky has always been synonymous with the Spring season, and his tone poem is a tribute both to Kentucky and to Spring. Harris himself has explained that he intended his music to have "a general programmatic feeling of Spring without any literal quotation from Dame Nature's Springtime orchestra." This work was commissioned by the Louisville Orchestra, which introduced it in Kentucky on April 5, 1949.

Harris has described the structure as a kind of scherzo in A-B-A- form "in which the middle part would correspond to a trio." He adds: "There is a little dance figure which runs through the work and finally becomes a fugato after the middle section." This dance figure, appearing in three trumpets immediately after the opening measures, makes a hasty allusion to Stephen Foster's melodic phrase in "My Old Kentucky Home" to the words "weep no more today." Harris concludes: "At the very close of the work, as a short codetta, the strings state a broad consonant chorale which suggests "Oh, the Sun Shines Bright in My Old Kentucky Home."

1955 SYMPHONY NO. 7.

The first version of Harris's Seventh Symphony was introduced in Chicago on November 20, 1952, after which it received the Naumburg Prize. In 1955, Harris revised it extensively, a definitive version in which it received its world première in Copenhagen, on September 15, 1955, Eugene Ormandy conducting. In a single movement, the symphony employs an idiom based on the twelve-tone technique. The composer goes on to explain: "In one sense it is a dance symphony; in another sense it is a study in harmonic and melodic rhythmic variation. The first half is a passacaglia with five variations. The second half is divided into three sections—contrapuntal variations in asymmetrical rhythms; contrapuntal variations in symmetrical meter, and further statement and development of the preceding two sections, wherein the original passacaglia theme is restated in large augmentation and orchestration, while ornamentation develops the melodic and rhythmic materials of the second section. A final variation of the rhythmic materials of the work serves as a coda. . . . The first half of the work is contemplative and traditional, predominantly harmonic in technique; however, with each successive variation, the mood becomes more dynamic and rhythmically free. . . . The second half of the work is an expression of merry-making America, predominantly contrapuntal in technique; however, the return of the passacaglia subject in the third section brings back the mood of contemplation which is absorbed in the vigorous coda. In this work I have hoped to communicate the spirit of affirmation as a declaration of faith in Mankind."

1961–1965 SAN FRANCISCO SYMPHONY (SYMPHONY NO. 8).

SYMPHONY NO. 9—1963. I. Prelude. II. Chorale. III. Contrapuntal Structures.

ABRAHAM LINCOLN SYMPHONY (SYMPHONY NO. 10). I. Lonesome Boy in the Wilderness. II. The Young Wrestler. III. Abraham Lincoln's Convictions. IV. Civil War, "Brother Against Brother." V. Praise and Thanksgiving for Peace.

Harris wrote his Eighth Symphony in 1961 on a commission from the San Francisco Symphony for its fiftieth anniversary. "Since St. Francis of Assisi is the patron saint of San Francisco," the composer explained, "I thought it fitting to write a symphony about the life of St. Francis." The symphony received its world première in San Francisco on January 17, 1962.

Here is the composer's own description of the symphony:

"The work has been conceived to express the moods of the five dominant periods of the life of Saint Francis:

"1. Childhood and Youth. 2. Renunciation of worldly living for the mantle of spiritual aspiration. 3. The building of the chapel, with his own hands. 4. The joy of pantheistic beauty as a gift of God. 5. A final period of ecstasy after his premonition of death.

"In the first section I have hoped to express the gradual transformation of carefree and unrestrained childhood to the ever-increasing energy and vigor of youth.

"In the second section I have hoped to capture St. Francis's mood of profound sorrow for the suffering of mankind and to transform this gradually toward a mood of abiding faith.

"The third section is conceived as a vigorous mood of physical activity; it is a fugal movement in which the theme is evolved in variations and contrapuntal textures of bright consonance.

"The fourth section is fantasy—pantheistic in nature—in which the piano (amplified and projected into the auditorium by speakers) enters prominently.

"The fifth section is in the nature of a Gloria in which the joyous sounds of harp and chimes and large shining chords of consonance (piano and brass) predominate.

"The entire work is a self-generation form (like life itself), with no stopping."

Commissioned to write his Ninth Symphony by Eugene Ormandy and the Philadelphia Symphony, Harris dedicated the work "to the city of Philadelphia as the cradle of American democracy." He completed it in 1962, and its world première took place in Philadelphia on January 18, 1963.

Bearing in mind that Philadelphia was the birthplace of American democracy, Harris "searched in the Preamble to our strong and radical Constitution, for appropriate guidance in form and substance for my Ninth Symphony," as Harris himself has explained. "It came simply and clearly. 'We the People,' the beginning of everything we are. 'To form a more perfect Union,' the hope of those wise statesmen who had the courage to believe that Mankind is essentially good. 'To promote the general welfare,' that men may cooperate in their endeavors for the common good."

Harris then goes on to say: "As I went to work, 'We the People' became in my mind the beginning, a Prelude, a swift moving panorama of all kinds of people in their basic drives and emotions—a kind of quick Dance of Life, of rhythms, melodies, dynamics and instrumental colors. 'To form a more perfect Union' became a long flowing chorale in which the harmony was emphasized. 'To promote the general welfare' meant a more formal planning of clearly interrelated functions. I found the contrapuntal structure of Fugue, Canon and Stretto most clearly stated such purpose. Consequently, I selected three mottos from the inscriptions of Walt Whitman, who spent the last years of his life in Camden.

"(1) 'Of Life Immense in Passion, Pulse, Power';

"(2) 'Cheerful for Freest Action Formed';

"(3) 'The Modern Man I Sing.'

"Three subjects were conceived to express the musical counterpoint of those three mottos. The third movement was built in three sections of the development of all three subjects."

Harris had written a *Gettysburg Address Symphony* (No. 6) in 1944. He returned to Abraham Lincoln for his Tenth Symphony, indeed named it *Abraham Lincoln Symphony*. Completed in 1965, it was introduced in Los Angeles on April 14, 1965.

"This work," the composer informs us, "has been contemplated for a quarter of a century, and was finally written for the occasion of the one hundredth anniversary of Lincoln's assassination on April 14, 1865. The five-movement work was strongly influenced by Carl Sandburg's monumental study of the times and life of Abraham Lincoln. I have chosen two moods from the youth of Lincoln, and three moods expressing his profound concern for the destiny of our democratic institutions."

The symphony is scored for a women's chorus, a men's chorus, a mixed chorus, brass choir, two amplified pianos and percussion. The text for the first, second and fifth movements are by the composer himself; in the third movement, the text is drawn from Lincoln's speeches and writings, while the movement is based on the Gettysburg Address.

HANS WERNER HENZE 1926–

Hans Werner Henze—one of the most significant opera composers to come out of Germany since Richard Strauss, and one of Germany's most important symphonists—is an anomaly among twelve-tone composers in that he is an eclectic. As Wolf-Eberhard von Lewinski has noted, Henze does not make "the new ordering of musical material a goal for itself. Speculative musical thought is always subordinated to the will of expression. . . . Henze . . . does not fear breaks in style, takes suggestions and ideas where he finds them, and writes passages that could appear indiscriminate and heterogeneous from a style-critical point of view."

His early enthusiasm for Stravinsky, Hindemith and Bartók led him to neo-classicism, linear writing and unresolved discords. This is the style of his earliest mature works, all of them completed by 1947: a violin sonata; a flute sonata; the Chamber Concerto, for piano, flute and strings; and his First Symphony. Then, influenced by his Parisian teacher, René Leibowitz, Henze became interested in the twelve-tone technique, his first such experiments taking place with his Violin Concerto, introduced at Baden-Baden on December 12, 1948. But the compulsive need for extending the horizons of twelve-tone music led him to adopt a highly free and personal manner of serial composition in which many varied styles and techniques are assimilated, including polytonality, neo-classicism, romanticism, at times even a Puccini-like lyricism and elements of jazz. "Out of these elements," explains Joseph Machlis, "he has forged an original language marked by brilliance of instrumentation, rhythmic urgency, and lyric intensity. . . . He achieved an individual approach to twelve-tone technique, within a framework that combines tonal, bitonal, polytonal and atonal elements."

"What is so striking about Henze," says Howard Klein, "is the vigor and spontaneity of his imagination. Although we are reminded here of Stravinsky, there of Berg or Mahler, the reminiscences are only faintly derivative. . . . But his net reaches wide and deep. It encompasses and fathoms a world of music investigated by other composers only in isolated bits. There is the overwhelming orchestrational ability which takes in the sonorities of Wagner and the colors of Boulez and Messiaen. The rhythmic drive and force of form rival Berg. In short, Henze is somebody. He may even be the foremost composer of our day."

Henze was born in Gütersloh, Westphalia, Germany on July 1, 1926. His principal music study took place in Heidelberg with Wolfgang Fortner and with René Leibowitz in Paris. Through Leibowitz, he was made aware of the artistic potential of the twelve-tone technique. Eclectic elements, however, soon began appearing in works like the *Piano Variations* (1948), the *Ballet Variations* for orchestra (1949), and his first ballet, *Jack Pudding*, the last of which exploited jazz idioms and was produced in Wiesebaden on June 5, 1951. Henze achieved international fame with his opera *Boulevard Solitude* in 1952, and this fame solidified with subsequent operas which placed him with the world's foremost composers for the stage.

In 1948, Henze was appointed musical director of Heinz Hipert's German Theatre in Constance. Between 1950 and 1952, he was the musical advisor on ballet for the Wiesebaden State Theatre, where his first two ballets were produced. In 1951, he was the recipient of the Robert Schumann Prize for his piano concerto, heard first at Düsseldorf on September 11, 1952. In 1952, Henze left Germany for good to live henceforth in Italy. Nevertheless, he continued to gather honors in Germany, including the Nordrhein Westphalian

Award in 1957, the Berlin Kunstpreis in 1959, and the Grand Prize for Artists in Hanover in 1962. He visited the United States for the first time in 1963 to attend the world première of his Fifth Symphony, which he had written on a commission for the New York Philharmonic. During the summer of 1967 he was composer-in-residence at Hopkins Center at Dartmouth College in Hanover, New Hampshire. Since 1961, Henze has served as professor of composition at the Mozarteum in Salzburg.

1951 BOULEVARD SOLITUDE, opera in seven scenes, with text by Grete Weil and the composer. First performance: Hanover Opera, February 17, 1952.

It was with *Boulevard Solitude* that Henze first commanded world attention. He had earlier written some works for the stage: two radio operas and a musical melodrama, as well as two ballets. *Boulevard Solitude* was his first work designed for the opera house, and it proved a sensation. At the première it inspired an ovation, though many in the audience were also expressing their loud resentment through catcalls and hissing. Loud dissent once again mingled with approbation when the opera was introduced in Italy (in Naples on March 4, 1954), and then was mounted in Rome, in April of 1954, and in London on June 25, 1962. The American première took place in Santa Fe, New Mexico, on August 2, 1967, performed by the Santa Fe Opera.

The text was an adaptation of the Manon Lescaut romance, a story previously made into successful operas by Massenet and Puccini. But with a difference. Henze's opera has a modern setting and modern characters, and its principal character is not Manon but Armand des Grieux. Here is how Erwin Stein summarized the action of the opera: "The undergraduate Armand meets Manon at a railway station. They fall in love, and, instead of traveling to her Swiss boarding school, Manon goes off with Armand to Paris. The subsequent idyll in Armand's attic ends when money is short and her brother Lescaut procures a rich, old lover, M. Lilaque. He, however, turns her out when Lescaut plunders his safe. Manon flies back to Armand, but their happiness is short: Armand turns to drugs, and Manon becomes the mistress of Lilaque's son. Lilaque's father discovers Manon, Armand and Lescaut in his house, misses a picture Lescaut has stolen and calls the police. Lescaut thrusts a revolver in Manon's hand and she kills Lilaque. The last scene shows Armand broken-hearted before Manon's prison."

The opera is in a single act, divided into seven scenes which, in turn, are made up of twenty-four musical numbers. All the musical material is derived from a twelve-tone row, but the later eclectic tendencies of the composer can already be detected. Dance elements (even jazz rhythms) play a prominent part in the overall musical texture. Formal arias and choral numbers (in one of the latter Massenet's *Manon* is quoted) are combined with Alban Bergian *Sprechstimme,* Stravinsky's neo-primitivism, Boris Blacher's variable meters, and even Puccinian lyricism. H. H. Stuckenschmidt, in reviewing the première for *Musical America,* pointed out that one of the remarkable features of this opera is the way in which Henze finds "a characteristic vocal style for each of the figures of his opera." For the hero, the style suggests traditional Italian opera with its emphasis on lyricism and its understanding of the voice. For Manon, Henze assumes a light, delicate style, which finds its happiest realization in a letter aria. For Manon's brother, the composer turns to the "brio style of the typical Italian baritone," while for old Lilaque the writing assumes the "dry pertness of operetta, a style admirably suited to the doggerel verse of the libretto at this point." Stuckenschmidt singles out as perhaps the most effective episode in the entire opera that which takes place in a den of thieves, "an original and bold conception . . . both musically and dramatically a stroke of genius." Here we find a combination of varying musical elements: "jazz forms, a song in C minor by young Lilaque, a delicate pantomime by the dancers intoxicated by drugs, a choral ensemble with a quotation from Massenet. Armand is transformed into Orpheus, as Manon's voice from a distance reads a letter that a beautiful dancer brings to him, and as he sinks into a dream only the whispered words, 'Beloved Armand,' remain in his consciousness."

1955 KÖNIG HIRSCH (THE STAG KING), opera in three acts, with text by Heinz von Cramer based on Gozzi's *Il Re Cervo*. First performance: Berlin State Opera, September 23, 1956.

When *König Hirsch* received its world première, one of the German critics, unidentified, described the performance as "one of the most important operatic events since the great Strauss premières." In sending in a report to *The New York Times,* Paul Moor revealed that the opera was given a "tempestous reception. . . . Irascible japes and heated counter-endorsements flew between top gallery and parquet before the first act had been ended and subsided only a full half-hour after final curtain. Literally overnight, Henze became page-one news all over Germany."

The text, adapted from a Gozzi fable, combines characteristic elements of allegory and fantasy. A prince, Leandro, abandoned in the forests by Governor Trataglia, has been raised by wild beasts. Reaching manhood, he returns to claim his throne and to find a bride, but the conniving of the Governor finally sends him back to the forests—a haven of truth as compared to the decay of so-called civilization. In the forests, the young man turns into a stag. Meanwhile, the Governor assumes the young man's body, takes over rule, and becomes a despot. The Governor orders that all forest stags be slain, but the young prince-turned-stag is saved by protecting animals. Soon the prince-turned-stag becomes homesick. He returns to the city, where the despot is slain by assassins and where the prince finally reverts to human form.

"Henze has set this fanciful stuff with an imaginativeness which is at times dazzling slapstick and quite genuinely touching," says Moor. "His scoring for an enormous orchestra incorporating harpsichord, accordion, mandolin, guitar and a thunderous percussion section . . . shows an imagination and skill that few living composers can match."

A revised, shortened version of the opera, renamed *Il Re Cervo,* was produced in Kassel, Germany, in 1963.

The American première of *König Hirsch* was given by the Santa Fe Opera Company in New Mexico on August 4, 1965. In his review for *The New York Times*, Raymond Ericson singled out the second act for special praise. "Set in a forest [it] has a wonderful atmosphere of poetic mystery. He [Henze] clothes the song-speech of the alchemists with music that is now playful, now gently sad." Ericson also praised the love scenes of Leandro and Costanza, which "are quietly tender," and the "little solos for Checco and Coltellino, with the barest of accompaniments, that form two of the most touching moments in the opera."

1960 DER PRINZ VON HOMBURG (THE PRINCE OF HAMBURG), opera in three acts, with text by Ingeborg Bachmann based on a drama of the same name by Heinrich von Kleist. First performance: Hamburg Opera, May 22, 1960.

Henze's growing success as an opera composer continued on the ascent with his third formal opera, *Der Prinz von Homburg,* which scored a triumph when introduced. To Gerhart von Westerman, the *Prinz* is "more personal in expression and more concentrated than *König Hirsch,* with its lush colors, while the orchestration is much more transparent and economical." Von Westerman explains that in this opera, Henze's "range of musical expression spreads from the restraint of a dream to the outburst of ardent passion. . . . It is Henze's music, with its effortless flow of arias and duets, fugues and passacaglias, which really turns it into operatic material."

The central character is a semi-historical Prince—Friedrich von Homburg—who becomes derelict in his military and official duties because of his passion for the Princess of Oranien. Though he comes home from the war victorious, he is arrested, tried and condemned to die. At the trial, the Prince confesses he is guilty and deserves death. But at the moment of execution, the Princess arrives with the Elector of Brandenburg, with whom she has interceded on the Prince's behalf. They come with a pardon, and the Prince is restored to his former high military station.

The opera shows a growing concern in Henze for lyricism and romantic expression, probably the result of having lived in Italy for a number of years. H. H. Stuckenschmidt remarked in *The New York Times*: "In the first act, Henze introduces his melodic materials, progressing from relatively simple and mostly tonal harmonies to more and more complicated textures. Voices are treated in a mixed recitative and arioso manner. Pentatonic scales and broken triads are gradually integrated into twelve-tone rows. The stylistic idea is to make the music increasingly complex to suit the growing dramatic tension, a doubly exciting process which carries through to Homburg's climactic farewell in the third act."

Der Prinz was given outside of Germany for the first time at the Festival of Two Worlds, in Spoleto, Italy, during the summer of 1960.

1961 DIE ELEGIE FÜR JUNGE LIEBENDE (ELEGY FOR YOUNG LOVERS), opera in three acts, with libretto (in English) by W. H. Auden and Chester Kallman. First performance: Schwetzingen, Germany, May 20, 1961 (in a German translation); Glyndebourne, England, July 13, 1961 (in the original English.)

When Henze's *Elegy* was produced in the United States in 1965, Conrad L. Osborne said in *Musical America*: "I may sum up by saying that it seems to me far and away the most important new opera to be introduced in New York for many years. I would rank it with *Peter Grimes* and *The Rake's Progress* as the most important since World War II." This judgment only continued the consensus of critical opinion in Europe when *Elegy* was first given. The opera proved such a sensation at its world première at Schwetzingen that, before the year ended, it had been produced at Glyndebourne, at the Munich Festival and at the Berlin Arts Festival; at the last of these, it was judged to be "the best new opera production" of the festival.

The excellent libretto (the work of the same men who had written the text of *The Rake's Progress* for Stravinsky) is richly poetic, and at times deeply symbolic. It is set in the Austrian Alps in the year of 1910. The central character is an egocentric genius, a poet named Gregor Mittenhofer, who comes each year with an entourage to the Schwarzer Adler in the Alps. There, through the years, the poet finds inspiration in the visions of Hilda Meck, a widow who for forty years has been awaiting the return of her husband who had vanished on the mountains during their honeymoon. When the body is finally recovered in a thaw, Hilda recovers, too. The poet now finds a new inspiration in the love affair that has developed between his stepson, Toni, and his own mistress, Elisabeth. He sends them off to the mountains to gather Edelweiss where they become victims of a violent snowstorm. This was an accident that could have been averted had the poet been ready to report their absence. Their death in the storm inspires the poet to write his *magnum opus,* entitled *Elegy for Young Lovers,* which, at the close of the opera, he reads to a Viennese audience.

Peter Davis explains that the work is an opera of "set pieces: the acts are divided into many small, titled sections, each a self-contained musical unit." Such a construction, Davis continues "results in a profusion of arias, duets, and ensembles. Perhaps the most striking feature of the score is the spellbinding beauty of its vocal lines—positively Italianate in their warmth and spontaneity. In the ensemble 'Out of Eden' from the second act, the solo lines melt and flow into one another with an irresistible effect. The character painting shows the touch of a born opera composer. Mittenhofer is one of the great musical creations of the contemporary operatic stage."

In discussing Henze's lyricism, Conrad L. Osborne said: "The vocal line takes off, on the one hand, from the late Strauss (the Strauss of the last songs) and on the other from Orff, but it elaborates on both and melds them into a kind of recitative-arioso alternation which solves . . . the problems of form and prosody that everyone finds so perplexing." Osborne finds the instrumentation equally "amazing." Using a huge and varied percussion section, together with the standard woodwinds and a small string section, Henze manages to produce "a continuity of truly beautiful sound—sound that is capable of a full range of emotion. This alone would rank him ahead of his contemporaries."

The *Elegy* was first seen in the United States on April 29, 1965, in a performance by the Juilliard Opera Company.

1955–1963 SYMPHONY NO. 4. I. Genesi (Introduction). II. Sonata. III. Variations. IV. Capriccio. V. Ricercar.

SYMPHONY NO. 5. I. Movimentato. II. Adagio. III. Molto pereptuo.

In the fall of 1963, Henze conducted the Berlin Philharmonic in two concerts in which all five of his symphonies were played. These performances were then recorded in a single album released by Deutsche Gramophon. Thus, an enviable opportunity was given to study the growth and development of Henze's symphonic style, a study which led many critics, both in Europe and in the United States, to come to the conclusion that Henze's significance does not rest on opera alone—indeed, that he is probably one of the most important symphonic composers alive.

Henze wrote his First Symphony in 1947 under the stimulation of Stravinsky and Bartók. Introduced at Darmstadt in the year of its composition, it was a failure; in 1963, the composer revised the work radically, scoring it for chamber orchestra. The Second Symphony was given at Stuttgart on December 1, 1949, and the Third Symphony, at the Donaueschingen Festival on October 7, 1951. "The Second and Third Symphonies," says Howard Klein, "show a progression away from the big gestures of the 1930s which pervaded the symphonic output of such composers as Hindemith, Copland, Harris or Sessions. The scoring, too, reflects the development procedure typical of an older line in the doublings and thickly scored melodies."

The Fourth Symphony, whose world première took place in West Berlin on October 9, 1963, is a curiosity in that, note for note, it had been previously used (1955) as the second-act finale in the opera *König Hirsch*. This is the reason why the symphony was subtitled *Il Re Crevo*. Peter G. Davis regards this as Henze's "greatest achievement" in the symphonic form. He describes the operatic action, of which this music is an interpretation, as follows in *High Fidelity Magazine:* "As the finale begins, King Leandor has been transformed into a stag and, disillusioned by the world of man, he longs to escape into nature. In the Genesi he calls upon the forest to disclose its secrets and each of the subsequent four movements represents one of the seasons as the stage picture portrays a stately panorama of nature. The King witnesses this ceaseless, unchanging cycle and realizes that the forest conceals nothing but the forest—he must return to mankind. As the King turns his back on the woods in silent acceptance of his mortality, the full orchestra wells up in a symphonic fabric of the most moving intensity."

The Fifth Symphony was written on a commission from the New York Philharmonic to help celebrate its opening season at Philharmonic Auditorium at the Lincoln Center for the Performing Arts. That orchestra, under Leonard Bernstein, introduced the work on May 16, 1963.

In his program notes for the New York Philharmonic, Edward Downes explains that the themes of the opening movement are "strongly colored by melodic half steps, although this is often disguised by octave displacements and rearrangements of notes reminiscent of twelve-tone procedures." One of the most important of these themes is a "four-note figure centering around one note" that is played early in the movement "very softly by muted violins against even softer woodwind chords." The second movement is a "delicate interlude in chamber-music style, punctuated by a series of cadenza-like unaccompanied solos for flute, solo viola, and English horn." In the finale, "the flying rhythms of this 'perpetual motion' . . . are established at the outset by soft muted strings." Midway in the movement, we hear a "series of slow-motion melodies which, by contrast, emphasize its restless perpetual-motion rhythm in the other instruments."

1966 DIE BASSARIDEN (THE BASSARIDS), opera in one act, with text by W. H. Auden and Chester Kallman based on Euripides's *The Bacchae*. First performance: Salzburg Festival, August 8, 1966.

When, one day, Henze revealed to Auden and Kallman his interest in writing a full-scale musical drama, they suggested Euripides's *The Bacchae* as possible material. With Henze responding favorably to this idea, the two men (who had previously provided the composer with the text for his *Elegy for Young Lovers*) went to work to prepare a libretto. Robert Breuer reveals in the *Saturday Review* that "the Greek drama underwent drastic dramaturgical changes. As finally conceived . . . the basic conflict between the 'orderly world' of King Pentheus of Thebes and the triumphantly acclaimed reign of the 'new god' Dionysus became the fundamental pattern for a huge historic canvas of similar spiritual, religious and political clashes." Peter Heyworth further explains in *The New York Times* that Auden and Kallman shifted Euripides's emphasis on the chorus to individual characters "who between them represent a whole range of attitudes to the irrational cult of Dionysus that sweeps the city of Thebes and drives it to destruction. In doing so, they have underpinned the story with a web of psychological motivation that is absent from Euripides but that gives *The Bassarides* an essentially contemporary flavor."

The opera is in a single uninterrupted act that takes about two and a half hours for performance. Its structure is unusual in that it is made up of four extended symphonic-like movements, almost like those of a mammoth symphony. "But," writes Heyworth, "if this use of symphonic form determines the outlines of the score, its essential detail stems from the systematic use of motives developed in the Wagnerian manner. In *The Bassarides,* Henze has finally made his peace with the whole tradition of German music drama. As a direct result, his music gains a flexibility and thematic richness that enable him to do justice to the tightly woven threads of the libretto. The influence of Wagner goes further: it is reflected in the whole weight and dramatic accent of this massive score."

In *High Fidelity*, Peter G. Davis says that Henze's score "abounds with excellences: an aria for Dionysus of bewitching Puccinian beauty; Agave's lyrical description of her first exposure to the joys of the new cult; the dark lament of Pentheus' omniscient nurse Beroe; and the choral writing which is uniformly effective." He points to the "wild hunt of the Bassarides (all armed with flashlights), followed by Pentheus' aria and destruction and appearance of the crazed Agave carrying her son's head" as the "dramatic peak of the opera . . . reached with thrilling results." And he finds that the most original moment in the opera arrives at the conclusion where "with disorder triumphant, Pentheus dead, Cadmus and his court banished from Thebes, and Dionysus in total command with the populace at his feet, the music suddenly becomes peaceful and soothing—more terrible in its calm acceptance of chaos than the wildest Dionysian orgy."

PAUL HINDEMITH 1895–1963

Those writers who enjoy finding a spiritual kinship between one famous composer and another have described Hindemith as a "twentieth-century Bach." The relationship between these two composers is not difficult to trace. Hindemith's *Ludus Tonalis* has a strong similarity of purpose and method to the *Well-Tempered Clavier*; and the works grouped under the title of *Kammermusik,* or *Chamber Music,* can loosely be described as contemporary Brandenburg Concertos. The bond that ties Hindemith to Bach is—counterpoint. With both composers, polyphony is the basis of their thinking; with both, polyphony serves as the material out of which mighty architectural structures are built. Yet one might say for Hindemith what Deems Taylor once said of Bach: "The best way to listen to Bach's music is to forget the word *counterpoint* and listen just for the music."

Early in his career, Hindemith came under the influence of the "back to Bach" movement—or "*Neue Sachlichkeit*" (New Objectivity)—which had been set into motion by composers like Busoni and Reger. With Hindemith, counterpoint was never an end in itself, the way it often was with Reger, but the starting point. Hindemith was not a composer to live in the past, but a very modern composer belonging to our own times. Though counterpoint was his method, and though he was partial to classical structures, there is independence in his thinking. His music is linear, by which we mean that the voices move with complete freedom of harmonic relationships. It has intensity, concentration, energy—qualities that we associate with contemporary expression rather than with Bach. It is often dissonant, sometimes atonal. This is music characterized by "intense and almost impersonal objectivity," says Edwin Evans, "with a concentration on counterpoint, the effect of which was sometimes dry and mechanical, though even then not inexpressive."

Hindemith's music is highly complex, even though a certain amount of simplification entered into some of his later works. His music is not easy to comprehend at first hearing. But as one gets to know a Hindemith work intimately, the resourcefulness and skill that the composer brings to polyphony, rhythm and the free use of tonality are of secondary importance. We become fascinated by the vigor and originality of his language, the subtlety of his intellectual processes, the high-minded idealism of his purpose. We become enthralled by the inexorable logic of his thinking. In the last analysis, Hindemith is perhaps a composer's composer, for the professional above all others can best appreciate Hindemith's remarkable powers.

There was about him a good deal of the Baroque composer, above and beyond his interest in polyphony. Baroque is the way in which he favored the concerto structure. The concerto became the means "through which Hindemith best expresses the dual ideal of polyphony and dynamic force," his biographer, Heinrich Strobel, explains. "The nineteenth century erred, according to Hindemith, in degrading the concerto by reducing it to an exercise in uncontrolled virtuosity, and by disfiguring it with the introduction of symphonic tensions. Hindemith utilizes all the possibilities of solo playing for his concertos. But even where the figuration is richest and most detailed, it is always incorporated in the thematic organism and is always part of the polyphonic play."

And like the Baroque composer, Hindemith wrote abundantly in every possible form and medium. He never felt that each and every composition is a hothouse flower to be nursed into life carefully and fastidiously, but rather that compositions had to sprout out of the rich soil of his imagination like some uncontrolled wild growth. It is the Baroque in Hindemith that made it possible for the creator of complex, cerebral, at times even esoteric exercises in linear counterpoint to undertake, with his other hand, numerous functional pieces for mass consumption. In the 1920s, Hindemith felt strongly the responsibility of the composer to society and to the times in which he lived. Consequently, he produced a great number of works for mechanical organ, radio, pianola, motion pictures, theatre, music for the home, and so forth. This music was baptized by its composer as *Gebrauchsmusik,* or functional music. One of Hindemith's most significant achievements in this field was a little opera about children and for children, intended to be performed by children. It was called *Wir bauen eine Stadt,* or *We Build a City,* and its première took place in Berlin on June 21, 1930.

Hindemith was born in Hanau, Germany, on November 16, 1895. As a boy he supported himself by playing the violin in café-houses, theatres and dance halls. At the same time, he attended Hoch's Conservatory in Frankfort, where he was a pupil of Arnold Mendelssohn and Bernhard Sekles. In Frankfort, Hindemith distinguished himself as a violinist (he was concertmaster of the Frankfort Opera orchestra) and as a violinist (of the Amar String Quartet, which he helped to found and which specialized in modern music). He also helped organize the Donaueschingen Festival at Baden-Baden dedicated to new music. It was there that his early chamber-music works were heard between 1921 and 1923, and attracted attention. In the half-dozen years that followed, Hindemith became recognized as one of the major creative figures in Germany,

In 1924, Hindemith married Gertrud Rottenberg, daughter of a conductor at the Frankfort Opera. They left Frankfort in 1927 and made their home in Berlin, where Hindemith was appointed professor of composition at the Berlin High School for Music, a post he retained until the time of Hitler. The Nazis did not look with favor on Hindemith, since he was married to a half-Jewess, and he had given performances with Jewish musicians. In addition, they regarded Hindemith's music as decadent or degenerate. Hindemith became the center of an explosive political controversy when Wilhelm Furtwaengler planned to produce and conduct the world première of the opera,

Mathis der Maler, an episode described in the section on that composition (*see*—1934). As an aftermath of this controversy, Hindemith left Germany, and his music was banned from German concert programs.

He first went to Turkey on the invitation of the government to help reorganize its musical life and its educational methods in music. In 1940, he made his home permanently in the United States and joined the music faculty of Yale University. He became an American citizen in 1946. He made outstanding contributions to the teaching of composition and harmony, his ideas on these subjects being incorporated into an important theoretical treatise, *The Craft of Musical Composition,* published between 1937 and 1939, and regarded by some musicologists as one of the most significant contributions to musical theory since Rameau.

In 1953, Hindemith decided to reestablish his home in Europe. He went to live in Zurich, where he had been a member of the University since 1948. Nevertheless, he made several return visits to the United States. Early in 1963, he participated in a four-day Hindemith festival in New York where his last opera, *The Long Christmas Dinner,* received its American première—having previously been introduced in Mannheim on December 17, 1961.

Hindemith made his last public appearance in Berlin on November 12, 1963, when he conducted the world première of his last composition, a Mass, for a cappella chorus. He died of a circulatory ailment in Frankfort, Germany, on December 28, 1963.

Among the world honors heaped on Hindemith were the Sibelius Prize of $32,000 in 1955, and the Balzan Prize in Rome for distinguished contributions to music in 1962.

1920 SONATA IN D MAJOR, FOR VIOLIN AND PIANO, op. 11, no. 2. I. Lebhaft. II. Ruhig und gemessen. III. In Zeitmas und Charakter eines geschwinden Tanzes.

The influence of Brahms and Reger can still be detected in this early Hindemith violin sonata, whose writing is essentially post-Romantic. Yet the discerning ear can already detect a suggestion of Hindemith's coming linear practice, in the presentation of the main subject of the first movement, which the score explains should be played "with great stubbornness." In this movement, there is also a hint of free tonality. The second movement is the one in which the composer clings most stubbornly to his Romantic upbringing. It is dominated by a Brahms-like melody of calm and stately beauty. The finale is a quick dance movement.

1922 STRING QUARTET NO. 3 IN C MAJOR, op. 16. I. Fugato. II. Quickly and Energetically. III. Calm and Flowing. IV. Lively. V. Rondo.

STRING QUARTET NO. 4, op. 22. I Allegro. II. Lento. III. Kleine Marsch. IV. Passacaglia.

KAMMERMUSIK (CHAMBER MUSIC) NO. 1, for chamber orchestra, op. 24, no. 1. I. Very Fast and Wild. II. Very Strict in Rhythm. III. Very Slow and with Expression. IV. As Animated as Possible.

KLEINE KAMMERMUSIK (LITTLE CHAMBER MUSIC), for flute,

oboe, clarinet, horn, and bassoon, op. 24, no. 2. I. Playful, Moderately Fast. II. Waltz. III. Placid and Simple. IV. Rapid, Very Lively.

In the Third Quartet, introduced at the Donaueschingen Festival in Baden-Baden on November 4, 1922, Hindemith crystallized his linear writing. The first movement is an atonal fugato in which the various voices achieve complete freedom of movement. No time value or key signature is designated. The scherzo bursts in without a break; this is sharply accentuated and powerfully propelled music, often in irregular rhythms. The longest of the movements, the third, brings to polytonality singular expressiveness. After a fantasialike section, virtuoso in character, the final movement, a rondo, enters without interruption.

The Fourth Quartet represents some of the most brilliant and complex contrapuntal writing of Hindemith in the quartet form. A fugue and a double fugue appear in the first movement, while in the second the contrapuntal writing is developed with remarkable inventiveness and variety of mood. A brisk march brings a measure of relief from these polyphonic elaborations, but the relief is only temporary. The closing passacaglia, which consists of twenty-seven variations of a theme, is an elaborate web that ends in a climactic fugato.

Hindemith's linear writing was further developed in seven important works for chamber orchestra, or for solo instrument and chamber orchestra, in which his break with post-Romanticism and Reger becomes complete. The first of these was introduced at the Donaueschingen Festival at Baden-Baden on July 31, 1922. Its main interest lies in the freedom of tonality and the compulsive momentum of the first movement; in the forty-five measure canon of the third movement where the time changes continually, almost with each measure; and in the finale, entitled "1921," which has a sardonic humor concealing the despair of the bitter post-World War I era. In that finale, Hindemith quotes a tune popular in Germany that year, *Fuchstanz*, a final vigorous statement of which brings the *Kammermusik* to its conclusion.

The *Kleine Kammermusik* is one of the composer's most ingratiating compositions of his early years. At the same time, it is still one of more popular works in the literature for chamber-music winds. And with good reason. From the first movement to the last, it overflows with humor, irony and delightful parodies. Arthur Cohn says that its "dance-hall attitude, in typical post-World War I style, equals a musical hedonistic view of life presented in cameo style." In the second movement, a piccolo replaces the flute.

1923 DAS MARIENLEBEN (THE LIFE OF MARY), song cycle for soprano and piano, op. 27. I. Geburt Mariä. II. Mariä im Tempel (Passacaglia). III. Mariä Verkündigung. IV. Mariä Heimsuchung. V. Argwohn Josephs. VI. Verkündigung über den Hirten. VII. Geburt Christi. VIII. Rast auf der Flucht in Ägypten. IX. Von der Hochzeit zu Kana. X. Vor der Passion. XI. Pietà. XII. Stillung Mariä mit dem Auferstanden. XIII. Vom Tode Mariä I. XIV. Vom Tode Mariä II (Thema mit Variationen). XV. Vom Tode Mariä III.

In 1923, Hindemith wrote the music for fifteen poems by Rilke, describing the life of the Virgin Mary. The cycle was presented at the Donaueschingen

Festival on June 17, 1923, where it made a profound impression. Nicolas Slonimsky described the work as music "in a neo-medieval idiom of great harmonic strength and high emotional content." The enormous demands the music made on the singer's technique and physical stamina discouraged further performances.

In 1941, Hindemith decided to rewrite the cycle completely, to make it more in the image of his now mature and fully realized style and at the same time to pay closer attention to the requirements of the singing voice. The revision proved a giant operation taking about seven years. Only one of the fifteen songs was allowed to stay as it had been. All the others were completely rewritten. "In this version," the composer has explained, "the vocal line has always and without exception been the point of departure for the composition, even in those songs in which the counterpoint is most highly developed." He adds: "The old version was essentially a series of songs held together by the text and the story unfolded to it, but otherwise not following any composition plan. There was no urge toward overall order serving to concentrate and strengthen this loosely organized potpourri sufficiently for the purely formal side of the composition to offer the listener a heightened aesthetic pleasure. Wiser distribution of forces, calculation of the high and low points—such considerations were unknown to the composer of the old version." In the revision "all these factors have been taken into account."

The revised *Marienleben* was first sung in New York by Jennie Tourel on January 23, 1949.

The fifteen songs fall into four groups, as the composer himself explained. In the first group (which ends with the fourth number), we find all the songs about Mary's personal experiences "be the treatment lyric . . . or epic." The second group comprises the more dramatic songs, beginning with "*Argwohn Josephs*" and ending with "*Hochzeit zu Kana*"; only "*Geburt Christi*" has some of the idyllic character of the numbers in the first group. "In these songs a considerable number of persons, actions, scenes and circumstances are shown, and only in the last of them does our central figure again actively appear." The third group concentrates on Mary's suffering. Here, says the composer, we encounter "the greatest intensity of expression and the awakening of the sublimest mood in the listener." In the fourth and final group, we come to "the point of highest abstraction, in which purely musical ideas and forms prevail. This is an epilogue in which persons and actions no longer play any role."

Hindemith also explains that the "dynamic climax" of the entire cycle—"that is, the song which in volume of sonority, in the frequency of harmonies employed, in variety and power of tonality, and in lapidary simplicity of form represents the highest degree of physical effort in the whole work"—is "*Hochzeit zu Kana*". He maintains that the "highest degree of expression tension" is achieved in "*Pietà*." And he points out that "*Vom Tode Maria II*" is the "high point in the intellectual, compositional part of the creative process" and "by far the most complicated of all the songs."

1924 STRING QUARTET NO. 5 IN E-FLAT MAJOR, op. 32. I. Very Quiet and Expressive. II. Lively and Very Energetic. III. Quiet; Variations. IV. Broad and Energetic; Allegretto grazioso.

Hindemith here designated a key, a not altogther frequent procedure with him. But the tonality, though stated, is not too restricting. Throughout the work it is free, marked by abrupt modulations and even by occasional polytonality. Counterpoint does not play quite the important role here that it did in earlier quartets. The emphasis is rather on thematic material and its development. This increased bent for lyricism, together with a simplification of writing and refinement of texture, makes this quartet more pleasurable on first contact than any of his preceding works in the form.

1926 CARDILLAC, opera in three acts, op. 39, with libretto by Ferdinand Lion based on E. T. A. Hoffmann's *Das Fräulein von Scuderi*. First performance: Dresden, November 9, 1926 (original version); Zurich, June 20, 1952 (extensively rewritten version).

In his rejection of Romanticism, and in his search for objectivity, Hindemith reverted to the classical opera of Handel with its separate musical numbers. "Not only is each number a distinct, clearly organized musical unit," says Donald Jay Grout, "but the music is constructed purely according to its own laws, the themes being straightforwardly developed in the manner of a concerto, undeflected by any attempt to illustrate more details of the text." Taking his cue from the then-recently produced *Wozzeck* of Alban Berg, Hindemith applied the forms of instrumental music to various sections of the opera (fugue, canon, passacaglica); and to emphasize further the significance of instrumental music, concert pieces were interpolated into various parts of the opera. So concerned is Hindemith with his musical (as opposed to dramatic) problems that the music seems to have a life of its own, independent of the text. And the musical problem is solved primarily by an austere linear style and occasionally by a dry accompanied recitative which represent a complete break with Romantic attitudes. One of the most controversial episodes pinpoints this anti-Romantic ideal, the love scene between the young cavalier and the prima donna, which is accompanied only by two solitary flutes, each progressing independently of the other.

The main character is a Parisian goldsmith who, in the closing decade of the seventeenth century, is so unable to separate himself from the jeweled creations he has fashioned that he murders his clients in order to regain the purchased items. The opera opens in a city square which becomes electric with the news that another murder has been committed; as in earlier murders, a piece of jewelry has been stolen from the victim. One of those present is a young cavalier who is in love with a prima donna. To win her favor he purchases for her a gold belt created by Cardillac. In the singer's bedroom, the cavalier comes to present his gift. A masked figure appears through the window, kills the cavalier, and snatches the belt away. In the second act, Cardillac's partner is suspected of the murders and is apprehended by the police. Then the prima donna arrives with a new suitor, a Marquis. They have come to purchase a jewel. Suddenly, the prima donna sees and recognizes the gold belt that had caused the cavalier's death. In the third act we are in the Opera where Lully's *Phaéton* is being produced, the prima donna singing the principal female role. Behind the scenes, Cardillac's partner, having escaped from prison, has warned the prima donna that her life is in danger. It is at this point that the prima donna comes to grips with the truth that Cardillac is a murderer. In the last act, Cardillac is fleeing from the police. Outside the opera house, crazed by fear, he confesses his crimes. The crowds fall upon him and kill him.

A quarter of a century after he had written *Cardillac,* Hindemith revised it completely. He discarded the old text and wrote a new one; then he set about rewriting the musical numbers, adding a few new ones. His aim now was to create a musical drama in which the music helped intensify the dramatic action and deepen the psychological interest. Besides rewriting some of the arias and ensemble numbers, to adapt them better to his new text, he added new recitatives and vocal numbers. Understatement now becomes an important means to attain heightened dramatic interest, as when Hindemith completely dispenses with music in the first act during the murder of the cavalier. Rhythm is exploited to increase the dramatic interest. Gerhart von Westerman notes that the two "cornerstones" of the revised opera are two huge and contrasting choral episodes, one opening the opera in a wild and savage mood, and the other closing it with tranquillity.

The American première of *Cardillac* took place at Sante Fe, New Mexico, during the summer of 1967, in a performance by the Sante Fe Opera.

1928 KAMMERMUSIK NO. 7, for organ and chamber orchestra, op. 46, no. 2. I. Not too Fast. II. Very Slow and Quite Peaceful. III. Fugue.

The seventh *Kammermusik*—actually a concerto for organ and chamber orchestra—has unusual scoring in that it utilizes two wind choirs (woodwind and brass), and, except for cellos and basses, has no strings. E. Power Biggs regards the first movement as the strongest. "Flamboyant themes with fragments sounding all around," he writes, "are set forth in an irresistible rhythm." The second movement is a canon for the organ over a recurring pedal. Trumpet flourishes bring on the finale which is dominated by a fugal theme that "circles up in an arpeggio over an augmented octave to scatter into chattering fragments."

1930 KONZERTMUSIK (CONCERT MUSIC), for strings and brass instruments, op. 50. I. Moderately Fast with Force. II. Lively; Slowly; Lively.

Concert Music was written on a commission for the fiftieth anniversary of the Boston Symphony, which introduced it under Koussevitzky's direction on April 3, 1931. It is scored for four horns, four trumpets, three trombones, tuba and a full string orchestra.

Arthur V. Berger has prepared the following analysis: "The first theme, powerfully announced by trumpets and trombones in unison, is declamatory, with strings weaving independent figures around it. The second section of the first movement, introducing a smoother, rhythmically less abrupt theme, is for brass alone. This prepares us for the extreme contrast of the third section, which is for strings alone. . . . A section for full ensemble follows, based on the second theme. . . . There is a final broad section for full ensemble with strings declaiming the first theme originally announced by brass.

"In the second movement, the three-voiced fugue is typical string material and the brass is thus excluded from an active part in it. But after the three voices enter, the brass punctuates the running material of the strings with a motive remotely suggesting 'blues.' . . . After a free development there is a sustained section and the fugue then returns, leading to a coda."

1932 PHILHARMONIC CONCERTO, variations for orchestra.

In 1932, the Berlin Philharmonic celebrated its fiftieth anniversary. For this occasion Hindemith wrote an orchestral concerto in the variation form, dedicating it to Wilhelm Furtwaengler, the musical director of the orchestra. The first performance took place in Berlin on April 15, 1932.

The work consists of a theme and six variations. The theme is in two parts, "each," explains Leopold Stokowski, "a transformation of the fundamental melodic curve and rhythm of the basic theme. As the whole composition unfolds, this basic theme assumes many variations of form and expression, ending with fantastic versions by the woodwind, heroic by the horns, and triumphpant by the whole brass choir." The six variations have the following tempo markings: Moderately Fast; Very Quiet; Moderately Lively; Quietly Animated; Proceeding in a Lightly Animated Way; In Marchlike Tempo.

1934 MATHIS DER MALER (MATTHIAS THE PAINTER), opera in seven scenes, with text by the composer. First performance: Zurich, May 28, 1938.

MATHIS DER MALER, Symphony. I. The Concert of the Angels. II. The Entombment. III. Temptation of St. Anthony.

What is perhaps Hindemith's most famous and successful work has known two lives. It originated as an opera. Writing his own libretto, the composer developed the few known facts about Matthias Grünewald, the early sixteenth-century painter, into a romantic story set against the turbulent background of the Peasants' War of 1524. Matthias (Mathis), employed by Cardinal Albrecht, abandons his lifework (painting religious pictures) to join the cause of Hans Schwalb, leader of the uprising peasants against the Church. Once plunged into the revolutionary struggle, Matthias is assailed by doubts. He sees on his side as much injustice, murder, pillage, as he had formerly witnessed on the other. He escapes with his beloved, the beautiful Regina, daughter of Schwalb, to seek peace of mind in the Odenwald. Ugly apparitions come to haunt him. They disappear. Then beautiful visions appear to bring him back to his art and are the inspiration for his panel designs on the Isenheim Altar. Matthias is back in his studio working. His beloved Regina is no longer with him. With quiet and peaceful resignation, he gives up the outside world.

Hindemith completed his opera in 1934. Its première was scheduled for that year at the Berlin State Opera, Wilhelm Furtwaengler directing. But the theme of the opera—the defeat of German liberalism—was too delicate for the times; and the details of the plot had overtones too sensitive for the ears of the Nazis. They expressed opposition to the forthcoming première while denouncing Hindemith viciously as representing those "decadent and degenerate" forces in music of which the Nazis hoped to purge Germany.

In spite of the opposition of the Nazi powers to Hindemith and to his opera, Wilhelm Furtwaengler presented the world première of a three-movement symphony, which the composer had adapted from his opera score. This concert by the Berlin Philharmonic on March 12, 1934, was an overwhelming success. The audience was reacting to a symphonic masterwork. But even more than that, aware as it was of the Nazi disapproval of Hindemith and *Mathis,* the audience was also expressing its denunciation of the Third Reich in the only way it could.

Still hopeful that he could win over the approval of the ruling powers, Furtwaengler published an open letter in the *Deutsche Allgemeine Zeitung* on November 25, 1934, entitled "The Hindemith Case," in which he pleaded for a more sympathetic attitude towards this great composer. When, that same evening, at a performance conducted by Furtwaengler, the conductor was given a massive ovation when he first made his way to the stage, Hitler personally ordered Furtwaengler to abandon all plans to produce the Hindemith opera. More than that—Furtwaengler was relieved of his various posts as a disciplinary measure, and was not allowed to leave the country. And Hindemith's music was henceforth banned from all programs in Germany.

It was several years before the opera was introduced. This took place not in Germany, since the Nazis were still in power, but in Zurich, in 1938, under Robert Denzler's direction. The opera was a formidable success. On March 9, 1939, the Zurich company presented it in Amsterdam. One week later, the opera was given in a concert version in London; and in 1946, with the Nazis defeated and the war ended, *Mathis* was finally seen for the first time in Germany, in Stuttgart. After that, La Scala presented it in 1957, the Vienna State Opera in 1958, and the Berlin State Opera in 1959. The American première took place in Boston on February 17, 1956.

When *Mathis der Maler* was introduced in the United States, Cyrus Durgin, the Boston critic, said it exerted "much power, and there is eloquence both of subject and treatment. . . . *Mathis* is a heavy, German-style opera in the unique musical manner of the composer. The score, instrumentally, is a torrent of the bold and vigorous harmonic complexity, dissonance, rhythmic vitality and powerful melody for which Hindemith has become world-famed. The melody is correct, for although Hindemith often treats the voice as an instrument, and gives it taxing intervals, what comes out is real melody."

In the symphony, which has become a modern classic, the composer endeavored to re-create the emotions aroused in a sensitive viewer by the three celebrated Grünewald paintings on the Isenheim Altar at the Museum of Colmar. Utilizing a flexible style that ranges from medieval modes to suggestions of twelve-tone system, but always emphasizing linear writing, Hindemith has created tonal symbols that are extraordinarily expressive without being programmatic or pictorial. The pervading mysticism and religious intensity of the paintings have been caught in the music. As Heinrich Strobel remarked, polyphonic writing here acquires a "symbolic force which is something entirely new for Hindemith. . . . Effects are obtained here which could not have been realized by dramatic expressiveness."

The first movement. (Ruhig bewegt; Ziemlich lebhafte Halbe) is the overture of the opera. The principal theme, presented by the trombones in the eighth measure, is a melody utilized throughout the entire opera—"*Es sungen drei Engel.*" A rapid main section contains three parts: first a lively theme, modal in structure, in flute and violins; then a serene and mystical theme in strings; finally, a fugato based on the two themes, while the trombone remembers the Angel or "*Engel*" melody.

The second movement (Sehr langsam) is derived from the sixth scene. Its first theme is in a purely linear structure, in muted strings and woodwind. The second is characterized by the intervalic leaps of fourths and fifths—first in oboe, then in flute accompanied by plucked strings.

The final movement (Sehr langsam, frei im Zeitmass; Lebhaft) comes from the intermezzo of the opera's final scene, which describes the painter's mellow resignation and his dismissal of the world outside his own workshop. This is the most powerful and dramatic part of the symphony. It opens with unison strings which leads to a brass chorale; and it ends with an exultant Hallelujah.

"The development of the three movements is singularly clear," says Strobel. "The dynamic curve descends from the festive and happy 'Concert of the Angels' of the beginning, to the quiet elegy of 'The Entombment,' and then proceeds, after the music of the Saint's ordeal, to the concluding Hallelujah hymn of the final visionary exaltation."

1935 DER SCHWANENDREHER (THE ORGAN-GRINDER), concerto on old folk melodies for viola and orchestra. I. Langsam—Mässig bewegt mit Kraft. II. Sehr ruhig; Fugato. III. Finale: variations on *Seid ihr nicht der Schwanendreher*—Mässig schnell.

The name of this concerto is derived from the melody which appears, and then is varied, in the last movement, "*Seid ihr nicht der Schwanendreher.*" The translations of the word *Schwanendreher* are varied, the most familiar being organ-grinder.

On November 14, 1935, this concerto was introduced by the composer and the Amsterdam Concertgebouw Orchestra, Mengelberg conducting.

The following explanatory note appears in the published score: "A minstrel, joining a merry company, displays what he has brought back from foreign lands: songs serious and gay, and finally a dance piece. Like a true musician, he expands and embellishes the melodies, preluding and improvising according to his fancy and ability. This medieval scene was the inspiration of the composition."

Folk melodies of the fifteenth and sixteenth centuries represent the kernel of the composition. The first movement is based on the song, "*Zwischen Berg und tiefem Tal.*" A ten-measure solo for viola opens this movement. After the appearance of the orchestra, there comes the main body of the movement, "a typical Hindemith Allegro," says H. H. Stuckenschmidt, "somewhat in the manner of the earlier 'motorized' passages—powerful, positive music, carried forward with a logical feeling for form, relentless in the interweaving and rhythmic interpretation of a few plastic motives."

There are two parts in the second movement, each of which uses a song. The first is an Adagio based on "*Nun laube Lindlein laube,*" introduced in a duo for solo viola and harp. A ten-measure viola solo leads to the second part, a vigorous five-voiced fugato based on the melody "*Der Gutsgauch auf dem Zaune sass.*"

The finale is a series of five variations on the tune, "*Seid ihr nicht der Schwanendreher.*" H. H. Stuckenschmidt explains that the "vigorous eighth-note opening phrase of the melody leads rondo-fashion through all five variations."

1937 SYMPHONIC DANCES, for orchestra. I. Langsam. II. Lebhaft. III. Sehr Langsam. IV. Mässig bewegt mit Kraft.

In 1937, Hindemith was commissioned by Serge Diaghilev to collaborate with the choreographer Léonide Massine in the writing of a ballet for the Ballet Russe. Before a subject was decided upon, Hindemith started making musical sketches, which he then found unsuitable when a decision was reached to build the ballet-scenario around St. Francis. He decided to elaborate his sketches into an independent symphonic work. Though he named it *Symphonic Dances,* there is very little terpischorean interest in the music, despite its motor action and its compelling rhythmic drive.

Symphonic Dances was introduced in London on December 5, 1937. At that time the following analysis was provided: "The music opens with a slow introduction based on a march-like theme which is repeated with varying orchestration. This leads into the main first movement . . . based on three themes of similar character. The first is introduced by the first violins and is treated fugally by the strings. The second is given mainly to the woodwind; the third is heard first on solo strings.

"The second movement corresponds to the scherzo of a symphony. It opens with a striking motif, immediately followed by a theme of irregular rhythmic formation. Another subject is introduced by the first clarinet and is developed, leading to some fine chords in the brass. After a recurrence of the first theme, a slower section is introduced, consisting of three parts, each punctuated by pause on the common chord.

"The slow movement begins with a passage for strings over which the first clarinet has an elaborate arabesque type of melody. Another melody is introduced as a flute solo.

"A rather slow introduction to the last movement has a vigorous theme for the strings and woodwind. . . . A theme of more purely harmonic character . . . leads into the Allegro. The main subject is a long melody given out by the cellos, violins, bassoons, and horn, accompanied by quick repeated notes. A subsidiary section leads to some forceful unison and octave passages on the strings, punctuated by outbursts on the wind. A quieter section follows in which the long melody appears as a bassoon solo, strings accompanying pizzicato. After some development of this theme, the introduction is reintroduced and its material subjected to further treatment, culminating in a brilliant passage for the whole orchestra, with which the work ends."

1938 ST. FRANCIS (NOBILISSIMA VISIONE), ballet in five scenes, with choreography and scenario by Léonide Massine. First performance: Ballet Russe de Monte Carlo, London, July 21, 1938.

NOBLISSIME VISIONE, suite for orchestra. I. Introduction; Rondo. II. March. III. Passacaglia.

When the ballet *Nobilissima Visione* was first presented, it bore the title of *St. Francis*. It described the mystical experiences of Saint Francis from the time he renounced material values until he found spiritual peace through the guidance of Poverty, Obedience, and Chastity. In the end, Poverty becomes his mystical bride. The ballet was introduced to America by the Ballet Russe in New York on October 14, 1938.

One year after the première of the ballet, Hindemith extracted several sections from the ballet score—those that in his words were "self-sufficient and comprehensible in concert music, and which do not depend upon supplementary stage action"—and developed them into an orchestral suite which he called *Nobilissima Visione*. The suite was heard for the first time in Venice in September, 1938. On March 23, 1939, its American première took place in Los Angeles, with the composer conducting the Los Angeles Philharmonic.

Hindemith's own description of this orchestral suite follows: "The Introduction consists of that part of the original music during which the hero of the action is sunk in deep meditation. The Rondo corresponds to the music in the stage score for the mystic union of the Saint to Mistress Poverty, the scene having been inspired by an old Tuscan legend. The music reflects the blessed peace and unworldly cheer with which the guests at the wedding participate in the wedding feast—dry bread and water only. The second movement pictures the march of a troop of medieval soldiers. First heard but distantly, their gradual approach is observed. The middle portion of this movement suggests the brutality with which these mercenaries set upon a traveling burgher and rob him. The third and closing movement corresponds to the portion of the ballet score representing the Hymn to the Sun. Here all the symbolic personifications of heavenly and earthly existence mingle in the course of the different variations through which the six-measure long theme of the Passacaglia is transformed."

1939 CONCERTO FOR VIOLIN AND ORCHESTRA. I. Mässig bewegte Halbe. II. Langsam. III. Lebhaft.

This work is not to be confused with *Kammermusik No. 4*, op. 36 (1925), which is sometimes programmed as a Concerto for Violin and Chamber Orchestra.

The 1939 violin concerto is the last major work Hindemith completed in Europe before settling in the United States. It was introduced in Amsterdam on March 14, 1940.

Though Hindemith does not abandon his contrapuntal style in this piece, he recognizes the lyrical nature of the solo instrument by indulging in long and expansive melodic ideas. One of these is heard in the very opening of the first movement; another, the principal theme of the second movement, has an even greater span. The slow movement has perhaps the most expressive and intense of these melodic ideas, heard in the solo instrument after a few introductory measures by the woodwind. The pace changes in the last movement, as soloist and orchestra indulge in music of sprightly character. An elaborate cadenza employing earlier material is heard towards the end of the work.

1940 THEME WITH VARIATIONS ACCORDING TO THE FOUR TEMPERAMENTS, for strings with piano.

In this music, originally intended as a score for a ballet that never materialized, Hindemith tried to give musical expression to the different moods of melancholic, sanguine, phlegmatic and choleric people. The "four temperaments" consequently are variations on the theme of human nature. The work is described as a theme with variations, but actually consists of three themes projected in three different sections; each variation, in turn, appears in the same order as the themes, and is divided into three sections of its own.

Themes: The first subject is heard in the strings (Moderato); the second is played by the piano (Allegro assai); the third appears in the entire orchestra (Moderato).

Variation I. Melancholic. Against a piano background, a muted violin is heard in a supple melody. A presto passage for orchestra follows, after which the variation ends with a slow march for piano.

Variation II. Sanguine. A delightful waltz melody is played by the piano and strings.

Variation III. Phlegmatic. A subject for strings alone (Moderato) is followed by a sprightly idea for piano (Allegretto). Strings and piano bring the variation to its end (Allegretto scherzando).

Variation IV. Choleric. A succession of vigorous chords in the piano are answered just as vigorously by the orchestra. After a Vivace section for the orchestra, a passionate and emotional passage is heard. The section ends Maestoso.

This work was heard for the first time in Boston on September 3, 1943, with Richard Burgin conducting members of the Boston Symphony Orchestra, and Lukas Foss playing the piano obbligato.

1940 SYMPHONY IN E-FLAT, for orchestra. I. Sehr lebhaft. II. Sehr langsam. III. Lebhaft. IV. Mässig schnell halle.

Though the symphony has a specific tonality—E-flat major—it is written with Hindemith's customary tonal freedom; there is no key signature in the music itself, beyond that on the title page. It was introduced by the Minneapolis Symphony Orchestra under Dimitri Mitropoulos on November 21, 1941.

Two principal themes dominate the first movement. The first is a vigorous and rhythmic subject heard in the horns; the second, which is much more lyrical, is set against the pizzicati of the strings and introduced after the development of the first. The second movement opens with the principal idea stated by the English horn, clarinet and trumpet against the quarter-note background of the tympani. The subsidiary subject is played by the oboe accompanied by violin chords, later to be taken up by the entire orchestra. The third movement has the nature of a scherzo, which develops into the finale without pause. The principal subject of this last movement, similar in some respects to the principal theme of the first movement, is announced by the first violins; following its development, a subject of decided strength and energy is heard in the brass. After a climactic development there comes a lull in the form of an intermezzo; but the earlier unrest returns and slowly grows in strength and proportion into a dynamic close.

1943 SYMPHONIC METAMORPHOSIS ON A THEME BY CARL MARIA VON WEBER, for orchestra. I. Allegro. II. Moderato. III. Andantino. IV. March.

Hindemith borrowed four Weber themes from the master's more obscure works in this elaborate "symphonic metamorphosis"; and in their order, the four movements suggest a symphony. The first, third, and last of the movements are derived from themes taken from eight pieces for four-hand piano entitled *All' Ongarese,* op. 60; the second movement, a scherzo, utilizes a subject from Weber's overture to incidental music to Schiller's *Turandot.* Hindemith took pains to explain that none of these Weber excerpts represents the composer at his best and that they are, consequently, altered and elaborated by him whenever necessary.

The theme is heard at once in the first movement. A second, more vigorous and abandoned, is presented, before both themes are briefly elaborated upon. Olin Downes described the second-movement scherzo as "*chinoisserie*." Here the flute is heard in highly decorated melody, which lower strings take over in a livelier tempo. In the Andantino, the main theme is heard in the wind instruments. The finale, which enters without pause, is brisk, march-like music to which the percussion instruments contribute a vigorous rhythm.

The *Symphonic Metamorphosis* was introduced in New York on January 20, 1944, with Artur Rodzinski conducting the New York Philharmonic Orchestra.

1943 LUDUS TONALIS (TONAL PLAY), for piano.

Ludus Tonalis is Hindemith's *Art of the Fugue,* a monumental exercise in the polyphonic technique. Subtitled by the composer "Studies on Counterpoint, Tonal Organization and Piano Playing," the *Ludus Tonalis* consists of twelve three-voiced fugues, each in one of the keys of the chromatic scale. The entire work begins with a Praeludium and concludes with a Postludium (the latter being the Praeludium inverted and in retrograde). Interludes are placed between the fugues. These interludes provide contrast to the weighty material of the fugues through their simplicity and lightness of mood; in song form, they consist of such varying material as a pastorale, waltz, march, cakewalk, and so on. The whole work takes about forty-five minutes to perform.

This is the plan of this giant conception:

Praeludium: Moderate—Arioso: Solemn, Broad.
Fuga prima in C: Slow.
Interludium: Moderate, with Energy.
Fuga secunda in G: Gay.
Pastorale: Moderate.
Fuga tertia in F: Andante.
Interludium: Scherzando.
Fuga quarta in A: With Energy—Slow, Grazioso—Tempo primo.
Interludium: Fast.
Fuga quinta in E: Fast.
Interludium: Moderate.
Fuga sexta in E-flat: Quiet.
Interludium: March.
Fuga septima in A-flat: Moderate.
Interludium: Very Broad.
Fuga octava in D: With Strength.

Interludium: Very Fast.
Fuga nona in B-flat: Moderato, Scherzando.
Interludium: Very Quiet.
Fuga decima in D-flat: Moderately Fast, Grazioso.
Interludium: Allegro pesante.
Fuga undecima in B (canon): Slow.
Interludium: Valse.
Fuga duodecima in F-sharp: Very Quiet.
Postludium: Solemn, Broad—Arioso: Quiet, Moderate.

In reviewing this work, a critic for the New York *Herald Tribune* wrote: "The *Ludus* is entirely tonal, being written in the type of twelve-tone scale Hindemith now champions, which is based on acoustic laws. Even the key order in which the fugues are arranged is the result of this system, one that leads to such harmonic freedom that among its consequences is the possibility of answering subjects in the fugues at intervals taboo in the past, such as the third and the tenth. The composer displays his unusual contrapuntal mastery in this opus. . . . There is a double fugue, No. 4, in the nature of a canzona. Fugue No. 9 is especially rich in contrapuntal devices, and in another, Fugue No. 3, the last half reverses the first."

The world première of *Ludus Tonalis* took place at the University of Chicago in February 15, 1944, Willard MacGregor performing. At that time *Modern Music* described the work as "staggering . . . the purely technical level—both as an instance of contrapuntal skill probably unequalled since Bach and as an investigation of the possibilities of the piano as a virtuoso instrument. . . . This aspect of Hindemith's power probably surprises no one. But the depth of expressiveness and the variety of moods are qualities for which some, unaware of the continual ripening of Hindemith's musical personality in the last decade, may have been unprepared."

1945 WHEN LILACS LAST IN THE DOORYARD BLOOM'D: *A Requiem for Those We Love,* for soprano, contralto, baritone, chorus and orchestra.

The Collegiate Chorale, and its founder-director, Robert Shaw, commissioned Hindemith to write a large choral work. The year was 1945. Hindemith found his inspiration in the sudden death of President Franklin D. Roosevelt, and his stimulus in his profound grief at this tragedy. He found a ready-made text in Walt Whitman's threnody on Abraham Lincoln, which he used in its entirety. The work, which takes about an hour to perform, was introduced in New York on May 14, 1946.

It has four sections. A slow and stately prelude precedes the opening number, "When lilacs last in the dooryard bloom'd," for baritone and chorus. A tender soprano arioso, "in the swamp, in secluded recesses" follows, leading to an eloquent march for the chorus ("Over the breast of the spring, the land, amid cities"), accompanying the journey of Lincoln's coffin from Washington, D.C., to its burial place in Springfield, Illinois.

The second part comprises an extended section for baritone and chorus ("O western orb, sailing the heaven"), an arioso for soprano ("Sing on, there in the swamp"), two additional numbers for baritone and chorus ("O how shall I warble myself for the dead one there I loved?" and "These and with these, and the breath of my chant"), and a mighty fugal close for chorus.

The soprano opens the third section with a moving air in which a gray-brown bird becomes the symbol for the poet's soul ("Sing on, sing on, you gray-brown bird"). A recitative for baritone, a hymn for baritone and orchestra ("And I knew death, its thought, and the sacred knowledge of death") and a duet for soprano and baritone ("I fled forth to the hiding, receiving night that talks not") are climaxed by the deeply moving death-carol for chorus, "Come lovely and soothing Death."

The final section is possibly the highest flight of eloquence to which the entire work soars. It begins with the exhortation of the baritone "To tally of my soul" and continues with the poignant chorus, "And carried hither and yon through the smoke, and torn and bloody."

When this work was first introduced, Howard Taubman described it as follows in *The New York Times*: "It has passages of true grandeur, like the climax of the fugue that concludes the second of the four movements. It has pages of touching, intimate lyricism, like the arioso fashioned out of the lines beginning, 'Sing on, there in the swamp.' It has a fine atmospheric orchestral prelude. And when the composer brings together the full potential of chorus and orchestra, he sometimes achieves an unforgettable effect. Such a passage is the choral section on the lines following 'coffin that passes through lanes and streets.' "

1945 CONCERTO FOR PIANO AND ORCHESTRA. I. Moderately fast. II. Slow. III. Medley on the Medieval Dance, *Tre Fontane.*

Hindemith composed this concerto on a commission from the pianist Jesús Maria Sanromá, who introduced it with the Cleveland Orchestra, George Szell conducting, on February 27, 1947.

There are three principal subjects developed in the first movement: a theme played in the very opening of the section by the clarinet, and then taken up by the solo piano; a lyrical idea brought up by two clarinets and bass clarinet; and a subject for muted trumpet. The second movement, in simple three-part form, is interesting for its orchestral color and appealing for its pure melodic writing. For his finale, Hindemith created a medley on the fourteenth-century dance theme, *Tre Fontane,* which he found in Volume I of the *Archiv der Musikwissenschaft.* This section opens with a canzone (solo piano) and develops into a march and a slow waltz. The melody of *Tre Fontane* returns in the piano and orchestra to conclude the work.

1946 SYMPHONIA SERENA, for orchestra. I. Moderately fast. II. Geschwindmarsch by Beethoven, Paraphrase. III. Colloquy. IV. Gay.

Antal Dorati, then music director of the Dallas Symphony Orchestra, commissioned Hindemith to write a new orchestral work for his organization. On February 2, 1947, Dorati introduced it with the Dallas Symphony Orchestra in Dallas.

For this première Dorati provided an analysis of the work which is complete and authoritative: "The first movement is in sonata form. . . . It is very alive and vivid music, with contrasting and strong themes . . . developed in the usual symphonic fashion. . . . The second movement takes the place of the scherzo. Under a fluent and steady current of woodwind passages, which provide a continuous thematic background, the Beethoven theme (a military march composed by Beethoven between 1809 and 1810) is stated in little bits at a time first, and gradually becomes stronger, more and more coherent, and develops into a very fast march, with which the scherzo closes brilliantly. The third movement is written for string orchestra divided into two groups. The first puts forth a serious and tender slow theme. The second group plays a faster scherzando passage, pizzicato. These two sections are connected by a recitative-like passage for two solo violins, one of them playing backstage. . . . The finale is the most complex and challenging of the four movements. It introduces a wealth of new thematic material, and . . . is of tremendous impact, and at the same time, full of enormous contrapuntal detail. Its form is quite new and individual, yet the roots are clearly entrenched in the classical symphony finale form, which is a mixture of the old sonata and rondo forms."

1949 CONCERTO FOR WOODWINDS, HARP AND ORCHESTRA. I. Moderately Fast. II. Grazioso. III. Rondo: rather Fast.

This concerto was the fruit of a commission from the Alice M. Ditson Fund of Columbia University, but it was written as a birthday gift for the composer's wife. The first performance took place in New York on May 15, 1949, Thor Johnson conducting. Klaus Roy, program annotator for the Cleveland Orchestra described this work as essentially a "fun piece," somewhere between chamber and orchestral music. He sees the first movement as a "leisurely musical stroll" with each of the participants contributing "his busy share of linear energy. . . . The solo instruments have brief but virtuosic cadenzas, in a section marked 'free.' The 'head-theme' of the beginning becomes inevitably the closing phrases." The second movement dispenses with trumpets and trombones, while the horns at one point double the lower strings. "The *idea* prevailing in the outer sections is that of the canon—imitations of voices at close range. . . . In the middle section, the woodwinds have a broad unison melody over a tapestry of agile strings; then the roles are reversed." The concluding rondo reminds us that the concerto was the composer's gift to his wife in that it playfully quotes, in solo clarinet, the "Wedding March" from Mendelssohn's *A Midsummer Night's Dream* suite.

1950 SINFONIETTA IN E, for orchestra. I. Fast. II. Adagio and Fugato; Allegretto. III. Intermezzo and Ostinato; Presto. IV. Recitative and Rondo.

The Louisville Orchestra in Kentucky commissioned Hindemith to write this Sinfonietta, which it introduced under the direction of Robert Whitney on March 1, 1950. Like the Concerto described above, the music makes a frequent excursion into humor. H. W. Hauschild, in his review, described the first movement as "polyphonic in the manner of a concerto grosso"; it proceeds in the continuous sweep of an opening movement in a Bach Brandenburg Concerto. The second movement has two parts, the first "reminiscent of the slow movement of *Mathis der Maler* and the second a scherzo-like fugato for woodwinds and brasses." The subject for the third-movement ostinato passes from one group of instruments to another. The concluding movement "abounds in vivacity and light humor that suggests the playing of children."

1950 DIE HARMONIE DER WELT (THE HARMONY OF THE WORLD), opera in five acts, with text by the composer. First performance: Munich, August 11, 1957.

DIE HARMONIE DER WELT, Symphony. I. Musica Instrumentalis. III. Musica Humana. III. Musica Mundane.

The setting of this opera is the Thirty Years' War and its main character is the renowned astronomer and mathematician, Johannes Kepler, and his relationship to the social and political problems of his time. The five acts are subdivided into fourteen scenes in portrarying what H. H. Stuckenschmidt described as "an action about the life and work of Kepler and about all the events that either furthered or hampered the astronomer's quest for harmony. . . . Kepler is shown on his eternal wanderings through Prague, Linz, Güglingen, Sagan, and Regensburg. Three female characters play an important part in his life: his mother Katharina, a mystical woman well versed in herbology, accused of being a witch, sentenced by court and saved by her own son; his little daughter Susanna by his first marriage; and his second wife, also named Susanna, a carpenter's daughter, whom he married against opposition, but who chose to share the life of the great astronomer."

"This is . . . no opera in the usual sense," said Everett Helm in *The New York Times,* "but rather a pageant of events and conditions. . . . Kepler is treated almost symbolically, as are other figures as well. A strong philosophical, speculative and ethical tendency underlies and motivates the work. It is in a sense a grandiose essay in music on the subject of cosmic order."

H. H. Stuckenschmidt regards the following as some of the striking features of the opera: "It strange division into symphonic, highly contrapuntal movements of a massiveness reminding us of Bruckner, and folk-melodies reflecting the spirit of the Baroque age. . . . Hindemith's great musicianship lies in his polyphony, in his fugue-like choruses, in his arias without obbligato accompaniments (such as the Venus aria in the final scene). . . . The magnificent final scene, when the very signs of the zodiac come to life and march across the stage, is based on a passacaglia theme with rising and falling fifths—an inspiration of Bruckner-like pathos and majestic grandeur."

As he had done previously with *Mathis der Maler,* Hindemith extracted some of the music of his opera score and adapted it into a symphony, which was introduced in Basle, Switzerland, on January 24, 1952, Paul Sacher conducting. The first movement describes Kepler's unhappy childhood, its main theme being announced by trumpets. This is followed by a march and a fugato. The second movement discourses on his spiritual evolution. Strings and clarinets present a broad and stately melody. The ensuing oboe solo is marked in the score as "quiet with elegiac expression" and an epilogue in waltz-time is "like a wistful dance sounding from afar." The third movement, a passacaglia, treats of mundane existence. A fugal subject, with which this movement opens, becomes the nine-measure theme for an extended passacagalia consisting of nine variations. An interruption comes with a gentle interlude for flute, answered by bassoon, and a passage marked in the score as "slow, mysterious, and delicate." The passacaglia theme then returns with twelve additional variations. The movement, and the symphony, ends with a coda.

GUSTAV HOLST 1874–1934

Literary influences played an important part in Holst's earliest works. Always an avid reader of poetry, his passion for Walt Whitman and his admiration for William Morris are discernible in the *Walt Whitman Overture* (1899), *The Mystic Trumpeter,* for soprano and orchestra (1904), and the second movement of the *Cotswolds Symphony* (1900), which he dedicated to the memory of William Morris.

In or about 1905, religious philosophy—as found in Sanskrit literature—began influencing Holst's musical thinking. *Sita* (1906), an opera based on an episode from the *Ramayana;* four groups of choral hymns composed to texts from *Rig-Veda* (1912); and an opera di camera, *Savitri,* based upon an episode from *Mahabharata* (1908) are all products of this period. Not the methods of Indian music (though the exotic scales and irregular rhythms of Eastern music can be detected) but the mysticism, poetry and spiritual overtones of Eastern philosophy interested Holst.

By 1915, Holst had more or less abandoned the oriental trend to arrive at his own identity. He now completed two works which were instantly successful, and which to this day remain his most frequently played works—*St. Paul's Suite* and *The Planets,* both for orchestra. With skill in harmonic and rhythmic writing, a wealth of orchestral color, and a genuinely affecting melody evolved from English folk music, Holst here arrived at full maturity.

After World War I, Holst's style became more austere. His interest in English folk music, first aroused in 1906, finally made him seek out a simpler style, a purer and more objective approach, compression and condensation. He never did attempt to imitate English folk songs; and only on rare occasions did he actually incorporate folk materials in his works. It is the artistic impulses behind the English song that impressed him. At the same time, he became drawn more and more to non-harmonic counterpoint and to the utmost freedom in the use of tonality. The strength and passionate speech and brilliance of color which were found in *The Planets* now gave way to the lean, concise and restrained music of the *Twelve Songs*; to lyrics of Humbert Wolfe (1902); and the Concerto for Two Violins and Orchestra (1929), the latter introduced in London on April 3, 1930. The music of this last period of Holst's creative life, however, has never gained either the circulation or the popularity of some of his earlier efforts.

Holst was born in Cheltenham, England, on September 21, 1874. His mother, a concert pianist, taught him the elements of music. In 1893, Holst entered the Royal College of Music, where he won a scholarship in composition. After completing his studies, Holst played the trombone in several orchestras. In 1901, he married Isabel Harrison, a singer in a chorus which Holst was then directing. Two years later, he assumed his first teaching post. For about two decades, Holst was active as a teacher of music at the St. Paul's Girls' School, at Morley College, and at the Royal College of Music.

During World War I, he helped organize the musical activities of British troops stationed in the Near East. In February of 1923, he suffered a concussion as a result of a fall. His physical deterioration compelled him to give up all musical activities except composing. Nevertheless, he was able to make a brief visit to the United States to lecture at the University of Michigan at Ann Arbor and at Harvard. For the next decade, he lived in seclusion, from which he emerged briefly in 1932 to revisit the United States, where he conducted a concert of his compositions with the Boston Symphony and lectured at Harvard. He died in London on May 25, 1934.

1913 ST. PAUL'S SUITE, for orchestra, op. 29. no. 2. I. Jig. II. Ostinato. III. Intermezzo. IV. Finale.

This delightful music was written for the school orchestra of St. Paul's Girls' School in Hammersmith of which Holst was musical director. It was written as an expression of gratitude for the new music wing, with a special soundproof studio, which the school had built that year for Holst.

The influence of the English folk song is strongly felt in this music. Occasionally, actual folk themes are quoted; most often, however, the music derives both its rhythmic impetus and the simplicity and modal character of its melody and harmony from folk tunes.

The opening Jig (Vivace) presents a robust theme in octave unison; the time changes frequently between 6/8 and 9/8. A contrasting subject follows. The second movement (Presto) has the character of a perpetual motion, with the second violins setting into motion a figure that runs continuously throughout the movement. A beautiful cantabile melody in solo violin, over plucked string chords, dominates the third section (Andante con moto). A contrasting animated part follows (Vivace). In the finale (Allegro), two famous English folk songs are quoted: "The Dargason" (which is repeated thirty times with various harmonic and rhythmic variations) and the ever-popular "Greensleeves," which appears as a contrapuntal countersubject in the cellos.

1916 THE PLANETS, suite for orchestra. op. 32. I. Mars, the Bringer of War. II. Venus, the Bringer of Peace. III. Mercury, the Winged Messenger. IV. Jupiter, the Bringer of Jollity. V. Saturn, the Bringer of Old Age. VI. Uranus, the Magician. VII. Neptune, the Mystic.

What is unquestionably Holst's most popular work in the United States and one of his finest, was written between the years of 1914 and 1916. A private performance conducted by H. Balfour Gardiner on September 29, 1918, introduced it to a select audience. Five of the seven movements ("Venus" and "Neptune" were omitted) were publicly introduced on February 27, 1919, with Sir Adrian Boult directing the London Philharmonic. The complete suite was heard on November 15, 1920, under Albert Coates.

In an interview, Holst explained: "These pieces were suggested by the astrological significance of the planets; there is no program music in them, neither have they any connection with the deities of classical mythology bearing the same names. If any guide to the music is required, the subtitle to each piece will be found sufficient, especially if it be used in a broad sense. For instance, Jupiter brings jollity in the ordinary sense, and also the more ceremonial kind of rejoicing associated with religious or national festivities. Saturn brings not only physical decay, but also a vision of fulfillment. Mercury is the symbol of the mind."

Strong rhythms and counterrhythms, and a vigorous melodic subject stated by trumpets and horns, bring up the martial character of the first section. A gentler mood is evoked with "Venus"—a soft horn call, answered by the delicate music of flutes, immediately brings up an atmosphere which to Richard Capell suggests "cool, clear air." Swift-winged movement is evoked in the third part, a fleet scherzo. Good spirits abound in "Jupiter," which has been called "an overture for an English country festival"; the core of this part is a fully articulated folk song which spans some forty bars. According to Capell, "a profound peacefulness" pervades the fifth movement. Bright-faced humor returns in "Uranus," who, Capell explains, "might have been called the god of laughter if after a point the prodigiousness of his pranks did not pass a joke." *The Planets* ends in an atmosphere of quiet mystery. "Neptune" is a movement that is played entirely pianissimo, "its hushed interrogation," says Capell, "coming as a beautiful relief, slackening the strain set up by the dynamic assertiveness that we have heard in the hour." In the final pages, a hidden choir of women's voices is heard on a sustained note, with the flute and clarinet as a background.

ARTHUR HONEGGER 1892–1955

Honegger first became known (at the close of World War I) as a member of the so-called school of young composers known as "The French Six." (The history of the origin of "The French Six" is described in the section on Georges Auric.) Honegger might mingle socially with the other members of "The Six"; he might even allow his works to be played with theirs. But he never wholeheartedly subscribed to some of the principles and directions to which, for a while at any rate, they were dedicated. For one thing, their partiality for jazz and music-hall idioms never intrigued him (though even he succumbed briefly to the vogue for "everyday music" with his Piano

Concertino, and one or two less notable items). He said at that time: "I do not have the cult of the carnival and the music hall, but on the contrary that of chamber and symphonic music in all their most grave and austere aspects." Nor could he adopt their fetish for neo-classic simplicity. Strong-willed, artistically independent, Honegger listened to the aesthetic discussions of his friends (who were influenced and inspired by Erik Satie) and to their music. Then in his composing he went his own way, in those directions to which his own conscience led him—now backwards in time to a neo-Handelian style in *Le Roi David,* now forward in his highly discordant symbol of the machine age, *Pacific 231.*

During the 1920s, he developed a style that was muscular in rhythm, spiced with discord, occasionally made stark and austere by polytonality and linear writing. The tonality tends to be free. Yet lyricism is not abandoned. Even before *Pacific 231*, his writing had become crystallized—in his incidental music to *Le Dit des jeux du monde,* heard in Paris on December 2, 1921, and in the powerful "mimed symphony" *Horace victorieux,* introduced at Lausanne on October 30, 1921. After *Pacific 231*, which had come in 1923, the style became increasingly bolder and more individual, with the Biblical opera, *Judith,* mounted at Monte Carlo on February 13, 1926, and with the orchestral *Rugby.*

Then, in the 1930s, Honegger began to touch his music with mysticism, with spiritual values, with deep religious conviction. This tendency first became evident in two oratorios in the 1930s, still regarded among Honegger's masterworks: *Jeanne d'Arc au bûcher* and *La Danse des morts.* And this new vein was tapped particularly in his last symphonies, to which he confided his deepest and most personal thoughts.

"The bulk of his work," says Allen Hughes, "represents a continuation of the late nineteenth-century tendency to create effect through the piling up of sound on sound, to add the organ (and even powerful electronic instruments) to the conventional orchestra, and to combine them with multiple choirs and soloists. Honegger's aesthetic was, in short, derived from the age preceding that in which he lived. But he made use of virtually all the musical materials the twentieth century offered him. Polychordality, polytonality, and atonality appear freely in his works as aids to expression. None of them, however, interested him as ends in themselves or as objects of experimentation."

Honegger was born in Le Havre, France, on March 10, 1892. His parents were Swiss, and though Honegger was born and lived most of his life in France, he remained a Swiss citizen until the end of his life. He received his early musical training from his mother and local teachers. For two years, he attended the Zurich Conservatory, and after that, he was a pupil of Gedalge, Widor and Vincent d'Indy at the Paris Conservatory. While still there, he wrote several songs in which he was influenced by Debussy. Performances of several piano pieces, his first string quartet, the orchestral prelude *Aglavaine et Sélysette,* and his first violin sonata took place in Paris between 1916 and 1917. He was a member of the *Nouveaux Jeunes*, a group of young French composers who gave a concert of their works on January 15, 1918. (The other members were Roland-Manuel, Honegger, Tailleferre, Poulenc and Auric.) And he attracted publicity and attention when his name was linked by the critic, Henri Collet, with those of Durey, Milhaud, Auric, Tailleferre and Poulenc as "The French Six." Honegger's fame throughout the music world first came about through the success of his oratorio *Le Roi David*.

On May 10, 1926, Honegger married Andrée Vaurabourg, the concert pianist who for a number of years had been introducing his piano compositions. In 1929, Honegger paid his first visit to the United States; between January 2 and March 28, he appeared in thirty concerts. During World War II, Honegger remained in Paris where he was active in the Resistance movement. He paid a second visit to the United States in 1947 to teach a master class in composition at the Berkshire Music Centre at Tanglewood, but was unable to fulfil this obligation because of a heart attack. His health deteriorated after that. In spite of this, he was able to complete several major works, all of them on the highest possible artistic level. Honegger died in Paris on November 27, 1955.

1921–1923 PASTORALE D'ÉTÉ, for orchestra.
PACIFIC 231, for orchestra.

Several conductors (Toscanini was one) liked to program these two compositions together on the same program as a study in contrasts. *Pastorale d'été* (1921) is quiet and bucolic, while *Pacific 231* (1923) is discordant and full of motor energy. The former was introduced in Paris on February 12, 1921. It is a gentle Nature etching. Two themes comprise its musical material: one for the horn, heard immediately after three introductory measures; the other, more vivacious, for clarinet.

Pacific 231 was one of the earliest musical compositions interpreting the machine age to achieve international renown. It glorified the locomotive. As a child in Le Havre, Honegger used to watch trains for hours at an end. His passion for trains persisted on into his manhood.

In writing *Pacific 231*, he did not try to imitate locomotive noises but, as he told an interviewer, to translate into music "the visual impressions made by the locomotive, and the physical sensation of it." Honegger explained further: "*Pacific 231* sets forth the objective contemplation; the quiet breathing machine in repose, its effort in starting, then gradual increase in speed, leading from the lyrical to the pathetic condition of a train of three hundred tons hurling itself through the night at a speed of one hundred and twenty kilometers an hour."

Despite the composer's avowed intentions, the work is a realistic portrait. What we get in this music is not so much the composer's emotional reactions to the locomotive as a picture of the locomotive itself—its puffings, snortings and increased momentum. It is for this reason that Constant Lambert put in a minority vote for *Pacific 231* when he wrote: "A little more thought might have told the composer that music which depends on varying degrees of stylized noise and speed for its expression is, on the face of it, the last medium in which to attempt an evocation of non-stylized noise and speed."

Pacific 231 was introduced in Paris at a Koussevitzky concert on May 8, 1924. It was a huge success. In 1924, the discords of *Pacific 231* were exciting and provocative. Today, of course, there is not much about them that is startling; and the reproduction of the sounds and movement of a train now seems almost naïve in its realism.

Honegger followed *Pacific 231* with two other short works for orchestra with the intention of creating a three-movement symphonic suite. The second was *Rugby* (1928), a description of a rugby contest. Its world première took place on December 31, 1928, in a soccer stadium in Paris during the intermission of an international rugby match between France and England. The third composition was *Mouvement symphonique No. 3* (1933), its first performance taking place in Berlin on March 27, 1933.

1921 LE ROI DAVID (KING DAVID), oratorio for narrator, soloists, chorus and orchestra.

Early in 1921, Honegger was commissioned to write music for *King David,* a "dramatic psalm" by René Morat, scheduled for performance at the Théâtre du Jorat at Mézières (near Lausanne), Switzerland, on June 11, 1921. He adopted a conventional pattern and wrote a formal oratorio. Though on occasion brusque harmonies and atonality bring suggestions of the later Honegger, the form and approach are reminiscent of Handel. The première performance was outstandingly successful. For the time being, anyway, Honegger became a favorite of the conservative group of French composers.

In 1922, Honegger reorchestrated the oratorio and adapted it for concert performance. Introduced on February 2, 1923, at Winterthur, *King David* once again proved a huge success. It was heard in Paris in 1924, in New York in 1925, and in Zurich and Rome in 1926. Then it virtually encircled the rest of the music world.

Varied elements go into the makeup of Honegger's polyglot style: some of the music is Hebraic or oriental in its intervallic structure and in the contour of the melodies; some of the music is Handelian, particularly in the polyphonic writing for the chorus; some of the tunes have the simple and direct appeal of folk songs. What gives this music its immense effect is its consistent deep religious conviction, regardless of what style is employed, and at times its deeply moving spiritual overtones.

The oratorio is made up of three large sections, which, in turn, are parceled out into twenty-eight smaller segments. In the first part, we confront David as a young shepherd and trace his career through his battle with Goliath and his conflict with King Saul. Here fourteen sections are separated by spoken narrative, beginning with an atmospheric orchestral introduction in which an oboe offers a haunting melody that derives its oriental personality through the consistent use of augmented seconds. In this section, we find the following noteworthy episodes: David's shepherd's song in the style of a folk melody; a psalm sung by unison chorus, Bach-like in its nobility; the stirring march of the Philistines, with its original orchestral timbres; and the poignant Jewish song of mourning.

There are only two extended numbers in the second part: a festive song and the dance before the Ark to celebrate the crowning of King David. In the closing part of this segment, we hear a stirring and joyous Alleluia.

In the concluding part, King David is carried up to the time of his death. Here we find two deeply moving songs of penitence; an impressive instrumental march of the Israelites; and a dynamic psalm. The work ends with a return of the Alleluia that closed the second part, but sung contrapuntally against a chorale to produce a stunning effect.

"The nobility of the subject," says Arthur Hutchings, "and Honegger's sincerity in its treatment (his first Biblical setting) carry us through this long procession of scenes, for which he provides apt and often simple music. Many of the choruses are only in two parts and predominantly diatonic. Atmosphere is evoked in a few bars, as in the opening (the barbaric march of the victorious army). . . . In the final section, David sings two penitential psalms (musically welded together by a common theme) . . . and these are among the most moving parts of a work that is far more human than any other by Honegger."

King David was staged as an opera in Paris on October 21, 1960.

1924 CONCERTINO FOR PIANO AND ORCHESTRA I. Allegro molto moderato. II. Larghetto sostenuto. III. Allegro.

This disarmingly pleasing little concerto is one of Honegger's few works to simulate a popular music-hall idiom. It is the kind of jaunty, insouciant music the French wrote so well in the 1920s—occasionally impudent and malicious, but always ingratiating for its simple approach, fresh lyricism and rhythmic vitality.

On May 23, 1925, the concertino was introduced in Paris. Andrée Vaurabourg (then Honegger's fiancée, later his wife) was soloist, and the orchestra was conducted by Serge Koussevitzky.

The first movement begins with a sustained dialogue between piano and orchestra. A syncopated theme for piano appears after a run. Following a brief fugal development, the opening material is repeated. The principal material of the second movement is a piquant little melody for the piano, with various embellishments by the orchestra. The interest here is exclusively lyrical, just as the interest in the finale is primarily rhythmic. In the closing movement, both piano and orchestra participate in highly syncopated passages as the music gathers force and grows into a telling climax, which, however, is dissipated.

1935 JEANNE D'ARC AU BÛCHER (JOAN OF ARC AT THE STAKE), dramatic oratorio for two narrators, solo voices, chorus and orchestra.

Honegger wrote this oratorio for Ida Rubinstein, who appeared in the title role when the work was introduced, in Basle, Switzerland, on May 12, 1938. In 1939, it was heard in Orléans and Paris; in 1940, in Brussels. After successful performances in most of the principal cities of Europe, it was introduced in the United States on January 1, 1948, by the New York Philharmonic Orchestra, directed by Charles Munch. Vera Zorina appeared as Joan of Arc.

The composer has designated the oratorio as a *mimodrame,* by which he meant that he intended it as a stage production, with scenery and costumes. However, the work has been heard more frequently as a concert-oratorio, though sometimes with slight concessions to stage procedures as to lighting and costuming.

When *Joan of Arc* was introduced in Basle, Roger Secretain provided the following notes: "The work . . . is in an unusual dramatic form, on two separate stages. From the beginning to the end of the spectacle Joan is seen fastened to the stake. Her bonds permit her to make the Sign of the Cross only with difficulty—this sign, which, Claudel says, "is the development of the four cardinal points of the human race . . . which is also the quartering of Joan between her earthly destiny and her divine vocation.' The cross is the struggle between earth and heaven. But Joan never flinches for a moment before the death which will clearly be conquered at last—at last convinced. She obeys the injunction of the Virgin who, from the top of the pillar, conjures her to let herself be embraced by her 'Brother Fire' . . . to let herself be drawn into heaven.

"As well as Joan's stake—symbol of the final sacrifice, where she stands immovably throughout the oratorio—one can see the unfolding of various images of Joan's life, as through Joan's own eyes. The synthetic vision typifies the genius of Claudel. Through his function as a poet, he sets the action in the past as well as the present. She is a presence simultaneously in all corners of the earth, in possession of time and space, exposed to all earthly temptation. The hour has come for this sublime heroine, he says, 'to understand what she has done; to utter the supreme *Yes!*"

The part of Joan is exclusively a speaking role; so is that of Frère Dominique, who opens the book of Joan's life and recalls episodes which float in and out of the drama—her heroism, her prosecution, her martyrdom—so that the past becomes the present. Joan is puzzled at the evil things for which the Church has condemned her; but Frère Dominique reveals that these are not ministers of God but beasts in the spurious trappings of divinity. Since the Paul Claudel drama has aspects of a miracle play—with emphasis on mysticism and symbolism—symbolic figures appear in the guise of animals performing human judicial functions, potentates are labeled Pride, Ignorance or Avarice, and cards in a card game appear as the game of war and state intrigues. The bestial scenes (symbols of the earthy aspects of France and her people of that time) are reenacted and against them is set the purity and faith of Joan, culminating in her triumphant release from the bonds of flesh in the agony of fire.

Honegger's score is a remarkably integrated network of music, spoken dialogue, dialogue with musical background, choruses, choral readings and so forth. Dialogue is often set over the most expressive orchestral background, in which the composer utilizes the fullest resources of his technique and creativity to point up every changing mood and nuance of his text. Extraordinarily effective, too, is the way in which, in some of the passages, lyricism is blended with recitative to achieve an effective song-speech.

There are a prologue and eleven scenes in the oratorio. The scenes have the following titles: I. The Voices of Heaven; II. The Book; III. The Voices of Earth; IV. Joan Delivered to the Beasts; V. Joan at the Stake; VI. The Kings, or the Invention of the Card Game; VII. Catherine and Marguerite; VIII. The King Who Goes to Rheims; IX. Joan's Sword; X. "Trimazo"—Rehearsal of the Merry Month of May; XI. Joan of Arc in Flames.

In the prologue, an extended choral narrative describes the chaos of ideals and consciences in France. The people are crying out to be saved. Throughout this episode, there is a recurring refrain: "In France there was a girl whose name is Joan." An atmospheric orchestral interlude then precedes a wordless chant which ends with the cries, "Joan, Joan, Joan." After that, through flashbacks, commentaries, asides, and dramatic scenes, the various highlights of Joan's life are detailed; at the same time, pointed criticisms are made of the integrity of church and society, and the low state of the people's morality.

Some of the most eloquent music is heard in the closing two sections. The first begins with children's voices exclaiming, "'This May, the month of May." This is immediately followed by a little folk tune chanted by Joan in recollection of her girlhood in Lorraine. It is a girlish little tune, combining folk song and dramatic recitative. This leads into the final part of the oratorio, "The Burning of Joan." Bitterly, the chorus comments on the fact that "Joan, the holy Joan" has been condemned as a sorcerer and a disbeliever. Joan replies with wonder that she should be accused by the people of France who stand ready to burn her. Soon she expresses her fear of the flames. But when the Virgin and the Saints call down to her from Heaven, what Joan feels is not fear but triumph. "I feel delight rising triumphant," she exclaims proudly. "Now I feel God rising triumphant." To this, the chorus of the saints and children's voices contribute the final comment: "Greater love hath no man than this—to give his life for those he loves."

1938 LA DANSE DES MORTS (THE DANCE OF THE DEAD), dramatic oratorio for solo voices, chorus and orchestra.

In the Spring of 1938, Paul Claudel (who three years earlier had provided Honegger with the text for *Jeanne d'Arc au bûcher*) became fascinated in Basle with various pictures of Death, particularly woodcuts by Holbein the Younger. These pictorial images about death gave him the idea for a new oratorio. After returning to Paris, he completed a text, combining his own mystical and religious thoughts with excerpts from both the Old Testament (Ezekiel and the Book of Job) and the New. Three choral exhortations provide the essence of Claudel's text. They are:

"Remember, man, that you are dust and to dust you will return."

"Remember, man, that you are spirit, and that the flesh is more than the outward dress, and that the spirit is more than the flesh, and that the eye is more than the face, and love is more than death."

"Remember, man, that you are stone, and on that stone will I build my church."

The oratorio has seven parts played without interruption. Here is how Arno Huth described the work in detail in *Modern Music*: "Prolonged thunderclaps (nineteen measures and fortissimo) precede the first exhortation and the Dialogue of the prophet and God; a march macabre, opening pianissimo, announces the awakening of the dead and leads with a resounding fortissimo to the apparition of a great army. Sotto voce, the small chorus intones the second exhortation, repeated several times, even when the large chorus is singing *La Danse des morts,* the central part of the work. The cries of the declaimer, 'The Pope! . . . The Bishop! . . . The King! . . . The Chevalier! . . . The Philosopher!' . . . recall the Holbein pictures and are a poetic counterpoint. The rhythms of the old popular song '*Sur le pont d'Avigon*' and of '*Carmagnole*' inspire the dance. United and opposed, they create an orgy which is finally interrupted by the theme of '*Dies Irae*'. . . . A Lamento, over an overlong monologue by the baritone over a transparent orchestra, represents repentance. Then follows the '*Sanglots,*' a strange choral song in which the men's and women's voices exchange vocalizations on a Latin text. . . . New thunderclaps . . . announce the '*Reponse de Dieu,*' a prophecy of the Resurrection and the return of the people of Israel to the Promised Land. Anticipating the 'promise themes,' the music develops in an ecstatic and mystic movement, '*Ésperance dans la Croix,*' related in its parables and solo parts to the Passion. Meanwhile the chorus prophesies that Israel shall be chosen, and then, in a powerful declamation by the voices in unison, comes the Revelation of the Lord (also recited in Latin). The epilogue, '*L'Affirmation,*' underscores the Christian element of the poem; stressing each syllable and shouting the word 'Pierre,' the whole chorus sings the last exhortation. After a sudden decrescendo, the work ends with vocalizations by the solo soprano to evoke the '*rire celeste.*' "

Huth goes on to describe Honegger's music in the following way: "His amazing use of different mediums—the speaker, soloists, choruses, orchestra and organ—as well as his sureness of forms, again prove his mastery. No matter how various the form elements, they are all incorporated into one entity, subordinated to a dramatic will and used for dramatic effect. The dance of the dead and the final choruses have a sweeping, expressive power, the air is surcharged with emotion."

The world première took place in Basle, Switzerland, on March 2, 1940.

1941 SYMPHONY NO. 2, for string orchestra. I. Molto moderato; Allegro. II. Adagio mesto. III. Vivace non troppo.

Honegger's Second Symphony was written in the gray year of 1941, when the Nazi troops were in Paris. Willi Reich believes that the music has caught "much of the mood of occupied Paris." Few other Honegger works are so deeply felt, or reach for such emotional heights.

An ostinato figure for violas, heard early in the first movement and repeated throughout, provides an atmosphere of gloom, which is intermittently interrupted by dissonances and vigorous sweep of defiant rhythms. Despair is also evident in the second movement, a passacaglia consisting of eight variations on a ground bass. This part opens gently enough in the violins, but midway grows in intense suffering until uncontrolled grief erupts. The finale, however, has overtones of good spirits, as one theme after another is nimbly projected before the presto-like coda is realized. Optimism is sounded loud and clear in the chorale of the closing page.

The Second Symphony was dedicated to the Swiss conductor Paul Sacher, who introduced it in Basle on May 18, 1942.

1946 SYMPHONY NO. 3 ("Liturgique"). I. Allegro marcato. II. Adagio. III. Andante con moto.

Honegger dedicated his Third Symphony to Charles Munch, who introduced it in Zurich on August 17, 1946. Munch believes that this work "poses the problem of humanity vis-à-vis God," expressing as it does the revolt of man against a Higher Will, then his voluntary subjugation to and acceptance of that Will.

The composer has provided explanatory Latin subtitles to the three movements. The first is a "*Dies Irae*" which, to Arthur Hoerée, "is irresistible in its fulguration, in its abruptness, its panic and trepidation, its ever-present lyricism." To Hoerée the second movement, a "*De Profundis*," is a "long cry of distress"; and the closing movement. '*Dona nobis pacem*,' aspires to "new peace through a long phrase in the violins whose inspiration borders upon the sublime."

In his program annotations for the New York Philharmonic, R. C. Bagar described the symphony as "dissonant, although not excessively, and a good deal of its structure is polyphonic. It is quite rhythmical in two end movements, impressively so in the first, with its vigorously syncopated phrases, the marked accents and the swift give-and-take, while in the third the rhythm subsides after the excitement. The second movement is songful, perhaps prayerful."

1946 SYMPHONY NO. 4, "DELICIAE BASILENSES" ("BASLE DELIGHTS"). I. Lento e misterioso Allegro. II. Larghetto. III. Allegro.

The subtitle for this symphony springs from the fact that this work makes use of old popular melodies from Basle, Switzerland. The symphony was written to honor the twentieth anniversary of the Basle Chamber Orchestra of which Paul Sacher was the conductor. When the symphony was introduced by that organization and conductor, on January 21, 1947, Honegger explained that the symphony gave "evidence of a connection with Haydn or Mozart in spirit and form. The instrumentation . . . virtually relates it to chamber music. The writing is transparent and, above all, linear."

Honegger continued: "The first movement . . . expresses a 'state of spirit.' In the midst of odious and stupid conditions of life which are imposed upon us, it raises the hope of an escape from such an atmosphere, as, for instance, to spend a summer in Switzerland surrounded by affectionate friends for whom the musical art still plays a major role. This expectation instils in the composer the urge to create.

"The second movement is based on the old popular song of Basle, '*Z'Basel an mi'm Rhi*, which towards the end of the movement is cited entirely in its original and ingenuous form (horn).

"The finale is of polyphonic construction, a bit complex, perhaps . . . in which the various components are progressively superimposed. The form contains elements of rondo, passacaglia, and fugue. From all of these superpositions there leaps forth the tune of '*Basler Morgenstreich*,' which soars over the stretto of the principal theme, and after a reference to the slow episode of the middle of the movement, there is a quick conclusion, like a cloud of dust which disappears."

1950 SYMPHONY NO. 5, "DI TRE RE." I. Grave. II. Allegretto. III. Allegro marcato.

Honegger's Fifth Symphony came four years after the Fourth, and was heard for the first time in Boston on March 9, 1951, with Charles Munch conducting the Boston Symphony Orchestra.

A mighty chorale for full orchestra opens the symphony, succeeded by a gentler idea, stated first by the clarinets, then by the English horn. The original chorale returns in a gentler vein, after which the movement ends softly. A staccato theme, appearing as a duet for clarinet and first violins, opens the second movement. Following a climax, an Adagio section appears. This Adagio section brings the movement to a close after the original subject has been stated. The third movement is in the nature of a perpetual motion, opening with a staccato phrase for trumpets soon to be taken up by the strings. Despite the rhythmic agility of this movement there is a pronounced suggestion of tragedy.

An interesting integrating feature of this symphony is the recurrence of a drum tap in D, pianissimo, as the last note of each movement. This is the reason why Honegger called his symphony "Di Tre Re," —"Re" being the note "D" in the nomenclature of France, and the phrase itself meaning "the three D's."

ALAN HOVHANESS 1911–

In view of Alan Hovhaness's total involvement with the Eastern world, it is important to remember that he was born in the United States, and that his musical training was thoroughly of the Western world. Nevertheless, from the early 1940s, he felt himself ineluctably drawn to the culture, legends, philosophy, languages, art and music of the East—so much so that he was impelled to destroy all the Western-type music he had thus far produced. From then on, he found the Near East, the Middle East and the Far East a bountiful source of inspiration. Most of his works—including symphonies and concertos—now assumed exotic titles, just as they were musical interpretations of exotic subjects. And his musical writing was now based on Eastern modes; assumed the highly individual stylistic approaches of Eastern music; exploited Eastern instruments. His style was modeled after oriental *ragas* and *talas*. Oriental, too, were his spiraling melodies with their elaborate figurations and arabesques; or the way in which repetition replaced development or variation, and an uninterrupted emotional climate was created through absences of climaxes.

"Its expressive function," Virgil Thomson once said about Hovhaness's music, "is predominantly religious, ceremonial, incantatory, its spiritual content of the purest. . . . The high quality of this music, the purity of its inspiration, is evidenced in the extreme beauty of the melodic material, which is original material, not collected folklore, and in the perfect sweetness of taste that it leaves in the mouth. . . . It brings delight to the ear, and pleasure to the thought. For all its auditory complexity—for ornateness is of the essence—it is utterly simple in feeling, pure in spirit, and high-minded. . . . Among all our American contributions to musical art, which are many, it is one of the most curious and original."

Hovhaness was born in Somerville, Massachusetts, on March 8, 1911. His father, an Armenian, was professor of chemistry at Tufts College. Hovhaness received his early musical training at the piano with Adelaide Proctor and Heinrich Gebhard. Between 1932 and 1934, he attended the New England Conservatory, where he was a composition pupil of Frederick Converse; and in 1942, he studied composition with Bohuslav Martinu at the Berkshire Music Center at Tanglewood.

A symphony, completed in 1933, was introduced at the New England Conservatory and received the Samuel Endicott Prize. Another symphony (1936) was introduced by the BBC Symphony under Leslie Heward in London on March 26, 1939. These and hundreds of other similar works—many of them markedly influenced by Sibelius—were destroyed after Hovhaness became interested in Eastern culture, philosophy and art. An early influence has been the works of an Armenian composer-priest, Gomidas Vartabed. A performance of Indian dances and songs by the Uday Shankar Company in Boston stimulated him further. In 1940, Hovhaness came into direct contact with Armenian liturgical music as organist of the Armenian church of St. James in Watertown, Massachusetts. From this time on, he devoted himself completely to the study of Eastern music, the influence of which can be detected in his three Armenian rhapsodies for orchestra, the piano concerto entitled *Lousadzak*, and the flute concerto called *Elibris*—all completed in 1944. On June 17, 1945, an all-Hovhaness program in New York first drew attention to his unusual compositions. Recognition followed, with a grant from the National Institute of Arts and Letters in 1951, Guggenheim Fellowships in 1953 and 1955, two honorary doctorates in 1958, and in 1959, a Fulbright fellowship for research in oriental music. He was given a hero's welcome in India and Japan during his world tour between 1959 and 1960, where he was the recipient of numerous honors and commissions. He became the first Western musician invited to participate at the annual festival at Madras, India, and to be asked to write music for an orchestra comprising Indian instruments. Hovhaness returned to Japan in the summer of 1962, on a Rockefeller grant, once again to do research. In 1965, he visited the Soviet Union.

1955 MYSTERIOUS MOUNTAIN, for orchestra, op. 132. I. Andante. II. Moderato; Presto. III. Andante con moto.

This is one of Hovhaness's most frequently played works for orchestra. He was commissioned to write it by Leopold Stokowski for the conductor's first appearance with the Houston Symphony. That performance took place in Houston on October 31, 1955, and was also heard by a nationwide audience on an NBC telecast. It was immediately successful. Hubert Roussel wrote in the Houston *Post* that in this composition Hovhaness produced "a texture of the utmost beauty, gentleness, distinction and expression potential. The real mystery of the *Mysterious Mountain* is that it should be so simply, sweetly, innocently lovely in an age that has tried so terribly hard to avoid these impressions in music." Soon after the première, the work was given by major orchestras throughout the United States. During the summer of 1958, Leopold Stokowski introduced it in the Soviet Union.

To the composer, mountains represent "symbols, like pyramids, of man's attempt to know God. Mountains are symbolic meeting places between the mundane and spiritual worlds. To some, the Mysterious Mountain may be the phantom peak, unmeasured, thought to be higher than Everest, as seen from great distances by fliers in Tibet. To some it may be the solitary mountain, the tower of strength over a countryside."

The composer then goes on to describe his music as follows: "The first and last movements are hymn-like and lyrical, using irregular metrical forms. The first subject of the second movement, a double fugue, is developed in a slow vocal style. The rapid second subject is played by the strings with its own counter-subject and with strict four-voice canonic episodes and triple counterpoint episodes. . . . In the last movement a chant . . . is played softly by muted horns and trombones. A giant wave in a thirteen-beat meter rises to a climax and recedes. . . . A middle melody is sung by the oboes and clarinets in a quintuple beat. Muted violins return with the earlier chant, which is gradually given to the full orchestra."

1957 MAGNIFICAT, for four solo voices, chorus and orchestra, op. 157.

The Magnificat—Mary's song of Thanksgiving on being told by the angel Gabriel that she will bear the Son of God—is based on a text from the first chapter of St. Luke. "I have tried," the composer says, "to suggest the mystery, inspiration and mysticism of early Christianity." To give greater authenticity to this expression, Hovhaness here makes extensive use of the non-metrical melodic line of the plainsong.

The work is made up of twelve sections: Celestial Fanfare; Magnificat (chorus); Et Exsultavit (tenor); Quia Respexit (soprano); Omnes Generationes (women's chorus); Quia Fecit Mihi Magna (baritone and chorus); Et Misericordia (soprano); Fecit Potentiam (alto); Esurientes Implevit Bonis (tenor and male chorus); Suscepit Israel (women's chorus); Sicut Locutus Est (baritone and chorus); Gloria Patri (chorus).

The composer provided the following description:

"No. 1. The music opens with a Celestial Fanfare, an introduction beginning with a murmuring passage in the basses which rises to a climax and recedes. Trombone, horn and trumpet sound a long melodic line of religious mood.

"No. 2. Magnificat is for chorus. The organum for all voices leads to a brief fugato, ending again in an organum.

"No. 3. Et Exsultavit is a tenor solo accompanied by murmuring pizzicato passages in the violas.

"No. 4 and No. 5. Quia Respexit is a soprano solo leading to a women's chorus in three parts (Omnes Generationes). The chorus is accompanied by a rhythmless murmuring in the lower strings and harp.

"No. 6. Quia Fecit Mihi Magna is for bass solo and chorus accompanied by a free rhythm in the basses. . . . A wild and stormy rhythmless passage in the strings rises to a thunderous climax and recedes to a pianissimo.

"No. 7. Et Misericordia for soprano solo. Violas and cellos hold a four-note cluster throughout. The oboes play a rapid melody which is taken up by the soprano voice.

"No. 8. Fecit Potentiam for alto voice. . . . A solemn trombone solo sounds the prelude and postlude.

"No. 9. Esurientes Implevit Bonis for tenor solo and men's chorus. A free-rhythm passage in the strings from fortissimo to pianissimo leads to the held 'A' in the men's chorus. In Byzantine style the tenor sings a florid melody over the held 'A.'

"No. 10. Suscepit Israel, for four-part women's chorus. Oboe, string and harp accompany the voices.

"No. 11. Sicut Locutus Est. Bass solo and chorus. An introduction for oboes and horns leads to a passage in the strings. The chorus enters, every voice chanting in its own time, like the superstitious murmuring of a great crowd, rising like a wave of sound and receding again into the distance. A similar passage in the lower strings becomes the background to a bass solo. Later oboes and horns lead to a rhythmless passage in the violins. Again the murmuring chorus rises to a fortissimo climax in free rhythm and diminishes to pianissimo.

"No. 12. Gloria Patri. An introduction for trombone solo accompanied by murmuring basses leads to a rhythmless climax in the strings. 'Gloria' is sounded by the sopranos and then the entire chorus. A heroic melody in the style of a noble galliard is sounded by first and second trumpets and is taken up later by the chorus. The music builds to a final climax."

When the *Magnificat* was given in New York in January of 1964, Miles Kastendieck wrote in the *Journal-American*: "[It] is a beautiful, inspired work, full of haunting melody, mystical harmonic effects, and strong religious feeling. It is music that reaches the listener almost immediately, communicating some of the mysticism surrounding religion and particularly early Christianity. A timeless quality pervades it for Hovhaness blends antiquarian and contemporary sounds ingeniously. Perhaps this very fluidity is the secret of its fascination. There is, of course, the singular idea of murmuring strings to fashion mood and meaning. This combines with free-rhythm passages to create fluid effect. . . . What makes the work particularly interesting is the division between vocal and instrumental writing; the opening celestial fanfare supplies the key, and the vocal organum that follows shows the way."

1964 FLOATING WORLD—UKIYO, ballade for orchestra, op. 209.

"Floating world," the composer informs us, "is an old Japanese Buddhist concept of uncertainty, change, undependability, insubstantial qualities of the world, the only joy being the hope of salvation in the next world. However, a new concept was superimposed during the prosperity of the seventeenth century, when the transitory world became associated with ideas of pleasure, delight and adventure. These two ideas become united. This music is an abstraction of these thoughts, inspired by the genius of the great Japanese playwright, Chikamatsu."

The ballade is dominated by a single dramatic theme. Whirlpools of sound in free rhythms are created by the orchestra, over which fragments of this theme are sounded. A ghostly march intrudes in the middle section, begun softly in percussion alone, then built up powerfully "like the mysterious procession of past civilizations and heroes, breaking off in a cry," the composer tells us. After an outburst of free rhythmic sound in the entire orchestra, the main theme is recalled in bells and brass as a prayer of supplication for salvation. The composition ends in a whirlwind crescendo.

This composition was written for and dedicated to André Kostelanetz. Its world première took place in Salt Lake City on January 30, 1965.

1965 FANTASY ON JAPANESE WOODPRINTS, for xylophone and orchestra, op. 211.

This composition consists of a number of mood pictures inspired by woodblock prints of old Japan, which are "evocations," the composer explains, "of his love for Japan, its extraordinary art, and vitality." This work was introduced in Chicago on July 4, 1965, with Yoichi Hiraoka as xylophone soloist and Seiji Ozawa, conducting. A few months later, under the direction of André Kostelanetz, it was introduced in the country that had inspired it—first in Tokyo, and then in Nagoya.

Edward Downes, program annotator for the New York Philharmonic Orchestra, informs us that "the opening picture, of the greatest delicacy, consists of alternating tone colors: the first an ethereal xylophone against the background of his sustained strings and murmuring pizzicatos, the second an ensemble of chromatically sliding oboes and clarinets against murmuring harp figures and, again, high sustained string tone. The third picture, of a more ceremonial cast, employs solemn brass with slow moving strings and percussion." A series of vignettes follows—described by the composer as "humorous, clown-like" leading towards a "wild festival scene" in which the orchestra imitates an orchestra of ancient instruments with microtonal slides.

JACQUES IBERT 1890–1962

The lighter side of Jacques Ibert expressed itself in music that has gaiety as well as levity, sardonic humor as well as wit. This is the style in which he wrote several of his most popular orchestral compositions (the *Divertissement*, for example, and the *Concerto da camera*), as well as the satirical opera *Le Roi d'Yvetot,* produced in Paris on January 15, 1930, and in the United States, at Tanglewood in Lenox, Massachusetts on August 7, 1950. The serious Ibert (beginning with his most popular orchestral work, *Escales*) utilizes impressionistic writing and methods the way Maurice Ravel did. Here Ibert was a neo-impressionist, partial to colorful orchestration, subtle effects, chords moving in parallel motion. His writing had clarity, deftness and refinement; his technique was self-assured. He was ever, as André George said of him, "an artist of breeding. . . . His musical temperament expands with singular felicity in the orchestra, where he revels in the subtlest management of exquisite sound values. . . . His music is always found to reflect his apt sense of color and his gifts of contriving those iridescent effects which are so striking a feature of his work."

Ibert was born in Paris on August 15, 1890. Since his father wanted him to be a businessman, he objected to a thorough musical training for Jacques. Nevertheless, Ibert studied the piano with his mother and then, in 1910, enrolled in the Paris Conservatory, where his teachers included Gedalge and Fauré. World War I interrupted these studies. During this period, Ibert served in the Navy, and after that was an officer in the French Naval Reserve. Despite the demands made on him by his naval duties, he was able in 1915 to write his first orchestral work, a tone poem entitled *Noël en Picardie*. The war over, Ibert returned to music study at the Conservatory, winning the Prix de Rome with the cantata *Le Poète et la fée*. He married Rose-Marie Veber, daughter of a famous artist, and spent with her his three-year period at the Villa Medici in Rome, where he completed his first two successful compositions for orchestra: *The Ballad of Reading Gaol* and *Escales*. His first opera, *Angélique*, was successfully given at the Opéra on January 28, 1927.

In 1937, Ibert was appointed director of the Academy of Rome, the first musician ever to hold this post. After World War II, he became the assistant director of the Paris Opéra, dividing his time and energies between Paris and Rome. He resigned from the Academy in Rome to become director of the combined management of the Paris Opéra and Opéra-Comique, but he retained this post only two years. During the summer of 1950, Ibert paid his only visit to the United States, to conduct a master class in composition at the Berkshire Music Center at Tanglewood. During this visit, his first opera to get produced in the United States was given at Tanglewood—*Le Roi d'Yvetot*. Ibert's last two major works for orchestra were commissioned in the United States: the *Louisville Concerto,* introduced by the Louisville Orchestra in Kentucky under Robert Whitney on February 17, 1954; and the *Mouvement symphonique,* written in 1956 for the seventy-fifth anniversary of the Boston Symphony. Ibert died in Paris on February 5, 1962.

1921 THE BALLAD OF READING GAOL, tone poem for orchestra.

This was Ibert's first successful composition. It was introduced at a Colonne concert in Paris, Gabriel Pierné conducting, on October 22, 1922. Its program is based on Oscar Wilde's famous poem describing the abuses suffered by prisoners in an English jail.

Here is how Arthur Hoerée described the programmatic content of Ibert's tone poem:

"This symphonic poem comprises three episodes. The first depicts the strange march, light and gay, of one who, drunk with the sun, forgets his enormous debt against society for having killed the thing he loved. The merry round of phantoms animates the second episode with its mad arabesques, in an instrumentation rich with color . . . [while] holding back . . . the diabolic frenzy of the movement. . . . The movement has vanished, but the bass emerges mysteriously, and the last vibrations link up with the last episode which suddenly becomes tragic: a milky day, the wailing of a fresh wind. The prayer of the criminal is choked with a poignant cry. And the body is left to rot in a hole."

1922 ESCALES (PORTS OF CALL), suite for orchestra. I. Rome—Palermo. II. Tunis—Nefta. III. Valencia.

During his duties in the Navy in World War I, Ibert visited many Mediterranean ports. They attracted him for their local color and their native popular tunes. In 1922, he wrote a musical travelogue of three such ports. The atmosphere and individuality of each is re-created musically. A free-flowing Italian melody beginning in the flute in the second measure brings up the picture of an Italian port. A chromatic theme (oboe) set against an oriental rhythm in divided strings and tympani transports us to Africa. In the last section, a languid and sensual Hispano-Moorish subject in the strings, developed in an improvisatory manner, evokes Spain.

Escales was heard for the first time on January 6, 1924, at a Lamoureux Concert in Paris. Since its première, it has become one of its composer's most frequently played works.

1930 DIVERTISSEMENT, for orchestra. I. Introduction. II. Cortège. III. Nocturne. IV. Valse. V. Parade. VI. Finale.

Like the *Concertino da Camera* described below, the *Divertissement* finds Ibert in one of his lighter and happier moods. The music was drawn from the score of a musical comedy, *Le Chapeau de Paille d'Italie,* produced in 1929. The Suite was introduced in Paris on November 30, 1930.

Following a lively Introduction built out of a single theme, there comes a march made up of two ideas: one is fast, played by the strings; the second is a vigorous subject for the trumpet. A powerful climax develops, after which, suddenly, there is heard an amusing quotation from the "Wedding March" of Mendelssohn's *A Midsummer Night's Dream.* The Nocturne is a short and simple melody. Infectious moods are posed by the Valse (in which there is an amusing passing reference to Johann Strauss's *The Blue Danube Waltz*) and the Parade, after which there comes the Finale, in which an effective climax is achieved with a characteristic Offenbach "can-can." The piano adds to the gaiety of the proceedings by interpolating strident and dissonant notes into the harmonization.

1934 CONCERTO FOR FLUTE AND ORCHESTRA. I. Allegro. II. Andante. III. Allegro scherzando.

This concerto was written for the eminent flute virtuoso, Marcel Moyse, who introduced it in Paris on February 25, 1934. In the first movement, a four-measure introduction precedes the appearance of the solo flute in the first half of the principal theme; the second half is played by the violins. A brief transition then leads into the second subject, more lyrical and expressive than the first; this, too, first appears in solo flute. The development opens with a fugato before the two main themes are developed; while the recapitulation is brought on with a repetition of the first theme in the strings and a descending scale passage. Flutes above muted strings offer the haunting melody of the poetic slow movement. The finale is a rondo made up of a twenty-four measure introduction and two main subjects, both assigned to the flute.

1935 CONCERTINO DA CAMERA FOR ALTO SAXOPHONE AND ORCHESTRA. I. Allegro con moto. II. Larghetto—animato molto.

This charming chamber concerto is not an excursion into jazz, as the solo instrument might suggest. Tart modern harmonies and cross-rhythms appear within the old chamber-concerto structure with delightful effect. The music is brisk and witty. Its artistic intent may be slight; but what it sets out to do—namely, to produce a workmanlike and aurally pleasing vehicle for an unorthodox solo instrument—it does successfully. There is skilful virtuoso writing for the saxophone. There is buoyant, lyrical material that is fresh and singable: the principal themes of both the first and the Larghetto movements, each one introduced by the soloist. In the Larghetto, Ibert's melodic writing grows mellow and thoughtful. But besides being lyrical, the concertino is witty, as in the fugato of the first movement, in which the various voices take part in a kind of rowdy abandon; or as in the leapfrog pranks of the rhythms in the closing page.

The Concertino received its first performance in Paris on May 2, 1935.

VINCENT D'INDY 1851–1931

As a passionate Wagnerian who made regular pilgrimages to Bayreuth, beginning with its very first festival, Vincent d'Indy might be expected to carry the master's torch in his lyric dramas. He did so—in *Fervaal,* produced in Brussels on March 12, 1897; in *L'Étranger,* also introduced in Brussels, on January 7, 1903. But this is one of two faces which d'Indy's music presents us. The other face, and the more familiar one, bears a resemblance to his teacher, César Franck. That influence on d'Indy can be found in his use of the cyclic form, which Franck had crystallized and perfected; in his emulation of Franck's high-minded thinking and the radiance that so often touches Franck's speech. To these qualities, learned from Franck, d'Indy added some of his own: an objectivity and detachment which did not permit his music to indulge in dramatics or emotional extravagances. D'Indy never tried to overwhelm his listeners with powerfully projected climaxes; he does not excite them with splendors of color or overpowering sonorities. His appeal is more to the intellect than to the emotion. The processes of his thinking provide aesthetic pleasure to those willing to follow them in all their subtle configurations.

"Clarity is the hallmark of his mind," said Romain Rolland in *Musicians Today*. "There are no shadows in him. The need for clarity is the main law of his artistic sense. In his music are displayed the qualities that go to the making of an army leader: a clear knowledge of the goal, a patient determination to reach it, a perfect knowledge of available means, a spirit of order, a thorough mastery over work and mind. The result is always clear—one might, if one wished, say that it is at times almost too clear."

D'Indy was born in Paris on March 27, 1851. He began his music study early—harmony with Lavignac, piano with Diémer and Marmontel. His first two opuses, written when he was nineteen, were *Trois Romances sans paroles* for piano and *La Chanson des aventuriers de la mer,* for baritone and chorus on a text by Victor Hugo. After the Franco-Prussian War—in which he served with the 105th Battalion and saw action in the battle of Val-Fleuri—he became a private pupil of César Franck, whose influence on the younger man has already been discussed. From 1872 to 1876, he was organist at the St. Leu Church. During the summer of 1873, he traveled in Germany where he met Liszt and Wagner; and in 1874, his overture, *Les Piccolomini,* became his first orchestral work to get a performance, introduced at a Concert Pasdeloup in Paris on January 25, 1874. (Several years later, d'Indy retitled this composition *Max et Thécla* and used it as the second part of the symphonic trilogy, *Wallenstein.*) From 1873 to 1878, he was chorusmaster of the Colonne Orchestra, where he had previously served as tympanist. In 1876, he made the first of many pilgrimages to Bayreuth, where he attended the inaugural Wagnerian festival held there, featuring the world première of the entire *Ring* cycle. In 1886, he assisted in the preparation of the first Paris production of *Lohengrin.*

Fame as a composer first came with what is one of his most famous compositions, the *Symphonie cévenole,* or *Symphony on a French Mountain Theme*; it was written in 1886 and was introduced by the Lamoureux Orchestra in Paris on March 20, 1887. The principal melodic idea of this symphony, recurring throughout the work in various transformations, is a mountain air the composer had heard in his native Cévennes mountain region. A decade later d'Indy completed the *Istar Variations,* which is also still very popular. The inspiration here was the Babylonian poem, *The Epic of Izdubar,* which describes the seven gates through which the daughter of Sin passes; at each gate, she takes off one of her garments, until at the seventh one, she is nude. We find here an unorthodox treatment of the theme-and-variations structure. The theme is not heard at the beginning, as is customary, but is allowed to grow and develop from embryo until, after the final variation, it is finally heard in its entirety. The first performance of *Istar Variations* took place at a Ysaÿe concert in Brussels on January 10, 1897.

With Franck, d'Indy helped found the Société Nationale de Musique in Paris in 1871 to perform contemporary French music. The Société was responsible for bringing about the premières of works by most of the important younger French composers. D'Indy was its secretary from 1876 to 1890 and, on Franck's death, became president.

In 1893, d'Indy was invited by the French government to serve on a committee to reform the Paris Conservatory. His plan proved so revolutionary it had to be shelved. In 1894, d'Indy founded the Schola Cantorum, a school for the study of church music which, six years later, extended its curriculum to every branch of music. The Schola Cantorum became one of France's great musical institutions; and d'Indy, who taught there many years, was one of France's most influential teachers, his pupils including Satie, Honegger, Roussel and Auric, among many others. In 1912, d'Indy was appointed professor of the ensemble class at the Paris Conservatory.

D'Indy also distinguished himself as a conductor by appearing as a guest with major orchestras, mainly in performances of his own music. He made his American debut with the Boston Symphony on December 1, 1905, in a French program. He made a second tour of the United States sixteen years later.

His reputation went into a decline after World War I, and performances of his music grew increasingly fewer. Nevertheless, d'Indy enjoyed a triumph in January of 1931, when he conducted in Paris a performance of his *Symphony on a French Mountain Theme*. He died in Paris of a heart attack on December 2, 1931.

1903 SYMPHONY NO. 2 IN B-FLAT MAJOR, op. 57. I. Extrémement lent; Très vif. II. Modérément lent. III. Modéré; Très animé.

Seventeen years separated d'Indy's two symphonies, the first one, the *Symphony on a French Mountain Theme* (or *Symphonie cévenole*), having been written in 1886. The Second Symphony was introduced in Paris by the Lamoureux Orchestra on February 28, 1904.

Here d'Indy makes consummate use of the cyclical form evolved by his teacher César Franck, a form in which ideas stated in one movement are repeated in subsequent sections to give the work greater integration. The thematic material of the Second Symphony is found in the first four measures of the introduction to the first movement: the first theme, rather somber, is heard in the cellos and double basses; the second, a phrase for the flute, features an ascending flight of the interval of seventh. These two ideas are varied and elaborated; they constitute the kernel of all the melodic materials of the symphony.

A slow introduction opens the work. A dramatic quasi-lyrical section follows. The second movement is a song for orchestra, the second section of which has the character of a funeral march. A folk-like melody opens the last movement and passes without interruption into the finale, which is made up of an introduction, fugue and finale.

D'Indy's style in this symphony consists mainly of chromatic harmonies and occasional excursions into whole-tone writing. There is little in the symphony to shock or arouse the listener—even in the year in which it was written. It is reserved and objective, rather than iconoclastic. Yet when the symphony was heard in America for the first time—on January 7, 1905, with the composer conducting the Boston Symphony Orchestra—Louis Elson wrote as follows in the *Boston Advertiser:* "D'Indy's symphony (????) is so unutterably shocking to us that we hesitate to express our frank opinion. It is evident that harmony books are now mere waste paper, that there are no more rules, that there is to be an eleventh commandment for the composer—'Thou shalt avoid all beauty,'" Philip Hale, however, was much more discerning. "We believe," wrote Hale, "that this symphony is one of the most important works of modern times.

. . . It contains deep and impressive thoughts, pages of beauty that is almost unearthly."

1905 JOUR D'ÉTÉ À LA MONTAGNE (SUMMER DAY ON THE MOUNTAIN), rhapsody for piano and orchestra, op. 61. I. Dawn. II. Day. III. Night.

This effective triptych of Nature portraits (which Daniel Gregory Mason once described as d'Indy's "masterpiece in the realm of programmatic music") is a veritable *Symphonie pastorale*. We find painted in the first movement the break of dawn, as Nature gently awakens from her slumber. In the second section, a picture of Nature—as drawn by a sensitive artist reclining under the shade of a pine tree—is vividly reproduced. Night comes. As the country becomes enveloped in serenity and darkness, the music takes on a pastoral character.

The work is alternately pictorial and impressionistic. It was introduced by the Colonne Orchestra in Paris on February 18, 1906.

1924 PIANO QUINTET IN G MINOR, op. 81. I. Assez animé. II. Assez animé. III. Lent et espressif. IV. Modérément animé.

The Piano Quintet, says M.D. Calvocoressi, is "remarkable for its clarity, simplicity and conciseness." The principal subject of the first movement is stated at once by all five instruments. A modulation into the key of E-flat major leads to the lyrical subject, in the piano. The second movement is in scherzo form, and in quintuple time, graceful and gentle in outer sections, rhythmic in its F major trio. In the slow movement, "the beautiful, introspective subject is introduced by the strings," M.D. Calvocoressi explains, "the piano coming in later to announce in D-flat major the second subject (which is the second subject of the first movement, broadened, but otherwise unaltered)." The finale is brisk and vivacious, highlighting a rhythmic theme which is soon treated canonically and which receives prominent attention in the concluding section.

1927 CONCERTO FOR PIANO, FLUTE, CELLO AND STRING ORCHESTRA, op. 89. I. Modéré mais bien decidé. II. Lent et espressif. III. Mouvement de ronde française.

In the last decade of his life, d'Indy was drifting more and more to neoclassical objectives and procedures. This tendency is found in the lean, objective, restrained writing of this concerto, introduced in Paris on April 2, 1927. "The first movement," explains Nicolas Slonimsky, "opens in the brisk fashion of the eighteenth-century concerto grosso, with the solo instruments, the concertino group, giving the tone to the musical proceedings. The string orchestra answers in the dominant, confirming the impression of an old form. It is with the entrance of the second songful theme in the flute in a key enharmonically arrived at, that the old form begins to be filled with new matter." The slow movement is "set in a gently swaying rhythm, with the flute, then the cello, intoning a recitative-like musical phrase." In the finale, we encounter "the meter of 5/8 and the melodic pattern follows agile scale runs. The essential rhythm of the five beats remains in a subsequent section, in a calmer mood, with the flute, followed by the cello, playing a free rhythmic phrase by way of a brief interlude."

CHARLES IVES 1874–1954

In the "Song for the Harvest Season" which Ives wrote in 1894 when he was twenty, we find startling polytonal combinations: this song is set for voice, cornet, trombone and organ, and each part is written in a different key. A string quartet and a symphony, in each instance his first in those forms, followed in 1896. Here the traditional concepts of harmony, tonality and rhythm acceptable to most other composers of this period are abandoned in favor of discords, polyrhythms and polytonality. And as Ives kept on writing after that, his daring and iconoclasm grew.

That all of Ives's music was written before 1928, and most of it in the first decade of the twentieth century, presents an interesting (and possibly inexplicable) phenomenon. Before Stravinsky, Ives worked with polyrhythms; before Bartók, he utilized agonizing discords; before Stravinsky and Milhaud, he employed polytonality; before Schoenberg, he ventured into atonality; before Alois Hába, he experimented with quarter tones; before Henry Cowell, he exploited tone clusters; and long before Boulez, he introduced music of chance.

Strange as it is to contemplate, the complex scores that were lying dusty and neglected on his shelves for so many years—their startling contents known only to Ives's wife and a handful of friends—contained often fully realized innovations which other and more famous composers arrived at years later and with which they are now identified.

From his beginnings as a composer, Ives believed in endowing music with wings so that it might soar over conventions, rules, habits and traditions. He was interested in music as a great and vital human experience—and principally an American experience—and not for the pretty sounds it could produce to delight the ear. "My God," he once exclaimed, "what has sound to do with music!" He was searching for what he himself once described as "the inner invisible activity of truth." For Ives, musical truth meant the full freedom of expression. Nothing must stop his flights of creativity. To the argument that some of his songs were unsingable he replied: "A song has a few rights the same as other ordinary citizens. . . . If it happens to feel like trying to fly where humans cannot fly—to sing what cannot be sung—to walk in a cave on all fours—or to tighten up its girth in blind hope and faith and try to scale mountains that are not—who shall stop it?" It was this fierce belief in the necessity of an artist to be free to speak and write without inhibitions that impelled him to interpolate a brief theme for trumpet in a sonata for violin and piano; to permit a violin obbligato to intrude inexplicably in a song for voice and piano; and to stop a bassoon midway in its part to inform it that "from here on, the bassoon may play anything at all."

And if he was an ultramodern, even an avant-garde, composer long before this species came so strongly to the fore in the twentieth century, he was also an authentically American composer at a time when most composers were producing European music. With a sublime disregard for European examples and traditions—to which virtually all other American composers of the period seemed bound—Ives wrote music which drew its breath and soul from American backgrounds and experiences. Almost everything American inspired him: American culture as found in the New England school of writers a century ago; American customs, as uncovered in revival meetings, camp meetings, barn dances, town meetings; American scenes such as one sees in picturesque New England; American history, holidays, politics, and—most of all—American tunes.

He was driven by American experiences to write music which in its austerity, independence, strength, brusqueness and motion could have come from nowhere but America. It is the intrinsic Americanism of Ives's music that gives it its significance and assures its permanence in our cultural heritage. When he realized his identity in music fully, Ives did much more than create new idioms and techniques and point to new horizons. He created a vibrant American art, and was probably the first to do so.

Ives was born in Danbury, Connecticut, on October 20, 1874. His musical iconoclasm was a heritage from a remarkable father—George E. Ives, bandmaster of the First Connecticut Heavy Artillery during the Civil War. The older Ives was also one to seek out new horizons for music. He was always experimenting: now with acoustics, now even with a system of quarter tones. He had his son sing "Swanee River" in one key while he himself played the accompaniment in an opposing tonality, in order to train the boy's ears to new sound relationships. He was Charles's first teacher. After that, Ives studied the organ with Henry Rowe Shelley, and during the four years he attended Yale, from 1894 to 1898, he continued his music study there with Horatio Parker and Dudley Buck. While still at Yale, Ives played the organ in churches and did some composing. After receiving his Bachelor of Arts degree, he went to work as an insurance clerk in New York City, supplementing his salary by serving as a part-time organist at the Central Presbyterian Church. In 1906, he founded the insurance firm of Ives and Company which, three years later, became Ives and Myrick, an organization that grew into one of the most successful of its kind in the United States. In 1908, he married Harmony Twichell, daughter of a clergyman.

He remained in the insurance business until 1930, all the while combining this successful activity with the writing of music. He insisted upon retaining an amateur status as a composer, never trying to get any of his works performed or published. When he himself published two of his opuses—the *Concord*

Sonata and *114 Songs*—it was merely to distribute them free to his friends. He was completely oblivious to public or critical reaction. For forty years, he lived in almost total creative obscurity, producing one remarkable work after another. Fame caught up with him just before his life was over; but when it did, it was through none of his own doing or seeking. His music, written some forty years earlier, was beginning to get heard, and getting heard, it was beginning to gather accolades. All this mattered little to him. He still avoided interviewers, photographers, newspapermen and organizations eager to honor him. He even refused to attend performances of his works. He was completely indifferent to the Pulitzer Prize in music bestowed upon him in 1947 for his Third Symphony. He remained a recluse to the very end, dying in a hospital in New York City on May 19, 1954.

1888–1921 114 SONGS, for voice and piano.

When, in 1922, Ives published his *114 Songs* for private distribution, he said in his preface: "Various authors have various reasons for bringing out a book. . . . Some have written a book for money; I have not. Some for fame; I have not. Some for love; I have not. Some for kindlings; I have not. I have not written a book for any of these reasons or for all of them together. In fact, gentle borrower, I have not written a book at all—I have merely cleaned house. All that is left out on the clothes-line. . . . " By "cleaning house" he meant that he had assembled all the songs he had been writing since the time he was fourteen. In publishing them in a single volume, he reversed the chronological order by going backwards in time. The first song in the volume is "Majority," written in 1921; the last of the one hundred and fourteen songs is "Slow March," which he had written in 1888.

The one hundred and fourteen songs are greatly varied in style, methods and content. Some songs are romantic; some are in syncopated ragtime rhythm; some are dramatic; some are satiric; some are ballads; some are war songs; some are church hymns; some are cowboy songs; some are songs of protest, and some are street songs. Some were adaptations of his own instrumental numbers. Some are the last word in simplicity and directness, while others are extraordinarily complex. "Majority" (1921) utilizes tone clusters, the first published piece of music to do so (the clusters to be played with the help of a ruler). "The Cage" (1906) is partly atonal. "Walking Song" (1902) is discordant, its simulation of church bells anticipating Debussy with adventurous harmonies. In "Charlie Rutledge" (c. 1900), where cowboy tunes are quoted, an intriguing ragtime effect is achieved through syncopation.

Not the technique but the artistic content distinguishes still other songs written in or about 1900. "The White Gulls," poem by Maurice Morris, is memorable for the subtlety and delicacy of its atmosphere. "Where the Eagle," which is only a single page in length, is to Aaron Copland "remarkable for its depth of feeling, its concision, its originality. Certainly no other American composer at the turn of the century was capable of producing a song of this worth." Copland also singles out "Berceuse" for its "rich harmonies and sensuous line"; "The Children's Hour," for its "charming flow and imagination." He adds that in songs like these "one knows oneself to be in the presence of a composer of imagination, a real creator."

1901 FROM THE STEEPLES AND THE MOUNTAINS, for orchestra.

SYMPHONY NO. 2. I. Andante moderato. II. Allegro. III. Adagio cantabile. IV. Lento maestoso. V. Allegro molto vivace.

Charles Ives's father experimented with acoustics by sending different sections of his band to different parts of the town. One section played from a steeple; a second section, on a building on Main Street; a third section, on the village green. He then studied the effect realized when all performed together a hymn or a march.

The son made a similar experiment in *From the Steeples and the Mountains.* Scored for two sets of church bells or chimes (each with a high and low part) and for four trumpets and trombones, each playing in unison, this short orchestral piece tried to simulate the sound of church bells as they might sound coming from different steeples. The effect is both polytonal and discordant. At the end of the score, the composer added the following comment: "After the brass stops, the chimes sound on until they die away. . . . From the Steeples —the Bells!—then the Rocks on the Mountains begin to shout!"

This composition did not get heard until sixty years after it had been written. Its première took place during a French-American Festival at the Lincoln Center for the Performing Arts, with Lukas Foss conducting the New York Philharmonic on July 30, 1965.

It also took half a century for the Second Symphony to get its initial hearing. This took place in New York on February 22, 1951, with Leonard Bernstein conducting the New York Philharmonic. Bernstein invited Ives to attend this première but the Connecticut recluse was not interested. He would not even attend a special performance that Bernstein wanted to arrange for Ives alone. But Ives did hear the work broadcast on his maid's radio in the kitchen, and was so delighted that when the symphony ended he performed a jig.

Ives said of the symphony: "It expresses the musical feelings of the Connecticut country around here (Redding and Danbury) in the 1890s, the music of the country folk. It is full of the tunes they sang and played then, and I thought it would be a sort of bad joke to have some of these tunes in counterpoint with some Bach tunes."

In *Modern Music,* Bernard Herrman gave the following description of this symphony: "Unconventionally, a slow prelude, somber and introspective in mood, forms the first movement. An organ-like melody is followed immediately by a theme whose startling harmonies suggest Prokofiev. It is at the end of this movement that Ives makes his first symphonic use of American material. A quotation from 'Columbia, the Gem of the Ocean,' appears as a countertheme in the horns. A brief oboe recitative links the Andante to the gay and rollicking Allegro, whose simple tunes and galloping rhythms recall the village band.

"Ives has described the third movement as a 'take-off,' a 'reflection of the organ and choir music of the *Long Green Organ Book* of the sixties, seventies and eighties.' To close this restful piece, of such deep feeling, the flute plays a quotation from 'America, the Beautiful.'

"The finale's Maestoso introduction is based on a proud born motive.

It builds up to a full sonority which introduces the Allegro, originally part of a previously composed *American Overture.* Against an exhilarating barn-dance tune, fragments of 'De Camptown Races' are heard. Ives calls the second subject, a variant of 'Old Black Joe,' . . . 'a kind of reflection of Stephen Foster and the old barn dance fiddling over it.'

"The first theme returns to overwhelm everything. Then the whole pattern is repeated with subtle variations in color and harmony. Now it is decorated by fragmentary quotations from folk and patriotic themes. Some are not easy to identify, since only a few notes of the original melody are preserved, and they are quickly caught up in the rushing speed of the dance. Then at the coda the trombones proclaim the entire 'Columbia' song with a loud, thumping hurrah on the bass drums. It is as though Ives were telling the whole world of his proud heritage. . . . The symphony orchestra has been swept aside to make way for country fiddlers and the firemen's band, for a Fourth of July jubilation, the shouting of children, a politician's speech and Old Glory."

1904 SYMPHONY NO. 3. I. Andante maestoso. II. Allegro. III. Largo.

It is with this symphony that, in his old age, Ives finally achieved the recognition he long deserved. It was heard for the first time forty-two or so years after Ives had finished writing it, when Lou Harrison conducted it in New York with the New York Little Symphony on April 5, 1946. On May 11 of the same year it was repeated on an all-Ives program in New York, at which time it was acclaimed by the critics. It received a special citation from the New York Music Critics Circle and, in 1947, the Pulitzer Prize in music.

The symphony was inspired by the camp meetings once rampant in the town of Danbury, Connecticut. Its melodic ideas are drawn from actual old hymn tunes: *O for a Thousand Tongues,* which is treated fugally in the first movement; and *Just as I Am* introduced in the last movement. The middle section of the symphony has been described by the composer as a game played by children at camp meeting while their elders listen to the Holy Words.

As one might expect in a work by Ives, the symphony is unorthodox. It is filled with unusual progressions and cross-rhythms. But it does not give the appearance of being exclusively an experimental work, filled as it is with a speech that is strong and personal, authentically American in every accent. What Lawrence Gilman wrote about another Ives composition applies even more strongly to this one: "This music is as indubitably American in impulse and spiritual texture as the prose of Jonathan Edwards."

1914 THREE PLACES IN NEW ENGLAND, for orchestra. I. The St. Gaudens in Boston Common; Colonel Shaw and His Colored Regiment. II. Putnam's Camp, Redding, Connecticut. III. The Housatonic at Stockbridge.

Whereas New England hymns had been the inspiration for the Third Symphony, New England geography provided the stimulation of *Three Places,* upon which Ives worked between 1903 and 1914. Of technical interest is the use of polyrhythm and polytonal discord in the second section describing the approach of two different bands from different directions, each band playing a different melody in a different tempo, key and rhythm. Of aesthetic interest is the exquisite and subtle impressionistic tone-painting of the Housatonic at Stockbridge with which the work ends.

The composer provided information regarding the programmatic background for this music. The first movement (Very Slowly) was inspired by *The St. Gaudens in Boston Common,* of which the following are the opening lines:

> Moving—Marching—Faces of Souls!
> Marked with generations of pain.
> Part-freers of a Destiny,
> Slowly, restlessly—swaying us on with you
> Towards other Freedom!

No American tunes are quoted in this section; nevertheless, as Joseph Machlis has written, "the melodic line unmistakably suggests the world of Stephen Foster and the range of emotion attached to the Civil War." The writing is consistently polyrhythmical and polytonal.

The setting of the second movement (Allegro: Quick Step Time) is a small park near Redding, Connecticut, which served as the winter quarters of General Putnam's soldiers in 1778–1779. A fourth of July picnic is being held under the auspices of the First Church and the Village Cornet Band. A child wanders off to the hillside where he tries to bring to mind what had happened in this very place during the Revolutionary War. Then, the dreams over, the child returns to his little friends to join them in dances and games. Nicolas Slonimsky described this section as a "musicorama of the American Revolution." Snatches of Revolutionary War songs and marches are interpolated; and at one point there is an intriguing polyrhythmic and polytonal clash between two marches supposedly played by two bands simultaneously. The music begins with a waltz, continues with a fox-trot, and ends up with the polytonal and polyrhythmic march.

For the third movement (Adagio molto), Ives quoted Roberts Underwood Johnson's poem, *The Housatonic at Stockbridge:*

> Contented river! in thy dreamy realm—
> The cloudy willow and plumy elm. . . .
>
> Thou hast grown human laboring with men
> At wheel and spindle; sorrow thou dost ken. . . .
>
> Thou beautiful! From every dreamy hill
> What eye but wanders with thee at thy will,
> Imagining thy silver course unseen
> Conveyed by two attendant streams of green. . . .

Strings provide a haunting background for a serene, hymn-like melody divided between horn and English horn. Though a sensitive picture is here being drawn, a strong and powerful climax is built up and then allowed to subside. Paul Rosenfeld described this movement as a "sonorous cataract, easily the jewel of the suite and one of the thrilling American orchestral compositions. . . . [It] includes a rhythm for solo violin quite independent of that of the rest of the orchestra, and atonal and polytonal figures that clash with the tonic harmonies of the brass and the woodwind."

This suite was heard first in New York City on January 10, 1931, with Nicolas Slonimsky leading members of the Boston Symphony.

1915 SONATA NO. 2 FOR PIANO ("Concord, Mass: 1840–60"). I. Emerson. II. Hawthorne. III. The Alcotts. IV. Thoreau.

In his now famous *Concord* Sonata, Ives drew the essence of his musical thought from the school of Concord writers. Actually, this composition is not a sonata at all, but a set or suite of four pieces which, the composer explains apologetically, "is called a sonata for want of a more exact name." The four movements are not four separate entities but are unified by a common method, concept and outlook. What Ives does here is to superimpose one structure upon another in the four successive sections to create an overall tension which makes the four parts an inextricable unity.

The structure is not the only thing unusual about this work. In his opening movement, "Emerson," Ives instructs the performer that the tempo should vary with the mood of the day and the mood of the performer himself. "The tempi need not be precisely the same," Ives explained. "The same essay or poem of Emerson may bring a slightly different feeling when read at sunrise than when read at sunset." Other unusual methods are followed elsewhere in the sonata. In the "Hawthorne" section, a ruler or a strip of wood must be used to play an expansive two-octave cluster. In "The Alcotts," the first four notes of Beethoven's Fifth Symphony are quoted because the Alcott children used to practice Beethoven's music tirelessly. In the closing section, a flute is introduced and allowed to play throughout a page because, Ives explained, Thoreau "much prefers to hear the flute over *Walden*."

The essence of Emerson's transcendental philosophy is captured in the mystery and the revelations of the first movement. This music was not planned to interpret any specific Emerson passages, but Ives did explain that some parts of the first movement relate to Emerson's poetry, while other parts refer to Emerson's prose. Emerson's sudden call for a Transcendental Journey is interpreted at one point with a loud and abrupt discord. The mystical ending of the movement is supposed "to reflect the overtones of the soul of humanity."

In the second movement, Hawthorne's "fantastical adventures into the half-childlike, half-fairylike phantasmal realms," (in Ives's words) are interpreted in music that is almost primitive in its wildness. A more idyllic and gentle vein is tapped in the music for "The Alcotts" and "Thoreau."

Nicolas Slonimsky described the *Concord Sonata* as "transcendental music in the philosophical conception of the word. It is a new type of impressionism in which ideas and convictions, even politics, are used as programmatic content."

The sonata was written between 1909 and 1915 and was published privately in 1920. Its first complete performance was given in New York City on January 20, 1938, by John Kirkpatrick.

To explain this complex and formidable work, Ives published a slim pamphlet entitled *Essays Before a Sonata,* lines from which are quoted above. With his customary wit, Ives dedicated this volume to "those who can't stand his music—and the music for those who can't stand the essays; to those who can't stand either, the whole is respectfully dedicated."

1913 STRING QUARTET NO. 2. I. Discussions. II. Arguments. III. The Call of the Mountains.

Ives often indulged in a Satie-like whimsy. It is found in the second movement of this quartet, in which he names the second violin "Rollo." At one point, where the second violin stops playing, Ives contributes the following comment: "Too hard to play—so it just can't be good music, Rollo." In a succeeding passage he informs the violin: "Join in again, Professor, all in the key of C. You can do that nice and pretty." A sentimental passage is marked "Andante emasculata" and a vigorous one "con scratchy" or "con fistiswatto."

The quartet as a whole was described by the composer as music "for four men—who converse, discuss, argue (politics), fight, shake hands, shut up, then walk up the mountain side to view the firmament." The first movement contains quotations from such popular tunes as "Dixie," "Marching Through Georgia" and "Columbia, the Gem of the Ocean"; but within the texture of this music, the keen ear can also detect fleet and passing allusions to other compositions, including Tchaikovsky's *Symphonie pathétique,* Brahms's Second Symphony, Beethoven's Ninth Symphony, and the hymn, "Nearer My God to Thee."

In reviewing a recording of this work, Howard Taubman said: "The composer lays aside his wit and bitterness . . . and writes music of depth and feeling. Here is music of character. When jokes pall and are forgotten, this expressive communication will remain to give us the measure of Charles E. Ives as a composer who did not deserve neglect."

1916 SYMPHONY NO. 4. I. Prelude: Maestoso. II. Allegretto. III. Fugue: Andante moderato. IV. Largo maestoso.

Ives's fourth and last symphony was his most complex one, scored for an immense orchestra (including a brass band), a large percussion section (including five tympani, two pianos, organ, and so on), and a chorus. Enormous rhythmic combinations are used: at one point twenty-seven different rhythms are played simultaneously. Numerous quotations of famous American tunes are used polytonally with Ives's own material. Three conductors are needed to keep the forces together.

The symphony is actually a combination of movements which Ives wrote at different times for various non-symphonic works. The last movement consisted of a mass of sometimes illegible manuscripts with missing pages located in an old trunk. Ives stuffed parts of this movement in desk drawers, parts were scribbled in notebooks. After Ives's death it took musicologists two years to bring order out of this chaos. This was done so skilfully that a unified artistic work emerged in which, as Irving Kolodin said, we find a "consistency of substance as well as a profundity of mood that are rarely to be found with such concentration in his orchestral work."

The second movement had been heard in New York on January 29, 1927 —thirty-eight years before Leopold Stokowski was able to present the whole symphony for the first time. It took a special grant of almost $8,000 from the Rockefeller Foundation to pay for all the rehearsals needed to master the technicalities of this mammoth score. Finally, on April 26, 1965, the American Symphony Orchestra under Stokowski (assisted by David Katz and José Serebrier) performed the world première. It received a special citation from the New York Music Critics Circle. It was recorded for Columbia (expenses paid for by the Samuel Rubin Foundation) and was put on video-tape for telecasts over the country by National Education Television.

Ives endowed the composition with a philosophic program, "that of the searching questions of What? and Why? which the spirit of man asks of life," he explained. "This is particularly the sense of the prelude. The three succeeding movements are the diverse answers in which existence replies." The second movement is "a comedy in which an exciting, easy and worldly progress through life is contrasted with the trials of the Pilgrims in their journey through the swamps and rough country," while the third "is an expression of the reaction of life to formalism and ritualism." The finale is "an apotheosis of the preceding content in terms that have something to do with the reality of existence and its religious existence."

The first movement opens with a somber, fatalistic theme in the basses. A special chamber ensemble (placed in the rear of the regular orchestra) gives soft reply. Violins contribute the strains of "The Sweet Bye and Bye." Then, as violins and flutes provide a reminder of "Nearer My God to Thee," a chorus is heard in the hymn, "Watchman, Tell Us of the Night" to end the movement. This is the text:

Watchman, tell us of the night,
What the signs of promise are:
Traveler, o'er yon mountain's height,
See that Glory-beaming star!
Watchman, aught of joy or hope?
Traveler, yes; it brings the day,
Promised day of Israel.
Dost thou see its beauteous ray?

The second movement was suggested by the "Hawthorne" movement of Ives's *Concord Sonata,* though it is by no means an orchestral transcription. It opens with a cacophonous blaring of "Marching Through Georgia," while above and under these strains individual instruments seem to proceed their own respective ways, now thinking about "Yankee Doodle," now about "Turkey in the Straw," now about "Columbia, the Gem of the Ocean." The effect, says Alfred J. Frankenstein, "is often one of a wild, senseless frenzy of noise, from which emerge, like flying fragments from an explosion, snatches of familiar tunes."

The third movement is an adaptation of a movement of Ives's First String Quartet. It is a double fugue in which two hymns are used prominently: "From Greenland's Icy Mountains" and "All Hail the Power." The finale originated as a *Memorial Slow March,* for organ; most of it is based on the familiar hymn, "Nearer My God to Thee." "Once again," says Frankenstein, "we are in the world of simultaneous but only vaguely related streams of sound—one stream in the percussion, one in the winds and strings, one in the chorus, now wordless." Here music seems once and for all to be freed from all restrictions. We find here no recognizable themes, no formal rhythmic procedures, no distinguishable harmonic schemes. Instruments go their separate ways. Suddenly a chorus enters with a wordless chant. All is abstract sound.

"The idea of the finale as a triumphant summation and spiritual affirmation," says Frankenstein, "here meets its most profound and significant challenge. In many ways, this may well be the most original and important movement in any of the symphonies by America's greatest composer."

LEOŠ JANÁČEK 1854–1928

Some critics have described Janáček as "the Moravian Mussorgsky," a phrase that puts the finger squarely on Janáček's creative manner. His indebtedness to Moravian peasant music was profound—he even used old Slavonic scales—just as Mussorgsky's debt to Russian folk music was profound. "The whole life of man is in folk music—body, soul, environment, everything," Janáček once said. "He who grows out of folk music makes the whole of himself. Folk music binds people together, linking them with other peoples and uniting mankind with a spiritual bond of happiness."

But more than this binds Janáček to Mussorgsky. Like Mussorgsky, Janáček tried to evolve his melodies out of speech patterns which he called "melodies of the language." The inflections, cadences, rhythms peculiar to the Bohemian language provide the contours for his melodic line. Janáček felt that under different circumstances—among different kinds of people, and under different stresses and strains—speech patterns change; and, he insisted, so must the melody. "After having studied the musical side of language," he said, "I am certain that all melodic and rhythmic mysteries in general are to be explained solely from rhythmical and melodic points of view on the basis of the melodic curves of speech. No one can become an opera composer who has not studied living speech. I wish that this could be understood once and for all." There is consequently a personal element in the harsh, stark declamations of his operas, and in the short, terse, oft-repeated phrases that overflow in his instrumental music. And the personal manner is also evident in his strong, robust harmonizations, in his ever-present feeling for dramatic effect, and in his avoidance of thematic development. He was not always a skilful or sophisticated workman (once again, there is here a striking resemblance to Mussorgsky!); but there are times when he seems to gain force and passion and individuality because of the comparative crudity of some of his methods and techniques.

Hans Hollander, Janáček's biographer, divides the composer's creative life into four distinct periods. During his first period, Janáček "though never entirely conventional, is generally indebted to classic-Romantic models and in particular to Dvořák's national traditionalism." In this phase, Janáček produced a Suite for strings (1877), the six *Lachian Dances* (1890) and the Suite for Orchestra (1891). During his second period, Janáček created his masterwork, the opera *Jenufa* (1903). "His absorption of the musical qualities of human speech and the consciousness of his congenital affinity with the folk music of his native Lachian district were the generating forces in this process." The third period coincides roughly with World War I and the period of national liberation of the Czech people. This is the time when he "proved flexible enough to absorb various traits of contemporary music outside the sphere of native folklore and rustic realism. . . . Whole-tone melody and polyrhythm are used to produce atmospheric effect. . . . and an occasional colorful *al fresco* treatment of the orchestral scoring enhances the impressionist feeling of the music." We encounter all this in his opera *The Excursions of Mr. Brouček* (1917) and the song cycle, *The Diary of One Who Vanished* (1919). Janáček's final creative period came in the last five years of his life. "The melodic, rhythmical and dynamic contrasts, often ruthlessly employed in former works, mellowed. . . . Janáček has learned by now how to economize his powers and achieve the greatest possible dramatic effect by means of a subtler psychological differentiation. . . . Janáček has reverted to classicism." This final period saw the writing of the monumental *Slavonic,* or *Glagolitic Mass* (1926), the second string quartet (1928) and his last opera, *The House of the Dead* (1928).

Janáček was born in Hukvaldy, Moravia, on July 3, 1854. Music study was begun with his father, was continued with Father Pavel Krizkowski at the Augustine Monastery, and was completed at the Organ School in Prague and Conservatories in Leipzig and Vienna. In 1881, Janáček became principal conductor of the Czech Philharmonic, holding this post for seven years; he also founded the Brünn Organ School, with which he remained associated for forty years. His first compositions included a Suite for strings (1877) and sundry other compositions. These were highly derivative. But a more personal attitude could be discovered in his first opera *Šarka* (1887), the six *Lachian Dances* for orchestra (1890), and the ballet *Rákocz Rákoczy*, produced in Prague on July 24, 1891.

Three trips to Russia, the first in 1896, interested him in the language, literature and the people, and led him to draw creative stimulation from Russian backgrounds and subjects. An even greater influence was his contacts with Moravian folk music, of which he made extensive studies and which led him to evolve a musical system of his own derived from folk songs and dances. His first masterwork was the opera *Jenufa* (1903), much of it written under the influence and impact of the tragic death of both his children. Since it was not immediately successful, *Jenufa* failed at first to lift him from his obscurity. But eventually, it was responsible for bringing him into the international limelight, following a highly successful revival in Vienna on February 16, 1918.

Some of Janáček's finest music came in his old age. These included his last four operas, all of them introduced in Brünn: *Kate Kavanova,* on November 23, 1921; *The Cunning Little Vixen,* on November 6, 1924; *The Makropoulos Case,* based on the Karel Capek fantasy, on December 16, 1926; and *From the House of the Dead,* based on the Dostoyevsky novel, produced posthumously on April 12, 1930. During the 1920s, Janáček also wrote two string quartets, the *Slavonic Mass,* and the Sinfonietta for orchestra.

Janáček's seventieth birthday was commemorated in Brünn and Prague with a production of a cycle of his operas. One year after that, he was given an honorary degree from the University of Brünn. He died in Ostrau, Moravia, on August 12, 1928. Comprehensive cycles of his works were given throughout Czechoslovakia to commemorate the twentieth and thirtieth anniversaries of his death.

1903 JENUFA, opera in three acts, with text by the composer based on a story by Gabriela Preissova. First performance: Brünn, January 21, 1904 (under the title, *Her Foster Daughter*).

Jenufa was the composer's third opera, and the first of his full length operas to get staged. Many of Janáček's later works for the stage were on Russian subjects. But his chef d'oeuvre, *Jenufa,* is entirely based on Moravian peasant life. The composer's lifelong researches into the folk music of Moravia provided him with the necessary tools with which to build a mighty folk opera. He was stimulated by a peasant story of lust and murder, for which he provided strong expressive melodies, many of them in a powerful declamatory style. But, as Rosa Newmarch has pointed out, not all of Janáček's melodies here follow speech patterns. "Sustained passion and tenderness forget their own melodies. . . . Jenufa's opening song, the 'Ave Maria' and the final duet are all 'singable' music." Tension is built up through nervous accompanying figures, and power is generated through primitive rhythms, many derived from Slovakian folk sources. Though use is made of folk songs and dances, realism rather than romanticism is emphasized, with a highly personal and virile approach towards harmony and orchestration. "At first they fall strangely on the ear," wrote Howard Taubman. "But the oddness takes on an agreeable pungency. The score fills out the naive, slushy libretto with a dignity and passionate feeling that makes one react to the characters as Janáček himself did."

Jenufa, a peasant girl of Moravia, has been loved by two stepbrothers, one of whom, Stewa, is the father of her child. But Stewa no longer loves Jenufa; he has found pleasurable company elsewhere. The other stepbrother, Laca, is ready to accept Jenufa as his bride. Jenufa's mother notices the instinctive horror of Laca towards accepting a son who is not his own. She gives Jenufa a sleeping potion, and while the girl is asleep, drowns the baby in the river. When Jenufa awakens, she is told by her mother that the baby has died naturally. Jenufa marries Laca. The wedding ceremony is interrupted by the discovery of the dead body in the river. For a while, Jenufa is accused of murder, until the mother confesses her crime and is led away. Jenufa is ready to call off the marriage, but Laca remains true to her.

When the Brünn Opera first introduced *Jenufa,* it was a failure. For the next twelve years the opera was not heard from again; but Janáček used this interval to good advantage by revising his score extensively. This revision was produced by the Czech Opera in Prague on May 26, 1916, the occasion upon which the opera used its now permanent title of *Jenufa.* But its success did not begin until it was heard in a German translation (by Max Brod) at the Vienna Opera on February 16, 1918. It was then given in most of the leading opera houses of Europe (where it has since become a fixture); on December 6, 1924, it was mounted at the Metropolitan Opera in New York. It was not again seen in the United States until November 2, 1959, when it was revived by the Chicago Lyric Opera.

1918 TARAS BULBA, rhapsody for orchestra. I. Death of Andrey. II. Death of Ostap. III. Prophecy and Death of Taras Bulba.

Russian literature provided Janáček with considerable artistic stimulation. He wrote operas based on a novel by Dostoyevsky, a drama of Ostrovsky, a poem of Lermontov. His String Quartet in E minor was inspired by Tolstoy's *Kreutzer Sonata.*

The epic novel of Nikolai Gogol about the fifteenth-century Cossack, Taras Bulba, and his two sons, Ostap and Andrey, was the spark to set Janáček's musical imagination aglow in this rhapsody. In the conflicts between the Ukrainian Cossacks and the Poles, Bulba's son, Andrey, turns traitor because of his love for a Polish girl. Captured, Andrey is brought before his father who, without hesitation, shoots him as a traitor. Bulba's second son, Ostap, is captured, tortured and executed in the presence of his father, who has come within the enemy lines to rescue him. Seeking revenge, Taras Bulba descends with his troops on Polish towns, wreaking havoc. He is captured and burned alive; with his last gasps, Bulba prophecies that a Czar will arise to bring complete victory to the Russian Orthodox faith.

From this novel, Janáček drew the three major tragic episodes to set to music—the respective deaths of Andrey, Ostap and Taras Bulba. The music throughout is dramatic, highly expressive, vivid with colors and dynamics. Turbulent, vehement, sometimes full of terror, this music nevertheless acquires contrasts by lapsing from time to time into elegiac moods. The first movement (Moderato quasi recitativo) first presents a tender melody for English horn accompanied by strings. A second lyrical subject is subsequently given by the oboe (Adagio—dolcissimo), descriptive of Andrey's love for the Polish girl. A strong phrase for first violins, over arpeggios in the harp and a soft chord in the woodwind, opens the second movement (Moderato). Contrast comes with a beautiful song for the violins. The main thought of the final movement (Con moto) is a melody for violins and solo horns. A turbulent Allegro section then precedes the concluding coda (Andante—Maestoso), which comes to a magnificent climax with full orchestra and organ.

Taras Bulba received its world première in Prague on November 9, 1924.

1923–1928 STRING QUARTET NO. 1. I. Adagio; Con moto. II. Con moto. III. Con moto; Vivace; Andante. IV. Con moto; Adagio.

STRING QUARTET NO. 2 ("Intimate Pages"). I. Andante. II. Adagio. III. Moderato. IV. Allegro.

These two string quartets present two different faces of love. The first string quartet (1923) was inspired by Tolstoy's famous story, *The Kreutzer Sonata.* In the quartet, we encounter the more emotional and passionate side of love, together with some of its tragedy. Joseph Suk, at whose instigation this composition was written—and whose Quartet introduced it in Prague in October of 1924—interpreted this music as a protest by the composer against man's iron-hand rule over women. But, perhaps, Max Brod arrives at a truer interpretation in saying that this music "ranges over the whole gamut of the emotions, the ceaseless agitation swelling to a yearning cry, and finally in the last movement to tragic despair." Since Beethoven's *Kreutzer Sonata,* for violin and piano, had been inspiration for the Tolstoy story, it is surely no coincidence that, in the third movement of the Janáček quartet, we hear an echo of the second theme from the first movement of the Beethoven sonata.

The second string quartet (1928) is more tender and more personal. Janáček originally planned to call the quartet *Love Letters,* then decided to subtitle it *Intimate Pages.* He wrote this music for Kamila Stöslova, a woman forty years younger than he, with whom he had been in love many years. Informing her of his intention to create an autobiographical quartet in which he could speak freely and openly, Janáček told Kamila: "You know, sometimes feelings are so strong and powerful that the notes hide under them and escape. A great love, a weak composition. But I want it be a great love—a great composition." Each of the movements is intended as a love letter. For example, the third movement, as Janáček revealed to Kamila, is gay music "which will resolve into a vision of your image." He also disclosed that "I wrote in tones my most tender desire. . . . You are giving birth. What would have been the destiny of that son in life? What will be your destiny? Just as you are, falling from tears into laughter, that is how it sounds."

1924 MLÁDI (YOUTH), suite for flute (or piccolo), oboe, clarinet, bass clarinet, bassoon and horn. I. Andante. II. Moderato. III. Allegro. IV. Con moto.

In its consistently pastoral character, and in its frequent expression of joy and ebullience, this sextet reveals the composer's love of nature. Rosa Newmarch wrote: "The freshness of thought, the suggestion of outdoor life, the happiness rarely overshadowed by pensive memory which we find in this sextet recall Dvořák; but the rhythmic subtlety, the original savor of the harmony, the unexpected developments of its thematic material, and the color contrasts derived from his six instruments, these are peculiar to Janáček's genius." A lighthearted and joyous tune dominates the first movement, while the principal material of the second and third movements suggests the peace and serenity of a rural scene.

1925 CONCERTINO FOR PIANO AND ORCHESTRA, with two violins, viola, clarinet, horn, bassoon and piano. I. Moderato. II. Più mosso. III Con moto. IV. Allegro.

Like the sextet commented upon above, the Concertino is essentially pastoral music. In fact, it has been described as a "hymn to Nature." Dr. J. Vogel says of it: "It is as though through some steep laborious path we suddenly heard the voices of the forest; as though we suddenly beheld, stark and unconcealed, the life of the world creature in it; as though we suddenly looked across a limitless expanse of country, steeped in hot sunshine."

Structurally, this composition is built from intradas, or preludes, each of which is complete and self-sufficient in itself, but which, nevertheless, relates to the preludes of the other movements, with the second and third movements being transformations of the first. In the first movement, piano and horn are dominant. The strong opening figure in the piano recurs throughout the movement, accompanied by a lyric line in the horn. In the second movement, the principal material is shared by piano and clarinet, with the latter highlighting a dance tune accompanied by chords in the piano. The third movement utilizes the full ensemble in varied tempos and moods. A running figure in the piano, which opens the finale, becomes the material out of which the principal theme is built.

1926 SLAVONIC MASS (or GLAGOLITIC MASS), for solo voices, chorus organ and orchestra.

Janáček was not a religious man: in fact, he was violently opposed to "organized religion" and openly expressed his contempt of churches. In writing this, his greatest work for chorus, he was, therefore, not producing a liturgical composition, but rather a composition that was pantheistic, patriotic and festive. Though his text was a sacred one—following the general pattern of the Roman Mass, though using an ancient Slavonic language instead of Latin—his aim was secular. He said: "I wanted to perpetuate faith in the immutable permanence of the nation, not on a religious basis but on a rock-bottom ethical basis, which calls God to witness." He had no intention of producing "medieval dungeon gloom, echoes of scholastic imitation, Bachian polyphony, Beethovenian pathos, Haydnish frivolity." Then he added: "In the tenor solo I hear a high priest, in the soprano solo a girlish angel, and in the chorus our folk."

He intended this Mass to help celebrate the tenth anniversary of the founding of the Czechoslovak Republic, but the Mass was given its first performance somewhat earlier—in Brünn on December 5, 1927. The music made such a deep impression that it was soon heard in Switzerland, Germany and England; its first performance in the United States took place in New York on October 26, 1930.

The Mass is in eight sections, five of which are choral. As was the custom in Czech church services, the five choral sections are preceded and followed by instrumental fanfares, to whose music the priests used to enter and depart; but just before the concluding fanfare, or intrada, the organ offers an extended joyful solo.

The Mass is made up of the following parts: an instrumental introduction; "Lord, Have Mercy" (the equivalent of the Kyrie); "Glory to God" (or Gloria); "I Believe" (or Credo); "Holy, Holy, Holy" (or Sanctus); "O, Lamb of God" (or Agnus Dei); an organ solo; and an instrumental intrada.

In reviewing the Mass for *High Fidelity* magazine, Alan Rich described it as follows: "The composer works with huge blocks of tone color . . . along with great inky washes. The mood is barbaric and exultant, no less pagan than Christian, a reminder that God is worshiped in many ways. In the Credo, for example, there is a kind of timeless abandon, in the chorus' recurring shouts of 'I Believe!' which punctuate the various divisions of the text. The final 'Amen' of this section also comes on with a wild sense of desperation, as though every member of the congregation were crowding forward to show his own hand and heart to the Almighty. . . . At times the work seems to stretch its sounds towards infinity. This is outdoor music, and the quiet, unearthly chant that begins the Sanctus seems to summon up images of an endless forest."

1925 SINFONIETTA, for orchestra. I. Allegretto. II. Andante. III. Moderato. IV. Allegretto. V. Allegro.

This sinfonietta originated as a series of fanfares for brass instruments, intended for open-air performance at an athletic meet in Prague. Hearing his fanfares, Janáček felt they deserved more extended musical treatment. He revamped them into a five-movement Sinfonietta. The origin of this work is revealed in the use of fanfare music for brass at the opening and close of the first movement, and in the fanfares of the last two.

Each movement is composed of several sections (some of them only a few bars), which proceed from one to another without much development, and often with the most tenuous transitions. The melodic and rhythmic ideas are all derived from Moravian folk songs and dances—and much of the work radiates peasant health and vigor.

The first movement presents one main theme, which is developed through three episodes. Two subjects are treated in the second movement, a dance tune and a contrasting lyric thought. The third movement opens with a haunting theme for muted violins and cellos against broken chords in harp. A polka-like theme for three trumpets in unison, followed by a countersubject in the strings, are the main ideas of the fourth movement, while the fifth serves as a climax to the entire work; this finale is episodic, with several brief new subjects in varied rhythms and tempi.

The Sinfonietta was introduced in Prague by the Czech Philharmonic on June 29, 1926.

DMITRI KABALEVSKY 1904–

Like so many other Soviet composers, Kabalevsky has utilized music to glorify the political and social ideologies of his country, as well as to pay tribute to the historic and cultural past of the Russian people. Even when his music does not have a stated program, its intention usually is to portray some phase of Soviet life and aspirations. He is satisfied to write in traditional forms, using stout harmonies, broad rhythms, compelling sonorities. He fills his music with subjective feelings; at the same time, he often draws deeply from the well of Russian folk song. A vein of pleasing wit is sometimes tapped to provide his writing with an infectious charm. Uncomplicated, direct, forceful, always aurally agreeable, always strongly identified with his country and people, his music makes an immediate appeal on listeners.

Kabalevsky was born in St. Petersburg on December 30, 1904. Though he early revealed a marked talent for music, he did not begin intensive study until his fourteenth year, when he entered the Scriabin School of Music in Moscow, specializing in piano; at the same time, he studied composition privately with Vassilenko and Catoire. He completed his music study at the Moscow Conservatory with Miaskovsky (composition) and Goldenweiser (piano). Upon his graduation in 1930, his name was inscribed on the honor plaque in the hall of the Conservatory.

Meanwhile, in 1925, he was appointed by the government to a teaching post in a children's school, where he composed several delightful works expressly for children's use. He maintained his interest in and contact with children for many years thereafter. Subsequently, he taught briefly at the Scriabin School. In 1932, he was appointed instructor of composition at the Moscow Conservatory, where he later became full professor. In 1939, he was elected president of the Organizing Committee of the Union of Soviet Composers, and in 1940, he received the Order of Merit. He was awarded the Stalin Prize three times: in 1946, for his second string quartet; in 1949, for his violin concerto; and in 1951, for the opera *The Family of Taras* (describing the Russian fight against Nazi invaders during World War II), whose first performance was in Moscow on November 2, 1947. He was honored with the Order of Lenin in 1965. Kabalevsky paid a visit to the United States in November of 1959.

1934 SYMPHONY NO. 2, op. 19. I. Allegro quasi presto. II. Andante non troppo. III. Prestissimo; Scherzando; Molto agitato; Allegro.

Kabalevsky's Second Symphony is actually his Third. The so-called Third Symphony, subtitled *Requiem for Lenin,* had been written in 1933, one year before the Second. He completed the Second, op. 19, in 1934, and it was introduced in Moscow on December 25 of that year, Albert Coates conducting the Moscow Philharmonic. It proved so successful that it was soon heard throughout Europe and the United States, its American première taking place over the NBC radio network on November 8, 1942, with Toscanini conducting the NBC Symphony.

In his First Symphony (1932), Kabalevsky spoke of man's adjustment to life after numerous inner conflicts. In the Second Symphony, he is more positive in his ideological approach. Man takes an active part in the reconstruction of his society, and thereby achieves his salvation.

The cogent first movement might be interpreted as man's triumph over the obstacles placed in his way in the building of a new society. The movement opens with a loud chord, much like the thrust of a clenched fist against possible opposition. A virile theme in the clarinet and a more lyrical second subject undergo dramatic development. Serenity comes in the second movement, which is beautifully melodic—as if man had found peace within himself. This movement opens with a flute solo accompanied by strings. Soon the orchestra bursts into song, and a new lyrical thought is later projected by solo trombone over plucked strings. But this inner peace develops into an exultant feeling of triumph in the last movement, which glows with brilliant orchestral color and is swept by powerful rhythmic forces. The finale opens with a scherzo section in which a vivacious tune is shared by two clarinets. Following a climax, a new subject is introduced by violins ana piccolo. Bassoon and clarinets recall the opening material before a new part is ushered in by a crescendo. Here we get a vigorous subject in trombone. A prestissimo section is developed climactically before the final Allegro reintroduces some of the earlier material. Then the second theme of the first movement helps bring the symphony to a joyful conclusion.

1936 CONCERTO NO. 2 IN G MINOR FOR PIANO AND ORCHESTRA, op. 23. I. Allegro. II. Andante. III. Allegro molto; Alla breve.

Kabalevsky's Second Piano Concerto is one of his finest and most successful works. It was written soon after the Second Symphony and was introduced in the United States over the radio on May 9, 1943. Leo Smit was the soloist, and the NBC Symphony was directed by Frank Black.

The concerto is classical in form, and filled with bright, vigorous melodies. The principal theme of the first movement is aggressive, contrasting with a second theme of singing character; both themes are ingeniously synthesized at the end of the movement. The entire second movement is melancholy; there are two main themes, one tender, the other passionate. A toccata-like third movement moves precipitously to impressive climaxes. The principal idea of this section is an adaptation of the first theme of the first movement.

1937 OVERTURE TO COLAS BREUGNON, for orchestra, op. 24.

COLAS BREUGNON, suite for orchestra. I. People's Rebellion. II. People's Calamity. III. People's Festival.

A novel by Romain Rolland, adapted by V. Bragin into a libretto, was the source for Kabalevsky's famous opera, *Colas Breugnon,* subtitled *The Master of Clamecy*. The character of Colas Breugnon—the witty, cunning Burgundian craftsman of the sixteenth century, who had such a laughing, lusty view of life—dominates the Rolland novel. And it dominates the opera, but with a difference. The Rolland tale consists more of the reflections of the hero, of his attitudes to situations, incidents and characters with which he is brought into contact; it has no particular social or political philosophy. But in Bragin's libretto, the story becomes a social criticism of the sixteenth century, with many interpolations of proletarian concepts. When the opera was introduced at the Leningrad State Opera on February 22, 1938, some Soviet critics—strange to report!—took the composer to task for the liberties he took with the Rolland story. But Rolland himself seemed highly pleased with the result and wrote to the composer: "You possess the gift of dramatic development which is absent in so many good composers. You also have your own harmonic language."

In preparing to write the opera, Kabalevsky made an intensive study of French folk songs—Burgundian folk songs in particular. "My aim was to convey the local color and nature of the epoch." Though only two brief themes are borrowed directly from Burgundian folk music, much of the score has retained the distinct flavor and personality of the French folk songs, even where the melodies are Kabalevsky's own. For this procedure, Rolland particularly commended the composer. "The folk songs are highly successful. You have grasped their essence perfectly and have given them form in your music."

The overture to this opera has often been performed by American symphony orchestras, and is probably the best-known single work by Kabalevsky. It is, in miniature, a characterization of the principal character—his "rich, laughing philosophy of life," in the description of Gerald Abraham, "his wise, salty humor, his wit, his fire, his pride in his craft, his cunning, his sturdy bearing of misfortune."

The sparkling, laughing measures of the overture are an admirable portrait of a man who loved the good things of life. A single bustling, good-humored and energetic melody is the foundation of the entire piece.

Kabalevsky extracted three orchestral episodes from his opera for an orchestral suite that is sometimes heard at symphony concerts.

1940 THE COMEDIANS, suite for orchestra, op. 26. I. Prologue. II. Galop. III. March. IV. Waltz. V. Pantomime. VI. Intermezzo. VII. Little Lyrical Scene. VIII. Gavotte. IX. Scherzo. X. Epilogue.

Kabalevsky wrote incidental music for a children's play, *The Inventor and Comedians,* produced in Moscow in 1940. The play centered around a band of itinerant comedians and their often amusing escapades as they travel from town to town, appearing in public squares, at fairs, and so on. In writing the music for this play, Kabalevsky assumed a simple and direct style, now witty, now pictorial, now nostalgic, now ingenuous. From this score, Kabalevsky prepared an orchestral suite comprising ten numbers. Since then, the suite has been heard with equal success at children's concerts and on symphony programs for adults.

1946 SONATA NO. 3 FOR PIANO, op. 46. I. Allegro con moto. II. Andante cantabile. III. Allegro giocoso.

Kabalevsky's Third Piano Sonata was heard for the first time in Moscow, at the Moscow Conservatory, in a performance by Yakov Zak on January 27, 1947.

A pleasant little tune opens the sonata. The sonority grows and the harmonic texture becomes detailed before the appearance of the second theme—another delightful melody. Both of these themes are quiet and restrained, but an incidental theme, march-like in character, has rhythmic strength and dissonant harmonies. The original material then returns, though sometimes in accelerated tempo and sharply accentuated rhythms.

A song of haunting beauty unfolds in the second movement; it has the simplicity and poignancy of a folk melody. But, almost as if the composer felt that such peace is ephemeral, the music suddenly becomes stormy and febrile as great power is generated. Then the original vein comes back: beauty triumphs over ugliness.

A martial mood is created in the last movement—music of galvanic power and great rhythmic surges, which makes one suspect that the recent war was still in the composer's mind. This suspicion is further strengthened by the outcries of jubilation that follow, the uninhibited joy of total victory.

1948 CONCERTO FOR VIOLIN AND ORCHESTRA, op. 48. I. Allegro molto e con brio. II. Andantino cantabile. III. Vivace giocoso.

CONCERTO FOR CELLO AND ORCHESTRA, op. 49. I. Allegro II. Largo molto espressivo. III. Allegretto.

Kabalevsky's violin concerto has become one of the most popular such works in the modern repertory. It received a dual world première, having been introduced simultaneously in both Leningrad and Moscow on October 29, 1948. In 1949, it was given the Stalin Prize.

Louis Kaufman, the violinist who introduced this concerto in America (over the NBC Pacific radio network on May 14, 1950), prepared the following succinct analysis:

"The first movement, in the fresh, unconstrained and sincere language of Kabalevsky, is an Allegro con brio which is candidly traditional in form and lively and ingratiatingly warm in content. The Andantino cantabile opens with a beautiful melody worthy of the great Russian romantic tradition, which is immediately contrasted with a rhythmically developed motive of capricious character that leads back to the first subject intoned by the orchestra. This is gracefully accompanied by the solo violin in muted scale and trill passages and ends with the soloist singing the basic theme simply, without the slightest deviation. The concluding third movement is . . . full of vitality and good-natured zest. This infectiously gay section includes a witty homage to Mendelssohn in the cadenza, after which the headlong pace is resumed to terminate in a brief and triumphant coda."

The Cello Concerto was first heard in Moscow on March 15, 1949, with Sviatoslav Knushevitzky as soloist. The first movement opens with a plucked string introduction which prepares the stage for the appearance of the solo instrument in a fulsome melody. The mood then passes from gaiety to yearning before the movement ends with a coda, in which the opening plucked section is recalled. In the second movement, the solo cello is heard in a doleful melody over syncopated string chords, and later on in a brilliant cadenza. The finale opens with a lively folk dance in the solo instrument. A more lyrical episode comes as a contrast, but the rest of the movement is lively, with at times electrifying virtuoso writing for the solo cello.

Actually, the violin and cello concertos are the first two parts of a trilogy in which the composer sought to "represent a manifold revelation of the ideas of our Soviet youth." In such a trilogy, the violin concerto assumes the character of a first-movement Allegro in a symphony or concerto; the cello represents the slow movement. The third concerto in this trilogy—serving as the finale for this overall symphonic concept—is the Piano Concerto No 3, op. 50, subtitled *Youth,* completed in 1952.

1956 SYMPHONY NO. 4, for orchestra. I. Lento; Allegro molto e fuoco. II. Largo. III. Scherzo. IV. Lento; Allegro.

Kabalevsky's Fourth Symphony came twenty-two years after its predecessor, the so-called Second, which was actually the composer's Third. The world première took place in Moscow in October of 1956. The symphony is well integrated; material from the first movement recurs in one guise or another in succeeding movements, and is used to bring the work to a rousing culmination in the concluding Allegro.

Without being specific, or assigning a definite and detailed program to his music, the composer hinted that his Fourth Symphony was autobiographical. He further explained that it embodied his basic ideas on life. "What do I believe? Life is good, even if sometimes death passes by. No matter what difficulties there may be, life is stronger than death." Then the composer described his music this way: "The first part is very dramatic. A lyric theme wants to break through and take its place, and there is great contrast between light lyricism and drama. But the section ends almost in a tragic way. The second part is like a funeral march but still a lyric theme penetrates it—like man's character. The third part is a light scherzo, almost fantastic. . . . Finally, in the fourth part the lyric part asserts itself."

1963 REQUIEM, for solo voices, chorus and orchestra.

For four years, Kabalevsky had been "obsessed," as he said, with the idea of writing a major work in memory of those Soviet heroes who fell in World War II. He sought a text that would "combine deep emotion with a penetrating idea, grand form with simplicity of expression, modernity with the universal humanist theme of the immortality of heroic exploits performed by man for the sake of victory of life over death." The verses were finally written for him by the poet, Robert Rozhdestensky.

The *Requiem* is in three long movements which, in turn, are divided into eleven independent episodes. Kabalevsky explained that the principal element of the first movement (after a short, concentrated introduction) is the melody "Glory Forever," the symbol of undying life, a life that is stronger than death. The second movement opens with questions man asks a gravestone at the tomb of the unknown soldier; but the gravestone remains silent. Then a mother's wail rises, in the style of a folk lamentation. The movement ends with a glowing tribute to childhood and youth. The concluding movement opens with an extended symphonic episode, based on the melody "Glory Forever." The exhortation "Remember," which had been heard throughout the first movement, is extensively developed. And it is with this exhortation that the work ends.

The world première of the *Requiem* took place in Moscow on February 9, 1963, Vladislav Sokolov conducting. Performances in other major Soviet cities followed. The American première took place at the Eastman School of Music in Rochester, New York, on December 9, 1965, Walter Hendl conducting. For this presentation, the text was translated into English.

The Soviet critic, A. Medvedev wrote: "The *Requiem* arouses in us layer upon layer of feelings, thoughts and images. The work develops not so much on the principle of dramatic contrast between the movements as on the evolution of one leading idea which grows and expands from episode to episode. This idea is the call 'Remember.' It is reiterated throughout the work, now as if spoken by the author; now uttered by the departed heroes; and again through live and active musical pictures. The general impression from the music of the *Requiem* is clarity and simplicity."

ARAM KHATCHATURIAN 1903–

Up to the time of his twentieth year, when he began music study, the only music Khatchaturian knew was the folk songs and dances of his native Armenia. The first piece he wrote, and had performed, the *Dance* for violin and piano (1926), drew its stylistic traits from the folk art of the trans-Caucasian peoples. And though for a brief period he was attracted to and influenced by the modern style and techniques of the contemporary French school, he soon rejected them and developed his personal idiom through the absorption of the folk elements found in the music of his people.

The intonations, the rhythmic patterns, the oriental colorings, and the dramatic emotional contrasts found in Armenian folk songs and dances are the predominant traits of Khatchaturian's music. The improvisational character of the songs of the *ashugs*—Armenian bards—is caught in his rambling melodies. Highly lyrical, rich in colors and dynamics, endowed with a powerful rhythmic momentum, his music has a forceful impact even on first acquaintance.

Khatchaturian was born in Tiflis, Armenia, on June 6, 1903, and began the study of music twenty years later at the Gnessin School of Music in Moscow. Six years after that, he entered the Moscow Conservatory, where his teachers included Miaskovsky and Vasilenko. His First Symphony, written in 1932 to commemorate the tenth anniversary of the Sovietization of Armenia, brought him his first recognition. His success became solidified with his Piano Concerto in 1937, Violin Concerto in 1938 (for which he received the Stalin Prize) and the ballet *Gayane* in 1942 (which brought him the Stalin Prize for the second time). Meanwhile, in 1939, he received the Order of Lenin and, soon after that, had his name inscribed on an honor plaque in the hall of the Moscow Conservatory. During World War II, he wrote and had performed his Seond Symphony, which had been influenced by that turbulent period. Along with other significant composers of the Soviet Union, Khatchaturian was condemned by the Central Committee of the Communist Party for his indulgence in "anti-popular trends" and "bourgeois formalism" on February 10, 1948 (*see* Prokofiev). A half-year after Stalin's death, Khatchaturian published in *Soviet Music* a much publicized article condemning the Central Committee for its action of 1948 and urging Soviet composers to seek out "creative innovation." This finally led to a decision by the Central Committee that composers must now be permitted greater creative freedom; at the same time the Committee placed Khatchaturian with Shostakovich and Prokofiev as the three foremost Soviet composers of the twentieth century.

In 1951, Khatchaturian was appointed professor of composition at the Moscow Conservatory and the Gnessin School; a few years later, he was given the Lenin Prize for the ballet *Spartacus*. His sixtieth birthday, in 1963, was celebrated throughout the Soviet Union.

Khatchaturian made several tours of Europe conducting his music. He paid his first visit to the United States in March of 1960. His American debut as conductor took place in Washington, D.C., on January 23, 1968. He is married to Nina Makarova, regarded by many Soviet critics as the foremost woman composer in the Soviet Union.

1932 SYMPHONY NO. 1. I. Andante maestoso; Allegro mon troppo. II. Adagio sostenuto. III. Allegro risoluto.

The first of Khatchaturian's major works was written to honor Soviet Armenia on its fifteenth anniversary. It was introduced the same year by Eugene Szenkar and the Moscow State Philharmonic Orchestra, scoring a decided success, and bringing the composer to the limelight for the first time.

Though it does not utilize actual folk songs, the symphony is rich with the colors, rhythms and personality of Armenian folk music. The improvisational character of the introduction (which contains the basic thematic ideas of the entire symphony) is derived from the bardic songs of the *ashugs*. This first movement is of epical structure. Khubov, who described it as "monumental," considers it a "perfectly independent symphonic poem." The first theme, Khubov continues, develops "immediately and organically" out of the prologue, while the second, an Armenian melody in a different tempo, "emerges against a background provided by the dying away of a metamorphosis of the principal theme." These same ideas are found in the next two movements, worked out with deep feeling in the slow section and with powerful dramatic impulses in the closing movement.

1935 CONCERTO FOR PIANO AND ORCHESTRA. I. Allegro ma non troppo e maesto. II. Andante con anima. III. Allegro brillante.

With his Piano Concerto, which Khatchaturian wrote one year after his First Symphony, and which was introduced in Moscow on July 5, 1937, with the composer as soloist, he solidified his success as a composer. The concerto enjoyed extraordinary popularity in the Soviet Union. After its American première on March 14, 1942, when it was performed by Maro Ajemian and the Juilliard Orchestra under Albert Stoessel, it became one of Khatchaturian's most frequently heard and widely admired works in the United States.

Its popularity is understandable. Its folk character endows it with rhythmic and harmonic vitality and an exotic oriental personality. It is brilliant in its virtuoso writing. The fast movements have an electrifying momentum, and are suggestive of Borodin and Liszt in their breadth and scope. The middle section catches its breath from the athletic movement which precedes it, to give way to introspective and poetic brooding; a fascinating contrast to the drive of the outside movements is thereby provided.

The vigorous and joyous theme with which the first movement opens (a theme characteristically Armenian in its cadential structure) dominates the entire section, returning in the finale with a renewed burst of energy. "The exotic romanza-like effect of the Andante," wrote the Soviet critic Khubov, "is achieved through a combination of fresh harmonies, folk mood, and laconic expression, the whole giving an impression of severe simplicity."

1938 CONCERTO FOR VIOLIN AND ORCHESTRA. I. Allegro confermezza. II. Andante sostenuto. III. Allegro vivace.

Three years after he wrote his Piano Concerto, Khatchaturian wrote a Concerto for Violin which is no less attractive in its use of engaging folk materials and no less brilliant in its exploitation of the virtuoso possibilities of the solo instrument. Like its predecessor for the piano, this concerto opens with a powerfully rhythmic first movement. The first theme sweeps with a heroic stride; the second subject, equally virile, is also intensely passionate. The second movement resembles a lament; it is one of the most poignant pieces of music written by this composer. The singing and romantic quality of the violin is utilized with great effect. A vertiginous finale has gypsy abandon.

The Violin Concerto was performed for the first time in Moscow on November 16, 1940, following which it earned for its composer his first Stalin Prize.

1942 GAYANE, two ballet suites for orchestra.

No. I: I. Sabre Dance: II. Dance of Ayshe; III. Dance of the Rose Maidens; IV. Dance of the Kurds; V. Lullaby; VI. Dance of the Young Kurds; VII. Variations; VIII. Lezghinska.

No. II: I. Russian Dance; II. Introduction; III. Gayane's Adagio; IV. Fire.

Gayane (or *Gayaneh,* as it is known abroad) is a patriotic folk ballet with libretto by K. N. Derzhavin. On December 9, 1942, it was introduced by the Kirov Theatre for Opera and Ballet (which is connected with the Leningrad State Academy) in the city of Molotov. N. A. Anisimova was the producer and principal ballerina. In 1943, it received the Stalin Prize, first degree.

The action takes place in a collective farm, with its everyday work and play activity providing much of the background material. Giko, a traitor to the Soviet Union, joins up with a group of smugglers. He sets fire to his own collective farm and attempts to murder his wife, Gayaneh, and their daughter. They are saved by Kazakov, who is in love with Gayaneh, and who marries her when Giko meets the fate that is his due.

Khatchaturian's score is a veritable cornucopia of Armenian folk dances, of which he later gathered twelve into two orchestral suites that have achieved considerable popularity on orchestral programs and in recordings. The dances have a wide variety of pace and mood, ranging from the tender and the nostalgic (as in the famous "Lullaby") to the corybantic (as in the even more celebrated

"Sabre Dance"), to the exotic (as in the "Dance of the Rose Maidens"). Shepherd dances, peasant dances, a Ukrainian *hopak* and a Georgian *lezghinka* are also represented.

"Lullaby" has a gentle, swaying tune in solo oboe, set against a decisive rhythm in harp and bassoon; flutes take up this subject, after which the melody grows and expands in full orchestra, then subsides. The impact of the "Sabre Dance" arises from its barbaric rhythmic strength and vivid sonorities; midway, relief from rhythmic tensions comes through a broad folk song in violas and cellos. "Dance of the Rose Maidens" offers a delightful oriental melody in oboe and clarinet against a pronounced rhythm.

Three of these dances ("Lullaby," "Sabre Dance" and "Dance of the Rose Maidens") were first heard in the United States in 1945, in a performance by the Kansas Philharmonic Orchestra under Efrem Kurtz. When these dances were first heard in New York at the Lewisohn Stadium, the "Sabre Dance" had to be repeated. This dance was then heard so frequently over the radio in 1948—even in arrangements for the piano and for popular orchestras—that, for a time, it enjoyed the status of a hit number.

1942 SYMPHONY NO. 2. I. Andante maestoso. II. Allegro risoluto. III. Andante sostenuto. IV. Andante mosso; Allegro sostenuto.

Khatchaturian's Second Symphony was a child of World War II. He began writing it soon after the Nazis invaded the Soviet Union. The "superhuman sufferings caused to the Soviet people by the Nazi monsters," said Khatchaturian, "are portrayed in the third movement." In the fourth, the heroism and unconquerable spirit of the Soviet people are powerfully delineated.

Khubov, who subtitled the work *Symphony with a Bell,* has written the definitive analysis of this work:

"The first movement has an introduction consisting of two elements—a bell motive, which shudders loudly through the entire orchestra, and a following theme for strings. The principal subject of the movement appears first in the lower strings, and with its statement there ensues a rather headlong development, embodying some harking back to previous material, plus hints of things to come. A brooding song now comes through the musical web, and it is intertwined with earlier themes. On the heels of this we enter into a march episode, introduced, however, by a repetition of the 'bell' idea. The march persists almost to the end of the section.

"The second movement presents an insistent rhythmic figure which grows to the dimensions of an irresistible danse macabre. The sinister quality of the music suddenly changes to a more genial section in a tune which comes floating into the scene. It lives its rather brief life, soon to be supplanted by the preceding business. . . .

"The third movement is of tragic import. Basically, it is a funeral march featuring a doleful theme of Azerbaijan folk origin. Shouted quite frenetically over the march is the *Dies Irae*. The music increases in power, and it ends in a great climax with the 'bell' motive.

"In the fourth movement, exultation is the feeling. Piercing fanfares open the section. The brass hurls out what is perhaps aptly described as a 'Brass Chorus of Glory.' Some softer fragments follow with the echoings of previous themes. Then a grand climax is attained as the 'bell' theme and the 'Brass Chorus' thunder out an idea symbolic of triumph."

The symphony was heard for the first time on December 30, 1943, with Boris Khaikin conducting the Moscow Conservatory Orchestra. The symphony, as it was heard in this country for the first time, on April 13, 1945, with Leonard Bernstein directing an improvised orchestra, was somewhat different from that introduced in Moscow. There were various revisions by the composer in the score, the most important being the shifting of the Andante sostenuto from the second movement to the third, and putting the Scherzo in its place. This revision was introduced in Moscow on March 6, 1944.

1944 MASQUERADE, suite for orchestra. I. Waltz. II. Nocturne. III. Romance. IV. Mazurka. V. Galop.

In 1939, Khatchaturian composed incidental music for a play by Mikhail Lermontov, *Masquerade,* dealing with the licentious life of the Russian upper classes in the 1830s. From this score, the composer prepared a concert suite of five numbers, which the Moscow Radio Orchestra introduced in 1944. The music is throughout lilting and infectious—of the summer "pop" variety—full of engaging melodies and whirling rhythms. Gentle lyricism characterizes the second and third movements, the "Nocturne" and the "Romance." The first and last movements are essentially rhythmic.

1946 CONCERTO FOR CELLO AND ORCHESTRA. I. Allegro moderato. II. Andante sostenuto. III. Allegro.

This vigorous work—like the concertos for the piano and for the violin—is indebted to Armenian folk music for its personality and stylistic traits. An impressive orchestral prologue inaugurates the first movement. The soloist then presents the principal theme, which is allowed to develop in a virtuoso manner throughout the movement (the longest and most fully developed of the three). A prolonged orchestral introduction, in which a flute solo is prominent, also opens the second movement. The cello then appears with a languorous oriental melody, which passes on to the orchestra. A climax follows. After the return of the principal melody, the third movement enters without any interruption. This part is highly rhythmic, containing flashing passages for the cello.

This concerto was introduced in Moscow on October 30, 1946.

1946 RUSSIAN FANTASY, for orchestra.

In 1944, Khatchaturian wrote a *Russian Fantasy* for native Russian instruments. This was the original source of his *Russian Fantasy* for symphony orchestra, a seven-minute composition, completed and published in 1946. The American première took place on April 1, 1948, with Leopold Stokowski directing the New York Philharmonic. The composition opens with a Maestoso section in which an eight-measure folk tune is prominently treated. After the tempo changes to Allegro, a second folk melody, livelier than the first, is introduced. The sonority develops, and the rhythmic drive is intensified until a stirring climax is reached.

LEON KIRCHNER 1919–

As early as 1950, Aaron Copland had said of Kirchner in *Notes:* "The impression carried away from a Kirchner performance is one of having made contact, not merely with a composer, but with a highly sentient human being; of a man who creates his music out of an awareness of the special climate of today's unsettled world. Kirchner's best pages prove that he reacts strongly to that world; they are charged with an emotional impact and explosive power that is almost frightening in intensity. Whatever else may be said, this music is music that most certainly is 'felt.' "

Such words still hold true today. Kirchner has passed from the Bartókian discords and rhythmic momentum of his earlier works to the austerity of the serial technique and linear writing of his later ones. But he still maintains contact with his listener through the power he always generates and the romantic feelings he communicates. His style reflects the impact of Schoenberg and Stravinsky as well as Bartók; nevertheless, it is his own. For all its complexity, it manages to have sensitivity and grace, for all its motor energy and strength, it manages to possess infectious lyricism.

Kirchner was born in Brooklyn, New York, on January 24, 1919. He was raised in Los Angeles, to which his family moved when he was nine. In Los Angeles, he studied the piano with John Crown and attended Schoenberg's composition class at the University of California in Los Angeles. In 1940, he received a Bachelor of Arts degree from the University of California at Berkeley, and in 1941, he did graduate work there in composition with Albert Elkus and Edward Strickland. For a while, he was also a pupil of Ernest Bloch. In 1942, he received the University's highest award, the George Ladd Prix de Rome. The war prevented him from going to Europe. Instead, he came to New York, where, in 1943, he wrote a choral piece, *Dawn* (text by García Lorca). For three years, he saw active service in the United States Army. Between 1947 and 1954, he was a member of the music faculty at the University of California at Berkeley. This period saw the writing of his first major works: the Duo, for violin and piano (1947), introduced at a concert of the League of Composers in New York on March 6, 1949; and his first string quartet, which received the New York Music Critics Circle Award in 1950. In 1951, he was given an award from the National Institute of Art and Letters; in 1956, his first piano concerto was given the Naumburg Award; and in

1959, he was once again a recipient of the New York Music Critics Circle Award, this time for his second string quartet.

In 1948, and again in 1949, he received Guggenheim Fellowships. From 1954 to 1961, he was professor of music at Mills College in Oakland, California. In 1961, he succeeded Walter Piston as professor of music at Harvard University. One year after that, he was elected a member of the National Institute of Arts and Letters and the National Academy of Arts and Sciences. In 1967, Kirchner received the Pulitzer Prize for his String Quartet No. 3, for strings and electronic sound; this composition was written for the Beaux Art Quartet, which introduced it in New York City on January 27, 1967.

1949 STRING QUARTET NO. 1. I. Allegro ma non troppo. II. Adagio. III. Divertimento and Trio. IV. Adagio.

Kirchner's first string quartet was influenced partly by Bartók and partly by Schoenberg. But, as Alfred J. Frankenstein remarked, it nevertheless has "its own immensely individual profile." Introduced in the year of its composition in New York, it received the New York Music Critics Circle Award in 1950 and was recorded for Columbia. The work was acclaimed in Budapest, Hungary, when the Juilliard String Quartet presented it there on September 24, 1958.

In analyzing the structure, Alexander L. Ringer points out that the opening Allegro is "interrupted by an Andante which anticipates material of the first Adagio, and the final slow movement has a fast conclusion." The tempo, therefore, alternates continually from fast to slow, as a nervous tension is sustained, exotic instrumental effects are achieved, and a powerful rhythmic momentum is built up.

1952 SONATA CONCERTANTE, for violin and piano.

Kirchner's style became crystallized with this one-movement composition, which Jay C. Rosenfeld described as "really a concerto for each instrument." The première took place in New York in November of 1952, in a performance by Tossy Spivakovsky and the composer. The music is rhapsodic and improvisatory, opening with a long, dramatic discourse by the violin in double stops (a section that returns several times later). A brief Adagio follows. The work ends with a coda, in which violin and piano take turns in bringing the composition to an effective denouement.

1953 CONCERTO NO. 1 FOR PIANO AND ORCHESTRA. I. Allegro. II. Adagio. III. Allegro ma non troppo.

This concerto was commissioned by the Koussevitzky Music Foundation and the Library of Congress in Washington, D.C. The first performance took place in New York on February 23, 1956. The composer was the soloist and Dimitri Mitropoulos conducted the New York Philharmonic. On June 4, 1957, this concerto was heard at the festival of the International Society for Contemporary Music in Zurich.

A ten-measure solo introduction for the piano, in the style of a toccata, precedes the presentation of the exposition section by the orchestra. When the piano enters, it takes over this material to a light orchestral accompaniment.

A slow section with an expressive melodic part follows, after which a brilliant cadenza brings the movement to its conclusion. The slow movement, says Alexander Ringer, is "a fascinating discourse between the lyrical contemplations of the piano and a dramatic recitative-like idea in the orchestra." In the rhythmic finale, "the dotted motif attains its inevitable triumph. It is heard immediately in the first measures of both the orchestra and the piano and returns in various guises on nearly every page of the score."

1955 TOCCATA, for woodwinds, percussion and strings.

This toccata was commissioned for the San Francisco Symphony, which introduced it on February 16, 1956. Though in a single movement, it is made up of four sections: an exposition, development, slow movement and a recapitulation with coda. Here is how Harold Rogers described it in the *Christian Science Monitor*: "It opens with dirge-like winds and eerie string harmonics, quickly picking up drive and frenzy. The tension is then relaxed into a mood of lyrical reminiscence, after which the tension builds again; but with each surge and each falling away the poetry changes in mood."

Paul Hume noted in the *Washington Post* that the main interest in this music lies in its rhythmic vitality. "Kirchner seizes our attention almost immediately by virile rhythmic devices, and by a sense of strongly guided motion that has no flagging, no lack of clarity of purpose or of achievement." But the sonorities are also of considerable interest, "expertly handled to maintain clarity, whether in the sound of four violins, or the usual string quartet . . . while the wind intruments add point and thrust to the silkier sounds."

ZOLTÁN KODÁLY 1882–1967

Like his friend and compatriot, Béla Bartók, Zoltán Kodály went on extensive expeditions throughout Hungary in search of authentic folk music. In a few years' time, Kodály had collected between three and four thousand of these melodies, many of which he published jointly with Bartók. These melodies were far different from the puling, sentimental gypsy songs that the world up to then had accepted as Hungarian folk music. The Hungarian folk-song and folk-dance music which Kodály and Bartók uncovered in different parts of the country lacks (as Paul Rosenfeld once wrote) "the meretriciousness of gypsy music, and is not sinuous, sliding or suggestive as that is. It is much severer, earthier, and homelier . . . and has some of the strength and savorsomeness of Mussorgsky's folk-born Slavic music."

Intimacy with this folk music was an influence on Kodály's development as a composer. Formerly, he had written works that betrayed stylistic traits of Brahms: a sonata for cello and another for violin, and a piano trio. Now (beginning with the *Summer Evening,* for orchestra, in 1906), his melodic language acquired the rhythm and inflection of the Hungarian language. The brusqueness of accent, the modal quality of the tonality, the persistent repetition of a melodic or rhythmic pattern, the narrative recitative-like character of his writing—all this became the identifying qualities of his own music, just as they were the qualities to distingush Hungary's musical folk art.

When Arthur Bliss said that "Kodály is the voice of Hungary in music," he was making an assessment that in some respects is truer of Kodály than it was of Bartók. Bartók used folk music as the point of departure for his own individual creative journey; though the folk-song influence was thoroughly absorbed, Bartók did not rely on quotation and in fact evolved a style that is Bartók through and through, and only incidentally Hungarian. Kodály, all his life, depended on actual folk songs for his material. He used native melodies from the towns of Marosszék and Galanta for orchestral dances; he built an entire opera, *Spinnstube* (first performance in Budapest on April 24, 1932), with actual folk songs and dances. His *Peacock Variations* borrowed its main theme from a Hungarian folk song. His most famous opera, *Háry János,* at times quotes folk tunes, and at other times has melodies and dances modeled so closely after native patterns that they seem to be actual folk material.

Actually, Kodály stands at a pole opposite to Bartók. Bartók took the severity of line in folk songs and went on to make it more severe; its complexity of rhythmic structure was magnified; its primitivism, intensified. Kodály, on the other hand, softened the hard lines, simplified the complex, and minimized the primitive. Kodály's misic is tonal, and his writing is often subjective or introspective, where Bartók veered towards atonality, and his writing for many years was thoroughly objective. The singing line of Kodály's lyricism is like the natural outpouring of the human voice. Where Bartók could be bitter and acrid, Kodály could be gentle and sweet. Where Bartók leaned towards expressionism, Kodály is at times even partial to impressionism.

Kodály was born in the town of Kecskemét, Hungary, on December 16, 1882. As a boy he sang in a church choir and began writing choral pieces; an orchestral overture, written in 1897, was performed by a high-school orchestra. In 1900, he enrolled in the Royal Academy of Music in Budapest, where he studied composition with Hans Koessler and where he began writing chamber music in a Brahmsian style. He was graduated from the Academy in 1905. He also attended the University, where in 1906 he received his doctorate.

His intensive researches into Hungarian folk music had begun in 1905 in collaboration with Bartók. He embarked upon numerous expeditions throughout Hungary, writing down and recording the native melodies and dances of different localities, then editing and publishing them. The impact of this research was reflected in his compositions, which deserted Brahms for a more national Hungarian personality. International fame arrived in 1923 with the *Psalmus Hungaricus,* and was extended with the opera *Háry János.* Thereafter, he became one of Hungary's major musical personalities—influential as a teacher, music critic and musicologist as well as a composer.

During World War II, in Nazi-occupied Hungary, he was influential in helping numerous refugees escape the hands of the invaders. Though his activities were uncovered by the Gestapo, his enormous popularity with the Hungarian people saved him from the concentration camp. In the winter of 1946, Kodály paid his first visit to the United States, arriving as an official delegate to the Congress of International Confederation of Authors' Societies, meeting in Washington, D.C. From the middle 1940s on, Kodály was venerated in Hungary as one of its giant cultural figures, and he has gathered honor after honor. He became president of the National Arts Council, a member of the National Assembly, and was three times recipient of the Kossuth Prize. On his sixty-fifth birthday he was given the Grand Cross of the Order of the Hungarian Republic. He was responsible for revolutionizing music education in Hungary through the formation of singing schools for children and the development of a new method of sight reading based on hand signals.

His wife, Emma, whom he had married in 1910, died in 1958. One year later, Kodály married Sarolta Péczeli, a nineteen-year-old student at the Musical Academy. During this period, Kodály completed the writing of his First Symphony, upon which he had been working for decades. His eightieth birthday was celebrated throughout Hungary with concerts tracing his entire creative career. In the summer of 1965, Kodály paid a second visit to the United States to serve as composer-in-residence at Dartmouth College, in Hanover, New Hampshire, during that college's third annual Congregation of the Arts. A feature of this festival was a series of four concerts, all devoted to Kodály's music. Zoltán Kodály died in Budapest, Hungary, on March 6, 1967.

1906 SUMMER EVENING, for orchestra.

The first composition in which Kodály's liberation from the influence of Brahms allowed him to evolve a nationalist style was a tone poem for chamber orchestra first performed in 1906 at a student's concert at the Musical Academy. Toscanini liked this early Kodály piece so much he asked the composer to revise it. Kodály did so in 1929, now scoring it for an orchestra of nine wind instruments and strings. The première of the new version took place in New York on April 3, 1930, with Toscanini conducting the New York Philharmonic. Lawrence Gilman described the music as an "extended revery" in which the composer "recalls the moods of the countryside—not without emotion." It opens with an eight-measure solo for English horn (Andante assai), which muted strings soon take over. Later on, an important new melody is introduced, one with the contours and spirit of a Hungarian folk song. It is heard in the oboe, accompanied by a staccato figure in flute, clarinet and plucked strings. After a crescendo, this folk melody is repeated in the violins, and in an altered form becomes the basis of a powerful climax.

1923 PSALMUS HUNGARICUS, for tenor solo, mixed chorus, children's chorus (ad libitum) and orchestra.

In 1923, Kodly was commissioned by the Hungarian government to write a work for performance in conjunction with festivities commemorating the fiftieth anniversary of the union of Buda and Pest. Kodály selected an old Hungarian text dating from the sixteenth century in which the poet,

Michael Veg, had adapted the Fifty-Fifth Psalm but had filled it with so many personal and national associations that it had become a Hungarian psalm. By interpolating his own lines, the poet was voicing a lamentation at the sad fate of Hungary under Turkish dominance and hurling a challenge at the oppressors. "Better it were to dwell in the desert," reads one of his lines, "than live with wicked liars and traitors who will not suffer that I should speak the truth."

In setting this text to music, Kodály drew copiously from old Hungarian modes and folk idioms, producing a work of singular power and eloquence. Lyrical passages are assigned to the chorus, while the main body of the psalm is sung by a tenor. It is not only one of his finest works but also one of the outstanding choral works of the twentieth century. Its first performance took place in Budapest on November 19, 1923. After that it was translated into numerous languages and given hundreds of performances throughout the world. The American première took place in New York on December 19, 1927, with Willem Mengelberg conducting the New York Philharmonic.

The work opens with a sixteen-measure orchestral introduction, after which altos and basses enter with an unaccompanied unison passage: "Sad was the king, dismal and downcast." This is a refrain that recurs throughout the composition. The tenor then sings a poignant song of supplication to God, imploring Him not to turn away from the misery of the Hungarian people ("God of my fathers, bow Thine ear to me, Turn not away the light of Thy countenance"). This plea is continually interrupted by the return of the unison chorus chanting, "Sad was the king, dismal and downcast." An Adagio orchestral intermezzo of compelling beauty precedes a final solo for tenor, "Now does the French courage enter my soul." The concluding section, for chorus ("Thou art Our one God, righteous in judgment") sings the praises of the Lord, who in His wisdom and justice must surely bring about the destruction of Hungary's enemies.

1925 HÁRY JÁNOS, opera in five parts, with prologue and epilogue (sometimes given in three acts), with text by Béla Paulini and Zsolt Harsányi, based on a poem by János Garay. First performance: Budapest, October 16, 1926.

HÁRY JÁNOS, suite for orchestra. I. Prelude: The Fairy Story Begins. II. Viennese Musical Clock. III. Song. IV. The Battle and Defeat of Napoleon. V. Intermezzo. VI. Entrance of the Emperor and His Court.

Kodály's most famous work is an opera centered around the character of Háry János, a figure familiar in Hungarian folklore. Háry János is a picaresque fellow, boastful, somewhat pompous, and addicted to fabulous lies, which he himself soon believes to be the truth. In Kodály's opera, János moves against the background of the Vienna of more than a century ago. To a group of incredulous listeners, he spins a yarn that Marie Louise, daughter of Emperor Francis and the wife of Napoleon, is arriving in Vienna. Indeed, she *does* arrive, and during her visit falls in love with Háry and wants to take him back with her to Paris. Háry is willing, but only on condition that his sweetheart, Orze, joins them. Thus Háry is the center of a situation he enjoys no end: Two women compete for his affections, while Napoleon is enraged with jealousy. Napoleon's anger leads him to declare war on Austria, a war in which Háry—who is on the side of the Austrians, of course—is a hero; single-handed he destroys the enemy. Napoleon is put in the humiliating position of begging for mercy. Marie Louise, repelled by Napoleon's cowardice, is more than ever convinced of her love for Háry and is eager to marry him. Háry, meanwhile, is welcomed back to Vienna in triumph. But in Vienna, he suddenly realizes that it is Orze he loves. With a magnificent gesture, he rejects Marie Louise, returns her to Napoleon, and accepts Orze as his wife, taking her back with him to his native village. There (in the final scene of the opera) we find Háry János telling his tall tales to the villagers, as Orze arrives to take him home for dinner.

Háry János was produced with outstanding success at its world première in Budapest. It was staged in Cologne, Germany, on September 26, 1931, in a German translation. When it was first heard in the United States—in New York on March 18, 1960—the text was translated into English. Reviewing the American première in *The New York Times,* Howard Taubman wrote: "Kodály's score has its roots in folk music. Either it quotes folk tunes bodily—and these are the finest passages—or it seeks to capture their spirit. There are some lively numbers and they help to give the work what beguiling, fanciful atmosphere it has."

Some of the finest pages in the operatic score were used by the composer for an orchestral suite, which was heard for the first time anywhere in New York on December 15, 1927, in a performance by the New York Philharmonic, conducted by Willem Mengelberg. This suite has since then become one of Kodály's most frequently played orchestral compositions. It opens with an orchestral glissando representing a sneeze: a Hungarian superstition has it that a statement is true if the speaker sneezes as he talks. In the first part, "Prelude: The Fairy Tale Begins," Háry tells his wondrous story; as his imagination grows, so do the orchestral sonorities and dynamics. Háry comes to Vienna. In "Viennese Musical Clock" he stands in front of the Imperial Palace and listens to the chimes of the musical clock, at the same time watching the rotating mechanical figures. In "Song," he nostalgically recalls the gentle evening that would descend on his little village and touch it with peace. The fourth section, "The Battle and Defeat of Napoleon," is war let loose in the orchestra: a march rhythm sets the armies into motion; they clash; a funereal melody ends the section, speaking of the dead enemy. In the fifth part, "Intermezzo," a Hungarian dance is heard—vital, electrifying, full of gypsy blood. The concluding movement, "Entrance of the Emperor and his Court," finds Háry at the height of his triumph, contemplating the grandeur of Viennese royalty.

1930 DANCES OF MAROSSZÉK, for orchestra (also for piano).

Marosszék is a town in the province of Szekely, Hungary, which Kodály visited during his intensive researches into Hungarian folk music. Here he found a valuable storehouse of autochthonous songs and dances. Six of these native melodies were woven by the composer, in 1927, into an integrated work for piano, which in structure resembles a rondo. "In this form," says Percy M. Young, "the brilliance of the keyboard realization is positively Lisztian."

At the suggestion of Toscanini, Kodály orchestrated his piano work in 1930. The orchestral version was heard in Dresden, Germany, on November 28, 1930—two weeks before Toscanini conducted this music in New York. In the orchestral piece, says Edward Kilenyi, "one visualizes . . . these Szekelys in their quaint costumes, singing and dancing at their holiday celebrations." The symphonic texture, still in rondo form, makes use of six dance tunes, the principal one being a subject heard at the beginning of the composition in violas, cellos and clarinets, accompanied by chords in bassoons, horns and double basses (Maestoso, poco rubato).

1934 DANCES OF GALANTA, for orchestra.

These dances were written for the eightieth anniversary of the Budapest Philharmonic; but the world première took place in the United States on December 11, 1936, at a concert of the Philadelphia Orchestra.

In the published score, Kodály appended the following information: "Galanta is a small Hungarian market town known to travelers between Vienna and Budapest. The composer passed there seven years of his childhood. There existed at that time a gypsy band which has since disappeared. Their music was the first 'orchestral sonority' which came to the ears of the child. The forebears of these gypsies were known more than a hundred years ago. About 1800, some books of Hungarian dances were published in Vienna, one of which contained music 'after several gypsies from Galanta.' They have preserved the old Hungarian traditions. In order to continue it, the composer took his principal subjects from these ancient editions."

There are here five gypsy dances, played without interruption. A breathtaking momentum is achieved in these *Dances*. The composition opens sedately, but as it progresses the tempo is accelerated until the music erupts into an orgiastic outburst. Though each dance is independent, thematic ideas are repeated throughout to give the work integration.

The work opens with an introductory subject for the cellos, which is soon repeated by horns. The first dance (Andante maestoso) is then played by solo clarinet. The second dance, more rhythmic than the first, appears in solo flute (Allegro moderato). The third dance (Allegretto con moto) is an outgrowth of a flowing theme first heard in solo oboe before being taken over by the woodwind, and after that by full orchestra. The fourth dance (Allegro) is a simple tune for strings, while the fifth (Allegro vivace) is a passionate gypsy melody shared by violins, violas and solo flute. Following this fifth dance, a motive from the fourth is recalled, The coda features the first dance and a cadenza for solo clarinet.

1936 TE DEUM, for solo voices, chorus and orchestra.

This profoundly religious work—one of the composer's masterworks for chorus—combines power with spirituality. Power is generated through the frequent use of discords, and varying rhythms and meters; spirituality, through the utilization of old church modes. Two basic motives are prominent throughout the composition: a trumpet call with which it opens, and the expressive melody accompanying the words "Pleni sunt" ("The Heavens and Earth Are Filled with the Majesty of Thy Glory") which appears as a brief fugue. Despite the religious character of the music, elements of Hungarian folk songs and dances are introduced into the texture. Two principal lyric passages—both luminous in their beauty, and both for soprano—have an unmistakable Hungarian identity. The first is heard to the text "Tu Rex gloriae Christe" ("Thou Art the King of Glory"), with the three other solo voices joining in polyphonically at the words "Tu partis sempiternus" ("Thou Art the Everlasting Son of the Father"). The second comes at the end of the work, quietly accompanied by the chorus.

The *Te Deum* was written to commemorate the two hundred and fiftieth anniversary of the delivery of Budapest from the Turks. It was first heard at the Budapest Cathedral on September 11, 1936.

1939 VARIATIONS ON A HUNGARIAN FOLKSONG ("Peacock Variations"). I. Introduction. II. Theme. III. Sixteen Variations. IV. Finale.

Kodály wrote these orchestral variations to help celebrate the fiftieth anniversary of the Concertgebouw Orchestra in Amsterdam, which introduced it on November 23, 1939, with Willem Mengelberg conducting. The American concert première took place under the composer's direction during his first visit to the United States—in Philadelphia on November 22, 1946.

The folk melody on which the entire work is based is "Fly, Peacock, Fly," which comes from the County of Somogy in the western end of Lake Balaton. The tune is heard in the oboe, accompanied by muted strings and harp, following a brief introductory section. Sixteen variations follow, which, says Percy M. Young, are "both extension and commentary; extension, because the foundation melody, ever present, is adapted and modified through a sequence of mood phrases; commentary, because these mood phases seem to be endemic in the natural function of folk art, direct the varying rhythmic, harmonic and instrumental patterns." The finale opens with a variant of the melody, built up climactically and concluding with a stirring coda in which the brass is prominent.

1939 CONCERTO FOR ORCHESTRA. I. Allegro risoluto. II. Largo. III. Allegro risoluto. IV. Largo. V. Allegro risoluto.

Kodály's orchestral concerto was commissioned by the Chicago Symphony for its fiftieth anniversary. The plan was to have the composer himself direct the world première. The composer's sickness, however, delayed the writing of the work so that the first performance had to postdate the anniversary year. And the outbreak of World War II made it impossible for Kodály to come to America to conduct the première. This took place on February 6, 1941, with Frederick Stock conducting the Chicago Symphony.

The work is an attempt to revive the Baroque concerto-grosso form by pitting a solo group against, and combining it with, the larger orchestral body. Reminiscent, too, of the Handelian concerto grosso is the alternation of fast and slow movements. The entire work is played without interruption.

The first movement opens with a forceful, Hungarian-like theme in unison strings. A secondary subject is later heard in horns. A tympani roll and a sustained note in solo cello leads into the next movement, which is built up from a motive heard at the beginning in solo cello and answered in imitation by a second solo cello, a solo viola and clarinet. In the third movement, the first theme of the opening Allegro risoluto is recalled in the violins, repeated by woodwinds, and then by full orchestra. This theme is given a fugato treatment. Once again a roll of tympani and a sustained note (this time in clarinet) serve as a transition to the next movement, a Largo in which the cello motive of the second movement is remembered. In the finale, the concerto's opening theme is recalled once again. The music gains strength and quickens in tempo towards a mighty climax in full orchestra.

1961 SYMPHONY IN C MAJOR. I. Allegro. II. Andante moderato. III. Vivo.

Kodály's only symphony took many years to germinate. The first thematic ideas occurred to him late in the 1930s, while he was traveling on a trolley in Budapest. He kept gathering sketches for many years after that. By the end of World War II, he began working more intensively and concentratedly, and by the early 1950s, was able to complete two movements. Several tragic events delayed the writing of the other movement: first the death of his wife in 1958, and then his own serious illness in 1960. Recovering from both, he threw all of his energies into the symphony, completing the work in 1961, in his seventy-ninth year. But, as Willi Reich reported, "the three-part work is by no means a tired old man's opus luxuriating in melancholic retrospection, but a piece of irresistible life and vigor, truly new and compelling in thematic invention and original handling of the symphonic form."

The world première took place in Lucerne, Switzerland, on August 16, 1961, Ferenc Fricsay conducting. George Szell conducted the American première with the Cleveland Orchestra on January 4, 1962.

John Weissman explained that "the two outer movements may be considered precedent and denouement respectively of the central idea conveyed in the slow movement, whose importance is emphasized by the variation form." There is no pause between the second and third movements; the slow movement emphasizes folk elements, while the finale is a joyous dance.

The symphony opens with an extended introductory section, which projects an atmosphere of mystery. In the main body, the first principal theme is stated by cellos and basses. A rhapsodic episode for flute, oboe and clarinet leads to the second main thought: a folk-song tune in clarinets over a pulsating figure in violas and a four-note ostinato in basses. In the slow movement, a five-measure introduction by horns precedes a haunting folk melody in muted violas, punctuated by plucked strings in the basses. A forceful statement by the horns is the first principal theme of the finale, which comes following a short preface. The theme is repeated in the strings, then is extensively elaborated upon. One of the unusual structural features of this movement is the emphasis on the interval of the fourth, which is the basis of the introductory episode, which recurs throughout the movement, and then becomes the core of the climactic coda.

ERNST KRENEK 1900–

Krenek's music has not always been so complex and cerebral as it is today. He came to the twelve-tone system, which he has favored for over thirty years, and to electronics and musico-mathematics, which are recent interests, by a long and devious route. His earliest compositions were written in the post-Romantic style of his teacher, Franz Schreker. These works included his first three symphonies (between 1921 and 1922), and his first three string quartets (between 1921 and 1923). Then, for a brief period, jazz fascinated him, the style in which he achieved international renown in 1927 with the opera *Jonny spielt auf!* After that, he tried to arrive at a simple romanticism in the vein of Franz Schubert. This tendency is first found in the song cycle, *Reisebuch aus den Österreichischen Alpen* (1929). After that, the need for "an ever freer and more incisive articulation of musical thought," as he phrased it, the artistic necessity to arrive at emotional restraint, compressed thinking, precision and economy led him to embrace the twelve-tone system. His first significant use of the twelve-tone row can be found in the historical opera *Karl V* (1932), produced in Prague on June 15, 1938. Most of his major works since then are based on the twelve-tone system, which he employs with technical astuteness and considerable dramatic effect. With *Sestina* (1957), he embraced total serialism; with *Spiritus Intelligentiae* (1958), he began to experiment with electronics; and with *Fibonacci-Mobile* (1965), he ventured into musico-mathematics.

Krenek was born in Vienna on August 23, 1900. He was a pupil of Franz Schreker in Vienna and Berlin between 1916 and 1923. The Romantic warmth and emotional appeal of his early chamber and orchestral compositions attracted some attention immediately after World War I. Krenek turned to opera in *Zwingburg,* libretto by Franz Werfel, produced in Berlin on October 16, 1924. In 1925, Krenek became the coach of the Prussian State Theatres in Cassel and Wiesebaden, resigning from the post two years later, after he had achieved his formidable success with the jazz opera, *Jonny spielt auf!* In 1929, he settled in Vienna. There, his personal contact with the atonalists and twelve-tonalists gave him a new direction and a new technique.

Though he was Aryan, he was found unacceptable to the Nazis and had to leave Austria in 1938. He made his permanent home in the United States (which he had visited for the first time one year earlier as conductor of the touring Salzburg Opera Guild); in 1945, he became an American citizen. From 1939 to 1942, he was head of the music department, then dean of the School of Fine Arts, at Hamline University, in St. Paul, Minnesota. He went to live in Los Angeles in 1947.

Krenek was extraordinarily productive in the United States, completing major works in all media, including operas; of the last, the most significant was *Pallas Athene Weint,* whose world première took place on October 17, 1955, during a festive week inaugurating the opening of a new opera house in Hamburg, Germany. A later important opera, *The Golden Ram* (*Der goldene Bock*), a travesty on the classical legend of the Argonauts, was introduced at the International Congress of Contemporary Music in Hamburg, Germany on June 16, 1964.

Krenek received the Grand Prize of Austria in 1963. During the summer of 1965, he was composer-in-residence at Dartmouth College in Hanover, New Hampshire, where an all-Krenek concert took place at the Congregation of the Arts on July 7, 1965.

1926 JONNY SPIELT AUF! (JOHNNY STRIKES UP THE BAND!), op. 45, opera in two parts (eleven scenes), with text by the composer. First performance: Leipzig Opera, February 10, 1927.

In the 1920s, the popularity of American jazz spread like a contagious disease throughout Germany and Austria. Many of the serious composers of those countries were so fascinated by jazz rhythms, harmonies and instrumentation, as well as by ragtime and blues melodies, that these stylistic details were exploited to the full in major concert and operatic works. This was part and parcel of the *Zeitkunst* movement ("Contemporary Art") which infected the intellectual climate of the Germanic countries in the 1920s.

One of the first European composers to achieve immense success by using jazz within the framework of opera was Ernst Krenek. He wrote libretto and music of *Jonny spielt auf!* "to interpret," as he explained, "the rhythms and atmosphere of modern life in this age of technical science." His hero was a Negro bandleader and violinist named Johnny, who steals the precious violin of the virtuoso, Daniello. He conceals the instrument first in the room of Daniello's girl friend, Anita, and then in the lodgings of another of Anita's lovers, the composer, Max. All four find themselves at a railway station en route to Amsterdam. Daniello is fatally crushed under the wheels of a train, while Max is rejoined with Anita on the Amsterdam-bound express. Johnny climbs atop a railway signal and proudly waves his violin. Suddenly, the station clock is transformed into a globe of the world. Johnny bestrides it like some conqueror, playing his jazz tunes on his violin, while the people respond to his dynamic fiddling by dancing frenetically.

For 1926, this was a novel libretto. And the music Krenek created for it—made up of music-hall melodies, blues, kinesthetic jazz rhythms slightly diluted—was no less novel. But the sensation that *Jonny spielt auf!* caused throughout Europe following its première in Leipzig came not only from a racy text and a spicy musical score. There were a number of things in the opera capable of causing surprise or shock: the appearance of a locomotive on the stage; the use of radio sounds, a whistle, automobile horns in the orchestration, together with such more or less unusual instruments as a rattle, a xylophone, saxophones. Indeed, *Jonny spielt auf!* became one of the most sensational operas produced in Germany in the era between the two World Wars, and one of the most successful: within three years of its première, it was mounted in over one hundred cities.

The American première took place at the Metropolitan Opera on January 19, 1929. On that occasion, W. J. Henderson pointed out in his review in the *New York Sun* that its greatest attraction lay in the fact that it was basically "keen satire and a theatre show. . . . His aim was to travesty the kind of recitative so often heard in very grand opera. . . . Krenek does not confine his burlesque attacks to opera; all conventions of music are his target. Naturally [he] does not miss the opportunity to employ parody. The grand opera music is frequently dissonant in the approved style of the day and there are some peppery instrumental combinations. . . . Let it be said that this is pretty good musical comedy with some outstanding moments, and that if you don't take it too seriously you can have a pleasant evening at its performance."

1946 CONCERTO NO. 3 FOR PIANO AND ORCHESTRA, op. 107. I. Allegro con passione. II. Andante sostenuto. III. Allegretto scherzando. IV. Adagio. V. Vivace.

Krenek completed his first two piano concertos (opp. 18 and 81) in 1923 and 1937 respectively. The third came nine years after the second. On November 22, 1946, the work was introduced by the Minneapolis Symphony Orchestra, with Dimitri Mitropoulos filling the dual role of piano soloist and conductor.

Unlike so many other Krenek works of the 1940s, this concerto does not employ the twelve-tone system. But it is, nevertheless, austere music. It is in five movements, played without interruption. A unique instrumental characteristic is the use of a different section of the orchestra as background for the solo instrument in each of the five movements. In the first, it is the brass and tympani; in the second, a fugue, the strings; in the third, the woodwinds; in the fourth, for the most part a cadenza, for solo piano, harp and percussion; and in the fifth, a rondo, full orchestra. In the concluding movement, the thematic ideas of earlier movements are repeated.

1947 SYMPHONY NO. 4 op. 113. I. Andante tranquillo; Allegro appassionata; Allegro vivace. II. Adagio. III. Allegro pesante; Allegro agitato; Allegro deciso.

Krenek's Fourth Symphony was introduced in New York by the New York Philharmonic Orchestra, Mitropoulos conducting, on November 27, 1947. This is complex and cerebral music, austerely objective. The writing is in the twelve-tone technique.

The composer has provided the following analysis:

"First movement. Technically, the movement consists of a quiet, fairly slow introduction, an agitated transition and a sonata-allegro with two themes, a brief development section and an abridged recapitulation. . . .

"Second movement. This movement consists of alternating variations on two themes. The general mood is one of resignation, in an essay of getting along without fighting for the 'ideal.'. . .

"Third movement. A long, elaborate introduction and a dramatic Allegro with some characteristics of a rondo appear in this movement, which is the longest of the three and contains the dramatic climax of the whole work."

1949 SYMPHONY NO. 5, op. 119.

While Krenek's Fifth Symphony is not in the twelve-tone technique, it is atonal music. It is classical in its concept of form; the material is developed concisely and economically. Played without interruption, the symphony is in five sections: I. Introduction. II. Sonata. III. Rondo. IV. Theme and Variations. V. Fugue. The concluding fugue is used as a kind of summation.

Material is repeated throughout the five movements: the theme of the fourth section (which undergoes eight variations) is derived from the coda of the third; and the thematic subjects (which become the basis of the concluding double fugue) are likewise derived from earlier ideas.

This symphony was introduced by the Albuquerque Symphony under Kurt Frederick on March 16, 1950.

1965 FIBONACCI-MOBILE, for string quartet, two pianos and "coordinator."

Krenek's interest in musico-mathematics has resulted in a number of stimulating compositions, including *Pentagram,* op. 163, for woodwind quintet, which he originally wrote in 1952 and revised in 1958. and the *Fibonacci-Mobile.* The latter received its world première at the Congregation of the Arts at Dartmouth College in Hanover, New Hampshire, on an all-Krenek program on July 7, 1965.

The "Fibonacci" in the title refers to the Fibonacci mathematical series, a row of numbers each of which is the sum of its two antecedents (1–1–2–3–5, and so on). In the *Saturday Review,* Oliver Daniel goes on to explain: "Against the complete material, consisting of eighty-one measures, as played by the two pianists, the individual strings play various melodies which can easily be arranged in numerous juxtapositions; then against a different set of eighty-one measures played by the two pianists, the strings entering at different points play their own complex fragments." Ernst Krenek himself goes on to explain: "Either complex consists of five sections of thirty-four, twenty-one, eight and five measures respectively. The musical material of these sections is the same, progressively condensed. The work is called 'mobile' because numerous combinations of the various elements may be used."

"The material itself is fascinating," reported Oliver Daniel. "It becomes completely intriguing to hear how the different melodies are pitted against one another. It is really a maze of mobile counterpoint and, while the result is not dissimilar to various aleatoric processes, it is the product of complete control."

ANATOL LIADOV 1855–1914

"Art," Liadov once wrote, "is the realm of the non-existing. Art is a figment, a fairy tale, a phantom. Give me a fairy tale, a dragon, a water sprite, a forest-demon—give me something unreal and I am happy."

In his music, Liadov lived continually in that make-believe world of enchantment peopled by unearthly spirits. It was his escape from the reality around him, which he found to be "tedious, trying, purposeless, terrible." Thus he succumbed to the spell of folklore; his music is most original and virile when it draws its ideas from that source.

A national composer, Liadov belongs to that group of Russian composers, beginning with Glinka and continuing with the "Russian Five," who built an art out of folk-song materials. Liadov's sphere is essentially a more limited one than that of his celebrated compatriots. He worked exclusively in the less ambitious forms—tone poems and adaptations of folk songs. In the best of his work, he revealed elegance of style and fine taste.

He was incorrigibly lazy. Rimsky-Korsakov has told us that Liadov was suspended from the St. Petersburg Conservatory because he not only refused to do any studying but, in time, even avoided classes. The same inertia and lethargy remained with him throughout his life. In certain seasons—when it was warm and fair—he could do no work at all. In others, he preferred doing tomorrow what he had planned for today. Ambitious projects, like an opera, never reached beyond the planning stage. He drove himself to complete other ventures, slighter in scope than operas. He avoided assignments like the plague; when he did accept them, he was never quite certain when he would complete them, or *if* he would.

It is a fascinating footnote to the musical history of our times that it was due to Liadov's indolence that the most dynamic and influential composer of our time was able to realize his first success. For it was to Liadov that Diaghilev came for a score to *The Fire-Bird;* and it was only because Liadov was dilatory that the assignment was finally turned over to Igor Stravinsky.

Liadov was born in St. Petersburg on May 10, 1855. He was the grandson and son of famous Russian conductors. From 1870 to 1878, Anatol Liadov attended the St. Petersburg Conservatory. After an unfavorable period in which he was suspended, he emerged as an outstanding student. Just before his graduation, he wrote his first orchestral work, *The Bride of Messina* (1877), which so impressed the Conservatory authorities that they appointed him instructor in harmony and theory. Besides his successful activity as a teacher (his pupils including Prokofiev and Miaskovsky), Liadov also distinguished himself as the conductor of the Musical Society which was responsible for giving performances of works by the younger Russians. As a member of the Ethnographic Society, Liadov made valuable researches into Russian folk music. He himself made some excellent adaptations of Russian folk songs and dances. He died in Polyanovka, near Novgorod on August 28, 1914.

1904–1909 FAIRY TALES FOR ORCHESTRA:
BABA-YAGA, op. 6.
THE ENCHANTED LAKE, op 62.
KIKIMORA, op. 63.

Liadov wrote three fairy tales for orchestra. The first, *Baba-Yaga* (1904), was heard in St. Petersburg on March 18, 1904. Baba-Yaga is a witch whose home is protected by a fence constructed out of the bones of human beings. Her swift flight through space, as she sweeps her path with a broom, is picturesquely described in this music, which is a literal portrayal in tones of air-locomotion.

The Enchanted Lake or *Le Lac enchanté* (1909) is a companion piece to *Kikimora,* both originally being sketches for an opera that never outgrew the outline stages. Unlike *Kikimora, The Enchanted Lake* has no program. But it is descriptive music, easily lending itself to programmatic interpretation. The opening rippling theme for muted strings (the principal melodic idea of the entire work) tells of the magic lake in which the grim encircling forests are reflected. Sprightly rhythmic subjects bring up suggestions of the water nymphs who inhabit the lake. *The Enchanted Lake* was heard for the first time on February 21, 1909, in St. Petersburg.

The source of *Kikimora* (1909) is a folk tale by Sakharoff; this orchestral fairy tale got its first hearing on December 12, 1909, in St. Petersburg.

The published score provides the following program:

"Kikimora (the phantom) is brought up by a sorceress in the mountains. In her youth she is beguiled from early morn to late at night by the tales of foreign lands told by the sorceress's Magic Cat. From night to dawn, Kikimora is rocked in a crystal cradle. In seven years the phantom grows up. Tiny and black, her head is small as a thimble, and her body as thin as straw. Kikimora makes all manner of noises from morning to night, and then whistles and hisses from early evening to midnight. Then the phantom spins until daylight—spins and stores up evil in her mind against all mankind."

After an introduction for muted strings, a melancholy strain is sounded by the English horn, flute and oboe over tremolo strings. When this idea has been developed, a presto section carries the work to its exciting conclusion.

1906 EIGHT RUSSIAN FOLK SONGS, suite for orchestra, op. 58. I. Religious Chant. II. Christmas Carol. III. Plaintive Melody. IV. I Dance With a Mosquito. V. Legend of the Birds. VI. Cradle Song. VII. Round Dance. VIII. A Village Dance Song.

This orchestral suite is a by-product of the composer's intensive researches into Russian folk music. For Liadov, these studies and researches represented a labor of love. All his life, he had passionately admired folklore and folk music. Out of the treasure house of this native art he selected eight tunes, and integrated them into a single composition, while clothing them in a rich harmonic and instrumental dress.

The first song is a religious chant sung by children in a procession; its main theme is presented by English horn and bassoons. The second is a Christmas carol, with oboes and clarinets offering the main melody; the third is a plaintive village song. In the fourth, a humorous tune is accompanied by an amusing dance of young peasants with a mosquito. This is a scherzo in which muted strings imitate the buzzing of mosquitoes. The bird song of the fifth movement is heard in the woodwind; chirpings and pipings of birds are here simulated. A tender cradlesong, in the sixth part, unfolds in the strings, followed by a rhythmic dance movement. The suite ends with a village dance, music accompanying the crowning of May Queen.

CHARLES MARTIN LOEFFLER 1861–1935

Though Loeffler spent the last fifty-four years of his life in the United States, became an American citizen, and wrote all of his works in this country, he rarely attempted to endow his music with an American identity. (One or two experiments with a jazz idiom represented only minor, negligible exercises.) His background was international. He was Alsatian by birth; he spent his boyhood in Russia; he received his musical training in Germany and France; and he served his professional apprenticeship in France. His music was also international. His first work for orchestra, *Les Veillées de l'Ukraine* (which the Boston Symphony introduced on November 20, 1891) was Russian in character, mood and material; and so was his more popular *Memories of My Childhood,* written over thirty years later. Other compositions revealed stylistic traits of Scriabin, and principally of Debussy. All of his work showed a Germanic respect for architectonic structure. He was at his best when his poetic temperament found expression in a post-impressionist style, at which time his writing had singular beauty and aristocracy.

Loeffler was born is Mulhouse, Alsace, on January 30, 1861. As a boy he lived in the Russian city of Kiev, where his father (a scientist and writer) had come to work for the Russian government. There, the boy Loeffler assimilated many vivid impressions of Russian life and folk music. In his fourteenth year, Loeffler came to Berlin, where he studied the violin with Rappoldi and Joachim, and harmony with Kiel. Further study took place in Paris with Massart (violin) and Guiraud (composition). After playing the violin in the Pasdeloup Orchestra in Paris, and in a private orchestra of Baron von Derwies in Lugano and Nice, Loeffler came to the United States. In 1882, he joined the violin section of the Boston Symphony, and from 1885 to 1903, he shared the first-violin desk with Franz Kneisel. After leaving the Boston Symphony in 1903, he devoted himself to composition. The Boston Symphony, which presented all of his early orchestral works, was also responsible in 1907 for the world première of *A Pagan Poem,* with which Loeffler achieved his greatest success. The last thirty years of his life were spent in retirement and seclusion on a farm in Medfield. He was made Chevalier of the Legion of Honor in 1919, and in 1926, he received an honorary doctorate from Yale. He died in Medfield, Massachusetts, on May 19, 1935.

1901 LA BONNE CHANSON, poem for orchestra.

La Bonne chanson received its first performance at a concert of the Boston Symphony, Wilhelm Gericke conducting, on April 11, 1902. Following that performance, Loeffler reorchestrated it, the new version getting heard in Boston on November 1, 1918, under Pierre Monteux. The composition was suggested to the composer from reading the fifth poem in Paul Verlaine's *La Bonne chanson,* beginning with the line "Before you fade and disappear, pale morning star."

The poem is rhapsodic in feeling and structurally is in a free theme and variation form. "The music opens with a passage suggestive of the opening verse of the poem," says Lawrence Gilman. "Harp, glockenspiel and strings evoke the thought of the early dawn, the fading and disappearing star. The strings sing the principal theme. After an Allegro passage . . . there is a return to the serener mood of the opening; antique cymbals hint at the sparkle of the dew on the hay. The music keeps pace with the mounting eagerness and desire of the poet-lover; the excitement grows, reaching its climax in an effulgent outburst of the full orchestra, announcing the rising sun."

1906 A PAGAN POEM, for orchestra, with piano, English horn and three trumpets, op. 14.

Among Loeffler's impressionist compositions, the most successful is *A Pagan Poem.* Rarely in his music does he achieve such refinement of writing as here; rarely is his feeling for beauty so sensitively realized. There is serene music, aglow—as Philip Hale once put it so well—with a "cool fire," and a cool fire that "is more deadly than fierce, panting flame."

The literary source of this music was Virgil's eighth eclogue, in which a Thessalian maiden calls upon her necromantic gifts to restore to her a deserted lover. The music does not attempt to follow this program literally, but strives to suggest through impressionistic means the emotions and moods evoked by the poem.

Originally, *A Pagan Poem* was scored for a small chamber orchestra, comprising a piano, two flutes, oboe, clarinet, English horn, two horns, three trumpets, viola and double bass. Two years after it appeared in this form in 1903, Loeffler scored it again, this time in an even more unorthodox manner: two pianos and three trumpets. Still dissatisfied, Loeffler finally rewrote it for full orchestra and the obbligato of piano, English horn and three trumpets. On November 22, 1907, this definitive version was introduced by the Boston Symphony Orchestra under Karl Muck.

The work opens with an atmospheric Adagio from which a brief theme and its inversion return throughout the composition. Viola and three flutes then present a solemn melody, which is elaborated upon. The piano enters forcefully with an inversion of the opening brief subject, then points to an Allegro section with a glissando. Here a new thought is soon projected, in first violins, harp and piano. After this material has been developed, a piano cadenza brings on a Lento assai section in which an idyllic melody unfolds in the English horn. The tempo then quickens into an Allegro vivace to provide a contrast of mood. The pace now alternates from fast to slow. Three offstage trumpets provide a dramatic interpolation. The composition ends with a powerful Allegro—an uninhibited expression of pure joy.

1923 MUSIC FOR FOUR STRINGED INSTRUMENTS. I. Poco adagio; Allegro comodo. II. Adagio ma non troppo; Allegro. III. Moderato; Andante quasi allegretto; Allegro vivo; Tempo di marcia; Allegro; Adagio.

Religious mysticism fills the pages of this work to give it its identifying character. Loeffler wrote the quartet to honor the memory of an American aviator, Victor Chapman, who died in World War I. The melodic ideas are derived from the Gregorian chant, providing the work with a remote, spiritual quality. The "Resurrexi" contributes a motto theme that recurs throughout the composition. The slow sections are among the most poignant in the entire composition, reflecting a funereal strain often found in Loeffler's writings. The slow second movement was inspired by the Easter services of the Catholic Church. The vividly pictorial third movement conjures to Carl Engel's mind "troops on the march to the front, braving death in the face of that resurrection which nature perennially proclaims with the return of Spring. But it is not only the reawakening of all things growing, it is the spiritual resurrection, the abandoning of what, after reaching perfection, must again decay."

1924 MEMORIES OF MY CHILDHOOD (LIFE IN A RUSSIAN VILLAGE), tone poem for orchestra.

In this orchestral work, the composer remembers nostalgically his Kiev childhood and his association with Russian folk music. It won the first prize of one thousand dollars in a competition sponsored by the Chicago North Shore Festival, and received its first performance in Evanston on May 30, 1924, Frederick Stock conducting.

The composer provided the following information:

"Many years ago, the composer spent more than three years of his boyhood in a Russian small town. . . . He now seeks to express by this music what still lives in his heart and memory of those happy days. He recalls, in the various strains of his music, Russian peasant song, the Yourod Litany prayer, 'the happiest of days,' fairy tales and dance songs. The closing movement of the tone poem commemorates the death of Vasinka, an elderly Bayan, or story-teller, singer, maker of willow pipes upon which he played tunes of weird intervals, and the companion and friend of the boy who now, later in life, notes down what he hopes these pages will tell."

The composer also provided the following analysis:

"Accompanying the distant sound of church bells, the cellos and double basses give out the first theme—a Russian peasant song, this, in its turn, being taken up by the violas and violins. A short melodic and rhythmical diversion leads to a short ecclesiastical section in which the litany, 'God Have Mercy Upon Us' prepares the way for the exultant nod of childhood happiness—an episode in E major. 'A Fairy Tale,' which follows, is succeeded by a 'Dance,' whose theme is sustained by four harmonies. The Dance subject, which is of Russian origin, is introduced by the clarinet and piccolo alternately, the violas then taking up the subject, Molto tranquillo. The trombones twice repeat the opening theme, its mood being one of sorrow for the death of a beloved friend—the peasant Vasinka. The conclusion of the work has for its basic motive the same opening subject, given to cellos and double basses. Fifteen measures later, there is heard the distant music of a cheerful character."

1930 EVOCATION, for speaking voice, women's chorus and orchestra.

On February 5, 1931, Severance Hall, the new home of the Cleveland Orchestra, was dedicated with a special concert. For that concert, Loeffler composed his *Evocation,* the text of which was taken from T. W. Mackail's *Epigrams of the Greek Anthology.*

The following paragraph, printed in the preface of the published score, can serve as a program for the music: "The imagined form of this music is to tell the building of a beautiful temple of the Muses; of the god Pan's rhapsodic lay and the nymphs' love for him; of their vain endeavors to fetter him to their beloved sunny fields whence Echo is listening for the pure fun of answering; of Syrinx, Pan's most beloved naiad, whom Artemis metamorphosed into a reed to save her from Pan's amorous pursuit; of the strange account given by the Singing Stone of itself; awed by solemn wonder at it we now seek the little stream running down the hills to meet us, the reeds bowing to us in the breeze. The nymphs are still calling, 'Pan, abide here on these sunny greens.'"

The work opens with a slow, stately fugue, symbolic of the temple of music (Severance Hall), its subject rising from the piano, double basses and tympani to the woodwinds, This fugue is shortly interrupted by a motif of the Singing Stone, in flutes and bassoons. There then comes a lyrical passage for the English horn describing the nymphs enjoying their Arcadian happiness and meeting the great god Pan. This interlude over, the principal theme (which grew out of the opening fugue) returns to lead to the encounter with the Singing Stone. The final scene takes place in the favorite stream of the nymphs and naiads where Artemis metamorphosed Syrinx. Pan's rustic lay is heard from the distance.

The narrator who speaks the lines of the Singing Stone is heard in a hushed voice offstage.

ROLF LIEBERMANN 1910–

Though Rolf Liebermann has identified himself with the twelve-tone school, he is by no means a strict adherent of that cult. He is ready and willing, at different points in an opera, to sidestep dodecaphony when the situation calls for a romantic, impressionistic, neo-classical or even Baroque approach. And he can abandon dodecaphony entirely when it is out of place in a comedy like *The School for Wives,* a one-act opera based on Molière, introduced in Louisville, Kentucky, on December 3, 1955. His writing can be lyrical and romantic as well as dramatic and atonal; it can be comic and satiric as well as humanistic. He can draw from the past to write formal arias, ensemble numbers and choruses. But always he maintains a sound respect for his text, and uses all the musical resources at his command to cater to that text. As Willi Reich noted, Liebermann's musico-dramatic approach is to use "purely musical means (tonal, polytonal and atonal harmonies, changes in timber, old forms) to symbolize and represent the dramatic conflicts."

His first two stage works have been designated as "*opera semiseria*" by which is implied a format in which satiric or humorous episodes are blended with human and dramatic values. This was true of Liebermann's music as well as the texts for which it was written. Each is made up of many different approaches, idioms and methods, with no attempt at achieving a basic stylistic unity. But the overall theatrical impact is inescapable, and from the first to the last, Liebermann remains a surpassing musical dramatist.

Liebermann was born in Zurich, Switzerland, on September 14, 1910. He studied law and music simultaneously: law at the University of Zurich; music at the Academy of Music with Hermann Scherchen (conducting) and Wladimir Vogel (composition). His early works—beginning with the *Polyphonic Studies* for chamber orchestra, introduced in Berlin in 1943—were in a tonal framework, and brought him an award from the municipality of Zurich. The twelve-tone system became part and parcel of his technique in 1947 with *Furioso,* for orchestra, and became basic to it with the Symphony, in 1949, introduced that year in Milan at the International Congress for Dodecaphonic Music.

He achieved international recognition with his first opera *Leonore 40/45,* produced in 1952. His later stage works solidified his position in twentieth-century opera. But he also wrote a number of provocative instrumental works, the most successful being the Concerto for Jazz Band and Orchestra (featured at the Donaueschingen Festival in Germany on October 17, 1954). And he has written experimental works, such as *Échanges,* scored for fifty-two industrial machines (teletypes, cash registers, staplers, and so forth), whose sounds were reproduced on magnetic tape; its first performance took place at the Swiss Exposition Nationale in Lausanne on April 24, 1964.

For a number of years, Liebermann was on the musical staff of the Swiss Radio Corporation in Zurich. In 1962, he became director of the Hamburg State Opera. Liebermann paid his first visit to the United States in 1955 to help prepare the world première of his opera *The School for Wives*. He paid a second visit to the United States in 1963 on a grant from the Ford Foundation.

1946 SUITE ON SWISS FOLK MELODIES (VOLKSLIEDER SUITE), for orchestra.

This was one of Liebermann's most successful works before he adopted the twelve-tone system. It is not only within a traditional tonal framework but also in a more or less conventional harmonic idiom. The suite makes use of six Swiss folk songs, each heard first in its original form; then each is varied and recalled. In writing the suite, the composer felt impelled to give "Swiss folklore a *niveau* it had not yet attained in Swiss concert halls." This is the reason he found it necessary "not to prejudice the unity of the work by inappropriate harmonizations."

The suite was first performed on January 10, 1947, on an English-French-Swiss broadcast by the BBC Theatre Orchestra.

1947 FURIOSO, for orchestra. I. Allegro vivace. II. Andante. III. Allegro vivace.

Liebermann's first work for orchestra to utilize the twelve-tone system received its première performance at the Darmstadt Music Festival in 1947, when it was described as "the first Existentialist composition." Leopold Stokowski introduced it to the United States in Dallas on December 9, 1950. It is made up of two series of twelve-tone rows, used in contrast with one another, then combined in the finale. "The series are not used according to the strict dodecaphonic theory or Schoenberg's aesthetic," we learn from *Forty Contemporary Swiss Composers*. "This is rather a free and personal combination, integrating purely tonal values."

1953 LEONORE 40/45, "*opera semiseria*" in seven scenes with prologue and prelude, text by Heinrich Strobel. First performance: Basle, Switzerland, March 26, 1952.

The opera proceeds on two levels. One is satirical, flippant, witty. The other is serious, dramatic, with strong humanistic feelings. The "Leonore" in the title is intended to draw comparison with the heroine of Beethoven's opera *Fidelio*. Liebermann's heroine is a French girl, symbolizing European culture and civilization during World War II, who falls in love with a German soldier. In a prologue, a Monsieur Émile explains in a light, humorous vein that his function is to explain what happens on the stage, when the authors are unable to do so for themselves. This is followed by a Prelude. In a German living room, in 1939, a radio performance of *Fidelio* is interrupted by the announcement that Albert's class has been called into the army—Albert being a young music student. At the same time, in a French home, Yvette, also a music student, is shocked to learn from her mother that a world war is imminent. The main action begins during the war years of 1941 and 1942, with Albert (now in the Germany army) and Yvette meeting at a concert hall. They fall in love and arrange clandestine meetings. They are separated when Albert is taken prisoner. At this point, Monsieur Émile intrudes to inform the audience that all turns out well for this romance. Yvette and Albert have found jobs in Epernay, and try to get married. But a tribunal of "the eternal bureaucracy" refuses to recognize the legality of this marriage, and are deaf to Yvette's appeal for humanity and compassion. Monsieur Émile, however, comes to the rescue with papers bearing heavenly seals sanctioning the marriage; the judges now give their grudging consent.

Though the satirical implications of the text are there for all to recognize, *Leonore 40/45* is, nevertheless, a work with very serious humanistic intent. Everett Helm, in his review in *Musical America,* even sees in it "the story of European civilization between the years of 1939 and 1947." He added: "Behind the action on the personal plane there are ideas such as mutual understanding and appreciation between so-called enemy peoples; the power of love to conquer the powers of darkness; the necessity of holding to one's ideas in the face of seemingly hopeless odds."

The text uses two languages, German and French, sometimes alternately, sometimes even simultaneously, The music is basically in the twelve-tone system, but lyricism is not sacrificed. Lyricism at its best can be found in the love duet of Albert and Yvette in the second scene, and in Albert's expression of longing for Yvette in the fourth. Effective ensemble and choral numbers are also represented, with the last scene closing with a traditional operatic finale.

Satire provides welcome spice, as in the delightful first-scene choral episode in which a concert audience expresses its disgust with modern music (in a musical setting written bitonally). A good deal of innocent merriment is contributed through the subtle way in which the music of other composers is quoted from time to time—Liszt, Wagner, Stravinsky, Schoenberg, Leoncavallo and, of course, Beethoven. Beethoven's *Fidelio,* which is briefly heard in the Prelude in a radio broadcast, returns to the final scene through the four stirring opening measures of the *Fidelio Overture,* music announcing in the opera the arrival of the guardian angle.

1954 PENELOPE, "*opera semiseria*" in two parts, with text by Heinrich Strobel. First performance: Salzburg, August 17, 1954.

Just as *Leonore 40/45* progresses on two different stylistic levels—the serious and the satiric—so *Penelope* progresses on two different levels in time. The opera is a modern treatment of the Homeric legend, but the outer frame of the opera is set in antiquity, while the inner frame takes place in modern times. "In the framing action," the librettist has explained, "we see barbaric antiquity, colorful, bizarre and artful like the late Cretan-Mycenaean culture. . . . The actual drama of homecoming is enacted as an opera seria in modern costumes and decor."

The libretto places the time of the drama during "the afternoon and evening of the 3,649th day after the end of the Trojan War." The opera, however, opens in antiquity, with three comical military characters wooing Penelope, who is awaiting Odysseus's return from the Trojan War. In order to frighten away her ludicrous suitors, Penelope brings up a picture of what the future will be like; the time and action now shift to the present day. A twentieth-century Penelope, thinking Odysseus is dead, has married Marchese Ercole only to discover that her former husband is very much alive and is about to come home with some of his friends. She rushes to the marketplace to meet him when, much to her relief, she discovers that Odysseus is dead after all, having succumbed to heart attack en route home. She can now resume her happy marital status with Marchese Ercole, only to discover—upon returning from the marketplace—that he has committed suicide. The opera ends with an apotheosis in which Odysseus, through the power of great poetry, returns to life and to Penelope. Now the world of today and the world of antiquity become one. The opera ends with an exultant hymn to art.

The antiquity sequence is treated in opera-buffa style; the modern action, as an opera seria, with the twelve-tone system dominating the writing. Thus graceful lyrical pages, pleasing Baroque-like arias, recitatives, ensemble numbers, satirical episodes and a large choral finale are juxtaposed with atonal, bitonal and twelve-tonal music.

In reviewing the première of the opera, Max Graf found Liebermann's structure a delightful mixture of the old and the new, with allowance even for the intrusion of boogie-woogie, to whose compulsive rhythms the friends of Ulysses perform a frenetic dance upon returning from captivity. "The essential part of the music," said Graf, "is in the melodies for voices, but not melodies in terms of the beloved tunes of Puccini or Verdi. The pandiatonic harmony is handled by the Swiss composer with energy. It gives impressive strength to the color of the orchestra which has its woodwinds, trumpets and trombones strengthened threefold, in addition to kettledrums, percussion, xylophone, celesta, harp and piano. The theatrical talent of Liebermann is among his greatest gifts. He knows how to get results, matching effective music to the stage episodes, and in particular contributing strong endings in his acts. The mixture of Greek antiquity and modernity is nothing new, but there is in the form of Liebermann's opera, which placed the Homeric Penelope alongside one in evening clothes, something spirited, unusual, and effective."

NIKOLAI LOPATNIKOFF 1903–

With several minor exceptions, Lopatnikoff has devoted himself to instrumental music. Like the two composers he admires most, Stravinsky (the Stravinsky between 1925 and 1955) and Hindemith. Lopatnikoff is a neo-classicist, who merges contemporary thinking and techniques with structures of the past. It is revealing to compare Lopatnikoff with both Stravinsky and Hindemith. Like Stravinsky, Lopatnikoff is lean, economical and objective in his writing, while employing forms of comparatively modest proportions. But in spirit, he is even closer to Hindemith.

Lopatnikoff, however, is not a stencil of any other composer. His polyphonic thinking and his linear style are basically his, even where they have been influenced by others. His melodic writing, sometimes touched with a Russian personality, is personal, and so are the compact textures and compressed structures he favors.

Lopatnikoff was born in Reval, Estonia, on March 16, 1903. He attended the St. Petersburg Conservatory, where he studied the piano with Sacharoff and theory with Shitomirsky. Further music study followed with Ernst Toch, Rehberg and Grabner. His first string quartet, introduced in Carlsruhe in 1924, and his first piano concerto, heard in Cologne on November 3, 1925, first drew attention to his creative gifts. While thus engaged in musical activity, he attended the Technological College of Carlsruhe, where he was graduated with a diploma in civil engineering in 1927. A year or so later, he decided that music rather than engineering would be his life's work. In this determination to follow music as a career, he was encouraged by a number of successful performances: The Boston Symphony under Koussevitzky introduced his *Introduction and Scherzo* on April 27, 1928. On January 8, 1929, his First Symphony was a major success at the German Music Festival in Carlsruhe, winning the German Radio Corporation Prize. He was also encouraged by the fact that his second string quartet received the Belaiev Prize in 1929.

For about a decade and a half, Lopatnikoff wandered over Europe, living at different times in Berlin, Helsinki and London. In 1939, he established his home permanently in the United States, becoming an American citizen in 1944. In 1945, he was appointed associate professor of composition at the Carnegie Institute of Technology in Pittsburgh, becoming full professor in 1948. His first major successes following his arrival in America came with the world premières of his Violin Concerto in Boston in 1942, and with the *Opus Sinfonicum,* which won a prize of $1,000 from the Cleveland Orchestra in 1943. Lopatnikoff received two Guggenheim Fellowships, and a grant from the National Institute of Arts and Letters. In 1963, he was made a member of that Institute. In 1966 he completed an opera, *Danton,* excerpts from which were introduced by the Pittsburgh Symphony Orchestra under William Steinberg on March 25, 1967.

1941 CONCERTO FOR VIOLIN AND ORCHESTRA, op. 26. I. Allegro moderato. II. Andante. III. Allegro con brio ma non troppo.

Lopatnikoff's Violin Concerto was introduced by Richard Burgin and the Boston Symphony Orchestra, Serge Koussevitzky conducting, on April 17, 1942. Three ideas comprise the first movement, which is soundly constructed and marked by a powerful rhythmic force. The lyrical second movement has a Russian personality. Vigor returns to the third movement, is occasionally infectiously gay, to be contrasted midway with a contemplative melody for two clarinets.

1942 SINFONIETTA, for orchestra, op. 27. I. Allegro II. Andantino. III. Allegro molto.

OPUS SINFONICUM, for orchestra, op. 28.

The Sinfonietta is an intimate work, which has the texture of chamber music. It is in its composer's most successful neo-classic vein. Within the structure of a classic concerto grosso, the composer injected modern linear writing in which the instrumental effects and sonorities help to contribute both irony and wit. Against the background of the orchestra, seven wind instruments (trumpet, horn, oboe, clarinet, flute, bassoon and piccolo) provide the melodic materials. A lively theme opens the first movement; this, and a countertheme heard in the clarinet, are the main threads out of which the composer weaves his polyphonic fabric. In the second movement, an ensemble of wind instruments is effectively set against the orchestra in the style of the concerto grosso. The finale, a rondo, gives vigorous play to the full orchestra, with emphasis on the family of percussions; this movement has been described as a true Russian dance.

The première took place on August 2, 1942, at the festival of the International Society for Contemporary Music at San Francisco.

The *Opus Sinfonicum* received a prize of $1,000 from the Cleveland Orchestra in a contest helping to celebrate that organization's twenty-fifth anniversary. The world première was given by that orchestra, under Erich Leinsdorf, on December 9, 1943. The composer explains that this composition was planned as a short piece of symphonic music, free in form, "a kind of abstract symphonic poem with a program." An introductory section for full orchestra is heard before the appearance of the main subject in solo oboe, flute and English horn. A lively Allegro follows, comprising two rhythmic ideas. A quiet middle section precedes the development of the basic themes. After a climax, the serene atmosphere of the introduction is restored. The music ebbs away into silence with several pianissimo measures for solo tympani.

1944 CONCERTINO FOR ORCHESTRA, op. 30. I. Toccata. II. Elegietta. III. Finale.

Lopatnikoff wrote this orchestral Concertino on a commission from the Koussevitzky Music Foundation. It is dedicated to the memory of Mme. Koussevitzky. The world première was given by the Boston Symphony under Koussevitzky on March 2, 1945. The first movement (Allegro molto) places emphasis on rhythmical interest, while the middle movement, as the title indicates, is a lyrical elegy with a Russian personality. The finale, in more or less rondo form, gives prominence to the piano in a series of varied episodes including an inverted fugato.

1958 VARIAZIONI CONCERTANTE, for orchestra, op. 38.

Commissioned by the Pittsburgh Symphony through a grant of the Pittsburgh Bicentennial Association for a major orchestra work, Lopatnikoff wrote most of the *Variazioni concertante* at the MacDowell Colony in Peterboro,

New Hampshire, during the summer of 1957, completing it in 1958, the year in which it was introduced by the Pittsburgh Symphony under William Steinberg. The theme is heard in plucked strings alternating with wind, after two introductory chords. This introductory section (Moderato) extends for fifty-three measures and highlights solos for flute, violin, English horn and clarinet. Four variations follow (Allegro molto; Allegro marcato; Andantino quasi allegretto; and Lento e molto rubato). At the end of the fourth variation, the original theme is once again recalled by plucked strings. The work ends with a vigorously rhythmic finale (Allegro energico).

1960 FESTIVAL OVERTURE, for orchestra.

This composition was the result of a commission from industry. The Pittsburgh Plate Glass Company asked Lopatnikoff to write an orchestral piece saluting the United States auto industry. *Festival Overture* was the result, and it was introduced by the Detroit Symphony under Paul Paray on October 12, 1960.

"The music," explains the composer, "seeks to reflect the atmosphere of a festive occasion without being in any way descriptive. . . . After a few measures of introductory nature, the horns and trumpets present a theme which is to play an important part in the course of the work. The subsequent thematic material in the first part is of a generally vigorous and energetic character, culminating in a climax which leads the way to the quiet, contrasting middle part. . . . Solo woodwinds and the string choir carry the materials of this lyrical interlude until it fades out in a bass clarinet solo. A distant solo drum rhythm announces the transition to the third part with its return to the lively mood of the opening. The motives of the first part are here developed and manipulated until the music reaches an explosive tension relieved by the transition to the coda. The musical ideas of the coda are treated in a concertante manner, with solo woodwinds and the piano coming to the fore. The pace of the music quickens continually and relentlessly toward the end, and the overture concludes in a buoyant and exuberant mood."

WITOLD LUTOSLAWSKI 1913–

Lutoslawski is the most significant composer of present-day Poland. He first attracted attention with his Symphony, which was introduced in Katowice on April 6, 1948. This work represented a break with former romantic tendencies towards a leaner and more concise style that had Polish national overtones. He further explored the possibilities of using Polish folk music as the starting point for his own strong and original speech with the *Triptych silésien,* for soprano and orchestra, whose world première took place in Warsaw on December 2, 1951; and this manner achieved its fullest crystallization with the Concerto for Orchestra in 1954. Then in 1958, he was temporarily attracted to the twelve-tone system, beginning with the *Funeral Music,* or *Musique funèbre.* Then, starting in 1961, Lutoslawski became absorbed with the creative potential of aleatory music, or music of chance, a field which he explored with considerable success in a number of exciting compositions, beginning with the *Jeux vénitiens,* in 1962, and continuing on with the *Trois Poèmes d'Henri Michaux,* for chorus and orchestra (first performance in Zagreb on May 9, 1963), the *Postludium,* for orchestra (1963), and the *Paroles tissées,* for tenor and orchestra (1965).

Lutoslawski was born in Warsaw on January 25, 1913. He attended the Warsaw Conservatory, where he studied the piano with Jerzy Lefeld and composition with Witold Maliszewski. He also studied higher mathematics at the University of Warsaw for two years. While attending the Conservatory, he wrote a piano sonata (1934). Soon after his graduation from the Conservatory with a diploma in composition, he completed a major work for orchestra, the *Symphonic Variations,* introduced by the Polish Radio. During the war, Lutoslawski served for a while in the Polish army as chief of a field radio station. After the war, he became active in the musical life of Poland by becoming a member of the committees of the Union Polish Composers and of "Autumn of Warsaw" festivals; he also served with the Radio Council and the Polish Musical Publications. In 1955, he received a first prize from the government for his contributions to Polish music. Four years later, he was elected to the Committee of the International Society for Contemporary Music. He paid his first visit to the United States in 1962 to conduct a master class in composition at the Berkshire Music Center at Tanglewood. He returned during the summer of 1966 to serve as composer-in-residence at Dartmouth College in Hanover, New Hampshire, at the invitation of the Hopkins Center Congregation of the Arts. Seven of his compositions were presented at Hanover at this time, four of them American premières. In 1963, a Polish recording of his *Trois Poèmes d'Henri Michaux* won the Koussevitzky International Award, and in 1964, it won first place at the International Rostrum of Composers of UNESCO in Paris.

1954 CONCERTO FOR ORCHESTRA. I. Intrada. II. Capriccio, Notturno ed Arioso. III. Passacaglia, Toccata et Chorale.

One of the strongest influences upon Lutoslawski in the late 1940s and the 1950s was Béla Bartók, whose partiality for discords and atonality, as well as his personal approach to musical nationalism, gave Lutoslawski direction for his own creativity. This Bartók influence is noticeable in the Concerto for Orchestra, which was introduced in Warsaw on November 26, 1954. Here, as Stefan Jorcinski has remarked, "folk motives are used as raw material completely subjected to the larger pattern of the work, and not as a form-determining factor."

Describing this work in the *Saturday Review,* Oliver Daniel wrote: "It is brilliant, inventive and professional *in excelsis.* In fact, it is really slick. It has enough low-key melodic interest to hold attention, but that is not its strong point. Its forte is color. Here, Lutoslawski, working in a somewhat anachronistic ambience, has written a work of old-fashioned vigor that does not seem merely carbon copied. It is an orchestral cousin to the virtuoso orchestral works of Boris Blacher and the late Béla Bartók. Indeed, his relationship to Bartók is more than superficial."

In the first movement (Allegro maestoso), the principal subject is given by the cellos, accompanied by basses, bassoons and harp. The second movement has the structural and stylistic character of a scherzo with trio. The finale first offers a passacaglia theme canonically (Andante con moto), and then a vigorous toccata episode (Allegro giusto). A majestic chorale for brass is prominent towards the end of the composition.

1958 MUSIQUE FUNÈBRE (FUNERAL MUSIC), for string orchestra.

The strong spiritual tie that bound Lutoslawski to Bartók is reflected in this elegy, which was written in memory of Béla Bartók. Its world première took place in Katowice, Poland, on March 26, 1958. A year later, it was heard at the Warsaw Autumn Festival and at the Venice Festival in Italy.

Here Lutoslawski experiments with the twelve-tone system, which he uses with such freedom that there are times when he achieves tonal results. Though played without interruption, the work is in four sections: Prelude, Metamorphoses, Apogee and Epilogue. The gentle music of the Prologue opens with a tone row constructed entirely of tritones and halftones. This becomes the basis of a flowing melody for solo cello. The subject is treated canonically, then one voice is added to another until a climax emerges. The Metamorphoses consists of varied episodes which reach naturally towards the discordant climax of the Apogee. The Epilogue brings back material from the Prologue. The orchestra now becomes reduced and refined until only a solo cello is heard.

1962 JEUX VÉNITIENS (VENETIAN GAMES), for chamber orchestra.

When Lutoslawski visited the United States for the first time, during the summer of 1962, he told an interviewer: "I have just made what I regard as a new beginning, or at least, a new concretization of everything I believe about music. My new style dates from my *Jeux vénitiens*. . . . That work makes considerable use of the techniques of chance, or aleatoric music, and now I am working solely in that direction." What had influenced Lutoslawski in this new direction was a performance by John Cage and his chance music at Darmstadt in 1961. "The experience provided a spark that ignited a powder keg in me," he reveals. "I was a mature composer with many things to express but in fifteen minutes I had an insight into new possibilities open to me by incorporating into my music Cage's ideas."

Jeux vénitiens was introduced at the Venice Festival in Italy on April 4, 1961, where it was regarded by some commentators as the high point of the festival. After the première, the composer revised the composition, the new version getting heard at the Warsaw Autumn Festival in the fall of 1961. Eleazar de Carvalho conducted the American première at the Berkshire Music Festival on August 13, 1965.

The work is in four parts, the first and last of which make the most extensive use of aleatory methods.

In his highly revealing program notes for the Boston Symphony, John N. Burk discloses that the score opens "to a folded double page on which are five panels with notes for various groupings of instruments." One group is the woodwinds; a second, brass; a third, tympani; a fourth, other percussion; a fifth, piano for two performers. "The music on these five panels is performed simultaneously. Since there are no bar lines and no rhythmic signature, the conductor can do no more than give the opening down beat. The music in the different panels being given a fixed duration (which nevertheless varies in each of them), a shorter group will come to the end of its part and is instructed at this point to repeat from the beginning against the longer continuing ones. This is the first of eight consecutive sections in the first movement, those following being mostly confined to the strings." The second section introduces the strings, for which the composer provided the instructions that "the bar lines, rhythmic values and meter are intended merely for orientation; the music should be played with the greatest possible freedom." The third movement is a flute solo which begins and ends pianissimo, accompanied by percussion. The last movement, says Burk, "has a regular bar beat except when the various sections are juxtaposed with overlapping. Again the tempo of certain phrases is determined by an indicated number of seconds. The work ends softly with an extended string chord and a piano punctuation."

GUSTAV MAHLER 1860–1911

Mahler once wrote: "All music since Beethoven is program music." He was probably influenced by the kind of music he himself was writing. Most of his works are programmatic, not as realistically as are the tone poems of Richard Strauss, but suggestively, in the vein of Beethoven, who in his last works tried to make music speak abstract ideas.

Mahler was a complex individual. His entire life was obsessed by inner turmoil and conflicts, spiritual doubts, *Weltschmerz*. Restlessly he searched for a meaning to life. And in his music he continually posed metaphysical questions. He sought to probe the meaning of life and death, to seek out the mysteries of Nature. Above all else, he wanted to resolve the cosmic questions that continually troubled him. In a way, his music is a spiritual autobiography.

Those who dislike Mahler (and they are as passionate as those who worship him) find him bombastic and garrulous. It is not difficult to uncover his weaknesses. He was given to profusion. His works are often mammoth in size and orchestral equipment. They indulge in emotional extravagances.

His melodies, often stemming from Austrian folk sources, are sometimes naïve and sentimental.

But at his best Mahler could rise far above his defects and arrive at an eloquence found in few other musical works. His music, when it is good, is shattering in emotional impact. It is full of human qualities, yet profound in its extramusical implications. Like the man who wrote it, it is uncompromising in its artistic ideals, passionate in sincerity, high-minded and noble in thinking. It is the last word in technical mastery, displaying a knowledge of the orchestra that few other composers have been able to match.

Though Mahler has written remarkable music in the form of the song and the song cycle, the essence of his art is to be found in his symphonies, of which only the first three were written before 1900. Like Beethoven, Schubert and Bruckner, Mahler wrote nine symphonies (a tenth was left uncompleted); like Beethoven, Schubert and Bruckner, he belongs with the great symphonists of all time. These nine Mahler symphonies fall into three distinct groups. The first, including the first four symphonies, was subjective; here, as Paul Stefan wrote, there took place "a great and intensely personal struggle with the world and the universe." In the second group, embracing the fifth through the eighth symphonies, the musician-philosopher became a tone-poet. "As though moving in lofty spheres," wrote Stefan, "he has now mastered his own musical language, penetrating into it more intensely, spiritualizing it, so that he now no longer needs human language." The final group includes the Ninth Symphony and that song cycle which Mahler liked to designate as a symphony, *Das Lied von der Erde*. The composer no longer drew his inspiration from the emotions and struggles of his life. As Bruno Walter remarked, he had now disassociated himself spiritually "from the sphere of life—a loosening of all former connections had changed the entire aspect of his feelings." He was now bidding the world farewell, sometimes with sorrow (as in *Das Lied von der Erde*), sometimes with peace and resignation (as in the closing movement of the Ninth Symphony).

A good deal of Mahler's music is an extension of Beethoven's last period; some of it goes back to Schubert. All of it, as Abraham Skulsky once noted, is thoroughly Viennese. "Every possible element of Viennese folk music can be found in his works, the waltz, the Ländler, the popular song, even the military march. These folk elements are used as basic materials, and are emphasized by Mahler's characteristically sharp and clear sonorities. The scope of his employment of folk materials sets him apart from the Viennese composers who merely explore the waltz, and his handling of the materials distinguished his music from the national music of other composers, in which the folk element is developed in traditional and conventional language. Mahler's emphasis on folklore has led many listeners to consider his music banal, and I do not consider this charge a justifiable one. A piece is not truly banal unless all its elements are banal, and this is far from the case of Mahler."

In a penetrating essay on Mahler published in *High Fidelity Magazine,* Leonard Bernstein wrote that Mahler is a colossus with "his left foot . . . firmly planted in the rich, beloved nineteenth century, and his right, rather less firmly, seeking solid ground in the twentieth." Then Bernstein adds: "All of Mahler's testing, experiments, incursions were made in terms of the past. His breaking-up of rhythms, his post-Wagnerian stretching of tonality to its very snapping point (but not beyond it!), his probings into a new thinness of texture, into bare linear motion, into transparent chamber-music like orchestral manipulation—all these adumbrated what was to become twentieth-century common practice; but they all emanated from those nineteenth-century notes he loved so well."

Mahler said: "My time will yet come." In the first decades of the twentieth century his music was kept alive by such devoted conductors and disciples as Bruno Walter, Otto Klemperer, Richard Strauss, and Willem Mengelberg among others. But only barely kept alive! However, since the end of World War II, and especially in the late 1950s and 1960s, Mahler's music achieved ever wider audiences throughout the world. Cycles of his symphonies were given with immense success in New York, London, and Vienna; and all nine symphonies were recorded in a single Columbia album under Leonard Bernstein's direction, who is perhaps the most passionate Mahler disciple of them all. The Mahler cult, once an esoteric group, has grown to prodigious proportions as more and more music lovers came to realize that in Mahler the world of music possessed not only the greatest symphonist since Brahms but also a prophet and a seer. As Bernstein remarks, Mahler's music foretold many of the harrowing experiences through which the twentieth century has gone. "And . . . in the foretelling, it showered a rain of beauty on this world that has not been equalled since."

Mahler was born in the Bohemian town of Kalischt, on July 7, 1860. At the age of fifteen, he entered the Vienna Conservatory where he remained for three years, a pupil of Julius Epstein in piano, Robert Fuchs in harmony, and Franz Krenn in composition. He won prizes for piano playing and composition. He began conducting immediately after his graduation from the Conservatory, and achieved his first major success with a performance of Mendelssohn's *St. Paul* in Leipzig in 1885. Subsequently, he conducted in opera houses in Prague, Pest and Hamburg, before coming to the Vienna Royal Opera, where his regime, from 1897 to 1907, proved to be one of the most lustrous in the history of that opera house. His importance as a conductor was an accepted fact; his incandescent performances of both operatic and symphonic music set a standard few have equaled. From 1908 until 1911, Mahler conducted in New York at the Metropolitan Opera House and with the New York Philharmonic Orchestra.

Despite his activity with the baton, Mahler found time and energy for composition. He wrote his First Symphony in 1888, and on November 20, 1889, it was introduced in Budapest. Mahler, who subtitled the symphony "The Titan," regarded it as an adventure of the soul. It was a highly subjective work into which Mahler poured his turbulent feelings regarding life, youth, nature, death. The audience that heard this symphony for the first time did not respond sympathetically; it regarded Mahler's overwhelming outpourings as pretentious, and was vocally hostile.

The audience reacted somewhat more favorably to Mahler's Second Symphony, "Resurrection," which he completed in 1894 and the première of which was conducted by Richard Strauss in Berlin on March 4, 1895. But the critics were still hostile. Mahler's "tonal allegory into the life of man," as the Second Symphony was described, his probing into the "whys" of human existence and the purpose of human suffering, along with his reaffirmation of life, seemed pompous stuff; one of the critics described Mahler as "cynical" and "brutal."

Nor was Mahler's Third Symphony (1896) received any more enthusiastically by the critics, when introduced in Krefeld, Germany, on June 9, 1902, the composer conducting. Scored for solo contralto, women's chorus, boys' chorus and orchestra, this symphony was a mighty hymn to Nature, the voice of the composer's Pantheism.

Hostility followed Mahler's creative work almost to the end of his life. Notwithstanding these attacks, he continued to write ambitious symphonies, song cycles and songs, in which his *Weltanschauung*, his philosophical questionings, his search for truth, found expression. Even in that field in which his greatness was generally accepted—conducting—he met bitter enemies. His high-minded principles, his intransigence, his driving will, his refusal to curry favor with anyone, made him a victim of numerous cabals and intrigues. His physical collapse in New York on February 21, 1911, was as much a result of the attacks of his enemies as it was of hard work. He was taken to Paris for serum treatments, then returned to Vienna, where he died on May 18, 1911. He was survived by his wife, the former Alma Maria Schindler, whom he had married on March 10, 1902, and a daughter, Anna Justina, who had been born in 1904 and who, in 1923, married the composer, Ernst Krenek.

1901 SYMPHONY NO. 4 IN G MAJOR. I. Gay, Deliberate, Unhurriedly. II. With leisurely motion. III. Peacefuly. IV. Very easily.

The darkness and the despair we find in so many of Mahler's symphonies are not to be found in this music. This symphony is sunshine and warmth. The shortest of the Mahler symphonies, and the lightest in orchestral texture, it is also the most good-humored and bright-faced. Its première took place in Munich on November 25, 1901, the composer conducting. As was the case with most of Mahler's symphonies, it was poorly received. One critic described it as a "musical monstrosity."

Both themes in the first movement are Schubertian in their pure lyricism and fresh spontaneity. The first is heard at once in the first violins. The second, preceded by a horn call, is given by the cellos. "In the course of the movement," Abraham Skulsky explains, "the themes undergo changes that in many ways prefigure contemporary techniques of development. They are used in reverse form, or broken into sections and superimposed; occasionally Mahler enlarges an interval in one theme or the other, giving it thus a personal romantic flavor. The orchestration likewise progresses from the simplicity of the beginning to greater and greater complexity. One entire section might even be called impressionistic in atmosphere, when over a pedal point of piccolo and basses the flute plays a serene melody; the first bar of this melody is then developed in dissonant fashion, with high notes in clarinets answered by muted trumpets and cymbals."

The second movement opens with a horn call, after which a solo violin enters with a ghostly tune, the instrument being tuned one tone higher to give an eerie effect and to simulate the strummings of a village fiddler. The middle Trio, however, is by contrast in a merry mood. In the third movement, we get a broad and stately theme in low strings which reappears in various guises, Mahler's only use of a variation form in a symphony. A soprano is heard in the fourth movement in a setting of a poem from *Des Knaben Wunderhorn* (ten verses from which he had set for voice and piano, or orchestra, in 1888). The text describes in simple and direct fashion a child's concept of heaven as a gingerbread place with simple attractions, an ingenuousness which Mahler carried over in his vocal setting by adding the following instructions over the music: "With childlike, bright expression, always without parody!" "The music," Bruno Walter explains, "depicts in words the atmosphere out of which the music of the Fourth grew. The childlike joys which it portrays are symbolic of heavenly bliss, and only when, at the very end, music is proclaimed the sublimest of joys, is the humorous character gently changed into one of exalted solemnity."

1902 SYMPHONY NO. 5 IN C-SHARP MINOR ("The Giant"). Part One—I. Funeral March: In a Stormy Measured Step. II. Stormily Agitated With Great Vehemence. Part Two—III. Scherzo: Vigorously, Not Too Fast. Part Three—IV. Adagietto: Very Slowly; V. Rondo—Finale: allegro giocoso.

This symphony is so gargantuan in size (though not the largest of the Mahler symphonies) and so overladen in its instrumentation that it has been called "The Giant." Mahler was dissatisfied with his original scoring and revised it repeatedly up to the year of his death, when he reorchestrated it completely. In its original version, it was introduced in Cologne on October 18, 1904, with Mahler conducting. It was unsuccessful.

Numerous programs have been superimposed upon this highly descriptive and dramatic music. But Bruno Walter informs us that Mahler had insisted to him that "not a single note points to the influence of extramusical thoughts or emotions upon the composition of the Fifth." Walter goes on to describe the music of the symphony as "passionate, wild, pathetic, buoyant, solemn, tender, full of the sentiments of which the human heart is capable—but still 'only' music, and no metaphysical questioning, not even from very far off, interferes with its purely musical course."

The symphony opens with a funeral march, music of such grandeur that it might well serve to describe the passing of a hero. Its main theme is announced immediately by solo trumpet. There is a contrasting middle section in B-flat minor, about which Lawrence Gilman said "the music, grown suddenly and passionately vehement, breaks in upon the measured tread of the Funeral Music like an uncontrollable outburst of shattering, maniacal, wild-visaged grief."

The second movement is in a stormy, rebellious mood, and brings the first part of the symphony to a close. Its principal disturbed subject is given out by the woodwind, while a subsidiary idea is of a more lyric character.

The second part consists of a rather whimsical scherzo, the spine of which is a horn solo that returns in various transformations. This movement is made up of waltz tunes, connected by passages for horns or trumpets.

The third part opens with what is perhaps the most famous section of the entire work, a charming, delicate Adagietto, soulful and romantic, a song for string orchestra. There follows the climax of the symphony, a rondo-finale movement, the rondo theme heard in the wind instruments, after which it is subjected to various changes. There are hasty reminders of themes from earlier movements, with the crowning section a grandiose triple fugue.

1904 KINDERTOTENLIEDER (SONGS OF DEAD CHILDREN), song cycle for voice and orchestra. I. "Once More the Sun Would Gild the Morn." II. "Ah, Now I Know Why Oft I Caught You Gazing." III. "When My Mother Dear." IV. "I Think Oft They've Only Gone Aboard." V. "In Such a Tempest."

Those who have been moved by the immense grief of this music, and who are familiar with the fact that Mahler lost his daughter in 1906, are likely to infer that this work was stimulated by the composer's personal tragedy. Actually, Mahler wrote the *Kindertotenlieder* several years before the death of his child. He was inspired by the moving elegies that the poet Friedrich Rückert wrote on the loss of his children. Of these he selected five and set them to music of profound sadness. Incidentally, following the death of his own child, Mahler was continually haunted by the superstition that death had come to his daughter because he had written this elegiac music!

Paul Stefan has provided the following admirable guide to this cycle of songs in his biography of Mahler: "The first . . . seeks in vain for consolation in the Universe. Again and again a double stroke of the glockenspiel sounds like a doleful reminder . . . and dies away gently with the greeting to the sun. . . . In the second, the eyes of the dead children brighten again—*only* eyes before, *only* stars now. In the third, the voice with its empty fourths, deep, muted, as though speaking alone, joins the sorrowful cor anglais melody. The glance seeks the vanished child on the threshold beside the entering mother. A violent outbreak of grief, and all becomes silent again; only a low G of the harp is struck. Then violins and horns begin a hurrying melody. . . . A furious storm; the children would never have been allowed in this weather. Anxiety is vain today. The glockenspiel is heard again, and over the celesta and violins sounds in major 'like a cradle song' the message of hope and lasting peace."

The first performance took place in Vienna in 1905 under the composer's direction.

1905 SYMPHONY NO. 6 IN A MINOR ("Tragic"). I. Allegro energico, ma non troppo: heftig, aber markig. II. Wuchtig. III. Andante moderato. IV. Allegro moderato.

Though Mahler avoided programmatic allusions to his symphonies he permitted the Sixth Symphony to be called *Tragic* when it received its world première at Essen, Germany, on May 27, 1906, the composer conducting. The tragedy here is found mainly in the monumental finale. However, the tread of Fate stalks ominously through the first movement, symbol of impending catastrophe.

The symphony meant much to the composer, as his wife, Alma, explained in her reminiscences. She herself regarded the work as Mahler's most personal symphony. Both Mahler and his wife wept when he played through the score for the first time. "None of his works moved him so deeply," she recalled. "When it [the rehearsal] was over, Mahler walked up and down in the artist's room, sobbing, wringing his hands, unable to control himself. . . . On the day of the concert, Mahler was so afraid that agitation might get the better of him that, out of shame and anxiety, he did not conduct the symphony well. He hesitated to bring out the dark omen behind the terrible last movement."

The first movement begins with a march subject with an octave drop in the violins, over a steady rhythm in the drum. This is the main theme. After it has been stated and developed, there comes a six-note rhythm in the tympani which Mahler intended as a fate motive, and which recurs with overpowering impact in the finale. A roll of the snare drum, taps of the tympani, a motto in trumpets—all this helps to bring on a chorale-like episode in the winds. This is followed by the movement's second principal subject, a melody in the violins. A dramatic development section unfolds and grow into a climax, after which distant sounds of cowbells are sounded.

The second-movement scherzo has a grotesque quality which is created by such interesting instrumental effects as having the strings play "*col legno*" (rapping bows on the strings with the wooden backs rather than with the hair) or having xylophones simulate the rattling of bones. The middle section, marked "in olden style," is lighter and more graceful. The slow movement is a sustained song, beginning in first violins and continuing in English horn, French horn and flutes. The peaceful atmosphere, thus projected, continues, as harps, celesta and high-string harmonics join in. But eventually, a passionate mood is aroused and erupts into a climax. Then the movement ends as serenely as a benediction, finally ebbing into silence.

And now comes the giant thirty-minute finale, the apotheosis of the entire work, often described as music of utter despair. The motto theme recurs three times at climactic points. The composer described them as "hammer-strokes" and instructed that they be "short, powerful, with a dull rather than metallic sound." The first such blow takes place when a forceful tutti interrupts the first development section. After a second development has progressed awhile, the full orchestra once again enters with a mighty exclamation, accompanied by the second hammer blow. The third hammer blow—it has been described as a "death blow"—appears in the coda. Alma Mahler has revealed that in the last movement "Mahler describes himself and his downfall, or, as he later said, that of his hero, 'the hero who undergoes three strokes of destiny, the third of which fells him like a tree.' These were Mahler's words."

The finale opens with a solemn declamation by first violins. Then the fate theme is announced. The main material of the first movement is remembered, together with ideas from other earlier movements. They become the basic part of two monumental developments, which are rudely interrupted by hammer blows. An air of mystery is introduced with a passage dominated by the sounds of cowbells, deep bells, harp, celesta and muted horns. The despair grows deeper and deeper. Tympani bring back the hammer blows for the last time, while a trombone quartet adds to the solemnity.

This has been one of Mahler's most neglected symphonies. In fact, it took over forty years for the work to get heard for the first time in the United

States. It was finally introduced to America by the New York Philharmonic under Dimitri Mitropoulos on December 11, 1947.

1906 SYMPHONY NO. 7 IN D MAJOR. I. Langsam: allegro con fuoco. II. Nachtmusik: allegro moderato. III. Schattenhaft: fliessend, aber nicht schnell. IV. Nachtmusik: andante amoroso. V. Rondo-Finale: allegro ordinario.

The tonality of Mahler's Seventh Symphony is somewhat ambiguous. Some critics have fixed E minor to it, some, B minor. Dika Newlin explains: "In this symphony, Mahler returned to the ideal of 'progressive tonality' which he had abandoned in the Sixth. The first movement itself progresses from B minor to E major, while the brilliant finale is in C major." The second movement is in C minor and C major; the third, in D minor and D major; and the fourth, in F major."

The structure also helps to set this symphony apart from others by Mahler. There are five movements, two of them Serenades (*Nachtmusik*). The scherzo is made up of what one analyst describes as "a strange fabric of melodic fragments and jogging dance sequences held together by one propulsive rhythm," and the two serenades, and scherzo that comes in between, as "a kind of symphony within a symphony." Alma Mahler, the composer's wife, discloses that as Mahler wrote the two serenades he was "beset by Eichendorff-ish visions—murmuring springs and German Romanticism" (Eichendorff being, of course, the famous German Romantic poet). And she adds: "Apart from this, the symphony has no program."

The symphony was introduced in Prague on September 19, 1908, the composer conducting. "The Seventh was scarcely understood by the public," recalled Mahler's wife, "it had a *succès d'estime*."

The first movement has a somber introduction in which tenor horn presents a triplet motive in the second measure, of which considerable use is made later on. In the main body of the movement, the principal theme is given by cellos and horns. This subject is elaborately developed, while there are constant reminders of the introductory motive. The second theme is given by first and second violins in octaves, part of which is accompanied by arpeggio figures in the cellos. Another elaborate development follows, with lyric passages entering for contrast.

The second-movement serenade begins with a haunting horn call, to which a second horn gives response. A chromatic passage leads to a slow subject for horn and to a march-like episode in double basses and double bassoons. The slow horn subject is taken over by the violins. A pastoral atmosphere is evoked through cowbells and flute passages, the flutes instructed by the composer to sound like "bird voices."

In the "shadow-like" scherzo that follows, the main thought (made up of a triplet figure) is presented by first violins, cellos and tympani. There are four contrasting trio sections, in which a ghost-like, almost grotesque, mood is created through various unusual instrumental effects.

Mandolin and guitar introduce the second serenade, whose main melody is heard in horn, accompanied harmonically by clarinet, harp, guitar and bassoon. New material is subsequently offered by cellos and horns. The overall effect of the movement is that of intimate chamber music, refined in texture, subtle in orchestral colorations.

A solo for tympani and a horn fanfare brings on the finale, preparing the ground for the main theme, in trumpets and horns. A march-like melody is now projected, to which flutes and clarinets provide an intriguing background in sixteenth-notes. An electrifying episode for strings and woodwind, followed by a dramatic pause, precede the appearance of a new melody—in flutes, oboes, English horn and clarinets. All this material is worked out dramatically. Before the movement ends, we get a recall of the first movement's principal subject, first in horns, then in trombones accompanied by thrusts by the tympani. This material helps to bring the symphony to a proud, sonorous conclusion.

1907 SYMPHONY NO. 8 IN E-FLAT MAJOR ("Symphony of a Thousand Voices"), for eight solo voices, two mixed choruses, boys' choir and orchestra. I. Veni Creator Spiritus. II. Final Scene from Goethe's *Faust.*

Because of the giant forces required to perform the Eighth Symphony, it has been nicknamed "Symphony of a Thousand Voices." Mahler regarded this as his masterwork, "the greatest thing I have done so far," he told Willem Mengelberg, the conductor, "and so unusual in form and content that one has difficulty in writing it. Imagine to yourself the entire universe suddenly beginning to sound and sing! These are no longer human voices, but revolving suns and planets." Elsewhere Mahler spoke of his earlier symphonies as "only preludes to this one," adding: "In those works everything is still tragically subjective; this one is a mighty dispenser of joy."

The first half of the symphony, "*Veni Creator Spiritus,*" is in the traditional sonata-allegro structure (Allegro impetuoso). This is a setting of a ninth-century Latin text by the Archbishop of Mayence, which later became part of the Roman Catholic liturgy for Pentecost. To Mahler, the "*Creator Spiritus*" represented not only God or the Holy Ghost but also the creative spirit of an artist which contained within itself elements of the divine. Mahler regarded this first half of the symphony as "a song of yearning, of rapturous devotion in invocation of the creative spirit, the love that moves the worlds." Three main subjects are presented. The first is the cry of the two massed choruses, "*Veni Creator Spiritus,*" repeated by trombones and trumpets and by two separate choruses. Then comes a contrasting melody (Dolce, espressivo) for soprano solo ("*Imple superna*"). The third main thought comes in the orchestra when the choruses are heard in the hymn's third strophe, "*Infirma nostri.*" A development of monumental proportions follows, with a climax reached in a giant double fugue.

Structurally, the second half may be described as an Andante, Scherzo and Finale, with coda. Its text is taken from the closing scene of the second part of Goethe's *Faust.* Here the music is entirely dramatic, at moments even operatic. Dika Newlin has explained in *Bruckner, Mahler, Schoenberg:* "Needless to say, Mahler has taken full advantage of the dramatic possibilities of his material, and the imaginative listener (placed in a receptive mood by the atmospheric introduction, with its one hundred and sixty-four bar pedal point in E-flat) may well visualize the scene laid before him at the beginning."

Miss Newlin notes that despite the Romanticism of Mahler's orchestration, and the unquestionable symphonic style of his developments, the Eighth Symphony is "in spirit a Baroque composition. The grandiose elan of its opening chorus has the quality of a Handelian oratorio. The literary form of any oratorio must of necessity be a narrative one; in the Eighth Symphony, on the other hand, we are confronted with the triumph of musical logic over verbal logic, the combination of texts in two different languages (German and Latin). No symphonist had yet dared to combine two different languages in a choral-symphonic work; that Mahler could do it without sacrificing unity is a striking tribute to the strength of the musical structure."

To Bruno Walter, no other work by Mahler expresses so fully "the impassioned 'yes' to life. 'Yes' resounds here in the massed voices of the hymn wrought by a master hand into a temple-like structure of a symphonic movement; it peals from the *Faust* words and from the torrent of music in which Mahler's own emotion is released."

The world première of the Eighth Symphony was the greatest triumph Mahler had known as a composer. It took place in Munich on September 12, 1910, the composer conducting. "Never again would Mahler see a night like this," says Dika Newlin, not only of the audience reaction to the première, but of the festivities that followed. The first American performance of this symphony took place in Philadelphia on March 2, 1916, Leopold Stokowski conducting.

1908 DAS LIED VON DER ERDE (THE SONG OF THE EARTH), "symphony" (or song cycle) for tenor, contralto and orchestra. I. Drinking Song of the Misery of Earth. II. The Lonely One in Autumn. III. Of Youth. IV. Of Beauty. V. The Toper in Spring. VI. The Farewell of a Friend.

Das Lied von der Erde and the Ninth Symphony represent Mahler's farewell to the world. Though there appears to be a tranquil resignation in the symphony, there is only the profoundest pessimism in the song cycle. In what is perhaps one of his most personal works, Mahler expresses his maladjustment to the world around him, and his bitter renunciation of it. "Dark is life, dark is death," is only one line in the cycle; but it might serve as the motif for the entire work.

Das Lied is a cycle of six songs, alternately sung by tenor and contralto. It is based on Chinese poems by Li-Tai-Po, Tchang-Tsi, Mong-Kao-Yen and Wang-Wei, which Hans Bethge adapted in his *Die Chinesische Flöte*. The somber mood of the poems, and the rich Chinese imagery, inspired Mahler to write music that is persistently dark and brooding in feeling and yet occasionally touched with vivid oriental colors.

Mahler referred to *Das Lied* as a "symphony"—though its relation to the classical symphonic form is, at best, remote. Keeping Mahler's designation in mind, Eric Blom finds the first song serving as the opening movement of the symphony; the second (poignantly elegiac music) is, then, the slow movement; the third (the only section that is not pessimistic) might be the scherzo; the fourth is in the nature of a minuet and trio; the fifth assumes the form of a rondo; and the last might approximate a slow-movement finale such as is found in Mahler's Ninth Symphony. In the last song, the despair of the preceding movements achieves a heartrending and climactic intensity.

One unidentified commentator, quoted in the program book of the New York Philharmonic Orchestra, contributed the following illuminating description:

"It is not the earth that sings, and the poems deal less with the aspects of nature than with the philosophy of human existence. The first poem is epicurean, a drinking song—the world is full of woe, the skies are eternal, earth will endure, but man's life is but a span. . . . The second poem describes nature in the pall of autumnal mists. . . . The lamp of life burns low, the poet's heart is filled with gloom, for it despairs of ever again seeing the sun of love which might perchance dry his tears—and he longs for rest. No. 3 is the song of youth, and its imagery is authentically Chinese—the picture of a bridge across a pond, a gay pavilion, people making merry, and reflected upside down in the watery mirror. No. 4 describes a scene of lovers wandering through an enchanted landscape, picking flowers and bestowing languishing looks upon one another. . . . The pessimistic mood returns: (No. 5). All life is a dream, full of woe; so, therefore, wine again: let us sleep the sleep of drunkenness. Finally (in No. 6) two poems are united: the poet sees the world in a drunken sleep, longs for his friend that he may say farewell, resolves no more to seek happiness away from home, and awaits the end while Spring wakens the world anew."

Das Lied von der Erde received its world première posthumously: in Munich on November 20, 1911, Bruno Walter conducting.

1910 SYMPHONY NO. 9 IN D MAJOR. I. Andante comodo. II. Im Tempo eines Gemächlichen Ländlers. III. Rondo burleske. IV. Adagio.

Mahler wrote his last complete symphony realizing that his life was drawing to a close and with the feeling that this would be his final work in the symphonic form. The music of the Ninth Symphony is filled with sadness and world-weariness, the conflicts of a man searching restlessly for the peace and tranquillity life has thus far denied him. There is a great deal of soul-searching in the music, and the drama of inner turmoil; but there is also a note of resignation, particularly in the radiant music of the closing Adagio.

The first movement, described by Alban Berg as the most beautiful ever written by Mahler, opens in an atmosphere of foreboding and mystery. It continues in a somber vein to project the most intense sadness and yearnings of the composer. There are two principal melodic ideas: one has the calmness of resignation and is given by the second violins, while the other (twenty measures later) is passionate and intense, its expression of agony stressed by piercing chords for the trumpets. In the second movement, one might reasonably expect an escape from this mental anguish, for here Mahler writes a Viennese Ländler, a peasant dance which, in the hands of Schubert, had lightness and gaiety. But Mahler writes his dance music with a suggestion of mockery, as if to comment with scorn on wordly pleasures. Irony, too, is injected into the third movement, which, Paul Bekker says, "is also a backward glance upon life with its indomitable activity, in which the song of creation is but an undercurrent to the always renewing changes of surging power. The artist mocks himself in a mockery which gives voice to the feelings of all those whose home is not in this world and its errors, who yearn for other shores. A movement of burning scorn."

But the mockery and the irony die on the lips, and in the final movement—

one of the most incandescent pages ever written by Mahler—comes resignation. This is music of ethereal serenity and of other-worldly beauty. Mahler, having gone through his herculean struggle with himself, has at last found peace of soul. About this closing movement, Paul Bekker wrote: "The violins soar slowly, and with heavy accent—a profound, beatific Adagio lifts its voice. . . . There are measures of a godlike love. But it is the love, not of a budding, flowering nature, but of a nature dying. D major, key of life's fulfillment, gives way to D-flat, key of sublimity. The mighty Pan appears no longer as creator but as god of release. Becoming is transformed into ceasing. Death is the godlike love; its majesty possessing the string choir in full songfulness. The melody is placid, yet wrought with the highest intensity of feeling. It is no song of mourning, but a noble affirmation, the unfolding of a final vision."

The first performance of the Ninth Symphony took place in Vienna on June 26, 1912—a little more than a year after Mahler's death—with Bruno Walter conducting the Vienna Philharmonic.

1911 SYMPHONY NO. 10 IN F-SHARP MINOR (performing version by Deryck Cooke). Part One—I. Adagio. II. Scherzo: schenelle Vierteln. Part Two—I. Allegretto Moderato. II. Scherzo: allegro pesante. III. Finale: lento non troppo; allegro moderato; tempo primo.

Mahler did not live to complete his Tenth Symphony. But what he had left behind were not just mere fragments and random sketches, but a comprehensive and detailed full-length draft of a five-movement symphony. Two of the movements were in a sufficiently advanced stage of completion to get performed in Vienna on October 12, 1924, Frank Schalk conducting, the performing score prepared by Ernst Krenek.

In a biography of Mahler published in 1913, Richard Specht said that Mahler had asked that the manuscript of his Tenth Symphony be destroyed after his death. But eleven years later, Specht modified this statement by saying that Mahler had made his request in a fit of depression, but had later instructed his wife she could do with the manuscript whatever she wished. Mahler's widow suggested to Arnold Schoenberg that he complete the symphony, but Schoenberg, after examining the manuscript in 1949, felt he was unable to do so because of his advanced years. The monumental job of developing Mahler's draft into a full-length symphony finally fell to the English musicologist, Deryck Cooke. "It is not intended as a 'completion' of the Tenth," Cooke explained, "but as a 'performing version' of Mahler's draft, as far as he had taken it." Mahler's elaborate harmonic and thematic material was reproduced without change and, aside from the orchestration which was found necessary, what was added were a few subsidiary harmonies and inner parts to the two scherzo movements. Cooke's performing version, which received the approval of Mahler's widow, was heard for the first time in London on December 19, 1960, over the BBC. Berthold Goldschmidt conducted a concert performance in London with the London Symphony on August 13, 1964. The American première took place on November 5, 1965, with Eugene Ormandy conducting the Philadelphia Orchestra.

When the symphony was repeated by the Philadelphia Orchestra in New York, Raymond Ericson described the work as "long and fascinating."

He added: "The final movement ends with an extended passage of such beauty that it alone would make the work's completion worthwhile." Ericson found the second and fourth movements, the two scherzos, "full of tricky rhythms, mordant passages and earthy dance-like sections—all characteristic of the composer." The third movement, called *Purgatorio,* is a short and eloquent interval between the two scherzos. "Then comes the last movement which seems to gather up the ideas of the earlier portions of the symphony only to resolve them in its final serene, other-worldly pages."

GIAN FRANCESCO MALIPIERO 1882–

Malipiero's painstaking and monumental researches into the music of Italy's past—which have resulted in definitive editions of Monteverdi, Vivaldi, Cavalieri, Galuppi, etc.—have had an inescapable influence on his own musical thinking. Without sacrificing modern techniques, he reaches into Italy's past for subtle stylistic qualities and suggestions; these set his music apart from those of other contemporary Italians by endowing it with a kind of medieval quality. Like that of Monteverdi, his melodic line frequently resembles a recitative, carrying powerful dramatic impact. Like those of Vivaldi and Tartini, his slow passages often have serenity, even spirituality. And like so many of the old Italians, Malipiero emphasizes counterpoint; indeed, he was one of the first Italians of our times to do so. His style frequently carries reminders of old Gregorian chants.

Not only old Italian music, but old Italian culture as well, has left its imprint on his music. Sometimes Malipiero models his themes after the strophes and cadences of old Italian poetry; sometimes his musical structures are imitative of poetic forms. And there are occasions when he successfully re-creates in his music the atmosphere and spirit, the social and cultural backgrounds, of the Italian Renaissance.

What Georges Jean-Aubry wrote of Malipiero in 1919 held true for many years after that: "His tendencies direct him unceasingly towards an economy of means which leaves nothing to chance but which gives no impression of painful restraint. His personality is attractive in its combination of ardor and abandon, of austerity and grace, of feeling and reason. . . . Malipiero's music is in no sense systematic, being given neither to exasperating harmonies nor to repeated rhythmic singularities. It utilizes the newest or oldest forms according to the necessities of feeling. Turn by turn, the melody is light, frail, or concentrated."

To Henri Prunières, Malipiero's harmonic style "never gives the impression of deliberateness, or of adherence to a system. The dissonances are the result of a very free polyphony. Malipiero does not hesitate to have recourse to the most consonant chords when he considers it necessary. At the same time he is the slave of no modal system and never seeks . . . to keep himself aloof from all definite tonality. He uses largely of the treasures of the ancient modes, exotic or modern, without any preoccupation other than that of expressing his ideas in a form as concrete as possible."

Malipiero was born in Venice on March 18, 1882, a descendant of an old Venetian family that numbered several famous musicians. For a year, in 1898, Malipiero attended the Vienna Conservatory. But most of his training was received from Enrico Bossi, first at the Liceo Musicale Benedetto Marcello in Venice, then at the Liceo Musicale in Bologna. While attending the latter school, Malipiero completed his first work for orchestra, *Dai sepolcri,* introduced at a Conservatory concert in 1904. A protracted stay in Paris, where he absorbed progressive cultural ideas and the latest musical idioms, influenced his technique, just as his studies in old Italian music, begun in 1902, helped to crystallize his style.

Malipiero attracted attention in Europe during and soon after World War I with several distinguished works. *Pause del silenzio,* for orchestra (1917), reflected the shattering impact the war had had upon him. It proved an outstanding success when introduced in Rome on January 27, 1918, Molinari conducting. This was followed by an opera, *Sette Canzoni,* part of a stage trilogy collectively entitled *L'Orfeide.* He completed it in 1919, and its world première took place at the Paris Opéra on July 10, 1920.

In 1920, Malipiero received the Elizabeth Sprague Coolidge prize of $1,000 for *Rispetti e Strambotti,* for string quartet. Since then his major chamber-music and orchestral works have had extensive hearings in the United States, including several significant world premières. Malipiero also distinguished himself as a teacher. From 1921 to 1923, he was professor of composition at the University of Parma. He later held a similar post at the Liceo Musicale Benedetto Marcello in Venice, where he became director in 1939, a post held for about two decades. Since the end of World War I, Malipiero has spent most of his time in the seclusion of a little town, Asolo, where he has devoted himself assiduously to composition, musicology, and to teaching a few private pupils.

1920 RISPETTI E STRAMBOTTI, for string quartet.

Rispetti and *Strambotti* are two ancient Italian forms of poetry. The former is an address of love from a gentleman to a lady; the other is a kind of roundelay.

In adapting these two forms of poetry to music, Malipiero attempted to sketch a varied picture of society against the background of the Renaissance, from the peasant to the clergy. In one movement, this quartet contains twenty loosely connected episodes in which two themes are prominent: one, based on the plainchant, suggests the clergy; the other, consisting of acrid chords, speaks for the peasantry.

This quartet received the Elizabeth Sprague Coolidge prize of $1,000.

The world première took place at Pittsfield, Massachusetts, on September 25, 1920, in a performance by the Letz Quartet.

1920 SAN FRANCESCO D'ASSISI (ST. FRANCIS OF ASSISI), mystery (or cantata) for solo voices, chorus and orchestra.

Malipiero's first significant choral work was a musical interpretation of the personality of St. Francis since, as the composer explained, that personality "is so musical in itself that one had only to cull it." The cantata consists of four tableaux or scenes which were "dictated by the same thought; these scenes breathe a musical life from which they cannot be disassociated, and I had contemplated a scenic setting which would reproduce the frescoes of Giotto." The composer explains further: "The words proclaimed by a single voice in the Prelude represent the basic principle of the Franciscan Order and are taken from the Evangel of St. Matthew. The text of the first scene is the *Canzone della Poverta* of Jacopone da Todi. "The Sermon to the Birds" is taken directly from the sixteenth chapter of the *Fioretti* of San Francesco. The following third scene is also taken from the *Fioretti*, chapter fifteen. The last scene is taken from *The Life of San Francesco* as written by San Bonaventura, where it even told that San Francesco improvised the Strophe for Our Sister, the Death in the Body, on the day of his death, after having begged his brothers to sing him the Canticle of the Sun."

The world première took place in New York City at a concert of the Schola Cantorum, Kurt Schindler conducting, on March 29, 1922.

The work includes four symphonic fragments, that are sometimes performed independently at symphony concerts. The first is a "Prelude" (Lento) which precedes the sentence from St. Francis's Hymn to the Sun: "Praised be my Lord God, with all creatures, and specially our brother in the sun." This is followed by "The Sermon to the Birds" (Lento), "The Supper of St. Francis and St. Claire" (Molto mosso) and "The Death of St. Francis" (Lento ma non troppo).

1927 SONATA A TRE, for violin, cello and piano. I. Allegro impetuoso. II. Ritenuto. III. Allegro impetuoso.

In 1927, Malipiero was commissioned by Elizabeth Sprague Coolidge to write a chamber-music work. In conceiving a trio for violin, cello and piano, Malipiero arrived at an original scheme. He wrote the first movement for cello and piano and the second for violin and piano; only in the concluding movement is the trio heard. The writing is impressionistic, with alternations of turbulent and placid moods. There is a richness of melodic ideas throughout. Themes used in the first two movements are repeated in the last.

Here is how the composer himself described this work in a letter dated January, 1950: "Three instruments, three human beings, have come together. The cello speaks first, alone; it is followed in the second movement by the violin. Each instrument retains its own character, expresses its own ideas, but in the last movement they finally come to an understanding. The piano constantly supports and helps first the cello, then the violin, like a good friend who acts as a moderator. There is not the faintest intention of a program idea in this *Sonata a Tre*. It was conceived in a spirit of peace and love."

The first performance, by the Elshuco Trio, took place at Pittsfield, Massachusetts, on September 20, 1928.

1935 LA PASSIONE, oratorio, for soloists, chorus and orchestra.

Malipiero has composed two oratorios which set to music the sixteenth-century mystery play by Pierozzo Castellani, *Rappresentazione della Cena e Passione,* the first being *La Cena,* composed in 1927. *La Passione* was introduced successfully at the Augusteo in Rome on December 15, 1935.

The text is a primitive one; for it, Malipiero produced music that has an archaic quality, derived from medieval Italian folk songs and Gregorian chants. It is simple to a point of being, at times, stark and bare. The melodic writing is fluid, with little difference between actual lyricism and recitative.

"In the main," wrote Raymond Hall, reporting the première performance in Rome, "the music adheres closely to the text . . . since the composer is dominated by the pictorial conception of the fresco. . . . Thus the outward dramatic events of the opening, such as Judas' betrayal, the arrest and trial, are not given much relief, and the characters themselves—the angel, Judas, the captain, the high priest, Pontius Pilate, Herod—are scantily differentiated in the score, but are rather reduced to a synthetic common denominator, Mary excepted. The orchestra . . . in its accompaniments and brief interludes creates the atmosphere of each situation in a few masterly strokes. . . . The concentration of subject and medium reaches a high degree of expertness."

1936 SYMPHONY NO. 2 ("Elegiaca"). I. Allegro non troppo. II. Lento non troppo. III. Messo. IV. Lento; Allegro; Lento quasi andante.

The year of 1936 was a tragic one for Malipiero. Though he tried to keep music outside the periphery of his own emotional crises, he could not help endowing the symphony he was writing with an elegiac character. "The first movement," wrote the composer, "is the least elegiacal, for the principal theme is full of vigor. The last movement, almost more than the second movement, justifies the character of an elegy. The third movement has a groundwork of ill-conceived melancholy."

The entire symphony has many pages of gentleness, and it is the opinion of Malipiero's wife that it has absorbed the quiet and serene character of the Italian countryside at Asolo, where it was written.

The symphony received its world première in the United States on January 25, 1937, in a performance by the Seattle Symphony Orchestra under Basil Cameron.

1947 SYMPHONY NO. 4 ("In Memoriam"). I. Allegro moderato. II. Lento funèbre. III. Allegro. IV. Lento.

World War I inspired Malipiero to write the bitter music of *Pause del Silenzio.* Out of World War II (and its aftermath) came the Fourth Symphony, a veritable elegy. "This terrible postwar period," Malipiero wrote, "is a huge cemetery in which is brought together all that is no more, so that one's soul has been disposed to draw into itself and make its own the grief of a friend."

The great tragedy through which Malipiero and his fellow Italians went during the years of World War II sets the mood for the entire symphony. The composer has explained that in the first and third movements he attempted to speak of hope; in the second and fourth movements, the mood is that of resignation. A theme first heard in the middle of the first movement—a forceful outburst—is the dominating thought of the entire symphony and makes constant reappearances. The second movement is almost uninterruptedly funereal, while the third is a conventional scherzo, an escape from the pessimism and grief of the preceding movement. The fourth movement, which brings up the image of a funeral procession, utilizes the pealing of church bells as the principal theme; this is subjected to six variations. This theme occurred to the composer thirty-six years before he put it into this symphony, and remained in his mind "until the day when I found its rightful place in the fourth movement of the symphony."

1954 FANTASIE DI OGNI GIORNI (FANTASY OF EVERY DAY), for orchestra.

Commissioned by the Louisville Orchestra in Kentucky, this orchestral fantasy was introduced by that organization on November 17, 1954. The composer described it as "a daily journey into the realm of fantasy." He wrote it at a time when he was seriously thinking of abandoning symphonic composition for good. As a substitute for symphonic writing, he decided to note down all ideas, themes, musical expressions that sprang to his mind for possible use at a later day. He put down these musical thoughts methodically day after day, as if in a diary. One day as he glanced through these ideas, he realized that they represented not unrelated fragments but a more or less artistic continuity. He gathered this material into a unified composition which he entitled *Fantasy of Every Day*.

FRANK MARTIN 1890–

Though Frank Martin has long been regarded as one of Switzerland's outstanding composers, recognition in the United States has been slow in coming. In Europe he has enjoyed a long record of successful performances. But not until 1939 did a major work of his receive an American performance: the *Ballade* (for saxophone, piano, percussion and strings), heard on an all-Swiss program. And not until a decade after that did he realize a success of major proportions in the United States. It came with the *Petite Symphonie concertante,* which most major American orchestras performed and which to this day has remained one of its composer's most popular compositions.

Since then, major works by Martin have had frequent representation on American concert programs, and his opera, *The Tempest,* was produced in New York.

Through the years of his rich creative activity, Martin has permitted his style to undergo several transformations. At first, he wrote somewhat academically, faithful to French traditions, strongly affected by Franck and Fauré. Between 1925 and 1928, he began to explore rhythmic problems, in compositions like the *Rhythmes,* for orchestra (1926), first performance at the festival of the International Society for Contemporary Music at Geneva on April 6, 1929. The next major development came in 1930, when he embraced the twelve-tone system in compositions like his piano concerto (1934) and his symphony (1937). In the early 1940s, beginning with the cantata *Le Vin herbé,* Martin finally arrived at a style identifiably his, in which he was to produce his most important works. Lyricism and expressive feelings, and at times mysticism, were now able to assert themselves strongly.

"Returning, as it were from an unreal, gravitationless tone world," wrote Paul Boepple, "Martin found tonality to be no longer the yoke against which he had once revolted, but a positive force which he was eager to harness. While it could be said that his music is atonal, tonality has become for him an active principle which he never takes for granted as an initial fact. The logic of his harmonic palette is no less compelling. In its sweeping completeness it reminds of the periodic table, being equally full of strangers and of old friends doing new things. Martin uses these seemingly all-inclusive resources with the utmost taste and skill so that his music usually sounds deceptively simple."

Jacques de Menasce succinctly summed up Martin's style as "broad melodic lines of chromatic nature, subtle harmonic and rhythmic patterns, and a sustained contrapuntal texture."

Martin was born in Geneva, Switzerland, on September 15, 1890. He studied music there with Josef Lauber and received his first public performances with the *Trois poèmes payens,* for baritone and orchestra, heard at a festival of the Association of Swiss Musicians in 1911. From 1923 to 1925, he lived in Paris, where he studied and assimilated progressive tendencies in music. He returned to Geneva in 1926, and from then on assumed a place of first importance in Swiss music. He helped organize the Société de Musique de Chambre, serving as its pianist and harpsichordist from 1927 to 1937. He taught music at the Dalcroze Institute, ultimately becoming its director. Between 1933 and 1939, he was director of the Technique Moderne Musique, which he had helped to organize; and from 1943 to 1946, he was president of the Association of Swiss musicians. International fame as composer came with *Le Vin herbé* in 1942, and the *Petite Symphonie Concertante* in 1946. He established permanent residence in Amsterdam in 1946, staying there twelve years, and traveling from that city regularly to Germany to teach at the Cologne Conservatory between 1952 and 1958. Since then, he has made his home in Leiden. Meanwhile, he made his mark as an opera composer with *The Tempest* in 1956. He later wrote a comic opera, *Monsieur de Pourceaugnac,* based on Molière, produced in Geneva on April 23, 1963. His oratorio, *Le Mystère de la nativité,* based on a fifteenth-century mystery play, introduced over the Swiss radio on December

24, 1959, was given a staged production at the Salzburg Festival during the summer of 1960. In 1960, Martin received honorary doctorates from the Universities of Geneva and Lausanne. During the summer of 1967, Martin was composer-in-residence at Dartmouth College fifth annual Congregation of the Arts at Hopkins Center.

1940 LE VIN HERBÉ (THE MAGIC POTION), cantata for solo voices, chorus and orchestra.

The text of *Le Vin herbé* is an adaptation of the legend of Tristan and Isolde as retold in the novel of Joseph Bédier published in 1900. The composer took three chapters from this book and used them with little alteration. Stylistically, in its restraint, subtle suggestions, mysticism and atmospheric writing, *Le Vin herbé* springs more naturally out of *Pelléas et Mélisande* than it does out of *Tristan and Isolde*. Its modest dimensions are, indeed, a far cry from the Wagnerian music drama, since this work is scored for a small chorus and an orchestra comprising only eight instrumentalists (piano, double bass, two violins, two violas and two cellos). The vocal writing is essentially declamation, with most of the lyric interest centered on the chorus, which is used with particularly telling effect in both the prologue and the epilogue.

The cantata is in three sections. The first is reminiscent of *Tristan and Isolde* (first act), except that the love potion is drunk by accident rather than design. The second part finds the lovers in the forest of Moret, having fled from the jealous rage of King Mark. The King finds them there asleep, with Tristan's sword lying between them. A change of heart leads the king to spare their lives. He substitutes his own sword for that of Tristan, a sign that he has forgiven them. In the concluding part, Tristan, married to another woman, is dying. He is calling for Isolde, who arrives only after Tristan has died. In the epilogue, the chorus comments that this is a tale "for those who are troubled and those whose hearts are glad, the discontented, the weary in spirit, those whose hearts rejoice, those who are sorely afflicted, and those who love."

Le Vin herbé received its world première in Zurich on March 26, 1942. It was produced at the Salzburg summer festival six years later. The American première was given in New York by the Schola Cantorum, Hugh Ross conducting, on February 26, 1961. On that occasion, Ross Parmenter called it in *The New York Times* "one of the loveliest works that has been composed in this century."

1945 PETITE SYMPHONIE CONCERTANTE, for harp, harpsichord, piano and two string orchestras. I. Adagio; Allegro molto. II. Adagio; Allegretto alla marcia.

This work reveals the influence of the twelve-tone system, but traditional procedures are not altogether abandoned. The blend of the old and the new is achieved gracefully. This little symphony is in two movements, each with a slow and fast section. The opening forty-six measure Adagio contains the thematic material utilized throughout the work. "The following Allegro," explains Jacques de Menasce, "which is set off by this Adagio after the briefest of transitions, is developed on the lines of a symphonic movement with two themes. Dying down gradually, however, it leads, after a moment of suspension, to the second Adagio, a quiet and mysterious fountainhead from which emerges the dance-like final Allegro."

The symphony is dedicated to Paul Sacher of the Basle Chamber Orchestra. That orchestra, under Sacher, introduced the work on May 17, 1946. On December 27, 1947, it was heard in the United States—Ernest Ansermet conducting the NBC Symphony over the NBC radio network.

1949 CONCERTO FOR SEVEN WIND INSTRUMENTS, PERCUSSION AND STRING ORCHESTRA. I. Allegro. II. Adagietto. III. Allegro vivace.

This work was introduced by the Musical Society of Bern, Luc Balmer conducting, on October 25, 1949. It scored such a success that performances followed immediately in the leading cities of Switzerland, as well as in Amsterdam, Berlin, Cologne and New York. The American première took place on December 28, 1950, with George Szell conducting the New York Philharmonic.

The three movements begin with the same syncopated theme which serves as a kind of motto. In the first movement, this motto theme introduces each of the seven wind instruments, which appear in the following order: oboe, clarinet, horn, trumpet, trombone, bassoon, flute. A principal lyrical idea appears in the clarinet and is developed by the flute; a second major subject is later heard in the trombone. This second subject, transferred to the violins, introduces the recapitulation section. A reentry of the respective solo instruments in their original order concludes the movement. The second movement consists of a variation and development of an atmospheric melody in the violins. The finale, in free rondo form, begins with a vivacious scherzo theme, with a secondary important subject later found in the trumpet. Both themes are worked out in great detail and then repeated. The movement ends with a variation of the scherzo theme.

1955 THE TEMPEST (DER STURM), opera in nine scenes with epilogue, the Shakespeare drama (with minor alterations) serving as the text. First performance: Vienna, June 17, 1956.

"What tempted me in Shakespeare's *Tempest,*" Martin has revealed, "is the infinite psychological richness of the characters. There is an entire gamut of human types as in no other play; and his gamut which transcends the human octave—from the pure spirit to the bestial monster—seems to me particularly suited to musical reproduction. There are so many different worlds: Ariel's world, the world of Prospero, Miranda and Ferdinand, the world of the courtiers, and finally the drunkards' and Caliban's world—each requiring music entirely different from the others."

Shakespeare's play served Martin so well as a libretto that, except for some necessary deletions, he used it in its entirety. He made only one basic change: Ariel becomes primarily a dancing role, the spirit's singing parts performed offstage, sometimes by a chorus, sometimes by a single voice. The choral pages had been written by the composer some years before he went to work on his opera, and were published in 1950 as a cycle of unaccompanied choral pieces entitled *Cinq Chansons d'Ariel.* These were incorporated into the opera almost unchanged, except that a few instruments were used to provide a sparing accompaniment.

The Tempest, which has been described as a "fairy opera," is a happy marriage of opera, pantomime and ballet. Though the vocal numbers are mainly in a declamatory style—and though a modified twelve-tone system is employed —lyricism remains the opera's strong suit. Rudolf Klein pointed out in the *Oesterreichische Musikzeitschrift* how well lyricism serves the text. "Take, for instance, the second scene between Miranda and Prospero. The long melody on which Miranda's recitative is superimposed has already appeared during the middle part of the overture. Its characteristic narrow melodic steps express Miranda's concern over the shipwreck. The further development of this melody is achieved solely through emotional elements and the retention of certain typical intervals. . . . Prospero begins with a repetition of the same melody, now transposed; this, however, serves only as a transition; for now comes Prospero's account of his own fate. He begins in the same melody which, through slight changes in its first eight notes, has a twelve-tone effect. At the point where he speaks of his faithless brother, a seemingly new melody emerges, which, however, shows some characteristic connections with the second part of the first melody. Its first eight notes, too, are dodecaphonic. So is the cello solo, which underpaints this part of Prospero's story in a sort of free cadenza. . . . This technique of unending melody combined with recitative, particularly expresses the world of Prospero and Miranda into which later Ferdinand is admitted."

Rudolf Klein shows how other musical elements are successfully exploited for character portrayal and atmosphere. "The world of faithless courtiers has mostly rhythmic accents, even some attributes of jazz, and it culminates in a tango. Caliban's sub-humanity is suggested by cacophonous intervals, while the world of drunkards, so far as there is any singing at all, is set in simple stanzas, couplets and the like. (When the three are completely drunk there is boogie-woogie.) Finally the apparitions of Ceres, Juneo and so forth are accompanied by a suite in Baroque style."

The American première of *The Tempest* was given by the New York City Opera on October 11, 1956, Erich Leinsdorf conducting.

1956 ETUDES, for string orchestra.

Martin wrote these *Etudes* at the request of Paul Sacher, conductor of the Basle Chamber Orchestra in Switzerland, which introduced it. At that time, the composer provided the following description: "The *Etudes* . . . are preceded by an Overture that serves to make the orchestra play at full strength without at first meeting excessive difficulties. The first Study is called 'For the connection of links.' These links pass, at first surreptitiously, from the cellos to the violas, to the second violins, then to the firsts, and descend again by the same path. The writing is essentially in one voice, or in two, very chromatic. . . . All is muted in this mysterious, fleeting little Scherzo.

"The first demand of the second Study is that the players put down their bows. It employs every means of plucking the strings—in chords, espressivo, with vibrato and glissando. In the middle section, while the cellos play a vibrant, rhythmical, somewhat Spanish melody over a simple double-bass accompaniment, the other instruments weave their high tracery as swiftly and lightly as possible.

"The third Study brings repose; it is very expressive and sustained, and is played by divided violas and cellos.

"Finally, the fourth Study, 'in fugal style,' has the general appearance of a double fugue, in which the first subject is essentially rhythmical and the second subject expressive. . . . In the middle part of this study, after a section in close canon, there is a figured chorale. Then the fugue takes over again, mixes the first and second subjects and leads to a broad conclusion."

1966 CONCERTO FOR CELLO AND ORCHESTRA. I. Lento; Allegro moderato; Lento. II. Adagietto. III. Vivace.

Martin wrote this cello concerto for Pierre Fournier who introduced it in Basle, Switzerland, in January of 1967 (Paul Sacher conducting), and in the United States on October 26, 1967, at a concert of the Cleveland Orchestra conducted by George Szell. The concerto opens with a slow and meditative recitative for the solo instrument in which the orchestra soon joins. A vigorous fast section follows, but the movement reverts to the sedate, pensive mood with which it had begun. A mournful melody for the solo cello, taken over by several solo woodwind instruments in turn, is the basis of the slow movement. The finale is marked "savage and rough." This is the style of the music both in the orchestra and in the solo instrument until about midway in the movement when solo cello and flute enter with an idyllic cantabile section. But the earlier roughness and savagery soon return to bring the concerto to a dramatic and vigorous conclusion.

BOHUSLAV MARTINU 1890–1959

The music of Martinu was subjected to two important influences. One is found in his use of form, in his partiality to the Baroque structure of the concerto grosso. The other is discernible in his style, so often dependent on Czech folk elements.

Though he drew copiously from Czech folk music (not so much from actual melodies as from the stylistic traits of these melodies), Martinu was by no means a present-day Smetana. The Czech influence is subtle, sometimes elusive; it is not possible to regard Martinu's music as a glorification or extension of Czech folk art, for the French manner had also contributed much to his writing in the way of clarity, economy, refinement, precision.

The Swiss conductor, Ernest Ansermet, has remarked that any pithy characterization of Martinu's music is not easy. Martinu's forms are, for the most part, traditional. His harmonic language (though sometimes complex) is also usually orthodox. His melodies, even when they have assimilated Czech elements, are not unique. But Ansermet goes on to put a finger on the essential quality that distinguishes Martinu's music—its expressiveness, attained "through media of his very own." There are few composers of our times who have achieved such true sentiment as is found in many Martinu works without resorting to conventional Romanticism.

Martinu was born in Polička, Bohemia, on December 8, 1890. His musical talent revealed itself early, encouraging some of his townspeople to create a fund to send him to Prague. There, first at the Conservatory and then at the Organ School, he was not an outstanding success. In fact, he was expelled several times for minor infractions, failed some of his examinations, and never received a diploma. In 1913, he joined the violin section of the Czech Philharmonic. During World War I, he lived mainly in his native city, where he taught music at the local high school and violin privately. Back in Prague, in 1920, he returned to the Czech Philharmonic. In 1922, he attracted the limelight as a composer with a ballet, *Istar,* and a tone poem, *Vanishing Midnight.* Despite these successes, he decided to return to music study, reentering the Conservatory, where he became a pupil in composition of Joseph Suk. In the fall of 1923, he came to Paris, where he stayed sixteen years. There he wrote a number of provocative compositions, including *Half-Time,* for orchestra (inspired by a football game between Czech and French teams), and *Bagarre,* a tonal description of a crowd, inspired by Charles Lindbergh's arrival at Le Bourget after his historic solo flight across the Atlantic. The latter received its world première in Boston, under Koussevitzky, on November 18, 1928. He received additional encouragement from the United States, including some more world premières, and the winning of the Elizabeth Sprague Coolidge Award in 1932 for his string sextet.

His reputation grew further with the premières of his ballet, *Špaliček* in Prague in 1932, and of his medieval miracle play with music, *The Miracle of Our Lady,* in Brünn in 1934. When the Nazis took Paris, Martinu escaped to Southern France. Then, by way of Lisbon, he came to the United States in 1941, establishing his home permanently in New York and becoming an American citizen. Some of his most ambitious and most successful compositions were written in the United States, including all of his six symphonies. Twice he received the New York Music Critics Circle Award: in 1952, for his opera, *Comedy on the Bridge*; and in 1955, for his Sixth Symphony, the *Fantaisies symphoniques.* He also distinguished himself as a teacher of composition at Princeton University, the Berkshire Music Center at Tanglewood, and the David Mannes School of Music in New York. In 1946, he returned to Czechoslovakia for a brief period, when he served as professor of composition in the Master School of the Prague Conservatory. In 1957, he was composer-in-residence at the American Academy in Rome. He died in Liestal, Switzerland, on August 28, 1959.

1937 CONCERTO GROSSO, for chamber orchestra. I. Allegro non troppo. II. Lento. III. Allegretto.

The composer has written: "The traditional form of concerto grosso has not been followed here, but rather the characteristic alternation of 'soli' and 'tutti,' which I have given to the pianos, woodwinds, and strings. The violins are divided into three sections in order to diffuse the full sonority of the strings and to provide more polyphonic activity. . . . In the first movement I work with a little rhythmic germ of a half-measure which binds the different developments of the other motives and which appears in the most diversified forms up to the end, where there remains nothing but this little germ within the fullness of the orchestra. The Lento of the second movement is an extended song by the cellos and other strings, which continues forceful and expressive. But a few measures before the end, the song subsides into tranquillity. In the third movement, of lively character, the two pianos take the foremost place as soloists, setting forth the themes (somewhat rhythmic) of a rondo. At first they are enveloped always by the polyphony of the orchestra; then the orchestra takes them up, relegating the contrapuntal ornamentation to the pianos."

This work has had a strange and involved history. It was scheduled for publication in Vienna, but the project was abandoned with the *Anschluss* in 1938. A Paris première was canceled because the music could not be procured from Vienna at this time. A performance then scheduled for Prague had to be canceled because of the Munich crisis. Now earmarked for a Paris première, the work once again had to be abandoned, this time because the Nazis had entered the city. In all the ensuing confusion, the manuscript appeared to be lost, only to be discovered in the United States in the possession of the conductor George Szell, who had brought it from Prague. At long last, the first performance did take place—in Boston, on November 14, 1941, with Serge Koussevitzky conducting the Boston Symphony Orchestra.

1938 DOUBLE CONCERTO, for two string orchestras, piano and tympani. I. Poco allegro. II. Largo. III. Allegro.

Martinu was working on this concerto in 1938, when the tragedy of Munich descended cataclysmically on the Czech people. Into his music, the composer transferred the tremendous impact that this historic event had on him; the concerto is actually the musical expression not only of Martinu but of all the Czech people during this period of crisis. "Its notes," says the composer, "sang out the feelings and sufferings of all those of our people who, far away from their home, were gazing into the distance and seeing the approaching catastrophe. . . . It is a composition written under terrible circumstances, but the emotions it voices are not those of despair but rather of revolt, courage and unshakable faith in the future. These are expressed by sharp, dramatic shocks, by a current of tones that never ceases for an instant, and by a melody that passionately claims the right to freedom."

This is one of Martinu's most emotional works, and one of his best. The power and feeling of this music were immediately recognized at the first performance, which took place in Switzerland, on February 9, 1940, with Paul Sacher conducting the Chamber Orchestra. R. Aloys Mooser, the Swiss critic, wrote: "We find in the Double Concerto miraculous fantasy, irresistible dynamism, and an exceptional sense of construction. But we also find here a tragic sentiment and fascinating expression in which this talent attains its ripeness, today in full blossom."

Though the première performance went well, the rehearsals that preceded it were not without incident. It seems that the orchestral musicians rebelled against the complexity of the music. "Gentlemen," the conductor said firmly, "you do not realize that this is a masterpiece." The musicians agreed to work further on the music and were eventually won over completely by the concerto.

1942 SYMPHONY NO. 1. I. Allegro. II. Scherzo. III. Largo. IV. Allegro.

Martinu did not undertake the writing of his First Symphony until after his fiftieth birthday. The symphony was, as a matter of fact, his first composition for a large orchestra in fourteen years. But if the composer approached his most ambitious artistic task up to that time with any degree of uncertainty, technical or otherwise, it is not apparent in the music. The symphony was Martinu's most significant production up to that time, a work of fine integration, forceful expression, sound workmanship. It was written on a commission from the Koussevitzky Music Foundation and was introduced in Boston on November 13, 1942, by the Boston Symphony Orchestra, directed by Koussevitzky.

"My symphony," wrote the composer, "follows the classical division into four parts. . . . In preserving this plan, I have also followed an aesthetic plan which my conviction dictates, and this conviction is that a work of art must not transcend the limits of its possibility in expression. . . . I have avoided elements which seem to me alien to the expressive purpose of the work. The basis of the orchestra is a quintet of strings, which does not prevent solo passages for woodwinds, while the brass and percussion fulfill their due part. I have tried to find new sound combinations and to elicit from the orchestra a unified sonority in spite of the polyphonic working which the score contains. It is not the sonority of impressionism, nor is there the search for color, which is integral in the writing and the formal structure. The character of the work is calm and lyric."

1943 CONCERTO FOR VIOLIN AND ORCHESTRA. I. Andante; Allegro. II. Poco moderato. III. Poco allegro.

CONCERTO FOR TWO PIANOS AND ORCHESTRA. I. Allegro non troppo. II. Adagio. III. Rondo.

In 1941, Martinu had written a chamber-concerto for violin and orchestra—the *Concerto da Camera* in F minor—with an unmistakable Czech identity. A more ambitious work for violin and orchestra followed two years later. In 1943, Mischa Elman, the violin virtuoso, attended a concert of the Boston Symphony Orchestra in which a new symphony by Martinu was performed. This music made such an impression on him that he contacted the composer after the concert and asked him to write a violin concerto for his use. Subsequently, Elman gave an informal recital for Martinu; it is said that in writing his concerto, Martinu kept in mind the individual style of the violinist. Mischa Elman introduced the concerto in Boston on December 31, 1943, with the Boston Symphony Orchestra under Koussevitzky.

This concerto is essentially lyrical, just as its predecessor had been dramatic. The composer explained his artistic intentions as follows:

"The idea for the concerto presented itself to me with the following order—Andante, a broad lyric song of great intensity which leads to an Allegro, exploiting the technique and the virtuosity of the instrument, and has the aspect of a single-movement composition. The definitive form complies with concerto structure. I have preserved its grave character, lyric in the first part; and even in the middle Allegro, the Andante theme returns to end the movement. The second part is a sort of point of rest, a bridge progressing towards the Allegro finale. It is almost bucolic, accompanied by only a part of the orchestra and progressing *attacca* into the finale, which is Allegro. . . . The concerto ends with a sort of stretto, Allegro vivace."

The Two-Piano Concerto was another product of Martinu's fruitful year in 1943. It was given for the first time anywhere in Philadelphia on November 5, 1943, with Luboschutz and Nemenoff as soloists with the Philadelphia Orchestra under Ormandy. The composer explained: "I have used the pianos for the first time in a purely solo sense, with the orchestra as accompaniment. The form is free; it leans rather towards the concerto grosso. It demands virtuosity, brilliant piano technique, and the timbre of the same two instruments calls forth new colors and sonorities."

In his analysis for the Boston Symphony Program, John N. Burk said: "The first movement exploits contrapuntal possibilities . . . as the pianists weave into the pattern a texture of sixteenth-note figures, or shifting arpeggios." In the second movement, the soloists are heard mostly unaccompanied. "The orchestra at length insinuates itself in phrases, and then more strongly, deferring once more to the pianists before the close." The finale, in rondo form, is "dance-like in character. The orchestra pauses while the soloists have a joint cadenza in slow tempo."

1943 MEMORIAL TO LIDICE, tone poem for orchestra.

SYMPHONY NO. 2. I. Allegro Moderato. II. Andante moderato. III. Rondo.

In June of 1942, the little Czechoslovakian town of Lidice was obliterated from the face of the earth, and its inhabitants shot, by the Nazis, in reprisal for the assassination in Prague of Heydrich, the Nazi Gauleiter. The civilized world was shocked. Jo Davidson created a statue on this subject, and Edna St. Vincent Millay wrote an epic poem. Martinu's tone poem was the result of a commission from the League of Composers, which asked seventeen composers to write works commemorating events in World War II.

The world première of Martinu's tone poem took place in New York on October 28, 1943, Artur Rodzinski conducting the New York Philharmonic in a concert commemorating the twenty-fifth anniverary of the Czechoslovak Republic. The tone poem was first heard in Prague on March 14, 1946, when the Czech Philharmonic, under Rafael Kubelik, performed it on the eve of the seventh anniversary of the Nazi occupation of Czechoslovakia.

Klaus G. Roy, the program annotator for the Cleveland Orchestra, described the tone poem as follows: "The composer remarked that his music was in the nature of a religious chant, constructed along the lines of a prayer and response based on a theme which resembles in style the ancient Czech church melodies. The opening tempo is Adagio, succeeded by an Andante moderato, with the first tempo returning at the close. Whether the reminder, near the end, of the aspiring theme in the "Tomb Scene" of Verdi's *Aïda* combined with a hint of the "fate" theme in Beethoven's Fifth Symphony is accidental or purposeful, we do not know; but it would make associative sense. Here, too, death is seen as the gate to everlasting life."

The Second Symphony is more pastoral than Martinu's First, having been conceived as intimate music with the proportions of a chamber-music work. It approaches the simplicity of a classic symphony. The principal theme of the first movement, reflective and tender, sets the mood for the entire work. This tranquillity is extended in the second movement, which assumes the personality of a Moravian folk song and is a pastoral poem. Only in the third movement is the intimacy temporarily abandoned with a rousing march for full orchestra. A transition leads to the finale (a rondo) in which the texture and sensitive expression of the earlier movement returns. A broad and simply constructed melody, also like a Moravian folk song, is the basis of the final movement.

The symphony was introduced by the Cleveland Orchestra under Erich Leinsdorf on October 28, 1943. Dedicated "to my fellow countrymen in Cleveland," this work was performed to commemorate the twenty-fifth anniversary of the founding of the Czechoslovak Republic.

1946 TOCCATA A DUE CANZONE (TOCCATA AND TWO CANZONE), for piano and chamber orchestra.

In many of his compositions, Martinu reverted to the concerto-grosso structure. In this work, the Baroque forms of toccata and canzona intrigued him. This composition was written for the Basle Chamber Orchestra which introduced it, under Paul Sacher, on January 21, 1947. The toccata is a bravura piece whose most significant idea is a lively dance tune, developed into a rousing waltz melody. There are pastoral interludes before the dance tune is remembered by the strings. Two Canzone follow, the canzona being a several-section sixteenth-century instrumental composition in contrapuntal style. The first canzona is built from a seven-note motive and features fugal episodes. The second is less polyphonic than the first and more harmonic. Effective use is here made of pedal points and symmetrical patterns of figurations.

1948 CONCERTO NO. 3 FOR PIANO AND ORCHESTRA. I. Allegro. II. Andante poco moderato. III. Moderato; Allegro (poco).

Martinu wrote his third piano concerto for the famous Czech concert pianist, Rudolf Firkusny, who introduced it in Dallas, Texas, on November 20, 1949, with the Dallas Symphony under Walter Hendl.

Martinu's manuscript contains no tempo indication for the first movement, but by its nature it is presumed to be an Allegro. A four-note motive appears in the second measure. It is developed dramatically before the solo piano appears with a vigorous subject. Flutes soon enter with a second idea. An orchestral tutti extending for thirty-six measures precedes the return of the solo piano in bravura music, whose brilliant character is maintained throughout the movement.

In the second movement, tremolo passages in orchestra precede the arrival of the piano in the ninth measure which is soon heard in a stately pronouncement, its material occasionally recalling the first movement. In the finale, a four-measure horn call is followed by the woodwind suggesting the main subject, which is stated by the piano thirteen measures later. This is a polka-like tune recurring throughout the movement, at times developed along symphonic dimensions. The principal theme of the first movement is recalled later in this finale, which ends with a vigorous coda.

1955 FANTAISIES SYMPHONIQUES (SYMPHONY NO. 6), for orchestra. I. Lento; Allegro; Lento. II. Allegro. III. Lento; Allegro.

The composer provided the following explanation about the origin of his Sixth Symphony. "I wished to write something for Charles Munch. I am impressed and I like his spontaneous approach to the music where music takes shape in a free way, flowing and freely following its movements. An almost imperceptible slowing down or rushing up gives the melody a sudden life. So I had the intention to write for him a symphony which I would call *Fantastic*; and I started my idea in a big way, putting three pianos in a very big orchestra. This was already fantastic enough, and during work I came down to earth. I saw it was not a symphony, but something which I mentioned before, connected with Munch's conception and conducting. I abandoned the title and finally I abandoned also my three pianos, being suddenly frightened by these three big instruments on the stage.

"I called the three movements *Fantaisies,* which they really are. One little fantasy of mine is that I use a few bars' quotation from another piece, from my opera *Julietta,* which, to my mind, fitted in perfectly well. This is of the nature of fantasy. I did it somehow for myself because I like the special orchestral color in it, and thinking that I shall never hear my opera again, I could listen once more to these few bars, which I rewrote by memory."

The work opens with trumpets in a sustained-note motive over woodwind figures. An ascending horn passage leads to the Allegro in which an effective melody is heard first in strings alone. With other parts of the orchestra entering, a climax is reached. An important later episode is a rapturous subject for solo violin. The movement ends with a return of the opening Lento section.

The second movement is an Allegro, in which a vigorous brief subject in strings is carried to a climax. A broader treatment of this material concludes the movement. In the finale, the orchestra is heard in a broad melody. Midway comes an Andante section followed by an Allegro for full orchestra. The finale, and the symphony, ends quietly.

The symphony was introduced by the Boston Symphony under Charles Munch on January 7, 1955, as part of the orchestra's celebration of its seventy-fifth anniversary. The work received the New York Music Critics Circle Award.

1958 PARABLES, for orchestra. I. The Parable of Sculpture. II. The Parable of a Garden. III. The Parable of a Labyrinth.

Martinu dedicated *Parables* to Charles Munch, who presented its world première with the Boston Symphony on February 13, 1959. The first two parables were inspired by Antoine de St. Exupéry's *Citadella*; the third, by Georges Neveux's *Voyage de Thesée.* In the first parable, the composer speaks of the way in which sculpture arouses in the observer the impulse that led to the creation of a work of art. The second is atmospheric impressionistic writing explaining that the cycle from fruit to seed and rebirth is part of life's plan. The third speaks for the strength of man to conquer a monster and also of his softness before a woman.

"Out of these programmatic materials," said John Briggs in *The New York Times,* "Martinu has fashioned an imaginative, richly expressive musical work. The slow movement . . . is especially striking for the aptness with which it employs the rich, sensuous musical vocabularly of the turn-of-the-century impressionism.

NICOLAS MEDTNER 1880–1951

Though Medtner wrote several fine songs and three sonatas for violin and piano, he is most important in his works for the piano. He has been called the "Russian Brahms"—the implication being that, like Brahms, his music is classical in structure, and that it has some of Brahms's austerity and power.

Though Medtner was himself an outstanding virtuoso of the piano and consequently knew the instrument as perhaps only a performer can—his writing is not always pianistically grateful. His music tends to get involved in its harmonic and contrapuntal textures, in its rhythmic play, to a point where it becomes somewhat cumbersome, even for virtuoso hands. But though his music may not come easily to the performer—and sometimes, due to its intellectual concentration, it does not come easily to the listener either—it is music which deserves the effort it must get. For at its best, it has grandeur and passionate sweep.

Medtner was particularly successful in the smaller forms: *Arabesques, Novellen, Fairy Tales, Improvisations, Marches, Musical Pictures, Etudes, Caprices, Moments Musicaux Romantic Sketches,* etc. These pieces are filled with fine melodies, deeply felt emotion, and a gift for conveying varied tone colors and atmospheres. Technically, these pieces are derived from the piano music of Schumann, and are Schumannesque in their imaginativeness and subtle suggestions, and in their delicate poetry.

Medtner was born in Moscow on January 5, 1880. He entered the Moscow Conservatory when he was only twelve years old, studying composition with Arensky and Taneiev and piano with Safonov. Before his graduation, which took place in 1900, he wrote some songs and piano pieces which first revealed his creative talent. In 1902, Medtner began the first of his many concert tours, which, in the years that followed, were to bring him around the world and establish his reputation as a virtuoso of first importance. He left Russia in 1921, stayed for a while in Germany and Paris, and then, in 1936, settled permanently in England, where he lived in comparative seclusion. In 1946, he appeared as soloist with the London Symphony under George Weldon in performances of all three of his piano concertos. In 1948, the Maharajah of Mysore provided the funds to record Medtner's entire creative output, most of it in Medtner's own performance—the first time that the entire lifework of a composer was put on records.

Medtner made two extended tours of the United States as pianist, often in performances of his own music—in 1924–1925 and in 1930. His American debut took place on October 31, 1924, when he appeared as soloist with the Philadelphia Orchestra under Stokowski in a performance of his Piano Concerto No. 1 in C minor.

Medtner died in London on November 13, 1951.

1905–1929 FAIRY TALES, for solo piano.

Op. 8: C minor; C major.
Op. 9. F minor; C major; G major.
Op. 14: F minor; E minor.
Op. 20: B-flat minor; B minor.
Op. 26: E-flat major; E-flat major; F minor; F-sharp minor.
Op. 34: B minor; E minor; A minor; D minor.
Op. 35: C major; G major; A minor; C-sharp minor.
Op. 42: F minor, "Phrygian"; G-flat major.
Op. 48: "Dance Fairy Tale"; "Elf Fairy Tale."
Op. 51: D minor; A minor; A major; F-sharp minor; F-sharp minor; G major.

Of all the forms utilized by Medtner, he was perhaps best in the one which he himself invented—the fairy tale. In these fairy tales, his music unfolds like a narrative. While they have no definite program, they are so rich in dramatic and emotional content that it is not difficult to find some extramusical interpretation in them, though what that interpretation is each listener must decide for himself.

Leonid Sabaneyev points out that a Medtner fairy tale does not re-create the world of elves and witchery, or the romanticism of enchantment. It is, rather, "the poetry of ancient heroic legends, and most of all an echo of the underworld Nibelungs, gnomes, and mountain kings. . . . It has no brightness or radiance, but dusk and darkness. Occasionally, it has an ominousness, and a certain closeness. In his *Fairy Tales,* Medtner is neither heavenly nor ethereal, nor in the clouds, but earthly, even earthy—subterranean."

1918 CONCERTO NO. 1 IN C MINOR FOR PIANO AND ORCHESTRA, op. 33.

Medtner wrote this one-movement concerto between 1916 and 1918, and it was introduced in 1918 in Moscow with Medtner appearing as soloist with the Koussevitzky Orchestra. Its American première and Medtner's American debut came simultaneously, in Philadelphia on October 31, 1924.

In structure it is an elaboration of the classic sonata form, consisting—as the composer explained—of "an exposition, a series of variations on two chief themes constituting the development, and a recapitulation."

The principal theme is heard in the violins after three strong measures of introduction by the piano. The cellos give the second theme against an ascending passage of chords and octaves in the piano. After a rhapsodic passage for piano, which is soon taken up by a solo horn, a brief development takes place. A short cadenza for the piano follows, after which come the nine variations. A coda, in which the two principal themes are combined, arrives after a recapitulation, and the concerto ends brilliantly.

PETER MENNIN 1923–

In Mennin's music, we generally encounter strength rather than sweetness, hypertension rather than serenity, rhythmic and polyphonic complexity rather than affecting lyricism. What the critics had to say about his Sixth Symphony (first performance in Louisville on November 18, 1953) applies to other Mennin works as well. "It has a solid foundation, a sure classical grip, and yet an exhilarating sense of freshness, too," said the critic of the New York *World-Telegram*. "It was an exciting composition, confident of direction and dramatic in the way it swept up themes and fragments of themes in its restless plunge." And the critic of the Louisville *Courier-Journal* wrote: "It is vigorous music with intense motor energy and clashing harmonic lines. The whole is a big, complicated work of intricate construction."

Peter Mennin was born Peter Mennini in Erie, Pennsylvania, on May 17, 1923. He first attended Oberlin Conservatory for two years, where he studied with Normand Lockwood. Then, after serving in the Air Force during World War II, he entered the Eastman School of Music, where his teachers included Howard Hanson and Bernard Rogers. While still at Eastman, he completed his Second Symphony, one movement of which received the Gershwin Memorial Award and was performed on March 27, 1945, Leonard Bernstein conducting. The entire symphony was given the Bearns Prize of Columbia University. After receiving his Bachelor of Music and Master of Music degrees, Mennin received a fellowship in orchestration at the Eastman School. When, in 1947, he got his doctorate, he was appointed to the faculty of the Juilliard School of Music, where he remained for a decade. Meanwhile, a number of major works, including several symphonies and concertos, were given significant performances by major musical organizations, many of them the result of commissions. In 1946, Mennin received awards from the National Institute of Arts and Letters and the American Academy of Arts and Letters; in 1949, and again in 1957, he received Guggenheim Fellowships; in 1950, the University of Rochester presented him with a centennial citation for distinguished contributions to music. From 1958 to 1963, Mennin was the director of the Peabody Conservatory in Baltimore. In 1962, he was appointed president of the Juilliard School of Music. He also became president of the Naumburg Foundation. During the summer of 1966, he was composer-in-residence at the Hopkins Center Congregation at Dartmouth College in New Hampshire.

1946 SYMPHONY NO. 3. I. Allegro robusto. II. Andante moderato. III. Allegro assai.

This symphony, completed when the composer was only twenty-three, was the first to achieve wide recognition. Its world première took place on February 27, 1947, with Walter Hendl conducting the New York Philharmonic. Olin Downes reported that the audience gave this work "a rousing reception. The young conductor led the young composer back to the stage to bow." Virgil Thomson described the symphony as "an accomplished work."

The composer provided the following terse analysis: "The first movement . . . makes use of two ideas which are developed polyphonically. Rhythmic and melodic extensions finally lead to a canon for full orchestra. The movement ends quietly. The second movement . . . is an extended song which moves along expressively, making use of sustained voice-weaving. The third movement . . . is . . . full of rhythmic impulse and with broad lines set off by polyphony of the orchestra."

1949 SYMPHONY NO. 5. I. Con Vigore. II. Canto: andante arioso. III. Allegro tempestuoso.

Mennin wrote this symphony on a commission from the Dallas Symphony, which under Walter Hendl, introduced it on April 2, 1950. At that time, the composer provided the following analysis:

"Each of the movements has its own basic character, and achieves contrast within itself through the musical materials and textures rather than from changes in tempo. The basic aim of the work is expressivity. Therefore, there is a great emphasis placed on the broad, melodic line, and little use of color for color's sake. Orchestrally speaking, the colors used are primary rather than pastel in quality. . . .

"The first movement opens dramatically in a declamatory fashion, with heavy punctuation. A broad melodic line follows, which spins out autogenetically, and which allows itself different textural presentations. These ideas are developed polyphonically, with occasional interruptions by the opening declamatory idea.

"The second movement, as the title 'Canto' suggests, is an extended song bringing out the singing qualities of the orchestra. Much use of sustained string writing is used. After a quiet opening section, the polyphonic weaving of the orchestral textures culminates in a broad passage in unison strings and climaxes one of the most intense moments in the symphony. The work slowly returns to the calm opening and ends quietly. . . .

"The last movement is one of rapid and bare linear writing set off by brass and percussive punctuation. It makes greater technical demands than the earlier movements. The basic girder of the movement is an idea in canon which has numerous variations in rhythm and mood. The movement closes with sounds similar to the opening of the last movement."

1963 SYMPHONY NO. 7, "VARIATION SYMPHONY."

Mennin's Seventh Symphony is in a single movement, but it comprises five sections. The composer explains that this work, though subtitled *Variation Symphony,* "has little relationship to the consecutive variation principle, but instead uses techniques of variation resulting from overall structural and dramatic concept."

It opens with a declamatory Adagio, in which, as the composer says, "a ruminative, slow movement melody" rises from "the darkest depths of the string section." The composer points out that from this opening melodic idea spring many of the symphony's most important themes. The Allegro that follows has elements of a Scherzo, and is dramatic in mood. After that comes an Andante with contrasting parts "emphasizing duality of opening material." Then comes a Moderato with cumulative variations, the basis of which is a passacaglia theme of eight measures derived from the basic subject of the opening Adagio. The work ends with an Allegro vivace, which is not only a summation but which introduces some new thoughts. The conclusion is reached with an overpowering climax.

Mennin was commissioned to write this symphony by George Szell and the Cleveland Orchestra. They introduced it in Cleveland on January 23, 1964.

GIAN CARLO MENOTTI 1911–

Through the years, the lament has been sounded periodically that opera is a dying—or a dead—art form. And through the years, there has always emerged some new composer to give opera a new lease on life, to prove that it is still a vibrant form. Sometimes a composer has done this by the application of new techniques and approaches, as was the case of Debussy, Alban Berg and Carl Orff. Less frequently, opera has been revitalized only because the composer has brought to it the freshness and vigor of a strong creative talent. The latter is the case of Menotti.

The opera as a form changed little with Menotti. When he writes in a comic vein, he carries on the traditions of Italian opera buffa, established through the centuries from Pergolesi to Wolf-Ferrari. In his more serious manner, he takes the torch of Verismo from the hands of Puccini. And yet with Menotti, opera has acquired pulse and heartbeat; it is living theatre.

Menotti's feeling for the stage is an instinct which he has revealed from the very first, both in his librettos (which he has always written himself—*Amelia Goes to the Ball* and *The Last Savage,* in Italian, and the rest in English), and in his scores. The music meets the most fastidious and subtle demands of his text. It has brisk pace, contrasts, moods of varying shades and hues, dramatic thrust. Menotti has a born gift for characterization; and in the painting of an atmosphere or the suggesting of a mood, he is virtually unique. He can be melodramatic and sardonic, realistic and fanciful, sordid and poetic. In one and the same opera, he can pass from song-speech to a Puccini-like lyricism; from pleasant and humorous ditties and choruses to discordant and polytonal writing; from impressionism to Verismo. He is, as Robert Sabin has written, "a diverse musical personality—a skilful and witty comedian who nonetheless writes grim and horrible tragedies; an heir to the past who does not hesitate to satirize his beloved masters; a realistic social commentator who bursts out into the most fantastic impossibilities; a musical traditionalist who commits hair-raising musical heresies without the flicker of an eyelash." More than anything else, Menotti is a man of the theatre who is always capable of finding the musical *mot juste* with which to point up an emotion, a conflict, a climax.

Menotti was born in Cadegliano, Italy, on July 7, 1911. A prodigy, he began composing at the age of six, wrote his first opera when he was eleven, and soon after that became a favorite in the salons of Milan. In 1928, he came to the United States where he has since remained. He attended the Curtis Institute on a scholarship; later, he succeeded his teacher, Rosario Scalero, as head of the composition department. He was only twenty-three when he wrote *Amelia Goes to the Ball,* which forthwith established him as an important operatic composer. Subsequently, operas—performed extensively throughout the world—justified the high promises of this maiden effort.

In 1945, Menotti received a grant from the National Institute of Arts and Sciences and the American Academy of Arts and Sciences. In 1946 and 1947, he was the recipient of Guggenheim Fellowships. He was awarded the Pulitzer Prize and the New York Drama Critics Circle Award twice (for *The Consul* and *The Saint of Bleecker Street*). In addition to his works for the stage, he has written a number of ambitious instrumental compositions, and a cantata, *Death of the Bishop of Brindisi.* He also provided Samuel Barber, the composer, with the libretto for his opera *Vanessa.* In 1958, Menotti founded the "Festival of the Two Worlds" at Spoleto, Italy, an annual summer event, of which he was artistic director until 1967. At that time he created the new post of general manager for the festival, appointed Thomas Schippers musical director and retained for himself the post of president.

1934 AMELIA GOES TO THE BALL, opera buffa in one act, with text by the composer. First performance: Philadelphia, April 1, 1937.

As a boy pianist, Menotti was the darling of Milanese society. From the intrigues and the banter of the salon, he drew his inspiration for this gay and impudent comedy—his first major effort in the operatic form, and his first important success. He wrote it when he was only twenty-three years old. It was introduced by members of the Curtis Institute of Music, under Fritz Reiner's direction, in Philadelphia. The same group brought the opera to New York a few days later. Its success was immediate. It was not long before it entered the repertory of many major opera companies, including that of the Metropolitan Opera Association on March 3, 1938.

Menotti wrote his own libretto, in rhymed Italian meter; it was translated into English by George Mead. In Milan, Amelia is dressed for a ball. Her husband discovers a love letter addressed to her. On learning that the culprit is his downstairs neighbor, he storms out with threats of murder. While he is gone, the lover enters through the window, pouring out his love for Amelia, whom he begs to run away with him. When the husband returns, the two rivals discuss the triangle. This discussion irritates Amelia, for it is making her late for the ball. In despair, she throws a vase at her husband, and calls to the police to arrest her lover for attacking his rival. The husband goes to the hospital; the lover to jail. And Amelia (in the company of the police officer) goes to the ball.

It is a witty, tongue-in-cheek little play. For it, Menotti wrote an infectious score, engaging for its lightness and gaiety. It oozes with blood-rich melodies; and it is made piquant with a discreet use of dissonance. Within the formal pattern of the opera buffa (aria, romanza, duet, trio, recitative, etc.), Menotti produced a work that is abundantly fresh and spirited; and a work which, though revealing the influence of Puccini and of Verdi's *Falstaff*, nevertheless possesses highly personal accents.

When *Amelia Goes to the Ball* was produced at the Metropolitan Opera Pitts Sanborn called it an "agreeable example of modern Italian opera, vivacious and tuneful." Its first performance in Italy—and its first performance in the Italian language—took place at San Remo on April 4, 1938.

1939 THE OLD MAID AND THE THIEF, radio opera in one act, with text by the composer. First performance: NBC radio network, April 22, 1939; Philadelphia, February 11, 1941 (staged production).

Written on a commission from the National Broadcasting Company, *The Old Maid and the Thief* is a comic opera in the vein of its immediate predecessor. It is in the traditions of opera buffa: witty, brisk, satiric, infectious, and formal with its arias and ensemble numbers. And, like its predecessor, its boasts a broad farce as a libretto. Miss Todd and her servant—starved for a man—eagerly welcome a tramp in their house, and prevail on him to remain indefinitely. He is treated royally. Miss Todd even goes to the length of stealing, to satisfy the ever-increasing demands of her lodger; on one occasion she raids a liquor establishment to get him a drink. The neighbors, ascribing the recent thefts to the tramp, demand that the police raid the house and arrest the culprit. Miss Todd begs him to escape. When the tramp learns that she has been stealing for him, he insists that she go to jail for her crimes. Upset by his lack of gratitude, Miss Todd goes to the police. During her absence, the tramp and Miss Todd's servant elope, stealing from the house whatever they can carry away. Thus is demonstrated—so says the author in his subtitle —"how a virtuous woman made a thief of an honest man."

"The score," says William L. Crosten, "is leaner than *Amelia*. The musical apparatus is smaller and the style considerably simpler. On the whole, this reduction of means was all to the good, for it seems to have bred a more personal sounding music, particularly in the three main lyric episodes. Still, as in *Amelia*, Menotti is at his best in the more active sections of dialogue. The formalities of a tea party are amusingly handled, something on the order of the scene in *Falstaff* at the Garter Inn."

1944 SEBASTIAN, ballet in one act, with choreography by Edward Caton. First performance; New York City, October 31, 1944.

SEBASTIAN, ballet suite for orchestra. I. Adagio. II. Barcarolle. III. Street Fight. IV. Cortège. V. Sebastian's Dance. VI. The Courtesan's Dance. VII. Pavane.

Sebastian is a melodramatic ballet set in Venice in the 1600s. Two sisters try to enlist witchcraft in an effort to destroy a courtesan with whom their brother is in love. They take the courtesan's veil, drape it around a replica of her figure, into which they plunge a knife, hoping that the courtesan might thereby be fatally wounded. But Sebastian, a Moorish slave belonging to the sisters, thwarts them. Since he, too, is in love with the courtesan he drapes the veil around himself and becomes the victim of the stabbing.

Menotti's theatrical sense served him well—even in ballet. At turns dramatic, atmospheric, subtly suggestive, descriptive, and sentimental, Menotti's score meets every demand of the ballet scenario. The best pages from this score have been used for a delightful orchestral suite sometimes heard at symphony concerts.

When *Sebastian* was revived in New York City on May 27, 1957, it was completely restaged, and utilized new choreography by Agnes de Mille.

1945 THE MEDIUM, opera in two acts, with libretto by the composer. First performance: New York City, May 8, 1946.

That the gifted composer of opera buffa was equally adept in a more somber and dramatic vein was eloquently proved with *The Medium,* which had been commissioned by the Alice M. Ditson Fund and which was introduced at a festival of contemporary music at Columbia University in New York.

The strange theme for this opera came to Menotti when he was visiting Austria in 1937. He was invited by a baroness to accompany her to her private chapel, where she spent an hour in communion with her dead daughter. "Though skeptical myself," Menotti has confessed, "I was impressed by her faith. Skepticism is a barren thing compared to faith. I try to show this in the opera."

In writing his macabre play, Menotti planned to describe the "tragedy of a person caught between two worlds, the world of reality which she cannot wholly comprehend, and the supernatural world in which she cannot believe." Madame Flora, a medium, defrauds her clients with fake séances—with the aid of a mute, Toby, and her daughter, with whom the mute is in love. During one of these séances, a cold, clammy, supernatural hand reaches for Madam Flora's throat. Terrified, she confesses to her clients that she is a fake—only to find that they do not believe her. Believing that the hand was that of Toby, she beats him and drives him out of the house. Then, as an escape, she takes to drink. In a stupor, she hears Toby returning to her home to claim her daughter. Lifting a revolver, she shoots Toby dead.

Though the play is rather contrived, it achieves dramatic strength through the originality and power of the music, which abounds with discords, polytonal combinations and recitatives that have the severity of song-speech. With an infallible theatrical instinct, Menotti skilfully contrasts his somber colors with bright ones. His score, while essentially tragic, has sardonic overtones; it introduces notes of gaiety and levity, which come as a blessed relief from the gruesome proceedings. Structurally and stylistically, the opera may stem from Puccini; but in its alternation of light and shade, the somber and the fanciful, it is a characteristic product of Menotti's theatrical talent.

When first produced, *The Medium* was received by the critics with a number of reservations. But two young, astute showmen—Chandler Cowles and Efrem Zimbalist, Jr.—became convinced that the opera could be a success on Broadway. They made that transfer on May 1, 1947, where, after a slow start, the opera began to attract curiosity and interest. It became a resounding box-office success and for the first time established Menotti's reputation as an opera composer on a solid foundation. After that, *The Medium* was given more than a thousand performances within a few years, both in the United States and in Europe. It was recorded in its entirety; was made into a successful motion picture in 1951, filmed in Italy under Menotti's direction; and in 1955, it toured Europe under the auspices of the State Department.

Menotti confesses that this opera is "the key work in my development as an operatic composer. It was with *The Medium* that I discovered what I could do in the lyric theatre. It contains the potentialities of my style."

1946 THE TELEPHONE, one-act comic opera, with libretto by the composer. First performance: New York City, February 18, 1947.

This amusing one-act, two-character opera has been described as a "skit with music." Subtitled by the composer, "*L'Amour à Trois,*" this play is slight indeed. But it is treated so deftly, and so admirably does it provide a stimulus for Menotti's satirical and always appropriately descriptive music, that it serves well the composer's operatic purposes. Music and text, song and stage action, are wonderfully integrated, so that a "trite gag," as one New York music critic referred to it, becomes a fresh and well-paced composition.

A young lover tries to propose to his girl, only to be repeatedly frustrated by the ringing of the telephone. In despair, the lover rushes to the corner drugstore to propose to his girl—by telephone.

Introduced in New York City in a small uptown theatre on February 18, 1947, *The Telephone* was so well received that it was transferred to the Broadway stage on May 1, to settle down for an extended and successful run paired with *The Medium.* Once again as a companion piece to *The Medium,* it toured Europe in 1955 under the auspices of the State Department.

1949 THE CONSUL, opera in three acts, with text by the composer. First performance: Philadelphia, March 1, 1950.

Out of the tragedy of our times has come a poignant musical drama—the most ambitious operatic work Menotti has produced up to this time. The reading of a newspaper account which told of a European woman committing suicide because she could not get a visa to the United States provided Menotti with the theme for his play. In a police state, Magda is seeking a visa for another country (both countries remain unidentified) in order to join her husband. She haunts the offices of the consul as frequently and as relentlessly as the secret police haunt her own home. The consul himself never appears on the scene; as a kind of disembodied spirit, never seen—but whose presence is always felt—he becomes the very personification of Fate itself, against whom the victim is helpless. The visa is never granted. The husband returns from his freedom to join his wife, who commits suicide.

In the creation of the grim parts of this opera, such as the overpowering closing suicide scene, Menotti again demonstrates the powerful gift for drama and atmosphere that made *The Medium* so effective. *The Consul* is macabre—but much more than that. Throughout the entire play there courses a profound feeling of pity which brings a humanity and emotional depth found in no other opera by Menotti. The composer feels intensely the tragedy of his characters, and the helpless situation in which they find themselves; and he projects the tragedy with crushing effect.

The resources of grand opera, together with the techniques of contemporary music, serve Menotti in his search for the appropriate musical counterpart for his moving text. Now he utilizes the crisp and cogent lines of song-speech, much as an atonalist might; and then, as in the magnificent aria sung by Magda to close the second act ("To This We've Come"), or the exquisite lullaby the grandmother sings to the dying child (also in that act), he allows his melodic fancy to soar without inhibition. In the same way, he passes without warning from formal harmony and counterpoint to polytonality, dissonance, free rhythms, etc., as the text develops from pathos to bitterness, from the diaphanous world of dream fantasies into sordid reality. And the same extraordinary technique that blends text and music into an indissoluble whole coalesces the varied styles and techniques into an inextricable unity.

The Broadway run of *The Consul* (after tryouts in Philadelphia) began at the Ethel Barrymore Theatre in New York City on March 15, 1950. There were cheers after the première performance; and the cheers were echoed by the critics. Virgil Thomson described the work as "a music drama of great power." Olin Downes wrote ecstatically: "He has produced an opera of eloquence, momentousness, and intensity of expression unequalled by any native composer . . . written from the heart, with a blazing sincerity and a passion of human understanding." *The Consul* received the Pulitzer Prize and the Drama Critics Award. Such success proved several things: that a vibrantly contemporary subject can be the basis of an effective opera; and that a serious opera need make no artistic concession to public taste to be box-office magic on Broadway.

The Consul has enjoyed a wide circulation in Europe. In 1951, it was produced in London, Zurich, Berlin, Vienna and at La Scala. In 1952, it was mounted in Hamburg; and in 1954, it was revived in London by the Sadler's Wells Company. It was unsuccessful only at La Scala, where Communists helped to create a disturbance, interpreting the text as an indictment of Iron-Curtain countries. It was also attacked by patriotic Italians who resented the fact that Menotti had become an American (though he had never renounced his Italian citizenship).

1951 AMAHL AND THE NIGHT VISITORS, opera in one act, with libretto by the composer. First performance: NBC-TV, December 24, 1951; Bloomington, Indiana, February 21, 1952 (staged version).

This is the first opera written expressly for television; and since the broadcast was sponsored, it is also the first opera whose world première was financed by a commercial organization. That première took place on Christmas Eve, 1951, over the television network of the National Broadcasting Company, which had commissioned the work. The opera was repeated over television the following Easter, and was also successfully presented as a stage production by several opera organizations, including the New York City Opera Company, and in 1953, at the Florence May Music Festival. For many years it was an annual feature on television at Christmas time.

The inspiration for the opera came to Menotti from the Flemish painting of Hieronymous Bosch, *The Adoration of the Magi.* Settings and costumes of the opera were directly influenced by it, as were the planned simplicity and naiveté of Menotti's text. The story centers around the crippled boy, Amahl, who is miraculously healed when he gives his crutches to the Three Wise Men, on their way to the manger in Bethlehem, as a gift to the Holy Child.

In reviewing the opera for *The New York Times,* Olin Downes remarked that "television, operatically speaking, has come of age." His analysis of Menotti's score follows: "The music is written often in recitative but with intensifying beauty at climactic moments, as when the child walks and the king chants of the power and majesty of the Savior. . . . The choruses of the approaching and departing shepherds and other ensemble pieces are always poetical and atmospheric, never obvious or banal. Mr. Menotti has used no folk-airs or Christmas chants in this score, but he has written delightfully and characteristically in his music for the peasant dances. His tune of the beggar boy's pipe which begins and ends the play . . . is one of his happiest ideas."

1954 THE SAINT OF BLEECKER STREET, opera in three acts, with libretto by the composer. First performance: New York, December 27, 1954.

When *The Saint of Bleecker Street* was introduced on Broadway, it was acclaimed by the critics both for the tense and taut drama of the libretto and the highly effective musical setting. Brooks Atkinson called it "the most powerful drama of the season," and Olin Downes reported that the music "dexterously underscores every word of dialogue, and every instant of action." *The Saint of Bleecker Street* received the Drama Critics Award as the best play of the year, the Music Critics Circle Award as the best opera, and the Pulitzer Prize in music.

The setting is the Italian quarter of New York City; the time, the present. Annina, who lives on Bleecker Street, is a sickly girl who is a religious mystic. When she receives the stigmata on her palms, she inspires the religious devotion of all her Catholic neighbors. But her brother, Michele, is an agnostic who regards all religious dogma as superstition. Devoted to Annina, he tries vainly to convert her to his irreligious ways. His sweetheart, Desideria, is jealous of Michele's attachment to his sister. In a bitter fight between them, Michele kills Desideria and is forced to go into hiding. But he cannot resist the temptation of returning to Bleecker Street to attend the festive ceremonies in which Annina is accepted by the Church as the Bride of Christ. Thus he is a witness when Annina, overwhelmed by the emotional experience and joy during the ceremony, falls dead.

As in his earlier musical dramas, Menotti skilfully combines contemporary techniques and idioms—with which he projects the tensions and the gripping dramatic climaxes of his play—with a lyricism that often has the sentiment and the tenderness of Puccini. Together with vividly realistic writing, the score embraces florid songs that mingle humor with emotion (the three wedding songs in the second act), humorous ditties (Corona's tune in the third act), dance tunes (the juke-box melody in the second act), gripping recitatives (the Saint's stirring narrative in the opening scene) and religious chants (the San Gennaro procession in the first act).

The Saint of Bleecker Street was given its first production in Italy at La Scala, Milan, on May 8, 1955. In 1956, it was telecast in London over BBC.

1956 THE UNICORN, THE GORGON, AND THE MANTICORE, a "madrigal fable," for chorus, ten dancers and nine instruments. First performance: Washington, D.C., October 21, 1956.

Subtitled "The Three Sundays of a Poet," and described as a "madrigal fable," this intimate and charming chamber opera (which had been commissioned by the Elizabeth Sprague Coolidge Foundation) represents a radical departure in technique and style from the more grim and realistic dramas for which the composer has become famous. The work requires a chorus, ten dancers and nine instruments; and the score embraces an introduction, twelve madrigals almost in the style of Monteverdi and often a cappella, and six orchestral interludes.

The central character is a lonely, retiring poet who is looked upon with suspicion by his neighbors. One day he emerges from his solitary castle retreat to lead a pet unicorn in a Sunday promenade. The women of the town now demand of their husbands pet unicorns of their own. But on another Sunday, the poet emerges with a pet manticore, and after that with a pet gorgon, always to the envy of the women who want similar pets. The three pets are at the poet's deathbed—symbolizing, in turn, the poet's youth, middle age and old age—as the poet, with his last dying words, upbraids his neighbors for their foolishness in trying to feel what other men have suffered and who are the destroyers of the poet's dreams.

"All this," says William L. Crosten, "is depicted most charmingly through sight and sound, the chorus being the mouthpiece for the characters while the dancers represent them in action. Everything conspires to make this one of Menotti's happiest inventions. The text is imaginative and amusing; the dances have style; and the choruses throughout are interesting for the variety of their vocal textures and the deftness of their settings."

1958 MARIA GOLOVIN, music drama in three acts, with text by the composer. First performance: Brussels, August 20, 1958.

In *Maria Golovin,* we once again find those ingredients for which the composer has long been famous and which always add up to compelling theatre: melodrama and suspense; a principal character who is physically afflicted, and who with the others is subjected to violent emotional torment; penetrating psychological insight; an eclectic style that wanders freely from enchanting Italian-like lyricism (such as the love music of the third act and the trio in the second) and formal arias and ensemble numbers, to realistic tone painting, programmatic writing, and dramatic recitatives. The setting is a town near a European frontier; the time, a few years after "a recent war." Maria Golovin, a wealthy and attractive woman, is the wife of a man who for four years has been a prisoner of war. She has found a home with her son in an apartment in a villa owned by Donato, a blind maker of bird cages. Since both she and Donato are emotionally starved, they fall in love. The affair fills the blind man with an all-consuming apprehension for the future, and with self-doubts. When Maria's husband is released from prison, she informs Donato she is leaving him to reestablish a home with her husband for the sake of their son. As she leaves, Donato fires a shot at her, but misses aim. However, he is deluded into believing he has killed her and that no other man will ever possess her.

Maria Golovin was commissioned by NBC for the Brussels Exposition in Belgium, where it was introduced. On November 5, 1958, it received its American première at the Martin Beck Theater but was able to survive only five performances. Nevertheless, early in 1959, it was presented over television by NBC and shortly thereafter revived by the New York City Opera Company. Menotti then revised the opera in many fundamental details; the new version was given its world première in Washington, D.C., on January 22, 1965.

In reviewing *Maria Golovin* in *The Saturday Review,* Irving Kolodin said: "From the atmospheric prelude . . . to its effective end, the ideas are strong and fresh. Moreover, Menotti's flow is cleverly diverted into some channels and areas he has not previously been able to navigate, in conversational vocal exchanges while the orchestra carries the melodic undercurrent, or in the evolution of a trio into a quartet in Act II."

1963 DEATH OF THE BISHOP OF BRINDISI, cantata for soprano, basso, children's chorus, chorus and orchestra.

The textual material for this, Menotti's first dramatic cantata, was derived from a medieval legend. In the year of 1212, a children's crusade of several thousand set out from Germany just before the Fifth Crusade, the aim being to free the Holy Land. With poor direction and equipment, the crusade was foredoomed to disaster. The youngsters never reached the Holy Land. Some say they were killed in a shipwreck; others, that they were captured by a pirate ship and sold as slaves.

Just before the children set sail from Brindisi, they received the blessings of the Bishop. In the Menotti text, which he himself prepared, we find the Bishop at his deathbed attended by a Nun. He is tormented by his conscience. "I blessed them to their doom," he laments. He wonders if he was right in having given his blessing to the children; if he should not have been more persuasive in trying to prevent them from undertaking such a quixotic adventure; if he is not guilty of this wholesale calamity.

A basso sings the part of the Bishop, while the part of the Nun, who is trying to comfort him, is undertaken by a soprano. The children are represented by a children's chorus. The regular mixed chorus speaks now for the angry

Brindisi townspeople, who hurl bitter accusations against the Bishop; and now for the Judgment of Heaven, in which he is absolved of guilt. The work ends with this eloquent absolution as the chorus sings: "Nothing is purposeless, nothing. . . . Sleep, sleep, at last, O gentle pilgrim. Sleep, sleep into dawn."

In this score, as in his operas, Menotti makes masterful use of theatrical effects. A storm at sea is realistically portrayed in the orchestra with ascending and descending chromatics; the denunciation of the townspeople is punctuated with discords; the agony of the Bishop is reflected in austere recitatives. At the same time the plea of the children seeking help ("O man of God, help us, help us") is portrayed through expressive choral writing. But in other choral pages for the children, Menotti can write with disarming simplicity that achieves the most affecting poignancy; and it is in pages like these ("Far in my town of towers" and "I shall kiss our Lord's Tomb") that this music is particularly effective. Harriet Johnson reported in the *New York Post*: "The music is more compassionate than powerful."

The cantata was commissioned by the Cincinnati Musical Festival Association, and was introduced in Cincinnati on May 18, 1963, Max Rudolf conducting. The following August, the work was successfully presented at the Berkshire Music Festival at Tanglewood; and in the fall of 1964, by the Boston Symphony in Boston and New York. The first European presentation took place at the Vienna Festival Weeks, on June 15, 1963.

1963 LABYRINTH, opera in one act, with libretto by the composer. First performance: NBC-TV, May 3, 1963.

Labyrinth was Menotti's first opera in six years, and the second he wrote expressly for television broadcast (the first having been *Amahl and the Night Visitors*). It was commissioned by the NBC Opera which introduced it. Since the production employs numerous trick camera effects, this opera's production must be confined exclusively either to television or to motion pictures. The work has been described as "opera's first adventure in photographic surrealism" and as "a spoken drama that could only exist in an electronic medium."

Menotti's text is replete with symbolism. Bride and Bridegroom come to an eerie hotel to spend their honeymoon. The hotel represents the world. Each character they meet is a symbol of some facet of life. A spy stands for science or philosophy trying to explain life's meaning. A bellboy represents dreams; an old chess player, the past; an executive woman, the present; an astronaut, the future. After encountering numerous adventures, the Bridegroom finally manages to reach the hotel desk, whose manager is Death. The manager urges him to lie down on a bench, then swiftly and expeditiously he builds a coffin around him, "nailing down the lid with ferocious hammer strokes." When the coffin is carried away, the Bridegroom is left lying on the bench, since the coffin has no bottom. Upon becoming convinced that the manager has left, the Bridegroom opens his hand and finds he is holding the key to his hotel room.

Menotti described his opera as an "operatic riddle" adding that "perhaps it is more of a riddle than an opera." And, as Irving Kolodin pointed out in *The Saturday Review,* "the riddle of *Labyrinth* is simply the mystery of life." Kolodin adds: "To its examination, Menotti has brought many artful expressions of his own fertile imagination, verbal and musical. His Groom. . . is an attractive figure, and the Bride . . . is an appealing one. She has a charming arietta ('I shall never, never see my home again' is its theme). There is a deft waltz strain for the spy (*'Lieber, sois tranquille'* about paying the bill is a sample of its internationally flavored text) and the Groom sings a kind of tango refrain while simulating weightlessness. A chamber orchestra is utilized with economy and judgment just right in this context. So far—and this applies to two-thirds of its forty-five minute length—Menotti has suited subject and treatment resourcefully to the chosen medium, with sometimes slyly humorous elaboration of his thesis. Traditional opera is spoofed broadly and subtly."

1963 THE LAST SAVAGE, opéra bouffe in three acts, with libretto by the composer. First performance: Opéra-Comique, Paris, October 21, 1963.

The Last Savage was commissioned by the Paris Opéra. Not for a century, not since Verdi, had that opera company contracted a non-French composer for a new work. The original request from the Opéra was for a spectacle. But with the changing of the directors at the Opéra, new specifications called for a reduction of dimensions. Finally, Georges Auric—who had by now become the head of both the Opéra and the Opéra-Comique—decided that an opéra bouffe would be far better at the Opéra-Comique than at the Opéra, and Menotti agreed.

These changing plans led to an operatic structure which the composer described as "a funnel." That is, the first act is the largest of the three, written when the intention was still to create a spectacle. The second is smaller than the first, written after the decision had been reached to reduce the opera's dimensions. And the third act, written with a small theatre in mind, was the most economical and sparing of the three. Menotti wrote his libretto in Italian (the first time he did so since his maiden effort, *Amelia Goes to the Ball*). He then translated it into French for the Paris première. George Mead translated it into English for the United States.

The Last Savage was intended as a satire on contemporary life and mores. It provides amusing and at times sardonic appraisals of such niceties of twentieth-century living as cocktail parties, abstract painters, composers who use the serial technique, beatniks, and so forth. Two acts are set in the splendors and jungles of India, and one act transpires in Chicago.

Kitty, an anthropologist, and the daughter of an American millionaire, is bent on finding the legendary Abominable Snowman in India. There she meets the son of the Maharajah who falls in love with her. Both the Maharajah and Kitty's father are deeply concerned over their respective economic futures. The father is appalled by the threat of government bureaucracy, taxes and trade unions in the United States, while the Maharajah is apprehensive about social reforms. Both are happy over a possible union between the two families through the marriage of their respective children. Kitty, however, refuses to consider matrimony until she has found her legendary Snowman. In order to bring about the marriage, the Maharajah invents the legendary figure by transforming Abdul, a stable boy, into the Snowman, or "the last savage."

In tune with the frivolities of his text, and its frequent tongue-in-cheek allusions to contemporary "civilization," Menotti created a twentieth-century opéra bouffe that is structurally and stylistically more or less old-fashioned. It is consistently consonant, consistently melodious, consistently studded with delightful arias and ensemble numbers ranging all the way from a trio to a septet. Harold C. Schonberg described the opera in *The New York Times* as a "Broadway musical masquerading as an opera."

The Last Savage received its American première at the Metropolitan Opera House on January 23, 1964. Soon afterward, the opera was mounted in Italy—at La Fenice in Venice when it was presented in the Italian language and under the title of *L'Ultimo selvaggio.*

1964 MARTIN'S LIE, opera in one act, with libretto by the composer. First performance: Bristol, England, June 3, 1964.

Martin's Lie is a "church opera" of modest proportions requiring a small cast, a boy in the leading role, and a chamber orchestra of thirteen instrumentalists. Commissioned by the Columbia Broadcasting System, the opera was introduced at the Bath Festival in England, at the ancient cathedral of nearby Bristol. After this performance, the opera was taped for television, with Menotti serving as producer; this version was telecast in the United States on January 24, 1965.

The central character is a twelve-year-old orphan in medieval England. He is so hungry for a father that when a heretic comes to him for shelter, he identifies the man as his own parent, and even at the threat of torture refuses to reveal where the man is hidden. Having to choose between love and truth, the child selects love.

Much of the emotional impact of this little opera comes from "its sensitive evocation of a child's innocence" as one correspondent from England remarked. "There are lovely passages for boys' voices, particularly the final dirge."

OLIVIER MESSIAEN 1908–

On June 3, 1936, there took place in Paris, at the Salle Gaveau, a concert of music by young (and then comparatively unknown) French composers. This concert marked the emergence of a new school of contemporary musicians, self-styled "*La Jeune France*" (phrase lifted from Berlioz). In its manifesto, published in the program of that concert, the school dedicated itself to "the dissemination of works youthful, free, as far removed from revolutionary formulas as from academic formulas." The manifesto said further: "The tendencies of this group will be diverse; their only unqualified agreement is in the common desire to be satisfied with nothing less than sincerity, generosity, and artistic good faith. Their aim is to create and promote a living music."

This school of young French composers comprised Daniel Lesur, Yves Baudrier, André Jolivet and—most important of all—Olivier Messiaen.

Though a member of a school, Messiaen has always gone his own way in his music, frequently venturing into foreign worlds of musical expression far removed from those in which his fellow composers moved. He is a complex and original thinker. His music abounds with complicated polymodal and polyrhythmic writing and with intricate ideas. He is not afraid to be expansive: he has written a ten-movement symphony, and a piano work of one hundred and seventy-five pages requiring two and a half hours for performance. He is partial towards the exotic: he calls upon rhythms derived from Hindu practice, archaic modes and scales, melodic ideas imitative of the plainsong. He has experimented with tone colors and timbres to produce unusual sonorities and instrumental textures. He has been influenced by the sounds and songs of birds. He has dabbled with electronic music and with *Musique concrète*. Rhythm has particularly occupied his attention. He has used it with the variety and flexibility of a virtuoso. His ten-movement symphony, *Turangalîla,* is indeed, a veritable apotheosis of rhythm. He even prepared a rhythm dictionary for rhythms of the Eastern and Western worlds as well as that of ancient Greece.

There have been several influences in Messiaen's artistic development. One has been of particular significance: the Catholic Church. Profoundly religious, Messiaen has often turned to the liturgy and Scriptures of his church for material for musical compositions, and often he has filled his writing with mysticism and spirituality. In his religious music, Messiaen's rhythmic writing is free and flexible, freed of restrictions from tempo or measure-demarcations. The melody thus tends to be continuous, built on modal scales. The concept of time is broken so skilfully that the music seems to have neither a beginning nor an end; it seems to move about in space with all sense of time destroyed. Thus, oblivious to time, the listener is drawn to contemplation, even to a kind of religious ecstasy. As the composer himself explained: "This music must be able to express noble sentiments and especially the noblest of all: the religious sentiments exalted by verities of our Catholic faith." In this music we find an escape, through religion, from temporal to spiritual values. Messiaen seeks out new reasons for life and hope, and is more concerned with finding spiritual ideals and expressing religious fervor than in devising a new musical language.

Since the middle 1950s, Messiaen has been absorbed with the sounds of bird songs and calls, some of which he had previously introduced into *Turangalîla*. He made an intensive study of this field with an ornithologist, and found considerable creative stimulation from it. More and more the sounds of birds dominate his music writing, beginning with the *Organ Book* (1952). The *Réveil des Oiseaux*, a piano concerto heard at the Donaueschingen Festival on October 11, 1953, utilizes some thirty different bird songs. *Oiseaux exotiques* and its successor, the *Première Catalogue d'oiseaux* (the latter a work for solo piano introduced on April 15, 1959), make further sophisticated use of bird sounds. Messiaen's most ambitious creation inspired by birds is the *Chronochromie* (*Color of Time*); here, songs of birds from many lands, including the Orient, are basic.

"If ever a composer was a slave to inspiration it is Olivier Messiaen," says David Drew in the *New Statesman*. "Perhaps the supreme gift is that he is morally and even technically incapable of performing an act of mere robbery: morally, because for him the manufacture of a single unfelt bar would be tantamount to blasphemy; technically, because although his *equipment* is probably unsurpassed in the history of French music, he does not possess the kind of routine that would simply 'get him through' a piece, even if his temperament could accept such a lowly ideal."

To Francis Poulenc, Messiaen can be compared to the painter Georges Rouault. "Both possess, indeed, that prodigious divination of color, that same visionary tone, that pride that often makes their mysticism border upon exacerbated paganism."

Messiaen was born in Avignon, France, on December 10, 1908, son of Cécile Sauvage, a famous poet. He attended the Paris Conservatory for eleven years (beginning with 1919), where he was a pupil of Dukas and Dupré among others; he won numerous prizes. In 1928, he wrote a piece for organ, *Le Banquet céleste,* in which his later religious bent is foreshadowed. This bent became even more evident in 1931, in *Les Offrandes oubliées*, his first orchestral work to get published; and in 1934, in *L'Ascension,* his most frequently heard symphonic composition. In 1931, he became the organist of the Trinité Church in Paris; from 1936 to 1939, he taught composition at the Schola Cantorum and the École Normale de Musique. During World War II, he served in the French army, was taken prisoner, and for two years was interned in a prison camp. There he wrote his deeply moving quartet, *Quatuor pour la fin du temps*, which received its world première in the camp on January 15, 1941. In 1942, Messiaen was released from prison and repatriated. He resumed his organ post at the Trinité and became professor of harmony at the Conservatory where, in 1947, a special class in rhythm was formed for him. During the summer of 1949, he taught a master class in composition at the Berkshire Music Center at Tanglewood—his first visit to the United States. He returned to the United States a few months later to attend the première of his symphony, *Turangalîla*, in Boston. After writing this mammoth symphony, he suffered a period of creative frustration, which kept him musically silent for a while. He entered a new rich phase of creativity in compositions like the *Oiseaux exotiques*, for orchestra, the *Première Catalogue d'Oiseaux*, for piano, and the *Chronochromie*, for orchestra in 1960. His second wife is the famous concert pianist, Yvonne Loriod, who for many years had performed his major piano compositions. In 1963, the Académie des Beaux-Arts presented him with the Florent Schmitt Prize.

1930 LES OFFRANDES OUBLIÉES (FORGOTTEN OFFERINGS), for orchestra.

In the published score there appears the following paragraph, intended by the composer as a clue to the emotional content of this music:

"With arms extended, sad unto death, on the tree of the Cross, sheddest

Thou Thy blood. Thou lovest us, Gentle Jesus, but we had forgotten. Urged onward by madness and the sting of the serpent, in a frenzied, panting race that gives no release, fell we into sin as into a tomb. Behold the table pure, the spring of charity, the banquet of the poor; behold adorable compassion, offering the bread of life and love. Thou lovest us, Gentle Jesus, but we had forgotten."

Les Offrandes oubliées was Messiaen's first major work to be performed. It was first heard on February 19, 1931, in Paris at a Straram concert, Walter Straram conducting. It was also the first of his works to give an indication of the extent of his talent.

Les Offrandes oubliées, described in the published score as a "symphonic meditation," was the composer's first published work for the orchestra. It was also the first of his compositions to gain an important performance, the first to reveal his creative potential, and the first work in a larger design to reflect his profound religious feelings.

1933 L'ASCENSION: QUATRE MÉDITATIONS SYMPHONIQUES (THE ASCENSION: FOUR SYMPHONIC MEDITATIONS), for orchestra. I. Très Lent et majestueux. II. Pas trop modéré et clair. III. Vif et joyeux. IV. Extrémement lent, ému et solennel.

The Ascension draws its text from Catholic liturgy and Scripture, comprising Christ's prayers to the Father and the emotional responses of his followers to his words. The composer provided each movement not only with a title but also with an explanatory caption, the latter serving as his program for the music:

I. Majesty of Christ Beseeching His Glory of His Father. "Father, the hour is come; glorify Thy Son, that Thy Son may glorify Thee."

II. Serene Hallelujahs of a Soul That Longs for Heaven. "We beseech Thee, O Lord . . . that we may dwell in Heaven in the spirit."

III. Hallelujah on the Trumpet, Hallelujah on the Cymbal. "God is gone up . . . with the sound of a trumpet. . . . O clap your hands, all ye people; shout unto God with the voice of triumph."

IV. Prayer of Christ Ascending to His Father. "Father . . . I have manifested Thy name unto men . . . and now I am no more in the world, but these are in the world, and I come to thee."

The first movement, scored for brass and woodwinds, is hymn-like. An archaic mannerism enters in the second part, in which a serene and spiritual atmosphere is evoked mainly by the woodwinds. The expression of joy becomes unconfined in the third section, for full orchestra. Only the strings (some muted) are used in the concluding part, which is a devout prayer.

The Ascension was introduced at a concert of the Paris Conservatory Orchestra, Charles Munch conducting, in 1935. The composer transcribed the work for solo piano, and for solo organ.

1941 QUATUOR POUR LA FIN DU TEMPS (QUARTET FOR THE END OF TIME), for violin, clarinet, cello and piano. I. Liturgie de cristal. II. Vocalise pour l'ange qui annonce la fin du temps. III. Abime des oiseaux. IV. Intermède. V. Louange à l'eternité de Jésus. VI. Danse de la fureur pour les sept trompettes. VII. Fouillis d'arc-en-ciel, pour l'ange qui annonce la fin du temps. VIII. Louange à l'immortalité de Jésus.

This quartet is its composer's most significant chamber-music composition, and one of the most deeply moving pieces of music to come out of and be inspired by World War II. Messiaen wrote it while he was a prisoner of war in Stalag VIII-A in Görlitz, Silesia. "Only music," he said, "made me survive the cruelty and horrors of the camp." The world première took place in this place of internment, on January 15, 1941, before an audience of five thousand fellow-sufferers. The composer officiated at the piano. "Never," says the composer, "was I listened to with such rapt attention and comprehension." The quartet was heard in the United States on an all-French program in New York on January 30, 1946. Six months later, on July 10, it was heard at the festival of the International Society for Contemporary Music at London.

Here is how Howard Taubman described the Quartet in *The New York Times* following its American première: "It is impossible to say whether the imagery or the musical thought comes first in Messiaen's workshop, but it is clear that his writing is quickened by large, and perhaps concrete, sacred images. And as is often the way with visions, they fluctuate between something that is close to revelation and something else that seems little more than deliberately whipped-up excitement. . . . This Quartet has memorable things—long-breathed passages full of mystery and poetry as well as pages of vibrant yet controlled fervor."

1943 VISIONS DE L'AMEN, for two pianos. I. Amen of the Creation. II. Amen of the Stars, of the Planet Saturn. III. Amen of the Agony of Jesus. IV. Amen of Desire. V. Amen of the Angels, of the Saints, of the Song of the Birds. VI. Amen of Judgment. VII. Amen of Consummation.

This is one of Messiaen's major works, and one of the most important works for two pianos written in our time. Davidson Taylor, who heard a private performance in Paris, described the music as follows in *Modern Music*:

"*Visions* is full of the music of bells, mellow bells and cracked harsh bells like those of Rennes, near bells and distant bells, deep bells and high delicate bells, and there is no trace of monotony in the music. . . .

"The first section of this grand and dramatic sevenfold Amen bears the quotation, 'Let there be light, and there was light.' The Amen of the stars quotes Baruch, 'God calls them and they say, Amen, we are here!' It is a savage dance. The final movement is headed '*De clarté en clarté*.' The two sections which remain most acute . . . are the one about the angels and the birds, with a long, serene melody decorated by the most intricate fretwork, and the one about the judgment, in which futile supplications are broken by great frozen chords like pronouncements from the throne of God."

The composer collaborated with his pupil (and later his second wife), Yvonne Loriod, in presenting the world première at one of the Concerts de la Pléiade on May 10, 1943. They also performed it throughout Europe after that; by the time they had given the composition its New York première on December 12, 1967, they had played it over sixty times.

1944 TROIS PETITS LITURGIES DE LA PRÉSENCE DIVINE

(THREE LITTLE LITURGIES OF THE DIVINE PRESENCE), for orchestra. I. Antienne de la conversation intérieure. II. Séquence du verbe, Cantique divin. III. Psalmodie de l'ubiquité par amour.

The text, prepared by the composer, was conceived "at the same time as the music," the composer has explained, "and the music, with the same rhyme and rhythm, takes on a very special aspect. . . . To write it the author has reread the Apocalypse, Saint Paul, Saint Thomas, the Imitation, the Song of Songs, Paul Éluard, and works on medicine, botany, geology and astronomy." The composer further said that he employed an unusual instrumentation for this unusual composition: "celesta, vibraphone, maracas, gong, tam-tam, piano, Ondes Martenot, and string orchestra. Not a chamber orchestra, still less a full orchestra grouped in a classical fashion, it is rather a Europeanized Hindu or Balinese instrumentation." The composer concludes that he "utilizes the language which is his own, and the procedures which are dear to him, but with increased tenderness. The three pieces seek great variety through polymodal or polyrhythmical modulations."

Here is how Edward J. Pendleton described this music: "Opening with a 'tender' chant accompanied by bird-like figures on the piano, the first piece, '*Conversation Intérieure,*' contrasts this prayer-like theme with contrapuntal commentaries of great freedom and suppleness. The second piece, 'Sequence of the Word,' contains a refrain, joyful and relatively simple, repeated again and again by the chorus to varied accompaniments. . . . The third section, 'Dedicated to God,' present in all things, opposes two ideas: the accumulation of various fragments and themes into a vast symbolical ensemble . . . with a quiet interior sentiment. . . . The adding up of polyrhythms, harmonies, and melodic fragments heard simultaneously . . . finally creates for us mortals a good deal of mere noise topped off by glissandos on the Ondes Martenot and fortissimo drum and cymbal rolls."

The world première took place at a Concert de la Pléiade on April 21, 1945, Roger Desormière conducting.

1945 HYMNE (HYMN), for large orchestra.

Messiaen made sketches for this work as early as 1932, but its actual composition came thirteen years later. Leopold Stokowski conducted the world première in New York with the New York Philharmonic on March 13, 1947. The composer provided the following analysis: "The work is based on two themes with a middle and final development. The first theme ends with a burst of winds. . . . The second theme, more dreamy and very singing, built on the '*modes à transposition limitées*' utilizes only violins and violas soli. The middle development is polymodal, alternating with and opposing the more belligerent first theme and the more passionate second theme. The final development resumes the martial character and the polymodality of the first development and concludes on a joyous fanfare of brass, surrounded by a brilliant shimmering of all the instruments of the orchestra in the tonality of B major."

1948 TURANGALÎLA, symphony for piano, Ondes Martenot and orchestra. I. Introduction. II. Chant d'amour, I. III. Turangalîla. IV. Chant d'amour, II. V. Joie du sang des étoiles. VI. Jardin du someil d'amour. VII.

Turangalîla, II. VIII. Développement de l'amour. IX. Turangalîla, III. X. Final.

This giant symphony, one of the most ambitious ever conceived, was commissioned by the Koussevitzky Music Foundation. The world première took place in Boston with Leonard Bernstein conducting the Boston Symphony on December 2, 1949. The composer attended this performance.

The title is a poetic term for a love song in the Indian language, but a love song with a strong rhythmic pulse. The composer confesses he was more intrigued in the sound of the title than in its meaning. He used the title for a ten-movement work requiring about two hours for performance. It is the apotheosis of rhythm, the culminating point of his lifelong interest in the study of the rhythms of the Eastern and Western worlds. As he himself explained in an awesome analysis: "The *Turangalîla* Symphony is written in a special rhythmic language and makes use of several new rhythmic principles—quantitative, dynamic, cinematic, phonetic, added values, non-reversible rhythms, asymmetric augmentations with several rhythmic identities, rhythmic modes, and the combination of quantitative and sounding elements in reinforcing the values and the timbre of each percussion instrument by chords which form the resonance of these timbres."

A huge orchestra is employed, greatly augmented in its percussion section. Besides the traditional woodwind, strings and brass (brass featured prominently in the last group), the orchestra includes three keyboard instruments, the glockenspiel, the celesta, and the vibraphone which the composer explains "has a special role similar to that of an East-Indian gamelan." In addition, the orchestra includes an Ondes Martenot (a radio-electric instrument) which "dominates the orchestra with its expressive voice," and a piano solo "designed to point up the orchestra with brilliance, with chord clusters and bird songs." The percussion family includes temple blocks, wood block, small cymbal, suspended cymbal, Chinese cymbal, tam-tam, tambourine, triangle, maracas, side drum, snare drum, bass drum, tubular bells.

The composer provided the following guide to his symphony: In the Introduction (Modéré un peu vif), "the first two cyclic themes are heard: one in ponderous thirds from the trombones, the other in gentle arabesques from the clarinets. Two Hindu rhythms are superimposed in pedals." The first Love Song (Modéré, lourd) begins "with the superimposing of three rhythmic successions of values in unequal augmentation. The theme is a refrain evoking two aspects of love in violent contrast: impassioned earthly love—ideal and tender love." The first Turangalîla movement (Presque lent, rêveur) receives "a nostalgic theme from the Ondes Martenot and a heavier theme from the trombone." The second Love Song (Bien modéré) is a scherzo with two trios. "The trios are very songful. . . . In the da capo, the scherzo and two trios are superimposed, thus erecting a three-fold music." The movement marked "Joy in the Blood of the Stars" (Un peu vif, joyeux et passioné) represents "the peak of carnal passion expressed in a long and frenetic dance of joy. . . . The full orchestra is released. The piano solo, brilliant and vehement, participates in the dynamic exacerbation of the terrible love." The sixth movement, entitled "Garden of the Sleep of Love" (Très modéré, très tendre) is a "long and slow melody of the Ondes Martenot and strings, infinitely tender and gentle, ornamented by the vibraphone and the songs of birds in the piano solo." The second of the three movements marked Turangalîla (Piano solo, un peu vif; orchestre, modéré) once again features bird songs in the piano solo, with twitterings in the woodwind. "The Development of Love" (Bien modéré) is "a canon in non-reversible rhythms. . . . This part develops the three cyclic themes with a passion constantly increasing." The third Turangalîla (Modéré) is "most complex in rhythm and orchestration. It makes use of a mode on a rhythmic chromaticism of seventeen values. . . . Chords played by the quintet of solo strings create the resonance of each percussive timbre. . . . The melody is expressed in normal values by the celesta, in augmentation by the Ondes Martenot, and in diminution by the piano solo. All this simultaneously." The finale (Modéré, avec une grand joie) opens with a "joyous fanfare of trumpets and horns." The second theme is the love theme in diminution. . . . "After the glorification of the 'love theme' fortissimo, an exuberant and brilliant coda ends the work in a delirium of love and passion."

1956 OISEAUX EXOTIQUES (EXOTIC BIRDS), for piano solo, two clarinets, small wind orchestra, xylophone, glockenspiel and percussion.

The resurgence of Messiaen's creative powers, after several years of quiescence, and his increasing fascination for transferring the sounds and songs of birds into his composition, came simultaneously. He had made such experiments earlier, in the *Turangalîla* symphony for example, and in several other compositions. *Oiseaux exotiques* was his most significant work in this vein up to this time. It exploited the sounds and voices of birds from exotic lands and climes.

Oiseaux exotiques received its world première in Paris on March 10, 1956. "Part of the novelty," wrote Harold C. Schonberg in *The New York Times,* when this composition was heard in New York on November 8, 1962, Gunther Schuller conducting, "lies in the closely repeated dissonantal patterns. They lead to an ornithological nightmare but at the same time a hypnotic one, where the attention is seized and held during a specified series of patterns that never seem to let go. If nothing else, the music is different from all other music. There is something actually pagan about it: Gauguin gone wild in tone."

1960 CHRONOCHROMIE (COLOR OF TIME), for large orchestra. I. Introduction. II. Strophe I. III. Antistrophe I. IV. Strophe II. V. Antistrophe II. VI. Épôde. VII. Coda.

This is Messiaen's most ambitious composition up to this time with material inspired by bird songs. Messiaen has explained in an interview that in utilizing bird songs he is not interested in realistic descriptions. What concerns him are "voices and rhythms." He explained: "It is material of extraordinary richness which nature offers me."

Chronochromie was commissioned by Heinrich Strobel and the South-West German Radio (Südwestfunk) in Baden-Baden. The world première took place at Donaueschingen on October 16, 1960, with Hans Rosbaud conducting the Südwestfunk Orchestra.

There are two basic elements in this composition as revealed by its title:

"color" and "time." The composer has explained that "the 'temporal' or rhythmic material consists of thirty-two different durations which are used in symmetrical interversions, while always retaining their original order. The permutations thus obtained are heard either separately and fragmentarily, or superposed three by three. The sonorities or the melodic material make use of bird-song from France, Japan and Mexico, as well as the sound of water notated in the French Alps." As for color: "The very complex mixture of pitch and timbre serves to underline and color the rhythmic durations: thus, 'color' clarifies the divisions of 'time.' "

The composer then provides a detailed analysis:

"*Chronochromie* is constructed in the same way as the choruses of ancient Greek tragedy, but with the Strophes repeated, and with the addition of an Introduction and Coda. There are seven sections, which are played without a break.

"INTRODUCTION. Throughout this movement, the orchestration is extremely varied and timbres are continually changing. Thus: the multi-speed string glissandi representing a gust of wind, the massive chords, the combination of rotating figures suggesting the complex sonority of water in the falls and streams of the Alps; finally, symmetrical permutations of durations and the songs of two Japanese birds: the Kibitaki and the Uguisu. The section ends with the strong cries of the White-tailed Eagle.

"STROPHE I. The structure of this section decided the title of the whole work. There are three superimposed symmetrical permutations of the thirty-two durations. These durations are colored in three ways. Firstly, by melodic counterpoints drawn from the songs of French birds and played on woodwind and keyed instruments. Secondly, by three metallic timbres: gongs, bells, suspended cymbals, Chinese cymbal, and tam-tam. Thirdly, by three differently colored chordal streams, one for each permutation level. . . . All this is played by twenty-two solo strings.

"ANTISTROPHE I. The opening section contrasts the two best songsters among French birds: the Song Thrush and the Skylark. The Song Thrush is always represented by the woodwind ensemble and, in order to reproduce its characteristic timbre, each note is provided with a different chord of a different color; there are thus a multitude of chords. Its song is characterized by short, strongly rhythmical phrases, which are repeated three times, in the manner of an incantation. The Skylark is represented by xylophone and marimba, punctuated by bells and accompanied by a haze of sound. . . . After a contrasting section—a slow melody spreads across all the strings—and a powerful brass chorale, three new symmetrical permutations of the thirty-two durations mingle with a melody of timbres and of various bird songs. These birds are all Mexican: the Slate-colored Solitaire, the Tropical Mockingbird, the Gray Salator, the Mexican Blue-Mockingbird and the famous Montezuma Oropendola. . . .

"STROPHE II AND ANTISTROPHE II. These contain the same basic elements as Strophe I and Antistrophe I, although the music itself is different.

"ÉPÔDE. As in the Greek choruses, this is quite unlike the other sections. Firstly, it is different in the instrumentation, since it is scored for eighteen solo strings: six first violins, six second violins, four violas, and two cellos. Then it differs in rhythm, since it is the only passage with the permutations of the thirty-two durations. Lastly, as music: here, there is no longer any sense of color or of harmony—there is nothing but the song of French birds, forming a free counterpoint of eighteen individual voices: Blackbirds, Garden Warblers, Golden Orioles, Goldfinches, Chaffinches, a Chiffchaff, a Yellowhammer, a Whitethroat, a Lesser Whitethroat, a Greenfinch, a Nightingale, and a Linnet. . . . "CODA. Elements from the Introduction appear in a different order and with other music."

NIKOLAI MIASKOVSKY 1881–1950

Miaskovsky was the most prolific of today's composers of symphonies. He wrote in all, twenty-seven works in that form. In his earliest symphonies (of which the Sixth is the best example), he was the subjective composer who imparted personal thoughts and feelings into his music. A more objective approach becomes evident with the Seventh Symphony. Influenced and inspired by the revolution in his native land, Miaskovsky turned to Soviet life and activity for his inspiration. Thus his Twelfth Symphony is known as the *Collective Farm Symphony*. In the next six symphonies—from the Thirteenth to the Eighteenth—an attempt is made to reconcile subjective and objective expressions. This was not satisfactory, as Miaskovsky himself realized. With the Nineteenth Symphony, still another approach is perceptible. From now on, the composer aims for simplified writing, consciously attempting the kind of music that is easily assimilable and can have immediate and direct appeal to large masses. His Twenty-First Symphony, generally credited as his best work, is the most successful realization of this point of view.

Though Miaskovsky was prolific in writing symphonies, he was also able to produce music in other forms as well, and with no diminution of quantity. His works include thirteen string quartets and nine piano sonatas together with symphonic poems, concertos, sinfoniettas, piano pieces and songs.

His earlier works are, for the most part, melancholy. In the description of Igor Glebov, this is music of "utter darkness—a gray, awesome, autumnal darkness, transformed into a moonless night, a tenebrous darkness." But his later works radiate optimism, though once in a while a melancholy strain does intrude. To continue Glebov's metaphor, the sun is allowed to pierce the darkness and bring warmth and light. This warmth and light comes from the frequent use of melodic phrases which Alexei Ikkonikov has described as "in the berceuse manner" and through the use of dance themes whose melodies are "reminiscent of the traditional long drawn-out Russian songs . . . clear in outline, lilting, broad and flowing." However, at times an exotic atmosphere is projected through the use of an "immense diapason of intricate modal harmonic formations" which brings to Miaskovsky's writing a "peculiar close-grained and dense quality."

Miaskovsky was born in Novogeorgievsk, near Warsaw (then Russia), on April 20, 1881. His father, an army engineer, directed him to engineering. In 1893, Miaskovsky entered the Cadet School in Nizhny Novgorod, and from 1895 to 1899, he was a pupil at a military school in St. Petersburg. Music study, however, was not altogether neglected. He received his early training as a pianist from his aunt and from Stuneyev, after which he studied harmony with Kazanli. At fifteen, Miaskovsky began composing music, his first efforts being piano preludes imitative of Chopin. In 1903, he took a six-month course in harmony with Glière, which made him change the course of his life from engineering to music. For three years, he studied theory and composition with Kryzhanovsky, and from 1905 to 1911, he attended the St. Petersburg Conservatory, where his teachers included Liadov and Rimsky-Korsakov. While still a Conservatory student, he wrote a piano sonata and his first symphony.

During World War I, Miaskovsky served in the Russian army, and was wounded and shell-shocked. In 1917, he was transferred to Reval to work on military fortifications, and from 1918 to 1921, he was a functionary in the Maritime Headquarters in Moscow. Demobilized, he was made, in 1921, professor of composition at the Moscow Conservatory, a post he retained till the end of his life; his pupils included Khatchaturian and Kabalevsky. In 1926, the title of Artist of Merit was conferred on him; an honorary Doctorate of Arts was given him in 1940.

As a composer, Miaskovsky specialized in instrumental music, and particularly in the writing of string quartets and symphonies. His Twenty-First Symphony received the Stalin Prize in 1941; so did his Cello Concerto in 1945, after being introduced in Moscow by Sviatoslav Kushentzky on March 17 of that year. However, when the Central Committee of the Communist Party denounced the leading Soviet composers for "decadent formalism" in February of 1948 (*see* Prokofiev), Miaskovsky was not exempt. He was brought to task for the strain of pessimism that he permitted to enter his writing, and for introducing as a teacher "inharmonious music" into the educational system. Miaskovsky died in Moscow on August 9, 1950.

1922 SYMPHONY NO. 6 IN E-FLAT MINOR, op. 23. I Poco largamente; Allegro feroce. II. Presto tenebroso. III. Andante appassionato. IV. Finale.

The Sixth Symphony was written in 1922 and received its first performance in Moscow on May 4, 1924, Golovanov conducting. Like all the early symphonies of Miaskovsky, this is highly personal music. The composer himself has provided the following information regarding its origin:

"The first impulse was given to me by the singing of the French revolutionary songs, *Ça ira* and *Carmagnole,* by a French artist, who sang them exactly as they do in the workers' districts of Paris. I made notes of his version, which was different from the printed versions, and I was particularly impressed by the rhythmic energy of *Carmagnole*. When, in 1922, I started my Sixth Symphony, these themes naturally found their place in the music.

The confused state of my world outlook at that time had inevitably resulted in a conception of the Sixth Symphony, which sounds strange to me nowadays, with the motives of a 'victim,' 'the parting of the soul and body,' and a short apotheosis symbolizing 'beatific life' at the end; but the creative ardor I then felt makes this work dear to me even now."

Further information regarding the emotional impulses that led to the writing of this music is found in the published score:

"At the time of its writing, Miaskovsky was deeply impressed by the passing of two persons particularly dear to his heart. . . . Some portions of the symphony are also influenced by *Les Aubes* of Emile Verhaeren, the Belgian poet."

Generally speaking, the symphony is somber in character, brooding in the slow movement and passionate and virile in the fast pages. Even in the last movement, aflame with Miaskovsky's revolutionary ardor, there is a strange feeling of portentous doom as a quotation of the *Dies Irae* appears. In this movement, a chorus, singing a wordless chant, adds to the despair, and the symphony closes as it began, with quiet melancholy.

1929 SINFONIETTA IN B MINOR for string orchestra, op. 32, no. 2. I. Allegro pesante e serioso. II. Andante. III. Presto.

Of Miaskovsky's two sinfoniettas for string orchestra, this is the one heard most frequently. With the Symphony No. 21, it shares the distinction of helping to bring its composer international fame. It was written eighteen years after the first, and was introduced in Moscow in May of 1930. It is pleasingly melodious, yet vitality and strength are not sacrificed. The first movement is robust, the principal melody being heard in unison strings. A gentle touch of melancholy enters the second movement with a melody for solo violin which undergoes four variations. Spirit and vigor return in the last movement. It proceeds at a brisk pace from beginning to end, the richness of the tonal texture enhanced by the use of divided strings.

1932 SYMPHONY NO. 12 IN G MINOR, op. 35. I. Andante. II. Presto agitato. III. Allegro festive o maestoso.

Miaskovsky wrote his Twelfth Symphony to commemorate the fifteenth anniversary of the October Revolution. It received its world première in Moscow on June 1, 1932. The work opens with a broadly flowing melody in clarinet which the English horn continues. After a change of tempo, a new subject is heard in basses and bassoon, soon to be adopted by clarinet and then by the complete orchestra. The main body of the movement enters with a sprightly idea for flute. This and earlier material are developed and altered. The movement ends with a final recall of the introductory first theme, once again in clarinet, but this time unaccompanied.

The trumpet brings on the second movement. The double basses present a subject which becomes the material for a fugato. After some excitement, an important staccato theme is given to the English horn, and carried on in a more flowing style by the oboe. Agitation ensues, and the orchestra erupts into a sonorous outburst. The movement ends as it began, with the voice of the trumpet.

In the finale, a five-measure introduction precedes the statement of the loud, vigorous first theme, in the full orchestra. A contrasting mood is then established with a lyrical, expressive thought for the cellos. A new idea is projected by the double basses when the tempo slows down; but with a return of a quickened pace, a subject from the second movement is recalled by the double basses, to be treated imitatively by other strings. The two main themes of the finale are then reviewed before the trumpets are heard in a new idea, accompanied by plucked strings. This idea is worked up into a powerful climax. A pause precedes the concluding coda in which the vigorous first subject is repeated by the first violins, creating a momentum that carries the symphony to a spirited conclusion.

1938–1940 STRING QUARTET NO. 5 IN E MINOR, op. 47. I. Allegro. II. Scherzo. III. Andante. IV. Finale.

STRING QUARTET NO. 6 IN G MINOR, op. 49. I. Elegy. II. Burlesque. III. Tristesse. IV. Rondo.

It is easy to see why the fifth string quartet (1938) is one of Miaskovsky's most popular works in this medium. It is consistently lyrical, with melodies that are fresh, inventive and often of a Russian identity; and it boasts intensity and passion to stir the emotions. The lyric line remains virtually unbroken in the first movement, which, says Ikkonikov, is written in "bright water-color tones." The second movement opens and closes "with a fantastic 'rustling' effect, with two song episodes in the middle." The third movement has a singularly arresting narrative quality. Says Ikkonikov: "It seems to tell in its principal theme a story of bygone days, rather melancholy and listless. In the middle section . . . the composer effects, as it were, a return to himself with an appassionata theme." The finale "puts us in mind of a romantic symphonized waltz" and makes a powerful impact through its rhythmic vitality.

The music of the fifth quartet, says I. I. Martinov, "contains a great wealth of emotion, and the score is remarkable for its clean lines and for the plasticity of its themes, with their unmistakable tonal relationship to the traditions of Russian folk song."

Martinov finds that the sixth quartet (1940) is "unusual, both in the character of its different movements and in their mutual relationships." He explains: "Thus the first movement (Moderato) is an elegy . . . [with] luminous strains of sadness." The second movement (Allegro giocoso) is a miniature toy march. The culminating point of the whole quartet is reached in the third movement, a rather somber composition of great harmonic complexity. The fourth movement concludes the work in a cheerful and lighthearted mood."

1940 SYMPHONY NO. 21 IN F-SHARP MINOR, op. 51.

This is both the best and the most successful of Miaskovsky's symphonies. It was completed in 1940 on a commission from the Chicago Symphony, and was introduced on November 16 of the same year by the Moscow Philharmonic under Alexander Gauck, under the title of *Symphonie-Fantasie.* It was successful from the first. Gregory Schneerson reported: "There were shouts of *bis*, demands for repetition, a rare case in the symphonic annals." The symphony was selected to inaugurate a ten-day festival of Soviet music; one year later, it received the Stalin Prize, first degree.

This comparatively short work (requiring only fifteen minutes for performance) is in a single movement, pleasurable music from the opening bar to the last. A meditative introduction contains the material of the entire work; the principal idea, out of which the other thematic subjects are evolved, is stated by the clarinet. With varied moods (repeated alternation between fast and slow sections) the symphony gains in power and brilliance until, after a fugal development, it arrives at a "festive and triumphant culmination," as Schneerson described it. In concluding the symphony, the composer returns to the material and mood of the introduction. "It is as though," Schneerson commented, "the composer returns to the initial mood of lyric reflection, which has now acquired a deeply transfigured character."

The American première took place in Chicago on December 26, 1940.

FRANCISCO MIGNONE 1897–

From the rhythms, melodies, instrumental colors and personality of Brazilian folk music (which, in turn, has assimilated Indian, African and Portuguese traits), Mignone has acquired both the inspiration and the materials for many of his compositions, and for some which have brought him his recognition. Interest in the folk music of his native land came to him early, even before his official emergence as a composer; and it has remained a vital influence throughout his creative career. However, other influences have also been discerned in his music: religious and social ones and, in his later works, those of progressive musical tendencies. But it is principally those works with a pronounced national identity that continue to be performed widely and that have placed him with Villa-Lobos as an outstanding musical spokesman of Brazil. Mignone's best music, like the best music of Brazil, is harmonically colorful, strongly rhythmic, sometimes exotic in character, and always imaginatively conceived.

Mignone was born in São Paulo on September 3, 1897. For a while, he combined the study of music at the São Paulo Conservatory with the playing of the piano in a local theatre. In 1918, his official debut as composer took place when he himself introduced a few piano pieces and his father conducted the première of *Suite campestre,* for orchestra. A seven-year grant from São Paulo enabled Mignone to go to Europe in 1920, where he stayed nine years. There he studied, composed, and assimilated musical influences. An opera strongly influenced by Brazilian folk music was written in Europe—*O Contratador dos Diamentes,* introduced in Rio de Janeiro in 1924; this score contains an orchestral interlude that brought Mignone performances throughout the world of music, the *Congada.*

After returning to Brazil, Mignone became one of Brazil's most influential musicians. He helped organize the Rio de Janeiro Conservatory, and in 1941, he played a major part in revamping the musical life of his country. Between 1950 and 1952, he was the director of the Teatro Municipal; in 1958, he was the conductor of the Brazilian Symphony; between 1962 and 1964, he served as musical director of the Radio Station of the Ministry of Education and Culture. For several years, he has been professor at the School of Music at the University of Rio de Janeiro.

In 1946, when his ballet *Iara* was first produced, Mignone was named Brazil's "best composer of the year," and in 1954, he was made honorary citizen of Rio de Janeiro. He received a government prize for his Concerto for Violin and Orchestra, which was introduced in Rio de Janeiro on April 23, 1961. Other significant late works included a piano concerto (world première in Rio de Janeiro on July 10, 1958); the orchestral *Imagens do Rio de Janeiro,* written to commemorate the fourth centennial of Rio de Janeiro and introduced in that city on April 7, 1965; together with three Masses, two piano sonatas and a violin sonata.

Mignone visited the United States in 1942 on an invitation from the American Department of State.

1920 CONGADA, dansa Afrobrasileira, for orchestra.

In 1920, Mignone went to Italy on a government grant to study with Ferroni. Coming in contact with Italian opera in its native setting had its effect on the young composer, who proceeded to write an opera in the traditional Italian manner: *O Contratador dos Diamantes*. The setting was eighteenth-century Brazil; the theme, the exploitation taking place in the Brazilian diamond mines. But it is not the voice of a Brazilian deeply concerned with folk idioms that is heard in this score; rather, it is an apprentice composer imitating a foreign style.

However, there are intermittent passages in which Mignone's nationalism asserts itself; and these are the best pages of the opera. One such section is the Afrobrazilian dance, "*Congada,*" found in the second act. This is vertiginous music, adopting the ingenious rhythms, brilliant colors and exotic character of Brazilian Negro music.

This piece is one of Mignone's most famous works. It was introduced in São Paulo on September 10, 1922, under the composer's direction, and since that time has been extensively performed.

The world première of the opera took place in Rio de Janeiro on September 20, 1924. Its success led the São Paulo Conservatory to name one of its music rooms after Mignone.

1940 FOUR CHURCHES (FESTA DAS IGREJAS), symphonic poem for orchestra.

In this symphonic poem, the composer attempted to evoke in music the feelings and ideas inspired by the festivities of the Catholic Church in Brazil. Though the music is inspired by the Brazilian Church, it is not religious music. The composer took pains to explain that these Brazilian religious fiestas combine the sacred with the profane, blending the religious chant of the church with the superstitious song of the Negro.

The first section brings up the hubbub of a fiesta day, as street noises mingle with the pealing of organ music from within the Church of Saint Francis of Bahia. The plainchant is heard; also the music of choir, organ and church bells. The fiesta comes to an end. Colonial Brazil is now described; the Negro slaves are building a church. Here Negro song mixes with the religious chant. There follows a portrait of the Gloria Church in Rio de Janeiro, in music that is serene and gentle. Then the church bells ring and the organ sounds its majestic voice to honor Our Lady of Brazil. All the people are united by their common devotion to the Church, and to Nossa Senhora Aparecida do Brasil, whose image looks down on them from her corner in the wall.

Four Churches was introduced in the United States on April 22, 1942, with Mignone himself conducting the NBC Symphony over the NBC network.

DARIUS MILHAUD 1892–

Like the old Kapellmeisters of the sixteenth and seventeenth centuries, Darius Milhaud writes music as naturally as he breathes. He is not one of those composers who pours his very lifeblood into every work he produces, to whom the creative process is a life-and-death struggle. Nor is he a composer to work so painstakingly on every bar and note that a year's effort usually results in a single major work. Milhaud writes music all the time, writes it with such extraordinary facility and ease that nothing seems able to stem the tide of his production. He has been crippled and immobilized by arthritis; he has lived through the trials of two world wars, the second of which uprooted him from his native land and sent him to find a new home in a new country; he has traveled frequently and extensively. And yet, despite circumstances which have often stultified the efforts of others, he has kept on writing abundantly.

He has written so many works that to catalogue them would be a futile task, one which—even if accomplished—would forthwith become out of date, in view of the many new compositions that would have been written in the interim. He has written and published well over four hundred compositions, in every possible form of music, and he has utilized many different styles. The remarkable part of it all is that he is not a superficial composer. His music rarely betrays carelessness, haste or glib thinking. What he has written invariably has revealed consummate mastery of technical equipment—that and the enviable capacity to arrive at the most felicitous musical expression with economy. Even when he adopts a popular vein—which he has done on many occasions—he brings to his writing such a personal charm and such a wealth of musical inventiveness and ingenuity that this music rises above popular appeal to achieve artistic dignity.

He was one of the six composers whom Henri Collet gathered into the school now known as "the French Six" (*see* Auric). But Milhaud has never marched under any banner other than that of complete artistic independence. He has always gone his own way. With amazing flexibility, he has employed now one style, now another, bringing to each assignment a completely fresh approach. He has written works in the idioms of South American folk music and American jazz; he has produced Hebrew music; he has written music that is ultramodern in technique (he may be called one of the first successful polytonalists); and he has created everyday and functional music. But through whatever vein he chooses for a given work, he sends the rich flow of lyricism—for lyricism is his hallmark. He has said: "The important thing in a musical work is the vital element—the melody—which should be easily retained, hummed and whistled in the street. Without this fundamental element, all the technique in the world can only be a dead letter." Paul Collaer noted: "In his creative act, the invention of the melody is the crucial, the decisive point, and once the melody is discovered, the composition itself flows spontaneously from his gifted nature." This melodic invention, together with the inexorable logic of his thinking and an engaging feeling of spontaneity, are the traits that give his music the great appeal it enjoys both with connoisseurs and amateurs.

Milhaud was born in Aix-en-Provence, France, on September 4, 1892. After studying music with private teachers and being graduated from the Lycée Mignet, he came to Paris in 1909. There he enrolled in the Paris Conservatory, where his teachers included Gedalge, Dukas, Widor and Vincent d'Indy. While at the Conservatory, he completed a violin sonata in 1911. In 1912, two sets of songs to poems by Francis Jammes became his first published work. In these, he was most strongly influenced by Debussy. His formal musical training ended with World War I. Rejected for military service, he concentrated on composition, producing a sonata for two violins and piano that won the Lepaulle Prize in 1915. He also now began developing the technique of polytonality, one of the idioms with which he has become identified, making it a basic tool in his opera *Les Choëphores* (1915), the second of a trilogy of operas collectively entitled *L'Oresteia,* text by Paul Claudel. This is the work with which he emerged as one of the most powerful and imaginative young French composers of the period. When Claudel became French ambassador to Brazil in 1916, he invited Milhaud to accompany him and serve as an attaché at the Legation. Milhaud stayed in Brazil from early 1917 until the end of 1918, a period in which he came into contact with and was affected by South American folk and popular music, idioms of which he started to incorporate into his own writing. After returning to France in February of 1919, Milhaud became affiliated with a group of five other young French composers into a "school" identified as "The French Six" (*see* Auric). It was in association with these colleagues that many of his works now got heard. In 1922, he toured the United States as pianist, composer and lecturer; in 1925, he married his cousin Madeleine in Paris. Between the two world wars, his reputation as composer swelled until there were few to deny him the position as France's foremost composer when Ravel died.

When World War II broke out, Milhaud came to the United States and joined the faculty at Mills College in Oakland, California. Though seriously crippled by arthritis he was able to make many appearances as guest conductor with major American orchestras in performances of his own music. In 1947, he returned to France and became professor of composition at the Paris Conservatory. Since then, he has divided his year between France and the United States. On his seventieth birthday, a festival of his music was presented at Mills College. He has received honorary degrees from several American universities, was made Commander of the French Legion of Honor, and officer of the Order of the Southern Cross in Brazil.

1915 LES CHOËPHORES (THE LIBATION BEARERS), op. 24. opera in seven sections, with libretto by Paul Claudel based on Aeschylus. First performance: Paris, March 8, 1927 (concert version); Théâtre de la Monnaie, Brussels, March 27, 1935 (staged version).

For twelve years, Milhaud had been occupied with the giant task of writing music for Paul Claudel's *L'Oresteia*, a trilogy based on Aeschylus. The first opera of this trilogy, *Agamemnon,* was completed in 1913 (first performance, Paris, April 16, 1927). The second opera was *Les Choëphores*. The concluding opera, *Les Euménides,* was written between 1917 and 1922 and was introduced in Antwerp on November 27, 1927. The entire trilogy was not produced in its entirety until 1963, when it was featured at a festival in West Berlin.

Les Choëphores is the finest of the three operas, and the first of Milhaud's compositions to indicate the extraordinary range, flexibility and depth of his creative powers. As the work of a young man of twenty-three, it is truly an astonishing achievement—astonishing not only for the maturity of its conception, for the strength of its dramatic interest, and its bountiful lyricism, but also for its effective innovations.

The opera opens with "*Vociferation funèbre,*" a chorus of libation bearers lamenting the murder of Agamemnon. "In the orchestra," explains Collaer in his biography of Milhaud, "beneath the declamation of women, there presently resounds the clamor of men's voices. The orchestra piles up blocks as if to build a cyclopean wall. . . . Lulls in the strophes, recurrences of terror in the antistrophes bring a culminating point of mighty instrumental power."

This is followed by "Libation," a brief section for solo soprano accompanied by a mixed-part chorus. This is music, says Collaer, "of sorrowful tenderness, punctuated by the mystery of the ritual, 'Ious.'" In this section we find an effective use of polytonality when in the a cappella chorus a different key is used for the male and female voices.

The "Incantation," which comes next, is the largest of the seven sections. To Robert Sabin this is "the crux of the dramatic development and the keystone of the musical arch." It opens with a majestic invocation of the Fates by sopranos and ends with the proclamation by Orestes and Elektra, supplemented by the voices of the libation bearers, that vengeance for Agamemnon's murder must be sought. "At the peak," says Collaer, "the music rises to the central point of the drama as by a gigantic stairway of which the theme forms the steps."

In the next two scenes—the "*Présages*" and the "Exhortation"—we find new and novel approaches both as to melody and instrumentation. Here, where the tensions have mounted and become almost excruciating, Milhaud replaces song with what he has described as "measured speech." He had "the words spoken in time with the music by one woman narrator, while the chorus uttered words or disjointed rhythms . . .", as he explained. The choruses are spoken rather than sung and are accompanied by percussion instruments, including such noisemakers as whistles, a board and hammer, a whip, and so forth. "One is never conscious of preciosity or the objectional intrusion of sound effects used merely for sensationalism," says Robert Sabin. "Everything is subordinated to the dramatic flow of the speech and the terrifying animal and nature sounds that give the spoken part a superhuman aura."

A "Hymn to Justice," for choir and orchestra, and a spoken "Conclusion," for voices and percussion, follow. "After the almost hysterical outburst of mass emotion," explains Robert Sabin, "the hymn to Justice and Light has an indescribable effect of majesty. A subtly orchestrated passage of polytonal splendor leads to the wonderful invocation, '*Parais, lumière, te voici!*'. . . . The sonorities lighten and diffuse until the atmosphere actually seems to be flooded with a bright but soft luminosity. After this visionary musical interlude, *Les Choëphores* ends with the terrible question that sets the stage for a final drama of the trilogy, 'Where will the wrath of heaven cease?' "

Les Choëphores received its American première in a concert version. This took place on November 16, 1950, with Dimitri Mitropoulos conducting the New York Philharmonic.

1918 STRING QUARTET NO 4, op. 46. I. Vif. II. Funèbre. III. Très animé.

Milhaud's fourth string quartet is his first to achieve wide circulation. He wrote it while he was still in Rio de Janeiro, and its première took place in Paris in 1919 by the Delgrange Quartet. The composer explains that his first movement is of a "pastoral character. The first idea is exposed in F major, then in A major, with these two tonalities expressed together. . . . After some developments, the second idea is expressed by the viola, sustained by the other instruments. The developments which follow are based on both themes together, in different rhythmic forms, in canon or successively, leading to a quiet end in F."

The second movement is "slow, heavy, somber. At the beginning the harmonies are vague but the rhythm has the preciseness of funeral-march elements. . . . Then the cello takes the rhythmic figure which gives the unity to the piece, and the other instruments have a kind of chorale which will bring a climax fortissimo, immediately followed by a pianissimo. Then comes a fugue-exposition on the new theme in which progressively the rhythmic idea will come again, reaching another climax. . . . As a recapitulation comes the coda, with a rapid review of the beginning and the chords of the chorale, ending on a D minor chord with an F-sharp in the bass."

The finale is "joyful," its first theme presented in violins against a strong rhythm in viola and cello. A gentler subject in two tonalities follows. "A development superimposes two elements of the first theme, leading to a climax with dissonant chords fortissimo, followed by a pianissimo third idea in the first violin, then in the viola."

1918 PROTÉE, symphonic suite no. 2, op. 57. I. Ouverture. II. Prélude et Fugue. III. Pastorale. IV. Nocturne. V. Finale.

In 1913, Milhaud wrote incidental music for Paul Claudel's satiric drama, *Protée;* he scored it for chorus and orchestra. Three years later, he rescored this material for small orchestra for a new production of Claudel's comedy. However, when a presentation was planned for the Théâtre au Vaudeville in Paris in 1919 (but never realized), Milhaud rewrote his music, adding many new sections, and using a large orchestra. The suite, which has been frequently presented at symphony concerts, is derived from this 1919 version; it was first performed in Paris on October 24, 1920. Monteux conducted the American première in Boston on April 22, 1921.

The overture is in a tango-habanera rhythm. This is followed by a very fast prelude, and a fugue for brasses supported by the orchestra. The pastorale uses the rhythm of 3-3-2, and the Nocturne is in 5/8 time. The finale has been described by the composer as "of a strong and bright character."

Claudel's satire concerns the pathetic and futile love of Proteus (an aged prophet inhabiting an island in the Aegean Sea) for a young girl.

1919 LE BOEUF SUR LE TOIT (THE NOTHING-DOING BAR), op. 58, pantomime or farce with music in one act, with text by Jean Cocteau. First performance: Paris, February 21, 1920.

There is a famous bar in Paris called Le Boeuf sur le Toit. It is sometimes believed that Milhaud's pantomime was named after the bar; actually, the reverse is true.

It is also interesting to point out that the text (or synopsis) was written *after* Milhaud had composed his music. Jean Cocteau heard a two-piano version of a score which Milhaud had written with the possibility of having it accompany a Charlie Chaplin movie. Cocteau was so taken with its stage possibilities that he offered to adapt a fantastic pantomime to it. The pantomime was introduced with the clown Fratellini in the principal role; Vladimir Golschmann conducted.

Though the setting for Milhaud's ballet is an American speakeasy, and the characters (all of whom are required to wear masks three times the normal size) are all drawn from American life, the music is derived from Brazilian music—tangos, maxixes, sambas, and one or two popular tunes.

The Nothing-Doing Bar, noisy and crowded, is filled with a strange assortment of people: a huge Negro boxer who puffs at an enormous cigar; a Negro dwarf; a flashy bookie; a woman with paper hair; and another with a dashing red evening gown. During a crap game, the fashionable lady slings the dwarf over her shoulder and takes him to the nearby billiard room. The boxer makes a play for the other woman, but is knocked out by the bookie. After the bookie goes through a tango, the sound of a police whistle is heard. Since this is the era of prohibition, everyone in the bar is upset. But the bartender calmly removes the liquor from view and hangs a sign reading: "Only Milk Served Here." The policeman enters, sniffs around, tastes the milk, and proceeds to do a dance. As he is dancing, a huge revolving fan falls on his head and decapitates him. If the patrons are upset by these events, they do not betray it. The dwarf sings a romance; the bartender presents the head of the policeman to the fashionable lady, who dances around it. The principal characters then make their exit, including the Negro boxer, who has since been restored to consciousness. When the dwarf refuses to pay his bill, the bartender replaces the head on the body of the policeman. Revived, the policeman is given the dwarf's bill—two feet long.

1921 SAUDADES DO BRASIL, suite for orchestra, op. 67. I. Sorocabo. II. Botofogo. III. Leme. IV. Copacabana. V. Ipanema. VI. Gavea. VII. Corcovado. VIII. Tijuca. IX. Sumaré. X. Paineras. XI. Laranjeiras. XII. Paysandú.

A "saudade" can be translated as a "nostalgic recollection." In these twelve saudades, the composer brings to mind memories of Brazil, where he lived for two years during World War I. The rhythms of Brazilian dances—principally that of the tango—are evoked. Actual Brazilian dances, however, are not reproduced, but merely suggested: Milhaud regarded these saudades as a kind of composite and idealized portrait of Brazilian dances. The twelve movements derive their names from different districts of Rio de Janeiro.

The *Saudades* were first introduced in Paris in 1921, Vladimir Golschmann conducting. At this performance, the dancer Loie Fuller interpreted the music.

1922 STRING QUARTET NO. 6, op. 77. I. Souple et animé. II. Très lent. III. Très vif et rhythmé.

Milhaud's Sixth Quartet, dedicated to Francis Poulenc, is one of his tersest and most compact works in this form. The first movement opens with a theme for viola (against a cello accompaniment) which progresses to the second theme, introduced by the cello. The development treats both themes succinctly. The recapitulation that follows is virtually a duplication of the opening exposition. The second movement grows out of a long-flowing melody, gentle in mood. A pastoral theme (violin and viola) opens the closing movement. This theme is followed by an extended quiet section. The music becomes more animated and complex in the development of these ideas. After a brief return to the opening theme, the quartet ends in a burst of sonority.

The quartet was introduced in Brussels by the Pro Arte Quartet in 1923.

1923. LA CRÉATION DU MONDE (THE CREATION OF THE WORLD), ballet in one act, op. 81a, with scenario by Blaise Cendrars and choreography by Jean Borlin. First performance: Paris, October 25, 1923.

During this visit to the United States in 1922, Milhaud visited the Harlem section of New York City and spent many hours listening with fascination to the jazz music of Negro bands. This was not his first association with American jazz. He had been fascinated by it in London in 1920, when he heard Billy

Arnold and his band at a dance hall. But in Harlem, he heard authentic New Orleans jazz played in an authentic manner for the first time and, as he confessed, it "was a revelation to me."

When he was asked to write music for an African-Negro ballet, *La Création du monde,* he decided to use the jazz idiom. He scored the music for eighteen solo instruments (including the saxophone). His style was that of jazz: the opening theme was a plangent blues melody set against an intriguing accompaniment that combined major and minor keys; there was a fugue based on a jazz motive; there was syncopation and ragtime. So admirably did Milhaud re-create the jazz style that Paul Rosenfeld called this work "the most perfect of all pieces of symphonic jazz," while Aaron Copland remarked that symphonic jazz had here succeeded in producing "at least one authentic small masterpiece." Equally important is it to remember that *La Création du monde* was one of the first large works in this genre, antedating Gershwin's *Rhapsody in Blue* by a year.

The story of the ballet concerns the creation of the world—but as seen through the eyes of an aborigine. The action takes place in semidarkness. Some of the dancers, portraying herons, appear on stilts; others, representing animals, clamber about on all fours.

An orchestral suite from the ballet score is better known than the ballet itself, having been performed frequently in this country and abroad. The suite comprises the following sections:

Overture.

I. The chaos before Creation. Giant deities of Creation hold council.

II. The confused mass begins to move. Suddenly a tree appears, and then various animals.

III. The animals join in a dance during which two bodies emerge limb by limb from the central mass.

IV. While the pair performs the dance of desire, the remaining mass dissolves into human beings, who join in a frenetic round to the point of vertigo.

V. The crowd disappears in little groups, leaving the Negro Adam and Eve embraced in a lasting kiss. It is springtime.

The entire work is played without interruption. The overture (Modéré) is atmospheric, with a haunting melody for saxophone accompanied by piano and strings; a jazz feeling is introduced through syncopated figures in trumpets, slides on the trombones, and flatted thirds in the harmonies. In the first part, the subject of a jazz fugue is presented by the double bass, with the trombone, saxophone, trumpet entering in turns. Full orchestra builds the motive into a powerful climax. A sudden quiet, and descending thirds in flutes and clarinets, lead to the next movement, in which the flute repeats the haunting melody of the overture, while the cello remembers the jazz-fugue subject, in augmentation. After that, we hear a blues in the oboe. The third movement has a saucy tune in violins, which is built up to an effective climactic point, then allowed to subside. In the fourth part, a dance melody is given by the clarinet against a syncopated accompaniment. Once again, the haunting melody of the overture is recalled, this time in oboe, after which another strong climax emerges. The finale has the oboe repeat the blues melody before it is quoted by the other instruments. A last recall of the opening haunting tune precedes a blues cadence, with which the suite ends.

1926 LE PAUVRE MATELOT (THE POOR SAILOR), opera described in the score as "lamentations" in three acts, op. 92, with text by Jean Cocteau. First performance: Opéra-Comique, Paris, December 12, 1927.

Jean Cocteau's somber text was inspired by a story item he had read in a newspaper at Le Piquey, where he was then spending his holiday. In making his poetic dramatization of this true-to-life episode, Cocteau stuck to the basic facts. In a twentieth-century French port, a sailor's wife has been waiting faithfully for fifteen years for her husband to return. She refuses to listen to her father's advice that she forget him and remarry, insisting that he will some day return. The husband does return—but in order to test his wife's fidelity he poses as a wealthy friend of the "husband." As such, he tells the wife that the "husband" is sick and impoverished. At the same time, he boasts how rich he is. He asks to spend the night, and the wife agrees. While he is asleep, the wife kills him with a hammer, hoping to rob him of his money which she can then use to save her husband. The curtain descends before she realizes that she has killed her own husband—for she sings ecstatically about his imminent return home.

In his review, Henri Prunières wrote: "Darius Milhaud has set this old tale to music of very melodic style which constantly calls to mind ancient sea songs and folklore. . . . The vocal parts are always grateful and melodious, with no recitatives. The polyphonic writing, at times very light, and again of extreme richness, accompanies the voices in a compact symphonic commentary. The orchestration is occasionally too heavy, covering the voices—the outstanding fault of a score which is rich in musical material and is truly interesting in its novelty."

Though *Le Pauvre matelot* became Milhaud's first successful opera, it had an unhappy beginning. It was a dismal failure at its première. One reason for this was that it was paired with *Tosca,* an unhappy marriage it seemed to that first-night audience. For another, it was poorly performed. But a presentation the same year at the Théâtre de la Monnaie in Brussels (where it was paired with Honegger's *Antigone*) went much better, and was acclaimed. Before long, *Le Pauvre matelot* became Milhaud's most widely played opera, getting heard in Berlin and about twenty other German cities, in Vienna, Salzburg, Prague, Barcelona and New York. The American première was given in Philadelphia on April 1, 1937, in a joint bill which offered the world première of Menotti's first opera, *Amelia Goes to the Ball.*

1928 CHRISTOPHE COLOMB, opera in two parts (twenty-seven scenes), op. 102, with text by Paul Claudel. First performance: Berlin State Opera, May 5, 1930 (in German).

Before *Christophe Colomb,* Milhaud had written a number of chamber operas including *Le Pauvre matelot,* discussed above. *Christophe Colomb* was his first in a grand design; and there are many musicologists who regard this as one of Milhaud's masterworks. It is the first of a trilogy of grand operas on American subjects. The second was *Maximilien,* op. 110, produced in Paris on January 3, 1932. The third, *Bolivar,* op. 236, created a scandal when given its world première in Paris on May 12, 1950.

Some of the novel techniques and procedures which Milhaud had used so successfully in *Les Choëphores* return in *Christophe Colomb*, including rhythmical speech, percussion accompaniment to a spoken narrative, and polytonal choral writing. Several new ones also appear: choral singing on a single vowel; staging the action on three different stage levels; and combining drama and music with pantomime, ballet, and even motion pictures.

In telling the Columbus story, Claudel uses symbolism and allegory with ample religious, philosophic and mystic touches. "Instead of merely recounting the discovery of America," explains Abraham Skulsky, "he chose to consider and interpret the ideas, questions, and emotions that four centuries of history have raised concerning Columbus's actions." Columbus's story is told by a narrator who reads to a chorus from a large book. The chorus represents the people who comment on what has happened, criticize, accuse, praise, and ask questions. "Each time the narrator arrives at a certain episode his words fade and the action is re-created before the chorus of people and before Columbus himself who, after the sixth scene, is seated in the chorus."

There are two parts. The first has nineteen scenes, the second, eight. In front of the stage, we find the narrator and chorus. In center, the dramatic action transpires. The rear consists of a screen on which motion pictures are flashed either to supplement the stage action or to contribute symbolic illustrations.

Abraham Skulsky has found in Milhaud's score all the outstanding traits of his style up to this point. "His natural gift of lyric inspiration, the refinement of his polytonal harmonic language, his greatness of conception in monumental scenes, and even his occasional quest for folkloristic elements are to be found in this work." Since the opera is made up of a succession of situations—rather than an integrated story unfolding logically and in sequence—and since each situation is self-sufficient, Milhaud had to contrive suitable music which was not dependent on what had gone before or what would come later. "Milhaud's strength lies exactly in this gift for continuous invention."

The first performance of *Christophe Colomb* in the United States took place on November 6, 1952, when the New York Philharmonic presented a concert version directed by Dimitri Mitropoulos.

1934 CONCERTO NO. 1 FOR VIOLONCELLO AND ORCHESTRA, op. 136. I. Nonchalant. II. Grave. III. Joyeux.

Milhaud wrote his First Cello Concerto for the French virtuoso, Maurice Marechal, who introduced it in Paris on June 28, 1935. The first movement opens with a cadenza-like introduction for solo cello that provides a contrast to the music that follows. The orchestra assumes the theme quietly, to plucked string accompaniment; the cello joins in. Then the momentum grows, but soon the cello is left to return unaccompanied. The interplay between solo instrument and orchestra continues for the rest of the movement, which sustains a placid atmosphere for the most part. The slow movement is played quietly, opening with somber sonorities in muted brass, drums and string tremolos, and dominated by a meditative, even gloomy, song for the solo instrument. The third movement is in a lively dance style, with the cello playing a prominent part in joyous escapades.

1936 SUITE PROVENÇALE, for orchestra, op. 152. I. Animé. II. Très modéré; Vif. III. Modéré. IV. Vif. V. Modéré. VI. Vif. VII. Lent. VIII. Vif.

In this infectious and simply written suite of eight dances, Milhaud has gathered a few of the eighteenth-century folk tunes of his native Provence (most of then by Campra) and dressed them with a pleasing orchestral raiment, adding an occasional piquant color of polytonal writing. The suite was first heard in Venice on September 12, 1937, the composer conducting. In 1938, it was used as background music for a ballet produced at the Opéra-Comique in Paris.

The first movement of the suite opens with a folk-like melody, a polytonal effect being realized by having the melody in the key of A major over a pedal bass in D. The second movement opens with a brisk march tune over a steady dance rhythm, its pace and momentum increasing to a lively "Vif." A vivacious tune maintains this vigor in the fourth movement (which is the shortest of this set), though some effective slow measures are interpolated before the end. Trumpets present the main folk tune in the fifth part, after which the entire orchestra takes command. A contrasting tune contributes a religious mood as variety. The sixth part offers a staccato melody whose sharply accented rhythm has ironic overtones, while the seventh is a slow episode with a poignant thought for English horn, trombones and horns. The finale, the longest of the movements, presents the full orchestra with stunning coloristic and polytonal effects, and with intriguing syncopations in the woodwinds. The original theme is given a stately final hearing, after which the suite ends abruptly.

1937 SCARAMOUCHE, suite for two solo pianos, op. 165b. I. Vif. II. Modéré. III. Brasileira.

Scaramouche has become a favorite with two-piano teams. Milhaud wrote it for Ida Jankelevitch and Marcelle Meyer, but was so doubtful about its success that he advised the publisher not to issue it since it could not possibly have any popular appeal. The publisher went ahead with the release in spite of the composer's warning, and was rewarded with a substantial hit as orders began to pour in from the United States and elsewhere. The suite was first introduced at the World's Exposition in Paris in 1937. Milhaud later adapted it for saxophone (or clarinet) and orchestra.

The first movement is characterized by its rhythmic vitality and motor energy. A tender song, in A-B-A structure, comprises the middle movement. The finale is the most popular of the three movements and is often heard as an encore independently of the rest of the suite. It is an exciting samba whose jaunty, gay melody is set against a pulsating, infectious rhythm.

1939 SYMPHONY NO. 1, op. 210. I. Modérément. II. Très vif. III. Très modéré. IV. Animé.

Milhaud completed his First Symphony during the first weeks of World War II, while he was still in France. It was completed in Aix-en-Provence and introduced by the Chicago Symphony on October 17, 1940.

If the cataclysmic events of the times had any effect on the composer, they reveal no traces in this music, which is, for the most part, serene and poetic. The composer has described the first movement as "very melodic, and quiet, with a great feeling for nature." The first principal theme is stated by the flutes and first violins; the second, by the woodwinds. The second movement, comprising three subjects, is "rather dramatic and robust, with a fugue in the middle." Tranquillity returns in the third part, which "begins with a theme like a chorale, the character of the movement being deeply tender; the chorale theme alternates with a melody very expressive and clear." The symphony ends as it began, in a placid mood, though touched now with slightly more joyous feelings. It is built out of three principal themes (the first for woodwinds, harp and plucked strings; the second for strings and woodwinds; the third for woodwinds, horns and trumpets).

1941 CONCERTO NO. 2 FOR PIANO AND ORCHESTRA, op. 225. I. Animé. II. Romance. III. Bien modérément animé.

The Second Piano Concerto came five years after the first. It was heard for the first time in Chicago, on December 18, 1941, with Milhaud as soloist and Hans Lange conducting the Chicago Symphony.

The concerto opens with a nervous, rhythmic theme that is used extensively throughout the movement. An extended section for orchestra follows in which a new idea is unfolded against a background utilizing the rhythmic pattern of the first subject. Another rhythmic passage is introduced and given considerable importance before the original material is repeated.

Twelve measures of piano solo introduce the second movement, following which the orchestra enters with the same theme, but stated canonically. Variations of the theme are at the same time heard in the piano. The orchestra then enters with the second theme, after which the piano injects a new idea. The two main themes are used in conjunction just before the coda.

Three ideas are utilized in the closing movement: a dialogue between piano and orchestra; a second theme set against a rhumba rhythm; and a third subject which comes in the orchestra in canonic form. The three ideas are heard independently, then mingled one with another. The concerto ends brilliantly.

1944 SYMPHONY NO. 2, op. 247. I. Paisible. II. Mystérieux. III. Douloureux. IV. Avec sérénité. V. Alléluia.

Milhaud wrote his Second Symphony in the United States on a commission from the Koussevitzky Music Foundation. He himself conducted the première performance in Boston with the Boston Symphony Orchestra on December 20, 1946.

Throughout the five movements, the composer maintains an atmosphere of serenity which at times develops into mystery and melancholy. Only occasionally does an eruption of dynamic power take place, and only to give greater emphasis to the expressive sadness and tranquillity of the music that precedes and follows it.

The composer described the first movement as "quiet and peaceful." It has an idyllic principal theme in flute, and a more virile secondary subject in the trumpet. In the second movement, another haunting subject is prominent, this time in the oboe. "This movement," says John N. Burk in his program notes for the Boston Symphony, "hovers for the most part in the high range of the orchestra, probing the harmonics of the violin and the trilled notes from the flutes or muted trumpets." Of the third movement, the composer said that "it is very expressive and of a sad and dramatic mood." Its prime material consists of a melancholy melody for English horn. Before the movement ends, one of the few tonal outbursts in the symphony occurs. But the placidity of earlier movements comes back in the fourth movement, which emphasizes the sylvan voice of the flute, and ends with an extended saxophone solo. The finale is a fugue, its subject stated at once by the full orchestra.

1944 SUITE FRANÇAISE, for orchestra (also for band), op. 248. I. Normandie. II. Bretagne. III. Isle de France. IV. Alsace-Lorraine. V. Provence.

LE BAL MARTINIQUAIS, for orchestra, op. 249. I. Chanson Creole. II. Biguine.

Folk music provided Milhaud with his materials for both the *Suite française* and *Le Bal Martiniquais*—materials which he utilized with the utmost creative freedom. The composer wrote in explanation: "The five parts of this suite (*Suite française*) are named after the French Provinces, the very ones in which the Americans and Allied armies fought together with the French underground for the liberation of my country." The composer adds further that his purpose in writing this work was to have young Americans "hear the popular melodies of those parts of France where their fathers and brothers fought to defend the country from the German invaders."

This suite was written both for band and for symphony orchestra. In the former version, it was introduced by the Goldman Band under Edwin Franko Goldman in New York on June 13, 1945. As a work for orchestra, it was heard for the first time on July 29, 1945, at a concert at the Lewisohn Stadium in New York, Maurice Abravanel conducting.

Le Bal Martiniquais is based on folk tunes of the French West Indies, which came to Milhaud's attention when the French West Indies was liberated in 1943. This material led him to write *La Libération des Antilles,* two Creole songs for voice and piano (op. 246), as well as *Le Bal Martiniquais*. The latter originated as a work for two pianos, but as the composer has said, "I thought these two pieces could be orchestrated. As a matter of fact, following the *Suite française,* which is based on French folk tunes, it makes a normal suite to end my little fantasy on folk tunes of the French Empire." *Le Bal Martiniquais* was given its world première in New York on December 6, 1945, with the composer conducting the New York Philharmonic.

1945 CONCERTO NO. 2 FOR CELLO AND ORCHESTRA, op. 255. I. Gai. II. Tendre. III. Alerte.

The Second Cello Concerto followed its predecessor by eleven years. It was commissioned by the cello virtuoso Edmund Kurtz, who introduced it with the New York Philharmonic Orchestra under Artur Rodzinski on November 28, 1946.

In the first movement, a music-hall theme plays a prominent part. It is heard in the nine-bar introduction, and is repeated by the solo cello in its first entrance. Immediately after the first theme has been unfolded, a second theme enters, as gay as the first. In the development, the playful atmosphere created by the two delightful themes is maintained. The second movement is very lyrical and very expressive: the main melody is introduced by the cello. The second theme of the movement is first heard in the orchestra and then repeated by the cello. The two themes are integrated into one in the closing page of this movement. The sprightly closing movement opens with a six-bar statement by the solo cello, after which the vigorous first theme is heard. The music then develops into fleeting passages, with effective virtuoso writing for the solo instrument, before coming to a decisive climax.

1946 SYMPHONY NO. 3 ("Hymnus Ambrosianus"), for chorus and orchestra, op. 271. I. Fièrement. II. Très recueilli. III. Pastorale. IV. Te Deum.

Soon after the liberation of France, the French government commissioned Milhaud to write a *Te Deum* to commemorate the event. The composer decided to extend the idea to symphonic proportions. He arrived at the following procedure: the first and third movements were for orchestra alone; the second, for orchestra and chorus, but without any text; the fourth, for chorus and orchestra, setting the complete text of the *Te Deum*.

The music, owing as it does its origin to the liberation of France from the Nazi invaders, is a work of great emotional force. The varied feelings of the composer, inspired by this momentous event, are reflected throughout the work. The first movement is stately, as if to suggest the indomitable spirit of France, unbowed after several years of oppression and degradation. A more introspective mood is caught in the second movement, music of quiet reflection ("*très recueilli*" meaning "wrapped in meditation"). The third movement was intended by the composer as a "return to the earth, to grass roots." Exultantly, the symphony erupts in music of religious ardor and consecration in the closing movement.

This symphony was first heard at a Milhaud festival in Paris on October 30, 1947.

1947 SYMPHONY NO. 4: 1848, op. 281. I. Insurrection. II. To the Dead of the Republic. III. The Peaceful Joys of Liberty Regained. IV. Commemoration, 1948.

Milhaud wrote his Fourth Symphony on a commission from the French government as part of the centenary celebration of the 1848 revolution against Louis Philippe, "the citizen king," which set up the Second Republic. The symphony was written during a forty-day ocean trip from San Francisco to Le Havre aboard a freighter during the summer of 1947. On May 20, 1948, the composer conducted the première performance over the France Radio.

Henri Mahlerbe, the eminent French critic, provided the following definitive analysis of the symphony for the French première performance:

"In the first movement (Animé), composed of fragments of song of popular aspect, interlaced, entangled, embroiled and penetrated with seditious cries, the composer portrays for us the joyful exaltation of the armed mob, as first scattered, then gradually united to struggle and triumph in an explosion of joy. The second movement (Lent) is simply a long lamentation, of a sad and intimate intensity, constantly sustained. Its pathetic effect is the more profound in that the composer marshals his potent forces with moderation and tellingly employs but a very few instruments. The third movement (Modérément animé) shows us, between bucolic episodes, the noble and tender emotion that prevailed in every heart at the triumph of liberty. Finally, in the last movement (Animé), the popular and heroic themes of the beginning are resolutely recapitulated and, with impressive mastery, varied, transformed, enriched, expanded, and, as it were, projected towards the future."

1948–1949 STRING QUARTET NO. 14, op. 291. I. Animé. II. Modéré. III. Vif.

STRING QUARTET NO. 15, op. 291. I. Animé. II. Modéré. III. Vif.

Milhaud devised the original scheme of writing two string quartets, each of which has an independent identity and is self-sufficient as an artistic product, which can also be played simultaneously as an octet for strings. The two quartets were played separately and together at the same concert by the Paganini Quartet at Mills College in Oakland, California, on August 10, 1949.

The two quartets were planned to contrast each other. The opening movement of the Fourteenth is lively and highly accented, while that of the Fifteenth has sustained lyricism; the middle movement of the Fourteenth seems like an accompaniment to that of the Fifteenth, which is a delicate melody of sensitive beauty; against the bright syncopation of the closing movement of the Fifteenth is the robust and animated vigor of the Fourteenth.

1954 DAVID, Biblical opera in five acts, op. 320, with text by Armand Lunel. First performances: Jerusalem, June 2, 1954 (concert version); La Scala, Milan, January 2, 1955 (staged version).

A visit paid to Israel by Serge Koussevitzky was the origin of Milhaud's Biblical opera. Dr. Koussevitzky was so impressed by the land, the people and its Biblical past that he conceived an idea for a pageant to link Israel's past with the present. After returning to the United States, he commissioned Milhaud to write an opera on the life and times of David, founder of Jerusalem, to help commemorate in 1954 the three-thousandth anniversary of that city as the capital of Judea.

When Milhaud's opera received its world première in Jerusalem, it was given in oratorio form, without costumes or scenery. The staged version took place at La Scala about half a year later. When first heard in the United States, this opera once again was given in concert form—at the Hollywood Bowl in California on September 22, 1956.

Lunel's text traces the story of David from the time the prophet Samuel calls at his father's house, to the anointment of the boy Solomon as the new king of Israel. "It is told," Peter Gradenwitz reported from Israel, "in simple but poetic words and in the form of scenes showing the episodes from the life of David the shepherd, the poet and musician, the soldier, the king, and the statesman."

To give cohesion to these varied scenes, a chorus named "Israelites of the Year of 1954" is seated outside the stage, dressed in twentieth-century clothing, to provide commentary and, from time to time, to draw a parallel between episodes in David's life and historic incidents in modern Israel. The felling of Goliath with a stone is compared to the successful struggle of young Israel against enemies of far superior power and resources; and when the Biblical youth returns from the vineyards with song and dance, they are heard chanting and dancing to a modern-day Israeli hora.

"Milhaud has here determined on the grandiose," writes Cynthia Jolly in *The New York Times*. In spite of his Biblical subject, Milhaud remained "within the realm of neo-classicism and polytonality without any concessions to Hebrew psalmody, oriental melos or instrumentally suggested local color," she adds. The opera emerges as powerful drama with considerable musical interest "full of deeply lyrical passage and dramatic action," says Walter Arlen, "in which the composer's sure and experienced hand evokes an atmosphere of uncanny realism without indulging in crass tone painting."

1955 SYMPHONY NO. 6. I. Calme et tendre. II. Tumultueux. III. Lent et doux. IV. Joyeux et robuste.

Milhaud was commissioned to write this symphony by the Koussevitzky Music Foundation for the 75th anniversary of the Boston Symphony. That orchestra, under Charles Munch, introduced it in Boston on October 7, 1955. The first movement, in 6/4 time, has two ingratiating lyric ideas. The first appears immediately in the strings, while the second is heard in a fuller orchestra. A lively movement follows, mainly in full orchestra, but it ends in a subdued vein to prepare the emotional climate for the third movement. That movement is a highly lyrical section in traditional three-part song form; its middle section is dominated by a chromatic subject in 3/4 time. Vigor returns in the finale with a stout, joyous theme for full orchestra in 12/8 time and continues in this energetic fashion until the conclusion of the symphony.

1960 SYMPHONY NO. 10. I. Decidé. II. Expressif. III. Fantasque. IV. Emporté.

In 1959, Milhaud was commissioned by the Oregon State Centennial Commission to write a symphony. He completed it early in 1960, and its world première was given by the Portland Symphony, Piero Bellugi conducting, on April 4, 1961. The opening movement, in the key of E-flat, opens with a motto theme that dominates it and which also brings it to its conclusion. The second movement in A-flat begins with a haunting solo for piccolo over muted strings, harp and tam-tam. An energetic rhythmic section comes midway, then the piccolo returns with its song. The third movement, in C minor, is a sensitive scherzo; while the finale, which returns to the opening movement key of E-flat, is a vigorous outburst of sound and a robust release of energy. In the middle of the movement, strings, trumpet and trombone are heard in a theme intended to spell out the word "Oregon." "The theme is arrived at by the ingenious process of laying out the alphabet like a scale, one letter to each note starting on the middle 'C' and proceeding upwards," explains Edward Downes in his program notes for the New York Philharmonic. "The result of spelling out 'Oregon' is a sort of disheveled fanfare, a hectic, bouncing theme, startling and emphatic enough to be easily recognized."

1962–1963 OUVERTURE PHILHARMONIQUE, for orchestra.
MURDER OF A GREAT CHIEF OF STATE, for orchestra.

The *Philharmonic Overture* (1962) is one of several works which the New York Philharmonic commissioned from distinguished composers to help celebrate its opening season at the Lincoln Center for the Performing Arts. Its world première took place there in December of 1962, with Sir John Barbirolli conducting the New York Philharmonic. It is in a three-part structure, with a slow section flanked by fast ones. Integration is achieved by having the work's vigorous opening two-measure subject repeated several times at the end.

One day after the assassination of President Kennedy in Dallas, Milhaud was commissioned by the Oakland Symphony for a memorial piece. Deeply moved by the tragedy, Milhaud lost no time in putting his feelings down on paper. He completed the score of *Murder of a Great Chief of State* one day after that, and it took him only one more day to score it. The world première took place on December 3, 1963, less than two weeks after the commission had been given, the Oakland Symphony being conducted by Bernard Samuel. Milhaud's music is more dramatic than elegiac. It is a short piece of music that takes only three and a half minutes for performance. It is described by Richard D. Freed as music that is "by turns stark and lyrical, a manly and profound lament, free of histrionics and eminently worthy of its subject."

ITALO MONTEMEZZI 1875–1952

In the half-dozen or so operas that Montemezzi contributed to the modern Italian lyric theatre, he demonstrated that he completely absorbed, and was satisfied with, the accepted traditions of Italian opera. Like the great Italians who preceded him, his principal concern was for lyricism, an abundant stream of which courses through his best operas. His secondary interests were emotion, dramatic action, atmosphere. He was, on the other hand, unsympathetic to realism or to the opening up of new vistas for the operatic form.

A certain enrichment to Italian operatic writing comes in Montemezzi's works through his interpolation of Debussy's sensitive atmospheric etchings, and through the Wagnerian enlargement of symphonic scope found in his orchestrations. But, for the most part, Montemezzi was quite content to walk in the footsteps of the mighty Verdi; and it is greatly to his credit that he was able to do this gracefully.

Montemezzi was born in Vigasio, Italy, on August 4, 1875. He was originally intended for a career in engineering. But in Milan, where he went to complete his technical studies, he entered the Conservatory and made rapid progress with Saladino and Ferroni. On January 28, 1905, his first opera, *Giovanni Gallurese,* was produced in Turin and proved an outstanding success. (Its American première took place at the Metropolitan Opera in New York on February 19, 1925.) His second opera, *Hellera,* was a failure when presented in Turin on March 17, 1909. But with his third opera, *L'Amore dei Tre Re,* Montemezzi achieved international fame and immortality. In 1920, Montemezzi married an American woman, Katherine Leith, and in 1939, they settled for a decade in Beverly Hills, California. There Montemezzi completed his last opera, *L'Incantesimo,* a one-act radio opera transmitted over the NBC network on October 9, 1943, the composer conducting. But this and his other earlier operas failed to repeat either the triumph or the high artistic standard of *L'Amore dei Tre Re.* In 1949, Montemezzi returned to Italy, and on May 15, 1952, he died in his native city of Vigasio.

1913 L'AMORE DEI TRE RE (THE LOVE OF THREE KINGS), opera in three acts, with text by Sem Benelli based on his tragedy of the same name. First performance: La Scala, Milan, April 10, 1913.

L'Amore dei Tre Re is the acknowledged masterpiece among Montemezzi's operas, the rest of which are now in total discard. It has deservedly been called one of the finest products of the Italian lyric theatre in the twentieth century. To Olin Downes, it was "the most poetical and aristocratic of modern operas." Some critics go even further and call it the finest opera since Verdi (with a sublime disregard of Puccini).

The text by Benelli—excellent theatre throughout, and sometimes filled with rare poetic imagination—is a powerful stimulant for a composer. Montemezzi confessed that he was "gripped by the beauty of this Benellian tragedy," and that he knew at once that he had "embarked on a work of great importance." He added further: "The tragedy responded absolutely to my conception, which was to construct an art work, different from anything done before—a real Italian music drama, with dynamism, drama, poetry—all of it bathed in an atmosphere of musical rapture."

When Montemezzi first contacted Sem Benelli it was to acquire the operatic rights for *The Jest.* But Benelli had just sold those rights for a paltry hundred dollars; in place of *The Jest,* the dramatist offered to write a new tragedy expressly for the composer. He outlined his idea to Montemezzi, who was so taken with it that then and there he took Benelli to his publisher, Ricordi, who signed both dramatist and composer to a contract.

It took Montemezzi more than two years to write his score. The opera was heard for the first time at La Scala in Milan, Tullio Serafin conducting. It was outstandingly successful. Nine months after that, on January 2, 1914, it was performed at the Metropolitan Opera House under Arturo Toscanini. After that, it entered the repertory of virtually every major opera house.

Montemezzi brought to his score not only his fully developed and original lyricism (at times, as in the last act, achieving incandescent beauty), but also a sense for dramatic effect (which in the climactic scenes of both the second and third acts has shattering force) and a keen sense for characterization. The portrait of the blind King Archibaldo is touched with pity and grandeur, compassion and terror—surely one of the great characterizations in all operatic literature.

Archibaldo's son, Manfredo, is married to the princess Fiora, who, in turn, is in love with Avito. When Fiora confesses that she loves someone else and not Manfredo, Archibaldo strangles her. Then, in an attempt to punish her guilty lover, he puts poison on her dead lips. Avito comes upon the dead Fiora, kisses her lips passionately, and dies. But Manfredo also sees the dead body of his wife. He, too, kisses her—and dies. Archibaldo momentarily succumbs to a feeling of triumph when, coming on the scene, he feels he has trapped the dead man. But when he recognizes his son Manfredo and sees him dead, his grief becomes overpowering.

Here is how Olin Downes described the opera in one of his reviews for *The New York Times:* "It has no sob arias for the tenor, or choral hits, or fat passages for the persecuted soprano, or villainous baritone. There are all kinds of male voices in it, but they are not there for vocal display. There are no set pieces, nor a single bid for the approval of the house. Here is a tone poem for voices and orchestra made from the patrician verse and the symbolic conception of Sem Benelli and a wholly exceptional creation it is."

Mr. Downes then added: "It is symphonic, owing something to the *Tristan* technique, but nothing to the Wagnerian style. For this lyricism is Italian in the highest sense of the world. The form is that of the continuous melody and not the set song. The symphonic orchestra carries the voices on its crest, but never usurps their proper office. . . . He never descends beneath the loftiest level. He never forsakes his ancestral heritage of beauty."

DOUGLAS MOORE 1893–1969

It is not easy to classify Douglas Moore. He has often used modern techniques but by no stretch of the imagination is he an ultramodern composer. He has frequently turned for stimulus and materials to American scenes and backgrounds, yet he cannot accurately be identified as a nationalist composer. He has used popular styles and tunes, yet he is hardly a popularist. On occasion, he is not at all reluctant to give free rein to his emotions, yet it would be difficult to regard him as a Romanticist.

The truth is that Moore belongs in the more conservative camp of American composers who like to work in clearly defined, established structures, to write singable melodies and dress them up in conventional harmonies. In his operas, his most successful medium, he works with set numbers, good tunes, and effective ensemble pieces. He is particularly adept here in projecting American backgrounds and characters. He once said: "The particular ideal which I have been striving to attain is to write music which will not be self-conscious with regard to idiom, and will reflect the exciting quality of the life, traditions, and country which I feel all about me." His technique, as Wilfred Mellers pointed out, is "basically nineteenth-century and Teutonic," and he has no hesitancy in using a "nineteenth-century European idiom to deal... with American subjects..... Puritan hymnody, hillbilly songs, military music, primitive ragtime are embraced with the 'regressive' style: so the pieces tend to sound like tasteful, superior film music."

Moore was born in Cutchogue, Long Island, on August 10, 1893. His education took place at Hotchkiss School and at Yale University; at the latter place, his musical ambitions were stimulated in the classes of David Stanley Smith and Horatio Parker. While at Yale, Moore wrote a still-popular football song, "Good Night, Harvard." In 1915, he was graduated with a Bachelor of Arts degree, and in 1917, with a Bachelor of Music degree.

He served in the Navy during World War I, after which he went to Paris and became a pupil in composition of Vincent d'Indy at the Schola Cantorum, and a private pupil of Nadia Boulanger at the organ. In 1921, he was appointed director of music at the Art Museum in Cleveland, a period during which he studied composition with Ernest Bloch. Between 1923 and 1925, he was organist at Adelbert College of Western Reserve University. After returning to Europe on a Guggenheim Fellowship he wrote his first opera, *White Wings,* with Philip Barry's play serving as libretto, its first performance finally taking place at Hartford, Connecticut, on February 2, 1949. He then joined the music faculty of Columbia University. In 1940, he became head of the music department, retiring in 1962 to become MacDowell Professor Emeritus.

His first successful composition was the orchestral suite, *P. T. Barnum,* in 1924. His first significant opera was *The Devil and Daniel Webster,* in 1939. Since then, he has become one of America's leading opera composers. *Giants in the Earth* received the Pulitzer Prize in music in 1951. Its text, by Arnold Sundgaard, was based on O. E. Rolvaag's novel about the early Norwegian settlers of the Dakotas; its world première took place in New York on March 28, 1951. It was not successful and went into a prolonged discard; but a decade after its première, Moore revised the opera extensively. *The Ballad of Baby Doe,* which entered the permanent American opera repertory, received the New York Music Critics Circle Award. Subsequent full-length operas included *The Wings of the Dove,* a major success, and *Carrie Nation,* a minor one. The latter—written to help celebrate the centenary of the University of Kansas in Lawrence—received its world première on April 28, 1966.

From 1946 to 1952, Moore was president of the National Institute of

Arts and Letters; between 1960 and 1963, he was president of the American Academy. He died in Greenport, Long Island, on July 25, 1969.

1924 THE PAGEANT OF P. T. BARNUM, suite for orchestra. I. Boyhood at Bethel. II. Joice Heth. III. General and Mrs. Tom Thumb. IV. Jenny Lind. V. Circus Parade.

With this delightful orchestral suite, which the Cleveland Orchestra introduced on April 15, 1926, Moore achieved his first substantial success as a composer. It is witty music, spontaneous, fresh, and rich with American flavor. In relating episodes in the fabulous career of a great showman, Moore first describes Barnum's boyhood, introducing the village music of country fiddles and bands, which Barnum no doubt heard in Bethel. Joice Heth was the 160-year-old Negress who was the first of Barnum's attractions; legend had it that she was the first person to put clothes on George Washington. In this section, there is a skilful interpolation of a Negro spiritual—a version of *Nobody Knows de Trouble I've Seen.* The General and Mrs. Tom Thumb, midgets, were another of Barnum's attractions; the music has mock military air about it. Jenny Lind was, of course, one of the greatest triumphs of Barnum's career; a melody for the flute suggests the incomparable coloratura voice of the Swedish nightingale, as she must have sung at her first American appearance in Castle Garden. In the concluding section, the circus of Barnum is described—with spirited, even raucous circus-parade music suggesting animals, clowns, acrobats and calliope.

1933 STRING QUARTET. I. Allegro comodo. II. Allegro giusto III. Andante cantabile. IV. Allegro.

This chamber-music work—successfully introduced by the Roth Quartet in 1936—is one of Moore's finest compositions. Graceful in its construction, melodically fresh, endowed with a spontaneous feeling, this quartet is a distinguished contribution to contemporary American chamber music.

Otto Luening succinctly described this quartet in *Modern Music:* "The first movement is polymodal, remarkably lucid, with a great feeling for transparent part-writing. Carefully spaced dissonances augment the natural resonance of the quartet in a unique manner. The lyric mood is personal and poetic. In the second movement, a march-like, American, folkish tune is clearly developed. Both movements reveal a growing mastery of form. The third is less definite in outline, but the melodic lines are in themeselves expressive. The finale is dance-like in character, carefully developed and in sharp rhythmic contrast to the others."

1938 THE DEVIL AND DANIEL WEBSTER, one-act folk opera, with libretto by the composer based on the story of the same name by Stephen Vincent Benét. First performance: New York City, May 18, 1939.

The protagonist of Benét's story (which in 1941 was made into a successful motion picture starring Walter Huston and Edward Arnold), is a New Hampshire farmer, who Faust-like, sells his soul to the devil—but for the coin of material prosperity which will enable him to get married. The wedding festivities are interrupted by the devil, who arrives (in the person of a Boston attorney) to claim the soul. Daniel Webster pleads the case for the farmer—before a jury composed of resurrected traitors and blackguards of the distant past; and he pleads it so eloquently that the farmer is released from his bargain.

Moore's approach to the opera form is a traditional one, and *The Devil and Daniel Webster* is pleasingly set in arias, ensemble numbers, etc. In his melodies, Moore frequently resorts to popular and folk idioms, with fine effect. The harmonic writing and orchestration are simply realized. The major appeal of the opera lies in its ingratiating lyricism, excellent writing for the voice, and dramatic strength.

1945 SYMPHONY NO. 2 IN A MAJOR. I. Andante con moto; Allegro giusto. II. Andante quieto a semplice. III. Allegretto. IV. Allegro con spirito.

The composer has provided the following analysis:

"First Movement: There is a lyric introduction in which features of the principal Allegro are gradually evolved. The Allegro giusto begins with the principal theme in the first violins. This theme consists of several ideas which are developed and varied in the music that follows. There is a transition in C-sharp minor, where a woodwind dialogue leads to a subsidiary theme in E major. These themes serve as the principal material of the movement, which follows the classical pattern of design. There is a short coda at an accelerated close.

"Second Movement: The mood . . . was suggested by a short poem of James Joyce which deals with music heard at the coming of twilight. This is a lyric movement in one long section. The principal elements are the introduction, a broad melody against a guitar-like accompaniment, and a third motive, which appears briefly at the end of each phrase of the principal melody and is heard in its entirety just before the conclusion.

"Third Movement: This is a polyphonic piece, somewhat resembling a minuet but more rapid, and if there is any elegance about it, it is of the rural rather than the court variety.

"Fourth Movement: The finale is an attempt to write an entertainment piece of the classic type rather than an apotheosis of the entire symphony. There is a four-bar introduction preceding the principal theme, which is heard in the first violins. This theme has a shifting rhythm of two and three which dominates the movement. There is a lyric theme for contrast, which, as it unfolds, contains a new rhythm that plays an important part in the development and coda."

The symphony is dedicated to the celebrated American poet, Stephen Vincent Benét, friend and, at times, collaborator of the composer. It was introduced in Paris—by the Paris Broadcasting Orchestra under Robert Lawrence—on May 5, 1946. After its American première in Los Angeles on January 16, 1947, it received honorable mention from the Music Critics Circle of New York.

1955 THE BALLAD OF BABY DOE, folk opera in two parts, with text by John Latouche. First performance: Central City, Colorado, July 7, 1956.

This American folk opera was commissioned by the Koussevitzky Music Foundation to honor the centennial of Columbia University in New York. Following its world première in Colorado, it was produced by the New York City Opera on April 3, 1957, when it received the New York Music Critics Circle Award. Since then the New York City Opera has frequently revived it; and in 1961, the Santa Fe Opera Company presented it in Berlin and Belgrade.

The libretto is based on historical fact. "The main points of the story," the librettist, John Latouche, has explained, "are lurid, earthy, human and deeply touching. Beginning with ostentation, even vulgarity, the lives of all three—Tabor, Baby and Augusta—had ended with tragic dignity that seemed very difficult to capture in dramatic form. And within the brief space of an operatic libretto, almost impossible. Yet the limitation of the form can be a virtue as well, forcing a selectivity and economy of diction impossible in a spoken drama. To use an awkward simile, the test of a libretto can be the conscious mind, while the musical setting can be compared to the unconscious mind, surrounding the sparse phrases with power, coloration and emotional currents arising from the creative focus of the work at hand."

The setting is Leadville, Colorado, during the gold-rush days of the late 19th century. Two central characters are Horatio Tabor and his wife, Augusta, who came to Colorado to prospect for gold and who for many years have suffered the direst poverty. Finally, Horatio becomes a partner in a rich silver mine and becomes a millionaire and a powerful political figure. It is at this point that he deserts his wife to marry a blond beauty from Wisconsin, Baby Doe. Towards the end of the century, Tabor loses all his wealth and power when government legislation impoverishes all the silver-mine owners of Colorado. But Baby Doe sticks with him faithfully and uncomplainingly until his death in 1899. For thirty-six years after that, she lives alone in a shack at the worthless silver mine left her by her husband. There she froze to death in 1935.

"The score," wrote Howard Taubman in *The New York Times,* "makes no attempt to pursue advanced techniques. It is full of tunes; it seeks to sing at all times. . . . In jubilation or sorrow it scales no heights. But it provides scenes of atmosphere and feeling. It serves the story well enough to cause it to hold the interest firmly." And in a later review, Mr. Taubman added: "At its liveliest it is just as gay as a musical comedy, and it has the advantage of dealing sympathetically with characters one can believe in. Since it is an opera, it does not hesitate to probe as deeply as it can into the emotions of its people."

Winthrop Sargeant reflected the general critical and public reaction to this opera when he wrote in *The New Yorker* that it is "very important even in the current history of music . . . a completely enchanting work of art." And he echoed the critical consensus when he had only the highest of praise for Moore's "distinguished melodic gift" and for his "vocal writing of the purest and most revealing sort. His arias and ensembles are all deft and graceful and they succeed in making you like, and sympathize with, the characters involved."

1961 THE WINGS OF THE DOVE, opera in six scenes (divided into two parts), with text by Ethan Ayer based on Henry James's novel. First performance: New York City Opera, New York. October 12, 1961.

Moore had been hunting for a suitable libretto for a number of years when, in the spring of 1959, Chalmers Clifton, the conductor, telephoned him. "I have a story for you that would be ideal for an opera," he told Moore. "Last night I saw the television adaptation of Henry James's *The Wings of the Dove*. Don't look any further. This plot has everything."

Ayer and Moore got a copy of the novel and "succumbed to the fascination of the story," as Moore recalls, "and we determined to see if we could make it work as an opera." They sketched out the libretto and the first scenes before bringing them to Julius Rudel, director of the New York City Opera. Rudel immediately accepted the work for his company. In addition, he recommended Moore for a Ford Foundation Commission, which enabled him to take a leave-of-absence from Columbia University and devote himself completely to his opera.

The basic material of the Henry James story has been retained. The setting is London and Venice in or about 1900. Milly Theale, a beautiful and fabulously wealthy American girl, is mortally ill. She has fallen in love with an impoverished journalist, Miles Dunster. Miles's sweetheart, Kate, urges him to encourage Milly's love and get married to her; for after Milly's death, they themselves would be able to get married and live in style. Miles consents, on the condition that Kate become his mistress. Milly, learning of this plan, is shocked to the point of physical collapse. Dying, she sends for Dunster to tell him she has left half her fortune to him anyway. This generosity so moves Dunster that he now has only hate for Kate, who realizes that all her scheming has come to naught.

In this opera, as in earlier ones, Moore works with traditional means, preferring set numbers in which his rich melodic vein could be tapped. He can be soaringly lyrical, as in Milly's wonderful song in the second act; and he can be light and tuneful and popular, as in the polka and waltz music pointing up the background of London in the 1900s. As Irving Kolodin wrote: "Moore holds firm to the precepts of melodic line, vocal suitability, and natural fall of verbal values."

In the New York *Post,* Harriet Johnson singled out some of the more powerful scenes in the opera, such as "the final one when Kate realizes that Miles no longer loves her." Miss Johnson continues: "The introduction to Scene IV is dreamily impressionistic, while by contrast the incisive instrumental punctuation at the end of Scene I . . . is apparently strident. It cuts with a carving, not a dinner knife."

Midway in his opera, Moore introduces a fanciful episode entitled "Masque of Janus," which is sung, danced and pantomimed. This takes place in the fourth scene, an entertainment for the guests come to the Palazzo Leporelli in Venice. The legendary story of the two-faced Janus serves as a focal point in the dramatic action, for it brings forcefully home to Dunster for the first time the extent of his duplicity.

Miles Kastendieck regards this as Moore's finest opera up to this time. Writing in the *Journal American* he said: "This is music drama in the best modern style. . . . From the outspoken notes of the prelude to the ingenious scoring of the closing pages, he writes dramatically as well as emotionally. . . . Perhaps its finest quality is the blend of the music and the drama. This is modern lyric theatre at its best."

CARL NIELSEN 1865–1931

The centenary celebration of Nielsen's birth in many of the music centers of the world, and particularly in the United States, has gone a long way towards bringing permanent recognition to an important composer. In Denmark, he has long been considered a leading creative figure in twentieth-century music and its most important symphonist of all time. But outside Scandinavia, Nielsen's music for a long time made little headway.

In the United States, an attempt to promote his symphonies began taking place in the early 1950s, when recordings made in Denmark were distributed, and when these symphonies were also widely performed by the Danish State Orchestra during its American tour. But this effort remained stillborn. The recordings soon disappeared from the catalogues for lack of demand, and the Nielsen symphonies still failed to invade American symphony programs. But a new impetus was made in 1965 that gained momentum. With performances of Nielsen's symphonies and other orchestral works by the New York Philharmonic under Leonard Bernstein, the Boston Symphony under Leinsdorf, the Philadelphia Orchestra under Ormandy, and many other major orchestras —and with a number of important new recordings released and taking hold in the catalogues—Nielsen's star began to rise. Leading articles now appeared to point up the fact that here was a composer whose place on the concert programs should be permanent.

"There have probably been different reasons for the difficulty of Carl Nielsen's music until now to win friends outside Scandinavia," explains Eric Tuxen, distinguished Danish conductor. "His music is very closely associated with the nature of his country as is Sibelius's. The Finnish composer had a very inspiring background for his dramatic tone poems in the landscape of Finland, with its thousand lakes and big, mysterious forests. Carl Nielsen's music is born out of the ethereal and calm Danish nature, with its soft colors and lack of dramatic accents. There is no pathos or flamboyant instrumentation to tickle the ear, but if one is able to catch the special, near ascetic language of his music, a door will soon be opened to a world of strange beauty, warm love for nature, and deep cosmic feeling."

Nielsen started out as an unashamed Romanticist who took his cue from Grieg and Niels Gade without indulging in their specific national practices.

Then he strengthened and enriched his language through the infusion of modern methods, including polytonality, which amazingly enough he began using in the first years of the twentieth century (or a decade or so before Stravinsky and Milhaud did so). At the same time, in its frequent polyphonic exercises, the music also looked backwards into the past. Vigor, breadth and virility became the hallmarks of Nielsen's style, but with them enters a most engaging pastoral quality that springs from the composer's intense love of nature. It is a love of nature, however, with religious and philosophical overtones. But as Richard Freed noted so well, Nielsen's pantheism "is more primitive than that of Vaughan Williams, more genial than that of Sibelius, less lyrical and polished than Dvořák's, more succinct and straightforward than Mahler's. Real tunes fill his symphonies without apology, set off in solid orchestral textures (despite frequent 'conflicts' between tonalities) bringing to mind such adjectives as hearty, robust, virile, confident, and, without exception, vital."

Nielsen was born in Nörre Lyndelse on the island of Funen, in Denmark on June 9, 1865. He began studying the violin mostly by himself, and at the age of fourteen was able to perform with a band in the Odense garrison. Formal training took place at the Copenhagen Conservatory with V. Tofte in violin, with O. Rosenhoff in composition; he also studied composition privately with Niels Gade. Between 1886 and 1890, he earned his living by playing in a theatre orchestra. This was the period in which his first opus appeared and was performed, a *Little Suite* in A minor for strings (1888). Winning the Ancker stipend enabled him to travel throughout Europe, where, in Paris, he married Anne Marie Brodersen, a young sculptress. After returning to Copenhagen, which he now made his permanent home, he played the violin in the court orchestra until 1905. From 1908 to 1914, he was musical director of the Copenhagen Royal Opera, and from 1915 to 1927, of the Copenhagen Musical Society; during this time, he was also heard as conductor in guest performances throughout Europe. Beginning with 1915, he became associated with the Conservatory, first as director and teacher of theory, and in 1930, as chairman of the Conservatory managing committee.

His first opera, *Saul and David,* was produced in Copenhagen on November 28, 1902. This was soon followed by the opera *Masquerade,* which many musicologists regard as the most important Danish national opera. These efforts, and the mounting success in Denmark of his symphonies (the first of which was completed in 1894) placed him with the foremost Danish composers of his time. Nielsen suffered a heart attack while conducting a concert of his music in Odense in 1926. He survived five more years, until becoming a victim of a second heart attack in Copenhagen on October 2, 1931. He received many honors. He was made Knight of the Dannebrog and a member of the Royal Academy of Stockholm. A five-day festival of his major works took place in Copenhagen in 1953; while his centenary twelve years after that was not only honored with an extensive festival in Copenhagen but also with commemorative performances throughout the world of music.

1906 OVERTURE TO MASQUERADE, for orchestra.

Nielsen wrote his opera *Maskarade,* or *Masquerade,* between 1904 and 1906. Its world première took place only one week after he had put the final touches on his manuscript—at the Royal Opera in Copenhagen on November 11, 1906. It was a giant success and went a long way towards establishing Nielsen's reputation in Denmark; since then, it has come to be regarded as one of the most significant national operas to come out of Denmark. Vilhelm Andersen's libretto was based on a comedy by Ludvig Holberg. The story was a light and amusing episode during a masquerade in eighteenth-century Copenhagen in which a young man and a young girl meet and fall in love, only to discover that this is the match their parents had been arranging and which they had been bitterly resisting all the while.

The gay, lighthearted mood of the opera is immediately caught in the sprightly overture, which opens with a dance-like tune (Allegro non tanto) and continues with a lyrical episode in low strings and bassoon. A new sprightly idea is introduced in the middle section.

1911 SYMPHONY NO. 3, "SINFONIA ESPANSIVA" ("Expansive Symphony"), op. 27, for soprano, baritone and orchestra. I. Allegro espansivo. II. Andante pastorale. III. Allegretto un poco. IV. Allegro.

The idea for this symphony occurred so suddenly and unexpectedly to the composer one day in 1910 that he had to jot down some of his ideas on a cuff while riding in a trolley car. Then he went to work with a will and passion, completing his symphony by April 1911. Its première took place in Copenhagen on February 28, 1912, with the composer conducting; it proved a major success. This was Nielsen's first symphony to attract critical accolades as well as public acceptance.

To Peter Garvie, the Third Symphony is a "further commentary on the nature of man, for it is expansive only in its human qualities—its sanity, geniality and freedom from distrust and reserve—not in its length. . . . Accordingly, the clashing rhythm of the opening bars is deceptive. We expect them to eject a series of dissonant motives, and, instead, as the rhythm settles, a long assured melody forms itself and expands. The development section reconciles fugato and waltz." To Garvie, the slow movement is "a study of expanding texture. The thematic material is austere and remains so to the climax. Then, as the tension relaxes, the texture becomes steadily richer and wordless voices are added. The means are contrapuntal but the effect is atmospheric." It is in this movement that the soprano and baritone are heard. "The third movement is the most clouded tonally and its climax is built on rhythm. . . . The finale opens with the greatest possible contrast: an extended, carefully balanced, yet continually growing melody. Elements of it generate the development and at the end are resumed into the context of the full theme."

In his biography of the composer, Robert Simpson takes pains to emphasize that the subtitle "*Espansiva*" is not to be taken programmatically; the term is used to signify the "outward growth of the mind's scope and the expansion of life that comes from it." To Simpson, this symphony "breathes a vivid gaiety that is created by no rose-tinted glasses, but by an irresistible sense in the composer's self of the corporate strength of all the healthy-minded people with whom he feels as one."

1916 SYMPHONY NO. 4, "THE INEXTINGUISHABLE," for orchestra, op. 29. I. Allegro. II. Poco allegretto. III. Poco adagio quasi andante. IV. Allegro: tempo giusto.

Nielsen's Fourth Symphony was first performed in Copenhagen on February 1, 1916, only two or so weeks after he had completed its writing. The symphony was acclaimed, was soon performed outside Denmark, and won for its composer a membership in the Swedish Academy and the Berlin Academy of Art.

To the published score, the composer appended the motto: "Music is life and, like it, inextinguishable." The symphony, consequently, was intended to point up the indestructibility not only of great art but also of the human spirit.

Though in four movements, the symphony is played without interruption, and is, in actuality, all of one piece, an inextricably unified concept. Here is how Harris Goldsmith described it in *High Fidelity:* "Violent eruptions of brass, tympani, and a recurring note motif in the strings constitute Nielsen's depiction of the forces of discord and evil. Finally, at the work's very end, a passionate reiteration of one of the more serene themes from the first movement triumphantly asserts the victory of the life force." Goldsmith goes on to emphasize that the symphony is "first and foremost a superbly rich specimen of absolute music which can be heard with no knowledge of the underlying programmatic implications. It makes a splendid sound."

1922 SYMPHONY NO. 5, op. 50. I. Tempo giusto; Adagio non troppo. II. Allegro; Presto; Andante un poco tranquillo; Allegro.

The Fifth is Nielsen's most famous symphony. Its first performance took place in Copenhagen on January 24, 1922, the composer conducting. Begun soon after the end of World War I, this music reflects some of the tragic events that had recently transpired. Some annotators see here the conflict between the constructive instincts of man and the destructive forces he faces, and find that, in the end of the symphony, the human will's determination to survive against any disaster is underlined. "One perceives a gigantic fight between the principles of good and evil," explains Eric Tuxen, "the latter especially being characterized by the snarling and persistent attempts of the snare drum to disturb and tear the melodic structure. The victory of light over the powers of darkness heralded already at the end of the first movement is completed in the second, with its manful belief in will and vitality in all their manifestations."

The symphony opens with tremolo violas, into which join first the bassoons, then the violins, and after that the other strings and woodwind. The distant roll of the snare drum is heard, and a powerful fortissimo is built up. After the tempo slackens into an Adagio, divided violas, cello and bassoons present an effective subject that receives contrapuntal treatment. Some of the material of the opening is then recalled, followed by a new outburst is heard, ending in a nine-measure cadenza for snare drum. (In the score, the composer advises the percussion player to improvise his art, "as if at all costs he wanted to stop the progress of the orchestra.") A climax is achieved, after which the movement ends quietly. The second movement opens with a forceful Allegro section, after which there comes a demoniac part. Flutes bring on a third section which is gentle and introspective, and in a contrapuntal style. The movement ends with a return of material from the first part.

1925 SYMPHONY NO. 6, "SINFONIA SEMPLICE" ("Simple Symphony"), I. Tempo giusto. II. Humoreske. III. Proposta seria. IV. Tema con variazioni.

The Sixth was Nielsen's last symphony. Its première took place in Copenhagen on December 11, 1925, the composer conducting. At that time, Nielsen told an interviewer that in writing this music he was trying to compose for each of the instruments, bearing its individuality in mind. "Each instrument is like a person who is sleeping, whom I have to wake into life. I think through the instruments themselves, almost as if I had crept inside them." He went on to explain: "I have in my new symphony a piece for small percussion instruments—triangle, glockenspiel, and side drum—which quarrel, each sticking to his own taste and liking. Times change. Where is music going? What is permanent? We don't know. This idea is found in my little Humoreske, which is the second movement of the symphony, and in the last movement, a theme and variations, which is jolly. In the first and third movements, there are more serious problematical things, but as a whole, I have tried to make the symphony as lively and gay as possible."

Robert Simpson described the first movement as follows: "It starts with four soft D's on the glockenspiel, introducing a lyric violin phrase. The mood of the music gradually becomes stormy, building to a tremendous climax for full orchestra. After some extended development the movement ends in a more tranquil spirit with a quiet passage in octaves for first and second violins."

In the second movement, use is made of triangle and drum taps, while trombone glissandos interpolate sounds which the composer intended to be contemptuous. The slow movement opens with a fugal episode, and the finale is a theme and variations, with the theme stated by solo bassoon. A brass fanfare introduces the concluding coda. A climax is reached, and subsides. The symphony ends with a quiet recall of the opening theme.

1926 CONCERTO FOR FLUTE AND ORCHESTRA. I. Allegro moderato. II. Allegretto; Poco adagio; Tempo di marcia.

Nielsen wrote three concertos for solo instruments and orchestra. The first, in 1911, was for the violin. The flute concerto followed in 1926, and a clarient concerto in 1928. The flute concerto belongs with the composer's significant compositions. He wrote it for Holger Gilbert Jesperson, to whom the work is dedicated, and who introduced it in Paris on October 21, 1926, Emil Telmanyi conducting.

The concerto has only two movements. The initial subject of the first movement, stated by the orchestra with the flute replying, is built from a descending scale of which much use is made throughout the movement. A brief cadenza precedes the entrance of the second theme in the orchestra; its opening four-note motive becomes prominent from this point on. A cantabile passage sets the stage for the return of the opening subject and for a cadenza for the flute.

The second movement has a forceful, rhythmic opening. After this energy has been dissipated, and the dynamics have been reduced to pianissimo, the solo flute is heard in a folk-song type of melody; here, too, as in the second subject of the preceding movement, a four-note motive is prominent. An Adagio section carries on this tranquil mood, but a march-like section eventually restores vigor.

CARL ORFF 1895–

Orff is one of the most original, forceful and inventive composers for the contemporary stage. He believes that music, in the long-accepted classical or romantic tradition, has come to the end of its development; that the contemporary composer must seek out new forms, new avenues of expression. He also feels that the stage is the only fruitful medium of artistic self-expression left to the present-day composer. Therefore, since 1935—when he completely disowned and withdrew almost everything he had written up to then—he has dedicated himself to the stage. His most significant such works (since he has fastidiously avoided calling them operas, so must we) are almost elementary in technique, style, approaches and idioms, in a conscious effort to reduce the stage and its appurtenances to their barest essentials. His musical writing is equally bare and primitive, consisting mainly of a rhythmic declamation (sometimes unaccompanied) that often consists of little more than repeated notes, or repeated phrases. His thematic material reveals dependence on plainsongs and Gregorian chants. Orff emphasizes rhythmic procedures so strongly that he likes to enlist the resources of a huge and varied percussion section which dominates the musical proceedings. In this respect, he is a neo-primitive, whose indebtedness to the Stravinksy of *The Rite of Spring* is obvious and freely acknowledged. Lighter, more popular, and at times comic elements may be introduced for folk-tale texts, but even here an adherence to a primitive style persists.

Henry Pleasants makes the observation that through Orff's works for the stage there runs "a certain detachment." He adds: "One does not wholly participate. There is rather a spectacle seen from a great distance in time, if not a great distance in space, and regarded with more than a trace of affectionate cynicism. It is an idealized world, but nobody is fooled, least of all the composer." Pleasants also notes that Orff's is an art "of distortion—stylization he calls it. Which is what keeps it from being antiquarian. It is a vision of times past, sentimental perhaps, excessive certainly, but all done with a conjurer's finesse—and with a conjurer's motive."

Orff was born in Munich, Germany, on July 10, 1895, to a family of Bavarian nobility. Orff began music study early, and in 1911, published a number of songs. He was graduated from the Academy of Music in Munich in 1914. For four years, he was employed as coach and conductor in German theatres. Then he returned to music study with Heinrich Kaminski. In 1925, he helped found the Gunther School of Music in Munich, where he taught for eleven years and evolved a system of teaching music to children through rhythm, bodily movements, and involvement in musical games; this system has been formalized by him in a five-volume study, *Schulwerk,* adopted by several leading musical institutions, and used as the basis of a class he conducted for many years for public schools over the Munich radio. Between 1925 and 1935, he wrote some orchestral and vocal music, besides making adaptations of stage works by Monteverdi. In 1935, he discarded most of what he had written up to that time to embark in a new direction, with a new set of values, and a new orientation. This approach was first crystallized with *Carmina Burana* in 1936, the first of a trilogy of works for the stage, collectively entitled *Trionfi. Carmina Burana* was extraordinarily successful and has remained Orff's most frequently performed work. Since then, Orff has pursued his goal with a passionate single-mindedness. In July of 1962, he paid his first visit to the North American continent as a guest of the Conference of Elementary Musical Education at the University of Toronto in Canada. The German government has decorated him with Pour le Merité, for arts and sciences.

1936–1951 TRIONFI (TRIUMPHS), a trilogy of "scenic cantatas":
I. CARMINA BURANA (SONGS OF BUREN), text by the composer, partly in medieval Latin and partly in medieval German, based on thirteenth-century poems of unknown authorship. First performance: Frankfort, Germany, June 8, 1937.

II. CATULLI CARMINA (SONGS OF CATULLUS), text by the composer based on poems of Catullus. First performance: Leipzig, Germany, November 6, 1943.

III. TRIONFO DI AFRODITE (TRIUMPH OF APHRODITE), text by the composer based on poems by Catullus, Sappho and Euripides. First performance: La Scala, Milan, February 13, 1953.

In 1935, one of Orff's friends told him about a collection of thirteenth-century poems which had been discovered a century earlier in the archives of the Monastery at Benediktbeuren in Upper Bavaria. These medieval poems aroused Orff's imagination and gave him the material with which, for the first time, he could embark on his radical experiments with a new, simpler approach to the musical theatre; a theatre in which, in the words of Henry Pleasants, he could "return to the fundamentals of song and dance, to a music more closely related to speech and gesture and situation."

There is no plot and no dramatic action in *Carmina Burana* (1936). The verses describe the activities of wandering students who, as minstrels, sing the praises of nature, love, the tavern and the free life. The work is made up of three parts, carrying the titles of "Springtime," "In the Tavern" and "The Court of Love." Scored for soprano, tenor and baritone solos, chorus and a large orchestra, the work, in text and music, is the final word in bare simplicity and the reduction to essentials. Orff did not specify in his score the precise nature of scenery, costuming or staging, preferring to leave these matters in the hands of producers. The singers are required to sit in the pit with the orchestra, while the stage is turned over to the dancers. As for Orff's music, it is concerned primarily not with melody or harmony but with rhythm. He uses a greatly expanded percussion section that includes two pianos, five kettledrums, three glockenspiel, xylophone, castanets, wood blocks, small bells, triangles, two small cymbals, three bells, chimes, celesta, tambourine, two side drums and a bass drum. His lyric line is a declamation usually formed from repeated notes, sometimes without any accompaniment, occasionally in the style of a plainchant. It has the most rudimentary harmony, and no polyphony or thematic development. Vocal parts are often sung in unison, octaves, thirds and fifths.

The work opens with a ninety-seven measure chorus invoking the goddess Fortune, over an ostinati figure that builds up to a passionate peak of intensity. A second chorus follows, lamenting "fortune's blows," in which there is a dramatic change of meter. All this is the prologue. In the ensuing choruses and solos, the joys of spring are extolled; then the joys of the tavern and the gaming table; then the joys of love, culminating in a mighty hymn. The composition ends with the chorus to fortune with which it had begun.

The American première of *Carmina Burana* took place in San Francisco on October 3, 1954 (though the work had previously become known to many American music lovers through a successful recording). This performance was a huge success. Alfred J. Frankenstein called the work "one of the most vivid, picturesque and richly tuneful choral pieces of modern times." When Leopold Stokowski conducted the Eastern première in Boston on November 19, 1959 (repeating the performance in New York one day later), Olin Downes spoke of the music as "one of the most fascinating and delightful choral works that this century has produced on either side of the water." *Carmina Burana* received the New York Music Critics Circle Award.

The second work in the trilogy is *Catulli Carmina*. Here the music is made up principally of a cappella choruses (sung once again from the orchestra pit), with only the prelude and postlude requiring the instrumental background of four pianos and percussion. Based on Catullus, the text opens with a love episode for young girls and boys, while the elders try to remind them that Catullus had died of love. Then, in the next three scenes, his story is told as a warning to young people. A chorus sings some of Catullus's verses while a dancer performs the part of Lesbia on the stage. Lesbia is unfaithful to Catullus, having gone to the arms of Catullus's friend, Caelus. Then, repentant, she tries to return to her first love, who rejects her even though he is still in love with her. The choral parts are divided into three sections designated as Actus I, Actus II Actus III.

The trilogy ends with *Trionfo di Afrodite*. This is not a dramatic production with music half so much as the description of a ritual. Young girls and boys are waiting for a couple to arrive for their wedding ceremony. They are led to the wedding tent in an impressive procession, where they submit to the laws of Aphrodite. When Aphrodite makes an appearance, everybody raises a voice to a culminating song of praise.

Techniques perfected by Orff in two earlier dramatic works are once again used effectively in the projection of this spectacle. As Howard Taubman said in *The New York Times:* "There are the fierce, pounding rhythms, used in such passages as 'Hymn to Hymen' and 'Nuptials Before the Wedding Chamber.' There is the expected device of loud and soft in choral writing. There is some use of spoken lines. And, for contrast, in much of the music for bride and bridegroom, there are elaborate melismatic phrases. It has to be conceded that Orff's techniques generate excitement and overwhelming waves of sound. By now all the devices he has developed he uses with commanding skill."

The American première of *Trionfo di Afrodite* took place in Houston, Texas, on April 2, 1956, Leopold Stokowski conducting.

1942 DIE KLUGE (THE WISE OLD WOMAN), fairy tale with music in six scenes, with text by the composer based on a fairy tale by Grimm. First performance: Frankfort, Germany, February 20, 1943.

Of Orff's works for the stage, *Die Kluge* is one of the most palatable on first contact. Though procedures previously perfected have not been abandoned—including declamation, rhythmic vitality, repetition of single notes or phrases, reliance on a single key or chord as the cornerstone of an entire scene—there is so much refreshing lyricism (particularly in the music for the old woman), so much colorful orchestration, such engaging comic episodes, that the play with music remains consistently entertaining. Music then is beautifully attuned to the demands of a charming fairy tale. *Die Kluge* has enjoyed successes throughout Europe; it has been recorded; and on several occasions, it has been produced in the United States, following its American première in Cleveland on December 7, 1949.

The play begins when a peasant has found a gold mortar which, over the protests of his daughter, he brings to the king. The king imprisons him, insisting that the peasant had hidden the pestle. In his cell, the peasant bemoans his fate. Again and again he cries out, "Had I only listened to my daughter!" The king hears these moans and, becoming interested in the daughter, summons her to court. Upon her arrival, the king promises to free the father if the daughter is wise enough to solve three riddles. She solves them. Not only is the father freed, but the king decides to marry the daughter. Then, when she arouses the king's displeasure, he sends her away for good, but not before he has presented her with a chest which she can fill with whatever treasure she wishes. She puts her husband to sleep with a draught, and stuffs him in the chest. When the king awakens, she tells him he is the treasure she most desires, a confession that helps bring about a tender reconciliation.

1948 ANTIGONAE (ANTIGONE), tragic play with music in one act, with text based on the Sophocles tragedy adapted into German by Friedrich Hölderlin. First performance: Salzburg, Austria, August 9, 1949.

In *Antigonae,* Orff reverts without digression to the primitivism of the *Trionfi* by emphasizing rhythmic speech, monotone chants and the varied sounds of a large percussion family. The last includes six pianos (not only played in the traditional manner but also with hammers and plectra), seven tympani, three xylophones, stone slabs, small wood drum, two bells, three glockenspiel, three Turkish cymbals, small anvil, two bass drums, six tambourines, six pairs of castanets and ten large Javanese gongs. "There is not a definable tune nor a harmonic progression," reported Henry Pleasants after the world première. "Instead, there is interminable declamatory recitative of so little melodic variety that there are literally pages on end devoted to a single note. In one passage picked almost at random, the note G is sung two hundred consecutive times. . . . The accompaniment is exclusively percussive and has recourse to all the modern percussion instruments. . . . The result is not as noisy as one might expect, but neither is it expressively helpful."

"What Orff has done with astonishing success," explained Ernest Newman, "is to dispense with most of the harmonic and contrapuntal resources that music has won for itself during the last thousand years and convey his meaning to us by means of melodic phrases of a quite primitive kind and often no more than a note-to-note syllabic inflection of the short . . . lines—standing out against a well-defined though not elaborate rhythmic background."

The Sophocles drama is adhered to basically. In mythical times, during the siege of Thebes, two brothers, fighting on opposite sides, are killed. King Creon decrees that Polynices, who had fought with the enemy, should not be buried. But Polynices's sister, Antigone, defies the command, tries to bury her brother, and is condemned to die. All the efforts of Haemon, King Creon's son, to save his beloved Antigone are to no avail. But the king is forced to change his mind when old Tiresias prophesies doom for the entire kingdom if Polynices is not buried. But this change of heart came too late. Antigone and Haemon have killed themselves, and so has Creon's wife.

VINCENT PERSICHETTI 1915–

Though Persichetti has successfully followed neoclassical procedures, particularly in some of his instrumental serenades, and though he is an eminently skilful writer of polyphony, he is essentially an eclectic composer who combines many different styles. Some of his writing is rooted in the past, while much of it utilizes some of the more advanced techniques of our time. This is the point which Robert Everett emphasized when he wrote in the *Juilliard Review:* "Persichetti enjoys the almost unique distinction of never having belonged to the Right, or Left, or for that matter, the Middle of the Road. . . . He has deliberately exchanged the advantages of a single system for the challenges imposed by the critical acceptance of several systems. In having done this, he is one of the composers who, so far, has challenged the parochial narrowness of the major segments of contemporary musical thought."

Persichetti was born in Philadelphia on June 6, 1915. He attended the

Combs College of Music, from which he received a Bachelor of Music degree in 1936. For two years after that, he studied conducting with Fritz Reiner at the Curtis Institute; and from 1939 to 1941, he was a scholarship student at the Philadelphia Conservatory, a pupil of Olga Samaroff Stokowski in piano and Paul Nordoff in composition. Additional study of composition took place for two summers with Roy Harris at Colorado College. In 1941, Persichetti received a Masters degree, and in 1945, a doctorate from Philadelphia Conservatory. From 1939 to 1942, he was head of the composition department of Combs College; and from 1932 to 1948, he was musical director of the Arch Street Presbyterian Church in Philadelphia.

Impatient with the music he had written before 1938, Persichetti destroyed most of it and embarked in a new direction with his first string quartet and piano sonata in 1939. His first symphony was completed in 1942 (première in Rochester, New York, on October 21, 1947). His first significant appearance as a composer came with *Fables,* for narrator and orchestra (text based on Aesop's *Fables*), which was introduced in Philadelphia on April 20, 1945, Eugene Ormandy conducting. A success of substantial proportions was achieved in 1947 with his Third Symphony. After that, Persichetti produced works in many different categories, except opera, showing an ever increasing mastery of means and maturity of thought and style. He received a grant from the National Academy of Arts and Letters in 1948, a Guggenheim Fellowship in 1958–1959, and a medal from the Italian government in 1958.

Between 1942 and 1962, Persichetti was head of the composition department at the Philadelphia Conservatory. During this period, in 1947, he joined and eventually headed the composition department at the Juilliard School of Music. Since 1952, he has been editorial consultant for the publishing house of Elkan-Vogel.

Persichetti married Dorothea Flanagan in 1941. She is a pianist who has made concert appearances and has taught at the Philadelphia Conservatory. She has given numerous performances of her husband's piano works.

1946 SYMPHONY NO. 3, op. 30. I. Somber. II. Spirited. III. Singing. IV. Fast and Brilliant.

Though he had previously written and had performed a number of works that revealed unusual talent, Persichetti first emerged as a significant composer with his Third Symphony, which took him four years to complete. Its world première was given in Philadelphia on November 21, 1947, Eugene Ormandy conducting.

A succinct analysis has been prepared by Dorothea Persichetti:

"The first movement, built on two dotted-note figures, is dark and inhibited music. These figures grow into a brighter melody which is overtaken by a return to the somber spirit of the beginning. The movement ends ambiguously on a twelve-note woodwind chord, with most of the instruments arriving at different conclusions about what has gone before.

"The air is cleared considerably in the gay, almost naïve, second movement. The dance rests momentarily in a quieter middle section and returns. The third movement begins hesitantly with a slow rhythmic figure in the strings, which becomes a background for a sustained English horn melody.

This is interrupted by the trombones in a mood reminiscent of the first movement. There is a climactic development of all the material, and an ending much like the beginning. The fourth movement is a virtuoso piece which sees each section taking its turn alone and in combination with the others in variations of the fast theme. Each exceeds the last in exuberance until a chorale in the woodwinds is presented and developed. The symphony ends with the chorale in the bass combined with the opening thematic material."

1950 SERENADE NO. 5, for orchestra, op. 43. I. Prelude. II. Poem. III. Interlude. IV. Capriccio. V. Dialogue. VI. Burla.

Persichetti has been partial to the serenade structure, having produced eleven such works. The first of these also happened to be his first opus as well (1929), scored for ten wind instruments.

The fifth Serenade was commissioned by the Louisville Orchestra in Kentucky, which introduced it under Robert Whitney's direction on November 15, 1950. The composition opens with a massive Prelude for full orchestra energized by a vital rhythmic pulse. The second movement features a poignant melody for oboe, muted trumpet and the strings playing sul ponticello. After that, comes a dance-like section in 3/4 time, introduced by flutes, followed by a lively section in which woodwinds are assigned virtuoso passages. "Dialogue" opens with the violas; the oboes give reply and other instruments join in. The work ends with a lively "Burla" in 2/4 time.

1951 SYMPHONY NO. 4, op. 51. I. Adagio; Allegro. II. Andante. III. Allegretto. IV. Presto.

The symphony was introduced by the Philadelphia Orchestra under Eugene Ormandy on December 17, 1954. The opening section offers two ideas: a motive in plucked strings, and a harmonic phrase in trombones, clarinets and bassoon. In the ensuing Allegro, a powerful momentum is created while the material of the introduction is extended and varied. In the slow second movement, the violins are heard in an expressive melody over a strongly rhythmic background. Later materials include two tender passages, the first for woodwinds, and the second for violins and violas. The Allegretto, in a three-part form, maintains a serene atmosphere. A lively opening brings on the concluding Presto, followed by a string melody. After that, subject matter from earlier movements is recalled. The symphony ends with a powerful final statement of a theme from the first-movement introduction.

1954 QUINTET NO. 2, FOR PIANO AND STRINGS, op. 66.

Commissioned by the Koussevitzky Music Foundation, the Second Piano Quintet received its world première at the Library of Congress in Washington, D.C., on February 4, 1955. The work is in a single movement, and constructed, Dorothea Persichetti explains, "from the germinal material presented in the non-vibrato first violin passage.... Various tempo changes indicate the motion of the piece." These tempo markings are as follows: Adagio assai; Andante sostenuto; Con mosso; Meno mosso; Adagio con gravita; Andante affettuoso; Presto con fuoco; Andante doloroso; Allegro giusto; Lento ma non troppo. The germinal idea is a falling motive found in the fourth measure.

1955 PIANO SONATA NO. 10, op. 67.

The Tenth Piano Sonata had been commissioned by the Juilliard School of Music for its fiftieth anniversary festival of American music in 1956. The original thought was to have Persichetti write music for a ballet, but when a mutually acceptable project did not present itself to both the composer and the Juilliard dancers, the commission, at the composer's request, was changed to a major work for piano. The sonata was introduced by Josef Raieff in New York on February 20, 1956.

Like the Piano Quintet, commented upon above, this sonata is a one-movement work derived from a single germinating source motive. The germinal material is heard at the beginning: a descending scale line in thirds. The composer's wife explains: "This music is closely related to the Piano Quintet. It was an introspective tune compositionally and much of the music of this period has, in some ways, a quieter feeling than do the earlier works. There is, if anything, more passion, but along with it there is more control, and with control, more freedom."

Though in a single integrated movement, the work has four sections: Adagio ("statement of the source motive, declamation and development"); Presto ("driving rhythmic transformation of the source motive"); Andante ("lyric 6/8 transformation of the source motive"); and Vivace ("the material in full bloom, a clear Sonata Allegro form, positive and direct, as though written first").

1958 SYMPHONY NO. 7, op. 80. I. Lento. II. Allegro. III. Andante. IV. Vivace. V. Adagio.

This symphony—which received its world première on October 24, 1959, in St. Louis, Eduard von Remoortel conducting—is built from material from the *Hymns and Responses for the Church Year,* op. 68, which Persichetti had written in 1955.

The first movement opens with an introduction, "a prayer in low strings suggesting the profile of the cantus firmus of the symphony," Dorothea Persichetti explains. The cantus firmus appears in the thirteenth measure in the horns ("Who Art One God"). This is followed by the first and second Kyrie responses, the second combined with the cantus firmus. Low strings and woodwinds bring on "The Lord is in His Holy Temple," a contemplative section. Later on, a tuba solo on the cantus firmus leads to the hymn, "Now in the Tomb is Laid."

The second part is the development movement which "brings the cantus firmus minor-major elements into tonal conflict." This movement is finally dominated by the Shakespeare response, "My ending is despair, unless I be relieved by prayer, which pierces so that it assaults Mercy itself and frees all faults."

The third movement opens with a flute solo over four muted horns which "unravels the cantus firmus material, revealing . . . the true melodic core and heart of the work, the e. e. cummings hymn, 'Purer than purest pure whisper of whisper so big with innocence' . . . The movement closes on echoes of the first Kyrie.

The fourth movement is built on the Wallace Stevens response, "We say God and the imagination are one, how high that highest candle lights the dark." This movement is dominated by two important fugal episodes, and ends with "a tempestuous section of defiance hailing the triumphal entrance of the eleventh-century Easter words of Peter the Venerable."

The final movement is made up of a succession of Amens, with brief references made to material from earlier movements.

GOFFREDO PETRASSI 1904–

Petrassi's instrumental works of the early 1930s were in a neo-classical idiom, with a strong leaning towards Hindemith; his choral compositions of the same period were rooted in the Baroque masterworks of the Roman school headed by Palestrina. Then, beginning with the *Notte oscura,* for chorus and orchestra (1951)—introduced at the Strasbourg Festival in June of 1951—Petrassi began to show an interest in the twelve-tone technique. From then on, his creative ideal was to create a compromise between serialism and his earlier neo-classical and neo-Baroque tendencies. He achieved that compromise through a most free and flexible handling of dodecaphonic techniques and making structural compromises in the concerto-grosso form which he so favored. Thus he has evolved an approach and style uniquely his, and with such a mastery of means and maturity of expression that he has come to be numbered with the foremost Italian composers of the twentieth century.

Petrassi was born in Zagarolo, near Rome, Italy, on July 16, 1904. As a boy he sang in various church choirs, becoming acquainted with and fascinated by the choral masterworks of the Roman polyphonic school. His initial training in music came with Vincenzo di Donato. From 1928 to 1933, he attended the Santa Cecilia Academy in Rome, where his teachers included Bustini and Germani; he received diplomas in composition and organ. Personal association with Alfredo Casella was responsible for interesting him in neo-classicism, a style found in such early Petrassi compositions as the Partita, in 1932, which was his first work to attract recognition; and his first orchestral concerto, in 1934. Succeeding instrumental works were also in a neo-classical vein, while the choral music of this period reflected his profound religious convictions as well as his intense admiration for sixteenth-century choral music. Among these choral compositions were the *Psalm IX* (1936), the *Magnificat* (1940) and the highly successful *Coro di morti* (1941). After 1950, Petrassi assimilated the twelve-tone system into his writing.

Between 1937 and 1939, Petrassi was the superintendent of La Fenice,

Venice's leading opera house. From 1947 to 1950, he was the artistic director of the Accademia Filarmonica in Rome; and from 1954 to 1956, president of the International Society for Contemporary Music. Since 1939, he has been professor of advanced composition at the Santa Cecilia Academy. In December of 1955, Petrassi paid his first visit to the United States to attend the world première of his Fifth Concerto for Orchestra in Boston. During the summer of 1956, he held a master class in composition at the Berkshire Music Center at Tanglewood, in Lenox, Massachusetts. On August 2, 1967, Dartmouth College's fifth annual Congregation of the Arts at Hopkins Center presented the world première of Petrassi's *Estri,* a chamber symphony completed in 1967.

1932 PARTITA, for orchestra. I. Gagliarda. II. Ciaconna. III. Giga.

This is the earliest Petrassi composition to gain universal recognition, and it is the one is which his neo-classic style was first realized. It won two prizes, one from the Sindacato Nazionale dei Musicisti, and another in an international contest sponsored by the Fédération Internationale des Concerts in Paris. A highly successful performance took place at the festival of the Society for Contemporary Music at Amsterdam on June 13, 1933. The work consists of three Baroque dance forms. "The bold thematic material and the lithe contrapuntal writing," writes Joseph Machlis, "powered by driving rhythms, set forth the composer's kinship to the neo-classic aesthetic, as did his penchant for a flexible diatonic idiom flavored with dissonance."

1941 CORO DI MORTI (CHORUS OF THE DEAD), dramatic madrigal for four-part male chorus, three pianos, brass, double basses and percussion.

The *Coro di morti* is one of Petrassi's earliest important works for chorus, and one of the first such of his compositions to have sustained its interest and importance through the years. It was first heard at the Venice Festival in September of 1941, the composer conducting, when it enjoyed a substantial success. In the United States, it has been performed in institutions of higher learning, such as the University of California in Los Angeles, the University of Illinois and the University of Indiana. When Petrassi came to the United States to teach composition at the Berkshire Music Center at Tanglewood during the summer of 1956, this composition was revived at a concert of the Berkshire Music Festival, Hugh Ross conducting.

The text is a poem by Leopardi in which the thought is expressed that to the dead the living are as mysterious and as terrifying as the dead are to those alive. "The work as a whole," a reviewer said in *High Fidelity,* "communicates a kind of macabre lyricism, with touches of the grotesque and satiric. Stravinsky is often recalled, especially in the tough rhythmic texture; but the music also has an Italianate drama and urgency altogether its own and it ends in a tenderly exalted mood."

1952 CONCERTO NO. 3, for orchestra, "RECRÉATION CONCERTANTE." I. Allegro sostenuto ed energico. II. Allegro spiritoso. III. Moderato IV. Vigoroso e ritmico; Adagio moderato.

Petrassi wrote his first orchestral concerto in 1934; here he helped revive the concertante style of the Baroque concerto grosso. This style persisted in his second orchestral concerto in 1951, though his writing is now characterized by what he has described as "an unrestricted freedom of invention."

In his third orchestral concerto, the twelve-tone technique is employed, once again without abandoning the eighteenth-century concertante style. This concerto had been commissioned by the Sudwestfunk of Baden-Baden for the Aix-en-Provence festival in France, where it was first heard in July of 1953. The four movements are played without interruption. In this composition, much more than in his earlier two orchestral concertos, the composer arrives at his goal of achieving a style for each instrument. He explained: "My instrumentation is based on the timbres of the instruments themselves. I seek to create new sonorities based on pure instrumental sounds rather than a big, muddy ensemble. It naturally follows that every instrument has its own direct responsibility; it cannot hide behind other instruments." As for his use of the twelve-tone technique, he said: "I am to some extent a dodecaphonist, but not a dogmatic one."

1955 CONCERTO NO. 5, for orchestra. I. Molto moderato; Presto. II. Andante tranquillo; Mosso con vivicita; Lento e grave.

This work was commissioned by the Koussevitzky Music Foundation for the 75th anniversary of the Boston Symphony, which introduced it in Boston on December 2, 1955, Charles Munch conducting. In writing works for orchestra, Petrassi has shunned the symphonic form, preferring to create orchestral concertos. But unlike the classical concerto grosso, these works contain no solo or concertino passages; and the style is in the twelve-tone technique. The first two movements are based on two fundamental themes comprising the twelve-tone series. The first theme is heard in a six-note sequence in the opening of the first movement, in violas *ponticello;* the remaining six-note sequence occurs in muted trumpet. The second theme is derived from the composer's own *Coro di Morti.* The second movement uses the second six-note sequence. The concerto ends serenely.

HANS PFITZNER 1869–1949

Though Pfitzner lived until 1949, artistically he never outgrew the late nineteenth century. He had no sympathy for the newer voices and the newer methods in twentieth-century music (although at one time in his career he himself had been condemned by some of his critics for being a modernist). In his music, he remained true to the spirit and traditions of Brahms and Wagner. He was the last of the German post-Romantics. Though he wrote four operas, many oratorios and other choral works (of which *Von deutscher Seele,* completed in 1921, was most famous), symphonies, concertos, chamber music and hundreds of songs, he is remembered today for his opera *Palestrina,* which had a vogue in central European opera houses for many years and which is still highly esteemed by German and Austrian musicologists.

Pfitzner was born to German parents in Moscow, Russia, on May 5, 1869. His father was a professional violinist, who brought his family back to Germany when Hans was a child. Hans Pfitzner received his musical training at Hoch's Conservatory in Frankfort, of which his father was then director, where his teachers included Kwast in piano and Knorr in composition. (In 1899, Pfitzner married Kwast's daughter.) In 1892, Pfitzner taught piano at the Coblenz Conservatory; and from 1894 to 1896, he was conductor at the Municipal Theatre at Mayence. In 1893, a concert of his works was successfully given in Berlin. For a long period, beginning with 1897, he resided in Berlin, where he taught composition at the Stern Conservatory and was conductor at the Theater des Westens. There, on April 2, 1895, his first opera, *Der arme Heinrich,* was produced with extraordinary success, following which it was mounted by some of the leading opera houses in Germany. *Palestrina* followed in 1917. His most successful choral work, *Von deutscher Seele,* was given its world première in Berlin in 1922, and revised in 1937.

Following the triumph of *Palestrina,* Pfitzner successfully followed three careers—those of composer, conductor and teacher. Making his home mainly in Munich, he led concerts of the Konzertverein between 1919 and 1920; and from 1930 to 1933, he was professor of composition at the Akademie der Tonkunst. In 1920, he was appointed Bavarian General Music Director, and in 1925, was decorated by the Prussian Academy of Arts and Sciences with the Award for Merit.

During the early years of the Nazi regime, Pfitzner affiliated himself wholeheartedly with Nazi ideologies. But he eventually dissociated himself from some of the racial and musical policies of the Third Reich, and even had a serious falling-out with Hitler and Goering. Deprived of his property, savings and income, he became destitute. After the war, he was found in an old-age home in Munich, from which he was brought to Vienna by the Vienna Philharmonic and given a pension. In 1948, a denazification court in Munich exonerated him of Nazi associations and sympathies. Pfitzner died in Salzburg, Austria, on May 22, 1949.

1917 PALESTRINA, "a musical legend" in three acts, with text by the composer. First performance: Munich, June 12, 1917.

THREE PRELUDES TO "PALESTRINA," for orchestra. I. Rühig. II. Mit Wucht und Wildheit. III. Langsam, sehr getragen.

Palestrina—with which its composer became one of the last significant exponents of the post-Romantic movement in German opera—is a legitimate child of the Wagnerian music drama. It is strongly reminiscent of *Parsifal,* with its emphasis on spiritual values, its strong religious overtones, and its suggestions of a consecrational festival play. There are some German critics, in fact, who do not hesitate to put it on a par with *Parsifal.*

The subject of the opera is the legend (long accepted as fact) that Palestrina, and his masterwork, the *Missa Papae Marcelli,* were responsible for saving contrapuntal music from being banished by order of high church dignitaries.

In the first act, Palestrina is told by Cardinal Barromeo that all music, except the Gregorian chant, would be prohibited by the Council of Trent. Refusing to fight the edict, Palestrina vows he will compose no more. But he is visited by the spirits of nine composers who prevail on him to return to music. An angel even sings to him a theme which Palestrina later uses in the Kyrie of his *Missa Papae Marcelli.* Palestrina seizes a pen and feverishly writes a Gloria, then falls into a deep sleep. His son, Inghino, and his pupil, Silla, find him the next morning—sheets of music scattered all around him. They assemble the papers, and as they do so, they become fully aware that the master has here written one of his greatest compositions.

In the second act, the Council of Trent is in a stormy session, as it tries to solve the problem of church music. Then, in the concluding act, Palestrina's Mass is brought to the Pope, who is profoundly impressed. He blesses Palestrina and appoints him director of the Sistine Chapel choir. Outside, a crowd is cheering the composer. As the shouts die down, and after Palestrina has been left alone in his chamber, he goes to the organ and begins playing.

Some writers have pointed out that in this opera the composer identified himself with his chief protagonist; that Pfitzner uses Palestrina's victory over the Council of Trent as symbolic of his own artistic victory over his critics and enemies. In any event, the text is as rich with symbolism as the music is with religious ardor and spirituality; some of the noblest pages in the score are those in which a deep religious note is sounded, as when the angels sing to Palestrina, or when Palestrina puts down on paper his Gloria music, or when the Pope addresses Palestrina in noble and solemn accents.

When *Palestrina* was first performed (Bruno Walter was the conductor), it proved so successful that it was sent on tour through Switzerland, despite the fact that this was the time of World War I and travel for an opera company was extremely difficult to arrange. It also proved successful when first given in Vienna (March 1, 1919) and in Berlin (October 11, 1919). Paul Bekker described the opera as "lofty art." Willi Schuh wrote: "In his *Palestrina,* Pfitzner creates his own monument: composer and subject blend as almost never before in the history of opera." He also described the music as "austere and sublime" and "unforgettable." In his autobiography, Bruno Walter later referred to *Palestrina* as "the mightiest musical dramatic work of our time." However, the world outside Germany and Austria was never strongly attracted to the opera. This may have been because the opera has no love interest and its action moves slowly, at times even drearily. There is no record of a staged performance in either the United States or England.

To non-Germanic countries, *Palestrina* is familiar through three orchestral preludes, each serving to introduce an act; these are sometimes represented on symphony programs. The first time these preludes were heard in the United States was on November 11, 1926, when Willem Mengelberg conducted them at a concert of the New York Philharmonic.

The first prelude is solemn and mystical. A soaring motive (symbolic of Palestrina's creative personality) is the first main theme; a second, in the flutes, is also symbolic of Palestrina, and is the music which Palestrina plays at the organ to close the opera. A third theme, for solo violin, suggests the splendor and majesty of the church.

The second prelude is powerful music describing the clash of minds at the Council of Trent. The main theme is presented loudly by horns and is built up to a dramatic climax. Woodwinds then introduce a gentler idea as a contrast.

The third prelude is spiritual music, with a tender and reverent singing subject for muted strings followed by a second expressive idea for the clarinet.

GABRIEL PIERNÉ 1863–1937

One can say of Gabriel Pierné what has often been said of some of the other conservative French composers of our time. He had technical skill; his style was elegant; sensitivity and refinement characterized his speech; his thought was touched by poetic beauty. What he lacked in originality and independence, he compensated for in charm. While discovering no new world, while content to live in a familiar one, he said what he had to say with freshness and appeal. Charles Malherbe put it this way; "The talent of Gabriel Pierné is above all touched with elegance and grace; without pain, he has elevated himself to the heights of the subject he handles; he has become almost a classicist with his works for harp and his Piano Concerto in C minor (op. 12, 1887); he has attained dramatic intensity with certain scenes of *Vendée* (Lyons, March 11, 1897) and finds in his *La Nuit de Noël* (1896) the precise note and the true emotion. Endowed with a fertile imagination, with a supple spirit, Gabriel Pierné sketches melodies full of charm and reveals himself expert in giving these melodies shape and form because, within him . . . is concealed a very substantial science, together with an intimate knowledge of the classics and a profound understanding of counterpoint."

Pierné was born in Metz, France, on August 16, 1863. At the Paris Conservatory, which he attended between 1871 and 1882, he was Debussy's classmate; his teachers there included César Franck, Marmontel and Massenet. Pierné won the highest honors, including the Prix de Rome for his cantata *Édith* in 1882. In 1890, he succeeded Franck as organist of the Sainte-Clotilde in Paris. After eight years in this post, he became assistant conductor, then full conductor, of the Colonne Orchestra, in which post he won international renown over a period of almost a quarter of a century. His first major appearance as composer came with the opera *La Coupe enchantée,* produced in Royan, France, on August 24, 1895. Fame arrived with the cantata, *The Children's*

Crusade, in 1905. After that, he was a prolific contributor to the literature of opera, ballet, instrumental, choral and vocal music. Paradoxically enough, despite his rich production in large structures, he is today perhaps best remembered for several comparative trifles: the *Entrance of the Little Fauns* from the ballet, *Cydalise and the Satyr;* the Serenade in A major, op. 7 (1875), originally for piano but popular in transcriptions; and the *March of the Little Lead Soldiers,* (*Marche des petits soldats de plomb*), op. 14 (1887), also first for the piano, then transcribed by the composer of orchestra. In 1925, Pierné was elected to the Académie des Beaux-Art, and in 1940, he was made Chevalier of the Legion of Honor. His death took place at Ploujean, in Brittany, on July 17, 1937.

1902 LA CROISADE DES ENFANTS (THE CHILDREN'S CRUSADE), cantata for children's and adults' choruses and orchestra.

With his Flemish legend, *The Children's Crusade*—text by Marcel Schwob—Pierné achieved international recognition as a composer; and to this day, it remains one of his most distinguished works. In 1905, it won the City of Paris prize of ten thousand francs, and on January 18 of the same year, it was introduced with outstanding success by the Colonne Orchestra, directed by Edouard Colonne. Soon after its première, it was heard throughout the world of music.

Pierné has told the legend of the thirteenth-century crusade of children to the Holy Land with poetic sensitivity. In the published score the following introductory explanation is found: "About that time, many children, without leader and without guidance, did fly in a religious ecstasy from our towns and from our cities, making for the lands beyond the seas. And to those who asked of them whither they were bound, they did make the answer: 'To Jerusalem, in search of the Holy Land.' . . . They carried staves and satchels, and crosses were embroided on their garments. . . . They traveled to Genoa, and did embark upon the seven great vessels to cross the sea. And a storm arose and two vessels perished in the waters. . . . And to those who asked of such of the children who were saved, the reason for their journey, these replied: 'We do not know.' "

The cantata is divided into four sections, or scenes: I. The Departure of the Children. II. Their Journey to Genoa. III. The Scene by the Sea. IV. The Savior in the Storm.

In the first scene, the heavenly hosts summon the children to their crusade, a summons they answer enthusiastically in spite of the pleading of their parents to ignore it. In the second scene, the children are on their way, marching through meadows and countrysides during the warm mornings of spring. The delight of the children at seeing the sea is described in the third scene, while in the fourth, the storm, shipwreck, the children's prayer for help, and the celestial vision of the Savior are reproduced.

The subject of the children's crusade was also used by Gian Carlo Menotti for his cantata *Death of the Bishop of Brindisi* (1963).

1913 CYDALISE ET LE CHÈVRE-PIED (CYDALISE AND THE SATYR), ballet in two acts, with scenario by G. A. de Caillavet and Robert de Flers based on Rémy de Goncourt's *Lettre d'un satyr,* and choreography by Léo Staats. First performance: Paris Opéra, January 15, 1923.

CYDALISE ET LE CHÈVRE-PIED, ballet suite for orchestra, No. 1.: I. The School of the Fauns (or The Entrance of the Little Fauns); II. The Lesson of the Pandean Pipes; III. March of the Nymphs; IV. The Dancing Lesson.

CYDALISE ET LE CHÈVRE-PIED, ballet suite for orchestra, No. 2: I. Ballet of the Sultan of the Indies; II. Entrance; III. Pantomime; IV. Dance of the Apothecaries; V. Dance of the Slaves; VI. Variation of Cydalise; VII. Finale.

Pierné's most famous ballet, *Cydalise and the Satyr,* was written in 1913. Though accepted immediately by the Paris Opéra, its première was delayed for several years by the outbreak of war. When finally performed, it achieved a great success. Émile Vuillermoz wrote as follows: "Gabriel Pierné has written . . . a score of extraordinary youthfulness and allurement; he has brought into play all the subtleties of modern instrumentation, as also a great knowledge and routine without the aggressive audacities of our modern experimenters. . . . This score abounds in coquetries of excellent quality, and is of vivacity and freshness which will enchant the public."

The scenario combines classic mythology with eighteenth-century French court life. An old satyr conducts a class in dancing and in the playing of Pandean pipes. Styrax, one of the pupils, is mischievous, and is expelled. He wanders into the woods, where he is met by a coach bearing a group of dancers, one of whom is Cydalise. Falling in love with Cydalise, Styrax hides in the coach and is brought into a French royal court. There he reveals himself to his beloved, makes love to her, and is about to win her over when, from the distance, come the voices of satyrs calling him back to the forests. Torn between his love for Cydalise and his desire to rejoin his companions, Styrax finally succumbs to the latter.

The opening movement of the first suite—*The Entrance of the Little Fauns,* or, as it is sometimes called, *The School of the Fauns*—is outstandingly popular. It is a sprightly piece in which a piquant tune (muted trumpets) is heard against the background of piccolos. An infectious rhythm is provided by snare drum, tambourine and violinists tapping lightly on the strings with the wood of their bows.

WILLEM PIJPER 1894–1947

Teacher, critic, editor, composer—Willem Pijper was one of the dominating figures in contemporary Dutch music. As a composer, he stood in the vanguard of the ultramodern school in Holland. He was one of the first Dutch composers to write in a polytonal style, this idiom appearing in his first string quartet (1914). After 1918, he progressed towards linear counterpoint. He also tried to break with what he regarded as the tyranny of the bar line through the employment of polymetric and polyrhythmic procedures. And he perfected a technical method, which he dubbed the "germ cell theory," in which a large work was built from a melodic or rhythmic or harmonic germ cell: a chord in his Piano Concerto (1927); a four-note sequence in his two-piano sonatinas (1925); a three-note melodic sequence and two rhythmic motives in his Third Symphony (1926). But these techniques were always for Pijper a means to an artistic end, never an end in themselves. As M. D. Calvocoressi said: "He is radical in his methods, yet temperate in their application. The attention he devotes to polyphonic devices and structural correspondences may be characteristic of his ancestry or of his study of old Dutch music; his sense of color and his diction are, in the main, unquestionably Latin; but his personality is distinctly his own. Its most personal feature is perhaps his capacity to express an aural, even impressionistic imagination, by a strictly deductive method."

Pijper was born at Zeist, Utrecht, Holland, on September 8, 1894. A sickly child, he was not allowed to go to school until he was fourteen. His childhood was a solitary one, given to omnivorous reading, the study of biology and the practice of music. Formal music study took place with Johan Wagenaar at the Utrecht Music School. His first important work was a string quartet in 1914, followed by the song cycle *Fêtes galantes* (1916) and his First Symphony (1917); the song cycle had been influenced by Debussy, the symphony by Mahler. But experimentation was begun even in those early works and continued more boldly after 1918, until Pijper evolved an idiom of his own, which became fully realized with his Third Symphony in 1926, and his opera *Halewijn,* which was introduced in Amsterdam on June 13, 1933. Meanwhile, Pijper was also pursuing careers as critic and teacher. He was music critic of the *Utrechts Dagblad* from 1918 to 1925, and editor of *De Muziek* from 1926 to 1929, a journal he had helped to found. After three years as teacher of harmony and composition at a high school in Amsterdam, Pijper became professor of composition at the Amsterdam Conservatory in 1925. From 1930 until his death, he was the director of the Rotterdam Conservatory. He was working on an opera, *Merlijn,* when he died at Leidshendam, near The Hague, on March 19, 1947.

1926 SYMPHONY NO. 3.

Pijper's last symphony is the one work by which he is best known in the United States. It has enjoyed numerous performances by many of America's major symphonic organizations. It is also one of Pijper's most important compositions. On October 28, 1926, it was introduced by the Concertgebouw Orchestra of Amsterdam under Pierre Monteux (who also introduced it to the United States at a concert of the Philadelphia Orchestra on February 17, 1928). A quotation from *The Aeneid,* which appears on the flyleaf of the published score, gives a clue to the composer's emotional intentions: "If I cannot influence the Gods, I will move the powers of Hell."

Though in three distinct sections, the symphony is played without interruption. The main theme comes at the very outset and consists of phrases that ascend and descend in intervals of the fourth. This is the "germ cell" of the entire work. A countersubject is a piquant melody for violins and flutes. A fermata leads to the slow movement (Adagio), music of great emotional depth, reflecting the composer's state of mind during a period of personal tragedy. The quiet and expressive sorrow is punctuated with orchestral outbursts, but at the conclusion of this section tranquillity returns. A solo violin introduces the return of the opening theme, now heard in the basses, after which the final movement (Molto allegro) brings music of herculean strength and defiance. The symphony ends in a sudden and frenetic climax, fortissimo.

WALTER PISTON 1894–

Some critics (mindful perhaps of his long career as professor of music, or aware that he has shown a marked partiality for such traditional forms as the symphony, the concerto, the suite, etc.) have described Piston as an academic or a classical composer. He is neither. There is no suggestion of the schoolroom or the textbook in his music. And though he likes classical forms, he is very often vibrantly contemporary in his idiom. But when he writes atonally, or when he uses dissonant counterpoint, he absorbs such modern techniques completely into writing which, for the most part, is derived from older styles.

It is not easy to classify a composer who at times is complex and at other times simple, at times coldly logical and at other times emotional. Piston writes as he pleases, adapting his style to the aesthetic requirements of the music he is writing. He is usually strongly melodic, with an extraordinary feeling for the large classical forms and for architectonic construction. He is thoroughly American without quoting native materials, just as he is thoroughly modern without flaunting avant-garde techniques. "His is the consolidating type of mind that assimilates the most significant trends in the art of an epoch," says Joseph Machlis, "welds them into a personal language, and sets upon them the seal of stylistic unity. His works are elegant, mature, architecturally clear, and self-contained."

Piston was born in Rockland, Maine, on January 20, 1894. While attending Mechanic Arts High School in Boston, he studied the violin and played in the school orchestra. He went to the Normal Art School from 1912 to 1916 to specialize in drawing and painting. After 1916, he devoted himself to intensive music study with Harris Shaw (piano), and Fiumara, Theodorowicz, and Winternitz (violin). During World War I, he played in the Navy band. After the end of the war, he enrolled in Harvard, specializing in music, and graduating in 1924 summa cum laude, and with a Phi Beta Kappa key. On a John Knowles Paine Fellowship he spent the next two years in Paris studying composition with Paul Dukas at the École Normale de Musique and privately with Nadia Boulanger, His first compositions to get an important performance were heard in Paris at this time—a piano sonata and *Three Pieces,* for flute, clarinet and bassoon, both written in 1926.

Following his return to the United States in 1926, he became a member of the music faculty at Harvard, where he stayed until 1960, serving as full professor from 1944 on. In 1928, he first attracted attention in the United States when his *Symphonic Piece* was introduced by the Boston Symphony under Koussevitzky on March 23. Major orchestral works, many of them introduced by the Boston Symphony, added to his reputation. His first major success was realized with his score to the ballet, *The Incredible Flutist,* in 1938. He subsequently received two Pulitzer Prizes in music (for his Third Symphony in 1948, and his Seventh Symphony in 1961), and two awards from the New York Music Critics Circle (for his Second Symphony in 1945, and his Viola Concerto in 1959). In addition, he received a Guggenheim Fellowship in 1935; was appointed a member of the Institute of Arts and Letters in 1938, and of the American Academy of Arts and Sciences in 1940. In 1966, Dickinson College presented him with its Arts Award. He has also been given four honorary doctorates.

1938 THE INCREDIBLE FLUTIST, ballet suite for orchestra. I. Introduction. II. Siesta Hour in the Marketplace and Entrance of the Vendors. III. Dance of the Vendors. IV. Entrance of the Customers. V. Tango of the Four Daughters. VI. Arrival of the Circus and Circus March. VII. Solo of the Flutist. VIII. Minuet and Dance of the Widow and Merchant. IX. Spanish Waltz. X. Eight O'Clock Strikes. XI. Siciliano, and Dance of the Flutist and the Merchant's Daughter. XII. Polka Finale.

Piston has preferred writing abstract music, feeling freest when he can permit his musical ideas to grow, develop and become transformed because of the musical logic involved rather than because of the demands of some text or program. Thus, he has written little that has programmatic interest, a notable exception being his score for *The Incredible Flutist.* To this ballet, he brought such a rich fund of wit, such vivid imagery, such an uncanny gift for translating the subtle innuendos of his ballet scenario to their musical equivalent, that it becomes obvious he has avoided program music, not because he is less gifted in that vein, but out of artistic preference and compulsion.

The Incredible Flutist was written in collaboration with the dancer Hans Wiener, who—with his dancers—introduced it at one of the concerts of the Boston Pops Orchestra on May 30, 1938. The action takes place in a village marketplace, which early in the morning awakens and becomes alive with activity. A circus enters: at its head, a juggler, a clown and a flutist. The miraculous piping of the flutist is able to charm snakes—and women. It charms one of the merchants' daughters. Suddenly, the clock strikes eight. Romance is in the air, and it infects all those in the marketplace. Couples are seen whispering tender sentiments. A rich widow kisses a merchant and, discovered by her lover, passes away into a swoon. The flutist strikes up one of his pretty tunes, and the widow recovers. A march is suddenly struck up. The circus leaves town.

An orchestral suite from the ballet score, introduced on November 22, 1940, by the Pittsburgh Symphony under Fritz Reiner became Piston's first major success and the first of his compositions to gain wide circulation among major symphony orchestras.

1943 SYMPHONY NO. 2. I. Moderato. II. Adagio. III. Allegro.

The Alice M. Ditson Fund of Columbia University commissioned Piston to write a symphony. On March 5, 1944, Hans Kindler conducted its première with the National Symphony of Washington, D.C. Following its performance in New York City by the New York Philharmonic Orchestra, the work received the New York Music Critics Circle Award.

A broad legato subject in the violas and cellos opens the symphony; this is the major theme of the first movement. It is subjected to elaborate development, and at the end of the movement appears in canonic form (pianissimo). A second idea—rhythmic rather than melodic—is heard in the oboe, clarinet and bassoons. In the Adagio, a delicate melody is given by the bassoon and sinuously winds its way throughout the movement, which is continuous and fluid rather than sectional. Three themes are heard in the concluding section of the symphony: one is robust and rhythmic (cellos and horns); a second is a march (clarinets and bassoons), and a third is melodic (English horn and clarinet).

1947 STRING QUARTET NO. 3. I. Allegro. II. Lento. III. Allegro.

Piston's Third String Quartet was written on a commission from Harvard University for its Symposium of Music Criticism. The work was introduced by the Walden Quartet in Cambridge, Massachusetts, on May 1, 1947. The first movement is vigorously rhythmic with occasional passages of lyric interest; the second theme calls for a rubato style. The slow movement is based on a single melodic phrase played by the viola. This melody undergoes several variations, is developed to a dramatic climax, and then is allowed to end quietly. A rondo, based on three themes, constitutes the closing movement. Light and spirited throughout, this is ingratiating music from beginning to end; the first of the three themes undergoes considerable fugal treatment.

1947 SYMPHONY NO. 3. I. Andantino. II. Allegro. III. Adagio. IV. Allegro.

The Third Symphony, which followed the Second by four years, was commissioned by the Koussevitzky Music Foundation. It is one of Piston's most important and successful works up to this period. Music of exceptional communicative power, it has a wider emotional range than most of Piston's work, passing from an almost delicate wit to a pastorale-like serenity, from introspective calm to dramatic intensity.

The first movement is based on three thematic ideas (the first in the oboe; the second in the horn, clarinet and English horn; the third, in the brass) which are developed singly and in combination. The second movement is a three-part scherzo, with the principal theme played by the violas and bassoons. The

Adagio comprises four large and closely connected sections of musical development: in the first, the theme is stated; in the second, it is presented in varied form; in the third, it rises to a climax; and in the fourth, it returns in its original form. A three-part finale consists of two major themes, one treated fugally, the other march-like in character.

Serge Koussevitzky conducted the first performance of the Third Symphony with the Boston Symphony Orchestra on January 9, 1948. It was outstandingly successful from the first. Late the same year, the symphony received the Hornblit Award and the Pulitzer Prize.

1948 TOCCATA, for orchestra.

Piston wrote this showpiece for orchestra at the request of Charles Munch for performance with the Orchestre National de France, scheduled to make an American tour. "Many memories of student days in Paris returned during the composition of this piece," the composer explains, "and I continually sought to bring out in the music those qualities of clarity and brilliance which are so outstanding in the playing of French musicians." The Toccata received its world première in a performance over the radio by the Orchestre National de France, Charles Munch conducting, during the late summer of 1948; the first public performance was given by this same orchestra and conductor in Bridgeport, Connecticut, on October 14, 1948. It was then performed on each of the forty-one programs given by the orchestra on its coast-to-coast tour. The composer described the work as "in simple three-part form and, as its nature implies, in brilliant and rhythmic style, except for the middle part, which is slower and more lyric in character."

1950 SYMPHONY NO. 4. I. Piacevole. II. Ballando. III. Contemplativo. IV. Energico.

Piston was commissioned to write his Fourth Symphony by the University of Minnesota to help celebrate its centenary. The world première took place in Minneapolis on March 30, 1951, Antal Dorati conducting the Minneapolis Symphony. The composer described the first movement as "easy going, in large two-part form." There are two main themes, the first heard at the beginning in the first violins, while the second, a more subdued subject, is given by the clarinet supported by other woodwind. A version of the first theme is the basis of a brief coda. This is followed by "a dancing movement in rondo A-B-A-C-A-B-A. The principal theme, A, is characterized by free rhythms and irregular meter. The B section is a waltz, and the middle section, C, is reminiscent of country fiddling."

The slow movement is "a continuous Adagio . . . growing by means of new aspects of the melodic phrase at the opening by the clarinet alone, then in varied form by violas and English horn. The climax is marked by a statement of this theme in chordal form by the brass." The finale is in sonata form. "The first theme is rugged and rhythmic, the second being by contrast more songful in character, and easily identified when first played by the oboe. There is a short development and a recapitulation building to a climax.

1954–1955 SYMPHONY NO. 5. I. Lento; Allegro con spirito; Lento. II. Adagio. III. Allegro lieto.

SYMPHONY NO. 6. I. Fluendo espressivo. II. Leggerissimo vivace. III. Adagio sereno. IV. Allegro energico.

The Fifth Symphony (1954) was the result of a commission from the Juilliard School of Music for a festival of American music planned for 1955, but postponed until the spring of 1956. The première of the symphony was given in New York on February 24, 1956, by the Juilliard Orchestra, Jean Morel conducting. The composer explains that "in the slow introduction may be found the origins of all the musical ideas subsequently developed in the symphony. The main body of the movement is in sonata form." In the slow movement, "cellos and basses outline in pizzicato a basic melodic pattern and against this the violins play a melody, the theme of the movement. There follow three variations, or transformations of the theme, each section growing out of the preceding. These variations are not greatly contrasting, but rather form a continuous whole, finishing with a coda recalling the start of the first variation." The finale is "a gay and rhythmic movement, in form resembling a rondo (A-B-A-B-A) in which there is considerable 'working out' of the second A."

Piston's Sixth Symphony (1955) was commissioned by the Koussevitzky Music Foundation for the seventy-fifth anniversary of the Boston Symphony. That orchestra, directed by Charles Munch, introduced it in Boston on November 25, 1955. The composer provides the following succinct description:

"The first movement is flowing and expressive in sonata form with two melodic themes alternating, the first for strings, the second for woodwind. The second is a fast and light scherzo in fugato style, with soft and delicate percussion and muted strings. The third is a serene Adagio with main theme for solo cello and second theme for flute. After variations and development of the main theme, the second theme returns in violas and is developed. The first theme then returns and the solo cello ends the movement. The fourth movement is an energetic rondo with two themes, dancing or march-like in style."

When the Boston Symphony toured the Soviet Union in 1956 (the first American orchestra to do so), the Piston Sixth Symphony was featured prominently on its first and subsequent programs.

1957 CONCERTO FOR VIOLA AND ORCHESTRA. I. Con moto moderato e flessible. II. Adagio con fantasia. III. Allegro vivo.

Piston wrote his viola concerto for Joseph De Pasquale, first violist of the Boston Symphony, who introduced it with that orchestra, Charles Munch conducting, on March 7, 1958. The concerto received the New York Music Critics Circle Award.

The composer explains that the first movement is "in sonata form with an animated second theme in contrast with the quietly expressive principal melody"; that the second movement is a "rhapsodic and improvisatory Adagio on a single theme in solo viola; the string choir is throughout muted"; and that the finale is a "lively and brilliant rondo on two themes, the first a lively dance-like melody for solo viola; the movement ends with a cadenza and a closing fanfare."

In the Boston *Herald,* Rudolph Elie reported that Piston "has, in one giant step, provided the world with a viola concerto worthy of the instrument.

. . . The Concerto displays the instrument in all of its special marvelous capacities, but at the same time makes its mark as a unified and deeply felt composition in which the viola does not merely contend with the orchestra, but rises out of it as an integral part of the communication."

1959 THREE NEW ENGLAND SKETCHES, for orchestra. I. Seaside. II. Summer Evening. III. Mountains.

This orchestral suite represents one of its composer's rare excursions into descriptive music with programmatic implications. The composition was commissioned by the Detroit Symphony Orchestra, which introduced it at the Worcester Festival in Massachusetts on October 23, 1959.

The composer reveals that the subtitles of his suite "serve in a broad sense to tell the source of the impressions, reminiscences, even dreams, that pervaded the otherwise musical thoughts of one New England composer." The Boston music critic, Cyrus Durgin, describes the work as follows: "Piston has produced three symphonic movements that are healthy with the free play of rhythm, muscular in the effect of their lively contrapuntal melodies, and well-built, with small sturdy skeletons of musical structure fleshed out by fascinating and expert instrumentation. . . . *Seaside* begins in a coloristic manner, including a hushed roll on a suspended cymbal. . . . *Mountains* is big music, with the giant tread of kettledrums beneath the powerful strings. There is a fine fugue, or at least a fugato, in the movement."

1960 SYMPHONIC PRELUDE, for orchestra.

This short orchestral piece was commissioned by the Association of Women's Committees for Symphony Orchestras, which gathered in Cleveland in April of 1961 for its thirteenth biennial conference. Its world première was given during that conference, on April 20, 1961, in a performance by the Cleveland Orchestra under George Szell. It proved so successful that in short order the composition was performed in Chicago, Philadelphia, New Orleans, St. Louis, Minneapolis and Houston, among other cities.

The composer says that the Prelude "might be characterized as a kind of discourse about a melody given out by the violas and a clarinet. There are a dozen or so aspects of this theme, each growing out of its predecessor making a continuous movement based on the variation principle, although the metamorphoses are not differentiated in the manner of a theme and variations. In overall design, the Prelude shows four facets. The first presents the melody mainly through violas, violins, woodwinds, then brass. The second is of thinner texture, chiefly woodwinds, starting with the oboe. In the third facet, thirty-second note motion begins in the lower strings, and there is a development to a climax. And in the fourth, a final statement of the theme occurs in the strings with a close in an extended cadence."

1960 SYMPHONY NO. 7. I. Con moto. II. Adagio pastorale. III. Allegro festevole.

Piston's Seventh Symphony brought its composer the Pulitzer Prize in music for the second time. He wrote it for the Philadelphia Orchestra, which introduced it on February 10, 1961, Eugene Ormandy conducting. The composer has explained that in writing this symphony he was conscious of the orchestra for which it was intended. Probably bearing in mind the famous Philadelphia Orchestra sound, he emphasized the lyrical and expressive elements rather than the dramatic—as in the expansive first subject of the first movement, which is heard in the strings without preliminaries, and in the touching melody (dolcissimo) in which the oboe is heard beginning with the third measure of the second movement. Harold C. Schonberg called the symphony "a typical Piston work," when he reviewed it, following its New York première on February 14, 1961, "smoothly constructed, well-orchestrated, shapely in form and always well-bred. . . . The melodic material—Mr. Piston composes in the orthodox vein, with relatively few dissonances or harmonic problems—is always to the fore."

ILDEBRANDO PIZZETTI 1880–1968

That Pizzetti's music is not heard more frequently in the United States is an irreparable deprivation. Few composers in our time achieved such a sensitive fusion between intellect and emotion, between old ways and new, as Pizzetti has done. Always music of high principles, his works have a character all their own, in the dramatic expressiveness of his melodic line, which is often more declamatory than lyrical; in his unique harmonic atmosphere, achieved at times through the use of modes; in the force and originality of his musical thinking. In whatever medium he chooses to write, he reveals a master's hand and the aristocratic intellect of a scholar. His passion for liturgical music and for the voice, first stimulated and developed in his early manhood, has made him most effective when he writes for chorus (whether for the opera house or the concert hall). However, he has also produced a good deal of distinguished instrumental music, though even here the tendency to use an instrument as if it were a singing voice can be detected.

Three influences have shaped his creative evolution. The first was Gabriele d'Annunzio, whose poems and dramas he set to music. This was the period that saw the writing of the remarkable song, "*I Pastori*" (1908), the incidental music to *La Pisanella* (first performance in Paris on June 11, 1913), and his first opera, *Fedora,* whose world première took place at La Scala in Milan on March 20, 1915.

Then Pizzetti turned to the Bible for material and stimulus. This phase resulted in the opera *Debora e Jaele,* which took him six years to write and which was mounted by La Scala in Milan on December 16, 1922; a setting of a fifteenth-century morality play, *La Sacra Rappresentazione di Abram e d'Isaac,* first heard in Florence in 1917. Finally, he found his inspiration in Italian history, the results of which were his most famous opera *Fra Gherardo* in 1926, together with *Orsèolo* (Florence, May 5, 1935) and *Vanna Lupa* (Florence, May 4, 1949).

He has probably been most significant in opera, a field to which he has contributed about a dozen works. Here Pizzetti sought to realize a more intimate association between the musical theatre and life itself. He put it this way: "Dramatic music should express life in action—conflicts of matter and mind, of instincts and aspirations, of egotism and moral duty; and lyrical music should express the transcendence, the overcoming of these conflicts." In Pizzetti's operas, as in life itself, action is combined with repose, dramatic conflict with introspection.

Pizzetti diverged sharply from the traditions of Italian opera that had hardened into stereotyped patterns. The singer in his opera is only one of many elements and is never assigned exaggerated importance, Nor is the music ever allowed to become dominant; it must be inextricably wedded to the text so that to separate the one from the other is to lose something vital. There are no formal arias in Pizzetti's operas. His melodic line usually consists of strong, expressive declamations (molded after the inflections of the Italian language); and when he allows greater freedom of flight to his lyricism, it must always grow naturally out of the texture of the play. The choruses, too, are never allowed to assume unusual importance (even though frequently his finest and most eloquent writing is reserved for the chorus), but are integrated into the whole design and must always serve a dramatic purpose. The fluidity and continuity of the opera as a whole is more important to Pizzetti than the effect of any one scene. His operas, consequently, may occasionally appear static in their action, but they have a unity of conception and purpose (realized partly by the fact that after *Fedora* he was his own librettist), which is one of their strongest attributes. Guido M. Gatti put it this way: "He has attained a perfection of rapport between verbal and musical aspects that is seldom encountered. The language of Pizzetti's operas cannot be described adequately as being either primarily verbal or primarily musical. It is essentially dramatic, and results from a fusion of the two elements that the composer has achieved through fifty years of tenacious study and absolute dedication to his artistic beliefs."

Pizzetti was born in Parma, Italy, on September 20, 1880. He received his musical training at the Parma Conservatory, which he entered in 1895 and from which he was graduated with honors in 1901. Following his graduation, he held various minor posts as conductor and teacher. In 1909, he became professor of theory and composition at the Conservatory of Florence, where eight years later he became director. In 1925, he was made director of the Verdi Conservatory in Milan; in 1936, he succeeded Respighi as professor of composition at the Santa Cecilia Academy in Rome; and from 1948 until his retirement in 1951, he was director of Santa Cecilia. His first opera, *Fedora,* was at first a failure, though after a revival in Rome and several performances elsewhere its subtle and classic beauty gained some measure of appreciation. *Debora e Jaele* was a success when introduced in 1922 at La Scala under Toscanini's direction, and *Fra Gherardo* in 1928 was a triumph. In 1930, Pizzetti paid a visit to the United States, appearing as conductor and pianist in performances of his compositions. He received the international Italia Prize in 1950 for his one-act opera *Ifigenia* (first performance over the Turin Radio on September 18, 1950). He was a member of the London Royal Academy of Music and the Académie des Beaux-Arts in France, and president of the Italian Society of Composers and Authors. He died in Rome on February 13, 1968.

1919 SONATA IN A MAJOR FOR VIOLIN AND PIANO. I. Tempestoso. II. Preghiera per gli innocenti. III. Vivo e fresco.

The reaction of the composer to World War I is revealed in the poignantly tragic music found in this sonata. One of the composer's most personal utterances, the sonata is among his more emotional creations, and among his unquestioned masterpieces. Grief unrelieved—grief in all its unrestrained intensity and piercing sting—is heard in the tempestuous first movement. The first theme, heard in the piano, is intense and passionate; the second theme, following immediately in the violin, is elegiac. The second movement is a "prayer for the innocents." Appended to the opening measures is the following line: "O Our Lord, have pity upon all the innocents who do not know why they must suffer." Against modern chords, and with altered rhythms, comes a melody of sustained beauty—"a gospel of charity," Castelnuovo-Tedesco called it. An element of joy comes at last in the concluding movement, a rondo, almost as if, after the grief and suffering, a reaffirmation of life comes. The principal theme resembles a folk song.

The sonata was introduced in the year of its composition by Ernesto Consolo and Mario Corti, to whom the work is dedicated.

1927 FRA GHERARDO, opera in three acts, with text by the composer based on the thirteenth-century Chronicles of Salimbene da Parma. First performance: La Scala, Milan, May 16, 1928.

Fra Gherardo is Pizzetti's fourth opera, and with it he achieved his first major international success for the stage. This opera belongs to the third of Pizzetti's creative periods, in which he tapped the veins of Italian history.

The hero of the opera is a weaver who rescues the lovely Mariola from attack, falls in love with her, and takes her to live with him. He repents this indiscretion and is driven to join the Flagellant Order. Nine years later, he is known as Fra Gherardo of the White Friars, a saintly man worshiped by the masses. He becomes the spearhead of the attack of the citizens of Parma against the nobility. Meanwhile, Mariola comes to him to confide that, some years back, she has given birth to their child, who has died. Fra Gherardo would like to make amends by devoting himself to Mariola. But she reminds him that his first duty is to the people of Parma in their uprising. The uprising is aborted when Fra Gherardo is arrested for heresy. For her part in the insurrection, Mariola is condemned to burn at the stake. Only one thing can save Mariola: Gherardo's expression of allegiance to the state. This he cannot give. Mariola rushes to him to be with him when they die. Gherardo is burned, and Mariola becomes the victim of an insane woman.

In a penetrating analysis of the opera in the Boston *Transcript,* H. T. Parker wrote: "As stringently as Debussy, Pizzetti holds that in music drama there should be no songful expansions, no lyrical effusions of emotion with all else at a pause. Rather, let the music publish and enforce the verse of the drama, phrase by phrase, period by period. With Mussorgsky, he agrees that a musical speech can compass the contours, the shadings, the emphases of the spoken word and so become semi-humanized discourse. With the Italian inventors and founders of opera—Peri, Monteverdi and the other pioneers—he would hark back to a declamation that defines precisely the significance of the verse in a given situation; while the orchestra, in measure, sustains it, in ampler degree it gives it background of emotion and atmosphere. These orchestral voices are the harmonic complement of the declaiming singers, yet intrinsically they go their own way. With the longest of leaps to the other extreme, Pizzetti . . . would have these two tonal streams, the orchestral and the vocal, converge however wide apart, in illusory and emotional impact upon the hearer. Again like Mussorgsky, Pizzetti passions himself for choruses that shall be the very voice of the people under single or divided sensation and emotion. . . . Finally, self-disciplined as Pizzetti is, absorbed as he is in his own theory and practice of music drama, he has not quite purged himself of the Old Adam which is Italian opera. From certain pages exhales for the instant a distinct Puccinian odor. In that unfortunate incident, compared to the rest of *Fra Gherardo*—the death of Mariola—she dies in plain Puccinian grace."

Fra Gherardo received its American première at the Metropolitan Opera in New York on March 21, 1929.

1928 CONCERTO DELL'ESTATE, for orchestra. I. Mattutino. II. Notturno. III. Gagliarda e finale.

Though Pizzetti confesses modeling this work after the concerto grosso of Vivaldi, there is little in the writing (which is modern in spirit and impressionistic in character) or even in the architectonic construction to remind us of the eighteenth-century classical form, beyond the rather superficial fact that two vigorous movements are separated by a lyrical one. The first part of this concerto is built around five themes, three appearing at once and almost simultaneously; the fourth is an oboe solo; the fifth, a largamente for full orchestra. Unaccompanied violins voice the lyric and poetic melody which comprises the entire middle section. For his closing part, Pizzetti re-creates an ancient dance, with brusque and dynamic rhythms.

On February 28, 1929, Arturo Toscanini gave the première performance of the Concerto in New York City with the New York Philharmonic Orchestra.

1929 RONDO VENEZIANO, for orchestra.

In the published score of this work, the composer himself provides an admirable analysis: "This composition consists of three 'strophes,' preceded and followed by a less extensive musical period in the guise of a 'ritornello' (refrain); whence the title *Rondo*. But just as there are, in Italian poetry, songs and odes in rondo form whose strophes differ in content as well as in expression, so the three 'strophes' of this rondo differ, not only in thematic material, but in movement and character.

"If the musical period that serves as a ritornello (opening and closing the composition) be regarded as an expression of the fundamental and immutable traits of the Adriatic city, the first strophe might be considered an expression of aristocratic Venice, luxurious and pompous (but without particular reference to any specific period of the past) and the third strophe as an expression of plebeian Venice. The middle strophe is a sort of intermezzo, both idyllic and impassioned.

"The architecture of the work is intentionally regular and symmetrical. The length of each repetition of the ritornello is virtually the same. Both the first and third strophes consist of two extensive periods, equally long, connected by an intermediate passage. In the case of the first strophe, this passage has almost the character of a minuet (quartet of strings with harpsichord, over a pedal of violoncelli and contrabassi); in the case of the third strophe, the connective passage has the character of a dance, quasi pastoral, inserted into the movement more joyous even than the Forlana: as if an enamored visitor in Venice, emerging from a square filled with a roistering, noisy crowd, should find himself in a secluded piazzetta looking upon a small gathering of youths and maidens dancing to the sound of two pipes, an accordion, and a bass viol under a pergola of grapes outside a rustic tavern."

The world première of *Rondo Veneziano* took place in New York City on February 27, 1930. Arturo Toscanini conducted the New York Philharmonic. The composer, on his first tour of the United States, was present at the performance.

1958 ASSASSINIO NELLA CATEDRALE (MURDER IN THE CATHEDRAL), opera in two acts and interlude, with text by the composer based on T. S. Eliot's poetical drama, *Murder in the Cathedral,* in an Italian version by Albert Castelli. First performance: La Scala, Milan, March 1, 1958.

This is Pizzetti's most important and most highly acclaimed opera since *Fra Gherardo.* The central character is the twelfth-century Archbishop, Thomas à Becket, who was assassinated in Canterbury Cathedral. In the opera, the setting is transferred from medieval England to what Irving Kolodin has described as "the dateless operaland of Italy. . . . What the work has lost in transference . . . is exemplified by a reference to the *Dies Irae* as events close in upon Thomas à Becket—or, more specifically, L'Arcivescovo Tommaso Becket, as the score identifies him. . . . It [the *Dies Irae*] adds little to the meaning of this content."

While the action of the opera often proves static, and dramatic interest often tends to lag, Pizzetti's musical writing achieves such power and eloquence that the opera remains a compelling emotional experience.

Most of the opera is written in a skilful accompanied recitative style which succeeds magically in capturing the mystical mood of the play. But the melodic element is not altogether absent, and is found particularly in the moving arias of the Archbishop at the end of the first act, and of the First Corifea at the beginning of the second. But as in Pizzetti's earlier operas, the most significant music is reserved for the chorus, for the moving choruses of the priests and of the Canterbury women. "It may be doubted," wrote Francis Toye, "whether he has ever done anything better. . . . The fear, the misery and the horror of the women are reflected to perfection in their music."

One musical theme dominates the opera, a motive that recurs whenever the Archbishop is on the stage. Generally, this idea is heard in the orchestra, but once it is given vocal treatment.

The American première of the opera took place in Carnegie Hall, New York, on September 17, 1958.

QUINCY PORTER 1897–1966

Porter's is the kind of music that suggests intimate confidences, the kind of music that demands smaller forces: now delicately playful, now amiable and charming, now tender and gentle, now moody and thoughtful. Though his music is always realized masterfully, with the fullest technical resources, there is an almost effortless quality about it—in the presentation of the melodic ideas, in their development, and in the transparent texture of his harmonic and contrapuntal writing—which gives it an engaging feeling of spontaneity. Herbert Elwell put it well when he said that Porter had acquired the skill of the professional without losing the enthusiasm of the amateur. Elwell wrote further: "Imagine music so lithe and well-tailored as to suggest a trim sloop taking the breeze and you have a hint of the clean, clear-headed sort of thing Quincy Porter has been turning out. . . . It has both form and expressiveness. It is forthright, vital and uninhibited, yet compact, terse and trenchant. It ranges emotionally from a sort of nervous exuberance in the fast movements to a wistful, tender serenity in the slow movements. When it is not buoyant and hopeless, it is likely to be nostaligic, with a touch of exotic color. . . . Its implications are often witty, its abbreviations and understatements, genial and stimulating. For all its meticulously polished workmanship, it is never content within the limitations of its chosen course. . . . It forges ahead with fine, fresh independence, yet it remains in unbroken continuity with the past. He achieved orientation and progressiveness, not by scuttling tradition, but by conserving those things which, because of their power to bring people together in agreement, are perhaps the most valuable things that could be nurtured in a world torn apart by uncertainty and confusion."

Porter was born in New Haven, Connecticut, on February 7, 1897. He is a descendant of Jonathan Edwards, the New England theologian, and the grandson and son of Yale professors. After extensive preliminary music study, he entered Yale in 1914, where he studied composition with Horatio Parker and David Stanley Smith at the School of Music. He was graduated from Yale in 1919 and from the School of Music in 1921. He also studied music in Paris between 1920 and 1922 at the Schola Cantorum with Vincent d'Indy (composition) and Capet (violin). Upon being graduated from the Yale School of Music, he wrote and performed a violin concerto (1921) which received honorable mention in the first American Prix de Rome; he also won the Osborne and Steinert Prizes for other compositions. Upon returning to the United States in 1922 he became a pupil of Ernest Bloch. In 1923, he was appointed to the faculty of the Cleveland Institute of Music, where he later became head of the theory department. This was the beginning of a long and fruitful career as teacher. For six years, he was professor of music at Vassar College; from 1938 to 1946, he was the dean, then director, of the New England Conservatory. In 1946, he became professor of music at Yale, holding this post until his retirement in July of 1965.

In 1928 and 1929, Porter was the recipient of Guggenheim Fellowships. He received the Coolidge medal for chamber music in 1943, was elected a member of the National Institute of Arts and Letters in 1944 (becoming its treasurer in 1964), and was awarded the Pulitzer Prize in music in 1954. From 1958 he was chairman of the board of directors of the American Music Center which he had helped to found in 1939.

Quincy Porter died at his home in Bethany, Connecticut, on November 12, 1966.

1931 STRING QUARTET NO. 4. I. Allegro moderato. II. Lento. III. Allegro molto.

This quartet was introduced by the Cleveland Institute Quartet in Cleveland on November 15, 1931. It is predominantly lyrical, with long spans of melody in the first movement, decorated by small rhythmic cells which jump from one instrument to another. The slow movement is built on one single theme. The form is contributed more by the motion of the rhythm, which increases to a climactic point before returning to the theme in its original form. The last movement has irregular rhythms, with a long theme for the cello.

1943 STRING QUARTET NO. 7. I. Allegro moderato. II. Adagio molto. III. Allegro moderato; Allegro molto.

Porter's Seventh String Quartet was commissioned by and dedicated to Elizabeth Sprague Coolidge. It was first performed at the Founder's Day Concert at the Library of Congress by the Coolidge Quartet on October 30, 1943.

The chief interest of the first movement is in the variety of rhythmic feeling that is worked into a consistent meter of 3/8 time, which does not change till the coda, which is in 2/8 time. A number of themes are woven together, but not treated in strict sonata form. The slow movement is somber and built on long dynamic lines, with frequent use of crossing instrument timbres. At the climax, the chief theme of the first movement is heard. The last movement begins with an energetic introduction, but soon settles into a fast triplet movement. It includes some references to themes from the first movement.

1948 CONCERTO FOR VIOLA AND ORCHESTRA. I. Adagio; Allegro. II. Largo. III. Allegro giusto.

Though Porter is at his best in smaller forms for more intimate combinations, he has produced effective music in the symphonic and concerto forms. The viola concerto is possibly his best work in the larger forms. On May 16, 1948, it was introduced in New York by Paul Doktor and the CBS Symphony Orchestra, Dean Dixon conducting, during the American Music Festival held at Columbia University.

The three movements are played without pause. The first movement (Adagio) contains much of the melodic material used later on, especially the main theme announced by the horn at the beginning. The viola plays in quasi obbligato, but introduces a number of melodic elements which are also made much of throughout the concerto. The Allegro that follows is in fast 6/8 rhythm, but with considerable lyric melody of the viola, interspersed with virtuoso passages. The slow movement (Largo) is meditative, and contains an important cadenza for the solo instrument. The last movement (Allegro giusto) is gay and contains some dance rhythms, a climactic return to the material of the opening of the first movement, and a fast, brilliant coda.

1950 STRING QUARTET NO. 8. I. Lento. II. Allegro. III. Adagio.

Porter's Eighth String Quartet was commissioned by the University of Michigan for the Stanley Quartet, which introduced it at Ann Arbor in the year of its composition. Though in three movements, each with a different tempo and mood, the work is actually a single, integrated composition in which one idea flows into the next, as Ross Lee Finney has said, "and the lovely arch of the entire work, ending where it began." The opening slow movement is in a continually changing meter. It has, says Joseph Machlis, "the quality of introspective lyricism—faintly tinged with nostalgia." The middle movement "takes its point of departure from a theme of distinctive profile which contains several usable motives" while the concluding Adagio is eloquently expressive, though charged with nervous energy.

1953 CONCERTO CONCERTANTE, for two pianos and orchestra.

Originally entitled Concerto for Two Pianos and Orchestra, this work was commissioned by the Louisville Orchestra in Kentucky, which introduced it on March 17, 1954. The soloists were Dorothea Adkins and Ann Monk, and Robert Whitney conducted. The concerto brought Porter the Pulitzer Prize in music.

The work is a unified one-movement composition which, as Howard Boatwright has written, "maintains tensions and variety by juxtaposition of expressive and lyrical elements and dance-like or energetic rhythmic elements." Mr. Boatwright goes on to explain: "Its pattern, in the broader sense, consists of a series of interruptions—the energetic elements interrupt the lyrical elements, and the lyrical element suddenly appears as the energetic sections come to abrupt endings. . . . But the real organization of this work is not a series of contrasting and thematically unrelated sectional blocks. It is . . . a fluidly conceived, subtly interrelated construction on the basis of a few simple motives. These motives appeared in varied disguises and forms throughout the whole piece—fast and slow, loud and soft, tender and wild." The tempo markings of the various sections are: Lento; Poco allegro; Lento; Allegro; Lento; Allegro.

FRANCIS POULENC 1899–1963

The music of Francis Poulenc has two faces. One is smiling, the other serious. He achieved his first success with tongue square in cheek, with the *Rapsodie nègre* in 1917. He followed this in 1918 with another gay escapade, the *Mouvements perpétuels* for piano in which his indebtedness to Satie is obvious; and in 1919, with two song cycles, *Le Bestiaire* and *Cocardes,* both characterized by a rich irony. Soon after that, as a member of the "school" of young French composers that came to be known as "The French Six" (*see* Auric), he produced other works in the "everyday" musical style with which "The French Six" was most often identified: witty, satiric, whimsical, occasionally impudent. In such a manner, Poulenc proved himself a master.

He never completely abandoned this pose of levity. From time to time he continued to produce compositions in which laughter and mockery were the keynotes. The smiling face is found in compositions like the Concerto for Two Pianos and Orchestra in 1932; the Allegro giocoso movement of the G minor Concerto for Organ and Strings in 1938; the Sinfonietta in 1947; the Presto giocoso movement of the Piano Concerto in 1949; and in the little surrealist opera, *Les Mamelles de Tirésias,* introduced at the Opéra-Comique in Paris on June 3, 1947 (in the United States at Waltham, Massachusetts, on June 13, 1953).

Nevertheless, beginning with the middle 1930s, the more serious Poulenc began to take precedence over the smiling one. In some of his compositions, his deeply religious nature—which had laid dormant for thirty-five years—expressed itself in music that is exalted and spiritual, beginning with the *Litanies à la Vierge noire* in 1936 and the Mass in G in 1937. In his songs, an art form to which he had become particularly partial in 1936 and which he continued to favor for the next twenty years, he betrayed an extraordinarily expressive lyricism and a deeply felt emotion. So remarkable was his song output, both in quality and quantity, that many critics consider him the foremost song composer of the twentieth century. In still other compositions he gave voice to a noble tragedy as in *Figure humaine* (1943), which was inspired by the tragedy of Paris under the heels of Nazi invaders and oppression. In the opera, *Les Dialogues des Carmélites* (1956), religious ardor and poetic expressiveness, lyric beauty and an exalted sense of tragedy are combined to produce a masterwork that has come to be regarded as a crowning achievement in twentieth-century opera.

Poulenc was born in Paris on January 7, 1899 to wealthy parents. Study of the piano began when he was five. In his sixteenth year he became a pupil of Ricardo Viñes. Poulenc's first composition, a piano piece, came early in 1917 followed soon by the *Rapsodie nègre.* For a number of years, Poulenc served in the French army, a period in which he managed to complete a number of works, including the two satirical song cycles, *Le Bestiaire* and *Cocardes,* and the *Mouvements perpétuels* for piano, all reflecting a Satie influence. Following Poulenc's release from the army, he continued music study for three years with Charles Koechlin. At about this time, his name became linked with those of five other young French composers who came to be known as "The Six." But like the other members of this group he went his own way which, in the middle 1930s, often led him to the poetic and the religious. In 1935, he appeared at the Salzburg Festival as piano accompanist to the renowned French baritone, Pierre Bernac. This marked the first of many highly acclaimed song recitals in Europe and the United States, his first appearance in America taking place in 1948 in such a performance. During World War II, Poulenc was active in the French Resistance movement. After the war, he became universally recognized as one of the world's foremost composers. Poulenc died suddenly in Paris on January 30, 1963.

1917 RAPSODIE NÈGRE (NEGRO PHAPSODY), for baritone, piano, string quartet, flute and clarinet.

Of the several influences that were so strongly brought to bear on Poulenc's early development as a composer, the most influential was that of Erik Satie. Satie's whimsy, wit, flair for satire and love of absurdity are all reflected in Poulenc's early works which brought him into the limelight. The first such was *Rapsodie nègre,* and it represented Poulenc's first taste of success.

In the middle 1910s, Paris enjoyed a vogue for all things Negro. One day, while browsing in a bookshop, Poulenc came upon a Negro poem in gibberish entitled *Les Poésies de Makoko Kangourou,* supposedly the work of a Liberian Negro. Actually it was a hoax intended to mock the interest of Parisians in Negro art, and it consisted of nonsense verses. Poulenc was so amused by these poems that he decided to write music for one of them, "Honoloulou." The words made no sense at all, its first lines reading:

"Honoloulou, poti lama
Honoloulou, Honoloulou,
Kati moki, mosi bolou,
Ratakou sira, polama."

Three verses of this poem were used as a vocal episode which made up the main body of the Rhapsody.

The Rhapsody was introduced in Paris on December 11, 1917. "The youthful charm of the work," says Henri Hell, "the musical instrumentation, and the streak of genuine humor in Poulenc made an immediate impact. It was a roaring success."

1918 TROIS MOUVEMENTS PERPÉTUELS, for piano.

Like the *Rapsodie nègre* which had preceded it, the *Mouvements perpétuels* (Poulenc's first successful composition for the piano) was influenced by Satie. When Ricardo Viñes introduced it in Paris in 1919, it created a mild sensation. The work is made up of three short, simple pieces, the first of which (in C major) has proved the most popular and has often been performed and recorded apart from the other pieces. All three pieces are fresh, spontaneous and melodious in which twentieth-century discord is married to the graceful and elegant style of eighteenth-century French harpsichord music.

1919 LE BESTIAIRE, OU LE CORTÈGE D'ORPHÉE (THE BESTIARY), cycle for mezzo-soprano, string quartet, flute, clarinet and bassoon. I. Le Dromadaire. II. La Chèvre du Thibet. III. La Sauterelle. IV. Le Dauphin. V. L'Ècrevisse. VI. La Carpe.

COCARDES (THE COCKADES), cycle for voice, violin, cornet, trombone, bass drum and triangle. I. Miel de Narbonne. II. Bonne d'enfant. III. Enfant de troupe.

While still under Satie's spell, Poulenc completed his first two major works for voice, each a song cycle, and each in a satirical or ironic vein. In *Le Bestiaire,* Poulenc displays the same apt gift for animal characterization, and with equally economical strokes, that Saint-Saëns had shown in his *Carnival of Animals,* or, for that matter, that Poulenc himself would later (1941) exploit in his *Les Animaux modèles,* a ballet adaptation of La Fontaine's fables introduced at the Paris Opéra on August 8, 1942. To words by Guillaume Apollinaire, Poulenc describes in *Le Bestiaire* six specimens of animal and marine life: the dromedary, goat, grasshopper, dolphin, crawfish and carp.

In *Cocardes* we get three ironic imitations of three popular songs to poems by Jean Cocteau. Poulenc felt that the isolated words of Cocteau's verses hopped around "like birds from tree to tree." "On these enigmatic poems composed of words liberated, as it were from their normal association . . . Poulenc wrote a series of biting sarcastic pieces," explains Henri Hell. Hell considers the last song, "*Enfant de troupe*" the best of the trio. "There are two bars reproducing some kind of barrel-organ refrain leading directly into a trumpet fanfare reminiscent of Bastille Day celebrations." Hell also points out that the second song, "*Bonne d'enfant,*" provides a premonition of Poulenc's later strong gift for tender melody.

1923 LES BICHES (THE HINDS), ballet in one act, with choreography by Bronislava Nijinska. First performance: Monte Carlo, January 6, 1924.

LES BICHES, ballet suite for orchestra. I. Rondeau. II. Adagietto. III. Rag-Mazurka. IV. Andantino. V. Final.

Serge Diaghilev, the artistic director of the Ballet Russe de Monte Carlo, planned a modern-day *Les Sylphides* for his company. Having heard and been delighted with Poulenc's *Mouvements perpétuels,* he commissioned the young composer to write the music for such a ballet. Once he started working, Poulenc had his own ideas on the kind of ballet he wanted to write. He sought a work, he said, "in which you may see nothing at all or into which you may read the worst. . . . In this ballet as in certain of Watteau's pictures, there is an atmosphere of wantonness which you sense if you are corrupted but which an innocent-minded girl would not be conscious of."

Nothing much happens in this ballet. The setting is a houseparty (the reason why, in English-speaking countries, the ballet has been presented under the title of *The Houseparty*). Men and women are drifting towards each other, some romantically inclined. One of these is the hostess herself who is attracted to one of her male guests. The guests perform various dances. Poulenc's score consists of a suite of such dances beginning with an Overture and ending with a Finale. Each dance is a complete, self-sufficient piece of music. They are: Rondeau, Chanson dansée, Adagietto, Jeu, Mazurka, Andantino, and Petite chanson dansée. A chorus accompanies the "chanson dansée" with a text taken from anonymous seventeenth-century poems.

"*Les Biches*," says Cyril W. Beaumont, "is a half playful, half malicious comment on that contemporary social entertainment known as the house-party. . . . The music, setting and dances are all conceived in the essence of sophistication. The ballet is subtle and beneath all the froth and muslin and choreographic badinage there are many piquant comments for those who choose to look below the surface." Beaumont points out that in the Adagietto, which is danced by the girl in blue, a "new style in choreography" is introduced. "Although the steps have a classical ballet foundation, the placing of the arms in angular positions which have a strange and unexpected grace, and the novel use of the shoulders which dip and rise in a wave-like rhythm, are quite new."

In its original conception, the ballet score comprised three pieces for chorus and orchestra together with orchestral episodes. Poulenc reorchestrated his score in 1940, abandoned the choral numbers and overture, and arranged the remaining orchestral episodes as a five-movement suite. The first, "Rondeau," opens with a slow introduction. The entrance of the trumpet brings on an acceleration of the tempo; it presents the rondo theme accompanied by woodwinds and string chords. The "Adagietto" was suggested by a phrase from Tchaikovsky's ballet music to *The Sleeping Beauty*. First we hear a melody for solo oboe, accompanied by flutes and bassoons. The trumpet takes this melody over, after which a strong climax is built up. The melody then returns in the oboe. In the "Rag-Mazurka" we have an amusing marriage of the rhythm of the Polish dance with syncopations of American ragtime. The "Andantino" offers a phrase in bass clarinet and plucked cello strings answered by cellos and bassoons. A contrasting subject is then offered by flutes, oboes and violins. The music grows animated and subsides into a gentle passage in which clarinets and harps are represented. The movement concludes with an energetic outburst. The "Final" is a brisk presto with the rhythm of a tarantella, its theme heard in flutes and violins.

1928 CONCERT CHAMPÊTRE, for harpsichord (or piano) and orchestra. I. Adagio; Allegro molto. II. Andante (Mouvement de sicilienne). III. Finale: presto (très gai).

In writing this delightful work for the harpsichordist Wanda Landowska, Poulenc had a double mission. For one thing, he tried to show that the harpsichord was by no means an archaic instrument. Besides this, he tried to re-create in modern terms the style of seventeenth-century French keyboard music, in the way Ravel did in the *Tombeau de Couperin*. "I decided to use the full orchestra against the harpsichord," the composer has said. "If they carry on a dialogue, the one does not harm the other. As soon as they play together I extract from the mass isolated instruments, and in turn each group strengthens, without crushing, the sonority of the harpsichord."

Except for the peroration, which is dignified and expressive, the entire work is replete with delightful tunes, sometimes set against tart harmonies, and—particularly in the last movement—is filled with the laughter and light-heartedness which we invariably associate with Poulenc. The spirit of the seventeenth century is preserved in the freshness and delicacy of the music, but there is never much doubt that this is the work of a contemporary composer.

The work was introduced by Wanda Landowska and the Paris Philharmonic Orchestra under Pierre Monteux on May 3, 1929.

1932 CONCERTO IN D MINOR FOR TWO PIANOS AND ORCHESTRA. I. Allegro ma non troppo. II. Larghetto. III. Finale.

This slight but highly ingratiating work has become one of Poulenc's most frequently heard compositions. It is in his finest witty vein, and is full of simple and engaging little tunes and droll rhythmic effects, many of which belong in the music hall rather than the concert auditorium. It was first heard at the festival of the International Society for Contemporary Music, held in Venice, on September 5, 1932. The composer and Jacques Fevrier were the soloists, and the La Scala Orchestra was directed by Desiré Defauw.

Two powerful chords introduce the composition, after which the first piano enters with a brilliant passage which is soon taken up by the second piano. There then comes a sprightly first theme—a staccato four-note phrase. The second theme is of the music-hall variety, and is introduced by the woodwinds and solo horn. The music then becomes sentimental, and after a brief cadenza for the two pianos the thematic material is revived. The movement ends quietly. In the Larghetto, the principal theme is a melody of great charm and wistfulness, announced first by the first piano. The second piano repeats the melody against an ingenious accompaniment provided by its partner. The tempo quickens, a climax is reached, and then the first theme returns to restore the original mood. The concerto closes with music-hall tunes, one of them resembling a march, another more lyrical. The music passes from melody to virtuosity, and the movement ends with an outburst of exuberance.

1936–1937 LITANIES À LA VIERGE NOIRE (LITANIES FOR THE BLACK VIRGIN), for women's or children's voices and organ.

MASS IN G MAJOR, for four-part a cappella chorus.

Though his father had been a devout Catholic, though his uncle had been the curé of Ivry-sur-Seine, and though he himself had received a rigorous religious training until his eighteenth year, Poulenc remained aloof from religion in his adult years. Then in his thirty-sixth year, a profound religious awakening took place, brought about by the sudden death of his friend Pierre-Octave Ferroud, a gifted composer who was killed in an automobile accident. This tragedy shook Poulenc to his roots and sent him on a pilgrimage to the sanctuary of Rocamadour. Here he was deeply moved by the sight of the chapel in its beautiful surroundings of rocks and mountains. On the evening of this experience, he began writing the *Litanies à la Vierge noire* (1936), his first significant religious composition, using for his text a recitation by one of the pilgrims. To Henri Ghéon, the opening three notes, on the words "*Ayez pitié*" represents a revelation of the composer's inner soul. And to Henri Hell "the rustic musical prayers of which the organ accompaniment recalls the chapel harmonium, display the simple fervor, the mingled sweetness and humility that are to emanate from all of Poulenc's religious works."

For the rest of his life, Poulenc remained fervently devout; and for the rest of his life, he continued to produce from time to time major religious works in which could be found some of his noblest and most spiritual writing. One of the most significant of these is the Mass in G major, dedicated to the memory of his father, completed in 1937. "The purity of the serene music," says Hell, "suggests the composer's almost human conception of God. At the opposite extreme from the flamboyant examples of religious music of the nineteenth century, this beautiful Mass, suggesting the unadorned architecture of a Romanesque church, requires nothing but the unaccompanied choir to make its telling effect of fervor and simplicity." The opening Kyrie is sung by the women's voices in which a Latin text is energized by strong rhythms. Basses sing the Gloria loudly, with sopranos and contraltos giving reply. The Sanctus, once again for women's voices, "is extremely light in texture," says Hell, with its concluding Hosanna in Excelsis "creating the impression of a vast, watery expanse." The Benedictus is "withdrawn in mood" while the closing Agnus Dei, highlighted by expressive solos for soprano and contralto, "reaches out to the chaste and truly disembodied ideal of the Catholic Mass."

1937–1943 SONGS, for solo voice and piano:

"Au-delà" from *Trois Poèmes*; "C" from *Deux Poèmes*; "Tu Vois le feu du soir" from *Miroirs brûlants*.

Tel Jour, Telle Nuit, song cycle: I. Bonne Journée; II. Une Ruine Coquille Vide; III. Le Front Comme un Drapeau Perdu; IV. Une Roulotte Couverte en Tuiles; V. À Toutes Brides; VI. Une Herbe pauvre; VII. Je n'ai envie que de t'aimer; VIII. Figure de force brûlante et farouche; IX. Nous avons fait la nuit.

Banalités, song cycle: I. Chanson d'Orkenise; II. Hôtel; III. Fagnes de Wallonie; IV, Voyage à Paris; V. Sanglots.

Two significant influences, one early and the other comparatively late, helped mold the future of one of the greatest songwriters the twentieth century has known. The first was a copy of Schubert's song cycle, *Die Winterreise,* which fell into Poulenc's hands while he was still a boy. He memorized these songs; they obsessed him. He became forcefully aware of the artistic potential of the song form. Then, in 1935, Poulenc became piano accompanist to the concert baritone, Pierre Bernac, in his song recitals. They continued giving recitals in Europe and America for many years, an experience which Poulenc confesses taught him more about the art of the song that he had formerly known. It is, therefore, no coincidence—but rather cause and effect—that he should have written his first song cycle in the same year that he appeared with Bernac for the first time.

That cycle was his first song masterwork—*Tel Jour, Telle Nuit,* a setting of nine poems by Paul Éluard. "Tragic and deeply tender of sentiment," is the way a critic for the New York *Herald Tribune* described these numbers, "richly varied of musical fancy, the whole work is an expressive ensemble piece for voice and piano that amplifies the literature of the combination."

Poulenc wrote almost a hundred songs after that, most of these settings of the poems by the surrealists, Éluard, Guillaume Apollinaire and Max Jacob. Here he proved himself the legitimate successor to Debussy and Fauré as one of the most sensitive French song composers of his generation. His natural and ever evident lyric gift had a seemingly inexhaustible palette of colors, variety of mood, and subtle shades of emotional expression. They span the entire gamut of feelings from the coquettish charm of "*Au-delà*" (second in the *Trois Poèmes*, to verses by Louise de Vilmorin, in 1937) through the subtle enchantment of "*Tu vois le feu du soir* (second of two numbers in *Miroirs brûlants,* poems by Éluard, in 1938) and the nostalgic recollection of days gone by in "C" (from *Deux Poèmes*, poems by Louis Aragon, in 1943), to the deep-rooted tragedy of what is possibly his greatest and most deeply moving song of all, "*Sanglots,*" from the *Banalités* song cycle.

Banalités, poems by Apollinaire (1940), is another of Poulenc's song masterpieces. Here we find the popular "*Hôtel,*" which Hell describes as a "lazy, sweet tune, a mere two pages of lyrical melody perfectly brought off"; "*Voyage à Paris,*" an amusing doggerel, and the already commented upon "*Sanglots,*"which Hell calls "one of the most penetrating poems of Apollinaire, exposing the mystery in the hearts of all men." About Poulenc's music for "*Sanglots,*" Hell adds: "The remarkable modulations in the piano accompaniment, which somehow reveal the inner pulsation of the poem, and the sensitive coordination of vocal and poetical inflections, establish a unity of poetry and music reaching far beyond the idea of a simple 'setting.' "

Poulenc's art in the song form, says Irving Kolodin in the *Saturday Review,* "consists in making each element—voice and piano—an interrelated but independent aspect of a single poetic impulse. . . . The resources that Poulenc developed embraced all the usual variants and some that he discovered for himself. But, at best, they were techniques that would have been little more than artifice without the vitalizing flow of emotion that Poulenc poured into the tonal design."

Awareness of Poulenc's greatness as a song composer first came after World War II, in an all-Poulenc song recital at the Salle Gaveau in Paris in 1945. To Americans, recognition came during the two tours Poulenc made with Bernac, the first in 1948, the other in 1950.

Poulenc's last song, appropriately entitled *Dernier Poème* (text by Robert Desnos) came in 1956. He explained to an interviewer in 1960: "Apollinaire, Éluard, Jacob are all dead, and somehow I understood their poetry extremely well. I was able to read between the lines of their poems; I was able to express all that was left unsaid in musical terms. Today, poets do not write in a manner that inspires me to song. . . . I have written well over a hundred songs and to write more would be to force myself in a direction in which I really have nothing further to say."

1941 CONCERTO IN G MINOR FOR ORGAN, STRINGS AND TYMPANI.

Charles Munch, who conducted the public world première of this organ concerto on June 10, 1941 (Maurice Durufle was the soloist), finds an allusion to Bach's famous G minor organ fantasia in the opening phrases. He feels that this quotation is deliberate; that in writing a major work for organ, Poulenc was paying tribute to the greatest master of organ music the world has known. In any event, those opening phrases are built from a four-note motto which recurs throughout the work. The concerto, in a single movement, has four sections. The first is an Andante—Allegro giocoso, the slow part being a solemn declaration, highlighting an organ recitative. The organ provides the transition to the lighter, more jovial Allegro giocoso part, whose main theme is presented by the strings. The second section is an Andante moderato, which appears after a stirring climax. This is the longest of the four sections, one which makes effective use of contrapuntal devices. Massive chords set the stage for a vigorously paced Allegro molto agitatio section. We now get a recall of the lighthearted music of the Allegro giocoso. But the levity is finally dispensed with. The concerto ends soberly and introspectively in the same solemn atmosphere with which the composition opened.

1943 SONATA IN D MAJOR FOR VIOLIN AND PIANO. I. Allegro con fuoco. II. Intermezzo: très lent et calme. III. Presto tragico.

This sonata was dedicated to the memory of Federico García Lorca, the celebrated Spanish poet who was killed by the Franco fascists in 1936. It is one of the most intensely and deeply felt of Poulenc's works, and one of his most lyrical effusions. The first movement goes from outright vehemence to sentimentality and back to vehemence. To the second movement, the composer appended the following Lorca quotation: "The guitar makes dreams weep"—a reminder that Lorca was also famous as a guitarist who accompanied himself in the singing of Spanish folk songs. Plucked violin strings give a faint suggestion of the guitar, but the body of the movement consists of a broad languorous melody, gentle rather than intense in its sadness; this is as tender and expressive a lyric page as can be found in Poulenc's works. The spell is broken: the turbulent, passionate third movement is the expression of grief at the contemplation of tragedy.

The first performance of the sonata took place in Paris on June 21, 1943. Ginette Neveu was the performer, and the composer was at the piano.

1943 FIGURE HUMAINE, cantata for unaccompanied double mixed choir.

Out of the turmoil and tragedy of World War II, and the occupation of Paris by the Nazis, came one of Poulenc's most poignant works for orchestra, the *Figure humaine,* dedicated to Pablo Piccaso. The text, by Paul Éluard, told of the suffering of the French people, but ended on a note of triumph with a mighty paean to liberty. Words and music were printed secretly in Paris under the very eyes of the invading Nazis. Soon after the liberation of Paris, the score was flown to London, where the work was introduced over BBC in London in January of 1945. The American première was given in New York by the Schola Cantorum on January 17, 1950. At that time Virgil Thomson said: "It is plain in meaning, lilting of meter and both fanciful and familiar as imagery. Irresistibly touching in sentiment, it is also a work of no mean literary sophistication, a devotional and patriotic text. Francis Poulenc's music, no less straightforward in melodious contours and dramatic accents, is its match for both simplicity and inventive workmanship."

Henri Hell notes that the more intimate pages of this cantata can be found in the fourth part, "*Toi ma patiente*" for the first choir alone, and in the sixth part, "*Le Jour m'étonne et la nuit me fait peur*" for the second choir. "Here the long soprano melody, accompanied by murmurs from the other voices, recalls the beautiful song, "*Une Herbe pauvre*" (from the cycle, *Tel Jour, Telle Nuit*). The most dramatic episode is found in the seventh part, in which "the contraltos of the first choir open with a fugal passage taken up by both choirs and developed to a climax as the words '*La Pourriture avait du coeur*' burst forth with tremendous fierceness. A long silence follows the close of this majestic movement, and the final Hymn to Liberty then opens quietly."

1947 SINFONIETTA, for orchestra. I. Allegro con fuoco. II. Molto vivace. III. Andante cantabile. IV. Finale: très vite et très gai.

This unpretentious, witty little orchestral work, which is in the vein of the Concerto for Two Pianos and Orchestra, was heard for the first time over the BBC in London, Roger Desormière conducting, on October 24, 1948.

It is a delightful excursion into levity, aptly described by G. H. L. Smith as "amiable without being banal, popular without concession, haunted with nimble dances and songs that each hearer will think he remembers, but which are new, nevertheless." The first movement is made up of several episodic ideas presented in a spirit of gaiety. The scherzo that follows carries on this carefree attitude. A lyrical third movement makes no pretense at profound emotion, but is pleasantly tuneful. The closing movement opens with a piquant little theme which injects insouciance; a second theme is more lyrical.

1949 CONCERTO FOR PIANO AND ORCHESTRA. I. Allegretto. II. Andante con moto. III. Rondeau à la française.

Poulenc himself introduced this concerto during his first visit to the United States in 1948–1949. This event took place at a concert of the Boston Symphony on January 6, 1950, Charles Munch conducting. The piano is here treated not as a solo virtuoso instrument but as an integral part of the orchestra. The main theme, a rhythmic subject, is heard at once in the solo piano, followed later on by a lyric secondary theme in the English horn over piano arpeggios. A tender melody in the strings to a march-like background provided by the horns opens and closes the slow movement. The finale is a Presto giocoso whose charming and tuneful main melody is presented by the piano unaccompanied. Poulenc interpolated into this final movement a recollection of an old French song that came to be known as "*À la claire fontaine*" and which bears a faint resemblance to the opening refrain of Stephen Foster's "Swanee River."

1950 STABAT MATER, for soprano, five-part chorus and orchestra.

One of Poulenc's major religious works, the Stabat Mater was written in memory of Christian Bernard, the painter. Its first performance took place at the Strasbourg festival on June 13, 1951, after which it was heard throughout

Europe and in the United States; it received the New York Music Critics Circle Award.

The composition has twelve sections of contrasting moods and feelings. It opens gently with the "Stabat Mater Dolorosa," progresses to the tragic in the "Cuius anima." Then, says Henri Hell, the work "encircles the whole range of religious experience from grace to drama and majesty." Of particular significance are the passages for solo voices. Says Hell: "The two soprano arias are magnificent lyrical outbursts."

1956 LES DIALOGUES DES CARMÉLITES (THE CARMELITES), opera in three acts, with text by Georges Bernanos based on Gertrude von le Fort's novel *Die letzte am Schafott,* and a motion picture scenario by the Rev. Bruckenberger and Philippe Agostini. First performance; La Scala, Milan, January 26, 1957.

The *Dialogues of the Carmélites* is Poulenc's first full-length tragic opera, and it is one of his unqualified masterworks. His deep religious convictions, his gift for soaring lyricism, his remarkable expressiveness in writing for chorus, and his wonderful compassion and humanity here find a single meeting place. Utilizing a continuous lyric line which reaches heights in the a cappella "Ave Maria" of the second act and the "Salve Regina" of the Carmelites, to which the crowd adds musical strains of its own in the closing scene, Poulenc has produced a drama touched with radiance, and which progresses towards a shattering conclusion with unrelenting dramatic force.

He wrote this opera because La Scala originally asked him to write a ballet on the subject of St. Margaret of Cortona. This idea did not appeal to him. Then the publishing house of Ricordi brought to his attention Georges Bernanos's *Les Dialogues des Carmélites.* One day, in a café in the Piazza Navone in Rome, he read the play at a single sitting and at once became convinced he had found the ideal libretto. He started working in August of 1953. The piano and vocal score was completed by September of 1955, with the full orchestral score was ready in June of 1956.

The setting is Paris during the French Revolution. The plot details the tragic fate of sixteen nuns who prefer to meet death rather than dissolve their order. These are dedicated women, to be sure, but women with weaknesses as well as strength, with doubts as well as faith. One of the main characters is the Mother Superior who succumbs to paralyzing fear when she must meet her death; by contrast, a noblewoman, who has become a nun because of her distaste for the outside world, proves herself a heroine at the guillotine.

The opera was a triumph when introduced at La Scala. Soon afterwards it was produced in major music centers throughout the world. The American première was given by the San Francisco Opera on September 22, 1957. On that occasion Howard Taubman reported in *The New York Times:* "When he is dealing with emotion, particularly with the spiritual feelings of the nuns, Poulenc is a rare artist. For the part of Mme. de Croissy, the Prioress who at her death is more concerned with her suffering than with God, he has written an agonizing scene. . . . For Mme. Lidoine, the New Prioress, he has composed music with richness and purity of tone. . . . In the final scenes, when the Carmelites face destruction at the hands of the fanatics of the Revolution, the opera becomes broadly dramatic. Poulenc rises to the occasion without theatricalism. Here his orchestra, which has been conservative and restrained, breaks forth with harsh harmonies. But he does not make uncontrolled use of the modern vocabulary of dissonance. He prefers suggestion to remonstrance."

In 1958, the opera was telecast by the NBC Opera over the NBC-TV network. It received the New York Music Critics Circle Award.

SERGE PROKOFIEV 1891–1953

Not many contemporary composers write music which has such an unmistakable identity as that of Prokofiev. What is particularly interesting is that Prokofiev's music, stylistically, changed little over the decades; the same qualities and mannerisms by which his later works are recognized can be found in many of his earlier productions. A saucy, infectious impudence is the attitude usually associated with his music. The mocking reeds, the mischievous leaps in the melody, the tart and often disjointed harmonies, the sudden fluctuation from the naïve and the simple to the unexpected and the complex—these are a few of the fingerprints that can be found in most of Prokofiev's works. Certain little idiosyncracies appear and reappear: for example, beginning a theme in a rather hackneyed pattern and then having it suddenly and inexplicably leap to an unexpected interval; or consciously setting a trite tune against a piquant and original harmony; or utilizing simple schoolbook chords in unorthodox relations. Somehow, whenever these and other similar devices emerge—though they are expected—they manage to bring surprise and delight.

In his attempt to free music from literary, metaphysical, or mystical associations and to have it appear as music and nothing else, Prokofiev's ironic and satiric vein has, of course, become famous. But it would be a mistake to assume that his is a one-string lyre—that he is witty and sardonic, and nothing more. As a matter of fact (and particularly in his later works), Prokofiev is also capable of music of great dramatic power, of sensitively projected emotions, of meditative moods, and of noble concepts.

Here is how Prokofiev himself described his approach to composition and his personal creative mannerisms in an autobiographical sketch published in 1941: "The principal lines which I have followed are these: The first is classical, its origin lying in my early childhood when I heard my mother play the sonatas of Beethoven. It assumes a neo-classical aspect in the sonatas and concertos, or imitates the classical style of the eighteenth century, as in the gavottes, the *Classical Symphony,* and to a certain extent in the Sinfonietta. The second is innovation [which at first] consisted in the search for an individual harmonic language, but was later transformed into the desire of finding a medium in which to express the stronger emotions. . . . This innovating strain has affected not only the harmonic idiom but the melodic inflection, the orchestration, and the stage technique as well. The third is the element of the toccata, or motor element; it was probably influenced by Schumann's Toccata, which impressed me greatly at one time. . . . This element is probably the least important. The fourth element is lyrical, appearing first as lyric meditation, sometimes unconnected with melos . . . but sometimes found in long melodic phrases, as in the opening of the First Violin Concerto, the songs, and so forth. This lyric strain has for a long time remained obscured, or perceived only in retrospect, and, since my lyricism has long been denied appreciation, it has developed slowly. . . . I should like to limit myself to these sour expressions, and to regard the fifth element, that of the grotesque, with which some critics try to label me, as merely a variation of the other characteristics. In application to my music, I should like to replace the word 'grotesque' by 'scherzoness,' or by three words indicating its gradations: 'jest,' 'laughter,' and 'mockery.' "

Prokofiev was born in Sontsovka, Russia, on April 23, 1891. Extraordinarily precocious, he began studying music early with his mother and with Glière and Taneiev. At five, he wrote his first piano pieces, and at eight, a complete opera. In 1903, he entered the St. Petersburg Conservatory, where he was a pupil in composition of Liadov, Rimsky-Korsakov and Nicholas Tcherepnine, and in piano of Annette Essipov. He was graduated with highest honors seven years later. When he made his first public appearance—on December 31, 1908—he introduced his still popular *Suggestion diabolique,* for piano. His *Scythian Suite,* whose discords at once established him as an *enfant terrible* of Russian music, was written in 1914. In the next few years, he was performed and published, and his original music began to make its influence felt in Russian music circles.

In the Spring of 1918, Prokofiev left the Soviet Union to circle the world. By way of Siberia, Japan and Honolulu, he came to the United States, arriving in August of 1918. He made his American debut in a piano recital in New York City on November 20, 1918. While in America he received a commission from the Chicago Opera Company to write an opera—*Love for Three Oranges*—produced in that city in 1921. Prokofiev also gave the world première of his famous Third Piano Concerto in Chicago during that first tour.

In October, 1923, Prokofiev began a ten-year residence in Paris. During this period he established his world reputation as one of the most powerful, original and provocative composers of our time. His native land did not forget him. Reports on Prokofiev's works appeared continually in the Soviet press; his music was published by the State Publishing House; and the Soviet critics did not hesitate in acclaiming him one of Russia's greatest composers. When, in 1927, Prokofiev returned to the Soviet Union for a three-month visit, he was given a hero's welcome.

At last, in 1932, Prokofiev decided to return to his native land for good. In explaining his long absence, he said: "I had not grasped the significance of what was happening in the U.S.S.R. I did not realize that the events there demanded the collaboration of all citizens—not only men of politics, but men of art as well." Before long, he assumed a position of first importance in Soviet musical life, a position he maintained for the next sixteen years. And, as Nicolas Slonimsky remarked, his music became "probably the greatest single influence in Soviet music." During World War II, he became a national hero by writing functional pieces and major concert works inspired by the conflict. His seventh piano sonata, *Stalingrad,* brought him the Stalin Prize for the first time, in 1943.

And then suddenly and without warning—as such things happen in a totalitarian state—he was in disgrace.

On February 10, 1948, the Central Committee of the Communist Party of the U.S.S.R. issued a public resolution denouncing the leading composers of the Soviet Union for "decadent formalism." or "cerebralism." The Committee felt that Russian composers had allowed themselves to be infected by Western musical thinking, with the result that the complex, dissonant, iconoclastic music they wrote was far removed from the masses. The principal targets for this attack were Prokofiev, Khatchaturian, Shostakovich, Miaskovsky, Shebalin, Muradeli and Popov.

The resolution was specific in its denunciation. Characteristics in these composers which it found lamentable were "the negation of the basic principles of classical music; a sermon for atonality, dissonance, and disharmony, as if this were an expression of 'progress' and 'innovation' in the growth of musical compositions as melody; a passion for confused, neuropathic combinations which transform into cacophony, into a chaotic piling up of sounds.... Many Soviet composers, in pursuit of falsely conceived innovation, have lost contact with the demands and the artistic taste of the Soviet people, have shut themselves off in a narrow circle of specialists and musical gourmands, have lowered the high social role of music and narrowed its meaning, limiting it to a satisfaction of the distorted tastes of esthetic individualists."

The Soviet composers thus rebuked did not lose time in trying to regain official favor. All of them rushed to admit that they had been at fault, that they now saw the truth and would mend their ways. Here is the way Prokofiev put it in a letter to Khrennikov: "As far as I am concerned, elements of formalism were peculiar to my music as long as fifteen and twenty years ago. Apparently the infection was caught from contact with some Western ideas. When formalistic errors in Shostakovich's opera *Lady Macbeth* were exposed by *Pravda,* I gave a great deal of thought to creative devices in my own music, and came to the conclusion that such a method of composition is faulty. As a result, I began a search for a clearer and more meaningful language.... The existence of formalism in some of my works is probably explained by a certain self-complacency, an insufficient realization of the fact that it is completely unwanted by the people. The Resolution has shaken to the core the social consciousness of our composers, and it has become clear what type of music is needed by our people, and the ways of the eradication of the formalist disease have also become clear.... This is the direction which I intend to take in my new opera on a contemporary Soviet subject, *A Tale of a Real Man* by Polevoy. I am highly gratified that the Resolution has pointed out the desirability of polyphony, particularly in choral and ensemble singing.... In my above-mentioned opera, I intend to introduce trios, duets, and contrapuntally developed choruses, for which I will make use of some interesting northern Russian folk songs. Lucid melody, and as far as possible a simple harmonic language, are elements which I intend to use in my opera."

But Prokofiev was too honest a creative artist and too independent a musical thinker to be able suddenly to write his music to measure. *A Tale of a Real Man,* introduced in concert form in Leningrad in 1948, did not quite turn out the way he had planned; in fact, that style remains unmistakably that of Prokofiev. Consequently, on December 29, 1948—at the conclusion of a nine-day discussion of Soviet music by the Union of Soviet Composers—Prokofiev came in for another stinging attack in a resolution drawn up by Khrennikov. "The plenum concedes that the creative reorientation of these composers proceeds very slowly, as revealed by the presence of some unliquidated formalistic elements in their music. Defeated ideologically, formalism still lives in the music of Soviet composers. This is demonstrated by the new opera of Prokofiev, *A Tale of a Real Man.*"

Eventually, however, he was able to rehabilitate his position in the Soviet Union. He wrote an oratorio, *On Guard for Peace,* which bitterly condemned the Western "warmongers" while extolling the Soviet "international peace movement." He also wrote a vocal-symphonic suite, *Winter Bonfire,* which (like the oratorio) adopted the realistic and pleasing style demanded by the new Soviet aesthetics. These works, introduced in Moscow on December 19, 1950, brought Prokofiev the Stalin Prize again early in 1951. To emphasize still further his return to the good graces of the ruling clique, there took place on April 23, 1953, a special Prokofiev concert celebrating the composer's sixtieth birthday. And when his Seventh Symphony was introduced on October 11, 1952, he was the recipient of a tumultous ovation.

Prokofiev died of a cerebral hemorrhage on March 5, 1953 (the same day Stalin passed away). Prokofiev's last major work was the ballet, *The Stone Flower,* which received its world première in Moscow posthumously, on February 12, 1954.

Prokofiev was twice married. His first wife was Lina Llubera, a Cuban singer whom he had met in California and whom he wed in 1922. They were divorced in 1939, following which Prokofiev married Mira Mendelson, a literary scholar and linguist.

Four years after the death of Prokofiev, the dictum of the Central Committee against decadent formalism was officially revoked. The first sign of thaw in this prolonged cold war against musical modernism appeared late in 1953 (a half-year after Stalin's death) in an article by Khatchaturian in *Soviet Music,* condemning the Central Committee of the Communist Party for its 1948 stand on music. "A creative problem cannot be solved by bureaucratic means," he said. Then, on May 28, 1958, the Central Committee passed a resolution to permit composers greater freedom in the selection of their subject matter and style, and to allow them greater latitude in the use of modern techniques and idioms.

1909–1917 COMPOSITIONS FOR SOLO PIANO:

Sarcasms, op. 17; *Suggestion diabolique,* op. 4, no. 4; Toccata, op. 11; *Visions fugitives,* op. 22.

SONATA NO. 1 IN F MINOR, op. 1.

SONATA NO. 2 IN D MINOR, op. 14. I. Allegro ma non troppo. II. Allegro marcato. III. Andante. IV. Vivace.

SONATA NO. 3 IN A MINOR, op. 28.

SONATA NO. 4 IN C MINOR, op. 29. I. Allegro molto sostenuto. II. Andante assai. III. Allegro con brio ma non leggiere.

Suggestion diabolique (1908) is Prokofiev's first composition to become successful and survive in the twentieth-century piano repertory. He himself introduced it when he made his piano debut on December 31, 1908. What is remarkable about this piece is the fact that already we confront some of the basic stylistic elements that characterize the mature Prokofiev; his percussive use of the piano; the quixotic intervallic leaps in the melody; the grotesquerie of the manner.

Sarcasms and the Toccata were both written in 1912. Prokofiev's original title for the first of these was *Sarcastic Pieces,* but several critics thought *Sarcasms* a better title, and Prokofiev yielded to their judgment. Nicholas Tcherepnine, Prokofiev's teacher who was generally unsympathetic to Prokofiev's experiments, praised this music highly as a successful "search for a new musical language." As a healthy reaction to so much of the romantic sentimentality of the late nineteenth-century piano literature, the importance of *Sarcasms* can hardly be overestimated.

Prokofiev was inspired to write the Toccata—a brilliant bravura piece built on repeated notes—from a hearing of Schumann's Toccata. The eminent Russian composer, Miaskovsky, described it as "devilishly clever, brisk, biting music, and Prokofiev to the life."

The *Visions fugitives* (1917) is a set of twenty short pieces, each a brief tonal impression. These numbers are far in advance of their time for their polytonal writing and unconventional harmonies. Nos. 1, 7, 16 and 20 are thoughtful and introspective, their lyricism occasionally touched by a Russian personality. No. 19 describes the crowd during the February Revolution; it has a powerful rhythmic momentum. Prokofiev himself introduced this set in a recital at St. Petersburg on April 15, 1918.

Prokofiev's first four piano sonatas came between 1908 and 1917. To James Lyons they "fairly represent the formative, reluctantly romantic Prokofiev. On the evidence, he was a kind of would-be Schubert in whose music the typical extremes of yearning and exuberance were as omnipresent, thinly disguised, as the malicious irony that bound them."

The first sonata was Prokofiev's first published composition. It originally had four movements, but only one of these was retained by the composer, the opening Allegro. The work is orthodox in style and structure and is faithful to the tonality of F minor. Warnings of Prokofiev's later percussive and whimsical style are found in the second sonata, which was written almost entirely in 1912, though its scherzo movement was based on an exercise Prokofiev had produced in 1907. The third sonata, based on material Prokofiev had sketched in 1907, was completed in 1917. It is in a single movement and is probably the most familiar of this quartet of compositions. It is of special interest for its rich sonorities and its pyrotechnical writing. The fourth sonata, taken from material sketched in 1908, was also completed in 1917. It is most distinguished for its brilliant bravura writing for the keyboard in its fast movements, and the poetic introspection of the slow one.

1911–1913 CONCERTO NO. 1 IN D-FLAT MAJOR FOR PIANO AND ORCHESTRA, op. 10 I. Allegro brioso. II. Andante assai. III. Allegro scherzando.

CONCERTO NO. 2 IN G MINOR FOR PIANO AND ORCHESTRA, op. 16. I. Andantino; Allegretto; Andantino. II. Vivace. III. Intermezzo: allegro moderato. IV. Allegro tempestoso.

Prokofiev's two piano concertos were written while he was still a Conservatory student. The first came in 1911, and was introduced by the composer in Moscow on August 7, 1912. This is the concerto that Prokofiev played for his graduation exercise at the Conservatory in the Spring of 1914 and which brought him the coveted Rubinstein Prize. But the critics did not like it. Sabaneyev described it as follows: "This energetic, rhythmic, harsh, coarse, primitive cacophony hardly deserves to be called music. In his desperate search for 'novelty' utterly foreign to his nature, the author has definitely overreached himself." What upset Sabaneyev and some of the other critics was Prokofiev's percussive writing, discords, and his highly personal lyricism which at times negated romantic tendencies. "This is a work," Nicolas Slonimsky says today, "in which Prokofiev's definitive style is clearly outlined. There is the familiar boisterousness, the 'football' quality that aroused so much admiration (and indignation) among Russian musicians and critics. The concerto is episodic in its development, but its episodes are firmly interconnected following, with some modifications, the form of a sonata."

The concerto, which is played without interruption, opens with three loud orchestral chords, following which the piano presents the main subject, a strident and dramatic subject in octave. A march-like theme for the brass is later used to built up a climax. The slow movement that follows is mainly concerned with a lyrical thought which has a nocturne-like character; it is heard in muted strings, clarinet and horn. After that, we get the finale, which has whimsy and satire and in which material from earlier movements is recalled.

The second concerto was completed in 1913. Its première—in Pavlovsk on September 5, 1913, the composer appearing as the soloist—was a fiasco. Here is what one unidentified critic wrote: "The audience does not know what to think about it. . . . Indignant murmurs are heard. One couple gets up and runs toward the exit. 'Such music is enough to drive you crazy' is the general comment. The hall empties. The audience is scandalized. The majority hisses." However, the concerto as heard today is not the one Prokofiev introduced. The original score was lost during the Revolution. Fortunately, Prokofiev's working sketches were found. In 1923, Prokofiev rewrote the entire concerto from the sketches, and this version was given at a Koussevitzky concert in Paris on May 8, 1923.

The concerto opens with a reflective melody in the piano. This is taken up by the woodwinds, which then enter into a conversation with the piano. A characteristic Prokofiev tune invades the middle part of the movement. The

Scherzo has the character of a perpetual motion, with whirling and pyrotechnic passages for the piano. This is followed by an intermezzo, which opens with a strongly accented ostinato figure, once again in Prokofiev's identifiable manner. Embellishments are provided by the piano. The finale is, for the most part, brilliant virtuoso music for the piano, with relief provided by an extended piano section. After a climax in piano and orchestra, the piano engages a cadenza before the concerto ends brilliantly and loudly.

1915 SCYTHIAN SUITE ("ALA AND LOLLI"), for orchestra, op. 20. I. Invocation to Veles and Ala. II. The Evil God and the Dance of the Pagan Monsters. III. Night. IV. The Glorious Departure of Lolli, and the Cortege of the Sun.

Soon after being graduated from the St. Petersburg Conservatory, Prokofiev planned a ballet about a legendary race known as the Scythians, and their gods. The Scythians were said to have inhabited a region southeast of Europe near the Black Sea, and to have become extinct in or about 100 B.C. Prokofiev outlined his ideas to Diaghilev, who was not impressed. Consequently, the composer revised his plans and decided to write an orchestral suite instead.

The first movement (Allegro feroce), in music of brilliant colors and vehement passion, describes an invocation to the Sun, leading deity of the Scythians. A sacrifice to Ala, daughter of Veles, follows. In the second section (Allegro sostenuto), a frenetic dance by the Evil God takes place. He is surrounded by the seven pagan monsters he has evoked. Night descends. The Evil God comes to Ala in the third section (Andantino) and brings her great harm. The Moon Maidens descend to console her. The suite ends (Tempestuoso) with the Scythian hero, Lolli, setting forth to save Ala. He is no match for the Evil God and would be overcome but for the help given him by the Sun God. Sunrise comes like a benediction; and the suite comes to an end.

The suite was heard for the first time on January 29, 1916, in St. Petersburg, with the composer conducting. Its advanced harmonic and rhythmic writing and its dissonances disturbed many who heard this music. It was treated harshly by the critics. One such criticism was written by Leonid Sabaneyev, and thereby hangs a tale. The original date set for the première had been postponed at the last moment—too late for Sabaneyev to retract the devastating criticism which he had sent in for publication. To make matters worse for the critic, he had not only written the review without having heard the music, but also without any possibility of having had access to the manuscript score. This incident created considerable disturbance against Sabaneyev and drew some sympathetic interest to the composer.

1917 CONCERTO NO. 1 FOR VIOLIN AND ORCHESTRA, op. 19. I. Andantino. II. Vivacissimo. III. Moderato.

Prokofiev's First Violin Concerto is not a concerto in the traditional meaning of the term. The virtuoso character of the solo instrument is never exploited (there are no cadenzas or passages of bravura writing), just as the orchestra is never allowed to assume the subsidiary role of an accompanying body. Solo instrument and orchestra are treated as a symphonic unit, both used inextricably in the development and embellishment of the musical ideas.

The concerto (which is sometimes played without interruption) opens in a contemplative mood set by the plaintive and lyrical opening subject in the solo violin. The movement gains in force as the solo instrument becomes more energetic; but the general feeling of repose is not altogether abandoned. The flashing Scherzo that follows has those characteristic leaps in the melody and nervous accentuations that make for Prokofievian whimsy. Intriguing effects are created by *sul ponticello* passages, left-hand pizzicati, and glissandi that end in harmonics. Broad lyricism returns in the concluding movement, beginning with a theme for bassoon that leads into the main theme for solo violin. The concerto ends as it began, with the plaintive opening subject soaring in the upper register of the solo violin, a piquant effect being introduced by having each note trilled.

The concerto waited half a dozen years for its première, which took place in Paris on October 18, 1923. Marcel Darrieux was the soloist, and Koussevitzky conducted.

1917 CLASSICAL SYMPHONY (SYMPHONY NO. 1), op. 25. I. Allegro. II. Larghetto. III. Gavotte: non troppo allegro. IV. Molto vivace.

As a successful attempt to adapt the classical symphony of Haydn and Mozart to twentieth-century techniques and idioms, Prokofiev's first symphony appropriately entitled *Classical*, represents one of the earliest examples of neo-classicism. The form and the instrumentation are of classical proportions; classical, too, are the economy and transparency of the orchestral writing and the brevity of the developments. But the harmonic progressions, the angular melodic lines with their capricious octave leaps, and the Prokofievian whimsy belong to our times. The strange blend of the past and the present, however, offers no contradiction. With all his customary mastery, Prokofiev has admirably synchronized old styles and new to create a living artistic product. This music is so simple and direct in its approach, so precise in the presentation of its thematic materials, and so terse and logical in its development that it can readily be assimilated at first hearing; and for these reasons it has been one of the most popular of Prokofiev's works.

The two principal subjects of the first movement are heard in the first violins: the first, heardstrong and impetuous, opens the movement; the second, gay and brisk with capricious octave leaps, follows after a brief transition in the flute. In the second movement, a piquant melody—characteristically Prokofievian—rises in the violins against a murmuring background. A running passage for pizzicato strings in the middle section leads to the return of the violins with their haunting song. In the Gavotte, the fusion of an old form with new writing is perhaps most brilliantly realized. A twelve-measure opening section offers the main theme in strings and woodwind. The middle part is a musette, its main theme heard in flute and clarinets over a pedal point in low strings. The closing movement opens with a loud chord, after which the music erupts with élan and exuberance in the strings and progresses with uninterrupted momentum until the end of the work.

On April 21, 1918, the composer conducted the première performance of his symphony in St. Petersburg.

1919 LOVE FOR THREE ORANGES, opera in four acts, op. 33, with text by the composer based on a tale by Gozzi. First performance: Chicago Opera, December 30, 1921.

LOVE FOR THREE ORANGES, suite for orchestra, op. 33-bis. I. Les Ridicules. II. Scène infernale. III. Marche. IV. Scherzo. V. Le Prince et la princesse. VI. La Fuite.

Prokofiev was commissioned by Cleofonte Campanini, general director of the Chicago Opera Company, to write the *Love for Three Oranges.* Campanini, finding the work too difficult to mount and perform, shelved it. When the opera company came under Mary Garden's direction, she decided to go ahead with the project. The opera, now somewhat revised, was finally given in 1921. It was repeated once in Chicago, and once in New York. It was not successful. While a good spectacle to the eye, its complicated and ironic libretto and the modern harmonies and lyricism of the daring score proved too puzzling. "After intensive study and close observation at rehearsal and performance," reported Edward Moore in the Chicago *Tribune,* "I detected the beginnings of two tunes. . . . For the rest of it, Mr. Prokofiev might well have loaded up a shotgun with a thousand notes of varying lengths and discharged them against the side of a blank wall." The opera passed into oblivion until the New York City Opera Company revived it on November 1, 1949.

For his libretto Prokofiev took an eighteenth-century fantastic tale by Carlo Gozzi and converted it into a knife-edged satire on grand opera. On the stage he placed an opera audience of twenty-four, comprising Glooms, Joys, Cynics, Empty-Heads—each group with its own pet aesthetic theories—who, from time to time, interrupt the play with comments and suggestions. The stage within the stage unfolds the fantastic story of a Crown Prince, long ill, who can be cured only through laughter. A sorceress comes to prevent his recovery. Attacked by the palace guards, her struggles prove so comical that that prince bursts into laughter. Though now recovered, his woes are not over: the sorceress has stricken him with a curse of having to fall in love with three oranges. The prince now goes in quest of his love. He finds two oranges and opens them up, only to find the beautiful princesses within them dead from thirst. In the third orange, the princess lies dying. The Cynics from the stage audience rush with a pail of water and revive her. The prince gets his love—while the stage audience takes the sorceress as prisoner.

For this strange, and often nonsensical play, Prokofiev created music that passes from wit to whimsy, from drollery to burlesque, with particularly brilliant writing for the orchestra. There is a great deal of impudence in his frequent quotations from Russian and French operas. The sum total is not only a broad burlesque of opera plots, so often both confused and confusing, but also something of a parody of romantic operatic composition. One critic put it this way in 1921: "He strips grand opera of its glamour and makes it no longer grand."

The critics sang a different tune about the *Love for Three Oranges* when the New York City Opera revived it in 1949. "It is a . . . most original piece . . . a most distinguished work of art," said Olin Downes in *The New York Times.* "The orchestra is simply amazing all the time, in its swift and mordant commentary, its scherzo movements, which are the quintessence of fantasy and humor, its savage accentuations of this or that piece of foolery."

Six sections from the opera were assembled by the composer into an orchestral suite, three having become popular and now often heard independently of the other three numbers. The first is the "March," with its characteristic Prokofiev intervallic leaps in the melody; for many years this number was popularized in the United States as the theme song for the radio program, "The F.B.I. In Peace and War." Whimsy and grotesquerie characterize the two other popular numbers, the "Scherzo" and the "*Scène infernale*." The entire suite was introduced in Paris on November 29, 1925.

1920 CHOUT (BUFFOON), ballet suite for orchestra, op. 21. I. Le Bouffon et sa bouffonne. II. Danse des bouffonnes. III. Les Bouffons tuent leurs bouffonnes. IV. Le Bouffon travesti en jeune femme. V. Troisième entr'acte. VI. Danse des filles des bouffons. VII. L'Arriveé du marchand; la danse des révérences et le choix de la fiancée. VIII. Dans la chambre à coucher du marchand. IX. La Jeune femme est devenue chèvre. X. Cinquième entr'acte et l'enterrement de la chèvre. XI. La Querelle du bouffon avec le marchand. XII. Danse finale.

Chout was commissioned by Serge Diaghilev, who wanted a ballet on a Russian subject for the Ballet Russe de Monte Carlo. Poring through several volumes of Russian folk tales, Diaghilev and Prokofiev seized upon two stories about a buffoon. They collaborated in combining the two stories into one, then in adapting the story into a ballet scenario. Prokofiev began writing his score in 1915. His final version, fully orchestrated, was not completed until 1920. Presented in six scenes, *Chout* was produced by the Ballet Russe in Paris on May 17, 1921. The composer then extracted the basic sections of his score and collated them into an orchestral suite, which was heard for the first time in Brussels on January 15, 1924.

The plot of *Chout* concerns the efforts of a buffoon and his wife to perpetrate a trick on seven other buffoons. Chout pretends he has killed his wife and then that he is able to restore her to life by whipping her. His purpose is to convince the visitors that his whip has magic powers and thus must command a huge price for its purchase. After the buffoons have purchased the whip, they kill their own wives only to discover they are unable to restore them to life. Infuriated, they seek vengeance. When Chout disguises himself as a woman cook, the avenging buffoons kidnap "her" as a hostage, unaware that "she" is actually Chout in disguise. Later on, Chout is chosen by a wealthy merchant to become his wife. Chout makes a discreet escape through the window and reappears as himself, demanding the return of the "cook." Since the merchant is unable to produce the "cook," he buys Chout off for a hundred rubles. The ballet ends in a joyous celebration in which Chout, his wife and his friends participate.

"*Chout* is not to be considered as popular music in the manner of Russian composers borrowing constantly from folk tales," wrote P.O. Ferroud. "But the story of the jester and his mate is drawn so directly from primitive art that it cannot belie its sources. Nevertheless, unlike so many other ballets, this one might be styled 'anti-magical.' It suggests the people in every turn, but a people of realistic and skeptical outlook, which does not believe, even in the face of a moral fable, that the miraculous is possible. The wonder-worker is but a sham. The burlesque effect is produced precisely because the jester knows the limits of his trickery, and his comrades do not. And the music refuses to help us. Full of life, mockery, and caprice, the music enjoys the fun just as we do and only intensifies its truculence."

The ballet suite opens with a portrait of the clown and his wife (Andantino scherzando). This is followed by the dance of the buffoons' wives (Andantino; Allegretto, ma non troppo). The buffoons kill their wives (Fugue; Allegro sostentuo; Vivace), following which Chout masquerades as a young girl (Andantino innocente). A third entr'acte (Un poco andante) is followed by a dance of the buffoons' daughters (Moderato scherzando; Vivace). The seventh section represents the arrival of the merchant, and the dance of obeisance and his choice of his fiancée (Andante gravissimo; Andantino; Allegro espressivo; Andante maestoso). Part eight takes place in the bedroom of the merchant (Moderato tranquillo), while in the ninth section a young girl is transformed into a goat (Moderato con agitazione). Section ten represents the fifth entr'acte and a description of the burial of the goat (Lento con tristezza). Following the quarrel of the buffoon and the merchant (Allegro marziale), we arrive at the finale and the concluding dance (Moderato; Allegro).

1921 CONCERTO NO. 3 IN C MAJOR FOR PIANO AND ORCHESTRA, op. 26. I. Andante; Allegro. II. Theme and Variations: andantino. III. Allegro ma non troppo.

For many years, Prokofiev had been accumulating the themes he was to develop in this concerto: the principal theme of the second movement came to him in 1913, while an episode in the first movement dates from 1911. He began to work with concentration on the concerto in the summer of 1921, completing it on September 28. The world première took place in Chicago on December, 1921, with the composer as soloist and Frederick Stock conducting the Chicago Symphony Orchestra. The work was well received; and ever since its première it has been one of Prokofiev's most successful and frequently heard compositions.

The composer's own analysis, as published in the score, follows: "The first movement opens quietly with a short introduction. The theme is announced by an unaccompanied clarinet, and is continued by the violins for a few bars. Soon the tempo changes . . . which leads to the statement of the principal subject by the piano. . . . A passage in chords for the piano alone leads to the more expressive second subject, heard in the oboe with a pizzicato accompaniment. This is taken up by the piano and developed at length. . . . At the climax of this section, the tempo reverts to Andante, and the orchestra gives out the first theme, *ff*. The piano joins in, and the theme is subjected to an impressively broad treatment. On resuming the Allegro, the chief theme and the second subject are developed with increased brilliance, and the movement ends with an exciting crescendo.

"The second movement consists of a theme with five variations. The theme is announced by the orchestra alone. In the first variation the piano treats the opening of the theme in quasi-sentimental fashion. . . . The tempo changes to Allegro for the second and third variations. . . . In variation four, the tempo is once again Andante, and the piano and orchestra discourse on the theme in a quiet and meditative fashion. Variation five is energetic (Allegro giusto). It leads without pause into a restatement of the theme by the orchestra, with delicate embroidery in the piano.

"The finale begins with a staccato theme for bassoons and pizzicato strings, which is interrupted by the blustering entry of the piano. . . . Eventually, the piano takes up the first theme and develops it into a climax. With a reduction of tone and slackening of tempo, an alternate theme is introduced in the woodwinds. The piano replies with a theme that is more in keeping with the caustic humor of the work. This material is developed and there is a brilliant coda."

1924 LE PAS D'ACIER (THE AGE OF STEEL), ballet suite for orchestra, op. 41-bis. I. Train of Men Carrying Provision Bags. II. Sailor with Bracelet and Working Women. III. Reconstruction of Scenery. IV. The Factory. V. The Hammer. VI. Final Scene.

Serge Diaghilev outlined to Prokofiev the idea for a ballet about Soviet life, with a specific plan: the first part would describe the crumbling of the old order, while the second part would be devoted to the building of a new Soviet world. He had engaged Georgi Yakulov to write the scenario, and he wanted Prokofiev to prepare the score.

The ballet was in essence a glorification of the growth and development of industrialization in the Soviet Union. It called for strident and realistic music in which factory noises and the rhythms of machines and engines in motion were to play a prominent part. Prokofiev's score fulfilled the assignment completely. It was highly dissonant, and with an almost stark naturalism. The occasional flavoring of Russian melodies, in which Prokofiev simulated the folk songs of his land, did not conceal the acrid bitterness of the music as a whole. This music was as tense as steel, an "apotheosis of machinery," as one unnamed critic described it.

At its première performance, which took place in Paris on June 1927, the ballet was received with comparative apathy. Diaghilev expected a scandal, but he received neither riots nor enthusiasm. However, when the ballet was introduced in London, the following July 4, it scored a decided success, and was played eight times. The *Musical Times* called it the most powerful Diaghilev ballet since *Les Noces,* and the *Empire News* felt that it expressed the spirit of modern Russia better than all the efforts of orators and writers.

The ballet suite for orchestra was introduced in Moscow on May 27, 1928.

1928–1930 SYMPHONY NO. 3 IN C MINOR, op. 44. I. Moderato. II. Andante. III. Allegro agitato. IV. Andante mosso.

SYMPHONY NO. 4 IN C MAJOR, op. 47. I. Andante; Allegro eroica. II. Andante tranquillo. III. Moderato. IV. Allegro risoluto.,

Prokofiev's Third Symphony (1928) was first heard in Paris on May 17, 1929. Pierre Monteux conducting the Orchestre Symphonique. For some of his basic melodic material, Prokofiev lifted themes from his opera, *The Flaming Angel,* op. 37 (1919), whose world première took place in a concert version broadcast over the Paris radio on January 13, 1954. However, the symphony makes no attempt to carry over any of the story or episodes from the opera and must be regarded as absolute music. Prokofiev's biographer, Israel V. Nestyev considers this as the most dramatic of the composer's four early symphonies. He finds three sharply contrasted themes in the first movement: "the first two are those of Renata's mental anguish in *The Flaming Angel*—the chromatic ostinato theme of the introduction (her despair) and the agitated melody of the main theme (the Leitmotiv of her love for Madiel)." The subordinate subject is, by contrast, quiet and gentle. The slow movement is mystical and otherworldly with what Nestyev describes as "an archaic quality." The Scherzo, on the other hand, is demoniac, suggested by the finale of Chopin's B-flat minor Sonata. Midway in the movement, however, a gentle and restful theme provides welcome contrast. The finale "brings back the world of medieval mysticism with images of suffering, torture and monstrous exorcisms. Funereal rhythms contrast with tense, piercing themes." In the recapitulation, the composer recalls the subordinate theme of the first movement, combining it with the principal theme of the finale.

The Fourth Symphony (1930) was commissioned by the Boston Symphony for its fiftieth anniversary. Its first performance took place in Boston on November 14, 1930, Koussevitzky conducting. In his last year, Prokofiev revised the symphony, now assigning it the opus number of 112. Its Western hemisphere première was given in Philadelphia on September 27, 1957, under Eugene Ormandy.

Some of the thematic material comes out of Prokofiev's ballet *L'Enfant prodigue,* op. 46 (1928), introduced in Paris on May 21, 1929. The composer felt that the demands of choreography had restricted his musical thinking and felt impelled to expand and develop his ideas within a symphonic structure.

A slow introduction, its main idea built out of descending sixth intervals, precedes a strong, rhythmic heroic section. A vigorous statement is followed by a contrasting theme, first in solo flute accompanied by clarinet, then in solo clarinet accompanied by two bassoons. In the slow movement, Prokofiev makes extended use of a haunting melody for solo flute, which is repeated by the strings; divided and plucked strings, joined by piano and cymbals on the off-beat, provide a change of mood. In the third movement, oboe and bassoon are heard in a tune which the strings soon expropriate. In the middle trio section, the main theme is given by the oboe and plucked strings. The finale opens with a dramatic proclamation by woodwind and strings in unison. Solo cellos are then heard with another strong thought. A section marked "grazioso" for brass contributes the contrast.

1930 STRING QUARTET NO. 1 IN B MINOR, op. 50. I. Allegro. II. Andante molto. III. Andante.

The personal confidences that are usually spoken by the composer within the intimate form of the string quartet are to be found in this music. In few of his works has Prokofiev written music in which he plumbs his own feelings so deeply. In place of the customary wit and satire that we have come to expect in Prokofiev, we find serene beauty (the second theme of the first movement) and the profoundest emotions (the opening of the scherzo). Perhaps in none of his other works has he maintained such a high level of spiritual and aesthetic beauty as in the whole of the closing movement. The quartet is characterized by Israel Nestyev as "predominantly deep, calm, and contemplative."

Prokofiev wrote this quartet for the Library of Congress in Washington, D.C., where it was introduced on April 25, 1931.

1931 CONCERTO NO. 4 FOR PIANO AND ORCHESTRA IN B-FLAT MAJOR, op. 53, for the left hand. I. Vivace. II. Andante. III. Moderato. IV. Vivace.

Prokofiev's fourth piano concerto (for left hand only) is the least known of the composer's five piano concertos. He wrote it for Paul Wittgenstein, the Austrian pianist who, having lost his right arm during World War I, gave concerts of music for the left hand. To provide himself with concert material, Wittgenstein commissioned composers to write works for him, one of whom was Ravel who produced his Concerto for the Left Hand and Orchestra for Wittgenstein. Prokofiev was another composer approached by Wittgenstein. But when Prokofiev delivered his manuscript, Wittgenstein did not like it, deeming it too modern in style for his tastes, and he would not perform it. This reaction led Prokofiev to put the concerto into discard. It was never played during the composer's lifetime. Then, Siegfried Rapp, a German pianist, received permission from Prokofiev's widow to play it in public. He did so in West Berlin in September of 1956. Thus, a quarter of a century after it had been written, the concerto was finally introduced.

Here is how Prokofiev himself described the plan of his concerto: "Four movements, the first swiftly running, built mainly on finger technique; the second an Andante developing with calm solemnity; the third a kind of sonata Allegro—not quite true to form—and the fourth a reversion to the first but cut short and piano throughout."

In their biography of Prokofiev, Lawrence and Elisabeth Hanson regard the opening as the "finest movement he was ever to write, with running passages of a decorous, classical gaiety for the pianist against a slower orchestral theme." In the slow movement, the Hansons find a "straining after the 'calm solemnity' he speaks of." The third movement opens "with a characteristic Prokofiev theme." The Hansons described the finale as "a stroke of genius... lasting less than two minutes." It provides a "bird's-eye view of the piano material from the first movement and cheerfully rounds off the work."

1932 CONCERTO NO. 5 IN G MINOR FOR PIANO AND ORCHESTRA, op. 55. I. Allego con brio; Meno Mosso; Tempo Primo. II. Moderato ben accentutato. III. Allegro con fuoco. IV. Larghetto. V. Vivo; piu mosso.

The melodic ideas for this composition (as in the case of the Third Piano Concerto) had been in existence long before the composer sat down to write his work. Actually, there have been two Fifth Concertos. One was written in 1918, and having been left in Russia when Prokofiev came to the United States, went astray. The other was developed in 1932 from the piano sketches of the original work, which the composer had preserved. The première of the concerto took place in Berlin on October 31, 1931. The composer was the soloist, and the Berlin Philharmonic was directed by Wilhelm Furtwaengler.

The composer's analysis follows:

"The first movement is an Allegro con brio with a Meno mosso as middle section. Though not in sonata form, it is the main movement of the concerto and fulfills the function and maintains the spirit of the traditional sonata form. The second movement has a march-like rhythm. I would not think of calling it a march because it has none of the vulgarity or commonness which is so often associated with the idea of march, and which actually exists in most popular marches. The third movement is a toccata. This is a precipitate, displayful movement of much technical brilliance and requiring a great virtuosity; it is a toccata for orchestra as much as for piano. The fourth movement . . . is the lyrical movement of the concerto. It starts off with a soft, soothing theme; grows more and more intense in the middle portion, develops breadth and tension, then returns to the music of the beginning. The finale has a decided classic flavor. The Coda is based on a new theme, which is joined by the other themes of the finale. There is a reference to some of the material of the preceding movements in the finale.

1934 LIEUTENANT KIJE, symphonic suite, op. 60. I. The Birth of Kije. II. Romance. III. Kije's Wedding. IV. Troika. V. Burial of Kije.

The first music written by Prokofiev after his permanent return to his native land in 1933 was for a film, *Lieutenant Kije*. The witty screen play concerns a mythical character, Lieutenant Kije, created by Tsar Nicholas I through the misreading of a military report. Rather than tell the Tsar that he has made a mistake, the courtiers are compelled to fabricate all sorts of military exploits for the invented character. Finally, pressed by the Tsar to bring the hero into the court, they bring about his noble death on the battlefield.

For this merry story, Prokofiev wrote a score in his best satirical vein. The character of Kije is virtually caricature; his exploits are told with tongue-in-cheek malice.

In 1934, the composer wrote a symphonic suite based on some of the best music of the motion-picture score. In the first part (Allegro), a fanfare of cornets and rolls of the drum evoke the character of the military hero, Lieutenant Kije. A march of somewhat hollow pomp is heard. In the succeding part (Andante), our hero succumbs to love. This section calls for a baritone solo, but most of the time Kije's song of love is assumed by the tenor saxophone. With a great deal of ceremony—and with no less sentiment—Kije gets married in the third movement (Allegro fastoso). A Moderato section brings up the Russian winter with sleigh bells. Within a tavern a lusty song is heard. (Once again the tenor saxophone substitutes for the singing voice.) Poor Kije is put to rest with full military honors in the concluding pages (Andante assai), as high points of his career are reviewed. Prokofiev's music emphasizes the fact that for the courtiers this is not an occasion for grief, but for constrained rejoicing: Kije has become a trial to them, and his death is a blessed relief.

The suite was introduced in Paris under the composer's direction on February 20, 1937.

1935 CONCERTO NO. 2 IN G MINOR FOR VIOLIN AND ORCHESTRA, op. 63. I. Allegro moderato. II. Andante assai. III. Allegro ben marcato.

The Second Violin Concerto followed the First by eighteen years. It was written for a French violinist, Robert Soetens, who introduced it in Madrid on December 1, 1935, with the Madrid Symphony Orchestra under Arbós. Prokofiev originally intended this work to be a sonata for violin and piano; but as his ideas grew more and more spacious, he realized that the concerto form was more suitable.

The Second Concerto is more melodic than the First and more romantic in its approach. The first movement (in sonata form) opens with a highly expressive melodic idea in the solo violin unaccompanied. This idea— the principal theme of the movement—is extended, after which a second melody, equally eloquent, is also proclaimed by the solo instrument against a background of soft strings. The working out of these two themes is elaborate, with the solo violin frequently indulging in pyrotechnical passages which decorate the melodies taken up by the orchestra. The second movement is classic in its emotional restraint and purity of writing. After two bars of prelude, the violin enters with the principal material—a moving and poetic melody out of which the entire movement develops. The concluding section of the concerto— a rondo in three sections—is more rhythmic than melodic, and gives play to Prokofiev's natural bent for satire.

1935 ROMEO AND JULIET, two ballet suites for orchestra, op. 64ter.

SUITE NO. 1: I. Dance of the People; II. Scene; III. Madrigal; IV. Minuet; V. Masques; VI. Romeo and Juliet; VII. Death of Tybalt.

SUITE NO. 2: I. Montagues and Capulets; II. Juliet, the Maiden; III. Friar Laurence; IV. Dance; V. The Parting of Romeo and Juliet; VI. Dance of the West-Indian Slave Girls; VII. The Grave of Romeo and Juliet.

Prokofiev wrote the music for this ballet for the Bolshoi Theatre in Moscow. The score received a concert hearing before the ballet was produced—in Moscow in October of 1935. When the ballet première took place, it was mounted not in the Soviet Union but in Brünn, Czechoslovakia, in 1938; on January 11, 1940, it was presented at the Kirov Theatre in Leningrad. The ballet was not successful. The Soviet critics did not like the inconsistencies in the scenario, and its submission to what one of them described as "the worst traditions of the old form." There was also some resentment over the imposition of a happy ending (so much so that after a trial performance the original tragic ending of the drama was restored). Prokofiev's music was described as hard, cold, incongruous to the text. Prokofiev himself said: "I have taken special pains to achieve a simplicity which, I hope, will reach the hearts of listeners, If people find no melody and no emotion in this work I shall be very sorry. But I feel sooner or later they will."

Israel Nestyev noted that "the composer employs the most expressive melodic images with extreme economy of timbral and harmonic embellishment. It is no wonder that, after the passionate chromatic sensuousness of Wagner's love themes, Prokofiev's lyricism . . . may seem a shade too passionless. It is not until one grows accustomed to this music that its amazing purity of emotion and power of conviction can be appreciated to the full."

The second suite is popular. The first movement (Andante) begins with a discordant introduction that is a premonition of coming tragedy. When the tempo changes to Allegro, the music offers a portrait of the proud Veronese nobles. A middle section (Molto tranquillo) brings a picture of Juliet dancing with Paris. In the second movement (Vivace), Juliet is portrayed, while in the third, Friar Lawrence (Andante espressivo) is described by two subjects, the first in bassoons, tuba and harp, and the other in divided cellos. Snare drum, harp, piano and plucked strings set the stage for a lively dance tune in the oboe in the fourth movement (Vivo). The fifth part is a haunting and poetic description of Romeo and Juliet before their parting (Lento). This part opens with a beautiful subject for flute, while later on a solo viola is heard in Romeo's love music. Prokofiev himself described the sixth movement (Andante con elegenza) as follows: "Paris presents pearls to Juliet; slave girls dance with pearls." The seventh and last part (Adagio) is funereal music for the tragic last scene of the drama.

The second suite was first heard in Leningrad on April 15, 1937. The première of the first suite took place in Moscow on November 24, 1936. Prokofiev also prepared a third suite from his ballet score, made up of the following sections: I. Romeo at the Fountain; II. The Morning Dance; III. Juliet; IV. Nurse; V. Morning Serenade; VI. Juliet's Death.

1935–1936 SUMMER DAY, suite of children's pieces for orchestra, op. 65-b. I. Morning. II. Tag. III. Waltz. IV. Regrets. V. March. VI. Evening. VII. Moonlit Meadows.

PETER AND THE WOLF, symphonic fairy tale for narrator and orchestra, op. 67.

Prokofiev liked writing music for children. Since he had an unusual gift for it, he did this often throughout his career. *Summer Day* originated in 1935 as a set of twelve easy pieces for the piano under the title of *Music for Children,* op. 65. It was heard in Moscow in 1936. In 1941, Prokofiev orchestrated seven of these compositions and provided them the new title of *Summer Day*. The orchestral adaptation was given in Moscow in 1946. In the first movement (Andante tranquillo), a quaint tune for first flute, accompanied by other woodwinds, is contrasted with a somber melody for bassoons, horns and cellos. This is followed by a section in which a capricious tune in violins and flutes is shared by the bassoons (Vivo). The waltz that follows (Allegretto) is introduced by the violins, after which comes another melody for the violins, this time with octave skips. The fourth part (Moderato) consists of a tender theme for cellos with several transformations. The march melody of the fifth part (Tempo di marcia) is shared between oboes and clarinets and the horns. Solo flute is heard in the main thought of both the sixth and the concluding movements, marked respectively Andante teneroso and Andantino.

Unquestionably, Prokofiev's greatest success as composer of music for children came with his remarkable symphonic fairy tale, *Peter and the Wolf* (1936), now familiar to young and old the world over. Prokofiev's intention in this work is to teach children the sounds of the different instruments of the orchestra. As the narrator informs the listener in the opening monologue:

"Each character in this tale is represented by an instrument in the orchestra: the bird, by a flute; the duck, by an oboe; the cat, by a clarinet in the low register; grandpapa, by the bassoon; the wolf, by three French horns; Peter, by the string quartet; and the hunter's rifle shots, by the kettledrums and bass drums."

The story then unfolds—in words and music. The narrator speaks the text, pausing to allow the music to give a tonal interpretation of what he has just described. During the recital, Leitmotifs in the different instruments appear and reappear, and are woven into the orchestral fabric with extraordinary ingenuity. The themes for the various animals are highly descriptive; and the melodic subject describing Peter has all the insouciance and impudence of the reckless youth who goes unafraid to capture the wolf and who succeeds in dragging the animal back to the zoo.

Peter and the Wolf was introduced in Moscow on May 2, 1936.

1938 CONCERTO NO. 1 IN E MINOR FOR CELLO AND ORCHESTRA, op. 58. I. Andante. II. Allegro giusto. III. Reminscenza.

Though originally sketched in 1933, Prokofiev did not complete his First Cello Concerto until 1938. It was introduced on November 26, 1938 at a festival of Soviet music in Moscow. This work is of a more slender structure than Prokofiev's other concertos for other instruments. The first movement is more of a prelude than a movement in sonata form, made up of a single theme. dramatized by dissonant harmonies. The second movement, a scherzo, has two subjects in the infectious grotesquerie style Prokofiev favored. The finale is in the theme-and-variations form. After the last variation, subject matter from the first and second movements is reviewed.

When the concerto received its American première on March 8, 1940, it was heard with a new cadenza which the composer had added, together with various revisions. A dozen years later, Prokofiev rewrote this concerto completely, calling it at first Concerto No. 2; it has since been heard and become known as *Symphony-Concerto*, the title that appeared in the published score when it was issued posthumously in 1959 (*see* 1952).

1939 ALEXANDER NEVSKY, cantata for mezzo-soprano, chorus and orchestra, op. 78.

Prokofiev's ability to write music for a comparatively popular medium and yet to maintain the highest artistic integrity and standards was proved by *Alexander Nevsky*. Though originating as motion-picture music, it is nevertheless one of the composer's finest creations, a work of great dignity and power.

The motion picture, directed by Sergei Eisenstein (in collaboration with Vasiliev), was built around the Russian defense of Novgorod in 1242 against the invading Knights of the Teutonic Order. The hero of this defense was Prince Alexander Yaroslavich Nevsky. Called to save his land, the Prince gathered around him a fighting force, met the enemy on the frozen waters of Lake Chud, and dealt them a disastrous defeat. (It must be recalled that when this motion picture was produced, in 1938—one year before the Soviet-Nazi pact—the sentiment against Germany was intense in the Soviet Union.)

The eloquent descriptive music that Prokofiev wrote for this motion picture impressed the composer, who realized that he had here the materials for a major musical composition. He extracted the most graphic pages of his score, amplified and extended them, and developed the whole into a cantata. In this form, *Alexander Nevsky* was introduced in Moscow (and with extraordinary success) on May 17, 1939, with the composer directing the Moscow Philharmonic Orchestra and Chorus.

The American première of *Alexander Nevsky* took place in a radio performance over the NBC network conducted by Leopold Stokowski on March 7, 1943. The first concert performance came on March 23, 1945, with Eugene Ormandy conducting the Philadelphia Orchestra. After the latter performance, Olin Downes wrote: "The music is built on grand lines with great mass effects. . . . The work has a master's simplicity, orchestral music of extraordinary power, and in the choral writing the racial accents of the people and of the composer who is here a true descendant of Mussorgsky. . . . The orchestral coloring is very remarkable and so is the superb writing for the voices. . . . The battle on the ice is in essence, perhaps, moving-picture music—but what moving-picture music! . . . Then there is the contralto solo . . . the lament of the field of the dead. Here again is a real simplicity, a real emotion, expressed in a radical way, with fine art."

The cantata is divided into seven sections, or "pictures."

I. "Russia Under the Mongolian Yoke." In somber music the composer evokes the feeling of desolation that seizes Russia following the Tartar invasion in the middle of the thirteenth century.

II. "Song of Nevsky." With ringing, soaring lines of music the chorus raises its voice in praise of the hero, Nevsky, who has helped bring about the defeat of the Swedes on the Neva River.

III. "Crusaders in Pskov." The Teutonic Knights, masquerading as religious crusaders, are depicted in music that pointedly combines Gregorian cadences (an ecclesiastical Latin text is set for chorus) with brutal, modern harmonies and sonorities.

IV. "Arise, Ye Russian People." The people of Russia are urged to rise against the invaders, the music now reflecting the intensity of this sentiment.

V. "The Battle on the Ice." A gruesome, realistic picture is drawn of the savage battle on Lake Chud.

VI. "Field of the Dead." Grief for the dead, expressed in a song by a Russian girl, mingles with the exaltation of patriotism.

VII. "Alexander's Entry into Pskov." A grandiose hymn of triumph is sounded by chorus and orchestra to celebrate the victory of Nevsky as he enters with glory into the city of Pskov.

1940–1944 THE "WAR SONATAS" FOR PIANO:

SONATA NO. 6 IN A MAJOR, op. 82. I. Allegro moderato. II. Allegretto. III. Tempo di valzer lentissimo. IV. Vivace.

SONATA NO. 7 IN B-FLAT MAJOR, op. 83. I Allegro inquieto. II. Andante caloroso. III. Precipitato.

SONATA NO. 8 IN B-FLAT MAJOR, op. 84. I. Andante dolce; Allegro. II. Andante sognando. III. Vivace.

Prokofiev himself dubbed these three compositions as "war sonatas," since all three were written when the impact of the Nazi invasion of the Soviet Union was most strongly felt by the Russian people in general, and Prokofiev in particular. About these three works, Abram Chasins has written in the *Saturday Review*: "They reveal a man in discord with the world and himself, a musician trying to find expression for the anxiety and instability of his epoch and of his own afflicted soul, an instinctive poet in revolt against rude realities. They also reveal a master craftsman who rarely fails to achieve some striking result even when he wavers. Twisting and turning back and forth he is sometimes freed, sometimes fettered; sometimes victorious and sometimes defeated; now bravely blazing paths into the future, now timidly following well-trodden mediocrity."

The most significant of this trio of sonatas is the seventh, which Svyatoslav Richter introduced in the Soviet Union in 1943, when it was so successful that it was awarded the highly coveted Stalin Prize. This sonata has acquired the sobriquet of "The Stalingrad Sonata" because it was written during the heroic stand and victory of the Red Army. An event of such magnitude inevitably left its impress at the time on the Russian people, who sensed that the turning point of the war had come; and it left its influence on the sonata Prokofiev was writing.

There is no programmatic analysis appended to this music; but it is not hard to find here the tensions and exaltations of the time. The powerful dynamism and the precipitous rhythmic sweeps of the first movement re-create the emotional disturbances that every Soviet citizen must have experienced at this historic hour. A disturbed chromatic opening precedes two subjects, the first dramatic and percussive, the second lyrical. The shattering power and force of the closing movement, with its theatrical ostinati, are like the iron wall of flesh and steel set up by the Red Army against the besieging enemy. Felix Borowski put it this way: "Something of the inexorable rhythm of the finale . . . gives a suggestion of the heroic inflexibility of a people who are not to know defeat. In between these two large and tempestuous movements, there is a slender one: songlike music of rare delicacy which comes as a lull between two storms."

1941–1942 WAR AND PEACE, opera in eleven scenes, op. 91, with text by the composer and his wife (Mira Mendelson) based on Tolstoy's novel. First performance: original version (thirty scenes), Leningrad, June 12, 1946; revised version (eleven scenes), Leningrad, April 1, 1955.

For many years Russian composers had been attracted to Tolstoy's epic novel as a subject for an opera, only to be discouraged by the seemingly impossible task of reducing the monumental proportions of the novel to libretto size. The year of 1941, which saw the invasion of the Soviet Union by the Nazis, gave new impact and significance to the Tolstoy classic. Prokofiev, who had long eyed the story covetously for a possible opera, was driven by the momentous events of the times to creative action. His biographer, Israel Nestyev, remarks that the speed with which Prokofiev wrote the opera, and the "dimensions and form of execution," may well be among the most amazing phenomena of the composer's career.

The libretto by Mira Mendelson written in prose (much of which was directly expropriated from Tolstoy), concentrates exclusively on the Napoleonic invasion of Russia in 1812. In five acts (eleven scenes), the opera is intended for performance on two consecutive nights: the first part, Acts I and II, are called by the composer "scenes of peace," while the remaining three acts are the "scenes of war." "In the first six scenes," the composer has explained, "I wanted to depict the main characters' peaceful life, their smiles and tears, their thoughts and dreams. These scenes deal with the relationships between Natasha Rostova, Andrei Volkonsky, Anatoli Kuragin and Pierre Bezhukov—what Tolstoy himself in one of his letters called 'the novel's core.' The libretto is written in such a way that the foreboding of war grows gradually stronger from the first to the seventh scene. Peaceful life is interrupted by Napoleonic invasion. Beginning with the seventh scene, interest is focused on the Russian people's struggle, their sufferings, wrath, courage and victory over the invaders. In this part the people themselves constitute the hero of the opera in the person of the peasants of the popular militia, the regular Russian army, the Cossacks, and the guerillas. Field Marshal Kutuzov, the soldiers' and people's favorite, appears on the scene. The destinies of the main characters introduced in the first six scenes are closely linked with war events. I was particularly anxious to stress the profound changes which occurred in their mental and moral make-up as a result of the danger threatening the country. . . ."

Sixty characters are employed in the opera, though most of them appear only once. There is the central love theme of Natasha and Andrei running through the entire work as a kind of coalescing agent, providing much of the lyrical interest in the opera (as, for example, the spring nocturne of Scene One). There are big mass scenes in which the historic events are projected on a vast scale (the chorus of the Smolensk refugees or the battle scene of Borodino). And there are subtle and highly picturesque orchestral tone-portraits (the picture of ruined Moscow that opens Scene Nine, and the vivid battle between the partisans and the French in Scene Eleven).

One of the outstanding qualities of Prokofiev's score is its gift for sharp character delineations. One Soviet critic elaborated on this point in the publication *Soviet Music:* "The principal characters of the opera have their own clearly defined idiom—one might almost say their own dialects, marking not only their aria passages but also their recitatives. . . . In this way Prokofiev may be said to give unity to separate groups of characters . . . and, with all that, to distinguish between the social classes to which they belong. . . . Thus the composer attains an unusual expressiveness and psychological realism."

A few scenes of *War and Peace* were presented in concert form at the Moscow Conservatory on June 7, 1945, S. Samosud conducting. One year later, the first part of the opera was presented at the Maly Academic Theatre in Leningrad. At that time, the Soviet critic A. Khokhlovkin exlcaimed that it "is a work of tremendous significance." But that, of course, was before 1948—when Prokofiev and most of his major works came in for severe criticism (and proscription) by the Central Committee of the Communist Party.

Prokofiev kept on revising his opera up to the time of his death, most of this revision consisting mainly of compression and condensation. The final version was completed in 1952 and was the one in which the opera was presented for the first time to the world outside the Soviet Union—in 1953 at the Florence May Music Festival. This version (in an English translation by Joseph Machlis) was also the one which introduced the opera to the United States, when it was broadcast by the NBC Opera Company over the NBC-TV network on January 13, 1957.

1941 STRING QUARTET NO. 2 IN F MAJOR, op. 92. I. Allegro sostenuto. II. Adagio. III. Allegro.

Prokofiev himself has said that this quartet combines "one of the least-known varieties of folk song with the most classical form of the quartet." The variety of folk song alluded to is that heard and preserved in the region of Kabardino-Balkaria, in the East Caucasus, where Prokofiev was vacationing in the war year of 1942.

The melos of the Caucasian folk song dominates the entire quartet. It is found in the almost naive initial theme of the first movement, which sounds like a nursery tune; the second theme is more sophisticated, but the entire movement has a down-to-earth character. In the second movement, a Caucasian love song is heard in the cello against oriental embellishments in the other instruments. This song is plangent in character, but as the movement progresses some gaiety is injected, and the song returns devoid of sentimentality. The abrupt and varied rhythms of Caucasian folk dances bring vitality to the closing movement. A lyric strain enters in the second section, though the rhythmic energy is not controlled; but in the third section, rhythm gives way to a deeply felt melody. After a solo passage for the cello, a new section is introduced. But the earlier rhythmic and melodic material is soon repeated, and the movement ends with a return of the opening section.

The Quartet was introduced in Moscow on September 5, 1942.

1944 CINDERELLA, two ballet suites for orchestra, op. 87.

SUITE NO. I.: I. Introduction; II. Pas de chat; III. Quarrel; IV. Fairy Godmother and Fairy Winter; V. Mazurka; VI. Cinderella Goes to the Ball; VII. Cinderella's Waltz; Midnight.

SUITE NO. 2: I. Cinderella Dreams of the Ball; II. Dancing Lessons and Gavotte; III. Fairy Spring and Fairy Summer; IV. Bourrée; V. Cinderella and the Castle; VI. Galop.

In 1940, the Kirov Theatre of Opera and Ballet in Leningrad asked Prokofiev for music for a ballet on either one of two subjects, the Snow Maiden, or Cinderella. Prokofiev chose the latter, and went to work at once. Hitler's attack on the Soviet Union, and Prokofiev's intense preoccupation with his opera *War and Peace,* delayed the completion of his score until 1944.

Nikolai Volkov prepared the scenario for the ballet based on Perrault's famous fairy tale. Volkov explained that though he kept Perrault continually in mind, "new images of the prince and the drudge rose before my eyes. The prince acquired the features of a passionate and an impetuous youth who longed to escape from the confining influence of the stagnant court life. . . . In our imagination, Cinderella was shrouded in the mist of dreams, a girl who lived on the foretaste of love. The result of this interpretation of the chief characters was that the ballet acquired the features of a love story. The fairy tale, while preserving its mood of fantasy, was filled with psychological and lyrical content. In Prokofiev's music this found expression in a profoundly moving Adagio, in the sweeping melodies of the waltz, and in the concluding Amoroso."

Prokofiev explained: "My music has three basic themes: first theme, Cinderella, the abused and the ill-treated; second theme, Cinderella, the chaste, pure and pensive; the third and main theme, Cinderella, in love, radiant with happiness. I also took a great deal of trouble to establish every character through the music—the sweet, shy, Cinderella, her timid father, her bad-tempered stepmother, her selfish sisters, the gay and passionate young Prince—in such a way that the audience felt caught up in their joys and sorrows. . . . I decided to write *Cinderella* in the tradition of the old classical ballet: I gave it pas de deux, adagios, gavottes, several waltzes, a pavane, passepied, bourrée, mazurka, and a galop. The fairy tale presented a number of fascinating problems to the composer—the atmosphere of magic surrounding the Fairy Godmother, the twelve fantastic dwarfs who pop out of the clock as it strikes midnight to remind Cinderella that it is time to go home, the swift changes of scenes as the Prince journeys over the earth in search of her, and the poetry of nature personified by the four fairies of Spring, Summer, Autumn and Winter and their retinue."

Cinderella was introduced not by the Kirov Theatre in Leningrad but by the Bolshoi Theatre in Moscow, on November 21, 1945; Galina Ulanova was Cinderella. When the Royal Ballet presented its own version at Covent Garden on December 23, 1948, Moira Shearer was Cinderella; and Margot Fonteyn danced the part with the Royal Ballet Company when *Cinderella* was first seen in the United States, in New York on October 18, 1949. (Miss Fonteyn also appeared in the ballet when it was televised over the NBC-TV network on April 29, 1957.)

To Lawrence and Elisabeth Hanson, *Cinderella* "is not only Prokofiev's greatest work as a cosmopolitan musician, it is also his greatest work as a Russian. In it he displays fully for the first time what is perhaps the finest of all fine qualities of the Russian genius—a manly poetic tenderness. . . . Not only is Prokofiev never at a loss for a first-class tune but the middle sections of his waltzes sometimes even surpass the main waltz theme in originality and charm. . . . The humor, it goes without saying, is enchanting. . . . The elegance . . . pervades the entire score."

1944 SONATA NO. 2 IN D MAJOR FOR VIOLIN AND PIANO, op. 94. I. Moderato. II. Scherzo. III. Andante. IV. Allegro con brio.

On one of the highly infrequent occasions that Bernard Shaw returned to his early role of music critic, he described this sonata as a "humorous masterpiece of authentic violin music." Shaw was only partly right. Humorous this sonata occasionally is—especially in the fleet, capricious scherzo, and in the playful and saucy impudence of the closing movement. But instead of humor, lyricism and tender feelings are the predominating traits of this work. It abounds in wonderful melodies. The sonata opens with one of these—a long, full, flowing song that dominates the entire first movement; and the graceful and delicate Andante is as gentle a piece of music as Prokofiev has written.

As for its being "authentic violin music": this sonata was *not* originally written for the violin, but for the flute and piano, a version heard in Moscow on December 7, 1943. Prokofiev then adapted his flute sonata for the violin, and David Oistrakh performed it in Moscow on June 17, 1944.

1944–1947 SYMPHONY NO. 5 IN B-FLAT MAJOR, op. 100. I. Andante. II. Allegro marcato. III. Adagio. IV. Allegro giocoso.

SYMPHONY NO. 6 IN E-FLAT MINOR, op. 111. I. Allegro moderato. II. Largo. III. Vivace.

In writing his Fifth Symphony (which arrived in 1944, fifteen years after his Fourth), Prokofiev voiced a hymn to the spirit of man—a spirit that could not be permanently subjugated by either oppression or war. This symphony was written in a single month during the summer of 1944 (though Prokofiev had been gathering sketches for it for several years), and reflects in many of its pages the impact of the war on the Russian people.

It opens with a majestic slow movement built around two themes; it grows in power and grandeur until the themes are evolved into a coda of epic stature. A scherzo-like section follows, nervous and abrupt in its sudden accentuations (some writers find this music expressive of the horrors of war). The third movement is a threnody of compelling emotional intensity—possibly what Prokofiev had here in mind was the terrible price that the Russians were paying for their heroic resistance to the Nazi invaders. The mood throughout is one of grief; at climactic moments, the tragedy becomes heartrending. But Prokofiev does not succumb permanently to pessimism. In the last movement, gaiety asserts itself through the ominous atmosphere and speaks for the future, in which the fruits of victory can be enjoyed.

The symphony was introduced in Moscow on January 13, 1945, with the composer conducting. When Serge Koussevitzky introduced this symphony in the United States, in November, 1945, he described it as one of the greatest works of our generation, and broke precedent by performing it twice in New York in the same season.

The Sixth Symphony (1947) is slighter in texture than the Fifth, more economical in its means, more transparent in its writing, lighter in mood, and more melodious. Written simply and emotionally, it is one of the most graceful of Prokofiev's later works, and is the kind of music that can be appreciated at first hearing. It is therefore strange to remember that this symphony was also severely condemned as "formalist" (or "cerebral") by the Central Committee of the Communist Party when it hurled a blanket denunciation at most of the major Soviet composers in February, 1948. After its première performance (in Leningrad on October 11, 1947), it was put on the proscribed list and shelved.

Prokofiev's own description of this symphony is as terse and direct as the music itself. "The first movement, of agitated character, is lyrical at times, and austere at others. The second movement is brighter and full of song. The finale, rapid and major, is near in character to my Fifth Symphony, but for the austere reminiscences of the first movement."

When this symphony received its American première (New York City, November 24, 1949, Leopold Stokowski conducting the New York Philharmonic), Mr. Stokowski provided the following analysis: "It is in three parts—

the first moderately quick, the second slow, and the third very animated. The first part has two themes—the first in a rather fast dance rhythm, the second a slower song-like melody, a little modal in character, recalling the old Russian and Byzantine scales. Later this music becomes gradually more animated as the themes are developed, and after the climax of the development there is a slower transition to the second part. . . . The harmonies and texture of the music are extremely complex. Later there is a theme for horns which is simpler and sounds like voices singing. This leads to a warm cantilena of the violins and a slower transition to the third part, which is rhythmic and full of humor, verging on the satirical. The rhythms are clear-cut, and while the thematic lines are simple, they are accompanied by most original harmonic sequences, alert and rapid. Near the end, a remembrance sounds like an echo of the pensive melancholy of the first part of the symphony, followed by a rushing, tumultuous end."

1952 SYMPHONY-CONCERTO IN E MINOR, for cello and orchestra, op. 125. I. Andante. II. Allegro giusto. III. Andante con moto; Allegro marcato.

This major work for cello and orchestra started out as Prokofiev's first cello concerto, op. 58 (*see* 1938). Between 1950 and 1952. Prokofiev went to great pains to rewrite it, while retaining basic material. He now considered it a new work and for this reason identified it as his second cello concerto. When the score of the later work was published posthumusly in 1959, it bore the new title of *Symphony-Concerto,* apparently following the composer's wishes. He wished to point up the symphonic rather than the concerto nature of this composition. The world première was given by Mstislav Rostropovich in Moscow on February 18, 1952.

This is Israel Nestyev's analysis: "The first movement is a kind of lyrical introduction to the whole work. The two principal themes of this unpretentious three-part movement are fine examples of the pensive but singing lyricism so typical of Prokofiev's later writing. . . . The first theme, the more vigorous of the two, has a fervent, impassioned quality, while the second is noble and tender. . . . A purely coloristic supplementary episode of descending chords in the muted strings creates the atmosphere of a strange, shadowy dream.

"The second movement is the most important, for it is here that the main musical ideas of the work are concentrated. From the moment the cello enters with an introductory cadenza, it is clear that it will play the protagonist's role in this movement. The compelling and dramatic opening theme, which first appears in angular, instrumental form, suddenly assumes the character of a transparent Russian melody. Another sharp contrast occurs in the bridge passage, where unadorned epic lyricism is replaced by a comic, semi-fantastic dance. . . . Immediately preceding the shortened recapitulation, an ominous harsh-sounding episode, marked pìu animato, is introduced. After appearing even more prominently in the extended coda, this episode is superseded by a powerful restatement of part of the first theme, which brings the classically worked out sonata-allegro to a close.

"The finale is written in an interesting form—a three-part variation movement containing two themes. The first of these is a slow instrumental melody; not satisfied with strict variation techniques, the composer later transforms it into a playful dance with amusing accents and humorous orchestration. The second theme is in the style of a rhythmic folk dance. . . . After another set of variations on the first theme, there follows a dramatic coda in which elements of the second movement's grotesque theme appear in substantially altered guise."

1952 SYMPHONY NO. 7 IN C-SHARP MINOR, op. 131. I. Moderato. II. Allegretto; Allegro. III. Andante espressivo. IV. Vivace.

This is Prokofiev's last symphony. It was heard in Moscow on October 11, 1952, a performance that proved so successful that the symphony had to be repeated a few months later for the Composers' Union. At that time, *Pravda* explained that Prokofiev here aimed "to create in music a picture of bright youth in answer to the call of the party of composers to create beautiful, delicate music able to satisfy the aesthetic demands of artistic tastes of the Soviet people." *Pravda* said further that the first movement spans the distance from a child's fairy tale and romantic dreams "to the first active aspirations of youth." The second movement is a symphonic waltz, while the third is a romantic effusion, at turns emotional and pensive, with the cellos heard in an expressive subject, while the bassoons and clarinets follow with a countersubject. The fourth movement passes from a dance to a march, and is consistently vivacious.

The American première was given by the Philadelphia Orchestra under Eugene Ormandy on April 10, 1953. The American critics were less enthusiastic than their Russian colleagues. Olin Downes said: "This is by no means Prokofiev's strongest symphony. Its movements are uneven in quality and inspiration. . . . The first and last movements are best, and the first, the strongest and loftiest of them all. . . . The second movement . . . becomes . . . tenuous, hanging in places, so to speak, by a thread as though the hand that held the pen had weakened in nerveless fingers. The finale is very gay, perhaps insolently so, in a jocose 'popular' vein. . . . The symphony must remain an enigma to the warmest admirers of Prokofiev."

GIACOMO PUCCINI 1858–1924

The last opera of the mighty Verdi, *Falstaff*, was produced in Milan in 1893. Less than a decade earlier the first opera of the twenty-five-year-old Puccini, *Le Villi,* was seen, also in Milan. Thus Italian opera did not have to wait long for Verdi's successor; the imperial line of Italian opera composers that began with Monteverdi remained unbroken.

Not that Puccini was another Verdi! He had little of Verdi's nobility and grandeur and sustained inspiration. The blemishes in Puccini's operas (which even his most enthusiastic admirers will not deny) could never have been perpetrated by Verdi: the excessive sentimentality; the often thin material with which he worked; the comparatively weak counterpoint; the excessive love for the voice which made him inflate an aria out of proportion to the requirements of the drama. Yet when these subtractions are made, there is enough value left in Puccini's operas to place them among the most important and successful operatic creations after Verdi; enough to endear them permanently to an entire generation of music lovers as few other operas have succeeded in doing.

On a scale more limited than Verdi (or than Wagner, whom he admired so profoundly), Puccini was a master. He had a consummate understanding of the theatre, its requirements, its strengths and weaknesses. He knew how to build a climax or big scene with a telling, often shattering effect. He knew how to transmute into his music, and often with the most economical means, every theatrical effect of the stage, however subtle or elusive—so much so that in his hands the music often became throbbing drama. He was a skilful hand at characterization—female characterization particularly. He could transform his style to simulate French music or Japanese music or Chinese music, when the text required it, without losing his identity. He was fastidious in his workmanship, and always elegant in his style. Beyond all this, he had a born gift for Italian melody—fluid, warm, passionate, of a rapturous beauty.

He always took from other composers whatever served his artistic purpose and so ingeniously integrated it into his own style that it became an inextricable part of his own idiom. Thus he always kept amplifying his technical resources, always kept extending the gamut of his artistic expression—and always kept growing as a creative artist.

He was first attracted to the new naturalism—or *Verismo,* as it is known in Italian opera—that appeared in Mascagni's *Cavalleria Rusticana* (1890) and Leoncavallo's *Pagliacci* (1892), and which had in turn been an outgrowth of operas like Bizet's *Carmen. Verismo* favored everyday settings, situations and characters, rather than historical subjects. It was partial to violent, passionate episodes treated in a realistic manner. Musically, *Verismo* substituted melodramatic arias for florid or soaring lyrical ones; and it emphasized naturalistic recitatives that sometimes sounded like exaggerated speech, choral passages and orchestral tone painting to establish moods and project atmosphere. Into his own operas, Puccini brought the freshness and vitality of realism, both in his selection of librettos and in his music for them. To *Verismo* Puccini brought the Italian lyricism he had inherited from his predecessors; Wagner's enriched harmony; and—as the years passed—the subtle tints of Debussy's impressionism (even to the use of the whole-tone scale), a discreet use of dissonance and unorthodox progressions and tonalities learned from the moderns, and even (in his last opera) a suggestion of Schoenberg's atonality.

Puccini was born in Lucca on December 22, 1858, descendant of a long line of musicians who had been famous in Lucca. He began to study music early, and completed his musical education at the Milan Conservatory, where his teachers included Bazzini and Ponchielli. His first opera, *Le Villi*—written soon after his graduation from the Conservatory, and submitted in a competition which was won by Mascagni's *Cavalleria Rusticana*—was heard in Milan on May 31, 1884, and was successful, winning for Puccini the support of the powerful publisher, Ricordi. His second opera, *Edgar* (1889)—commissioned by Ricordi—was a failure; but *Manon Lescaut,* which followed on February 1, 1893 was a veritable triumph and established Puccini's reputation. That reputation swelled to formidable proportions in the years that followed, as Puccini produced two of his masterpieces: *La Bohème* (adapted from Murger's *La Vie de Bohème*) was introduced in Turin on February 1, 1896, under the baton of Arturo Toscanini; *La Tosca* (from the drama of Sardou) was first witnessed in Rome on January 14, 1900. Each opera was extraordinarily successful, and made their composer both internationally famous and wealthy. Since *La Bohème* and *La Tosca* were written before 1900, they are not discussed below.

Madama Butterfly, which followed *La Tosca* by four years, was at first a decided failure—but only for a while. After undergoing extensive revisions, it returned to conquer. Thereafter, Puccini's status as the leading Italian composer of his time was never again questioned. When he visited the United States in 1907 to attend the American première of *Madama Butterfly* at the Metropolitan Opera House, he was given a thunderous welcome. The result of this American visit was a commision from the Metropolitan Opera to write an American opera, *The Girl of the Golden West* (based on the play by David Belasco). Introduced at the Metropolitan on December 10, 1910, the opera was a triumph; but it has since become recognized as one of Puccini's lesser works. Other operas followed: *La Rondine* (1917), and the trilogy, *Il Tabarro, Suor Angelica,* and *Gianni Schicchi* (1918). None of these were of the stature of his earlier masterpieces, but they had enough charm and musical interest to enjoy a measure of success.

In 1924, a throat ailment developed into a cancer, necessitating an operation for Puccini. The operation itself was successful, but a heart ailment developed. On November 29, 1924, Puccini died of a heart attack in Brussels. He was survived by his common-law wife, Elvira Gemignani, with whom he had fallen in love when he was twenty-six. She left her husband to live with Puccini, bearing him a son, Antonio, in 1886.

Two years after his death, Puccini's last opera, *Turandot,* was performed in its unfinished state at La Scala under Toscanini. Subsequently, it was completed by Franco Alfano and was performed throughout the world.

1903 MADAMA BUTTERFLY, opera in three acts, with text by Giuseppe Giacosa and Luigi Illica based on the drama by David Belasco, in turn an adaptation of a story by John Luther Long. First performance: La Scala, Milan, February 17, 1904.

The fact that *Madama Butterfly* was one of the most decisive opera failures of our time at its première performance, and that it is today one of the best-loved operas in the repertory, is not entirely a paradox. For the *Madama Butterfly* we know and love today is not the same opera that was heard at La Scala in Milan.

When the news of the fiasco was told to Arturo Toscanini over the telephone, the conductor was not surprised. Toscanini had already pointed out to the composer some of the glaring faults of the opera, the most important being the second act, requiring an hour and a half for performance, which was much too long and much too static. There were other irritants in the opera: the annoying reminder of *La Bohème* in the music accompanying Butterfly when she appears in her wedding dress; and the unpleasant spectacle of the scene involving Butterfly's drunken uncle.

But Toscanini also knew that the opera, at its best, possessed a beautiful score and could, with revisions, become an opera of great tenderness and appeal. And to prove his faith, Toscanini offered to conduct the work in South America—despite its failure at La Scala—if Puccini made the necessary changes. Puccini—who loved his *Butterfly* more than any other of his operas and who was convinced of its ultimate success—went to work with a will. The two acts of the original score now became three; the unpleasant moments were deleted; the action was heightened; and the music was made more lyrical, with the inclusion of an entirely new aria, "*Addio, fiorito asil!*"

The new version was first heard in Brescia, Italy, on May 28, 1904, with Campanini (who had conducted the première performance) once again the conductor. The opera was now a triumph; Puccini was called to the stage ten times. The next month, Toscanini directed it in Buenos Aires, where the success of the opera was even greater. And thereafter *Madama Butterfly* conquered the world. The American première took place in Washington, D.C., on October 15, 1906. A few months later, on February 11, 1907, it was given at the Metropolitan Opera in New York.

But when the opening night audience in Milan had revolted against the opera (the hissing became so great that it finally erupted into a violent uproar that shook the house), it had not only been alienated by the faults of the first version, but—ironically—by the virtues of the opera as a whole. For *Madama Butterfly* was Puccini's most original score up to that time, and it had proved too novel for ears accustomed to *La Bohème* and *La Tosca*. Harmonically, Puccini had taken a bold step forward, using Debussy's unusual suspensions, unresolved discords, and the exotic whole-tone scale to project the kind of atmosphere the Japanese play required; he even employed special instrumental and harmonic effects to simulate Japanese music, and he interpolated snatches of American melody to heighten the American context of the play.

In later performances, operagoers were to take this opera to their heart for its sentimentality, lyricism and poignant drama. But the true strength of the opera lies in the original conception of the music as a whole, and the wonderful way in which music serves the drama. Arias like "*Un bel di*" and "*Addio, fiorito asil!*" may remain the tours de force of the opera whenever it is performed. But to the sensitive opera lover, there are greater and more original moments in the opera; the exquisite lullaby, "*Dormi amor mio,*" the picture of dawn painted by the orchestra, the shattering impact of the dissonant chords that end the opera.

The pathetic story of the love of an American naval lieutenant and a Japanese girl is a familiar one. In Nagasaki, Japan, early in the 1900s, B. F. Pinkerton, a lieutenant in the United States Navy, confides to the American consul, Sharpless, how he has becomes infatuated with Cio-Cio-San, a Japanese girl known as Madama Butterfly ("*Amore o grillo*"). Cio-Cio-San appears, accompanied by friends and relatives whom she proceeds to introduce to

Pinkerton ("*Spira sul mar*"). She confides to her beloved that for his sake she stands ready to renounce her religion. Cio-Cio-San's uncle bitterly condemns her for discarding her religion and people, which sends the girl into tears. Tenderly, Pinkerton takes her into his arms, and as night begins to fall, the lovers exchange gentle confidences ("Viene la sera").

The second act brings us into Butterfly's house where Suzuki, Butterfly's servant, is praying before an image of Buddha. Pinkerton has gone off with the American fleet on maneuvers. But Butterfly is confident of his love and certain he will return to her, in what is undoubtedly the most famous aria in the opera, "Un bel di." Sharpless now arrives with a letter, but before Butterfly can read it, a marriage broker appears to suggest a wealthy suitor for Butterfly, whom she rejects decisively. She tells Sharpless that she belongs to Pinkerton alone and that if he were to desert her she would kill herself. A sound of distant cannon is the first indication that the American naval forces have returned, and Pinkerton with them. Overcome with joy, Cio-Cio-San and her friends prepare for Pinkerton's return by decorating the house with cherry blossoms ("Scuoti quelle fronda"). Cio-Cio-San then puts on her wedding dress and waits for Pinkerton to arrive.

With the arrival of dawn, with which the third act opens, Pinkerton and Sharpless finally appear. With them is the American woman who is Pinkerton's wife. After Sharpless has successfully convinced Pinkerton not to see Butterfly, the lieutenant bids a poignant farewell to the house that holds such tender memories for him ("Addio fiorito asil"). By the time Butterfly comes into the room, Pinkerton has gone, but Sharpless and the American woman have remained. They entreat Butterfly to surrender to Pinkerton the son that had been born to her during Pinkerton's absence. In the end, Butterfly consents to do so, but only on the condition that Pinkerton himself make the request. When Sharpless and the American woman depart, Butterfly bids her little son farewell ("Tu, tu, piccolo iddio"). She gives him a doll and an American flag to play with while she goes behind a screen where she pierces a dagger into her bosom. By the time Pinkerton appears, she is dead. Pinkerton gives vent to his grief, while Sharpless gently leads the boy out of the house.

1910 LA FANCIULLA DEL WEST (THE GIRL OF THE GOLDEN WEST), opera in three acts, with text by Guelfo Civinni and Carlo Zangarini based on David Belasco's play of the same name. First performance: Metropolitan Opera, New York, December 10, 1910.

In 1907, Puccini came to the United States to supervise the Metropolitan Opera production of *Madama Butterfly*. He was profoundly impressed by America and he expressed the wish to write an opera for America, with an American background. "If I could get a good Western libretto," he confided at the time, "I would undoubtedly write the music for it." Attending a performance of David Belasco's play, *The Girl of the Golden West* (adapted from a story by Bret Harte), which was then having a successful run in New York, Puccini realized that he had finally found the libretto for which he had been searching. The Metropolitan Opera commissioned him to write the opera.

It took him three years to complete the project. The world première in New York was a splendiferous affair. Prices of admission were doubled. The Metropolitan Opera spared no expense in making the production as lavish as possible, assembling a remarkable cast that included Caruso, Destinn and Amato, and assigning the baton to Toscanini. A glamorous audience was present and proved most enthusiastic. As Richard Aldrich reported in *The New York Times:* "The house was filled to its utmost capacity, and the audience was repeatedly brought to a high pitch of enthusiasm and, as it seemed, could hardly give sufficient acclaim to those who were responsible for the production and those who participated in it." He then said: "In setting this drama to music, Mr. Puccini undertook a task that not so many years ago would have been deemed impossible, almost a contradiction in terms of all conceptions of what the lyric drama could or should be. . . . This treatment involves a more or less detached and formless paragraphic, sometimes a rapid and staccato vocal utterance, projected against an equally expeditious and hastily sketched orchestral background, to which is given the task of accentuating, emphasizing and intensifying—if it can—the significance of the dialogue with points or broad stretches of color, thematic fragments, quickly shifting kaleidoscopic harmonies. . . . This is interrupted now and again, however, by pages in a broader style—lyric movements of psychologizing, when the music is given more opportunity to rise to its true task of expressing emotion or passion or sentiment. Here the voices may likewise sing in a broad arioso, in phrases that at least have melodic outline and shapeliness."

The Girl of the Golden West, despite auspicious performance beginnings, is not one of Puccini's most successful operas. It is only intermittently revived—and with good reason. The long stretches of conversation invite dullness. The marriage of Italian lyricism to an American Western setting is frequently incompatible, a fact emphasized by the unconvincing interpolation of snatches of syncopated rhythms and musical material lifted from America's West. The extensive use of impressionistic devices and particularly of the whole-tone scale, and the novel innovations in the orchestration, seem out of place. And a good deal of the lyricism is just commonplace. Perhaps most damning of all, as Richard Aldrich notes, was the fact that "this music seems almost like an adjunct of the scenery, a kind of heightening of scenic setting, rather than interpretation or a voicing of the significance of the drama."

The drama is set in the foot of Cloudy Mountain in California during the gold-rush period. Minnie, owner of the Polka saloon, is the darling of the miners. She is loved by Jack Rance, the sheriff. He speaks to her of his feelings in the aria "*Minnie, dalla mia casa*" then tries to force his attentions upon her. She rebuffs him. At this point, a stranger appears. He is Dick Johnson of Sacramento, whom Minnie recognizes as the man to whom she had once been strongly attracted. What she does not know is that, under the name of Ramerrez, he is an outlaw come to hold up the saloon. When Minnie is put in charge of the gold, Dick Johnson is willing to forget all about his intended holdup. They become lovers. Then, discovering he is an outlaw, she sends him on his way. No sooner does he leave Minnie's cabin when he is shot by the sheriff. Minnie drags him back into her cabin, where they are followed by Jack Rance, the sheriff. In desperation, Minnie proposes to play a hand of poker with Jack. If he wins, he can bring the outlaw to justice and she will then be ready to marry Jack. But if he loses, he must give up his pursuit of the outlaw. Minnie wins the hand by cheating.

In the third act, Johnson, recovered, has been captured and is about to be strung up. In *"Ch'ella mi creda libero"* he prays that Minnie will eventually believe him in his now determined effort to mend his ways and find a new life. Minnie appears on horseback to plead with the sheriff and the miners to save the life of her beloved. They are so moved that they set Johnson free and allow him and Minnie to begin a new life together.

1917 LA RONDINE (THE SWALLOW), opera in two acts, with text by Alfred Maria Willner and Heinrich Reichert, adapted and translated into Italian by Giuseppe Adami. First performance: Monte Carlo, March 27, 1917.

In his biography of Puccini, George R. Marek reveals that there were two reasons why Puccini wrote *La Rondine*. One was for money, and the other because of anger. The money came from the director of the Karlstheater in Vienna who wanted Puccini to write several numbers for an operetta with spoken dialogue and was willing to pay a handsome price. Anger was the result of sharp differences between Puccini and his publisher, Ricordi. To spite Ricordi, Puccini decided to write *La Rondine* for Vienna, and have it published in that city.

The outbreak of World War I delayed both the writing and the production. Meanwhile, Puccini lost interest in writing an operetta for which he had neither the talent nor the temperament. He asked Adami to rewrite the play (originally the work of Willner and Reichert) into a libretto. The opera, naturally, would be light and gay, but it would be an opera nonetheless. This is the text that Puccini finally set. Since the war disrupted the activities of most of Italy's opera houses, the world première of Puccini's new opera was scheduled for Monte Carlo, where it was well received. This reaction was not repeated when this opera was first given in Italy, Vienna and New York (the American première taking place at the Metropolitan Opera on March 10, 1928). As W. J. Henderson said in the New York *Sun, La Rondine* was "neither grand opera nor the kind of comic opera familiar to this town, but just a vivacious, high-class play mingling humor, farce, tender emotions in delectable proportions. . . . It must be accepted for what it is. . . . It will not bear rough usage; it is slender and feminine. The score must be scrutinized as if it were graven in the smoke of the midnight lamp. It is the afternoon off of a genius. . . . The whole score is fragile and shallow."

The story is as slight as Puccini's music. During the second French Empire, Magda is the mistress of the wealthy banker, Rambaldo. At one of their parties, the poet, Prunier, suggests that sentimental love is once again coming into vogue, a statement that leads Magda to reveal to him that in times past she had had a romance with a student she had met in a dance hall. Prunier then reads Magda's fortune: She has left her home like a swallow, and like a swallow she will return to it. Some time later, Magda meets and falls in love with Ruggero, for whom she deserts Rambaldo, and with whom she goes off to the Riviera. When Magda discovers that Ruggero's mother had insisted that the young man's wife must have an untarnished reputation, she is forced to leave him and to return to the rich banker.

Except for one or two arias (notably those of Magda in the first act, *"Che il bel sogno di Doretto*" and "*Ora dolci e divina*") there is little in *La Rondine* to reveal the hand of a master. And if the opera is occasionally revived, it is mostly due to the role of Magda, an appealing one for sopranos.

1913–1918 IL TRITTICO (THE TRIPTYCH), three one-act operas. First performance: Metropolitan Opera, New York, December 14, 1918.

I. IL TABARRO (THE CLOAK), text by Giuseppe Adami based on Didier Gold's play, *Le Houppelande.*

II. SUOR ANGELICA (SISTER ANGELICA), text by Giovacchino Forzano.

III. GIANNI SCHICCHI, text by Giovacchino Forzano.

Puccini's trilogy of one-act operas is an interesting study in contrasts. The first, *Il Tabarro,* is a rather sordid drama of lust, jealousy and murder; this is a true child of *Verismo.* On a barge on the Seine River, Michele, a skipper, suspects that his wife, Giorgetta has been unfaithful. Actually, she is carrying on an affair with Luigi, using a lighted match as a signal for a rendezvous. When Michele lights his pipe, Luigi, mistakes it for the signal, and makes an appearance. Michele kills him and hides his body under his cloak. Upon Giorgetta's arrival, Michele tears the cloak from the dead body and hurls his faithless wife on her dead lover.

Puccini's music has force and bitterness. Says George R. Marek: "The music rises with the drama in a strong and uncompromising crescendo, breaking at the point of the murder. There is not a moment's let-down. . . . The style is terse and extremely effective. Michele's monologue leading up to the murder is first-class music drama. So is the murder."

The second, *Suor Angelica* (exclusively for women's voices) is a tender little opera in which the peace of convent life is caught in music that is consistently sensitive and delicate. The time is the seventeenth century, the place a convent, to which Sister Angelica has come to expiate an old sin. She had given birth to a child and had abandoned it. Upon learning from her aunt that the child has died, Angelica prays for forgiveness, and commits suicide.

George R. Marek points out that the music for this poignant story is "religious," but "operatically religious." "It is well designed, the design leading up to the beatific finale, the appearance of the Virgin." An orchestral intermezzo and the beautiful arioso of Angelica, "*Senza mamma,*" are among the more popular excerpts.

The last—and most famous—of the three operas is *Gianni Schicchi,* an excursion into wit, with the comic elements of the text carried over into music that chuckles warmly, occasionally erupts into burlesque humor, but moves from first bar to last with brisk gaiety. On occasion (as in the aria "*O mio babbino caro*") Puccini even writes subtle satire—parodying his own sentimental vein in earlier operas!

The libretto, by Giovacchino Forzano, is in the best traditions of opera buffa. The action is set in thirteenth-century Florence. The relatives of the recently deceased Buso Donati, wealthy Florentine, gather to mourn his death—and to learn the terms of his will. To their horror, they discover that Donati has bequeathed all his possessions to the Church. Heartbroken, they seek out the crafty lawyer, Gianni Schicchi, who devises an ingenious plan. Nobody but his relatives as yet knows of old Donati's death. They are sworn to strict secrecy, with the additional warning that, by Florentine law, they are all liable to severe punishment if their ruse is ever detected. Thereupon the body of the dead man is removed and Schicchi goes into Donati's bed. Simulating the dying man, he calls for two notaries and two witnesses and dictates a new will. The new will, however, is not what the relatives had expected—since crafty Schicchi gives them trifles and bequeaths the bulk of the dead man's fortune to himself! Afraid of the Florentine law which would hold them guilty as accomplices to a fraud, the relatives are helpless. After the will is drawn up, they attack the lawyer with fists and angry condemnations. But Schicchi disperses them with a club. Proud owner of Donati's fortune, he is able to realize the marriage of his daughter to her lover.

1924 TURANDOT, opera in three acts (completed by Franco Alfano), with text by Giuseppe Adami and Renato Simoni, based on Gozzi's play in and adaptation by Johnn Friedrich Schiller. First performance: La Scala, Milan, April 25, 1926.

Puccini's last opera, left unfinished by his death, has the most original score he ever wrote—the most inventive in its orchestral effects, the most daring in its harmony and tonality, the most original in its melodic ideas. Dissonances, unusual timbres and colors, novel scales, even at times startling bitonalities are here integral parts of Puccini's style, and he uses them—together with his sentiment and lyricism—with overpowering effect. Chinese melodic ideas are interpolated to add local color—at times, as in the funeral music for the Persian Prince, with unusual effect; but the character of the music is not Chinese, but unmistakably Puccinian. Some critics go so far as to call *Turandot* Puccini's greatest opera, and Turandot herself Puccini's most eloquent characterization. This may be excessive praise; but there can be no doubt that in *Turandot,* more than in any other preceding opera, Puccini revealed the artistic potentialities which he might have realized had he lived.

In Peking, in legendary times, the beautiful, frigid Princess Turandot consents to marry anybody of noble birth who can answer three questions, but who stands ready to forfeit his head if he fails. A Persian prince is the first victim; as he is led to his execution, the crowd pleads in vain for mercy ("O giovinetto"). The Princess Turandot appears, and as she does so, an Unknown Prince, who is actually Prince Calaf, curses her for her cruelty. But, suddenly, he is so overwhelmed by her beauty that he is determined to make a try for her. Liù, a slave girl in love with Calaf, pleads with him to desist from such folly ("Signore, ascolta"). Calaf is sympathetic to her; indeed, he consoles her tenderly ("Non piangere, Liù"). But his mind cannot be changed.

In a square, outside the palace, Princess Turandot explains the reason why she chose to play her fatal game: She is avenging the cruelty the Tartars had inflicted on her mother by being no less cruel to any man wishing to make love to her. She now stands ready to pose the three questions to Calaf. He answers them easily; the crowd acclaims him ("Gloria, o vincitore"). The Princess, however, reneges on her bargain. No man, she announces icily, will ever possess her. Calaf chivalrously offers her a way out: If by the following morning she can uncover his real identity (since all the while he has been presenting himself as the Unknown Prince), he will die willingly; if she fails to do so, she must stick to her bargain. By royal edict, the emperor orders his heralds to seek out the identity of the Unknown Prince; nobody in the realm can sleep until this task has been accomplished. In "*Questa notte,*" Calaf comments on this development, while musing over the fact that the Princess must truly be disturbed. He would like to resolve her problems with a kiss ("Nessun dorma"). Liù is brought before the Princess and tortured so that she might reveal the Calaf's identity. But true love has sealed her lips. When she feels that the torture is about to make her weaken, she commits suicide. Now Calaf steps forward boldly and takes the Princess in his arms. This gesture forces upon Turandot the realization that she is really in love with him. Magnanimously, the Prince is willing to reveal his identity to Turandot—is willing to accept death in order to release her from her promise. But when Turandot learns he is the Prince of the hated Tartars, her love turns to hate and she orders his death. In the closing scene, Turandot has had a change of heart. She announces to the Emperor she has uncovered the Prince's true name, and that the name is "Love." The Prince and Princess embrace, while the people sing a hymn to love.

Puccini did not live to finish *Turandot.* His death came after he had completed the poignant music of Liù's death. Franco Alfano was selected to put the final touches on the opera, which he did with exceptional skill, and with a remarkable sympathy for Puccini's methods and style. It is with Alfano's ending that the opera is now performed. However, Puccini had confided to Toscanini that, were he to die before he finished writing his opera, he would like to have it produced just as he has written it. Consequently, at the world première, with Toscanini conducting, the opera was performed in its unfinished state. In the middle of the third act—just after Liù's suicide—Toscanini put down his baton, turned to the audience, and with tears streaming down his face, announced; "Here—here—the master laid down his pen."

The American première was given at the Metropolitan Opera on November 16, 1926. It was a failure, mainly due to poor casting. It stayed on in the repertory a number of seasons; then, for three decades, went into discard as far as the Metropolitan Opera was concerned. On February 24, 1961, the opera was revived under the direction of Leopold Stokowski (who was then making his Metropolitan Opera debut) to score the major success it so well deserved.

SERGEI RACHMANINOFF 1873–1943

In an artistic statement which Rachmaninoff once dictated to this author, he said: "I try to make my music speak simply and directly that which is in my heart at the time I am composing. If there is love there, or bitterness, or sadness, or religion, these moods become part of my music, and it becomes either beautiful, or bitter, or sad, or religious. For composing music is as much a part of my living as breathing and eating. I compose music because I must give expression to my feelings, just as I talk because I must give utterance to my thoughts."

Rachmaninoff inherited the artistic mantle of his distinguished predecessor Tchaikovsky, whom he admired so profoundly; he wore that mantle with such dignity and grace that it never appeared to be a borrowed garment. Like Tchaikovsky, Rachmaninoff was temperamentally opposed to composers who wrote music to dogmas or creeds or who tried to endow their works with mystic concepts; and so he never had much sympathy for the school of the "Russian Five" or the works of Scriabin, whose impress on Russian musical thinking was so far-reaching in the early years of Rachmaninoff's career. Like Tchaikovsky's, Rachmaninoff's roots were embedded in tradition. While he was intellectually stimulated by the innovations of Stravinsky and Prokofiev, he could never bring himself to think as they did. Like Tchaikovsky, Rachmaninoff was always a sad and lonely man, a man whose intense melancholy and perpetual feeling of desolation echo and re-echo in the music he wrote.

Rachmaninoff did not bring to music that which it did not have before him. He was satisfied that the materials he had acquired as a student served his artistic purposes fully. But how admirably he used those materials, with what mastery of formal structure and variety of lyrical expressiveness and harmonic beauty! With techniques and traditions acquired from others, Rachmaninoff nevertheless was able to bring to music a creative vein that was his own. He was never the innovator, never the original thinker. But what he felt so sensitively he was able to put down on paper—and in music of often surpassing sentiment and beauty.

Rachmaninoff was born in Onega, Novgorod, on April 1, 1873, to a wealthy landowner who dissipated his wealth and sent his family into bankruptcy when Rachmaninoff was only nine. At the St. Petersburg Conservatory (which he entered in 1882), Sergei was more or less apathetic to his music studies. Not until he had been aroused by the imaginative teacher, Sverev, and subjected to severe discipline, did Sergei begin to realize the potentialities of his remarkable native gifts. In 1885, he entered the Moscow Conservatory. There as a pupil in composition of Taneiev and Arensky, and in Siloti's piano class, he revealed the true scope of his talent, which was recognized by Tchaikovsky among others. While still a Conservatory student, Rachmaninoff completed his first piano concerto, in F-sharp minor, which he performed at the Conservatory on March 17, 1892. Soon after that, as a graduation exercise, he wrote a one-act opera, *Aleko,* which won him a gold medal; when it was produced at the Bolshoi Theatre in Moscow on May 9, 1893, it was acclaimed. Soon after his graduation, Rachmaninoff achieved international popularity with his Prelude in C-sharp minor, for piano, op. 3, no. 2 (1892), which he himself introduced at a recital in Moscow on September 26, 1892.

But though success had come this early, it did not stay. The première of his Symphony No. 1 in D minor—in St. Petersburg on March 27, 1897—was a fiasco. This proved a traumatic experience for the composer, inducing a morbidity that made further composition impossible for a number of years. Not until 1901 was he able to emerge from this period of utter futility and despair; but when he did so, he wrote one of his greatest works, and one of the most popular piano concertos in the twentieth century, that in C minor, in 1901. On April 29, 1902, he married his first cousin, Natalie Satina, a gifted young pianist.

Having found his stride as a composer, Rachmaninoff soon proved himself an extraordinary pianist and an unusually gifted conductor. After the turn of the twentieth century he began concertizing as pianist throughout the world, soon to achieve a place of preeminence among the virtuosos of his generation. Between 1904 and 1906, he was the principal conductor of the Bolshoi Theatre in Moscow. In 1907, he decided to give up his permanent conducting post to concentrate on composition. He went to live in Dresden, Germany, where he completed two of his finest works for orchestra, the Symphony No. 2 in E minor, and the tone poem, *The Isle of the Dead.*

In 1909, Rachmaninoff began the first of several tours of the United States. His American debut took place at Smith College, in Northampton, Massachusetts. on November 4, 1909. On November 28, 1909, he appeared in New York in the world première of his third piano concerto in D minor. During the rest of the tour he frequently appeared in the triple role of conductor, pianist and composer.

Unsympathetic to the Soviet regime, Rachmaninoff left his native land towards the end of 1917, never to return. He established his home first in Switzerland, then in the United States, where he ultimately became an American citizen. An outspoken foe of the Soviets, Rachmaninoff was for a long time violently attacked in his own country. In the closing years of his life, however, he found himself and his music glorified in the Soviet Union; and after his death he was singled out as a model for Soviet composers to emulate.

In the winter of 1939, the Philadelphia Orchestra, presented a three-concert cycle of his works, with Rachmaninoff once again appearing in the triple role of composer, conductor and pianist. His last major work, the *Symphonic Dances,* for orchestra, was completed one year later. He was embarking on a concert tour of the United States when he was stricken by his last, fatal illness. He died at his home in Beverly Hills on March 28, 1943.

1900–1916 SONGS, for voice and piano:

"Before My Window," op. 26, no. 10; "Christ Is Risen," op. 26, no. 6; "Daisies," op. 38, no. 3; "Fate," op. 21, no. 1; "How Fair This Spot," op. 21, no. 7; "Lilacs," op. 21, no. 5; "To the Children," op. 26, no. 7; "Vocalise," op. 24, no. 14.

The romantic ardor, the long-sustained melodic line, the richly sensuous harmonies, the sentimentality and pathos which course so freely in Rachmaninoff's instrumental compositions can, to be sure, be encountered in his songs. This is a medium calculated to exploit these qualities to best advantage. Here, too, as elsewhere, Rachmaninoff is the spiritual heir of Tchaikovsky. Most of Rachmaninoff's songs, says Richard Anthony Leonard, "are hymns of passionate longing or desire, or lovely landscapes." Leonard then explains that Rachmaninoff's song procedures, for the most part, are not unlike those of Schumann. "The accompaniment . . . is seldom a mere prop or means of underlining the vocal line. By going along on a contrapuntal track of its own, the piano collaborates with the voice in stating the poetic thought." Leonard notes that in Rachmaninoff's earlier songs, the accompaniments are often "overwhelmingly dramatic or even flamboyant," while in the later ones they are "far more laconic, spare, subtly understated."

A number of Rachmaninoff's famous songs came before 1900. These include two exquisite items from opus 4: "In the Silent Night," words by A. Fet (1889) and "O Cease Thy Singing," also known as "The Songs of Grusia," words by Pushkin (1893). Also familiar among his pre-1900 creations is "Floods of Spring," op. 14, no. 11, words by F. Tyutchev (1896).

Though some of these early songs are of particular interest for their strong dramatic content or for their pronounced Russian personality, the best of Rachmaninoff's post-1900 songs have what Leonard describes as "a far purer and subtler strain": for example, "Before My Window" (1906) and "How Fair This Spot" (1900), both of them to words by G. Galina; "Lilacs," words by E. Beketova (1900); and "Daisies," words by I. Severyanin (1916). Some have a poignant nostalgia that is unforgettable—"To the Children" (1906), where T. Khomyakov's poem describes a now empty nursery which once quivered with the happy presence of children; some have a moving religious character—"Christ Is Risen" (1906), poem by D. Merezkhovsky; some have an ominous feeling—"Fate" (1900), poem by A. Apouchtine, melody inspired by Beethoven's Fifth Symphony.

One of Rachmaninoff's most celebrated songs has no words at all, since it is a "Vocalise," or a vocal exercise (c. 1915). The soaring melody is sung on a vowel. Rachmaninoff himself transcribed it for orchestra, a now familiar version; other musicians have transcribed it for the piano, and for various instruments and the piano.

1901 CONCERTO NO. 2 IN C MINOR, for piano and orchestra, op. 18. I. Moderato. II. Adagio sostenuto. III. Allegro scherzando.

When the fiasco of his First Symphony sent him into a despondency that stultified all creativity for several years, and seemed to warn of an impending nervous breakdown, Rachmaninoff consulted a prominent physician by the name of Dr. Dahl, who effected cures through the powers of autosuggestion. Patiently, the physician worked on Rachmaninoff to renew self-confidence and to convince him that his natural gift for creativity had not died. Eventually, the physician managed to restore Rachmaninoff's faith in himself and his music. With the return of such reassurance came the will to compose.

One of the works Rachmaninoff wrote in this period of revived self-confidence was the Second Concerto for Piano and Orchestra. Appropriately enough, it was dedicated to Dr. Dahl, who had made it possible. The concerto proved to be one of Rachmaninoff's greatest works, and one of his most successful. More than any other of his compositions—except perhaps for the fabulous C-sharp minor Prelude—it helped to spread his reputation throughout the world of music. Its first performance, on November 9, 1901 (the composer was the soloist with the Moscow Philharmonic Society), was a triumph. Three years later it won the Glinka Prize. Since then it has been heard more often than any other of Rachmaninoff's large works. After Rachmaninoff's death, the popularity of the concerto continued to swell in the United States. One of its principal melodies became a popular song and reached the "Hit Parade"; the concerto itself was used as the basis of three major motion pictures, including Noel Coward's *Brief Moment.*

The concerto opens with a ten-measure introduction for solo piano in which full chords grow in sonority until, at last, the strings erupt into the passionate first theme, accompanied by arpeggio figures. The second theme is of a more tender, of a more feminine beauty; it is presented by the solo piano. For the next sixty-two measures this material is amplified. The development section concentrates on the first theme, as does the concluding coda, in the latter instance embellished by intriguing passage work in the piano.

An atmosphere of surpassing peace and loveliness is projected in the second movement, which opens with gentle chords for muted strings, woodwinds and horns, over which the piano soon traces a haunting song. A quickening of the tempo brings on a development of this subject and is followed by a brief cadenza for the solo instrument. A new idea is suddenly interpolated by the piano in the coda.

The concluding movement begins with a twenty-measure orchestral preface to a subject introduced by the piano. The rhapsodical song for strings that follows is the heart of the movement. (It was lifted in 1946 for the American popular song hit, "Full Moon and Empty Arms.") This same melody, majestically proclaimed by full orchestra and supported by piano chords, brings the concerto to an exciting conclusion.

1903–1910 COMPOSITIONS FOR SOLO PIANO:
VARIATIONS ON A THEME BY CHOPIN, op. 22.

PRELUDES, op. 23, I. F-sharp minor; II. B-flat major; III. D minor; IV. D major; V. G minor; VI. E-flat major; VII. C minor; VIII. A-flat major; IX. E-flat minor; X. G-flat major.

PRELUDES, op. 32: I. C major; II. B-flat minor; III. E major; IV. E minor; V. G major; VI. F minor; VII. F major; VIII. A minor; IX. A major; X. B minor; XI. B major; XII. G-sharp minor; XIII. D-flat major.

For the theme in his *Variations on a Theme by Chopin* (1903), Rachmaninoff takes the melody from Chopin's Prelude in C minor, op. 28, no. 20. This receives twenty-two variations, many of which are short, some of which are brilliant virtuoso passages, and some of which are by themselves self-sufficient pieces suggesting such forms as the etude, prelude or nocturne. An extended transition leads to the concluding coda.

If there is a single piece of music that is inextricably associated with the name of Sergei Rachmaninoff it is surely the Prelude in C-sharp minor, the second in the *Five Pieces,* op. 3, no. 2 (1892). The composer could hardly have guessed that this little item—effective though it is—would blaze his name throughout the music world; that, as a matter of fact, it would haunt him for the rest of his life. In performances and in publication, it traveled around the world. It was even responsible for some of Rachmaninoff's early successes as a pianist. Audiences everywhere came to hear him play his own prelude whenever he gave a recital! Yet, regrettably, the composer could not profit directly from this success: He had sold the piece outright to his publisher for a few rubles.

It is a vividly descriptive piece of music which, though without a program, invites extramusical interpretation. And it is characteristic of the best preludes that Rachmaninoff would write later in his career. These preludes are more like miniature dramas than mood pictures or atmospheric vignettes. They are so vibrantly graphic that they encourage programmatic interpretation.

The Preludes, op. 23, were written in 1903; the op. 32 set, in 1910.

Almost a rival in popularity to the C-sharp minor Prelude is the one in G major, op, 32, no. 5 (Moderato). This is music of stirring martial character that seems to portray the marching of men to war; the contrasting lyric section almost suggests the poignancy of homesickness. Other preludes offer dramatic surges and conflicts—notably the E-flat minor, op. 23, no. 9 (Presto), and the F minor, op, 32, no. 6 (Moderato). The yearning and anxiety of the F major Prelude, op. 32, no. 7, is equally expressive. Occasionally, however, these preludes arrive at a simple, classical beauty, as those in E-flat major, op. 23, no. 6 (Andante) and G-flat major, op. 23, no. 10 (Largo).

1907 SYMPHONY NO. 2 IN E MINOR, op. 27. I. Largo; Allegro moderato. II. Allegro molto. III. Adagio. IV. Allegro vivace.

Rachmaninoff composed his First Symphony, in D minor, op. 13, in 1895. The first performance, conducted by Glazunov in St. Petersburg, on March 27, 1897, was a fiasco. The performance was a slipshod affair; besides, the music itself did not seem to have much of an appeal. The failure of this symphony, followed by that of the First Piano Concerto, brought the composer to the brink of a nervous breakdown. Out of this period of silence and morbidity, Rachmaninoff emerged creatively revitalized. He composed his first masterpiece, the Second Piano Concerto. Then, retiring to Dresden in 1907 to devote himself to creative work entirely, he wrote his Second Symphony and *The Isle of the Dead.*

Completed in 1907, the Second Symphony was heard on February 8, 1908, in Moscow under the composer's direction. It was an unqualified success. It won the Glinka Prize (the second time the composer was thus honored).

The symphony—often music of intense melancholy—reflects Rachmaninoff's debt to Tchaikovsky. The long opening introduction (Largo) is the kind of plangent music that reminds us of the closing movement of the *Pathétique* Symphony. It is, perhaps, more introspective than Tchaikovsky; but the Russian pain is there. Powerful chords destroy the mood, and the violins begin the Allegro moderato section with a hint of the main theme, which, when fully realized, is somewhat excitable in nature. Strings and wind bring the second subject, quieter than the first. A shattering climax, in which the principal melody of the movement is quoted by the solo violin, is gradually evolved before the development begins. The return of the principal ideas follows, after which comes an elaborate coda.

The first movement is generally introspective and sad. The second, a scherzo, is, on the other hand, vigorous. It comprises two themes and a trio. The main scherzo subject, first heard in horns and then in violins, later becomes material for an effective fugal passage. The slow movement is rich with expressive ideas: one for the violins; another for the clarinet; a third for violins and oboe. This is the mood of the opening Largo, once again reflective music touched with an indefinable yearning. A lively, rhythmic introduction sets the finale into motion. A march melody is played by the wind instruments, after which a beautiful thought for the violins in octaves is presented. An extended working out of this material leads to the recapitulation and the coda. Material from earlier movements is recalled at the end of the symphony, the main thought of the Adagio being placed contrapuntally against the lively subject of the finale.

1909 THE ISLE OF THE DEAD (DIE TOTENINSEL), tone poem for orchestra, op. 29.

Between 1906 and 1908, Rachmaninoff lived in seclusion in Dresden, a refugee from his many activities in Russia as pianist and conductor. He had come to Germany to devote himself entirely to creative work.

In an art gallery in Leipzig one day, Rachmaninoff saw the Arnold Böcklin painting, *The Isle of the Dead.* The grim picture gripped the imagination of the composer. The tall, ghostly cypresses and menacing cliffs stood brooding over the waters, on which there approached a Stygian boatman conveying a flag-draped coffin and a lonely mourner. Rachmaninoff decided to set this picture to music. He completed his tone poem in 1908. On May 1, 1909, he himself conducted its première performance in Moscow.

The gentle lapping of the waters is heard throughout the work in a musical figure in alternating rhythms, first played by the cellos, then by other instruments. The main theme, invoking an atmosphere of tranquility, is given by the horns. But a plangent note is soon interpolated by a solo violin. Divided strings then bring up subdued expressions of mourning. The cellos suggest the Catholic Requiem, with a brief quotation of the *Dies Irae.* The despair deepens, the emotions become more tortured as woodwinds and brass bring the music to a climax. Then the intense feelings are relaxed. The thematic material of the opening returns to bring back dark serenity: the boat disappears into the blackness, and the lapping waters continue to murmur to the cypresses.

1909 CONCERTO NO. 3 IN D MINOR FOR PIANO AND ORCHESTRA, op. 30. I. Allegro ma non troppo. II. Adagio. III. Alla breve.

The Third Concerto followed the Second by eight years. In 1909, Rachmaninoff came to the United States for the first of many tours. Having just completed his Third Concerto, he decided to introduce it during his visit. On November 28, 1909, he performed it in New York City under Walter Damrosch's direction.

Two introductory measures for orchestra usher in the piano with the first major theme, which is Slavic in character. After this idea has been discussed, the second theme enters pianissimo in the strings, and is then elaborated in a passionate section. A rather detailed development follows, leading into a cadenza for piano which is one of the finest pages in the entire work; this cadenza, incidentally, is accompanied. Thematic material of the preceding pages returns, and the movement ends in a subdued mood.

The second movement is an intermezzo, the principal idea of which is a lovely Russian melody, first heard in the woodwinds, then repeated in turn by the strings and the piano. This melody is worked out extensively before a new theme (clarinet and bassoons) enters against the background of a waltz rhythm in the strings.

The final movement comes without pause, with an energetic passage for the piano. The orchestra replies with equal vigor. Music of considerable restlessness follows. There is a relaxation of this nervous energy as ideas from the first movement are recalled. But the agitation is soon resumed, and the concerto ends with a fiery and brilliantly sonorous idea.

1911–1916 ÉTUDES-TABLEAUX, for solo piano:

Op. 33: I. F minor; II. C major; III. E-flat minor; IV. E-flat major; V. C minor; VI. C-sharp minor; VII. E-flat major.

Op. 39: I. C minor; II. C major; III. F-sharp minor; IV. B minor; V. E-flat minor; VI. A minor; VII. C minor; VIII. D minor; IX. D major.

The Étude-Tableau is a structure devised by Rachmaninoff. It is a piano miniature in either binary or ternary form in which a picture or a scene is poetically interpreted in music marked by brilliant pianism. Rachmaninoff did not reveal what images he had in mind when he wrote these compositions. But when Ottorino Respighi orchestrated five of them, the composer revealed the pictorial source of these specific items. The Etude in E-flat major, op. 33, no. 4 (Allegro con fuoco) describes a fair; the C major, op. 39, no.2 (Lento assai), which has also been transcribed for violin and piano by Heifetz, brings us the picture of sea and sea gulls; the A minor, op. 39, no. 6 (Allegro) tells the fairy-story of Little Red Riding Hood; the C minor, op. 39, no. 7 (Lento lugubre) is a funeral march; and the D major, op. 39, no. 9 (Tempo di marcia) is an oriental procession. In the Etude in A minor, op. 39, no. 6 (Allegro molto) the composer quotes the *Dies Irae* (which he had previously used in his orchestral tone poem, *The Isle of the Dead,* and which he would later interpolate into his *Rhapsody on a Theme by Paganini*).

In addition to the seven numbers in op. 33, Rachmaninoff wrote two more Études-Tableaux, which he finally decided not to publish; they were issued posthumously in 1948.

1927 CONCERTO NO. 4 IN G MINOR FOR PIANO AND ORCHESTRA, op. 40. I. Allegro vivace; Alla breve. II. Largo. III. Allegro vivace.

Like the Third Piano Concerto, the Fourth received its première in the United States. On March 18, 1927, Rachmaninoff introduced it with the Philadelphia Orchestra, Leopold Stokowski conducting. Eleven years after the première, Rachmaninoff revised the concerto.

After six measures of introduction, the piano enters with a characteristic Rachmaninoff theme, a broad, majestic melody. Some subsidiary ideas are then contributed, after which the tempo changes to Moderato and the piano enters with the second lyrical theme, less spacious than the first and more poignant. The slow movement opens with five introductory bars by the piano. The strings then voice the principal melody, full of Russian pathos, which is soon taken up by piano with some elaboration. After the strings, woodwinds and horns continue with this theme, a brief agitated section is interpolated.

A new idea is momentarily introduced (piano with accompaniment by clarinets), but the original melody soon returns. The third movement enters without interruption. A movement full of brilliant colors and dynamic rhythmic drive, it reintroduces thematic material heard in the preceding two movements.

1931 VARIATIONS ON A THEME BY CORELLI, for solo piano, op. 42.

In Rachmaninoff's second set of piano variations, the theme is taken from Corelli's twelfth violin sonata in D minor, better known as *La Folia.* Here, Rachmaninoff's writing has greater cohesion, and the overall structure is better integrated than was the case in his first set of variations for solo piano, that on a theme by Chopin (*see* 1903–1910). Twenty variations, some of them bearing only a distant relationship to the Corelli melody, are followed by an impressive coda.

1934 RHAPSODY ON A THEME BY PAGANINI, for piano and orchestra, op. 43.

Though Rachmaninoff designated this work a "rhapsody," it is actually a set of twenty-four variations on a Paganini theme. The theme—taken from the Caprice No. 24 for solo violin—is the same one which served Brahms for his *Variations on a Theme by Paganini,* for piano, op. 35. Boris Blacher also used it for his *Variations on a Theme by Paganini* (1947).

In Rachmaninoff's *Rhapsody* (his last work for piano and orchestra), the theme is first heard in its entirety (violins, later taken up by the piano) only after the completion of the first variation. The brief orchestral prelude that opens the work, however, gives a hint of it.

It is interesting to note that in this rhapsody (as in his earlier *Isle of the Dead* and the Étude-Tableau, op. 39, no. 6) Rachmaninoff interpolates quotations of the liturgical melody *Dies Irae,* which appears in Variations 7, 10 and 24. The climax of the entire work, as a matter fact, comes with a brilliant and majestic statement of the *Dies Irae* in full orchestra. Rachmaninoff never explained the significance of this interpolation.

A nine-measure introduction (Allegro vivace) precedes a suggestion of the Paganini theme. After that come the first two variations, the first violins reflecting on the theme to a rhythmical accompaniment by the piano, and then the piano taking the center of the stage, accompanied by brass, woodwinds, and then strings (L'Istesso tempo). Between these two variations, the theme is projected.

Lawrence Gilman has singled out those variations that have particular interest. "In Variation VII (Meno mosso, a tempo moderato) the piano expiates on a melody derived from that of the *Dies Irae* . . . while the cellos and bassoon concern themselves with the Paganini theme in augmentation." In the tenth variation, "the sinister tones of the *Dies Irae* are heard again, at first in double octaves for piano, against the Paganini theme in the second violins and a countersubject for clarinets." In the fifteenth variation, "the orchestra is silent for twenty-seven measures, while the piano alone (Più vivo scherzando) executes a florid interlude." The eighteenth variation is "distinguished by an extensive cantilena for the solo instrument (developed from an inversion of the characteristic sixteenth-note figure of the theme)." In the finale, "the intervals and rhythms of the theme are heard in the piano and woodwinds against an ominous recurrence of the *Dies Irae* . . . by brass and strings. But the piano has the last word, with a concluding assertion of a fragment of the theme."

On November 7, 1934, the *Rhapsody* received its first performance in Philadelphia. The composer was the soloist, and the Philadelphia Orchestra was conducted by Leopold Stokowski.

1936 SYMPHONY NO. 3 IN A MINOR, op. 33. I. Allegro moderato. II. Adagio non troppo. III. Allegro.

Thirty years elapsed between the second and third symphonies. The latter was written between 1935 and 1936. On November 6, 1936, it was introduced with Leopold Stokowski conducting the Philadelphia Orchestra.

Lawrence Gilman characterized this symphony as a "profusion of those sweeping cantabile phrases, darkened by moods of melancholy and brooding and impassioned stress. . . . Somber, lyrical, defiant, it is a work wholly representative of the Slavic genius and Rachmaninoff in particular."

The symphony opens in a melancholy vein. A headlong movement of the strings and woodwinds invokes the first subject (oboes and bassoons). The second subject is a broad, mobile melody for the cellos.

A ten-measure theme for horn opens the second movement. Then there comes one of the most eloquent pages in the entire symphony—a melody for solo violin, set against chords in the woodwinds and brass. The melody grows in beauty and richness as it is taken up by all the violins in unison. A solo flute then enters with the second theme. The music now becomes more passionate and virile, but the movement ends as it began, moody and somber. The finale is impetuous music. The first theme is uncontrolled energy (violins and violas). The surge is kept in check for a while, as a somewhat more lyrical page of music is presented, but only for a while. The original momentum is re-created and reaches a climax. An elaborate fugue follows, the theme of which is derived from the first subject. There is a brief return of lyricism, and then the symphony ends in an orgiastic outburst of energy.

1941 SYMPHONIC DANCES, for orchestra, op. 45. I. Non allegro. II. Andante con moto: tempo di valse. III. Lento assai; Allegro vivace.

Rachmaninoff's apotheosis of the dance was his last major work. He completed it in Huntington, Long Island, in 1940. On January 3, 1941, it was heard for the first time in Philadelphia, with Eugene Ormandy conducting the Philadelphia Orchestra.

The work was not intended by the composer as dance music, but rather as music inspired by the dance. It is essentially symphonic in its writing, devoid of any program. The composer originally intended appending the subtitles "Midday," "Twilight," and "Midnight" to the respective movements, but discarded this idea because he wanted the music to be disassociated from all extramusical suggestions. The hint of the dance is brought up, however, in the use of the waltz rhythm in the second movement, and in the exploitation of the rhythms of popular music in the closing movement. But the interest in the work lies exclusively in the music itself, in its rhythmic ingenuity and brilliant instrumental colors.

MAURICE RAVEL 1875–1937

When Ravel's sardonic *Histoires naturelles* was introduced in Paris on January 12, 1907, a storm of controversy—long brewing—suddenly erupted. Some critics, headed by Pierre Lalo, accused Ravel outright of plagiarizing Debussy, of buying fame with the counterfeit coin of imitating a fashionable composer. It was not so much that the declamation of *Histoires naturelles* made these critics recall the melodic line in *Pelléas et Mélisande,* nor that Ravel's harmonic language borrowed chords identified with Debussy. The simple truth was that they simply did not like *Histoires naturelles*—Lalo called it a "café-concert with ninths"—and, provoked by this dislike, they launched an attack on Ravel's derivativeness. Other critics—of whom M. D. Calvocoressi and Georges Jean-Aubry were the most vocal—insisted that though Ravel had been influenced by Debussy, he had a pronounced artistic personality of his own.

From the perspective of time, it is not difficult to decide on which side the truth lay. Ravel's music is no more Debussy (even in those works which have such striking titular similarity to compositions by his celebrated contemporary) than it is Chabrier, Fauré or Saint-Saëns, three other composers who had influenced him. Whatever Ravel has written—and this goes even for his early Quartet in F major—is characterized by his own individual approach to technique and style. Precise, direct, transparent, intellectual, almost classical in form, and at times witty and sardonic, Ravel was actually the antithesis of Debussy, whose writing by comparison was vague, sensuous, loose in formal construction. Rollo H. Myers put it this way: "Where Debussy's music is wrapped in a kind of sensuous haze, Ravel's outlines are hard and clear-cut; where one shimmers, the other glitters. Debussy's pantheism colored everything he wrote; he vibrated in sympathy with the forces of nature—the sun, the sea, the wind—whereas Ravel would have been more likely to vibrate in the presence of some stylized imitation of sun or sea; a forest oak would have stirred his imagination far less than a Japanese dwarf tree with its artificial implications."

Debussy had been an influence, to be sure; it was hardly possible for a young composer to function in the Paris of the early twentieth century without reacting to the impact of Debussy's music. But actually there were other influences in Ravel's development which were more pronounced, as for instance Chabrier. In addition, there was the influence of Spanish music, to which Ravel had been susceptible from the very first, and which was responsible for works ranging from his early *Habanera* (1895) to such later masterpieces as *Rapsodie espagnole, Bolero, L'Heure espagnole, Alborada del gracioso* and *Don Quichotte à Dulcinée.* There was the influence of Erik Satie, which resulted in the wry irony, subtle humor and delicate wit of *Histoires naturelles, L'Enfant et les sortilèges, L'Heure espagnole.* There was the influence of the Viennese waltz: *La Valse* and *Valses nobles et sentimentales.*

But in spite of these influences—and all the others—Ravel was no imitator of any existing style. These influences represented the starting point for his own thinking; and the processes of that thinking—and the final thought—became distinctly Ravel's own. Hoerée put it well when he wrote that in subjecting himself to varied influences, Ravel was actually an innovator. "He works 'on a motif' like a painter. He installs himself before a Mozart sonata or a Saint-Saëns concerto as an artist does before a group of trees. When his work is finished, it is usually impossible to find any traces of the model." Or, to carry the idea still further, where the traces of the model are still evident, they have undergone such transformation that the model itself is completely forgotten. The personality of his melody (which often acquires an exotic character through the use of Phyrygian or Dorian modes), his bold and adventurous harmony, his extraordinary skill at instrumentation, his exquisite workmanship, his delicately projected moods, from wit and satire to outright enchantment, are the fingerprints by which his works are always readily identifiable.

His music is consistently objective, a conscious effort at all times to be reserved and detached from the subject it is treating. In this he was almost sui generis. André Suares elaborated on this point in *La Revue Musicale.* "Nothing could be more objective than the art of Ravel, or more deliberately intended to be so. If music is capable of painting an object without first revealing the painter's feelings towards it, then Ravel's music achieves this more than any other. . . . Ravel is always a more or less ironical spectator, even when he is moved; for when his feelings are aroused he disguises them in order, as it were, to throw the hearer off the scent. Everything in Ravel's music indicates deliberate self-effacement, a determination to indulge in no confidences. His harmonies, his search for and discovery of new effects, the nervous tension and superstitious smile, the trembling of the lips in his melodies, the hidden fever and agitation of his rhythms are sufficient proof of his sensibility; but he conceals it; he covers it with a veil that allows nothing to appear; he is not only ashamed of it but almost hates it; he denies its existence; and so he abjures all rhetoric and, from fear of excess, he is capable of putting up with what might seem to be indigence. He prefers dryness to abundance. In short, he is so reticent with regard to his feelings that he would prefer to appear to have none at all rather than reveal them."

Maurice Ravel was born in Ciboure, in the Basque region of France, on March 7, 1875. His father was Swiss by birth, while his mother was Basque. The Ravel family moved to Paris when Maurice was three months old. There, at seven, he began piano lessons with Henri Ghys, and at eleven, studied harmony with Charles René. Beginning with 1889, he spent fifteen years at the Paris Conservatory, where he proved an exceptional student under such teachers as Gedalge, Charles de Bériot and Gabriel Fauré. Ravel's first composition, a piece for the piano, came in 1893; it was influenced by Chabrier. His first published works followed in 1895: *Menuet antique* and *Habanera,* the latter of which (for two pianos) already betrayed some of the composer's mature, later tendencies. His first work to get performed was *Les Sites auriculaires,* for two pianos, introduced in Paris on March 5, 1898. Success came with two piano compositions, the *Pavane pour une Infante défunte,* written in 1899, still one of Ravel's most popular compostitions, though more so in the composer's orchestral transcription than in its original piano version; and *Jeux d'eau,* written in 1901. His String Quartet in F major, in 1903, the Sonatine and *Miroirs,* both for piano, in 1905, the *Rapsodie espagnole* for orchestra and the one-act comic opera *L'Heure espagnole,* in 1907, placed him in the front rank of French composers.

In the early 1900s, Ravel identified himself with a group of other young composers who identified themselves as the "Société des Apaches"; this group included Stravinsky and Manuel de Falla among others. They called themselves "apaches" since an apache was a social outcast, and they regarded themselves as musical outcasts because of their progressive tendencies. They met regularly to exchange ideas on music and to listen to each other's compositions, an association which helped Ravel to develop creatively.

Despite his extraordinary talent and impressive achievements, Ravel failed four times to win the much coveted Prix de Rome. The fourth such attempt was in 1905. The injustice of denying the Prix to a composer of such gifts created a scandal which brought about the resignation of Theódore Dubois as director of the Paris Conservatory, to be replaced by Gabriel Fauré.

By the time of World War I, Ravel had produced several of his masterworks. These included the suite, *Mother Goose,* the *Valses nobles et sentimentales,* and what is generally accepted today as Ravel's crowning achievement, the ballet *Daphnis et Chloé.*

During World War I, Ravel served at the front in a motor corps. In 1921, he acquired a villa, "Le Belvédère," in Montfort l'Amaury, where he lived in comparative seclusion for the rest of his life. A slow workman who was painstakingly fastidious about details, he did not produce numerous works; but what he did create was always of the first order. In 1928, Ravel paid his only visit to the United States, making his American debut with the Boston Symphony on January 12, 1928.

An automobile accident in France brought about a lesion of the brain and partial paralysis. An operation proved fatal. Ravel died in a hospital in Auteuil, on the outskirts of Paris, on December 28, 1937.

1901 JEUX D'EAU, for piano.

A line from a poem by H. de Regnier—"a river god laughing at the waters as they caress him"—stirred Ravel's imagination and impelled him to write a descriptive piano piece. "This piece," explained the composer, "inspired by the sound of water and the music of fountains, cascades, and streams, is founded on two motifs, after the fashion of the first movement of a sonata, without, however, being subjected to the classical plan."

Jeux d'eau is not only a gem of descriptive writing in which the water is made to laugh and play in scintillating cascades of tones. It is also the source of a new technique for the writing of piano music from which many of Ravel's contemporaries (even Debussy) were to profit. It brought to the piano sonorities resonances and colors it had not known before; and its sensitive use of the highest register of the piano was revolutionary.

Ricardo Viñes introduced *Jeux d'eau* at a concert of the Société Nationale in Paris on April 5, 1902. At this same concert he introduced still another Ravel gem for the piano: the delicate and tender *Pavane pour une Infante défunte,* written in 1899.

Jeux d'eau was well received; and in performances and in publication it soon traveled triumphantly throughout the world of music, making the name of its composer famous. Regrettably, Ravel himself thought so little of the commercial possibilities of this piece that he did not bother to copyright it; its phenomenal worldwide success, therefore, brought him few returns.

1903 STRING QUARTET IN F MAJOR. I. Allegro moderato. II. Assai vif. III. Très lent. IV. Vif et agité.

Ravel's Quartet, the first of his chamber-music masterpieces, was written when he was only twenty-eight. It is one of his most spontaneous works. Many years later, at the height of his mastery, Ravel regarded this youthful work with satisfaction; he said that though his later chamber music revealed greater technical adroitness, he preferred the Quartet for its freshness.

The Quartet, which Ravel dedicated to Fauré, was Ravel's first major success. Introduced by the Heyman Quartet on March 5, 1904, at a concert of the Société Nationale in Paris, it was a triumph. Some critics did not hesitate to call it a masterpiece. "In the name of the gods of music and of my own," Debussy wrote to the young composer, "do not change one thing in your Quartet!"

It is a melodious work. abundant in its lyric ideas. There is nothing remote or obscure about it; its charm is evident even with a casual acquaintance. The first movement, in sonata form, consists of two main themes, both suave and aurally pleasing, and built up with great effect. The scherzo that follows opens with a delightful pizzicato section; a broadly melodic middle section provides contrast. The slow movement is a poem of gracious moods and tender sentiments that makes us think of Debussy. The work ends effectively with music that alternates between storm and calm.

1903 SHÉHÉRAZADE, three poems for voice and orchestra. I. Asie. II. La Flûte enchantée. III. L'Indifférent.

Ravel himself acknowledged the two influences that helped mold *Shéhérazade*. "Debussy's spiritual influence at least is fairly obvious," he confessed, "and I have succumbed to the profound fascination which the East has held for me since childhood."

He first planned *Shéhérazade* as an opera, but then, in 1898, contented himself by merely writing an orchestral overture, his first symphonic composition. It was performed at a concert of the Société Nationale in Paris on May 27, 1899.

Then, in 1903, Ravel read a series of poems by Tristan Klingsor, collectively entitled *Shéhérazade.* He decided to set three to music. Using some of the melodic material from his early overture, he scored his composition for voice and piano, and then orchestrated it. The set of three songs was introduced in Paris on May 17, 1904. Jane Hatto (to whom the first song is dedicated) was the soloist, and Alfred Cortot conducted. The vocal line was mainly declamatory, over a richly colored orchestral background. An exotic oriental atmosphere contributed a piquant flavor. The first song, "Asia," is a haunting dream of an imagined continent which the poet wished to visit and from which he hoped to return with a storehouse of wondrous tales. "Each phase of this fantastic oriental kaleidoscope," says R. H. Myers, "is underlined with a marvelous musical commentary that changes to fit each passing mood." "The Enchanted Flute" describes the emotions of a girl as she watches her master asleep at her side, while she listens to the sounds of a flute serenade. "Here," says Myers, "a flowing counterpoint is maintained between the voice and the flute over muted strings, creating a languorous, almost conventionally oriental atmosphere." "The Heedless One" tells of a mysterious youth who is indifferent to the woman who watches him passing by. "With complete sureness of touch and the simplest means, Ravel suggests discreetly the ambiguous charm of the mysterious passerby."

1905 SONATINE IN F-SHARP MAJOR, for piano. I. Modéré. II. Mouvement de menuet. III. Animé.

MIROIRS, suite for piano. I. Noctuelles. II. Oiseaux tristes. III. Un Barque sur l'océan. IV. Alborada del gracioso. V. La Vallée des cloches.

The Sonatine, written for a competition conducted by a music journal, is one of Ravel's finest works for the piano. "The passionate surge of the first movement," writes Roland-Manuel, "the tender, nostalgic grace of the minuet and the nervous vivacity of the finale bear the double imprint of youth and mastery. The almost meridional brightness and clear outline . . . the concise lyricism, the ingenuity of the melodic style, emphasized rather than hindered by the structural austerity, give it a classic character." To Maurice Delage, the first theme of the first movement is reminiscent of some "beautiful Roman melody." An inversion of the first two notes of this theme helps to introduce the minuet, while the finale has irresistible motor energy.

The Sonatine was introduced in Lyons by Mme. de Lestang on March 10, 1906.

With *Miroirs,* Ravel entered a new phase in his development. The harmony becomes so daring that Ravel felt that it would "put many musicians out of countenance who up to now have been most familiar with my style." The modulations are freer; the rhythmic patterns more varied; the developments more extended.

The five pieces are tone pictures reflecting, rather than duplicating, their subjects, and completely divorced from the emotions of their creator. They are inspired by some external image mirrored in sound.

Ravel considered "*Oiseaux tristes*" the most typical of the group. "In it, I evoke birds lost in the torpor of a somber forest, during the most torrid hours of summertime." The music is said to have been inspired by the singing of birds in the Fontainebleau forests. Despite trills, arpeggios and descending thirds suggesting the call of a cuckoo, the music does not try to imitate the song of birds. The entire piece has a symbolic character, with a consistently repeated note contributing an eerie atmosphere.

"*Une Barque sur l'océan*" is a shimmer of varying colors in its description of the changing sea. It is one of Ravel's most sensitive portraits. But to the French critics of 1905 it proved a baffling piece of music. Gaston Carraud thought that because the "spectacle changes every instant," it was a "bewildering kaleidoscope. One does not know what sort of weather is to be found on this ocean." (In 1908, Ravel orchestrated this piece.)

The most famous number of the entire suite is the "*Alborada del gracioso.*" *Alborada* is a morning serenade; and *gracioso* implies buffoonery. Utilizing a characteristic Spanish rhythm, Ravel brings about a delicate blend of irony and vivid tone painting. This work is as famous in the orchestral transcription, which Ravel himself prepared in 1912, as in its original piano version.

Each of the five pieces is dedicated to a different member of the "Apaches" —young Parisian intellectuals (of whom Ravel was one) who met regularly to discuss art, music and literature.

The first performance of *Miroirs* took place in Paris on January 6, 1906, at a concert of the Société Nationale. The pianist was Ricardo Viñes, to whom "*Oiseaux tristes*" is dedicated.

1906 INTRODUCTION AND ALLEGRO, for harp with string quartet, flute and clarinet.

Ravel wrote the *Introduction and Allegro* for the Parisian harpist, Micheline Kahn. She introduced it in Paris on February 22, 1907, at a concert of the Cercle Musical.

The Introduction opens with a duet for flute and clarinet. The principal melodic idea of this section is an extended melody for the cello against the background of violin, flute and clarinet. The intensity of the music grows, the tempo quickens, the sonority expands. The Allegro now enters without interruption, opening with a long and appealing harp solo. This melody is soon taken up by the flute, then by the other instruments. A rather involved development follows. Towards the end of the work a harp cadenza recalls some of the principal melodic ideas.

1907 RAPSODIE ESPAGNOLE (SPANISH RHAPSODY), suite for orchestra. I. Prelude à la Nuit. II. Malagueña. III. Habanera. IV. Feria.

This rhapsody is one of several works in which Ravel's fascination for Spanish subjects is reflected. And it is one of his major creations. On March 15, 1908, it was introduced at a Colonne concert, Eduard Colonne conducting; its success was so great that the second movement had to be repeated.

A four-note motif in muted strings brings up a tranquil scene. (This motif is used several times throughout the work.) One by one the sections of the orchestra pick up this theme. A cadenza for clarinets, and another for bassoon, lead into the second section, the main theme of which is heard in the double basses and after some evolution is repeated by bassoons, and then by muted trumpets. After a brief pause, the English horn enters with an improvisation. The Habanera movement (which is an adaptation of the *Habanera,* for two pianos, which Ravel wrote in 1895) is interesting for its rhythmic cogency. The Habanera rhythm (first projected in the clarinets) dominates the entire movement. In the concluding section, the music erupts with vital colors and spirited animation; the music is made rhythmically alive through an adroit use of the percussion. The gaiety subsides somewhat in the middle section (a song for English horn, followed by a repetition of the principal theme of the first movement). Then the excitement returns, and the music moves energetically to a whirlwind climax.

1907 L'HEURE ESPAGNOLE (THE SPANISH HOUR), comic opera in one act, with text by Franc-Nohain (Maurice Legrand). First performance: Opéra-Comique, Paris, May 19, 1911.

Ravel, who was always ineluctably drawn to Spanish subjects, Spanish rhythms and Spanish melodies, came upon Franc-Nohain's mocking little comedy *L'Heure espagnole,* and was intrigued by it. Having just completed the sardonic *Histoires naturelles,* Ravel was in the mood to write another work in a similar vein; and *L'Heure espagnole* seemed to provide a desirable subject.

It is a gay comedy of illicit love. Concepción is eager for her husband, the clockmaker Torquemada, to leave the shop, because she is expecting her lover. She reminds Torquemada that he must be off to regulate the town clock. No sooner is he gone when one of Concepción's lovers enters; then a second and a third. With Torquemada soon to return, Concepción insists that two of the lovers hide in the huge clocks. Torquemada finds them, but they have a ready explanation: they are customers and are only inspecting the insides of the clocks; indeed, they even buy the clocks to prove their integrity. A gay and impudent quintet ends the opera, in which the characters remind the audience that, after all, this takes place in Spain.

Ravel described his little opera as "a sort of musical conversation." It is an opéra bouffe—but with a difference. The touch is lighter, the mood gayer and more ironic, and the feeling more intimate than those in opéra bouffes. There is some exaggeration for the sake of humor and burlesque, but it is always in good taste; the text never presses its wit too hard. The musical writing, much of it in expressive declamation, is crystal clear; the harmonic texture, refined; the instrumentation, subtle.

The opening and closing pages are among its strongest suits. The opening is impressionistic writing into whose orchestral texture are woven the sounds of bells and chimes and the voice of a cuckoo clock, creating what Cecil Smith once described as a "world of lyric fantasy into which the misbehavior and prattle of the human characters intrude a harsh and disturbing note." The closing part is a Habanera for quintet of voices mocking the traditional closing scenes of Italian operas. "It evokes old-fashioned Italian operas with their trills, warblings, advances hand on heart . . . besides furnishing a springboard for the tenor to launch his high C on tiptoe," says Helene Jourdan-Morhange. Among the more memorable passages between the opening and closing are Gonzalve's Malaguena and Concepción's spirited diatribe against timid lovers.

Though completed in 1908, *L'Heure espagnole* was not performed until 1911. At that time it was received coldly. One critic called it "a miniature pornographic vaudeville"; another maintained it was "obscene." One or two, however, managed to sense that the work had genuine merit. Henri Ghéon wrote in the *Nouvelle Revue Française* that "it is miraculous to see how Franc-Nohain's buffoonery, whose comedy lies in gestures rather than words, becomes the jumping-off ground for those unexpected and unrestricted arabesques, based on the spoken word, but melodic all the same; to see how an art so concentrated and absorbed by the problems of expression can give the impression of being so natural. His grace and gaiety, in my opinion, are supremely vocal."

The American première took place in Chicago on January 5, 1920, with performances in New York following soon afterwards. It was first performed at the Metropolitan Opera House on November 7, 1925.

1908 MA MÈRE L'OYE (MOTHER GOOSE), suite for orchestra (also for piano, four hands). I. Pavane of the Sleeping Beauty. II. Hop o' My Thumb. III. Laideronnette, Empress of the Pagodas. IV. Conversations of Beauty and the Beast. V. The Fairy Garden.

In 1908, Ravel wrote a piano suite for four hands based on tales from Mother Goose for Mimi and Jean, two children of his friend, Godebski. "The idea of conjuring up the poetry of childhood in these pieces," wrote Ravel, "has naturally led me to simplify my style and clarify my writing." The four-hand version was introduced at a concert of the Musicale Indépendante in Paris on April 20, 1920; the performers were six-year-old Christine Verger and ten-year-old Germaine Duramy. In 1912, Ravel orchestrated the music for a ballet, which was presented at the Théâtre des Arts in Paris on January 21 of that year

The suite is in five sections. The first is a sad and stately dance of twenty measures. For the second, Ravel quoted the following passage from the Perrault tale to describe the music: "He believed that he would easily find his path by means of his bread crumbs, which he had scattered wherever he had passed; but he was very much surprised when he could not find a single crumb; the birds had come and eaten everything up."

In the third part, the story of Laideronnette is told. Laideronnette, daughter of a king, is cursed with ugliness by a wicked princess; her beauty is restored through the love of a prince.

The conversation between Beauty and the Beast consists of a little waltz melody, alternating with (then set against) a vulgar and brusque theme in the lower register. The suite ends with an enchanting theme for strings, out of which the entire concluding section is developed.

1908 GASPARD DE LA NUIT, three "poems" for piano. I. Ondine. II. Le Gibet. III. Scarbo.

Ravel was inspired by the poems of Aloysius Bertrand to write a suite of three descriptive pieces for the piano under the collective title of *Gaspard de la nuit*. It is one of his finest creations in which he succeeded not only in producing music of "transcendental virtuosity" (in his own description) but also music full of the "fascination of dreams" and "the pervading enchantment of nocturnal visions" (Roland-Manuel).

"Ondine," the most famous of this trilogy, reproduces the sound of water with delicate broken chords. *"Le Gibet,"* a musical portrait of the gallows, sounds the knell of doom in a persistent pedal point. *"Scarbo"* is an ironic scherzo describing a will-o'-the-wisp.

Gaspard de la nuit was introduced by Ricardo Viñes at a concert of the Société Nationale in Paris on January 9, 1909.

1911 VALSES NOBLES ET SENTIMENTALES (NOBLE AND SENTIMENTAL WALTZES), suite for piano (also for orchestra). I. Modéré. II. Assez lent. III. Modéré. IV. Assez animé. V. Presque lent. VI. Assez vif. VII. Moins vif. VIII. Lent.

Valses nobles et sentimentales had its roots in the infectious piano waltzes of Franz Schubert. It comprises seven waltzes and an epilogue played without interruption. The rhythms have the pulse and lilt of the Vieennse waltz; but the harmonies are bold.

The waltzes were introduced by Louis Aubert at a concert of the Société Indépendante in Paris on May 9, 1911. That concert was unusual in that all compositions were presented anonymously. The intention was to confuse not only those academicians and reactionary critics in Paris who were continually attacking the new and the original, but also those admirers who indiscriminately praised the music of their friends. Emile Vuillermoz revealed: "Ravel himself was seated in a loge in the midst of a group of society dilettantes who habitually swooned when they heard the sounds of Ravel's music. Heroically faithful to his oath as a conspirator, the composer of *Valses nobles et sentimentales* had not warned them that his work was included in the program. When they heard it, they began to jeer in the hope of pleasing Ravel by assailing this composition which they believed to be by someone else. Ravel accepted these manifestations in silence."

One year later, Ravel orchestrated the waltzes for a ballet, *Adélaide, or The Language of the Flowers*. It was presented at the Théâtre de Chatelet on April 22, 1912, with Mlle. Trouhanova as prima ballerina. The program for the ballet première contained the following synopsis: "Paris about 1825 at the house of the courtesan Adelaide. A salon furnished in the style of the period. At the back a window looking out on a garden. On each side vases full of flowers are placed on stands.

"I. A ball at her house. Couples are dancing as the curtain rises. Others seated or walking are talking tenderly. Adelaide goes and comes among her guests, breathing the odor of voluptuousness.

"II. Enter Loredan, elegant and melancholy. He goes toward Adelaide and offers her a buttercup. Simpering, she accepts the tribute and fixes the flower in her bodice.... She takes a black iris and puts a finger on her mouth.

Intoxicated, he falls at her feet, waving a sprig of heliotrope. She plucks two daisies and gives one to Loredan.

"III. She strips the flower she has kept and sees that the young man loves her sincerely. . . . Again Loredan declares his passion. . . . Little by little all the couples join in the play. . . . As Loredan entreats her, Adelaide again puts the flower to the test. This time its answer is favorable.

"IV. The lovers dance, showing their sentiments, but at the end of the pas de deux, Adelaide sees the duke enter; she stops, confused.

"V. Fanning herself with her handkerchief, she resumes the dance, but this time with an affected ingenuousness. The duke hands her a bouquet of sunflowers, then a casket containing a diamond necklace, with which she adorns herself. At the end of the dance, she takes the flower that enriched her bodice and lets it fall at his feet. The duke picks it up.

"VI. Despair of Loredan. Ardent pursuit. Adelaide repulses him coquettishly.

"VII. The duke begs Adelaide to grant him this last waltz; she declines his offer and goes in search of Loredan. . . . She invites him to dance. At first he refuses, but won gradually by the tender persistence of the courtesan, he allows himself to be persuaded. All the guests join in the dance.

"VIII. The guests withdraw. The duke advances to take his leave, hoping that he will be restrained. Adelaide . . . presents him with a bunch of acacia. The duke leaves showing somewhat his vexation. Loredan comes up, sad unto death. Adelaide offers him a cornpoppy. He refuses the consolatory flower and runs out with gestures of an eternal farewell. Left alone . . . Adelaide inhales voluptuously the odor of the tuberose. . . . Loredan appears, wrapped in a cloak, wild-eyed, with dishevelled hair. He walks toward Adelaide, who seems to be unconscious of his presence. He falls on his knees . . . and, taking a pistol from beneath his cloak, he puts it to a temple. Smiling, she draws a red rose from her breast, lets it drop carelessly, and falls into the arms of Loredan."

The first concert performance of the orchestrated version of *Valses nobles et sentimentales* was given in Paris on February 15, 1914, Pierre Monteux conducting. A motto by Henri de Regnier appears in the published score as a dedication: "To the delicious pleasure of useless occupation."

1912 DAPHNIS ET CHLOÉ, ballet in three scenes, with scenario and choreography by Michel Fokine. First performance: Ballet Russe, Paris, June 8, 1912.

DAPHNIS ET CHLOÉ, two ballet suites for orchestra. First Series: I. Nocturne; II. Interlude; III. Warlike Dance. Second Series: I. Daybreak; II. Pantomime; III. General Dance.

The impresario of the Ballet Russe, Serge Diaghilev, who was responsible for discovering the genius of Stravinsky, Manuel de Falla, and Prokofiev, also recognized Ravel's pronounced gifts early. In 1909, Diaghilev heard several Ravel works; immediately he sensed the promises they held. When, one year later, Fokine presented him with a scenario for a ballet about Daphnis and Chloë, Diaghilev went to Ravel for the music. Ravel took two years for the assignment. Strange to report of Diaghilev, whose musical instincts were so sound, he did not like Ravel's music. (A decade or so later, he was again to dislike a work that Ravel had written for him on commission—*La Valse*!) For a while, Ravel was tempted to abandon the entire project, but was prevailed upon not to do so by the music publisher Durand. After delays, caused mainly by internal dissensions in the ballet company, the Ballet Russe presented *Daphnis et Chloé* with Pierre Monteux conducting. Nijinsky, Karsavina and Bohm were the principal dancers. The choreography was by Fokine; the decor by Leon Bakst. The performance was not successful.

But there were some critics who recognized the distinction of Ravel's score. Jean Marnold wrote in the *Mercure de France:* "The score abounds in tableaux of the most exquisite plastic beauty. . . . *Daphnis et Chloé* really constitutes a 'musical drama' which offers the coherence and unity of a vast symphony. All of this music holds itself together and lives its own autonomous existence, to such an extent that the preliminary introduction of the Leitmotifs would make even a blind man understand and follow the scenic action."

The source for the ballet scenario was a Greek pastoral, believed to have been written by Longus. But the original version was subjected to considerable change. In the ballet, the shepherd Daphnis dreams that Pan saves Chloë out of the memory of his love for the nymph Syrinx. Imitating Pan and Syrinx, Daphnis fashions a pipe out of reeds, and begins playing for Chloë, who dances until she falls into his arms. A general dance and a joyous tumult follow.

Even more famous than the ballet (which some now regard as one of the finest in the French repertory) are the two orchestral suites, or "series," which Ravel prepared from the score, and which have been extensively performed.

The first suite, or "series," carries the following synopsis: "A little flame suddenly burns on the head of one of the statues. The nymph comes to life and leaves her pedestal. Others descend, come together, and begin a slow and mysterious dance. They see Daphnis, bend over him, and dry his tears. Reanimating him and leading him to the rock, they invoke the God Pan. Little by little the form of the god assumes definite shape. Daphnis kneels in supplication. All is dark. Behind the scene, voices are heard, far off at first. And now there is a dim light. The pirates' camp is disclosed. There is a bold cast; the sea is in the background, with rocks to the right and left. A trireme is near the shore. Cypresses are here and there. The pirates, laden with booty, run to and fro. Torches are brought, which at last throw a strong light on the stage."

The second "series" is even more celebrated than the first. The following synopsis appears in the score: "No sound but the murmur of rivulets fed by the dew that trickles from the rocks. Daphnis lies stretched before the grotto of the nymphs. Little by little the day dawns. The songs of birds are heard. Afar off a shepherd leads his flock. Another shepherd crosses the back of the stage. Herdsmen enter, seeking Daphnis and Chloë. They find Daphnis and awaken him. In anguish he looks about for Chloë. She at last appears encircled by shepherdesses. The two rush into each other's arms. Daphnis observes Chloë's crown. His dream was a prophetic vision; the intervention of Pan is manifest. The old shepherd Lammon explains that Pan saved Chloë in remembrance of the nymph Syrinx, whom the god loved.

"Daphnis and Chloë mime the story of Pan and Syrinx. Chloë impersonates the young nymph wandering over the meadow. Daphnis appears as Pan and declares his love for her. The nymph repulses him; the god becomes more insistent. She disappears among the reeds. In desperation he plucks some stalks, fashions a flute, and on it plays a melancholy tune. Chloë comes out and imitates the accents of the flute with her dance. The dance grows more and more animated. In mad whirlings, Chloë falls into the arms of Daphnis. Before the altar of the nymphs he swears on two sheep his fidelity. Young girls enter; they are dressed as bacchantes, and shake tambourines. Daphnis and Chloë embrace tenderly. A group of young men appear on the stage. Joyous tumult. A general dance. Daphnis and Chloë."

In "Daybreak," flickering woodwind in upper register suggest the murmur of rivulets. An arching melody rises from lower strings, swells and ebbs away. Finally, an opulent song unfolds, as flutes and piccolo provide delightful arabesques. Strings expand this melody, as the colors become richer and deeper through the addition of harp glissandos, a violin solo, celesta, and woodwinds in the upper register. The music becomes rapturous. Once again the arching melody rises from lower strings towards a point of climax in which the brass join. The entrance of the brass is like the first burst of the sun in the morning. It is dawn.

The whole "Pantomime" section has a pastoral character, this mood being created at once by oboe and flute who engage in a soft dialogue. Muted strings join in. Harp arpeggios and divided strings set the stage for an extended flute solo over a rhythm in plucked strings. This is the song of Pan. Then the mood is briefly dramatized. But the pastoral scene returns with the solo flute involved in a fast dance, and the violin engaging a solo.

In "General Dance," a colorful ripple in the woodwind precedes the outburst of a bacchanale. From this point on, changing meters, chromatic scales create a voluptuous mood. Into this dance, Ravel brings his remarkable virtuosity at instrumentation. Descending chromatic scales and kinesthetic rhythms remind us of Borodin's *Polovtzian Dances*. The excitement mounts and a stirring climax is reached.

1914 TRIO IN A MINOR, for piano, violin and cello. I. Modéré. II. Pantoum: assez vif. III. Passecaille; Très large. IV. Finale: animé.

Ravel once confessed that in this piano trio he was influenced by the early trios of Saint-Saëns; and what impressed Ravel particularly was Saint-Saëns's clarity and economy. Ravel's trio is a work reduced to essentials. It is a masterpiece of form and technique in its avoidance of all superfluous details.

Roland-Manuel wrote that the trio is a work "at once serious and impassioned, in which each instrument is clearly outlined in the enhancement of the melody." The best movements, according to Roland-Manuel, are the first (for the ingenuity of structure and the originality of metrical design) and the passacaglia (in which the problem of the opposing sonorities of piano and strings is solved "with consummate lightness and distinction"). The second movement, a scherzo, is called a "pantoum," after a Malayan poetic form calling for two independent thoughts moving in parallel lines.

1917 LE TOMBEAU DE COUPERIN, suite for piano (also for orchestra). I. Prélude. II. Fugue. III. Forlane. IV. Rigaudon. V. Menuet. VI. Toccata.

During World War I, Ravel planned the writing of a musical composition honoring the memory of friends who had died in battle.

He had in 1914 begun work on a musical tribute to the great French composer of harpsichord music, François Couperin-le-Grand (1668–1733). It was a suite comprising seventeenth-century forms and dances and written with seventeenth-century economy and transparency. Work on this suite was interrupted when Ravel enlisted in the French Army. But in 1917, back in civilian life, Ravel resumed work on the suite, and at that time he decided to make this composition the gesture of homage to the war dead that he had been planning for some time. Though written for the war dead—and at a time when Ravel was further depressed by the death of his beloved mother—there is no undercurrent of either pity or sorrow beneath the serene classic surface of this music. It is music of tranquillity which has caught the spirit of an age long gone.

The suite was introduced in Paris in April, 1919. Some time later, Ravel transcribed the music for small orchestra (omitting the fugue and toccata movements). The orchestral version was heard for the first time on February 28, 1920, in a performance of the Pasdeloup Orchestra, Rhené-Baton conducting.

Nicolas Slonimsky's analysis follows: "The first movement Prelude (Vif) begins in a murmuring hurly-burly of the woodwinds, punctuated by plucked strings. A chromatic descending line helps to sustain the even motion, in which the strings soon join. A feeling of stability comes from the pedal point in the transition; the hollow fifths in parallel progressions suggest an archaic detachment. The dynamics are subdued, and then a sudden crescendo wells up to a climactic chord of the thirteenth. After a few scattered figurations and a protracted trill, the Prelude comes to an end."

The Forlane (Allegretto) is a "stylization of an old dance of Italian origin that is close to a gigue in rhythm. It is a gay dance, and Ravel keeps its original gaiety in soft instrumental colors as a nostalgic reminiscence of another era."

The Minuet "has a characteristically recessive bass, leading to a cadential construction every fourth bar. The tonic-dominant pedal point is the ground for the middle section, following the classical formula."

In the Rigaudon (Assez vif), the "harmonic texture is pandiatonic, so that not a single accidental mars the initial eight bars in the score. The middle section approaches the rhythm of a polka. The Rigaudon ends with a decisive flourish in clear C major."

1920 LA VALSE, choreographic poem for orchestra.

Ravel loved the Viennese waltz, particularly the waltzes of Schubert and Johann Strauss. The piano waltzes of Schubert had been the stimulus for the *Valses nobles et sentimentales* (*see* 1911). For many years he was planning to write a Viennese waltz of his own for use as a ballet, but this time a waltz inspired by Johann Strauss II. A commission by Diaghilev in 1919 set Ravel working on this idea. He conceived the ballet "as a kind of apotheosis of the Viennese waltz," as he later wrote, "linked, in my mind, with the impression of a fantastic whirl of destiny."

In the published score, the following descriptive paragraph is found: "Whirling clouds give glimpses, through rifts, of couples dancing. The clouds scatter, little by little. One sees an immense hall peopled with a twirling crowd. The scene is gradually illuminated. The light of the chandeliers bursts forth, fortissimo. An Imperial court, in or about 1855."

The waltz opens vaguely in the basses. Suddenly a waltz rhythm springs to life. It grows until a fully developed Viennese waltz is heard, in the best traditions of Johann Strauss. But suddenly the music becomes bitter as a few strident chords break the gay spell. The waltz returns, but it is now harsh and dissonant. The music grows more and more feverish. The mood is now that of despair. Discords bring the work to a close. In this transformation of the waltz from gaiety to tragedy, Ravel has portrayed Vienna itself, from its prewar abandon and light heart to its postwar futility and despair.

Diaghilev did not like *La Valse,* felt that it did not have choreographic possibilities, and refused to perform it. (Diaghilev's harsh opinion of the work brought about a permanent rupture between him and the composer.) But, perhaps as vindication for the work, it was extraordinarily successful when the Lamoureux Orchestra performed it on December 12, 1920, with Camille Chevillard conducting. Some years later, Ida Rubinstein included it in her repertory with equal success.

1925 L'ENFANT ET LES SORTILÈGES (THE CHILD AND THE SORCERERS), fantasy in two parts, with text by Colette. First performance: Monte Carlo, March 21, 1925.

During World War I, the director of the Paris Opéra approached Colette, the novelist, to write a stage work—a *divertissement féerique* (a comedy of magic) that could be set to music. When this assignment was completed, both Colette and the director agreed that Ravel was the logical candidate to write the music. A copy of the text was dispatched to the composer. At that time, however, Ravel was at the front, in the motor corps, and the text never reached him. After the war, the comedy was brought to his attention. Though he reacted favorably to it (he always had a special weakness for fantasies of all kinds) he did not get around to the job of composition until 1924.

Colette's little play was, indeed, made to order for Ravel's temperament and talents. The fairy tale takes place in Normandy, where a mischievous boy, severely upbraided by his mother for his refusal to do his lessons, avenges himself by breaking up the furniture in the room and torturing domestic animals. The furniture suddenly comes to life and taunts the boy. Out of one of the books he has destroyed—his favorite—the Princess of a fairy tale comes into being to say she will have nothing more to do with him. Suddenly the child finds himself outside of the house. The trees, the squirrel and the tree frogs arrive to threaten him. But in the ensuing confusion, the squirrel is hurt. The boy tends to the animal. This kind act appeases the boy's attackers; the animals carry him back to his home, where his mother is waiting for him.

Ravel wrote his music, as he said, in the spirit of an "American operetta" —with an abundance of tongue-in-cheek humor. In one of his most provocative scenes he has a duet in cat language: the mewing of the cats grows out of the melodic line. In another scene—the dance of the cup and the teapot—he burlesques American fox-trot music. But Ravel's music is not exclusively satirical. At other places he evokes a world of enchantment—the child's magic world of imagination—in music of the greatest delicacy. He has given us few pages of music that are realized with such exquisite finesse as his musical description of the garden and its animal inhabitants in the opening of the second scene.

L'Enfant et les sortilèges was so successful at the première that the following season the Opéra-Comique presented it in Paris under Albert Wolff's direction. This time the reaction was a mixed one. There were those who liked it greatly and spoke of it as a work of genius (Henri Malherbe, for example). Those who disliked it—André Messager was one of these—denounced the music for its ingenuous imitativeness as in the duet of the cats. *L'Enfant* received fifteen performances in two seasons and could hardly be called a success. The American première took place in San Francisco on September 19, 1930.

1924 TZIGANE, rhapsody for violin and orchestra (also violin and piano).

Ravel wrote *Tzigane* in 1924 for the violinist Yelly d'Aranyi. Conscious of her Hungarian nationality, Ravel wrote a stylization of Hungarian gypsy music. He did not intend to satirize or burlesque it. He meant to write a bravura piece of music that was Hungarian in personality and temperament. *Tzigane* exploits many of the well-known conventions of the Hungarian rhapsody form. It opens with a long slow cadenza for solo violin. After a second cadenza, this time for the harp, the main section begins with a fiery gypsy melody for the violin. Other gypsy tunes and dances follow, developed in a rhapsodic manner, and culminating in a whirlwind finish.

Tzigane was originally written for violin and "lutheal," a "lutheal" being an organlike attachment to the piano. In this version it was introduced in London on April 26, 1924, by Yelly d'Aranyi. Subsequently, Ravel orchestrated the accompaniment.

1927 SONATA FOR VIOLIN AND PIANO. I. Allegretto. II. Moderato. III. Allegro.

This sonata is the first of several major works in which Ravel was markedly influenced by American jazz, and specifically by the music of George Gershwin. The jazz influence is found in the second movement "blues," a saucy tune being heard in the violin after an introduction of strongly accented chords in plucked strings of the violin. The first movement is more traditional Ravel, with two main subjects and three subsidiary ideas. The main theme is stated first. Three subsidiary subjects follow. Then, after a change or mood, a second melody is heard. Before the movement ends, a third lyrical thought is projected briefly by the violin. In the finale, thematic material from earlier movements is recalled.

1928 BOLERO, for orchestra.

Bolero is a remarkable feat of compositional virtuosity; and as a matter of fact, it was intended as such by the composer. For a long time Ravel had been intrigued by the idea of writing a piece of music consisting entirely of a single theme allowed to grow through harmonic and instrumental ingenuity.

In the summer of 1928, the dancer Ida Rubinstein asked Ravel to orchestrate for her Albéniz's *Iberia*. When Ravel discovered that the orchestration rights to *Iberia* belonged to Arbós, he offered to write a work of his own which would be Spanish in character. It was then that Ravel decided to experiment with his long-held idea. He took not one theme but two (a subject and its countersubject), both in the bolero rhythm. Without any development, variation or modulations, these themes were permitted to develop through change of instrumentation and sonority, reaching seventeen minutes later towards an overwhelming climactic statement in full orchestra. The result was a musical tour de force. It was a success when Ida Rubinstein danced to it at the Paris Opéra on November 20, 1928. It was a sensation when Arturo Toscanini introduced it with the New York Philharmonic Orchestra in New York City on November 14, 1929.

Since 1929, *Bolero* has become one of Ravel's most famous works. It has been heard in many different versions, including transcriptions for jazz band, harmonica, and two pianos; it has been incorporated into a Broadway revue; and it was the inspiration for a Hollywood movie.

Ravel himself described the work as follows: "It is a dance in a very modern movement, completely uniform in melody as well as harmony and rhythm, the latter marked without interruption by the drum. The only element of diversity is brought into play by an orchestral crescendo."

1931 CONCERTO IN G MAJOR FOR PIANO AND ORCHESTRA. I. Allegramente; Andante a piacere. II. Adagio assai. III. Presto.

CONCERTO IN D MAJOR FOR PIANO LEFT HAND AND ORCHESTRA.

In the dusk of his career, Ravel contributed two works to the piano-concerto literature, one for piano and orchestra, and the other for left-hand piano and orchestra. In the first of these, in G major (which took the composer two years to write and sometimes kept him at his desk ten hours a day) he felt he had expressed himself most completely and perfectly. Ravel explained that he conceived the work as a "concerto in the strict sense, written in the spirit of Mozart and Saint-Saëns." He completed it in 1931. On January 14, 1932, he conducted its première (as part of a Ravel festival) with the Lamoureux Orchestra; Marguerite Long was the soloist.

Henri Prunières, the eminent French critic, has provided the definitive analysis of this concerto:

"The first movement is constructed on a gay, light theme which recalls Ravel's early style. It appears first in the orchestra, while the piano supplies curious sonorous effects. . . . The development proceeds at a rapid pace with a surprising suppleness, vivacity, and grace. This leads to an Andante a piacere, where the piano again takes the exposition of the theme, while the bassoons, flutes, clarinets, and oboes surround it one after another with brilliant scales and runs. Then begins a grand cadenza. The orchestra enters again discreetly, at first marking the rhythm and then taking up the development, leading to a brilliant conclusion.

"The second movement consists of one of those long cantilenas which Ravel knows so well how to write. . . . Evolving over an implacable martellato bass, the melody is developed lengthily at the piano; then, little by little, the orchestra takes possession of it while the piano executes fine embroideries and subtle appoggiaturas.

"The Presto finale is a miracle of lightness and grace, and recalls certain scherzi and prestos of Mozart and Mendelssohn. The orchestra marks a syncopated rhythm while the piano leads the movement. The spirit of jazz animates this movement . . . but with great discretion."

The Left-Hand Concerto was written simultaneously with the Concerto in G major. Ravel did it on commission for the one-armed pianist, Paul Wittgenstein, who introduced it in Vienna on November 27, 1931. A serious altercation between composer and performer, created by Wittgenstein's demand for certain changes in the music, drove Ravel to coach another pianist in this work: Jacques Février, who performed it in Paris on January 17, 1933.

In one movement (Lento; Allegro; Lento), this concerto utilizes jazz effects with exceptional skill. The composer explained the structure as follows: "After an introductory section, there comes an episode like an improvisation, which is succeeded by a jazz section. Only later is one aware that the jazz episode actually is built up from the themes of the first section."

1932 DON QUICHOTTE À DULCINÉE, three songs for baritone and orchestra. I. Chanson romanesque. II. Chanson épique. III. Chanson à boire.

These three songs (text by Paul Morand) became Ravel's last completed composition. He wrote it on commission from a motion-picture company which planned a film about Don Quixote starring Feodor Chaliapin. Ravel's delay in producing the score, combined with his disagreements with the film company on the kind of material he should prepare, caused a change of plan. When the movie was released, the Morand poems were sung to Jacques Ibert's music. Ravel first released his own songs with piano accompaniment; then he provided the orchestral background. The world première of the latter took place in Paris at a Colonne concert on December 1, 1934. Martial Singher was the soloist, and Paul Paray conducted.

In the first song, Don Quixote offers to give up his life for his lady, if she so requires. The rhythms here are Spanish and Basque. The second song was described by Glenn D. McGeoch as "a confident prayer to the Madonna, full of great tenderness and haunting beauty"; its rhythm is based on the 5/8 time of the Zortizico, a Basque dance. The concluding number is a rousing drinking song in the style of an Aragonese Jota.

ALAN RAWSTHORNE 1905–

It is not easy to characterize Rawsthorne's music. He is a modernist in that he often dispenses with key signatures, uses discords and a severe melodic line, and achieves the feeling of atonality. Yet he also has some of his roots deep in Baroque soil, in his interest in the chaconne, variation, and concerto grosso structures, and in his occasional partiality for cantilena or aria writing. He is also a Romantic, capable of expressing deeply personal emotions. To Carolyn Wilson, in judging Rawsthorne's music, "two things come instantly to mind. . . . They are his imaginative range harnessed to wonderful craftsmanship, and the conclusive answer which he seems to have found for himself in the consolidation of his intensely personal idiom."

Alan Rawsthorne was born in Haslingden, Lancashire, England, on May 2, 1905. He did not begin formal music study until he was twenty-one, having originally planned to become a dentist, a profession for which he prepared himself accordingly. Between 1926 and 1930, he attended the Manchester College of Music, and after that he studied the piano privately with Egon Petri. From 1932 to 1934, he was a member of the faculty of Dartington Hall in South Devon. After marrying Jessie Hinchliffe, a violinist, in 1935, he settled in London to devote himself to composition. Performances of his early works at festivals of the International Society for Contemporary Music first brought him to the limelight: the *Theme and Variations,* for two violins, in London on June 18, 1938, and the *Symphonic Studies,* for orchestra, in Warsaw on April 21, 1939.

During World War I, Rawsthorne served in the British Army writing music for army films. His reputation as a serious composer grew perceptibly during the war years, with premières of his first piano concerto and his *Cortèges,* for orchestra, at the Promenade Concerts in London in 1942 and 1945 respectively. This reputation was solidly established after the war with the successful presentation of his First Symphony on November 15, 1950, and the première of his second piano concerto half a year later. In the seclusion of his home in a village in Essex—where he lives with his second wife, Isabel Lambert, a painter—Rawsthorne has since produced a second and third symphony (1959, 1964), a second and third string quartet (1954, 1965), a *Concerto for Ten Instruments* (1962), the orchestral *Variations on a Theme by Constant Lambert* (1961) and the Concerto for Cello and Orchestra (1965).

1951 CONCERTO NO. 2 FOR PIANO AND ORCHESTRA. I. Allegro piacevole. II. Allegro molto. III. Adagio semplice; Poco allegro. IV. Allegro.

This concerto was commissioned by the Arts Council of Great Britain for a national festival in 1951. The work was introduced in London on June 17, 1951. Clifford Curzon was the soloist, and the London Symphony was directed by Sir Malcolm Sargent. It achieved an extraordinary success and helped to carry its composer to the forefront of twentieth-century British composers.

This is the composer's own analysis of his concerto: "The first movement consists of three main sections. The first opens quietly, with the piano playing a flowing accompaniment while a solo flute announces the melody from which most of the movement is derived. This melody lasts for eighteen bars. . . . The piano then continues with another statement of the melody accompanied by florid figurations widely distributed over the keyboard. Another paragraph is started by the entry of the cellos and basses who proceed to develop the various phrases of the melody in a rather darker mood. . . . The second section continues with a light scherzando theme in a gayer mood while the third section consists of a recapitulation of the first eighteen bars of the movement and a coda.

"The Scherzo is a rondo-like structure whose principal subject is announced at the outset by the piano accompanied by spasmodic interjections by the orchestra.

"The slow movement opens without break with an orchestral introduction announcing the three phrases from which most of the music is derived. The first phrase, played by a solo bassoon, is based on the notes of the chord which finishes the Scherzo. The second appears on a horn, and the third on the flute.

"In the last movement, the mood of the slow movement is dispelled by a brassy fanfare preparing the way for the tune which forms the basis for most of the movement. The tune is played by the piano alone. . . . It provides the material for a number of episodes. . . . The work ends with a fugato passage which works up into an energetic climax."

1959 SYMPHONY NO. 2, "PASTORAL."

The Second Symphony reveals the romantic facet of the composer's many-sided creative personality. The composer has explained that this music sprang "from the various sensations aroused by life in the country." The third movement was described by the composer as a country dance with "sinister elements appearing from time to time, as so frequently happens during rustic pursuits." In the finale, in which the voice enters, the composer has set a poem about Spring by Henry Howard, Early of Surrey, of the sixteenth century.

When the symphony was introduced in the United States, in New York on May 1, 1962, Raymond Ericson reported in *The New York Times:* "The music reflects the pastoral atmosphere in an alternating brooding and lyrical fashion. The alternation can be pinpointed in the English composer's overlay of major and minor triads for his harmonic and melodic material, in his use of a march-like theme as an interruption of the rhapsodical slow movement."

GARDNER READ 1913–

"I feel," Read once wrote, "it is a greater test of a composer's technique and abilities to cultivate as many different styles as he feels necessary rather than pursue only one." So speaks an eclectic, who in an industrious lifetime has produced over one hundred and twenty-five compositions in all forms and media. Read has, at turns, been Romantic, neoclassic, impressionistic; he has used popular tunes and folk melodies in compositions like the *First Overture* (1943), where Stephen Foster is quoted, and *Pennsylvaniana Suite* (1946), where the folk music of Western Pennsylvania provides basic material. Yet, since within such frameworks he has not hesitated to use polyharmonic combinations, discords and polytonal writing. He remains a voice of the twentieth century.

Read was born in Evanston, Illinois, on January 2, 1913. When he was ten, he was a choir boy at St. Luke's Church in Evanston. Music study began five years later after he had entered high school. He attended the Eastman School of Music, graduating with a Bachelor of Music degree in 1936, and receiving a Masters degree in composition one year after that. In 1936, he completed his first symphony, recipient of first prize in a competition sponsored by the New York Philharmonic; it was introduced by that orchestra, under John Barbirolli's direction, on November 4, 1937. In 1938, he received the Cromwell Fellowship for travel in Europe, which made it possible for him to study with Sibelius in Finland and Pizzetti in Italy. Returning to the United States, he was a student in composition of Aaron Copland at the Berkshire Musical Center. He completed a second symphony which was given its world première by the Boston Symphony on November 26, 1943, and which received the Paderewski Award. Since then, many of Read's orchestral works have been widely presented by major orchestras. Read has had a long and active career as a teacher of composition: at the St. Louis Institute of Music from 1940 to 1942; the Kansas City Conservatory, where he was head of the composition department from 1943 to 1948; at the School of Music at Boston University where, since 1948, he has been composer-in-residence and professor of composition; and at the University of California in Los Angeles where, in 1966, he was visiting professor of composition. The Boston University celebrated Read's fiftieth birthday with a festival of his music in 1963. In 1957, and again in 1964, Read received grants from the U.S. Department of State to lecture and conduct in Mexico.

1936–1947 COMPOSITIONS FOR ORCHESTRA:
PRELUDE AND TOCCATA, op. 43.
NIGHT FLIGHT, tone poem, op. 44.
PENNSYLVANIANA, suite, op. 67. I. Calmly and with Deliberation. II. Slowly with Pleading Earnestness. III. Lively with Spirit.
PARTITA, for small orchestra, op. 70. I. Allegro giusto, con anima. II. Larghetto con semplicita. III. Allegro molto energico.

The *Prelude and Toccata* (1937) was first heard in Rochester, New York, on April 29, 1937. It was Read's first success as an orchestral composer, having enjoyed over forty performances both in the United States and in South America.

An eight-note figure rises in the lower woodwinds over a pedal point, gaining in volume and momentum as it progresses. Against this is placed a four-note motive for horn, which, in various transformations, is the source of the entire composition. The Toccata uses such traditional devices as canon and stretto. At a climactic point, the main theme of the Prelude is combined contrapuntally with that of the Toccata.

Night Flight, though begun in 1936, was not completed until 1942. It owes both its title and inspiration to the celebrated novel of Antoine de Saint-Exupéry. Its world première took place in Rochester, New York, on April 27, 1944, Howard Hanson conducting. While the novel deals with the flight of mail planes over the South American Andes, the tone poem makes no attempt to provide a literal description of aerial transportation. "I have sought," the composer explains, "to express the loneliness and mysterious beauty of the space in which these planes must fly." He adds: "A constantly reiterated note on a fixed pitch gives the illusion of the radio beam signal sent to all pilots during their flight." In reviewing this composition for *Modern Music,* Bernard Rogers said: "It seems virtually barren of line or thematic growth; all is color. . . . This is an attractive experiment, showing a resourceful hand and an alert mind."

Pennsylvaniana (1947) was introduced by the Pittsburgh Symphony, under Fritz Reiner, on November 21, 1947. This is a suite making effective use of folk-song materials from Western Pennsylvania. Each of the three movements is built out of a different folk song. The first movement is based on the tune "Dunlap's Creek," whose melody is heard in strings before it is taken over by the other sections of the orchestra. The second movement is derived from the Evangelist song, "I'm a Beggar," played by the English horn following a short introduction. In the third movement, an old British ballad, "John Riley," provides the material; it is given by the strings and piano after several introductory strokes of the tympani.

The *Partita,* completed in 1946, was heard for the first time at the American Music Festival in Rochester, New York, on May 4, 1947. The composer provides the following description: "The first movement is in sonatine form, with the rhythmic patterns of the main and subsidiary themes reversed in the recapitulation. The second movement is based on a ground bass idea which ascends chromatically with each repetition, passes to the upper voice, and descends chromatically, ending as it began in the lower voice. The third movement is a free rondo, the second section of which is a fugato, with successive entries at the third rather than the fifth."

1948 SYMPHONY NO. 3, op. 75. I. Introduction. II. Scherzo. III. Chorale and Fugue.

Fourteen years separated the completion and the performance of Read's Third Symphony. Read began writing it in August of 1946, and completed it during the summer of 1948. But the world première had to wait until March 2, 1962, when William Steinberg directed the Pittsburgh Symphony. At that time the composer contributed the following analysis: "The Third Symphony . . . employs contrapuntal forms not usually associated with the traditional symphonic design—the passacaglia with its series of variations on a ground bass, and the sonata-allegro design, with its two or three contrasted themes. The passacaglia subject becomes the principal theme, while the counterpoints of the first two variations become, respectively, subsidiary and closing themes. The variations are interrupted by a development section based on all three melodic ideas. As a recapitulation, the passacaglia variations resume, and the three thematic elements are simultaneously restated. The movement ends with a simple and quiet statement of the passacaglia subject.

"As a dramatic contrast in texture as well as in mood, the second movement is a *sotte voce* scherzo. The thematic ideas are purposely fragmentary, in opposition to the well-defined melodic material of the passacaglia and of the fugue to come. The rhythm fluctuates between a 6/8 and 5/8 meter, and the harmony is almost entirely bitonal—largely a combination of two minor triads whose roots are an augmented fourth apart. The violins employ an unusual and rare device during the course of the brief movement by tapping the string with the ivory tip of the bow stick.

"The final movement comprises a chorale as an introduction, the harmony based upon the bitonal progressions of the scherzo, followed by an elaborate fugue based on the opening passacaglia subject. Thus the last movement of the symphony is linked in very specific ways to the preceding movements. At the end of the fugue both the original passacaglia theme and the chorale material are announced together with the fugal permutations, and the symphony ends in an exultant mood."

1957 STRING QUARTET, op. 100. I. Allegro brioso e molto energico. II. Adagio espressivo, molto cantando. III. Vivace e grottesco. IV. Allegro con spirito.

This string quartet, Read's first, was commissioned by the Kindler Foundation of Washington, D.C. The world première took place in that city in 1958 in a performance by the Classic String Quartet. The first movement is in the traditional sonata-allegro structure. The composer explains that it is "driving and highly rhythmic and makes much use of polyharmony." The second movement is introspective in mood and canonic in design. In the scherzo, a serial construction is followed but, the composer informs us, "as the basic row is triadic, the music has a more polytonal than atonal flavor." The finale is rondo-like, with exuberant moods; the quartet ends in a dramatic vein.

MAX REGER 1873–1916

Though he was extraordinarily partial to the polyphonic style of Johann Sebastian Bach and to the structures of Baroque music (passacaglia, toccata, fugue, variations), Max Reger was, surprisingly enough, regarded by some of his contemporaries as a revolutionary. This is because, in his attempt to extend music's articulateness, Reger utilized formidably complex harmonic and contrapuntal structures, generally too intricate for their own good; he developed monumental structures, often fussy with details; he was free in his use of modulation and sometimes abstruse in his notation.

Today we are more apt to consider Reger an academician than an iconoclast, an academician in whose music a fabulous technique and equally fabulous scholarship are more often ends in themselves rather than the means to an end. If Reger's music is not heard frequently, it is because it is often too elaborate and ponderous. As one English critic put it: "He stifles music with too many notes." Yet it has a significant role in twentieth-century music, and it has exerted an influence.

He liked to use the old contrapuntal forms, which he did with outstanding skill, because he believed in abstract music and felt that counterpoint made possible the purest kind of music. He was perhaps at his best in writing variations on the themes of other composers (which would invariably end up in a giant fugue). Then he could give free play to all his technical adroitness and ingenuity by transforming a comparatively simple idea through all the resources of harmony, counterpoint, rhythm and instrumentation into truly monumental structures.

His God was Johann Sebastian Bach, whom he regarded as "the beginning and end of all music." An unidentified music critic for the London *Times* noted this fact when he said: "Unlike any of his contemporaries, he based his style deliberately on the Teutonic Baroque counterpoint of Bach, and the hallmark of his style is a creative reinterpretation of Bach's methods along romantically expressive lines. . . . His veneration of Bach is most obviously to be found in his organ works, two hundred and sixteen in number, but also in his addiction to fugues. . . . He was a renowned contrapuntist, and almost automatically ended his bigger works with a gigantic fugue. . . . It must be argued that twentieth-century neo-classicism, the Back-to-Bach movement among composers, derives from Reger." This "Back-to-Bach movement" which came to be known as "*Neue Sachlichkeit*" ("New Objectivity") found eager disciples in Germany, among them the young Hindemith.

"To the same degree that Reger succeeded in digesting Bach's substance—the polyphonic character, the unique tension and compression of harmony, and not least the sordid religious foundation—to that degree he became the great teacher for the future," says his biographer, Otto Eberhard.

Reger was born in Brand, Bavaria, on March 19, 1873. The son of a schoolmaster, he was at first intended for the teaching profession, even though he had shown unusual ability in his early music studies. He passed the necessary teaching examinations. But before assuming his first post, he heard Wagner's *Die Meistersinger* and *Parsifal* in Bayreuth, which fired him with the ambition of becoming a composer. He sent some of his compositions to Hugo Riemann, who accepted him as his pupil at the Sonderhausen Conservatory and had him live in his home. When Riemann transferred to Wiesbaden, Reger continued his music study for four years at its Conservatory.

His studies ended, Reger taught piano and organ in Wiesbaden in 1895–1896. In 1896, he had to enter military service, an experience that broke his health and kept him an invalid for a number of years. In 1901, he settled in Munich, where he married Elsa von Bagensky, and began to make headway as a concert pianist. In 1905–1906, he taught counterpoint at the Musical Academy in Munich and conducted a choral group. In 1907, he was made director of the Leipzig Conservatory and conductor of its chorus, and from 1907 until his death, he taught counterpoint there. He also conducted the Meiningen Orchestra between 1911 and 1915. All this while he was exceptionally prolific as a composer. In 1911, he was appointed Hofrat in the city of Jena, and in 1915, he was made the musical director of that city. The King of Saxony conferred on him the honorary title of Professor. During World War I, Reger tried to enlist in the German army but was turned down because of his poor health. He died of a heart attack in Leipzig on May 11, 1916.

1910 CONCERTO IN F MINOR, FOR PIANO AND ORCHESTRA, op. 114. I. Allegro moderato. II. Largo con gran espressione. III. Allegro con spirito.

Early in his career, Reger had worked on a piano concerto in F minor for Eugène d'Albert, which he revised four times, and then abandoned in 1897. His second attempt at writing a piano concerto (once again in the key of F minor) came in 1910, intended for the virtuoso Frieda Kwast-Hodapp. When he sent his manuscript to the pianist, it bore the following inscription: "This beastly stuff belongs to Frau Kwast. The Chief Pig, Max Reger, confirms it." Frau Kwast-Hodapp introduced the concerto in Leipzig on December 15, 1910, with Artur Nikisch conducting the Gewandhaus Orchestra. Apparently, the work met with favor, for Mme. Kwast-Hodapp played it about thirty times more. Then it went into discard. It had to wait a long time before getting a hearing in the United States. This took place in Minneapolis on November 16, 1945, with Rudolf Serkin soloist, and Dimitri Mitropoulos conducting. Serkin's interest in the concerto has helped to keep it alive both in Europe and the United States.

The concerto opens with an impressive twenty-three measure orchestral introduction. The wind instruments, over rolls of the tympani, are heard in the main theme. The piano enters with the powerful stride of unaccompanied octaves and chords. A lyric section (Molto tranquillo) follows. The second movement has romantic interest, the main melody being given to the unaccompanied piano. Romantic ardor gives way to a good humor and irresistible spirits in the finale, which is dominated by a tune in a dance rhythm and several subsidiary thoughts; these are treated in the development section in fugato style. A dramatic coda concludes the concerto.

1912 A ROMANTIC SUITE, for orchestra, op. 125. I. Notturno. II. Scherzo. III. Finale.

Poems by Joseph Freiherr von Eichendorff were the inspiration for the *Romantic Suite*. A quotation from *Nachtzauber* appears at the head of the first movement. It reads:

Hears't thou not the brooklets streaming
Where sweet spring her blossom strewed,
Where the woodland lakes are dreaming,
By the marble icons gleaming
In sweet nature's solitude?

This movement, a nocturne, begins (Molto sostenuto) with an important motive for two flutes. Muted divided first violins repeat it. Then an expansive passage introduces a new idea in the violins. Later on, the romantic spirit of the movement is heightened and intensified with a beautiful thought for the first violins on the G string. A climax is built up, then subsides. The movement ends quietly.

The second-movement scherzo is based on a poem entitled *Elfe*. It reads as follows: "Stay with us! The dancing place down in the valley is bedecked with shining moonbeams. Glow worms luminate the hall, and the crickets chirp dance tunes. Joy, that lovely child, is cradled in the evening breezes. Most beautiful is it where the silver flows on shrubs and bushes." In this movement (Vivace), a sprightly tune is presented by the woodwinds over tremolo violins. This is followed by a lyrical thought in clarinets and violas, and by a waltz-like melody in oboe, accompanied by harp and strings.

In the finale, the composer quotes two stanzas from the poem *Morgengruss*:

Rise, O Sun on high!
Trembling in the sky,
Earth quivering with ecstasy.
Boldly from the night
The wooded splendor bright
Is drawn in dreams still stirring.

This movement begins (Molto sostenuto) with the same subject that was heard at the beginning of the first movement. Nine measures later, a stately melody is played by cellos and English horn, followed without much delay by a subject begun by the horns and continued by the woodwind. An extensive working out of this material takes place, rising towards a powerful climax. Then comes a change of mood with a passage for three horns over string tremolos. Another climax is built up. The suite ends on a strong, sonorous note.

The first performance took place in Dresden, on October 11, 1912, von Schuch conducting.

1913 FOUR TONE POEMS AFTER BÖCKLIN, for orchestra, op. 128. I. Der geigende Eremit. II. Im Spiel der Wellen. III. Die Toteninsel. IV. Bacchanal.

Arnold Böcklin is the Swiss painter whose *Isle of the Dead* (*Die Toteninsel*) was the source of inspiration for Rachmaninoff's famous tone poem of the same name, written in 1907. Reger, too, set that painting to music, in the third section of the *Four Tone Poems*; the other three sections also owe their origin to famous Böcklin paintings.

The first, "The Hermit with a Violin," shows an old bearded friar playing on a violin for the Madonna; angels listen to him appreciatively. To give his music an ecclesiastical character (Molto sostenuto, doch nie schleppend), Reger uses the Phrygian mode. The music of the friar is played by a solo violin.

The second of Böcklin's paintings, "Sport among the Waves," shows Bacchic figures sporting in the waters. This music (Vivace) is a delicate, lively scherzo. A vigorous theme for horn describes the male figures; a gentle subject for strings speaks for the females.

"The Isle of the Dead," the third Böcklin painting, has been described in the section of Rachmaninoff which discusses the tone poem of that name (1907). Reger re-creates the mystery and desolation of the painting in a brief but highly atmospheric piece of music (Molto sostenuto).

The concluding painting, "The Bacchanal," is laid outside a Roman tavern, where carousing and noisy merrymakers are involved in a tavern brawl. The music (Vivace) is high-tensioned and nervous, full of contrasts, climaxes, abrupt changes of tempi, in reproducing a febrile atmosphere.

On October 12, 1913, Reger directed the première performance in Essen.

1914 VARIATIONS AND FUGUE ON A THEME BY MOZART, for orchestra, op. 132.

The theme that Reger developed in this pretentious set of variations is the subject which opens Mozart's Piano Sonata in A major, K. 331, and which in the original setting is also subjected to variation treatment.

In Reger's work there are nine variations. The Mozart theme (Andante grazioso) is presented in two stages. The first is played by oboe and two clarinets, and repeated by the strings; the second, by oboe and clarinet, supported by violins and violas, and repeated by strings. In the first variation (L'Istesso tempo), there are decorative passages in the strings around the theme, which is stated by the oboe. The rhythmic character of the theme is carried over in the second variation (Poco agitato); while in the third (Con moto), a fragment of the theme, played by clarinets and bassoons, is elaborated upon. The fourth variation (Vivace) is turned over to horns, bassoons and clarinets. Woodwinds and strings present the idea in the fifth variation (Quasi presto), before it is developed. The principal melody returns in the strings in the variation that follows (Sostenuto), but in a different meter. The original rhythm of the theme reappears in the seventh variation (Andante grazioso), with the theme itself stated in the horns. After the eighth variation (Molto sostenuto), there comes a culminating fugue (Allegretto grazioso), in which the theme is presented by first violins and answered by second violins. The fugue is developed with great power, and a climax is reached with the principal melody proclaimed by the trumpets.

On February 5, 1915, Reger directed the première performance with the Berlin Royal Opera Orchestra.

1915 VARIATIONS AND FUGUE ON A THEME BY BEETHOVEN, for orchestra (also for two pianos), op. 86.

Reger originally wrote these variations as a two-piano composition. This was in 1904. Eleven years after that, he orchestrated it, omitting four of the variations; this is the version in which the music is today heard most often. The theme comes out of Beethoven's *Eleven New Bagatelles*, for piano, op. 119. The subject is heard first in strings alone, then in strings, woodwind and horns (Andante ma non troppo). The eight ensuing variations create a new personality for the simple tune, through Reger's extraordinary skill at polyphony and thematic transformation; each of the eight variations is in a different key, only two of them (the sixth and eighth) in the key of B-flat major, the tonality of Beethoven's theme. The tempo markings for the variations are as follows: Un poco pìu lento; Appassionato; Andantino grazioso; Vivace; Andante sostenuto; Allegretto con grazia; Poco vicace; Allegro pomposo. The eighth variation is a fugue, whose subject is not the Beethoven theme but rather one of Reger's own invention. This subject is heard in the first violins. At a climactic point, Reger's theme (in strings and woodwind) is combined contrapuntally with that of Beethoven.

OTTORINO RESPIGHI 1879–1936

Ottorino Respighi identified himself with the distant musical past. He made modern transcriptions and adaptations of old Italian music and pieces by the Baroque masters (*Old Airs and Dances for the Lute*, for example, and *The Birds*). In his own compositions, he sometimes utilized old modes and plain chants, as in the *Concerto gregoriano,* for violin and orchestra (first performance in Rome on February 5, 1922) and the *Concerto in the Mixolydian Mode*, for piano and orchestra (introduced in New York on December 31, 1925).

But if Respighi's name survives in twentieth-century music, it is not for his neo-modal music, nor even for any of his operas. His fame today rests securely on the trilogy of tone poems in which he interpreted three different facets of Rome: its fountains, pines and festivals. Here he is the modern composer who knows how to utilize contemporary idioms forcefully. Here he is the remarkable tone painter of pictorial images. Here he is the orchestrator with exceptional virtuosity. His idiom, in this trilogy of orchestral pieces, is, as Henri Prunières once noted "an able compromise between the counterpoint of Strauss, the harmony of Debussy and the orchestration of Rimsky-Korsakov —and the whole tinted with a little Italian melody."

It is through his tone poems for orchestra that Respighi earned the reputation of being one of Italy's most significant symphonic composers of the twentieth century. These successful works were responsible for encouraging Italian composers to return to cultivate the symphonic field (neglected for so many years for the sake of opera), and thus help bring about something of a symphonic renascence in Italy.

Respighi was born in Bologna, Italy, on July 9, 1879. His musical studies took place at the Liceo Musicale with Sarti and Martucci; and later on, with Rimsky-Korsakov in St. Petersburg. While still a student at the Bologna Liceo, he wrote a set of symphonic variations which was performed. But it was as a violinist and violist that Respighi began his professional career in music, by performing with the Mugellini String Quartet between 1903 and 1908. Drawn more and more to composition, he completed a comic opera, *Re Enzo*, produced in Bologna on March 12, 1905; a *Notturno*, for orchestra, introduced in New York City on January 6, 1905; and a lyric tragedy, *Semiràma*, influenced by Strauss's *Salome,* mounted in Bologna on November 20, 1910. In 1913, he was appointed professor of composition at the Santa Cecilia Academy in Rome. In 1919, he married Elsa Oliveri-Sangiacomo, a gifted singer and composer, and one of his pupils.

Between 1917 and 1924, he achieved international renown with his two symphonic poems, *The Fountains of Rome* and *The Pines of Rome*. In 1923, he was elevated to the post of director of Santa Cecilia, but occupied it only two years. He resigned to devote himself more completely to composition, to tour the world in performances of his works, and to teach composition to a select few at the Santa Cecilia. Respighi made his first tour of the United States in 1925–1926, his American debut taking place with the New York Philharmonic under Willem Mengelberg, on December 31, 1925, when he was heard in the world première of his Piano Concerto. He returned to the United States to attend the American première of his opera, *La Campana sommersa,* or *The Sunken Bell* (Metropolitan Opera, November 24, 1928), and the world première of his "mystery," *Maria Egiziaca* (New York, March 16, 1932, Toscanini conducting the New York Philharmonic). In 1932, Respighi was appointed to the Royal Academy of Italy. He died of a heart attack in Rome on April 18, 1936. His wife completed his last opera, *Lucrezia,* which was produced at La Scala on February 24, 1937.

1917 FOUNTAINS OF ROME (FONTANE DI ROMA), tone poem for orchestra. I. The Fountain Valle Giulia at Dawn. II. The Triton Fountain in the Morning. III. The Fountain of Trevi at Midday. IV. The Villa Medici Fountain at Sunset.

Though the *Fountains of Rome* is in four distinct sections, it is played without interruption; it is consequently to be regarded as an integrated symphonic poem in the manner of Richard Strauss.

In the published score, the composer explained that his purpose in writing this work was "to give expression to the sentiments and visions suggested . . . by four of Rome's fountains, contemplated at the hour in which their character is most in harmony with the surrounding landscape, or in which their beauty appears most impressive to the observer."

The composer also provides the program he was trying to interpret in his music: "The first part of the poem, inspired by the Fountain of Valle Giulia, depicts a pastoral landscape. Droves of cattle pass and disappear in the fresh, damp mists of a Roman dawn. A sudden loud and insistent blast above the trills of the whole orchestra introduces the second part. It is like a joyous call, summoning troops of naiads and tritons, who come running up pursuing each other and mingling in a frenzied dance between the jets of water.

"Next there appears a solemn theme, borne on the undulations of the orchestra. It is the Fountain of Trevi at midday. The solemn theme, passing from the wood to the brass instruments, assumes a triumphal character. Trumpets peal; across the radiant surface of the water there passes Neptune's chariot, drawn by sea-horses and followed by a train of sirens and tritons. The procession then vanishes, while faint trumpet blasts sound in the distance.

"The fourth part is announced by a sad theme which rises above a subdued warbling. It is the nostalgic hour of sunset. The air is full of the sound of tolling bells, birds twittering, leaves rustling. Then all dies peacefully into the silence of the night."

In the first section (Andante mosso), the pastoral mood is evoked by oboe, clarinet, French and English horns, while the morning is heralded by horn, oboe and bassoon. Following an acceleration of tempo, a haunting melody is presented by oboe and is repeated by clarinet. The second section (Vivo) opens with a horn call, to which the orchestra gives response. Flutes, clarinets and harp present the dance of naiads and tritons. A jubilant mood is created, but this part ends faintly with soft staccato notes of the trumpet. In the third part (Allegro moderato), a solemn melody is heard in woodwinds and horns as a preface to a vigorous section in which the brasses announce the passing of Neptune's chariot. The pageant is brilliantly described, then it disappears into the distance, as the sounds of undulating strings and horn-calls recede. The Finale (Andante) opens with a poignant subject for flute and English horn. Next we hear the violins in an expressive theme to harp glissandi, and a haunting thought for flute. The opening sad tune returns in violins and is faintly repeated by the flute. The music ebbs away gently.

The world première of *Fountains of Rome* took place in Rome on March 11, 1917.

1921 CONCERTO GREGORIANO FOR VIOLIN AND ORCHESTRA. I. Andante tranquillo; Allegro molto moderato. II. Andante espressivo e sostenuto. III. Allegro energico.

This violin concerto was introduced in Rome on February 5, 1922, with Mario Corti as soloist with the Augusteo Orchestra. When the concerto was heard in Paris a few years later, an anonymous program annotator provided the following information about the work: "The title . . . was given to this work by the composer not only because the music was inspired by the Gregorian chant, but also because he sought to imbue his music with the purity and sobriety of form peculiar to the religious music of the Middle Ages. It will perhaps at first seem strange that the composer chose the form of the violin concerto as a medium wherewith to transport his listeners into the atmosphere of the church music of the Middle Ages—music so remote from all the complexities and the virtuosity of musical form in the last two centuries; a form predominantly instrumental. But, on closer examination of this score, one perceives that the work has few of the traits which usually characterize the instrumental concerto. The connection between the solo instrument and the orchestra has in this case quite a different significance: the solo violin plays, so to speak, the role of cantor in the old religious service, while the orchestra represents the choir of believers."

A few bars of ecclesiastical music usher in the first theme, a tranquil melody for oboe, which is soon taken up by the solo instrument. After the tempo changes to Allegro molto moderato, the solo violin introduces a new theme, more virile in character. A cadenza for the violin leads into the second movement, the principal theme of which (announced by solo violin against muted strings) is recognizably Gregorian. A second important idea, also of medieval character, is stated by the oboe. The music grows impassioned, but the emotions soon subside and the movement ends gently with a brief recollection of the opening subject.

The composer designated his concluding movement an "Allelujah." It is, indeed, joyous, exultant music, the emotional climate for which is set by the opening powerful theme for four horns in unison.

1924 CONCERTO FOR PIANO AND ORCHESTRA (in the Mixolydian mode). I. Moderato. II. Lento. III. Allegro energico.

The Mixolydian is the seventh of the ecclesiastical modes. Respighi himself introduced his concerto at a concert of the New York Philharmonic Orchestra on December 31, 1925, Willem Mengelberg conducting. The theme of the first movement is derived from a Gregorian chant, *Omnes gentes plaudite manibus*. The second movement has the pervading atmosphere of medieval mysticism. The third movement—a passacaglia—follows without interruption.

1924 PINES OF ROME (PINI DI ROMA), tone poem for orchestra. I. The Pines of Villa Borghese. II. The Pines Near a Catacomb. III. The Pines of the Janiculum. IV. The Pines of Appian Way.

Like its celebrated predecessor, *The Fountains of Rome,* this tone poem is in four sections, but the entire work is played without a break. In the earlier tone poem, the composer sought to present a series of nature portraits. In *Pines of Rome,* nature is used as the stimulus to arouse memories and reveries in the composer.

The published score contains the following programmatic information, provided by the composer:

"I. 'The Pines of the Villa Borghese.' Children are at play in the pine grove of the Villa Borghese, dancing the Italian equivalent of Ring-around-the-rosy, mimicking marching soldiers and battles, twittering and shrieking like swallows at evening, and they disappear. Suddenly the scene changes to—

"II. 'The Pines Near a Catacomb.' We see the shadows of the pines which overhang the entrance of the catacomb. From the depths rises a chant which re-echoes solemnly, sonorously, like a hymn, and is then mysteriously silenced.

"III. 'The Pines of the Janiculum.' There is a thrill in the air. The full moon reveals the profile of the pines of Gianicolo's Hill. A nightingale sings (represented by a phonograph record of a nightingale's song, heard from the orchestra).

"IV. 'The Pines of the Appian Way.' Misty dawn on the Appian Way. The tragic country is guarded by solitary pines. Indistinctly, incessantly, the rhythm of innumerable steps. To the poet's fantasy appears a vision of past glories; trumpets blare and the army of the consul advances brilliantly in the grandeur of the newly risen sun toward the sacred way, mounting in triumph the Capitoline Hill."

In the first part (Allegretto vivace), the games of the children are described in brief motives for brass and woodwind. The hubbub is reproduced with piercing discords. A change of mood takes place in the second part (Lento) in which a serene scene is painted by muted and divided strings and a religious hymn is chanted by the orchestra. In the third part (Lento), an evening scene is suggested by a clarinet solo. Into the mysterious night pierces the song of a nightingale, reproduced through a phonograph recording; the sound of the recording is placed over tremolo strings. (This is probably the first instance in which a recording was used in an orchestral composition.) The fourth part (Tempo di marcia) presents a vigorous march tune built up powerfully into a thunderous climax.

The first performance took place in Rome on December 14, 1924; Bernardino Molinari conducted the Augusteo Orchestra.

1926 CHURCH WINDOWS (VETRATE DI CHIESA), four impressions for orchestra. I. The Flight into Egypt. II. The Archangel Michael. III. The Matin of Saint Chiara (St. Claire). IV. St. Gregory the Great.

The world première of *Church Windows* took place in Boston with Serge Koussevitzky conducting the Boston Symphony on February 25, 1927. This is a set of four orchestral preludes, or impressions, inspired by examples of stained-glass windows in various Italian churches. The composer himself gave a succinct résumé of the program for each of the sections.

The first is a "tonal representation of the little caravan on a starry night carrying the Treasure of the World." This is an evocative nocturne built from a theme resembling a Gregorian chant.

In the second, "Michael, with flaming sword in hand, drives from heaven the rebellious angels." The main subject is heard in the low orchestral register over an organ pedal point. In a contrasting middle section, the trumpet is heard in a variation of the opening theme.

The third is a picture of how St. Claire "being gravely sick and lamenting that she could not attend the Matin at church, was transported miraculously so that she could take part in the service." Here the music has an elegiac quality into which the bright tones of a celesta seem to bring solace.

The concluding impression is the blessing of the throng by St. Gregory the Great, "clothed in pontifical vestments. . . . He is represented in all his splendor at ceremonial services of the Church." Tolling bells precede a chorale melody taken from the Gregorian Mass of the Angels. A crescendo is enriched by the tones of the organ. Organ and orchestra then join to describe the splendors of a church ceremony.

1927 TRITTICO BOTTICELLIANO (A BOTTICELLI TRIPTYCH), for small orchestra. I. Spring. II. Adoration of the Kings. III. The Birth of Venus.

GLI UCCELLI (THE BIRDS), suite for small orchestra. I. Prelude. II. The Dove. III. The Hen. IV. The Nightingale. V. The Cuckoo.

IMPRESSIONI BRASILIANE (IMPRESSIONS OF BRAZIL), suite for orchestra. I. Notte tropicale. II. Butantan. III. Canzone e Danze.

In his *Botticelli Triptych*, Respighi presents tonal descriptions of three paintings of the distinguished Renaissance artist. A pastoral mood prevails in the first section, inspired by Botticelli's *La Primavera*. Sounds of nature are imitated, and snatches of Italian pastoral tunes are introduced to describe the dancing of nymphs. The second movement uses ecclesiastical modes to provide the proper religious mood for Botticelli's *L'Adorazione dei Magi*. In the third part, stimulated by Botticelli's *La Nascita di Venere,* undulating figures in the orchestra suggest the flow of the water as Venus is brought into view upon her vessel of sea shells. A sensuous melody speaks for Venus, and the undulating figures at the end of the section recall the flow of the waters as they carry Venus out of view. The *Triptych* was commissioned by the Elizabeth Sprague Coolidge Foundation and was introduced in Vienna in September of 1927.

In *The Birds,* Respighi freely adapts for orchestra music of four seventeenth and eighteenth century composers. The Prelude (Allegro moderato) is built from two themes by Bernardo Pasquini, the first heard in the flute, oboe and clarinets, and the other introduced by the oboe and continued by the other woodwinds. "The Dove" (Andante espressivo) is based on a melody by Jacques de Gallot, a subject heard in oboe, accompanied by harp and muted strings. "The Hen" is based on the popular piece, "*La Poule,*" by Rameau. The clucking of the bird is realistically reproduced by the violins. "The Nightingale" (Andante mosso) uses the melody of an anonymous English composer, heard in the woodwinds over a string accompaniment. In this section, Respighi parodies the "Forest Music" from Wagner's music drama *Siegfried,* in an accompanying passage. "The Cuckoo" (Allegro) is derived from a celebrated *Toccata on the Song of the Cuckoo* by Pasquini. At the conclusion of this section, the opening theme of the Prelude is sonorously recalled.

The Birds was introduced in São Paulo, Brazil, in 1927, the composer conducting. The music was used for a ballet mounted in San Remo, Italy, on February 19, 1933.

Respighi wrote his *Impressioni Brasiliane* for his Brazilian tour. He directed its world première in Rio de Janeiro in January of 1928. He planned a five-movement suite based entirely on Brazilian popular and folk melodies, but completed only three sections. In the first, Respighi offers an atmospheric picture of a tropical night (which had made a deep impression upon him during a trip between Tijuca and Rio de Janeiro). A serene mood is also found in the second part, which is a portrait of the city of Butantan, just outside São Paulo. A sinuous theme suggests the movements of a snake, because poisonous snakes were raised at a reptile institute in Butantan. The idea of poisonous snakes apparently brought up in the composer a feeling of horror, for this section quotes the *Dies Irae*. The third part is made up of a lush Brazilian song and a syncopated dance. Sensuality is heightened through the effective use of harp, celesta glissandi, and muted horns in the orchestration.

1928 ROMAN FESTIVALS (FESTE ROMANE), tone poem for orchestra. I. The Circus Maximus. II. The Jubilee. III. The October Excursions. IV. The Eve of the Epiphany in Piazza Navona.

The third work in the symphonic trilogy about Rome is devoted to Roman festivals. On February 21, 1929, it was introduced in New York with Toscanini conducting the New York Philharmonic Orchestra.

As in the cases of the two earlier symphonic poems, the composer himself prepared the programmatic text for *Roman Festivals*.

"I. 'The Circus Maximus.' A threatening sky over the Circus Maximus, but the people are celebrating: Hail Nero! The iron gates open, and the air is filled with a religious chant and the roaring of savage beasts. The mob undulates and rages: serenely, the song of the martyrs spreads, dominates, and finally is drowned in the tumult.

"II. 'The Jubilee.' Weary, in pain, the pilgrims drag themselves through the long streets, praying. At last, from the summit of Mount Mario, is seen the holy city: Rome! Rome! And the hymn of jubilation is answered by the clangor of multitudinous church bells.

"III. 'The October Excursions.' Fetes of October, in the castles engarlanded with vine-leaves—echoes of the hunt—tinklings of horse-bells—songs of love. Then, in the balmy evening, the sound of a romantic serenade.

"IV. 'The Eve of Epiphany in Piazza Navona.' A characteristic rhythm of bugles dominates the frantic clamor: on the tide of noise float now and again rustic songs, the lilt of saltarellos, the sounds of the mechanical organ in some booth, the call of the showman, hoarse and drunken cries, and the stornello in which the spirit of the populace finds expression: 'Let us pass, we are Romans.'"

1928 TOCCATA, for piano and orchestra. I. Prelude. II. Adagio. III. Allegro.

In this neo-classic work, Respighi adopted the toccata form of Frescobaldi, filling it (as he himself put it) "with the modern spirit, and modernized through the character of the harmonies." It is in three sections played without pause.

The composer provided the following analysis:

"The prelude is based on a principal theme which is followed by a number of small episodic ideas of rhythmic character, and in the form of a cadenza-recitative. The Adagio consists of a melodic idea which is developed at great length in a sustained dialogue between piano and orchestra. The final movement begins with a brilliant theme which is amplified through manifold rhythmic transformations, interrupted by a brief episode of scherzo character."

SILVESTRE REVUELTAS 1899–1940

The music of Revueltas is thoroughly, unmistakably Mexican, but his approach to musical nationalism is far different from that of his celebrated countryman, Carlos Chávez. Chávez found Mexico in his country's past and culture, while Revueltas found it in himself and in his everyday surroundings. Revueltas never went searching for old songs and dances in distant regions of Mexico. ("Why should I put on boots and climb mountains for Mexican folklore, if I have the spirit of Mexico deep within me?") He did not try to reproduce Mexico's dance rhythms and folk tunes within large sophisticated structures; and except for the percussion, he did not use Mexican instruments. What he did do was to simulate the melodic contours, rhythms, sonorities and spirit of Mexican popular music in his compositions. Nor did he ever seek into ancient Mexico for subject matter. It is Mexico itself—the Mexico that so fascinates the visitor—that we confront in the music of Revueltas: its exotic streets, byways, alleys; its marketplaces; its games and customs; its dives and resort towns; its people. His music evokes vivid sketches and mood pictures of Mexico, but only through the impress that the country had made on his own sensibilities.

His style is primitive, given to brusque rhythms, sharp contrasts in meter and sonority, vivid colorations in the orchestration. As for the last of these, the orchestration, it often derives its effects from imitating popular Mexican dance bands. Formal harmonic procedures and a concern for form or symphonic development did not overly concern him. But his style is powerful and imaginative, and his best music has dynamic impact. It is a Mexican art, even though it is a Mexican art which in character, spirit and purpose is a world apart from that of Chávez.

Revueltas was born in Santiago Papasquiaro, in the state of Durango, Mexico, on December 31, 1899. He began studying the violin when he was eight, and from 1913 to 1916, he attended the National Conservatory of Mexico City. Between 1916 and 1918, he attended the Saint Edward College in Austin, Texas; and from 1918 to 1920, he was a pupil of Felix Borowski and Samatini at the Chicago Musical College. For about two years after his studies had ended, he conducted theatre orchestras in Texas and Alabama. Then he became Chávez's assistant conductor with the then-newly organized Orquesta Sinfónico in Mexico City. He remained with that organization until 1935. Meanwhile, in 1933, he was made a member of the faculty of the National Conservatory in Mexico City, whose orchestra he conducted. In 1935, he founded an orchestra of his own, but it did not survive.

Encouraged by Chávez, Revueltas turned to serious composition in 1931. His first success came with *Esquinas,* or *Street Corners,* whose première he conducted on November 20, 1931. A number of orchestral compositions followed, all pointing up his great individuality and his personal approach to Mexican nationalism in music. In 1937, he went to Spain to join the Loyalist cause in the revolution, and to work in its Music Section. At a concert meeting of the Committee against War and Fascism in Barcelona, on October 7, 1937, he led the world première of his orchestral suite *Redes.* After his return to Mexico, he was victimized by an attack of pneumonia which proved fatal. He died in Mexico City on October 5, 1940, a few hours after the world première of his ballet *El Renacuajo Paseador* in that city.

1932 CUAUHNAHUAC, tone poem for orchestra.

This was Revueltas's first composition to gain recognition outside Mexico. Its première took place in Mexico City on June 2, 1933, in Mexico City, the composer conducting the Orquesta Sinfónico. "Cuauhnahuac" is the ancient Indian name for the Mexican resort town of Cuernavaca. "This is music without tourism," the composer has explained. "In the orchestra, the huehuetl (Indian drum) is used as a means of nationalist propaganda. Other instruments in the score are even more nationalistic." These other instruments also belong to the percussion family.

A writer for *Musical America* has written that in this work Revueltas makes brilliant use of a "*corrido* type of melody intoned by flutes and trumpets which gracefully oscillates between the tonic and dominant." He also says: "This work shows another factor of transcendental importance in Revueltas's style: the superimposing of different harmonic levels, as in the passage where the cellos play a motif in G major and the rest of the voices are definitely in the realm of E-flat."

1934 CAMINOS, tone picture for orchestra.

Caminos is a musical description of picturesque Mexican streets, those "rather tortuous byways," wrote the composer, "probably unpassed, over which limousines won't venture; short enough so that one doesn't feel their roughness, and gay enough so that one forgets it." It is a gay piece of music, full of verve and excitement. The principal theme (first heard in the oboe) is imitative of a Mexican folk tune.

On July 17, 1934, Carlos Chávez introduced *Caminos* with the Orquesta Sinfónica of Mexico City.

1937 SENSEMAYÁ, tone poem for orchestra.

Sensemayá ("Chant to Kill a Snake") is a poem by Nicolas Guillen, an Afro-Cuban poet. The opening lines are as follows:

Mayombe—bombe—Mayombe!

Mayombe—bombe—Mayombe! . . .
The snake has glossy eyes
The snake comes and coils itself around a tree
With its glossy eyes around a tree
With its glossy eyes around a tree.

"*Sensemayá,*" wrote Revueltas's sister, "is simply a fanciful, whimsical name; it has no interpretation and no sense. The poet used it solely as an idiomatic rhythm in his poem . . . and this poem inspired Revueltas to compose his tone poem of the same name."

In its original form, as written in 1937, *Sensemayá* was scored for voice and small orchestra. One year later, Revueltas rescored it for large orchestra without voice. It carries over the rhythmic pulse of the poem in strong accents, and in its primitiveness, this music is suggestive of a pagan rite. The rhythmic pattern which opens the work persists throughout. The basic theme is heard in tuba; then is taken over by muted solo trumpet; and after that, is passed on to other instruments. Cross rhythms, syncopations, changing meters all help to create tension and build up a powerful climax.

WALLINGFORD RIEGGER 1885–1961

As an apprentice composer, Riegger was partial to impressionism. But beginning with his *Rhapsody for Orchestra,* op. 5 (1925), he began to write in an atonal style. He said: "I felt the need to express musical ideas for which the older techniques were inadequate. I found the new atonal idiom, with its fresh possibilities in sonority and rhythm, creatively stimulating, and more expressive of the feelings I wished to convey in music." From atonality, the path led to the twelve-tone technique, which Riegger used for the first time, though only in part, in *Dichotomy,* for string orchestra, op. 12 (1932). His first composition in a rigid and consistent twelve-tone technique was his second string quartet, op. 30 (1940).

The fact that Riegger was one of the first American composers to become interested in atonality and the twelve-tone system left on him the permanent brand of *enfant terrible*. Actually, he wrote a good deal of music in other, more easily assimilable, styles and idioms: music with interest in vital rhythmic procedures, in rich sonorities, even in moving lyricism. The truth was that Riegger refused to be shackled to any one style or system. He had muscular vigor, dynamic power; he could be brusque, and discordant. He could also give way to romantic feeling, indulge in appealing wit and whimsy, and express himself with the utmost directness. Herbert Elwell put it well when he said: "There is no false emotionalism in Riegger, no academic padding, no pompous and untested certitudes that drive blindly toward vague conclusions. . . . Riegger is . . . an advanced and highly independent musical thinker, who speaks his piece with terse, uncompromising language that says exactly what it means and stops at the right place when it has no more to say."

Riegger was born in Albany, Georgia, on April 29, 1885. His music study took place mainly at the Institute of Musical Art in New York, where, in 1907, he became a member of its first graduating class; also in Europe, where he studied the cello with Robert Hausmann and Anton Hekking, and composition with Edgar Stillman Kelley. After marrying Rose Schramm in New York in 1910, Riegger played the cello for three years with the St. Paul Symphony. For a number of years after that, he conducted opera and symphony in Europe. Returning to the United States in 1917, he was made head of the departments of theory and cello at Drake University.

As a composer, he began attracting interest in the early 1920s by winning the Paderewski Prize in 1922 for his Piano Trio in B minor, op. 1 (1919), receiving honorable mention for his *American Polonaise,* op. 3, in a competition conducted by the Lewisohn Stadium Concerts in 1923, and by getting, in 1924, the Elizabeth Sprague Coolidge award for *La Belle Dame sans merci,* op. 4, the first American composition to gain this distinction. While serving as head of the cello and theory departments at Ithaca Conservatory, Riegger wrote the *Study in Sonority,* for strings, in which he developed his atonal style. In 1928, he left Ithaca to settle permanently in New York City. There he later held teaching posts at the Institute of Musical Art, Teachers College of Columbia University, and the Metropolitan Music School. During the 1930s, he devoted himself successfully to the writing of music for ballets performed by Martha Graham, Doris Humphrey, and Charles Weidman, among others. He received the New York Music Critics Circle Award for his third symphony in 1948. His seventieth birthday in 1960 was celebrated with programs of his works in Kansas City and New York and with representation of major compositions on various orchestral programs throughout the United States. In 1961, he received the Brandeis Creative Arts Award from Brandeis University. He died in New York City on April 2, 1961.

1927 STUDY IN SONORITY, for ten violins, op. 7.

This atonal exercise in violin sonority was written for ten violins, each violin having a different part. Necessity was the mother of this invention. When he wrote it, Riegger was a member of the faculty of Ithaca Conservatory where he led the school orchestra. During the summer, the orchestral forces became sadly depleted, with only the violins remaining. The necessity of getting some music for this ensemble to play led Riegger to write a piece for ten violins, which he originally called *Caprice.* "While the work has no hint of twelve-tone writing," the composer explained, "it is nevertheless completely atonal in the sense of being devoid of diatonic implications. Structurally speaking, after a rather free and capricious beginning, the initial motive, of slow, poignant character, becomes transformed into an incisive fugue-like theme. The plan of the work thereafter consists of building up of various backgrounds, against which this theme is from time to time projected. Interspersed are episodes, in which appear different rhythmic and harmonic patterns with interwoven counterpoint. The chords are generally composed of from eight to twelve different tones, and the compass of the violin is extended by tuning the G string down to E."

The *Study* received its first public performance at the hands of the Philadelphia Orchestra under Leopold Stokowski on October 30, 1929. On that occasion forty violins were used.

1941 CANON AND FUGUE, for orchestra, op. 33.

One day, in 1941, Riegger found a manuscript of a canon he had written during his student days. He was impressed with it and decided to use it in a new orchestral composition to which he would add a fugue "to give needed contrast and dimension," as he later explained. He wrote the work originally for strings, but in 1943, adapted it for large orchestra. The composer explained that the canon was "of stately character. The theme, or leader, begins in the horn, which is imitated below by the violas, always a measure later. An independent bass pizzicato gives weight and solemnity. After a close in major, the woodwinds begin a sprightly fugue, derived thematically from the canon. Gradually, the whole orchestra becomes involved, exploiting a large number of polyphonic devices, and eventually leading back to the canon, repeated in its entirety and culminating in a climactic close."

The *Canon and Fugue,* for strings, received its première at a festival of contemporary music at Berkeley, California, on August 1, 1942. The large orchestral version has been performed extensively—in Paris, Brussels, Moscow, Mexico City, Santiago, and Gothenburg, as well as in New York and at the Yaddo Festival at Saratoga Springs.

1947 SYMPHONY NO. 3, op. 42. I. Moderato. II. Andante affettuoso. III. Moderato; Allegro. IV. Passacaglia and Fugue.

If there is any single composition with which Riegger won wide acceptance with audiences and critics, it is with his Third Symphony. He wrote it on a commission from the Alice M. Ditson Fund, and its world première took place at the fourth annual festival of Contemporary American Music at Columbia University in New York on May 16, 1948. At that time, it received the New York Music Critics Circle Award as the best new orchestral work of the season; also the Naumburg Award, which brought with it a Columbia recording by the Eastman-Rochester Orchestra under Howard Hanson.

The following analysis of the symphony is by the composer:

"After a two-measure introduction, the arbitrarily arranged twelve tones of the chromatic scale are announced in a lyrical manner by the oboe . . . which is followed by the other woodwinds. The series is then taken up softly by the violins in a sixteenth-note continuous pattern, which serves as a background. After the brass has asserted itself rather positively and at some length, there is a simmering down to prepare for the subordinate theme, consisting of soaring chord blocks in the upper register of the violins. The movement is cast in a sort of truncated sonata form, as the second theme does not appear in the reprise. Its place is taken by a fugue-like treatment of the first seven notes of the series, which serves as a coda.

"The woodwind opening of the second movement is taken from *With My Red Fires,* a dance which I composed in 1936 for Doris Humphrey. Nothing has been changed for sixteen measures; then, instead of drum beats, the strings intercede to continue the mood. After various happenings, including a fortissimo restatement of the theme, there is a return to the beginning now played more intensively by the strings, followed by a subdued ending.

"The third movement is mostly scherzo-like in character in the course of which occurs another fugal section. In fact, all four movements contain fugal passages, the finale being a passacaglia and fugue. The passacaglia theme of five measures is characteristically announced in the basses, but is eventually taken up by other instruments, culminating in excited pizzicato passages (compressed statements of the theme) leading into the fugue. This is lively and energetic, with a hint of querulousness about it. Finally, the passacaglia theme reappears, this time in the violins, answered in the basses and leading into a sustained climax, with which the movement ends."

1957 SYMPHONY NO. 4, op. 63. I. Allegro moderato. II. Allegretto con moto; Allegro; Come prima. III. Sostenuto; Presto.

Riegger wrote his Fourth Symphony on a commission from the Fromm Music Foundation of Chicago for the Festival of Contemporary Arts at the University of Illinois. The world première took place at the University, in Urbana, on April 12, 1957. The symphony is dedicated to the memory of Riegger's wife, who died in 1957.

Klaus G. Roy provided the following illuminating program notes when the symphony was performed in Cleveland: "The first movement begins and ends on the tonality of B. One cannot call it major or minor; it is modal, and purposely fluid. The opening melody of the violas and cellos revolves around the tonic note in a sort of rocking motion, akin to that of Gregorian chant. What is yet more important than the tune itself is its entrance in the violins eight measures later, higher by an augmented fourth (or diminished fifth)—with F as its center. This interval, harmonically unsettled—built on sand, as it were—constitutes one of the basic ideas of the movement. We hear it recur in several of the themes and later spelled out in the sharp accents of the tympani. . . . Toward the close, the interval opens from that of the augmented fourth to that of the major seventh. Abruptly, as if questioning, the climax is broken off, and the shadow of the opening fragment is heard once more; it comes to rest on the tonic B."

In his second movement, Riegger used material he had written in 1936 for *Chronicle,* a ballet performed by Martha Graham; the dance described the suffering of the Spanish people during the civil war. This is the reason why this movement, midway, has a decidedly Spanish character; this is also the reason for the prevailing tragic mood of the movement as a whole.

"The music instantly offers us that equivocal interval of the augmented fourth once more," explains Klaus G. Roy. "The plaintive melody of the woodwinds, however—an eleven-tone row that is 'completed' by one note in the accompaniment—is answered by the major seventh interval of the plucked strings. . . . Important also is the rising scale of the strings, with its augmented intervals or whole-tone motion. A slow and ironic scherzando develops; the woodwinds play in sixths, but again over whole-tone patterns. . . . The Allegro which breaks in, the winds playing in thirds, has the air of a Spanish dance, a fandango perhaps; but its tone is one of forced gaiety, a bit hopeless in brevity. The opening motion soon recurs—with a kind of wry jocularity, a sadness in its smile.

"The Finale opens Sostenuto, with a serious and expansive melodic arch treated in free canon or imitation. The tempo quickens, and the same melodic outline is heard in compressed form from the flute; although the theme is not twelve-tone, it gives somewhat the feeling of it during its angular path. . . . The motion picks up further speed, and we find ourselves in a triple-time Presto, essentially a scherzo movement. . . . The general atmosphere is that of a satiric dance, with many intriguing juxtapositions of sonorities. . . . The distant intervals of the seventh and ninth are prominent also in a harmonic sense. This becomes more and more apparent as the arching theme begins to dominate in the scherzo-like movement, closing the music in a few slower and declamatory final measures. Revealingly, it is the dissonant or unresolved interval of the major seventh which rules the final chord, with F-sharp in the bass instruments and F-natural in the treble."

ALBERT ROUSSEL 1869–1937

As a young man, Roussel was attracted to the impressionist style of his provocative contemporary, Debussy; and as a former pupil of Vincent d'Indy, he tried to reconcile impressionism with classical structures. Roussel's earliest major works reveal the influence of both Debussy and d'Indy. This became evident in his first symphony, *Le Poème de la forêt,* op. 7 (1904–1906), a sensitive portrait of Nature, introduced in Brussels on March 22, 1908. But the influence was a passing phase. Next came his voyages as a sailor and as a tourist, which brought him into contact with the fascinating and exotic East. Highly impressionable, Roussel now turned to oriental subjects, and oriental musical materials, in his writing. In such a vein he completed a symphonic triptych for solo voices and chorus, *Évocations,* op. 15, heard in Paris on May 18, 1912, each of whose movements was a picture of a different facet of India. In such a vein, too, was his opera-ballet, *Pâdmâvati,* op. 18 (1914), mounted in Paris on June 1, 1923. Then he deserted exoticism and the East. With the Symphony No. 2 in B-flat major, op. 22—première in Paris on March 4, 1922—Roussel began exploring the possibilities of absolute music in modern idioms within a classical structure; and with the Suite in F major, for orchestra, he embraced neo-classicism.

Thus Roussel passed through various phases. His greatest and maturest works drew elements from each of these phases. His tendency toward a long, undulating melodic line and his interest in complex rhythms came from the oriental period. From his teacher, Vincent d'Indy, he acquired a healthy respect for classical structures as well as the occasional use of the cyclic form. Roussel used modern writing—be it polytonality or polyrhythm—when it served his artistic purpose; and he used it without abandoning the poetic language he had inherited from Debussy and d'Indy.

"His work is made in his own image," once wrote Georges Jean-Aubry, "which it reflects in all its aspects with the fidelity of a mirror, his love of an even life, his ardor continent but keen, his exquisite sense of the voluptuous, a thousand fine details without mannerism; and under this amiable delicacy a power gentle and firm, at times wistful. He reached self-realization slowly but with certainty, without restlessness or hesitation—also without ostentation, or the wish to draw upon the curiosity of anyone, applying himself solely to his art."

Roussel was born in Turcoing, France, on April 5, 1869. Planning a naval career, he was educated at the Stanislas College in Paris and at the Naval Academy at Brest. After that he served as an ensign, then as sub-lieutenant, on naval vessels ploughing the seven seas. The sea was a passion. But he had also been interested in music from childhood on, having begun piano lessons and having made tentative attempts at composition early. Recognizing the fact that he preferred music to the Navy, Roussel resigned his commission in 1894 and began studying music seriously in Paris, first with Eugène Gigout, then for nine years at the Schola Cantorum, where he came under the influence of Vincent d'Indy. Roussel's first work to get performed was *Two Madrigals,* for chorus, which received first prize in a competition sponsored by the Société des Compositeurs; the composer led the première performance in Paris on May 3, 1898. The year of 1898 also saw the appearance of his first publication, *Des Heures passent,* a suite for the piano. While still attending the Schola Cantorum, Roussel also completed several orchestral pieces, which were conducted in Paris by Alfred Cortot.

In 1908, Roussel was graduated from the Schola Cantorum, was married to Blanche Preisach, and met his first success as composer through the première of his first symphony, *Le Poème de la forêt.* In 1909–1910, he embarked on a sea voyage to the East with his wife. This was an experience that during the next few years led to the writing of compositions on oriental subjects. But his first major success did not come with any of these works but with a ballet inspired by Fabre's *Studies of Insect Life—Le Festin de l'araignée* in 1913.

Roussel filled the post of professor of counterpoint at the Schola Cantorum between 1902 and 1914. During World War I, he served for a while as transport officer in the artillery, seeing action at Verdun. His poor health brought about his separation from the service early in 1918. After the war, and until the end of his life, Roussel divided his year between his home in Paris and a villa in Vasterival, on the Normandy coast, where he spent his summers.

Roussel paid his only visit to the United States in 1930, on an invitation from Mrs. Elizabeth Sprague Coolidge to hear his Trio, op. 40—for flute, viola and cello (1929)—performed at a festival in Chicago. He also attended the world première of his Third Symphony in Boston.

His high station in French music was recognized in 1931, when he was given an honorary membership to the Santa Cecilia Academy in Rome; and in 1933, when the German city of Hamburg presented him with the Brahms Centennial Medal. Roussel was president of the music section of the Paris International Exhibition and a member of the French committee of the International Society for Contemporary Music. His last completed work was the String Trio, op. 58 (1937); its première was given posthumously at an all-Roussel concert in Paris on April 4, 1938. Roussel died in Royan on August 23, 1937.

1912 LE FESTIN DE L'ARAIGNÉE (THE SPIDER'S FEAST), op. 17, ballet-pantomime in one act, with scenario by Count Gilbert de Voisins based on Fabre's *Studies of Insect Life,* and choreography by Leo Staats. First performance: Théâtre des Arts, Paris, April 3, 1913.

LE FESTIN DE L'ARAIGNÉE, suite for orchestra. I. Prelude. II. Entrance of the Ants. III. Dance of the Butterfly. IV. Hatching of the Ephemera; Dance of the Ephemera. V. Funeral March of the Ephemera.

The ballet scenario is set in a garden dominated by a spider. First the spider lures a butterfly into its web, then celebrates his victory with a dance. Two mantises are the spider's victims. An ephemera, or mayfly, bursts out of its chrysalis to perform a dance of its own before expiring. The spider now begins to prepare a feast, but is destroyed by one of the mantises. The insects perform the funeral rites for the dead ephemera and move out of sight. Night falls. The garden is deserted.

The plot is allegorical, as Robert Bernard noted when he wrote that the ballet is "a bitingly ironical portrayal of the appetites, the passions and the destructive folly of mankind, to which is opposed the carefree happiness of the poet, who runs to meet his ineluctible destiny without time for reflection."

Basil Deane points to the simplicity of means with which Roussel achieves each of his effects in a remarkable score. "For example, the entry of the ants is accompanied by a miniature march on the horns and woodwinds, combined with a quick ostinato figure, high on the violins. Nothing could more aptly illustrate the organization and bustling energy of these tiny insects." In the same way, the mourning rites of the insects is expressed by "short, drooping melodic phrases, monotonous rhythms, repetitive Phrygian harmonies, and the somber color of low strings and English horn." And the "slow and painful emergence of the ephemera" is depicted in "vague harmonies and fragmentary orchestration" just as the "joyous confidence of its brief maturity is conveyed by a tuneful and diatonic waltz."

Though the ballet is little known in the United States, much of its music is famous by virtue of a symphonic suite which Roussel prepared from the score and which has since become one of his most celebrated works. The suite was heard for the first time in New York City on October 23, 1914, with Walter Damrosch conducting the New York Symphony Society.

The Prelude describes a garden on a summer afternoon. In the second section, the ants, in the words of the composer, "industriously explore the garden until they find a rose petal, which they carry off with great difficulty." The Dance of the Butterfly follows. "The gay creature dances into the spider's web, where she dies after a brief struggle." After the hatching, the dance, and the death of the ephemera, "all the insects join with great pomp in the funeral procession. . . . Night falls on the solitary garden."

1925 CONCERTO FOR SMALL ORCHESTRA, op. 24. I. Allegro. II. Andante. III. Presto.

In writing this concerto, Roussel, the neo-classicist, was reverting to the Baroque structure of the concerto grosso, in which a group or groups of solo instruments are set off against, or combined with, the rest of the orchestra. But the materials Roussel used are of the twentieth century. The concerto was introduced in Paris on May 5, 1927, conducted by Walter Straram, to whom the work is dedicated. When the concerto received its first American hearing —in New York on October 5, 1928—Lawrence Gilman provided the following illuminating analysis:

"The opening Allegro . . . is evolved from a pervasive figure so woven into the texture of the score that the movement has almost the character of a passacaglia. . . . This integrating and persistent theme is the decisively rhythmed figure introduced by two sixteenth notes and an eighth which is heard at the beginning of the movement in the violas, fortissimo. . . .

"The slow movement . . . is patterned chiefly upon a subject adumbrated by the flutes at the beginning, under long sustained octaves of two muted solo violins, against which a solo bassoon projects a melody conspicuous for the widely spaced intervals of the latter. Solo horn and solo trumpet and other strings spin a contrapuntal web of long-breathed melodies. A flute embroiders a phrase from the opening song of the bassoon, now heard from the strings. The intertwining of lyric voices brings an end on a long-held dissonant chord, *ppp*.

"The finale is a jocose and vigorously rhythmed Presto, in triple time, based on contrasting and juxtaposed fragments of the subject enunciated forte by the trumpet at the fifth measure against a staccato figure for the strings which in itself supplies material for the movement. There is use of the effect of a drone bass, followed by a quieter section. . . . A meno presto passage is followed by a resumption of the first tempo, with a variant of the chief subject appearing as a heavily accented bass. There is a *fff* climax, and a diminuendo, with the scale motive in wave-like figures for the clarinet, the chief theme singing above it in oboe and flute. There is a pianissimo close."

1926 SUITE IN F MAJOR FOR ORCHESTRA, op. 33. I. Prelude. II. Sarabande. III. Gigue.

With this suite, written for the Boston Symphony Orchestra, Roussel abandoned impressionism, orientalism, modernism—styles which he had been cultivating—in order to enter the neo-classical world, grown so inviting to composers in France at that time. The first performance of the Suite took place on January 21, 1927, in Boston, with Serge Koussevitzky conducting the Boston Symphony Orchestra.

The composer's own analysis follows:

"The Prelude is conceived after the manner of the instrumental toccata of ancient days. The first theme is based upon a continued rhythm of rapid eighth notes, announced by the strings and with rhythmic punctuation by the woodwinds and the horns. Then by successive expositions this principal motive gives birth to various countersubjects. . . .

"The violins in octaves sing the principal phrase of the Sarabande, which is later doubled by solo flute. A second melodic phrase appears in the clarinet, and the violoncellos and double basses provide a rhythmic background based on the first subject. . . .

"The final movement is built on the rondo form. The violins present a bright and lively motive, the basis of the couplet, while the answering motive of the recurring refrain is obviously related to the first. These two ultimately combine to develop a conclusion at once brilliant and vigorously rhythmical."

1930 SYMPHONY NO. 3 IN G MINOR, op. 42. I. Allegro vivo. II. Adagio. III. Vivace. IV. Allegro con spirito.

Roussel's Third Symphony was written on a commission from the Boston Symphony Orchestra to honor its fiftieth anniversary. Completed in 1930, it was introduced by the Boston Symphony under Koussevitzky on October 24 of that year. The composer—on his first visit to this country—attended the first performance.

The symphony is integrated through the repetition of a five-note motive in three of the four movements. The first movement is in sonata form. Three measures of introduction are followed by a highly rhythmic first theme (violins and woodwinds); introduction and first theme are written in the Phrygian mode. Brief ideas follow each other, each highly lyrical until the second main theme is heard in the flute. Development proceeds in the accepted manner, rising to a climax in which the five-note motive emerges resplendently.

The second movement opens with the motif theme. The tempo develops from Adagio to Andante to Più mosso, when a huge fugue, based on the motto theme, is launched by the flutes.

The third movement was described by the composer as a kind of valse-scherzo. It is diaphanous and light-footed. The finale opens with a vigorous theme for flute and continues with an expressive idea for strings. The music becomes very lyrical. At the end, the motto theme returns twice.

1930 BACCHUS ET ARIANE, op. 43, ballet in two acts, with scenario by Abel Hermant and choreography by Serge Lifar. First performance: Paris, May 22, 1931.

BACCHUS ET ARIANE, Suite No. 2, for orchestra.

Roussel wrote music for two classic ballets, the first of which was *Bacchus and Ariadne*. (The second classic ballet, *Aeneas*, op. 54, was written in 1935 and introduced in Brussels on July 31 of that year.) Hermant's scenario is a retelling of the celebrated Greek legend. On the island of Naxos, to which Theseus has abducted Ariadne, daughter of Minos, youths and virgins are celebrating their deliverance from the monster, Minotaur. Suddenly a mysterious personage descends on the celebrants, creates panic, and seizes Ariadne.

The conqueror is the god, Bacchus. Ariadne proceeds to forget all about Theseus and to enjoy herself in the company of fauns and the bacchantes.

When the ballet was first seen in Paris, Henri Prunières described it as "one of the happiest and most original productions of the Gallic school in this genre during these many years." He went on to say: "It gripped us at the very opening measures, and did not cease to hold us until the very end. The hand of the master, in full possession of his powers, is felt here. . . . I do not know of any other than Roussel who could have carried out the requirements with such fidelity and who could have worked in the ephebic choruses, the fauns and the bacchantes, with such telling and sprightly effect around the mysterious, sarcastic and passionate figure of the god."

Roussel prepared two orchestral suites from the ballet score, the second of which has become popular at symphonic concerts. Its première took place in Paris on November 26, 1936, with Charles Munch conducting the Orchestre Philharmonique. The published score of the second suite has outlined the action described by the music: "Introduction—Awakening of Ariadne—She looks around her, surprised—She rises, runs about looking for Theseus and his companions—She realizes that she has been abandoned—She climbs with difficulty to the top of a rock—She is about to throw herself into the stream—She falls in the arms of Bacchus, who has appeared from behind a boulder—Bacchus resumes with the awakened Ariadne the dance of her dreaming—Bacchus dances alone (Allegro; Andante; Andantino)—the Dionysiac spell—A group marches past—A faun and a Bacchante present to Ariadne the golden cup into which a cluster of grapes have been pressed—Dance of Ariadne (Andante)—Dance of Ariadne and Bacchus (Moderato e Pesante)—Bacchanale (Allegro brilliante)."

1932 STRING QUARTET IN D MAJOR, op. 45. I. Allegro. II. Adagio. III. Allegro vivo. IV. Allegro moderato.

Roussel had a profound respect for the string-quartet medium. He wrote in 1929: "Is not the string quartet . . . the supreme test which reveals, honestly and artlessly, the merit of the musician, the quality of the music within him?" And in 1932, he described the string quartet as "music's most significant expression." In view of such sentiments, it is not surprising to find that the only string quartet Roussel ever wrote came when he was in his full maturity, at the height of his technical and creative powers. The work was introduced in Brussels on December 9, 1932.

The opening movement is in a concise sonata form with the two themes in contrasting tonality and personality. Basil Deane says: "The development treats this material in the same sequence as it appears in the exposition, and the recapitulation repeats it in new guises. Thus the movement falls into three sections, the second two being variations of the first."

The slow movement is in ternary form, with "melodic angularity and contrapuntal complexity" employed "for the expression of intense emotion." In the middle section, Roussel makes use of bitonality with telling effect. The third movement is a scherzo, whose prevailing mood is described by Dean as "rather acid gaiety," while the finale is a fugue, whose subject has a "striking rhythm and angular contour." The final stretto of the fugue leads into an Allegro con brio episode which is highlighted by a spirited ascending theme. The Quartet comes to an end with a whirlwind Presto.

1934 SYMPHONY NO. 4 IN A MAJOR, op. 53. I. Lento; Allegro con brio. II. Lento molto. III. Allegro scherzando. IV. Allegro molto.

Four years separated Roussel's Third and Fourth Symphonies. The Fourth was introduced in Paris by the Pasdeloup Orchestra under Albert Wolff on October 19, 1935, and was so vigorously acclaimed that one of the movements (the third) had to be repeated.

After a slow introduction of seventeen measures, the Allegro con brio begins with a theme developed out of a phrase in the sixth measure. The subject undergoes development before the second theme is heard in the horn. The movement now quickens and a climax emerges. The original material then returns—the first theme now heard in the woodwinds and muted trumpets; the second, in the oboe.

The Lento molto is enveloped in mystery. It opens with a quiet melody for strings. The first oboe then enters with a recollection of an idea from the introduction of the first movement. The tempo quickens; the atmosphere becomes restless. But when the feverish agitation is dissipated, the clarinet brings back the opening melody against a contrapuntal background of a second melody in the bassoon. This material is extended. A climax is reached and dies down; the movement then ends gently.

Violins and cellos present a lively theme which is like a gigue to open the third movement. This is the integral material of this entire section, all other subsidiary ideas being derived from it.

A theme for oboe against a pizzicato background of strings brings in the finale, a vivacious rondo. After this theme has been adopted by the first violins, a new theme—moving in its eloquence—is presented by the first violins. The entire finale is spirited, but it is not without grace. It ends on a triumphant note with a proud and exultant restatement of the opening subject for full orchestra.

CARL RUGGLES 1876–

The span of Ruggles's creative life in music was about a quarter of a century, his last composition coming in 1945. In that period his output consisted of little more than half a dozen compositions. He was always a slow worker; he was always painstaking; and he always needed a strong stimulus or motivation to begin working. Yet in spite of his creative frugality, Ruggles is one of America's most vital, most independent, and most admirable composers. He stands with Charles Ives as one of the first Americans to embark on a fresh, new course in music.

Ruggles started out by writing homophonic music with broad melodic lines on a sound harmonic base. Before long he became the iconoclast who ventured into the then-rarely cultivated fields (at least in America) of dissonant counterpoint and atonality. He also achieved a new Spartan-like kind of economy by never doubling a note in his harmony or repeating a note or its octave either in the melody or in the inner parts until the tenth progression. His writing was full of tension; it was hard and muscular; it possessed an intensity which one critic described as "anguished." Time has not robbed this music of its original profile. His few compositions, says Theodore Strongin, "have become monuments to an uncompromising New England musical conscience. . . . Concentrated, dissonant, asymmetrical, logical, but spontaneous sounding, they are like eloquent . . . prose."

Ruggles was born in Marion, Massachusetts, on March 11, 1876. He studied the violin in boyhood, then continued his music study with Christian Timner and Joseph Claus, completing it in Boston with Walter Spalding and John Knowles Paine. In 1908, he married Charlotte Snell. Four years later he came to Winona, Minnesota, where he founded the Winona Symphony and taught at the Winona Conservatory. Five years after that, he came to New York, where he helped found the International Composers Guild to promote new music. Though he had been writing compositions for a number of years, the first work he was later ready to acknowledge was the song "Toys" (1919). *Men and Angels*, a suite for five trumpets and bass trumpet (1920), followed, subsequently revised as *Angels*. He produced only a handful of compositions after that, but each one is significant, and each is representative of his mature powers.

In 1937, he joined the faculty of the School of Music at the University of Miami in Florida, where he remained for about a decade. After *Organum* (1945), he gave up composition to devote himself to painting. In 1953, he received an award from the National Association of American Composers and Conductors; in 1954, he was made a member of the National Institute of Arts and Letters. For a long time, Ruggles divided his year between New York City and a summer home in Arlington, Vermont. After the death of his wife, in 1957, he went into seclusion in Arlington. His ninetieth birthday in 1966 was celebrated with a two-day festival sponsored by Bowdoin College in Maine, where his music was played and discussed, and his paintings exhibited.

1920 ANGELS, for four violins and three cellos (or four trumpets and three trombones).

Angels began life in 1920 as *Men and Angels*, a suite for five trumpets and one bass trumpet; it was introduced at the concert which launched the International Composers Guild in New York on December 17, 1922. It was then featured at the festival of the International Society for Contemporary Music in Venice on September 8, 1925. When Ruggles revised and rescored this composition in 1938, he called it simply *Angels*, and as such it was introduced in Miami, Florida, on April 24, 1939.

In this work Ruggles began to depart from the homophonic style that had characterized his song, "Toys," for his first experiments with dissonant counterpoint. The music is high-tensioned and discordant. Here is how Virgil Thomson described it in the *Herald Tribune* when the composition was revived in New York on February 27, 1949, after a twenty-year silence: "It is a sustained and tranquil motet for four trumpets and three trombones all muted. The texture of it is chromatic secundal counterpoint. Its voices, non-differentiated as to expressive function, are woven together by thematic imitation. The dissonance-tension is uniform throughout; hence, in the long run, harmonious, though that tension carries the maximum of dissonance possible to seven voices."

1924 MEN AND MOUNTAINS, for chamber orchestra (also for large orchestra). I. Men. II. Lilacs. III. Marching Mountains.

The dissonant counterpoint with which Ruggles had experimented in *Angels* is here employed with greater freedom, while the flight from any basic tonality becomes more pronounced. *Men and Mountains* owes its inspiration to the poet, William Blake, whose line "Great things are done when men and mountains meet" appears in the published score. As a composition for chamber orchestra, it was first heard in New York City on December 7, 1924. Ruggles later rescored it for large orchestra. This version was heard in New York City on December 19, 1936. Lawrence Gilman had this to say about this composition: "Mr. Ruggles is well suited to set Blake to music. . . . The wild, gigantic, tortured symbols of Blake's imagination, his riotous and untrammeled excursions in the world behind the heavens are all of a piece with Mr. Ruggles' thinking. There is a touch of the apocalyptic, the fabulous about his fantasies. . . . He is a master of a strange, torrential and perturbing discourse." About the middle movement, possibly the most eloquent section in the entire work, Gilman said: "He has found a strange new poignancy of harmonic and polyphonic speech, a translation into tones of that picture which evidently haunted the dweller among New England hills."

1926 PORTALS, for string orchestra.

Portals was first heard at a concert of the International Composers Guild in New York on January 24, 1926, Eugene Goossens conducting. In the version heard then, it was scored for an orchestra of thirteen strings. But Ruggles soon extended the scoring to a string orchestra.

Here the point of departure for Ruggles's music is a quotation by Walt Whitman: "What are those of the known, but to ascend and enter the unknown?" Ruggles's style here is even more linear and atonal than in earlier compositions. Harmonic emphasis is sidestepped for a style that is basically contrapuntal. As Charles Seeger noted, the counterpoint challenges "the chordal origins of the technique. The determining feature or principle of the melodic line as conceived by Ruggles is that of non-repetition of tone."

1933 SUN TREADER, for large orchestra.

Many critics regard *Sun Treader* as Ruggles's most important composition. It was first heard in Paris on February 25, 1932, Nicolas Slonimsky conducting.

Strange to say, it then took some thirty years for the work to get heard in the United States. Meanwhile, it was performed in Berlin, and on April 22, 1936, at the festival of the International Society for Contemporary Music at Barcelona. The American première was given in Portland, Maine, on January 24, 1966, during the festival commemorating Ruggles's ninetieth birthday; Jean Martinon conducted the Chicago Symphony.

The poetic source was *Pauline* by Robert Browning, a line from which appears in the published score: "Sun-treader, light and life be thine forever." Theodore Strongin in *The New York Times* found the music well suited to this motto. "The composition, he said, is light and life personified, but not sweetness and light. Craggy, rangy, it is all contained power. Its concentrated, close-knit dissonant lines surge and recede and finally rise to an apotheosis of a close."

Ruggles divides his large orchestra into independent choirs. "They follow each other in close counterpoint," says Strongin, "They support, prod, urge each other constantly. The speech of each mounts over extended periods, stops, continues on with greater emphasis, speeds up several times over a repeated tympani beat, restates itself from new standpoints."

1945 ORGANUM, for large orchestra.

Ruggles's last composition was introduced in New York on November 24, 1949, with Leopold Stokowski conducting the New York Philharmonic. The composition is in a ternary structure. John Kirkpatrick, the concert pianist who made a piano reduction of the score for *New Music*, has pointed out that the first twenty measures, "one long unified paragraph," presents a canonic imitation of the main melody beginning with seventh measure. After a six-measure interlude, we come to the fourteen-measure middle section, where the melody is heard in retrogression. A second interlude is the bridge to a return of the "original paragraph" with some modifications and condensation. A five-measure coda brings the work to its conclusion.

ERIK SATIE 1866–1925

It is not difficult to understand why so many of his contemporaries were puzzled by Erik Satie; why they were incapable of accurately measuring his importance. Here was a supposedly serious composer earning his living as a cabaret pianist in Montmartre, who did not hesitate to write popular tunes for music-hall entertainers or to introduce popular elements in his serious efforts. Here, too, was a composer who used outlandish titles for his compositions, then cluttered them with whimsical comments.

Here, finally, was a supposedly creative artist who insisted on making a mockery of artistic dignity, a shambles of artistic purpose. Was he a charlatan or a genius? Some musicians put him in the latter category—Debussy, Ravel, Milhaud, for example. Others dismissed him as a poseur, a buffoon, a pixy, a bad boy who refused to grow up.

And yet, for all his strange attitudes and frequent excursions into whimsy, Satie was a very serious artist, and one of the most significant forces in twentieth-century music. Even in the pieces he wrote for the piano before the twentieth century, at the dawn of his career, he demonstrated extraordinary independence of style, thought and purpose. In 1886, he wrote *Ogives*, the word meaning "pointed arch"; these pieces were the result of Satie's study of Gothic art. *Ogives* represented for Satie an attempt to suggest, through the rise and ebb of the melodic phrase, the contour of Gothic art; and its main interest lies in its exotic medievalism and the use of modal harmonies. The three *Sarabandes* followed in 1887, an effort to dress up a Baroque structure with new harmonies: chords of the ninth and eleventh which anticipated Debussy. The prevailing mood of these *Sarabandes* is mysticism; the melodic material has a liturgical character. After the Sarabandes came the three *Gymnopédies* in 1888. A "gymnopedia" was a religious festival in ancient Sparta in which naked youths worshiped their gods in song and dance. Satie was stimulated into writing this music by a decoration on a Greek vase. Each of the three pieces is in slow 3/4 time; in each, the medieval mode used is Aeolian; each opens with a four-measure introduction; each presents a grave and serene melody in the right hand. The progressions are particularly interesting, with a logic all their own. There is no feeling of concord following discord, no point of rest. But for all the novelty of the harmonic scheme, and for all its exoticism, *Gymnopédies* is simple, direct, concise music, representing an important break with the inflationary methods of the post-Romantic school. *Gnossiennes* (1890) is still another step forward, pieces inspired by a reading of Flaubert's *Salammbô*. Here Satie experiments for the first time with barless notation. The pieces have no key and no signature. Thematic construction is abandoned, modal cadences are emphasized. Here, too, we find Satie's first excursion into whimsy with verbal explanations like "open the head" or "play in a fashion to achieve a pit or hole." "All the essential features of Satie's style," says Rollo H. Myers of *Gnossiennes,* "are already apparent in these pieces—the obstinately melodic phrases, the modal cadences, the basic rhythm firmly established in the bass persisting till the end."

Satie rebelled against composers who took themselves and their art too seriously by bringing music down to earth and making it human. He was the apostle of "everyday music" ("*musique de tous les jours*"). By his revolt against excessive emotionalism, complexity, grandiose structures, pretentious metaphysical aims, he reduced music to simplicity with a clarity and freshness of writing and an infectious wit that were like a breath of pure air in a fetid atmosphere. Through his queer titles and queerer instructions, he mocked the preciousness of Debussy and his followers (even though he had been their stimulus and inspiration) and helped to rid impressionism of some of its less desirable traits. He sent music towards a healthy new direction, a direction which, because of the example he set, was taken by members of the "French Six" in their excursions into levity, and after that, by the School of Arcueil (who include Sauguet and Desormière) in their fetish for austerity and simplicity.

Satie might very well be singled out as France's first modernist; certainly he set into motion many of the methods, trends and innovations that characterized twentieth-century French music. He also anticipated many twentieth-century musical "schools" and cults that came to flower after his death. He was one of the first serious composers to make successful use of American ragtime. This is found in his ballet *Parade,* where he was also a pioneer in writing mechanistic music and in utilizing sounds and noises within a serious musical framework. He was one of the first to employ polytonality. He anticipated dadaism in *Le Piège de Méduse* (1913) and musical surrealism in *Relâche* (1924). He even suggested the later function of background music for motion pictures. This happened at an exhibition of painting in Paris on March 8, 1920, when his music—designed as "*musique d'ameublement*" ("furnishing music")—was played from a gallery as background to the business of looking at pictures. He meticulously explained in the program that the music was not to be listened to actively, was not even to be noticed; that the art patrons were to behave as if there were no music. When some of the patrons actually stopped to listen to the music, Satie went from one to the other begging them to continue what they were doing and not to pay any attention to the musical sounds, which had been intended to contribute a kind of subliminal background atmosphere.

Without Satie, French music would hardly have developed as it did in the twentieth century. No wonder, then, that Ravel once said: "Erik Satie occupies a very special place in the history of contemporary music."

Satie was born in Honfleur, Calvados, on May 17, 1866. He began music study in his tenth year with a local organist who inspired him with a love for old Gregorian plainchants which persisted all his life. This was soon supplemented by the study of piano and harmony with local teachers. In 1883, he entered the Paris Conservatory, but he was not happy there. His rebellious thinking brought him into continual conflict with his teachers, until, after a single year, he decided to desert the Conservatory and shift for himself in his music studies as best he could. He began writing his first piano pieces in 1885, and two years later, his first publication appeared. His first significant compositions, and his first innovations, were not slow in coming. They appeared between 1886 and 1890 with *Ogives, Sarabandes, Gymnopédies* and *Gnossiennes.*

After leaving the Conservatory, Satie earned his living playing the piano in such Montmartre cabarets as Chat Noir and Auberge du Clou. In the former, he met Josephin Péladan, leader of the Rosicrucian Society, a religious cult in which Satie interested himself for a number of years. Association with Péladan resulted in Satie's becoming the composer for the cult, a period in which Satie's writing was touched with mysticism and influenced by early church music. The most important compositions of this religious phase of Satie's creative life included the *Danses gothiques,* for piano (1893) and the *Messe des pauvres,* for solo voices and organ (1895).

At the Auberge du Clou, Satie met Debussy for the first time. Satie's ideas and music, his espousal of a French style and tradition in music as opposed to the German, and his unorthodox methods all had a profound impact on Debussy's development. As Debussy confessed, it was through Satie that he got "the aesthetic concept underlying *Pelléas*."

By 1895, Satie had freed himself of mysticism. He found a new direction in 1897 with the writing of *Pièces froides,* for piano, the first of many works with whimsical titles. Whimsy, wit, satire would dominate his writing for the piano during the next decade and a half, as he would continually seek out fresh, new idioms.

In 1898, Satie moved to Arcueil, a suburb of Paris, in a drab and impoverished apartment which he made his home for the rest of his life. As long as he lived, nobody was permitted to set foot into his home. He did his own housekeeping, fetched his own water in the public square, and would make frequent visits to distant Montmartre to visit his friends, always on foot (he never used a public conveyance). He became known as an eccentric; and by 1905, he had also become known as one of the most provocative and notorious figures in French music. Then, feeling his technique was inadequate, he returned to formal study by enrolling in the Schola Cantorum, where for three years he was a pupil of Vincent d'Indy and Albert Roussel. This period of study enabled Satie to embark on more ambitious creative assignments than just pieces for the piano. He now produced music for the ballet and for the stage, which included two masterworks, *Parade* in 1916 and the symphonic drama, *Socrate,* in 1918. Satie died in a hospital in Paris on July 1, 1925.

1903–1919 COMPOSITIONS FOR PIANO:

AVANT DERNIERS PENSÉES (NEXT TO LAST THOUGHTS). I. Idylle à Debussy. II. Sérénade. III. Rêverie.

CROQUIS ET AGACERIES D'UN GROS BONHOMME EN BOIS (PROVOCATIONS OF A BIG WOODEN SIMPLETON). I. Tyrolienne Turque. II. Danse maigre. III. Españaña.

DESCRIPTIONS AUTOMATIQUES (AUTOMATIC DESCRIPTIONS). I. Sur un vaisseau. II. Sur une lanterne. III. Sur un casque.

EMBRYONS DESSÉCHÉS (DESSICATED EMBRYOS). I. Holothurie. II. Edriophthalma. III. Podophthalma.

SPORTS ET DIVERTISSEMENTS (SPORTS AND DIVERSIONS). I. La Balancoire. II. La Chasse. III. Comédie italienne. IV. La Mariée. V. Colin-Maillard. VI. La Pêche. VII. Yachting. VIII. Bain de mer. IX. Le Carnaval. X. Le Golf. XI. La Pìevre. XII. Les Courses. XIII. Les Quatre coins. XIV. Pique Nique. XV. Water Chute. XVI. Le Tango. XVII. Traineau. XVIII. Flirt. XIX. Feu d'artifice. XX. Le Tennis.

TROIS MORCEAUX EN FORME DE POIRE (THREE PIECES IN THE SHAPE OF A PEAR). I. Manìere de commencement. II. Prolongation du même. III. Un en Plus; Redite.

TROIS PRÉLUDES FLASQUES (FLABBY PRELUDES). I. Sévère réprimande. II. Seul à la maison. III. On Joue.

The pixy in Satie revealed itself with his very first publication, a piano piece which he designated as opus 62! This was in 1887. But it was only after he had broken with religion and mysticism late in 1895, and sought out for himself a new creative direction, that he began adopting bizarre titles for his music. In 1903, when Debussy happened to comment that Satie's pieces were formless, Satie wrote, as refutation, *Three Pieces in the Shape of a Pear* to demonstrate that his music *did* have some kind of shape after all. After that, his titles grew more and more bizarre—partly, because he enjoyed placing tongue square in cheek; partly, as a revolt against the euphuistic titles chosen by the impressionists. At the same time, he began interpolating into his music all kinds of strange, quixotic directions to performers together with nonsensical program annotations and comments. The second piece in *Embryons Desséchés* (1913) quotes Chopin's *Funeral March*, but it is identified as a Schubert Mazurka; a phrase in the third number in the same set bears the following commentary, "like a nightingale with a toothache." *Sur un vaisseau,* the first piece in *Descriptions automatiques* (1913) contains the remark, "the captain says, a very good journey!" while the third piece contributes the following thought, "this is magnificent, light as an egg." The second piece in *Avant dernieres pensées* (1915) introduces a humorous text between the staves. Nonsensical program annotations appear in various compositions. One of them reads: "This is the case of the lobster; the hunters descend to the bottom of the water; they run. The sound of a horn is heard at the bottom of the sea. The lobster is tracked. The lobster weeps."

Despite the absurd titles and the ridiculous verbal asides—despite the occasional excursions into irony, satire and parody—Satie's piano music is often deadly serious. Continually it seeks out new techniques and methods, while trying to achieve an extraordinary economy of means and simplicity of style in music that carefully avoids the romantic and the sentimental. The *Trois Morceaux en forme de poire* (1903) might be intended as a caricature of classical pedantry or impressionist preciousness. At the same time, this music has such nobility and tenderness—a lyricism that Myers has described as Schumannesque—that Paul Collaër regards it as "one of the composer's most perfect, most beautiful, and most powerful works." He adds that it "strikes a new note with its resolute movement, its rhythmic breadth and through the use in some passages of rather coarse music in reaction to excessive elaborateness. ... It shows a development towards counterpoint—Satie was on the scent of what he lacked.... The only thing humorous about the work is its title."

And about the only thing "flabby" about *Trois préludes flasques* (1912) is the title. The music is muscular, with a severe linear technique that anticipates the neo-classic writing of Hindemith. And the only thing humorous about this work is its mock Latin directions.

One of the more remarkable of Satie's piano works, and one heard most rarely, is the suite, *Sports et divertissements* (1914) which Darius Milhaud has described as "one of the most characteristic works of the French school." Here we encounter twenty short pieces descriptive of various outdoor sports and diversions. The Satie whimsy may be uncovered in the fact that the composer had the composition published on music paper ruled with red lines. In his brief preface, Satie advises the performer "to turn the pages of this book with an amiable and smiling hand, for this is a work of fantasy that does not pretend to be anything else." But the music is neither fanciful nor whimsical. It consists of pieces, says Wilfred Mellers, "with the authenticity of

Japanese epigraphs, providing examples of almost every aspect of Satie's mature art." The work opens with a brief "Choral," a preamble, austere and concentrated music for which the composer provided the following comment: "I have put into it everything I know about Boredom. I dedicate this 'Choral' to those who do not like me—and withdraw."

Witty verbal comments are also found in many other pieces, while the music itself seems to maintain a contradictory pose of seriousness. "Through all these works," Mellers explains, "the subtlety increasingly depends on the pattern that is made out of lyrical fragments, rigid rhythms, harmonies that are in themselves transparently simple. The ease of the writing within the narrow restrictions of the material employed in each piece—two or three contrasted phrases, a clearly defined program, a couple of surprisingly related harmonies—is a triumph of technical dexterity." In this music, writes Rollo H. Myers, Satie "proves himself an artist of the finest quality, working to a scale which in itself would be a handicap to most writers, let alone musicians, but triumphing over his self-imposed limitations with the virtuosity of a marksman scoring a bull's eye with each shot."

1916 PARADE, a "realistic ballet" in one act, with text by Jean Cocteau and choreography by Léonide Massine. First performance: Ballet Russe de Monte Carlo, Paris, May 18, 1917.

In 1915, Satie became acquainted with Jean Cocteau, who had been impressed with the composer's *Trois Morceaux en forme de poire*. Cocteau suggested that Satie join him and Pablo Picasso in creating a ballet for Diaghilev's Ballet Russe. The result was *Parade*, sometimes described as a "cubist manifesto." Picasso's cubistic stage designs and costumes, Massine's at times cubistic choreography (in placing the Managers in wooden frames as a kind of human scenery, for example) was matched by Satie's attempt to arrive at a cubistic-like musical score. By piling up his lyrical phrases into a structure, much as if they were cubes or cones, and placing the phrases into fresh and at times unusual relationships, Satie had succeeded in carrying over into music some of the techniques of cubism. Joseph Machlis explained further: "Satie's music juxtaposed seemingly incompatible elements and recombined them in a formal integration: snappy fragments of music-hall melody with a strict fugato, lyrical phrases and driving ostinato rhythms, simple diatonic harmonies and clangorous polytonal effects."

Parade created a scandal at its première. Not comprehending the artistic aim of choreography, staging, costuming or music, many critics felt they were being mocked. Some newspapermen called the creators of this ballet "Boches," accusing them of trying subtly and surreptitiously to introduce German ideas into France, called an act of treason since France was then at war with Germany. So vitriolic was one of the critics that Satie was impelled to send him an insulting letter. Sued by the infuriated critic, Satie was sentenced to eight days in jail for "public insults and defamation of character." (The sentence however, was suspended.)

Parade is a satire on the touring companies of entertainers, playing in city streets, its attractions combining some of the features of music hall, the circus and American Negro bands. To draw attention to their show, these companies always preceded their performance with a parade of the cast. The principal characters of the ballet include a Chinese juggler, two acrobats, a little American girl, and three managers. On a Sunday outside a Paris music hall, there has taken place a parade of performers. The company managers are barking at passersby, trying to get them to attend the performance. But the Parisians think that the parade is the actual performance and ignore the solicitations. Some of the performers then join the managers in attracting the passersby to the show, but in vain. This is the main action of the ballet, which Cocteau likened to a Punch and Judy show.

For his musical background, Satie tried using the sounds of sirens, clicking typewriters, a discharged revolver, airplane motors, dynamos. Thus, almost a decade before George Antheil's *Ballet mécanique*, and Edgard Varese's experiments with "organized sound," Satie experimented with noise within a musical context and with mechanistic music. Technical difficulties, however, made it necessary, during the rehearsals of *Parade,* to eliminate almost all of these extramusical sounds. The few that remained (such as the clicking of typewriters) could not be heard at the actual performance. These clicking typewriters were recruited to provide an American background and atmosphere for the appearance and dance routine of the American girl. More significant, even, in realizing such an American profile was the interpolation of American ragtime music (in a theme strongly reminiscent of Irving Berlin's "That Mysterious Rag"). This interpolation represented one of the earliest successful attempts to use a popular American musical idiom within a serious musical design, and for serious artistic purpose. French music-hall tunes were also simulated; for example, the unpretentious little waltz tune with which the acrobats make their appearance. Though violently denounced in 1917, *Parade* has since come to be regarded as one of Satie's masterworks. Darius Milhaud has written: "The performance of Satie's *Parade* will stand in the history of French music as a date equally important with that of the first performance of *Pelléas et Mélisande*."

1918 SOCRATE, a symphonic drama in three parts for four voices and chamber orchestra, with text derived from the *Dialogues* of Plato translated by Victor Cousin. I. Portrait of Socrates. II. By the Banks of Ilyssus. III. Death of Socrates. First performance: Paris, February 14, 1920.

Socrate ranks with *Parade* as one of Satie's crowning artistic achievements, a masterwork in which the whimsical humorist and satirist of the piano pieces turns to the writing of richly poetic and deeply reflective music that rises to the heights of expressiveness and eloquence.

The sections are derived from three of the most famous of Plato's *Dialogues*: The Symposium, Phaedrus, and Phaedo. The first consists of a dialogue between Socrates and Alcibiades. The second is the dialogue between Socrates and Phaedrus. The third is Phaedo's narration. Here, as in his own piano pieces, Satie creates his own genre. The writing for the voices is mainly in recitatives, with each syllable accented equally, while the orchestral background moves independently of the narrative in anticipation of the linear technique of the later neo-classicists. "The simple and limpid style of this deeply reflective work," says Rollo H. Myers, "which flows quietly and inevitably along in an uneventful stream, flecked here and there by little eddies and whirls of subdued emotion, betokens a final mastery and controlled equilibrium to which all of Satie's previous works seem to have aspired with varying degrees of success." Myers also points out that Satie has here achieved "something that no one had hitherto attempted in music—the weaving of a kind of tapestry of sound to carry a long, melodic narration entrusted to four different voices, succeeding one another like runners in a relay race."

It is in the third part, where Phaedo describes the death of Socrates, that Satie scales the heights. Here is how Myers describes this part: "A grave note is struck in the very first bars in an ascending sequence of triads which recurs, suggesting the tolling of a bell. . . . There are passages of sheer musical beauty, as for example where Socrates takes a cup of hemlock and drinks it. . . . Almost the only touch of dramatic realism in the music occurs at the passage describing how the poison has begun to work; the stiffening and chilling of the body of Socrates is pressed in a harsh discord. . . . Satie moves on an aesthetic plane so detached and remote from normal experience that it does demand from the listener a concentrated effort and willingness to divest himself of preconceived notions about music before he can enter into the necessary state of receptivity."

FLORENT SCHMITT 1870–1958

In writing about Schmitt, music critics often speak of his allegiance to tradition and classical form. But though Schmitt's most famous works seem traditional enough today, they were highly original and adventurous in their time. It must be recalled that his three most famous works (*Psalm 47*, the Piano Quintet, and *The Tragedy of Salome*) were all written by 1908. For that time, these works were courageous enough in their use of compound meters, advanced harmonies, and exotic orchestration. Time, of course, has robbed this music of its daring. But since the music did not depend on its originality for its interest, time has not robbed it of its power to delight audiences. As we listen to these works today, what impresses us profoundly, is their eloquent expressiveness, their ardor, and their emotional force.

Schmitt was born in Blâmont, France, on September 28, 1870. His preliminary music study took place at the Conservatory of Nancy with Henri Hesse in piano and Gustave Sandré in harmony. When he was nineteen, he entered the Paris Conservatory. There he was a pupil of Fauré, Massenet and Dubois among others. In 1900, he received the Prix de Rome. While residing at the Villa Medici, he completed his first major work, the *Psalm 47*, in 1904. After extensive travels for a two-year period, he settled in Paris, where, on

December 27, there took place an all-Schmitt concert. This was soon followed by the successes of his Piano Quintet and *La Tragédie de Salomé.*

Schmitt identified himself closely with the new developments in French music as a founder and member of the executive committee of the Société Musicale Indépendante, and as a member of the Société Nationale. For two years, between 1922 and 1924, he was director of the Lyons Conservatory. In 1932, he visited the United States in guest appearances in performances of his works; during this period he participated in the world première of his *Symphonie concertante,* for piano and orchestra, which the Boston Symphony presented on November 25, 1932. In 1936, Schmitt was elected to the Académie des Beaux-Arts in succession to Paul Dukas. He was also made Commander of the Legion of Honor, and in 1957, he was awarded the grand prize in music by the City of Paris. His first symphony was written when he was in his mid-eighties. He attended its world première at a festival of the International Society for Contemporary Music at Strasbourg on June 15, 1958. Schmitt died at Neuilly-sur-Seine, near Paris, on August 17, 1958.

1904 PSALM 47 (Psalm 46 in the Vulgate), for chorus, soloists, organ and orchestra, op. 38.

Though this setting of the 47th Psalm ("O Clap Your Hands, All Ye People") is one of Schmitt's earlier works, it is also one of his best; and there are many French authorities who consider it a monument in contemporary French choral music. Schmitt wrote it in Rome while holding down the Prix de Rome. On December 27, 1906, it was introduced in Paris at an all-Schmitt concert. The critics were divided in their opinion. Some (like Arthur Pougin) spoke derisively of its "bizarre" orchestration, "ferocious" modulations, "infernal" dissonances. Others (notably M. D. Calvocoressi) described the music as of singular power and grandiloquence.

In *Le Temps,* Emile Vuillermoz provided a definitive analysis:

[The composition opens with a roll of the tympani. Trumpets join in, setting the stage for the chorus which enters with the majestic outcry: "Glory to God!"]

"The orchestra, which has supported this call with all its power, extends it in triumphal fanfares. The chorus sings with rhythmic insistence the words 'O Clap Your Hands, All Ye People.' The instruments respond with noisy chords . . . and follow it with a sort of barbaric ritual in five rhythms. But the dance seems to become a processional. . . . The brasses take up the heavy rhythm of barbaric exaltation. A rapid crescendo, and the orchestra pauses abruptly, while organ and divided chorus proclaim a fortissimo of chords as massive as the colonnade of a temple. The trumpets resound anew and a repetition of 'Glory to God!' brings in a majestic vocal fugato, 'For the Lord is Very Mighty.' This whole evocation of the human race saluting its Creator is music of power and sovereign beauty. . . . But the clamor subsides. . . . Over a caressing equilibrium of divided violas, a violin solo sings a supple and expressive phrase. . . . One by one the desks make their entrance to surround the simple voice which is exaltingly intoxicated and lost in its impassioned dream. We are in an oriental atmosphere. . . . The chorus murmurs in ecstasy while sinuous arpeggios of the harp rise like incense. Trumpets and muted horns, muted strings, with a soft roll on the cymbal, add a drab halo of sound. . . . The magic of the Far East evaporates. . . . Now the music becomes once more alert. The orchestra resumes its mighty voice. . . . Once more the portals of the celestial temples open, and the organ supports the enunciation, 'Because the Lord Is Very Formidable.' The crescendo mounts until all the forces of the orchestra and chorus proclaim, 'Glory to God!' The ending is a formidable tumult of transport in which the people fill the air with their savage and joyful cries."

1907 LA TRAGÉDIE DE SALOMÉ (THE TRAGEDY OF SALOME), suite for orchestra, op. 50. I. Prelude; Dance of the Pearls. II. The Enchantment of the Sea; Dance of Lightning; Dance of Fear.

Schmitt's most famous orchestral work was inspired by a lurid poem of Robert d'Humieres for which the composer produced sensual music that is at times exotic and at other times barbaric. Originally intended as a "mute drama" (in which form it was introduced by Loie Fuller in Paris on November 9, 1907, under the direction of D. E. Inghelbrecht), *The Tragedy of Salome* was first scored for chamber orchestra. Subsequently, Schmitt rewrote it for large orchestra, in which version it was heard for the first time at a Colonne concert in Paris on January 8, 1911.

After a gloomy Prelude in which the tragedy of Salome is foreshadowed, there comes a frenetic dance describing Salome's joy at the jewels she has just received from her mother. Moody music introduces the second part, bringing back the lugubrious atmosphere of the Prelude. Out of this rises a melody (oboe) derived from a folk song of Aica. Salome then dances by the illumination of lightning. She disappears, then returns with the head of John the Baptist on a tray. At first she appears ecstatic, but terror soon seizes her. She hurls the head into the sea, the waters of which soon change to blood. Lightning tears through the sky. A bolt strikes the palace of Herod and shatters it.

1908 QUINTET IN B MINOR FOR PIANO AND STRINGS, op. 51. I. Lent et grave. II. Lent. III. Animé.

Though Schmitt is at his best in the larger forms for orchestra or orchestra and chorus, he has produced at least one work of chamber music dimensions which is an unqualified masterpiece. This is his Piano Quintet, also one of his comparatively early works, begun as it was in 1901, though completed seven years later. Its first performance at a concert of the Société Nationale in Paris on March 27, 1908, was outstandingly successful, and did much to establish Schmitt's reputation. M. D. Calvocoressi spoke of it as "one of the most moving . . . and revealing creations of the past few years."

A slow and expressive introduction opens the quintet, after which comes the Allegro movement, orthodox in form, but full of vigorous ideas and unusual harmonies. The slow movement is the best of the three, high-minded and poetic in speech and full of sensitive beauty. An athletic final movement of impressive structural dimensions is rhythmically interesting.

ARNOLD SCHOENBERG 1874–1951

Not until after World War I did Schoenberg crystallize his thinking into that system of composition with which his name is inevitably associated: the twelve-tone technique or row (dodecaphony). The impact of this system on composers throughout the world for the next half-century can hardly be exaggerated.

In his earliest music, Schoenberg was a child of the post-Romantic movement in Austria, and was profoundly influenced by Wagner. Schoenberg's first large-scale work, an unpublished string quartet in D major (1897), was full of the kind of soaring and sensuous melodies and chromatic harmonies which were the carry-overs of the age of Wagner. The celebrated *Verklaerte Nacht,* or *Transfigured Night*—originally for sextet (1899), but become famous in the composer's transcription for chamber orchestra (1917, new revision, 1943)—was also strongly influenced by Wagner, while the mammoth *Gurre-Lieder* revealed a strong indebtedness not only to Wagner but also to those other post-Romantic giants who carried the Wagnerian torch, Richard Strauss and Gustav Mahler. But Schoenberg eventually exhausted the potentials of post-Romanticism. In reaction, he began searching for simplification, precision, brevity—in his pieces for the piano and for the orchestra. He came to the conclusion that the old methods of tonality and harmony had become obsolete; that the twentieth-century composer had to seek out new ways, methods and sounds. "Every tone relationship that has been used too often must finally be regarded as exhausted," he said. "It ceases to have power to convey a thought worthy of it. Therefore every composer is obliged to invent anew, to present new tone relations." Step by step, Schoenberg began to progress towards liberation from the tyranny of tonality, from slavery to a key center or tonic; towards the breakdown of any distinction between consonance and dissonance; towards the evolution of a new kind of lyricism; towards the realization of an expressionist style which sought out abstractions, and was completely divorced from extramusical connotations. His interest in expressionism and abstraction had been aroused by the work of the Viennese painter, Oskar Kokoschka, with which he had become fascinated in 1910.

In the *Eight Songs,* op. 6 (1905), Schoenberg began to experiment with the wide intervallic leaps in his melodic line that would later be basic to his style. His second string quartet, in F-sharp minor, op. 10 (1907), was the last time he used a key signature for about thirty years; its finale was the first completely atonal piece ever written, and for this reason the year of its composition has been described as "one of the most decisive turning points in the history of music." The tonal center is dispensed with in the *Three Piano Pieces,* op. 11 (1908), and discords predominate. With *Pierrot Lunaire* (1912), he arrives at a new kind of declamation: song speech, free in rhythm and unequal in its measures (*Sprechstimme,* or *Sprechgesang*), the pitch of each note indicated rather than sung, with the voice sliding up or down to the next indicated note. Here, and with the *Five Pieces for Orchestra* (1912), Schoenberg arrives at musical expressionism, as atonality (a term he disliked as a description for this style, preferring "non-tonality") becomes a fully realized method.

But atonality eventually represented to him not freedom but anarchy. He sensed the compelling need to devise a new set of principles to replace the old ones he had discarded—in short, to discipline his thinking. A period of creative silence during World War I enabled him to crystallize his thinking and to devise for himself a new method of composition, a method which he described as "composing with the tones of the basic motive." He explained further: "In contrast to the ordinary way of using a motive, I used it already almost in the manner of a basic set of twelve tones." Thus the idea of writing music derived entirely from a preconceived framework of twelve tones kept simmering within him.

Actually, Schoenberg was not the creator of the twelve-tone system. That distinction goes to another Austrian, Joseph Mathias Hauer (1883–1959). Hauer had a strong bent for mathematics as well as music. He devised a new precise system based on "tropes" or patterns without repeated notes, in themes spun out to twelve tones. In 1912, he published a piano piece called *Law,* which is the first known composition ever to embody the twelve-tone technique. He developed his theories further in a publication on tropes appearing in 1921. Since Schoenberg did not lay down the foundations of his system until 1923, Hauer protested passionately that he was the father of the idiom. This is certainly true—chronologically. But the twelve-tone technique with Hauer was just a bare statement, a suggestion. It was not developed with the fullest resources of contrapuntal and canonic devices until Schoenberg took it in hand and demonstrated all its artistic possibilities.

Schoenberg's first successful experiments with a twelve-tone row can be found in the concluding waltz of the *Five Pieces,* for piano, op. 23 (1923), and the fourth movement of his *Serenade,* op. 24 (1923). The first composition to be constructed entirely from a twelve-tone row followed in 1924 with the *Suite for Piano,* op. 25. From this point on, for the next two decades, the twelve-tone row became his creative tool for a succession of iconoclastic compositions which opened for twentieth-century music an entirely new world of sound and aesthetics.

A few of the salient features of the twelve-tone system can be succinctly explained. The twelve tones of the chromatic scale are arranged in a definite order or row; each composition is built out of its own row; the twelve tones can be arranged in a melodic pattern, provided that no tone is repeated before the others are used; each tone is given equal importance and independence, without subservience to a tonic; the whole composition consists of restatements of the series in any of its numerous formations, horizontal and vertical; the row can be used in its original form, inverted, in retrograde, and in retrograde and inverted; finally, all the four forms of the series can be transposed to any step of the chromatic scale, allowing in all for forty-eight variations.

Schoenberg used this system with consummate skill and ingenuity. But for many years there was something hard and cold about the logic of his music, something almost forbidding in this careful calculation, something even ugly about the sounds that were produced. Gone are the passions, intensity and flaming beauty of the *Verklaerte Nacht* and the *Gurre-Lieder,* gone even the dramatic power and expressiveness of *Pierrot Lunaire.* The twelve-tone compositions were the productions of a highly analytical brain that handled compositional problems as if they were mathematical equations, and dispensed completely with human feelings and experiences. Schoenberg might well say that a twelve-tone composer—like any other composer—may be "cold-hearted and unmoved as an engineer . . . or may conceive in sweet dreams, inspiration. What can be constructed with these tones depends on one's inventive faculty." (Indeed, his pupil and disciple, Alban Berg, was to prove that this was the case!) But the music that Schoenberg put down on paper in the 1920's, 1930s and early 1940s was arid, austere, heartless. The layman heard only baffling, seemingly disorganized, complexity. Even well-trained musicians listened without affection, while admiring the extraordinary technique and inventiveness that were involved.

Beginning with the *Ode to Napoleon* (1943), Schoenberg was able to bring human as well as intellectual values to music. Transplantion to the United States had proved to be healthy for Schoenberg. He was now taking his art out of its formerly cloistered isolation, making it not merely a brilliant application of his theories but also an expression of his inmost feelings towards the world around him. Thus he could now write musical works which drew their subjects, and their emotional impact, from the contemporary world. Thus he could write functional music for a school band. Thus he could produce a major abstract work and flood it with warmth and even *gemütlich* charm.

But besides bringing emotion and a human approach to the writing of music in twelve-tone rows, Schoenberg also managed to change his onetime ascetic approach to the technique. He no longer felt the compulsion to write exclusively in the style of his invention. In some of his last works, the twelve-tone technique is utilized in spasmodic pages; in others, it is not used at all. The gamut of expressiveness was, therefore, greatly extended. He even felt the urge to return to older Romantic styles—and yielded to that urge.

He could now say: "If a composer does not write from the heart, he simply cannot produce good music. . . . I get a musical idea for a composition. I try to develop a certain logical and beautiful conception, and I try to clothe it in a type of music which exudes from me naturally and inevitably. I do not consciously create tonal, atonal, or polytonal music. I write what I feel in my heart—and what finally comes on paper is what first courses through every fiber of my body."

Schoenberg was born in Vienna on September 13, 1874. Though he began studying the violin when he was eight, at the Realschule, and made his first efforts at composition when he was twelve, he did not at first show strong talent for music. It was only after he had become a pupil in counterpoint of Alexander von Zemlinsky, that his innate gifts began to flower. While earning his living playing the cello in an orchestra conducted by Zemlinsky,

Schoenberg began developing as a composer. He completed a string quartet and several songs in 1897; the string quartet made a good impression when introduced in Vienna in the winter of 1898. The songs, gathered in opp. 1, 2 and 3, become Schoenberg's first publications. A few of these songs were introduced in Vienna in December of 1900 by Professor Gärtner and were failures. From this time on, performances of his works in Vienna, Berlin and London (with one or two exceptions) provoked scandals.

During this first period of Schoenberg's career as composer, in which his ties to post-Romanticism were steadfast, he produced *Verklaerte Nacht* and *Gurre-Lieder*. On October 7, 1901, Schoenberg married Zemlinsky's sister, Mathilde. Schoenberg went to live in Berlin where he earned his living conducting an orchestra in a cabaret and doing other hackwork. In 1902, serious endeavors won him the Franz Liszt stipend, mainly through the influence of Richard Strauss. Schoenberg was back in Vienna in 1903, where he devoted himself to teaching. He gathered around him several highly gifted progressive-minded musicians who were to become his disciples, among them Alban Berg and Anton Webern. The adulation of his students was a measure of compensation for the violent hostility that greeted each new work of his when introduced. These scandals led him in 1911 to return to Berlin, where he taught composition at the Akademie für Kunst and lectured on aesthetics at the Stern Conservatory. With the outbreak of World War I, he was mobilized in the Austrian army. The war years was a period of creative inactivity, but a period of re-evaluation.

After the war, Schoenberg divided his activities between Vienna, in the suburb of Mödling where he made his home, and Berlin, where, in 1915, he received a life appointment as professor at the Academy of Arts in succession to Busoni. In Vienna he helped found the Society for Private Performances, where the music of Schoenberg and his circle could be performed under favorable auspices. In 1923, his wife, Mathilde died, after bearing him two children. One year later, Schoenberg married Gertrud Kolisch, sister of the famous violinist and founder of the Kolisch String Quartet; they had three children. She survived him by almost sixteen years, passing away in Los Angeles, California, on February 14, 1967.

With the rise of Hitler in Germany, Schoenberg was deposed from his professorship at the Academy of Arts in Berlin. Though he had been converted to Christianity in 1921, Schoenberg was regarded as undesirable by the Nazis because of his Jewish birth and his revolutionary methods in music. Recognizing the menace of Nazism, Schoenberg decided to leave Europe for good. En route to the United States, he returned to the Jewish fold in a religious ceremony in a Parisian synagogue. He came to New York in the fall of 1933 and for a few months taught composition at the Malkin School of Music in Boston. He then established permanent residence in Brentwood, a suburb of Los Angeles. From 1935 to 1936, he was professor of music at the University of Southern California, and from 1936 to 1944, at the University of California in Los Angeles. After 1944, his teaching activity was confined to a few select private pupils. His seventieth and seventy-fifth birthdays were celebrated with festive concerts of his works in Europe and the United

States. In 1947, he received a Special Award of Merit from the National Institute of Arts and Letters. He died at his Brentwood home in California on July 13, 1951.

1899–1917 VERKLAERTE NACHT (TRANSFIGURED NIGHT), for chamber orchestra (also for sextet), op. 4.

PILLAR OF FIRE, ballet in one act based on *Verklaerte Nacht,* with choreography and book by Antony Tudor, and with Schoenberg's music. First performance: New York, April 8, 1942.

Verklaerte Nacht is Schoenberg's most frequently heard composition. It started out in 1899 as a sextet for strings. In this form it received its world première in Vienna on March 18, 1902, when it was a failure. In 1917, Schoenberg transcribed it for chamber orchestra, the form in which the composition became world famous. A few additional stylistic changes were made by the composer in 1943.

What we hear in this music is not the apostle of atonality, or the high-priest of the twelve-tone system, but the ardent post-Romantic of the late nineteenth century, powerfully influenced by Wagner. Chromatic in its harmonies, sensuous in melodic content, hyper-emotional in feeling, *Verklaerte Nacht* is effective atmospheric music which catches magically the descriptive and emotional nuances of the poem that had inspired it. That poem was *Weib und die Welt* by Richard Dehmel. It tells of a walk through a moonlit grove by a man and a woman. The woman confesses she has been unfaithful, and is pregnant with another man's child. The man stands ready to forgive and forget. The two fall rapturously into each other's arms and resume their walk through the grove. Through the man's compassionate forgiveness, the world becomes transfigured.

Schoenberg divided his tone poem into two sections. In the first, the woman confesses her guilt; in the second, she is forgiven. The work opens in a quiet, nocturnal mood. The atmospheric music of the introduction, intended to describe the lovers walking through the moonlight, later becomes the transition between the two sections of the tone poem, and is brought back to end the composition. Tremolos in violins and violas set the stage for the first theme, which erupts turbulently, then subsides. The mood becomes passionate, and a powerful climax is reached. A recitative-like passage brings back the material of the introduction, but this time in loud and forceful accents. Atmospheric writing now suggests the night, the walk, the confession. The transfiguration is evoked in undulating figures, in a passage for solo violin in the upper register, and in a version of the main theme. Soon this main theme is used polyphonically with the music of the transfigured night. A crescendo describes an outburst of passion on the part of the lovers. The music of the introduction is recalled to suggest the resumption of the walk in the moonlight through the grove.

Pillar of Fire, the ballet inspired by *Verklaerte Nacht* and using its music, follows the story line of Dehmel's poem closely, placing the time in or about 1900, and the setting in an unidentified town. "Because it is a ballet," George Balanchine explains, "it takes the story and presents it dramatically, introducing additional characters, giving us a picture of the community in which such an event can take place, motivating the principal characters and their actions as completely as possible." *The Pillar of Fire* was a huge success at its première, receiving twenty-six curtain calls. It has since come to be recognized as Antony Tudor's finest dance creation. It was in this work that the American ballerina, Nora Kaye, first emerged as a star.

1901 GURRE-LIEDER (SONGS OF GURRE), cantata for narrator, solo voices, chorus and orchestra.

In the last and most ambitious of his post-Romantic compositions, Schoenberg produced ardent, beautiful music. The *Gurre-Lieder,* as Paul Rosenfeld once said of it, is "poetic, glamorous; the poetry is a fragile one, and an exquisite one, a sort of expression of the gleaming, evanescent moment of feeling." The style springs from the two mighty Richards—Wagner and Strauss—and a mighty Gustav (Mahler). It is prodigal in its use of chromatic harmonies, elaborate contrapuntal passages, sensuous surges of melody. After thus letting himself go emotionally and romantically without inhibitions, Schoenberg felt impelled to adopt a new creative style calling for discipline.

The *Gurre-Lieder* is the kind of super structure to which so many post-Romantics were addicted. The forces included a narrator, five solo voices, three male choruses, an eight-part mixed chorus, and a huge orchestra numbering one hundred and forty musicians. When Schoenberg wrote out the parts of his giant score, he had to order special note paper with forty-eight staves.

The *Gurre-Lieder* is a setting of nineteen poems by Jens Peter Jacobsen, narrating the story of the love of King Waldemar I of Denmark for Tove during the Middle Ages. It is in three sections. In the first, we are told that the king has presented his beloved with the castle of Gurre as a gift. An ecstatic love scene unfolds, Tristanesque in sensuality and in its premonition of death. This part ends with the celebrated "Song of the Wood Dove," an elegy in which the bird describes the murder of Tove at the hands of the Queen. In the second part, the king rejects God for having allowed the murder to take place. The third part is the most dramatic of all, depicting, in Paul Stefan's words, "a spectral vision of a ride of Death" followed by a "melodramatic interlude . . . and finally a magnificent chorus greeting the sun."

In the third part, Schoenberg anticipates his future as a composer. A narrator provides a transition between the description of the night-ride and that of the rising sun. This music is the first time that Schoenberg employed *Sprechstimme* or *Sprechgesang,* a technique of melodic writing which he would develop fully a decade later in *Pierrot Lunaire*. In spite of this forward glance, *Gurre-Lieder* belongs solidly in Schoenberg's first creative period, having been conceived between 1899 and 1901, except for the final chorus and orchestration which came in 1911.

The first performance took place in Vienna on February 23, 1913, Franz Schreker conducting. It was a huge success. After the majestic opening of the final chorus, "Behold, the Sun!" many in the audience arose and remained standing until the entire work was over. A tremendous ovation followed. Schoenberg, who had a seat in the gallery, was finally induced to come to the stage. He came, made a hurried bow to the conductor and orchestra, but refused to recognize the audience. He later explained: "For years, those people who cheered me tonight refused to recognize me. Why should I thank them for appreciating me now?"

1906 KAMMERSYMPHONIE NO. 1 (CHAMBER SYMPHONY), for fifteen solo instruments, (also for full orchestra), op. 9-b.

The first *Kammersymphonie* is a transitional work. It has been described as a two-faced mirror, one face looking into Schoenberg's post-Romantic past, and the other looking forward into Schoenberg's expressionist future. This is one of the last works in which Schoenberg uses a basic tonality (it opens and closes in the key of E major); to some of its harmonic writing and scoring Schoenberg's earlier post-Romantic tendencies still cling. But this music is also a voice of the future. As Egon Wellesz noted: "Already in the opening bars a chord consisting of five superimposed fourths appears, which harmonically heralds the first theme of the principal section, a passionate theme of aspiration for the horn." This theme, Wellesz adds further, "made up of fourths, plays an important part in the course of the symphony: it appears at all the important points of departure in the development, and thanks to its peculiar composition it is capable of discarding tonality and also, through its fanfare-like character, of bringing into the polyphonic texture of the voices a contrast that has immediate effect."

The première took place seven years after it had been written, in Vienna on March 31, 1913. As was now almost habitual with Schoenberg premières, a riot developed in the auditorium. Before the music ended, the audience expressed its resentment by whistling, banging the seats, hissing, laughing. Some left the hall noisily, expressing their anger as they left. In order that a better understanding of this complicated music be possible, the work was played a second time at this concert, but without favorable results. As a correspondent for the *Musical Courier* reported: "The audience sat perfectly silent as if stunned. One Berlin critic compared the harmonic structure of the work to a field of weeds and turnips mixed together, and the general opinion was that the composition was a most unaccountable jumbling together of abnormalities." The critic of the Berlin *Signale* described the work as a "horror chamber symphony."

Schoenberg rescored the composition for full orchestra in 1935; this was introduced in Los Angeles on December 17, 1935, the composer conducting.

1907 STRING QUARTET NO. 2 IN F-SHARP MINOR, with soprano voice, op. 10. I. Mässig. II. Sehr rasch. III. Litanie: langsam. IV. Entrückung: sehr langsam.

In his second string quartet (which followed the first in D minor, op. 7, by three years), Schoenberg is still bound to the past by his adherence to a basically classical structure, by his use of a specific key signature. But before the work ends, Schoenberg embarks on a major revolution. The finale is completely atonal (the first piece of music of its kind), and for this reason the year of its composition has been described as one of the most decisive turning points in the history of music.

The work starts off in a traditional manner, with a first movement in sonata form. The scherzo is also traditional for the most part, its ironic overtones having been interpreted as a satire on the more or less conventional attitudes of the first movement. Here Schoenberg quotes briefly the famous Austrian drinking song, "*O du lieber Augustin.*" The third movement introduces a soprano voice in a setting of a Stefan George poem, "Deep Is the Mourning that Wraps Me in Darkness." Here the composer's material is derived from the main themes of the two preceding movements. The voice is again heard in the epoch-making atonal finale, once again in a poem by Stefan George. "With the first notes corresponding to the words 'I feel the air of other planets,' the hearer is at once in a new tone-world," says W. W. Cobbett.

1909 FIVE PIECES FOR ORCHESTRA (5 ORCHESTER STÜCKE), op. 16. I. Vorgefühle. II. Vergangenes. III. Farben (Der wecheselnde Akkord). IV. Peripetie. V. Das obligate Rezitativ.

Schoenberg's first complete works in an atonal style were the 3 Klavierstücke, for piano. op. 11 (1909), and the *Five Pieces for Orchestra.* The latter is among his most significant productions in the second phase of his development. Since it is a major pioneer work in the atonal style, it was described by Virgil Thomson in 1948 as "among the more celebrated works of our century. . . . It deserves every bit of its worldwide prestige and none of its worldwide neglect."

And it had been sorely neglected. The world première took place in London at a Queen's Hall Promenade concert, Sir Henry J. Wood conducting, on September 3, 1912. The critics were savage in their reactions. "Modern intellect has advanced beyond mere elementary noise," said the critic of the *Morning Post,* "Schoenberg has not." The critic of the *Daily News* said: "We must be content with the composer's assertion that he has depicted his own experiences—for which he has our heartfelt sympathy." And a reviewer for the *Daily Mail* remarked: "If music at all, it is music of the future and, we hope, a distant one."

The work was played again in London on January 17, 1914, with Schoenberg conducting, and in the United States on December 18, 1914, with Karl Muck conducting the Boston Symhony. After that, performances came few and far between. When Dimitri Mitropoulos led the composition at a concert of the New York Philharmonic, in the fall of 1948, it had been played twice before in New York, and on one of these occasions only three of the five movements had been given.

Here is how Egon Wellesz described the work: "The first movement, 'Presentiments,' is the simplest harmonically. It is constructed on a logical and consistent bass motive which is sometimes augmented, sometimes diminished." The second movement, "The Past," is lyrical and reflective. "The middle section is unusually soft and tender; it begins with a theme for solo viola which is taken up later by the cello. Then begins an episode in which the celesta plays an imitative figure, accompanied by two flutes alone. Into this texture there is brought a theme, light and staccato, for the bassoon, which later becomes prominent and forms a counterpoint to the first lyrical theme of the middle section." This is followed by "Colors" or "The Changing Chord," a pictorial piece of harmonic interest in which the same chord is seen in a continually changing light. Here is how Schoenberg himself described this piece of music: "The change of chords which runs through the entire piece without any thematic development, produces an effect comparable to the quivering reflection of the sun upon calm water." The fourth piece, "Peripetie" is agitated music. "Peripetie" is defined as a "sudden reversal of circumstances in a drama, or, by extension, in actual affairs." Here, says Wellesz, we find "lively passages for the woodwinds and impetuous figures for the trumpets and trombones." The concluding number, "The Obbligato Recitative" is both lyrical and polyphonic. René Leibowitz describes this movement in the following way: "A principal melody, perpetually new, which never repeats a previously heard figuration, runs throughout the piece. . . . The melody is constantly accompanied by parts of great expressive force and utter independence. . . . The astonishing counterpoint which results from this, combined with the instrumental variety . . . makes this piece one of the richest examples of polyphony in all music."

1909–1913 ERWARTUNG (EXPECTATION), monodrama in four scenes, with text by Marie Pappenheim. First performance: Prague, June 6, 1924.

DIE GLÜCKLICHE HAND (THE LUCKY HAND), a drama with music in one act, with text by the composer. First performance: Vienna, October 14, 1924.

Schoenberg's first stage work was a one-character opera that he wrote in seventeen days in 1909. It takes half an hour for performance. There is no dramatic action, the music following "the course of inner emotions," as Abraham Skulsky explained, "and suggests the world of Freudian psychoanalysis." In place of action Schoenberg gives us "the expression of inner emotion in almost a minute to minute development." The single character is a woman who, in the first scene, is searching for her lost lover. She has come to the edge of a forest; since it is night, she is overwhelmed by fears. She, nevertheless, penetrates the forest in the second scene. She stumbles over an object she thinks is a body but which actually is just the trunk of a tree. In the third scene, her terror mounts as she approaches the edge of the forest. The concluding scene finds her outside the forest. Once again she stumbles, but this time over the body of her beloved. "From this moment on," says Skulsky, "the drama reveals her subconscious states and hallucinations. In quick succession we pass from despair to hope, from love to hate, from reality to dreams. Her last words, sung in a state of ecstasy are, 'Oh, are you here? I was searching.'"

While not in the twelve-tone technique (the device was not to be formulated by Schoenberg for another fourteen years), the work is, nevertheless, constructed from the twelve tones of the chromatic scale, though not in any preconceived sequence. Consequently, this little opera anticipates Schoenberg's later concept of the twelve-tone row. "A striking example of this prophetic treatment," says Skulsky, "may be found in the middle of the fourth scene where the woman sings of her love for the man whose body she has found. At the words '*Nun kuss ich mir an di zu Tode*' the voice starts a twelve-tone theme which is directly taken over by the bassoon." Another spot where the twelve-tone row is anticipated is the beginning of the opera. "Eight notes of the scale constitute the melodic line, three additional notes are placed vertically in the harmony, and the twelfth is an enharmonic tone used previously."

The world première of *Erwartung* was given at a festival of the International Society for Contemporary Music in Prague. The American première came in the form of a concert presentation by the New York Philharmonic under Dimitri Mitropoulos on November 15, 1951. The first American staged version followed in Washington, D.C. on December 28, 1960.

Written immediately after *Erwartung* (between 1910 and 1913), *Die glückliche Hand* is "the counterpart of its stage predecessor," says Paul Collaer. "In this drama, the destiny of a life in its entire span is condensed into a few decisive and supreme moments. There is no realism here, either, and we are transported into that dream-state which reflects the almost visionary state Schoenberg lived in for the whole period from 1910 to 1914."

The cast comprises a man (baritone): a man and a woman who have silent roles; a chorus of six women; and a chorus of six men. On a darkened stage, a man is lying on the floor, while a mythological monster is holding him down under a giant paw. The chorus is dimly seen through gaps in the backdrop. In a chant, that is half speech and half song, the chorus laments the fate of the man for trying to achieve that which is unattainable. After the monster and chorus disappear, the man is found in a series of tableaux, seeking a woman who symbolizes for him earthly happiness, but who prefers another who represents power and wealth. Other disappointments and frustrations overwhelm the hero. In the concluding scene, he is once again found on the floor, as the monster bites him in the neck. The opera ends with the questioning chant of the chorus: "Must you once again suffer? Don't you know the meaning of sacrifice? Must you go through all this again?" Finally, the chorus exclaims sympathetically: "Poor thing!"

"The music," says Collaer, "is even more unreal than *Erwartung,* and is lit with almost heavenly colors. . . . [It] achieves, even more completely than *Erwartung,* the ideal of dramatic expression: all motion is confined to the spirit."

In *The World of Opera,* Wallace Brockway and Herbert Weinstock point out that in the staging Schoenberg intended "that color dynamics should parallel musical dynamics—increasing orchestral volume being accompanied by a shift in colors from red to brown to green to dark blue to purple."

The American première of *Die glückliche Hand* took place in Philadelphia on April 11, 1930, under the auspices of the League of Composers. Leopold Stokowski conducted.

1912 PIERROT LUNAIRE, song cycle for speaking voice, piano, flute (or piccolo), clarinet (or bass clarinet), violin (or viola) and cello, op. 21. I. Modenstrunken. II. Colombine. III. Der Dandy. IV. Eine blasse Wäscherin. V. Valse de Chopin. VI. Madonna. VII. Der kranke Mond. VIII. Nacht. IX. Gebet an Pierrot. X. Raub. XI. Rote Messe. XII. Galgenlied. XIII. Enthauptung. XIV. Die Kreuze. XV. Heimweh. XVI. Gemeinheit. XVII. Parodie. XVIII. Der Mondfleck. XIX. Serenade. XX. Heimfahrt. XXI. O alter Duft.

In setting the decadent symbolism of Albert Guiraud's "three-seven melodramas" (or short poems), Schoenberg passed over the threshold of expressionism. This is abstract music completely divorced from extramusical connotations, in spite of the fact that he is setting a verbal text; its interest and force spring exclusively from musical values. It is not necessary to know the poems to respond to Schoenberg's taut, intense music, or to appreciate its capacity to reflect the many different moods and shades of feeling. As a matter of fact, the composer at times consciously made his music antithetical to the words—as in the nineteenth song in which the text speaks of a viola, but the music is written for the cello.

New avenues of expression are traveled upon. There is no identifying tonality, the music passing freely from one key to another; discords predominate; the melodic writing is tense and concentrated; the solo voice—*Sprechstimme* or *Sprechgesang*—almost becomes a musical instrument, an integral part of the instrumental texture, as it glides from one note to the next.

In the first song, "Moonstruck" (piano, flute, viola and cello) the poem describes how the moon pours its wine on the sea night after night—wine to be drunk with the eyes. "Colombine" (piano, flute, clarinet, viola) praises the pale blossoms of the moonlight, and the white wonder roses. "Dandy" (piano, piccolo, clarinet) discusses Pierrot as he stands by a fountain in the moonlight. "A Pale Washerwoman" (flute, clarinet, violin) tells of the whiteness of the washerwoman's arms and the linen she is washing; this entire piece has no piano accompaniment, is throughout pianissimo, and is marked "without any expression." "Waltz by Chopin" (piano, flute, clarinet) touches on the sad and wistful charm of a waltz, which is compared to the pale drop of blood that colors the lips of a sick man. "Madonna" (flute, bass, clarinet and cello) is a poetic prayer to the Madonna; here, the piano accompaniment is heard only in the last measure. "The Sick Moon" (speaking voice and flute) is a poignant description of a sick man. "Night," subtitled "Passacaglia" (piano, bass clarinet and cello) is an invocation to the black night; the narrator is assigned only three singing tones in low register. "Prayer to Pierrot" (clarinet and piano) is a plea for the restoration of life's gaiety to one who now knows only terror. "Theft" (flute, clarinet, violin and piano) speaks of Pierrot's nightly adventures in stealing the ducal rubies, symbol of the bloody drops of a past fame. "The Red Mass" (piccolo, bass clarinet, viola, cello and piano) is Pierrot's blasphemous attack on dusk. "The Song of the Gallows" (piccolo, viola, cello and piano) is the condemned man's last sight of a mistress who is about to murder him. In "Decapitation" (bass clarinet, viola, cello and piano) Pierrot catches a glimpse of the crescent moon, which appears to him like a Turkish sword about to decapitate him. "The Crosses" (piano, flute, clarinet, violin and cello) symbolizes the verses as crosses on which the poet bleeds. "Homesickness" (clarinet, violin and piano) compares Pierrot's cries to the sighs of an old Italian pantomime. "Outrage" (piccolo, clarinet, violin, cello and piano) once again gives voice to Pierrot's outcries, this time when he bores a hole into Cassander's skull into which he stuffs Turkish tobacco;

sticking a reed into the base of the skull, Pierrot puffs with contentment. "Parody" (piccolo, clarinet, viola and piano) shows a matron in love with Pierrot, exposed by the moonlight. In "Moonspot" (cello and piano) Pierrot takes a walk in the moonlight when the moon throws a white spot on Pierrot's jacket which will not come off. "Serenade" (cello and piano) finds Pierrot playing on a viola with a huge bow. Cassander seizes him by the collar and begins to fiddle a tune on his bald head. "Journey Home," subtitled "Barcarolle" (flute, clarinet, viola, cello and piano) speaks of Pierrot's trip to Bergamo, a water lily serving as his boat, and the moonbeam as his rudder. "Oh, Olden Fragance" (flute, clarinet, violin, cello and piano) nostalgically recalls the charm of old tales.

Because this music was both so complex and so unorthodox, *Pierrot Lunaire* needed forty rehearsals before it could get performed. The première in Berlin on October 16, 1912, provoked a scandal. "If this is music," wrote Otto Taubman in the *Boersen Courier,* "then I pray my Creator not to let me hear it again."

1924 SUITE FOR PIANO, op. 25. I. Praeludium. II. Gavotte. III. Musette. IV. Intermezzo. V. Minuet. VI. Gigue.

This is the first Schoenberg composition in which the entire composition is built from a twelve-tone row (E, F, G, D-flat, G-flat, E-flat, A-flat, D, E, C, A, B-flat). The first movement (Rasch) is twentieth-century vitality, while the next two movements (Etwas langsam; Nicht hastig und Rascher) return to the world of Baroque. An expressive melodic line is found in the Intermezzo. The minuet (Moderato) has for its opening and closing sections another sustained melodic line while the trio makes use of an inverted canon. The concluding part (Rasch) contains a good deal of bravura writing and electrifying changes of tempo.

1926 STRING QUARTET NO. 3 op. 30. I. Moderato. II. Adagio. III. Allegro moderato. IV. Molto moderato.

In Schoenberg's first string quartet (1905), the writing, for the most part, was post-Wagnerian. The second quartet (1908) was his first departure from traditional tonality. The third quartet was the first in the twelve-tone technique, the technique here being used with a certain amount of freedom, since repetition of notes is permitted in introductory and transitional pasages. This quartet was introduced in Vienna by the Kolisch Quartet on September 19, 1927.

The structure is classic, not only in its use of the four traditional movements but also in the way each is developed. The first movement is identified by a rhythmic ostinato that courses throughout the section, frequently serving as the background for the terse themes. The first principal theme is given in the fifth measure by the first violin, which later also presents the second theme. In the second movement, the theme and variations form is utilized. Two ten-measure themes are varied three times. The last two movements have powerful rhythmic momentum, while the melodic material is austere. The third movement is an intermezzo, the main thought assigned to viola, with second violin and cello providing the accompaniment. The finale is a rondo, the key to which is the opening twelve-measure subject in the violin.

1928 VARIATIONS FOR ORCHESTRA, op. 31.

This is Schoenberg's first work for orchestra constructed from a twelve-tone row. Its première was given by the Berlin Philharmonic under Wilhelm Furtwängler on December 2, 1928. "The majority of the audience was silent," wrote Max Marschalk in *Die Vossiche Zeitung,* "but two excited minorities engaged in combat. The give-and-take of remarks for and against the piece grew to greater dimension and took more unfortunate forms than we ever experienced at a Schoenberg première. And we are accustomed to almost anything." At the American première in 1929 (performance by the Philhadelphia Orchestra under Stokowski), the audience broke out into hissing.

The work is made up of an introduction, the theme, nine variations and a finale. The introduction is subdued (Misterioso) in which the tone row is introduced, together with its inversion. This introduction ends with a motive built on the name of Bach (the notes, B, A, C, H—"H" representing in German B-natural, and "B," B-flat). It is presented by the trombone. The theme that follows is given by the cello over a chordal accompaniment; it has three sections, each utilizing one form of the twelve-tone row. Schoenberg has explained that the nine variations on this theme are "formal or developing variations, inasmuch as everything develops from the theme and its individual features, and there is, as usual, a general tendency towards quicker movement. But they are also 'character' variations, in that each of them at the same time develops some particular 'character.' Each of the first four variations contains an exact repetition of the theme in one part, with only rhythmic variations." The finale serves as a development. The theme never appears here in its entirety; instead, it is offered in fragments. The B-A-C-H motive makes frequent appearances.

1932 MOSES UND ARON, opera in two acts, with text by the composer based on *Exodus*. First performance: Hamburg Radio, March 12, 1954 (concert version); Zurich, June 6, 1957 (staged presentation).

Moses and Aaron is a twelve-tone opera. Schoenberg completed two acts in 1932, intending a third, for which he completed the text but not the music. In his last months, in 1951, he returned to the opera, hoping to complete it, but he did not live to do so. He left instructions, however, that, if the music remained unwritten, the opera be produced with the third act played as spoken drama.

This is the composer's most ambitious stage work. Some musicologists place it with the most important operas written since *Pelléas et Mélisande.* Nevertheless, it had to wait more than twenty-two years to get performed—partly because it was not finished, partly because it offered prodigious musical and staging problems. When first heard, it was given in a radio presentation, in oratorio fashion. Then the Zurich Opera produced it. Three hundred and fifty choral rehearsals, and thirty orchestral rehearsals were needed to bring the work into shape. Neither performance, however, proved a completely satisfactory realization of the composer's intentions. It was mainly through the efforts of Hermann Scherchen that the opera finally emerged into the limelight of critical and public acceptance. He conducted stage performances in Milan, Vienna, Berlin and Paris. Then, on June 28, 1965, the opera was mounted at Covent Garden, where it proved a success of the first magnitude.

The action is taken out of chapters 3 and 4, and 20 through 32, in *Exodus,* beginning with the calling of Moses from the voice in the burning bush and reaching a climax in the second act with the orgy before the Golden Calf. In that orgy, naked virgins engage in promiscuous sexual practices; live bears are sacrificed, their blood-drenched carcasses being thrown over the heads of the revelers. This scene caused a good deal of concern in England before the Covent Garden première, inviting some unwelcome sensationalism attending that performance. At the request of the censors, the virgins were made to wear loin cloths and have their backs turned to the audience during the carnal episodes. The Corybantic around the gold calf was understressed. Since fire is not permitted on the stage of Covent Garden, the burning of live animals was dispensed with. "But," reported Jan Maguire to the *Herald,* "the orgy was quite evident—little was left to the imagination—and the most realistic scene was the sacrifice of the animals."

In *The New York Times,* Peter Gradenwitz explained that "Schoenberg tried to give his own answers to the eternal questions of morals, religion, belief, idolatry. His Moses is the bearer of great spiritual ideas, which he feels impotent to express in words. His younger brother, Aaron, is the man of deeds—a born orator and leader. God speaks through Moses; Moses wants Aaron to convey the message to the people. . . . The second act . . . ends on a tragic note, and no answer is given to the problem." The third act, for which no music exists, shows "spirit to triumph over matter, Moses over Aaron, the idea over the word. The opera, when performed only as a monumental fragment, without the final act, puts Schoenberg's own credo into a somewhat faulty perspective."

A single twelve-tone row serves as the basis for the entire opera. Extensive use is made of *Sprechstimme,* with Moses's part being entirely spoken, while Aaron's is sung, ranging from declamation to expressive melody. The variety of musical means employed is highlighted by the effective use of polyphony: the double fugue of the Interlude between the first and second acts, for example; or the strict canon climaxing the hymn of the people at the end of the first act. Orchestral sonorities help build up tensions, or to arrive at points of climax, particularly, as Hans F. Redlich wrote in *Opera,* "the wiry screech of the woodwinds in their highest register, and also the low moan of the trombones, tuba and double bassoon." Particularly significant and unique for Schoenberg was the "rhythmic resource and incisiveness, which contrasted starkly with the impressionistically veiled presentation of much of Schoenberg's early orchestral music. Thoroughly dramatic motifs, such as the barbaric shout of the four horns at the beginning of the 'Dance Around the Golden Calf' reiterated later backstage by trombones at the entry of the Ephraimites and the tribal leaders, have an immediate scenic appeal, like nothing in Schoenberg's earlier works for the stage."

In summing up his overall reaction to the opera, Redlich concludes: "Its very sound—mysterious, visionary, frenzied, triumphant in turns—is as unique as its mixture of elements of opera, oratorio and cantata, serving together in the transmission of a tremendous religious experience. When the music ebbs away prematurely at the end of Act II—with Moses despairing of his vocation in a moving passage combining instrumental melody and *Sprechstimme*—an artistic and a human experience has reached its consummation, which may well represent to future generations the musical high-water mark of this century."

1936 CONCERTO FOR VIOLIN AND ORCHESTRA, op. 36. I. Poco allegro. II. Andante grazioso. III. Allegro.

The Schoenberg concerto is not often heard for two good reasons. It is not easy to listen to, and it is not easy to perform. As for the latter, the concerto is probably one of the most difficult in the repertory, as the composer himself realized when he remarked: "I believe that in my violin concerto I have created the necessity for a new kind of violinists."

The form is more or less traditional, with the first movement a sonata-allegro, the second in ternary structure, and the finale a rondo. The entire work is in the twelve-tone technique. The row on which the concerto is based is as follows: A, B-flat, E-flat, B, E, F-sharp, C, C-sharp, G, A-flat, D, and F. In the opening of the concerto, the row is shared by solo instrument and orchestra. After this, however, the row is heard in its entirety in the solo violin.

The world première took place in Philadelphia on December 6, 1940. Louis Krasner was the soloist, and Stokowski conducted the Philadelphia Orchestra. The concerto is dedicated to Schoenberg's pupil and disciple, the dedicated dodecaphonist, Anton Webern.

1936 STRING QUARTET NO. 4, op. 37. I. Allegro molto; energico. II. Comodo. III. Largo. IV. Allegro.

In his Fourth Quartet, Schoenberg was able to realize what Lou Harrison described in *Modern Music* as a more delicate balance of forms, "which allows for greater differentiation of musical idea and intense dramatic contrast." This, as Harrison explains, made it possible for Schoenberg to "reintroduce the special expressive features of his early expressionist style without inferring either an esthetic regression or an upset in the solidity of his works."

Almost classic in form, this quartet has a simplicity and clarity which have distinguished some of Schoenberg's later works. Two themes comprise the first movement, the first energetic, the second highly syncopated. The second movement, a scherzo, opens with a swaying subject for viola which yields to melodic material strangely reminiscent of the old Viennese Ländler—heavy-stamping waltz music. The expressive third movement opens with the four strings playing in unison to create a highly effective mood; there then follows a melody of dark, rich character which bears some resemblance to the Hebraic *Kol Nidrei.* (Schoenberg had made a setting of the *Kol Nidrei* two years earlier.) A rhythmically forceful movement brings the quartet to a close.

1942 ODE TO NAPOLEON, for speaking voice, piano and string orchestra, op. 41.

The *Ode to Napoleon* is a setting of Byron's *Ode to Napoleon,* a bitter denunciation of the autocrat. It is Schoenberg's first musical work with political implications. Byron's poem was used by the composer as a protest of man against tyranny and dictatorship. Schoenberg's view of the German dictator, whose hordes were sweeping triumphantly across Europe in 1942, was no different from Byron's view of Napoleon. Byron's final lines of invocation to George Washington—who represented to the poet the very opposite of Napoleon—were to Schoenberg a veritable paean to democratic freedom.

Schoenberg's music is in the twelve-tone technique, but without the mathematical rigidity of his earlier works; a definite twelve-tone row is not readily recognizable. The music for the speaking voice is the *Sprechstimme* of *Pierrot Lunaire,* but much more elastic, since no indication of pitch is given and many of the inflections are left to the performer. There is less austerity to Schoenberg's melodic writing in this score. Many of the melodic ideas are, indeed, rich with symbolic implications: that of Napoleon (ascending fourths, followed by descending minor seconds) gives a suggestion of the ruthlessness of the autocrat; that of Washington (fifths) represents, through harmonic inversion, the very antithesis of the dictator. Besides, there are pages in this music in which Schoenberg has brought genuine emotional warmth: the invocation to Washington is music of grandeur in breadth and feeling.

The *Ode to Napoleon* was introduced by the New York Philharmonic under Artur Rodzinski on November 23, 1944.

1942 CONCERTO FOR PIANO AND ORCHESTRA, op. 42.

Though this concerto is played without interruption, it is actually divided into four sections. The first is a waltz-like Andante consisting primarily of an extended lyrical passage for solo piano, following which the orchestra enters to participate in the development. This lyrical subject is the embryo out of which the entire concerto grows, and is subjected to numerous transformations and developments. A delightful scherzo-like section follows, in which the composer utilizes a wide gamut of colors and instrumental effects. An emotional Adagio ends in a cadenza, which serves as the transition to the concluding vigorous rondo.

The concerto is written entirely in the twelve-tone technique; but here Schoenberg's style is much less severe and forbidding than in earlier works. Indeed, pleasing sounds are achieved, along with romantic feelings and occasionally even an infectious charm.

On February 6, 1944, this concerto was introduced by Eduard Steuermann and the NBC Symphony under Stokowski.

1943 THEME AND VARIATIONS, for orchestra, op. 43-b.

During the last decade of his life, Schoenberg occasionally departed from the twelve-tone technique to write music in a more traditional style. As he said in *The New York Times* on December 19, 1948: "A longing to return to the older styles was always vigorous in me; and from time to time I have to yield to that urge."

It may have been just such an urge—or it may have been the particular purpose for which the work was intended—that led Schoenberg to adopt both a definite key center (G minor) and the resources of accepted harmonies for the *Theme and Variations*. For the work was intended for use by high-school bands, and Schoenberg never expected his twelve-tone technique to be the musical diet of youngsters. The band version was completed in 1943. Soon afterward, it was arranged by the composer for full orchestra, in which form it was introduced by the Boston Symphony Orchestra under Serge Koussevitzky on October 20, 1944.

The work consists of a theme (which is march-like in character, befitting a band) and seven variations. "In general," explained Schoenberg, "the variations proceed in the traditional manner, using motival and harmonic features of the theme, thus producing new themes of contrasting character and mood. In the first two variations, the tempo increases considerably. Variation III is an Adagio of a more songful character. Variation IV is a stylized waltz. Variation V, Molto moderato cantabile, is a canon in inversion. Variation VI is very fast (Alla breve) and violent in character, while the texture is contrapuntal. Variation VII approaches the style of a chorale prelude. The finale, as usual in classical music, adds a number of ideas which vary only part of the theme. The treatment is mostly contrapuntal."

1947 A SURVIVOR FROM WARSAW, cantata for narrator, men's chorus, and orchestra, op. 46.

Out of one of the ghastlier pages of the history of World War II—that concerning the Nazi concentration camps—Schoenberg has created one of his most stirring works. In the text, written by Schoenberg himself, the narrator begins with the following words: "I cannot remember everything. I must have been unconscious most of the time." He then describes grimly the clubbing of the old and the sick, and the lining up of the healthier ones for the gas chamber. The Nazis shout their orders in German. But above these cries there arises the traditional Hebrew prayer, "Hear O Israel"—first softly, but then growing in intensity until it becomes at once a shout of defiance and a promulgation of undying faith.

The realism of the text, which is one of its most striking features, is matched by the equally stark realism of Schoenberg's music, much of it written in his twelve-tone technique. Rarely before has he endowed his technique with such a wealth of human values. The atonality becomes expressive of mental anguish; the complex rhythms re-create the emotional turmoil; and the ascetic melodic line assumes cogent dramatic power.

"Into a rhapsodic musical structure that appears loose at first glance," says Kurt List, "Schoenberg infuses an atmosphere of horror and fear by purely musical means. This is accomplished in the first place—and on the surface—by impressionistic orchestral devices. More than in any other of Schoenberg's works the instruments are here exploited for all their coloristic potentialities, with their individual techniques pushed to the limit by such devices as tremolos in the strings, *Flatterzunge* (flutter-tongue) in the winds. . . . Rhythmically, the atmosphere of horror is created by repetitive, almost obsessional, metric patterns of a kind that Schoenberg had not made use of since his *Five Pieces for Orchestra*."

Though commissioned by the Koussevitzky Music Foundation, *A*

Survivor from Warsaw was not introduced by the Boston Symphony under Koussevitzky, but by the Albuquerque Civic Symphony under Kurt Frederick —on November 4, 1948.

GUNTHER SCHULLER 1925–

Gunther Schuller belongs in the camp of the avant-garde by virtue of his provocative, and frequently successful, experiments. He is the creator of "third-stream music," a term he devised in 1957 to describe compositions trying to bring about a fusion between jazz improvisations and the twelve-tone technique. It is in this style that he wrote not only his highly provocative and much publicized opera, *The Visitation,* in 1966. He has been involved with the problem of acoustics, by rearranging the seating of the orchestra to arrive at stereophonic projection better able to meet the needs of twentieth-century orchestral resources. He has assumed a place all his own by using serialism with such variety and effect that he has won wide public approval for at least a few of his serial compositions, even before his opera made him an international figure in music. He is a virtuoso of orchestration; he possesses an extraordinary ear for timbre and a remarkable gift to exploit the finest potential of instruments. Discussing this very point, John Rosenfeld has written: "He has one of the highest talents since Rimsky-Korsakov for placing instruments in the most euphonious and inviting registers." Schuller has a sense of humor. He can write simply and with clarity. And he has proved, as Irving Lowens noted in *Musical Quarterly,* "that melody and the most advanced serial technique are by no means incompatible."

Schuller was born in New York City on November 22, 1925. His father was a violinist in the New York Philharmonic for over forty years. When he was twelve, Gunther became boy soprano at the St. Thomas Choir School in New York. He also started studying the flute, but two years later transferred to the French horn, which he mastered. For a while he attended the Manhattan School of Music where he studied theory. Beyond this, he has been self-taught.

In 1943, he played the horn in the orchestra of the Ballet Theatre. Between 1944 and 1945, he was the first horn of the Cincinnati Symphony, and from 1945 to 1959, he played the horn in the orchestra of the Metropolitan Opera (nine of these years as first horn). In Cincinnati, he made his debut as composer with a horn concerto. In New York, he later achieved his first successes with the *Symphony for Brass and Percussion* (1950), introduced in the year of its composition by the Cincinnati Symphony; also the *Romantic Overture,* written in 1951, and performed successfully in Darmstadt, Germany, and in New York between 1954 and 1958. In 1959, he completed and had introduced his most successful work for orchestra, *Seven Studies on Themes of Paul Klee.*

After leaving the Metropolitan Opera orchestra, Schuller devoted himself to conducting and teaching, besides composition. In 1960, he received awards from the National Institute of Art and Letters and Brandeis University. One year later he became the first American composer commissioned to write a work for the modern-music festival at Donaueschingen, in Germany, for which he produced the *Contrasts,* for orchestra, introduced on October 22. He was twice recipient of Guggenheim Fellowships. He was sent by the State Department of the United States as special visitor to West Germany, Yugoslavia and Poland. In 1964, he received the Darius Milhaud Prize for his score to the Polish-made motion picture *Yesterday in Fact.* In 1965, he became composer-in-residence in Berlin on a Ford Foundation. He used this period to write the opera that achieved international renown, *The Visitation,* which had been commissioned and introduced by the Hamburg Opera. In 1966, he received the Hornblit Award.

In 1964, Schuller was appointed associate professor of music at Yale. In 1965, he succeeded Aaron Copland as head of the composition department at the Berkshire Music Center at Tanglewood. He resigned from Yale in 1966 to become president of the New England Conservatory in Boston.

1958 WOODWIND QUINTET, for flute, oboe, clarinet, French horn, and bassoon. I. Lento. II. Moderato. III. Agitato.

The *Woodwind Quintet* was one of the most successful chamber-music compositions Schuller had written up to this time. In the first movement, there is a continually dramatic contrast between agitated moods and placid ones. As Samuel Baron wrote in his liner notes for a Concert-Disc recording: "Whereas the 'calm' music gives the impression of absolute control (there is a long melody treated as cantus firmus, with a counterpoint of fragmented commentaries), the 'agitated' music gives the impression of wild abandon." Baron describes the second movement as a "sound piece" because of its interest in sonorities. "There is a *klangfarbenmelodie* on the note A. . . . There are sections that alternate vibrato playing with non-vibrato playing. There are violently changing versions of the same tone clusters. . . . The final drawn-out chords are dazzlingly scored to give the most eerie sense of space." Jazz elements are introduced in the closing movement. "The beginning and concluding sections . . . are in a strict and steady jazz beat. . . . The middle section, however, is in free rhythm and consists of a series of cadenzas for clarinet, bassoon, and horn."

1958 SPECTRA, for orchestra.

In *Spectra,* Schuller undertakes two experiments. The first concerns structure. Convinced that the conventional forms of symphonic music had outlived their usefulness for twentieth-century composers, Schuller created in *Spectra* a one-movement structure which, as he has explained, had "no preconceived formal mold into which the music could be formed. In terms of form, the work in a real sense unfolds itself."

The other experiment was of a "physical-acoustical nature." New techniques of writing for the orchestra, Schuller felt, demanded a new seating arrangement in the orchestra. In *Spectra,* he "devised a seating plan which conforms more to the variegated color possibilities of the modern orchestra, thus making performance more practical. The seating plan for *Spectra* also splits the orchestra into seven groups—five of them of various chamber-music sizes—which can operate independently or be joined at any time into a single unit." For example, a bass flute was placed in the very front, and tubas were given a new place of prominence to the right of the conductor, while to the conductor's left, woodwinds took over the place usually assigned to strings. This new arrangement of the orchestra not only helped to produce a stereophonic projection of the music ("causing sounds literally to travel from one side of the stage to the other") but also made possible the incorporation "into the very structure of the work (not as mere effects) antiphonal ideas."

The composer explains that the title of this composition suggests "an analogy with the color spectrum." It refers "to the use of various color series in an important all-pervading structural element of the work."

Spectra was commissioned by Dimitri Mitropoulos and the New York Philharmonic, who presented the world première in New York on January 14, 1960.

1959 SEVEN STUDIES ON THEMES OF PAUL KLEE. I. Antique Harmonies. II. Abstract Trio. III. Little Blue Devil. IV. The Twittering Machine. V. Arabian Town. VI. An Eerie Moment. VII. Pastorale.

This is one of the rare works in a serial technique which, from its first performance on, has won public approval. Having been written for the Minneapolis Symphony on a Ford Foundation grant (in conjunction with the American Music Center), this composition was received most enthusiastically when it was introduced in Minneapolis, under Antal Dorati's direction, on November 27, 1959. In short order, it was performed by major American symphony orchestras, receiving almost unqualified praise everywhere. It also represented the United States at the festival of the International Society for Contemporary Music at Cologne, Germany, on June 12, 1960.

Schuller interests himself here in the problem of finding the musical equivalent for the visual arts. Paul Klee, to be sure, is the celebrated Swiss modernist (1879–1940) with dadaist and surrealist tendencies. Seven of his paintings provided Schuller with material for his tonal explorations. The composer himself contributed the following information about each of the seven sections in an article published in the Minneapolis *Star* on November 26, 1959:

"Each of the seven pieces bears a slightly different relationship to the original Klee picture from which it stems. Some relate to the actual design, shape or color scheme of the painting, while others take the general mood of the picture or its title as a point of departure. . . . In *Antique Harmonies,* I tried to preserve not only Klee's amber, ochre and brown colors, but also the block-like shapes over which, in constant variation, Klee builds this remarkable painting. Over a dark, dense background, blocks of lighter-colored fifths gradually pile up, reaching a climax in the brighter yellow of the trumpets and high strings. A repeated cadence, common in the fourteenth-century music, and the organum-like open fifths establish the 'antique' quality of the harmonies.

"The music for *Abstract Trio* is played almost entirely by only three instruments at any given time. But the three instruments change during the course of the piece, changing from the bright color of the woodwind through the grainier texture of the muted brass and bassoon to the somber hues of low woodwind and tuba.

"*Little Blue Devil* is transformed into a kind of jazz theme. A perky angular theme (my musical impression of the geometrically conceived head in Klee's painting) is combined with a blues progression, altered to nine bars instead or the conventional twelve, and occasionally distorted asymmetrically. Various shades of 'blue' are maintained through the use of muted brass and low register clarinets.

"A piece based on Klee's famous *The Twittering Machine* should, it seems to me, do primarily one thing: twitter. The mathematical constructive element in present-day serial technique seemed to lend itself with special logic to such a pointillistic musical presentation.

"Klee's *Arab Village* is an abstracted serial view of a town baking in the bright North African desert sun. A beholder of such a scene—floating, as it were, above the village—might hear the often simultaneous chant of Arab melodies; the melancholy distant flute, blending with throbbing drums and the nasal dance tunes of the oboe. . . .

"The music of *An Eerie* (or *Ominous*) *Moment* is a musical play on the title more than on Klee's actual pen drawing. . . . I have tried to convey the atmosphere created by the slinking shapes of the picture. The strange, ominous tension of the opening finally finds sudden release in two terrified outbursts, only to sink back into oblivious calm.

"*Pastorale* was subtitled *Rhythms* by Klee. It is one of the many works of the artist employing a variation principle. It is also a painting that cannot be understood by a single glance. As in Klee's painting, several rhythmic-melodic shapes occur on various register and speed (temporal) levels. The pastoral quality of the clarinet, French horn and English horn underlines the suspended mood of the music."

1960 MUSIC FOR BRASS QUINTET. I. Moderato. II. Scherzo-Like. III. Slow.

This work was commissioned by the Elizabeth Sprague Coolidge Foundation for the Library of Congress in Washington, D.C., where it was introduced in January of 1961. The entire composition is improvisational in style. The first movement, explains the composer, "develops an organic continuity by means of fragmentation." In the second movement, the melodic and rhythmic material evolves "an initial maximum of fragmentation which produces an almost completely suspended time feeling, giving way to an intensification and thickening of texture." The finale is in the A-B-A structure, but with cadenzas in the "B" section.

1964 AMERICAN TRIPTYCH: STUDIES IN TEXTURE. I. Four Directions. II. Out of the Web. III. Swing Landscape.

In *American Triptych,* Schuller continues the experiment of the *Seven Studies on Themes of Paul Klee* to translate visual arts into musical sound. But in *American Triptych,* he goes a step further by seeking out those musical sounds that best approximate the texture of the painting he is interpreting in his music, rather than trying to portray the subjects themeselves. For this purpose he chose three abstract or non-objective paintings: *Four Directions* by Alexander Calder; *Out of the Web,* by Jackson Pollock; and *Swing Landscape,* by Stuart Davis.

American Triptych was introduced in New Orleans on March 9, 1965, the composer conducting.

The composition is short, lasting only fourteen minutes in all, and it is that blend of serialism and jazz for which the composer has coined the term "third stream."

1966 THE VISITATION, opera in three acts, with text by the composer based on Franz Kafka's *The Trial.* First performance: Hamburg Opera, October 12, 1966.

In 1963, Rolf Liebermann, director of the Hamburg Opera, commissioned Schuller to write a jazz opera for his company, scheduling the première for October of 1966. Schuller had no intention of writing another *Porgy and Bess.* Nevertheless, he was convinced that a jazz opera—even the kind of jazz opera in which he was interested, namely in a "third-stream" style—called for an American-Negro subject and characters. The search for a suitable libretto was on. His first choice fell on Ralph Ellison's *Invisible Man.* He had already completed a number of sketches, musical as well as literary, when he discovered that negotiations for the Ellison story had fallen through. With the October 1966 première date looming ever nearer, Schuller's search for a libretto became more frantic. Material by Genet and William Faulkner was considered and rejected. Finally, during the summer of 1965, reading about the racial riots in the South—and the injustices and inhumanity they bred—Schuller was struck with the possibility of adapting Kafka's surrealistic drama, *The Trial,* by transplanting the setting to the United States and using Negroes as main characters. The fact that the Austrian composer, Gottfried von Einem, had made an opera out of *The Trial* posed no insuperable problem, since von Einem voiced no objections. The deal with the Kafka estate proceeded smoothly. And Schuller went to work, developing his own libretto.

The principal character in Schuller's opera is an American Negro University student, Carter Jones. He occupies a nebulous world, since he is rejected by his own people and has not been accepted by the whites. "He is not better or worse than the people who surround him," explains James H. Sutcliffe, "a very human creature who falls victim to his own sensuality (there are three jazzy seduction scenes) at every point in the plot where a way out of his dilemma seems to be opening up for him. He is questioned, threatened, tried by a kangaroo court, bullied, and finally lynched . . . all for crimes he is not aware of having committed. The opera traces his frustrated attempts to find justice in a nightmare world of corruption and misunderstanding. Jones alone appears in every scene. The rest of the large cast forms a kaleidoscopic living background to his private world or helpless terror."

The opera opens with a recording of Bessie Smith singing a blues,

"Nobody Knows You When You're Down and Out." Thus a jazz note is sounded without preliminaries. After that, throughout the opera, a jazz ensemble of seven instrumentalists is used both in conjunction and in opposition to the symphony orchestra, and at times as background to the singers. From time to time, Schuller makes use, says Paul Moor, of "the kind of tonal jazz association with juke joints, with sleazy nightspots and at the end with old-time New Orleans funerals." But basically, Schuller's score is more in a twelve-tone or serial technique than in a jazz idiom.

The Visitation was the first opera sung in the English language to receive a world première in Germany. This did not prevent the work from achieving a fabulous reception. There was a twenty-two minute ovation after the opera was over, and some fifty curtain calls. The following morning the newspapers hailed the work and its performance as a triumph. Reaction from the world outside Hamburg was immediate. The Hamburg Opera received numerous invitations to bring the new opera to major capitals in Europe. Three companies bid for recording rights, while the performing rights were sought after, both in Europe and the United States. Two German opera houses offered Schuller commissions for new operas, and BBC made an offer for a new television opera. Few operas in the twentieth century have enjoyed the immediate and universal acclaim of the *Visitation,* and few composers have emerged the way Schuller did, as a major creative figure in the musical theatre with a maiden effort.

Strange to say, when *The Visitation* received its first American hearing on June 28, 1967 at the hands of the Hamburg Opera then visiting New York, the reaction of both audience and critics was in sharp contrast to that of Hamburg, Germany. Some in the audience left the opera house after the second act; others booed loudly at the end of the opera. The critical consensus was virtually unanimous in denouncing both the text and the music. The libretto was found to be an awkward presentation of cliches about civil rights; the characters seemed caricatures; the emotion appeared maudlin; and the sexual episodes lacked convincing motivation. The score was treated just as harshly. "The serial cliches," to Harold C. Schonberg in *The New York Times,* had "very little profile. The music never seems to go up or down. It plods along in a determined manner, like an old man walking down the street and mumbling to himself." Schonberg summed up: "The entire opera has a feeling of amateurism. . . . He [Schuller] is a long way from tackling a large-scale serious subject."

The question was inevitably posed why this opera should have been evaluated so much more enthusiastically on foreign soil than on home grounds. The reason in all probability is that German audiences are partial to the use of jazz in opera and are fascinated by the subject of racial discrimination in America. Besides there was a good deal in the often sordid text on which many a German could focus his anti-American sentiments.

When *The Visitation* was produced by the San Francisco Opera in October of 1967, it was received far more enthusiastically than it had been in New York. Typical of the critical reaction was the comment of the reviewer for the *Chronicle*) "The opera made impressive impact and established itself as an important work."

WILLIAM SCHUMAN 1910–

In discussing Schuman's music, many writers point out its invigorating, robust movement. Leonard Bernstein noted many years ago that Schuman's early compositions were characterized by "energetic drive, vigor of propulsion," while Alfred M. Frankenstein singled out their "nerves, virtuosity, drive." Motor energy is still one of the engaging qualities in Schuman, bringing buoyant enthusiasm and overpowering strength to each of his major works. But Schuman's music is by no means exclusively dynamic. Other traits are hardly less appealing: his expressive counterpoint, complex in texture, sometimes linear, but warm and intense; his long-breathed melodies, often of a classical beauty; his sure feeling for clear architectonic structure; and the production of an orchestral sound that is unmistakably his. His is music, as Flora Reta Schreiber and Vincent Persichetti have said in their biography of the composer, "that gets under the notes and in the blood stream. It breathes lyric beauty and stamps a vivid impression upon the listener. The pages of the scores are complex but the music that is projected from this complexity is clear and forceful. The control of emotional drive and the clarity of formal thinking bring the music directly within the reach of the listener. Logic is at no point outrun by invention and the architectural pattern is devoid of any feeling of experimentation."

Schuman was born in New York City on August 4, 1910. His academic education took place in the city public schools. His early musical training was haphazard, consisting mainly of some lessons on the violin. At high school he formed a jazz ensemble, in which he played violin and banjo and sang; at a boy's camp, during the summer, he created scores for stage productions and had his first serious piece of music played, a tango for violin and piano. After that, he wrote music for popular songs that were published and used as special material by night-club performers and vaudevillians. One of these songs, "In Love with You," had lyrics by Frank Loesser, later become one of America's most successful popular composers and lyricists; this was his first publication.

Hearing a symphony concert convinced Schuman to pursue music more seriously. After some preliminary study at the Malkin School of Music, he was taught counterpoint by Charles Haubiel and, for two years, composition by Roy Harris. Schuman's First Symphony and first string quartet were heard at the W.P.A. Composers Forum in New York in 1936; neither work satisfied the composer and he withdrew them permanently. His Second Symphony, introduced at a W.P.A. concert in New York, after which it was performed by the Boston Symphony under Koussevitzky on February 17, 1939, was also withdrawn after receiving unfavorable notices. But with the *American Festival Overture* and the third string quartet in 1939, the Third Symphony in 1941, and the cantata, *A Free Song,* in 1942, Schuman emerged as a composer not only of enormous potential but also of impressive achievements. The symphony got the New York Music Critics Circle Award, and the cantata received the Pulitzer Prize in music, the first time the award was ever given. In addition, Schuman received Guggenheim Fellowships in 1939 and 1940, the Award of Merit from the National Association of American Composers and Conductors in 1941, and an award from the National Institute of Arts and Letters in 1943. Since that time, he has been performed extensively. He has also gathered innumerable awards, tributes and other forms of public recognition. These include several honorary doctorates, and in 1957, the Bicentennial Anniversary Medal from Columbia University and the Brandeis University Creative Arts Award in music. He was made Fellow of the National Institute of Art and Letters and given an honorary membership to the Royal Academy of Music in London.

Between 1935 and 1945, Schuman was a member of the music faculty of Sarah Lawrence College in Bronxville, New York. In 1945, he was appointed director of publications of G. Schirmer, but he resigned this post after a few months to become president of the Juilliard School of Music. During the seventeen years he held this office, he instituted major reforms, changes of curriculum and other innovations which made the Juilliard School one of the foremost of its kind in the world. In January of 1962, Schuman withdrew from Juilliard to become president of the Lincoln Center for the Performing Arts in New York.

1939 AMERICAN FESTIVAL OVERTURE, for orchestra.

An incisive three-note phrase opens this authentically American piece of music, Schuman's earliest composition to become a repertory piece. This phrase was intended to simulate a familiar call—the syllables "Wee-awk-eem" which were used by boys in the New York City streets to convoke the gang for play. "This call," Schuman explained, "very naturally suggested itself for a piece of music being written for a special occasion—a festival of American music."

Schuman's own analysis of the piece follows: "The first section of the work is concerned with the material discussed above and the ideas growing out of it. This music leads to a transition section and the subsequent announcement by the violas of a fugue subject. The entire middle section is given over to this fugue. The orchestration is at first for strings alone, later for woodwinds alone, and finally, as the fugue is brought to fruition, by the strings and woodwinds in combination. The climax leads to the final section of the work, which consists of the opening materials paraphrased and the introduction of new subsidiary ideas."

The overture was introduced by the Boston Symphony Orchestra under Koussevitzky on October 6, 1939.

1941 SYMPHONY NO. 3. I. Passacaglia; Fugue. II. Chorale; Toccata.

Schuman wrote his First Symphony in 1935, and his Second four years after that. It was with his Third Symphony that he achieved his first major success as a symphonic composer. Its première—by the Boston Symphony Orchestra under Koussevitzky on October 17, 1941—was a triumph; the audience was enthusiastic, and the critics, virtually rhapsodic. The symphony received the New York Critics Circle Award in 1942, and after that was performed by virtually every major American symphony orchestra; it was also played with considerable success in London, Paris, Copenhagen, Berlin, etc.

Though seventeenth-century forms are utilized by Schuman, there is nothing archaic about the music, which is modern in idiom. There is polyphonic writing here of great complexity and dexterity, but this polyphony frequently has vertical beauty and dynamic power, and is often warm and human in its expressiveness. The theme of the Passacaglia is heard in the violas in the low register—a sturdy theme that dominates the entire movement. It is then altered melodically and rhythmically in a series of inventive variations. The Fugue comes without pause; its theme (approximately four measures long, marked Vigoroso) is heard in horns. A short introduction in violas and cellos leads to the Chorale that opens the second part (Andantino). It is derived from the passacaglia theme and is presented by solo trumpet. It is treated in several different ways before the music flows naturally into the Toccata section. As its name implies, the Toccata is a display piece featuring brilliant virtuoso writing for the entire orchestra.

1942 A FREE SONG, secular cantata no. 2, for chorus and orchestra. I. Too Long America; Look Down, Fair Moon. II. Song of the Banner at Daybreak.

For the text to his second secular cantata, Schuman went to Walt Whitman, couching three Whitman poems (as Nicolas Slonimsky put it so well) "in a propulsive rhythmic style as a twentieth-century counterpart of old Handelian forms." The writing is elaborately contrapuntal (the second part opens with an involved fugue), but the counterpoint generates considerable power. The overall effect is one of strength and brilliance.

On March 26, 1943, the cantata was introduced by the Boston Symphony Orchestra—in collaboration with the Harvard Glee Club and the Radcliffe Choral Society—under the direction of Serge Koussevitzky. Soon after this première performance, the cantata was awarded the Pulitzer Prize in music.

1943 SYMPHONY FOR STRINGS (SYMPHONY NO. 5). I. Molto agitato ed energico. II. Larghissimo. III. Presto leggiero.

Schuman's Fifth Symphony, scored for strings alone, was commissioned by the Koussevitzky Music Foundation and was introduced by the Boston Symphony under Koussevitzky on November 12, 1943. It is among the composer's most economical works in the symphonic form, comprising only basic materials made up of concentrated harmonic and contrapuntal thoughts. A brilliant, incisive theme, fortissimo, opens the first movement; it is presented by violins in unison on the G string. The secondary subject, derived partly from the first, is given loudly by the violas. This material is developed and varied with rhythmic and harmonic skill, as the powerful surge that set the movement into motion is maintained. Broad muted chords, in the second movement, precede the statement of the main melody in muted strings. The concluding movement is in a more or less rondo form. This is lively music, dominated by a robust theme that gets varied with each reappearance.

1945 UNDERTOW: CHOREOGRAPHIC EPISODES FOR ORCHESTRA. I. Prologue—Birth and Infancy. II. The City—Adolescence and Manhood. III. Epilogue—Guilt.

Undertow was Schuman's first ballet score. It was introduced by the Ballet Theatre in New York on April 10, 1945, described in the program as "a psychological murder story." Actually, it is the case history of a psychopath. The scenario (in three scenes) and the choreography is by Antony Tudor, based on a suggestion by John van Druten.

The following summary was prepared by both Schuman and Tudor: "The ballet . . . concerns itself with the emotional development of a transgressor. The choreographic action depicts a series of related happenings, the psychological implications of which result in inevitable murder. The hero is seen at various stages, beginning with his babyhood when he is neglected by his mother. . . . Frustrations . . . are heightened during boyhood by his sordid experiences in the lower reaches of a large city. He encounters prostitutes, street urchins, an innocent young girl, a bridal couple, dipsomaniacs, and a visiting mission worker whose care and friendship he seeks. The emotions aroused in the abnormal youth by these episodes . . . result in climax after climax, reaching a peak in the murder of a lascivious woman. It is only when he is apprehended for this crime that his soul is purged."

For this grim scenario, Schuman produced a powerful score, which derives much of its effect from continual reiteration, and in which the darker and more dramatic pages are offset by passages of gaiety and irony.

Schuman said: "In the symphonic version of *Undertow* I have attempted to maintain the continuity of the ballet score while at the same time keeping in mind the comparative demands of the theatre and concert hall. With the exception of the opening music for 'The City' all the principal episodes of the original score are maintained, but for concert purposes the music has been telescoped. Also, the orchestra for the concert version is larger than that used for the ballet."

The symphonic version was first performed in Los Angeles, Alfred Wallenstein conducting the Los Angeles Philharmonic, on November 29, 1945.

1947 CONCERTO FOR VIOLIN AND ORCHESTRA. I. Allegro risoluto; Molto tranquillo; Agitato—fervente. II. Interlude: andantino. III. Presto leggiero; Adagio; Alla marcia; Cantabile alternando con presto.

This concerto was introduced in Boston by Isaac Stern and the Boston Symphony Orchestra under Charles Munch on February 10, 1950. An expansive melody for the violin opens the concerto, undergoing some development and then being succeeded by a second melody, tranquil in mood, also played by the soloist. A rhapsodic passage for the violin is then heard. After a large cadenza, the movement ends dramatically. The second movement is intended as an interlude, consisting of a long, rhapsodic melody for the violin; it is intense in feeling, broad in design. A four-voice fugato introduces the final movement. After a climax for orchestra, the solo instrument enters. A short cadenza and a powerful climax then bring the concerto to an end.

Schuman revised this concerto twice, in 1954 and again in 1958.

1948 SYMPHONY NO. 6.

In 1948, the Dallas Symphony Orchestra commissioned Schuman to write an orchestral work. On February 27, 1949, it was introduced by that organization under Antal Dorati in Dallas, Texas.

Though in one uninterrupted movement, the symphony conisists of six parts, marked: Largo; Moderato con moto; Leggieramente; Adagio; Allegro risoluto—Presto; Larghissimo. The framework of the symphony is the two outside slow movements, while the other four movements have a suggestion of the classical symphonic form. The major subject is presented in the opening section, with a contrasting theme appearing contrapuntally. After the material has been offered, there comes the march-like music of the second section, in which the themes appear in variation. A kind of cadenza for kettle-drum leads into the third part, which is vivacious. After a slow passage for strings, there comes the Adagio, built out of a chorale-like melody. A violin solo comes as a transition to a highly rhythmic development section. There then emerges the turbulence of the Allegro risoluto passage, whose concluding Presto is in the nature of a coda. After a climax, an intermediary passage leads to the concluding Larghissimo, eloquent music with suggestions of mysticism.

1949 JUDITH: CHOREOGRAPHIC POEM FOR ORCHESTRA.

The Louisville Orchestra commissioned Martha Graham to prepare a solo dance with orchestra and asked her to suggest a composer for the music. Schuman had recently worked with Miss Graham in the ballet *Night Journey* (first performance at Harvard University, May 1, 1948). She asked him to write an orchestral piece she could use for a dance routine. The result was *Judith,* sometimes described as a "concerto for dancer and orchestra." It was introduced on January 4, 1950, with Robert Whitney conducting the Louisville Orchestra in Kentucky, and Miss Graham as dance soloist. The work made an extraordinary impression. When it was heard the following year in New York, it received the New York Music Critics Circle Award.

For his subject, Schuman went to the Book of Judith in the Old Testament Apocrypha. The famous Biblical story relates how the Bethulia are besieged by the Assyrians, headed by the general, Holofernes. On the pretext that she has come to betray her city, Judith gains access to the camp of the enemy, where she manages to murder the general during his drunken sleep. When she has delivered the head of the general to her people, they dance before her with joy.

Freda Rheta Schreiber and Vincent Persichetti say: "This dramatic and mature work contains numerous episodes and outbursts that are integrated by potent thematic material. The themes are introduced early in the work and never wait for each other to disrobe. . . . On the contrary, the presence of two or three themes is often used to press a point, and when a whole section is based on a few notes of a specific theme, the motif grows to resemble other themes in the work."

1950 STRING QUARTET NO. 4. I. Adagio. II. Allegro con fuoco. III. Andante. IV. Presto.

The composer instructed his performers in his score to be "calm and relaxed" in playing the first movement. But as Nicolas Slonimsky has remarked, this is made difficult by "the harsh frictional discords in the movement," cast as it is in two-part counterpoint. The second movement, to Slonimsky, "illustrates Schuman's technique of divergent harmonic progressions; in the opening bars, the cello moves consistently in contrary motion to the first violin." This movement is skilful in polyphonic technique, particularly in the work out of the fugal second theme. The third movement "establishes at the outset a solemn hymn-like mood; the harmony is strong and dissonant; a powerful progression in the cello in double stops, provides the tonal support." The finale "contains interesting rhythmic developments of thematic fragments."

1955 CREDENDUM (ARTICLE OF FAITH), for orchestra. I. Declaration. II. Chorale. III. Finale.

Credendum is probably the first orchestral composition commissioned by the United States government. It was contracted for by the United States National Commission for UNESCO, through the office of the Department of State. The world première took place in Cincinnati on November 4, 1955, Thor Johnson conducting the Cincinnati Symphony.

Here is how the composer described the music:

"The first movement is scored for wind instruments and percussion with the exception of occasional support from the string basses. As its title implies, the musical materials of this movement are 'oratorical' in nature. In the second movement, the chorale melody is heard first in the string section of the orchestra where it is developed at some length. As the movement progresses, the chorale is stated by the brass instruments, while the strings begin filigree of a contrasting nature. The music gains in intensity and the woodwinds join in the figurations set against the chorale. The movement ends quietly with reference both to the choral theme and the contrasting figurations.

"The finale opens with scherzo-like material given to the string basses and bass clarinet. The gradual development of this material leads to the establishment of characteristic figures. Against these figures a long melody emerges in the cellos joined as it continues its course by the first violins. These two melodic lines together with the figures set against them lead to a return of the opening section. As the music gains momentum, a vigorous subject derived from the melody originally heard in the cellos is announced and developed contrapuntally. A brief reference to music heard earlier in the movement leads ultimately to a return to the Chorale. . . . The work ends with the music of the 'Declaration' now paraphrased and leading to a peroration."

1956 NEW ENGLAND TRIPTYCH (THREE PIECES FOR

ORCHESTRA AFTER WILLIAM BILLINGS). I. Be Glad Then, America. II. When Jesus Wept. III. Chester.

On several occasions Schuman utilized material from the music of William Billings—Billings being the famous American eighteenth-century composer of psalms and fuguing tunes, and of "Chester" often described as the *Marseillaise* of the American Revolution. In 1943, Schuman wrote the *William Billings Overture,* which the New York Philharmonic under Artur Rodzinski introduced on February 17, 1944. A dozen or so years later, he produced a band arrangement of Billings's "Chester." During the same year he also composed the *New England Triptych.* Here Billings's melodies are used freely, merely as a point of departure for Schuman's own musical thought. In this work we encounter more of Schuman than of Billings.

The composer described his treatment of three Billings tunes as follows:

"In the first movement, "Be Glad Then, America,' a solo for tympani, begins the short introduction which is developed prominently in the strings. This music is suggestive of the 'Hallelujah' heard at the end of the piece. Trombones and trumpets begin the main section, a free and varied setting of the words, 'Be glad then, America, shout and rejoice.' The tympani again solos, leads to a middle fugal section stemming from the words, 'And ye shall be satisfied.' The music gains momentum and combined themes lead to a climax. There follows a free adaptation of the 'Hallelujah' music with which Billings concludes his original choral piece and a final reference to the 'Shout and rejoice' music."

In the second movement, the setting of "When Jesus Wept" is in the form of a round. "Here Billings's music is used in its original form as well as in new settings with contrapuntal embellishments and melodic extensions."

The triptych ends with Billings's most famous hymn turned into the war song "Chester"—America's first great martial tune. "The orchestral piece derived from the spirit both of the hymn and the marching song."

The *New England Triptych* was commissioned by André Kostelanetz, who introduced it with the University of Miami Symphony, in Miami, Florida, on October 28, 1956.

1961 A SONG OF ORPHEUS, for cello and orchestra.

The Ford Foundation commissioned Schuman to write a composition for Leonard Rose, the eminent cellist. Looking about for some idea around which to build his composition, Schuman recalled something his friend and biographer, Vincent Persichetti, had once advised him: namely, to use a song, "Orpheus with His Lute," which Schuman had written in 1944, as a theme for a set of variations. In the end, Schuman did not actually write a set of variations for cello and orchestra, but a fantasy in which, as he explained, "all the music grows out of the melodic line of the song, which is stated at the very beginning of the composition."

The solo cello presents the melody. The oboe appropriates it in an eloquent exchange with the cello. When the oboe reaches the concluding held-note of the song, the cello embarks on a cadenza—the transition to the middle section in which the melody is developed and transformed. After another cadenza for the solo instrument, the composition reverts to the mood and tempo of the song, as it was presented in the opening measures.

The world première of this fantasy took place in Indianapolis on February 17, 1962. Leonard Rose was the soloist, and the Indianapolis Symphony was conducted by Izler Solomon.

1962 SYMPHONY NO. 8. I. Lento sostenuto; Pressante vigoroso; Lento. II. Largo; Tempo più mosso; Largo. III. Presto; Prestissimo.

For its opening season at the Lincoln Center for the Performing Arts, the New York Philharmonic commissioned Schuman to write a symphony. That symphony, the composer's eighth, was performed under Leonard Bernstein's direction on October 4, 1962.

Here is how a reviewer described the symphony in *Musical America:* "The opening is ominous, with subterranean chords tolling out a dirge that is exemplary in its scoring. It is a keen lament, all sorrow and genuinely tragic. Intervallically, it embraces the third, in its major and minor forms, with great ingenuity. And even when it turns fast there is sadness to its melodic gestures.

"The second movement, too, is pensive and brooding, and it is full of deep thoughts. This is not meant to indicate, however, that it is austere, for, in fact, the interlaced string writing is especially attractive. Even when it grows agitated, convulsed by twisting its previous motto ideas, it maintains its warmth. And when at the close there is a return to tranquillity, replaced by a few measures of anguish, there is still an affirmation of faith to calm the spirit.

"The third movement is exciting, elaborately scored and melodically disjunct, but always with a purpose. There is, in addition, considerable byplay between solo winds, and the massed brass sound that Mr. Schuman has always favored. The work ends with a wild climax that makes sense in every way. It finishes with a roar and concludes a piece that does credit to its creator, who, in my opinion, is America's greatest symphonist."

1964 AMARYLLIS, variations for string trio.

This thirty-minute compostion is a set of variations on an old English round. As Paul Hume remarked in the Washington *Post,* the composer examines the round "from every angle. In purposeful simplicity, he let the three players walk around the tune, setting it forth in a variety of direct ways. Gradually, however, and almost always at a soft, softer, or softest level of sound, Schuman began to carry the ancient melodies into regions of harmonic thought far removed in actuality, if not in implication, from those in which it began." When the variations are completed, a novel, intriguing touch was introduced with the entrance of three singers who come out chanting the English round, in its original version. "From this point to the conclusion," says Hume, "they continued their song while around them the strings wreathed old and new harmonies, those that were new now sounding strangely right with the older melody."

Amaryllis represents on the part of the composer an interesting and successful attempt to discuss a melody from the distant past in terms of the advanced techniques and methods of the twentieth century.

ALEXANDER SCRIABIN 1872–1915

Before he became a devotee of mysticism, Scriabin was a composer of exquisite miniatures for the piano which have been favorably compared to the best of Chopin. These miniatures are truly Chopinesque in poetic content, felicitousness of form, long drawn-out soulful melodies, and reflections of magic moods; they belong with the very best in Romantic piano music.

But then Scriabin succumbed to a grandiose religion-philosophy which he called "The Mystery," and tried to make his music at least a partial expression of such a philosophy. He evolved his own harmonic system, whose spine was the "Mystery Chord"—built not out of thirds but fourths. His writing grew increasingly involved, remote and rarefied, until it became difficult for the listener to follow him in his strange, mystic dreams.

In or about 1900, Scriabin was drawn to the mysticism of Prince S.N. Trubetskoy, with whom he attended meetings of the Philosophical Society, whose discussions impressed him profoundly. Scriabin was particularly impressed by Trubetskoy's idea of the oneness of love and God. Two years later, Scriabin was drawn to Nietzsche's philosophy which made him identify himself with the concept of the Superman. (He even planned at this time an opera about a Nietzschean hero who, through art, conquers the world.) From Nietzsche, he went on to theosophy and pantheism. Thus as the years passed, he immersed himself ever deeper in the nebulous world of mysticism until he arrived at solipsism. The creative ego became all important. "The external world is the result of my subjective spiritual activity," he wrote. "The world is nothing else than an antithesis of my personal consciousness. The 'not I' which is opposed at will by the 'I' is necessarily only so, so that the 'I' in the 'I could create' can create. . . ." "I am the apotheosis of creation; I am the aim of all aims; I am the end of all ends." Art, he became convinced, must be a "transformer of life," a means of converting life into "a kingdom on earth."

His vision was not merely a new kind of music but a new kind of *Weltanschauung*: a unity of all social, religious, philosophic and artistic thinking into a new system. "Art," he said, "must unite with philosophy and religion in an indivisible whole to form a new Gospel which will replace the old Gospel which we have outlived. I cherish the dream of creating such a 'Mystery.'" He wanted that "Mystery" to summarize the whole history of mankind from the beginning of time to the final cataclysm which he felt would some day be at hand to purge the world and make room for a new race of nobler men. He wanted to use every artistic means at his disposal: dancing, music, poetry, colors, even smells. He even thought of devising a new language for his "Mystery," made up of sighs and exclamations rather than words.

For the practice of that "Mystery," he envisioned a special globe-shaped temple in India, situated on a lake—for he knew that his immediate world was not ready for his concept. He was convinced that the human race as he knew it was doomed, and he felt that his "Mystery" would be the final expression of the dying race and the transition to the new race of man.

When World War I broke out, Scriabin saw in it the purification the world was waiting for, after which the new race could emerge. And he had no doubt that he himself was the Messiah pointing the way to the new world.

Scriabin never did get around to writing the "Mystery," which he planned over a great number of years. He merely finished the text and some musical sketches for a cantata called *L'Acte Préalable* (*Preliminary Act*), which was to have been the introduction to the entire philosophy. He called the Introduction "Propylaea," just as the entrance to the Acropolis in Athens was so named. But the idea of the "Mystery" penetrated more and more into his writing after 1900 until it obsessed him entirely.

Scriabin was born in Moscow on January 6, 1872. His mother was an excellent pianist, a graduate of the St. Petersburg Conservatory. She died when Alexander was still an infant. Since the father was a consul stationed in the Near East, the boy was placed with his grandmother and aunt, who pampered and over-protected him, keeping him from play with other children. Scriabin became a spoiled child haunted by all kinds of fears and neuroses, and given to excessive display of emotions. His aunt gave him his first piano lessons, but he was impatient with exercises, doting on improvisations. In 1882, he entered the Military School in Moscow, a period in which he continued to study the piano with Conus and Zverev. After leaving the School, he decided on music rather than the army as a career. In 1885, he became Taneiev's pupil in composition. Three years later, he entered the Moscow Conservatory, where he was a pupil of Safonov, Arensky and Taneiev. Upon graduating from Safonov's class in piano in 1892, he received a gold medal. But he was a poor student in theory, failed his examinations, and never received a diploma in composition. In spite of this, he was already producing highly gifted pieces for the piano in the style of Chopin.

In 1894, Scriabin gave a recital in St. Petersburg, when he played some of his own compositions. This performance made a strong impression on Belaiev, publisher and patron. Belaiev now stood ready to publish all of Scriabin's music and to finance his career as a concert pianist. A successful tour of Europe followed.

In 1897, Scriabin married Vera Isakovitch, a pianist. She devoted her career to promoting Scriabin's music, often appearing with him in two-piano recitals. From 1898 to 1903, Scriabin taught the piano at the Moscow Conservatory. He abandoned teaching to concentrate on composition and on appearing as pianist. In 1903, he deserted his wife for young Tatiana Schloezer (sister of the music critic, Boris de Schloezer). Since Vera refused to grant Scriabin a divorce, Tatiana lived with him as common-law wife, bearing him three children. (The children were legitimatized after Scriabin's death.) Late in 1906, Scriabin came to the United States for his first American tour, making his debut in New York on December 20, 1906, as soloist with the Russian Symphony under Altschuler in his own piano concerto. The tour was aborted when a scandal erupted over the fact that Scriabin was traveling with a woman who was not his legal wife. To avoid prosecution on the grounds of moral turpitude, Scriabin and Tatiana left the United States hurriedly.

Belaiev's death in 1904 left Scriabin without a patron. For a time, he was supported by a wealthy pupil. Then, in 1908, he found a new patron in the young conductor, Serge Koussevitzky, who not only stood ready to publish all of Scriabin's music but was willing to promote Scriabin's orchestral music at his concerts. When Koussevitzky and his orchestra embarked on their tour of the Volga in 1910, Scriabin went along to give eleven performances of his piano concerto. It was for Koussevitzky that Scriabin wrote his *Prometheus* Symphony. Before long, however, clashing egos and temperaments caused a permanent break between the two artists. Nevertheless, Koussevitzky continued to perform Scriabin's music up to the end of his long and rich career as conductor and was largely responsible for popularizing it to the western world. Scriabin made his last public appearance at a recital in St. Petersburg on April 15, 1915. Soon after his return to Moscow, a carbuncle on his upper lip developed into gangrene. He died in Moscow on April 27, 1915.

1903–1914 SONATAS, for piano:

No. 4, F-sharp major, op. 30; No. 5, F-sharp major, op. 53; No. 6, G major, op. 62; No. 7, F-sharp major, *White Mass,* op. 64; No. 8, A major, op. 66; No. 9, F major, *Black Mass,* op. 68; No. 10, C major, op. 70.

PRELUDES, for piano:

Op. 31: No. 1, D-flat major—C major; No. 2, F minor; No. 3, E-flat major; No. 4, C major.

Op. 35: No. 1, D-flat major; No. 2, B-flat major; No. 3, C major.

Op. 37: No. 1, B-flat minor; No. 2, F-sharp major; No. 3, B major; No. 4, G minor.

Op. 39: No. 1, F-sharp major; No. 2, D major; No. 3, G major; No. 4, A-flat major.

Op. 48: No. 1, F-sharp major; No. 2, C major; No. 3, D-flat major; No. 4, C major.

Op. 67: No. 1, Andante; No. 2, Presto.

Op. 74: No. 1, Douloureux, déchirant; No. 2, Très lent, contemplatif; No. 3, Allegro drammatico; No. 4, Lent, vague, indécis; No. 5, Fier, belliqueux.

Scriabin wrote ten sonatas for the piano. The first three (in two movements, with introduction and main section) reveal his indebtedness to Chopin and Liszt; all were written before 1900. With the Fourth Sonata (1903), Scriabin adopted the one-movement form which he would henceforth utilize. The Fourth Sonata is programmatic; the first movement is intended to be the motive of desire, and the second, the motive of anguish. Technically, this sonata is of interest because its harmonic construction—with its building up of the intervals of the fourth—suggests the later "Mystery Chord."

With each succeeding sonata, Scriabin penetrated ever deeper into mysticism. The Fifth Sonata (1908) bears the following quotation from *The Poem of Ecstasy*—intended as the program for the music:

I call to life, O mysterious forces,
Submerged in depths, obscure!
O thou creative spirit, timid of life,
To you I bring courage!

The music is, for the most part, turbulent in the introduction, while in the prologue that follows it becomes at different times tender, mysterious, impetuous.

The Seventh Sonata (1911) was the composer's favorite, possibly because of its rich vein of mysticism. The music is mostly harsh, ending with a frenetic dance. The Eighth Sonata (1913) is the longest. It begins with an expressive introduction, following which comes the complex main section built out of three principal ideas. The Ninth Sonata (1913) has been called *The Black Mask*. It opens in an atmosphere of mystery and proceeds with the main section, in which four ideas are heard in succession, then developed. The peroration of this work, wrote Hull, "is masterful and striking, and the sonata ends in that dim and mysterious light in which the dream opened."

Scriabin's last sonata (1913) is probably the most elusive in content, the most obscure in thought, and the most complex in technique.

Scriabin wrote eighty-nine preludes for the piano. Up to op. 31 (1903), the preludes are Chopinesque in the delicacy of melody and refinement of style. The best of these preludes—they are among the finest short work for the piano in twentieth-century music—traverse a flexible range of emotions. There is serenity in op. 11, no. 5; contemplation in op. 11, no. 2; lyric poetry in op. 22, no. 1; and gentle sadness in op. 11, no. 3; on the other hand, there is febrile restlessness in op. 11, no. 14; dramatic power in op. 11, no. 1; and intensity and turbulent feeling in op. 27, no. 1.

After op. 31, the harmonic writing becomes more involved and sometimes more acrid, and the atmospheric effect more subtle. With the last preludes, two in op. 67 (1913) and five in op. 74 (1914), the style reaches—as Sabaneyev said of all Scriabin's later piano music—"an extraordinary exquisiteness and refinement, the harmony a rare complexity, along with a saturation of psychological content. . . . We observe a dissolution of rhythm, a reduction of melody to the minimum, a severance of the musical web and line which turns into a series of spasmodic exclamations and destroys the impressions of unity and wholeness."

The op. 74 preludes were Scriabin's last compositions. James Bakst described them as "nervous, enigmatical and mystical." He notes here "an abundance of peculiar sound effects," and finds the second prelude expressing "complete emotional prostration. The music seems to become an indistinct mumble."

1904 THE DIVINE POEM (LE DIVIN POÈME), Symphony No.

3 in C major, op. 43. I. Struggles. II. Delights. III. Divine Play.

The merging of music with philosophy was one of Scriabin's pet ideals. In this he was abetted by his common-law wife, Tatiana Schloezer, who wrote a programmatic text, rich with theosophic implications, which became the basis of *The Divine Poem*.

In this symphony (it is actually a tone poem and not a symphony) Scriabin attempted to represent, as Tatiana's text explains, "the evolution of the human spirit which, torn from an entire past of beliefs and mysteries which it surmounts and overturns, passes through pantheism and attains to a joyous and intoxicated affirmation of its liberty and its unity with the universe (the divine 'Ego')."

Tatiana's text of the three movements follows:

"*Struggles*. The conflict between the man who is a slave of a personal god, supreme master of the world, and the free, powerful man—the man-God. The latter appears to triumph, but it is only the intellect which affirms the divine 'Ego,' while the individual will, still too weak, is tempted to sink into pantheism.

"*Delights*. The man allows himself to be captured by the delights of the sensual world. He is intoxicated and soothed by the voluptuous pleasures into which he plunges. His personality loses itself in nature. It is then that the sense of the sublime arises from the depths of his being and assists him to conquer the passive state of his human 'Ego.'

"*Divine Play*. The spirit finally freed from all the bonds which fastened it to its past of submission to a superior power, the spirit producing the universe by the sole power of its own creative will, conscious of being at one with this universe, abandons itself to the sublime joy of free activity—the 'Divine Play.' "

The three sections are played without interruption. An introductory section offers the main theme in basses, to which trumpets give reply. After the theme is assumed by first violins and woodwinds, the main body of the first movement begins with the same subject built up to a dramatic climax. A hymn-like episode is then offered by muted strings, followed by a subject in the woodwinds to accompaniment of violas and basses. The recapitulation recalls the theme in the horns. The second movement follows with a slow, eloquent melody in woodwinds and horns, which the strings soon take over. This is given an intense treatment, occasionally interrupted by exclamations in the horns. Basses lead into the lively finale, which presents a vigorous subject in the strings. After that we hear a second melody, in oboes and cellos, to which the woodwinds and horns provide the harmony. A return of the first melody precedes the development. The main theme of the first section is remembered just before the close of the symphony.

The Divine Poem was introduced in Paris on May 29, 1905, with Artur Nikisch conducting.

1907–1913 ETUDES, for piano:

Op. 42: No. 1, D-flat major; No. 2, F-sharp minor; No. 3, F-sharp major; No. 4, F-sharp major; No. 5, C-sharp minor; No. 6, D-flat major; No. 7, F minor; No. 8, E-flat major.

Op. 65: No. 1, B-flat major; No. 2, C-sharp major; No. 3, G major.

The twenty-six etudes for piano which Scriabin wrote are usually in the grand manner, of which the dramatic op. 8, no. 2, is both a famous and a characteristic early example—the op. 8 set having been written in the early 1890s. The influence of Brahms can be detected in two of the op. 8 etudes (nos. 2 and 3), while that of Chopin is prevalent in the sixth of the set. In op. 42, rhythmic problems are explored with considerable virtuosity, while two of the etudes in op. 65 are characterized by unusual intervallic and harmonic procedures.

1908 POEM OF ECSTASY (LE POÈME DE L'EXTASE), Symphony No. 4 in C major, op. 54.

Here Scriabin discusses the "Joy in Creative Activity," and the "Ecstasy of Unfettered Action." Five motives are used to symbolize various emotions or actions: yearning (flute), protest (muted trombone), apprehension (muted horns), will (trumpet), and self-assertion (trumpet). The two themes heard in the prologue (Andante, Lento) describe respectively the pursuit after an ideal and the Ego theme realizing itself. A sonata-form section follows (Allegro volante), beginning with an ecstatic theme depicting the soaring flight of the spirit, to which the two themes of the prologue are joined contrapuntally. After a repetition of the two prologue themes, a Lento passage tells of human love. A trumpet subject calls to the Will to assert itself, and the creative force is let loose. All these melodic and rhythmic ideas are now developed with great variety, "at times spending dreamy moments of delicious charm and perfume," as A. Eaglefield Hull wrote, "occasionally rising to a climax of almost hilarious pleasure; at other moments experiencing violent stormy emotions and tragic cataclysms."

Scriabin played parts of the symphony to a select group of Russian musicians which included Rachmaninoff, Glazunov and Rimsky-Korsakov. This eminent jury denounced the work in no uncertain terms. Rimsky-Korsakov said bluntly: "He's half out of his mind." Nevertheless, the Belaiev publishing house accepted it and even awarded the composer the second Glinka Prize.

The first performance took place in New York on December 10, 1908, Modest Altschuler conducting. "The nerves of the audience were worn and racked as nerves are seldom assailed, even in these days," said W. J. Henderson in the *Sun*. "Scriabin's *Le Poème de l'extase* was the cause. This composition was heralded as a foster child of theosophy. Certainly it conveyed a sense of eeriness and uncanny connotation. Most of the time, the violins were whimpering and wailing like lost souls, while strange undulating and formless melodies roved about in the woodwinds. . . . It all seemed far more like several other things than ecstasy." Yet others were of a different mind. After the symphony had been introduced to Russia (in St. Petersburg on February 1, 1909), Boris de Schloezer maintained that the first six notes taught "the essence of the creative spirit." A Scriabinite (Y. D. Engel), who attended a rehearsal in St. Petersburg, described how "excitement reigned. Perfect strangers who happened to get into conversation quarreled warmly or shook each other's hands in delight. Sometimes there were even more unrestrained scenes of agitation and enthusiasm."

1910 PROMETHEUS: THE POEM OF FIRE, Symphony No. 5 in F-sharp major, op. 60.

Prometheus is Scriabin's last work for orchestra. Here we find the roots of the grandiose "Mystery" which he was beginning to conceive at that time. Man (represented by the piano) is set against the Cosmos (the orchestra). Adapting a later version of the Prometheus legend, Scriabin sets out to show how mankind, in primitive stages, lacked the Promethean spark; it was consequently without will or self-consciousness. Prometheus then gave mankind the divine spark, bringing into existence the power of the Creative Will. But the gift of fire is both a curse and a blessing; there are those who use it for good, while others make it an instrument of evil.

"We have here," says Rosa Newmarch, "the elements of a fairly definite and infinitely varied psychological program: the crepuscular, invertebrate state of Karma-less humanity; the awakening of the will to create, in both its aspects; the strange moods of bliss and anguish which follow the acquisition of consciousness; probably, also, the last, fierce rebellion of the lower self preceding final ecstasy of union, when the human mingles with the divine—with *Agni,* the fire which receives unto itself all other sparks in the ultimate phase of development."

The mystical atmosphere is created with a typical Scriabin "Mystery" chord at the opening of the work. The emergence of the Creative Will is suggested in a trumpet call, after which the piano enters with a theme suggesting the Creative Will. The music grows in passion and sensuousness as self-consciousness is born, and with it human love. There are conflicts; but eventually Humanity merges with the Cosmos. The work ends ecstatically as a chorus of mixed voices joins the orchestra in a wordless chant.

One of the novel features of this composition is its marriage to actual colors; for Scriabin had intended having a keyboard instrument throw colors on a screen while the music was being played. However, when *Prometheus* was introduced (by the Koussevitzky Orchestra under Koussevitzky, with Scriabin at the piano, on March 15, 1911, in Moscow) the colors were dispensed with, as they invariably are when the work is heard nowadays. A performance of *Prometheus* with colors, by the Russian Symphony Orchestra under Modest Altschuler, took place in New York City on March 20, 1915.

ROGER SESSIONS 1896–

It is not easy to pigeonhole Sessions into any single serviceable classification. He is not, strictly speaking, a polytonalist, an atonalist, a serialist, or a neo-classicist—though each of these styles can be uncovered in his writing. In his early years, he used to be a Romantic, but the rejection of this phase is proved by the fact that Sessions destroyed or withdrew most of the music he wrote at that time. Since the middle 1930s, Sessions has been one of the most complex of living American composers. His music is high-tensioned and discordant. Generally written around more than a single tonal center, it emphasizes highly complicated rhythmic patterns, linear counterpoint and dissonant harmonies rather than melody, the last of which is most often declamatory rather than lyrical. His musical ideas are as involved as they are original, abounding with subtle processes of thought, not easily followed. Complexity of technique and involved thinking, however, do not obscure the vigor and independence of his writing, and the excitement it generates. Nor have they kept him from ascending to the highest level of significance in American music.

In commenting on Sessions's complexity, Alfred J. Frankenstein has observed that its erudition "is always servant of big lyric and dynamic ideas. It is complex, but its complexity is a special form of eloquence. It is elaborate, but elaboration is always of the intellectual and emotional pressures that bring it to being. It consequently urges and commands the hearer rather than soothes him, and it leaves you rather breathless when it has finished with its sharp intensities, its expressive depths, its rugged epical bigness."

Sessions was born in Brooklyn, New York, on December 28, 1896, of New England ancestry. As a child he was brought to Massachusetts, where he began studying the piano. At thirteen he tried writing an opera. Academic education was received at the Kent School in Connecticut. At fourteen, he matriculated at Harvard where, four years later, he received a Bachelor of Arts degree; there he was the editor of the *Harvard Musical Review*. He then enrolled in the Yale School of Music, a pupil of Horatio Parker. He also studied composition privately with Ernest Bloch. When Bloch became director of the Cleveland Institute of Music in 1921, Sessions followed him, first to continue his studies of composition, then to serve as Bloch's assistant. During this period, he completed his first composition to gain significant performances, the incidental music to Andreyev's *The Black Maskers,* introduced in Northampton, Massachusetts in June of 1923. As an orchestral suite, first heard in Cincinnati on December 5, 1930, *The Black Maskers* gained wide circulation. For eight years, after 1925, Sessions lived in Europe, receiving two Guggenheim Fellowships, a two-year fellowship at the American Academy in Rome, and a Carnegie grant. In Europe, he wrote his First Symphony, in E minor, introduced by the Boston Symphony under Koussevitzky on April 22, 1927. After returning to the United States, Sessions held various important teaching posts. These included two years at the School of Music at Boston University; at Princeton between 1935 and 1945, where he rose to the post of associate professor; at the University of California in Berkeley, where between 1945 and 1954 he was professor; from 1953 to 1965, as full professor at Yale; and in 1966, as a teacher of composition at the Juilliard School in New York. His first major success as composer came with his Second Symphony in 1947. Never a prolific composer, Sessions forged slowly forward to a top rank among American composers. He was made a member of the National Institute of

Letters, the American Academy of Arts and Letters, the American Academy of Arts and Sciences, and the Berlin Akademie der Künste. In 1958, he was sent by the State Department to the Soviet Union, where his music was successfully performed. In 1964, he received an honorary doctorate from Harvard.

Since 1927, when he helped Copland to found the Copland-Sessions concerts in New York, Sessions has been active in promoting modern music. He has served as a member of the board of directors of the League of Composers in New York and as president of the United States section of the International Society for Contemporary Music.

1935 CONCERTO IN B MINOR FOR VIOLIN AND ORCHESTRA. I. Largo e tranquillo, con grande espressione. II. Scherzo. III. Andante. IV. Molto vivace e sempre con fuoco.

This violin concerto is a comparatively early work of Sessions; it was begun in 1931 and completed four years later, Sessions considers the concerto one of the earliest works in which his later characteristic style is evident. The first performance of the concerto took place in 1935 at a concert at the New School for Social Research in New York; Serge Kotlarsky was the soloist, and the composer accompanied him at the piano. The première with orchestra was given by the Illinois Symphony Orchestra, Izler Solomon conducting, with Robert Gross, violinist, on January 8, 1940.

The first movement is divided into three large sections, each of which is introduced by a theme which opens the concerto (trombone, answered by trumpet). The second movement is a vigorous Scherzo, the principal theme of which begins with two staccato chords and continues energetically in clarinet and flute; the second theme is even sprightlier. A middle trio section is tranquil in character. An involved melody, heard for the most part in the solo violin, dominates the Romanza section. An unaccompanied passage for violin heralds the approach of the final movement, which is the longest and most complex of the entire work. Sessions described the character of this movement as "that of ever-increasing intensity, relieved by a waltz-like episode which forms a large portion of the middle section."

The orchestration dispenses with the violins in order to emphasize the role and personality of the solo instrument. The wind section, however, is expanded, and enrichment of string writing comes from splitting up violas and cellos into subdivisions.

1946 SYMPHONY NO. 2. I Molto agitato. II. Allegretto capriccioso. III. Adagio tranquillo ed espressivo. IV. Allagramente.

Though the ideas for this symphony date as far back as 1934, Sessions did not set to work on it until 1944, when he was commissioned by the Alice M. Ditson Fund. He completed it two years later, and on January 9, 1947, it was introduced by the San Francisco Symphony under Pierre Monteux. It was then heard at the festival of the International Society for Contemporary Music in Amsterdam in June of 1948, Eduard van Beinum conducting. The symphony is dedicated to the memory of Franklin Delano Roosevelt, whose death occurred when the composer was writing the Adagio movement, its solemn mood reflecting the composer's reaction to this tragic event.

The composer has this to say about the work: "With reasonable accuracy it may be considered as in the key of D minor—the movements being in D minor, F minor, B-flat minor, and D major respectively. . . . Those who would like a clue to what is sometimes called the 'emotional content' I would refer to the tempo indications of the various movements, which give a fair idea of the character of each—though the hearer may perhaps feel that the Adagio is predominately dark and somber, and find that the last movement is interrupted, at its climax, by a blare of trombones, introducing an episode which contrasts sharply with the rest of the movement, which returns to its original character only gradually."

The first movement is in five distinct sections, a Molto agitato part being heard at the opening, closing, and in the middle, and two tranquil sections (Tranquillo e misterioso) providing a contrast. The second movement is a brief intermezzo which John Veale described as "nimble, ironical, and dance-like." Its basic thought is the theme heard early in oboe and English horn. Three ideas, all of them introspective and moody, comprise the slow movement. The first appears in the third measure in muted violas (accompanied by muted strings); the second is given by oboe, accompanied by the woodwinds; and the third is presented by solo clarinet, accompanied by the piano. The concluding movement is a seven section rondo.

After the symphony was introduced in New York by the New York Philharmonic under Mitropoulos, it received the New York Music Critics Circle Award. This performance was recorded for Columbia under a grant from the Naumburg Foundation.

1947 THE TRIAL OF LUCULLUS, opera in one act, with text by Bertolt Brecht. First performance: Berkeley, California, April 18, 1947.

Brecht's libretto started out as an anti-Hitler radio play in 1939. "In setting the text," explained the composer, "I have been guided . . . by my strong convictions, first, that the opera can become once more, as it has so often been in the past, a vital dramatic medium; that music and drama are essential ingredients which must be welded into an ensemble in which neither is subservient to the other, and both essential elements of an indissoluble whole; and finally that the opera is, first of all, vocal music, and that characterization becomes stereotyped and one-dimensional if it is entrusted mainly to instruments."

In Brecht's libretto, the individual is placed vis-à-vis to society. The shade of Lucullus, the Roman general, comes to trial in the realm of the dead before a jury of humble people before he can gain entrance to Elysium. Lucullus pleads his case by pointing to his achievements: seven kings dethroned; fifty-three cities destroyed; the Roman Empire extended to Asia; the booty and spoils of war brought back to Rome. But the jury interprets these victories in terms of the dead, the wounded, the suffering, and the lands pillaged and laid waste. And the final judgment of the jury is a foregone conclusion.

"The remarkable feature of the opera from a purely aesthetic point of view is the unparalleled suppleness of its declamation," wrote Alfred J. Frankenstein in the San Francisco *Chronicle*. "Through an exquisitely perfect adjustment of tone and word, Sessions achieves an incredibly clear-edged musical characterization of individuals, so that the music of each role projects its personality with the utmost definition and point."

1950 STRING QUARTET NO. 2. I. Lento. II. Allegro appassionato, alla breve. III. Andante tranquillo. IV. Presto. V. Adagio.

The five movements are played without interruption and although, as the composer has said, there is a "psychological sequence . . . at the core of the conception," no themes are repeated through the movements.

The composer's description follows: "The first movement may be roughly described as a 'double fugue.' . . . The second movement presents two strongly contrasted sections, one fast and one quieter and more rhapsodic; the fast section returns three times, the last time in the form of a coda." The third movement is a theme and variations, the theme being "relatively long"; five variations follow which "although they differ in character, even in tempo and rhythm, do not range very far from the theme itself." The fourth movement is in the form of a scherzo. "The first part of the 'return' presents the principal theme in a more concentrated form and at a different pitch. The contrasting themes, the climax and the coda, however, are, after their very first measures, repeated literally in the da capo section. . . . The last movement is the shortest and least elaborate of the three slow movements, and has in a sense the character of an epilogue. . . . It is dominated by the melodic phrase of the opening measures, which returns on three later occasions. . . . The final measures, a kind of coda, do not lead to a sharply defined, cadential close, but trail, as it were, into space."

1962 MONTEZUMA, opera in three acts, with text by G. A. Borgese. First performance: Berlin, April 19, 1964.

In the middle 1930s, Sessions first discussed with Borgese the idea of writing an opera about Montezuma, the Aztec emperor, who was worshiped by his people as a god. Borgese, however, did not finish writing his text until 1941. The fact that, in the composer's opinion, it was too long and cumbersome, and that the death of the librettist prevented any revisions, kept Sessions from working on the opera for almost two decades. Then he himself laboriously rewrote and shortened the libretto, completing this task in 1959. It took him three more years to produce the score. The opera was originally intended for the Florence May Music Festival, but procrastination on the part of the festival authorities coupled with a request from the Deutsche Oper in Berlin for its production brought about a change of scene for the world première. The response of German audiences and critics to the new opera was divided, some denouncing it, others calling it a masterwork.

The setting is Mexico in the early sixteenth century, during the invasion by the Spaniards under the leadership of Fernando Cortez. At first the Mexican natives, together with their emperor Montezuma, regard the white conquerors as legendary heroes. But admiration turns to hate when the Spaniards defy Cortez's orders and give way to murder, plunder and pillage, led by the ambitious and avaricious Alvarado. The disenchantment of the natives finally leads them to turn on their own emperor and to kill Montezuma.

Heinz Joachim notes that Sessions "constantly employs new rhythmic and thematic variations for the musical characterization of various situations. The voices are used mainly in a declamatory style. . . . Especially effective are some of the choruses, particularly the final 'Chorus of the Clouds,' with which the three-hour work seems to dissolve into timelessness."

In a report to *The New York Times,* Peter Maxwell Davies singles out some of the other memorable pages in the score: for example, "the ritual murder of the slaves by the Aztec priests . . . helped by harmonies that create an almost unbearable tension"; also "the final section where the Aztec emperor is killed by the Spaniards." Mr. Davies goes on to say: "The Sessions characteristic is heard to full advantage at the close of Act I, in the almost Tristanlike passion of the duet between the Spanish captain, Cortez, and Malinche, the Aztec slave girl, and later in Montezuma's final aria, in Act III."

But in the last analysis, as Joachim takes pains to point out, this work is "not so much an opera as it is epic music theatre. . . . Without dramatic action, the historical material is treated as a monumental chronicle . . . with large scenic tableaux. Chief among them are the second-act meeting between Montezuma and Cortez, with its religious-philosophical discussions; the Aztec ritual of human sacrifice; the Christian ceremony of baptism; the battle ordered by Alvarado; and, finally, the betrayal of Montezuma. A masked dance at the emperor's court and a love scene between Cortez and the slave girl Malinche (who converts to Christianity but finally returns to Montezuma) bring softer colors to Sessions's otherwise dark painting, which is richly endowed with symbolism."

1963 SYMPHONY NO. 5. I. Tranquillo; Allegro molto. II. Lento. III. Allegro deciso.

Sessions's Fifth Symphony was commissioned by Eugene Ormandy and the Philadelphia Orchestra, who introduced it in Philadelphia on February 7, 1964. This is the shortest symphony Sessions has written, and the only one in which the movements are played without pause.

At the time of its première the composer contributed the following analysis:

"The symphony begins very softly . . . with a gently swaying figure, around which various instruments, beginning with the piccolo in the low medium register, enter in turn with short melodic fragments. . . . This forms a sort of introduction. . . . It occurs very briefly between the Allegro molto which follows and the Lento which constitutes the main slow section of the piece—and also, less briefly, at the very close. . . . The Tranquillo of the opening leads directly to the Allegro molto, which opens with a sharply defined phrase, descending in the violins and woodwinds from the high to the middle register. This phrase, together with contrasting subsidiary phrases, forms the material of the main three sections of this movement. A contrasting section, which appears twice, begins softly and more quietly in the flute, over triplets in the marimba, and soft low tones of the bass clarinet.

"The second movement, Lento, begins with a solo for trombone over a soft roll on the bass drum. The trombone passage is continued by low bassoons, over which muted trumpet and horns develop a phrase somewhat of the type frequently described under the term 'chorale.' The movement is for the most part a kind of dialogue between these instruments. . . . and passages of a more rhapsodic character on the violins over woodwinds. After the third entrance of this dialogue, however, occurs an interlude in which the woodwinds predominate at the beginning, and which leads to a strong climax. The concluding phrase of the dialogue is followed by the resumption of the monologue of the opening of the movement, this time on a solo trumpet, followed by violins and other instruments, and descending to a three-toned chord in the cellos and basses. This chord gradually becomes rhythmically animated, and over it the trumpet enters with the opening phrase of the third movement. . . . Two sections, which are both massive and energetic in character, are separated by a somewhat shorter episode, of lighter texture and shorter phrases, Meno mosso e giocoso."

DMITRI SHOSTAKOVICH 1906–

No other composer of our time has commuted from acclaim to denunciation in quite the way that Shostakovich has—particularly in his own land. As the composer of the brilliant First Symphony—and the passionate advocate of music of Soviet ideology—Shostakovich early became the darling of Soviet officialdom, the object of much praise, honor and important performances. Then, with his position seemingly secure, he experienced the first of his setbacks. An opera based on a satirical play by Gogol, *The Nose,* was produced at Leningrad on January 13, 1930, only to be soundly denounced by the Association of Proletarian Composers as a product of "bourgeois decadence." It took Shostakovich a little time to rehabilitate his position in Soviet music—but rehabilitate it he did, particularly with the success of his first piano concerto. Then once again savage attack descended on him. His opera, *Lady Macbeth of Mzensk*—which had been running with considerable success for two years!—suddenly became the victim of a critical blitz. In an article in *Pravda* entitled "Confusion Instead of Music," the opera was described as vulgar, "the coarsest kind of naturalism. . . . The music quacks, grunts, growls, and suffocates itself in order to express the amatory scenes as naturalistically as possible." Hardly had the echoes of this attack died down when (one week later) another Shostakovich work came in for similarly rough treatment. The ballet *The Limpid Stream,* about a collective farm in Kuban, was described as "without character. . . . It jingles, it means nothing. The composer apparently has only contempt for our national songs."

Two such attacks within one week, and in an organ like *Pravda,* could mean only one thing: the pet of Soviet music had lost favor with the powers.

Shostakovich was now avoided by other leading Soviet composers. His Fourth Symphony in C minor, op. 43, was dropped after a rehearsal and was denied performance. (Its première did not take place until January 20, 1962.) He was henceforth not given much attention in the press in 1936 and 1937, and when he was, it was always unfavorably. Those who had formerly been warmest in their praises—and these included intimate friends—were now contemptuous of him.

But with the most amazing resiliency, Shostakovich once again bounced back to success, abetted by the major success of his Fifth Symphony in 1937. When his Piano Quintet received the Stalin Prize in 1940, there could no longer be a doubt that he was once again the leading composer of his land. With the outbreak of the war, he became even more than that—a national hero, particularly after the triumph of his Seventh Symphony, the *Leningrad,* which again earned him the Stalin Prize.

Now, surely, it appeared that his position was unassailable! But Shostakovich was still to experience storm and stress. In 1946, his Ninth Symphony was denounced by *Culture and Life* for its "ideological weakness" and for its failure to "reflect the spirit of the Soviet people." In a totalitarian state, unfavorable criticism directed against a composer of Shostakovich's stature and prestige is usually the warning of greater attacks to come; and the denunciation of the Ninth Symphony was only the beginning. On February 10, 1948, Shostakovich was one of several major composers to be officially denounced by the Central Committee of the Communist Party for "decadent formalism" (*see* Prokofiev). The term "formalism" had been hurled at Shostakovich in 1936; it was now applied not only to him but to other major Soviet composers as well.

And yet once again Shostakovich was to return to grace! He beat his breast publicly and confessed his guilt: "I know that the Party is right; I know that the Party shows solicitude for Soviet art. . . . All the directives of the Central Committee . . . and in particular those that concern me personally, I accept as a stern but paternal solicitude for us, Soviet artists. . . . I shall try again and again to create symphonic works close to the spirit of the people." And he turned to the writing of music fulfilling the new aesthetic requirements of the Committee. In 1949, his oratorio *The Song of the Forests* received the Stalin Prize for the third time (in conjunction with his score for the motion picture *The Fall of Berlin*). This and the fact that a few months earlier he had been sent by the Soviet government to the United States as a member of the Cultural and Scientific Conference for World Peace, was stout evidence that Shostakovich was once again favored.

In the post-Stalin era, when the 1948 musical doctrine of the Central Committee was abrogated and a new latitude was given Soviet composers in self-expression, Shostakovich once again assumed an imperial position in Soviet music. But even now, he was not altogether safe from attack. This happened again on December 18, 1962, when his Thirteenth Symphony was introduced. Its concluding movement was a setting of the provocative poem *Babi Yar* by Yevutchenko, in which anti-Semitism in the Soviet Union was indicted. The audience and critics reacted to Shostakovich's new symphony with such hostility that he revised the text to omit some of the more controversial lines and suggestions. Heard again in this new version in February of 1963, the symphony now proved a huge success.

In the Soviet Union, where musical criticism is so often dictated by political expediency and has very little to do with the quality of the music under discussion, these frequent changes of official attitude to Shostakovich's music are more interesting than significant. What is significant, however, is that Shostakovich has often been subjected to wide divergence of public reaction in the world outside the Soviet Union. He has been widely publicized, praised and performed; and he has been severely criticized, too. His music has been described as vital, fresh, spontaneous, infectious, powerful; it has also been called vulgar, trite, commonplace. Frequently these disparate points of view have been expressed by one and the same critic; and frequently, too, they have been expressed about one and the same work.

The sad truth is that few major composers of our time have been so uneven in their production. In his best satirical vein, Shostakovich is inimitable; his scherzos are fleet-footed, rhythmically dynamic, aglow with wit and malice, full of spice and sting. Sometimes he achieves moments of genuine majesty. And in his more recent symphonies, he has written expressive melodies. But it often happens that after a grandiose page of music he suddenly becomes as naïve as a schoolboy, almost as if he cannot discriminate between the good and the bad. At his best, he is a powerful and original voice; at his worst, he is synthetic, given to disturbing clichés, a strained striving for obvious effects, and a bending of the knee to political expediency.

Shostakovich was born in St. Petersburg (now Leningrad) on September 25, 1906. He began music study at the piano with his mother when he was nine. Soon afterwards, he attended the Glasser School of Music, where he wrote his first piece of music, a *Theme and Variations,* for piano. He attended the Leningrad Conservatory from 1919 to 1925, a pupil of Nikolaiev in piano and Maximilian Steinberg in composition. For his graduation piece in composition he completed his First Symphony, with which he achieved international renown.

He was only eleven when revolution changed the political and social structure of his country. He consequently knew no other society than that of the proletariat, to which, of course, he subscribed wholeheartedly. From the very first, he traveled under the banner of proletarian music, as articulated first by the Association of Proletarian Musicians (organized in 1924), and then by the Society for the Encouragement of Proletarian Composers (founded in 1925). "We are revolutionaries," Shostakovich said in an interview, "and as revolutionaries we have a different concept of music. Lenin himself said the 'music is a means of unifying broad masses of people.'" Music was to interpret the social and political ideals of the people; it was to reflect the pride of the people in their industrial and social achievements; it was to "reflect [as the platform of the Association of Proletarian Musicians noted] the rich, full-blooded psychology of the proletariat," and to penetrate "into the innermost masses of workmen and peasants, unite the thought and will of these masses and raise them for further struggle and construction."

The fluctuations of Shostakovich's fortunes as the people's composer have been described in preceding paragraphs. Notwithstanding these fluctuations, he has remained a crowning figure in Soviet music. He received the Stalin (or Lenin) Prize five times, and has been decorated with the Order of Lenin twice. When he was sixty he got the highest accolade a Soviet citizen can get, the title of Hero of Socialist Labor, the first musician ever to receive this honor. His sixtieth birthday was also celebrated in Leningrad with a series of concerts providing a cross-section of his creative achievements. In addition to all this, Shostakovich earned the International Sibelius Prize in 1958, and the Silver Insignia of Honor from the Austrian Republic in 1967.

Shostakovich visited the United States twice: in 1949, as a member of a committee representing the Soviet Union at the Cultural and Scientific Conference for World Peace in New York; and in 1959, on the cultural exchange program instituted in 1955 between the Soviet Union and the United States. In 1962, he attended the Edinburgh Festival, where a series of concerts was devoted to his major works, including all of his string quartets and most of his symphonies.

On May 13, 1932, Shostakovich married Nina Varzar, a physicist. They had two children, one of whom, Maxim, became a concert pianist. Nina died in 1954, and in 1956, Shostakovich married Margarita Kainova.

1926 SYMPHONY NO. 1 IN F MAJOR, op. 10. I. Allegretto. II. Allegro. III. Lento. IV. Allegro molto.

When the First Symphony was rehearsed prior to its première performance, Glazunov voiced amazement at the composer's virtuosity in orchestration. Others were impressed by its freshness and kinetic drive; still others expressed amazement that so completely and maturely realized a work could be found in a "first symphony" by so a young composer. When the symphony was introduced by the Leningrad Philharmonic under Nikolai Malko on May 12, 1926, there was an exceptional ovation for the composer. In a letter to a friend, Shostakovich's mother wrote: "The audience listened with enthusiasm and the scherzo had to be played twice. At the end, Mitya [Dmitri] was called to the stage over and over again. When our handsome young composer appeared, looking almost like a boy, the enthusiasm turned into one long thunderous ovation." Performances followed in Moscow; in Berlin (conducted by Bruno Walter); in Philadelphia and New York (conducted by Leopold Stokowski). Each performance was a major success. By the time Shostakovich had reached his twenty-third birthday, the symphony had been heard in most of the world's music centers; and he had become, despite his youth, an international figure in music.

There are many who consider this youthful symphony one of the best Shostakovich has ever written; certainly it has remained one of the most popular. It never fails to magnetize audiences with its electric energy, or to delight with its wonderful spontaneity, freshness and youthful enthusiasm. Derivative though it occasionally is (sometimes from Tchaikovsky, at other times from Prokofiev), it still has a basic personality of its own. In fact, Nicolas Slonimsky found in this symphony the following characteristics of the composer's style and technique which subsequently formed his creative trademark: (1) a highly rhythmic opening subject, fundamentally diatonic, but embellished with chromatics; (2) individualized instrumentation with frequent division of the strings, and special effects, such as violin glissandi; (3) exploitation of the lowest and highest registers, particularly the low reaches of the brass and high notes in the strings; (4) independent role of the percussion; (5) inclusion of the piano in the orchestral score; (6) inverted pedals in tremolos in the violins; (7) extensive scale runs; (8) sudden modulations, directly into the tonic.

A muted trumpet opens the first movement, the principal theme of which is a tripping melody for the clarinet; the second theme is a sentimental idea in the vein of Tchaikovsky, heard in flute against pizzicati of the strings. The themes stated, the atmosphere becomes feverish and a sudden climax erupts. The movement ends gently, however, with a restatement of the opening bars in clarinet and cellos.

The music of the second movement is Shostakovich in a familiar pose of irresponsibility—spirited music full of joyful impulsiveness. Its main subject is given by the strings and repeated by the piano; the theme of the trio is heard in two flutes. The Lento that follows, is in an entirely different manner —romantic, and touched with sadness, dominated by a tender song heard at the opening of the movement in an oboe against string tremolos. A crescendo in side drum begins the finale, which arrives without interruption. It has stirring emotions and sharp contrasts. First, we get a restrained theme (Lento), which is soon succeeded by a turbulent Allegro molto section. The main ideas include a tune for the clarinet, which is built up into a climax, and a strong theme for strings and woodwind. The movement then passes from slow to fast, from tranquillity to drama. The music ends brilliantly with a whirlwind presto.

1930 THE AGE OF GOLD, ballet in three acts, op. 22, with scenario by A. V. Ivanovsky and choreography by E. I. Kaplan and V. I. Vainonen. First performance: Leningrad. October 27, 1930.

THE AGE OF GOLD, suite for orchestra, op. 22-a. I. Introduction. II. Waltz. III. Adagio. IV. Polka. V. Danse russe.

In 1929, a competition was held in the Soviet Union for a ballet on a Soviet theme. Young Shostakovich emerged the winner with his first ballet score, in which he successfully tapped the veins of mockery and satire. The first act takes place at an international exposition in an unidentified capitalist city. A Fascist representation is being welcomed with pomp and ceremony, while the arrival of a Soviet football team goes unnoticed. A boxing match involves a white man (a Fascist) and a Negro, the white man emerging the victor through a fraudulent decision by the referee; this arouses the anger of the spectators. The scene shifts to a cabaret, where Deva, a famous Fascist dancer, performs a number of dances, one of them intended to attract the interest of the captain of the football team. When the captain refuses to drink a toast to Fascism, he is attacked by a group of Fascists. After the riot is quelled, tensions are released through the dancing of a fox-trot.

In the first scene of the second act, a Negro eludes the clutches of the police; in the second scene, a procession of workers, a dance of pioneers, a football game, and an exhibition of motion pictures all take place in a workers' stadium. The third act shifts the action into a music hall where a festival called "The Age of Gold" is performed. Fascism is denounced. A common front of mutual understanding is established between the workers of Western Europe and the Soviet football team.

The ballet was not a success, mainly due to its cumbersome and often confused scenario. But Shostakovich's music was liked. The finest sections of the ballet score were assembled by the composer into a five-movement orchestral suite, which received its first performance even before the ballet itself was produced—in Leningrad on March 19, 1930. The introduction is made up of some of the basic melodic material of the ballet score. This is followed by a lilting waltz tune. The "Adagio" is the music accompanying the dance with which Deva tries to gain the interest of the captain of the football team. It highlights cantilena passages for soprano saxophone, euphonium and piccolo. The "Polka" that follows is the most famous part of this suite, intended as a satire on the Geneva Disarmament Conference following World War I. Here an impudent little tune is given by solo xylophone, to which the saxophone contributes a saucy melody of its own. A rollicking country dance is given by the trumpet and tuba, mocking brass-band music. (Shostakovich transcribed the "Polka" for solo piano.) Soon the entire orchestra joins in the merriment. The suite ends with a vigorous "Trepak," or "Russian Dance," in which accordion-like harmonies are exploited and in which the percussion play a prominent role. A noisy climax is built up before the dance (and the suite) comes to a sudden end.

1932 LADY MACBETH OF MZENSK, opera in four acts, op. 29, with text by the composer and A. Preis based on a story by Leskov. First performance: Moscow, January 22, 1934; revised version, entitled *Katarina Ismailova,* Moscow, January 1963.

In adapting Leskov's tale of lust, murder, adultery and suicide for operatic presentation, Shostakovich introduced political and social implications calculated to conform to Soviet ideologies. At times brutally realistic, at times satiric—so much so that the opera assumed a kind of dual personality—*Lady Macbeth* became an indictment of provincial middle-class life in Czarist Russia, and its heroine was shown to be a helpless victim of a morally bankrupt and decadent bourgeois society. The heroine, Katarina Ismailova, falls passionately in love with Sergei, a worker, in nineteenth-century Russia. She murders her father-in-law, and then her husband; when the latter's body is found, she and Sergei are arrested just as they are about to get married. They are sent to a transit camp for convicts where Sergei becomes attracted to young Sonya. Inflamed by jealousy, Katarina throws Sonya over a parapet into the river, then commits suicide by diving into the water.

In translating stage action into music, Shostakovich frequently commented sardonically or sarcastically on the tragic events transpiring. As Peter Heyworth remarked in *The New York Times*: "The father-in-law expires in agony to music as coolly detached as anything in Hindemith's *Cardillac*; the husband's body is hidden to the jolliest of little tunes. . . . A good deal of the satire rubs off on Katarina herself, so that it becomes increasingly difficult to take her seriously as a tragic heroine." At other times, Shostakovich translated action as literally as possible into appropriate musical sounds, notably in the bedroom scene where glissandi of trombones describe all too vividly what is happening. Thus the opera had a kind of schizoid personality, which one Soviet critic sought to explain away by referring to it as a "new genre of satiric tragedy."

The early up-and-down turbulent history of *Lady Macbeth* was described in the opening paragraphs of this section on Shostakovich. A few more details might be sketched in here for further clarification. When first performed in the Soviet Union, the critics were virtually unanimous in their praises, describing it as "a work of genius," "a great masterpiece," and so forth. The opera had a successful run of two years, when suddenly it was victimized by violent attack. What caused this sudden change of attitude? It is believed that Stalin attended a performance and was revolted by the lurid realism of the love scenes both on the stage and in the music. A few days later, the press let loose a barrage against the opera (which sent it into discard for some thirty years) and against the composer (which almost destroyed his career).

As a matter of cold fact, a reaction similar to Stalin's was expressed by some of the critics when *Lady Macbeth* was introduced in the United States—on January 31, 1935, in Cleveland, and about a week later, in New York. Olin Downes found the opera "lurid." More violent still was W. J. Henderson's report in the *Sun:* "*Lady Macbeth of Mzensk* is a bed-chamber opera. We see much of the coarse embraces of the two sinners mumbling and fumbling about in bed with the side of the house removed so we shall miss nothing. For their first embraces the composer has written music which for realism and brutal animalism surpasses anything else in the world. . . . Shostakovich is without doubt the foremost composer of pornographic music in the history of the art."

During the Khrushchev era, in which many of the restrictions formerly imposed on Soviet composers were relaxed, Shostakovich returned to his long-neglected opera. He revised the musical content slightly (interpolating two new orchestral entr'actes), but made radical changes in the text to remove many of the more objectionable carnal episodes. To avoid any confusion with the earlier version, he gave his opera a new name, that of the heroine, *Katarina Ismailova*. (Actually this is the title that was used when the opera was produced in Moscow and several other Russian cities in the early 1930s.)

Following the revival of the opera in Moscow early in 1963, productions took place at Covent Garden later in 1963, in San Francisco in 1964, and New York in 1965. In discussing the London performance, Peter Heyworth said in *The New York Times* that the score possessed "huge gusto and invention . . . while Katarina's unhappiness and final despair is most touchingly depicted. What is more, the score has real symphonic energy." After the San Francisco production, Alexander Fried said: "Shostakovich's music—blatantly inconsistent as it is—is music only a man of vital, masterly gifts and craftsmanship could have written. And more than once it attains inspired beauty."

Katerina Ismailova was made into a Soviet motion-picture opera, released in 1967.

1933 TWENTY-FOUR PRELUDES, for piano, op. 34.

Shostakovich's set of piano preludes is in the tradition of Chopin, Scriabin and Rachmaninoff rather than that of Debussy. For the Shostakovich prelude is a psychological rather than an impressionistic sketch.

There is a wealth of emotional feeling in these preludes, though it must be confessed that their quality is uneven, ranging from "the sublime to the downright banal," as Ivan Martynov points out. Martynov singles out the following preludes as outstanding: the somber and tragic E minor Prelude, which "calls to mind the lofty portals of a Gothic church"; the structurally interesting E-flat minor Prelude, a fugato; the D major ("Velocity Étude") Prelude, with its effective passage writing; and the jazzy D minor Prelude, the last of the set.

The composer himself presented the première of the twenty-four preludes in Moscow on May 24, 1933.

Leopold Stokowski made an effective orchestral transcription of the E-flat minor Prelude.

1933 CONCERTO NO. 1 IN C MINOR FOR PIANO AND ORCHESTRA, op. 35. I. Allegro moderato. II. Lento. III. Moderato. IV. Allegro.

One of the unusual features of this piano concerto is its instrumentation: it is scored for string orchestra and a single trumpet. The trumpet ushers in the first movement with a simple, almost ingenuous little melody. The piano then enters with the first theme; the piano also introduces the second theme, after the pace has quickened into an Allegro vivace. The development is frequently contrapuntal, growing all the while in sonority; it ends with a restatement of the first theme, set against low groans of the trumpet.

A waltz rhythm is prominent in the second movement, with the main melody—a long, sustained song—heard in the violins, then answered by the piano. The tempo quickens; the sonority grows to fortissimo. The melody is later taken up by the trumpet, and after that by the piano.

The third movement is a brief twenty-nine-bar intermezzo, in which two cadenzas for the piano are prominent, one of them accompanied. The final movement brims over with good spirits, with the trumpet assuming almost a harlequin's role. The tunes are gaily mocking, and there is even a witty parody of the kind of melodic material found in the classical sonatas, and a mischievous quotation of a Beethoven melody (from the rondo, *Rage Over a Lost Penny*); the latter is found in the cadenza towards the close of the concerto, the only place in the entire work where a cadenza is featured.

The concerto was introduced on October 15, 1933, by the Leningrad Philharmonic under Fritz Stiedry; the composer was soloist.

1934 SONATA IN D MINOR FOR CELLO AND PIANO, op. 40. I. Moderato. II. Moderato con moto. III. Largo. IV. Allegretto.

This early cello sonata is one of its composer's most lyrical works. The two themes of the first movement are rich in melodic interest. The first is elegiac in mood and made interesting by its unmetrical flow and its avoidance of a specific tonality. The second, which comes after a change of key from

D minor to B major, is romantic. The second movement presents a rustic-type waltz with satirical suggestions. The trio part is dramatized by electrifying scale passages, arpeggios and glissandi. A depressive mood pervades the Largo, in which the cello chants a beautiful song of sorrow after a twenty-measure muted introduction. This despair is abandoned in the finale, a rondo, which has irrepressible good spirits, arrested midway by a soaring and expressive melody for cello and piano.

The première of the sonata took place in Leningrad on December 25, 1934. V. Koubatzki was the soloist, with the composer at the piano.

1937 SYMPHONY NO. 5 IN D MINOR, op. 47. I. Moderato. II. Allegretto. III. Largo. IV. Allegro non troppo.

The huge success of Shostakovich's Fifth Symphony—one of the greatest he has known—came at a critical moment in his career. For one thing, Shostakovich had up to now failed to write a symphony that could repeat the triumph and inspiration of the youthful First. The Second Symphony in B major ("To October") op. 14, written in 1927, was a failure when introduced in Leningrad on November 6 of that year. If the Third Symphony in E-flat major ("May Day"), op. 20—which came two years later and was heard in Leningrad on January 21, 1930—did not duplicate the fiasco of the Second, it could hardly be considered a success either; it has rarely been heard. The Fourth Symphony in C minor, op. 43, was so badly received by the musicians at the first rehearsal that it never reached public performance at that time. In fact, it had to wait until January 20, 1962, for its world première!

The première of the Fifth Symphony, therefore, did not promise much.

But even more ominous to the possible success of the Fifth Symphony than the outright failure of its three predecessors was the fact that at this time, 1937, Shostakovich was out of favor. The official blasts in *Pravda* against his opera *Lady Macbeth of Mzensk* and his ballet *The Limpid Stream* had discredited him. His works were now being rarely performed, while he himself was ignored. But in spite of such an unfavorable climate for the introduction of his new symphony, it was a success of the first magnitude when heard for the first time in Leningrad on November 21, 1937. The next morning *The New York Times* ran a report of the première with the following headlines: "Composer Regains His Place in Soviet Music. Dmitri Shostakovich Who Fell From Grace Two Years Ago, On Way to Rehabilitation. His New Symphony Hailed. Audience Cheers as Leningrad Philharmonic Presents Work." The Soviet critics—frigid to Shostakovich for the past year and a half—hurled about superlatives without inhibitions. Gregory Schneerson wrote: "This is Shostakovich's day of triumph! The symphony is a work of extraordinary profundity, by a mature artist who has successfully overcome the childhood disease of leftism. This is, indeed, a joyous occasion." Alexei Tolstoy exclaimed in *Izvestia*: "Glory be to our people which produce such talents!"

The symphony opens powerfully with a big, wind-swept theme, in octaves divided between low and high strings, treated canonically; this sets the stage for music of dramatic interest and striking contrasts. Violas are heard in the second important theme over a strong rhythmic pulse in cellos and basses. A forceful entrance by the horns brings on the development section which has epical design. The second movement is slighter in texture, a scherzo resembling a waltz in Shostakovich's satirical style. There are two waltz melodies, one in the cellos and double basses, the other in the woodwind. The slow movement is one of the most emotional and profound pieces of music that the composer had thus far produced. First, we get a doleful, extended song in the violins; after that, an elegiac melody in oboe over tremolo strings. This material grows and develops into a moving apostrophe. Music, march-like in character, is heard in the concluding movement presented by the brass over rhythms in the tympani. Material from earlier movements is remembered midway in the movement, then the march melody returns to bring the symphony to a powerful conclusion.

1939 SYMPHONY NO. 6 IN B MINOR, op. 54. I. Largo. II. Allegro. III. Presto.

The Sixth Symphony was heard for the first time (and received none too enthusiastically) on November 5, 1939, in Leningrad. Shostakovich had originally intended it as a tribute to Lenin, and conceived it along monumental lines for a large chorus, orchestra, and soloists, with texts provided by peasant poets. But somewhere during the writing of the music, Shostakovich abandoned the Lenin idea, as well as the ambitious scheme, and created a symphony for orchestra alone without any program.

The symphony opens in an unorthodox way: The usual sonata-allegro first movement is absent, and we have in its place the second-movement Largo. This slow movement is long, involved and emotional, opening with a lyric section for low strings and woodwind, which the violins carry over to a high register. This is followed by an equally lyric theme in the strings, more elegiac in character. The scherzo that follows is light and frivolous with occasional sardonic commentary interpolated by a xylophone. The symphony ends with a highly rhythmic Presto, in rondo form, with march and dance music taking turns in expressions of restrained mockery.

1940 PIANO QUINTET IN G MINOR, op. 57. I. Prelude and Fugue. II. Scherzo. III. Intermezzo.

The piano quintet is one of Shostakovich's foremost successes in the field of chamber music. On November 23, 1940, it was introduced and acclaimed at the Moscow Festival of Soviet Music. Soon after this, it won the Stalin Prize of one hundred thousand rubles.

Lyrical and human, the quintet (despite its unorthodox form) is easily appreciated at first hearing. It opens with a Prelude and Fugue. The form may be that of Bach; but the style is unmistakably Shostakovich. This introductory movement is in three parts (Lento, Poco più mosso, Lento), with the thematic material presented in the first section; the Fugue derives its melodic idea from one of the melodies of the Prelude, and is charged with feeling. The Scherzo finds Shostakovich in a recognizable impish attitude. The rhythms are impulsive; the melody has infectious gaiety. The last movement has been described by Victor I. Seroff as "ballet music with a march rhythm"; one of the themes is a traditional melody of the Russian circus, announcing the approach of the clowns.

1941 SYMPHONY NO. 7 IN C MAJOR ("Leningrad"), op. 60. I. Allegretto. II. Moderato; Poco allegretto. III. Adagio. IV. Allegro non troppo.

Divorced from the stirring times in which it was created, the Seventh Symphony loses much of its emotional and dramatic interest. Recent hearings have confirmed the original suspicion that this is, for the most part, a vulgar work compounded of cheap and obvious effects. It can hardly hope to survive for its musical interest. But it is a piece of contemporary history, and as such may remain an interesting musical curiosity.

It was begun (it will be recalled) in July, 1941, a grim period for the Soviets. The Nazi hordes, which had invaded the land one month earlier, were sweeping relentlessly across the land, bringing defeat and devastation, searing the principal Russian cities with fire, and laying siege to Leningrad. Shostakovich, in Leningrad, planned his symphony as an expression of what he called "the majestic ideas of the patriotic war. Neither savage raids, German planes, nor the grim atmosphere of the beleagured city could hinder the flow of ideas. I worked with an inhuman intensity I have never before reached."

When the government fled to Kuibyshev, Shostakovich followed. There he completed the symphony in December. The première performance took place in Kuibyshev on March 5, 1942, with the Bolshoi Theatre Orchestra conducted by Samuel Samosud. This concert was a gala political, as well as musical, occasion. High diplomatic and military officials attended, and responded enthusiastically to the new work.

The symphony was soon after this heard throughout the Soviet Union, acclaimed wherever it was performed. The score was microfilmed and flown by air to the Unites States. On July 19, 1942, Arturo Toscanini conducted the première American performance with the NBC Symphony over the radio.

Shostakovich has described his symphony in the following way:

"The first and longest movement bears a dramatic and, I would say, tragic character. Our peaceful life has been broken up by a threatening event, war, and everything has to be subordinated to its laws. The music also has another theme: a requiem expressing the people's sorrow over their dead heroes.

"The next two movements were intended as an intermezzo. They confirm life in opposition to war. I tried to express the thought that art, literature, and science must advance in spite of war. It is, if you like, a polemic against the statement that 'when the cannons roar the muse is silent.'

"The fourth movement is dedicated to our victory. It is an immediate continuation of the second and third movements; their logical outcome. It is the victory of light over darkness, wisdom over frenzy, lofty humanism over monstrous tyranny.

"On the whole, I feel that the Seventh Symphony is an optimistic conception. As a composition it is closer to my Fifth Symphony than to my Sixth; and it is a continuation of the emotions and moods of the Fifth Symphony."

Here is Nicolas Slonimsky's illuminating description:

"The first movement opens with a vigorous C major theme, in powerful unisons, punctuated by the rhythmic spurts of the trumpets and kettledrums.

This is the theme of the Leningrad citizen, who had become the hero of the siege. The tonality darkens when an E-flat is introduced in the melodic ascent. The music softens; there is a moment of lyrical lassitude. Suddenly, out of nowhere, a little puppet-like tune is heard in the strings pizzicato and col legno against the steady beat of the drum. Relentlessly it grows, it takes on body, spreads all over the orchestra, magnified, yet unchanged in its melodic pattern. A Soviet writer described it as a 'psychological portrait of the enemy.' . . . The theme of the citizen hero struggles through, integrated, from the melodic allusions into a powerful restatement. But the enemy leaves a path of destruction in its march. The victims are mourned in a threnody intoned by a bassoon solo.

"The second movement . . . is . . . a rather unusual one for Shostakovich. It opens with a simple modal subject in the second violins in 4/4 time. The scherzo proper gives prominence to a solo for E-flat piccolo clarinet, played against a contrasting subject in the lower woodwind."

In the third movement, "after a chorale-like introduction in full chords, the music swims into clear D major. A nervous, gypsy-like dance is heard, a recollection of carefree gaiety, and the movement is concluded in optimistic clarity.

"The finale follows the slow movement without pause. It begins with a broad descriptive melody. Imperceptibly the music comes to rhythmic life, becomes fugal, and increases its dynamic energy. . . . The finale summons all the resources of the orchestra, ending in a crushing C major."

1942 SONATA NO. 2 FOR PIANO, op. 61. I. Allegretto. II. Largo. III. Moderato.

Shostakovich's Second Piano Sonata was heard for the first time in Leningrad on November 11, 1943, with the composer performing. In reviewing the American première, Robert Bagar wrote in the *New York World-Telegram*: "The last movement is the great joy of the work, though there is joy unconfined in the beauties that unreel almost every second through it. . . . To contrast with the resolute and decisive feel of the first and third sections, there is the Largo, with its delicately exotic flavor. Some low chords are utilized in a kind of pallid and bleak rhythmic background against fragments of melody that fall gracefully and softly on the ear."

1943 SYMPHONY NO. 8 IN C MINOR, op. 65. I. Adagio. II. Allegretto. III. Allegro non troppo. Iv. Largo. V. Allegretto.

The Eighth Symphony came one year after the Seventh, and was heard for the first time at a festival of Soviet music in Moscow on November 4, 1943, with Eugene Mravinsky conducting the State Symphony Orchestra.

Shostakovich explained that this symphony was an attempt "to look into the future, into the postwar epoch." "Life is beautiful," Shostakovich wrote in explaining the mood of this work, "and all that is dark and ignominious will disappear. All that is beautiful will triumph." But though the composer intended it as an optimistic utterance, the symphony has a pervading feeling of deep tragedy, as though Shostakovich could not forget the war that was raging so bitterly all around him.

It opens with a long and very lyrical Adagio movement, The principal subject is a soaring melody for the first violins. This basic theme is preceded by a pleasing duet for high and low strings which opens and closes the movement. The second movement has a march-like character. The next three movements proceed without interruption. The third carries on the rhythmic momentum of the second, the march-like tune being heard first in the violas. The fourth is in a form suggesting the passacaglia, the bass of which recalls the opening theme of the symphony. The fifth is pastoral music in which a series of melodic ideas is presented by different solo instruments. The symphony subsides into a quiet revery and ends in a subdued C major chord.

1944 PIANO TRIO IN E MINOR, op. 67. I. Andante; Moderato. II. Scherzo. III. Largo. IV. Allegretto.

The elegiac character of many of the pages in this piano trio is due to the fact that it was written in memory of one of Shostakovich's close friends who had died—the musicologist Ivan Sollerinsky. Its world première took place in Leningrad on November 14, 1944. When the work was heard in America for the first time—in New York City on April 27, 1945—Noel Straus described it as follows: "The first movement . . . was introduced by a short and striking Andante which started most unconventionally with unaccompanied harmonics on the cello, stating a theme taken up next by the muted violin and then by the piano. This resulted in a strangely effective color combination that added to the brooding mood of the prefatory measures. . . . The following movement . . . gained in interest as it reached its despairingly wild concluding section but was overshadowed by the last two divisions . . . meant to be played without pause and really form a single entity. The Largo, in which the violin and cello move in broad melodic lines over an ostinato bass of sustained harmonies on the piano, is one of the most poignant of Shostakovich's inspirations, while the Allegretto, built up on themes of folk-dance nature, but always with an undercurrent of sorrow, is the crown of the whole work."

1944 STRING QUARTET NO. 2, op. 68. I. Overture. II. Recitative. III. Romance. IV. Waltz and Variations.

Shostakovich's Second String Quartet came seven years after the First (op. 49). It was introduced by the Beethoven Quartet in Leningrad on November 14, 1944. Ivan Martynov described the quartet as a "romantic poem" full of "light and space."

A propulsive theme, given an exotic character by use of plagal cadences, opens the quartet; a second important subject, tender and expressive, occurs in the high register of the violin against pizzicati of the other strings. In the next two movements, as Martynov notes, the listener is carried into "the sphere of lyrical contemplation." The Recitative reminds Martynov of the classical recitatives of Bach, while the Romance is a "calm song," interrupted briefly by passionate episodes. The waltz that follows is in the traditions of Glinka and Tchaikovsky (rather than the Viennese waltz); the melody is introduced by the cello.

1945 SYMPHONY NO. 9 IN E-FLAT MAJOR, op. 70. I. Allegro. II. Moderato. III. Presto. IV. Largo. V. Allegretto; Allegro.

The Ninth Symphony is the most joyous of Shostakovich's works in that form, "a merry little piece," as he himself described it. It is also the shortest and simplest. It was heard on November 3, 1945, in Leningrad, with Eugene Mravinsky conducting the Leningrad Philharmonic Orchestra.

There are some commentators who like to consider the Ninth Symphony as the third in a symphonic trilogy inspired by the war. The Seventh expressed the martial spirit of a people rising to defend its land; the Eighth echoed the tragic overtones of a grim war; the Ninth was the gay and uninhibited voice of victory.

Gregory Schneerson, the eminent Soviet critic, has prepared the following analysis:

"The opening bars of the first movement transported us at once to a bright and pleasant world. There was joyous abandon, the warm pulsation of life and the exuberance of youth in those whimsical dance themes and rhythms. There was something about the classical purity of form, the dynamic development of the themes, and the rich expressiveness emanating from a sheer pleasure in the interplay of sound images that reminded us of Haydn. . . . As the symphonic action developed, Haydn associations grew gradually fainter until at last we came to the kernel of the music, to Shostakovich himself. Shostakovich—ever original, ever fresh, ever the clever, witty narrator, eager and sincere.

"The second movement introduces a new mood, one of warm and gentle lyricism, faintly touched by wistful meditation. The Scherzo, built on the variational development of several dance melodies, is perhaps the culmination of the emotional content of the entire symphony. It is music of radiant joy, an almost childlike abandon to happiness. The swift movement of the Scherzo is interrupted by a brief but extremely significant episode—the Largo. Here, it seems to me, is a key to the understanding of the single idea uniting the three parts of this symphonic trilogy. The Largo is the link that joins the separate parts in spite of stylistic differences of musical idiom and emotional content.

"The finale scintillates with humor and inventiveness. Radiant in mood and simple in design, the theme passes through masterful elaboration until it reaches the whirlwind coda that completes the symphony. A brief upward scale . . . and the symphony is ended."

Though the audience and critics liked this symphony, Soviet officialdom soon frowned upon it as "ideologically weak" and a poor reflection of the true spirit of the Soviet people. I. Nesteyev denounced the cynicism and the cold irony of the music in *Culture and Life,* and found that these traits were the results of Stravinsky's influence. In reply to this denunciation, Serge Koussevitzky expressed the opinion in Boston that the Ninth Symphony was "one of the most beautiful of our contemporary works." He gave the American première with the Boston Symphony at the Berkshire Music Festival at Tanglewood on July 25, 1946.

1949 SONG OF THE FORESTS, oratorio for children's choir, mixed choir, soloists, and orchestra, op. 81. I. At the War's End. II. In Forests Let Us Clothe Our Land. III. Remembrances of the Past. IV. Children Plant the

Forests. V. Arise to Great Deeds All Ye People. VI. Promenade in the Future. VII. Glory.

With this oratorio (Shostakovich's first large work for chorus), he reestablished himself as a leading composer in the Soviet Union after the destructive attacks leveled against him in 1948 by the Central Committee of the Communist Party. When it was introduced in Leningrad on November 26, 1949, it was acclaimed in the Soviet press as a prototype of the kind of subject and the kind of music to which Soviet composers were expected to devote themeselves, and the Stalin Prize was conferred on it. The text, by Eugene Dolmotovsky, glorifies the program of reforestation undertaken by the Soviet Union after World War II to reclaim desert areas.

Shostakovich's score makes extensive use of two principal melodic subjects. The first is a cyclical theme which is heard at the opening in the orchestral introduction. The second is a germ motive, appearing first in the bass solo to the words "With victory came the end of the war," which undergoes considerable transformation and development throughout the entire oratorio. Both subjects are heard simultaneously in chorus and orchestra in the concluding "Glory."

The oratorio is in seven sections. The first tells about the end of World War II and the project to reclaim the desert lands in central Russia. The second part echoes the joyous reaction of the people to this plan. A melancholy mood is evoked in the third movement as the wastelands, and the misery they create for the people, are described. A lighter part follows: The children join in the activity of planting the trees, singing as they work. The sixth part is a pastoral poem, evoking the beauty of Nature in the springtime. All the vocal and orchestral forces are combined with immense power and brilliance of color in the finale, a mighty fugal paean to the glory of reforestation.

1953 SYMPHONY NO. 10 IN E MINOR, op. 93. I. Moderato. II. Allegro. III. Allegretto; Lento; Allegretto. IV. Andante; Allegro.

Shostakovich's Tenth Symphony was his first new work in that form in almost ten years. It was introduced in Leningrad on December 17, 1953. Following its American première by the New York Philharmonic conducted by Dmitri Mitropoulos on December 14, 1954, it received the New York Music Critics Circle Award. The composer has explained he hoped to make his music express the "thoughts and aspirations of our contemporaries," and specifically their thoughts about and aspirations for peace. But he did not provide a specific program. The work opens with a slow introduction in which a six-note theme is prominent in cellos and basses; this subject recurs several times throught the symphony. After fifty measures, the pace quickens and a lyric thought is projected by the clarinets. A more rhythmic idea, in flutes, but equally lyrical, is still another important subject in this movement. The brief scherzo that follows as a second movement is brisk, rhythmic and charged with motor energy. Then comes the slow movement, opening with a folk-song-like melody in strings in imitation. A solo horn is later answered by the strings in a new version of the six-note opening theme. There then ensues a poetic nocturne in which a horn solo over plucked strings is prominent. This is followed by an English horn giving important treatment to the opening material of the movement. The finale opens leisurely and meditatively with an oboe solo of oriental character. The main theme that follows is a martial melody. There then take place a brief recall of material from the scherzo and slow movements, and a final repetition of the six-note motive, after which the work rushes on towards an exciting conclusion.

1955 CONCERTO IN A MINOR, for violin and orchestra, op. 99. I. Nocturne (Moderato). II. Scherzo (Allegro). III. Passacaglia (Andante). IV. Burlesca (Allegro con brio).

Shostakovich wrote this violin concerto for David Oistrakh who introduced it in Leningrad on October 29, 1955, Eugene Mravinsky conducting. One of the unusual features of this work is its four movements; another, its sensitive and transparent scoring, through the omission of heavy brass and emphasis on such instruments as the celesta, harp and xylophone.

The main thought of the first movement comes after a Moderato opening when the violin presents a flowing melody in shifting meters against a contrapuntal background of a bassoon. In the scherzo, a light subject for flute and bass clarinet, with interpolations by the solo violin, provides the first main subject. A change of key brings on a dynamic and dramatic episode, after which the earlier graceful material is brought back by the solo violin. The third movement, a passacaglia, is built from an ostinato subject in cellos and basses answered by horns. The violin appears with a sustained song. In the cadenza considerable prominence is given to the ostinato figure. The finale enters without pause. A gay dance-like tune in orchestra, in the composer's identifiable vein of mockery, appears in the orchestra. From then on, the music progresses with numerous brilliant virtuoso passages for the violin and dramatic episodes for the orchestra.

1957 CONCERTO NO. 2 IN E MAJOR FOR PIANO AND ORCHESTRA, op. 102. I. Allegro. II. Andante. III. Allegro.

Shostakovich wrote his second piano concerto for his nineteen-year-old son, Maxim, who introduced it in Moscow on May 10, 1957. It is an intimate work of modest proportions, requiring a small orchestra, utilizing a chamber-music style, and emphasizing a consistently light and graceful touch. The first movement presents two lighthearted subjects, the first heard in the piano after a brief orchestral introduction, and the second more lyrical in character. After the Andante opens with a subdued orchestral preface, the piano arrives with a nostalgic song with a strong Russian personality. This is the heart of the movement. The finale enters without interruption to give play to gaiety, and healthy animal spirits.

1957 SYMPHONY NO. 11 IN G MINOR: 1905, op. 103. I. Palace Square (Adagio). II. January 9 (Allegro). III. Eternal Memory (Adagio). IV. Alarm (Allegro non troppo).

In Shostakovich's Eleventh Symphony, descriptive titles for each of the four movements provide a clue to the intent of the music. He wrote the symphony to commemorate the Russian Revolution of 1905, for whose fiftieth anniversary this work had been commissioned. Shostakovich placed considerable emphasis on virile, martial-like melodies, brass fanfares, and percussion effects imitating the marching of men and the firing of shots. The symphony comes to a theatrical conclusion with a finale dramatized by the pealing of chimes.

"As history transcribed in music, the symphony has its points," said Ross Parmenter in *The New York Times*. "With its sounds of people assembling from far off, and of their sad retreat, with its dramatic agitation in the depiction of the massacre, and with its evocation of the people rising successfully, it is certainly vividly pictorial."

For his melodic material, the composer drew from folk songs and songs of the Revolution; also, two themes appropriated from his own earlier works commemorating the same revolution.

The world première took place in Moscow on October 30, 1957, and was given a rousing ovation. It earned for its composer the Lenin Award.

1959 CONCERTO FOR CELLO AND ORCHESTRA, op. 107. I. Allegretto. II. Moderato. III. Cadenza. IV. Allegro con moto.

Shostakovich wrote this concerto for the distinguished Soviet cellist, Mstislav Rostropovich, who introduced it in Leningrad on October 4, 1959. He was also the soloist when the work received its American première—in Philadelphia with Eugene Ormandy conducting on November 7, 1959; on that occasion the composer was in the audience, on his second visit to the United States.

The concerto opens with a four-note motto theme that in one form or another recurs throughout the work; it is presented by the solo cello. Later on in the movement the solo cello is heard in the second subject, a melody in the instrument's high range. The second movement has a placid string introduction, with a motive for horn that remembers the second theme of the first movement. Then the cello arrives with a soaring song, to which muted violins soon provide contrast. After a recall of earlier material in the French horn the movement ends quietly. The third movement, which appears without pause, is an extended cadenza for the solo instrument. Then, once again without pause, comes the finale, its basic theme introduced by oboes and clarinets accompanied by strings. Solo cello takes over this melody and then contributes a tune of its own. The concerto ends with effective repetitions of the opening-movement motto theme by the French horn, by high woodwinds, by solo cello, and finally by the woodwind choirs.

1963 STRING QUARTET NO. 9 IN E-FLAT MAJOR. I. Moderato. con moto. II. Adagio. III. Allegretto. IV. Adagio. V. Allegro.

Lyricism is emphasized in this one of Shostakovich's best string quartets of his later period. The world première took place in Moscow on November 20, 1964.

The mood of the first movement is established by the first violin with a wistful phrase. This subject is taken over by the lower strings and is worked out briefly. A more virile, dance-like tune serves as the second subject; it is played by the cello, accompanied by string instruments pizzicato. Later on another important theme is introduced by the first violin—a spacious idea spanning two octaves; it is heard in counterpoint to the first theme.

There are two slow movements. The first is dominated by an expressive melody for viola over a chordal accompaniment. The third movement is a scherzo with a polka-like character. The second of the two slow movements follows, made up of a chorale with recitatives. The finale is the longest and most complicated of the five movements. A vigorous scherzo-like opening theme (which later receives fugal treatment) and a simple folk song in the first violin are the basic materials. A brief recall of the spacious two-octave theme of the first movement precedes a vigorous conclusion.

1964 THE EXECUTION OF STEPAN RAZIN, vocal-symphonic poem for basso, chorus and orchestra.

Shostakovich wrote this extended work for solo voice, chorus and orchestra to commemorate the fiftieth anniversary of the October Revolution. It received its world première in Moscow on December 28, 1964, and scored a major success. For his text, the composer used a poem by Yevtushenko, whose hero is the notorious Cossack who led a peasants' revolt in seventeenth-century Russia and met his doom at the hands of the Czar's troops. Even in death, Stepan Razin is a formidable foe, since his severed head has such piercingly angry eyes that the Czar becomes frightened, and fright turns to terror when the dead head begins to laugh.

A Soviet publication (author not identified) provides the following description of Shostakovich's music: "The soloist's part is closely interwoven with that of the chorus. The latter now voices its sympathy with the protagonist, now expresses the feelings of the people, now again comments on the events that unfold in the poem. The composer makes the chorus express what is going on within Stepan's soul, and this enables him to bring into relief the emotions of his hero. Elements of Russian folk songs are treated in a true symphonic manner. The chorus in particular is written in folk tradition; it is mostly two-part, its melodic line close to folk-song intonations and in a strict rhythm. The orchestra is highly expressive and colorful."

1966 STRING QUARTET NO. 11. I. Introduction. II. Scherzo. III. Recitative. IV. Study. V. Humoresque. VI. Elegy. VIII. Conclusion.

The eleventh string quartet was written in memory of Vasili Shirinsky, a member of the Beethoven String Quartet in the Soviet Union, and a musician who had often performed Shostakovich's works. It was introduced in Moscow on June 6, 1966. The quartet, which has the character of a suite, is dominated by a single mood, which the Soviet critic, D. Blagoi, describes as "grief at irreparable loss." He adds: "Undergoing various emotional treatments in the course of its seven brief movements, this main idea lends to the Quartet's exceptional unity." Blagoi also finds the division and nomenclature of the separate movements as "rather symbolic . . . while the leading dramaturgic principle is the uninterrupted flow of music." He also feels that "improvisation seems the best word to define it. Yet this improvisatory freedom, a hallmark of true art, presupposed meticulous attention to every detail."

JEAN SIBELIUS 1865–1957

Sibelius has proved once again that no musical structure or style becomes dated or obsolete if a composer can bring to them freshness, creative strength and a personal point of view. Sibelius never completely broke with tradition. He invented no new idioms and fashioned no new forms. He used modern devices most sparingly, if at all. Yet his music is recognizably his. There is no mistaking the hand that fashioned those healthy, irresistible melodies in the fast movements, or the bucolic songs of tranquillity often touched with sadness in the slow ones. There is no mistaking, either, the hand who built those architectural monuments of his symphonies—cathedrals of tone, built idea by the idea, the way cathedrals are stone by stone. Sibelius's music is like none other heard in our concert hall. It is the music of the North; music influenced by Northern geography, climate, temperament, ideals and legendary backgrounds. As David Cherniavsky remarked, we encounter "not only the ethnical influence of the Nordic race and the austere grandeur of the Northern landscape, but also the vital stimulus of the new progressive spirit of Scandinavia and Finland in modern culture."

When Sibelius began composing, Brahms dominated the world of symphonic music; and Brahms influenced the young Sibelius profoundly. They met in Vienna in 1890, the young man coming to pay reverent tribute to the master. In his first orchestral works—two overtures written between 1890 and 1891—Sibelius imitated the post-Romantic style of Brahms's music.

But it was not long before a new Sibelius emerged from the shell of the old, a Sibelius with a manner and message all his own. Returning to his native land following travels in Germany and Austria, Sibelius was fired with patriotic ardor that influenced his musical writing. He now sought to express the soul of his land in music deriving its character from Finnish folk songs and often inspired by the old Finnish epic, the *Kalevala*: in *Kullervo,* op. 7 (1892); *En Saga*, op. 9 (1892, revised 1901); *Karelia,* op. 11 (1893); the four orchestral *Legends*, op. 22, that includes the poignant tone poem *Swan of Tuonela* (1895), and *Finlandia*, op. 26 (1899, revised 1900).

Just before writing *Finlandia,* Sibelius composed his first symphony, in E minor, op. 39 (1899), which was introduced in Helsinki on April 26, 1899. With it he launched his career as one of the most celebrated symphonists of the twentieth century, possibly the most famous since Brahms. The First Symphony, and the Second which followed it in 1901, were true to the Germanic post-Romantic traditions, with a strong echo of Tchaikovsky added. But with the Third Symphony, Sibelius began deviating slightly from the accepted symphonic structural procedures. With the Fourth Symphony, he achieved more conciseness, economy, and a greater intensity than heretofore. In the next three symphonies he reduced the orchestral forces, often sacrificing long and spacious melodies for short, epigrammatic ideas, replacing expansive emotions with sober and restrained reflections, and simplifying the orchestral fabric through a reduction of harmonic and contrapuntal resources.

The Sibelius symphonies have at times been overpraised. Writers like Cecil Gray and Constant Lambert regarded them as the greatest works in this form since Beethoven and felt that they would influence the entire future of music. The Sibelius symphonies have also been severely attacked: by Paul Henry Lang, who regards them as "obese," "turgid" and "redundant"; by Aaron Copland who considers them sympathetic "but not very significant"; by Virgil Thomson who maintained that Sibelius orchestrated badly and was capable of producing highly vulgar music. Surely the truth must lie somewhere between two such extremes. If Sibelius is not the greatest symphonist since Beethoven, and if he is not likely to influence the whole future of music—both opinions which we must consider as excessive—he was, nevertheless, a powerful, original voice in twentieth-century music; and his later symphonies are among the proudest adornments of twentieth-century symphonic literature.

In *Music, History and Ideas,* Hugo Leichtentritt finds that Sibelius's music has gone through three phases, which he identifies respectively as "the national, the European, the cosmic." He explains: "In the first phase Sibelius speaks and sings to the people of his country with tunes, dance rhythms and accents of Finland. This northern phase, to which almost all of his symphonic poems belong, is later expanded from a provincial dialect to the musical language of international validity." Leichtentritt finds that in his later symphonies, Sibelius "passes beyond this European phase toward a still vaster horizon, beyond Scandinavia and Europe to a spiritual world where the elect spirits of humanity meet on common ground, freely discoursing on the great themes around which all higher aspirations of mind and soul revolve eternally." Summing up, Leichtentritt concludes: "Here is an art of intrinsic worth and substance, instead of virtuoso showmanship, brilliant technical exhibitionism and revolutionary experimentalism. Here is music thoroughly modern in spirit, grown not in a hothouse but from its native soil, and fixed in the soil of Finland with far-reaching, firm, and densely knotted roots."

Sibelius was born in Hämmeenlinna (Tavastehus), Finland, on December 8, 1865, the son of a regimental doctor. In his ninth year, he began studying the piano, but soon transferred to the violin; at ten, he wrote his first piece of music, a duet for violin and cello. While attending the Finnish Model Lyceum, he supplemented violin lessons with the study of theory. In 1885, he came to Helinski to study law at the University. After a single year, he dropped law to to concentrate on music. He enrolled in the Institute of Music, where his teachers included Ferruccio Busoni (then on a visit to Finland) and Martin Wegelius. During this period in 1888, he published his first composition (a song) and had one of his works played for the first time, a *Theme and Variations,* for string quartet. A state grant, in 1889, enabled him to continue his music study in Berlin, with Adolf Becker, and in Vienna, with Robert Fuchs and Karl Goldmark. The chamber and orchestral music he now produced betrayed the impact of German post-Romanticism.

Back in his native land in 1891, Sibelius became aroused by national consciousness, and by the spirit of rebellion among his countrymen against Russian oppression. He absorbed the national epic of Finland, the *Kalevala*. He acquainted himself with the history and traditions of his country. He became fired with the dream of seeing Finland liberated. This national awareness entered his musical writing and motivated the production of his first ambitious compositions with a Finnish identity: *Kullervo,* inspired by the *Kalevala,* introduced in Helsinki on April 28, 1892; the first version of *En Saga,* heard in 1893; an overture and an orchestral suite, both of them entitled *Karelia,* also in 1893; and the *Four Legends,* one of which is *The Swan of Tuonela,* once again inspired by the *Kalevala,* heard first in Helsinki on April 13, 1896.

On June 10, 1892, Sibelius married Aino Järnefelt, daughter of the famous Finnish conductor and composer. Soon after this, Sibelius was appointed to the faculty of the Music Institute and of the Orchestral School, as teacher of theory, violin and composition. He was able to give up most of his teaching duties, and concentrate on composition, in 1897, through an annual government subsidy (the first such given to a composer in Finland). Stimulated by this new-found independence, Sibelius completed, in 1899, the original version of the tone poem that first made him famous, *Finlandia*; also his first symphony. In 1900, he toured Scandinavia, Germany, Holland and France with the Finnish Philharmonic, whose programs included some of his own compositions.

In 1904, Sibelius retired to the small town of Järvenpäa, twenty miles from Helsinki (Helsingfors)—to Villa Ainola, which remained his home from then on. For a while, he toured European capitals conducting his compositions. In 1914, he paid a visit to the United States to conduct at the Norfolk Music Festival in Connecticut, where he made his American debut on June 4, 1914; on this occasion he introduced his tone poem *The Oceanides,* written for this event. During his stay in the United States, he received an honorary doctorate from Yale University.

After World War I, Sibelius became a national figure as well as a composer of international stature. Anniversaries of his birth—particularly his eightieth and ninetieth years—became occasions for celebrations throughout Finland. They also inspired commemorative concerts in the rest of the world. But, creatively, he had come to a dead end, his last composition being *Esquisses,* a cycle of piano pieces, op. 114, in 1929. For many years rumors were circulated that he was working on an eighth symphony, but these were proved unfounded. In the last quarter century of his life, he withdrew from the world outside of Järvenpäa. He died there of a cerebral hemorrhage on September 20, 1957, and was buried in the garden of his villa.

1900–1901 EN SAGA, tone poem for orchestra, op. 9.

FINLANDIA, tone poem for orchestra, op. 26.

The first versions of both *En Saga* and *Finlandia* were written before 1900—*En Saga* in 1892, *Finlandia* in 1899. But these compositions are today heard in the revisions which the composer made later, that of *En Saga* in 1901, and that of *Finlandia* in 1900.

En Saga is Sibelius's earliest work to enter the permanent symphonic repertory, and it was one of Sibelius's first orchestral compositions to get performed. Heard in Helsinki on February 16, 1893, the composer conducting, it was a failure. Dissatisfied with it, Sibelius withdrew it from further performances until he had an opportunity to rewrite it, the major changes being made in the orchestration. Now heard again, *En Saga* proved a significant success—and deservedly so. It is the composer's first important work reflecting the spirit and personality of Finland; with it, Finnish national music achieved artistic significance for the first time.

A horn call over string tremolos is the summons to the first main subject. This is hinted at before it is fully realized in bassoons over string arpeggios. After this subject is developed and brought to a climax, a second principal idea is announced by violas. Once again a climax is reached. Now a dramatic change of mood is introduced with a bucolic section emphasizing an idyllic song for solo clarinet. A third climax follows, then the tone poem subsides into tranquillity.

Finlandia has had a dramatic career, closely tied in with Finnish history at the end of the nineteenth century. Intended by the composer as a reflection of the emotions of an exile returning to his native land, this stirring music owes its origin to the February Manifesto issued by the Russian government to abrogate the Diet and suppress free speech and press in Finland. To raise funds to fight this tyrannical move, a group of Finnish patriots inaugurated a series of entertainments, for one of which Sibelius wrote a suite, *Finland Awakes*. This was in 1899. The fourth movement was called "Suomi," the Finnish name for Finland. After this performance, this fourth movement was divorced from the suite, rewritten, retitled *Finlandia,* and reintroduced on July 2, 1900, Robert Kajanus conducting. This is the version that has become world-famous. After that, through the years, *Finlandia* became the musical voice of Finland, the expression of its aspirations and its spirit. The outside world came to identify it with Finnish idealism and its struggles for independence. Within Finland it did more, at the turn of the twentieth century, to bring about Finnish freedom than any speech, pamphlet, or published propaganda.

It is a vibrantly national piece of music, so much so that for a long time many believed that some of its melodies quoted folk sources. All the ingredients, however, are Sibelius's own. The stirring opening measures for the brass, and the disturbed music that follows it immediately, all suggest the unrest of a proud people in the face of dark tyranny. There next comes a tender melody in the woodwind, almost like a supplication. A tonal storm erupts, the struggle for freedom has begun. Suddenly a melody, like a folk song, is heard in the woodwinds; it sounds like a prayer for peace. This is the most famous melody in the score—indeed, probably the most famous Finnish melody ever written. The strings reply with another national theme, and the woodwinds and strings proceed to alternate in a paean to freedom and truth. The composition grows climactically into a grandiose proclamation of the triumph of the people over the forces of oppression.

1901 SYMPHONY NO. 2 IN D MAJOR, op. 43. I. Allegretto. II. Tempo andante ma rubato. III. Vivacissimo. IV. Allegro moderato.

Sibelius's First Symphony in E minor, op. 39, was completed in 1899, and introduced in Helsingfors on April 26 of the same year. The Second

Symphony was not slow in following the first. It was begun in Rapallo, Italy, in 1901, completed in Finland at the close of the same year, and given its première in Helsingfors on March 8, 1902, under the composer's direction.

The Second Symphony—though long a favorite with audiences—has come in for severe criticism among some critics for its emotional plenitude and extravagances of color and sonority. Virgil Thomson, writing his first criticism in the *New York Herald Tribune* on October 9, 1940, called the symphony "vulgar, self-indulgent, and provincial beyond all description." Maybe so. The sobriety and reflectiveness of the later symphonies are surely more artistically satisfying than the uninhibited outpouring of sound and feelings of the Second. But if the Second has indiscretions, they are those of impetuous, emotional youth; it has also the virtues of youth—drive, buoyancy, gusto, excitement.

Eight introductory measures in the strings preface the entrance of the first theme by oboes and clarinets. The theme has a rustic quality that made Georg Schneevoigt refer to the entire first movement as a picture of the pastoral life of the Finns. A second idea is briefly introduced by horns alone. After this material has been worked over, there comes a pizzicato passage for strings which serves as a prelude to the second theme—a passionate utterance for woodwinds which later grows in the strings into a song of intense longing.

A roll of the drums and a pizzicato passage for the strings usher in the first theme of the second movement, played by the bassoons. This is a somber theme. The tempo quickens, the sonority grows as a feeling of restlessness intrudes. Then another melody, no less plaintive than the first, is heard in divided strings. These two themes are developed in some detail, following which comes a sweeping climax, culminating in a pause. The beautiful, melancholy second melody returns, before a coda brings the movement to a close.

The exuberant and spirited third movement, which is actually a scherzo, is said by Schneevoigt to represent the awakening of the patriotic spirit of the Finns. Two themes are prominent, one for the violins, the other for flute and bassoon.

The symphony comes to an exultant close with majestic music. The principal theme is proclaimed by the trumpet, and receives prominent treatment throughout the movement. (Later on in the movement, in the recapitulation, it emerges with climactic force in the strings.) A second theme appears in the oboe and is developed by other woodwinds. To Schneevoigt this movement describes the hope for deliverance from tyranny that stirred in every Finn, and his confident belief that this deliverance was at hand.

1903 VALSE TRISTE, for orchestra, op. 44.

Sibelius wrote incidental music for a play by his brother-in-law, Arvid Järnefelt, entitled *Death* (*Kuolema*). Only one of these numbers was published, a sentimental piece called *Valse triste*. This number—one of Sibelius's least important and least representative compositions—achieved formidable success throughout Europe after Sibelius had conducted its première performance in Helsinki on April 25, 1904. It became a staple in the repertory of café-houses; sold sheet music in all kinds of arrangements by the hundreds of thousands; helped make Sibelius a household name. The composer, however, never profited from this success, which realized a fortune for the publishers: he had sold the composition outright for two hundred dollars.

The music literally describes the following program appearing in the published score:

"It is night. The son, who has been watching beside the bedside of a sick mother, has fallen asleep from sheer weariness. Gradually a ruddy light is diffused through the room: there is the sound of distant music . . . strains of a waltz melody [Lento, in the cellos] . . . . The sleeping mother awakens, rises from her bed, and begins to move silently. She waves her hands and beckons in time to the music. Strange visionary couples appear, turning and gliding to an unearthly waltz rhythm. . . . Then she seems to sink exhausted on her bed and the music breaks off. Presently she gathers all her strength and invokes the dance once more, with more energetic gestures than before. Back come the shadowy dancers, gyrating in a wild, mad rhythm. The weird gaiety reaches a climax; there is a knock at the door, which flies wide open; the mother utters a despairing cry; the spectral guests vanish. The music dies away. Death stands at the threshold."

1903 CONCERTO IN D MINOR FOR VIOLIN AND ORCHESTRA, op. 47. I. Allegro moderato. II. Adagio di molto. III. Allegro ma non tanto.

Sibelius's only concerto was completed in 1903 and revised in 1905. The revised version was introduced in Berlin by Karl Halir on October 19, 1905, Richard Strauss conducting; the first version had been heard in Helsinki on February 8, 1904.

This is a work filled with romantic ardor, containing many rhapsodic passages for the violin. It opens with the solo instrument intoning a melody against an accompaniment of divided muted strings. When this idea—the principal one in the movement—had been fully realized, there is some passage work for the soloist. The entrance of the orchestra marks the transition to the second theme—subdued and lyrical—also presented by the volin.

The second movement is in a poetic vein. Five measures in the woodwinds preface a beautiful, poignant subject for the solo violin over chords in horns and bassoons. The orchestra then appears with contrasting material, but the violin soon returns in the original mood.

The finale (which the composer once described as a "danse macabre") enters with an outburst of vitality, the rhythmic pattern being established at once by tympani and string basses. Above this rises the voice of the violin in a sinister dance tune. This movement is in the form of a rondo, and contains two themes. The first is played by the solo instrument. The second is heard in violins and cellos. This theme is elaborated upon by the solo violin which later embellishes it; it then returns in the orchestra.

1906 POHJOLA'S DAUGHTER, symphonic fantasy for orchestra, op. 49.

Like so many other of Sibelius's early works, this tone poem is a musical setting of an episode from the *Kalevala*. This episode is described in the score as follows: "Vainämöinen, the magician, while on a homeward journey, encounters the Maid of Pohjola, the North Country, seated on a rainbow.

Overwhelmed by her beauty, he beseeches her to descend and join him, which she promises to do, if he can perform various magic feats for her. The last of these, to make a boat for her out of the fragments of her spindle, is too much for him. He has to give up in despair. Louhi's daughter remains on her rainbow, and Vainämöinen jumps back into his sleigh and resumes the homeward trail."

The tone poem opens with chords for horn, bassoon and muted cellos (Largo), over which rises a subject for solo cello descriptive of Vainämöinen about to embark on his journey. A number of themes trace his thoughts and adventures. A crescendo in the brass brings on an important forceful subject which brings this section to a close. Now we get a picture of Pohjola's daughter on her rainbow. Divided violins and harp set the stage for an oboe solo to which the English horn, and then flutes and clarinets, reply. The music now becomes dramatized as Vainämöinen performs the various feats required of him. The tone poem ends gently as Vainämöinen, begins his homeward journey, his delusions and sufferings ended.

The composer conducted the world première at a Siloti concert in St. Petersburg on December 29, 1906.

1906–1917 SONGS, for voice and piano:

"In the Field a Maiden Sings," op. 50, no. 3; "O Were Thou Here," op. 50, no. 4; "Roses," op. 50, no. 6; "The Tree," op. 57, no. 5; "Slow as the Sunset Colors," op. 61, no. 1; "Flower Song," op. 88, no. 6.

Sibelius wrote over eighty songs. A handful have sufficient charm and appeal to have survived, but basically Sibelius's gift was symphonic rather than vocal. In his best songs, he was more often stimulated by Nature than by love. His melodies most often consist of expressive declamations which, says Astra Desmond, "has tapped some primeval source of inspiration, so here one feels he has gone back to a rhapsodic style that ancient minstrels may have used." In his piano accompaniments, he frequently yields to the temptation of using orchestral methods. "He is," says Desmond, "too fond of using the lower registers which, so effective in his orchestral writing, sound heavy and turgid on the piano."

Some of his most popular songs are found in the op. 50 set (1906). The third one, "In the Field a Maiden Sings" (poem by Susman), is one of Sibelius's finest. A haunting melody over syncopated chords describes the maiden as she sings in the field. The poet inquires: Is her song sad because her lover is dead? The song dies out. The red of the evening dies away. The fields become deathly still.

The fourth song in this set, "O Were Thou Here" (poem by Dehmel), is much more dramatic, while the sixth, "Roses" (poem by Ritter) has an infectious lightness of touch, its 3/4 times suggesting Johann Strauss II.

"The Tree" is the fifth number in a group of eight songs to poems by Josephson (1909). "I am a tree. . . . Now I stand naked among my fellows. O, when shall I die? O, how I long for you, you cold, white snow!" "Here," says Desmond, "is the real Sibelius. . . . After a short introduction a syncopated rhythmical background is heard supporting the voice in a fine long sweeping phrase which forms a whole verse."

"Slow as the Sunset Colors," poem by Tavatjerna (1910), is one of the few by Sibelius inspired by love, and possibly for this reason, one of the few boasting an exquisite melody. Here the poet describes the fading of the fisher-girl's song as the sunset colors fade and as the breeze dies down. "The accompaniment begins with a vague wandering single note figure in the bass, later joined by a pathetic melody in the right hand which breaks off as the voice enters," explains Desmond, adding: "The subtle cross-rhythms enhance the feeling of remoteness. Rhythm and tonality become more definite as the poet recalls the fisher-girl's song."

"Flower Song," poem by Ruenberg (1917), has a "nostalgic waltz-like rhythm" which has helped to make this a favorite.

1907 SYMPHONY NO. 3 IN C MAJOR, op. 52. I. Allegro moderato. II. Andantino con moto quasi allegretto. III. Allegro.

The writing of the Third Symphony took Sibelius three years. On September 25, 1907, it was introduced in Helsinki, the composer conducting.

The first movement opens in a rugged spirit, then passes from pastoral moods, with idyllic passages in the woodwinds or strings, to stormy ones in grandiose climaxes for full orchestra. There are two main themes: that with which the symphony opens, vigorous and restless, is scored for the lower strings; the other, of greater repose, is suggested first by horns and woodwinds, then emerges eloquently in the cellos. The second movement is characteristic Sibelius music—poetic, slightly elegiac, restrained. There are three basic ideas: the first opens the movement and is voiced by two flutes; the second is introduced by the clarinet; the third comes in the cellos. The concluding movement is a combination of scherzo and finale, with a heroic theme for horn serving as a kind of link between the two. The scherzo is vivacious and light-footed, with emphasis in the instruments on the woodwinds; the finale, grandiose and spacious, achieves eloquence with a majestic page for divided violas.

1906 NIGHT RIDE AND SUNRISE, tone poem for orchestra, op. 55.
IN MEMORIAM, funeral march for orchestra, op. 59.

Sibelius's most celebrated tone poems for orchestra is Finnish music frequently inspired by the *Kalevala.* Some of his less famous tone poems have neither national or literary affiliations but what Rosa Newmarch called "intelligible psychological significance." *Night Ride and Sunrise* and *In Memoriam* fall into this category.

Night Ride and Sunrise was introduced in St. Petersburg in January of 1909, Alexander Siloti conducting. Sibelius said he had no intention of producing here romantic music in the vein of Joachim Raff. This music, he explained, was "concerned with the inner experiences of an average man riding solitary through the forest gloom; sometimes glad to be alone with nature; occasionally awe-stricken by the stillness or strange sounds that break it; not filled with foreboding, but thankful and rejoicing in the daybreak."

The tone poem opens with an exclamation by the brass, and a subject in the woodwind to which the percussion provides an individual rhythmic background. In the eleventh measure, violas and cellos are heard in a motive which Rosa Newmarch regards as "the backbone of the entire work." This motive "moves up and down steadily and gracefully in the strings." With a change of tempo, solo flute and solo oboe "utter a lugubrious cry and other wind instruments echo the eerie phrase." The motive returns briefly in flutes, oboes and clarinets before there appears a change of subject, with the woodwinds heard in "undulating passages . . . against the sibilant effect of cellos playing sul ponticello." This is intended to describe the wind rushing through the forest trees just before dawn. The break of dawn is announced by a strong theme in the strings over a drum roll, into which oboe, flute and clarinet interpose the voice of birds. Sunrise is depicted in a short Largo section. Then the "welling of light is described in the clear brilliance of ascending and descending staccato passages for strings and woodwind."

In Memoriam is subtitled a "funeral march for orchestra," but it was not intended as an elegy for any one person. In this music, the composer meditates on the ephemeral quality of mortal things and on the problem of death. Cellos, double basses and tympani announce the funeral rhythm in the opening measures. Then woodwind, over harmonies in the horns, give the principal subject. This is interrupted by descending chromatic scales in strings and woodwinds. After this melody has been stated, a new theme is heard in the lowest register of violins and violas, completed by trills in the upper woodwinds. There is still another important thought: a plangent melody for violins, violas and English horn. The main material now having been presented, a dramatic climax is worked up to a peak of frenzy in the full orchestra. A diminuendo, based mainly on the third melodious subject, helps to bring the tone poem to a serene ending, with two quiet drum taps.

Im Memoriam was heard first in Helsinki on April 3, 1911, on the same program at which Sibelius's Fourth Symphony received its première.

1909 VOCES INTIMAE (INTIMATE VOICES) IN D MINOR, for string quartet, op. 56. I. Andante; Allegro molto moderato. II. Vivace. III. Adagio di molto. IV. Allegretto ma pesante. V. Allegro.

This is its composer's only string quartet. It has never gained wide circulation because, in the opinion of Harold E. Johnson, it "neither plays nor sounds like a string quartet. The impression produced on both players and listeners is that Sibelius wrote it with the strings of the symphony orchestra in mind." Yet it holds considerable fascination for students of Sibelius, since it is one of the composer's most personal documents, and also one whose linear style endows it with a modernity not often encountered in Sibelius. In structure, it is something of a compromise between the forms of the sonata and the suite.

It is in five movements, each, says Eric Blom, with a "clearly cut contour and none in the traditional quartet forms"; each differing "in its style and content from the others . . . linked together by no thematic affinity but rather by a subtly produced balance of contrast."

The first movement opens with a brief slow introduction in which an unaccompanied exchange between violin and viola represents the main subject. The whole movement is derived from it. The second movement enters without interruption. "The music," says Blom, "weaves a fabric of the lightest tremolos which, throughout the movement, are scarcely ever abandoned by all the instruments at once." The third movement is melodic and emotional. "The thematic threads that bind the music together are as freely spun as those in the first movement, but there is a slightly greater regularity of recurrence." This is followed by a scherzo-like movement, its main subject "rugged and splenetic," presented by first violin. To Blom, the finale is "perhaps the most deeply personal and representative movement of the whole quartet, and the one that reveals the nationality of Sibelius most unmistakably. It is as much a Finnish epic as any of his symphonic poems based on incidents from the *Kalevala*."

1911 SYMPHONY NO. 4 IN A MINOR, op. 63. I. Tempo molto moderato quasi adagio. II. Allegro molto vivace. III. Il tempo largo. IV. Allegro.

With the Fourth Symphony—one of the finest of the seven—Sibelius passes from the emotion, expressiveness, and frequent overstatement of the first three symphonies to greater sobriety and impersonality. If the quiet restraint of the Fourth makes it less exciting listening than the dramatics of the Second, for example, it offers other and probably greater rewards: a gentle autumnal beauty that reminds one at times of Brahms in the master's most poetic writings; a simplicity of approach and in the presentation of materials that can come only from the most consummate mastery of technique. To Gerald Abraham, in this symphony "the composer is most completely himself" while his symphonic methods are "most uncompromisingly employed. Sibelius here has carried compression so far that even many of those who feel the greatness of the music are apparently puzzled by its form and unable to grasp the inner logic which they are conscious is present."

Besides all this, the Fourth Symphony represents the most progressive writing that Sibelius had done up to this time—so much so that when it was first heard, the symphony was regarded as highly rebellious music, even by discriminating listeners. After hearing the Fourth for the first time, W. J. Henderson wrote: "He is as frankly dissonant as the worst of them. He has swallowed the whole-tone scale, the disjointed sequences, the chord of the minor second, the flattened supertonic and all the Chinese horrors of the forbidden fifths." But, in all fairness to Henderson, he did pronounce the work "a noteworthy composition," filled with "elemental imagination, courage of utterance, and fearlessness of style."

The symphony opens in the Lydian mode. A six-measure introduction offers a ponderous subject in the lower strings. This is the nucleus of the movement's main subject, which unfolds opulently in the cellos—a melancholy whose emotion is intensified when the other strings join in. The second theme, in the strings, is brought on by a brass fanfare. As these and lesser ideas unfold, the music gains in austerity and strength. A scherzo movement follows, gently touched with laughter as it begins with a lively tune for the oboe. From this light mood, we pass on to pastoral music evoking a world of serenity and beauty: the slow movement, built for the most part from the whole-tone scale, one of Sibelius's loftiest creations. It opens with a subject for the flute, which the clarinet continues. But the main idea is an autumnal song for the cellos. Other sections of the orchestra take it over. Then the coda brings on with the tolling of bells a new theme in bassoons and clarinets. Amplified, it becomes the principal subject of the finale. Among the other material found in this closing movement are a fanfare, a declamation and a chorale. Crude, ungovernable strength dominates this music, but in the end serenity is restored, as earlier material is recalled.

Sibelius conducted the world première of his symphony in Helsinki on April 3, 1911.

1915 SYMPHONY NO. 5 IN E-FLAT MAJOR, op. 82. I. Tempo molto moderato; Allegro moderato ma poco a poco stretto. II. Andante mosso quasi allegretto. III. Allegro molto.

Written in the second year of World War I, the Fifth Symphony came in a period of great trial and suffering for Sibelius. Since his publishers were German, the flow of royalties had been halted; and with Finland not a signatory to the Berne convention, performances of his music in the rest of the world brought him no fees. The annual grant he was getting from the government had lost much of its purchasing power through inflation. His financial situation, then, was serious. To keep food and heat at home, he had to do hack work. In spite of these trying conditions, Sibelius managed to write a new symphony. It was begun at a time when Sibelius was tempted into believing the war would be of short duration; but by the time the symphony was completed in 1915, Sibelius knew that the war would be long and bitter, with no end in sight. Its completion proved, as Karl Ekman wrote, "an expression of its creator's great optimism, gained through suffering; an elevating testimony, in an evil period, to an unshakable faith in the ever-renewing power of life." On Sibelius's fiftieth birthday, December 8, 1915, the new symphony was introduced in Helsinki, the orchestra conducted by Robert Kajanus. Subsequently, Sibelius revised the symphony extensively, not once but several times, so much so that after the final revision the composer considered the result practically a new work. The definitive version—the one with which we are familiar today—was heard for the first time in Helsinki on November 24, 1919, the composer conducting.

The first movement is built out of germinal ideas which are introduced early, developed from embryo to full growth as the music progresses. The first of these ideas is an ascending theme for first horn with which the movement opens; another is a stark motive for the woodwinds against quivering strings; a third is a bright, triumphant passage for three trumpets. A scherzo follows without pause, with a lilting tune for the woodwinds; the music gains in momentum until it erupts in a climax of shattering force. Two major themes provide the material for the concluding movement, the first, lyric, played by the violas, and the second, extraordinarily powerful, pronounced by the horns; this second theme is built into a climax of great dimensions toward the close of the movement.

1923 SYMPHONY NO. 6 IN D MINOR, op. 104. I. Allegro molto moderato. II. Allegretto moderato. III. Poco vivace. IV. Allegro molto.

The Sixth Symphony came almost a decade after the Fifth. It was introduced on February 19, 1923, with the composer conducting. Cecil Gray has remarked, in his biography of Sibelius, that the keynote of this symphony "consists in a sense of serenity and poise, avoiding every kind of extreme.

. . . The coloring . . . is neither opulent nor ascetic, neither bright nor somber, but in intermediate tones. . . . The tempi are neither conspicuously fast nor slow. . . . This suggestion of balance between extremes is further symbolically reflected in the tonality of the first movement, which is ostensibly that of D minor, but with the B-natural giving the impression of hovering ambiguously between major and minor. This modal atmosphere . . . can also be perceived in the other movements . . . imparting an underlying spiritual unity to the whole four movements."

The symphony opens with a polyphonic string passage in which, says Ralph Hill, "the melodic outlines suggest the basic descending figure upon which the development is constructed." This music is at turns subdued and rhapsodic, moods that dominate the entire movement. The fast section that follows is more brusque and restless, essentially modern in its use of discords and unrelated tonalities. Here we find a second group of themes "begun by flutes and oboes in thirds," exploiting "the descending motive once more." In the recapitulation this second group of themes is given in reverse order. Then a review of other earlier material takes place, following which the movement ends in a short and tranquil coda.

The slow movement (the shortest of the four) has the personality of folk music. This is simple, direct, sustained lyricism. "It begins with a series of syncopated 6/5 chords on flutes and bassoons. . . . Over this background the strings enter with two thematic motives."

The third movement is a short scherzo. "Of the opening group of themes, the introductory, galloping motive on the strings is most important later. A rushing semiquaver passage on the strings leads to the second subject or transitional theme on the flutes, repeated by the oboes." A long elaboration of the "galloping motive" and a free recapitualtion follow, ending up in a coda built from the "galloping motive." Episodic ideas, rather than a sustained lyric line, continue to dominate the finale, some of which have a decided folk character. This movement opens with a broad chorale in the violins, woodwinds and horns to which lower strings give an antiphonal reply. The thematic material of the entire movement is built from this episode. "The last section consists of a development and recapitulation of the chorale theme in its original form . . . followed by a coda in which a phrase from the chorale is heard in the cellos, with a free mirror inversion in the violins. The final bars, too, have a subtle relation to the opening bars of the movement."

1924 SYMPHONY NO. 7 IN C MAJOR op. 105.

The Seventh Symphony is the only one Sibelius wrote in a single movement. It has changes of mood and tempi, but these changes are not formalized. The music is organically unified, subjected to a logic of its own, but this logic is as inexorable as that of the classical symphony.

It was introduced in Stockholm on March 24, 1924, with the orchestra directed by the composer.

The symphony is built episodically. It opens with a lugubrious subject for the strings, of which much use is to be made throughout the work. An idea for woodwinds against tremolo strings follows, but it soon makes way for a heroic fanfare for trombone, which is also subsequently elaborated; this fanfare is the dominant thought of the entire work. The music passes from passion to grandeur with occasional passages of brutal strength. After a climactic page, the tempo becomes Vivace, and woodwinds and strings join in music of light-hearted gaiety. But the levity passes. Once again the moods become in turn passionate, savage, grandiose, poetic. A monumental climax emerges. The turbulent emotions dissipate and a gentle passage for flute and bassoon is heard against tremolo strings. A crescendo is built up for the conclusion of the work.

Cecil Gray, whose enthusiasm for the Seventh Symphony apparently knew no bounds, has written: "If the Fourth Symphony represents the highest point to which he attains in the direction of economy of material and conciseness of form, the Seventh shows him at the summit of his powers in respect to fecundity of invention and subtlety and intricacy of design. It is not merely a consummate masterpiece of formal construction, however, but also a work of great expressive beauty, of lofty grandeur and dignity, a truly Olympian serenity and repose which are unique in modern music and, for that matter, in modern art of any kind. It seems, indeed, to belong to a different age altogether, a different order of civilization, a different world almost—the world of classical antiquity."

1926 TAPIOLA, tone poem for orchestra, op. 112.

Tapio is the ancient forest god of Finland, and *Tapiola* is just one more name for the country which is described in this tone poem. The following four lines, appearing in the published score, give a clue to the music's meaning:

Widespread they stand, the Northland's dusky forests,
Ancient, mysterious, brooding, savage dreams.
Within them dwells the Forest's mighty god
And wood-sprites in the gloom weave magic secrets.

A theme descriptive of the forest is the principal idea of the work. It is heard at the opening in the strings, after a soft drum roll. From out of this basic subject, the entire work is evolved—the theme being allowed to grow, to change, chameleon-like, and to develop as the music becomes an eloquent and unforgettable portrait of Nature. Now melancholy, now idyllic, the music is finally driven by uncontrollable momentum to heights of dynamic power.

Ernest Newman wrote in his program notes for the first volume of the Sibelius Society recordings that "constant association with *Tapiola* will convince any imaginative listener that here is one of the greatest works in the whole range of symphonic music. The creation of it all, out of practically one fragment of melody, would be a tour de force of the first order had the composer ever thought of anything in the nature of a tour de force; but the fact is that the ingenuity is not there for its own sake, as a piece of technical calculation, but as the inevitable evolution of one central idea."

Tapiola received its world première in New York City on December 26, 1926, performed by the New York Symphony Society under Walter Damrosch (who had commissioned it).

ELIE SIEGMEISTER 1909–

Siegmeister first received recognition as a composer with a strong American folk identity. Having become a devoted nationalist, he traveled extensively to different parts of the United States gathering local folk tunes, putting them down on paper, and making arrangements and adaptations. As a result of his intensive diggings, he uncovered a veritable mine of American folk music, little known out of its own locale. He performed much of this music with the American Ballad Singers, an organization he founded in 1939; he also published some of it. Most important of all, in the 1930s and 1940s, he incorporated some of this material in his serious musical compositions, producing a number of works that re-created American scenes and backgrounds. Even in those of his works where folk songs were not quoted directly (and these were many), their influence was apparent. His melodies and rhythms acquired their identifying traits from folk, and at times popular sources, notably jazz.

The personality of folk or popular music sometimes penetrates into the writing he has done since 1950. But essentially he has devoted himself to the structures of absolute music—the symphony, the quartet, the sonata—to which he brought a modern Romantic style, frequently quite dissonant but always strongly lyrical and emotional. More than ever his music must serve as the reflection of his inner experiences and deepest feelings. Yet he is also capable of strength and dynamism. He remains today as he was yesterday: a composer of straightforward, communicative music—imaginative, evocative, melodic and unmistakably American.

Siegmeister was born in New York City on January 15, 1909. His boyhood and youth were spent in Brooklyn, New York. He began studying the piano when he was nine, his first important teacher being Emil Friedberger, a pupil of Leschetizky. As a student at Columbia College, which he entered when he was fifteen, he attended Seth Bingham's class in composition; he also studied counterpoint privately with Wallingford Riegger. After graduating from college he spent five years in Paris, where he was a pupil of Nadia Boulanger. Back in the United States, he studied conducting between 1935 and 1938 at the Juilliard School of Music. Hearing some Kentucky folk songs sung to him by Aunt Molly Jackson gave him the direction he now needed. He dedicated himself passionately to American folk music and towards achieving an American identity in his own compositions. This interest in folk music led him to edit, with Olin Downes, *A Treasury of American Song*, and to write for Broadway the score for *Sing Out, Sweet Land,* a Theatre Guild production in 1944 based on folk songs. His researches in folk music also inspired his first successful works for orchestra. Since 1949, Siegmeister has been a member of the music faculty of Hofstra University in Long Island, where he became full professor in 1965 and composer-in-residence in 1966. In 1963, he completed his most ambitious work, a full-length opera, *The Plough and the Stars,* based on the Sean O'Casey drama. It received its world première in St. Louis on May 15, 1963.

1943 OZARK SET, for orchestra. I. Morning in the Hills. II. Camp Meeting. III. Lazy Afternoon. IV. Saturday Night.

In *Ozark Set,* four scenes in the life of the Ozark mountain people of Missouri and Arkansas are described. The first movement paints the back country as it slowly awakens to a day of activity. The shouting, stamping and frenetic religious singing of a camp meeting are re-created in the second part, while the third evokes a picture of open fields and prairies baked in the sun. The set ends with a square dance on a Saturday night.

Siegmeister wrote this suite when the Theatre Guild of New York asked him if he had any music that could be utilized for a play set in the Ozarks. Not having any such music, the composer sat down to write some. The play never materialized, but the music became the basis of one of Siegmeister's best orchestral works. The *Set* was introduced by the Minneapolis Symphony Orchestra under Dimitri Mitropoulos on November 7, 1944.

1945 WILDERNESS ROAD, for orchestra.

In *Wilderness Road,* Siegmeister creates a musical picture of the West, for which he has provided the following program: "Through the dark, ancient forest and over the silent hills stretched the Wilderness Road—gateway to the West. Over it came a great caravan: tall, cheerful men with their axes and rifles, their women and children, their wagons, dogs and horses; pioneers, seekers and builders of a new land. The wilderness echoed with their coming; they passed, leaving quietness, a hope and a dream."

Wilderness Road was written between August, 1944, and April, 1945. It was introduced by the Detroit Symphony Orchestra in June, 1945.

1947 SYMPHONY NO. 1. I. Andante. II. Vivace brioso; Allegretto grazioso. III. Moderato cantabile. IV. Maestoso; Allegro spiritoso.

"My symphony," the composer has explained, "has no program. I might say simply that it deals with the spirit, the struggle, the hope of man. The music does not use any actual folk tunes, but some of the themes have a marked folk character and some sections have the feeling of American popular song and dance. I think this is natural for an American composer."

The first movement has two main themes; a slow and lyrical melody for solo clarinet, later joined by solo bassoon, with which the symphony opens; and a ballad-like subject for solo oboe. The second movement is robust, "in the general spirit of raising the roof," as the composer puts it. Its main subject is a strongly accented, at times syncopated, melody for bassoons and cellos accompanied by plucked strings. The middle trio has a blues-like melody in waltz rhythm, for viola and English horn. The third movement, slow and lyrical, adopts a popular style, starting with a quiet and dreamy song for oboe, and progressing towards an equally affecting theme for solo trombone. The concluding movement opens gravely. It then becomes, at turns, dramatic, dance-like and poetic. "The momentum of what sounds like the terrifically earnest urgency of 'getting religion,'" says the composer, "is driven home by American folk-dance rhythms, leading to a huge and triumphant climax."

The world première took place in New York on October 30, 1947, Leopold Stokowski conducting the New York Philharmonic.

1956 CONCERTO FOR CLARINET AND ORCHESTRA. I. Easy, Freely. II. Lively, Lightly. III. Blues, Slow Drag. IV. Fast and Driving.

Siegmeister waited a long time to write his first concerto. When he did so, he selected for his solo instrument not the violin or the piano, as might have been expected (particularly the piano since it is Siegmeister's instrument), but the clarinet. He explains why: The clarinet represents to him a personal, popular typical American voice; it is an instrument that expresses jazz in all its aspects as a deeply American speech; and to him it speaks the dreams, joys and sorrows of the American people better than any other instrument.

The first movement opens with a partly reflective rhapsodic section in a blues style. A lively section follows, but the movement returns to its opening introspective mood at the close. The second movement was described by the composer as "bouncy, perky." It presents the "dance-like aspects of jazz. It is humorous and full of surprising changes of rhythm and mood. The feeling is transparent, scherzo-like." In the third movement, the composer turns to the "deeper, more basic aspect of jazz—the blues. This is an outcry of pain: there is both bitterness and longing here." In the finale, rhythmic vitality becomes dominant, as complex rhythmic patterns are formed, while the solo instrument engages the orchestra "in a combat." The composer adds: "The music laughs, at times; and at times it is barbed and prickly. The feeling of a struggle mounts in violent rhythms—until, finally, a clear triumphant passage is reached. Jazz, emerging from the people, is seen by the composer as an affirmative life-breathing statement."

The concerto was introduced in Oklahoma City in 1956.

1957 SYMPHONY NO. 3. I. Moderato, pesante; Allegro ritmico. II. Lento, sostenuto. III. Ritmico, Allegro moderato.

This symphony was introduced over the radio by the Oklahoma City Symphony under Guy Fraser Harrison on February 8, 1959.

The symphony differs from the two earlier ones by the composer in that it is not in strict sonata structure but in a free variation form. The composer explains that his symphony "evolves out of three key ideas: the five-note opening; an upward-reaching chromatic figure; and a 'wedge' motive in trumpets. These undergo kaleidoscopic transformation throughout a structure involving three broad sections: 1. A terse declamatory introduction, then a fast movement in which insistent motivic statements alternate with dance-like elements; 2. A contemplative slow section, in which a long-lined lyricism dominates, despite explosive interruptions; 3. A scherzo-like closing section, over whose contrasting textures clear motivic designs are superimposed, as in a montage. In the hammering climax, the three root ideas are telescoped into one, culminating in a climactic return of the declamatory opening." The composer also said: "In this work, violent unisons in the entire orchestra are separated by complex interweavings of linear rhythms, widely-spaced and tighty-grouped textures spinning over new evolutions of the opening material."

In reviewing a recording of this symphony released by the Composers Recording Inc., a critic for the *American Record Guide* writes: "The symphony is no cold slice of abstract handicraft. It has a pungency of contemporary musical speech with sensitive and marvelous rhythmic interlarding. If the linguistics of a New Englander are combined with the clipped tongue of New Yorkese, one produces a national speech. Siegmeister seems to catch (though not deliberately) this urban-suburban in his music. The rhythms are asymmetrical but not nervous. These are natural rhythms, implanting the flavor of the present day—pulsative fricatives that spice the duple, triple and quadruple arrangements."

1960 STRING QUARTET NO. 2. I. Allegro con fuoco. II. Larghetto molto sostenuto. III. Allegro con spirito.

The second string quartet followed Siegmeister's first by a quarter of a century. It was introduced by the Galimir String Quartet at an all-Siegmeister concert at Hofstra University in Long Island on January 28, 1961. This performance was repeated in New York City on February 10, 1961.

The composer describes this work as follows: "The Quartet contains those elements of energy, lyricism, and wildness that have always been a part of my music, welded into a tight organic structure. The overall formal plan involves transformations of the root ideas of the first movement during the course of the two that follow. Thus the opening unison theme is metamorphosed into the secondary viola theme of the slow movement and again into what becomes the beginning of the third movement. The interweaving of such metamorphosed material throughout the quartet can be sensed by the listener who has heard the work two or three times, but complexities of structure can be discussed in detail only with score in hand. Nevertheless, these same complexities define the impact of the work as a whole and whatever challenge it may have for the listener."

1967 I HAVE A DREAM, cantata for solo baritone, narrator, chorus and orchestra.

This cantata was commissioned by Temple Beth Sholom, in Long Beach, New York, where it received its world première on April 16, 1967.

The text, by Edward Mabley, is based on a speech by Martin Luther King made at the civil-rights march on Washington in August of 1963. It is a call to justice, a plea for the brotherhood of all races. This message, the composer felt, held meaning to the Jewish people as well as to Negroes. In setting text to music, the composer wove together material from both the Negro and Hebraic traditions, incorporating both into his own personal musical speech.

A stark, brooding orchestral introduction brings on the voices of narrator and soloist in a cry for justice, with the chorus giving reply in "The Sound of Freedom," a vision of the future. "Exile" recalls the lamentations of ancient Jews banished to Babylon and, through a startling shift to cool jazz, the "exile" of modern Negroes from freedom. An obsessive, catching refrain, "Now is the Time" precedes the chorus in an angry, blues-like call for change. The narrator then recalls that the destiny of both races is intertwined, while the soloist introduces an ancient Hebrew chant. John Donne's famous line,

"No man is an island" serves as the text for an introspective, spiritual fugue, whose subject again recalls the blues; it is sung by a semi-chorus, largely a cappella. Soloist and chorus break in again with a rhythmic and dissonant affirmation. The "prophetic" statement is now heard. It is the refrain, "I Have a Dream" by the soloist, its main melody echoing an old Hebrew chant. A massive choral proclamation follows. The narrator calls for a faith enabling men to work together, and the chorus intones lines from the Declaration of Independence. The cantata concludes with a blend of speaking and singing voices calling for freedom to ring out from every hamlet, state and city. The chorus responds with an intensified version of the jazz-like quasi-spiritual, "The Sound of Freedom."

KARLHEINZ STOCKHAUSEN 1928–

Few composers since the end of the second world war have been so adventurous in opening up new frontiers for music as Stockhausen has been. To Stockhausen, the structures, systems methods and means handed down to us by centuries of evolution are obsolete. His point of departure was Webern and the serial technique. His early compositions, in this system (*Kontrapunkte No. 1*, in 1953, for example) perfected a pointillistic method in which individual tones are dabbed on the score the way a painter might put colors or spots on a canvas; and in which development, repetition, variation and contrast are dispensed with. From serialism, Stockhausen progressed towards new areas. New concepts had to be realized through new media, such as electronic instruments (to which he gave the identification of "sound objects"), within a new kind of structure ("open form"); in "open form," each new composition must create its own structure. A new kind of concert hall is needed with new concepts of time and space—a spherical auditorium with the audience in the middle and the music converging on the audience from all parts of the hall through loudspeakers ("spatial dimension in music"). He has explored elements of chance in constructivist pieces in which the performer is given the freedom to choose the succession of thematic ingredients and contrapuntal possibilities in a kind of controlled improvisation. He has devised a new kind of notation ("time fields") with all kinds of complex visual symbols to depict sound, color, tempo, and so forth. He represents a complete break with the past. "Each new work," says Arthur Cohn, "is unique and only tenuously related to a previous one. Each opus is new music. . . . His importance is not to be underestimated."

Stockhausen was born in Mödrach, near Cologne, Germany, on August 22, 1928. He studied the piano at the High School for Music in Cologne from

1947 to 1950, composition with Frank Martin in 1950–1951, and with Milhaud and Messiaen in Paris in 1951–1953. His affiliation with Pierre Schaeffer and "*musique concrète*" in Paris led him to explore the possibilities of electronics in music. Between 1952 and 1954, he studied physics and acoustics at the University of Bonn. In 1953, he became associated with the Cologne Radio, where he initiated his experiments in electronic music; he has been affiliated with Cologne Radio since then. In 1954, his *Electronic Studies* became the first published score of electronic music. Meanwhile, beginning with 1951, he began writing new music for traditional instruments. These compositions included *Kreuzspiel,* for oboe, bass-clarinet, piano and percussion (1951), and, in 1952, *Spiel,* for orchestra, and the *Schlag Quartet.* In *Kontrapunkte No. 1,* for ten instruments (1953), he adopted serialism. Experiments in "spatial dimension in music" were first successfully pursued in *Gruppen,* for three orchestras (1957). *Zeitmasse,* for flute, oboe, English horn, clarinet and bassoon and *Klavierstück XI*, both in 1956, sought out the creative potential of controlled chance. Electronic music became another fruitful source for Stockhausen's creative investigations, beginning significantly with the *Gesang der Jünglinge* in 1956.

1956 ZEITMASSE (TEMPI), for flute, oboe, English horn, clarinet and bassoon.

KLAVIERSTÜCK XI (PIANO PIECE XI), for solo piano.

Stockhausen has produced a number of constructivist pieces in what he terms "open form," in which controlled chance is a significant element. *Piano Piece XI* consists of nineteen fragments. The performer is allowed to play these fragments in whatever order he wishes. Further, the element of chance is extended when the performer is permitted to use any one of six designated tempi, dynamics, intensities, and types of touch in each of the fragments. When a fragment has been repeated three times, the composition is over. Thus the work becomes a fluid piece of music changing with every performance.

The music is printed on a large sheet of paper measuring thirty-seven by twenty-one inches. The music comes in three ways: in a roll packed in a cardboard carton; with a wooden stand for placement on a piano; and on a board.

This piano piece was introduced in New York on April 22, 1957, by David Tudor.

Chance is also a factor in *Zeitmasse,* first heard over the Munich radio in November of 1956. The performer can, at will, slow down or increase the tempo, sometimes in contrast to, and at other times in conjunction with, metronomically set speeds. The performer is also permitted to improvise in cadenza-like passages, though the materials he is to use in these improvisations have been established. Stockhausen's main concern, however, is the problem of what Arthur Cohn has described as the "splintering" of tempi. Tempo ceases to be a "basic premise" and becomes "disordered" as "metric continuity" is abrogated. "It makes," concludes Cohn, "tempo unrest the prime sensation. . . . The patterns within the music follow this disintegrative range, and for the most part consists of values disassociated from any fundamental time phase. . . . Stockhausen creates a species of musical atomization. He proves his statement that time is most experienced when all sense of time is lost."

1956–1960 GESANG DER JÜNGLINGE (SONG OF YOUTH), for human voice (boy soprano) and electronically taped sounds.

KONTAKTE (CONTACT), for piano, percussion and electronic sounds.

From the time he had affiliated himself with the Cologne Radio, where he helped develop one of the first important studios of electronic music, Stockhausen has become convinced that the music of the future belongs to electronics and no longer to traditional orchestras or combinations of instruments. In the *Gesang* (1956)—introduced at the international conference of musicologists in Cologne in 1958—he combines the voice of a boy soprano with electronic sounds to provide a musical setting for a text from the Book of Daniel.

Kontakte (1960), on the other hand, combines traditional instruments (piano and percussion), rather than a voice, with electronic sounds. It was heard at the International Festival for Contemporary Music at Cologne on June 11, 1960. The title, we are told in the liner notes of a German recording, "not only indicates contacts between electronic and instrumental sound groups but also contacts between autonomous, very characteristic, moments" by having the instrumental parts prerecorded. When *Kontakte* was first heard in New York (January 6, 1964), Raymond Ericson wrote: "The tape of electronic sounds, wholly prepared and controlled by the composer, suggested an aural landscape of considerable fascination." And in his review of the German recording, Irving Kolodin said: "There is no doubt at all that electronics . . . have given rise to a vast range of aural possibilities. Stockhausen's experiments have codified a good many procedures and elaborated an impressive range of techniques. So far, the aesthetic to make communicative use of the procedures and techniques is unformed, and lasting interest in the product thereof is minimal."

In both the *Gesang* and *Kontakte* spatial possibilities are also explored. The composer has instructed that *Gesang der Jünglinge* should be performed through a five-channel sterephonic system, and that the sounds of *Kontakte* should converge on the audience from four different sections of the auditorium.

Kontakte was used by the composer as background music for a neo-dadaistic play with music called *Originale,* seen in New York on September 8, 1964. Here we confront all sorts of absurd incidents and episodes. A chimpanzee plays the cymbals. One man sprays himself with a shaving cream while ducking in water. Eggs are dropped on a plastic sheet from the top of a ladder. A girl performs on a cello while seated on a balcony railing.

1957 GRUPPEN (GROUPS), for three orchestras.

The problem of exploiting the "spatial dimension in music," the presentation of music at concerts stereophonically, has absorbed Stockhausen's interest for years. *Gruppen* was his first significant experiment in this direction. Three orchestras are placed in different parts of the auditorium, "surrounding" the audience. Stockhausen explains further: "They play—each under the direction of its own conductor—partially independently in different tempi: from time to time they meet in common rhythm; they call to each other and answer each other; one echoes the other; for a whole period of time one hears only music from the left, from in front, or from the right; the sound wanders from one orchestra to the other."

Gruppen was introduced in Cologne on March 24, 1959.

1961 ZYKLUS (CYCLE), for percussion.

The element of controlled chance is significant in *Zyklus*. This is a composition for a single percussion player, but a variety of percussion instruments are used (marimbaphone, guero, two wood drums, suspended bunch of bells, side drum, four tom-toms, two cymbals, "hi-hat," triangle, vibraphone, four cow bells, gong, tam-tam). The instruments are grouped in a circle. The performer progresses from one instrument to the next until he has come to full circle. Chance enters in the fact that the performer can begin on any page of the score he wishes; but then he must run through all the remaining pages in the given order without interruption, and finish with the first stroke of the page on which he started.

The published score does not use formal notation but is filled with "time fields," all kinds of elaborate symbols, graphs, charts, and visual images to guide the player. "One difficulty," Eric Salzman has explained in *The New York Times,* "is that Stockhausen's percussion has almost no meaningful rhythm. There are shorts and longs, attacks and pauses, rolls and single blows. But the necessity of coming down with a particular stroke in a particular place—what one might call the absolute foundation of any rhythmic concept—is not there."

RICHARD STRAUSS 1864–1949

Strauss's career as a composer ended as it had begun: with the writing of music, classical in structure, Romantic in feeling, warm with pleasing melodies and gracious with conventional harmonies. After listening to his earliest and last works, it becomes difficult to remember that between these two periods Strauss produced works that shocked and outraged the world and made him one of its most provocative musical figures.

His early works were of Brahmsian vintage: the Piano Quartet in C minor, op. 13 (1884) and the Violin Sonata in E-flat major, op. 18 (1887). Hardly had the ink dried on the violin sonata when Strauss impatiently discarded his post-Romantic, Brahmsian manner to create a new kind of music—realistic, descriptive, utilizing the fullest modern resources of orchestration, adventurous in its use of structure, skilful in counterpoint, and magnetizing for its power and passion. This is the music of his tone poems. In this new direction, he had been influenced by the poet philosopher-musician, Alexander Ritter, not only Wagner's friend but also a member of his family, since he was married to Wagner's niece. In his many conversations with Ritter, Strauss became convinced that his destiny lay in carrying over to symphonic music dramatic expressiveness, or "*Musik als Ausdruck*" ("Music as Expression") to use a term favored by the Wagnerites; and to pour this expressiveness within the elastic form of the Liszt tone poem.

The transitions from his old ways to the newer ones came with the symphonic fantasy, *Aus Italien,* op. 16 (1886), whose discords dismayed not only critics and audiences but also Strauss's father and friends. *Aus Italien* was a failure when heard in Munich on March 2, 1887. But for Strauss, there was no turning back any longer. Here is how Strauss himself explained his change of creative attitude to Hans von Bülow, in a letter dated August 24, 1888.

"I have found myself in a gradually ever-increasing contradiction between the musical-poetic content that I want to convey and the ternary sonata-form that has come down to us from the classical composers. . . . If you want to create a work of art that is unified in its mood and consistent in its structure, and if it is to give the listener a clear and definite impression, then what the author wants to say must have been just as clear and definite in his own mind. This is only possible through a program. I consider it a legitimate artistic method to create a correspondingly new form for every subject, to shape which neatly and perfectly is a very difficult task, but for that reason the more attractive."

Macbeth, op. 23 (1887), was Strauss's first tone poem; it was heard first in Weimar on October 13, 1890. Then, in rapid succession, followed the series of orchestral masterworks, all of them tone poems, with which the name of Richard Strauss is inextricably associated:

Don Juan, op. 20 (1888), based on a poem of Nikolaus Lenau, introduced in Weimar on November 11, 1889.

Tod und Verklärung (*Death and Transfiguration*). op. 24 (1889), after a poem by Alexander Ritter, introduced in Eisenach on June 21, 1890.

Till Eulenspiegels lustige Streiche (*Till Eulenspiegel's Merry Pranks*), op. 28 (1895), inspired by a famous German legend about a practical joker, first heard in Cologne on November 5, 1895.

Also sprach Zarathustra (*Thus Spake Zarathustra*), op. 30 (1896), freely based on Nietzsche, performed at Frankfort-on-the-Main on November 27, 1896.

Don Quixote, "fantastic variations on a theme of knightly character," op. 35 (1897), performed at Cologne on March 8, 1898.

Ein Heldenleben (*A Hero's Life*), op. 40 (1898)—in which the composer identified himself as the hero by quoting from his own compositions in the section entitled "Works of Peace"—introduced in Frankfort-on-the-Main on March 3, 1899.

In these tone poems Strauss gave a new importance, as well as independence, to discords; in fact, it might well be said that he was one of the first important composers to make effective use of unresolved discords. He also enriched and extended the art and science of orchestration. With Strauss, the orchestra assumed the role of a virtuoso. Each instrument shared equal importance with every other instrument—even double basses, trombones, or tympani, all formerly used for support rather than for solo effects. He extended orchestral colorations by adding instruments rare or new to the symphonic ensemble: a quartet of saxophones; machines of his own invention, such as wind and thunder machines; cowbells. He made every instrument rise above limitations formerly set for it—writing for the trombone, as one critic said, as if it were a piccolo. Finally, there was his instinctive gift for using the proper form for the story he is telling. Each of his tone poems is of one piece with a beginning, a middle, and an end—as every good story should be. One after another, the descriptive motives are presented and then woven into an inextricable design, a design as remarkable for technical construction and subtle thematic transformations as that of Wagner. The tone poems made Strauss the storm center of the music world in the closing decade of the nineteenth century. Their stark realism, their discords, their flexible forms, their attempt to extract the last ounce of expressiveness out of tones, their layer upon layer of orchestral color, the multifarious changes and transformations to which his thematic ideas were subjected, his sensuality and his sentimentality—all this inspired dissension, praise and vituperative criticism, acclaim and satire. "This is not music," maintained César Cui, "but a mockery of music." Even so progressive a musician as Claude Debussy regarded one of Strauss's tone poems as "an hour of music in an asylum." But to music lovers the world over, these remarkable tone poems were a bountiful reservoir of musical wonders: power, passion, grandiloquent speech, orchestral wizardry, exalted poetic concepts, high flights of imagination and fancy.

At the same time that he was writing his tone poems, Strauss was also producing songs in which the traditions of the German Lied were brought to the threshold of the twentieth century. The more than one hundred songs he wrote are (like the tone poems) uneven in quality. But at their best they deserve a place at the side of the greatest lieder of all time. The finest Strauss songs were all written before 1900, and include the following jewels: "*Zueignung,*" or "Dedication" (von Gilm), op, 10, no. 1; "*Allerseelen,*" or "All Soul's Day" (von Gilm), op. 10 no. 8; "*Cäcilie*" (Hart), op. 27, no 2; "*Heimliche Aufforederung*" (Mackay), op. 27, no. 3; (*Morgen,*" or "Morning" (Mackay), op. 27, no. 4; "*Traum durch die Dämmerung,*" or "Dream in the Dusk," (Biernbaum), op. 29, no. 1; "*Wiegenlied,*" or "Cradle Song" (Dehmel), op. 41, no. I, and "*Freundliche Vision,*" or "Friendly Vision" (Biernbaum), op. 48, no. 1.

Strauss may not always have been discriminating in the choice of his poetic texts, some of which are truly pedestrian; he may have indulged too frequently in excessive emotion: he may not always have achieved the happiest of balances between voice and piano accompaniment. But he was truly a lord of soaring, expressive melody, a melody that reflected different shades of feeling and different atmospheres with great subtlety, and his piano accompaniments have a rich symphonic-like texture. His best songs, like the best pages of his tone poems, are the products of a master.

Since his tone poems and his most famous songs were all written before 1900, they are not discussed in the pages that follow.

In one department beyond all others—that of opera—was Strauss able to produce masterworks after 1900. His first opera, *Guntram,* op. 25 (produced in Weimar on May 10, 1894), was all too obviously the offspring of the Wagnerian music drama. It was a failure. *Feuersnot,* op. 50, introduced in Dresden on November 21, 1901, also failed to make a good impression. This work also sprang out of Wagner, though this time not the Wagner of the *Ring* cycle (as had been the case with *Guntram*) but the Wagner of *Die Meistersinger*. In *Salome,* in 1905, and *Elektra,* in 1908, Strauss found texts able to take full advantage of the sensuality and eroticism of his musical style and his extraordinary gifts at realistic writing. After *Elektra,* Strauss produced an operatic masterwork of quite a different personality, *Der Rosenkavalier,* in 1911—a comedy set in Vienna to the strains of infectious waltz melodies and an almost Schubertian kind of affecting lyricism. For the next thirty-five years and more, Strauss continued to produce major works, mainly for the stage.

"He laid the foundations, in the great sweeping melodies of his youthful *Don Juan*—which were something without parallel at that time in German or any other music—for a new melodic style, that of musical prose, which at its best can be as wonderful as the finest musical metric, surpassing this, indeed, in sweep of line, variety of phrasing articulation, and the shifting of actual footfall." So wrote Ernest Newman in the London *Sunday Times,* adding: "In *Salome* and *Elektra* in particular he proved that tonal harmony is still capable of new subtilizations. . . .Finally, in each of his orchestral works he cast his structures unerringly in a form appropriate to the subject. . . . The mere fusion of them all into an organic musical work would of itself have been a technical feat of the first order; but more astounding even than that is the imaginative power that somehow made a psychological unity of it all, a poignant expression of resignation and nostaliga. Yes, he was of the royal line, even if some queer kink of indolence and cynicism in him made him too often content to play the part of the Old Pretender."

Strauss was born in Munich on June 11, 1864, the son of a well-known horn player who had played under Wagner, and a wealthy mother who belonged to the prosperous Munich brewing family of Pschorr. A precocious child, Richard was given piano lessons when he was four, first by his mother, and then by August Tombo. When he was six, he started composing. Later music study included instruction on the violin from Benno Walter, and in composition from F. W. Meyer. Strauss's progress was so rapid that by the time he was eighteen, he had received performance for some of his songs, a string quartet, and a symphony; he had also published his first opus, a *Festival March*, for orchestra. His reputation even penetrated to the United States where his second symphony in F minor received its world première in New York on December 13, 1884, Theodore Thomas conducting. Academic education, however, was not neglected. After completing the courses at public and high schoools, Strauss entered the University of Munich in 1882 for the study of law. He left the University after a single year, determined now to devote himself completely to music. After his first horn concerto in E-flat major, op. 11, had been introduced by the Meiningen Orchestra on March 4, 1885, its conductor, Hans von Bülow, appointed Strauss as his assistant with the orchestra. This was in 1885. One year later, Strauss succeeded von Bülow as music director of the Meiningen Orchestra, an appointment that started him off on a long and successful career with the baton. This career included major appointments with the court opera in Munich, the court orchestra in Weimar, the Berlin Philharmonic, the Berlin Royal Opera and the Vienna State Opera.

Strauss's conductorial activity did not impede his creative efforts. Up to the time he had come to Meiningen, he was an echo of Brahms. But in Meiningen, his friendship with the musician-poet-philosopher, Alexander Ritter, opened up for him the direction which first brought him world fame, and notoriety, with his tone poems, and then with such early operas as *Salome* and *Elektra*.

In 1904, Strauss toured the United States for the first time, conducting the Wetzler Orchestra in programs of his own music; on this occasion, he presented the world première of his *Symphonia domestica.* He came to America a second time, in 1921, this time as a guest of major American symphony orchestras.

Though there was a perceptible decline in his creative powers after World War I, there was no diminution in either his fame or his significance. He was universally recognized as Germany's foremost composer, one of the undisputed greats of contemporary music. When the Nazis rose to power in 1933, Strauss openly allied himself with the new regime by becoming president of the Third Reich Music Chamber. It was not long, however, before he came to grips with the Nazi superiors, particularly after he had collaborated with Stefan Zweig, a Jew, in writing the opera *Die schweigsame Frau,* op. 80. Three weeks after the production of this opera, in Dresden on June 24, 1935, Strauss was removed from his official position. He went into retirement in Garmisch-Partenkirchen, where he had maintained a villa for many years. With the outbreak of World War II, which he opposed, he was for a while under house arrest. The war years, spent partly in Switzerland and partly in Garmisch-Partenkirchen, were difficult for Strauss, since his royalties had been impounded and he was living under the ominous cloud of government disapproval. He emerged from this prolonged retirement after the war by conducting, in 1947, a concert of his works in London during a Strauss festival. A denazification court in Munich, in 1948, cleared him of charges of Nazi collaboration, and fully restored him to the good graces of world opinion. His eighty-fifth birthday was celebrated in music centers the world over.

Strauss's last composition was the *Four Last Songs* (1948), with orchestra. Strauss died of uremia at his villa in Garmisch-Partenkirchen on September 8, 1949. He was survived by his wife Pauline—the former Pauline de Ahna, a famous singer who had appeared in his early operas, and whom he married on September 10, 1894; also by their only child, a son, Franz.

1903–1925 SINFONIA DOMESTICA, op. 53.

PARERGON TO THE SINFONIA DOMESTICA, for left-hand piano and orchestra, op. 73.

Though designated as a symphony, the work is actually a one-movement tone poem played without interruption. It was completed on the last day of 1903 and introduced in New York City on March 21, 1904, with Strauss conducting the Wetzler Orchestra during his first tour of the United States. This was Strauss's first major work for orchestra in the twentieth century.

When Strauss worked on this *Sinfonia,* he did not hesitate to explain that it was a piece of musical autobiography, illustrating "a day in my family . . . partly humorous—a triple fugue, the three subjects representing papa, mama, and baby." However, when the work was introduced, Strauss insisted that it must be listened to as pure music and refused to give any detailed programmatic explanations. Evidently he subsequently reconsidered the decision of passing this work off as absolute music. When it was played in Germany, Strauss sanctioned the use of the following descriptive subtitles:

"I. Introduction and development of the three chief groups of themes.

The husband's themes: (a) easygoing; (b) dreamy: (c) fiery. . . . The wife's themes: (a) lively and gay; (b) grazioso. . . . The child's theme: tranquil.

"II. Scherzo. Parents' happiness. Childish play. . . . Cradle song (the clock strikes seven in the evening).

"III. Adagio. Doing and thinking. Love scene. . . . Dreams and cares (the clock strikes seven in the morning).

"IV. Finale. Awakening and merry dispute (double fugue). . . . Joyous conclusion."

When the *Sinfonia* was introduced in London, Strauss allowed the following detailed analysis to be published in the program:

"The symphony continues without a break, but has four well-defined sections. . . . The Introduction is devoted to an exposition and treatment of the chief themes, or groups of themes, its most striking feature being the introduction of the child theme on the oboe d'amore. . . . The composer has spoken of this theme as being 'of almost Haydnesque simplicity.' On this follows a very characteristic passage, which has been interpreted as representing the child in its bath. The chief theme of the Scherzo is the child theme in a new rhythm. At its end the music suggestive of the bath recurs, and the clock strikes seven. We then come to the Lullaby, where we have another version of the child theme. . . . The elaborate Adagio introduces no new themes of any importance, and is really a symphonic slow movement of great polyphonic elaboration and superlatively rich orchestral color. The gradual awakening of the family is depicted by a change in the character of the music, which becomes more and more restless . . . and then there is another reference to the bath music, and the glockenspiel indicates that it is 7 A. M. In this way we reach the final fugue. . . . The subject of the dispute between father and mother is the future of the son. The fugue (the chief subject of which is another variant of the child theme) is carried on with unflagging spirit and humor and a great variety of orchestration, the introduction of four saxophones adding fresh colors to the score. . . . The father and mother, however, soon assert their former importance, and the whole ends with great spirit and in the highest good humor with an emphatic reassertion of the husband theme . . . suggesting that the father had the last word in the argument."

In 1925, Strauss took the first three measures of the child theme and elaborated it into a completely self-sufficient orchestral work which he entitled *Parergon to the Sinfonia Domestica,* op. 73. It was scored for left-hand piano and orchestra. having been written for the one-armed pianist, Paul Wittgenstein, who introduced it in Dresden on October 16, 1925. Paul Wittgenstein had this to say about this work: "Strauss told me that the first part describes the illness of the child and the second part his recovery. . . . What made him choose just the theme of the child, I do not know. Perhaps he felt that this theme had not been sufficiently developed in the *Sinfonia domestica.* All the other themes are new and not contained in the *Sinfonia.*"

A "parergon" is defined as a "subordinate activity or work: work undertaken in addition to one's main employment."

1905 SALOME, opera in one act, op. 54, its text being the drama of the same name by Oscar Wilde, translated into German by Hedwig Lachmann. First performance: Dresden. December 9, 1905.

A decade after he had written his first opera, *Guntram,* Strauss demonstrated to the music world that he had not lost his capacity to shock and outrage. The choice of Oscar Wilde's play *Salome* as a text for an opera—with its emphasis on the insane passion of Salome for John the Baptist—was in itself highly provocative. But in matching the sensuality and neuroticism of Wilde's play with music no less erotic (vivid in its musical characterizations, passionate in harmonic colors and instrumental effects, lasciviously suggestive in its rhythms and sinuous melodies), Strauss was producing a work that could not help but arouse moral indignation.

The planned première in Vienna was abandoned when the censors stepped in. For a brief period it seemed that no opera house would be courageous enough to present it, until Count Seebach, Intendant of the Royal Opera in Dresden, announced his intention of producing it. Despite an attempted strike by the principal singers because of the complexity of the music (Frau Wittig, the Salome, furiously asked how she could be expected to dance for ten minutes and follow it with the singing of exacting music for another quarter of an hour!) the first performance did eventually take place. Instead of the angry protests and expressions of disgust which had been anticipated, there were thunderous ovations by the audience; Strauss took twenty-five curtain calls. The critics were equally enthusiastic. But this decisive victory for *Salome* did not mean the end of its trials. The Berlin performance was at first forbidden by the Kaiser himself—and when it was finally heard, in 1906, it was denounced for its "perverse depravity," and described as "repulsive." A scheduled London performance was called off, once again as a result of censor trouble. And the American première set off a storm which is surely one of the dramatic pages in the history of American opera.

That American performance took place on January 22, 1907, with the Metropolitan Opera under the direction of Heinrich Conried. The present author has written as follows about this episode in his book, *Music Comes to America*:

"Conried was not too farsighted when he arranged a special dress rehearsal for an invited audience to take place on Sunday morning. Many came straight from church services, and the shock of contrast was more than most of them could stomach. They left the opera house denouncing the 'lewd' spectacle. After the first performance, a righteous-minded citizenry descended on Conried with fury for permitting such a display of obscenity on his stage. The clergy rose up in battle. The critics, too, joined in this universal chorus of outraged feelings. Krehbiel wrote that 'the stench of Oscar Wilde's play had filled the nostrils of humanity,' while still another writer spoke of the opera as a 'decadent and pestiferous work.' One critic vented his spleen as follows: 'As to the mind and morals, they were diseased. Not to emphasize disgust, their state was one of decomposition far advanced. As to the music, it fits. It makes worse that to which nothing but music could give added degradation.' A few musicians (like Emil Paur) tried to defend the Strauss music, but their voices were drowned by the furor of the opposition. Before the second performance could be put on the stage, Conried received a curt note from the directors of the Metropolitan informing him that they considered 'the performance of *Salome* objectionable and detrimental to the best interests of the Metropolitan Opera House,' and protesting 'against any repetition of the opera.' There was nothing for Conried to do but withdraw *Salome* after one performance."

On November 25, 1910, the opera was revived in this country by the Chicago Opera Company with Mary Garden in the title role. In Chicago, too, the temperature rose high. The chief of police, who was required to attend the performance, described the opera and Mary Garden as "disgusting." After a second performance, the protests grew more shrill, and further presentations were canceled.

The shock is gone, and with it moral indignation. Recent revivals of *Salome* have drawn attention only to the remarkable qualities of the music, its extraordinary character delineations, its dazzling orchestration, the power and richness of its melodic and harmonic writing, and the incomparable way in which it blends with the play into a single, indivisible work of art.

The story of *Salome*, coming to Oscar Wilde's play by way of the Scriptures, is well known. Salome, lascivious and perverted daughter of Herodias, has fallen in love with the prophet, John—a captive of her stepfather, Herod. She desires him and tries in vain to seduce him. When she fails, her love turns to lust and hate. Herod, who is in love with his stepdaughter, promises her anything she may desire if only she will dance for him. She dances—then demands the head of John. The prophet is killed, and his head is brought on a tray to Salome. Passionately, Salome caresses the head and kisses its lips as she delivers her final apostrophe. Realizing the extent of his stepdaughter's depravity, Herod orders her death.

Salome is still Wagnerian in its use of Leitmotiv technique, in the uninterrupted flow of the melodic line, in the symphonic character of the orchestral writing, in its harmonic progressions and elaborate use of polyphonic resources, and mostly in the way in which music and drama are one and indivisible. But *Salome* is also Strauss, in the way he matches Wilde's sensual moods and eroticism with sinuous melodies, orgies of orchestral and harmonic colors, abrupt and rapidly changing rhythms, and sometimes the most striking literalness in translating stage action or word into music. The piercing cries and trills of the E-flat clarinet, the violin tremolos, the double bass glissandos, the harrowing monotones in the trombones, the chromatic leaps in three-quarter time, the wide skips in the declamation—all this provides us with the varying nuances of Salome's passion for the prophet, and her perverted lust for the decapitated head. Descending fourths in trombones and cellos tell of the prophet's stern denunciation of Salome. A contrapuntal fugato suggests a theological discussion by the Jews. The shrieks and primitive rhythms of the opening measures of the Salome dance inform us of Herod's stimulation in witnessing this lewd exhibition. In his music, Strauss penetrates deeply into human motivations, into the deepest and darkest recesses of human psychology, into the abysses of human emotion in a way that no other composer before him had done.

The ending of the opera, beginning with Salome's sensual dance of the veils and culminating with her passionate apostrophe to the head of John the Baptist, is surely one of the most stirring climaxes in twentieth-century opera.

The dance, of course, is famous by itself as a symphonic repertory item. It begins at once in a frenzy with cries in the orchestra and kinesthetic rhythms. The frenetic mood subsides; violas and flute are heard in an exciting dance motive. Now, as Salome begins her sinuous motions, the music grows intense and passionate. A second dance melody now unfolds in the strings. This slow voluptuous melody is the heart of the composition. Once completed, it gives way to music that mounts impetuously towards a powerful climax in full orchestra. The ending of Salome's dance is accompanied by trills in the woodwind and tremolo strings. The music now rushes to an exciting and irresistible conclusion.

Her dance over, Salome's wish is granted. The head of the prophet is brought to her. Then, in a scene of horror, she yields to the perversion of necrophilism by making love to the head, surrendering completely to her obsession. "I have kissed your mouth," she cries. More and more excited grows the declamation and the orchestral background. "I am athirst for thy beauty, I am hungry for your body." Then a terrible weariness sets in—her voice plunges to the depths. Reminders of passions now spent are found in the clarinets with hurried quotations from Salome's dance music. The rapture is dissipated. An outcry in the orchestra, a shudder in drums and strings—a last reminder of the dance—tell of the horror that this scene has evoked in the spectators. Somewhere in the orchestra there grumbles an ominous trill. Herod has ordered the guards to seize Salome and kill her.

1908 ELEKTRA, opera in one act, op. 58, with text by Hugo von Hofmannsthal, based on the tragedy of Sophocles. First performance: Dresden, January 25, 1909.

Elektra was Strauss's fourth opera, and the first in which he collaborated with the Austrian dramatist, Hugo von Hofmannsthal. Hofmannsthal's adaptation of the famous Greek drama of Sophocles is a highly individual one, filled with lusts and passions the original never knew. In the Hofmannsthal adaptation Elektra becomes a shrieking and hysterical personification of hate, and her mother, Klytemnestra, a loathsome picture of depravity. The whole drama becomes morbid and neurotic; yet it is filled with power and passion. And the music Strauss wrote for it is one of his most vividly realistic and sensual scores. Drama and music are so ideally mated to one another that the net result is a work of pathos and beauty. It is one of Strauss's unquestioned masterpieces for the theatre, one of the mighty productions of twentieth-century opera.

The opera's setting is the inner court of the palace at Mycenae. Servants are talking about the strange and crazed behavior of Elektra. One of them tries to suggest that not madness but sorrow has afflicted Elektra. Elektra soon makes her entrance, mourning the murder of her father, Agamemnon, and vowing vengeance with the help of her brother, Orestes. Her sister, Chrysothemis, comes to warn her that her mother and her mother's lover, Aegisthus, are plotting to incarcerate Elektra. Elektra tries to win her sister's collaboration in the plot for vengeance, but Chrysothemis insists she lives not for hate but for love. An extended scene between Elektra and her mother, the Queen Klytemnestra, follows. When the Queen confesses she has been tortured by evil dreams and horrible nightmares, Elektra tells her that those dreams will end only when blood is shed—"the right blood." Then Elektra goes on to describe the coming death of the Queen. An attendant appears and whispers in the Queen's ear that Orestes is dead—news that brings the Queen relief and joy. Chrysothemis brings the same tidings to Elektra, who refuses to believe them. Overwhelmed by rage, Elektra digs in the earth to try to find the axe that had killed her father. She is interrupted by the arrival of a stranger come to tell her that Orestes is indeed dead. It is not long before Elektra recognizes that the stranger is none other than her brother, Orestes; he himself had spread the rumor of his death to put his mother off her guard. They begin to evolve a plan of action. Orestes enters the palace and slays first his mother then Aegisthus, as Elektra lurks in the shadows listening rapturously to their cries for help. Demented with joy, Elektra performs a Corybantic on her father's grave, then falls dead.

The play, with its decidedly psychoneurotic overtones was at turns grim and sensual; and the music followed suit. Strauss used a large orchestra (larger than the one for *Salome*) emphasizing the dark colors of the lower pitched instruments. He split up his strings to increase the sensuality of sound, with violins subdivided into three sections, violas into three sections, and the cellos into two.

When Elektra makes her first appearance as an unkempt, ragged vision of ugliness, the orchestra hurls a discord, which in its violence immediately sets the mood of lust for vengeance and hate that smolder in her heart. Then from the depths of the orchestra comes the ascending phrase that speaks her hatred of her mother and of her mother's lover. Horrifying, too, is the picture offered by Klytemnestra—particularly in the ominous harmonic clusters that accompany her arrival, their heaviness suggesting the way in which her corruption and feelings of guilt weigh on her conscience.

As the story progresses to its denouement, Strauss's music increases in demoniac frenzy, becomes increasingly high-tensioned and hysterical. More and more shattering are his discords; more and more sensual the lush of his harmonies and orchestral colors; more and more agonizing the cries of Elektra and Klytemnestra that replace arias. Then, as in *Salome,* the horror reaches its apex in the closing scene with a dance which frees Elektra of all her inhibitions. A grim motive, known as Elektra's hatred, is here given prime importance; then in the closing measures, as Elektra falls lifeless, the orchestra erupts into an anguished cry that throughout the opera (and beginning with the opening prelude) has personified Agamemnon.

In *Zeitschrift für Musik,* Alfred Kalisch calls Elektra's dance "the culminating point of the opera. . . . The mind has to travel far back to search for anything at all comparable to it in musical mastery and almost elemental power, and finds nothing till it arrives at the closing scene of *Götterdämmerung.* Not only is there colossal skill in the way in which all the previous threads are woven into one, not only is there great art in the way the climax grows and the orchestral color gradually changes from darkness to the bright light of noon day; but the result is achieved without sacrifice of euphony or beauty, and the whole conception of the scene betrays a creative power which is certainly without rival in the present day."

When the opera received its world première in Dresden, a correspondent for *The New York Times* reported: "It is a prodigious orchestral orgy, and makes superhuman demands upon the mental and physical powers of the singers and players. The marvelous imitative effects of the orchestra are blood-curdling, drastic, and gruesome to the last degree. It is fortunate for the hearers that the piece is no longer, for else it would be too nerve-wracking!" The German critics were appalled by what they heard and saw. "Lurid," "violent," "gruesome" were some of the adjectives they used to describe the startling new Strauss opus.

The American première came on February 1, 1910, at Oscar Hammerstein's Manhattan Opera House in New York (where it was sung in French). The reaction was compounded of shock, dismay and indignation. But the American reaction was far different when *Elektra* returned after more than a quarter of a century—this time to the stage of the Metropolitan Opera, on December 3, 1932. Lawrence Gilman remarked: "Apparently no one was outraged. A huge audience sat through the long, unbroken act with every indication of unbroken attention, and at the end of the performance there was an extraordinary scene of enthusiasm, with countless recalls for the singers, the conductor and their colleagues. Is it possible that the terrible *Elektra* has come to stay?"

1910 DER ROSENKAVALIER (THE ROSE CAVALIER), opera in three acts, op. 59, with text by Hugo von Hofmannsthal. First performance: Dresden, January 26, 1911.

Strauss expressed the desire to write a comic opera soon after finishing *Salome*. But not until after he had written *Elektra* did he set about realizing this ambition. He confided to his librettist, Hugo von Hofmannsthal, that he had in mind an opera combining the best qualities of Mozart and Johann Strauss; and Hofmannsthal proceeded to prepare a suitable text which, as he wrote to Strauss, "will to a certain extent correspond with your artistic individuality" in its "blending of the grotesque with the lyrical." He set his play in the eighteenth-century Vienna of Maria Theresa. Through his two principal characters—Baron Ochs and the Marschallin—he deftly mingled sentiment with broad comedy, tenderness with burlesque, lust with nobility. The result was one of the finest librettos in all opera.

The story is spiced with the intrigues of the roué Baron Ochs, cousin of the Marschallin (Princess von Werdenberg). The Marschallin herself is carrying on a flirtation with the seventeen-year-old Octavian. Their little tête-à-tête is interrupted by the entrance of Ochs; Octavian quickly disguises himself as a maid. The Baron has come to ask his cousin to find someone who can bear a silver rose (symbol of a marriage proposal) to Sophia. Coming upon the disguised Octavian, Ochs flirts with "her" and invites "her" to a private supper. Meanwhile, the Marschallin gets rid of the Baron by promising to get him a suitable rose-bearer; and the one she has in mind for this assignment is Octavian.

Octavian brings the silver rose to Sophia; they fall in love with each other. To Baron Ochs, Sophia is aloof, proof to the outraged roué that Octavian has stolen Sophia from him. He challenges his rival to a duel, in which he is slightly wounded. But the receipt of a letter from the Marschallin's "maid"—the disguised Octavian—soothes his pains and sends him dancing with joy; for the maid has written to remind him of their rendezvous. This takes place in a public tavern where the Baron makes impatient advances to the "maid." Things do not go well for the Baron. Strange faces appear in the windows of the tavern to haunt him. Suddenly there arrives a woman claiming him as her husband and the father of her children. A climax is reached when Octavian removes his female disguise and reveals himself. Baron Ochs leaves the tavern in fury. And the Marschallin, who in the meantime has made an appearance, magnanimously renounces Octavian to allow him to marry his beloved Sophia.

Some criticism has been leveled against the score Strauss wrote for this wonderful play—its length, verbosity, and occasional lapses into triteness and sentimentality. Much of this criticism is deserving. But in spite of these defects, *Der Rosenkavalier* (music *and* words) is one of the glories of comic opera, the finest example of this genre since *Die Meistersinger*. If there are weak moments in *Der Rosenkavalier,* there are also many pages of grandeur, magic, beauty, tenderness, wisdom, compassion and wit; and it is these pages that have assured the opera permanence in the repertory.

Lawrence Gilman once pointed out that a leading character in this opera—if not *the* leading character—is the symphony orchestra. "This laughing, rapturous, mocking and outrageous commentator, this witty and vivid and sometimes philosophical interpreter, now riotous with mirth and horseplay, now ravishing in the beauty and charm and tenderness of its voice, is the true vehicle of the play. And it is Strauss's orchestra . . . that gives it the final and exalting touch: it is the orchestra, at the end, that caps the rough-and-tumble poetic comedy and turns the horseplay into loveliness, crowning the drama with a quality of beauty that brought a new accent and an unsuspected eloquence into musical art."

Certainly the orchestra plays the major role in projecting the delightful waltz tunes that course through the opera and that are its most famous episodes. These waltzes are true Strauss—not Johann but Richard—in their ribaldry, good humor and satire, and in their spellbinding orchestral colors and harmonies. However, there are other pages in the opera even more significant, pages that must rank with the most exalted operatic writing in the twentieth century. There is the monologue in which the Princess, in love with a mere boy, must come to the sad realization she is no longer young. She must contemplate her faded beauty and her lost youth; she must accept the inevitability of having to give up Octavian for good, when he falls in love with a girl nearer his own age. The Marschallin's contemplative air is recognizable Strauss in the dramatic expressiveness of the melodic line—a semi-arioso which Strauss favored in this opera and which he once described as a "conversation style"—and in its profound psychological insight. Behind the voice, the orchestra moves with its Mozartean line, texture and subtlety.

Then there is the closing trio in which the Marschallin surrenders Octavian to Sophia. While the two lovers overflow with love and gratitude, Octavian cannot quite escape a feeling of guilt in leaving the Marschallin. This is a page of music that places Strauss solidly with the immortals. The three characters unwrap their most secret thoughts and feelings in a euphonious counterpoint.

An enharmonic change at the end points up the fact that the Marschallin's decision to give up Octavian is fixed and unshakable. Then with a final blessing to the lovers, the Marschallin leaves the stage with sorrow and dignity. A page of incomparable serenity and sweetness follows in the orchestra, with overtones of *Tristan* rapture. And then Sophia and Octavian sing their ecstatic love duet with which the opera closes. Some have likened this lyric beauty to Mozart at his greatest, some to Schubert. Actually, it is neither. This is Richard Strauss ecstasy and rapture in a musical dress all his own.

The Dresden Opera accepted *Der Rosenkavalier* in 1910, but problems of staging slowed down the rehearsals until it seemed that the new opera would be doomed to failure. The celebrated director, Max Reinhardt, was called in, and saved the day. The first performance went off magnificently; the new opera was an immediate success, and it stayed that way. The American première was given at the Metropolitan Opera in New York on December 9, 1913.

Soon after the première of his opera, Strauss collected the waltzes in an integrated orchestral work which has gained considerable popularity throughout the world of symphonic music. (Strauss made a new orchestral adaptation of these waltzes in 1946.) He also wrote an orchestral suite combining some of the opera's notable passages. The suite includes the Introduction, the entrance of the rose-cavalier, the duet of Sophia and Octavian, the waltz music, the trio, and the concluding love duet.

1912 ARIADNE AUF NAXOS (ARIADNE ON NAXOS), opera in one act, op. 60, with text by Hugo von Hofmannsthal. First performance: Stuttgart, October 25, 1912; Vienna, October 4, 1916 (revised version).

This sparkling little opera was originally written as a postlude for the Max Reinhardt production of Molière's *Le Bourgeois gentilhomme,* for which Strauss had written incidental music. Since this postlude required more than an hour for presentation, it was out of place in the Molière production and was never used. After being presented independently of the Molière comedy, this postlude was revised extensively, revamped into a one-act opera with prologue.

It is a play within a play. The prologue takes place in the private theatre of a wealthy eighteenth-century European, who arranges the performance of *Ariadne* for his own and his guests' delight. Its young and idealistic composer is asked by his patron to vary the seriousness of his opera with comedy, and the patron insists that broad burlesque scenes be interpolated into the classic story. The young composer is upset, but he is advised by his music master to follow instructions. While contemplating his sad fate, the young composer is accosted by Zerbinetta, queen of the comedians, who is flirtatious. At first the young composer mistakes her coquetry for an interest in his artistic problems; but he is soon disenchanted. He takes his music master severely to task for forcing him to make concessions with his ideals and escapes from the theatre.

Then the opera, *Ariadne,* begins for the patron and his guests. Ariadne, feeling alone and forsaken, lies sleeping in a cave on the island of Naxos in ancient times. Her slumber is accompanied by the singing of Naiad, Dryad and Echo. Awakening, Ariadne bemoans her sad fate. To dissipate her sorrow,

Zerbinetta and four clowns come to her with song and dance; but Ariadne is too absorbed in her sorrow to notice them. The arrival of another visitor is announced by Naiad, Dryad and Echo; he is young and handsome. Ariadne is ready to welcome him if he is Death—for she is weary of life and her sorrows. But he is Bacchus, who comes bringing with him the joy of life. Suddenly Ariadne's great sorrow passes. She joyfully falls into the arms of Bacchus.

Ariadne represents for Strauss one more step away from the harrowing realism of *Salome* and *Elektra*. It is light and gay, satirical and lyrical. It is also a step away from *Der Rosenkavalier,* in the economy of its means, simplicity of methods, modesty of structure. *Ariadne* is a chamber opera requiring a small orchestra in which each instrument has an important solo assignment. It also places considerable importance on the voice by offering several wonderful arias in the composer's most aristocratic and winning lyrical style. One of the best of these is that of Zerbinetta, "*So war es mit Pagliazzo,*" a brilliant coloratura number which, in its wit and spirit, is a reflection of her flirtatious personality; this number has become a favorite in the concert hall. Noteworthy, too, is Ariadne's aria, "*Es gibt ein Reich,*" in which, awakening from sleep, she describes a pure kingdom, a kingdom of the dead, where she yearns to go. Two ensemble numbers are also deserving of special attention: "*Es gibt, ob Tanzen, ob Singen,*" in which Zerbinetta and her companions try to cheer up Ariadne with song and dance; and the enchanting trio of the nymphs, "*Töne, Töne, süsse Stimme.*"

The American premiere took place in Philadelphia on November 1, 1928.

1912 LE BOURGEOIS GENTILHOMME, suite for orchestra, op. 66. I. Overture. II. Minuet. III. The Fencing Master. IV. Entrance and Dance of the Tailors. V. The Minuet of Lully. VI. Courante. VII. Entrance of Cleonte. VIII. Intermezzi: Dorante and Dorimene, Count and Marquise. IX. The Dinner.

On October 25, 1912, in Stuttgart, Max Reinhardt presented Hugo von Hofmannsthal's adaptation of Molière's *Le Bourgeois gentilhomme*. For this presentation, Strauss wrote the incidental music. The play was a failure. Neither the audiences nor the critics liked the way in which Hofmannsthal tampered with the Molière play. But there were no dissenting voices in the praise for the delightful music Strauss had written. Abandoning that gargantuan orchestra for which he had become famous, together with inflation of style, Strauss proved here that he could write directly, purely, and transparently. There is a great deal of charm and delicacy in this music; and delightful wit as well. Richard Specht has gone so far as to say that this is the most masterly music ever written for a dramatic play, incomparable for "its pseudo-archaic style . . . its sparkling hilarity, and . . . its fresh melodies."

Most of the orchestral music was assembled by Strauss into a successful suite in 1918. It received its first performance in Berlin on January 26, 1920. (The postlude was adapted by Strauss into the one-act opera *Ariadne auf Naxos*.)

The theme of the Molière play revolves around the *nouveau riche* Jourdain, who, impelled to rise in station, summons tailors to fit him out in finery and employs teachers to instruct him in the artistic graces. He even entertains the thought of engaging in a little affair with an attractive Marquise, as befitting a man of his importance—a venture that is brusquely frustrated by his wife. For his daughter, he contemplates, of course, a worthy marriage. But his daughter is in love with Cleonte, who conceives the idea of dressing himself in Turkish garb and posing as the son of a Sultan. Jourdain—elevated by the "Sultan" to the rank of *mamaouchi*—blesses this marriage and gives over his daughter to Cleonte in disguise.

Strauss's music, like the comedy for which it was intended, brims over with humor and satire. The suite opens with an Overture (Molto allegro), an amusing caricature of Jourdain. The music is brisk and spirited, opening with a rapid subject for strings and piano and progressing towards a broad section in which violas and cellos, accompanied by chords in the wind, participate. An allegretto section offers a melody for oboe, which other instruments take over.

There follows a dainty minuet (Moderato assai) with a graceful melody for the flute. Then comes an episode with the fencing master (Animato assai) describing Jourdain's grotesque efforts to learn the fine art of fencing. A heavy subject is heard in low strings and trombone, followed by brilliant passages, first for trumpet, then for piano, and after that for violins. A section for full orchestra rushes towards a climax.

The wit of the fencing episode is broadened into burlesque with the entrance and dance of the tailors (Vivace). First the woodwinds present a gavotte. Then a polonaise provides the music for the tailors' dance, its theme heard first in solo violin.

In "The Minuet of Lully" (Molto moderato), Strauss adapted a number which Lully had written for the original production of Molière's play. The main melody is assigned first to the oboe, then to the flute, and after that to strings and woodwind. Then comes another classic dance a courante (Vivace assai). Here the dance tune is encountered in strings and clarinet.

Cleonte enters with music that is now a bit solemn, now a bit gay—material once again borrowed from Lully. The eighth section (Andante; Galante e grazioso) brings up a picture of the rococo world of Louis XIV. The principal melodic material is given by the violins after introductory episodes in bass clarinets and bassoons. The concluding movement (Moderato, alla marcia; Allegro molto; Allegretto; Andante; Moderato; Presto) has an amusing interpolation of a phrase from Wagner's *Das Rheingold* to suggest Rhine salmon; also a quotation from Strauss's own *Don Quixote,* the bleating of sheep, to speak for the roast mutton. An andante section simulates tables conversation. The suite ends with a Presto, the energetic music accompanying a dance of the scullions.

The first performance of Molière's *Le Bourgeois gentilhomme* with *all* of Strauss's music including the postlude, *Ariadne auf Naxos,* was given at the Edinburgh Festival in Scotland in 1950.

1915 EINE ALPENSINFONIE (AN ALPINE SYMPHONY), op. 64.

This was Strauss's first symphonic work in a dozen years, the last having been the *Symphonia domestica* in 1903. The new work, like the older one, is not a symphony, but a tone poem. It is in a single movement describing incidents and experiences occurring during a day in the Alps. Throughout the score the composer fixed subtitles to provide a programmatic clue to the music. They read as follows: "Night—Sunrise—The Ascent—Entrance into the Forest—Wandering Beside the Brook—At the Waterfall—Apparition—On Flowery Meadows—On the Mountain Pasture—Lost in the Thicket and Brush—On the Glacier—Dangerous Moments—On the Summit—Vision—Mists Arise: The Sun Is Hidden—Elegy—Calm Before the Storm—Thunderstorm—The Descent—Sunset—Night."

A huge orchestra of one hundred and nine players is required, including such unusual instruments as a heckelphone (a kind of baritone oboe), a wind machine (which Strauss had invented for *Don Quixote*), a thunder machine (which Strauss now devised for this composition). The use of "Samuel's Aerophon" is optional. This is a device permitting woodwind instruments to sustain some of the long notes through a bellows operated by foot and attached to the instrument by a rubber tube.

The symphony was introduced in Berlin on October 28, 1915, the composer conducting. When the work was performed by the New York Philharmonic under Josef Stransky, in 1916, W. H. Humison provided the following illuminating analysis:

"Strings, bassoon, clarinets, and horns open with a descending motive—'Night'; almost immediately against a chord consisting of all the notes of the scale (B minor) sounded by muted strings, the 'Mountain' motive is intoned by trombones and tuba. Soon comes 'Sunrise,' for nearly full orchestra with an imposing theme. The 'Ascent,' an energetic theme, first played by cellos and basses, is made much of in this part of the work. Hunting horns announce the entrance into the forest, a 'flowing' theme (strings) suggests the brook, a marked theme with a 'Scotch Snap' is played by the brass as the waterfall is approached. Arpeggios, glissandos, rapidly descending scales, glockenspiel and triangle picture the cascade, a passage which, begun fortissimo, ends in extreme pianissimo. Woodwind instruments play a lively theme which represents 'Apparition.' This passes into the section 'On Flowery Meadows'—where the theme of 'Ascent' is heard from the cellos.

"Although this symphony is not divided into movements, the first section may be said to end at this point. Now comes the 'Alm' episode—cowbells are heard, and the 'Alpenhorn' is represented by the English horn. The principal theme of this episode, however, is a gentle melody played by the horn. 'Lost in the Thicket' is portrayed by a fugato movement, until the theme of 'Ascent' indicates escape from the entanglements, and again an open path toward the summit. The cold air of the glacier is suggested by a transformation of the 'Waterfall' theme, with new material added. 'Dangerous Moments' is a sort of intermezzo, which leads us to the 'Summit.' Here four trombones play a majestic motive, and as the magnificent view extends before one's imagination, the chief themes of the work are repeated in varying guise. The 'Vision' is a transformation of the 'View' theme, and the organ is heard in the 'Elegy.' The storm breaks, and we begin the descent, to an inversion, naturally, of the 'Ascent' theme. The 'Mountain' theme again is sounded, passing into 'Sunset' and 'Night'; and the work ends as it began, with 'Night' and a long-drawn-out B-flat minor chord."

1917 DIE FRAU OHNE SCHATTEN (THE WOMAN WITHOUT A SHADOW), opera in three acts, op. 65, with text by Hugo von Hofmannsthal, based on his own story. First performance: Vienna, October 10, 1919.

It took *Die Frau ohne Schatten* more than three years to get written, and more than two years after that to get performed. But it required a generation and more before the world of music came to realize what a truly remarkable opera this is, an opera deserving to stand at the side of Strauss's greatest works for the stage. At its world première, *Die Frau ohne Schatten* was a failure. It did not make a much better impression when it was heard in Dresden twelve days after its world première, and in Berlin on April 18, 1920. From then on, it was produced in different cities at greatly spaced intervals. But it is only of recent date that the opera has come fully into its own. Its American première by the San Francisco Opera on September 18, 1959, was a major success. And the first production by the Metropolitan Opera in October of 1966 (at its new home at the Lincoln Center for the Performing Arts) was a triumph. There are now many authorities who consider it Strauss's greatest opera of all, and regard Von Hofmannsthal's libretto as his most profound and sublime.

In conceiving his text for a Strauss opera based on his own fairy tale, Von Hofmannsthal wanted it to stand in the same relation to Mozart's *The Magic Flute* that the *Rosenkavalier* did to *The Marriage of Figaro*. In this effort, he conceived a play made up of folk lore, fairy tale and mythology—an allegory full of symbols to point up the moral of the power of unselfishness. The action takes place in legendary times. In the world of the spirits, a young Empress, offspring of the supernatural Keikobad, has no shadow—the shadow being symbolic of fertility. This is the reason why she cannot bear a child, though she has been married to the Emperor for a year. In three days' time her husband will be turned to stone, while she herself will be forced to return to her father. To forestall such developments, the Empress—accompanied by the malevolent Nurse—descends to earth for the purpose of buying a shadow from some mortal. They arrive at the hut of Barak, a dyer, who is afflicted with a nagging wife. While Barak is off to the market, the Empress and the Nurse stimulate the greed of Barak's wife to the point where she is ready and willing to part with her motherhood. Later on, during a storm, the wife reveals to Barak what she has done. This so arouses the dyer that he threatens to kill her. The Empress, moved by pity, cries out she will never accept a shadow stained with blood. At the same time, the dyer's wife is led to confess that she has not as yet actually sold the shadow, but is willing to die nevertheless. At this point the earth swallows up dyer and wife, and they are sucked into the world of the spirits. There they become reconciled. The Empress, because of her unselfishness and nobility, gains a shadow; at the same time, she saves her husband from ossification.

The symbolism is not far to seek. "The shadow is a symbol of fertility and, by extension, humanity," explains Harold C. Schonberg in *The New York Times*. "The Empress is a non-human who has to experience love and pity to fulfil herself. Barak, the dyer, is humanity raw, a good man who has not achieved spiritual values. The Nurse is supposed to represent the forces of darkness and diabolism. The dyer's wife is a symbol of unfulfilled womanhood. Everything in *Die Frau ohne Schatten* has several levels of meaning."

Die Frau ohne Schatten is Strauss's most Wagnerian opera, Wagnerian in its orchestration, Wagnerian in its dramatic arias, and Wagnerian in its network of Leitmotives. But as William Mann takes pains to point out, Strauss's Leitmotivs are "not always definitely associated with set persons, but rather with states of mind or action."

But the score is also Richard Strauss *in excelsis,* certainly in its greatest moments. George R. Marek singles out some of those moments. "Some of the orchestral interludes are superb, of great thrust and power," he writes. He finds that the "finest music occurs in Act III, Scene I, a touching monologue by the Dyer's Wife followed by Barak's soliloquy ('*Mir anvertraut*'), the two then uniting in a duet ending with Barak's words 'If I might see her once again and say to her, 'Do not be afraid!' Here one hears the Strauss who wrote '*Traum durch die Dammerung.*' " To Irving Kolodin, in the *Saturday Review,* the score contains "some of the freshest, sweetest, and most heartfelt music he ever wrote. It brings together not only the vocal resources he [Strauss] had derived from *Rosenkavalier* and *Ariadne* (and *Elektra* and *Salome* before them) but also the orchestral artifices he had been storing up for decades before *them.* It is a miracle of instrumental delicacy as well as richness, with almost any tint or shade available to him at will."

1930 ARABELLA, "lyrical comedy," in three acts, op. 79, with text by Hugo von Hofmannsthal. First performance: Dresden, July 1, 1933.

In May of 1916, Strauss, in a communication to von Hofmannsthal, suggested that his gift for writing music for tragic operas had by now been dissipated; that now what he wanted most was to concentrate on comedy. Strauss continued: "I am definitely the only composer alive who really possesses humor, wit, and a pronounced talent for parody. . . . Our way began with *Rosenkavalier* . . . I feel the greatest eagerness to undertake another work of its kind (sentimentality and parody are the perceptions most adequate to my talent)."

It was more than a dozen years before the collaborators got around to the business of writing another *Rosenkavalier.* That successor was *Arabella.* Both operas are set in Vienna. Both operas are light and gay. Both operas make effective use of waltz music. In both operas, going around disguised as the opposite sex is basic to the plot. But here the similarity ends. The humanity, wisdom, tenderness and compassion of *Der Rosenkavalier* cannot be found in *Arabella. Arabella* is froth—delicious froth—throughout. Rarely was Strauss's touch lighter and more graceful; rarely was his orchestral writing more delicate, sensitive and iridescent; rarely was his gaiety more heart-warming. "Perhaps the score does dream back a bit to the time of the Silver Rose," opined Robert Breuer, "but . . . hearers will find that it sounds more refined and restrained. The parlando style makes for transparency; the singing voices are not hindered by orchestral outbursts. There are remarkably melodic passages in each act."

The action takes place in Vienna in 1860. Count Waldner, an aristocrat deep in debt, hopes to marry off his daughter, Arabella, to a rich man. His other daughter, Zdenka, is being raised as a boy, since the father cannot afford to pay the bills for two girls. Zdenka is secretly in love with the officer, Matteo, who in turn is interested in Arabella. In spite of her own interests, and since she is unable to reveal she is a woman, Zdenka does her best to promote the affair between Arabella and Matteo. She sends him letters with Arabella's name. Meanwhile, the wealthy Mandryka, from another town, sees Arabella's photograph and falls in love with her. He comes to Vienna to ask for her hand and is welcomed by Waldner with open arms. But Mandryka decides to stay at the hotel until he is summoned. Mandryka meets Arabella at a coachman's ball and finds her even more beautiful than her picture. He tells her of his feelings and finds her sympathetic. Meanwhile, still determined to help Matteo, Zdenka gives him the key to Arabella's bedroom, advising him Arabella intends to meet him there. When Mandryka learns about this, he becomes convinced Arabella has betrayed him; he finds solace by flirting with the coquette, Fiakermilli. Waldner insists there must be some misunderstanding, and drags him off to the hotel to straighten things out. There they discover that the key is not for Arabella's room but for Zdenka's. Matteo now learns that Zdenka is a female, and what is more, that she is a highly desirable female. The opera ends with Arabella descending the hotel staircase, carrying a glass of water to Mandryka, symbolic of betrothal. Mandryka drinks, and Arabella falls into his arms.

Delightful Viennese waltz music, à la *Rosenkavalier,* found in the second act, is not the sole source of this opera's charm. Another is the Slavic folk music which Strauss tapped for two outstanding vocal numbers in the first act: the duet of Arabella and Zdenka, "*Er ist der Richtige,*" and Arabella's air, "*Mein Elemer!*" Still another of Arabella's airs has a haunting folk-song quality, "*Über seine Felder,*" which she sings early in the third act.

Other distinguished musical episodes include the love duet of Arabella and Mandryka, and the brilliant coloratura air of the coquette, Fiakermilli, both in the second act; and the closing scene of the opera, as Arabella descends the stairway with a glass of water for Mandryka ("*Das war sehr gut, Mandryka*").

Arabella was well liked when it was introduced in Dresden, and again when it was heard in Vienna and Berlin. But the American première—at the Metropolitan Opera in New York on February 10, 1955—was severely criticized. Olin Downes called the opera "prevailingly dull, uninspired, unoriginal." Paul Henry Lang said: "The substance of this music is disappointing. . . . The melodic line lacks a sharp profile." However, with later performances of *Arabella* in the United States, the critics proved increasingly receptive, and recognized the opera for what it really is: a minor opera, to be sure, but one with enchanting moments.

With *Arabella,* the fruitful collaboration of Strauss and Hugo von Hofmannsthal came to an end. Von Hofmannsthal died on July 15, 1929, a few days after completing the text.

1940–1947 CONCERTO NO. 2 IN E-FLAT MAJOR FOR HORN AND ORCHESTRA. I. Allegro. II. Andante con moto. III. Rondo.

CONCERTO FOR OBOE AND SMALL ORCHESTRA. I. Allegro moderato; Vivace. II. Andante. III. Vivace.

DUET CONCERTINO FOR CLARINET AND BASSOON, STRING ORCHESTRA AND HARP. I. Allegro moderato. II. Andante. III. Allegro ma non troppo.

In old age, Strauss, creatively speaking, was returning to the womb. In his two last concertos, the one for the horn (1940) and the other for the oboe (1946), he was once again the post-Romantic of his young years, using classical forms, and filling them with ardent, almost Brahms-like materials. The Horn Concerto was introduced at the Salzburg Festival on August 11, 1943; the Oboe Concerto in Zurich, on February 26, 1946.

Sixty years separate the two horn concertos, the first one, op. 11 (also in the key of E-flat major), having been completed in 1883 when Strauss was nineteen. The second concerto, explains Nicolas Slonimsky, opens "with a display of passages along the tonal row of natural harmonics. The fanfare-like melody in a heroic manner, is reminiscent of Strauss's early tone poems." In the development, the solo horn "is . . . homogeneously coalescent with the woodwinds and strings without losing its individuality and distinctive tone color. . . . The concluding section is also typically Straussian, with its telescoped canons, and rhythmic burlesquing in rapid figurations." The second movement is in the rhythm of "a swaying barcarolle. A pastoral theme in the woodwinds is projected against the background of softly murmuring strings." In the finale, the orchestra "gives the exposition a gigue-like movement; then the horn enters solo, with bouncing rhythms sliding along a harmonic row. After a resounding orchestral bustle, the horn resumes the foreground, sounding a repeated series of piercing B-flats, first in the low, then in the high, register, and does not let go until all the sonorous resources of E-flat harmonies are completely and satisfyingly exhausted."

The three movements of the oboe concerto are played without interruption. The solo instrument is heard at once in a vivacious subject characterized by semi-quaver runs; it also presents the second subject, in which agile intervallic leaps predominate. Two minor ideas are later introduced, followed by a cadenza. The slow movement opens with an extended song for the solo instrument, and ends with a cadenza. The Vivace is built out of material from earlier movements. New ideas are also introduced, including a shepherd's call and a melody for solo violin and solo cello.

The *Duet Concertino* (1947)—Strauss's last instrumental composition—is for the unusual solo combination of clarinet and bassoon accompanied by harp and string orchestra. The string orchestra makes use of five solo strings. Strauss wrote the concertino for the Radio Svizzera Italiana in Lugano, Switzerland, where it was introduced on April 4, 1948. In the opening movement, the solo clarinet is heard first; the bassoon enters in the thirty-ninth measure. The spirited thematic material is discussed vigorously now by one solo instrument, now by the other, and now by the solo instruments in juxtaposition to the orchestra. The clarinet leads into the slow movement without pause. Here the principal subject is assigned to the bassoon over tremolo strings and harp. The movement ends with a brief cadenza for both solo instruments. Once again there is no pause between movements. The finale, a rondo, begins with the main subject in both solo instruments. This idea is commented upon before a new thought is projected by the two instruments.

1941 CAPRICCIO, "a conversation piece for music in one act," op. 85, with text by Clemens Krauss. First performance: Munich, October 28, 1942.

Capriccio was Strauss's last opera. It is a curiosity, a kind of a last will and testament on the part of the composer in which he speaks to discriminating hearers about his ideas on the musical theatre. "I do not intend writing another opera," he said in discussing his plans for *Capriccio,* "but would love to create . . . a treatise on drama, a fugue for the stage." And this is what he accomplished. Carefully avoiding the term "opera," but designating it rather as a "conversation piece," Strauss concocted in *Capriccio* a two-hour discussion on what is more important in opera, the words or the music. There is no action, no conflict, no characterizations, no atmosphere—only a discussion. The conclusion hinted at is that the words and music have equal significance, and only when they are united into a single inextricable unity is the problem of opera solved.

The setting is a chateau near Paris in 1775, the period in which Gluck was reforming opera with his musico-dramatic experiments. Offstage, the Andante of a string sextet is played, the work of a composer named Flamand. The Countess Madeleine is listening to it attentively, and she is being watched for her reactions by composer Flamand and a poet, Olivier, each of whom is in love with her. They argue about the respective importance of their callings, and each tries to plead his own case with the Countess. The Countess is noncommittal, but her brother, the Count, denounces all opera as nonsense. At this point, a producer, La Roche, outlines plans for an elaborate series of entertainments to honor the Countess's birthday. Neither the musician nor the poet is impressed with these plans, and La Roche denounces them bitterly for their failure to create poetry and music that has truth as well as beauty. The Countess urges Flamand and Olivier to take up the challenge and create something so vital and significant that La Roche will be silenced by shame. The Count suggests a theme for their creative effort, the happenings of that day in this very chateau, with themselves as protagonists. Both men are excited by this idea and decide to develop it. When the stage is emptied, the Countess returns and sings a sonnet with verses by Olivier and music by Flamand. This leads her to look into a mirror and ask herself which of the two men does she really love, which of the two is superior to the other. She cannot find an answer, and with the problem unsolved, she goes off to supper.

Thus ends the opera, as the key of D-flat major is sounded in the orchestra. "Isn't D-flat major the best possible end to my theatrical life?" Strauss asked Clemens Krauss. "After all, one can only leave one last will and testament." No answer seems to have been given to the problem as to whether words (symbolized by the character of Olivier) is more important than the music (symbolized by Flamand), but the implication is there that both are equally significant.

Though intended as a kind of dissertation on opera for the composer's own pleasure, *Capriccio* has a good deal of audience appeal. For in spite of its non-dramatic qualities, the text did provide Strauss with opportunities to express his deep feelings and to tap the fund of his melodic gifts. The opera begins with an emotional string sextet, and later in the opera is again reflected in the beautiful love duet, in the unforgettable air sung by the Countess as she looks into her mirror at the close of the opera, and in the second of the two orchestral interludes. The opera also reveals moments of genuine strength and dramatic impulse and is brightened by the infusion of comic elements, such as the parody of eighteenth-century operatic duets.

The American debut took place in New York City on April 2, 1954.

1945 METAMORPHOSEN, study for twenty-three solo strings.

This unusual exercise in string sonority was introduced in Zurich by the Collegium Musicum under Paul Sacher on January 25, 1946.

The work, which assigns separate parts for ten violins, five violas, five cellos and three double basses, features solo instruments and groups of strings as well as the entire orchestra. There are three sections played without interruption: Adagio, Agitato, Adagio. The entire composition is built from two theme groups of three subjects each. They are subjected to considerable development and transformation, with groups of strings used frequently in contrast to each other, and with lyric passages of solo character punctuating the elaborate texture. The music is touched with tragedy, opening as it does with a lugubrious theme in two violins, which leads into somber chords reminiscent of the Funeral March from Beethoven's *Eroica Symphony*. The composition concludes with this theme played contrapuntally with the actual one from the Beethoven symphony. It must be remembered that, when Strauss wrote this music, Germany was collapsing in the closing months of the war. Indeed, at the conclusion of his manuscript, Strauss wrote the two words, "In Memoriam" —in memory, no doubt, of the dying Germany, then being occupied by the Allied forces.

1948 VIER LETZTE LIEDER (FOUR LAST SONGS), for voice and orchestra. I. Frühling. II. September. III. Beim schlafengehen. IV. Im Abendrot.

These four songs are the last pieces of music Strauss was destined to write. They were heard first in London on May 20, 1950, with Kirsten Flagstad as the soloist and Wilhelm Furtwaengler conducting.

The first three poems are by Hermann Hesse, the fourth by Josef von Eichendorff. The first poem "Spring," tells how the sweetness of life returns at the contemplation of Spring's sights and smells. The other three poems are in an elegiac mood, touched with a soft, gray autumnal light. In "September," the poet contemplates the falling of the leaves of flowers as summer stands by smiling at the sight of his garden growing wan and pale with grief. "Time to Sleep" is weighted down by the weariness that comes at day's end, as the poet seeks peace and rest in sleep. "At Dusk," the final song, continues in the same vein, yearning for a time to sleep, for a rest so long desired.

It is not difficult to equate both "Time to Sleep" and "At Dusk" with death, and the peace it finally brings—a thought which surely struck a personal chord with Strauss at the dusk of his life, writing what he knew would be his swan song. The very last words which Strauss was destined to set to music, the last words in the song "At Dusk," contains the question, "Is this really Death?" Here, Strauss interpolated an ascending phrase from his tone poem *Death and Transfiguration*. He completed writing this song in 1949, just before his death. In writing his last piece of music he was doing just as his beloved Mozart had done before him, creating his own elegy.

But quoting one of his early tone poems was not the only way in which, as he sounded his final notes, Strauss was returning to his youth. In all four songs, he reverted to the style that, in the end of the nineteenth century, made him one of the foremost composers of the lied since Hugo Wolf. Once again we encounter that soaring, expressive lyricism that takes its cue from Brahms; once again we find accompaniments of symphonic dimensions which are the equal partners of the voice in the projection of a mood or feeling, and often with Wagnerian overtones. As a composer, Strauss ended up as he had begun. He had come full circle.

IGOR STRAVINSKY 1882–

Like a colossus, Stravinsky has straddled the world of twentieth-century music for half a century.

He first became a cyclonic force in the music of his time with a series of masterworks for ballet which many still consider among his greatest achievements: *L'Oiseau de feu* (*The Fire-Bird*), *Petrouchka*, *Le Sacre du printemps* (*The Rite of Spring*). Though he drew his inspiration and stimuli from Russian backgrounds and folklore, Stravinsky nevertheless struck a path all his own into unexplored regions of musical sound. Orthodox harmonies made way for dissonance; traditional tonality for polytonality. A severe, often crude, melodic line, built from fragments, and often consisting of no more than a few notes, brought brutal strength. Rhythm was revitalized through the use of rapidly changing meters, displaced accents, polymeters, polyrhythms. Rhythm had never been a significant element in the music of the Romantics, post-Romantics, and impressionists. But with Stravinsky, rhythm became fully emancipated; in fact it displaced melody as the central point of interest. Stravinsky used units of seven, eleven, or thirteen beats. Continually, he shifted restlessly from one meter to another. Through subtle and often complex syncopations, he repeatedly dislocated the accent. Hand in hand with this virtuoso handling of rhythm came a new emphasis on percussion instruments, and the building up of brilliant, even orgiastic, orchestral sonorities. All this represented the neo-primitive movement: a return to the dynamic and elementary forces of primitive music within sophisticated structures.

This was, indeed, "the music of the future." On the post-Romantic, impressionistic and post-impressionistic world of 1911–1914, this music descended with a shattering impact. It created fierce dissension between those who envisioned its composer as a prophetic voice in music and others who saw in this revolution only sham, artifice or anarchy. Few works of music were so violently attacked in their own day as these three scores; and few works have had such a decisive influence on the musical thinking of an entire generation. Consciously or otherwise, composers began imitating this fresh, vital, dynamic speech. Younger men in all the arts accepted Stravinsky as the spearhead of their attacks against staid tradition, smug status quo, and outmoded practices. In Italy, the futurist Marinetti paraded the streets with a banner proclaiming: "Down with Wagner! Long live Stravinsky!"

Then, just when these revolutionary works began to gain acceptance, and when the name of Stravinsky had become fully identified with the avant-garde in contemporary music, a radical change of style took place with Stravinsky. It was the breaking away from the complexity, the dissonance and the orgiastic sounds of his neo-primitive phase, just as it was a break with his ties to Russian precedents. Seeking a more objective approach to his art, Stravinsky felt the need of greater clarity and lucidity in his writing, greater economy and simplicity. He wanted to free his music of all extramusical implications and interest. The drift towards this new trend came in 1918 with *L'Histoire du soldat* (*A Soldier's Story*), in 1919 with *Pulcinella,* and in 1920 with *Symphonies of Wind Instruments*. It became fully realized with the Octet in 1923. Polyphony replaced rhythm as a basic creative tool. The classical and Baroque structures of the concerto, oratorio, Mass, symphony, opera seria, and opera buffa were now favored. Transparency of texture, economy of instrumentation and the stripping bare of all emotion became an artistic necessity. Stravinsky had become a neo-classicist.

Once again controversy raged around the personality and music of Igor Stravinsky. Some critics insisted that the reservoir of Stravinsky's genius had now run dry; that his writing had become barren, desiccated, pedantic and contrived. Others were just as persuasive that this new phase was a logical, probably inevitable, development in the evolution of a great creative personality; that the neo-classic works lifted their creator to new and greater heights. To his doubting critics, Stravinsky insisted with calm self-assurance that just as they had refused to understand him when he first wrote his Russian ballets, but learned to lavish on them extravagant praise, so they would eventually come around to his new way of thinking. "Their attitude certainly cannot make me deviate from my path," he wrote firmly in his autobiography. "I shall assuredly not sacrifice my predilection and my aspirations to the demands of those who, in their blindness, do not realize that they are simply asking me to go backwards. It should be obvious that what they wish for has become obsolete for me, and that I could not follow them without doing violence to myself."

Stravinsky was right, and once again his severest critics were wrong. While not all the works of Stravinsky's neo-classical period have won full acceptance—and while some are singularly unpalatable and uninteresting—the best are deeply moving for intensity of expression, are eloquent in their simplicity and possess a grandeur all their own. Few will now deny that works like the *Symphony of Psalms,* or *Oedipus Rex,* or *Apollon Musagète* or *The Rake's Progress* are works of first importance.

With his opera, *The Rake's Progress,* in 1951, Stravinsky once again came to the end of a road. This was the last of his neo-classical compositions. Almost seventy years old, Stravinsky now felt the need for a new set of musical principles as radically different from neo-classicism as neo-classicism had been from neo-primitivism. He found those new principles in dodecaphonic music, music in the twelve-tone system, which for many years he had regarded with either indifference or disdain. Twelve-tone procedures were experimented with in the *Cantata on Four Poems by Anonymous English Poets* and the Septet, both in 1952, and in the ballet *Agon*, in 1956. From twelve-tone music to serialism was the next and final development, which came in 1956 with *Canticum Sacrum ad honorem Sancti Marci nominis*. Since then, the serial technique has been the tool with which Stravinsky has fashioned many ambitious compositions for ballet, for chorus, for solo voice, and for the orchestra. Whether or not one is ready and willing to embrace these compositions, the fact cannot be denied that today, as yesterday, Stravinsky remains one of the most influential musicians and one of the most representative composers of the twentieth century.

Stravinsky was born on June 17, 1882, in Oranienbaum, a suburb of St. Petersburg. He was the son of the leading basso of the St. Petersburg Opera. Law had been selected for him by his father. Though Igor detested it, and was by his own admission a poor student in academic courses, he managed to survive both the preparatory schools and the University. Meanwhile, he found himself more and more drawn to the making of music. He had begun piano study at the age of nine and had received most of his musical knowledge by poring through harmony and counterpoint texts. After that, he received instruction in instrumentation from Rimsky-Korsakov.

In 1906, with his course of law study at the University ended, Stravinsky married his cousin, Catherine Gabrielle, who encouraged him to surrender all thoughts of law and specialize in music. Under Rimsky-Korsakov's guidance, Stravinsky now completed his First Symphony, in E-flat major, and *Le Faune et la bergère,* a cycle of songs for mezzo-soprano and orchestra based on poems of Pushkin. These were Stravinsky's first works to get performed—in St. Petersburg on February 5, 1908. Two orchestral pieces followed: the *Scherzo fantastique* and *Feu d'artifice* (*Fireworks*). They were introduced in St. Petersburg on February 6, 1909, a concert attended by Serge Diaghilev. Recognizing a touch of genius in these pieces, Diaghilev engaged Stravinsky to write music for the Ballet Russe, which Diaghilev had then recently founded.

Stravinsky's first assignment was to orchestrate two pieces by Chopin for *Les Sylphides,* produced by the Ballet Russe on June 2, 1909. This project was not without significance: it brought Stravinsky a new creative medium, that of ballet, which helped make him a world figure in music. He became that world figure for the first time with his next ballet assignment, *L'Oiseau de feu* in 1909. With *Petrouchka* in 1911 and *Le Sacre du printemps* in 1913—all written for and introduced by the Ballet Russe—Stravinsky become one of the most provocative and widely publicized composers of his generation.

In 1919, Stravinsky permanently broke his ties with his native Russia and went to live on the outskirts of Paris; he become a French citizen on June 10, 1934. Besides his intensive preoccupation with compositions in his newly adopted neo-classical manner, Stravinsky now began touring the capitals of music as a conductor of his own works. He made his first tour of the United States in 1925, making his American debut on January 8 as a guest conductor of the New York Philharmonic.

Soon after the eruption of World War II in Europe, Stravinsky established his home permanently in the United States. In 1939–1940, he occupied a lecturer's chair at Harvard. Then he moved to Hollywood, California, to set up there his home with his second wife, Vera de Bossett, an artist whom he had married in April of 1940 (one year after the death of his first wife, Catherine). In America, where he became a citizen on December 28, 1945, Stravinsky remained remarkably productive as a composer, while at the same time intensifying his activities as a guest conductor. In the fall of 1962, he paid his first return visit to his native land in almost half a century to conduct several concerts of his compositions. Though his music had long been held in contempt in the Soviet Union, he now received a thunderous welcome.

Stravinsky's eightieth birthday inspired commemorative concerts the world over. In the United States, he received a gold medal from the Secretary of State, Dean Rusk, and was invited to the White House by President and Mrs. John F. Kennedy. Between June 30 and July 23 of 1966, the New York Philharmonic held a ten-day Stravinsky festival at the Lincoln Center for the Performing Arts. Among the many world honors heaped on Stravinsky were gold medals from the National Institute and American Academy of Arts and Letters, from the Royal Philharmonic Orchestra of London, and from Finland; the Sonning Award in Denmark; and the international Sibelius prize from Finland.

1908 FEU D'ARTIFICE (FIREWORKS), for orchestra, op. 4.

Fireworks was one of the two compositions which made such an impression on Diaghilev that he engaged the young and then still unknown composer to work for the newly-founded Ballet Russe. Diaghilev heard this piece at its world première—at a Siloti concert in St. Petersburg on February 6, 1909.

Stravinsky wrote *Fireworks* as a wedding gift for Rimsky-Korsakov's daughter. He had planned it as a surprise and as such despatched the manuscript to the master. Rimsky-Korsakov never saw the work; he died a few days before the manuscript arrived.

Fireworks is no impressionistic picture but the kind of pictorial representation which the Russians (Rimsky-Korsakov and Balakirev, particularly) did so well. The orchestra is a large one (the brass choir including six horns), but the structure is comparatively simple. A four-bar tune based on the chord of the dominant is the basic material from which the entire piece is built. First, we get this subject in fragments, measure by measure. Then it is stated in full canon. After that, a canon in retrogression leads to a reprise in the tonic. As this subject leaps from one part of the orchestra to another, various fascinating colors are discharged like the leaping flames of a pyrotechnical display. But there are also moments of repose in divided strings. In one of these brief quiet pages, we hear a descending passage which betrays how much Stravinsky admired Dukas's *The Sorcerer Apprentice*. The explosive rhythms, asymmetrical arrangement of the barring, displaced accents, the succinctness of the musical language, harsh contrasts of timbres and overall dynamic power—all this in *Fireworks* provides a prophetic glimpse at the composer's later neo-primitive methods.

1910 L'OISEAU DE FEU (THE FIRE-BIRD), dramatic ballet in one act, with choreography by Michel Fokine. First performance: Ballet Russe, Paris, June 25, 1910.

L'OISEAU DE FEU, Suite No. 2, for orchestra. I. Introduction—The Fire-Bird and Her Dance. II. Dance of the Princess. III. Kastchei's Infernal Dance. IV. Berceuse. V. Finale.

The Russian legend of the Fire-Bird was planned as a ballet for Diaghilev by Fokine even before the commission for writing the score went to young Stravinsky. Another Russian composer had been assigned the job—Liadov. But Liadov procrastinated so long in completing this commission that the impatient Diaghilev decided to entrust it to Stravinsky. It was a bold gamble on the part of the impresario—for, up to then, Stravinsky had written little to suggest that he was able to fulfill so ambitious a project.

Stravinsky devoted the winter of 1909 and the early months of 1910 to the writing of this music. He was guided by the indefatigable Fokine, who was ever at the composer's side with advice, criticism and valuable suggestions.

The Ballet Russe introduced *The Fire-Bird* at the Paris Opéra, with Fokine, Mme. Fokine and Karsavina as the principal dancers. The settings were designed by Bakst and Golovina. Gabriel Pierné conducted.

That première was a resounding success. It made Stravinsky famous overnight. It also brought to the repertoire of the Ballet Russe one of its most strikingly original and famous works.

The Fokine scenario developed the traditional Russian legend without much variation. Ivan Tsarevitch, roaming aimlessly one night, stumbles across the Fire-Bird and captures it as it is in the act of plucking golden fruit from a silver tree. As a reward for its release, the Fire-Bird presents Ivan with one of its glowing feathers, which he accepts. Suddenly, the thick darkness of the night dissipates. A castle comes into view, from whose doors thirteen maidens of surpassing beauty emerge. Little realizing that they are being observed, they play with the silver tree and its fruit. Emerging from his hiding place, Ivan receives from one of the maidens a golden fruit as a gift, and they dance out of sight. The night passes into dawn. Suddenly, Ivan realizes that the castle is the home of the dreaded Kastchei, who captures wayfaring strangers and subjects them to his will. Determined to conquer this ogre, Ivan enters the castle, which is guarded by terrifying monsters. Kastchei attempts to bewitch Ivan; but his power is impotent before the magic feather Ivan holds in his hand. Then the Fire-Bird comes into view, reveals to Ivan a casket, and informs him that Kastchei's fate is concealed in it. Ivan opens the casket and withdraws an egg, which he smashes to the ground. Death emerges from the smashed eggshell and obsesses the body of Kastchei. As Kastchei perishes, the castle suddenly disappears and the maidens are freed from their bondage. As a reward, Ivan receives in marriage the hand of the most beautiful of the captive maidens.

The music Stravinsky wrote for *The Fire-Bird* still owes a debt to Rimsky-Korsakov, as did all his earlier compositions. There is a good deal of *Le Coq d'or* here: the love of fantasy; the pseudo-oriental melodies; the rich harmonic texture and the well-sounding instrumental colorations; the interest in folk lore. The most popular single excerpt, the hauntingly beautiful "Berceuse," belongs to the Russian national school. But there is also much in *The Fire-Bird* to hint at things soon to come: the adventures in discords and the exercises in changing rhythms in an episode like "Kastchei's Infernal Dance." Other pages reveal a primitive force and offer audacious harmonic progressions that will soon become a part of Stravinsky's basic vocabulary. And it was the discords, the audacious harmonic progressions and the primitive force that outraged some of those who heard this music for the first time. Pavlova, who was supposed to have danced in the première, refused to be affiliated with such "horrible music." Others considered it noisy and vulgar. Some, however, recognized its importance, and knew that a new master had appeared. After one of the rehearsals Diaghilev confided to a friend: "Mark that man Stravinsky. He is on the eve of celebrity." And following the première, Debussy rushed over to the young Stravinsky to embrace him, almost as if to hail a worthy successor.

Stravinsky prepared three different orchestral suites from his ballet score. The second is the one heard most often. Stravinsky prepared it in 1919 (eight years after he had assembled the first suite). The second differs from its predecessor by being scored for a medium rather than a full orchestra, and by the deletion of several minor sections. The third suite retains the more sparing orchestration of the second suite and restores the Adagio and Scherzo movements from the first one; new transitional sections between respective parts are interpolated to provide greater cohesion.

In the popular second suite, the Introduction begins with a portentous subject in the low strings. An air of mystery is created. An episode for two flutes in imitation, over a sustained chord in horns, sets the stage for the dance of the princess, whose main melody is played first by oboe (accompanied by harp) and continued by solo cello, clarinet and bassoon. A piercing fortissimo chord in full orchestra brings on Kastchei's infernal dance. The abandoned melody is heard first in unison strings fortissimo. The music progresses towards a frenzied climax. Then a quiet transition in woodwinds, horns, piano and harp—followed by divided and muted cellos and violas—establishes the proper mood for the nostalgic and tender "Berceuse." The cradle song is assigned to the bassoon, accompanied by muted strings and harp. A horn solo over string tremolos brings on the finale; later on in this movement, this theme is given a radiant presentation by unison strings over ascending brass scale. The finale ends joyously, as Kastchei's victims are released and Ivan gets as his reward the hand of one of the beautiful princesses.

The ballet, *L'Oiseau de feu,* was mounted for the first time in the United States in New York City on January 17, 1916, presented by the visiting Ballet Russe. A successful revival of the ballet was given by the New York City Ballet in New York on November 27, 1949, with choreography by George Balanchine, and scenery and costumes by Marc Chagall.

1911 PETROUCHKA, ballet in one act, with choreography by Michel Fokine. First performance: Ballet Russe, Paria, June 13, 1911.

PETROUCHKA, ballet suite for orchestra.

Early in 1911, or some months after the successful première of *The Fire-Bird,* Diaghilev visited Stravinsky at Clarens, Switzerland, to listen to sections of a new ballet score upon which the composer was at work at that time. Diaghilev expected to hear the music for the ballet later known as *The Rite of Spring*. What he found Stravinsky immersed in was quite a different score: music of irony and capricious moods which, because the composer could not find a better name for it, he called a *Konzertstück*. What Stravinsky was trying to portray in this work was a pathetic sawdust puppet so frequently seen at Russian fairs: Petrouchka. Diaghilev was not only enthused with the portions he heard Stravinsky play, but immediately recognized the value of Petrouchka as a theme for a ballet. Together with the composer he now worked out the general lines of a scenario, setting the action in a Russian fair. With this as a working basis, Stravinsky developed and elaborated his *Konzertstück* into a ballet score, now named *Petrouchka*.

When *Petrouchka* was introduced in Paris by the Ballet Russe, Karsavina and Nijinsky were the principal dancers. Benois designed the scenery; Fokine prepared the choreography; Monteux conducted.

Philip Hale quotes the following admirable description of the action without crediting his source:

"This ballet depicts the life of the lower classes in Russia with all its dissoluteness, barbarity, tragedy, and misery. Petrouchka is a sort of Polichinelle, a poor hero always suffering from the cruelty of the police and every kind of wrong and unjust persecution. This represents symbolically the whole tragedy in the existence of the Russian people, suffering under despotism and injustice. The scene is laid in the midst of the Russian carnival, and the streets are lined with booths, in one of which Petrouchka plays a kind of humorous role. He is killed, but he appears again as ghost on the roof of the booth to frighten his enemy, his old employer, an allusion to the despotic rule of Russia."

Stravinsky's score is at turns vividly pictorial, subtle and revealing in its characterizations, humorous and sardonic, and vividly national. There are in this music carry-overs from Russian folk lore: for example, the liturgical chant in the woodwinds in the first scene and, in the fourth scene, the quotation of three well-known Russian folk songs. In spite of borrowings, the Stravinsky score spoke with a fresh, new voice. Bolder than ever is Stravinsky's use of unresolved discords. His experiments with polytonality are both brilliant and successful—so much so that henceforth polytonality becomes a favored idiom of some modernists. The long-flowing melodies of *The Fire-Bird* are replaced by terse, epigrammatic statements, loosely strung together. This was "new music"—bold and free.

In individuality, in sureness of technique, in variety of material and moods, *Petrouchka* represents a giant advance over *The Fire-Bird*. Stravinsky's natural bent for ironic and sardonic suggestions gave his new ballet score an intriguing, piquant flavor the earlier work did not possess. The tonal characterization of Petrouchka was subtler and more imaginative than any found in *The Fire-Bird*, and the evocation of ever-changing moods was achieved with a far more skilful and varied hand.

The following sections from the ballet score were adapted by Stravinsky into his frequently played orchestral suite: Carnival; The Magician; Russian Dance; Petrouchka; The Arab; Dance of the Ballerina; Nurses' Dance; The

Bear and the Peasant Playing a Hand-Organ; The Merchant and the Gypsies; The Dance of the Coachmen and the Grooms; The Masqueraders; The Quarrel of the Arab and Petrouchka; The Death of Petrouchka.

As a ballet, *Petrouchka* was first seen in the United States in New York on January 25, 1916, in a performance by the visiting Ballet Russe.

1913 LE SACRE DU PRINTEMPS (THE RITE OF SPRING), ballet in two parts, with choreography by Vaslav Nijinsky and book by Igor Stravinsky and Nicholas Roerich. First performance: Ballet Russe, Paris, May 29, 1913.

LE SACRE DU PRINTEMPS, suite for orchestra. I. The Adoration of the Earth. Introduction—Harbingers of Spring—Dance of the Adolescents—Spring Rounds; Games of the Round Cities—The Procession of the Wise Men—The Adoration of the Earth—Dance of the Earth. II. The Sacrifice. Introduction—Mysterious Circle of the Adolescents—Glorification of the Chosen One—Evocation of the Ancestors—The Sacrificial Dance of the Chosen One.

Soon after completing the writing of *The Fire-Bird*, Stravinsky had what he has described as "a vision." He saw a girl dancing herself to death in a sacrificial pagan rite. He reported this transport to Nicholas Roerich, who, impressed, agreed that it could be elaborated into a new ballet. Roerich helped Stravinsky work out a general outline in which images of pagan Russia were evoked.

The writing of this new ballet was delayed while another one, of quite a different character, engaged Stravinsky—*Petrouchka*. Not until *Petrouchka* was out of the way did Stravinsky return to *The Rite* and complete it.

The Rite of Spring has no detailed or specific program. In abstract terms it portrays a ritual of pagan Russia. Symbolic or anecdotal details are not permitted to intrude. A ritual is taking place: the adoration of Nature by primitive man. A haunting melody in the upper register of the bassoon describes the birth of Spring. Other woodwinds join in, and soon the orchestra is quivering to life as the earth awakens. Barbaric dances and games follow. A steady rhythm is pounded out; this primitive effect is heightened by the introduction of polytonal harmonies; displaced accents add to the excitement as eight horns interpolate syncopated rhythms. Soon the young girls and boys begin the games of Abduction, introduced by woodwinds and brass fanfare. The Spring Rounds follow, brought in by a gentle Russian-like subject for high clarinet and bass clarinet accompanied by flute trills. Drum rolls follow. Muted trumpets are sounded. An overwhelming crescendo brings on the Sage to consecrate the earth, after which a tumultuous dance of the earth takes place.

The second part of the ballet opens with a picture of a pagan night touched with mystery and awe. A Russian melody is heard in muted violins in harmonics. A dance of the mysterious circle of adolescents is succeeded by two exciting ritual dances. Now comes the climactic point of the ballet. A female dances herself to death in a Corybantic. The music reaches a pitch of frenzy. Then, with a last orgiastic outburst, the rite comes to an end.

Ever-changing rhythms, volatile meters, shattering discords, outbursts of orchestral sounds and colors create a tension that at times almost becomes excrutiating. Simple diatonic themes are stated, restated, and restated—the continual repetition having a kind of hyponotic effect. These simple phrases are set against the discordant complexity of the harmonic texture to create a nerve-wracking impact, an impact enhanced all the time by the way in which the composer uses an immense orchestra—and especially the percussion, to which an altogether new significance is assigned—for primitive effects. Stravinsky carefully planned every rhythmic effect, giving precise instructions to the tympanist when to change from a hard felt stick to a wooden one, and to the gong player on how to describe an arc with his stick on the surface of his instrument. Percussive effects, and dynamic rhythms, are fully exploited to achieve music of rare savagery and brutality, very similar to the canvases of wild beasts then being produced in Paris by the artists of the Fauve—the reason why Stravinsky's neo-primitivism is sometimes described as "music of the Fauve."

The première performance, at the Théâtre de Champs Elysées in Paris on May 29, 1913, created a scandal which has been frequently described. Nijinsky's exotic choreography and Roerich's bizarre settings and costumes were partially responsible. But it was Stravinsky's revolutionary score which, more than any single factor, stirred that first-night audience to dynamic reactions. The performance had not progressed very far when catcalls, shouts, and stamping of feet began to drown out the music. On the one hand, musicians like Maurice Ravel and Debussy arose to exclaim that this was a work of genius; on the other, people like the critic André Capu, the Austrian Ambassador, and the Princess de Pourtalès pronounced it a fake. Blows were exchanged. One woman spat in the face of a demonstrator. Pandemonium followed. Very little of the music could now be heard.

When *The Rite of Spring* was introduced in London at the Drury Lane Theatre on July 11, 1913, the audience was better mannered than the one which had witnessed the première performance in Paris. But the critics were just as savage. "It has no relation to music at all as most of us understand the word," one of them wrote Another remarked: "A crowd of savages . . . might have produced such noises."

Appreciation for this powerful and original music did not come suddenly. When the orchestral suite was introduced in this country by Pierre Monteux and the Boston Symphony in 1924, there was still profound antagonism to this music. One wit contributed the following verse to the pages of the *Boston Herald*:

Who wrote this fiendish *Rite of Spring*?
    What right had he to write this thing?
Against our helpless ears to fling
    Its crash, clash, cling, clang, bing, bang, bing!

If acceptance came slowly, it came inevitably as well. This score is now heard often—more often in the concert hall than in the theatre—and much of the original surprise is gone. Instead of shock, we get its extraordinary vitality, feeling of excitememt, audaciousness of thought and technique, all of which make an inescapable impact. By the time the ballet was mounted for the first time in the United States (in Philadelphia on April 11, 1930, Leopold Stokowski conducting, and Martha Graham in the leading dance role), there were few to deny that this was a masterwork. Additional evidence of the music's growing acceptance by the public at large came less than a decade later when it was incorporated into the Walt Disney animated motion picture, *Fantasia,* where it was seen and heard by millions.

On May 29, 1963, the fiftieth anniversary of the première of *Le Sacre du printemps* took place in London, with Pierre Monteux conducting the suite in the presence of the composer. A fifteen-minute ovation followed the conclusion of the performance. One London reviewer remarked: "In a long experience of London's music, I do not recall a scene to surpass this one."

1917 LE CHANT DU ROSSIGNOL (THE SONG OF THE NIGHTINGALE), tone poem for orchestra. I. The Palace of the Chinese Emperor. II. The Two Nightingales. III. Illness and Recovery of the Emperor of China.

The Song of the Nightingale exists in three different musical forms. It originated as an opera, inspired by Rimsky-Korsakov's *Le Coq d'or.* After that, it was transformed into a ballet for the Diaghilev repertory. Subsequently, it was revamped into a tone poem for orchestra, the form in which it is best known.

The delightful fairy tale of Hans Christian Andersen appealed to Stravinsky as early as 1909, when he planned a "lyric tale in three acts" to a libretto by his friend Mitusov, and actually completed the entire first act. Not until 1914, however, was he able to complete the opera. It was then introduced at the Paris Opéra on May 26, Pierre Monteux conducting. One month later, it received four performances in London. Then—as an opera, at any rate—it passed into oblivion.

Diaghilev suggested to Stravinsky the conversion of the opera into a ballet. For this purpose, the composer adapted the last two acts into an integrated orchestral piece which could be utilized as the musical background for a ballet sequence. It was as an orchestral piece—or symphonic poem—that this new version was first heard: in Paris, on December 16, 1917, with Ernest Ansermet conducting. As a ballet (scenery by Matisse and choreography by Massine), it was introduced by the Ballet Russe in Paris on Feburary 2, 1920, once again with Ansermet conducting.

The three sections of the symphonic poem are played without interruption. They describe the following program:

I. The Palace of the Chinese Emperor. The festivities attending the arrival of the Emperor into court are described. Following this—and with considerable pomp and ceremony—the nightingale, whose exquisite singing is world famous, is brought into the presence of the Emperor.

II. The Two Nightingales. The nightingale raises his voice in a song of such beauty that tears come into the eyes of the Emperor. A mechanical nightingale is then introduced into the court. It, too, sings beautifully, much to the chagrin of the live bird, who disappears. Angry, the Emperor orders the banishment of the live bird and gives the place of honor beside his bed to the mechanical nightingale.

III. Illness and Recovery of the Emperor of China. The Emperor is dying. Together with the pains of his illness come pangs of conscience for evils committed. Frantically he calls to his mechanical bird to sing, to drive out his thoughts and pains with beautiful music. But the mechanical bird is silent; the mechanism has broken. Suddenly the sweetest music is heard. It is that of the real nightingale, who has returned. The music so calms the Emperor that he falls into a deep sleep, from which he awakens fully recovered. A funeral march announces the arrival of the courtiers, who expect to find their Emperor dead. But they find instead a vigorous and healthy ruler.

The songs of the nightingale, played in turn by a solo flute, an E-flat clarinet, and a solo violin, are among the most eloquent pages in the score—a welcome relief from the recurrent dissonances and acrid sounds that precede and follow them. Subtle suggestions of irony give the work considerable spice: for example, the mock-heroic entrance of the Emperor in the first section (written, appropriately, in the pentatonic scale of oriental music); or, once again, the satiric funeral march in the last part for an Emperor who proves to be vulgarly healthy.

There are three main sections, played without interruption. The tone poem opens with bustling music which, in the opera, was used in the introduction to the second act. It tells about the preparations made by the courtiers for the Emperor's arrival. A Chinese march, constructed mainly from the pentatonic scale, brings the Emperor and his entourage to the scene. Now, with a flute cadenza, followed by a melody for flute and E-flat clarinet, we hear the singing of a live nightingale. In a presto section, the mechanical bird is brought to the Emperor and begins its own song, in piccolo, flute and oboe. A command in muted trombone banishes the live nightingale after which an elegiac song is played by trumpet over muted strings. Solemn music now evokes the picture of the dying Emperor. Suddenly, the voice of the live nightingale is heard once more in flute solo and solo violin. A mock funeral march brings on the courtiers, come to mourn a dead Emperor, only to find him hale and hearty again. The tone poem ends with a brief epilogue for solo trumpet accompanied by harp and muted strings.

1917 LES NOCES (THE WEDDING), cantata with dances, with text by Igor Stravinsky derived from poems by Kirievski, and choreography by Bronislava Nijinska. First performance: Ballet Russe, Paris, June 13, 1923.

Stravinsky adopted an unconventional form for his "Russian choreographic scenes," which he designated as a cantata. *The Wedding* is a setting in four tableaux of scenes describing a Russian wedding ritual. It is scored for solo voices (soprano, contralto, tenor and baritone), chorus and instrumentalists. The instrumental ensemble consists of the unusual combinations of four pianos and a battery of percussion that includes four tympani, bells, xylophone, tambourine, cymbals, small cymbals, triangle, bass drum, side drum, and drum without snares. Unusual, too, is the placement of the singers—not on the stage, but in the orchestra pit.

Several popular Russian poems, collected by Kirievski, an authority on Russian folklore, provided the subject for this cantata. While there is no integrated plot as such, the action can be readily described:

I. "The Tresses." The bride is being dressed and prepared by her friends for the wedding ceremony.

II. "At the Bridegroom's Home." A similar ritual takes place at the home of the groom. Friends of both families shower the parents of the bride and groom with congratulations. The marriage ceremony then takes place.

III. "The Bride's Departure." After being blessed by his parents, the groom joins his bride as voices of congratulation are heard. The married couple leave, followed by the guests.

IV. "The Wedding Feast." The parents of both the bride and the groom lament the loss of their children. The wedding feast begins. Revelry takes place as the bride is formally presented to the guests before being passed over to her husband. A couple are chosen to prepare the bridal room and (as was then customary) to warm the bed. The bridal pair are conducted to the room, while the parents dally outside. The voice of the bridegroom is heard through the closed door, in praise of love.

All this is a picture of rather primitive people with primitive customs. For it, Stravinsky conceived an equally neo-primitive score. Brief snatches of thematic ideas replace sustained lyricism. Harsh and complicated rhythms, monotonous tone colors, piercing sonorities bring elemental power. The awkward lines and abrupt phrases suggest the illiteracy of the characters. This is not music that makes for pleasurable listening. But it cannot be denied that this is powerful music, or that it achieves its effect with sledgehammer blows.

No other work by Stravinsky took so long to crystallize. The first sketches were begun in 1914, and the first draft was completed in 1917. But not until 1923 was the orchestration completed.

When it was introduced in London three years later (this performance was notable for the fact that the four pianos were played by composers—Poulenc, Auric, Dukelsky and Rieti), it created a minor scandal. The audience booed and jeered. The critics were poisonous. The music, however, found a stout-hearted protagonist in none other than H. G. Wells, who wrote an open letter declaring: "I do not know of any other ballet so interesting, so amusing, so fresh, or nearly as exciting as *The Wedding*. . . . I protest against this conspiracy of willful stupidity that may succeed in driving it out of the program. . . . The ballet is a rendering in sound and vision of the peasant soul, in its gravity, in its deliberate and simple-minded intricacy, in its subtly varied rhythms, in its deep undercurrent of excitement."

The first American hearing was in a concert version heard in New York in February of 1926, a presentation of the International Composers Guild. The first staged version followed in New York on April 25, 1929, when Leopold Stokowski conducted, and the performers at the four pianos were four distinguished American composers—Aaron Copland, Marc Blitzstein, Louis Gruenberg and Frederick Jacobi.

1918 L'HISTOIRE DU SOLDAT (A SOLDIER'S TALE), narrative ballet in five scenes "to be read, played and danced," with text by C. F. Ramuz and choreography by Ludmilla Pitoev. First performance: Lausanne, Switzerland, September 28, 1918.

L'HISTOIRE DU SOLDAT, suite for orchestra. Part I: I. Soldier's March. II. The Soldier's Violin—Music at the Brook. III. Pastorale. Part II: IV. Royal March. V. Little Concerto. VI Three Dances—Tango, Waltz, Ragtime. VII. The Devil's Dance. VIII. Little Chorale. IX. The Devil's Song. X. The Great Chorale. XI. Triumphal March of the Devil.

Only three dancers, a narrator, and seven instruments are required for the performance of this intimate ballet. This economy was dictated not so much by artistic necessity as by simple expediency. Many theatres and ballet companies had to suspend operations during World War I. Ambitious ballets, requiring large forces, had almost no chance of being produced. Such being the situation, Stravinsky, planning a ballet in 1917, decided to write one that made only limited demands on the production facilities of any theatre.

The Swiss poet C. F. Ramuz prepared the text, based on a Russian folk tale. A soldier, returning from the wars, meets a devil disguised as an amiable gentleman. The devil offers the soldier a magic book, capable of answering any question, in return for his violin. Eagerly, the soldier accepts the bargain, only to discover that knowing the answers to all the questions induces in him an insatiable wanderlust. He loves a Princess and loses her. Finally, when homesickness brings him home, he is seized on the border by the devil.

The score is made up of heterogeneous elements, but as Eric Walter White notes, "by brilliant manipulation, the composer obtains an effect of complete coherence and integration." The score includes a march, a tango, a waltz, chorales, even ragtime. The interpolation of ragtime music is one of the unusual and interesting features of this composition. Ernest Ansermet, the distinguished conductor who led the world première, had brought back from America examples of New Orleans jazz. Stravinsky was completely fascinated by them. Since he was then working on *L'Histoire,* he not only included a ragtime section but in his overall instrumentation even simulated a 1916 New Orleans Dixieland jazz band (particularly in the way he used his clarinet, trumpet, trombone and piano). His writing for percussion, not only in the ragtime section but elsewhere (it is the sole accompaniment to the tango), is also a carry-over of this New Orleans jazz influence.

Eric Walter White points out that all the instruments, except the double bass, are "treated on solo lines." The violin is prominent in Numbers 2, 5, 6, 7 and 11; the cornet and trombone, in Numbers 1 and 4; clarinet and cornet share the spotlight with the violin in Number 5; while clarinet, bassoon, cornet and trombone divide the four-part harmonies of Numbers 8 and 10, the two chorales. "This gives the various numbers great variety of character and coloring despite the limited number of instruments at the composer's command. . . . He encourages each solo instrument to develop an independent linear existence and then fits them together like pieces of a mosaic."

As a ballet, *L'Histoire du soldat* received its first American performance in New York on March 25, 1928, at a concert of the League of Composers.

1919 PULCINELLA, ballet with song in one act, with choreography by Léonide Massine and music based on melodies by Giovanni Battista Pergolesi. First performance: Ballet Russe, Paris, May 15, 1920.

PULCINELLA, suite for small orchestra. I. Sinfonia. II. Serenata. III. Scherzino; Allegro; Andantino. IV. Tarantella. V. Toccata. VI. Gavotta con due Variazioni. VII. Duetto. VIII. Minuetto; Finale.

SUITE, for violin and piano based on *Pulcinella.* I. Introduction. II.

Serenata. III. Tarantella. IV. Gavotta con due Variazioni. V. Minuetto; Finale.

SUITE ITALIENNE, for violin and piano based on *Pulcinella*. I. Sinfonia. II. Canzona. III. Danza. IV. Gavotta con due variazioni. V. Scherzino. VI. Moderato; Allegro vivace.

The music of Giovanni Battista Pergolesi (1710–1736)—discovered in manuscript form in Naples—provided the musical material for this Stravinsky ballet. Stravinsky wrote *Pulcinella* for Diaghilev. It was first produced by the Ballet Russe in Paris. Pablo Picasso designed the scenery and costumes; Massine prepared the choreography; the principal dancers included Massine and Karsavina; Ernest Ansermet conducted.

Pulcinella is a traditional character of the early Neapolitan theatre. In Stravinsky's ballet, he is the source of envy of all his neighbors because the girls are in love with him. They plot to kill him. Pulcinella simulates death. Believing they have achieved their aim, the Neapolitans assume Pulcinella's costume and proceed to make love to their respective girls. Meanwhile, Pulcinella puts on a sorcerer's robe and brings to life his double. However, vengeance is not in Pulcinella's heart. He attends the love-making of his neighbors and benevolently arranges for their respective marriages—while he himself weds Pimpenella.

An anonymous Swiss annotator remarked that, in adapting Pergolesi's music, Stravinsky "did more than transcribe. . . . In the case of some numbers, which he took as a point of departure, he elaborated a work which it is necessary to regard as to some extent original. . . . Feeling certain sympathetic affinities with the music of Pergolesi, Stravinsky reverted in his imagination to the environment of the Neapolitan music-makers of the early eighteenth century and provided what is, in effect, a 'portrait' of Pergolesi and his times. . . . He borrowed from Pergolesi not only the melodies and their characteristic harmonies, but also the strains of style and the form of these pieces."

Stravinsky adapted a concert suite for orchestra from his ballet score, which was introduced in Paris on December 22, 1922, Pierre Monteux conducting. The music from *Pulcinella* also provided Stravinsky with material for two different suites for violin and piano. One of these he entitled simply as *Suite* (1925). A second suite, called *Suite italienne,* was written in 1933.

As a ballet, *Pulcinella* was first seen in the United States in Chicago in 1933, with choreography by Laurent Novikoff.

1922 MAVRA, comic opera in one act, with text by Boris Kochno based on *The Little House at Kolomna* by Pushkin. First performance: Paris, June 3, 1922.

Stravinsky conceived this little opera (which takes only twenty-five minutes to perform) because, as he put it, he had "a natural sympathy . . . for the melodic language, the vocal style and conventions of the old Russo-Italian opera. This sympathy led me back to a tradition . . . which represented no tradition from the historical point of view and answered no musical necessity. . . . The music of *Mavra* is in the direct tradition of Glinka and Dargomijsky. I wanted merely to try my hand at this living form of opera buffa."

The plot is characteristic of Italian opera buffa. Parasha and Basil are in love. When Parasha's mother laments the loss of her cook, Parasha brings as replacement Basil, in woman's disguise and under the assumed name of Mavra. The ruse is discovered when Parasha and her mother return suddenly and discover their cook—shaving. The mother faints. When she recovers, Basil jumps out of the window and escapes, as Parasha calls after him.

For this gay text Stravinsky produced one of his most engaging scores, rich with wit and lyricism, and occasionally marked by novel treatment in the instrumentation. The scoring calls for twelve woodwinds, twelve brasses and some strings. Recitative is dispensed with altogether. The score consists of a continuous stream of melodies for solo voice and ensemble numbers, both varied in character. As Paul Collaer pointed out, four sources yielded the styles of Stravinsky's lyricism: Russian occidental melody as found in Glinka and Dargomijsky; classical Italian melody; gypsy melody; chromatic melody.

The first American performance took place in Philadelphia on December 28, 1934, in an English translation.

1923 OCTET FOR WIND, for two bassoons, two trombones, two trumpets, flute and clarinet. I. Sinfonia. II. Tema con variazioni. III. Moderato.

With this composition, Stravinsky's neo-classical style, which he would favor for the next thirty years, first came to full flower. Stravinsky himself conducted the world première—in Paris at a Concert Koussevitzky on October 18, 1923; this was the first time that the composer introduced one of his own works. Aaron Copland, who was in the audience, has described how shocked and confused the audience was upon hearing this music, having come expecting another example of Stravinsky's neo-primitivism. Instead, they were confronted with music that stood at a pole completely opposite to *Le Sacre du printemps.* For here, as Copland has explained, Stravinsky "posed a new universalistic ideal for music, based on classical forms and contrapuntal textures, borrowing his melodic material eclectically from all periods, yet fusing the whole by the indubitable power of his personality. . . . With the writing of the Octet, he completely abandoned realism and primitivism of all kinds and openly espoused the cause of objectivism in music."

Stravinsky has revealed that the idea to write this composition came to him in a dream in which he saw a group of wind players perform a chamber-music work. Stravinsky could not recognize the music, but he did identify the instruments. The following morning he began working on a composition for the same combination.

The opening movement is in two sections, Lento and Allegro moderato. The air in the second movement (Andantino) is a waltz, an episode which Stravinsky builds into five variations; the first of these variations is repeated several times. Stravinsky himself regards the last variation, a slow fugato, as the most interesting section of the entire composition. The concluding movement is interesting for its motor energy.

1924 CONCERTO FOR PIANO AND WIND ORCHESTRA. I. Allegro. II. Larghissimo. III. Allegro.

The scoring of this piano concerto is unorthodox, calling for a wind orchestra supplemented by double basses and tympani. This instrumentation is characteristic of Stravinsky's continual experiments with unusual combinations following World War I. In line with Stravinsky's neo-classicial thinking, the concerto re-creates the concerto-grosso style of the seventeenth century—but with modern idioms.

Stravinsky himself introduced this concerto in Paris on May 22, 1924, at a Concert Koussevitzky. He was also the soloist when this work was given its American première, in Boston on January 23, 1925.

The first movement is the most ambitious of the three. It is a toccata conceived along spacious lines; the main subject is a three-part invention in the vein of Bach. The slow movement is introduced by the piano with an expressive idea, which is then repeated by the orchestra before receiving elaboration. In the final Allegro, the first subject consists of the final cadence of the preceding movement, but in fast time; the theme is treated fugally, and then is allowed to assume various shapes and forms. This section carries reminiscences of musical ideas heard in the opening and slow movements.

1927 OEDIPUS REX, opera-oratorio in two acts, with text by Jean Cocteau translated into Latin by J. Danielou, based on Sophocles. First performance: Paris, May 30, 1927 (concert version); Berlin, February 25, 1928 (staged version).

In planning a major dramatic work based on the majestic tragedy of Sophocles, Stravinsky called upon Jean Cocteau to prepare a new text. Stravinsky felt that the language of the new text should be a dead one (Latin), in order to give the subject a kind of remoteness, or, as he put it, "a statuesque plasticity and a stately bearing entirely in keeping with the majesty of the ancient legend." When Cocteau completed his play in French, it was turned over to Jean Danielou for translation into Latin.

In order to make the play more comprehensible to the audience, Stravinsky adopted the device of having a narrator (in evening dress) appear on the stage at intermittent perods to sum up the action that is to follow.

It was as an oratorio that *Oedipus* was first performed. Stravinsky planned it as a surprise for Diaghilev, commemorating the twentieth anniversary of the impresario's activities. Since a dramatic presentation demanded Diaghilev's collaboration—and since funds for such a presentation were lacking anyway—Stravinsky decided to introduce it in concert form. Stravinsky himself conducted the première performance in Paris. That evening also included stage presentations of several ballets made famous by Diaghilev. *Oedipus* was not well received. Heard between two colorful ballets, it appeared dull and pretentious.

Subsequent performances—both in oratorio and operatic versions—have since proved that this music, for all its austerity, has an eloquence all its own. The first staged version was conducted by Otto Klemperer in 1928. It was outstandingly successful. No less successful have been the many concert performances this work has received, many of them under the composer's direction. The American première, presented in oratorio style, took place in Boston on February 24, 1928. A staged version followed in Philadelphia on April 10 and in New York on April 21, in 1931, Leopold Stokowski conducting.

Like the masterworks he had written a decade earlier, *Oedipus* is profoundly influenced by Russian music. The "Gloria" with which the first act closes, and which reappears at the opening of Act II, stems directly from the choral music of the Russian Orthodox Church. Eric Walter White further notes that the choral salutation to Creon "might be a literal quotation from Mussorgsky's *Boris*," while the air of the messenger has the "modal rusticity of a Russian folk song."

In reviewing a staged performance of *Oedipus Rex* by the New York City Opera on September 24, 1959, Howard Taubman said in *The New York Times*: "In *Oedipus Rex,* Stravinsky arrived at a monumental style, hewed, as it were, out of granite. This is neo-classicism raised on the shoulders of church traditions. It is tragedy and horror stated without agitated heroics, and its compassion assumes a timelessness that is right for this story based on Sophocles."

1928 APOLLON MUSAGÈTE (APOLLO, LEADER OF THE MUSES), classic ballet in two scenes, with scenario by Igor Stravinsky and choreography by Adolph Bolm. First performance: Washington, D.C., April 29, 1928.

Unlike so many other Stravinsky ballets, *Apollon Musagète* has virtually no plot. It is, says Eric Walter White, "one of the very few modern ballets of which it can be said that its music and choreography are completely classical both in conception and in execution." The ballet consist of two tableaux. The first describes the birth of Apollo, while the second tells of his association with the Muses Calliope, Polyhymnia and Terpsichore. "After a series of dances," the composer explains, "treated in the traditional style of ballet (Pas d'Action, Pas de Deux, Coda), Apollo, in the apotheosis, leads the Muses, with Terpsichore at their head, to Parnassus, where they are to live afterwards."

Elizabeth Sprague Coolidge commissioned Stravinsky to write this ballet for a modern music festival at the Library of Congress in Washington, where it received its première. This work was produced in Paris, with George Balanchine's choreography, in a Ballet Russe presentation on June 12, 1928.

In describing the style he assumed for the music of this classic ballet, Stravinsky has said: "It seemed to me that diatonic composition was the most appropriate for this purpose, and the austerity of its style determined what my instrumental ensemble must be. I at once set aside the ordinary orchestra because of its heterogenity, with its group of strings, woodwind, brass, and percussion instruments. I also discarded ensembles of wind and brass . . . and I chose strings."

1928 LE BAISER DE LA FÉE (THE FAIRY'S KISS), ballet-allegory in four scenes, with scenario by Igor Stravinsky, choreography by Bronislava Nijinska, and music based on melodies by Tchaikovsky. First performance: Paris, November 27, 1928.

DIVERTIMENTO (SUITE SYMPHONIQUE) FROM THE BALLET, LE BAISER DE LA FÉE. I. Sinfonia. II. Swiss Dances; Waltz. III. Scherzo. IV. Pas de deux.

When the dancer, Ida Rubinstein, commissioned Stravinsky to prepare for her a ballet score, the composer decided to do homage to one of his favorite composers, Tchaikovsky, by using Tchaikovsky's melodies. The title page of the published score of *Le Baiser* reveals that this music was "inspired by the Muse of Tchaikovsky." For his subject, Stravinsky went to Hans Christian Andersen, the story of the Ice Maiden, which the composer summarized as follows: "A fairy imprints her magic kiss on a child at birth and parts it from his mother. Twenty years later, when the youth has attained the very zenith of his good fortune, she repeats the fatal kiss and carries him off to live in supreme happiness with her ever afterwards." Stravinsky then adds: "This subject seems to me to be particularly appropriate as an allegory, the muse having similarly branded Tchaikovsky with her fatal kiss, and the magic imprint has made itself felt in all the musical creations of this great artist."

The principal motive used by Stravinsky is the Tchaikovsky song, "Lullaby in a Storm," from his *Sixteen Children's Songs,* op. 54. The ballet begins and ends with it. Among other Tchaikovsky melodies used prominently are the popular *Humoresque,* for piano, op. 10, no. 2; *Nata Waltz* from *Six Pieces for Piano,* op. 51, no. 4; and *The Peasant Plays Harmonica* from *Children's Album,* for piano, op. 54, no. 10. "Stravinsky," explains Herbert Fleischer, "takes as the basis of the composition the melodies and characterisic turns of expression of Tchaikovsky. He removed the often too sweet and rather feminine meltingness of Tchaikovsky's melos. He recasts the tones of the master, so reverenced by him, in his own rigid tonal language. Yet the lyrical tenderness of Tchaikovsky's melos is not lost."

Stravinsky was not happy with Ida Rubinstein's choreographic conception, and it was not often produced following the world première. More appealing to the composer is the choreography of George Balanchine, which the American Ballet presented in New York on April 27, 1937.

Salient sections of the ballet score were assembled by the composer into a four-movement symphonic Divertimento. The first, Sinfonia (Andante; Allegro; Vivace) describes a woman carrying her child through a storm. Fairy spirits abscond the child, and the Fairy plants a kiss on his forehead. The child is then abandoned, but is soon taken off by peasants. In the second movement (Tempo giusto; Poco pìu lento), peasants are dancing at the village fair. Among them are a young man and his betrothed. The girl departs, leaving her beloved alone. In the third section (Moderato; Allegro grazioso), the young man is conducted by the Fairy to a mill where he finds his betrothed playing games. The young man and his betrothed are then seen in the concluding fourth section (Adagio; Allegretto grazioso; Presto), where the betrothed puts on her wedding veil.

1929 CAPRICCIO, for piano and orchestra. I. Presto. II. Andante rapsodico. III. Allegro capriccioso ma tempo giusto.

Stravinsky's ironic vein is evident in this work, introduced in Paris on December 6, 1929, with Ernest Ansermet conducting the Orchestre Symphonique, and the composer playing the piano part.

"I had in mind the definition of a capriccio given by Praetorius," explained the composer. "He regarded it as meaning a fantasia—a free form made up of fugato instrumental passages. This form enabled me to develop my music by the juxtaposition of episodes of various kinds which follow one another, and by their nature give the piece that aspect of caprice from which it takes its name."

The first and last movements project a light, ironic mood. The middle part, however, is rhapsodic music in a Baroque style.

A strong, rhythmic idea is given by the piano and the tympani in the first movement following an equally vigorous introduction. Other succinct, and at times dance-like, statements follow. The vigorous introduction returns to end the movement. The second movement opens with an exchange between piano and woodwinds. A cadenza for piano and a solo for flute serve as a transition to the finale, which derives its vitality from a number of sprightly dance themes, some of them with a jazz personality.

1930 SYMPHONIE DES PSAUMES (SYMPHONY OF PSALMS), for chorus and orchestra. I. Prelude. II. Double Fugue. III. Allegro symphonique.

An intensely religious man, Stravinsky has here produced one of his most reverent compositions. It was written "to the glory of God," and is permeated from the first bar to the last with profound spirituality, though on occasion the beauty is austere and remote. It has the primitivism of early Christian art, and it has reminded Paul Rosenfeld of "mosaics in a Byzantine church."

Stravinsky produced this work to commemorate the fiftieth anniversary of the Boston Symphony Orchestra. It was, however, not introduced in Boston but in Brussels, on December 13, 1930, Ernest Ansermet conducting the Brussels Philharmonic. One week later, on December 19, Serge Koussevitzky conducted it in Boston.

For his text (sung in Latin), the composer went to the Vulgate: verses 13 and 14 of Psalm XXXVIII (Part I); verses 2, 3 and 4 of Psalm XXXIX (Part II); and the entire Psalm CL (Part III).

The composer has written: "The juxtaposition of the three psalms is not fortuitous. The prayer of the sinner for divine pity (prelude), the recognition of grace received (double fugue), and the hymn of praise and glory are the basis of an evolutionary plan. The music which embodies these texts follows its development according to its own symphonic law. The order of the three movements presupposes a periodic scheme and in this sense realizes a 'symphony.' For a periodic scheme is what distinguishes a 'symphony' from a collection of pieces with no scheme but one of succession, as in a suite."

Stravinsky's orchestration is unusual in that he dispenses with clarinets, violins and violas. His musical style leans heavily on polyphonic writing, equal prominence being given to orchestra and chorus. The three movements are played without a break.

The symphony opens, as Joseph Machlis has explained, with a "prelude-like section in which flowing arabesques are traced by oboe and bassoon . . . punctuated by an urgent E minor chord." The altos are then heard in a "chant-like theme consisting of two adjacent notes—the interval of a minor second (semitone) that has structural significance throughout." In the second-movement double fugue, for four voices, the oboe is heard in the main subject, which is characterized by wide leaps in the melody. The third movement opens with a sober Alleluia, which is followed by an Allegro "with Stravinskyan rhythms that project the spirit of the Psalm in dance-like measures," Machlis explains. A brief recollection of the Alleluia music closes the composition.

1931 CONCERTO IN D MAJOR FOR VIOLIN AND ORCHESTRA. I. Toccata. II. Aria. III. Aria. IV. Capriccio.

Stravinsky wrote his violin concerto for Samuel Dushkin, who introduced it in Berlin on October 23, 1931, with the Berlin Radio Orchestra, the composer conducting.

The work is integrated by an introductory series of chords in the solo violin which (slightly varied) preface each of the four movements. The first section has three principal themes, which are subjected to considerable, often complicated, development. Two arias follow, the first being a spacious melody first heard in the solo violin, while the second is more ornamental. The closing section consists of two main themes and has much virtuoso writing for the solo instrument.

In 1940–41, the music of this concerto was adapted by the De Basil Ballet Company for a ballet entitled *Balustrade,* choreography by Balanchine.

1934 PERSÉPHONE, melodrama in three parts, with text by André Gide. I. Abduction of Persephone. II. Persephone in the Underworld. III. The Rebirth of Persephone. First performance: Paris, April 30, 1934.

In 1933, the dancer Ida Rubinstein commissioned Stravinsky to set to music a poem which André Gide had written, a poem based on the Homeric *Hymn to Demeter*. In three parts, this poem describes Persephone's descent to the lower regions, following her breathing of the narcissus aroma, which gives her a vision of that world of which she is to be queen. She grows bored with that world and yields to nostalgia for the life she has deserted. At last she succumbs and returns to the upper regions.

This poem became the basis of a "melodrama," a veritable mélange of the arts, calling for music, singing, dancing, miming and recitation. The score utilizes a speaking voice, tenor, chorus and orchestra. The role of Persephone is mimed, spoken and danced. Eumolpus (a tenor) serves as narrator, while the chorus is used to represent the Nymphs, Shades and Danaïdes. A chorus of children is used in the third part. The full orchestra is used only twice, to accompany the appearance of Mercury in the second part, and in the introduction to Part Three.

The world première was given at the Paris Opéra by Ida Rubinstein. Kurt Jooss prepared the choreography and Stravinsky conducted.

Hugh Ross noted that the most commendable feature of the score is its "undisguised . . . melodies, such as those of the women's choral dance (Part I), the oboe solo at the beginning of Part II, and the seductive Scherzando of Eumolpus, the spring chorus, and the madrigal in Part III." Classical repose is another distinguishing trait of this music, as, for example, in the two opening choruses and in the chorus hailing Persephone's return to the upper world.

1936 JEU DE CARTES (CARD PARTY), ballet "in three deals," with scenario by Igor Stravinsky and M. Malaieff, and choreography by George Balanchine. First performance: New York, April 27, 1937.

In 1936, Stravinsky was commissioned by the American Ballet to write a new work for its repertory. That organization introduced *Card Party,* the composer conducting.

The composer has thus summarized the action: "The characters in this ballet are the cards in a game of poker, disputed between several players on the green baize table of a gaming house. At each deal the situation is complicated by the endless guile of the perfidious Joker, who believes himself invincible because of his ability to become any desired card.

"During the first deal one of the players is beaten, but the other two remain with even 'straights,' although one of them holds the Joker.

"In the second deal, the hand which holds the Joker is victorious, thanks to four Aces, who easily beat four Queens.

"Now comes the third deal. The action grows more and more acute. This time it is a struggle between three 'flushes.' Although at first victorious over one adversary, the Joker, strutting at the head of a sequence of Spades, is beaten by a 'royal flush' in Hearts. This puts an end to his malice and knavery."

The three "deals" of the ballet are divided as follows:

I. Introduction; Pas d'Action; Dance of the Joker; Little Waltz.

II. Introduction; March; Variation of the Four Queens; Variation of the Jack of Hearts and Coda, March, and Ensemble.

III. Introduction; Waltz-Minuet; Presto (Combat between Spades and Hearts); Final Dance (Triumph of the Hearts).

George Balanchine has explained that the ballet tried to show that "the highest cards—the kings, queens and jacks—in reality have nothing on the other cards. They are big people, but they can easily be beaten by the small cards. Seemingly powerful figures, they are actually silhouettes."

The ballet score is sometimes heard as a concert piece, in which form it is performed without interruption and without alteration.

1938 CONCERTO IN E-FLAT MAJOR ("DUMBARTON OAKS"), for fourteen instruments. I. Tempo guisto. II. Allegretto. III. Con moto.

Stravinsky wrote this composition for a Washington, D.C., music lover and named it after his patron's estate, which later achieved publicity as the scene of a celebrated international monetary conference. The style is contrapuntal in the vein of Bach's Brandenburg Concertos. The three movements are performed without interruption. Fugal writing predominates throughout, and becomes the climactic peak of the first and third movements. A graceful and gentle melodic middle movement, classic in its objective beauty, provides a serene interlude for two robust movements.

The Concerto received its first performance in Washington, D.C., on May 8, 1938.

1940 SYMPHONY IN C MAJOR. I. Moderato alla breve. II. Larghetto concertante. III. Allegretto. IV. Adagio; Tempo giusto.

There was a thirty-five year hiatus between Stravinsky's First Symphony in E-flat major and his Second, in C major. During these years Stravinsky passed from being an apprentice studying under Rimsky-Korsakov to being a composer of world significance in full mastery of his technique. Though the style of the Second Symphony is in Stravinsky's neo-classic vein, the form follows the First Symphony in its adherence to classical structures. The first movement is in strict sonata form, with two clearly stated themes, the first presented by oboe with string accompaniment, and the second, in oboe and bassoon repeated by strings. They are developed in classical style and then recapitulated. A beautiful song, written simply, forms the second movement: it is described by its composer as an "aria." It opens with a solo for oboe to a contrapuntal idea in violins. Two classical dances—the minuet and the passepied—form the third movement, which ends in a fugue, subject stated by trombone with horns offering the reply. The closing section begins with an impressive Adagio (bassoons, horns and other brasses) and continues with a robust section faintly suggesting the concerto-grosso style.

This symphony was written, as the composer has said, "to the glory of God, "and was dedicated to the Chicago Symphony to commemorate its fiftieth anniversary. That orchestra, under the composer's direction, introduced it in Chicago on November 7, 1940.

1943 ODE, triptych for orchestra. I. Eulogy. II. Eclogue. III. Epitaph.

Stravinsky was commissioned to write an orchestral work by the Koussevitzky Music Foundation. He decided on an ode—a eulogy to the late Natalie Koussevitzky, in appreciation of her "spiritual contribution to the art of the eminent conductor, her husband, Dr. Koussevitzky."

A chant in three parts, the ode opens with a song in sustained melody, treated fugally. A lively piece follows suggesting outdoor music; this was intended by the composer to be a tribute to Tanglewood, home of the Berkshire Music Festival, where Koussevitzky officiated each summer. A serene theme introduces the final section which is melancholy throughout.

The *Ode* was introduced by the Boston Symphony Orchestra under Serge Koussevitzky on October 8, 1943.

1945 SYMPHONY IN THREE MOVEMENTS. I. (Tempo indication not given.) II. Andante. III. Con moto.

Five years after he wrote his Second Symphony in C major, Stravinsky produced a third work in the symphonic form. A radical change in the composer's approach to the symphonic style is here evident. The *Symphony in Three Movements* is completely independent of formal symphonic structure. There is no sonata form, no development, no recapitulation. The music is conceived, as Ingolf Dahl wrote in his definitive analysis,"as the succession of clearly outlined locks, or planes, which are unified and related through the continuity of a steadily and logically evolving organic force."

The first movement is the most ambitious of the three. Though it has no marking other than metronomic, it is essentially an Allegro. It has been described as a toccata and is in three sections, the first and third being harmonic and the middle, polyphonic. Ingolf Dahl points out that this movement is constructed from thematic germs, identifying them as "the interval of the minor third (with its inversion, the major sixth), and an ascending scale fragment which forms the background to the piano solo of the middle part." A kind of "delicate intermezzo," with the concertino formed by harp and flutes, is heard in the second movement, which has a chamber-music texture. This movement dispenses with trumpets, trombones and percussion. A majestic theme in full orchestra prefaces the closing movement, which, like the first, is in three sections—though here the sections may be regarded as variations on the original theme. A fugue, unusual for its rhythmic and intervallic construction, leads to a coda-like finale, its subject stated by trombone and piano.

The symphony is dedicated to the New York Philharmonic Orchestra, which introduced it in New York on January 24, 1946, the composer conducting.

1946 CONCERTO IN D MAJOR FOR STRINGS ("BASLER CONCERTO"). I. Vivace. II. Arioso. III. Rondo.

The twentieth anniversary of the Basle Chamber Orchestra led its conductor, Paul Sacher, to commission Stravinsky to write a new work to commemorate the event. The result was a chamber concerto modeled after the classical concerto grosso. It was introduced in Basle, Switzerland, on January 21, 1947.

With a comparatively simple tone language, and with transparent instrumentation, the concerto utilizes the concerto grosso style by setting solo instruments alternately with and against the rest of the orchestra. One of the fine moments in the work is in the lyrical middle movement, as the sustained melody is first heard dolce espressivo in the first violins and cellos. A brisk Vivace opens the concerto, and the closing movement is marked by striking instrumental effects.

1948 MASS, for mixed chorus, boys' chorus and ten wind instruments.

Stravinsky's first major liturgical work was introduced in Milan on October 27, 1948 under the direction of Ernest Ansermet.

Stylistically, the music reaches back to the early contrapuntal Flemish school. But though the modal writing suggests the distant past, the dissonant counterpoint is of our times. This is one of Stravinsky's economically realized works. The texture is transparent; the writing, pure and refined; the mood, almost continually subdued. Effective use is made of the wind instruments, the work being scored solely for ten brasses and two woodwinds. These instruments are frequently heard alternating with the a cappella choruses. Solo voices are employed only in the Gloria and Sanctus sections.

When the Mass was introduced in the United States, on February 26, 1949 (it was heard twice on the same program, before and after the intermission), there was considerable difference of opinion among the critics regarding the success of the composer in producing religious music. Noel Straus wrote in *The New York Times* that, for the most part, the Mass "is singularly bereft of either spirituality or human feeling. . . . Nowhere, except in the few measures of the Hosanna, was there anything to imply that the music was intended for actual use in a religious service. Nothing could be further removed from the spiritual than the trivial march employed in the Christe Eleison."

On the other hand, Arthur V. Berger, critic of the New York *Herald Tribune*, found the work to be of "uncommon purity and remarkably unforced religious sentiment. . . . This Mass, as a whole, is a work of beauty and has the simple directness of truth."

1948 ORPHEUS, ballet in three scenes, with choreography by George Balanchine. First performance: New York, April 28, 1948.

In his ballet, Stravinsky follows closely the classic and well-known story of Orpheus and Eurydice, treating it with simplicity and directness.

The published score contains the following summation of the ballet:

"Scene I: Orpheus weeps for Eurydice. He stands motionless with his back to the audience. Friends pass, bringing presents and offering sympathy. Air de Danse. Dance of the Angel of Death. Interlude (the Angel and Orpheus reappear in the gloom of Tartarus).

"Scene II. Pas des Furies (their agitation and their threats). Air de Danse (Orpheus). Interlude (the tormented souls in Tartarus stretch out their fettered arms towards Orpheus and implore him to continue his song of consolation). Air de Danse (Orpheus). Pas d'Action (Hades, moved by the song of Orpheus, grows calm. The Furies surround him, bind his eyes, and return Eurydice to him.) Pas de Deux (Orpheus and Eurydice before the veiled curtain). Interlude. Pas d'Action (the Bacchantes attack Orpheus, seize him, and tear him to pieces).

"Scene III: Apotheosis of Orpheus. Apollo appears. He wrests the lyre from Orpheus and raises his song heavenwards."

The score is almost continually in a subdued mood, written with simplicity, avoiding ornamentation of all kinds, and achieving a deeply affecting eloquence through spare writing. A high degree of expressiveness and an almost gentle melancholy bring to this music a human quality not often encountered in the neo-classic Stravinsky—these, and a truly classic repose. However, though it is generally quiet and serene, *Orpheus* has (as Alfred Frankenstein points out) "its share of those prickly, dynamic dances, as if the body of the music rested on a bed of fine steel springs, that are a Stravinsky specialty. . . . *Orpheus* indicates that Stravinsky has finally suffused his classic ideal with a rich and sensitive humanism."

When *Orpheus* was introduced by the Ballet Society in New York, the principal dancers were Nicholas Magallanes and Maria Tallchief. Scenery and costumes were designed by Noguchi. Stravinsky conducted the première performance.

When performed in the symphony hall, the score of *Orpheus* is utilized without any changes whatsoever. The first concert performance took place in Boston on February 11, 1949, Stravinsky conducting.

1950 THE RAKE'S PROGRESS, opera in three acts and epilogue, with text by W. H. Auden and Chester Kallman based on engravings by Hogarth. First performance: Venice, September 11, 1951.

In 1922, Stravinsky had written the comic one-act opera *Mavra*. It took him twenty-nine years not only to return to the operatic stage but also to write his first full-length opera. Where *Mavra* looked back to opera buffa, *The Rake's Progress* reverted to the classic opera of Handel, Gluck and Mozart. Stravinsky himself revealed that while writing *The Rake's Progress* he continually listened to recordings of Mozart's music, and especially to *Così fan tutte*. The structure of *The Rake's Progress* follows the classic patterns of Mozart by utilizing arias, recitatives, ensemble numbers, choruses, and extended finales for grand ensembles. The style skilfully combines farce and wit with passion and even tragedy. As Howard Taubman noted in *The New York Times*: "He has used for the most part the gallant, elegant style of the eighteenth century." In so doing, he has "composed music that has gaiety, tenderness, simplicity and brilliance, incisive wit and honest feeling."

Stravinsky here uses a chamber orchestra (no trombones), for which he writes with a transparent texture. In line with his reversion to eighteenth-century methods, he calls upon a harpsichord to accompny the recitatives. But in spite of the classical structure, and the Mozartean or Gluckian suggestions, in spite of other eighteenth-century procedures, Stravinsky succeeds in achieving a modern point of view. Ronald Eyer wrote in *Musical America* that Stravinsky's "harmony, though by no means atonal, is mostly free and astringent; the rhythm also is free and in constant mutation among all the varieties of duple and triple meters." And though the opera abounds with refreshing lyricism, the melody is often "wide-striking and craggy."

The libretto was inspired by eight drawings of Hogarth. The plot is set in the eighteenth century, and revolves around Tom Rakewell. He abandons his sweetheart, Anne Trulove, squanders a recently inherited fortune on lust and carousing, and consigns his soul to Shadow (Mephisto). A last attempt to redeem himself makes him assume the futile role of a benefactor. He must now live up to his bargain and deliver his soul to Shadow, but he succeeds in convincing the devil to engage in a game of chance for it. Tom wins the gamble, but he loses his mind, and must wander in Bedlam. In the end, just before his death, his sweetheart Anne returns to him, and the lovers are finally reunited. In the epilogue, the four main characters appear in front of the curtain to underline the moral of the opera by saying: "For idle hands and hearts and minds the devil finds work to do."

The première of *The Rake's Progress* was an event of international significance. It took place in Venice, as part of the Venice Festival, which was reputed to have paid $20,000 for the performance rights. Tickets were at a premium, as music lovers from all parts of Europe as well as America converged on Venice to attend the première. It was an immense success. Before a year had passed, the opera was performed in Paris, Copenhagen, Antwerp, Brussels, Cologne, Düsseldorf, Frankfurt, Hamburg, Milan, Monte Carlo, Munich, Stuttagart and Zurich. The American première took place at the Metropolitan Opera House on February 14, 1953.

1952 CANTATA ON FOUR POEMS BY ANONYMOUS ENGLISH POETS, for soprano, tenor, female chorus and instrumental quintet. I. A Lyke-Wake Dirge—Versus I (Prelude). II. Ricercar I. III. A Lyke-Wake Dirge—Versus II (First Interlude). IV. Ricercar II. V. A Lyke-Wake Dirge—Versus III (Second Interlude). VI. Westron Wind. VII. A Lyke -Wake Dirge—Versus IV (Postlude).

The opera, *The Rake's Progress,* was Stravinsky's last composition in a neoclassic style. He now became interested in abstraction. In the *Cantata,* he began for the first time to think in terms of the twelve-tone technique. However, this technique is still used tentatively and intermittently.

The cantata is a setting of four anonymous fifteenth-and sixteenth-century English lyrics. Three of the poems are semi-sacred, while the fourth ("Westron Wind") is a love lyric. The instrumental accompaniment comprises two flutes, two oboes (a second interchangeable with English horn) and cello. Working successfully with the English language in *The Rake's Progress* had encouraged Stravinsky to provide settings to English words once again. The four poems were selected because, as he has said, they "attracted me not only for their great beauty and their compelling syllabification, but for their construction which suggested musical construction."

The work begins with a brief instrumental preface in the Phrygian mode. This instrumental prelude is heard again before the third, fifth and seventh stanzas. A choral episode, mainly modal, follows. In the first ricercar, a poem entitled "The Maidens Came," in canonic style. is set for soprano and instrumental quintet. The second ricercar is a setting of "Tomorrow Will be Dancing Day" for tenor, cello, flutes and oboes in pairs. "Westron Wind" is in a simple song form, for tenor and soprano without accompaniment. The composition ends in an instrumental quintet in which the English horn substitutes for the second oboe.

The Cantata was heard first in Los Angeles on November 11, 1952.

1953 SEPTET, for violin, viola, cello, clarinet, horn, bassoon and piano (or harpsichord). I. Allegro. II. Passacaglia. III. Gigue.

In the Septet, Stravinsky continues to explore the possibilities of the twelve-tone technique as a basis for his compositions, but this work is not as yet in a strict twelve-tone idiom. The Septet was introduced in Washington, D.C., on January 24, 1954. It opens with an expansive theme with an octave range which is developed by imitation. A contrasting twelve-measure episode, followed by a light and graceful section, precedes a fugato. The theme of the passacaglia is a transposition of the first five notes of the first movement's initial subject. It extends for eight measures and is succeeded by eight variations. A four-section gigue serves as the finale. Here each section is a fugue based on the subject of the passacaglia theme of the preceding movement.

1956 CANTICUM SACRUM AD HONOREM SANCTI MARCI NOMINIS (SACRED CANTATA IN HONOR OF ST. MARK, PATRON SAINT OF VENICE), for tenor, baritone, chorus and orchestra. I. Dedication: Euntes in Mundum. II. Surge aquilo. III. Ad tres Virtutes Hortatioes. IV. Brevis Motus Cantilenae. V. Autum Profecti.

Stravinsky was commissioned to write his sacred cantata by the Venice Festival. The world première was held in St. Mark's Basilica (by special permission of the Cardinal of Venice) on September 11, 1956, the composer conducting. At the composer's request, this seventeen-minute work was played twice at this performance, before and after intermission.

This is Stravinsky's first work of which parts are in a strict serial technique, namely the three middle sections. This is an economically conceived composition, transparent in instrumentation, spare in material. The orchestra here used is unorthodox in that it comprises flute, three oboes, three bassoons, four trumpets, four trombones, harp, violas and basses. The text is in Latin, chosen by the composer from the Vulgate.

The *Canticum* is in five sections, beginning with a dedication to "the city of Venice, in praise of the patron Saint, the Blessed Mark Apostle," for tenor and baritone. Three mystical sections follow: an aria for tenor with instrumental accompaniment; a central part for chorus and orchestra; and a solo for baritone concluding with a four-part canon for unaccompanied chorus. The composition ends with a slow Amen section.

"The work," as Christina Thoresby has explained in *Musical America,* "continually exploits different combinations of solo sonorities—the instruments and voices almost never being scored in tutti. . . . The dedication, sung in duet by tenor and baritone with two trombones, as well as the monumental opening and closing choirs, are diatonic. The first choir, which opens in typical Stravinskian fashion, is reflected in retrograde by the final one, the work ending on a low note from the bassoon. These two solid bastions, invoking the command to teach the Gospel, flank the three more mystical inner sections, written in the twelve-tone technique, which are concerned with spiritual faith. . . . The beautiful tenor solo, "Surge Aquillo' . . . and the introspective baritone solo . . . ending in 'Credo, Credo' . . . surround the central section for choirs and instruments—itself subdivided into three parts extolling Charity, Hope and Faith. Here are short organ interludes in passacaglia form . . . which make effective, beautiful points of repose in the intricate choral counterpoint."

1957 AGON, classic ballet in one act for twelve dancers, with choreography by George Balanchine. First performance: Los Angeles, June 17, 1957.

Agon is a classic ballet on the subject of a Greek dance competition, the word "Agon" being a Greek term for contest or struggle. The ballet, however, is devoid of any further plot or program, and is presented without decor or costumes. The music has also been reduced to barest melodic and harmonic essentials. It is based upon classic dance melodies uncovered by the composer in a seventeenth-century French dance manual, including the Sarabande, Galliard and Bransle. The idiom is in the "serial technique." The ballet was commissioned by the Rockefeller Foundation. When the ballet suite is given at symphony concerts, the entire eighteen-minute ballet score is used.

"*Agon,*" said Mildred Norton in the *Saturday Review,* "possesses the crystalline texture and rhythmic élan that vivify Stravinsky's writing for the theatre and in which a lively instrumentation gives the most calculated device the effect of sudden and sardonic caprice. The orchestration, in fact, appears to recapitulate all the more telling expressive sallies of the composer's later music. There is the persistently nervous staccati, and unremitting rhythmic tension, the quick febrile exchange of instrumental repartee which we have come to know." Miss Norton then explains that what individualizes this music is "its novel and exuberant use of timbres. Such interludes as harp staccati against the shimmer of mandolin, of flute configurations over castanets, or solo violin above trombones as well as silken harmonics in the upper strings are provocative highlights in a tonal palette of characteristic cleanliness and candor."

1958 THRENI (TEARS), LAMENTATIONS OF THE PROPHET JEREMIAH, for solo voices, chorus and orchestra.

Having used the serial technique in three of the five sections of *Canticum Sacrum,* Stravinsky proceeded inevitably towards the building of an entire composition serially on a single twelve-tone row. He did so in *Threni,* whose text was selected by the composer from the Vulgate (Lamentations of Jeremiah). This composition was commissioned by the Hamburg Radio. The world première was held at the International Festival of Contemporary Music in Venice on September 23, 1958; the performance over the Hamburg radio followed on October 13.

Eric Salzman points out that this work is "made up of short and distinct phrases (which, however, also fall into larger groupings), and the austere, ritualistic effect of the work is greatly the result of this pattern." Salzman also notes that we do not get here any "grandiose orchestral or choral sounds" since "only a few instruments out of the large orchestra are employed at any one time." The solo sections, are essentially contrapuntal, with one of them made up exclusively of unaccompanied canons "that are interpreted only by the chorus which introduces each line with the inevitable Hebrew letter."

When *Threni* was given its American première on January 4, 1959, Howard Taubman found that the second section is "a remarkable example of the composer's gift for saying much with few notes and voices." Here is how Taubman described this part: "It begins with a monody by the basso profundo. As additional soloists join, there are successive canons for two, three and four voices. Occasionally, the chorus interpolates a brief phrase. Otherwise, there is no accompaniment. The entire passage builds and sustains an unforgettable mood."

1961 A SERMON, A NARRATIVE, AND A PRAYER, for tenor, contralto, narrator, chorus and orchestra.

Paul Sacher, conductor of the Basle Chamber Orchestra, commissioned Stravinsky to write a new instrumental composition, but Stravinsky countered with the suggestion that he produce, instead, a religious work for voices and orchestra. *A Sermon, a Narrative, and a Prayer* was introduced in Basle under Sacher's direction on February 23, 1962. Described as a "meditation of the New Testament virtue of hope" and as a "personal expression of faith" this composition is divided, as the title suggests, into three sections. The first is based on St. Paul's sermon on the nature of hope; the second sets the account in the Acts of Stephen's martrydom, pointing up the virtue of action; and the final is a setting of Thomas Dekker's "Foure Birds of Noah's Ark."

Reporting to *The New York Times,* Peter Heyworth found the first section "remarkable for its intensity of line (the melodic writing throughout is as compelling as it is individual)." He added that the "tense contrapuntal working to which this is subjected reflected the involved implications that underlie the simplicity of St. Paul's language."

The *Narrative,* to Heyworth, "packs an immense variety of action and incident into an exceptionally brief space." Here the music "contains much that is strikingly dramatic, such as the momentary pause of violence that marks the fury of the Elders and Scribes who are trying Stephen."

The third movement "comes as a cry for mercy and grace." It conveys "a sense of rapt inner communion." Nevertheless, Heyworth points out that throughout "Stravinsky remains Stravinsky. There is no trace of loose emotionalism; the intensity of feeling is channeled in a rigorously sustained canonic form, and in its gentleness and strength this is one of the most impressive examples of twentieth-century religious art."

1963 ABRAHAM AND ISAAC, sacred ballad for baritone and chamber orchestra.

This ballad was commissioned by Israel for its fourth annual festival. It was introduced in Jerusalem on August 23, 1964. Robert Craft conducted, and Ephraim Biran was the baritone solo. Stravinsky here uses a Hebrew text drawn from chapters 22 and 23 of the *Genesis.* This tells the story of how God tested Abraham by asking him to sacrifice his son Isaac. It is interesting to remark that the world première of this composition took place in the very shadow of Mount Moriah, the place in the Bible where God's angel came to stop Abraham from sacrificing his only son. Stravinsky's style is in strict serial technique, with economy of forces, concentration of speech and brevity as the main attributes. The orchestra— comprising some strings, woodwinds and brass, but no percussion—is used sparingly as background for the narration.

1965 VARIATIONS, for orchestra.

VARIATIONS, ballet in three parts, with choreography by George Balanchine. First performance: New York, March 31, 1966.

Stravinsky wrote his orchestral variations in memory of the famous writer, Aldous Huxley; its world première took place on April 17, 1965, in Chicago, with Jean Martinon conducting the Chicago Symphony. Stravinsky suggested that this composition be played twice (which was done at the première), explaining that "one might think of these constructions as musical mobiles in that the patterns with them will seem to change perspective with repeated hearings." Clive Barnes explains that the score is based on "a series of notes making up the melody and grouped in two six-note formations. The halves of this melody are more or less symmetrical, permitting the composer to turn the sections upside down and inside out and by rhythmic changes and varying sonorities to create a series of continuous variations."

In developing a ballet for this music, George Balanchine created three sections, each of which is choreographed for the complete score, with the result that the score is heard three times. The first part is choreographed for twelve girls; the second, for six men; and the third, for a single girl.

1966 REQUIEM CANTICLES, for vocal quartet, chorus and orchestra.

Requiem Canticles was commissioned by Princeton University (in memory of Helen Buchanan Seeger). Robert Craft conducted the world première in

Princeton on October 8, 1966. Three sections (Prelude, Interlude and Postlude) are purely instrumental; they represent the first, fifth and last movements. The rest of the movements provide settings of texts taken from the Latin Requiem. The second, third and sixth movements ("Exaudi," "Dies irae" and "Rex tremendae") are scored for chorus and orchestra; the fourth movement ("Tuba mirum") is for bass solo accompanied by two trumpets; the seventh movement ("Lacrimosa") is for contralto and orchestra; and the eighth (Libera me") is for solo vocal quartet, with the chorus interpolating spoken parts.

In reviewing this composition for *High Fidelity,* Bernard Jacobson wrote: "It is . . . more expansive in scale than anything Stravinsky has written for a few years. . . . The delicacy of Stravinsky's ear and the fertility of his imagination have worked their customary wonders. In the instrumental movements and in the more lyrical vocal passages, the sap of musical invention still runs more copiously than in many composers a third his age."

KAROL SZYMANOWSKI 1882–1937

Szymanowski was the foremost composer of our time in Poland; Hugo Riemann goes so far as to consider him the greatest creative figure to emerge in Poland since Chopin.

Szymanowski found himself artistically when he began drawing his inspiration and material from native sources, producing a series of national works in which his land and its people are mirrored. But Szymanowski came to nationalism by a circuitous route. As a visitor to Berlin, in 1905, he was greatly affected by Germanic post-Romanticism; his works from op. 1 to op. 10 are imitative of Bruckner, Mahler, Reger, and, most of all, Richard Strauss. He then freed himself of Germanic influences to produce music that was subjective, feverish in moods, filled with dramatic or tragic pronouncements (opp. 11–23), the influence here being mainly that of Scriabin. For a brief period, he turned to mysticism and oriental philosophy, an interest that was responsible for the writing of his *Love Songs of Hafiz,* op. 24 (1914), the one-act opera *Hagith,* op. 25 (1922), and the symphony, *The Song of the Night,* op. 27 (1916). After that, came an interest in the post-impressionism of Ravel, discernible in such works for the piano or for the violin as *Métopes,* op. 29 (1915), *Mythes,* op. 30 (1915), and *Masques,* op. 34 (1917).

Obviously he was groping for a personal idiom. He found it soon after a visit to Zakopane, in the Tatras mountains of Poland. He listened to the songs and dance music of this region, with its free use of melody and harmony and its modality, and felt as if he had suddenly stepped into a new world.

"The music," he later wrote, "is enlivening by its proximity to Nature, by its force, by its directness of feeling, by its undisturbed racial purity." Back from this visit, he wrote his first mazurka. From that moment on, he was not only a composer from Poland but a *Polish* composer. "Each man must go back to the earth from which he derives," he wrote. "Today I have developed into a national composer, not only subconsciously, but with a thorough conviction, using the melodic treasures of the Polish folk." How overwhelming an experience this contact with native Polish music was, and how profoundly it affected his musical thinking, was soon demonstrated. Between 1926 and 1928, he produced two of his masterpieces—the ballet *Harnasie,* and the *Stabat Mater*—both of which are intensely national in feeling.

His music derives its rhythmic force and its rich harmonic colors, as well as its prevailing oriental sensuality, from Slavonic folk music; but to these qualities is often added a vein of mysticism.

He stands alone, apart from the other creative figures of the twentieth century. "Szymanowski's music belongs to none of the popular twentieth-century spheres of influence," says Scott Goddard. "It is worth remarking that at a time when Stravinsky on the one hand and Schoenberg on the other were the rage, there were still composers who, in that generation, kept their own way. They never were the rage, never taken by fashion or run by cliques; their music was comparatively seldom heard. But they did keep the quality that shows in Szymanowski's best music, the original vision of the alert-minded creative artist."

Szymanowski was born in Timoshovka, in the Polish Ukraine (where his parents owned an estate) on October 6, 1882—*not* on September 21, 1883, as was believed so long even by the composer himself. His was a cultured household where all the arts were appreciated; he early came into contact with good music. A leg injury suffered in childhood made it impossible for him to attend school, or to play games with other children. As a result, his childhood was lonely and introspective, given almost entirely to reading, making music, and the education given him at home by private teachers. His first lessons on the piano were given him by his father, then by an aunt. After that, he began studying theory with Gustav Neuhaus. By 1900, he had written a number of compositions for the piano, including a set of nine gifted preludes, which became his opus 1. In 1901, he went to Warsaw for more intensive training at its Conservatory, principally with Sigmund Noskowski. There he completed his first work for orchestra, *Concert Overture,* op. 12, and a piano sonata in C minor, op. 8, which won first prize in a Chopin competition in Lemberg. He was also thrown in with a group of other young Polish musicians who formed the Association of Young Polish Composers, later identified as "Young Poland in Music"; their aim was the promotion of new Polish music. On February 6, 1906, this group gave a concert at which several of Szymanowski's works were performed.

Early in 1906, Szymanowski arrived in Berlin, where he saturated himself with German music, While there he completed his First Symphony in F minor, op. 15 (1907), which was derivative from Mahler and Richard Strauss and which he later withdrew. In 1908, he left Berlin to divide his time between his native city and various European capitals. His major works now reflected the influence of Scriabin upon him; these included his Second Symphony in B-flat major, op. 19 (1909) and his second piano sonata in A minor, op. 21 (1910). Between 1912 and 1914, Szymanowski lived in Vienna. This was the period in which his fascination for oriental and Near-Eastern subjects is reflected in his writing. Just before the outbreak of World War I, while on a visit to Paris, he became impressed with Ravel's post-impressionism and allowed that style to affect his writing. During the war, Szymanowski lived in Poland, and visited Russia for a concert tour with the violinist, Paul Kochanski. The aftermath of war and revolution left him destitute. Settling in Warsaw in 1919, he earned his living playing the piano, and making guest appearances in European cities; in 1921, he paid his first visit to the United States.

After discovering the national songs and dances of Poland in the Tatras mountains, Szymanowski finally arrived at a national idiom in which he produced his masterworks. In 1926, he was appointed director of the Warsaw Conservatory. Three years later, he suffered a nervous breakdown which compelled him to resign from this post. Strengthened by a stay in a sanitorium, Szymanowski returned to composing, producing several distinguished works, including his second violin concerto and the *Symphonie concertante* for piano and orchestra. He also became president of the Academy of Music in Warsaw.

Suffering a physical relapse, Szymanowski was advised by his physicians to take a holiday in Switzerland and France. The continual deterioration of his physical resources forced him to return to a sanitorium, in Lausanne, Switzerland. He died there of laryngeal tuberculosis on March 28, 1937, and was buried in a vault in the Skalka Church in Cracow.

1909 SYMPHONY NO. 2 IN B-FLAT MAJOR, op. 19. I. Allegro moderato. II. Theme and Variations. III. Allegro moderato, molto energico.

Szymanowski wrote three symphonies. The first, in F minor, op. 15, was written in 1907 and was introduced in Warsaw on March 26, 1909. The second came in 1909, with its world première held in Warsaw on April 7, 1911. A third symphony is entitled *Song of the Night,* op. 19. Scored for tenor, mixed chorus and orchestra it was first heard in London on October 24, 1921·

The second symphony was its composer's most significant work during that early period when he was strongly influenced by Scriabin, and had not yet embraced Polish nationalism.

The first movement begins at once with a sensitive, poetic theme, in solo violin. This is the first principal subject. The second one, which has a melancholy character, is heard in the violas. There is a passionate working out of these ideas in the development, but in the coda the sensitive and at times ethereal mood projected in the early part of the symphony returns.

The second novement is in the form of theme and variations. The dolce theme is given by the cellos. Five variations follow. The first is slow and sedate, and the second is rhythmic, though the pace is not quickened. The third is a scherzando, the fourth a gavotte, and the fitth a minuet.

A powerful introduction sets the stage for the finale—a fugue whose subject is the virile counterpart of the sensitive first theme of the opening movement. With remarkable polyphonic skill, the composer proceeds to weave other thematic ideas from the earlier movements into his contrapuntal texture.

1915 MÉTOPES, three poems for piano, op. 29. I. The Island of Sirens. II. Calypso. III. Nausicaa.

Ravel's influence on Szymanowski is particularly evident in several piano works, of which *Métopes* is characteristic. It is a cycle of three sensitive tone poems, evoking pages from the *Odyssey* with vivid harmonic writing and languorous melodies. Three different moods are created: the first, describing the island of the sirens, is sensuous; a tender and wistful picture is etched in Calypso; and the final piece, telling of the games of maidens, is Corybantic. (The word "metope" represents carved work on the Doric frieze.)

1917 ÉTUDES, for piano, op. 33.

At different times in his early career, Szymanowski was influenced by different composers. The Études, written while Szymanowski was in Russia, stem not from Chopin but principally from Scriabin (though there are occasional suggestions of Debussy and Schoenberg). The Études, which the composer wished to be played in their entirety and without interruption, are not so much exercises in technique or virtuosity as they are brief impressions. Each is self-sufficient in its rhythmic or harmonic interest, yet gains in effect through contrast of mood or tempo, as the result of its juxtaposition to its neighbors. The often subtle interplay of rhythms, the refinement of speech, the involved chordal structures, are all derived from Scriabin.

1926 HARNASIE, ballet-pantomime in two acts, op. 51, with scenario by Jerzy Rytard. First performance: Prague, May 11, 1935.

A few years after coming into contact with the life, music and dance of the Tatras mountaineers, Szymanowski decided to interpret them in a national work for the stage. His ballet *Harnasie* derived its subject from legendary sources. The story is a simple and primitive one: a peasant bride is abducted from her wedding by the leader of the Harnasie, a wild mountain tribe; soon after this, love between them flowers. With the cogent rhythmic force, the coruscant harmonic colors, the exotic melodies and shifting tonalities of the peasant music of the Carpathian mountains, Szymanowski produced not only a score of immense power and originality, but also one of his most vital national creations.

In *Music and Letters,* H. H. Stuckenschmidt described *Harnasie* as follows:

"The music conjures up with the power of genius the wild and lonely landscape of the Carpathians. It is dominated by the thematic *idée fixe,* which is used in modified forms in nearly all the nine numbers of the score.... The peculiar orchestral texture, which gives preference to oboe or clarinet solos and avoids the thickness of earlier Szymanowski scores, contributes much to the impression of local color. Tenor solos and mixed choruses are added to the orchestral sound. Pieces like the march of the Harnasie, the Cossack-like drinking song, and the peasant dance (made famous by Paul Kochanski's violin arrangement even before the whole ballet was known) show Szymanowski as a masterly manipulator of nationalist melody and of intricate Slavonic rhythms."

1926 STABAT MATER, for soloists, chorus and orchestra, op. 53.

"For many years," Szymanowski has written, "I have thought of Polish religious music. I have tried to achieve first of all the direct emotional effect, in other words, the general intelligibility of the text and the fusion of the emotional substance of the word with its musical equivalent. I wanted the music to be as far as possible from the official liturgical music, from its elevated and former musty academicism."

The *Stabat Mater* was the composer's first venture into liturgical music. It is one of his finest works, and the first of his compositions to be acclaimed in his native land. Its première in Warsaw on January 11, 1929, was a tremendous success.

Within a highly flexible form, Szymanowski mingled religious and national feeling to produce a highly personal work: sixteenth-century polyphony (treated with freedom) is blended with Polish rhythm and melody. The result is music that is more pictorial and dramatic than spiritual. As the Italian critic, Guido Pannain, noted, "the drama of the Cross becomes a prophetic vision of a legendary epic. . . . It is not the heart of the believer that is wrung by emotion . . . but the fancy of a poet that conjures up an epic vision."

1932 SYMPHONIE CONCERTANTE NO. 2, for piano and orchestra, op. 60. I. Allegro moderato. II. Andante sostenuto. III. Allegro non troppo.

In calling his only work for piano and orchestra a *Symphonie concertante* instead of a concerto, Szymanowski was emphasizing the equal importance enjoyed by both the solo instrument and the orchestra in projecting the music. Some critics have, in fact, come to designate this work as Szymanowski's Fourth Symphony in recognition of the importance assigned to the orchestra. On October 9, 1932, with the composer at the piano, it was introduced in Poznan. Repeated soon after that in Warsaw by the Warsaw Philharmonic under Fitelberg, once again with the composer at the piano, it scored a major success. It has been performed extensively throughout the world of music, and has become one of the composer's most celebrated works.

In the first movement, the piano comes forth with the principal theme against quiet, syncopated chords in the strings. This theme is taken up by the orchestra, and is then developed. The second theme is heard in the flute against chromatic-scale passages in the strings—a whimsical idea which has been compared to an ancient Venetian dance. The flute opens the second movement with a feeling melody set against the piano and strings; the violas then join with a countermelody. The second theme, no less beautiful than the first, appears in muted horns and after that in the piano. A recall of the principal theme of the first movement serves as a transition to the third, which is vital with dance rhythms. The music develops with savage intensity until it erupts in a breath-taking climax, a "healthy liberation of energy," as Herbert Elwell described it.

1933 CONCERTO NO. 2 FOR VIOLIN AND ORCHESTRA, op. 61.

One of Szymanowski's most intimate friends was the violinist Paul Kochanski, for whom he wrote many works, including two concertos. Kochanski introduced the Second Concerto in Warsaw on October 6, 1933, with the Warsaw Philharmonic, Georg Fitelberg conducting.

Though divided into two sections (separated by a cadenza), the concerto is in a single movement. In the first part, the principal theme is heard in the solo violin after a brief prelude. After this idea has been imitated by several different instruments of the orchestra, the solo violin returns with the second melody, which is also taken up by parts of the orchestra. The music grows in rhythmic and emotional force until an Appassionato section is reached. The intensity is relaxed. A cadenza leads into the second section, which begins rhythmically, but then proceeds into the statement of a beautiful lyrical theme. The principal subjects of the first and second sections are then developed, after which the music is built up into a forceful climax.

ALEXANDER TANSMAN 1897–

Tansman has tried to reconcile modern techniques and styles with the identity of Polish national music. The dances of Poland have left their throb and rhythm in his works; but a strong and personal lyricism is equally evident. He indulges in extended melodic ideas that frequently assume the personality of a lied and which, after they are fully unfolded, are subjected to elaborate development. The setting for these melodies is a modern harmonic language, with frequent excursions into dissonance.

Tansman was born in Lodz, Poland, on June 12, 1897. He began his music study at the Lodz Conservatory and continued it at the Warsaw Conservatory with Pierre Rytel; at the same time he pursued the study of law at the University. He began composing early: he was only fifteen when he heard one of his own works performed in public, and only twenty-two when his compositions won the Grand Prize of Poland. In 1920, he established his home in Paris, became an integral part of its musical life, and, in 1938, a French citizen. On February 17, 1920, Vladimir Golschmann conducted a concert of Tansman's piano music in Paris, from which time on, Golschmann became instrumental in presenting many of Tansman's orchestral works both in Europe and in the United States. In 1926–1927, Tansman toured Austria and Germany in the triple role of pianist, conductor and composer. He made his American debut as soloist with the Boston Symphony on December 28, 1927, when he was heard in the world première of his Second Piano Concerto. In 1933, he toured the Far East. Tansman spent the years of World War II in the United States. Soon after his arrival in 1941, he received the Elizabeth

Sprague Coolidge medal for distinguished services to chamber music. During this stay, Tansman completed several major works, including three symphonies; he also wrote music for the movies. In 1946, Tansman returned to his home in Paris. His major later works include an oratorio, *The Prophet Isaiah* (1951); an opera *Le Serment,* produced in Brussels on March 11, 1955; and a ballet, *Resurrection,* mounted in Nice in 1962.

1930 TRIPTYQUE, for string orchestra (or string quartet). I. Allegro risoluto. II. Andante. III. Presto.

The *Triptyque,* or "three panels," was introduced in 1931 in Paris by the Brosa String Quartet. Tansman also scored the work for string orchestra; this version was heard on November 6, 1931, with Vladimir Golschmann conducting the St. Louis Symphony.

The composer has analyzed the work as follows:

"I. A marked and energetic theme is given out by the second violins, with the rhythmic emphasis clearly punctuated in the violoncellos. This is repeated and seized upon by the first and second violins and, in harmonic and rhythmic development, leads into a second theme based upon a rhythmic play on the interval of the third. In a closely woven exposition the two themes are superimposed in dynamic and harmonic development, which leads to an incisively rhythmic close.

"II. The movement begins with a fugal development of a theme of calm and serene character which rises in lyrical ecstasy to a climax and then returns a little slowly to the pianissimo of the beginning. . . .

"III. This movement develops in a sort of 'perpetual motion,' in which the rhythms are superimposed in a fashion sometimes playful, sometimes case-hardened and mechanistic. Into this rapid movement enters an interlude of grave character, but the whir of rhythms returns to develop into an interlacing of the several themes of the work, which finishes in a sort of Polish hymn."

1931 QUATRE DANSES POLONAISES (FOUR POLISH DANCES), for orchestra. I. Polka. II. Kujawiak. III. Dumka. IV. Oberek.

Some of Tansman's most effective compositions are in a Polish national idiom, of which the *Four Polish Dances* is representative. It was first heard at a Pasdeloup concert in Paris on December 12, 1933, Rhené-Baton conducting. Arturo Toscanini led the American première at a concert of the New York Philharmonic on October 6, 1934. The second movement, Kujawiak, is a variety of mazurka, but in a slow tempo; Dumka is a Slavonic form made famous by Dvořák, characterized by its elegiac lyricism. Oberek is another variety of mazurka, but in an accelerated tempo.

Irving Schweké wrote as follows about Tansman's use of Polish folk song and dance materials: "He follows a parallel line to that of the Spanish master, Falla. . . . He works in his surroundings, but never imitates them. All that the folk lore of his country can suggest is a melodic curve, a natural harmony; all that it contains is the very emotion of his race, which he has learned to capture and give expression to."

1941 RAPSODIE POLONAISE (POLISH RHAPSODY) for orchestra.

The inspiration for this rhapsody was the invasion of Poland by Nazi Germany with which World War II was launched. In his music, Tansman spoke not only of the tragic events attending the attack on Warsaw, and the impact it had on the Polish people, but also of hope for ultimate victory. Harry R. Burke described this music in the St. Louis *Globe-Democrat* as follows: "There is an inexorable tread as of tanks in the introduction, and a threnody in oboe, and later the clarinet mourns for material defeat. But Tansman perceives hope. . . . The music enters upon a polonaise—and suddenly one is aware of the implusive, the propulsive, the energizing tread to the dignity of a dream. It dies away then in reminiscent vaporings of woodwinds and its spirit thence emerges in string harmonies and woodwind melodies to become a mazurka in which are reassembled the gaiety of heart, the chivalrous tradition, which are Polish. But these are reasserted as determination. Spirit can still conquer."

The rhapsody was introduced on November 14, 1941, with Vladimir Golschmann conducting the St. Louis Symphony.

1942 SYMPHONY NO. 5 IN D MINOR. I. Lento; Allegro con moto. II. Intermezzo: andante sostenuto. III. Vivo. IV. Lento; Allegro con moto.

This is the first work written by Tansman in the United States after he settled here in 1941. On February 2, 1943, it was introduced in Baltimore by the National Symphony Orchestra (of Washington, D.C.), the composer conducting.

The symphony is classical in form, and is predominantly melodic. A slow introduction leads into the Allegro, in which the first theme is a lyric passage for strings; the second theme is also melodious. Both ideas are worked out polyphonically; in the stirring climax the two melodies are played simultaneously. The second movement is lyrical and introspective: the first theme is presented by the clarinet against divided violas, and the second is heard in the strings. The Scherzo movement is in song form, and is particularly interesting for its frequent changes of meter and rhythm. This movement makes an intriguing excursion into the world of jazz. A slow introduction ushers in the finale in which the principal theme—fully projected and developed in the ensuing Allegro con moto section—is suggested.

"The cyclic method is present in the structure," said Olin Downes in a review in *The New York Times*. "Themes and their transformations recur in different movements. The last movement is a summing up, and also a simplification in its harmonic style. One might discover in this symphony an inner program which hinted at such clarification and clearing of inner horizons on the part of the composer. The ending is tranquil and in the major, after much polyharmony."

1944 SYMPHONY NO. 7.

Tansman's Seventh Symphony was heard for the first time on October 24, 1947, with Vladimir Golschmann conducting the St. Louis Symphony. The movements are played without interruption. The lyrical element is emphasized throughout while the prevailing mood is meditative. It opens with a slow introduction in which the two principal themes are stated. The main part follows developing these two main ideas; then the slow introduction returns. The Andante cantabile movement is consistently quiet and contemplative, opening with a gentle subject for two flutes. A second theme, for horns and trombones, leads into a climax, following which the melody for the two flutes returns. This is succeeded by a scherzo with two basic melodic elements, the first satiric, the other with the characteristics of a folk song. The finale is lively. Towards the end of the symphony, strains of the first movement reappear gradually, and as the pace slackens, the symphony ends with a reiteration of the first-movement's slow introduction. Thus the work ends serenely.

1949 RICERCARI, for orchestra. I. Notturno. II. Danza. III. Intermezzo. IV. Toccata. V. Study in Boogie-Woogie.

Several modern composers have resurrected the form of the ricercare (the American, Norman Dello Joio, for example). The ricercare is a contrapuntal form, the instrumental counterpart of the vocal motet; it develops a basic idea, or several basic ideas, fugally. With different composers the ricercare form has undergone different transformations. With Tansman it consists of five contrasting movements: the first (Andante sostenuto) presents a placid melody, first heard in oboe, then repeated by flute, trumpet and clarinet; this is followed by a sprightly scherzo (Molto vivace) which develops into a mazurka-like dance. A brief intermezzo for muted strings brings temporary repose. After a robust toccata for full orchestra comes a boogie-woogie treatment of an earthy idea.

This composition was commissioned by the St. Louis Symphony to honor its seventieth anniversary. The orchestra, under Vladimir Golschmann, introduced it in St. Louis on December 22, 1949.

DEEMS TAYLOR 1885–1966

The music of Deems Taylor is not the kind to create new styles or influence new composers. Its function is to bring pleasure to the listener, which it usually does; and it brings pleasure through its logic, gracious wit and sentiment, suave sophistication, and grace. Taylor has never paid even lip service to any single style or trend, nor has he ever attempted to join any school of musical thought. He must write as his heart, not his intellect, dictates. His works consequently are romantically conceived, generously filled with pleasing melodies, attractive in their settings of warm harmonies and apt instrumentation. His music—whether for the symphony hall or opera house—may never transport us into a new world; but it will bring a brighter glow to the present one.

Taylor was born in New York City on December 22, 1885. He received his academic education at the Ethical Culture School and New York University. His formal musical training was slight, consisting of eight months of piano lessons when he was eleven; and later on two years of harmony and counterpoint with Oscar Coon. Taylor always considered himself a self-taught musician. He wrote his first piece of music, a waltz, when he was ten. In 1913, he received a prize for *The Siren Song,* an orchestral tone poem. In 1914, he completed writing two cantatas (*The Chambered Nautilus* and *The Highwayman*) and had his first publication, a song. After leaving college, he held various editorial jobs; during World War I, he was a war correspondent for the New York *Tribune.* In 1921, he initiated a highly successful career as music critic for the New York *World,* where he stayed four years. He subsequently was the editor of *Musical America,* and music critic of the New York *American.* He also achieved a national reputation as a musical commentator over the radio and for the Walt Disney motion picture production, *Fantasia.*

His first success as a serious composer came with his delightful orchestral suite, *Through the Looking Glass,* in 1919 and the tone poem, *Jurgen,* the latter introduced in New York City on November 19, 1925. Commissions from the Metropolitan Opera in New York for two operas made Taylor a nationally famous composer. They were *The King's Henchman* in 1926 and *Peter Ibbetson* in 1931. Taylor wrote two more operas after that: *Ramuntcho,* based on Pierre Loti, produced in Philadelphia on February 10, 1942; and *The Dragon,* based on a play by Lady Gregory, introduced in New York on February 6, 1958. In his last years, Taylor was crippled by arthritis. He died in New York City on July 3, 1966.

Taylor served as the president of ASCAP (The American Society for Composers, Authors and Publishers) between 1942 and 1948.

1919 THROUGH THE LOOKING GLASS, suite for orchestra. I. Dedication; The Garden of Live Flowers. II. Jabberwocky. III. Looking Glass Insects. IV. The White Knight.

Though this suite is the earliest of Taylor's major works for orchestra, it is also one of his best. Its spontaneity and wit assure it permanency in American symphonic literature. Taylor wrote it between 1917 and 1919 as a three-movement work for flute, oboe, clarinet, bassoon, horn, piano and strings; in this version, it was heard for the first time in New York on February 18, 1919, in a performance by the New York Chamber Music Society. Two years after that, Taylor scored this music for full orchestra and added two new movements. The orchestral adaptation—and the one by which this composition is now known—was introduced by the New York Symphony Society under Walter Damrosch on March 10, 1923.

The suite is, of course, inspired by the delightfully nonsensical fairy tale of Lewis Carroll. Taylor has written his own program notes for the music:

"I. Carroll precedes the tale with a charming poetical foreword, the first stanza of which the music aims to express. It runs—

> Child of the pure, unclouded brow
> And dreaming eyes of wonder!

Though time be fleet, and I and thou
 Art half a life asunder,
Thy loving smile will surely hail
The love-gift of a fairy-tale.

A simple song theme, briefly developed, leads to The Garden of Live Flowers. Shortly after Alice had entered the looking glass country, she came to a lovely garden in which the flowers were talking. . . . The music, therefore, reflects the brisk chatter of the swaying, bright-colored denizens of the garden.

"II. This is the poem that so puzzled Alice, and which Humpty-Dumpty finally explained to her. The theme of that frightful beast, the jabberwock, is first announced by the full orchestra. The clarinet then begins the tale, recounting how, on a 'brillig' afternoon, the 'slithy toves did gyre and gimble in the wabe.' Muttered imprecations by the bassoon warn us to 'beware the jabberwock, my son.' A miniature march signalizes the approach of our hero, taking 'his vorpal sword in hand.' Trouble starts among the trombones—the jabberwock is upon us! The battle with the monster is recounted in a short and rather repellent fugue, the double-basses bringing up the subject and the hero fighting back in the interludes. Finally his vorpal sword (really a xylophone) goes 'snicker-snack' and the monster, impersonated by the solo bassoon, dies a lingering and convulsive death. The hero returns to the victorious strains of his own theme—'O frabjous day! Callooh! Callay!' The whole orchestra rejoices—the church bells are rung—alarums and excursions. Conclusion. Once more the slithy toves perform their pleasing evolutions, undisturbed by the uneasy ghost of the late Jabberwock.

"III. Here we find the vociferous *diptera* that made such an impression upon Alice—the Bee-elephant, the Gnat, the Rocking-horse-fly, the Snap-dragon-fly, and the Bread-and butter-fly. . . .

"IV. The White Knight was a toy Don Quixote, mild, chivalrous, ridiculous, and rather touching. He carried a mousetrap on his saddle-bow, because 'if they *do* come, I don't choose to have them running all about.' . . . There are two themes; the first, a sort of instrumental prance, being the knight's own conception of himself as a slashing daredevil. The second is bland, mellifluous, a little sentimental—much more like the knight as he really was. The first theme starts off bravely, but falls out of the saddle before long, and has to give way to the second. The two alternate, in various guises, until the end, when the knight rides off, with Alice waving her handkerchief—she thought it would encourage him if she did."

1926 THE KING'S HENCHMAN, opera in three acts, with text by Edna St. Vincent Millay. First performance: Metropolitan Opera, New York, February 17, 1927.

Deems Taylor's first opera has known the fate of many another American opera. It was introduced with the loud fanfare of publicity bugles—so much so that its première assumed the proportions of a world-shaking artistic event; it was accorded the cheers of audiences and the extravagant praise of critics; it was the favored topic for parlor discussions; and then, after it was heard fourteen times in three seasons, it was relegated to an obscurity which appears to be more permanent than temporary.

The King's Henchman was not—as Lawrence Gilman said of it after the première performance—"the best American opera we have ever heard." Nor was its introduction at the Metropolitan as much of a red-letter day in musical history as the newspaper accounts at the time would lead us to believe. But it is also much better than its present neglect suggests. It is the work of a cultured musician who combines compositional skill with taste and refinement and a sensitive feeling for beauty. It may lack originality, with its frequent reminiscent echoes of Wagner and sometimes Debussy; it may lack an American personality; it may occasionally seem static in its movement. Yet the charm and freshness of its best pages make it a rewarding experience for the opera lover. There are many pages of fine music: the forest love scene; the simulation of English folk songs in the Bardic Song of Act I; the prelude to and the Incantation Song from Act II; the love duet in Act II; and the prelude to the last act.

What Olin Downes said in 1926 still holds true: "It has undeniable theatrical effect, conciseness, movement, youthful spirit and sincerity; its text is poetic and well adapted to the needs of the singers; its music has the impact, the expressiveness and color appropriate to music drama. . . . Mr. Taylor's score proves his melodic gift, his spirit and sense of drama. . . . He develops, combines, transforms his motives in his orchestra; he also writes broad and curving phrases for the singers, phrases reinforced by the surge and impact of the instruments. It need not be claimed in all this that he has always succeeded in hitting the dramatic target. The remarkable thing is Mr. Taylor's degree of success, the communicative and sensuous quality of his music, and above all, the direct and unaffected manner of his composing."

When the opera was commissioned from Taylor by the Metropolitan Opera Association, he called upon one of America's foremost poets for his libretto—Edna St. Vincent Millay. She produced a variation of the Tristan and Isolde theme. King Eadgar of tenth-century England is in love with Aelfrida, the Devon princess. To press his suit, the King sends his best friend, Aethelwold, to Devon. There Aethelwold goes to sleep in a forest at the same time that Aelfrida wanders through it, intoning an incantation that will bring her a lover. Because of the powers of this incantation, Aethelwold and Aelfrida fall in love with each other and get married; meanwhile, Aethelwold dispatches to King Eadgar the news that Aelfrida is much too unattractive for him. The arrival of the King in Devon uncovers the fraud and sends Aethelwold to his death by his own hand.

1931 PETER IBBETSON, opera in three acts, with text by the composer and Constance Collier, based on the novel of the same name by George Du Maurier. First performance: Metropolitan Opera, New York, February 7, 1931.

Taylor's second opera followed the first by four years, and—like its predecessor—was the result of a commission by the Metropolitan Opera Association. For his subject, he selected the famous novel of Du Maurier which—in collaboration with Constance Collier—he adapted into a workable libretto. The story is, of course, familiar. Peter Ibbetson is the victim of a tyrannical uncle who has adopted him, and, to escape from the grimness of reality, he yields to dreams about his childhood in which he meets his little sweetheart, Mary. But dreams are not enough to relieve Peter of his misery: in a fit of fury, he murders his uncle. Sentenced to life imprisonment, Peter once again seeks solace in dreams, and once again evokes Mary out of the past. After thirty years of imprisonment, Peter learns that Mary has died. The will to live has now gone from him. As he dies, the walls of his prison disintegrate; Peter is young again; he rises from his couch and turns to Mary, who is waiting for him.

The tender vein of melody in the opera—made colorful by the effective interpolation of French folk songs for children—the delightful orchestration, and the warm sentiment were the qualities that endeared *Peter Ibbetson* to its audiences when it was introduced at the Metropolitan Opera on February 7, 1931. It was heard sixteen times during the next four seasons (including the opening night of the 1933–1934 Metropolitan Opera season, the first time such a thing happened to an American opera) The critics did not like *Peter Ibbetson* as much as they had *The King's Henchman,* but they did single out several passages in the opera which were of great interest: the waltzes of Act I; the inn music of Act II; the dream music of Act III.

Taylor took the major orchestral passages of the opera and adapted them into two suites. The first includes two extended orchestral passages marked Molto allegro and Andante. This suite was heard for the first time on March 18, 1938, in Indianapolis, with the Indianapolis Symphony Orchestra conducted by Fabien Sevitzky. The second suite, comprising the waltzes, inn music, dream music, and finale, was introduced by the Baltimore Symphony Orchestra under Howard Barlow on January 7, 1940.

Peter Ibbetson was heard over the radio in the fall of 1927 in a coast-to-coast broadcast which marked the official opening of the Columbia Broadcasting System. On this occasion, the composer made his first appearance as a radio commentator, a role he would henceforth fill frequently and with remarkable success for other composers and with other compositions. The opera was successfully revived at the Empire State Music Festival in New York on July 22, 1961.

1945 ELEGY, for orchestra.

This short orchestral threnody was inspired by the death of an Egyptian princess who died at the age of twelve. When the work received its world première—in Los Angeles on January 4, 1945—the composer provided the following analysis:

"The first section, marked Lento, introduces a dirge-like main theme, heard as a horn solo. It is taken up by the strings and then by the full orchestra, which brings it to a climax. A long, descending subsidiary theme leads to the second section, marked Tranquillo. Its theme is simple and lyric in character, suggestive of youth and naïveté. It is developed at some length, but is interrupted by a grave reminder of the dirge theme. Then the lyric theme resumes, and is followed by two variants, one very lively and dance-like, the other, greatly augmented, intoned by the brass. The two variants alternate until they reach a climax that is cut across by the trumpets, playing a harsh reminder of the dirge. The music subsides, and the final section begins with the dirge theme, played by all the violins, on the G-string. After a last climax, the descending theme of the first section leads to a quiet close."

ALEXANDER TCHEREPNIN 1899–

Since the early 1920s, Tcherepnin has been a prolific contributor to all musical media. Some of his music reflects his Russian background; other music is influenced by his long residence in the Orient and his intense preoccupation with oriental music. In a good many of his compositions he has been partial to a nine-tone scale, which he himself devised and with which he is identified. This scale consists of a semi-tone, a whole tone, and a semi-tone repeated three times, and is particularly effective for satire, for the expression of anguished emotion, and for the description of grotesque situations. Tcherepnin has also employed a polyphonic method which he has designated as "interpoint." Willi Reich has explained that here the composer's aim is "to construct polyphonic form chiefly in broken, intersected lines, the thematic insertions being evoked and made clear simultaneously by breaks in the part-writing."

Whatever the style, idiom, or background, his music always reveals the hand of a masterful technician, and the voice of an artist who does not believe in either circumlocution or prolixity. What Cyrus Durgin said of a late Tcherepnin symphony applies equally to all his major creations, whatever their form or medium. His is music "of large stature, solid substance, much imagination in melody and harmony, and above all, original. There is constant motion, and the music lives and breathes in every measure." This is music "by an expert in the uses of counterpoint . . . [who] employs every instrument for coloring purposes and makes everything sound."

Tcherepnin—son of the distinguished Russian conductor and composer, Nicholas Tcherepnin—was born in St. Petersburg on January 21, 1899. He received his first lessons on the piano from his mother. By the time he was fourteen, he had written an opera, a ballet and a good deal of piano music, some of the last getting performed at a concert in St. Petersburg in 1913. For several months, he attended the St. Petersburg Conservatory, where he was a pupil of Sokolov in harmony and of Kobiliansky in piano. In 1918, he was brought to Tiflis, where his father had become director of the Conservatory. There Alexander continued his music studies with Ter Stepanova (piano) and Th. de Hartmann (counterpoint), while engaging in various musical activities, including the giving of piano recitals throughout the Caucasus. In 1921, he came to Paris. As a student at the Paris Conservatory, he completed his musical training with Vidal (composition) and Isidor Philipp (piano). In 1922, he gave a highly successful piano recital in London featuring some of his own music. Between 1923 and 1934, he established his reputation as a composer with the ballet, *Ajanta's Frescoes*, which Anna Pavlova had commissioned and which she introduced in London on September 10, 1923; with the *Rapsodie georgienne,* for cello and orchestra, op. 25, heard in Bordeaux in 1924; and his second piano concerto, op. 26, whose world première took place in Paris on January 26, 1924.

He made a world tour as composer-pianist in 1934, performing throughout the United States a year after that. Between 1934 and 1937, he made extended tours to the Orient, where he devoted himself to teaching, promoting the interests of young Oriental composers, and publishing oriental music in Western notation. In 1937, he married a Chinese-born pianist, Lee Hsien-Ming and in 1958 he became an American citizen. From 1949 to 1964, he was on the faculty of the DePaul University School of Music in Chicago. During these years, he divided his time between the United States and France. In May of 1967 Tcherepnin toured the Soviet Union in performances of his works—his first return visit to his native country in almost a half a century.

1924 CHAMBER CONCERTO FOR FLUTE, VIOLIN AND CHAMBER ORCHESTRA, op. 33. I. Allegro. II. Andantino. III. Vivace. IV. Vivace. IV. Allego molto.

In this early chamber-music composition, Tcherepnin already makes use of the nine-tone scale. The tonality of this composition is marked as D major, but the notes used by Tcherepnin are: D, E-flat, F, F-sharp, G, A, B-flat, B, and C-sharp.

"The interesting corollary of Tcherepnin's use of the nine-tone scale," says Nicolas Slonimsky, "is the creation of a double chord, both minor and major. Every one of the first three movements of the Chamber Concerto ends such a bitonal chord, which may sound to untutored ears like a tonic chord with a wrong note deliberately or accidentally thrown in. . . . Tcherepnin concludes the last movement . . . on a single unadulterated tonic in unison."

The first movement, Slonimsky adds, "maintains the lively tempo of a classical Allegro, and the angular intervals of the new-fangled scale add considerable zest to the music." The second movement is lyrical, with the solo violin heard in "the exotic-sounding abbreviated version of the scale reduced to six notes; then the flute plays its own solo using all the notes of the scale." The third-movement scherzo had "acrid harmonies composed from the dissonant ingredients of the scale." The finale is in a vigorous rhythm and once again makes use of the nine-tone scale.

The *Chamber Concerto* was introduced in 1925 at the Donaueschingen Festival in Germany, Hermann Scherchen conducting. The work received the Schott international prize.

1927 SYMPHONY NO. 1 IN E, op. 42. I. Maestoso; Allegro risoluto. II. Vivace. III. Andante. IV. Allegretto.

Tcherepnin wrote his First Symphony during a brief visit to the United States in 1927, while residing at Islip, Long Island. The symphony was introduced at a Concert Colonne in Paris on October 29, 1927, Gabriel Pierné conducting.

The nine-tone scale here used by the composer is: E, F, G, G-sharp, A, B, C, C-sharp, D-sharp. The first movement may be regarded in the sonata form, but, the composer adds, "the shortness of the Exposition, the entire new version of the Recapitulation and the large multisectional Development are far removed from classical form." The main theme (only three measures long) is given by four horns. The tempo changes to Allegro risoluto at the fourth measure, with a secondary theme presented by strings. The composer explains: "It becomes by degrees extended and developed until the whole orchestra takes part in many-voiced polyphony—the strings and woodwind in horizontal interpoint, the trumpets putting forward the theme in augmentation, the horns initiating the theme rhythmically, and the lower basses giving the whole a rhythmically moving foundation. The Development consists at first of alternating appearances of both themes, then in counterpoint with each other, then progressing in 'crab fashion' until the second development. A syncopated part follows, after a short repetition of the first exposition, to a quiet coda."

The second movement, a scherzo with trio, is unusual in that only the percussion instruments are used. This is followed by a slow movement based on three themes. "The first is announced by a trumpet, the horn in interpoint to it. The second is for clarinet, the tympani in interpoint, the strings giving out a tremolo with the bows played near the bridge. This is followed by a polyphonic development of both themes, serving as a bridge to the appearance of the third theme, played by a solo violin, with a double bass in interpoint. There is now further development, and at the end, the three subjects are joined in a six-voiced unaccompanied interpoint."

The fourth movement was described by the composer as "a species of the rondo form." The opening theme is presented by the strings, followed by a subsidiary idea beginning in brass and continuing in strings. The first idea, transformed, returns in the concluding coda before the symphony ends vigorously.

1957 SYMPHONY NO. 4 IN E, op. 91. I. Moderato. II. Allegro. III. Andante con moto.

This symphony was commissioned by Charles Munch and the Boston Symphony, who presented the world première on December 5, 1958, in Boston. It was the recipient of the historic Glinka Prize (which had formerly gone to such famous Russian composers as Rimsky-Korsakov, Scriabin and Glazunov, among many others).

Tcherepnin's son, Serge, prepared the following analysis for the Boston Symphony Program Notes:

"The first movement . . . is concise in form, based on three groups of thematic material. The second movement is in the sectional form of a valse. The third and last movement is of liturgical character: Tcherepnin introduced in it a theme '*Requiescat in pace*' from a medieval Russian church chant and uses it as cantus firmus. . . . One can find . . . the specific aspects of his musical speech: the use of the nine-step scale (which, when taken from E, reads, E, F, G, G-sharp, A, B, C, C-sharp, D-sharp); the use of the polyphonic proceeding which he terms 'interpoint'; and the rhythmic intensity characteristic of his works. There is also an aim for melodic expansion. And in the second movement, serial chromatic patterns are used as bridges between the movement's sections."

In reviewing the symphony for the *Christian Science Monitor,* Harold Rogers wrote: "In the opening . . . one was impressed at the outset by the melodies—peppery figures for the woodwind, or lovely lyrical lines weaving through the other choirs of the orchestra. Though these melodies are accessible, they are not trite. The transparent orchestration has been fashioned by a master hand; the architecture solidly and artistically built.

"There is a danceable quality in the first two movements. . . . The middle Allegro movement opens with a jolly theme stated by the piccolo—later restated, surprisingly by the tuba—while everything whirls in a rollicking three-time.

"But the element of mystery enters the last movement out of which a singing melody arises with aspiration. For a time there is restlessness; then the piece closes in a calm and unspectacular way."

1964 SERENADE, for string orchestra. I. Mesto. II. Allegretto. III. Vivace. IV. Lento. V. Allegro moderato.

The *Serenade* was commissioned by the Zurich Kammerorchester which introduced it under the direction of Edmond de Stoutz at the Venice Biennale on September 11, 1965. Orchestra and conductor then performed it extensively during a tour of Germany, Austria, Holland, Italy and Switzerland.

In five movements (played without interruption) this composition dispenses with all development of thematic material, preferring to present one new idea after another in striking procession: In reviewing the *Serenade* for the *Music Leader,* Bradley Martin said: "It abounds in musical ideas and formal inventions, such as themes which appear only once and are immediately chased away by others which have no musical relationship in the traditional sense, or the idea of short musical 'patterns' which appear, then reappear again unchanged, but set in totally different contexts."

RANDALL THOMPSON 1899–

Thompson himself has said that his works fall into two distinct categories. Some of them utilize melodic ideas with a decided national character, stamping these works as native products and their creator as an indigenous composer. But Thompson has pointed out that a great many other works are eclectic, with a universal appeal; instead of being *American* music, these compositions are music by an American.

But in whichever of these two categories his works may fall, they are all characterized by economy and simplicity of means and nobility of expression. Thompson has always felt the necessity for a composer to write music "that will reach and move the hearts of his listeners in his own day." Consequently, he has never had any interest in esoteric styles or intricate techniques and forms; but he has always tried to write with sincerity, high purpose, and depth of feeling within traditional forms that are impressive for their sound construction and inexorable logic.

Thompson was born in New York City on April 21, 1899. He attended Harvard, where he studied music with Spalding, Hill, and Davison, receiving a Bachelor of Arts degree in 1920 and a Masters degree in 1922. For a while, in 1920–1921, he studied composition privately with Ernest Bloch. In 1933, he received his doctorate in music at the School of Music at the University of Rochester. Meanwhile, in 1922, he won a fellowship for the American Academy at Rome where he spent three years and where two of his early orchestral compositions were introduced: *Pierrot and Cothurnus* on May 17, 1923, and *The Piper at the Gates of Rome,* on May 27, 1924. Upon returning to the United States, he held various teaching and directorial posts: at Wellesley College (from 1927 to 1929, and again in 1936–1937); University of California at Berkeley (1937–1939); the Curtis Institute in Philadelphia (where he was director from 1939 to 1941); the School of Fine Arts at the University of Virginia (which he headed between 1941 and 1946); Princeton University (1946–1948); and Harvard University (where he was professor of music from 1948 until his retirement in 1966, and head of the music department between 1952 and 1957).

Success as composer came first with the première of his Second Symphony in 1932. Thompson received Guggenheim Fellowships in 1929 and 1930, and the Elizabeth Sprague Coolidge Award for distinguished contributions to music in 1941. Many of his later works were written on commissions. These included *The Last Words of David,* for chorus and orchestra, introduced at Tanglewood on August 12, 1949; the orchestral fantasy, *A Trip to Nahant,* in Philadelphia on March 18, 1955; the Requiem, for double chorus and orchestra, presented at the Berkeley Festival of Music on May 22, 1958; and the oratorio, *The Nativity According to St. Luke,* introduced in Cambridge, Massachusetts, on March 28, 1965.

1931 SYMPHONY No. 2. I. Allegro. II. Largo. III. Vivace. IV. Andante moderato; Allegro con spirito; Largamente.

The Second Symphony was Thompson's first major work to stamp him as an outstanding American composer, and his first large work to achieve success. It was introduced in Rochester, New York, on March 24, 1932, by the Rochester Philharmonic conducted by Howard Hanson. Since then, it has become one of the most frequently heard American symphonies, receiving more than five hundred performances in the United States and Europe in a decade.

The following is the composer's own analysis of the symphony: "I. The principal theme is announced immediately by the horns, forte, and answered by the trumpets. From this motive is derived a series of rhythmic figures which form the toccata-like background of the entire movement. The subsidiary theme is of a more reticent nature, but the violoncellos accompany it in persistent rhythm. The development section begins quietly and forms a gradual crescendo, at the apex of which the first theme returns in an ominous fortissimo against a counter-rhythm of the kettledrums. A more extended transition leads to a sinister presentation of the second theme. At the close, a major version of the second theme in augmentation is sounded fortissimo by the horns and trumpets against the continuous pulse of the strings. The movement subsides, apparently to end in the major. An abrupt minor chord brings it to a close.

"II. The violins play a warm, quiet melody against pizzicato chords in the violoncellos. A contrasting melody is sung by the oboe. The movement is not long, but its mood is concentrated. It ends simply." (The composer might have added that the main melody resembles a Negro spiritual.)

"III. Scherzo with trio. The first section begins in G minor and ends in D minor. The trio progresses from B major to G major. The first section returns transposed. Now, beginning in C minor and ending in G minor, it serves as a kind of extended 'subdominant answer' to its former presentation. There is a short coda, making intensified use of material from the trio.

"IV. The slow sections which begin and end this movement serve to frame the Allegro, a modified rondo. The theme of the Allegro is a diminution of the theme of the first and last sections. The Largamente employs for the first time the full sonorities of the orchestra in a sustained assertion of the principal melody."

1936 THE PEACEABLE KINGDOM, for mixed chorus.

A painting by the eighteeth-century American, Edward Hicks—showing William Penn surrounded by peaceful Indians on one side of the canvas, and the Biblical Daniel surrounded by lions on another—was the stimulus for this choral work, which was commissioned by the League of Composers for its twenty-fifth anniversary. It was first performed in Cambridge, Massachusetts, on March 29, 1936, at a concert of the Harvard Glee Club and the Radcliffe Choral Society, G. Wallace Davison conducting.

There are seven choral sections, with the text taken from The Book of Isaiah:

"I. Say ye to the righteous, it shall be well with him; woe unto the wicked, it shall be ill with him.

"II. Woe unto them . . .

"III. The noise of a multitude in the mountain. . . . Everyone that is found shall be thrust through. . . . Their children also shall be dashed to pieces before their eyes. . . . Their faces shall be as the flames.

"IV. Howl ye, for the day of the Lord is at hand. Howl! O gate; cry! O city! Thou art delivered.

"V. The paper reeds by the brooks, and everything sown by the brooks, shall wither, be driven away, and be no more.

"VI. For ye shall go out with joy, and be led forth with peace.

"VII. Ye shall have a song, and gladness of heart, as when one goeth with a pipe to come into the mountain of the Lord."

1940 ALLELUIA, for mixed chorus.

This short and brilliant choral work—one of the finest in present-day American music—had an exciting, even breathless, origin. It was commissioned by Serge Koussevizky for the opening-day ceremonies of the first session of the Berkshire Music Center during the summer of 1940; and the time allowed for the composition was only three weeks. Thompson chose as his text the single word *Alleluia*—and set to work. G. Wallace Davision tells the rest of the story:

"On Saturday, forty-eight hours before the formal opening, we had not heard from Thompson nor seen the music. Mr. Judd telephoned to Philadelphia; Thompson assured us that the score had just been printed, and that three hundred copies would arrive in Lenox Monday morning. . . . At two o'clock on Monday afternoon the students assembled for the first time. . . . In the corner of the barn I had secreted our collection of Bach chorales, for one mail after another had arrived at the Lenox post office during the morning without the package from Philadelphia. But at just five minutes before two, Mr. Judd came in with the music. I tried it over once on the piano, and the chorus of two hundred and fifty, assembled from all over our country for the first time, went to work. By 2:45 it was time to go to the Shed for the exercises, and at 3:30 we had given the first performance of a work which has been heard hundreds of times in choral concerts from Boston to San Francisco. So sure was Thompson's technique, so expert his craftsmanship, and so masterly his grasp of the true genius of choral singing, that despite a blueprint of unique limitations, he had created one of the noblest pieces of choral music in the twentieth century."

1942 THE TESTAMENT OF FREEDOM, for men's chorus and orchestra.

The *Testament*—written to honor the two-hundredth anniversary of the birth of Thomas Jefferson—sets four passages from Jefferson's writings. It opens with the following declaration: "The God who gave us life gave us liberty at the same time; the hand of force may destroy but cannot disjoin them" (from *A Summary View of the Rights of British America,* 1774). The next part, taken from *The Declaration of Causes and Necessity of Taking Up Arms* (July 6, 1775), begins with the following line: "We have counted the cost of the contest and find nothing so dreadful as voluntary slavery." The third section is also taken from this *Declaration,* beginning with : "We fight not for glory or for conquest." The fourth part comes from a letter to John Adams (September 21, 1821): "I shall not die without a hope that light and liberty are on steady advance." The *Testament* concludes with the declaration that opened it.

With the hope of reaching large masses with this paean to freedom and democracy, Thompson utilized the simplest possible resources for his musical setting. The chorus is often heard in unison; and when it is divided, the part-writing has the directness of an anthem. The orchestral background is subdued, built on conventional harmonic schemes to set off the voices. As Olin Downes wrote after the first New York performance, he "has . . . written . . . as a most thoughtful and modest artist, seeking for the right notes to communicate something profoundly of his people that was in his heart. His musical instincts and honesty protected him from all the notes but the right ones."

The *Testament* was introduced on April 13, 1943, at the University of Virginia (which had been founded by Jefferson, and where, at this time, Thompson was serving on the music faculty). The University Glee Club was directed by Stephen Tuttle, while the composer played the accompaniment on the piano. This performance was broadcast over the CBS network and was transmitted by short wave by the OWI to the armed forces. On April 14, 1945, the *Testament* was performed at Carnegie Hall by the Boston Symphony Orchestra under Koussevitzky, to honor the memory of the recently deceased President Roosevelt.

1948 SYMPHONY NO. 3 IN A MINOR. I. Largo elegiaco. II. Allegro appassionato; Calmato ma triste assai. III. Lento tranquillo. IV. Allegro vivace.

The Third Symphony, commissioned by the Alice M. Ditson Fund, was completed almost two decades after the Second. It was begun in 1944, when the composer sketched the material for all four movements; but it took four years to complete the work. It was introduced by the CBS Symphony Orchestra under Thor Johnson in New York City on May 15, 1949, as part of the American Music Festival.

The following analysis of the symphony is by the composer: "The first movement is in sonata form, with only one principal theme and one principal rhythm. The prevailing mood is one of sadness. The second movement is full of action and defiance. The form is a modified rondo, in which the final statement of the principal theme is presented more slowly. Allusions to the theme of contrast, also greatly augmented, bring the movement to a desolate conclusion. The third movement is introduced by a phrase in the horn which later grows into a melody. The principal theme is song-like, and its three presentations are set off by plaintive passages in the woodwinds alone. The finale is in sonata form, and all the material is cheerful. There is no apotheosis of the themes nor any heroic peroration. The serious and even tragic elements of the earlier movements are dispelled in exuberance."

In his review in the New York *Sun*, Irving Kolodin wrote: "The third symphony . . . flows freely and powerfully from the source—in the composer's imagination—to the point where it joins the open seas of musical creation. The image, although a casual one, is not without relation to the kind of work it is. It begins with a trickle of thought, so to speak, and gathers its energies as other tributaries join it. It has power and logic, purpose and consummation;

all expressed in an idiom neither terribly new nor terribly old—rather than an idiom to suggest a derivation from such folk sources as Dvořák also heeded, enriched by the tonal and instrumental resources that have come into the musical language since."

VIRGIL THOMSON 1896–

In the middle 1920s, when so many composers were helplessly sucked into the vortex of their theories and inextricably enmeshed in the labyrinth of their techniques, Thomson set out to write music as simply and as lucidly as he could. He wanted to produce good tunes and good-sounding harmonies within clearly defined forms. He wanted to write the kind of music that audiences could listen to and respond to with their hearts. He had no desire to be impressive for his skill or erudition or courage; he merely wanted his works to provide the hearer with a pleasurable aesthetic experience.

Because he always tried to be entertaining and charming, Thomson was for a long time not taken very seriously by his fellow musicians. But as he produced one work after another, he achieved a considerable measure of success. Following the première of *Four Saints In Three Acts,* it became apparent that his simplicity was deceptive: that it required a consummate skill to arrive at the ease of expression and the precise logic found in Thomson's music; that because this music was so easy to listen to, it was not necessarily superficial or trite.

In whatever form he has chosen to write, Thomson continued to write simply. He has wit and he has feeling. He has a pronounced American identity: many of his healthy melodies are shaped after old American hymns and folk songs. He has charm and sophistication. By being himself and writing as he feels, Thomson is, as Aaron Copland said of him, "about as original a personality as America can boast, in or out of the musical field."

Thomson was born in Kansas City, Missouri, on November 25, 1896. In his childhood, he took lessons on the piano and organ and in theory, and at twelve, he officiated as organist at the Calvary Baptist Church in Kansas City. After serving in the army during World War I, when he was commissioned second lieutenant in the Military Aviation Corps, he entered Harvard. There he attended classes in music taught by Davison and Hill. During the summer of 1921, he was a member of the Harvard Glee Club which toured Europe. Thomson remained in Paris for a year at this time to study composition with Nadia Boulanger, on a John Knowles Paine Traveling Fellowship.

He was back in Harvard in 1922, filling the post of assistant instructor besides playing the organ at King's Chapel in Boston. He was graduated from Harvard with a Bachelor of Arts degree in 1923. For a year after that, he studied counterpoint with Rosario Scalero and conducting with Chalmers Clifton in New York. In 1925, he established permanent residence in Paris, where he remained until World War II, though making frequent visits back to the United States. In Paris, he became strongly influenced by Erik Satie and the "French Six" in the writing of "everyday music." In this manner he wrote the opera *Four Saints in Three Acts* in 1928, text by Gertrude Stein; its world première in 1934 brought him prominence for the first time. After returning to the United States, Thomson served as music critic of the New York *Herald Tribune* between 1940 and 1954, resigning in 1954 to devote himself to composition and conducting. He gathered his newspaper criticisms into three volumes: *The Musical Scene* (1945), *The Art of Judging Music* (1948), and *Music Right and Left* (1951). He has been a prolific composer, scoring major successes in all media. In 1949, he received the Pulitzer Prize for his score to the documentary motion picture *Louisiana Story*. He is the recipient of honorary degrees from Syracuse University (1949) and Rutgers (1956). In 1948, he was made a member of the National Institute of Arts and Letters, and in 1959, of the American Academy of Arts and Letters. In 1966, he received the Gold Medal of the National Institute of Arts and Letters. He has also been a successful teacher, having been a visiting professor in music at the University of Buffalo in 1963, and at the Carnegie Institute of Technology in 1966.

1928 SYMPHONY ON A HYMN TUNE. I. Allegro. II. Andante cantabile. III. Allegretto. IV. Alla breve.

American church hymns proved a bountiful source from which Thomson continually drew material for his compositions. In this, his first symphony, which he had begun writing in Paris in 1926, but which he completed two years later, he made use of a hymn that had become something of a theme song for the Southern Baptist Convention, "How Firm a Foundation, Ye Saints of the Lord." A second hymn, "Yes, Jesus Loves Me," becomes a significant subsidiary idea.

In writing his symphony, Thomson tried re-creating the atmosphere of farm life in mid-Western America in the nineteenth century. To do so he assumed a simple, homespun style. So successful was he in accomplishing this that Paul Rosenfeld likened the symphony to a Currier and Ives print.

Before the symphony received its world première, it was extensively revised. That première took place in New York on February 22, 1945, with the composer conducting the New York Philharmonic.

The composer has provided the following description:

"The Introduction is a conversational passage for solo instruments and pairs of instruments, followed by a statement of the hymn tune in half-in-and half-out-of-focus harmonization. The Allegro is a succession (and superposition) of dance-like passages derived from the main theme. Only the Introduction gets recapitulated. The movement ends with a cadenza for trombone, piccolo, solo cello and solo violin.

"The Andante cantabile is song-like and contemplative, a series of variations on a melody derived from the hymn tune, ending with the suggestion of a distant railway train.

"The Allegretto is a passacaglia of marked rhythmic character on the hymn-tune bass.

"The finale, a canzona on a part of the main theme, reintroduces the chief material of the symphony, including the hymn in full, and ends with a coda that recalls the Introduction."

1928 FOUR SAINTS IN THREE ACTS, "an opera to be sung" in four acts, with text by Gertrude Stein adapted by Maurice Grosser. First performance: Hartford, Connecticut, February 8, 1934.

In 1934, a group that called itself "The Society of Friends and Enemies of Modern Music" presented an experiment in opera in Hartford, Connecticut. Called *Four Saints in Three Acts,* it boasted an undecipherable libretto (frequently consisting only of unintelligible words and syllables, or intelligible phrases and words that had no seeming relation to their fellow phrases and words), the work of Gertrude Stein, apostle of alogical writing. The music was by the then-unknown American composer, Virgil Thomson. An all-Negro cast was dressed in cellophane costumes.

So unorthodox an opera inevitably invited interest. Soon after the world première, the opera moved to New York—to Broadway—on February 21. There it enjoyed a successful six-weeks run and attracted national attention. Later the same year, the opera was seen in Chicago. Since then, it has been revived several times in concert performances, was heard on a coast-to-coast broadcast over the CBS radio network in 1947, and was recorded by RCA Victor. As a stage presentation, it was revived on Broadway by ANTA with an all-Negro cast on April 16, 1952, and soon after that, this same production was included in the program of the "Masterpieces of the Twentieth Century" festival in Paris.

The setting is believed to be Spain, and the time is not specified. Thomson describes what happens as follows: "It shows Saint Theresa surrounded by women, and Saint Ignatius surrounded by men, all helping and working and studing to be saints. In the first act Saint Theresa is posed in a series of living pictures on the steps of the cathedral at Avila—a sort of Sunday school entertainment showing scenes from her saintly life. The second act is an outdoor party. The third act takes place in a monastery garden, with Saint Ignatius meeting the Holy Ghost ('Pigeons on the grass alas!') and drilling his Jesuit disciples in military discipline. In an epilogue called Act Four all the saints hold communion in heaven while the choir sings, 'When this you see remember me.' "

For all its unintelligibility, it proved to be a delightful opera—amusing, earthy, piquant, novel. What caused most surprise, however, was not the strange text, or the revolutionary staging and costuming, or even the unusual casting—but the very pleasing and melodious music that accompanied all these peculiar proceedings. The simplicity of the score (utilizing only the most elementary progressions and the most rudimentary harmonic language) had the naïve but robust quality of music derived from folk, popular and church-hymn sources. But within that simplicity, Thomson gave expression to an infectious wit, charm and even melodic beauty. It was, as Lawrence

Gilman said of it, a truly "suave and charming score." And Cecil Smith wrote after the 1952 revival: "*Four Saints in Three Acts* remained a masterpiece—wayward and ambiguous, alternately profoundly curious and tongue-in-the-cheek, but worthy of respect and affection as a piece far superior to the mere temper of the particular time in which it was first produced."

The most celebrated vocal excerpt comes in the third act when St. Ignatius describes his vision of the Holy Ghost ("Pigeons on the grass alas"). This is followed by another celebrated episode, when the chorus chants "Let Lucy Lily Lily Lucy Lucy let Lucy Lucy Lily Lily Lily Lily Lily." Another high vocal point is the famous interrupted solo of St. Theresa, "There are a great many persons and places near together."

1936 THE PLOW THAT BROKE THE PLAINS, suite for orchestra. I. Prelude. II. Pastorale (Grass). III. Cattle. IV. Blues (Speculation). V. Drought. VI. Devastation.

In 1936, Thomson wrote the background music for a documentary film produced by Pare Lorentz for the United States government pointing upon the way in which natural resources are abused, how the soil is exploited, and how havoc is caused by droughts. The six-movement symphonic suite which the composer prepared from his motion-picture music became his first successful orchestral composition; it has received extensive performances by major orchestras. *Modern Music* described this music as follows: "Simple, uninterrupted progression towards destruction provides a strong unifying factor. From the opening movement, with its mournful, broad sweep, prophetic of waste, there is a gradual build up to the final 'Devastation.' This movement is very similar to the beginning, yet the careful sequence of events which leads to its results in quite a different feeling, of consummated rather than implied loss. On the way there is a subtle stroke in the unhappy, almost querulous gaiety of the 'Blues,' a fine piece of understatement, of making a slight, apparently dissimilar mood a symbol of something more deeply tragic."

1937 FILLING STATION, "ballet document" in one act, with choreography by Lew Christensen, and scenario by Lincoln Kirstein. First performance: Ballet Caravan, Hartford, Connecticut, January 6, 1938.

Filling Station is the first successful modern ballet on an American subject which, in all its facets, is the work of Americans. The setting is an American filling station attended by Mac. First, a motorist comes asking road directions. Then two truck drivers are seen, followed by a state trooper come to accuse them of speeding. The motorist returns with his wife and daughter. A young couple drops in, slightly intoxicated, for they have just come from a party. Drama now intrudes with the presence of a gangster come for a holdup. In the ensuing scuffle, the girl is killed. Mac, the attendant, proves himself a hero by helping apprehend the gangster. The ballet ends as it had begun, with Mac quietly reading his newspaper in his filling station.

When *Filling Station* was revived by the New York City Ballet in 1952, the role of Mac was danced by Jacques d'Amboise, then only eighteen, a performance that first established him as a star. At that time, Walter Terry described the ballet as "unpretentious, lively, thoroughly entertaining and . . .

lovable." Terry found Thomson's score to be "infectious . . . delightful to the ear and an invitation to dance . . . based upon the popular rhythms (invigorated by some perennial folk memories) of the day."

1947 THE MOTHER OF US ALL, opera in three acts, with text by Gertrude Stein adapted by Maurice Grosser. First performance: New York City, May 12, 1947.

When Thomson was commissioned by the Alice M. Ditson Fund to write a new opera, he decided to revive his collaboration with Gertrude Stein, the librettist of his *Four Saints in Three Acts.* Stein agreed, and provided the composer with a somewhat more intelligible text than her first: a political fantasy based upon the career of Susan B. Anthony, pioneer in the woman suffrage movement, from her earliest struggles to her ultimate triumph after death. Somewhat obscure, rambling and poetic, the play was full of anachronisms and digressions into discussions of marriage, politics, love, etc.; the thirty-one characters included Ulysses S. Grant, Lillian Russell, Daniel Webster, Andrew Jackson, Thaddeus Stevens, John Adams and Anthony Comstock, as well as two other people thinly disguised as Gertrude S. and Virgil T.

The opera was introduced at Columbia University in New York City, during the American Music Festival.

The program for that performance carried the following excellent summary of the Stein libretto:

"The opera opens in the home of Susan B. Anthony, where she discusses with her supporter, Anne, her purposes and her difficulties. Virgil T. and Gertrude S. supply comment and interpretation... The second scene depicts a political rally, ending with a formal debate between Susan B. Anthony and Daniel Webster.

"The second act takes place on a village green beside Miss Anthony's house. Andrew Jackson and Thaddeus Stevens quarrel. Constance Fletcher and John Adams fall in love. The second scene of this act represents a daydream in which the suffrage leader reflects upon Negro suffrage, political celebrity, and the mystery of wealth and poverty. The third scene shows the wedding of Jo the Loiterer to Indiana Elliot, which is variously interrupted but eventually performed.

"The first two scenes of the third act take place in the drawing room of Susan B. Anthony. A delegation of politicians wishes her to speak for them at a meeting. She at first refuses, but finally accedes. In the next scene she is again at home. She has spoken, been successful, and foresees the final triumph of her cause. The last scene is a sort of epilogue, ending with the unveiling of Miss Anthony's statue in the Congressional Library."

The text obviously called for tongue-in-cheek music, and Thomson produced a score that met the demands of the play felicitously. It was witty, entertaining, satiric, even popular. It was filled with folksy melodies (though there were no actual set arias), some of them reminiscent of old waltzes, ballads and hymns.

In comparing the new opera with *Four Saints in Three Acts,* Olin Downes found that the later work is "more direct, more human in its approach, with more of characterization and, one would say, more of emotional reaction on the composer's part." Downes then described Thomson's music as "built upon the simple harmonic lines, with the admirable prosody of which he is a master, and a knowledge of singing use of the language. There is now and again a sustained melodic line that departs from the very close fitting of syllable and tone which prevails. The score has tunes closely related to America's past and even present . . . and there is a hymn tune, excellently conceived in the style of the old American hymns . . . which consititutes a really moving commentary on the scene of the wedding and, without sentimentalizing, brings home a certain pathos. . . . . There are, of course, the satirical contrasts. . . . Elsewhere one remembers old comic Italian madrigals with canonic imitations and all that. . . . The end of the opera, when Susan B. wonders whether the fight won has been important . . . is of a certain loftiness and resignation."

After completing the writing of his opera, Thomson wrote three orchestral numbers based on materials from his score. These three numbers—together with a fourth transcribed from the opera—became a symphonic suite which the composer introduced with the Knoxville Symphony on January 17, 1950. The first movement is the introduction to the opening act, its first sections and coda derived from the music in the opera identifying Susan B. Anthony, and the part just before the coda coming from the intermezzo describing Susan B. Anthony's dream. The second and third movements are vivid tonal pictures of a lively political rally (music taken from Act I, Scene II), and of a wintry day. The suite ends with the music in the opera accompanying the marriage of Jo the Loiterer to Indiana Elliott, and concludes with the funeral music attending the apotheosis of Susan B. Anthony.

The opera was revived in New York City by the American Opera Society on April 1, 1964.

1948 LOUISIANA STORY, Suite No. 1, for orchestra. I. Pastoral—The Bayou and the Marsh Buggy. II. Chorale—The Derrick Arrives. III. Passacaglia—Robbing the Alligator's Nest. IV. Fugue—Boy Fights Alligator.

ACADIAN SONGS AND DANCES, Suite No. 2 from Louisiana Story. I. Sadness. II. Papa's Tune. III. A Narrative. IV. The Alligator and the Coon. V. Supersadness. VI. Walking Song. VII. The Squeeze Box.

In 1948, Thomson was commissioned to write the music for a documentary film called *Louisiana Story,* produced by Robert Flaherty. The film told the story of an oil development project in Louisiana and its impact on the life of a single French-speaking family—all seen through the eyes of a fourteen-year-old boy. For this film, Thomson wrote a score that was influenced by the songs and dances of the Acadian region, deriving his sources from *French Folk Songs* edited by Irene Therese Whitfield. In 1949, Thomson was awarded the Pulitzer Prize in music for this score, the first time such an honor was given to music for a motion picture.

Thomson subsequently created two orchestral suites out of this music, the first of which has enjoyed great success. It was first introduced by the Philadelphia Orchestra under Eugene Ormandy on November 26, 1948.

Thomson has described the suite in the following way: "The orchestral suite . . . consists of four movements: the Pastoral, describing bayous, the boy in his rowboat, and the maneuvers of the 'marsh buggy,' an amphibious bulldozer which is part of the oil-prospecting machinery; a Chorale, which represents the boy playing in a tree with his pet racoon and his view from there of the drill barge's majestic approach; a Passacaglia, which recounts the boy's adventure in robbing an alligator's nest of its eggs, ending with the approach of the mother reptile; and a chromatic Fugue in four sections, which is used in the film to accompany the boy's fight to land an alligator that he has hooked with bait."

The last two movement are described by Dr. Frederick W. Sternfeld as follows: "The alligator fugue (finale) is an example of chromatic and dissonant music that fulfills a descriptive function and yet rises beyond that role by virtue of its inner logic and by its power to lay bare the core of events, not merely to reflect the surface. . . . All this is achieved with the utmost economy—the entire fugue takes less than five minutes—and the tension is never hysterical. . . . The passacaglia, which precedes the fugue, is broader in dimension and looser in structure. It forms the accompaniment to several of the alligator's attacks before the final tussle."

The second suite adapted by Thomson from his motion-picture score, and which bears the title of *Acadian Songs and Dances,* makes far more extensive use of folk material than did the first; here Thomson's own music is also often strongly influenced by the waltz and polka rhythms of Cajun folk tunes and dances.

1950 CONCERTO FOR CELLO AND ORCHESTRA. I. Rider on the Plains. II. Variations on a Southern Hymn Tune. III. Children's Games.

It took Thomson almost five years to complete his cello concerto, which he had begun in 1945. It was introduced on March 24, 1950, in Philadelphia. Paul Olefsky was the soloist, and Eugene Ormandy conducted the Philadelphia Orchestra. On August 27 of the same year, the work was heard at the Edinburgh Festival for its European première, with Anthony Pini, cellist, and the Royal Philharmonic conducted by Sir Thomas Beecham.

Thomson intended the concerto as a self-portrait, "the physical state," says John Cage, "of a healthy human being." The first movement (Allegretto) is in classical sonata form, with two cadenzas for the solo instrument. This music has been described as a "loping, lilting, open-air piece in six-eight time." The second movement (Andante) is based on an early nineteenth-century tune, "Tribulation." This melody is heard over a bass accompaniment, followed by ten variations. After the fifth variation, the solo instrument embarks on an introspective cadenza. The finale, in rondo form, quotes two melodies: the hymn, "Yes, Jesus Loves Me," and a theme from a Beethoven piano sonata. "He does this intentionally," said Olin Downes, "and the themes fit in well with the other scraps of folksy tunes that prattle along, side by side, or in combination, in this amusing finale."

1954 CONCERTO FOR FLUTE, STRINGS, HARP AND PERCUSSION: I. Rapsodico. II. Lento. III. Ritmico.

The world première of this concerto took place at the Venice Biennale on September 18, 1954. At that time, the composer explained in his program notes: "The chief problem for me in writing a flute concerto was to present the flute in a musical and orchestral texture becoming to the instrument. Naturally, I had already considered the expressive character of the work to be suitable to the flute. Otherwise I should not have composed it. My omission of wind instruments from the orchestral accompaniment was determined by the desire to make the solo part sound prominent and beautiful. The expressive content of the piece is double. It is first of all a portrait, but it is also bird music. That is to say, it is a portrait conceived as a concerto for nightingale and strings." While, in his extended series of portraits for various instruments or combinations of instruments, Thomson always identified his subject, he has refused to to do so in the case of this concerto.

The first movement is an unaccompanied flute solo extending for forty-one measures. John Cage explains that the form "is that of a continuous invention gradually becoming more and more florid." The composer notes that the second movement is "a study in dual chromatic harmonies, each of which is acoustically complete and wholly independent of the other." And the third movement is also based on double harmonies; but in this instance the contrast is between chromatic chords and diatonic chords. . . . The character of the harmonic contrast in this movement is aimed to accentuate, to dramatize, the rhythmic animation that is characteristic of the expressive content."

1960 MISSA PRO DEFUNCTIS, for double chorus and orchestra.

This is one of Thomson's most ambitious religious compositions, It was commissioned by the State University College of Education for the twenty-ninth annual Spring Festival of the Arts held at the College in Potsdam, New York, on May 14, 1960, the composer conducting.

There are nine sections. In place of vocal soloists, the composer has throughout the work interpolated brief instrumental passages engaging the services of individual instrumentalists. The composer explains that the two choruses—one male, and the other female—are "treated as a harmonic unit not always related harmonically to the other save by contrast. In this way certain sections of the work attain a highly dissonant result without confusion of sound within the choirs. . . . The separation of men and women into two choirs, each harmonious within itself, allows for a blending of sound in each that is not possible in any mixture of the two."

Though this is devotional music, the composer did not hesitate to borrow folk idioms and even popular strains. The score makes use of waltz rhythms, progressive jazz, boogie-woogie, tango, and American hymnology. "Within the religious framework," James Gruen has written in *Musical America,* "these Thomsonian devices have been placed on the side of the angels, as it were, and been given reverential status." Gruen singles out the "Dies Irae" as one of the summits of the work. "Here a host of musical ideas bring to life the reality of the Last Judgment, divine anger, divine grace, hell fire and the possibility of achieving preferential treatment through prayer. With emotional accuracy, the composer sustains the long section with all manner of vocal and orchestral subtleties."

1961–1962 A SOLEMN MUSIC, for orchestra (also for band).
A JOYFUL FUGUE, for orchestra.

A Joyful Fugue (1962) is a sprightly scherzo commissioned for the Philadelphia Orchestra by Edward B. Benjamin. The Philadelphia Orchestra, under Eugene Ormandy, introduced it in Philadelphia on February 1, 1962. The composer described this music as follows: "Exposure of the subject proceeds by canonic imitation, by inversion, and by stretto, as well as by varieties of simultaneous statement, though never by retrograde motion, since the subjects do not invite this usage. The final statement together of all four themes is followed by a coda evocative of organ virtuosities."

When the Philadelphia Orchestra introduced *A Joyful Fugue* it coupled it with an earlier Thomson piece for orchestra, *A Solemn Music*. This is a short funeral march written in 1949 for band in the twelve-tone style. It was inspired by the death of two close friends—Gertrude Stein and the painter, Christian Berard—and it was commissioned by the League of Composers. As a band composition, it was introduced by the Goldman Band in New York on June 17, 1949. The orchestral adaptation was made in 1961 for Nadia Boulager for her appearance as a guest conductor of the New York Philharmonic on February 15, 1962.

SIR MICHAEL TIPPETT 1905–

When he renounced and withdrew most of the compositions he had written before World War II, Tippett was not at the same time casting aside the strong Romantic feelings that pervaded those compositions. Beginning with his *Double Concerto,* for string orchestra (1939), Tippett began combining his former Romanticism with polyphonic structures. A strong contrapuntal style, with frequent use of a linear technique, has characterized Tippett's writing since that time. He also developed a stronger lyricism than heretofore, together with a complex rhythmic vocabulary and, in his latest works, an interest in fresh, new sonorities. Without being avant-garde, he has been an individualist who (as one unidentified English critic once said of his music) "gently disturbs the senses but nowhere violates them" and whose "purity and integrity of style . . . is deeper than appears on the surface." Many different strains coalesce in his music, from the Americanism of the Negro spiritual and jazz to the Celtic folk element. All this, as W. H. Mellers has remarked, merge "into the broader aspects of the European tradition—troubadour music, medieval polyphony, madrigal technique, the most rigid dance symmetry, and the Beethovenian 'drama' of thematic development." Tippett's music is "contemporary music which demands a contemporary approach," continues Mellers, "and at the same time it has a flexible relation to the evolution of the whole European tradition. Both lyrical and sophisticated, it holds the scales between the two *pis allers* of modern music—provinciality and cosmopolitanism."

Tippett was born in London on January 2, 1905. His childhood and boyhood were spent in a small Suffolk village, where he began taking piano lessons. In his eighteenth year, he came to London, where he enrolled in the Royal College of Music. There he studied composition with Charles Wood and R. O. Morris, and conducting with Sir Malcolm Sargent and Sir Adrian Boult. Though he undertook ambitious composition from his twenty-ninth year on, including a symphony, he rejected everything he had written before 1938, except for his first string quartet, which he had written in 1935 and revised in 1943. The *Double Concerto,* for string orchestra, in 1939, was his first major mature achievement which he stood ready to acknowledge; and from that time on, he worked slowly and painstakingly on large works in all media, for which recognition came slowly but inevitably. Between 1940 and 1951, he was the musical director of Morley College in London, where some of his major works were introduced.

A humanitarian from boyhood on, profoundly concerned with social injustice and human suffering, Tippett was a passionate pacifist, who during World War II accepted prison rather than disavow his convictions. This strong love of peace and social justice penetrated into the writing of some of his most successful works, beginning with the oratorio, *A Child of Our Time,* in 1942. Tippett's first opera, *The Midsummer Marriage,* was a failure when introduced at Covent Garden on January 27, 1955. A second opera, *King Priam,* was given at Coventry Cathedral in England on May 29, 1962.

Tippett's sixtieth birthday was celebrated both in England and the United States with performances of major works. In the United States, he was invited to participate at the music festival at Aspen, Colorado, an occasion marking his first visit to America. Tippett was knighted in June of 1966.

1939 CONCERTO FOR DOUBLE ORCHESTRA. I. Allegro con brio. II. Adagio cantabile. III. Allegro molto.

Tippett's orchestral concerto—scored for two string orchestras of equal size—was his first successful composition, and the first he regards as truly representative of his later mature style. He himself conducted the world première in London in April of 1940. It is in the concerto-grosso structure in which two instrumental groups alternate or combine in the presentation of thematic material and which makes elaborate use of polyphonic practices.

The composition is characterized by constantly changing tempo markings, shifting accents, syncopations, and the presentation of phrases of unequal length. Here is how Edward Sackville described this music in *The New Statesman:* "The Concerto is polyphonic in texture, but the weaving is mostly close enough to allow the extraordinary freshness and lyrical quality of the melodies and chordal structures to eliminate any dryness inherent in the style. The rhythmic intricacies are indeed considerable, but exist only to enhance the vitality of the composition, making the most expressive use of the arabesques suggested by the themes, as in the madrigals of the Renaissance. All three movements are related to one another by an anagrammatic figure, which in the slow movement takes an arrestingly lovely form."

1942 A CHILD OF OUR TIME, oratorio for chorus and orchestra.

No single work by Tippett has been heard so frequently and so widely as this deeply moving oratorio into which he poured so much of his own strong feelings against inhumanity and injustice. A tragic episode from the history of pre-World War II in Europe was Tippett's inspiration: the murder of a Nazi diplomat in Paris by a Jewish youth trying to avenge the persecution of his people in Germany. To a text of his own writing, Tippett used this incident to point up man's inhumanity to man, to lament the ascendancy of evil in the world, and to express the hope that justice might prevail. "Vast in scope . . . the work evolves as a compelling humanistic plea," says Allen Young. "Tippett's attention to the line of the work keeps it surging, and the freedom of his dissonances and contrasting harmonies establishes its inner tension."

To heighten the drama of his message, Tippett interpolated five Negro spirituals into his score, including "Nobody Knows De Trouble I've Seen" and "Deep River." He used these spirituals within his oratorio context the way Bach used chorales. The purpose of this quotation was to remind the listeners that the Negro, too, was despised, rejected and persecuted; that it was only fitting and proper that one persecuted people should speak out for another. "It is a silhouette of all persecuted humanity," says an unidentified critic for the *Times Educational Supplement.* "Jazz rhythms, madrigal and Negro spiritual have been absorbed and fused into a style which is unmistakably and uncompromisingly Tippett's own, yet gloriously happy; for all the complexity of texture its colors stand out as boldly as poppies in a field of green wheat."

The world première took place in London on March 19, 1944, Walter Goehr conducting.

1953 FANTASIA CONCERTANTE ON A THEME BY CORELLI, for string orchestra.

This composition was commissioned by the Edinburgh Festival Society. Its première took place at the Edinburgh Festival on August 29, 1953, at a concert of the BBC Symphony, the composer conducting.

The Corelli theme comes out of the Concerto Grosso in F, op. 6, no. 2. After the theme has been stated, a series of variations follow. "As the music gradually increases in complexity," wrote Malcom MacDonald in his program notes for the world première, "the harmonic style veers gradually from Corelli to Tippett. . . . The variations give way to a double ground bass. . . . A rather more lyrical middle section is based on a major version of the original theme, suitably extended; it gives way to a fugal section of extreme complexity . . . . A transition is made to the final section, a Pastorale owing something to that of Corelli in his *Christmas Concerto*. . . . The work concludes with a final variation of the original theme."

1965 THE VISION OF SAINT AUGUSTINE, for baritone, chorus and orchestra.

Commissioned by the BBC, *The Vision of Saint Augustine* (its composer's most ambitious and finest work for chorus) was introduced in London on January 19, 1966. The composer prepared his own text, basing it mainly on two mystical experiences from *The Confessions of Saint Augustine,* supplemented by material from the Vulgate, and Bishop Ambrose's hymn, "*Deus Creator Omnium*." The two Saint Augustine visions deal first with the one experienced with his friend Alypius in a garden near Milan, and then with the glimpse of eternity he gets with his mother, Monica.

The work is in three sections. The following admirable analysis was prepared by Anthony Payne in *Tempo*: "The first movement, which prepares the way for the second where the vision itself is described, is in a free rondo form in which the recurring section is a narrative speech-rhythmed chant for the chorus in close two-part harmony. The first sub-section is a magnificent setting of "*Deus Creator Omnium*" over a once-repeated isorhythmic bass. . . . Then the first really powerful climax bursts out . . . as reference is made to the window through which we may imagine the pair to be looking at the moment of vision. . . .

"The second movement describes the vision, in three broad melodic paragraphs, each punctuated by a short pause. . . . The climax is capped by a magnificent six-page Alleluia, one of the outstanding moments in the score. . . . The movement ends with a paraphrase of the opening three paragraphs, for orchestra alone. . . .

"The shorter final movement argues that eternal life of the saints may be a prolongation of the mystical moment experienced in the previous movement, and it works towards a climactic statement of the Alleluia which reappears almost unaltered. The variations that are introduced are significant though, for pauses are made in order that freshly superimposed solo lines may sound through, and each resumption of the Alleluia takes up quite boldly at the point it would have reached if it had continued behind the solo. One sees with a shock that the ecstatic vision is now incomplete and incapable of being sustained, so that the human fallibility, in the last courageous choral statement, 'I count not myself to be apprehended,' has been prepared for."

ERNST TOCH 1887–1964

Though Ernst Toch early shook off the influence that Brahms had had on him, he never rejected either Brahms's healthy respect for form, nor his Romantic disposition. The structural logic of Toch's music is one of its salient qualities, revealing at all times the hands of a master. Within these structures, Toch has produced music that successfully reconciles a Romantic temperament with a modern spirit. Articulateness combined with craftsmanship produced works that are generally lyrical, charged with feeling, original and forceful in the flowering of basic ideas, and strong with rhythmic momentum. As Oliver Daniel once wrote, Toch's music "is born of the best of the late Germanic tradition, but with an important freshness" and it possesses "naturalness and spontaneity."

Toch was born in Vienna on December 7, 1887. Though he began composing when he was six, and always showed an unusual interest for music which he learned through self-study, he was directed to a professional career outside music. From 1906 to 1909, he attended the University of Vienna as a medical student. Nevertheless, he never relaxed his musical activities, producing a good deal of chamber music. Winning the Mozart Prize in 1909 changed his direction from medicine to music. For a year, he lived in Frankfort-on-the-Main, studying the piano with Willy Rehberg. In 1910, he was awarded the Mendelssohn Prize and after that four consecutive Austrian State Prizes for composition. In 1913, he joined the faculty of the High School for Music at Mannheim as a teacher of theory. During World War I, he was an officer in the Austrian army. After the war, Toch established his reputation as composer with successful performances of major works, including his first piano concerto in Düsseldorf on October 8, 1926, and his comic opera, *Die Prinzessin auf der Erbse* (*The Princess on the Pea*), produced at the Festival of New Music at Baden-Baden on July 17, 1927.

He settled in Berlin in 1929, and in the Spring of 1932, he toured the United States as pianist in performances of his music. In 1933, with the rise of Hitler in Germany, he left that country for good. In the fall of 1934, he established residence in New York, where he taught composition at the New School for Social Research. In 1936, he transferred his home to California. There he became an American citizen and was appointed professor of music at the University of California in Los Angeles. During the next few years he wrote music for motion pictures. Between 1950 and 1958, Toch lived mainly in Switzerland, but in the latter year he reestablished his home at Santa Monica, where he had been living before 1950, and where he now stayed until the end of his life. In 1956, he received the Pulitzer Prize in music for his Third Symphony, and in 1957, he was elected a member of the National Institute of Arts and Letters and received the Grand Cross of the Merit Order from the West German Republic. His seventy-fifth birthday, in 1962, was commemorated with concerts of his works both in Europe and America. In 1963, he received the Cross of Honor for Science and Art from the Austrian government. He died in Los Angeles on October 1, 1964.

1932 SYMPHONY (OR CONCERTO) NO. 2 FOR PIANO AND ORCHESTRA, op. 61. I. Allegro. II. Lebhaft. III. Adagio. IV. Cyklus Variabilis.

Toch's second piano concerto is one of his finest works for solo instrument and orchestra. It was written six years after his first piano concerto, op. 38. The première performance took place on August 20, 1934, in London with the composer at the piano and Sir Henry J. Wood conducting.

The work is classical in its form and gives such equal importance to both the solo instrument and the orchestra that it has at times been described as a "symphony for piano and orchestra." The first movement is in sonata form, with both principal themes stated early and developed soon after they make their appearance; the first theme is treated fugally between piano and orchestra, while the second theme gets a more harmonic setting. The second movement has a marked dance rhythm and consists of two ideas, one in a tarantella rhythm, the other in waltz time. The slow movement is brief; it is full of feeling and reaches a climax with a long and impressive section for unaccompanied piano. The composer himself described the final movement as "Changeable Cycle," by which he meant that it utilizes a free-variation form, the last part of which carries memories of melodic ideas first stated in the first two movements.

1934 BIG BEN, variation-fantasy for orchestra, op. 62.

One foggy evening when Toch was in London, he crossed the Westminster bridge and heard the chiming of Big Ben. "The theme," the composer explained, "lingered in my imagination for a long while, and evolved into other forms, somehow still connected with the original one, until finally, like the chimes themselves, it seemed to disappear into the fog from which it emerged. I have sought to fix this impression in my variation-fantasy."

Toch did not write this work until he came to the United States. He completed it in the fall of 1934, and on December 20 of the same year it was heard for the first time in Cambridge, with Richard Burgin conducting the Boston Symphony Orchestra.

The Big Ben theme is heard somewhat disguised in the opening of the work. The variations that follow are of changing moods, ranging, as Paul A. Pisk once wrote, "from the heavy, peasant-like, almost Russian dance to the pastel colorings of a London fog." The climax of the work is a fugue, after which there comes a transitional passage to the concluding sounds of the chiming clock.

1936 PINOCCHIO, A MERRY OVERTURE, for orchestra.

This gay and sprightly piece of music was written soon after Toch had become acquainted with the story of Pinocchio at the home of Alvin Johnson, then director of the New School for Social Research. It was introduced by the Los Angeles Philharmonic under Otto Klemperer on December 10, 1936.

The following verse appears on the title-page of the score:

Italian lore would have us know
That gay marionette Pinocchio!
With deviltry and gamin grace
He led them all a merry chase.

The score then carries the following description of the tale, which serves admirably as the program for Toch's music:

"Pinocchio is a figure in Italian folklore created by Carlo Collodi. According to the story, he was fashioned by old Gepetto, a wood-carver, from a curiously animated piece of wood. His rascally demeanor and mischievous escapades gave his creator many an anxious moment. His particular failing was fibbing, each lie prompting his already long nose to grow longer. He is a sort of brother-in-mischief to the German Till Eulenspiegel. To this day children are warned by their elders that their noses will grow as long as Pinocchio's if they do not tell the truth."

1937 QUINTET FOR PIANO AND STRINGS, op. 64. I. Allegro non troppo. II. Con sordini. III. Adagio. IV. Allegro.

One of the composer's finest chamber-music compositions, the Piano Quintet was written on a commission from Mrs. Elizabeth Sprague Coolidge. Its première took place at the Berkshire Festival of Chamber Music in Pittsfield, Massachusetts, on September 23, 1938, performed by the composer and the Roth Quartet.

The composer himself identified the mood of each of the four movements by appending to each a descriptive word: "Lyrical" to the first; "Whimsical" to the second; "Contemplative" to the third; and "Dramatic" to the fourth. The first and concluding movements are in the sonata form. Each has two contrasting themes, the first dramatic, the second lyrical. In each instance the development is free with new material interpolated.

The second movement is in a cyclic form. Its middle section, says Nicolas Slonimsky, "presents . . . an antiphonal treatment of the instrumental disposition. The piano gives the exposition of the thematic material in 'free declamation'; the strings, playing in unison, give a 'reiterating response.' "

The third-movement Adagio opens with an expressive thought for strings alone, following which the piano embarks on a brief interlude. Slonimsky says that "the thematic development . . . is less compact than a classical form would demand; the motives follow one another in a rhapsodic manner. Yet the architectonic design . . . is never diffuse. Toch insists that in all circumstances he maintains the 'natural balance of tension and relaxation' to secure the logic of form within the free flow of melodic and rhythmic elements."

1947 HYPERION, dramatic prelude for orchestra, op. 71.

Toch wrote this dramatic prelude on a commission from the Kulas Fund in Cleveland. On January 8, 1948, it was introduced in Cleveland, with George Szell conducting the Cleveland Orchestra.

The composer provided the following description: "It begins in a somber, subdued mood, and though based on close unity of its thematic material, rises to a mood of hopefulness and assurance—somehow perhaps reflecting the idea of the Latin proverb '*Per aspera ad astra.*' "

The work opens slowly with a chromatic theme in the bassoons. The tempo then quickens, and a broad and spacious subject is heard in the bassoons and lower strings. The principal idea of the piece then arrives in the trumpets and trombones, derived from the opening bars of the work. The opening theme also serves as material for the climax, which is played by unison strings, bass and bassoon.

1955 SYMPHONY NO. 3, op. 75. I. Molto adagio; Agitato; Tempo primo. II. Andante tranquillo. III. Allegro impetuoso.

Toch's third and most famous symphony was commissioned by the American Jewish Tercentenary Committee of Chicago. Its world première took place in Pittsburgh on December 2, 1955, with William Steinberg conducting the Pittsburgh Symphony. In 1956, the symphony received the Pulitzer Prize in music.

One of the unusual features of this symphony lies in its instrumentation. Two sound-producing instruments, never before found in symphonic work, are required to produce novel noises. One of these is a tank of carbon dioxide that produces a hissing sound through a valve; the other, a wooden box in which croquet balls are set into motion to create a percussion sound by a rotating crank. Both these "instruments" are used backstage. The composer explained the presence of these noisemakers by revealing that he had long felt hampered by the limitations imposed upon him by the conventional instruments of the orchestra, and had always wanted to use sonorities and sound textures which conventional instruments were incapable of reproducing. "It must not be assumed," said a critic for *Musical America,* "that the symphony is merely a trick piece depending upon instrumental novelties for its effects. The odd instruments are used sparingly, though not timidly, nor just for textural reasons, and they fit artistically into the general orchestral design."

In addition to these sound makers, the orchestration calls for a Hammond organ, a pipe organ, an Armonicon (glass harmonica) and tuned glass bells, besides the usual orchestra.

The mood of the music is suggested by a quotation from Goethe's *The Sorrows of Werther* appended to the score: "Indeed am I but a wanderer, a pilgrim on earth—what else are you?" Two sections of the symphony are lyrical, one is dramatic. The composer explains his structure as a kind of "ballistic curve with an initial impulse, a steady line, and then a decline," found in each of the three sections.

VINCENZO TOMMASINI 1878–1950

Tommasini joined forces with such twentieth-century Italian composers as Respighi, Casella, Pizzetti and Malipiero in creating an Italian school of instrumental composers. In his apprentice works, he imitated first the German Romanticists, then the French impressionists. Gradually, however, he arrived at a nationalist style in which old Italian forms were stylized and old Italian songs and dances were simulated. Melody is the basis of Tommasini's works—but it is an *instrumental* melody as opposed to the operatic; the harmony, while never experimental, is allowed freedom of movement; the idea and form are inextricably synthesized so that it is often difficult to isolate one from the other.

Guido M. Gatti singles out the fine, sensitive, alive and vivid emotion in Tommasini's music for special attention. "This fine emotion, half sentient, half mystic . . . can be discerned in all his compositions, and the more we study the musician's work, the clearer and more luminous does it become. His score may be arduously wrought to the last stage of nobility and refinement, but his fundamental thought, the root of his emotion, remains simple and glowing with life."

Tommasini was born in Rome on September 17, 1878. His father, a well-known historian, insisted he receive a comprehensive academic education. While acquiring his musical training at the Santa Cecilia Academy in Rome (composition with Falchi, violin with Pinelli), Tommasini attended the public schools. He then specialized in the Greek language, literature and philology at the University of Rome. These studies over, Tommasini undertook extensive travel in Europe and the United States. In 1910, he completed the first work to point up his individuality—the String Quartet in F. In 1913, he received first prize from the city of Rome for his one-act opera, *Uguale fortuna,* which was produced that year at the Teatro Costanzi in Rome. Fame came with the sensitive orchestral tone poem, *Chiari di Luna,* introduced under Toscanini's direction in Rome on November 16, 1916, and with the ballet, *The Good-Humored Ladies,* in 1917.

Tommasini died in Rome on December 24, 1950.

1917 THE GOOD-HUMORED LADIES (LA DONNE DI BUON UMORE), choreographic comedy in one act, with choreography by Léonide Massine and scenario based on Goldoni's comedy of the same name. First performance: Ballet Russe, Rome, April 12, 1917.

THE GOOD-HUMORED LADIES, suite for orchestra. I. Presto. II. Allegro. III. Andante. IV. Tempo di ballo. V. Presto.

Tommasini's international fame came with this ballet, which was performed by the Ballet Russe with outstanding success throughout Europe. The ballet scenario was based on Goldoni's gay comedy set in eighteenth-century Venice during a carnival. Serge Diaghilev provided the following outline of the ballet scenario at the world première: "The Good-Humored Ladies can think of nothing but roguery. They send to the lovesick Rinaldo a note in which a lady wearing a rose-colored ribbon offers him a rendezvous. Five ladies, all wearing rose-colored ribbons, present themselves, and finally Rinaldo remains alone with old Silvestra. The soubrette, Mariuccia, in love with Leonardo, arranges for a supper with the little rake, Battista, during the course of which they play many jokes on the old Marquis Luca, who finally courts the two young people, both disguised as ladies. In the end, the Good-Humored Ladies give to old Silvestra as partner the inn-keeper Niccolo, whom they have dressed up as a lord. Through all this roguery passes the melancholy and charming figure of Constanza, fiancée of Rinaldo, with whom the other women are carrying on flirtations."

Tommasini's score is an adaptation of music by Domenico Scarlatti, the distinguished eighteenth-century composer of piano sonatas. These are the Scarlatti sonatas which appear in the orchestral suite adapted by Tommasini from his ballet score: G major, L. 388; D major, L. 361; B minor, L. 33, G major, L. 209; G minor, L. 499; D major, L. 463; F major, L. 385.

1922 TUSCAN LANDSCAPES (PAESAGGI TOSCANI), rhapsody for orchestra.

Tuscan Landscapes is a rhapsody on popular Tuscan folk melodies. It was introduced by the Augusteo Orchestra in Rome under Bernardino Molinari in December, 1923. The work is in two sections, played without interruption. The first (Andante sostenuto) is grave and dreamy; out of a nebulous background rises a melancholy Tuscan folk song. The second part (Vivace) is, by contrast, vital and gay, built out of two Tuscan folk tunes.

1927 PRELUDE, FANFARE, AND FUGUE (PRELUDIO, FANFARA E FUGA), for orchestra.

The three sections of this work are played without interruption. Two lyrical ideas comprise the first part, the Prelude: the first appears in muted strings and first horn in unison; the second in English horn and celli against the roll of tympani. A pianissimo passage for first and third horns against a roll of tympani and tremolo of low strings marks the beginning of the Fanfare. A flourish comes from the distance, growing into the Fanfare proper, which develops into a crashing fortissimo. A decrescendo follows, culminating in one trumpet sounding a long C. This note ties in with the first note of the ensuing fugue. The work ends with a dramatic climax for full orchestra.

The piece was introduced soon after its composition by the Augusteo Orchestra in Rome under Victor de Sabata.

1928 THE CARNIVAL OF VENICE (IL CARNEVALE DI VENEZIA), variations for orchestra.

Tommasini wrote these variations, "à la Paganini," in 1928, and they were introduced in New York by the New York Philharmonic Orchestra under Arturo Toscanini on October 10, 1929.

Tommasini's description of this work is as follows:

"The composition is an evocation of the Carnival of Venice in the manner of Paganini. On the thrice-familiar theme, the celebrated violinist composed twenty bravura variations for the violin, and in these he tried, it would seem, to describe various episodes and scenes of the Venetian festival.

"The orchestral composition begins with an introduction that depicts nightfall on the canals in the city of lagoons. After the exposition of the theme there follow thirteen variations, the substance of which is drawn from just so many selected from the twenty written by Paganini. Suddenly one hears a prolonged blare of brass on the chord of C major. This interrupts, as if in a startling vision, the series of variations. Forthwith one hears the striking of midnight. Then a brief finale, describing the return of festivities even more animated than before."

JOAQUIN TURINA 1882–1949

Turina belonged with the school of Spanish nationalist composers which came into being as a result of the inspiration and researches of Felipe Pedrell (*see* Albéniz). Like his celebrated fellow nationalists, Albéniz and Manuel de Falla, Turina spent many years in Paris; and the impress of French music is even more noticeable on Turina's work than on those of his forerunners and compatriots. As a pupil of Vincent d'Indy, Turina absorbed the influence of César Franck, whose stylistic traits (serenity and mysticism, particularly) and technique (the cyclic form, for example) are evident in some of Turina's music. The delicate impressionistic writing of Debussy, whom Turina knew personally, is also one of Turina's attributes as a composer. To these French mannerisms, Turina brought the rhythms, melodies and personality of his native land, producing a music that was distinctly his own. "He advanced Spanish style from its base of singular and ingrown nationalism," says Edward Cole, "toward a more universal expression by dint of his sound academic equipment and taste."

Turina was born in Seville on December 9, 1882. After preliminary study of theory and piano in Seville, and additional piano lessons with José Tragó at the Madrid Conservatory, he came to Paris in 1905. He remained there almost a decade, attending the Schola Cantorum as a pupil of Moszkowski in piano and d'Indy in composition. The Piano Quintet in G minor, successfully performed in 1907, marked Turina's official debut as composer; it became his first published work. Influenced by Albéniz and Manuel de Falla to turn to writing Spanish national music, Turina composed his first important work in 1912, *La Procesión del rocio,* for orchestra. In 1914, he returned to Spain, settling in Madrid, where he assumed a place of first importance in its musical life. He distinguished himself not only as a composer but also as a professor at the Madrid Conservatory, as a conductor of ballet performances, as a pianist with the Quinteto de Madrid, and as a critic for *El Debate.*

Turina died in Madrid on January 14, 1949.

1912 LA PROCESIÓN DEL ROCIO, for orchestra, op. 9.

Each season in June there takes place in Triana, a suburb of Seville, a colorful religious procession known as the "Procession of the Dew," in which the image of the Virgin is carried in a silver cart drawn by oxen. This procession is described in Turina's best-known orchestral work, written in 1912 and introduced by the Orquesta Sinfónica of Madrid on March 30, 1913. The orchestral piece is in two sections. The first describes festive Triana throbbing with song and dance and festivity. The second brings up the impressive procession. A religious melody appears and reappears throughout the work to solemnize the occasion. After a climax, in which the religious theme is prominent, songs and dances of Triana are heard anew, and then ebb away.

1917 MUJERES ESPANOLAS (SPANISH WOMEN), for piano, Set No. 1, op. 17. I. La Madrilena classica. II. La Andaluza sentimental. III. La Corena coqueta.

The bulk of Turina's music is for the piano, an area to which he became Spain's most significant contributor since Albéniz. *Mujeres espanolas,* as the title suggests, is a set of three portraits of Spanish women. The first describes a woman of classic beauty and personality; this is an Andalusian melody accompanied by chords simulating the strummings on a guitar. The second, depicting a sentimental lady, has a languid melody which midway is interrupted by a dance-like episode; the entire piece has the character of an improvisation. The third brings up a picture of a coquette in music made sprightly with Spanish dance rhythms.

Turina produced a second set of *Mujeres espanolas,* this time comprising five numbers, in 1932, op. 73.

1920 DANZAS FANTASTICAS (FANTASTIC DANCES), for orchestra (also for piano), op. 22. I. Exaltation. II. Musing. III. Orgy.

Out of the storehouse of Andalusian dance rhythms, Turina drew the material for this set of three Spanish dances—originally for piano, then adapted by the composer for orchestra. The first, which begins somewhat placidly with an introduction of flamenco character, develops frenetically into a jota. This music was inspired by the following quotation by José Mais: "It was like the feature of some incomparable picture, moving within the calyx of a blossom."

The sinuous movement of an Andalusian folk song provides the character for the second dance, which is full of oriental languor. The basic rhythm here is derived from the Basque dance, Zortzico, to which the composer was partial. For this movement, the following quotation was used by the composer: "The strings of a guitar sounding laments of a nature that remind one of nothing so much as the weight of sorrow."

An orgiastic outburst of energy marks the concluding dance, which is continually vitalized by dynamic rhythms. To this movement, the composer appended the following quotation: "The perfume of flowers is intermingled with the odor of the camomile, and the bouquet of tall chalices filled with incomparable wine. From this, like incense, the dance rises."

Danzas fantasticas, in its orchestral version, was introduced in Madrid in March of 1911.

1925 LA ORACIÓN DEL TORERO (THE BULLFIGHTER'S PRAYER), for string quartet (also for string orchestra), op. 34.

The Bullfighter's Prayer is marked by striking contrasts of mood and colors. It opens quietly: after progressing with impulsive rhythms to moods of impetuous character, an expansive melody unfolds to dominate the composition.

A forceful climax then arrives. The ideas stated in the beginning of the piece are repeated. The principal melody brings the work to a gentle conclusion.

EDGARD VARÈSE 1883–1965

Varèse once said: "Contrary to general belief, an artist is never ahead of his time, but most people are far behind theirs." His career has provided the necessary proof. In the 1920s and early 1930s, Varèse's music—voice of the machine age—inspired laughter, abuse and devastating criticisms. In the 1940s, Varèse was never played; he was the forgotten man of modern music. But the people finally caught up with him. By 1960, Varèse was the recipient of major performances and honors, as well as exalted praises. The younger generation of composers began to regard him as their patron saint. The critics hailed him as a prophet whose works anticipated by a good quarter of a century many of the tendencies crystallized in the avant-garde movement in music since the early 1950s. Now, in 1963, Stravinsky (who had previously shown little interest in Varèse) could say in *Dialogues and a Diary*: "Varèse's music will endure. We know this now because it was dated in the right way. The name is synonymous with a new intensity and a new concretion, and the best things in his music . . . are among the better things in contemporary music. More power to this musical Brancusi."

In reviewing an all-Varèse program in New York in 1961, Ross Parmenter asked the question as to whether Varèse had succeeded in organizing sound into music. Parmenter's answer was in the affirmative. "It is music that is fundamentally human, despite so many inhuman sounds. What it seems to demonstrate is the human condition that was always mysterious and strange because of natural forces and that has now been made more terrifying by man's own inventiveness."

Varèse was born in Paris on December 22, 1883. (Until the time of his death, the year of his birth had erroneously been given as 1885.) He was intended for engineering, and for this purpose was given a sound training in mathematics and science. Finally deciding upon music as a career, he attended the Schola Cantorum as a pupil of Vincent d'Indy and Albert Roussel, and then the Paris Conservatory, a pupil of Widor. In the latter institution, he received the first Bourse Artistique of the city of Paris.

Impatient with academicism, he soon left classroom study in Paris for Berlin, where he founded a chorus and did some orchestral conducting. A good many of the works written at this time he destroyed as unworthy.

When World War I broke out, he served briefly in the French army. Then, in December of 1915, he came to the United States to establish permanent residence in New York City; in 1926, he became an American citizen. From the first, he was a vital force for promoting the interests of new music and the modern composer. He organized the New Symphony Orchestra, and after that, the International Composers Guild and the Pan-American Society, all dedicated to the presentation of modern music. Beginning with 1923, his own provocative compositions began a stir in American music circles, beginning with *Hyperprism* in 1923 and continuing through *Equatorial* in 1934. For almost two decades after that, Varèse did no more composing, devoting himself to his scientific and mathematical studies and to the theoretical aspects of music. Then, in 1954, he returned to creativity with *Deserts,* and from this time on, he interested himself in the possibilities of electronic music.

In 1960, Columbia Records issued an album of his major works; and in 1961, and again in 1964, all-Varèse concerts were held and acclaimed in New York. In 1962, he received the Brandeis University Award in Music; in 1963, the first Koussevitzky International Recording Award; and in 1965, the Edward MacDowell medal.

Varèse died in New York City on November 6, 1965. He was survived by his wife, Louise, whom he had married in 1921 and who was a gifted translator.

1923–1934 HYPERPRISM, for wind instruments and percussion.

OCTANDRE, for flute, oboe, clarinet, bassoon, horn, trumpet, trombone and double bass.

INTÉGRALES, for small orchestra and percussion.

AMÉRIQUES, for large orchestra.

ARCANA, for large orchestra.

IONISATION, for forty-one percussion instruments and two sirens.

EQUATORIAL, for bass voice, trumpet, trombone, organ, percussion and Thereminvox.

Varèse described his own music as "organized sound." Beginning with the early 1920s, he made a complete break with the past by evolving his own forms—each composition finding that structure which best suited its material. He filled those forms with fragmentary thematic scraps built up sonorously for aural effect. Melodic themes, thematic development, thematic variation had no place in such a scheme of things. What had an important place were experimental sounds, discordant sounds, and sometimes produced by non-musical objects. Sonority fascinated him, together with timbres and sound textures. He was always searching for something new in those directions. He reproduced the sounds of sirens and machines, and he simulated the jungle sounds of birds and insects. He would use the usual instruments together with unusual percussions and noisemakers. "I fly on my own wings," he explained. In all this—as well as in his lifelong interest in spatial relationships—he was about a quarter of a century ahead of his time.

His compositions created shock and dismay each time one was introduced. Audiences were provoked to laughter, critics to violent abuse. When *Hyper-*

prism was first heard—in New York City on March 4, 1923—W. J. Henderson said in the New York *Sun*: "Bully Bottom in his proudest moments could not have given such imitations of the roaring of the lion, the shrieking of the wind, the pattering of hailstones and the swearing of distracted menagerie." The music made Olin Downes think of "election night, a menagerie or two, and a catastrophe in a boiler factory."

Octandre—first performance in New York on January 13, 1924—drew the following comment from W. J. Henderson: "An '*Octrandre*' is a flower having eight stamens. Mr. Varèse's *Octandre* was no flower; it was a peach. It cannot be described. It ought not to be. Such music must be heard to be appreciated. It shrieked, it grunted, it chortled, it mewed, it barked—and it turned all eight instruments into contortionists. It was not in any key, not even in no key. It was just a ribald outbreak of noise."

Intégrales—première in New York on March 1, 1925—led Ernest Newman (then a visiting critic for the New York *Post*) to say: "It sounded a good deal like a combination of early morning in the Mott Haven freight yards, feeding time at the zoo, and a Sixth Avenue trolley rounding a curve, with an intoxicated woodpecker thrown in for good measure." W. J. Henderson wrote: "If it be music to blow one piercing tone from the piccolo and a squeal from an E-flat clarinet for five minutes while other wind instruments in other keys make sounds like an injured dog's cry of pain or a cat's yell of midnight rage, and sundry instruments of percussion crash and bang apparently just for the sake of crashing and banging, then this is the real thing."

Varèse now began pursuing his experiments with sounds and sonorities with larger instrumental forces. *Amériques* (first performance on April 9, 1926 with Leopold Stokowski conducting the Philadelphia Orchestra) used a large orchestra. The style, Nicolas Slonimsky explains, is "in free dissonant counterpoint . . . [making use] of rigid mottoes as themes in place of developed motifs." Samuel Chotzinoff thought this music depicted "the progress of a terrible fire in one of our larger zoos." *Arcana* was also for large orchestra, and this, too, was introduced by the Philadelphia Orchestra under Stokowski—on April 8, 1927. Here is how a critic for *High Fidelity* Magazine described this music recently: "In its use of repeated-note figures, of rhythmic interplay and juxtaposition, of percussion instruments, and of harmonic and sonority build-up, it is . . . exceptionally original and personal in conception." But when *Arcana* was first introduced thirty-five years earlier, Edward Cushing said that the score was "long and infinitely wearying in its revelations of the unspeakably hideous," while Oscar Thompson maintained that the music "plunged the listener into morasses of sound which seemingly had little relation to music. . . . There was no mercy in its disharmony, no pity in its succession of screaming, clashing discords."

Varèse's greatest complexity of rhythmic and sonorous treatment was reserved for *Ionisation,* which he scored for percussion, friction and sibilation instruments. It was heard for the first time in New York on March 6, 1933. Here is how Nicolas Slonimsky describes it: "The first subject [is] given out by the tambour militaire (while two sirens glide over the whole range in opposite directions like two harp glissandos), the second by the tutti of percussion instruments, the development section being built on contrasting metal and wood percussion tone color, and the coda . . . introducing tubular chimes and low register pianoforte tone clusters (like pedal points)."

Varèse made his first use of an electronic instrument with *Equatorial,* which was scored for bass voice, trumpet, trombones, organ, percussion and the Thereminvox. The last of these produced sounds electronically. *Equatorial* was introduced in New York on April 15, 1934.

1954–1960 DESERTS, for wind instruments, percussion and electronically produced sounds.

POÈME ÉLECTRONIQUE, for electronically produced sounds.

NOCTURNAL, for soprano, men's chorus, chamber orchestra and electronically produced sounds.

In 1936, Varèse had said prophetically: "The future composer of symphonic music will consult the scientist in his laboratory instead of the violin maker in his garret."

Varèse had gone as far as he could in finding new sounds and new sonorities with the materials he had at hand in the 1930s. He had to bide his time until new resources became available. And so, for almost two decades, he wrote nothing. Then the world of electronics opened up a completely new world of sound possibilities. In Paris, in the late 1940s, "musique concrète" was developed by the radio scientist, Pierre Schaeffer, who produced new rhythms, new colors and new sound effects through electronic means on tape, and then created still other rhythms, colors and sounds by distorting or altering these recorded sounds. After that, in the early 1950s, laboratories and electronic research centers opened up new horizons for composers like Pierre Boulez, Karlheinz Stockhausen and others. Varèse now had new materials with which to work.

He now produced one of his most important works—*Deserts,* for wind instruments, percussion and sounds produced electronically on tape. When given its world première—in Paris on December 2, 1954—this composition created a sensation. In *Deserts,* as we learn from a reviewer for *High Fidelity* Magazine, "the thematic material has become abstracted to the barest figures of one or two repeated notes and intervals. The patterns of rhythm, accent, dynamics and sonority have achieved equal importance and actually emerge with 'thematic' significance. And all these powerfully imagined instrumental sounds are brilliantly dovetailed with the taped interludes through skilful use of percussion. The percussion mediates, so to speak, between the sophisticated, complex, pitched close sounds of the wind instruments, and the primitive, open, limitless power of the sounds on tape. Out of this opposition grows a good deal of the strength and shape of the work."

Poème électronique was created by Varèse for the Philips Pavilion at the Brussels Exposition, during the summer of 1957. This is electronic music projected stereophonically through four hundred and twenty-five loudspeakers. The music was used in conjunction with lights devised by the architect, Le Corbusier, flashed on the ceiling of the Pavilion. But no effort was made to realize a relation between lights and sounds; each was independent of the other. "The work started with a sound as of vast church bells tolling," was the way

Edward Downes described this music. "It came from all sides. . . . There followed sounds suggesting sirens, kettledrums, gunshots, skyrockets exploding into outer space, and then something like a slowed-down human voice seemed to sigh: 'Oh, god. . . ' the pitch of the final vowel sinking gradually into the bottomless depths of a booming echo chamber."

Varèse's last composition came in 1960—*Nocturnal,* for soprano and men's voices, a chamber orchestra and electronic sounds. The world première took place on an all-Varèse program in New York on May 1, 1961.

In commenting on Varèse's last works, Peter G. Davis said: "One day composers may equal and even surpass the vision of these remarkable conceptions; today, however, they are works by which the future must be measured."

RALPH VAUGHAN WILLIAMS

1872–1958

The debt that English folk music owes to Vaughan Williams is profound; and vice versa. There is no question but that his painstaking researches into the music of England's past, undertaken in the first years of the present century, and the tasteful adaptations he made of this music, have helped to lift it out of its undeserved neglect. But it is also true that this service has not been without compensations. For not until Vaughan Williams came upon the carols, madrigals, folk songs, and dances of the Tudor period—came upon them and absorbed them so completely that they became a part of his musical thinking—did he arrive at his destiny as a composer. Identification with his country and its music gave Vaughan Williams the direction he needed; from them he drew strength and inspiration. "Art, like charity," he said, "should begin at home. It is because Palestrina and Verdi are essentially Italian and because Bach, Beethoven and Wagner are essentially German that their message transcends their frontiers. The greatest artist inevitably belongs to his country as much as the humblest singer in a remote village."

More than this: from the music of the Tudor period, Vaughan Williams extracted and assimilated stylistic elements which gave shape and substance to his own music. The tendency toward modal writing, the robust rhythm, the transparent counterpoint, the serene melody, the restrained feelings are all qualities which Vaughan Williams's music acquired from folk sources. Not that there is a question of imitation or borrowing! The fusion of such traits with his own veins of mysticism, poetry and introspection is so inextricable and complete that what we have in the works of Vaughan Williams is not the resurgence of an old style but the emergence of a highly personal one. That style may be ineluctably tied up with the past; but—like a relay runner—it takes up the stick from its predecessor and forges ahead on its own power.

That Vaughan Williams's music is so thoroughly English in personality and ambience is not exclusively the result of its having been rooted in the country's folk music. The English element in Vaughan Williams, as Ernest Newman once said, takes two forms: "A realization that we get nowhere else in music of the brooding beauty of the quiet English countryside and an expression that has no rival anywhere in music of what thoughtful Englishmen regard as one of the most precious possessions of their race, the vein of mellow mysticism that runs through so much of our heritage or poetry and prose." Newman concludes: "I can conceive, of course, his *Pastoral Symphony,* and *The Lark Ascending,* and the *Serenade to Music,* and the Fifth Symphony, and *The Pilgrim's Progress* speaking to the heart of men of other races; but I cannot conceive them flooding their souls with the same complex of emotions as they set up in the souls of us whose minds have been molded by English poetry."

His nine symphonies, however—possibly his greatest single contribution to the music of our generation—are not hemmed in by national boundaries. They cover, says Michael Kennedy, "an extraordinary range of human experience. . . . Each is a necessary and inevitable extention of the composer's personality, a momentous personal statement. Each has a distinctive character. The last of them asserts that he remained unpredictable and independent to the end and that his mental vigor was astonishing."

Vaughan Williams was born in Down Ampney, in Gloucester, England, on October 12, 1872. He wrote his first piece of music when he was six. He began studying the piano in childhood with private teachers, continuing his studies at a preparatory school in Rottingdean, which he entered in 1882, and at Charterhouse, from 1887 to 1890. At the latter school, his Piano Trio in G was performed on August 5, 1888. From 1890 to 1892, and again from 1894 to 1899, he received a comprehensive training at the Royal College of Music in London from Hubert Parry and Charles Stanford, among others. For two years, between 1892 and 1894, he attended Trinity College at Cambridge, where he was active in all of its musical activities. While attending the Royal College of Music, he worked as an organist at St. Barnabas in South Lambeth.

On October 9, 1897, he married Adeline Fisher. He spent the next few months with his wife in Germany absorbing its musical experiences, and for a while studying composition with Max Bruch. Back in England, he supported himself by playing the trombone in various orchestras while devoting himself to composition. A Quintet—for clarinet, horn, violin, cello and piano—was heard in London on June 5, 1901; *Bucolic Suite,* for orchestra, was given in Bournemouth on March 10, 1902. In these and other compositions of this period, he was influenced by Brahms.

A more personal point of view entered his writing after he had become interested in the folk music of the Tudor period, in which he did a considerable amount of research in the early 1900s. Under the stimulus of this old English music, he began adopting a national style in composition which, at first, quoted freely from folk sources. This tendency first became evident in 1906 with three *Norfolk Rhapsodies,* for orchestra, the first of which, in E minor, has survived, while the other two were discarded by the composer.

A brief period of study in Paris with Ravel in 1908 strengthened his technical equipment and enriched and subtilized his gift at orchestration and harmonization. But his creative personality, long since formed by his studies of old English folk music, remained unchanged. That personality began revealing itself more strongly than heretofore in the song cycle, *On Wenlock Edge,* in 1909; in his first symphony, *The Sea Symphony,* text by Walt Whitman, and first performance at the Leeds Festival on October 12, 1910; and in the composer's first masterwork, *Fantasia on a Theme by Thomas Tallis* in 1910. With *A London Symphony,* in 1913, Vaughan Williams had taken his place with the foremost English composers of his time.

During World War I, Vaughan Williams served first in the Territorial Army Military Corps as a hospital orderly in France and Macedonia, and then at the front as an artillery lieutenant. The war ended, he joined the faculty of the Royal College of Music, where he taught composition up to the time of his death. Between 1920 and 1928, he was the conductor of the Bach Choir. A succession of important works in every possible medium raised him to a place of first importance in English music. In 1935, he received the Order of Merit. He remained richly productive up to the last days, in spite of old age and growing deafness. Past eighty, Vaughan Williams married his secretary, Ursula Wood, on February 7, 1953 (his first wife having died in 1951).

Vaughan Williams paid three visits to the United States. The first took place in 1922, when he conducted a program of his music at the Norfolk Festival in Connecticut. He returned in 1932 to lecture on national music at Bryn Mawr College, and again in 1955 to lecture at Yale and Cornell, and to conduct guest performances with various orchestras.

On August 26, 1958, Vaughan Williams died at his home in London. He was cremated two days later, and on September 19, his ashes were buried in Westminster Abbey.

1906 NORFOLK RHAPSODY NO. 1 IN E MINOR, for orchestra.

Some of Vaughan Williams's most popular works for the orchestra represent elaborate settings of English folk songs which he unearthed during his researches, and which he then collected and arranged. The first of his mature orchestral compositions is one of these. In 1906, he produced three orchestral rhapsodies based on folk tunes he had gathered at King's Lynn in Norfolk. Two of these rhapsodies he subsequently withdrew, and they have not been performed since the early 1900s. The first, in E minor, has survived. He had originally intended integrating the three rhapsodies into a folk-song symphony, with each of the rhapsodies serving as a movement. Dissatisfied with the second and third rhapsodies, he abandoned this project.

The first rhapsody was introduced at a London Promenade Concert on August 23, 1906. The following folk songs are used: "The Captain's Apprentice," "A Bold Young Sailor," "The Basket of Eggs," and "On Board a '93." The rhapsody opens with an Adagio section based on a motive from "The Basket of Eggs." A solo viola is heard in "The Captain's Apprentice" in the sixteenth measure; horns later take over. After a quickening of the tempo, flutes recall "The Basket of Eggs" melody in thirds. English horn, accompanied by harp, then is heard in "A Bold Young Sailor." Woodwinds and strings repeat the tune. A climax is built up ending with a vigorous statement of "The Captain's Apprentice." After this comes "On Board a '93" in the strings. The concluding coda is based on the second measure of the opening tune.

Vaughan Williams revised this rhapsody in 1913, giving new importance to "The Captain's Apprentice" and completely revising the coda.

1909 ON WENLOCK EDGE, cycle of six songs for tenor and string quartet and piano. I. On Wenlock Edge. II. From Far, From Eve and Morning. III. Is My Team Ploughing? IV. Oh, When I Was in Love with You. V. Bredon Hill. VI. Clun.

This is the first important work completed by the composer following his stay in Paris and his studies with Ravel. When this song cycle was introduced by Gervase Elwes and the Schiller Quartet in London on November 15, 1909, the critics expected to find French influences. However, the composer's English personality gave this setting of poems by A. E. Housman their distinct personality. The critic of the London *Times* found each of the poems "remarkable for accurate accentuation of the words and for genuinely deep expression, with an appropriate rustic flavor."

The six poems by Housman comprise two that reflect on life, three on love, and one on death. The first song (Allegro moderato) is significant for the way in which the music matches the text in descriptive details. Michael Kennedy considers the second song (Andantino) the most beautiful in the set, and points to the effective use of "wide consecutive common chords on the piano." The setting of the third song (Andante sostenuto, ma non troppo lento) is, to Kennedy, "more elaborate," while the fourth (Allegretto) has considerable lyrical freshness and charm. "Bredon Hill" (Moderato tranquillo) is "the most ambitious as well as the most pictorial" with the string quartet and piano describing "the lazy scene" while the voice "enters freely and softly." The concluding song (Andante tranquillo) is "a complete change of mood" suffused as it is with warm sunshine, far removed from "the sense of fatality" found in the poem.

In the early 1920s, Vaughan Williams arranged this song cycle for tenor and orchestra.

1910 FANTASIA ON A THEME BY THOMAS TALLIS, for string quartet and double orchestra.

Thomas Tallis was an English composer of contrapuntal music who lived in the sixteenth century and served as organist of the Chapel Royal during the reigns of Edward VI, Mary, and Elizabeth. In 1567, Tallis composed eight tunes in eight modes for the Metrical Psalter of Matthew Parker, Archbishop of Canterbury. The third of these tunes, "Why Fumeth in Fight," was adapted by Vaughan Williams for his *Fantasia*, which was introduced at the Three Choirs Festival in Gloucester on September 6, 1910, the composer conducting.

When first performed, the *Fantasia* was not successful. A critic for the *Musical Times* found the work "over-long for the subject matter." The composer took this criticism to heart, withdrew it, then condensed and reworked it. It was the revised version that took hold permanently—so permanently, in fact, that it has become one of the composer's most frequently played compositions. "The work," now said J. A. Fuller-Maitland in the London *Times,* "is wonderful because it seems to lift one into some unknown region of musical thought and feeling. Throughout its course one is never quite sure whether one is listening to something very old or very new. . . . That is just what makes this *Fantasia* so delightful to listen to. . . . It is full of visions which have haunted the seers of all time."

To bring out the antiphonal character of sixteenth-century music, Vaughan Williams divided his strings into two orchestras and a quartet of solo instruments. The tempo marking is Largo sostenuto. The Tallis theme is first heard in the orchestra against the tremolo of first violins, following a short introduction. The first violins repeat the melody. The two orchestras (one muted) discourse on this idea, after which it is passed on to the solo instruments. The melody is developed and transformed; then a forceful climax emerges. The melody is then heard in the solo violin against a contrapuntal background of a solo viola. The music comes to a serene close.

1912 FANTASIA ON CHRISTMAS CAROLS, for baritone solo, chorus and orchestra.

Vaughan Williams here uses four Christmas carols for fantasia treatment: "The Truth Sent from Above" and "There is a Fountain "which come out of Herefordshire; "Come All You Worthy Gentlemen" from Somerset; and "On Christmas Night" from Sussex. In addition to these, he quotes fragments from several other carols, including "The First Nowell," "The Virgin Unspotted" and "The Wassail Song."

The composer uses the chorus in four different ways: in the traditional manner of singing words and music; singing with half-closed lips on the syllable *Ah;* singing with closed lips; and singing with a "humming tone," that is, with open lips sounding a short "u" as in the word "but."

The *Fantasia* was introduced on September 12, 1912, at the Three Choirs Festival at Hereford, the composer conducting.

The work opens with a solo for violoncello. The baritone then enters with "The Truth Sent from Above"; after the baritone has sung the second verse, the solo cello relinquishes the role of accompaniment to the chorus, which hums softly in the background. (Here, as in other parts of this work, the chorus is used more like a part of the orchestra than as a vocal supplement to it.) In the final stanza, the chorus joins with the baritone.

The second carol, "Come, All You Worthy Gentlemen," is sung by tenors and basses, with the entire chorus participating in the sixteenth measure; sopranos and altos render the second stanza, while the entire chorus is again heard in the final four lines.

Four measures for orchestra serve as a prelude to the third carol, "On Christmas Night," which is sung by the baritone to an accompaniment of strings. Five measures later the chorus enters, the sopranos singing the text, while the rest of the chorus chants the syllable *Ah.* A climax is reached with the expression of exultation, in which the music for chorus and orchestra grows in sonority until a formidable fortissimo is evolved. The chorus repeats the last line of the carol diminuendo, after which the baritone returns to sing the final stanza of the *second* carol to a choral counterpoint of the final stanza of the *third.* Chimes and full orchestra proclaim a New Year's greeting during which the fourth carol, "There Is a Fountain," is heard in the orchestra.

1913 A LONDON SYMPHONY. I. Lento; Allegro risoluto. II. Lento. III. Allegro vivace. IV. Andante con moto: Maestoso alla marcia; Andante sostenuto.

Vaughan Williams's first two symphonies are programmatic. The first, the *Sea Symphony,* for soprano, baritone, chorus and orchestra (1910) has a text by Whitman; it was introduced at the Leeds Festival on October 12, 1910, the composer conducting. The second, provides a clue to its meaning in its title, *London Symphony.* Yet, notwithstanding this title, Vaughan Williams never actually intended the work to be descriptive. As he explained: "The title . . . may suggest to some hearers a descriptive piece, but this is not the intention of the composer. A better title would perhaps be *Symphony by a Londoner,* that is to say the life of London (including its various sights and sounds) has suggested to the composer an attempt at musical expression; but it would be no help to the hearer to describe these in words. The music is intended to be self-impressive, and must stand or fall as 'absolute' music. Therefore, if listeners recognize suggestions of such things as the Westminster chimes or the *Lavender Cry,* they are asked to consider these as accidents, not essentials of the music."

And yet the music of this symphony is so pictorial and, at moments, so realistic, that the listener cannot help bringing up to mind definite pictures of London as he hears the music. The composer must have finally recognized this fact, for he did not dissuade his friend, the conductor Albert Coates, from providing an elaborate verbal description of the intent of the music when the latter directed a revised version of the symphony in 1920.

The following has been accepted as the key to the meaning of this music:

I. London sleeps. The Thames flows serenely through the city. The city awakens. We get different glimpses of the city—its varied character—its good humor—its activity.

II. Portrait of the region known as Bloomsbury. It is dusk—damp and foggy twilight. There is poverty everywhere—poverty and tragedy. An old musician outside a pub plays *Sweet Lavender.* The gloom deepens. The movement ends with the musician still playing his sad tune.

III. Sitting late on Saturday evening at the Temple Embankment. On one side of the river are the slums; on the other, the stately majesty of the Houses of Parliament. The Thames River flows serenely.

IV. A picture of the crueler sides of the city: the unemployed; the unfortunate. The music ends with chimes of Big Ben on Westminster Tower. The Epilogue (Andante sostenuto) gives a picture of London as a whole. The symphony ends as it began—with the Thames flowing silently, serenely.

The symphony opens in an air of mystery, with a motive based on a figure from the striking of Big Ben. Muted strings, clarinet and horn are heard in a gentle subject, following which the flow of the Thames River is suggested by murmuring strings. The awakening of the city is suggested by motives in horns, trumpets and trombones. These ideas are discussed at length in the main body of the movement.

The second movement opens with parallel minor chords, There follows a sensitive melody for English horn accompanied by muted strings. "Sweet Lavender" is played by a solo viola.

The third movement is a scherzo which the composer designated as a nocturne. A lively dance tune is heard, first in clarinets, then in violins and woodwinds. After that, a new tune is introduced by flutes and oboes. The movement is carried to a climax, following which highly atmospheric music evokes a picture of fog descending on the Thames River.

The finale opens with a vigorous introduction, prefacing a march tune in violas, cellos, clarinets and bassoons. This theme is elaborated upon. Suddenly the harp plucks the chimes of Big Ben. After a short pause, an epilogue reviews some of the material originally heard in the first-movement introduction.

The first performance took place in London under Geoffrey Toye's direction on March 27, 1914. But this is not the version heard today. In July of 1914, the composer sent his manuscript to Fritz Busch in Germany. It got lost en route. The composer now had to reconstruct his score. The rewritten symphony was played in Bournemouth on February 11, 1915. After that, the composer revised his symphony three times. The first revision was heard in London on March 18, 1918, Adrian Boult conducting; the second, in London on May 4, 1920, Albert Coates conducting; and the third and final one, in London on February 22, 1934, Sir Thomas Beecham conducting.

1914 THE LARK ASCENDING, romance for violin and orchestra,

This composition was written in 1914, revised in 1920 and introduced in a violin and piano version in Shorehampton, England on December 15, 1920. Marie Hall and Geoffrey Mendham were the soloists. The orchestral version was given in London on June 14, 1921, with Marie Hall as soloist and Adrian Boult conducting.

The Lark Ascending is a poem by George Meredith, of which Vaughan Williams's music is an interpretation. The poem appears on the flyeaf of the published score.

> He rises and begins to round,
> He drops the silver chain of sound,
> Of many links without a break
> In chirrup, whistle, slur and shake.
>
> * * *
>
> For singing till his heaven fills,
> 'Tis love of earth that he instils,
> And ever winging up and up,
> Our valley is his golden cup,
> And he the wine which overflows
> To lift us with him as he goes.

* * *

Till lost on his aerial wings
In light, and then the fancy sings.

The composition opens Andante sostenuto with the principal melody stated by violin solo in a quiet cantabile passage. An Allegretto tranquillo (Quasi andante) section follows, more energetic than the earlier one. The opening melody returns at the conclusion, followed by a spirited passage describing the flight of the lark as it disappears into space.

1921 A PASTORAL SYMPHONY. I. Molto moderato. II. Lento moderato. III. Moderato pesante. IV. Lento; Moderato maestoso; Lento.

Vaughan Williams's third symphony was introduced in London on January 26, 1922, by the London Philharmonic Orchestra conducted by Adrian Boult.

Though Vaughan Williams provided this symphony with the sobriquet of "Pastoral," he once again emphasized (as he had done in the case of the *London Symphony*) that he wanted it to be listened to as pure music.

The symphony is not, as its name might indicate, a portrait of Nature; there are no descriptive passages of brooks or storms, such as one encounters in another *Pastoral Symphony*—that of Beethoven. Vaughan Williams's symphony is a contemplative work. All four movements are comparatively slow and melancholy and quiet, filled with the most personal musings. If there is little variety in either pace or feeling, there is, as Guido Pannain pointed out, considerable variety, nevertheless, "in the inner movement of the music, in subtle changes of mood rather than in the external program of the work." Pannain further remarks that in the final movement a clue is given to the meaning of the entire symphony: Here a voice enters singing a wordless chant—a "vocal liturgy"—speaking of "nature purified of the senses, absorbed in a greater faith and contemplation of itself—the tenderness of affection and the poetry of unvoiced prayers."

The contemplative character of the first movement is set forth in the expressive opening theme for basses and harp, accompanied by woodwinds in consecutive triads. "You think you have had contemplation in the first movement," wrote Herbert Howells, the English composer. "But what Vaughan Williams means by 'contemplative mood' you will only know when the second is reached." Introduced by a song for solo horn, the movement has a remote character due to its modal writing, which helps it achieve a plane of calm and eloquent beauty unique even in Vaughan Williams. The composer has designated the third movement as a 'slow dance'; it consists of three ideas, one for trumpets and trombone, another for flute, and a third for trumpet (the last in the Mixolydian mode). The fourth movement sensitively creates an atmosphere of peace and suggests the infinite. It opens with a slow section in which a wordless solo for voice (soprano or tenor solo) is heard above a drum roll. When the voice dies out, muted strings hint at the principal subject, which soon appears in the Moderato maestoso section in woodwinds, horns and harp. A bit of agitation follows only to be put to rest by a recall of the theme formerly given by the solo voice but now assigned to the orchestra. A mighty climax erupts and subsides. The symphony ends with the same quiet revery, the same hushed beauty, with which it began.

1930 JOB, a masque for dancing, in nine scenes and epilogue, with scenario by Geoffrey Keynes and Gwendolen Raverat based on Blake's *Illustrations of the Book of Job*. First performance: Norwich, October 23, 1930 (concert version); London, July 5, 1931 (staged version).

Geoffrey Keynes, an authority on Blake, was impressed by twenty-one of Blake's illustrations for The Book of Job as material for a ballet. He prepared a suitable scenario and invited Vaughan Williams to write the music. The English character of Blake's drawings led the composer to make a compromise between the Biblical character and subject on the one hand, and on the other, the masque, the popular seventeenth-century English stage medium that combined song, dance and dialogue. This compromise, in turn, encouraged the composer further to include in his score such old dance forms as the pavane, minuet, galliard and saraband.

Both Keynes and Vaughan Williams recognized that Blake's drawings were not essentially an interpretation of the Biblical story. The drawings were more in the nature of a personal drama involving a struggle with and a triumph over destiny; and it was this theme that was emphasized in the plans for a ballet. Keynes tried interesting Diaghilev in the project, but the artistic director of the Ballet Russe regarded it as too old-fashioned and too English for his tastes. Vaughan Williams, nevertheless, kept on working on his music, keeping the ballet scenario in mind, but always stimulated by Blake's illustrations. Vaughan Williams finally produced a score that was suitable for ballet, yet at the same time was an integrated symphonic creation suitable for concert performance.

The first performance of this music as a symphonic composition took place at the Norwich Festival in England, the composer conducting. When *Job* was staged in London in 1931, choreography was by Ninette de Valois, and settings and costumes by Gwendolen Raverat; Constant Lambert conducted. The first staged presentation in the United States took place at the Lewisohn Stadium in New York on August 24, 1931, in a performance by the Denishawn Dancers.

Frank Howes has noted that the music to *Job* utilizes three basic patterns. The first is that of Job, a pastoral theme "alternating triplets with even quavers"; the second is the theme of the Satan, "characterized by a background in G minor, from which leap chords in A major and B-flat minor suggesting disorder in harmony." The third is the motive of Godhead which combines an "irregular descending phrase with sweep and authority."

The ballet is in eight scenes, but the composer's score is in nine. In the Introduction to the first scene (Largo sostenuto), Job is found in quiet contemplation, surrounded by his flocks; shepherds and husbandmen come to do him homage. A Pastoral Dance of Job's sons and daughters follows (Allegro piacevole). Satan appeals to God. The Heavens open to reveal God surrounded by his Sons, with an entourage of Angels. A saraband of the Sons of God, introduced by soft sustained chords with rising arpeggios, follows (Andante con moto).

The second dance (Presto), whose music is dominated by a strong falling theme over a bass pedal, describes Satan's Dance of Triumph; the third scene, opening with a gentle and pastoral melody for oboes and flutes, is the Minuet of the Sons of Job and Their Wives (Andante con moto). In the fourth scene, introduced by pianissimo strings, Job's Dream is portrayed vividly (Lento moderato; Allegro). As Job sleeps, Satan stands over him, evoking visions of Plague, Pestilence, Famine, Murder and Sudden Death. In Scene Five, Job awakens and greets Three Messengers who inform him his wealth has been destroyed and his sons and daughters are dead (Lento; Andante con moto; Lento). An oboe episode awakening Job is here followed by processional music. Three of Job's Comforters perform a dance in the sixth scene (Andante doloroso). A recollection of the falling theme from Scene Two is recalled, now given by plucked strings. A saxophone episode points up the hypocrisy of Job's Comforters. Scene Seven, opening with a violin cadenza, is Elihu's Dance of Youth and Beauty (Andante tranquillo; Allegretto). The violin cadenza is followed by a pavane for strings, woodwinds, harp and tympani. In the eighth scene (Andante con moto; Allegro pesante; Allegretto tranquillo; Lento), the Sons of the Morning drive away Satan, as Job's household builds an altar and dance in front of it a galliard. The concluding scene (Largo sostenuto) brings back the music of the opening. Job, humble and chastened, sits in the midst of his family and blesses it.

1934 FANTASIA ON GREENSLEEVES, for harp (or piano) and strings, with optional flutes.

Of the many English folk songs which Vaughan Williams helped to popularize through his adaptations, few if any have gained such wide circulation as "Greensleeves." The melody dates from the sixteenth century. As "The Ballad of My Lady Greensleeves" it was registered at Stationer's Hall in 1575. Shakespeare mentions it in *The Merry Wives of Windsor*. In the seventeenth century, it was used as the party tune of the Cavaliers; while in 1957, it became a popular song hit in the United States. Vaughan Williams was so fascinated by this sad, sweet melody that he made several arrangements of it. He used it for the first time in his opera, *Sir John in Love,* a four-act opera based on Shakespeare's *The Merry Wives of Windsor,* performed in London on March 21, 1929. There the song is sung by Mrs. Ford in the scene where Falstaff comes to call on her (opening of the third act). In this version, the text is taken from "A Handefull of Pleasant Delites" published in 1584.

The instrumental fantasia (Lento) is an adaptation of the melody as it appears in *Sir John in Love,* but with amplification. This work opens and closes with the melody, stated simply, and beautifully harmonized for the strings. In the middle section, Vaughan Williams interpolates a second folk song, "Lovely Joan," which the composer found in Norfolk in 1908.

The *Fantasia* was first performed in London on September 27, 1934, the composer conducting.

1934 SYMPHONY NO. 4 IN F MINOR. I. Allegro. II. Andante moderato. III. Allegro molto. IV. Finale con epilogo fugato: allegro molto.

Of Vaughan Williams's symphonies, that in F minor, his fourth, is the first in which he experimented with modern idioms. The romantic and introspective poet of the *London* and *Pastoral* symphonies now uses complex rhythms, discords and angular melodies. When Eric Blom first heard this work, he described it in the Birmingham *Post* as "harshly and grimly uncompromising in its clashing dissonant polyphony." This symphony, then, is not the kind with which one associated the name of Vaughan Williams in 1934. Nevertheless, it is forceful and original music, characterized by a strong lyricism and a remarkable integration of form, polyphony and momentum.

When this writer visited Vaughan Williams before World War II, he expressed amazement that a work like this should have been written by the composer. Vaughan Williams shrugged his huge shoulders and remarked simply: "I wrote as I felt." He added that if he were never again to write a work in a similar vein, he still had to write the F minor Symphony at the time he did and the way he did. At a rehearsal, he remarked to his orchestra men: "I don't even know if I like it—but that is what I meant when I wrote it." To a friend, Vaughan Williams said further: "When you say you do not think my F minor Symphony beautiful, my answer *must* be that I do think it is beautiful—not that I did not *mean* it to be beautiful because it reflected unbeautiful times. . . . I wrote it not as a definite picture of anything external—e.g., the state of Europe—but simply because it occurred to me like this—I cannot explain why."

The two themes of the first movement become the basic materials of the entire symphony and are heard throughout, though often transformed. The first is stated by full orchestra, and the second by brass alone. The slow movement begins with a development of the second theme, played by the first violins; after considerable polyphonic development, the flute enters with a transformation of the first theme. The next two movements utilize fugal writing extensively; the concluding movement is the climax of the entire work. In this last movement, the culmination comes with an elaborate fugal epilogue, the subject of which is the first theme (trombones) combined polyphonically with other ideas. With a reminiscence of the opening measures of the first movement, the symphony comes to a close.

The symphony was introduced on April 10, 1935, in London by the BBC Symphony under Sir Adrian Boult. In spite of its unusual (for Vaughan Williams) style, it was a huge success.

1938 SERENADE TO MUSIC, for sixteen solo voices and orchestra.

In 1938, the eminent English conductor, Sir Henry J. Wood, celebrated the fiftieth anniversary of his debut with a concert in London on October 5. For this performance, and to honor Sir Henry, Vaughan Williams wrote a vocal Serenade to a text from Act V, Scene 1, from Shakespeare's *A Merchant of Venice*. This text begins with the Lorenzo lines: "How sweet the moonlight sleeps upon this bank!"

The reason why Vaughan Williams set his text to sixteen voices is that Wood had suggested that the score contain material that could be sung by the sixteen singers who had been closely identified with Wood's career. Vaughan Williams opened his composition with a gentle chorale for all the voices. Though the ensemble returns from time to time briefly, the composition concentrates basically on the solo voices, for each of which the composer wrote music that he felt was a reflection of the singer for whom it was intended.

The Serenade is basically a *pièce d'occasion*. Nevertheless, it is music of great beauty, "one of Vaughan Williams's most sensuous works," says James Day. "Its appeal is universal, as long as men are prepared to allow music gently to steal over them and glory in the sheer beauty of silken sound."

1943 SYMPHONY NO. 5 IN D MAJOR. I. Preludio. II. Scherzo. III. Romanza. IV. Passacaglia.

That it was only a temporary excursion into the realms of modernism that Vaughan Williams had made with the F Minor Symphony—and not a permanent visit—was proved with the Fifth Symphony, which came a decade later. Introspective moods, gentle serenity, sensitive balance between thinking and feeling—these and the predilection for modal harmony once again characterize Vaughan Williams's writing.

In this symphony, the composer incorporated ideas he had sketched for a subsequent opera, *The Pilgrim's Progress;* but he took pains to explain that—with the exception of the slow movement—none of the music has any spiritual affinity with the Bunyan allegory.

The four movements have a unanimity of mood. It is one of tranquillity and inner peace (such as prevails in the Concerto in A minor for Oboe and Orchestra, written in 1944 and introduced by Leon Goossens on September 20, 1944, Sir Malcolm Sargent conducting), incongruous with the period that produced it, the harrowing years of World War II. This mood is projected in the first movement (Moderato), the initial theme of which is stated by two horns. The entire movement has a contemplative character. In the Scherzo (Allegro) that follows, another meditative idea unfolds at some length in the strings. Neville Cardus described this movement as "a delicate piece of fancy, aerial and mysterious, with a bucolic middle section." The connection between the third movement (Lento) and Bunyan is emphasized by the following quotation from Bunyan's allegory, which appears in the published score: "Upon that place there stood a cross, and a little below, a sepulchre. Then he said: 'He hath given me rest by His sorrow, and life by His death.'" This is rhapsodic music, created out of two themes. The finale (Moderato) is a passacaglia in which the cellos provide the ground bass. The music gains in power and exultation until, as A. E. F. Dickinson wrote in his review of the work, it "seems to fill the whole world with its song of good will."

The symphony was introduced at a Promenade concert in London on June 24, 1943, with the composer conducting the London Philharmonic. The symphony is dedicated to Jean Sibelius.

1947 SYMPHONY NO. 6 IN E MINOR. I. Allegro. II. Moderato. III. Allegro vivace. IV. Moderato.

A product of Vaughan Williams's old age (completed in his seventy-fifth year), this symphony does not betray any weakening of the composer's creative powers. On the contrary, it shows them to be at their very height. It is one of Vaughan Williams's greatest works; and, perhaps as an inevitable corollary, it is one of the finest musical creations of our generation.

The turmoil of the war and the postwar period reverberates in this strong and powerfully felt music. The composer, who had managed to find eacape from the realities of war in such earlier works as the Concerto for Oboe and the Fifth Symphony, could escape no more from the world around him. In the lamentation which rises from the strings in the opening and closing of the first movement, we have an expression of the mighty tragedy of our times. In the second movement, the anguish makes way for philosophic evaluations, and there is momentary calm. But the Scherzo brings back the turmoil and the terror. Then comes the much-discussed last movement (the longest of the four). This is the most serene music that the imagination can conjure, a whisper from beginning to end, ebbing away into infinite silence. The soul has found peace, at last, within itself.

The four movements are played without any interruption, with each of the first three having "its tail attached to the head of its neighbor," as the composer put it.

Its polyphonic texture is one of the distinguishing traits of this symphony. The first movement opens with a lamentation that rises from the strings (a subject that also ends the movement). After this, curbed energy is permitted release, finding a resting place in the chord of E minor. Emotional turbulence returns with the descent of strings braced with cross accents. Out of this cross-accent design comes an impressive theme for brass.

In the second movement, we find a temporary calm, though the opening subject is a brisk, syncopated figure which subsequently grows into a new thought for the trumpets. The English horn leads into the third movement, a scherzo, which the composer explains is fugal in texture but not in structure.

The finale, marked in the score as an epilogue, is the high point of the entire symphony, and one of the most controversial pieces of music by this composer. This is music which begins quietly and continues *sotte voce* until the end. The music is deliberate, unhurried. First comes a long fugal contemplation, the first four notes taken from the symphony's first theme. Serenity soon gives way to desolation. But always the voice remains soft, the texture light, the pace deliberate. At last the music ebbs away "to the edge of silence," in Scott Goddard's happy phrase. It comes to rest on the indecisive chord of E minor, in a tone of questioning and speculation. For after the contemplation, the turbulence and the soul-searching have ended, life apparently still remains a question mark.

The symphony received its world première in London on April 21, 1948, Sir Adrian Boult conducting.

1949 FANTASIA (QUASI VARIAZIONE) ON THE OLD 104TH PSALM, for piano solo, with chorus and orchestra.

This composition comprises the celebrated psalm tune from the Ravenscroft Psalter, with six variations. An Introduction (Maestoso) offers a four-measure subject derived from the last line of the psalm tune. The piano arrives in the fourth measure. After the orchestra reaches towards a climax, the piano is heard in an improvisation on the first two and last two lines of the psalm. Only now is the full psalm melody heard—in piano, accompanied by full chords. Six variations follow, though the composer takes pains to explain that each of these sections does not necessarily bring the complete variation, just as each statement of the tune does not always insist upon a variation. In the last variation, the minor key is abandoned, as an elaborate fugal episode is worked out. Forceful chords for piano and orchestra and the composition on a note of triumph.

The first performance was a private one—at Vaughan Williams's house in Dorking, on November 20, 1949. The first public performance took place at the Three Choirs Festival in Gloucester on September 6, 1950; Michael Mullinar was the piano soloist, and the composer conducted.

1951 THE PILGRIM'S PROGRESS, a morality in four acts, a prologue and an epilogue, with libretto adapted by the composer from John Bunyan's allegory of the same name, with interpolations from the Bible and verses by Ursula Wood. First performance: Covent Garden, London, April 26, 1951.

The appeal of John Bunyan's *The Pilgrim's Progress* to the composer was of long standing. He first began putting sketches and ideas on paper for a possible opera based on the allegory as far back as 1909. Attending a church pageant in which a scene from *The Pilgrim's Progress* was produced, some time in 1920 or 1921, revived Vaughan Williams's interest in his project. In 1922, he wrote *The Shepherds of the Delectable Mountains,* a one-act pastoral based on *The Pilgrim's Progress*—first performance in London on July 11, 1922. (This episode was incorporated into his full-length opera in 1951.) In 1925, he began working on parts of the first and second acts of this full-length opera. It took him more than a quarter of a century to complete the assignment.

The prologue shows Bunyan in Bedford Gaol, where he completes his book and is visited by the Pilgrim. In Stephen Williams's succinct summary: "The Pilgrim starts on his progress from the City of Destruction. His neighbors try to stop him, but Evangelist urges him to pass on. He passes on through the Valley of Humiliation, where he fights with Apollyon, and to Vanity Fair, which is the main episode of Act III. In Act IV, we see the Delectable Mountains, towards which the Pilgrim marches with unimpaired fortitude. And after many misadventures he is admitted by a chorus of Heavenly Beings into the Golden Gate of the Celestial City. There is an epilogue in which we see Bunyan again holding out his book to us as a testimony of his spiritual pilgrimage."

Stephen Williams then goes on to describe Vaughan Williams's musical procedure: "Vaughan Williams does not make any striking use of the Leitmotif, but there are musical themes associated with various elements and events. A pentatonic trumpet call expresses the Pilgrim's Way and there is a 'valor' theme dominating Act II. Bunyan also has a hymn in the prologue and the epilogue. Naturally, the worldly characters sing and dance to sordidly sophisticated music, and Vanity Fair is indicated by the kind of strident, discordant scoring which is blatantly descriptive of it and yet suggests the contempt of the man of integrity for such 'new found gods.'"

Vaughan Williams disregards all the accepted conventions of both theatre and opera, Herbert Murrill pointed this out in *Music and Letters,* adding that the composer "throws to one side the nice delineation of character, the careful balance and adjustment of climax-points, the pointed underlining of the dramatic situation; and with a sort of humble self-confidence writes a loose-knit and contemplative score that succeeds by its sincerity, convinces by its integrity and becomes a unity by its single-mindedness."

1952 SINFONIA ANTARTICA, for soprano, women's chorus and orchestra. I. Prelude. II. Scherzo. III. Landscape. IV. Intermezzo. V. Epilogue.

In 1948, Vaughan Williams wrote the music for *Scott of the Antarctic,* a motion picture based on the ill-fated expedition of Sir Robert Scott to the South Pole in 1911–1912. The picture opened in London on December 30, 1948. The music was intended specifically to reflect the unspoken thoughts of the men as they made the journey, and symbolically to voice the spiritual qualities of man which enable him to "defy power which seems omnipotent." Much of the effect of the music came from its capacity to project the mood and atmosphere of the frozen landscape through austere tone colors and sounds produced by a large orchestra supplemented by a piano, organ, celesta, vibraphone, xylophone, glockenspiel and wind machine. Vaughan Williams adapted this film music into a symphony, his seventh, utilizing a wordless soprano solo and a female voice choir as well as the large orchestra. It was introduced in Manchester on January 14, 1953, Sir John Barbirolli conducting. The opposition of man and Nature is portrayed in the opening prelude (Andante maestoso) and concluding epilogue (Alla marcia moderato, ma non troppo). The scherzo (Moderato; poco animando) and Intermezzo (Andante sostenuto) represent pictures of animals found in the Antarctic regions, including the lumbering whales and the cumbersome penguins. The Landscape movement (Lento) is a portrait of the icy regions.

For his text, Vaughan Williams took lines from Shelley's *Prometheus Unbound* in the prelude; from Psalm CIV in the scherzo; from Coleridge's *Hymn before Sunrise in the Vale of Chamouni* in the Landscape; from John Donne's *The Sun Rising* in the Intermezzo; and from Captain Scott's journal in the epilogue.

1954 CONCERTO FOR TUBA AND ORCHESTRA. I. Prelude. II. Romance. III. Rondo alla tedesca.

This is one of the scattered few concertos (if indeed not the only one) for the tuba. "The concerto," the composer has explained, "is nearer to the Bach form than that of the Viennese school, though the first and last movements finish up with elaborate cadenzas, which allies the concerto to the Mozart-Beethoven form. The music is fairly simple and obvious. . . . The orchestration is that of the so-called theatre orchestra, consisting of woodwinds, two each of horns, trumpets and trombones, tympani, percussion and strings.

The first movement is in the form and style of a scherzo, with virtuoso passages for the solo instrument. The second movement is more romantic, with a haunting melody assigned to the solo instrument. The finale is spirited music throughout, with a good deal of vivacity; the cadenza just before the close once again taxes the virtuosity of the performer.

The world première took place in London on June 13, 1954. Sir John Barbirolli conducted the London Symphony, while Philip Catelinet was the soloist.

1955–1957 SYMPHONY NO. 8 IN D MINOR. I. Fantasia. II. Scherzo alla marcia. III. Cavatina. IV. Toccata.

SYMPHONY NO. 9 IN E MINOR. I. Moderato maestoso. II. Andante sostenuto. III. Allegro pesante. VI. Andante tranquillo; Poco animato.

The Eighth Symphony (1955) was introduced in Manchester on May 2, 1956, Sir John Barbirolli conducting. It is unusual in structure. The first movement (Moderato; Presto; Andante sostenuto; Allegretto; Andante non troppo; Allegro vivace; Andante sostenuto; Tempo I, ma tranquillo) has been dubbed "seven variations in search of a theme." The opening section suggests some figures that are later developed, but there is no basic theme as such, and the variations that follow are based on those figures. There are seven short sections in this movement, the seventh and last being a repetition of the third, though on a larger scale.

The second movement (Allegro alla marcia; Andante; Tempo I) is a rhythmic airy scherzo, scored only for the wind instruments. After the brief trio, in which the bassooons carry the main thought, there is no complete recapitulation of the first part of the scherzo, but rather a short stretto and an equally short coda.

The slow movement (Lento espressivo), scored for strings, is interesting for its lyric expressiveness, beginning with a twelve-measure cantilena passage for the cellos.

The finale (Moderato maestoso) is remarkable for its dramatic impact, heightened through the elaborate use of percussion, including such instruments as the vibraphone, xylophone, gongs and bells. The two-section main theme is heard first in the trumpet and then in the orchestra. A secondary idea is introduced by strings and horns.

The Ninth was Vaughan Williams's last symphony. He completed it in 1957, and revised it in March-April of 1958. The première was heard in London on April 2, 1958, Sir Malcolm Sargent conducting. A later performance (on August 5) represented the composer's last appearance in public; he died three weeks later.

The scoring calls for three saxophones, and a fluegel-horn in B-flat (the latter a kind of keyed bugle), besides the usual large orchestra. Commenting on the presence of the saxophones, the composer said: "This beautiful and neglected instrument is not usually allowed in the select circles of the orchestra and has been banished to the brass band, where it is allowed to indulge in the bad habit of vibrato to its heart's content. While in the orchestra, it will be obliged to sit up and play straight. The saxophones, also, are not expected, except in the scherzo, to behave like demented cats, but are allowed to be their romantic selves." As for the fluegel-horn, the composer explained that its presence is "very important, but if one is unobtainable, the part may be played in the tutti on a third trumpet, some solo passages being cued in for first trumpet or first horn."

This symphony is a personal utterance, sometimes described as the composer's summation of his artistic faith and principles. This is not music of either faith or optimism, but music of brooding despair. A haunting melody in the first movement recurs in various guises throughout the work. In the slow and eloquent finale, the voice of despair is sounded most strongly. Almost as if aware of this deep note of pessimism, the composer added after the final measure the single word "niente" ("nothing").

Here is how a reviewer for *Musical America* described this symphony: "After a solemn introduction the first movement develops a theme stated in the solo clarinet in a series of flowing free variations. At the close it comes to full circle with a reference to the opening. Throughout, one senses the composer's ease and casualness. . . . In the second movement . . . a leisurely theme is contrasted with a livelier figure in a dialogue that ends with a return to the tranquil mood and melody of the beginning. A brilliant and extended Scherzo dies into a mere wisp as it leads into the tranquil introduction to the fourth movement. Here again we encounter one of those winding figures, of which Vaughan Williams is so fond, which do not have a striking profile in themselves but which lend themeselves beautifully to contrapuntal treatment as well as to melodic variation. The finale is again vigorous, but by no means compressed."

HEITOR VILLA-LOBOS 1887–1959

Variety is the spice of Villa-Lobos's music. It was ever impossible to prejudge the kind of music one was likely to hear when one attended a première performance of one of his works. For there was hardly a composer anywhere who has written in so many different veins, in so many different forms, and for so many different combinations of instruments. He has been Romantic, impressionistic, and decidedly modern. In different works, he has been sardonic and witty or poignant and pathetic; grandiose and eloquent or introspective. He has been on occasion cerebral; and on other occasions popular. He has been entirely original; and he has utilized parody and quotation.

The common denominator of his amazing output—amazing not only for its variety but also for its quantity (he has written more than two thousand works)—is its national feeling. From the music of his country, its popular tunes and ditties as well as its folk songs and dances, Villa-Lobos has assimilated rhythms, melodies and instruments in the creation of music which, whatever its idiom may be, beats with the heart and pulse of his native Brazil. Since Brazilian music is for the most part highly rhythmic and syncopated (carrying within it the throb of the jungle), Villa-Lobos's music most often has vertiginous movement and momentum. Since Brazilian melodies are often tender, Villa-Lobos's lyricism is often filled with a pleasing sentimentality. Since Brazilian music is vivid with color, Villa-Lobos's music usually contains rich harmonic schemes and brilliant orchestral effects. As a sophisticated medium for his national outlooks and materials, he devised two new structures—the *Chôros* and the *Bachiana Brasileira*—each of which yielded some of his finest creations.

He was, in short, Brazil in music. More than any other composer, as Irving Schwerké once said of him, "he seems to be actuated by the interior flame of his race."

Nicolas Slonimsky has pointed out that Villa-Lobos is a "programmatic composer. Every piece of music he writes has a story, and every title he places over a finished work is a picture. Brazilian legendary epos particularly fascinates him. His music is more than individualistic; it is almost anarchistic in its disregard of the performer's limitations, When Villa-Lobos needs a certain sonority, he expects the player to produce it. . . . Yet Villa-Lobos's music is not unplayable; it is merely difficult in an untraditional way. To the technical complexity is added the complexity of rhythm, and aural perception. Villa-Lobos can write in an exceedingly clear manner, as witness his numerous, and successful, choruses and piano pieces for children; but when he needs utmost expressive power, he resorts to the harshest type of dissonance, and employs instrumental effects that seem to do violence to the instruments, at least in the view of conventional performers."

Villa-Lobos was born in Rio de Janeiro. While the year of his birth was long in doubt, it is now known to be 1887—on March 5. He did not have much schooling. Compelled to make his own living when he was still a boy, Villa-Lobos played in restaurant and theatre orchestras, thus coming into direct contact with Brazilian popular music, which remained a significant influence in his development. For a brief period in 1907, he attended the National Institute of Music in Rio de Janeiro, but he never took to studies, preferring to go his own way, gathering both musical knowledge and experiences haphazardly. His first published composition was *Salon Waltz*, for piano, in 1908. This was followed one year later by *Canticos Sertanejos,* a suite for small orchestra employing popular tunes and rhythms.

In 1912, Villa-Lobos went on an expedition to East Brazil, where he made a study of Indian music, rites and myths. For a number of years, he continued to roam Brazil in search of native songs and dances. The study of this music had a far-reaching impact on his growth as a composer. It was only after he had absorbed the native music of Brazil that he was able to arrive at his own creative personality. His first significant works for orchestra made use of Brazilian-Indian materials. These compositions included the *Dansas Africanas* in 1914, and the tone poems *Amazonas* and *Uirapurú* in 1917. Meanwhile, on November 12, 1915, there took place in Rio de Janeiro the first concert devoted entirely to his compositions.

In 1916, Villa-Lobos settled in Rio de Janeiro and married Lucilla Guimaraes, a Conservatory-trained pianist. Three years later, the eminent concert pianist, Artur Rubinstein, became impressed with some of his works and used his influence to get the young composer a government subsidy. This enabled Villa-Lobos to go to Paris in 1922, where he stayed four years, and where he first attracted world attention with his vital and original compositions through important performances. After returning to Brazil, Villa-Lobos became the director of musical education in São Paulo in 1930. Two years later, he moved on to Rio de Janeiro to hold a similar post. He revolutionized the methods of music teaching by encouraging children to sing folk songs and join choruses, and also by devising a unique method of hand signals by which illiterates could sing formal compostitions. As a conductor, he drew attention to the music of Brazilian composers. And as a composer of international importance, he gave significance and inspiration to a national movement.

In 1944, Villa-Lobos visited the United States for the first time, touring America as guest conductor in performances of his own music. He toured the United States again in 1947 and 1957, and Europe in 1949 and 1958. Though seriously ill in his last years, his creative energy remained extraordinary. He died in Rio de Janeiro on November 17, 1959.

1914–1917 DANSAS AFRICANAS (AFRICAN DANCES), for orchestra. I. Allegro vivo. II. Allegro molto. III. Allegro ben marcato.

AMAZONAS, tone poem for orchestra.

UIRAPURÚ (THE ENCHANTED BIRD), tone poem for orchestra.

These are Villa-Lobos's first successful works for orchestra. All three were the immediate results of his researches in Brazilian-Indian music, dance, rites and mythology.

The *African Dances* came first in 1914. This is a set of three dances, all making effective use of native Brazilian rhythms and percussion instruments. A brief eight-measure introduction to the first dance sets the stage for the main dance tune, stated forcefully in clarinets and cellos to plucked-string accompaniment. The second dance opens with a quiet subject for flute and bassoon, accompanied by a soft roll in the tympani. A few sonorous measures for the brass precede the principal melody, a syncopated dance tune for violins. In the third dance, woodwinds, horns and violas loudly present the main dance melody. After a pause, the violins take the melody over to a syncopated horn accompaniment. Muted trombones then contribute a countertheme, and an effective cantabile episode is contributed by the violins in octaves. A dramatic recall of the main theme in cornet and unison strings brings the dance to its conclusion.

The *African Dances* received its world première in Paris on April 5, 1928.

Amazonas (1917) owes its inspiration to a Brazilian-Indian legend describing how an Indian girl is pursued by gods and monsters in a dense tropical jungle. Together with his use of Brazilian rhythms, some of them projected by native instruments, we find in this unusual score such novel instrumental effects as harmonic-glissandos or string instruments played below the bridge. *Amazonas* received its first performance in Paris on May 30, 1929; it was subsequently used for a Brazilian ballet, *Miremis*.

Uirapurú, written in the same year as *Amazonas* (but revised in 1948) was also inspired by Indian legend and the jungle. The published score contains the following program:

"This is the story of the legendary Uirapurú, who, according to the fetishists, was the King of Love and the most beautiful Cacique in the world. The Uirapurú's nightly song lured the Red Indians into the Brazilian wild woods to seek the magic singer. An ugly Indian played with his nose a flute in a peaceful and serene forest. Suddenly a gay group of natives appeared. They were the most handsome inhabitants of Para. The unsightly Indian attempted to conceal himself, but the natives found him and showed their displeasure at his invasion of their forest by driving him away, kicking and beating him mercilessly.

"They then continued their eager search for the Uirapurú, leaving no spot in the forest unexplored in their efforts to locate him. They were confident that they would be rewarded by finding a youth more handsome than any ever seen by human eyes. All the animal kingdom which reigns at night —glowworms, crickets, owls, bacarus, enchanted toads, bats—were witnesses to this harried search.

"An occasional sweet trill in the distance encouraged them and spurred them on in their search.

"Lured by the touching song of the Uirapurú, a beautiful and charming Indian maiden appeared. She held a bow and arrow and looked like a capable huntress. The Uirapurú was suddenly transformed into a handsome youth, to the amazement of all the Indians who had been so anxiously seeking him. They discussed this transformation among themselves, while they happily and with a sense of victory followed the huntress who had fascinated the Uirapurú.

"When their discussions ceased they heard the sharp, shrill tone of a flute made of bones. The Indians feared the revenge of the ugly Indian and quickly tried to hide the handsome youth. However, the bloodthirsty and vindictive Indian came upon the unsuspecting youth in his hiding place and aimed an arrow which struck its mark and instantly killed the boy. The Indian maidens immediately took him into their arms and carried him to the brink of a fountain where he suddenly changed into a bird, became invisible, and left the sad and impassioned maidens. They heard his beautiful song as it died down in the silence of the woods."

1920–1929 CHÔROS, NOS. 1–14.

No. 1, for guitar solo; No. 2, for flute and clarinet; No. 3, for male chorus and seven wind instruments; No. 4, for three horns and trombone; No. 5, Alma Brasileira, for solo piano; No. 6, for orchestra; No. 7, for flute, oboe, clarinet, saxophone, bassoon, violin and cello; No. 8, for large orchestra and two pianos; No. 9, for orchestra; No. 10, Rasga o Coração, for chorus and orchestra; No. 11, for piano and orchestra; No. 12, for orchestra; No. 13, for two orchestras and band; No. 14, for orchestra, band and chorus; Chôros bis, for violin and piano.

The "chôros" is a musical form of Villa-Lobos's invention. Nicolas Slonimsky explains that a "chôros" is a street band which plays popular tunes;

subsequently, the term *chôros* was applied to the kind of music such a band played. However, in his works written in the form, Villa-Lobos extended the meaning of the word. It became, as he himself explained, "a new form in which are synthesized the different modalities of Brazilian, Indian and popular music, having for principal elements rhythm and any typical melody of popular character. . . . The word 'serenade' gives an approximate idea of the significance of the chôros."

Chôros No. 1 (1920) initiates this series with a work for guitar solo. This is an extended piece, with a recurrent folk-song type melody of plaintive character, but with an abundant supply of contrasting subsidiary material. The last Chôros, though it is not the last in the numerical series, is the twelfth (1941), for large orchestra, whose world première took place in Cambridge, Massachusetts, on February 21, 1945, with the composer conducting the Boston Symphony.

The following are characteristic works in this form:

Chôros No. 4 (1926) is an example of the composer's bent for instrumental experimentation, since it calls for the rare combination of three horns and trombone. The basic melody is popular and comes midway in the composition.

Chôros No. 5, better known as *Alma Brasileira* (1926), is one of Villa-Lobos's most famous compositions for the piano. It is in three-part song form, the outer sections being rhythmic, while the middle part is lyrical, reminiscent of a Brazilian popular tune.

Chôros No. 7 (1926) was introduced on July 15, 1942, in Rio de Janeiro under the composer's direction. This is melancholy music, opening as it does with a lament for the flute. After that, the composition employs a polyphonic treatment of several folk melodies with occasional quotations of popular tunes heard in small Brazilian towns. The composer explained that there are successive musical episodes "just as there are new episodes of life." The orchestra here enlists the services of several unusual members, including a guitar, a bombardine (a brass instrument resembling the tuba), and native percussion instruments.

Chôros No. 7, Settimino (1924), is a septet for wind instruments. "Popular song, unreserved national dances, and the improvisational take turns in appearing," Arthur Cohn explains. "Slow-paced, exotically colored sections merge into dance patterns (there is even an outright waltz in one place). Thus the primitive jungle accent is related to an almost savage keenness of tone color." Cohn takes note of a fact often disregarded: this septet is actually for eight instruments, a tam-tam being employed to produce nine sounds, after which it is abandoned.

Chôros No. 10, Rasga o Coração (1926), for chorus and orchestra, was introduced in Rio de Janeiro on December 15, 1926, the composer conducting. The composer described this work as follows in the published score: "This work represents the reaction of a civilized man to stark nature; his contemplation of the valleys of the Amazon and the land of Matto Grosso and Para. The vastness and majesty of the landscape enrapture and captivate him. The sky, the waters, the woods, the birds fascinate him. But little by little his humanity asserts itself; there are living people in this land, even though they are savages. Their music is full of nostalgia and of love; their dances are full of rhythm. The Brazilian song, 'Rasga o Coração' is heard, and the Brazilian heart beats in unison with the Brazilian earth."

1921 FANTASIA DE MOVIMENTOS MIXTOS (FANTASY OF MIXED MOVEMENTS), for violin and orchestra. I. Alma Convulsa. II. Serenidade. III. Contentamento.

Though most of this music was written in 1921, and introduced in Rio de Janeiro on December 15, 1922, Villa-Lobos revised it several times; the final version was heard on November 1, 1940, the composer conducting in Buenos Aires, with Oscar Borgerth as soloist. The titles provide the emotional climate for each of the three movements: "Torment," "Serenity," "Contentment." Lisa M. Peppercorn has described this work pithily as follows: "The first movement uses a number of themes, partly of Indian flavor, which appear only once or are repeated several times, without receiving symphonic handling. This is typical of Villa-Lobos's writing. His abundance of ideas leaves him little opportunity for development. On the other hand, the thematic material is conceived in such a way that it is less suited for the usual working-out technique."

1926 RUDEPOEMA, for piano solo (also for orchestra).

One of the fruits that grew out of the friendship of Villa-Lobos and the celebrated concert pianist, Artur Rubinstein, was a long and highly technical piece for the piano, written in 1926. Villa-Lobos intended it as a tonal portrait of Rubinstein's temperament—hence the title, which means "savage poem." Free in form and rhapsodic in character, the work has vertiginous rhythmic vitality and impetuous movement; it utilizes large sweeps of sound that tax the timbres and sonorities of the piano. Indeed, it is more orchestral than pianistic, a fact that must have occurred to the composer, since he orchestrated it in 1932. The orchestrated version was introduced in Rio de Janeiro, under the composer's baton, on July 15, 1942.

When the Boston Symphony Orchestra under Koussevitzky performed the orchestral version early in 1945, the program annotation described the music as follows: "There are broad effects such as glissandi, pedal bass chords, and a range which sometimes requires three or four staves. The poem is rhapsodic, free in form, with frequent changes of tempo."

1928 WOODWIND QUARTET; for flute, oboe, clarinet and bassoon. I. Allegro troppo. II. Lent. III. Allegro molto vivace.

WOODWIND QUINTET, for flute, oboe, English horn, clarinet and bassoon.

The woodwind quartet is a work of great concentration and economy. The first movement is based on a single theme, and a single rhythmic pattern. The second movement is in elementary A-B-A song form. Two melodic ideas, one rhythmic and the other lyrical, constitute the material of the finale.

The composer has explained that his woodwind quintet is in the style of a Chôros. It is in a single movement, but it comprises a number of sections. The work opens with a tranquil episode. Power is soon generated, and power is built up as several native Brazilian sounds are simulated—jungle cries, the voices of tropical birds, the rhythm of native drums. The frenetic mood subsides into tranquillity only to be built up again towards a climax.

1932–1945 BACHIANA BRASILEIRA, NOS. 1–9.

No. 1, for eight cellos; No. 2, for chamber orchestra; No. 3, for piano and orchestra; No. 4, for orchestra; No. 5, for voice and eight cellos; No. 6, for flute and bassoon; No. 7, for orchestra; No. 8, for orchestra; No. 9, for strings.

In his suites for various instruments, or for orchestra, to which he gave the title of *Bachiana Brasileira,* Villa-Lobos attempted a fusion of Bach's polyphonic style with the personality of Brazilian folk music. The composer frequently utilizes alternate sets of titles for the movements to emphasize this duality; one set suggests Bach, the other, Brazilian folklore. "His admiration for Bach has not led him to imitation," says Burle Marx, "but rather to a rendering of his style in the Brazilian idiom. . . . It is in scope and intensity of feeling that he approaches the spirit of Bach."

Bachiana Brasileira No.1 (1932) was introduced in Rio de Janeiro on September 12, 1932, Burle Marx conducting. It is in three movements: I. Introduction (Embolada); II. Prelude (Modinha); III. Fugue (Conversa). The first movement is essentially Brazilian in its rhythmic interest and in its evocation of popular tunes. The spiritual character of the melody for solo cello in the second movement—later carried on by the other cellos, often in unison—and the fugal writing of the third movement suggest Bach, though the subject of the third-movement fugue is based on a Brazilian rhythm.

Bachiana Brasileira No. 2 (1933) is in four movements: I. Prelude (Song of the Hoodlum); II. Aria (Song of Our Country); III. Danza (Woodland Memory); IV. Toccata (The Little Train of Caipira). The fourth movement is the most popular; it is, indeed,one of the composer's most famous compositions, having entered the permanent repertory of semi-classical literature. The first movement, an Adagio, contrasts a melancholy subject for baritone saxophone, trombones and cellos with a rhythmic episode of a strong Brazilian identity. The second part opens passionately in full orchestra before yielding to a song for solo cello. In the third movement, a solo trombone over string accompaniment precedes a scherzando section that is built up to a powerful climax. The popular fourth movement is a realistic picture of a little train puffing its way through Brazilian communities. Villa-Lobos is said to have written this music before the preceding three movements (in 1931) during an hour's train trip from one town to another in São Paulo. The percussion family in this movement includes four native Brazilian instruments: ganza, chucalho, matraca and reco-reco.

Bachiana Brasileira No. 3 (1934) was first performed in New York on February 19, 1947, with the composer conducting the CBS Symphony. This is a four-movement composition for piano and orchestra marked as follows: I. Preludio (Ponteio); II. Fantasia (Revery); III. Aria (Love Song); IV. Toccata (Woodpecker).

Bachiana Brasileira No. 4 originated as a piano composition in the 1930s but is more familiar in the orchestrated version made by the composer in

1941 and introduced in New York on June 6, 1942. Arthur Cohn described this music as "a partita . . . with much Bach and no semblance of folkloristic accompaniment until midway in the third movement."

Of all the *Bachianas Brasileiras,* the most celebrated is No. 5. It has two parts, an "Aria" and a "Danza." The first was written in 1938, the second in 1945. The Aria, introduced in Rio de Janeiro on March 25, 1939, is a three-part song for voice and eight cellos (pizzicato). The first and third parts consist of a wordless chant to the syllable *Ah,* and the middle section, which has a text, is in the style of a folk song. The song movement has been described as a "love-song dance."

Bachiana Brasileira No. 6 is scored for the contrasting voices of a flute and a bassoon. To Olin Downes, this music plunged him "into a primitive scene. He hears primitive sounds and pulsatile instruments; he thinks of the cries of villagers, their rude dances, their wild rhythms, and gyrations in the forest." Arthur Cohn explains that the first movement, an Aria (Chôro) is "constructed sequentially" while the second part, a Fantasia, has a "very segmented design, with very little freedom of flow."

Villa-Lobos's last three *Bachianas Brasileiras* are all for orchestra, though the ninth is for strings alone. The seventh (1942) was performed in Rio de Janeiro on March 13, 1944; the eighth, in Rome on August 6, 1947. The ninth was written in 1945.

The seventh opens with a rhythmic prelude and ends with a four-voiced fugue, which strays from the norm by introducing a horn episode. The middle parts are rhythmic, one of its movements being a Toccata in which a subject with a Bach-like rhythmic pulse and with Bach-like figurations is maintained by the strings, over which various subjects, some with a pronounced Brazilian identity, are introduced.

Arthur Cohn maintains that the highlight of the eighth one is its Aria (Modinha), while in the ninth, the emphasis in the last three movements is on Bach's polyphonic style, though Brazilian lyricism is established in the opening prelude.

1938 STRING QUARTET NO. 6 IN E MAJOR (Brazilian Quartet No. 2). I. Poco animato. II. Allegretto. III. Andante. IV. Allegro vivace.

Villa-Lobos wrote two string quartets which he subtitled *Brazilian* to point up their debt to the folk music of that country. The second is the more famous. The work opens with a movement full of animation and good spirits. In the second movement, the main theme is a broad and sensual melody. There follows an Andante which is a delicately atmospheric tone painting, subtly impressionistic, quivering with the sounds of a Brazilian jungle on a summer's night. A staccato theme for violins opens the final movement, which is alive and colorful with Brazilian rhythms and melodies.

1945 MADONA, tone poem for orchestra.

Madona was commissioned by the Koussevitzky Music Foundation. It was introduced in Rio de Janeiro under the composer's direction on October 8, 1946.

Dedicated to the memory of Natalie Koussevitzky, *Madona* was intended by its composer as a portrait of Mrs. Koussevitzky. Villa-Lobos wrote: "There was an indefinable expression in her features which at once inspired in me an intuitive and definite confidence, remaining as an inexplicable and enduring memory of a being possessed with rare gifts of kindness. . . . Since it would be impossible for me to describe her in a prolonged literary dissertation, objective, concrete or conventional, I depend upon the mystery of sounds, as embodied in the free songs of my country's birds and folk and natural surroundings by which my musical nature is inspired."

1946 MANDÚ-CARARÁ, symphonic poem (or ballet) for large chorus, children's chorus and orchestra.

Hugh Ross, who conducted the world première of *Mandú-Carará* with the Schola Cantorum in New York on January 23, 1948, wrote the following illuminating description:

"*Mandú-Carará* is a legend of the Nheengatu people, a Brazilian Indian tribe. The work is named for a famous young Indian dancer, and the climax is a triumphal dance led by Mandú-Carará in celebration of the happy ending of the story.

"The legend concerns the adventures of two children, and parallels in a Brazilian setting the story of Hansel and Gretel. Two greedy children have been left by their poor father in the woods as he is unable to feed them any longer. In their wanderings they come upon an ogre, Currupira, who lures them to his hearth. They ask him the way home, but he detains them and his wife begins stuffing them with food.

"A musical interlude then describes how the children outwit Currupira, telling him how they had just seen two far monkeys near his hut. He goes in search of them, and meanwhile the children kill his wife and run away.

"Currupira comes home and rushes madly about the wood, crying with fury. The children save themselves from him by swimming across a river and with the help of forest creatures find their way home. There they find Mandú-Carará with their father. This is the signal for a general celebration, culminating in the dance of Mandú-Carará.

"The story has elements both of symphony and ballet. The one-eyed Currupira with reversed ears and feet and his wicked Indian wife, the cotias and monkeys of the jungle, the children, Mandú-Carará and the Indians all find their musical embodiment in Villa-Lobos's score.

"The percussion instruments emphasize the rhythms of Mandú-Carará's dance. A heavy stumbling ostinato, soon after the entry of the chorus, represents the frightened children wandering in the jungle."

1954 CONCERTO NO. 2 IN A MINOR, for cello and orchestra. I. Allegro non troppo. II. Molto andante cantabile. III. Vivace. IV. Allegro energico.

In the twelve-measure introduction to the first movement the woodwinds and strings suggest a subject that is amplified into a dramatic statement by the solo cello. After an extended development, the solo cello also presents the second theme, a lyric idea contrasting the mood of the first theme. In the second movement, flutes, clarinets, muted strings and brass create the proper mood with which to introduce a beautiful folk-song-like melody of rhapsodic character in the solo cello. A light and capricious scherzo that culminates in a cadenza leads without pause to the finale, in which principal material from the first and second movements is recalled. A powerful momentum is then built up through varied rhythms, contrasting meters and expanding sonorities.

The concerto received its world première in New York on February 5, 1955. Aldo Parisot was the soloist and Walter Hendl conducted the New York Philharmonic.

1955 SYMPHONY NO. 11. I. Allegro moderato. II. Largo. III. Scherzo: molto vivace. IV. Molto allegro.

This work was commissioned by the Koussevitzky Music Foundation for the 75th anniversary of the Boston Symphony, which introduced it in Boston on March 2, 1956, the composer conducting. A stately subject for full orchestra leads to the main theme of the first movement in strings. The second main theme comes later in horns and trumpets over ostinato figures in strings and harp. The melody of the second movement is assigned to the flutes; a second section then begins with a subject in bass clarinet which is soon taken over by various woodwind instruments, a violin solo, and brass. The scherzo movement is made up of a succession of woodwind solo passages. The finale consists mainly of a vigorous, strongly accented subject developed with considerable force by the full orchestra.

SIR WILLIAM WALTON 1902–

Eric Blom has pointed out a salient trait that sets Walton apart from most living composers: his capacity "to create a musical work that is not only all of a piece, but remains unique and unrepeatable, for each time he tackles a new composition it turns out to be entirely different from the last."

However great is the stylistic difference between, say, *Façade* and *Belshazzar's Feast*, or *Belshazzar's Feast* and the Viola Concerto, or the Violin Concerto and the two symphonies, certain individual mannerisms remain: the long, sinuous melodic line; the detailed harmonic and contrapuntal writing, which never appears cluttered because of the transparency of the texture; the rich and brilliant orchestration; the irresistible drive of the rhythms and cross-rhythms. His extraordinary craftsmanship and articulateness, revealed from the very first, have enabled Walton to blend form and content, idea and style, into an inextricable unity. Though his works are comparatively few in number, they are all distinguished by technical mastery and a wide gamut of expressiveness;

and it is for these reasons that, ever since his early *Façade,* he has been one of the most significant and interesting composers in England.

Walton was born in Oldham, Lancashire, England, on March 29, 1902. His father, a church musician, gave him his first music lessons. At the age of five, William sang in the church choir which his father directed. Five years after that, he entered the Christ Church Cathedral Choir School at Oxford, where he studied under Sir Hugh Allen and received a Bachelor of Music degree in 1918. For a brief and unsatisfactory period, he attended Christ Church College, Oxford, but was expelled for failure to attend to his studies, since all of his time was dedicated to musical interests. At Oxford, he completed the writing of a string quartet and a piano quartet. The first of these was introduced at the festival of the International Society for Contemporary Music at Salzburg on August 4, 1923; the latter received a publication award from the Carnegie Trust Fund in 1924. In both these compositions he was influenced by Brahms and Fauré. Nevertheless, individual characteristics soon to become recognizable as his own could be detected. After leaving Oxford, he lived in London with the Sitwell family, an association that led to the writing of *Façade* in 1922, with which Walton achieved his first success. *Portsmouth Point,* for orchestra, in 1925, the viola concerto in 1929, and *Belshazzar's Feast* in 1931 helped to establish his reputation.

During World War II, Walton served in the Ambulance Corps in London. In uniform, he wrote the music for documentary films, the scores for two ballets, and the background music for several successful commercial motion pictures, including *Major Barbara, Hamlet* and *Henry V.* During the war, in 1942, Oxford conferred on him an honorary doctorate in music. After the war, a succession of major works, each one of first significance, placed Walton with the foremost composers of the twentieth century. In recognition of his achievements, he was knighted in 1951. In 1953, he wrote a Te Deum for the coronation of Queen Elizabeth II, and in 1954, he completed the writing of his first opera, *Troilus and Cressida.* He paid several visits to the United States, the first one just before World War II. He began a career as conductor of his own music soon after the end of World War II with a Scandinavian tour. In 1955, he appeared as conductor for the first time in the United States, leading a performance of his *Crown Imperial March* (1938) at the United Nations; on August 8, 1963, he led an all-Walton concert at the Lewisohn Stadium in New York.

Walton married Susan Gil in Buenos Aires in 1948. They subsequently established their permanent residence on the island of Ischia.

1922 FAÇADE, an "entertainment" for reciting voice and seven instruments (also for full orchestra). I. Hornpipe. II. En famille. III. Mariner Man. IV. Trio for Two Cats and Trombone. V. Through Gilded Trelises. VI. I Do Like to be Beside the Seaside. VII. Scotch Rhapsody. VIII. Lullaby for Jumbo. IX. Old Sir Faulk. X. By the Lake. XI. A Man from a Far Countree. XII. Country Dance. XIII. Swiss Yodeling Song. XIV. Black Mrs. Behemoth. XV. Popular Song. XVI. Polka. XVII. Valse. XVIII. Tarantella. XIX. Four in the Morning. XX. Something Lies Beyond the Scene. XXI. Sir Beelzebub.

FAÇADE, Suite No. 1, for orchestra. I. Polka. II. Valse. III. Swiss Yodeling Song. IV. Tango-Pasodoble. V. Tarantella sevillana.

FAÇADE, Suite, No. 2, for orchestra. I. Fanfare. II. Scotch Rhapsody. III. Country Dance. IV. Noche española. V. Popular Song. VI. Fox-Trot, Old Sir Faulk.

FAÇADE, ballet in one act, with choreography by Frederick Ashton. First performance: Sadler's Wells, London, April 26, 1931.

While attending Oxford, Walton befriended Sacheverell Sitwell. Upon leaving Oxford for London, Walton went to live with the Sitwells—that literary family that included Osbert and Edith as well as Sacheverell. Edith was a poet who, between 1920 and 1921, had put down on paper abstract poems. Before long, an idea was hatched to set some of these poems to music and present both in as abstract a manner as possible. The Sitwells entered into the project by suggesting all kinds of novel ideas for the performance. Thus *Façade* was born—conceived, as Sir Osbert Sitwell once revealed, "in high spirits . . . aiming at obtaining a new kind of beauty as well as gaiety." He explained further: "We sought to reach a country between music and poetry where, as on the border between waking and sleeping, new landscapes would show a brief but memorable vividness, and strange glimpses of fates, of mortals, and of immortals, could be captured within the world of a minute or two minutes."

Edith Sitwell's poems were sheer nonsense, but delightful nonsense, fresh and exciting examples of dadaism, concerned more with the value of sound than with meaning. She herself described these silly pieces as "technical experiments—studies in the effect that texture has on rhythm, and the effect that varying and elaborate patterns of rhymes and assonances and dissonances have on rhythm."

But the music young William Walton wrote for these verses was neither abstract, nor nonsensical, nor esoteric. With a down-to-earth sense of humor, he resorted to parody, burlesque, mock seriousness, tongue-in-the-cheek sentimentality, and calculated clichés to produce a score that was not only great fun through and through but also a tour de force of technical mastery. The music caricatured the popular song, the American fox-trot, and such European dances as the waltz and the polka. It mocked Rossini's *The Barber of Seville,* the Swiss yodel, and Mozart's *Don Giovanni* through parody. For all its irrepressible lightness of spirit, the score was, as Hubert Foss remarked, "accomplished stuff, indeed, well wrought and beautifully written." Sometimes, by way of delightful contrast, Walton became deadly serious in the haunting loveliness of his writing (in *By the Lake,* for example, or *A Man from a Far Countree*).

The project, first described as a "melodrama," was tried out at the Sitwell home early in 1922. At that time, the work consisted of an overture, an interlude and settings of sixteen poems, all scored for narrator and seven instruments. The first public performance followed on June 12, 1923, at Aeolian Hall in London. A curtain had painted on it a face with a megaphone-shaped mouth. As Edith Sitwell, concealed behind the curtain, recited her poems, her voice floated in sing-song fashion out of the large, distorted painted mouth. She was hidden from view and so were the accompanying instruments.

This concert aroused "an outburst of critical rage and hysteria in the audience," as Sir Osbert Sitwell later recalled. Noel Coward left the auditorium in the middle of the performance revealing obvious shock and anger. Edith Sitwell was warned to remain hidden after the concert to avoid molestation or attack. There was one important dissenting voice to all this opposition. It came from Ernest Newman in the *Sunday Times:* "I can only confess that, done as this brilliant group of people does it, the thing has an unholy fascination for me. As for Walton's music, nothing cleverer has been produced in that line by any composer in any country; the stuff is always nimble-witted, and the deftness of the craftsman is a joy."

After this performance, Walton revised his score, adding a fanfare and settings for several more poems, and rewriting the instrumental part for full orchestra. This adaptation was heard at the New Chenil Galleries in London on April 27, 1926, and proved a huge success. The work was then featured twice on the same program at the festival of the International Society for Contemporary Music at Siena on September 14, 1928. In 1942, Walton once again revised his music, limiting the number of poems to twenty-one. Before that, he had also prepared two suites for orchestra (1928, 1938). The first was introduced at the International Festival for Contemporary Music at Siena in 1928, and the second, in New York City on March 30, 1938. Both have gained wide circulation on symphony programs and in recordings.

Two ballet adaptations were made of *Façade*. The first was produced by Günter Hess in Germany in 1929. The more popular one, however, was that given in London in 1931, with Frederick Ashton's choreography, and with Lydia Lopokova, Alicia Markova and Frederick Ashton as principal dancers. It became a standard item in the ballet repertory at Sadler's Wells. It was introduced in the United States, in a Sadler's Wells production in New York on October 13, 1949, with Moira Shearer and Frederick Ashton. Ashton's choreography consisted of a series of nine humorous episodes in front of a façade of a Victorian house.

1925 PORTSMOUTH POINT, concert overture for orchestra.

Portsmouth Point, a British naval arsenal opposite the Isle of Wight, was the subject of a print by Thomas Rowlandson. A feverishly active and colorful waterfront scene is depicted. On the left is a money lender's shop, on the right a tavern, and at the dock several sailing vessels. Sailors are busily loading ships; loving couples are saying farewell; a lonely musician with a wooden leg is playing the piano.

This print inspired Walton to write his brisk overture. Syncopated themes, discords, frequent changes in time signature evoke a picture of feverish activity and confusion. The composition is filled with salty tunes suggesting nautical melodies of the eighteenth century and the vigorous rhythms of sailor dances; but Constant Lambert also finds the influence of Catalonia sardanas in some of the material.

The overture had an outstandingly successful première at the festival of the International Society for Contemporary Music at Zurich, on June 22, 1926, Volkmar Andrae conducting.

1927 SINFONIA CONCERTANTE, for orchestra with piano obbligato. I. Maestoso; Allegro spiritoso; Allegretto. II. Andante comodo. III. Allegro molto.

This composition represents a drastic change of pace for the composer—away from the levities of *Façade* and the spirited tunefulness of *Portsmouth Point* to a greater sobriety and deeper musical expressiveness. It was introduced in London by the London Philharmonic under Ernest Ansermet on January 5, 1928; York Bowen was the assisting artist.

After a slow introduction, the Allegro spiritoso movement arrives. It is built from several ideas which appear consecutively. In the section that follows, development and recapitulation are telescoped into one. The brass is used sparingly in the second movement for music of devotional character; Walton's talent for writing sensuous music of emotional impact here becomes evident. Gaiety comes in the concluding movement with several lusty tunes.

1929 CONCERTO FOR VIOLA AND ORCHESTRA. I. Andante comodo. II. Vivo con molto precioso. III. Allegro moderato.

Today this work is generally recognized as one of the most important viola concertos written in the twentieth century. But this evaluation represents no radical change of public or critical opinion, since the concerto was a success of the first magnitude at its première. This took place at a Promenade concert in London on October 3, 1929, with Paul Hindemith as soloist, and the composer conducting. The critic for the *Musical Times,* for example, wrote: "The success . . . might almost be said to have amounted to a sensation, were it not that the music made an impression, not a mere hit. It is one of the most remarkable of recent compositions, British or otherwise, the more so because it does not draw attention to itself by anything but sheer quality." It was again acclaimed at the festival of the International Society for Contemporary Music at Liège on September 4, 1930, with Lionel Tertis soloist. And when William Primrose performed it with the Philadelphia Orchestra in 1944, Olin Downes did not hesitate to call it "one of the best scores that the very adroit and accomplished Mr. Walton has given us."

Almost as if to emphasize that the frivolities of youth were over and that wisdom and noble sentiments were replacements, the concerto opens unorthodoxly with a deep-feeling slow movement. After a brief introduction for orchestra, the solo instrument is heard in a passionate subject (Espressivo), the main thought of the movement; muted strings provide a shimmering background with tremolos. The second subject is equally emotional (also marked Espressivo) and is once again presented by solo viola. As this material is discussed, it becomes dramatized, particularly in the orchestra. Towards the end of the movement, the woodwinds recall the first subject, with solo viola providing decorative figurations; the viola then remembers the second theme.

The second movement is a dynamic scherzo in which we are reminded that the thoughtful and passionate creator of the first movement is also capable of light humors. Such a mood persists into the third movement, with a lively main subject for bassoon. Intensity of feeling, however, returns with the lyrical second theme, a subject in double stops for the solo instrument. Dramatic interest is built up in an extended orchestral episode. A quiet tremolo in violins recalls the first theme of the first movement in the solo instrument to achieve for the concerto unity and integration.

1931 BELSHAZZAR'S FEAST, oratorio for baritone, chorus and orchestra.

The success of the Viola Concerto was followed by an even greater triumph. No choral work by an Englishman since Elgar's *The Dream of Gerontius* received higher praises from the critics and more unqualified enthusiasm from the audience than did *Belshazzar's Feast* when first heard. And with good reason. The breadth of design and the majesty of style of a Handelian oratorio are here combined with the violent surge of modern rhythms and the dramatic pulse of modern harmonies.

Walton's first work for chorus, *Belshazzar's Feast,* had been commissioned by the Leeds Festival, where it was introduced on October 10, 1931, Sir Malcolm Sargent conducting.

The text (prepared by Osbert Sitwell) is an adaptation of passages from the Bible (fifth chapter of the Book of Daniel), with the addition of Psalms 137 and 81. The oratorio opens with a fanfare prefacing the words, "Thus spake Isaiah." Isaiah's dire prophecy of the Babylonian captivity, sung by discordant male voices, follows. We then hear (to quote Colin Mason's fine analysis) "a short orchestral passage" succeeded by "a lament sung by chorus, 'By the Waters of Babylon We Sat Down and Wept,' which has often been praised as Walton's finest music. The magical change from the first mood to this, effected neither by a long transition nor by a distinct pause, takes place, it seems, inevitably, though we wonder afterwards how it was done. The passionate sorrow of the captives is expressed here as finely as the brutality of the prophecy, the repetition of words not being used in the classical ornamental way, but to give the impression of their echoing cries, lamenting for Jerusalem." The chorus then describes brilliantly the sumptuous feast, after which trumpets herald the arrival of Belshazzar, followed by the people singing his praises. An orgy develops; all the while, voices are raised high in praise of Belshazzar. "From this point on," continues Colin Mason, "the intensity rises until the dramatic moment of Belshazzar's death, after which Walton gradually changes it into an exultant hymn, with some passages almost of the beauty of the prisoners' chorus, and a massive Handelian Alleluia."

1935 SYMPHONY NO. 1. I. Allegro assai. II. Scherzo: presto, con malizia. III. Adagio con malincolia. IV. Maestoso; Brioso ed ardentemente; Vivacissimo; Maestoso.

It is perhaps indicative of the far-reaching interest of Walton's public in his music that the first performance of his First Symphony should have taken place even before it was completed. When the first three movements were finished in 1934, they were heard in a performance by the London Symphony Orchestra under Sir Hamilton Harty on December 3 of the same year—even though it was known that a fourth movement was being written. That fourth movement was completed the following summer; the entire symphony was then heard on November 6, 1935, in a performance by the BBC Symphony under Harty.

The symphony is a complex work which employs elaborate harmonic and contrapuntal textures and a profusion of terse themes. The first movement is not in the usual sonata form but passes fluidly from one idea to the next, by-passing the usual development and recapitulation sections found in conventional symphonies. There is an undercurrent of malicious irony in the Scherzo, which is markedly rhythmic and syncopated. But the slow movement that follows enters a world of calm and contemplation in which irony has no place; Walton's rich vein of lyricism is here tapped, beginning with a delicately spun melody for flute (Doloroso molto espressivo). The symphony ends in a broadly designed finale which is in four sections—the first and closing parts being somewhat declamatory, while the middle portions are vigorous, with a climax reached in a fugal exposition.

1939 CONCERTO FOR VIOLIN AND ORCHESTRA. I. Andante tranquillo. II. Presto capriccioso a la napolitana. III. Vivace.

Walton produced this work for Jascha Heifetz. The violinist introduced it in Cleveland on December 7, 1939, with the Cleveland Orchestra, Artur Rodzinski conducting. It was subsequently revised.

This concerto is music that is deeply felt and emotionally projected. It opens with a slow movement in which an atmosphere of tranquillity is evoked. A long, beautifully carved melody for the solo violin follows the introduction; subsidiary ideas are superimposed on this melody to provide contrapuntal interest. Later there appear some dramatic outbursts in the orchestra and assertive passages for the violin; but the initial mood is reestablished both in the orchestra and solo instrument, and new material is introduced to heighten the serenity and eloquent beauty of the opening passage. The movement that follows has spirited movement and boisterous spirit: an impetuous dance appears in the violin after a one-bar introduction by the orchestra; a second brief orchestra exclamation leads into a Neapolitan song, also heard in the solo violin; a third orchestral outburst brings on an infectious waltz.

The main theme of the finale is heard first in the lower strings and bassoons, and becomes the matrix for several subsidiary ideas; a second theme appears in the woodwinds, with embellishments by the violin. The music of this movement passes from whimsy to melancholy, from sensitive moods to passionate ones.

1940 SCAPINO, a comedy overture for orchestra.

This infectious and gay little overture is in the vein of *Portsmouth Point,* full of spirited melodies and rhythms. Scapino is, of course, a familiar character in the Italian commedia dell'arte. For his inspiration, Walton went to two etchings of Callot, reproductions of which he pasted into the manuscript score. The overture opens with a delightful character study of Scapino (Molto vivace); after a relaxed theme is heard in the horns and violas and then in the violins, there comes an interlude which is described by the composer as a "serenata." A playful section, in which earlier material returns, closes the work.

Walton wrote this overture on a commission from the Chicago Symphony Orchestra to commemorate its fiftieth anniversary; at that time, the composer was serving in the British Army. The première took place in Chicago on April 3, 1941, with Frederick Stock conducting the Chicago Symphony.

1947 STRING QUARTET IN A MINOR. I. Allegro. II. Presto. III. Lento. IV. Allegro molto.

This quartet is Walton's second, the first—an apprentice work—having been written in 1922. The Second Quartet came twenty-five years later, and was first performed in London on May 4, 1947, by the Blech Quartet.

This is one of Walton's most compact and economical works. Intense in feeling, subdued in expression, its best pages reflect a restrained melancholy. The main theme of the first movement, heard in the upper register of the viola, is elegiac, as is the entire third movement, in which muted strings speak of intimate and tender thoughts. Only in the final movement is the spell of sad revery shattered; the music now becomes turbulent and passionate.

1949 SONATA FOR VIOLIN AND PIANO. I. Allegro tranquillo. II. Variazioni.

Walton wrote this sonata for Yehudi Menuhin and Louis Kentner, who gave it a trial performance in Zurich in 1949. Walton then felt the need of further revision. The final and definitive version was introduced in London in 1950 by the same pair of artists.

The sonata has only two movements, The first is in sonata form, with a melodious first subject in the violin over chords in the piano, and the second a reflective melody in the piano. The development and the concluding coda concern themselves entirely with the first subject. The recapitulation is a shortened version of the exposition.

The second movement is a series of variations on a two-part expressive melody first heard in the violin. The seven variations bear the following tempo markings: Poco più mosso; A tempo, quasi improvisando; Alla marcia molto vivace; Allegro molto; Allegretto con moto; Scherzando; Andante tranquillo. The movement ends with a vigorous coda (Molto vivace).

1954 TROILUS AND CRESSIDA, opera in three acts, with text by Christopher Hassall based on the poem of the same name by Chaucer. First performance: Covent Garden, London, December 3, 1954.

The world première of *Troilus and Cressida* was attended with a good deal of pomp and ceremony. This was the first opera by a composer now universally recognized as a major voice in twentieth-century music. In fact, no opera aroused in London such advanced interest and publicity since Britten's *Peter Grimes* almost twenty years earlier. The performance of *Troilus and Cressida* became one of the most brilliant events of the season, the auditorium filled with leading representatives of government, industry, society and culture.

What was needed was a work of first significance to rise to such an august occasion. This is what *Troilus and Cressida* turned out to be—a majestic opera overflowing with wonderful lyricism and magnetized by powerful dramatic situations; an opera, searching in its characterizations both in text and music; an opera, frequently soaring to peaks of nobility and eloquence. The final curtain inspired a fifteen-minute ovation. The next day the critics were rapturous. Not since *Peter Grimes* had an English opera received such unanimous acclaim from public, critics and professional musicians.

It took Sir William almost seven years to write his opera. Hassall had completed his text for Walton in 1948, based on Chaucer's version of the legendary romance. During the siege of Troy, Colchas goes over to the Greeks, leaving his daughter Cressida behind. Troilus, son of King Priam, falls in love with her. Through Pandarus, Cressida's uncle, a meeting between the lovers is arranged. An obstacle is posed when Cressida is summoned by her father from Troy to join him, and when Cressida is successfully wooed by Diomede, the messenger sent to escort her to her father. In the end, Troilus is killed by Colchas and Cressida commits suicide.

The dramatic element is emphasized throughout. As Ronald Eyer noted in *Musical America:* "Sir William . . . knows how to build dramatic tension and how to hold an audience breathless through an emotional scene. The episode of Pandarus in a losing battle of wits with Diomede, which ends in the seizure of Cressida by the Greeks, is as climactic a first-act curtain as you are likely to see outside Italian melodrama. . . . The third and last act is pure Verdi as far as dramatic denouement is concerned—the outraged lover, the frustrated rival, the spurned maiden who prefers death to degradation, and the traitorous father who is sent back to his own people for his just deserts; all these are stock opera characters in stock situations. . . . The music is a different story. Here Sir William is rarely British, frequently Italian, but most consistently German and middle European in his derivations. . . . Sir William seems to have made of himself a crucible for the distillation of all the more effective operatic devices of two centuries."

The lyric element is also stressed. As Howard Taubman reported when the opera was first heard in the United States (in San Francisco on October 7, 1955): "It is not afraid to sing. The roles of Troilus and Cressida have sustained lyric passages integrated in such a way that they cannot be called set arias. These passages have a restrained sweetness and are noble in character. Thus perhaps the most moving and eloquent moment in the opera comes in the second-act love scene, with its impassioned orchestral interlude providing an appropriate commentary."

Troilus and Cressida was produced by the New York City Opera three weeks after the American première in San Francisco. The composer was present both in San Francisco and in New York.

1956 CONCERTO FOR CELLO AND ORCHESTRA. I. Moderato. II. Allegro appassionato. III. Lento; Allegro molto; Adagio.

Walton wrote his cello concerto for Gregor Piatigorsky, who introduced it in Boston with the Boston Symphony on January 25, 1957, Charles Munch conducting. The composer described the first movement as "lyrical and melodic." The soloist projects a lengthy lyrical discourse over divided strings and a harp chord. The tempo then quickens and the mood becomes dramatized, but the lyrical element is soon reassertive. About the second movement the composer has said that it is "technically more spectacular," based as it is on a perpetual-motion kind of rhythmic theme in the solo cello. The finale incorporates within itself the slow movement of the concerto, with an expressive melody for the solo instrument over a transparent accompaniment in an opening Lento section. An ascending passage in the solo instrument brings on the full orchestra with a section consisting of a theme and four improvisations. The second and fourth improvisations are for the solo cello alone. The fourth leads to an epilogue based on ideas from the first and third movements. The concerto ends quietly and majestically.

1957 PARTITA, for orchestra. I. Toccata. II. Pastorale Siciliana. III. Giga Burlesca.

This work was commissioned by the Cleveland Orchestra for its fortieth anniversary, and it was introduced in Cleveland on January 30, 1958, George Szell conducting. This is virtuoso music for the orchestra. Dazzling writing for orchestral forces is combined with witty statements in the flanking sections; a welcome contrast provided by the romantic Pastorale in which a beautiful melody for oboe and viola solo is highlighted.

"The eighteenth century forms are invoked but only as a frame of reference," said Howard Taubman. "Sir William's procedures have the tang of our century—the early part of it, one would say. Sir William can be crisp, impressionistic and . . . diverting. The Partita does not go deep and it is not meant to. It is an agreeable occasional piece, made to order for a fine orchestra."

1960 SYMPHONY NO. 2. I. Allegro molto. II. Lento assai. III. Passacaglia.

The Second Symphony followed the First by a quarter of a century. It was the result of a commission from the Royal Liverpool Philharmonic. Walton began his preliminary sketches in 1957; devoted himself to intensive composition in 1959; and completed the work in July of 1960. The world première took place at the Edinburgh Festival on September 2, 1960, with John Pritchard conducting the Liverpool Philharmonic.

The first movement, in sonata form, is monothematic—its single main subject heard at once in woodwind and repeated by first violins. A subsidiary thought is a derivation of this theme, presented by the woodwind. A bassoon solo introduces the development section, which gives complex treatment to the main idea. The movement ends with a return of the opening thought.

The second movement is lyrical and romantic, its melody presented first by solo woodwinds. As the music progresses, it gains in ardor and emotional intensity. The finale is a passacaglia, a short theme in octaves, in full orchestra, being followed by ten variations, a fugato, and a coda.

In reviewing the world première, Peter Heyworth wrote: "The usual hallmarks of his music are here—the syncopated rhythmic mannerisms, the rising and falling sevenths that so often recall Elgar, and that strangely bittersweet orchestral palette. If the years have brought any change of emphasis, it is that Walton has come to accept the basically romantic roots of his idiom with increasing frankness."

1963 VARIATIONS ON A THEME BY HINDEMITH, for orchestra.

Walton wrote this set of orchestral variations for the one hundred and fiftieth anniversary of the Royal Philharmonic Orchestra in London. The première took place on March 8, 1963, the composer conducting.

The Hindemith theme comes out of his Cello Concerto—a nine-measure subject. Hindemith is also represented in the seventh variation with another of his themes, this time from *Mathis der Maler*. This union of Hindemith and Walton is a marriage of true minds. The *Variations* is a skilful work, and an effective one; and surprisingly enough, though it is unmistakably Walton, it sounds a good deal as if Hindemith might have written it himself. "The piece," says Alfred J. Frankenstin, "is wonderfully witty, brilliant and ingenious; and if it has to quote Hindemith directly in order to attain few moments of deep feeling, these moments are wonderfully well managed." The composition ends in a spirited fugato.

ROBERT WARD 1917–

Robert Ward belongs with those traditionalists who have not lost faith in melody, well-sounding harmonies, and the capacity of both to project human emotions. In his operas, he follows the example of the Italians by placing prime importance on the voice, just as in writing his orchestral music, he remains faithful to Romantic traditions that dictate the necessity of speaking from the heart to the heart. What Glenn Dillard Gunn wrote in reviewing Ward's second symphony applies to all of Ward's major works, whatever the medium: "Ward is a modernist who is unafraid of melody. He has a gift for the lyric line which may be heroic in dimensions and content . . . grave and deeply poetic . . . or brisk and gay. This strong melodic expression is supported by an active and resourceful imagination for contrapuntal design, by a great talent for rhythmic variety and a gift to clothe his ideas in colorful orchestral sonorities. The sum of these excellences is greatness."

Ward was born in Cleveland, Ohio, on September 13, 1917. After two years of piano study with Ben Burtt in Cleveland, he received an intensive musical training at the Eastman School of Music, where he acquired a Bachelor of Music degree in 1939, and at the Juilliard School of Music. He also attended the Berkshire Music Center at Tanglewood, where he studied composition with Aaron Copland. During World War II, he was assigned to the Seventh Infantry Division as regimental, then division, band leader. He toured the army installations in the Pacific, for which he and his band were cited for outstanding service, and where he received a Bronze star. While still in uniform, he sketched two orchestral compositions, which became his first pieces of music getting significant performances: *Adagio and Allegro,* introduced in New York in May of 1944, and the overture *Jubilation,* heard in Los Angeles, on November 21, 1946. Following his release from the army, and the completion of his music study, he joined the faculties of the Juilliard School and Columbia University. He served as musical director of the Third Street Music Settlement in New York from 1952 to 1955; as assistant to the President of of the Juilliard School from 1954 to 1956; and since 1956, as vice-president and managing editor of the Galaxy Music Corporation.

His first major success as composer came with his second symphony in 1947. His first opera was *He Who Gets Slapped,* based on Andreyev's play of the same name, introduced under the title of *Pantaloon* in New York on May 17, 1956; it was presented under its now definitive title of *He Who Gets Slapped* by the New York City Opera on April 12, 1959. International recognition arrived with his second opera. *The Crucible,* in 1961. A third opera, *The Lady from Colorado,* was introduced in Central City, Colorado, on July 3, 1964.

Ward has been the chairman of the American Composers Alliance and subsequently chairman of its board of directors. In 1963, Sioux City presented a festival honoring Ward with performances of his major instrumental works, together with lectures on music and other festivities. In 1967, Ward was appointed president of the North Carolina School of Arts at Winston-Salem.

1947 SYMPHONY NO. 2. I. Fast and energetic. II. Slowly. III. Fast.

The symphony with which Ward achieved his first major success as a composer was his second in that form. He began writing it in 1941, but the basic composition was done during the summers of 1946 and 1947. The world première took place in Washington, D.C., on January 25, 1948, Hans Kindler conducting. It made such a good impression that soon afterwards it was repeated at the American music festival at Columbia University in New York; it also became Ward's first composition to get performed by the Philadelphia Orchestra.

"Though the melodies, harmonies and rhythms are definitely of the past few decades and have a strong American flavor," the composer has explained, "the structural principles employed can for the most part be found in music written before Beethoven. The first movement strives to combine the traditional fugue and sonata forms." The subject that receives fugal treatment is a boldly accented jazz tune in the strings. "The slow movement is a freely developed aria in which I depended on variation and increasing lyric tensions rather than contrast to build the form." Here the main melody is heard in muted strings, after which it is developed by woodwinds and horns. An emotional peak is reached, then the mood subsides. "The finale is a rondo with no particular complications. A strong passage, in which the snare drum is prominent, generates power, which, before long, engages the entire orchestra and which reaches towards a stirring climax."

1961 THE CRUCIBLE, opera in three acts, with text by Bernard Stambler based on the play of the same name by Arthur Miller. First performance: New York City Opera, October 26, 1961.

The Crucible is one of the most significant operas by an American—for the nobility, distinction and dramatic interest of Ward's music and also because it boasts an extraordinarily effective libretto derived from a major American play. When Ward saw an off-Broadway production of Arthur Miller's *The Crucible,* he immediately became aware of its possibilities for opera. What impressed him, as he has said, was the "rich orchestration of its language" and the "line of plot, which was projected so strongly that it would come through even when compressed into a singable libretto." Once Ward had brought Miller around to his own way of thinking, the distingushed playwright worked closely with Bernard Stambler, the librettist. The play required only minor changes—some compression, and the deletion of several minor characters—and these were made with Miller's assistance. A taut libretto, strong not only in dramatic interest but also in character delineations and philosophical and psychological implications, was the result.

In setting text to music, Ward placed first importance on the voice rather than the orchestra; in fact, he used only a small orchestral ensemble comprising paired winds, four horns, some strings and percussion. "I admire a work like *Wozzeck* in which the orchestra tells the story," Ward explained, "but for my style the best things happen when the voice becomes the center of the action." Then he explained his method: "I have tried not to impede the action with too many formal musical considerations. Certain moments begin as arias, like the speech of Rev. Hale in the first act, or John Proctor's final speech in the last, but then they melt into the surrounding ensemble, and lose their identity as set pieces."

Though his strong suit is melody—which in an earlier and in a later opera he developed into fully developed arias, duets and ensemble numbers—Ward here suppressed his lyric bent in favor of a powerful declamatory, or parlando, style that set the action into motion and kept it fluid. Thus text and music become one, indivisible—a single texture, an American texture since, by drawing from New England psalmody and hymnology, he helped to create and establish a strong American identity.

The play is compounded of lust, hatred, superstition, revenge, jealousy, bigotry—based on the infamous Salem witch trials of 1692 in New England. A group of hysterical girls create the fiction that they have consorted with the devil in a ritual in the woods, and that the devil has taken the town over. The superstitious and deeply religious Puritans become terror stricken, creating a climate in which hate and cruelty can flourish. The principal characters are John and Elizabeth Proctor. Their maid, Abigail, has carried on an affair with John that is long over. Abigail now seizes the opportunity to get rid of her rival, Elizabeth Proctor, by swearing she is a witch. Elizabeth Proctor is arrested. So is her husband, who can save himself from death if he is willing to admit dalliance with the devil and witchcraft, which he refuses to do. The play consequently places considerable emphasis on the question of freedom of conscience. "All the evil instincts of man—lies, hypocrisy, vindictiveness, greed, brutality, lust for power—rise to the surface when a populace is entangled in the snares of superstition," Arthur Holde has written. "The demagogic insinuations of degenerate, psychopathic men so whirl about as to evoke horror at every point. All the conflits of the story are made believable through the dialogue conceived in the dialect of the uneducated or half-educated inhabitants of Salem at the time. We live with these poor hysterical creatures tormented by their adversaries—creatures who, when confronted by that which has been defined for them as sin, sin that can be expatiated only by confessions exhorted from them, are eager to atone through death."

Irving Kolodin has pointed out that Ward's problem was to evolve a musical speech "equal to conflict that is inward and philosophical rather than outward and physical." Kolodin finds that Ward's resolution "leaves the listener-viewer with some sense of exaltation, a reasonable amount of conviction that the spirit has conquered the body and is a tribute to the skill with which he builds the tale of witchcraft . . . lechery and love to its fated, unhappy outcome. . . . He has a real feeling for the divided but complementary functions of voices and orchestra. The former are used mainly for exposition of the text, mostly in a kind of melodic sing-song with the orchestra a source of commentary and contrast. When appropriate, the vocal line flames into a strain of song not unrelated to the psalmody characteristic of the time and the place. . . . Also worthwhile is the harmonic 'tone' derived from clerical influence on the secular life of the time, though he is not averse to a jostle of tonalities when it suits expressive purpose."

Commissioned by the Ford Foundation, *The Crucible* proved a formidable success when introduced by the New York City Opera. It received the Pulitzer Prize in music and a citation from the New York Music Critics Circle. When the opera was given its première in Germany—in Wiesbaden in 1962—in a performance conducted by the composer, Ward became the first American ever to direct the German première of an American opera.

ANTON WEBERN 1883–1945

The twelve-tone system that Schoenberg and Alban Berg cultivated so passionately was also Anton Webern's method—beginning with the *Three Songs,* op. 17 (1924) and continuing on through the String Trio. op. 20 (1927). Then Webern felt impelled to go beyond his celebrated dodecaphonic colleagues. Where Schoenberg and Berg had confined their system merely to determine pitch, Webern began employing it for tone color, dynamics, rhythm. Thus the twelve-tone system developed into the serial technique, or serialism. This is a creative way of life which has had a cataclysmic impact on twentieth-century music. An entire generation of young composers of the world have embraced serialism—and not merely the young ones, since Stravinsky in his old age abandoned neo-classicism for serial music. To avant-garde composers like Pierre Boulez and Karlheinz Stockhausen, serialism meant the dawn of a new day for music; the careers of both these adventurous musicians began with the writing of serial music. Thus Anton Webern represents a revolution so immense and so far-reaching that Ernst Krenek was once led to maintain that Webern's music is the most complete break with tradition that music history has known in centuries; a break far greater than the one Schoenberg had made. For Schoenberg had poured his new wine into old bottles by employing classic forms, however flexibly. But with Webern all sense of structure seems gone, all consciousness of thematic presentation and development abandoned. Webern's music consists of a seemingly unrelated series of sounds—short, epigrammatic ideas sometimes no more than a few notes in length, one idea following another. There are passages in which each tone is a theme played by a different instrument, while the tones of a chord are distributed to different instruments playing in different registers. There are times when each tone is of a different color (harmonics, pizzicato, col legno, and so on). For what Webern considered of prime significance was the individual tone and the individual timbre. He explained: "Once started, the theme expresses all it has to say. It must be followed by something fresh." Henry Cowell has described this process as "a most frighteningly concentrated interest in the possibilities of each individual tone."

The idea of the expressionist composer to reduce music to barest essentials —to remove all the flesh and leave just the skeleton—was finally realized by Webern. In many places, a Webern theme is reduced to a single tone. At times, each instrument is not permitted to play two consecutive notes, but after sounding a note must wait until the other instruments have been heard from. Brevity had become a fetish. The *Six Pieces for Orchestra* lasts only ten minutes, its shortest movement requiring only fourteen seconds for performance. All of the six *Bagatelles,* for string quartet, extend for only fifty-eight measures, the shortest one being just thirteen measures long. Themes have been reduced to fragments. This process of fragmentation, of atomization, goes hand in hand with understatement. Webern's music is often pitched on the lowest possible level of dynamics. Passage after passage is spoken in a whisper. Individual tones are set off by such an abundance of rests that silence becomes an integral part of a composition.

Hand in hand with this reduction to essentials goes an interest and skill in canonic invention, which becomes fundamental to Webern's serial procedures.

When he died, Webern was rarely performed. Less than a quarter of a century since his death he has become not only "the prophet of a new movement in musical composition," as Ernst Krenek said of him, but also the most widely performed and the most highly revered of all dodecaphonic composers. All his works were recorded by Columbia in 1957. Major festivals of his music have been held in Seattle and in Salzburg, Austria. An International Webern Society was formed in 1962.

Today, Webern is no longer the unsung prophet. Egon Wellesz noted this fact when he wrote in 1966: "He was one of the last musicians of a great tradition—a great Austrian and fully aware of this spiritual inheritance, like Rainer Maria Rilke and like his favorite poet, Georg Trakl. An Austrian, who knew all the obstacles, all the enmities, all the jealousies to which he was exposed by living and working in Austria, he carried on saying *dennoch* ('nevertheless'). He was aware that fame would come only after his death—and so it was. Fame came abundantly when the book of life was closed."

Webern was born in Vienna on December 3, 1883. His family was titled, the reason why for many years Anton Webern prefixed "von" to his last name, a practice he abandoned late in his life. Some music study took place with Erwin Komauer in Klagenfurt during boyhood. At the University of Vienna, which he entered in 1902 as a student of philosophy, he attended classes in musicology taught by Guido Adler. Webern received a doctorate in music from the University in 1906. Between 1904 and 1908, he studied composition privately with Arnold Schoenberg, whose influence was decisive and permanent. Meanwhile composition (some songs) had begun when Webern was fifteen. This was followed by a ballad for voice and orchestra, *Siegfrieds Schwert* (1903) and *Im Sommerwind,* for orchestra (1904). In these, the influence of Wagner and Richard Strauss is pronounced. But association with Schoenberg carried Webern away from his post-Romantic tendencies and influences towards greater objectivity and abstraction, a tendency first to be noted in his *Passacaglia,* for orchestra, in 1908. After that, Webern was drawn more and more to atonality. In 1924, he embraced the twelve-tone technique. And, beginning with his Symphony, in 1928, he progressed to serialism.

For many years, Webern supported himself by conducting theatre orchestras. He married Wilhelmine Mörtl on February 22, 1911. After a brief period of military service during World War I, he went to Prague where he conducted symphony concerts. In June of 1918, he established his home in the Mödling suburb of Vienna. There he helped Schoenberg found and direct the Society for Private Musical Performances, which promoted the works of the Schoenberg school. Between 1922 and 1934, he conducted the Worker's Symphony Concerts in Vienna, and in 1927, he was the musical director of the Austrian Radio. In 1933, he entered the pedagogical field by accepting private pupils in composition.

First performances of his works invariably inspired hostility. Nevertheless, he kept on working, without deviating from the goal he had set for himself, confident that the victory of his music would some day be assured. World War II brought tragedy. First, his son was killed in a bombing raid. Then, seeking refuge from the war in Mittersill, in the Austrian Tyrols, Webern was accidentally shot on the evening of September 15, 1945, by an American soldier come to imprison Webern's son-in-law for black market operations. On the twentieth anniversary of Webern's death, plaques were fixed on the house in Mittersill where he had died and on the church which had served as his morgue.

The painstaking and dedicated Webern scholar, Hans Moldenhauer, came upon two rich finds of Webern manuscripts, whose existence had not been known even to Webern scholars. The first was found in 1961 in the possession of Webern's daughter; and the other, in 1965, in an attic of an old house in Vienna.

1908 PASSACAGLIA, for orchestra, op. 1.

This is Webern's first opus, but, of course, it is not his first composition. Earlier works, dating from the time he was fifteen, are in a post-Romantic style. The Passacaglia is Webern's first to hint at his later development. While looking back over its shoulder to the passacaglia in Brahms's Fourth Symphony (and further back still to Bach's C minor organ Passacaglia), this first opus, nevertheless, is marching into the future. Humphrey Searle points out some of Webern's later mannerisms in this early composition—in the "angular, leaping melody, exquisite subtle effects of scoring (much contrasting of muted and unmuted strings, division and subdivision of strings, *ppp* tremolo passages sul ponticello), the breaking-up of the essential contrapuntal texture into thematic scraps."

The theme on which the variations are based is heard in unison and octave strings muted (Sehr mässig) at the beginning of the composition. Webern's *Passacaglia* departs from convention by being in duple instead of triple time.

The composer himself directed the première performance—in Vienna in the year of the work's composition.

1910 SIX PIECES FOR ORCHESTRA, op. 6. I. Langsam. II. Bewegt. III. Mässig. IV. Sehr mässing. V. Sehr langsam. VI. Langsam.

With the *Five Pieces,* for string quartet, op. 5, and the *Four Pieces,* for violin and piano, op. 7—both written between 1909 and 1910—Webern grows increasingly sparing in the use of his resources, at the same time increasing the tension of his writing. Another significant step forward in this direction came with his *Six Pieces for Orchestra.* All six pieces take only ten minutes for performance. The texture is so refined, and so much attention is given to individual instruments, that the orchestra sounds like a group of solo performers. Also characteristic of the later Webern is the fact that thematic development and repetition are avoided. The structure consists of a succession of melodic fragments. For example: the procession of the ideas in the first piece is as follows—four low notes in solo flute, one note in muted trumpet, two chords on the celesta, three notes in the flute, one note in the French horn, three quiet chords in muted violas and cellos, and so forth.

The first performance took place in Vienna on March 31, 1913, Arnold Schoenberg conducting. The audience started to express its shock through laughter, and ended up with guffaws and shouts of disapproval. It soon became impossible to hear any of the music because of the hubbub in the auditorium.

1913 SIX BAGATELLES, for string quartet, op. 9.

FIVE PIECES FOR ORCHESTRA, op. 10. I. Sehr ruhig und zart. II. Lebhaft und zart bewegt. III. Sehr langsam und äusserst ruhig. IV. Fliessend, äussert ruhig. V. Sehr fliessend.

Webern's compelling need for ever greater concentration, condensation and rarification is met in the *Six Bagatelles* and the *Five Pieces for Orchestra.* This is music stripped down to its bones. Both the *Bagatelles* and the orchestral pieces are the final word in brevity. The entire six *Bagatelles* extend for just fifty-eight measures. The first piece has ten measures; the second and fourth, eight measures; the third and sixth, nine measures; and the fifth, thirteen measures. The five orchestral pieces take about six minutes to perform. The fourth is one of the shortest pieces of music ever created for orchestra, consisting of six and a third measures that take just nineteen seconds to perform. The other movements are, respectively, twelve measures, fourteen measures, eleven and a half measures, and thirty-two measures. In both works, a few unrelated tones express a basic idea. In place of statement, there is only the barest suggestion. As Schoenberg said of the *Bagatelles,* "a whole novel is expressed in a single sigh." Erwin Stein explains further about the *Bagatelles:* "Almost every note of a melody is given to a different instrument, and each one is a different tone color. . . . They are melodies in one breath. . . . The composer says only the barest essentials and his expression determines the form of the piece."

The *Bagatelles* was introduced in Donaueschingen, Germany, in July of 1924.

In the *Five Pieces for Orchestra,* sonority is reduced to a whisper, ranging from pianissimo to almost inaudible sounds. Only a single climax changes the dynamic range. This is found in the concluding measure of the second piece; but even in such a climactic moment, only eight instruments are used. Harmony is virtually non-existent. Nicolas Slonimsky explains that all five pieces are written in "pointillist manner, each instrument playing alone, and very little, so that the changing timbre assumes melodic value."

The world première of the *Five Pieces* took place fifteen years after it had been written—at the festival of the International Society for Contemporary Music at Zurich, on June 23, 1926. Originally, Webern provided programmatic headings for each of the five movements as follows: Primal Urge, or Concept (*Urbild*); Metamorphosis (*Verwandlung*); Return (*Rückehr*); Memory (*Errinerung*); and Soul (*Seele*). These titles were dropped in the published score.

1928 SYMPHONY, for chamber orchestra, op. 21, I. Ruhig schreitend. II. Variationen.

This symphony has been described as one of the most influential works in the twentieth century. The reason for this is that this is Webern's first composition to suggest a serial technique. "In it reside," says Roy G. Klaus in his program annotations for the Cleveland Orchestra, "all the aspects that have been adopted, with talent or without, with originality or imitation, with deftness or awkwardness, with comprehension or misunderstanding—by composers all over the world. . . . Here is that concision, fragmentation, distillation, hyperexpressivity of every note bordering on the obsessive; here is that apparent chaos that on analysis reveals the 'total organization' for which Webern's disciples have striven since."

Discussing this symphony, René Leibowitz has written: "Their bare bones frighten us. A few notes seem to have been scattered at random without any apparent reason. Hearing this music produces a similar impression. The music speech is chopped up by continual rests. There seems to be no melody, no harmony; as for the rhythm, it appears incomprehensible. The instrumental style, too, proves problematic, reduced as it is to the emission of isolated tones, without the slightest concern for sonority as such. The whole produces the effect of a world of chaos ruled in the most arbitrary manner."

The symphony is scored for string quartet, clarinet, bass clarinet, harp and two horns. It has only two movements. The first represents the bare outlines of a double canon. Two subjects are presented piecemeal, each instrument contributing one or two notes before the next instrument takes over for one or two notes more. The second movement is a theme and seven variations.

The symphony received its world première in the United States because it had been commissioned by the League of Composers in New York. That première was conducted by Alexander Smallens in New York on December 18, 1929. The audience expressed its amusement with raucous laughter—so much so that Smallens had to conduct the orchestra with one hand and use the other hand to try to silence the audience. The critical response was savage. Olin Downes suggested that the composition be called "The Ultimate Significance of Nothing." Oscar Thompson wrote: "What the audience heard suggested odd sounds in an old house when the wind moans, the floors creak, the shades rustle, and the doors and windows alternately croak and groan." Samuel Chotzinoff maintained that the symphony offered sounds "uttered at night by the sleeping inhabitants of a zoo."

1940 VARIATIONS FOR ORCHESTRA, op. 30.

This is the next-to-the-last composition completed by Webern. Its première took place at Winterthur, Switzerland, in February of 1943, Hermann Scherchen conducting. The composer attended this performance, the last time he was destined to hear one of his works played in public.

Webern described his music as follows to Willi Reich: "Everything in this piece is derived from the two ideas stated in the first two measures by the double bass and oboe. The second form of the idea is in retrograde: the second two tones are the retrograde movement of the first two, but are doubled in rhythmic length. Then the trombone states the first form of the double bass idea but in half notes. That is how I construct my row, with these three groups of four tones each, in the bass, oboe, trombone."

The composer added the following explanation to the poetess, Hildegard Jone: "There are six tones given in a shape determined through their order of succession and rhythm. . . . This shape now becomes the theme followed by six variations. The theme itself, however, is already nothing but variations, metamorphoses of this first shape. As a unit, it is the point of origin for further variations. But this theme, with its six variations, produces formally a structure. . . . Thus, although I have called the piece *Variations,* they are welded into a new unity. So, many metamorphoses of the first shape produce the theme. This, as a new unit, in turn undergoes as many metamorphoses; these, welded into a new unity, make up the form of the whole."

1940–1943 CANTATA NO. 1, for soprano, chorus and orchestra, op. 29.

CANTATA NO. 2, for soprano, bass, chorus and orchestra, op. 31.

Both cantatas are set to texts by the Austrian poetess, Hildegard Jone; each finds Webern at the height of his technical and expressive powers. Some musicologists regard these two cantatas as the composer's supreme achievements. Arthur Cohn is one of these, seeing in these two cantatas (and especially in the op. 31) that "Webern has transcended method. . . . The articulated expression of the cantatas bears testimony to his creative magic."

Both cantatas emphasize the voice. In the first one, the solo soprano appears in the second part. In the second cantata, three of the six sections are devoted to solo voices, while two other movements feature a solo soprano with a women's chorus, and a mixed chorus, respectively. The sixth part is for chorus and orchestra. "Notwithstanding the decisive serialism and the first objectivity of the music," says Cohn, "there is an eloquence far beyond the feeling that one is simply being led by the technical hand."

Both cantatas were introduced posthumously. The first was heard at the festival of the International Society for Contemporary Music in London on July 12, 1946; the second, at the festival of the same society, in Brussels, on June 23, 1950.

KURT WEILL 1900–1950

In the era between the two world wars, there arose in Germany an aesthetic cult in which Kurt Weill proved a major force and a vital spokesman. That cult was named "*Zeitkunst,*" or "Contemporary Art." It glorified an art form that was vibrantly contemporary in style and theme, speaking for and interpreting twentieth-century experiences in a light, breezey, and often popular style.

Weill began his career as composer with a symphony (1921), a violin concerto (1924) and various other compositions in advanced styles and techniques slanted towards a limited, highly sophisticated audience. But he soon became dissatisfied with his artistic isolation, and felt a compelling need to address masses with an easily comprehensible art. He said at the time: "I want to reach the real people, a more representative public than any opera house attracts." He wanted to write "for today" and not "for posterity."

And so, he evolved a new art form which he called a "song play." This was neither musical comedy nor opera, but a mixture of both. This was *Zeitkunst.* The librettos were usually as timely as the front page of a newspaper. And the musical style was also a legitimate offspring of the times, borrowing what it needed from jazz, music-hall ballads, dance tunes and other popular sources. At the same time, it drew just as deeply from the reservoir of classical and Romantic music.

Weill's first song play was *Der Protagonist,* text by Georg Kaiser, first performance in Dresden on March 27, 1926. During the next seven years, Weill wrote music for other song plays which opened new horizons for the German musical theatre. The most celebrated of these was, of course, *Die Dreigroschenoper* (*The Three-Penny Opera*), a sensation when first produced in Berlin on August 31, 1928, and became a stage classic. The text by Bertolt Brecht was based on John Gay's *The Beggar's Opera. The Three-Penny Opera* was a bitter, satirical commentary on social and political corruption in Germany; and Weill's music was a brilliant marriage of popular and serious elements. Arias, canons, operatic-type choruses, rubbed elbows with a shimmy, a fox-trot and popular tunes. In five years' time, *The Three-Penny Opera* received over ten thousand performances throughout Europe, translated into eighteen languages. And when it was revived in the United States in 1954 (text revised and modernized by Marc Blitzstein), it had a six-year run in New York, and was performed throughout the United States by two national companies. It was made into motion pictures several times.

Just as brilliant in its social and political criticism, and just as invigorating and captivating in its musical style, was *Aufstieg und Fall der Stadt Mahagonny,* or *The Rise and Fall of the City Mahagonny*—text once again by Brecht. It was introduced simultaneously in Leipzig and Frankfort on March 9, 1930. Since these and other Weill song plays belong more to the popular musical theatre than to the serious, their discussion does not come within the scope of this volume.

Weill also revealed his gift for creating *Gebrauchsmusik,* the term Hindemith had devised for "functional music." In 1930, Weill wrote an opera called *Der Jasager,* based on a Japanese *No* play, one of the first German operas written directly for schools.

Thus it can be seen that, as one of the foremost composers for the Broadway theatre after 1935, and as the composer of the educational one-act folk opera, *Down in the Valley,* Weill had not entered upon any new creative phase but was continuing an old one. With his delightfully lyrical scores for a long chain of Broadway stage successes, he proved himself to be one of the most resourceful composers for the popular theatre; but that talent had already been strongly in evidence in his German operas. And what he had done in Germany with *Der Jasager* he repeated in this country with *Down In the Valley:* writing functional music for schools, music which had such freshness and originality that its interest transcended the school auditorium and successfully penetrated the opera house.

Weill was born in Dessau, Germany on March 2, 1900. His musical education took place at the Berlin High School for Music, principally with Humperdinck. He later was a private pupil in composition of Busoni. Weill's early works for string quartet and for orchestra revealed a solid technique. But not until he turned to the writing of music for the theatre in 1927, and emerged as an apostle of *Zeitkunst,* did his creative gift unfold fully. In 1926, he married Lotte Lenya, who, two years later, starred in the song play which made Weill an international figure in music, *The Three-Penny Opera.*

When Hitler came to power, Weill and his wife fled from Germany.

For two years, they lived in Paris. Weill came to the United States in 1935, and in 1943, he became an American citizen. His first score for the Broadway stage was *Johnny Johnson,* an anti-war satire by Paul Green, which opened on November 19, 1936. Weill's long string of successes for the Broadway theatre included *Knickerbocker Holiday* (1938), *Lady in the Dark* (1941), and *One Touch of Venus* (1943), all three musical comedies; also, the musical plays, *Street Scene* (1947) and *Lost in the Stars* (1949), which were subsequently produced in the opera house.

Kurt Weill died in New York City on April 3, 1950.

1924 CONCERTO FOR VIOLIN AND ORCHESTRA, op. 12. I. Andante con moto; Un poco più andante; Tranquillo ma sempre andante. II. Notturno; Cadenza; Serenata. III. Allegro molto un poco agitato.

Weill's career as composer began with the writing of a number of works in which (as a favorite pupil of Busoni) he brought modern, and at times iconoclastic, attitudes to sound classical orchestras. The concerto was introduced at the Zurich Festival on June 23, 1926. For almost thirty years after that, it lay forgotten. Then, in March of 1955, it was revived by Anahid Ajemian in Indianapolis, Izler Solomon conducting.

A drum roll precedes a nocturnal episode in the wind instruments, an episode in which the solo instrument soon becomes involved. This romantic mood is destroyed by a dramatic section. After a climax, the violin embarks upon the brilliant second subject, but before long the conflict and drama return. Calm is restored before the movement ends.

A drum roll serves to open the second movement (Allegro un poco tenuto; Un poco tranquillo) which has three sections. In the first, the xylophone is heard in a capricious idea, followed by a dance tune in the violin. The middle part (Tranquillo; Vivace) is a cadenza for the violin, interrupted from time to time by trumpet fanfares. The final part is a melodious Serenata.

In the finale, a single subject is dominant. It is heard in violin and orchestra and has two contrasting parts, the first lyrical and the other, dramatic.

1929 DIE DREIGROSCHENOPER (THE THREE-PENNY OPERA), suite for orchestra. I. Overture. II. Die Moritat von Mackie Messer. III. Annstat—Das Lied. IV. Die Ballade vom angenehmen Leben. V. Pollys Lied. VI. Tango—Ballade. VII. Kanonen-Song. VIII. Dreigroschen Finale.

Weill's world-famous song play, *The Three-Penny Opera,* was produced in Berlin in 1928. In 1929, Weill adapted some of the principal sections from his score into a suite, which was introduced by the Berlin Philharmonic. After that, some of these movements, in Weill's basic orchestration, were heard in European night clubs and even used as dance music.

The music of the suite (just as the music of the entire song play) is a mixture of many styles: a fox-trot, a tango, the blues, mock chorales, music-hall tunes, ballads, jazz, ragtime. The most celebrated movement of the suite—even as it is the most famous song in the entire stage score—is "Moritat," more familiarly known in the United States as "Mack the Knife." A "moritat" ("*mord*" meaning "murder" and "*tat*" meaning "deed") was a popular tune sung by performers at street fairs describing the crimes of fiends. When *The*

Three-Penny Opera was in rehearsal for its world première, the actor portraying Macheath, the highwayman, insisted he needed an entrance song. Brecht, the librettist, produced some verses for such a number in which Macheath's history as a highwayman is described; and Weill created for these words a monotonous tune, accompanied by hand organ, which took Berlin by storm. This tune also became a hit song of major proportions in the United States, after *The Three-Penny Opera* was revived in the United States, off-Broadway, in 1954. In 1955, twenty different recordings of this number were issued, and the song appeared several times in the Number One position on television's Hit Parade. In a few years' time, it had been recorded in forty-eight versions, and had sold well over ten million discs. Bobby Darin's recording in 1959 sold over a million discs and was responsible for lifting an unknown singer to stardom.

1947 DOWN IN THE VALLEY, American folk opera in one act, with text by Arnold Sundgaard. First performance: Bloomington, Indiana, July 15, 1948.

In 1947, the dean of the School of Music of Indiana University turned to Weill for a student opera. At that time, Weill had in his drawer the score of a fifteen-minute radio opera, inspired by the American folk song *Down in the Valley,* the libretto of which had been prepared by Arnold Sundgaard; the opus had been turned down by prospective sponsors as too highbrow for public consumption. Weill decided to adapt and enlarge the radio piece into a musico-dramatic composition. Together with his librettist, he extended it into a forty-five-minute one-act opera and interpolated a great deal of new music.

This revised work was heard for the first time at Indiana University in 1948, Ernst Hoffman conducting. It proved to be so successful that one month later it was repeated at Ann Arbor by the University of Michigan, at which time it was broadcast over the NBC network. After that—and within a comparatively short period of time—the opera was presented by hundreds of organizations throughout the country, amateur and professional. It was featured at summer camps and festivals. It was televised and recorded. It was even incorporated into the repertories of several European opera houses.

It is not difficult to explain its immediate popularity. It is a charming opera, unpretentious in its simplicity and directness, at turns engagingly lyrical and dramatic. And it is as indigenous to the American scene as the folk song that inspired it. It calls for the most elementary forces: a small orchestra, or, failing that, two pianos; limited stagecraft and scenery; a small cast, on whom the vocal demands are not too exacting.

The tale is equally simple, succinctly summarized by the "Leader" in the following words sung at the opening of the work: "I'll sing of Brack Weaver, who died on the gallows one morning in May, he died for the love of sweet Jennie Parsons, he died for the slaying of Thomas Bouche." The story is then told in a series of flashbacks. Sentenced to death for the murder of Bouche, Brack Weaver feels he cannot face the gallows without seeing his beloved Jenny once more. He makes a break, and finds his loved one sitting on her porch. With her he recalls how they met and fell in love; how the villain, Bouche, tried to force his attentions on Jenny; how, at a square dance, he killed Bouche in a brawl. Convinced that Jenny still loves him, Brack can face his doom. He gives himself up to the posse that has come to hunt him.

The opera is filled with lovely songs for the principal characters and many dramatic passages for the chorus, which plays a prominent role both as commentator on the drama and as an actual participant in it. Five Kentucky mountain folk songs are interpolated in the score:

"Down in the Valley," "The Lonesome Dove," "The Little Black Train," "Hop Up, My Ladies," and "Sourwood Mountain."

JAROMIR WEINBERGER 1896–1967

The influences of three different countries shaped the style of Weinberger's music at different periods: France, Czechoslovakia and the United States. His apprentice works were written in the impressionist style of Debussy. Recognizing that in these early pieces he was imitative rather than creative, he destroyed most of them and set off in another direction. It was then that he subjected himself to the aesthetic aims of Smetana and Dvořák in the writing of Czech music with pronounced national traits. Soon after coming to the United States and becoming a permanent resident and citizen, he abandoned the Czech idiom for music inspired by the culture and backgrounds of his new land: he wrote compositions inspired by Whitman, Lincoln and Washington Irving, and even adapted the song "Dixie" into an orchestral prelude and fugue. In the early 1950s, he deserted all forms of nationalism for a more universal language.

His style may have changed at different periods in his life, but his basic creative approach never did. The shaping of new idioms and techniques he left to others. He was always the Romanticist who went in for well-shaped melodies and rich-sounding harmonies within sound classical forms. A superb craftsman and an elegant orchestrator, his music is the cultured speech of an artist who is not afraid to search the deepest recesses of his heart to express what he finds there.

Weinberger was born in Prague on January 8, 1896. He attended the Prague Conservatory, and in 1915, studied composition privately with Max Reger in Leipzig. In 1922, he came to the United States to serve as professor of composition at the Ithaca Conservatory in New York State. Upon returning to Europe in 1926, he held minor jobs in music at Bratislava and Eger. He first achieved international prominence with music steeped in Bohemian nationalism; and the first such work, and his most famous opera, is *Schwanda, the Bagpipe Player,* introduced in 1927, then circling the globe. After 1939, Weinberger made his home in the United States, where he became a citizen and maintained a permanent residence in Florida. In 1955, his *Préludes réligieuses et profanes* was successfully introduced in Rotterdam, and *Five Songs from Des Knaben Wunderhorn* was heard at the Vienna Music Weeks Festival in 1962. Weinberger died in St. Petersburg, Florida on August 8, 1967.

1927 SCHWANDA DER DUDELSACKPFEIFER (SCHWANDA, THE BAGPIPE PLAYER), opera in two acts, with text by Miloš Kareš adapted from a play by Josef Tyl. First performance: Prague, April 27, 1927.

Like its distinguished predecessor, Smetana's *Bartered Bride, Schwanda* went to Bohemian legend and folk song for text and music. The text, by Miloš Kareš, gracefully mingles fantasy with realism. The bandit Babinsky is hiding at Schwanda's farm, where he meets and falls in love with Schwanda's wife, Dorota. Schwanda, he feels, must be erased from the picture so that he, Babinsky, may have Dorota for himself. He tells Schwanda fabulous tales about the court of Queen Ice-Heart, where one can become rich and powerful; and Schwanda decides to go there with Babinsky. At the court, Schwanda plays his bagpipe, and with such eloquence that he wins the heart of the Queen, who desires to marry him. Dorota appears and frustrates the marriage—a fact which so infuriates the Queen that she orders Schwanda's death. Babinsky, however, saves Schwanda, who continues to delight the court with his wonderful music. But Dorota nags Schwanda about his affair with the Queen, while the bagpipe player protests his innocence. May he be consigned to the depths of Hell if the Queen ever even kissed him! Hardly have these words been spoken when the earth swallows Schwanda. But Dorota remains true to him, even though he has departed for other worlds. Babinsky recognizes that Dorota, after all, is not for him, and restores Schwanda to her—by winning him in a game of cards with the devil.

There can be no question that there are derivative echoes in the score Weinberger wrote for this merry tale. There are more than mere suggestions of Smetana and Rimsky-Korsakov in the music: on occasion there are even outright quotations. It is also true that the recitatives are often long and dull; that the harmonic writing is not always original. But in spite of these flaws, the music is a delightful experience—gay, infectious, tuneful. The melodies assume the character of Bohemian folk songs; the best of them—such as the recurring song of home sung by Dorota—have a distinctly personal flavor. The orchestral pages, such as the overture, the intermezzi, the rousing polka with which Schwanda sets the court a-dancing, and the fugue, are brilliantly scored and ingenious in their rhythmic and contrapuntal writing.

Strange to say, when this opera was heard for the first time it was not particularly successful. But the first German performance, which took place in Breslau on December 16, 1928 (in a translation into German by Max Brod), was a triumph. To the German audiences, *Schwanda* appeared as a delightful escape from the intellectualism with which so many German operas of the time were concerned; and they responded to it enthusiastically. That success set off the magnificent career of *Schwanda* in the opera houses of the world: within a four-year period, it was heard more than two thousand times in

Central Europe. It was introduced at the Metropolitan Opera in New York on November 7, 1931, when Pitts Sanborn found the score to have "verve, impetuosity and an engaging tunefulness."

The deservedly famous and popular "Polka" and "Fugue" from *Schwanda* are frequently heard at orchestral concerts. The Polka has a rousing peasant vigor and healthy good spirits which make it everlastingly appealing. Within the classic structure of the "Fugue," the folk elements of the music are magically retained; at the climax, the melody of the "Polka" is effectively joined with the principal theme of the "Fugue."

1929 CHRISTMAS OVERTURE, for orchestra and organ.

This is one of Weinberger's most successful works for orchestra in the Czech idiom. It is a delightful potpourri of Czech Christmas songs inspired by old Czech folk tales. Up to the time of World War II it was heard everywhere in Europe; it was a tradition in Czechoslovakia to play this work over the radio each Christmas eve.

It utilized three Christmas songs of the festival of Epiphany (Koledy) and fuses them with what the composer describes as "old organ mixtures."

1939 UNDER THE SPREADING CHESTNUT TREE, variations and fugue on an old English tune, for orchestra.

In the summer of 1938, Weinberger attended a cinema theatre in Juan les Pins, on the French Riviera, where he saw a newsreel of the King of England and a group of young people in a boy's camp, singing a popular song called *Under the Spreading Chestnut Tree*. The tune made a deep impression on the composer, who decided to write a major orchestral work based on it. It was not written, however, until early in 1939, after the composer had come to this country.

The published score carries a detailed analysis of the work by the composer himself. The melody is heard at the opening. After it has been stated, the piano creates a transition from the theme to the first variation (throughout the work the piano serves as a catalytic agent between the different parts of the work). Called "Her Majesty's Virginal," the first variation is a canon. In the second variation, "The Madrigalists," the composer pays tribute to the early English composers, while the third is entitled "The Dark Lady," after the heroine of the Shakespeare sonnets. The tune acquires a Scottish character in the fourth variation, "The Highlanders," as the orchestra simulates the quality of bagpipe music. In the "Pastorale" variation that follows, the composer attempts a description of the English countryside. The twenty-third chapter of Dickens' *Pickwick Papers* was the stimulation for the sixth variation, entitled "Mr. Weller, Senior, Discusses Widows With His Son, Samuel Weller, Esq." The concluding variation is a "Sarabande," for the Princess Elizabeth, Electress Palatine and Queen of Bohemia in the early seventeenth century, the unhappy daughter of James I, and the unhappy ruler of an unhappy country. A fugue, the theme of which has eight bars, brings the orchestral work to a culmination.

The first performance took place in New York on October 12, 1939, John Barbirolli conducting the New York Philharmonic.

1940 THE LEGEND OF SLEEPY HOLLOW, suite for orchestra. I. Sleepy Hollow. II. Katrina's Waltz. III. The Headless Horseman and Ichabod Crane. IV. Dutch Polka.

In 1939, Weinberger was commissioned by Nathaniel Shilkret to write this work, inspired by Washington Irving's famous story. On November 21, 1940, it was introduced in Detroit by the Detroit Symphony Orchestra, Victor Kolar conducting.

Quotations from Irving's *The Legend of Sleepy Hollow* preface each of the four movements in the published score and provide the programmatic clue to the music:

I. "Not far from the village of Tarrytown there is a little valley, or rather a lap of land, among high hills, which is one of the quietest places in the world. A small brook glides through it with just murmur enough to lull one to repose. . . ."

II. "Old Baltus van Tassel moved about among his guests with a face dilated with content and good humor, round and jolly as the harvest moon. . . . Ichabod prided himself upon his dancing . . . the lady of his heart was his partner."

III. "It was the very witching time of the night that Ichabod . . . pursued his travel homewards along the sides of the hills. The night grew darker and darker. . . . He was approaching the place where many of the scenes of his ghost stories had been laid."

IV. "Brom Bones, shortly after his rival's disappearance, conducts the blooming Katrina in triumph to the altar."

ERMANNO WOLF-FERRARI 1876–1948

Though one of his most successful operas, *The Jewels of the Madonna,* is tragic, the name of Wolf-Ferrari is almost always associated with the field of comic opera (opera buffa). He may often succumb to a conventional lyricism or stilted structures. But Wolf-Ferrari also possesses those qualities which make for successful opera buffa: spontaneity, freshness and a talent for pointing up comic situations with a few swift strokes of the pen. *Le Donne curiose* (1903) and his masterpiece, *The Secret of Suzanne* (1909), rank with the finest creations of twentieth-century opera buffa, and give their composer a deserving place with those great men, from Pergolesi through Rossini and Donizetti, who originated and developed the form.

Wolf-Ferrari was born in Venice on January 12, 1876, the son of a German father and Italian mother. At first, it was his intention to follow in the footsteps of his father by becoming a painter. But in his adolescence, he decided to specialize in music, going to Munich in 1893 to study for two years with Rheinberger. During this period, he heard a performance of Wagner's *Siegfried* which affected him so strongly that he became ill. In later years, adulation for Wagner's music dramas was displaced by outright revulsion; his own operatic writing was an attempt to negate everything for which Wagner stood.

After returning to Venice, he achieved his first significant performances with the oratorio *La Sulamite* performed in Venice in 1899. His first opera, *Cenerentola,* while none too successful when introduced in Venice on February 22, 1900, was exceptionally well received in Germany two years later. With *Le Donne curiose* in 1903, and *I Quattro rusteghi* in 1906, Wolf-Ferrari hit his stride as a composer of opera buffa.

For several years, he was director of the Liceo Benedetto Marcello in Venice. In 1912, he visited the United States to supervise the American première of *The Jewels of the Madonna* in Chicago. *L'Amore medico,* based on Molière—first performance in Dresden on December 4, 1913—was his last opera for a dozen years. Beginning with 1925, Wolf-Ferrari completed seven more operas, but none of these were successful, and none have survived.

Wolf-Ferrari died in Venice on January 12, 1948.

1901 CHAMBER SYMPHONY (KAMMERSYMPHONIE), for chamber orchestra, op. 8. I. Allegro moderato. II. Adagio. III. Vivace con spirito. IV. Adagio; Con fuoco.

Though Wolf-Ferrari's reputation rests almost exclusively on his works for the stage, he did produce a few creditable instrumental works, one of the best of which is a *Chamber Symphony*. Though his long, fully realized melodic lines remind us that he is essentially a composer for the voice, Wolf-Ferrari did possess a fine feeling for instrumental writing, a sound structural craftsmanship, and a highly developed harmonic sense.

The work opens with an introduction for the piano, following which the main theme is introduced by the clarinet; this and the secondary theme are broadly melodic. A bassoon solo, in an emotional theme, dominates the slow movement, which midway passes from a sentimental to a capricious mood. A majestic slow section opens the finale, yielding to a vigorous section; the moods alternate from the lyrical to the dramatic and back to the lyrical as contrapuntal writing and percussive effects are generously exploited.

1903 LE DONNE CURIOSE (THE INQUISITIVE WOMEN), opera buffa in three acts, with text by Luigi Sugana based on a comedy by Goldoni. First performance: Munich, November 27, 1903 (in a German translation by Hermann Teibler entitled *Die neugierigen Frauen*).

Le Donne curiose was Wolf-Ferrari's first opera buffa. Already he reveals here a unique gift in using an inconsequential play, filled with all varieties of trivia, as the pivot on which to spin a light and tuneful score to enchant ear and heart, music full of innocent merriment.

In eighteenth-century Venice, three women are certain their husbands are indulging in orgies at their men's club. They manage to gain admission, and from a hiding place see that all the men are doing at the club is to indulge in a hearty meal.

Spare material, indeed, to sustain three acts! It is no surprise, then, that this play fails to hold the interest of the spectator. The compensating feature, however, is the composer's genuine gift for reaching comic effect in his music, but for which the play's humor would fall flat on its face. The score maintains freshness, spontaneity, lyricism and wit—and it is for the score that this comic opera deserves revival.

The duet for soprano and tenor, "*Il cor nel contento,*" and the soprano aria, "*Tutto per te,*" are among the outstanding vocal excerpts; the main orchestral sections include the vivacious overture, and the Minuet and Forlana.

The American première took place at the Metropolitan Opera in New York on January 3, 1912. Richard Aldrich, writing in *The New York Times,* called Wolf-Ferrari a "master of moods in musical representation, and sentiment expressed with direction and without sentimentality."

1906 I QUATTRI RUSTEGHI (THE FOUR RUFFIANS), opera buffa in four acts, with text by Giuseppe Pizzolato based on a comedy by Goldoni. First performance: Munich, March 19, 1906 (in a German translation under the title, *Die vier Grobiane*).

Having demonstrated his talent at opera buffa with *Le Donne curiose,* Wolf-Ferrari lost no time in proving once again that comedy was his strong suit. *I Quattro rusteghi* came immediately after *Le Donne curiose.* Once again, what we have here is the slender thread of a slight, inconsequential plot. Lunardo refuses to allow his daughter and her fiancé to meet each other before the wedding ceremony. The fiancé, with the help of several other ruffians, thwarts Lunardo in typical opera-buffa manner: by putting on female clothes and feigning to be a woman.

In his music, Wolf-Ferrari not only betrayed his indebtedness to his distinguished predecessors in the art of writing comedy (notably Mozart, Donizetti and Verdi) but he even went to the lengths of interpolating into his score brief quotations from two of these masters. But the two most famous parts of the opera are Wolf-Ferrari through and through—the melodious orchestral intermezzo in Act II, and Filipeto's stirring romance, "*Luceta e un bel nome.*"

This comic opera had to wait almost half a century before getting heard in the United States. This première took place in New York on October 18, 1951. At that time, Cecil Smith found that "the chief felicities . . . were those of transparent texture and brightness of mood. . . . Wolf-Ferrari achieves an instrumental texture that is pellucid, yet warm and friendly. But although there are occasional sly comments from the instruments, as when the solo bassoon laughs at one of the garrulous ruffians, his orchestra characteristically plays more of a supporting role than the *Falstaff* orchestra, leaving most of the overt fun-making to the singers. . . . All the vocal parts lie beautifully for singers . . . but the musical ideas, while prevailingly melodic, are not always inventive. . . . The ensembles, however, are another matter—and fortunately they constitute the lion's share of the score. Wolf-Ferrari could write for three or four basses alone (the ruffians are all basses) without losing the thread of individual characterization in each part."

1909 IL SEGRETO DI SUSANNA (THE SECRET OF SUZANNE), opera buffa in one act, with text by Enrico Golisciani. First performance: Munich, December 4, 1909 (in a German translation by Max Kalbeck entitled *Sussanens Geheimnis*).

The changing mores of society have reduced to absurdity the one-act libretto of *The Secret of Suzanne*. A jealous Count detects the smell of tobacco in his house, and forthwith suspects his wife of having a lover. Suzanne soothes her irate husband and sends him off to the club. But still unconvinced, the Count hides outside the window of his house to spy on his wife. What he discovers is that she does not harbor a secret lover, but rather a secret passion—for smoking. Delighted that his wife is faithful to him, he comes inside to join her in a smoke.

But so vivacious and infectious is the music for this rather silly story that the "intermezzo" (as Wolf-Ferrari aptly called it) remains a jewel in the literature of comic opera. Unpretentious in its artistic aims, it remains from beginning to end a delightful excursion into lighter moods. The effervescent overture and its best arias (Suzanne's delightful air in praise of smoking, "*O, Gioio la nube leggera,*" and her aria, "*Via, così non mi lasciate*") are truly in the best traditions of opera buffa—fresh, witty, vital, effervescent music, which requires no familiarity or analysis to be fully appreciated, and which never seems to lose its appeal.

1911 I GIOIELLI DELLA MADONNA (THE JEWELS OF THE MADONNA), opera in three acts, with text by Enrico Golisciani and Carlo Zangarini. First performance: Berlin, December 23, 1911 (in a German translation by Hans Liebstöckl, entitled *Der Schmuck der Madonna*).

The Jewels of the Madonna is Wolf-Ferrari's only successful opera in a serious vein. While it lacks the spontaneity and charm of his lighter works, it does generate considerable dramatic power. It is excellent theatre, even when the music on occasion appears commonplace in inspiration. A product of the *Verismo* school of operatic writing, it employs realistic effects (even in the orchestration), and frequently with fine dramatic effect.

In present-day Naples, Gennaro, a worker, and Rafaele, leader of the Camorra, are rivals for the love of Maliella. When Gennaro overhears Rafaele boast that he will steal the jewels of the Madonna for Maliella—jewels on the statue of the Madonna which is carried throughout Naples in a religious ceremony—he decides to beat his rival to the game, even though the punishment for this crime is death. Eventually, when Maliella recognizes that she is an outcast because she is the possessor of the stolen jewels, she commits suicide by jumping into the sea. Gennaro, too, realizes the immensity of his crime: he atones for it by killing himself with a knife.

The most celebrated vocal excerpt in the opera is Rafaele's beautiful second-act serenade, "*Aprila, bella,*" with which he convinces his beloved to run off with him. Two of Gennaro's arias in the first act are also of interest: "*Madonna, con sospiri*" and "*Madonna dei dolori.*"

But some of the orchestral episodes have proved even more popular than the vocal ones, and are frequently heard at orchestral concerts of the semi-classical or "pop" variety. These include the Intermezzo between the first and second acts (which was written *after* the opera had been completed, and almost as an afterthought). This is music in a consistently languorous mood. A second intermezzo occurs between the second and third acts. This opens with a light, infectious tune followed by a broadly lyrical section. A third popular orchestral excerpt is the dynamic *Dance of the Camorristi* which opens the third act, a tarantella danced during a revel in the Camorristi hideout.

At the American première of the opera—on January 12, 1912, by the Chicago Opera in Chicago—it was presented for the first time anywhere in the English language. The composer paid his first visit to the United States to help supervise this production. On March 5, of the same year, the Chicago Opera introduced it to New York at the Metropolitan Opera House. The first production by the Metropolitan Opera company took place on December 12, 1925.

EUGENE ZADOR 1894–

Some of Zador's most frequently heard works for orchestra have the same national origin as their composer. Beginning with his *Variations on a Hungarian Folksong* (1926)—introduced in Vienna on February 9, 1927—Zador has frequently modeled his melodies and rhythms on Hungarian gypsy folk tunes and dances. But he neither borrows, nor paraphrases, nor adapts. His material is always his own.

Music with a Hungarian personality represents only one facet of his creativity. Another vein he has tapped richly is that of wit and bright-faced gaiety. A third is his programmatic music, where he reveals a pronounced gift for adapting his exceptional technique and creative resources to the pictorial or atmospheric demands of his subject.

He is, for the most part, a traditionalist, still faithful to the concept that music must sound well to the ear and find its response in the heart.

Zador was born in Bátaszék, Hungary, on November 5, 1894. He received his musical training at the Vienna Conservatory, mainly with Heuberger, and with Max Reger in Leipzig. Specializing in musicology with Hermann Abert and Arnold Schering in Leipzig, and after that with Fritz Volbach in Münster, Zador received his doctorate in music from the University of Münster in 1921. During this period, he served for five years as music critic for a Hungarian journal, and completed writing his first mature work, *Bánk Bán,* a tone poem for orchestra heard in Budapest in 1918. In 1921, he came to Vienna where he became professor of music at the Conservatory. There he completed his first symphony (1922), and his first opera, *Diana;* the latter was produced by the Budapest Royal Opera on December 22, 1923. Success came with the *Variations on a Hungarian Folksong* in 1927. In 1934, his Piano Quintet won the Hungarian National State Prize. A year later, he received an honorary title of "Professor" from the Royal Academy of Music in Budapest, and an honorary doctorate from the New York College of Music. He came to the United States in 1939. In 1940, he established residence in Hollywood, California, where he became an American citizen and where for almost a quarter of a century he orchestrated music for motion pictures; three of these scores were awarded "Oscars": *Spellbound, A Double Life,* and *Ben-Hur.*

1934 RONDO, for orchestra.

HUNGARIAN CAPRICE, for orchestra.

Following its première in Vienna in 1934 by the Vienna Symphony under Kurt Pahlen, the *Rondo* was widely performed throughout Europe and helped solidify its composer's reputation. A main theme is alternated with two contrasting subjects, with the main theme, amplified, returning in the concluding coda. This main theme (Allegro) is heard in the horn, with the first contrasting subject appearing in the woodwinds (Allegretto). A second contrasting subject is a quiet episode for the woodwinds, which the strings repeat. The composition ends with a powerful three-part canon built on the opening theme.

The *Hungarian Caprice* was introduced by the Budapest Philharmonic under Carl Schuricht on February 1, 1935. The opening subject, played by the strings, is an Allegro. It is followed by a slower theme in horns, then in violas and cellos. The middle part is a three-voice canon derived from the first and second themes. Following several repetitions of earlier material, the work ends with a tumultuous Vivace, exploiting the horn theme.

1940 CHILDREN'S SYMPHONY. I. Allegro moderato. II. Fairy Tale. III. Scherzo militaire. IV. The Farm.

The first version of Zador's popular *Children's Symphony* came in 1940. It had only a single performance, in New Orleans in 1940. Almost two decades later, Zador revised the work extensively. The new and final version was heard in Beverly Hills, California, on October 17, 1960, Herbert Weiskopf conducting. Since then, the work has had over one hundred performances in America, Europe and the Near East, directed by some of the world's foremost conductors.

The composer's description follows:

"The first movement is a regular symphonic opening in the form of a sonata, with a main theme and a side theme, a reprise and development of two themes. These themes have a playful charm, like a rondel, and the whole movement has a childlike gaiety.

"In *Fairy Tale,* it is easy to imagine that somebody's grandmother is telling a story—a pleasant story which becomes increasingly dramatic. Could it be that a witch appears and tries to kill the children? But then in the nick of time, the hero arrives and slays the witch, bringing happiness to all.

"*Scherzo militaire* tells of soldiers marching with trumpets and drums. Rank after rank of soldiers march forward till at last comes the great General. He gives sharp orders and the whole army comes to a sudden halt.

"*The Farm* begins with a sleeping farm at night. The sun rises and the farm awakes to the barking of a dog, the mooing of a cow, the crowing of a rooster and the cackling of geese, till the whole farm is alive and Nature shows her multi-hued and lively face. Playing children shout in the meadow and the echo repeats their shouts. Everything is gay and cheerful, rising to a climax of a happy song. As the sun sets and night falls, the animals return from the pastures. Again the mooing, barking, cackling. Then the chimes of the nearby church ring, calling all children to prayer and sleep. The work concludes with a few cheerful bars from the first movement."

1943 BIBLICAL SCENES, triptych for orchestra. I. Joseph. II. David. III. Paul.

This symphonic triptych was inspired by Thomas Mann's trilogy of novels collectively entitled *Joseph and his Brothers*. The composer originally intended only a tone poem based on the Biblical figure of Joseph. But as he worked, the musical material in his hands grew to monumental proportions. Upon completing the Joseph section, Zador decided to continue the work by adding portraits of David and the Apostle Paul. He says: "The music does not follow the events in detail; it rather endeavors to depict them in large contours and symbolic moods. The beginning of the first movement (Andantino) portrays Joseph as the symbol of Innocence. It develops with a brisk section which brings to our mind the crisis of Joseph's life, his imprisonment, and so forth, and terminates with the dream scene of its fulfillment.

"David's symbol is the harp. Therefore, it dominates the beginning of the second movement to give way later to the pastoral melodies of the oboe—the oboe characterizing David as a simple shepherd's boy. The next part of the movement is a musical phrasing of David's fight with Goliath and the victory of David over the giant. The people are ecstatic with joy and hail David their King.

"The 'Paul' movement (Moderato) is divided into two parts. In the first, Paul is characterized as the hard, austere persecutor of Christ. The second part gives us Paul's spiritual transformation and the triumph of Christ's teachings."

The world première took place on December 10, 1943, in Chicago, in a performance by the Chicago Symphony. After Dr. Mann had heard the work, he wrote to the composer: "You have succeeded admirably in doing with musical tones that which I attempted to do with words, namely to unite primitive, oriental sound with modern sensibility and understanding. It is real satisfaction to me to know that my story has inspired a master in the art which has ever been very dear to me, to create a work of such beauty and so full of the promise of permanency."

1958 ELEGIE, for orchestra.

FUGUE FANTASIA, for orchestra.

The *Elegie* was given its world première by the Philadelphia Orchestra under Eugene Ormandy on November 11, 1960; the *Fugue Fantasia* got its first performance in a radio performance in Sidney, Australia, in 1958, Tibor Paul conducting.

The *Elegie* is one of many works to derive its personality and stylistic details from Hungarian folk songs and dances. It was commissioned by Edward B. Benjamin of New Orleans who often sponsored the writing of "restful music that charms and soothes." The composer's original intention was to call the work *The Hungarian Plains,* then felt that a less descriptive title would better serve to indicate "the abstract universality of its moods." Edwin H. Schloss, the program annotator for the Philadelphia Orchestra, further describes this composition as follows: "The music is generally in a quiet and elegiac mood but in the course of development it reaches dramatic levels only, however, to return to the nostalgic mood of the beginning."

The composer described his *Fugue Fantasia* in the following way: "It is a short work, destined to open a concert. The introduction leads to a regular fugue on a chromatic theme. Later, it becomes a fantasia, when I take greater liberties, making a detour to other themes and developing them independently from the first time. Contrapuntal episodes contrast with free melodic lines in augmentations and inversions. The word 'fantasia' applies to the orchestration as well, inasmuch as I use sounds of unusual expression, such as the transition from the middle part to the first theme played by the brass and using a forceful solo for tympani."

1960–1961 RHAPSODY, for orchestra.

A CHRISTMAS OVERTURE, for orchestra.

The *Rhapsody* (1960) received its world première on February 12, 1961, in Los Angeles, with Laszlo Somogyi conducting the Los Angeles Philharmonic. The composer explains that his music "is highly colored by Hungarian folk style with the rhapsodic rhythm and gypsy-like figures of the clarinet suggesting Hungarian dance patterns." The work opens with a sonorous introduction, following which we hear the first principal subject, based on the interval of the fourth, suggested by the violins before it is stated fully by cellos. The second theme is also built from the same interval. This is a lively tune for violins over a plucked-string accompaniment. A slow middle section provides contrast. Eventually, the sonority grows to achieve a passionate climax.

As is the case with Zador's national compositions, *A Christmas Overture* (1961) is neither a potpourri nor an adaptation of famous tunes. All the melodies are Zador's own, but they do try to capture some of the basic characteristics and personality of Yuletide music. "These themes," the composer explains, "range in expression from joyful gaiety and a carefree Scherzo (Sleighride) to solemnity and pure simplicity (Nativity). The overture is climaxed by an almost liturgical atmosphere, exulting in the all-embracing Faith. It is a composition of melodic simplicity, contemporary only in its construction and orchestration."

Its world première took place in Glendale, California, on December 17, 1961.

1965 FIVE CONTRASTS FOR ORCHESTRA. I. Introduction. II. Autumn Pastorale. III. Phantasy. IV. Scherzo rustico. V. Finale.

VARIATIONS ON A MERRY THEME, for orchestra.

For the world première of *Five Contrasts,* which took place on January 8, 1965, with Eugene Ormandy conducting the Philadelphia Orchestra, the composer provided the following description: "Each movement differs from the next in mood, color and expression; and traditional basic unity is dispensed with. The first movement opens with a romantic horn theme, followed by a robust marcato phrase. After diversified development, it closes with a recapitulation of the opening horn theme. In the second movement, the oboe plays a lighthearted theme, colored by Hungarian folk idioms, against a dark orchestral background. The third movement is a free fantasy, entirely different from the two previous movements. A piano solo is followed by a nostalgic theme for the trumpet. After reaching a climax in the brass and higher strings, the movement ends with a return of the trumpet solo. The fourth movement is a stylized peasant dance, the Austrian Ländler, broadly melodic, robust and prankish. The last movement is an Introduction and Fugue, in which the fugue theme undergoes innumerable transformations, with a forceful climax at the end."

In a similarly light and often humorous vein is the *Variations on a Merry Theme,* whose first performance took place in Birmingham, Alabama, on January 12, 1965. The theme is a gay and lively tune played by the flute. It then reappears in different keys and instruments. It emerges augmented in rhythm, then abbreviated. Sometimes it is lyrical (in saxophone) and sometimes it is dramatic (trombones). The composition ends with a sprightly fugato based on this subject.

1966 ARIA AND ALLEGRO, for brass and strings.

Zador wrote the *Aria and Allegro,* intending it as an opening number for a symphony concert. Its world première took place on March 2, 1967, Hans Schmidt-Isserstedt conducting the Los Angeles Philharmonic. The composer calls this a "simple work. . . . The brass is thematically integrated in the piece not only giving rhythmic or dynamic accents, but also carrying the musical thoughts." The Aria offers a melody "accompanied by a vertical combination of chords, which gives the harmonization an almost bitonal character." This is followed by the Allegro, which is a rondo in structure, the main theme heard four times. In the middle part, a slower scherzo theme is presented by the strings. After the final reiteration of the rondo subject, a strong finale is heard in full orchestra.

SCHOOLS—STYLES—TECHNIQUES—IDIOMS—TRENDS—MOVEMENTS—TENDENCIES IN TWENTIETH-CENTURY MUSIC

Aleatory Music (*Chance Music*)*:* Music created spontaneously through chance methods rather than calculation.
See Boulez, Cage, Stockhausen.

Apaches: See Société des Apaches.

Arcueilists: A school of modern French composers founded by Satie (then living in the Parisian suburb of Arcueil) which included Henri Sauguet, Roger Desormière and Maxime Jacob, and which dedicated itself to simplicity.
See Satie.

Atonality: The absence of a basic tonality or key.
See Schoenberg, Berg, Webern.

Audio-Visual Music: Compositions combining dadaistic visual stage effects with music requiring electronic equipment, noisemakers, loudspeakers, as well as traditional instruments.
See Cage.

Cante Hondo (*Deep Song*)*:* A type of song popularized in Andalusia in Spain which has the tortuous contours and throbbing vibrations of oriental chants, and which discusses life's tragedies rather than joys.
See Falla.

Concrete Music: See Musique concrète.

Contemporary Art: See Zeitkunst.

Dadaism: An escape into nonsense as a cynical expression of disenchantment with life's realities.
See Introduction, Walton (*Façade*), Milhaud (*Le Boeuf sur le toit*).

Decadent Formalism: See Formalism.

Directional Music: See Spatial Dimension in Music.

Dodecaphony: See Twelve-Tone System.

Domaine musical: An annual series of concerts of avant-garde music founded by Boulez in Paris in 1954.

Dynamism: See Neo-Primitivism.

Evocación: A mystic portrayal of Spain as found in the music of Falla.
See Falla.

Everyday Music: See Musique de tous les jours.

Expressionism: The seeking of the very essence or inner soul-state of a subject through abstraction.
See Schoenberg, Berg, Webern.

Fauvism: See Neo-Primitivism.

Formalism (or *Decadent Formalism*)*:* The charge of cerebralism leveled against leading Soviet composers by the Central Committee of the Communist Party of the U.S.S.R. on February 10, 1948.
See Prokofiev, Shostakovich.

The French Six (*Les Six*)*:* A school of modern French composers that included Auric, Durey, Tailleferre, Honegger, Milhaud and Poulenc.
See Auric, Honegger, Milhaud, Poulenc.

Gebrauchsmusik: Functional Music.
See Hindemith.

Germ Cell Theory: A creative process developed by Willem Pijper in which a large work is constructed from a melodic, rhythmic or harmonic germ cell.
See Pijper.

I-Ching (*"Chinese Book of Changes"*)*:* A method in aleatory or chance music utilized by Cage in which Chinese dice are thrown to provide the materials, and the order of their appearance, in a musical composition.
See Cage.

Impressionism: The escape from realism and post-Romanticism in which emphasis is placed more on the impression or sensation aroused by a subject rather than on the subject itself; more on light, color and mood than on form and substance.
See Debussy.

Italian Manifesto Against Cerebral Music: A manifesto signed by several Italian composers (including Respighi and Pizzetti) on December 17, 1932, condemning cerebral music and composers.

Jazz: Jazz techniques and styles exploited by many composers in works of serious artistic intent.
See Gershwin, Copland, Gould, Grofé, Schuller.

La Jeune France (*Young France*): A phrase borrowed from Berlioz identifying a school of contemporary French composers including Jolivet, Daniel-Lesur and Messiaen.
See Messiaen.

League of Composers: An organization founded in New York in 1923 for the promotion of modern music and modern composers through concerts, broadcasts, receptions, commissions, and the publication of *Modern Music*. *Modern Music* stopped publication in 1947, and the League of Composers was dissolved a number of years after that.

Linear Music: Contrapuntal music in which the voices move independently of harmonic relationships.
See Hindemith.

"*Melodies of the Language*": The molding of the contours of declamation in folk opera by Janáček after the patterns of Moravian language and speech.
See Janáček.

Metrical Modulations: A polyrhythmic device in Elliott Carter's music in which contrasting rhythms abound horizontally and vertically.
See Carter.

Microtone: *See* Quarter-Tone Music.

Monday Group: A school of young Swedish composers influenced by Hindemith.
See Blomdahl.

Musico-Mathematics: A direct application of mathematical series to musical composition.
See Krenek (*Fibonacci-Mobile*).

Musik als Ausdruck (*Music as Expression*): The attempt to endow music with deepening expressiveness and increasing capacities to translate non-musical concepts into tones.
See Strauss.

Musique concrète (*Concrete Music*): Musical sounds reproduced on tape and sometimes including distortions or alterations of sounds already recorded. Different sounds and their electric manipulation thus form the composition of concrete music.
See Introduction, Boulez, Cage.

Musique d'ameublement (*Furnishing Music*): Music intended not for active listening but exclusively as background.
See: Satie.

Musique de tous les jours (Everyday Music): French music rebelling against post-Romantic attitudes and tendencies through simplicity, clarity, wit, and the exploitation of popular idioms and materials. A corollary movement in Germany was *Zeitkunst.*
See Satie.

Mystery: A metaphysical concept by Scriabin which was to be a synthesis of all the arts and which would embrace the whole history of mankind and even project a new religion.
See Scriabin.

Mystery Chord: A chord devised by Scriabin built from fourths in place of thirds.
See Scriabin.

Nationalism in Music: The reflection in music of the rise of nationalism in Europe in the late nineteenth century, a movement which gained impetus in Russia with the "Russian Five." Composers now made a conscious attempt to express national feeling in their music by banding into schools whose mission was to express their countries' backgrounds, history, culture, and people in music, and to exploit idioms derived from folk (and sometimes popular) sources.

Leading National Schools

Armenia: *See* Khatchaturian.
Bohemia: *See* Weinberger, Martinu.
Brazil: *See* Villa-Lobos, Mignone.
Finland: *See* Sibelius.
Hungary: *See* Bartók, Kodály.
Italy: *See* Casella.
Mexico: *See* Chávez, Revueltas.
Moravia: *See* Janáček.
Poland: *See* Szymanowski.
Rumania: *See* Enesco.
Soviet Union: *See* Shostakovich.
Spain: *See* Albéniz, Falla, Turina.
Sweden: *See* Atterberg.
United States: *See* Copland, Cowell, Ives, Siegmeister.

Naturalism: See Realism, Verismo.

Nazi Musical Policies: See Hindemith, Strauss.

Neo-Baroque Music: The reversion to the contrapuntal practices of the sixteenth and seventeenth centuries.
See Busoni, Hindemith, Reger.

Neo-Classicism: The reversion to old classical and forms of the Baroque era but with a twentieth-century approach.
See Busoni, Hindemith, Stravinsky (middle period).

Neo-Dadaism: A return to the dadaistic movement of the 1920s.
See Cage.

Neo-Mysticism: The imposition of religious implications into music that is Romantic in expression and usually Wagnerian in idiom.
See Scriabin.

Neo-Primitivism (or *Dynamism, Fauvism*)*:* The transfer of the dynamic and elemental force of primitive music into sophisticated musical forms, also known as Dynamism or Fauvism—Fauvism, because of the paintings of wild animals in vogue in Paris in the early 1910s.
See Stravinsky (first period).

Neue Sachlichkeit (*New Objectivity*)*:* The Back-to-Bach movement instigated by Reger which preceded neo-classicism.
See Reger.

New England School of Composers: A group of New England composers, conservative in their outlook, which included Foote, Chadwick, Henry F. Gilbert and Horatio Parker.
See Foote.

Nouveux Jeunes (*The New Young Men*)*:* A school of young French composers which was the immediate forerunner of "The French Six." This school embraced Auric, Honegger, Poulenc, Roland-Manuel, and Tailleferre.
See Auric.

Open Form: A term devised by Stockhausen to designate a musical structure which is shaped by the material, each new composition creating its own structure.
See Stockhausen.

Organized Sound: A term devised by Varèse for compositions exploiting noise-makers and various percussion sounds.
See Varèse.

Political Music: Music serving to propagandize political or social dogmas.
See Blitzstein.

Polymeters: Simultaneous use of different rhythms (also called polyrhythms).
See Stravinsky, Ives.

Polytonality: Simultaneous use of different tonalities.

See Milhaud, Stravinsky.

Popularism: The introduction into serious music of popular tunes, idioms, techniques.
See Satie, Gershwin, Gould, Milhaud, Weill.

Post-Romanticism: The reversion to the Romantic ideals of the middle nineteenth century through gargantuan forms, frequently elaborate programs and just as frequently philosophic or metaphysic implications. *See* Mahler, Scriabin, Strauss.

"*Prepared Piano*": The preparation of a piano is an innovation of John Cage in which dampers of metal, wood, rubber, felt, etc. are stuffed between the strings of a piano in carefully measured positions, to produce unusual percussive effects.
See Introduction.

Proletarian Music: Soviet music written for mass consumption which reflects the interests and ideologies of the people and which is readily assimilable.
See Shostakovich, Prokofiev.

Quarter-Tone Music (or *Microtone*): Music constructed from intervals equal to one half of a half tone (or one quarter of a whole tone), a method identified in the twentieth century with Alois Hába.
See Introduction.

Realism (or *Naturalism*): The simulation of realistic effects in music (see also Verismo).
See Strauss.

Secondal Harmonies: See Tone Clusters.

Serial Technique: A dodecaphonic process in which the twelve-tone system is applied not only to pitch but also to rhythm, tone color, dynamics, etc.
See Webern, Boulez, Stockhausen, Stravinsky (third period).

Société des Apaches: A group of rebel musicians who in 1904 promoted in Paris new ideas and methods and which included Falla, Stravinsky, Schmitt and Ravel.
See Ravel.

Song Play: A term devised by Weill for *Zeitkunst* opera, opera which incorporates popular elements in the music and racy subjects in the libretto.
See Weill.

Sound Objects: A term devised by Stockhausen for music produced electronically.
See Stockhausen.

Soviet Musical Policies: See Formalism, Proletarian Music.

Society for Private Performances (*Verein für Musikalische Privataffühhrungen*)*:* A society founded in 1918 by Schoenberg and his school for the performances of their music under favorable auspices.
See Schoenberg.

Spatial Dimension in Music (*Directional Music*)*:* An attempt to arrive at stereophonic effects in live performances either by scattering the musical forces in different parts of an auditorium—or electronically by scattering loudspeakers—so as to have the musical sound converge on an audience from many directions.
See Introduction, Stockhausen.

Sprechstimme (or *Sprechgesang*)*:* A declamation developed by the atonalists in which the pitch is indicated rather than sung with the voice swooping from one interval to the next.
See Schoenberg, Berg.

Stochastic Music: Music produced by computer, developed by Iannis Xenakis in Paris with IBM 7090.
See Introduction.

Synthesizer (or *Mark II Synthesizer*)*:* An electronic instrument devised by the David Sarnoff Research Center in the 1950s for Milton Babbitt.
See Introduction.

Third Stream: A term devised by Gunther Schuller for music combining serialism with jazz methods.
See Schuller.

Time Fields: A term devised by Stockhausen for a new kind of notation with all kinds of visual symbols to designate sound, color, tempo, etc.
See Stockhausen.

Triton: A group of French composers seeking moderation in style, including Henri Barraud and Rivier.
See Rivier.

Twelve-Tone System (or *Technique,* or *Row*)*:* The construction of a musical work from a set of tones, twelve in number, according to definitely set laws.
See Schoenberg, Berg, Webern.

Variable Meters: A devise developed by Blacher in which a rhythmic row becomes the basis of a musical composition, its pattern based on some arithmetical series.
See Blacher.

Verein für Musikalische Privataufführungen: See *Society for Private Performances.*

Verismo: A school of Italian opera composers, beginning with Mascagni and Leoncavallo, which developed naturalism in opera.
See Puccini.

Whole Tone Scale: A scale created out of whole tones, the octave being divided into six equal parts.
See Debussy.

Zeitkunst (*Contemporary Art*)*:* Art dealing with contemporary themes in a style employing popular elements.
See Weill.

SOURCES

ABRAHAM, GERALD, *Eight Soviet Composers*. London: Oxford University Press, 1944.

———, *This Modern Music*. New York: W. W. Norton, 1952.

ABRAHAM, GERALD (editor), *The Music of Sibelius*. New York: W. W. Norton, 1947.

ANSERMET, ERNEST, "Falla's Atlantída." *Opera News,* September 29, 1962.

ANTHEIL, GEORGE, *Bad Boy of Music*. Garden City: Doubleday & Co, 1945.

AUSTIN, WILLIAM W., *Music in the 20th Century*. New York: W. W. Norton, 1966.

BACHARACH, A.L. (editor), *British Music of Our Time*. London: Pelican Books, 1946.

———, *The Music Masters, vol. 4:* The Twentieth Century. London: Penguin Books, 1957.

BAKST, JAMES, *A History of Russian-Soviet Music*. New York: Dodd, Mead, 1966.

BALANCHINE, GEORGE, *Balanchine's Complete Stories of the Great Ballets*. New York: Doubleday & Co, 1954.

BEAUMONT, CYRIL W., *Complete Book of Ballets*. New York: Garden City Publishing Co., 1941.

BEECHAM, Sir THOMAS, *Delius*. New York: Alfred A. Knopf, 1960.

BERGER, ARTHUR, *Aaron Copland*. New York: Oxford University Press, 1953.

BERNARD, ROBERT, *Albert Roussel—Sa Vie, Son Oeuvre*. Paris: La Colombe, 1948.

BERNSTEIN, LEONARD, "Mahler: His Time Has Come." *High Fidelity Magazine,* September 1967.

BOEPPLE, PAUL, "Swiss Composers." *The New York Times,* January 13, 1952.

BRODER, NATHAN, *Samuel Barber*. New York: G. Schirmer, 1953.

CALVOCORESSI, M. D., "Willem Pijper." *Gamut* (London), July 1928.

CARDUS, NEVILLE, *A Composers Eleven*. London: Jonathan Cape, 1958.

———, "Ralph Vaughan Williams" in *Talking of Music*. London: Collins, 1957.

CARNER, MOSCO, *Puccini*. New York: Alfred A. Knopf, 1959.

CHASE, GILBERT, *America's Music*. Revised edition. New York: McGraw Hill, 1966.

———, *The Music of Spain.* New York: Dover, 1959.

———, (editor): *The American Composer Speaks.* Louisiana State University Press, 1966.

CHERNIAVSKY, DAVID, "Special Characteristics of Sibelius's Style," in *The Music of Sibelius,* edited by Gerald Abraham.

COHN, ARTHUR, *20th Century Music in Western Europe.* Philadelphia: Lippincott, 1965.

———, *20th Century Music in the Western Hemisphere.* Philadelphia: Lippincott, 1961.

COLLAER, PAUL, *A History of Modern Music.* New York: Grosset and Dunlap, 1961.

COWELL, HENRY and SIDNEY, *Charles Ives and His Music.* New York: Oxford University Press, 1955.

DANIEL, OLIVER, "The New Music of Poland." *Saturday Review,* July 30, 1966.

DAY, JAMES, *Ralph Vaughan Williams.* London: J. M. Dent, 1961.

DEAN, BASIL, *Albert Roussel.* London: Barrie and Rockcliffe, 1961.

DEL MAR, NORMAN, *Richard Strauss.* London: Barrie and Rockcliffe, 1962.

DEMUTH, NORMAN, *Albert Roussel: A study.* London: United Music Publishing, 1947.

———, *Ravel.* London: J. M. Dent, 1947.

———, *Vincent d'Indy.* London: Rockcliffe, 1951.

DENT, EDWARD J., *Busoni.* London: Oxford University Press, 1933.

DESMOND, ASTRA, "The Songs of Sibelius" in *The Music of Sibelius,* edited by Gerald Abraham.

DOWNES, EDWARD, "The Music of Norman Dello Joio." *Musical Quarterly,* April 1962.

DREW, DAVID, "Chronocromie." *New Statesman* (London), November 9, 1962.

EKMAN, KARL, *Jean Sibelius.* New York: Tudor Publishing Co., 1945.

ELWELL, HERBERT, "Quincy Porter." *Modern Music,* Winter 1946.

EVANS, EDWIN, "Arnold Bax." *Musical Quarterly,* April 1923.

EVERETT, ROBERT, "Persichetti." *Juilliard Review,* Spring 1955.

EWEN, DAVID, *David Ewen Introduces Modern Music.* Philadelphia: Chilton, 1962.

———, *A Journey to Greatness: The Life and Music of George Gershwin.* New York: Holt, Rinehart and Winston, 1956.

———, *Leonard Bernstein.* Revised edition. Philadelphia: Chilton, 1967.

EWEN, DAVID (editor), *The New Book of Modern Composers.* Revised edition. New York: Alfred A. Knopf, 1967.

FASSETT, AGATHA, *The Naked Face of Genius: Béla Bartók's American Years.* Boston: Houghton Mifflin, 1958.

Forty Contemporary Composers (no editor). Switzerland: Bodensee-Verlag Amriswil, 1956.

FOSS, HUBERT J., *Ralph Vaughan Williams,* London: Faber and Faber, 1963.

———, "William Walton." *Musical Quarterly,* October 1940.

GATTI, GUIDO M., *Ildebrando Pizzetti.* London: Dennis Dobson, 1951.

GLOCK, WILLIAM, "A Note on Elliott Carter." *Score* (London), June 1955.
GODDARD, SCOTT, "Szymanowski." *The Listener* (London), May 22, 1947.
GOLEA, ANTOINE, *Georges Auric*. Paris: Ventadour, 1958.
GOSS, MADELEINE, *Bolero: The Life of Maurice Ravel*. New York: Henry Holt, 1940.
GRADENWITZ, PETER, *Music and Musicians in Israel*. Tel Aviv: Israel Music Publishing Co., 1959.
GRAY, CECIL, *Sibelius*. Revised edition. London: Oxford University Press, 1945.
———, *A Survey of Contemporary Music*. London: Oxford University Press, 1924.
GRETCHANINOFF, ALEXANDER, *My Life*. New York: Coleman-Ross, 1952.
GROUT, DONALD J., *A Short History of Music*. Revised edition. New York: Columbia University Press, 1965.
HALL, JAMES HUSST, *The Art Song*. Norman: University of Oklahoma Press, 1953.
HANSON, LAWRENCE and ELIZABETH, *Prokofiev*. New York: Random House, 1964.
HARASZTI, EMIL, *Béla Bartók: Life and Works*. Paris: Lyrebird Press, 1938.
HARTOG, HOWARD (editor), *European Music in the 20th century*. New York: Praeger, 1957.
HELL, HENRI, *Francis Poulenc*. New York: Grove, 1959.
HERMANN, BERNARD, "Four Symphonies by Charles Ives." *Modern Music,* May-June 1945.
HESELTINE, PHILIP, *Frederick Delius*. London: Bodley Head, 1952.
HILL, RALPH (editor), *The Concerto*. London: Penguin Books, 1956.
———, *The Symphony*. London: Penguin Books, 1956.
HODEIR, ANDRÉ, *Since Debussy*. New York: Grove, 1961.
HOLLANDER, HANS, "Janáček's Development." *Musical Times* (London), August 1958.
HOLST, IMOGEN, *Benjamin Britten*. New York: Thos. Y. Crowell, 1966.
HORAN, ROBERT, "Samuel Barber." *Modern Music,* April 1945.
HOOVER, KATHLEEN and CAGE, JOHN, *Virgil Thomson: His Life and Music*. New York: Sagamore Press, 1959.
Honegger, Arthur, *I Am a Composer*. New York: St. Martin's Press, 1966.
HOWARD, JOHN TASKER, *Our Contemporary Music*. New York: Thos. Y. Crowell, 1941.
HOWES, FRANK, *The Music of Ralph Vaughan Williams*. London: Oxford University Press, 1954.
———, *The Music of William Walton*. London: Oxford University Press, 1965.
HULL, ARTHUR E., *A Great Russian Tone Poet: Scriabin*. London: K. Paul, Trench, Trubner, 1916.
HUTCHINGS, ARTHUR, *Delius: A Critical Biography*. New York: Macmillan, 1948.
———, "Arthur Honegger" in *The Music Masters,* vol. 4, edited by A. L. Bacharach.

HUTH, ARNO, "Dance and Death in Basle." *Modern Music,* Fall 1940.
IKKINIKOV, ALEXEI, *Nikolai Miaskovsky*. New York: Philosophical Library, 1946.
JACOB, ARTHUR (editor), *Choral Music*. London: Pelican Books, 1963.
JEAN-AUBRY, GEORGES, "Gian Francesco Malipiero." *Musical Times* (London), January 1919.
JOHNSON, H. E., *Jean Sibelius*. New York: Alfred A. Knopf, 1959.
KENNEDY, MICHAEL, *The Works of Ralph Vaughan Williams*. London: Oxford University Press, 1964.
KOBBE, GUSTAV, *The Complete Opera Book*. Revised Edition. New York: Putnam, 1954.
KOLODIN, IRVING, "The Merit of Poulenc." *Saturday Review,* February 23, 1963.
LANG, PAUL HENRY and BRODER, NATHAN (editors): *Contemporary Music in Europe: A Comprehensive Survey*. New York: G. Schirmer, 1965.
LANGE, KRISTIAN and ÖSTVEDT, ARNE, *Norwegian Music*. London: Dennis Dobson, 1958.
LAPLANE, GABRIEL, *Albéniz*. Paris: Milieu du Monde, 1956.
LARNER, GERALD, "Bluebeard's Castle." *Records and Recordings* (London), May 1966.
LATOUCHE, JOHN, "About the Ballad of Baby Doe." *Theatre Arts,* July 1956.
LEDERMANN, MINNA, "Memories of Marc Blitzstein." *Show,* June 1964.
LEIBOWITZ, RENÉ, "Alban Berg's Five Orchestral Songs." *Musical Quarterly,* 1948.
——, *Schoenberg and His School*. New York: Philosophical Library, 1949.
LEICHTENTRITT, HUGO, *Music, History and Ideas*. Cambridge: Harvard University Press, 1938.
LEONARD, RICHARD, *A History of Russian Music*. New York: Macmillan & Co., 1957.
LIESS, ANDREAS, *Carl Orff*. London: Calder and Boyar, 1966.
VON LEWINSKI, WOLF-EBERHARD, "The Variety of Trends in German Music" in *Contemporary Music in Europe* edited by Lang and Broder.
LOCKSPEISER, EDWARD, *Debussy: His Life and Mind.* New York: Macmillan & Co, 1962, 1965.
MACHLIS, JOSEPH, *Introduction to Contemporary Music*. New York: W.W. Norton, 1961.
MAINE, BASIL, "Elgar: An Appraisement." *The Nineteenth Century* (London), April 1934.
——, *Elgar: His Life and Music*. London: Bell, 1933.
MAISEL, EDWARD M., *Charles T. Griffes*. New York: Alfred A. Knopf, 1947.
MANN, WILLIAM, *Richard Strauss: A Critical Study of his Operas*. New York: Oxford University Press, 1966.
MAREK, GEORGE, *Puccini*. New York: Simon and Schuster, 1951.
——, *Richard Strauss: The Life of a Non-Hero*. New York: Simon and Schuster, 1967.
MARX, BURLE, "Brazilian Portrait." *Modern Music,* October-November 1939.
MAYER-SERRA, OTTO, "Falla's Musical Nationalism." *Musical Quarterly,* April 1934.

MARTYNOV, IVAN, *Shostakovich.* New York: Philosophical Library, 1947.
MELLERS, W. H., *Music in a New Found Land.* New York: Alfred A. Knopf, 1965.
———, *Studies in Contemporary Music.* London: Dennis Dobson, 1947.
MILHAUD, DARIUS, *Notes Without Music—An Autobiography.* New York: Alfred A. Knopf, 1953.
MYERS, ROLLO H., *Erik Satie.* London: Dennis Dobson, 1948.
———, *Ravel: Life and Works.* New York: Thos. Yoseloff, 1960.
NATHAN, HANS, "U.S. of America" in *History of Song,* edited by Denis Stevens.
NESTYEV, ISRAEL, *Serge Prokofiev: His Musical Times.* Stanford: Stanford University Press, 1960.
NEWLIN, DIKA, *Bruckner, Mahler, Schoenberg.* New York: King's Crown, 1947.
NEWMAN, ERNEST, "Berg's Wozzeck." *Musical Times* (London), March 1949.
———, "An English Composer and Universal Music." *The New York Times Magazine,* October 12, 1952.
PAHISSA, JAIME, *Manuel de Falla.* London: Museum Press, 1954.
PAKENHAM, SIMON, *Ralph Vaughan Williams.* London: Macmillan & Co., 1957.
PANNAIN, GUIDO, *Modern Composers.* New York: E. P. Dutton, 1933.
PAYNE, ANTHONY, "Tippett's The Vision of St. Augustine." *Tempo* (London), Spring 1966.
PERSICHETTI, VINCENT and SCHREIBER, FLORA, *William Schuman.* New York: G. Schirmer, 1954.
PROKOFIEV, SERGE, *Autobiography of Serge Prokofiev—Materials, Documents, Reminiscences,* edited by S. I. Schlifstein. Moscow, 1956.
PRUNIÈRES, HENRI, "Malipiero." *Musical Quarterly,* July 1920.
REESER, EDWARD (editor): *Music in Holland.* Amsterdam: Meulenhoff (no year).
REDLICH, HANS F., *Alban Berg.* New York: Abelard-Schumann, 1957.
———, "Schoenberg's Religious Testament." *Opera* (London), June 1965.
REICH, WILLI, *Alban Berg.* London: Dennis Dobson, 1954.
REID, CHARLES, "Britten at Fifty." *The New York Times Magazine,* November 17, 1963.
Reis, Claire (editor), *Composers in America.* New York: Macmillan, 1947.
ROBERTSON, ALEC (editor): *Chamber Music.* London: Penguin Books, 1957.
ROLAND-MANUEL, *Ravel.* London: Dennis Dobson, 1947.
ROLLAND, ROMAIN, *Musicians of Today.* New York: Henry Holt, 1914.
ROSENFELD, PAUL, *Discoveries of a Music Critic.* New York: Harcourt, Brace, 1936.
SAFRANEK, MILOS, *Bohuslav Martinu.* New York: Alfred A. Knopf, 1953.
SALZMAN, ERIC, *Twentieth-Century Music: An Introduction.* New York: Prentice-Hall, 1967.
SAMUEL, CLAUDE, *Panorama de l'art musical.* contemporain. Paris; NRF, 1962.
SCHONBERG, HAROLD C., "Forgotten Man—Busoni." *The New York Times,* December 8, 1963.
SCHWARTZ, ELLIOTT and CHILDS, BARNEY (editors), Contemporary Composers on Contemporary Music. New York: Holt, Rinehart and Winston, 1967.
SEROFF, VICTOR, *Debussy: Musician of France.* New York: Putnam & Sons, 1956.

———, *Rachmaninoff*. New York: Simon and Schuster, 1950.
———, *Ravel*. New York: Henry Holt, 1953.
Simpson, Robert, *Carl Neilsen, Symphonist*. London: J. M. Dent, 1952.
———, (editor), *The Symphony—Elgar to the Present*. London: Penguin Books, 1967.
Skulsky, Abraham, "Gustav Mahler." *Musical America,* February 1951.
Slonimsky, Nicolas, "Dmitri Shostakovich." *Musical Quarterly,* October 1942.
———, *Music of Latin America*. New York: Thos. Y. Crowell, 1945.
———, *Music Since 1900*. Revised edition. New York: Coleman-Ross, 1949.
Smith, Julia, *Aaron Copland*. New York: E. P. Dutton, 1955.
Stein, Erwin, "Boulevard Solitude." *Opera Annual—1954–1955*, edited by Harold Rosenthal. London: John Calder, 1954.
Stevens, Denis (editor), *A History of Song*. New York: W.W. Norton, 1960.
Stevens, Halsey, *The Life and Music of Béla Bartók*. Revised edition. New York: Oxford University Press, 1964.
Stravinsky, Igor, *Igor Stravinsky: An Autobiography*. New York: Steuer, 1958.
Strobel, Heinrich, *Paul Hindemith*. Revised edition. Mainz: B. Schott, 1948.
Stuckenschmidt, H. H., *Busoni*. London: Calder and Boyar, 1966.
———, "Hindemith Today." *Modern Music,* 1937.
———, *Schoenberg*. New York: Grove, 1959.
Suares, André, "Ravel." *La Revue Musicale* (Paris), April 1925.
Suckling, Norman, *Gabriel Fauré*. New York: E. P. Dutton, 1946.
Terry, Walter, *Ballet*. New York: Dell Publishing Co., 1959.
Thompson, Oscar, *Debussy*. New York: Dodd, Mead, 1937.
Thomson, Virgil, "John Cage Late and Lately." *Saturday Review,* June 30, 1960.
———, *Virgil Thomson*. New York: Alfred A. Knopf, 1966.
Trend, J. B., *Manuel de Falla and Spanish Music*. New York: Alfred A. Knopf, 1929.
Vaughan Wiliams, Ralph, *Nationalism is Music*. London: Oxford University Press, 1934.
Wellesz, Egon, *Arnold Schoenberg*. New York: E. P. Dutton, 1925.
———, "Early Days in Vienna." *Saturday Review,* May 28, 1966.
von Westerman, Gerhart, *Opera Guide*. New York: E. P. Dutton, 1965.
White, Erich Walter, *Benjamin Britten*. London: Boosey and Hawkes, 1954.
———, *Stravinsky*. California: University of California Press, 1966.
Wildgans, Friedrich, *Webern*. London: Calder and Boyar, 1966.
Yates, Peter, *Twentieth Century Music*. New York: Pantheon, 1967.
Young, Percy, *Zoltán Kodály*. London: Ernest Benn, 1964.

INDEX

A

B

C

D

E

F

H

I

J

K

L

O

P

Q

R

S

T

U

V

W

X

Y

Z